AutoCAD® 2008 and AutoCAD LT® 2008 Bible

AutoCAD® 2008 and AutoCAD LT® 2008 Bible

Ellen Finkelstein

Wiley Publishing, Inc.

AutoCAD® 2008 and AutoCAD LT® 2008 Bible

Published by
Wiley Publishing, Inc.
111 River Street

Hoboken, N.J. 07030
www.wiley.com

Copyright © 2007 by Wiley Publishing, Inc., Indianapolis, Indiana

Published by Wiley Publishing, Inc., Indianapolis, Indiana

Published simultaneously in Canada

ISBN: 978-0-470-12049-1

Manufactured in the United States of America

10 9 8 7 6 5 4 3 2 1

For general information on our other products and services, please contact our Customer Care Department within the U.S. at 800-762-2974, outside the U.S. at 317-572-3993, or fax 317-572-4002.

For technical support, please visit www.wiley.com/techsupport.

Wiley also publishes its books in a variety of electronic formats. Some content that appears in print may not be available in electronic books.

Library of Congress Control Number: 2007926385

About the Author

Ellen Finkelstein learned AutoCAD in Israel, where she always got to pore over the manual because it was in English. After returning to the United States, she started consulting and teaching AutoCAD as well as other computer programs, including Microsoft Word, Excel, and PowerPoint. She has also taught courses on Web writing and usability. Her Web site, www.ellenfinkelstein.com, contains tips and techniques for AutoCAD and PowerPoint, and she publishes a monthly AutoCAD Tips Newsletter. Ellen has written extensively on AutoCAD, including articles for Autodesk's Web site, such as three white papers on dynamic blocks, and features for AutoCAD's Help system. She is also the editor of Inside AutoCAD, a monthly newsletter published by Eli Journals.

Ellen's first book was *AutoCAD For Dummies Quick Reference*. Since then, she has written books on Word, PowerPoint, OpenOffice.org (*OpenOffice.org For Dummies*), Flash (such as *Flash 8 For Dummies*), and Web technologies (for example, *Syndicating Web Sites with RSS Feeds For Dummies*). You're holding the eighth edition of this book, which previously appeared for AutoCAD releases 14, 2000, 2002, 2004, 2005, 2006, and 2007.

To MMY for teaching me that there's more to life than meets the eye and that the deeper levels of life are the most powerful and blissful.

Credits

Acquisitions Editor
Stephanie McComb

Project Editor
Jade L. Williams

Technical Editor
Lee Ambrosius

Copy Editor
Marylouise Wiack

Editorial Manager
Robyn Siesky

Business Manager
Amy Knies

Vice President & Executive Group Publisher
Richard Swadley

Vice President and Executive Publisher
Bob Ipsen

Vice President and Publisher
Barry Pruett

Project Coordinator
Erin Smith

Graphics and Production Specialists
Joyce Haughey
Jennifer Mayberry
Barbara Moore
Heather Pope
Amanda Spagnuolo
Ronald Terry

Quality Control Technician
Todd Lothery

Permissions Editor
Laura Moss

Media Development Specialist
Steven Kudirka
Kit Malone

Proofreading and Indexing
Aptara Corp.

Foreword

Congratulations!

As someone interested in AutoCAD, or as someone who uses it to make a living as many do, you have truly made a worthwhile investment.

I have used Ellen's AutoCAD Bibles as guides and learning materials for some years now, and they have proved invaluable to me.

First of all, it's all there. You are not going to get a more comprehensive guide than the one that you hold in your hands. Everything from the basics of AutoCAD to programming in AutoLISP and VBA is covered.

Moreover, the information is well organized, making it easy for you to traverse the 1300 or so pages. Both the contents at a glance and a comprehensive index make retrieving information that you need a cinch.

My personal favorites are the real-world AutoCAD drawings that are available on the DVD. As every designer knows, there is no better way to learn than by doing, and the drawings are an excellent tool to guide you through a series of exercises that are available with each chapter in the book. Even more helpful is the fact that the drawings are available in both a before and after format, allowing you to use the after format as a reference.

Ellen has been doing this for so long that she is practically a household word in the world of AutoCAD. A true friend of the product development team, she is an active participant in our beta program and helps shape the direction of future releases of AutoCAD. You are truly learning from one of the finest professionals in the field.

Don't let the size of the book intimidate you. It is written to be comprehensive, but I don't believe that anyone uses all of the features in AutoCAD. Pick out the tools that you want to learn about and proceed from there, or if you are interested in learning new things, pick a different topic each week to learn about.

Whether you're new to AutoCAD or a veteran, you will undoubtedly find this book to be an excellent resource.

Now the only question left is: what will you design?

Abhi Singh

AutoCAD Product Manager

Autodesk, Inc.

Welcome to the *AutoCAD 2008 and AutoCAD LT 2008 Bible*. Whether you use AutoCAD or AutoCAD LT, you'll find complete explanations of all the powerful features that you need to know about to design and draw anything. This book is designed to be your comprehensive guide to both the AutoCAD and AutoCAD LT programs.

This book covers every significant AutoCAD and AutoCAD LT feature. If you're a beginning user, you'll find everything you need to start out; if you're already using AutoCAD or AutoCAD LT regularly, the book covers advanced material, as well. Although you can use this book as a tutorial if you're just starting out or learning a new set of features, it also provides a solid reference base to come back to again and again. The short tutorials on almost every topic will quickly have you creating professional-level drawings. The DVD is chock-full of drawings, a trial version of AutoCAD 2008 and AutoCAD LT 2008, and add-in programs (which are mostly for AutoCAD only). This book is all that you need to make full use of either program.

For AutoCAD 2008, the emphasis is on enhancing basic and important drafting tools, such as layers, text, dimensions, and blocks. Important enhancements for laying out a drawing for printing or plotting are also among the new features. Most of these new features are in AutoCAD LT 2008, as well.

Is This Book for You?

The *AutoCAD 2008 and AutoCAD LT 2008 Bible* covers all of the essential features of AutoCAD and AutoCAD LT and includes clear, real-life examples and tutorials that you can adapt to your needs.

Although I fully cover the basics, I have also included material on the many advanced features, such as external database connectivity, AutoLISP, Visual Basic for Applications (VBA), 3D modeling, rendering, and customization. (Most of the advanced features apply to AutoCAD only.) The following categories should help you decide whether this book is for you.

If you are a new AutoCAD or AutoCAD LT user

If you are new to AutoCAD or AutoCAD LT, the *AutoCAD 2008 and AutoCAD LT 2008 Bible* guides you through all that you need to know to start drawing effectively, whatever your field. Just start at the beginning.

If you are upgrading to AutoCAD 2008 or AutoCAD LT 2008

This book highlights all of the new features and helps you to make the upgrade transition as seamless as possible. Look for the New Feature icons.

If you are switching from another CAD program

You already know what CAD is all about. This book clearly explains the AutoCAD and AutoCAD LT way of drawing the models that you have already been drawing. In addition, you'll find a great deal of essential information about transferring files and data from other formats.

How This Book Is Organized

This book is divided into eight parts.

Part I: AutoCAD and AutoCAD LT Basics

Part I provides the background information that you need to start drawing. It starts with a "quick tour" that has you drawing right away, and then covers how to start a drawing, use commands, specify coordinates, and set up a drawing.

Part II: Drawing in Two Dimensions

Part II covers all of the commands and procedures for drawing and editing in two dimensions. In addition, I discuss how to control the drawing process with layers, zooming, and panning. Also included in this part is information about dimensioning, plotting, and printing.

Part III: Working with Data

Part III covers many ways to organize and share data, including blocks, attributes, external references, and external databases.

Part IV: Drawing in Three Dimensions

Part IV explains everything that you need to know to draw in three dimensions. It also discusses how to present 3D drawings using hiding, shading, and rendering techniques.

Part V: Organizing and Managing Drawings

Part V helps you to incorporate AutoCAD and AutoCAD LT into your work world by explaining how to set standards, manage drawings, and work with other applications. It concludes with a chapter on getting drawings on the Internet.

Part VI: Customizing AutoCAD and AutoCAD LT

Part VI introduces the tools that you need to customize commands, toolbars, linetypes, hatch patterns, shapes, fonts, and menus. You'll also find a chapter on script files, which you can use to create macros.

Part VII: Programming AutoCAD

Part VII introduces you to programming AutoCAD. It includes three chapters on AutoLISP and Visual LISP, and one chapter on Visual Basic for Applications. This part applies to AutoCAD only. Note: Chapter 37 has been moved to the DVD because of lack of room in the book.

Part VIII: Appendixes

Part VIII provides additional information for AutoCAD and AutoCAD LT users. Appendix A gives instructions for installing and configuring AutoCAD and AutoCAD LT. Appendix B covers additional resources for AutoCAD and AutoCAD LT users. Appendix C explains what you'll find on the DVD.

ON the DVD-ROM The DVD contains a complete copy of this book in nonprintable PDF format.

How to Use This Book

You can use this book in two ways: as a tutorial and learning tool, or as a reference.

As a tutorial

The overall organization of the book goes from simple to complex, and each chapter has several step-by-step exercises. This enables you to use the book as a tutorial, from beginning to end. You can always go back and redo any exercise when you need to refresh your memory on a particular feature.

For newcomers to AutoCAD or AutoCAD LT, Parts I (AutoCAD and AutoCAD LT Basics) and II (Drawing in Two Dimensions) are essential. After that, you can refer to chapters that interest you. Parts III (Working with Data) and V (Organizing and Managing Drawings) are also useful for beginners. Intermediate users will probably be familiar with most of the material in Part I and will be more likely to skip around, looking for the specific topics that they need. However, don't forget that many new features are introduced in Part I. Enough material appears in this book to bring intermediate users up to a fairly advanced level.

I have designed this book to be comprehensive and to include every significant feature of AutoCAD and AutoCAD LT. Therefore, do not be concerned if some of the material seems too advanced. It will be there when you are ready for it.

As a reference

The *AutoCAD 2008 and AutoCAD LT 2008 Bible* is organized as a reference that you can refer to whenever you are stuck, or when you try to do something for the first time. Each chapter covers a topic completely, making it easy to find what you're looking for. Each Steps exercise (with a few exceptions) can be done on its own without doing the other exercises in the chapter. You can easily look up a topic and complete a related exercise without having to go through the entire chapter. A complete index at the back of the book can also help you to find features and topics.

Doing the Exercises

AutoCAD is a very customizable program. To a lesser extent, AutoCAD LT can also be customized in many ways. This book assumes that you are working with the default setup. However, a number of changes may have been made to your system that could result in menus, toolbars, and drawings appearing or even functioning differently from those shown in this book. If you installed AutoCAD or AutoCAD LT yourself and made some adjustments, you know what changes you have made. However, if you are using a computer that was set up by someone else, it may help to talk to that person first, to see what changes they made.

In addition, as you work through some of the exercises in this book, you will make certain changes in the program's setup. Most of these are minor changes that any user would make while drawing. For safety, Cautions and Tips accompany all changes that could have serious consequences, such as customizing the menu. For example, when customizing the menu, you will be instructed to copy the menu file under a new name, and you will then work with the new menu file, not the original one. Nevertheless, if you are working on a network or sharing your computer with someone else, it is important to consult with others who may be affected by the changes that you make.

If you do the exercises, I recommend that you do them from the beginning. Important instructions are given during earlier exercises that may affect your system later. For example, one of the first exercises is to create a new folder to hold your drawings from the exercises. This folder keeps your exercise drawings separate from other drawings that have been created in your office. However, each exercise stands on its own so that you can go back and do only the exercise that you need.

CROSS-REF You can create your own configuration to help ensure that some changes that you make will not affect others. Instructions for doing this appear in Appendix A under the heading "Creating Multiple Configurations."

The exercises in the *AutoCAD 2008 and AutoCAD LT 2008 Bible* have been carefully checked by a technical editor to ensure accuracy. However, we cannot anticipate all situations, due to either varying hardware and software configurations or customization. If you have a problem with an exercise, contact me at the e-mail address listed at the end of this Preface so that I can correct the problem in the book's next edition. I will also try to give you the information that you need to complete the exercise.

Conventions Used in This Book

Given all the ways in which you can execute a command in AutoCAD and AutoCAD LT, you'll find it useful to read this section, which describes this book's typographical conventions. You will find this section helpful for doing the step-by-step exercises as well.

Using commands

AutoCAD and AutoCAD LT use standard Windows conventions for menus and toolbars. To indicate that you should choose a command from the menu, for example, I say, "Choose View ⇨ Viewports," which means that you should click the View menu with your mouse, puck, or stylus and then click the Viewports menu item. A few of the toolbar buttons have flyouts, which are equivalent to sub-menus. They are called flyouts because they fly out when you click and hold the button on the main toolbar, displaying even more buttons. Therefore, to indicate which button to choose, I may need to tell you to choose (or click) Zoom Extents from the Zoom flyout of the Standard toolbar. Although I haven't found a good alternative, this is not completely satisfactory for two reasons. First, it's a mouthful! Second, the flyout names do not appear, making it hard to know which is the Zoom flyout. However, in most cases, the button icon will make it obvious which flyout I'm talking about.

Every command also has a command name that you can type on the command line, which appears at the bottom of your screen. Command names are shown in capital letters, as in CIRCLE. AutoLISP functions (which apply to AutoCAD only) are shown in small capital letters, as in COMMAND.

Figures

In order to create clear, legible figures, I have used a white background in AutoCAD and AutoCAD LT. However, the default drawing area color is black. In Appendix A, I explain how to change this color. As you read through the book, you should be aware that you may see on your screen a negative image of what I show in the figures — a dark background and light-colored objects. Once you get used to this difference, you'll easily recognize what you see in the figures.

In AutoCAD, the new 3D environment further changes what you see on your screen. The default 3D background is gray. Again, I have sometimes changed the background color to white for the purpose of creating a clear figure.

Prompts, your input, and instructions

In the step-by-step exercises, most instructions are presented in the same font and style that you are reading now. However, when I reproduce the command line, the prompts appear in a `nonproportional font`. Other instructions (such as "*Type in the first coordinate*") are shown in italic. In any context, input that you need to type appears in **bold**.

The Dynamic Input feature shows prompts near your cursor, but additional options only appear if you click the down arrow on your keyboard. To make clear all of the available options, I use the command line format of prompts.

Here's a sample step-by-step section. In this exercise, you click the proper toolbar button, type the number shown in bold, press Enter where indicated by the bent arrow (⏎) symbol, and follow the instructions that appear in italic.

   7. To create a second rectangle inside the first one, choose Offset from the 2D Draw control panel of the Dashboard, and follow these prompts:

```
Specify offset distance or [Through/Erase/Layer] <Through>: 4 ⏎
Select object to offset or [Exit/Undo] <Exit>: Click the rectangle to
    select it.
Specify point on side to offset or Exit/Multiple/Undo] <Exit>: Click
    anywhere inside the rectangle.
Select object to offset or [Exit/Undo] <Exit>: ⏎
```

Often I refer to specific elements in a drawing. References to these elements appear in the text as numbers in circles, such as ❶, ❷, ❸, and so on. You'll find the corresponding number in the figure to which the text refers.

Mouse and keyboard terms

You can draw using a mouse or a puck. The mouse is familiar to all users. A puck (or sometimes a stylus) is used with a digitizing tablet. Because most users do not have a digitizing tablet, I do not directly refer to it in this book. If you have one, follow the instructions for using the mouse in the same way, but using your puck.

A mouse can have two or more buttons. Many users like using a mouse with at least three buttons because you can customize the buttons to suit your needs. However, because many mice have only two buttons, I assume only two. The left mouse button is used to choose commands and toolbar buttons, and to pick points in your drawing. For this reason, it is sometimes called the *pick button*. The right button usually opens a shortcut menu.

The time-sensitive right-clicking feature enables you to use the right button either to open a shortcut menu or as the equivalent of pressing Enter. Because this feature is not on by default, I do not assume that you have turned it on. I use the term *right-click* when you need to access a shortcut menu. If you have time-sensitive right-clicking turned on, you need to hold down the right mouse button more than 250 milli-seconds (by default) to display the shortcut menu. See Chapter 3 and Appendix A for more details.

If I say one of the following

- Choose Tools ⇨ Options
- Click Line on the Draw toolbar
- Select the circle in your drawing

it means that you need to use the left button of your mouse.

When I say to press Enter, it means that you need to press the key that is marked Enter, Return, or ↵ on your keyboard. Often I use the bent arrow symbol (↵) that you see on your Enter key to indicate that you should press Enter.

I also use the mouse terms listed in the following table.

Mouse Terms

Term	Description
Cursor	The shape on your screen that shows you where the mouse is pointed. It can take a number of shapes, such as crosshairs, pickbox, or arrow. It is also known as the mouse pointer.
Pickbox	A type of cursor consisting of a small box, used to select drawing objects.
Crosshairs	A type of cursor consisting of intersecting lines, sometimes with a pickbox at their center.
Pick	Point to a drawing object and click the left mouse button.
Click	Press the left mouse button once and release it.
Double-click	Press the left mouse button twice in rapid succession.
Click and drag	Click the left mouse button and hold it down while you move the mouse, dragging an object on your screen with it.
Choose	Click a menu item, toolbar button, or dialog box item. You can sometimes choose an item using the keyboard, as well. I also use this word when you need to choose a command option, which you can do by choosing from a shortcut menu with a mouse, but also by typing the option's abbreviation on the keyboard.
Right-click	Press the right mouse button once and release it. If you have turned on time-sensitive right-clicking, hold the right mouse button at least 250 milliseconds (by default) before releasing it.
Shift and click	While holding down the Shift key, press the left mouse button once and release it.
Shift and right-click	While holding down the Shift key, press the right mouse button once and release it.
Shift and mouse wheel	A new shortcut in AutoCAD for temporarily starting the 3DORBIT command requires you to press the Shift key and hold down the mouse wheel, using it like a button.
Select	Highlight an object in a drawing by picking it or by using another object selection method, or highlight text in a dialog box or text document.

What the Icons Mean

AutoCAD 2008 and AutoCAD LT 2008 Bible is liberally sprinkled with icons — symbols in the left margin that call your attention to noteworthy points.

AUTOCAD ONLY This icon means that the feature that I am discussing is not available in AutoCAD LT.

CAUTION The Caution icon means that you should pay special attention to the information or instructions because a possibility exists that you could cause a problem otherwise.

CROSS-REF Cross-References refer you to a related topic elsewhere in the book. Because you may not read this book straight through from cover to cover, you can use cross-references to quickly find just the information you need.

NEW FEATURE The New Feature icon means that a feature is new to AutoCAD 2008 or AutoCAD LT 2008 or has been significantly changed.

NOTE A Note icon alerts you to some important point that requires special attention, or additional information that may be helpful.

ON the DVD-ROM The On the DVD icon highlights references to related material on the DVD.

TIP A Tip shows you a way to accomplish a task more efficiently or quickly. You'll find plenty of practical advice here.

About the DVD

The DVD contains all of the drawings that you need to do the exercises in this book. These drawings are a great resource to help you learn using real-world drawings. In addition, the DVD includes the drawings that result after you finish an exercise or tutorial. In this way, you can check whether you have done an exercise correctly.

The DVD also contains many add-on programs that I hope you will find useful. I am especially pleased to include a 30-day trial versions of AutoCAD 2008 and AutoCAD LT 2008 on the DVD, as well as this entire book in (nonprintable) PDF format. Note that Chapter 37 has been moved to the DVD because of lack of room in the book.

Other Information

If you are already an advanced user but need tips and secrets for getting the most out of AutoCAD or AutoCAD LT, this book will probably not add too much to your already great store of knowledge. However, few people know everything about these complex programs, and so you may be surprised by what you can learn.

This book assumes that you know the basics of Windows, although the instructions that you'll read here are usually detailed enough to get you through any task.

If you do have AutoCAD and want a more basic book, look at *AutoCAD 2008 For Dummies*, by David Byrnes. Another option is *AutoCAD & AutoCAD LT All-in-One Desk Reference For Dummies* by David Byrnes and Lee Ambrosius. (Lee Ambrosius is also the technical editor for this book.)

AutoCAD 2008 and AutoCAD LT 2008 Bible covers AutoCAD 2008 and AutoCAD LT 2008. However, most of the information also applies to Release 2007 of both programs. I have used AutoCAD in Windows Vista, but almost everything also applies to Windows XP and 2000, although some of the screens will look different. If you are using AutoCAD LT 2008, again, some of the screens will look different. Where there is a significant difference between AutoCAD and AutoCAD LT, I explain the difference.

Contacting the Author

I would be happy to hear any comments that you have about this book. The best way to contact me is by e-mail at `ellen@ellenfinkelstein.com`. You can also use the United States Postal Service (a.k.a. snail mail) and write to me in care of Wiley. Please note that I can't provide technical support for my readers. The publisher maintains a page on its site that includes the drawings used in the exercises (in case you lose your DVD) and any errata at `www.wiley.com/go/autocad2008bible`. I have my own Web site at `www.ellenfinkelstein.com` that contains information on my books and on AutoCAD, including many AutoCAD tips. There you can also sign up for my AutoCAD Tips Newsletter.

Acknowledgments

I would like to offer special thanks to Tom Heine and then Courtney Allen, Jenny Watson, and Stephanie McComb, my acquisitions editors, who were very supportive throughout the writing of this book.

A huge thank-you goes to Jade Williams, whose infinite organizing power kept the book on track. Jade kept up with a seemingly infinite number of versions of text documents and images, coordinating the writing, editing, and production of the entire book.

My thanks to Lee Ambrosius, an AutoCAD consultant (www.hyperpics.com), and the highly knowledgeable technical editor for the book. Lee's comments improved the book throughout. I'm grateful to Melanie Perry for assisting me in updating several chapters.

I also thank Marylouise Wiack for her precise editing of this very technical book, and all of the people at Wiley who helped with the production of this book and its DVD.

Thanks to Abhi Singh, the AutoCAD Product Manager at Autodesk, Inc., for writing a great Foreword for this book. I also want to express my great appreciation to the members of Autodesk's beta and product teams who were very supportive throughout the alpha and beta period. They include: Shaan (the great) Hurley, Nate Bartley, and many others.

Many people contributed drawings and software for this book. I'd like to thank all of them. They have helped to make this book the most comprehensive book on AutoCAD and AutoCAD LT available.

Finally, I would like to thank my husband, Evan, and two kids, Yeshayah and Eliyah, who helped out around the house while I was writing, writing, and writing (and who wanted to see their names in print). Without their support, I could not have completed this book.

Contents at a Glance

Contents

Contents

Contents

Contents

Contents

Contents

Contents

Contents

Part V: Organizing and Managing Drawings · 887

Chapter 26: Keeping Control of Your Drawings · 889

Contents

Contents

Part I

AutoCAD and AutoCAD LT Basics

The six chapters in Part I provide all of the basics that you need to know to start drawing in AutoCAD or AutoCAD LT. These chapters are essential for the beginner, but even current users can find some new tips and pointers especially related to features that are new to AutoCAD 2008 and AutoCAD LT 2008. The Quick Start chapter is a beginner's tutorial to get you up and running immediately. You'll draw a window and have the opportunity to use many of the 2D features of AutoCAD and AutoCAD LT. This tutorial will provide a firm basis for the knowledge in the rest of this book.

Chapter 1 introduces you to AutoCAD and AutoCAD LT and surveys the main screen, including the menus, toolbars, command line, and status bar. You'll learn how to launch the program, execute a command in a variety of ways, save a drawing, close a drawing, and exit the program. Chapter 2 explains how to create and open drawings. Chapter 3 covers the many ways to use commands, while Chapter 4 discusses how to specify coordinates. Chapter 5 concludes Part I with an explanation of how to set up a drawing.

If you feel that you know enough to skip to Part II, skim this part for New Feature icons to find out about the latest developments in AutoCAD and AutoCAD LT.

Quick Start

Quick Start: Drawing a Window

Learning AutoCAD or AutoCAD LT is a bit like trying to decide which came first — the chicken or the egg. On one hand, you need to know the basics before you can start drawing. On the other hand, understanding the basics can be very difficult if you haven't had the experience of drawing something. In this Quick Start chapter, you resolve this problem by drawing, dimensioning, and printing a simple window in AutoCAD or AutoCAD LT.

This Quick Start chapter is meant for beginners. You'll get the feel of AutoCAD's precision drawing tools and experience how to build a drawing. The AutoCAD/AutoCAD LT interface, including the toolbars and menus, is very customizable. Note that the instructions for the exercise in this chapter assume that no one has made major changes to the default settings.

Chapters 1 through 5 fill you in on basic information that you need to move on to drawings that are more complex. By experiencing the drawing process first, you will find the initial learning curve to be easier and smoother.

> **NOTE** Don't worry if you don't immediately understand everything you're doing. It all becomes clear as you progress through this book. If you haven't read the Preface, now is a good time to go back and read the part that explains how to follow the exercises. When you type the X and Y coordinates (shown in bold), type the first number, a comma, and then the second number, with no spaces between them. The ⏎ symbol means to press Enter on your keyboard.

1. Start AutoCAD or AutoCAD LT.

   You may see a Workspaces dialog box. If so, choose 2D Drafting & Annotation from the list and click OK. You see the new drawing. (If you are prompted for a template, skip to Step 2, third sentence.)

2. Choose File ➪ New. The Select Template dialog box opens. Navigate to the `Drawings` folder of the DVD of this book, choose `abqs-a.dwt`, and click Open. You see a blank drawing. (I explain more about templates and opening drawings in Chapter 2.)

3. To save the drawing and give it a name, choose File ⇨ Save. In the Save Drawing As dialog box, use the Save In drop-down list to navigate to any convenient folder, such as the My Documents folder. Type **abqs-01** in the File Name text box and click Save. (I go into more detail about saving a drawing in Chapter 1.)

> **NOTE**   In Chapter 1, I provide instructions for creating a special AutoCAD Bible folder for all the exercises in this book. If you want to create this folder now, do so and save the drawing in that folder.

4. To free up the drawing area, close any windows or palettes that are open, by clicking their Close (X) button, so that your screen looks like Figure QS.2.

5. On the right side of the screen, you should see a palette, called the Dashboard, which contains the Layers *control panel* (section), as shown in Figures QS.1 and QS.2. If not, see the Note instructions following this step. From the Layer Control drop-down list on the Dashboard, click the down arrow and choose WINDOW, as shown in Figure QS.1. (Layers help you organize the objects in your drawing; I cover them in detail in Chapter 11.) Anything you draw will now be on the WINDOW layer.

> **NOTE**   If you don't see the Dashboard, choose Tools ⇨ Palettes ⇨ Dashboard. If you still don't see the Dashboard, it may be minimized to a thin, vertical bar, usually on the right side of your screen. Place your cursor over the bar, and the Dashboard should appear. For easier use during this tutorial, right-click the part of the vertical bar closest to the rest of the Dashboard; if the Auto-Hide item is checked, click it to uncheck it so that the Dashboard stays open. If you don't see the Layers control panel shown in Figure QS.1, right-click anywhere on the Dashboard and choose Control Panels ⇨ Layers.

FIGURE QS.1

Choose the WINDOW layer from the list of layers.

6. With your left mouse button (also called the *pick button*), choose Rectangle from the 2D Draw control panel of the Dashboard. The 2D Draw control panel should be above the Layers control panel that you used in the previous step. (Using the Dashboard is only one way to give AutoCAD and AutoCAD LT commands. I explain other ways in Chapter 3. You can find more about drawing lines and rectangles in Chapter 6.) Move your mouse so that the cursor is in the main drawing area. Your screen should look like Figure QS.2. (If you don't see the tooltip bar — also called the Dynamic Input tooltip — near the cursor, then click the DYN button on the status bar at the bottom of your screen.)

FIGURE QS.2

Starting to draw a rectangle.

Workspaces toolbar

Standard Annotation toolbar

2D Draw control panel

Layers control panel

Dynamic Input tooltip   Layer Control   Dashboard

7. Follow these prompts to draw a rectangle that is 44" wide and 80" high.

    ```
    Specify first corner point or
    [Chamfer/Elevation/Fillet/Thickness/Width]: 0,0 ↵
    Specify other corner point or [Area/Dimensions/Rotation]: 44,80 ↵
    ```

 NOTE   You see the full prompt shown here in the Command window at the bottom of your screen. You see an abbreviated version of the same prompt in the Dynamic Input tooltip that appears near the mouse cursor. In an architectural drawing, distances are assumed to be in inches, so you don't need to specify a unit (although you can if you want).

Notice that the text that you type in appears next to the cursor in the Dynamic Input tooltip. When you press Enter, the text that you typed is echoed in the Command Line window at the bottom of the screen.

8. To create a second rectangle inside the first one, choose Offset from the 2D Draw control panel of the Dashboard, and follow these prompts:

    ```
    Specify offset distance or [Through/Erase/Layer] <Through>: 4 ↵
    Select object to offset or [Exit/Undo] <Exit>: Click the rectangle's
    border to select it.
    ```

```
Specify point on side to offset or [Exit/Multiple/Undo] <Exit>: Click
anywhere inside the rectangle.
Select object to offset or [Exit/Undo] <Exit>: ↵
```

 9. You can draw from geometric points on objects such as endpoints and midpoints. (I explain how to specify coordinate points in Chapter 4.) To draw a line between the midpoints of the inner rectangle, choose Line from the 2D Draw control panel of the Dashboard and follow these prompts:

```
Specify first point: Press and hold the Shift key and right-click.
From the shortcut menu that opens, choose Midpoint. Place the cursor
near the midpoint of the left side of the inner rectangle. When you
see a triangle and the Midpoint tooltip, click.
Specify next point or [Undo]: Press and hold the Shift key and right-
click. From the shortcut menu that opens, choose Midpoint. This time,
place the cursor near the midpoint of the right side of the inner
rectangle. When you see the Midpoint tooltip and triangle, click.
Specify next point or [Undo]: ↵
```

Your drawing should now look like Figure QS.3. (Your window should be green.)

FIGURE QS.3

The beginning of a window.

 10. You will now draw a temporary construction line to help you find a starting point for the pane in the top of the window. From the 2D Draw control panel of the Dashboard, choose Line. Follow these prompts:

```
Specify first point: Press Shift and right-click. Choose Endpoint from
the shortcut menu. Pick the left endpoint of the last line you drew.
```

Specify next point or [Undo]: **4,4** ↵. (This notation specifies that the endpoint of the line is 4 units above and to the right of the first point. Chapter 4 explains more about specifying coordinates in this manner.)
Specify next point or [Undo]: ↵

11. Again, choose Rectangle from the 2D Draw control panel of the Dashboard. Follow these prompts:

Specify first corner point or [Chamfer/Elevation/Fillet/Thickness/Width]: *Press Shift and right-click. Choose Endpoint and pick the final endpoint of the diagonal line you just drew.*
Specify other corner point or [Area/Dimensions/Rotation]: **2'4",2'4"** ↵

> **NOTE** This notation specifies 2 feet, 4 inches in the X and Y directions.

12. Choose Erase from the 2D Draw control panel of the Dashboard. At the Select objects: prompt, click the short, diagonal construction line that you drew in Step 9. The Select objects: prompt appears again. Press Enter to end the command. (Chapter 9 explains the ERASE command as well as other simple editing commands.)

13. Click the ORTHO button on the status bar at the bottom of the drawing area if it is not already selected (indented). The ORTHO feature constrains drawing to right angles — either horizontal or vertical. (You can find more about ORTHO in Chapter 4.)

14. To finish the bottom of the window, choose Line from the 2D Draw control panel of the Dashboard. Follow these prompts:

Specify first point: **8",3'4"** ↵
Specify next point or [Undo]: *Move the mouse cursor down from the start point of the line. You see a temporary drag line. Then type the following length of the line.* **2'8-7/16** ↵

> **NOTE** You can see what you type in the Dynamic Input tooltip as you are typing. Therefore, you can check that you've typed the right numbers before you press Enter.

Specify next point or [Undo]: *Move the cursor horizontally to the right and type* **28** ↵.
Specify next point or [Close/Undo]: *Now try entering the distance using decimal notation, instead of feet and inches. Move the cursor up and type* **32.4375** ↵
Specify next point or [Close/Undo]: ↵

15. To draw shutters, first change the layer. Click the Layer Control drop-down list in the Layers control panel of the Dashboard, and choose EXWALL.

16. Choose Line from the 2D Draw control panel of the Dashboard. Follow the prompts:

Specify first point: *Press Shift and right-click. Choose Endpoint from the shortcut menu. Click the upper-left corner of the window.*
Specify next point or [Undo]: *Move the cursor to the left. Type* **1'6"** ↵
Specify next point or [Undo]: *Move the cursor down. Type* **6'8"** ↵
Specify next point or [Close/Undo]: *Type* **#0,0** ↵. (The pound sign ensures that your line goes to 0,0 no matter where you are.)
Specify next point or [Close/Undo]: ↵

17. To draw the opposite shutter, you'll mirror the first shutter that you just drew. (I cover the MIRROR command and many other editing commands in Chapter 10.) Choose Mirror from the 2D Draw control panel of the Dashboard and follow these prompts:

```
Select objects: Click the three lines that make up the shutter.
Select objects: ↵
Specify first point of mirror line: Press Shift and right-click.
Choose Midpoint from the shortcut menu.
Click near the middle of the top horizontal line of the window.
Specify second point of mirror line: (The ORTHO button should still
be indented. If it isn't, click it.) Move the cursor downward and
pick any point.
Erase source objects? [Yes/No] <N>: ↵
```

The window should look like Figure QS.4.

FIGURE QS.4

The completed window.

18. To add a dimension to the bottom of the window, you should first change the layer. From the Layer Control drop-down list on the Layers control panel of the Dashboard, choose DIMENSION. (Chapters 14 and 15 explain how to create and format all types of dimensions.)

19. To place the dimension, choose Dimension ➪ Linear from the menu. Follow the prompts.

```
Specify first extension line origin or <select object>: ↵ (Pressing
Enter lets you select an object to dimension.)
Select object to dimension: Pick the bottom horizontal line of the
window (the bottom of the rectangle).
Specify dimension line location or
[Mtext/Text/Angle/Horizontal/Vertical/Rotated]:
Move the cursor down until the dimension is nicely spaced below the
window. Click to place the dimension line.
```

NOTE If you don't have enough room to place the dimension below the window, click the down arrow of the vertical scrollbar as necessary. I explain additional techniques for changing the view of your drawing in Chapter 8.

20. Click Save on the Standard Annotation toolbar to save your work.

 21. To prepare for printing, click the Layout tab, A Title Block-Landscape, at the bottom of the drawing area. If you don't see any tabs, click the A Title Block-Landscape button at the right end of the row of buttons on the status bar below the drawing area. You then see the window inside a title block and border, as shown in Figure QS.5. This title block and border come with the template to help you easily prepare the drawing for printing. (Chapter 17 explains how to lay out and print/plot a drawing.)

FIGURE QS.5

The window with a title block as it appears on the Layout tab.

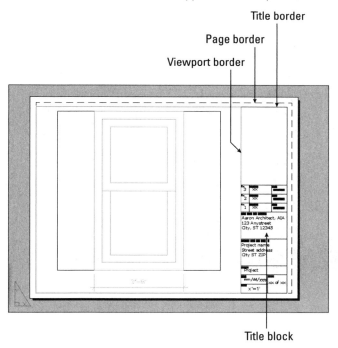

Title border

Page border

Viewport border

Title block

22. To set the scale for printing, click the magenta viewport border (labeled in Figure QS.5). Choose Tools ➪ Palettes ➪ Properties. In the Properties palette, click the Standard Scale item. (To see this item, you may have to scroll down in the Properties palette or enlarge it by dragging on its bottom and right edges. If the palette collapses to a thin bar, pass your cursor over the bar to expand it.) Click the down arrow that appears to the right of this item and check that the scale is set to 1" = 1'-0". Click the Close button at the top of the Properties palette. (I explain more about scales in Chapter 5.)

23. If the window and its dimension are not centered in the viewport window, double-click inside the viewport border. Then choose View ➪ Pan ➪ Realtime. Click and drag as necessary to center the window in the viewport. Press Esc to exit Pan mode. Double-click outside the viewport border to return to the layout.

24. To add some text to the title block, you need to zoom in. (I explain zooming in more detail in Chapter 8.) Choose View ➪ Zoom ➪ Window. Follow the prompts:

```
Specify first corner: Click slightly above and to the left of the
words Project Name.
Specify opposite corner: Click slightly below and to the right of the
words City ST ZIP.
```

These words should now appear very large in the drawing area. They are already placed and formatted, so all you need to do is replace them. (I explain all about how to create and edit text in Chapter 13.)

25. Double-click the `Project name` text. The Text Formatting toolbar opens, along with a ruler, as shown in Figure QS.6.

FIGURE QS.6

Editing text for a drawing.

26. Select the text by dragging from the upper-left corner to the lower-right corner. Type the following:

```
Double-hung window ↵
2010 Coral Lane ↵
Anytown, IA 12345
```

Click OK on the Text Formatting toolbar to close the In-Place Text Editor.

27. To return to your previous view, choose View ➪ Zoom ➪ Previous from the menu.

28. Click Save on the Standard Annotation toolbar to save your drawing.

 29. You're ready to print your drawing! Depending on your setup, either you can print directly to your printer, or if you have a plotter available, you can use that. (The layout is set up to fit on an 8½-x-11-inch or A-size paper.) Choose Plot on the Standard Annotation toolbar. The Plot dialog box opens. (I cover printing and plotting in Chapter 17. Appendix A explains how to configure a printer or plotter.)

30. In the Printer/plotter section of the Plot dialog box, click the Name drop-down list and choose the printer or plotter that you want to use.

31. Click the Preview button to open the preview window. You should see the window and its title block laid out as shown in Figure QS.7.

FIGURE QS.7

Viewing the window in Preview mode.

NOTE   If things don't seem right, click the Close Preview Window button and review the previous steps to see if you can find the problem. Also, see the sidebar, "Help! My Drawing Doesn't Look Like the Figure."

 32. Make sure your printer or plotter has an 8½-x-11-inch or A-size sheet of paper, and click the Plot button on the Preview window's toolbar. Congratulations! You've just created and printed your first drawing!

 33. Click the Close button at the upper-right corner of the AutoCAD application window to close both AutoCAD and the drawing. Click Yes to save your changes.

Help! My Drawing Doesn't Look Like the Figure

If your drawing doesn't look like the image shown in Figure QS.7, there could be several reasons. To fix the problem, try one of the following solutions:

- You may have made a mistake when creating the drawing. If you think that's the case, start over and follow the prompts again.
- You may have started AutoCAD or AutoCAD LT based on a template with different properties from the default. Be sure to use the template on the *AutoCAD 2008 and AutoCAD LT 2008 Bible* DVD, as explained in Step 2 of the previous exercise. Then follow the prompts again.
- If your drawing still seems wrong, put the DVD that accompanies this book in your DVD drive. Choose File ➪ Open and use the Open dialog box to find `abqs-01.dwg` in the `Results` folder on the DVD. This drawing contains the end result of the exercise. You can try to find the difference between this drawing and yours. You can also copy `abqs-01.dwg` from the DVD to your hard drive and print or plot it.

One of the preceding options should solve your problem.

NOTE It's important to understand that this Quick Start tutorial used techniques that are easiest to understand for beginners; as a result, the techniques were sometimes a little awkward. AutoCAD and AutoCAD LT have many capabilities that make drawing easier and faster. You learn all these features in this book.

Summary

In this exercise, you practiced many of the skills that you need to use AutoCAD or AutoCAD LT effectively. Most of your work in AutoCAD or AutoCAD LT builds on these basic skills. The rest of the chapters in this book explain these procedures in more detail as well as many features not covered in this Quick Start exercise.

Chapter 1

Starting to Draw

In this chapter, I explain the essentials that you need to start drawings. After a little background, I discuss the basics of the screen that you see when you open AutoCAD or AutoCAD LT, and how to use it. If you've never used AutoCAD before, do the Quick Start chapter first, "Quick Start: Drawing a Window."

AutoCAD and its younger brother, AutoCAD LT, are both created by Autodesk. Together they are the most widely used technical drawing programs anywhere. AutoCAD alone has more than 3,000,000 registered users. According to Autodesk, CAD stands for *computer-aided design*, but it can also stand for computer-aided *drafting* or *drawing*.

The first version of AutoCAD, running under DOS, came out in 1982. AutoCAD was the first significant CAD program to run on a desktop computer. At the time, most other technical drawing programs ran on high-end workstations or even mainframes. AutoCAD LT was introduced in 1993, as a less expensive alternative to AutoCAD, for people who don't need all of AutoCAD's advanced features.

IN THIS CHAPTER

Getting acquainted with AutoCAD and AutoCAD LT

Starting AutoCAD and AutoCAD LT

Creating a new drawing

Using the AutoCAD and AutoCAD LT interface

Saving your drawing

Closing a drawing and exiting AutoCAD and AutoCAD LT

AutoCAD's Advantages

AutoCAD's success has been attributed to its famous *open architecture* — the flexibility that the end user has to customize the program using source code files in plain text (ASCII) format — and programming languages (such as AutoLISP and Visual Basic for Applications).

As a result, AutoCAD is an extremely flexible drafting program, applicable to all fields. AutoCAD's support for languages other than English, including those using other alphabets, is unparalleled, making AutoCAD highly popular abroad. As a result, AutoCAD is used in all disciplines and in more than 150 countries.

Through a high level of technical innovation and expertise, Autodesk has created a program with advanced features and capabilities, including 3D surface and solid modeling and visualization, access to external databases, intelligent dimensioning, importing and exporting of other file formats, Internet support, and much more.

The major disciplines that use AutoCAD are:

- Architectural, Engineering, and Construction (AEC)
- Mechanical
- Geographic Information Systems (GIS)
- Surveying and Civil Engineering
- Facilities Management
- Electrical/electronic
- Multimedia

However, AutoCAD has many other lesser-known uses, such as pattern making in the garment industry, sign making, and so on. In this book, I try to provide examples from many fields. The world of AutoCAD is very broad, and you can learn from seeing the many approaches that AutoCAD makes possible.

Comparing AutoCAD and AutoCAD LT

AutoCAD LT's advantages are its lower cost and its compatibility with AutoCAD. The programming code that is used to create AutoCAD LT is a subset of the code used in AutoCAD. Here are the major differences between AutoCAD and AutoCAD LT:

- AutoCAD includes features that enable CAD managers to hold drawings to certain standards, such as for layer names and text styles. AutoCAD LT doesn't contain these features.
- AutoCAD LT is not as customizable as AutoCAD, which is both programmable and fully customizable.
- AutoCAD LT includes minimal options for 3D; AutoCAD includes a full-featured 3D capability.
- AutoCAD LT has fewer presentation features than AutoCAD, which includes gradient fills, true color display, and 3D rendering.
- AutoCAD LT is deployable on a network but does not have AutoCAD's network license management feature that includes reporting and flexible licensing.
- AutoCAD LT does not offer the database connectivity feature, but you can now use tables to connect to data in a Microsoft Office Excel file; AutoCAD offers the flexibility to connect to other types of databases, create labels from the data, and so on.
- AutoCAD LT does not include AutoCAD's quick-dimensioning feature, which allows you to quickly insert a number of dimensions, one after the other.
- AutoCAD LT does not come with Express Tools, a set of additional routines that ship with AutoCAD.
- AutoCAD LT does not include sheet sets and fields, two features that were introduced in AutoCAD 2005.

AutoCAD and AutoCAD LT have a few other minor differences, as well. Some of these differences are only in the user interface, so that you can accomplish the same task but the procedure is slightly different.

Starting AutoCAD and AutoCAD LT

This section starts a quick tour of AutoCAD and AutoCAD LT. The first step is to start the program.

ON the DVD-ROM The DVD contains a 30-day trial version of AutoCAD 2008 and AutoCAD LT 2008.

This book covers AutoCAD 2008 and AutoCAD LT 2008 running on Windows 2000, Windows XP Home/Professional, or Windows Vista. (Most of the figures were taken in Windows Vista.) Every computer is set up somewhat differently, so you may need to adjust the following steps slightly. If you didn't install the software yourself and are unfamiliar with the folders (also called *directories*) on your computer, get help from someone who is familiar with your computer system.

CROSS-REF If you need information on installing AutoCAD or AutoCAD LT, see Appendix A. Appendix A also covers configuring the software and printers or plotters.

By default, installing AutoCAD or AutoCAD LT places a shortcut on your desktop, as shown in Figure 1.1. You can double-click one of the shortcuts to launch the program that is installed on your machine, or you may choose one of the following:

- For AutoCAD: Start ⇨ (All) Programs ⇨ Autodesk ⇨ AutoCAD 2008 ⇨ AutoCAD 2008
- For AutoCAD LT: Start ⇨ (All) Programs ⇨ Autodesk ⇨ AutoCAD LT 2008 ⇨ AutoCAD LT 2008

FIGURE 1.1

A shortcut on the desktop provides a quick way to open AutoCAD or AutoCAD LT.

Creating a New Drawing

After you launch AutoCAD or AutoCAD LT, it automatically opens a new drawing named Drawing1.dwg. You can see the drawing name on the title bar. You can start drawing immediately. In Chapter 2, I explain how to start a drawing based on a template and how to open an existing drawing.

STEPS: Starting AutoCAD or AutoCAD LT

1. Click Start on the taskbar at the bottom of your screen.
2. Choose one of the following:
   - **For AutoCAD:** Start ⇨ (All) Programs ⇨ Autodesk ⇨ AutoCAD 2008 ⇨ AutoCAD 2008
   - **For AutoCAD LT:** Start ⇨ (All) Programs ⇨ Autodesk ⇨ AutoCAD LT 2008 ⇨ AutoCAD LT 2008

   You see a blank drawing named Drawing1.dwg.

If you are continuing with this chapter, keep this drawing open. I cover exiting from AutoCAD and AutoCAD LT later in this chapter.

Using the AutoCAD and AutoCAD LT Interface

AutoCAD offers three quite different preset *workspaces*, depending on how you want to work. For example, these workspaces determine the toolbars that you see. Also, AutoCAD offers both 2D and 3D environments. The 3D environment is quite different from the AutoCAD LT screen, but the AutoCAD 2D and the AutoCAD LT environments are similar. In this section, I discuss the 2D environment. Both AutoCAD and AutoCAD LT offer two 2D workspaces: 2D Drafting & Annotation and AutoCAD (or AutoCAD LT) Classic. These two workspaces offer different configurations of toolbars and other tools. The 2D Drafting & Annotation workspace is the default workspace.

NOTE AutoCAD's 3D environment includes the 3D Modeling workspace, and the drawing templates acad3D.dwt and acadiso3D.dwt. (I cover templates in Chapter 2.) I cover this 3D environment in Part IV, "Drawing in Three Dimensions."

Figure 1.2 shows the default screen that appears when you first open AutoCAD or AutoCAD LT. Your screen may look somewhat different — remember that AutoCAD and AutoCAD LT can be customized in many ways — but the general features will be the same.

NOTE If you see other items open on your screen, you can close all of these items by clicking their Close (X) button. Also, by default, the screen is black, rather than the white screen that you see in Figure 1.2. You can leave it that way or change the drawing area color, as I explain in Appendix A.

If you find yourself in a 3D environment in AutoCAD, you'll see a gray background and a perspective view. To work in 2D in AutoCAD, you need to switch to a 2D environment. To switch to a 2D environment, follow these steps in AutoCAD:

1. From the Workspaces toolbar, choose 2D Drafting & Annotation from the drop-down list. This displays the Dashboard with 2D commands.
2. Choose File ⇨ New. From the Select Template dialog box, choose acad.dwt and click Open. This places you in a 2D view and turns off the grid.

The AutoCAD and AutoCAD LT screens consist of four important areas. These are discussed in the following sections.

The drawing area

The blank area in the middle of the screen, called the *graphics window* or *drawing area,* is where you draw. You can think of this as a sheet of drafting paper, except that this piece of paper can be any size — even the size of a huge factory!

By default, you draw in *model space,* so called because that's where you draw your models. When you create a new drawing, by default, you are in model space, so that you can just start drawing. You can lay out your drawings for plotting in *paper space,* also called a *layout.* To switch from model space to a layout, use the tabs at the bottom of the drawing area. (See the section "Creating a Layout in Paper Space" in Chapter 17 for details.)

FIGURE 1.2

The AutoCAD and AutoCAD LT screens are very similar.

Drawing Minimize, Maximize, and Close button

Application Minimize, Maximize, and Close button

Workspaces toolbar   InfoCenter

Menu bar   Standard Annotation toolbar

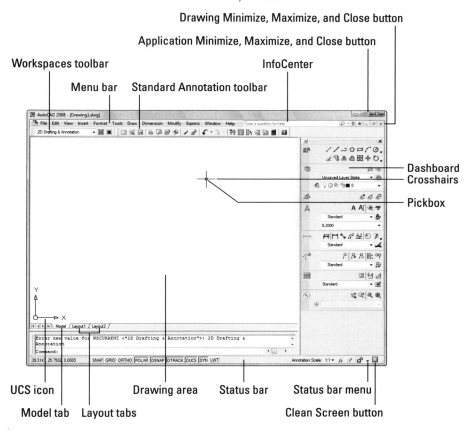

Dashboard
Crosshairs

Pickbox

UCS icon   Drawing area   Status bar   Status bar menu

Model tab Layout tabs   Clean Screen button

> **NOTE** Instead of the model and layout tabs, you may see two buttons on the status bar that you can use to switch between model space and paper space.

When you start to draw, you need to specify where to start drawing. One way is to use coordinates. To specify a coordinate, the universally accepted convention is to put the X coordinate first, followed by a comma, and then the Y coordinate. Examples are –3,5, 3,2, 6,–2, and –1,–1. These coordinates specify points in the drawing area.

> **CROSS-REF** Chapter 4 is devoted to explaining how to specify coordinates. To create three-dimensional models, you need to add a Z coordinate when specifying a point. Chapter 21 discusses three-dimensional coordinates.

> **TIP** If you want the maximum amount of free space for drawing, click the Clean Screen button at the right side of the status bar to remove the title bar, toolbars, palettes, and the status bar. Click the same button to get them back. You can also press Ctrl+0 to toggle between the two displays.

The UCS icon

Notice the symbol with two arrows in the drawing area in Figure 1.2. This symbol is called the User Coordinate System (UCS) icon. The arrows point to the positive directions of the X and Y axes to help you keep your bearings. (In a 3D environment, you see a Z axis as well.) You can change the look of this icon, and turn it on and off, as I explain in Chapter 8.

The crosshairs

In the drawing area of Figure 1.2, notice the intersecting lines with a small box at their intersection. The small box is called the *pickbox* because it helps you to select, or pick, objects. The lines are called *crosshairs*. They show you the location of the mouse cursor in relation to other objects in your drawing.

As you move your mouse around, the pickbox and crosshairs move with your mouse. At the bottom of your screen, at the left end of the status bar (described later), you can see the X,Y, coordinates change as you move your mouse.

The menus and toolbars

At the top of your screen is the title bar, and directly beneath the title bar is a menu bar. Below that are one or two rows of toolbars. In addition, on the right is the Dashboard, which you use to give AutoCAD or AutoCAD LT commands to draw, edit, display information, and so on. You also use the Dashboard to change settings. I explain how to work with toolbars and the Dashboard in Chapter 3.

> **NOTE** The AutoCAD Classic and AutoCAD LT Classic workspaces do not show the Dashboard; instead, you see three additional toolbars — the Draw, Modify, and Draw Order toolbars — which are usually docked at the left and right sides of the screen. From the Workspaces toolbar drop-down list, try switching between the 2D Drafting & Annotation workspace and the AutoCAD or AutoCAD LT Classic workspace to see which one you prefer. In Appendix A, I explain how to customize workspaces.

In the 2D Draw *control panel* (section) of the Dashboard or on the Draw toolbar, move the mouse cursor over the first button. You should see a tooltip that says Line, as shown in Figure 1.3. Also notice the status bar when the cursor is over the button on the toolbar, it tells you that this button creates straight-line segments. You use buttons on a toolbar or control panel to execute commands. For example, to draw a line, you click the Line button on the Draw toolbar. You get some practice drawing lines in the exercise that follows.

FIGURE 1.3

Moving the cursor over the Line button displays a tooltip.

> **NOTE** If you inadvertently start a command that you don't want to use, press Esc.

Because you can customize the menus, toolbars, and the Dashboard to suit your needs, your screen may appear somewhat different. AutoCAD and AutoCAD LT provide many more toolbars that you can display when you need them. Some examples of toolbars are Dimension, View, and Zoom. You learn about these, and more, later in this book.

TIP You can lock the position of toolbars and windows (palettes). On the right side of the status bar, at the bottom of the screen, is a lock icon. Click this icon to open a menu allowing you to individually lock floating toolbars, docked toolbars, floating windows (palettes), and docked windows (palettes). You can also choose the All option and lock or unlock all your toolbars and palettes. Locking these interface components prevents you from moving them inadvertently.

The command line and dynamic input tooltip

At the bottom of the screen, you see a separate window showing approximately three lines of text. (You can change it to show as many lines as you like by dragging the top edge of the window up or down.) Notice the word Command:. This is the *command line*. All commands can be executed by typing them on the command line.

Even if you use a menu item or toolbar button to execute a command, you may see a response on the command line. AutoCAD and AutoCAD LT often provide options that must be typed in from the keyboard. Text that you type appears on the command line. For example, when you type coordinates specifying a point, they appear on the command line.

The Dynamic Input tooltip allows you to see the text that you type at the cursor. This tooltip doesn't appear until you start typing a command. You can also choose options near the tooltip. (For more information, see the section "The Command Line and Dynamic Input" in Chapter 3.)

To see more of the command line, press F2 to open the AutoCAD or AutoCAD LT Text Window. You can scroll back through previous commands. Press F2 again to close the window. You can also simply hide the Text window by clicking in the AutoCAD or AutoCAD LT window for easy access to the Text window later from the Windows taskbar.

The status bar

At the very bottom of the screen is the *status bar* (refer to Figure 1.2). At the left are the X,Y coordinates. As you move your mouse, these coordinates change. (If they don't change, click them and move your mouse again.) The status bar also contains several buttons that I explain later in this book.

At the right side of the status bar is a small down arrow. Click it to open the status bar menu. This menu determines which buttons appear on the status bar. If you don't use a certain button, choose it on the menu to remove its checkmark and make it disappear. You can always go back and choose the item again to redisplay the button.

Creating a New Folder

For your work with this book, you should create a new folder so that you can save your exercise drawings where they won't get mixed up with other drawings. The following directions leave it up to you where to create this new folder. Each computer system is organized differently. If you aren't sure what to do, choose the drive (not the folder) where AutoCAD or AutoCAD LT is installed and create a new folder there.

CAUTION I do not recommend creating a subfolder in the AutoCAD 2008 or AutoCAD LT 2008 folder. This folder contains the files that make up the program. If you keep your drawings here, it is too easy to make a mistake and delete necessary program files. Some people create a subfolder in the My Documents or Documents folder.

STEPS: Creating a New Folder

1. Move the mouse cursor down to the taskbar at the bottom of your screen and right-click the Start button.

2. Choose Explore.

3. On the left pane of Windows Explorer, click the drive where you want to create the new folder. If you don't know where to create the folder, choose the drive where AutoCAD or AutoCAD LT is installed. If you're on a network, choose the drive that represents your computer. If you keep your work in subfolders of the My Documents (Documents in Windows Vista) folder, click that folder.

4. If you want to make a *subfolder* (a folder within a folder), choose the folder where you want to create the subfolder.

5. From the Explorer menu, choose File ➪ New ➪ Folder, or Organize ➪ New Folder. A new, highlighted folder, named New Folder, appears in the right pane. You may have to scroll down to see it.

6. Type **AutoCAD Bible** for the folder name and press Enter. (If you did the exercises from a previous edition of this book, such as *AutoCAD 2007 and AutoCAD LT 2007 Bible,* and you already have a folder named AutoCAD Bible, first rename the original folder to something such as ACAD2007Bible.)

Save all drawings that you create for this book in your AutoCAD Bible folder.

 Creating a folder for your drawings as described in the previous steps is essential before you go on to exercises in the rest of this book.

Using the Interface

If you did the Quick Start exercise, you had the experience of drawing a window, but I chose the simplest method of completing each task because I had not yet described the AutoCAD and AutoCAD LT screen. In the following exercise, you draw some simple objects, but experiment with all the features of the user interface to get a feel for how they work. (Chapter 3 explains in more detail how to use commands.)

For this exercise, simply follow the instructions exactly. When you type the X and Y coordinates (shown in bold), type the first number, a comma, and then the second number, with no spaces between them.

TIP Don't worry if you don't understand everything you're doing. It all becomes clear as you progress through this book. If you haven't read the Preface, now is a good time to go back and read the part that explains how to follow the exercises.

Follow the prompts shown next. As explained in the Preface, you type what appears in **bold**.

STEPS: Drawing a Line in Four Ways

1. Start AutoCAD or AutoCAD LT.

   You see a new drawing. (If you are prompted for a template, type or choose acad.dwt. or acadlt.dwt.)

2. From the menu, choose Draw ➪ Line.

3. Move your mouse to move the crosshairs cursor around the screen. Notice the Dynamic Input tooltip that follows the cursor around, as shown in Figure 1.4. (If you don't see the Dynamic

Input tooltip, click the DYN button on the status bar.) At the same time, notice the coordinates changing on the left side of the status bar.

FIGURE 1.4

When you move the mouse around, the Dynamic Input bar follows the cursor, displaying the current coordinates.

4. Anywhere on the screen, stop moving the mouse and click the left mouse button to pick a point. When you move the mouse again, the Dynamic Input bar changes to prompt you to specify the next point and to show you the angle and length of the cursor from the original point you picked, as shown in Figure 1.5.

FIGURE 1.5

After specifying the first point of a line, the Dynamic Input bar prompts you for the next point.

5. Pick any point to create a line segment. You see the same Dynamic Input tooltip as before, which means that you can continue to create more line segments. (Chapter 6 is all about drawing lines.)

6. Press Enter to end the command and finish your line.

7. For your second line, choose Line from the 2D Draw control panel of the Dashboard. Again, pick any point on the screen.

NOTE   Figure 1.2 labels the Dashboard. If you don't see the Dashboard, type **dashboard** at the command prompt. If you don't see the 2D Draw control panel, which is the top section in Figure 1.2, right-click anywhere on the Dashboard and choose Control Panels ➪ 2D Draw.

8. Move your mouse so you can see the length and angle tooltips. Notice the value for the length. Now type a different value and press Enter. For example, if the Length tooltip says 13.7638, type **5** ⏎.

9. Press Enter to end the command. The line's length is based on what you typed, not where the cursor was, but the line's angle is the same as it was before you typed in the length.

10. For your third line, type **line**. Notice that the text appears in the Dynamic Input tooltip as you type, but not in the command-line area.

11. Press Enter. You now see the command that you typed in the command line area as well as the Dynamic Input prompt to specify the first point.

12. Click in two places to pick a start point and an endpoint.

13. This time, to end the line, right-click anywhere in the drawing area. By default, this opens a shortcut menu, but it may end the command. If so, you're done. If you see the shortcut menu, choose Enter from the shortcut menu to end the command.

14. For your fourth line, if you don't see the Draw toolbar, right-click any toolbar that is already displayed and choose Draw from the list of toolbars. Click the Line button on the Draw toolbar. Move the mouse so that the cursor is in the drawing area. Pick two different points and press Enter.

15. Leave the drawing on your screen and read on to the next exercise to save the drawing.

You should now have four lines on the screen. You can see how the interface offers several ways to work. You can use the method that suits you best.

Saving a Drawing

Saving a drawing is similar to saving any other file in Windows. You should get in the habit of saving your work every 10 to 15 minutes to avoid losing your work in case the software or your computer system crashes.

Saving a drawing for the first time is different from saving it subsequently because you have to name the drawing the first time you save it.

To save a drawing, click Save on the Standard Annotation toolbar. If you're saving a drawing for the first time, the Save Drawing As dialog box appears, as shown in Figure 1.6.

FIGURE 1.6

The Save Drawing As dialog box.

Down the left side of the dialog box are several buttons to help you find a location to save drawings more quickly. Together, these buttons are called the *Places list*. Use the Places list as follows:

- **History** lists shortcuts to recently used drawings.

- **My Documents (Windows XP) or Documents (Windows Vista)** lists drawings and folders in the My Documents or Documents folder. Some people store files in this folder. (Windows 2000 may call this the Personal folder.)

- **Favorites** lists files and folders in the Favorites folder. You may have an Autodesk subfolder; if so, double-click the Autodesk subfolder to save a drawing there. Usually, this folder contains only shortcuts to files saved elsewhere. To put a shortcut to an already saved drawing in Favorites, choose File ⇨ Save As and click the Tools drop-down list; then click Add to Favorites. You can later open the file from the Favorites folder.

- **Desktop** shows drawings on your desktop.

- **FTP** switches you to the FTP locations folder, where you can find an FTP location that you have set up, as explained in the following discussion of the Tools drop-down list.

- **Buzzsaw** sends you to www.buzzsaw.com, the Autodesk business-to-business portal for the building design and construction industry. You can set up a new account or access existing projects.

 Conveniently, you can reorder the buttons in the Places list. Just drag any button to a new location.

Of course, you can also choose a location from the Save In drop-down list to which you want to save the file. To save a file, type a filename in the File Name text box and click Save to save the file.

Use the Views drop-down list of the dialog box to specify how you want to display files in this dialog box. List just displays the name; Details adds the file size, type, and date modified; Thumbnails and Preview add a preview image of the drawing.

Use the Tools drop-down list of the dialog box to do the following:

- **Add or Modify FTP Locations:** FTP sites are locations on the Internet for transferring files. To add or modify FTP locations, choose Tools ⇨ Add/Modify FTP Locations from the menu of the Save Drawing As dialog box. You need to list the name of the FTP site, choose a logon type (Anonymous or User), and specify your user name and password if you're logging on as a User. You can then save drawings (called *uploading*) to FTP locations by clicking the Save In drop-down list and choosing FTP Locations. This feature makes an intranet or any server with FTP capability as accessible as your own computer system.

- **Add Current Folder to Places:** If you save to a specific folder often, you can navigate to that folder and then choose Tools ⇨ Add Current Folder to Places. The Places Bar then displays a new button for that folder so that you can easily click the button to go straight to the folder.

- **Add to Favorites:** When you have navigated to a folder, you can add it to the Favorites folder by choosing Tools ⇨ Add to Favorites. You can also select a file in a folder and add it to the Favorites folder.

- **Options:** The Options dialog box opens, where you can specify certain settings relating to saving drawings. I discuss these options in Chapter 8 and Appendix A.

- **Security Options:** Choose this setting to set a password or attach a digital signature. I discuss these features in Chapter 26.

AUTOCAD ONLY The SAVEALL command of the Express Tools saves all open drawings, without closing them. Choose Express ➪ File tools ➪ Save All Drawings. If a drawing hasn't been saved, you are prompted for a filename.

ON the DVD-ROM The DVD includes a small program, savea.lsp, that automatically backs up your drawing to the floppy drive after you've saved it on your hard drive. If you like to back up to a diskette regularly for safety, this program can be useful. Look in \Software\Chapter 01\Savea. The file contains instructions for changing the drive to any letter you use, such as D:. (AutoCAD only.)

STEPS: Saving a Drawing for the First Time

1. The four lines you created earlier in this chapter should still be on your screen. Click Save on the Standard Annotation toolbar. The Save Drawing As dialog box opens.
2. Click the Save In drop-down list. If necessary, choose the drive where you created your AutoCAD Bible folder for this book.
3. Double-click the AutoCAD Bible folder.
4. In the File Name text box, select the filename. Type **ab01-01** and press Enter (or click Save).
5. Keep your drawing on the screen and go to the next exercise.

AutoCAD saves your drawing under the name ab01-01.dwg. This numbering system will help you organize your drawings from this book and find equivalent drawings on the DVD more easily. It just means that this is the first drawing from Chapter 1 of *AutoCAD 2008 and AutoCAD LT 2008 Bible*.

Closing a Drawing and Exiting from AutoCAD and AutoCAD LT

You can close your drawing and keep AutoCAD or AutoCAD LT open. The simplest way to do this is to use the drawing Close button just under the application Close button. You can also choose File ➪ Close.

TIP You can choose Window ➪ Close All to close all open drawings. If any of the open drawings have unsaved changes, AutoCAD or AutoCAD LT prompts you to save the changes. If you have AutoCAD, you can choose Express ➪ File tools ➪ Quick Exit, which closes all open drawings (prompting you to save if necessary) and then exits the program.

To exit AutoCAD or AutoCAD LT, click the Close (X) box at the top-right corner of your screen. You can also exit out of AutoCAD or AutoCAD LT by typing **quit** on the command line and pressing Enter. Another method is to choose File ➪ Exit.

If you've made any changes to your drawing since last saving it, AutoCAD or AutoCAD LT asks you if you want to save your changes. Choose Yes or No as your situation requires. Choosing Cancel returns you to your drawing. If you have opened more than one drawing to which you have made changes, you have a chance to save each drawing in turn so that you don't exit AutoCAD or AutoCAD LT without saving all the changes you've made in your open drawings.

STEPS: Closing Your Drawing and Exiting AutoCAD or AutoCAD LT

1. Your drawing should still be on your screen. Choose File ⇨ Close. You now see a gray screen with no drawing. (Repeat this process if you have other drawings open. Save or cancel the changes to these extra open drawings as you like.)

2. Click the Close button in the upper-right corner to exit AutoCAD or AutoCAD LT. The program closes immediately.

Summary

In Chapter 1, I explained how to start AutoCAD and AutoCAD LT and create a new drawing. I gave you a tour of the screen and explained how to save a drawing. This chapter provides the basis for all your work in AutoCAD and AutoCAD LT.

In this chapter, you learned the following:

- A brief history of AutoCAD and AutoCAD LT
- Some of the different disciplines that use AutoCAD and AutoCAD LT
- How to start AutoCAD and AutoCAD LT
- How to start a new drawing
- The user interface and its various sections, including the drawing area, the UCS icon, the crosshairs, the menus and toolbars, the command line, and the status bar
- How to start a command from a toolbar
- How to start a command from the command line
- How to start a command from the menu
- How to start a command from the Dashboard
- How to draw lines
- Several ways to pick points on the screen to specify coordinates
- How to save a drawing for the first time
- How to close a drawing
- How to exit AutoCAD and AutoCAD LT

You may have several questions at this point, but "well begun is half done." The next chapter explains all the ways to start a new drawing as well as how to open an existing drawing.

Chapter 2

Opening a Drawing

AutoCAD and AutoCAD LT offer a number of options for opening new and existing drawings. These options create a great deal of flexibility and save you time as well. You can create complex templates to avoid doing the same basic setup and drawing over and over.

Creating a New Drawing from a Template

A *template* is a special file that contains drawing settings and often objects (such as a title block and text). A template has a DWT filename extension. When you use a template as the basis for a new drawing, the drawing takes on all the settings and objects contained in the template. Use templates to avoid re-creating settings and redrawing objects for new drawings. AutoCAD and AutoCAD LT come with many templates that you can use as is or customize. You can also create your own templates.

> **NOTE** AutoCAD and AutoCAD LT offer a Startup dialog box that provides choices for starting a new drawing as well as opening existing drawings. To display the Startup dialog box whenever you open AutoCAD or AutoCAD LT, type **startup** on the command line and press Enter. Then type **1** and press Enter again.

To create a new drawing based on a template, choose File ➪ New to open the Select Template dialog box, which lists all the available templates, as shown in Figure 2.1. Click any template to see its preview, if any. Double-click a template to create a new drawing based on that template. Because AutoCAD or AutoCAD LT opens with `Drawing1.dwg`, the new drawing is named `Drawing2.dwg`. Subsequent drawings that you create are named `Drawing3.dwg` and so on. When you save and name your drawing, the original template file is unaffected.

The QNEW command is useful if you always start a new drawing based on the same template. You set a default template and then click QNew on the Standard toolbar to start a new drawing immediately, based on that default template. To set the default template, follow these steps:

1. Choose Tools ➪ Options and click the Files tab.
2. Double-click the Template Settings item.
3. Double-click the Default Template File Name for QNEW item.
4. Click the listing under the Default Template File Name for QNEW item (which says None by default).
5. Click Browse to choose the template that you want.
6. Click OK to close the Options dialog box.

You can specify whether this default template uses metric or imperial measurements by setting the MEASUREINIT system variable. (System variables are discussed further in Chapter 5.) On the command line, type **measureinit**. Enter **0** ↵ for imperial units and **1** ↵ for metric units.

The default template is `acad.dwt` for AutoCAD and `acadlt.dwt` for AutoCAD LT. Another default template is `acad -Named Plot Styles.dwt` or `acadlt -Named Plot Styles.dwt`, which refers to named plot styles. (See Chapter 17.)

FIGURE 2.1

Choose a template from the Select template dialog box.

STEPS: Opening a Drawing Based on the Default Template

1. Start AutoCAD or AutoCAD LT.
2. Choose File ➪ New.
3. From the Select template dialog box, choose `acad.dwt` (for AutoCAD) or `acadlt.dwt` (for AutoCAD LT) from the list.
4. Click Open. You now have a blank drawing named `Drawing2.dwg`, as shown in Figure 2.2.

FIGURE 2.2

When you create a drawing based on a template, AutoCAD or AutoCAD LT creates a new drawing.

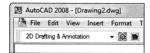

NOTE In AutoCAD, the default workspace is 2D Drafting & Annotation. However, you can choose another 2D workspace, AutoCAD Classic (for AutoCAD) or AutoCAD LT Classic (for AutoCAD LT), from the Workspaces toolbar. For 2D drawing, make sure that you're not in the 3D Modeling workspace if you are using AutoCAD. I discuss workspaces in Appendix A.

In both AutoCAD and AutoCAD LT, you may see palettes (windows) open that you don't want to use. You can close these by clicking their Close (X) button.

Working with Templates

A template contains ready-made settings to get you started drawing quickly. These settings include the size of the drawing (called *limits*), the unit type (such as *decimal* or *feet and inches*), and others. An important part of setting standards in an office where people work together on drawings is the creation of a template so that all users work with an identical setup.

CROSS-REF In Chapter 5, I explain the options available for setting up a drawing. In Chapter 26, I cover the process of setting standards for drawings.

A template may contain more than just settings — it often contains a complete title block, for example, and may include *boilerplate* (standardized) text as well.

Customizing the default template

Most people customize the default template to create one or more templates that suit their particular needs. After your templates are created, you don't have to worry about most settings; they are already available for you, and you can quickly start to draw.

To customize `acad.dwt` or `acadlt.dwt`, follow these steps:

1. Create a drawing based on a template as described in the previous section.
2. Make any changes you want.
3. Click Save on the Standard toolbar.
4. In the Save Drawing As dialog box, click the Files of Type drop-down list box. Choose AutoCAD Drawing Template or AutoCAD LT Drawing Template (`*.dwt`). In the list of template files, choose the template that you want to customize. Click Save.
5. When asked if you want to replace it, click Yes.
6. In the Template Options dialog box, revise the description as you like. (For information about the New Layer Notification option, see Chapter 26.)
7. From the Measurement drop-down list, choose English (Imperial) or Metric, depending on the type of units you plan to use.
8. Click OK.

CAUTION   If you're using someone else's computer, don't change the templates that come with AutoCAD or AutoCAD LT without first checking with the computer's owner. It can be a frustrating experience to start a drawing based on a template and find that all the settings have been changed. Also, if you create new templates, put them in their own folder to avoid losing them when you upgrade or reinstall AutoCAD.

Creating your own templates

You may want several templates to choose from on a regular basis. For example, you may create drawings of several sizes. AutoCAD and AutoCAD LT let you create as many templates as you want. To create your own templates, either start a drawing based on a template and make the changes you want or open an existing drawing that already has some of the settings you want and make any further changes you need. Follow these steps:

1. If you start a new drawing based on a template, choose Save from the Standard toolbar. If you open an existing drawing, choose File ⇨ Save As from the menu.

2. Make any changes you want.

3. In the Save Drawing As dialog box, click the Files of Type drop-down list box. Choose AutoCAD Drawing Template or AutoCAD LT Drawing Template.

4. In the File Name text box, type a name for your template. Click Save.

5. In the Template Options dialog box, enter the description as you want. From the Measurement drop-down list, choose English (Imperial) or Metric, depending on the type of units you plan to use. (I discuss the New Layer Notification item in Chapter 26.) Click OK.

TIP   Name your templates in a way that clearly differentiates them from regular drawings. You may want drawings set up for each of the standard paper sizes (A through E), with a title block in each. Useful names might be `tb-a.dwt`, `tb-b.dwt` (tb meaning title block), and so on.

Most AutoCAD and AutoCAD LT users take advantage of these techniques as a standard practice. You can usually make profitable use of a template as the basis for a new drawing.

Creating a Drawing with Default Settings

Occasionally, you may want to create a drawing without any settings. It is actually impossible for a drawing to have no settings at all, but you can create a drawing with the minimum possible presets. You might want to do this if you're working on someone else's computer and don't want to take the time to get rid of a large number of complex settings that aren't helpful for your work.

To create a drawing with the fewest possible settings, choose File ⇨ New. Instead of choosing a template, click the arrow to the right of the Open button (see Figure 2.1). Choose one of the following options:

- Open with No Template — Imperial
- Open with No Template — Metric

Opening an Existing Drawing

Often you need to open an existing drawing, either to complete it or to make changes. Opening a drawing in AutoCAD or AutoCAD LT is like opening a file in any Windows program. You can find existing drawings by name or by viewing a thumbnail, or preview image, of the drawing.

Choose Open from the Standard toolbar. The Select File dialog box appears, as shown in Figure 2.3. In the Look in drop-down list box, choose the drive where your drawing resides. In the main box, double-click the folder you need. Then choose your drawing. The Preview box enables you to quickly look at the drawing to see if it's the one you want. (If you don't see a preview, choose Preview from the Views drop-down list in the dialog box.) Click Open. The drawing opens.

When you open more than one drawing, by default, AutoCAD and AutoCAD LT display only one button on the Windows taskbar. You switch between drawings using the Window item on the drop-down menu. If you want to display a separate taskbar button for each drawing, type **taskbar** on the command line and press Enter. At the `Enter new value for TaskBar <0>:` prompt, type **1** and press Enter. Then you can click any drawing's button to display that drawing. You can view thumbnail images of all the drawings in a folder in the Select File dialog box (and other dialog boxes that enable you to choose a file) by clicking the Views button and choosing Thumbnails. Windows Vista automatically displays thumbnails in Windows Explorer; you can choose their size from the Views drop-down list.

FIGURE 2.3

The Select File dialog box is equivalent to the Open dialog box in most Windows programs.

You can also use the Places list at the left side of the dialog box to find drawings. The Places list is described in Chapter 1.

Using other ways to open drawings

You can double-click a drawing in Windows Explorer to open it. If AutoCAD or AutoCAD LT is not running, Windows loads the program and the drawing as well. If AutoCAD or AutoCAD LT is running and a drawing is active, the drawing opens as a second drawing within the program.

 You can also open a drawing from the DesignCenter — a feature for managing both drawing files and many of their components. First, choose Tools ➪ Palettes ➪ DesignCenter from the menu. The DesignCenter palette opens, displaying an Explorer-like list of drawings in the left pane. (If you don't see the list of drawings, click the Tree View Toggle button on the DesignCenter toolbar.) Navigate to the folder containing the drawing and choose the drawing's folder in the left pane. The drawings in the folder are listed in the right pane. Right-click the drawing of your choice and choose Open in Application Window. For more information on the DesignCenter, see Chapter 26.

You can open a drawing using the Sheet Set Manager (AutoCAD only). I cover sheet sets in Chapter 26.

Using shortcuts in dialog boxes

You can use several shortcuts when working in dialog boxes that open or save files, as follows:

- Double-click the drawing file to open it immediately without clicking Open.
- Click the Views drop-down list. Choose List to see a simple list. Choose Details to see the file size and the last date and time the file was saved.
- Right-click inside the dialog box to open a shortcut menu with more options.
- Click the name of a drawing to highlight it and then click it once more to rename it (but don't double-click it — that opens the drawing).

ON the DVD-ROM The drawing used in the following exercise on opening a drawing, abqs-01.dwg, is in the Results folder of the *AutoCAD 2008 and AutoCAD LT 2008 Bible* DVD. Place the DVD in your DVD drive.

STEPS: Opening a Drawing

1. If AutoCAD or AutoCAD LT is not open, start the program.
2. Click Open on the Standard toolbar.
3. In the Select File dialog box, choose the drive for your DVD in the Look in drop-down list box.
4. In the main box, double-click the Results folder.
5. In the main box, click abqs-01.dwg.
6. Click Open. The drawing opens. Keep this drawing open for the next exercise.

Using an Existing Drawing as a Prototype

Although a template can be very useful, if you plan to use the objects and settings in a drawing only a few times, you can simply use one drawing as a prototype for other drawings. You may often need to draw a series of related drawings — perhaps several related electrical schematics or a group of similar apartments in an apartment complex. When a significant part of the first drawing is applicable to subsequent drawings, don't start over — open an existing drawing, and immediately save it under a new name, as described in the next section. Make the necessary changes and resave the drawing.

Saving a Drawing under a New Name

Whether you want to use an existing drawing as a prototype or simply make a copy of a drawing, you need to save the drawing under a new name. First open the drawing and then choose File ⇨ Save As.

In the Save Drawing As dialog box, type a new name in the File Name text box. Then click Save. You may also want to change the location of the new drawing by changing the folder in the Save In drop-down list box.

ON the DVD-ROM The drawing used in the following exercise on saving a drawing under a new name, abqs-01 .dwg, is in the Results folder of the *AutoCAD 2008 and AutoCAD LT 2008 Bible* DVD.

STEPS: Saving a Drawing under a New Name

1. If you did the exercise in the Quick Start chapter, open abqs-01.dwg from the folder where you saved it. (I suggested the My Documents or the AutoCAD Bible folder.) Otherwise, open the drawing from the Results folder of the *AutoCAD 2008 and AutoCAD LT 2008 Bible* DVD.

NOTE For this exercise, choose the AutoCAD Classic (for AutoCAD) or AutoCAD LT Classic (for AutoCAD LT) workspace in the Workspaces toolbar. For both AutoCAD and AutoCAD LT, close any palettes that may be open.

2. Choose File ⇨ Save As. The Save Drawing As dialog box opens.

3. In the File Name text box, change the filename to ab02-01.dwg. Choose your AutoCAD Bible folder and click Save.

4. At the bottom of the drawing area, click the Model tab. (If your screen doesn't show this tab, on the status bar, click the button to the right of the LWT button; its tooltip reads Model.)

5. From the Layer Control drop-down list on the Layers toolbar, choose the DETAILING layer.

6. Choose Rectangle from the Draw toolbar. (If the Draw toolbar is not displayed, right-click any toolbar and choose Draw.) Follow the prompts, entering the text in the Dynamic Input tooltip:

```
Specify first corner point or
[Chamfer/Elevation/Fillet/Thickness/Width]: -15,3 ↵
Specify other corner point or [Dimensions]: 12,6'1 ↵
```

7. Again, choose Rectangle from the Draw toolbar. Leave the crosshairs to the right of the window and follow the prompts:

```
Specify first corner point or
[Chamfer/Elevation/Fillet/Thickness/Width]: 3'11,3 ↵
Specify other corner point or [Dimensions]: 12,6'1 ↵
```

Your drawing should look like Figure 2.4.

FIGURE 2.4

The window with added detailing.

8. Click the drawing Close box, which is just below the application Close box. Because you haven't saved the changes to the drawing, a message asks if you want to save them.

9. Click Yes. AutoCAD or AutoCAD LT saves and closes the drawing.

10. Click the application's Close box (X) to close AutoCAD or AutoCAD LT.

Summary

In this chapter, you explored the various ways of opening a drawing. You learned the following:

- Starting a new drawing based on a template
- Customizing a template
- Creating your own templates
- Starting a new drawing with no template
- Opening an existing drawing
- Using an existing drawing as a prototype for a new drawing
- Saving a drawing under a new name

In the next chapter, you read about using commands.

Chapter 3

Using Commands

utoCAD and AutoCAD LT have been around for a long time. As a result, the way you give the program commands — called the *user interface* — is somewhat unique. You can give the same command in several ways. In this chapter, you read about the various possibilities and start to get acquainted with all of them.

Commands are important. In a word processing program, you can simply start typing; in a spreadsheet program, you can begin by entering data, but in most cases nothing happens in AutoCAD or AutoCAD LT until you give it a command.

The AutoCAD and AutoCAD LT Interface

Many new commands have been added to AutoCAD and AutoCAD LT over the years. Often, older commands that were no longer necessary were kept to maintain compatibility with earlier releases. A number of these older commands, as well as certain rarely used commands, are not found in the menus. Other than this idiosyncrasy, the menus are similar to those of other Windows programs.

Using menus

A menu item can do three things — execute a command, open a submenu, or open a dialog box. As in all Windows programs, the menu items provide clues to let you know what is going to occur after you click a menu item, as follows:

- A right arrow opens a submenu with more options.
- An ellipsis (. . .) opens a dialog box.
- A plain menu item immediately executes a command.

The Screen Menu

In early releases, AutoCAD provided a menu on the right side of the screen, called the *screen menu*. If you're still using the screen menu, I suggest that you adjust to the new interface. You'll find its consistency with other Windows programs to be an advantage.

If you must have the screen menu, you can easily display it. Choose Tools ⇨ Options. Click the Display tab. In the Window Elements section, choose Display screen menu. Click OK.

AutoCAD's current default is to not show the screen menu, so I don't use it in this book. Therefore, the word *menu* always means the pull-down menu at the top of the AutoCAD screen. AutoCAD LT doesn't offer a screen menu.

Looking at the command line whenever you click a menu option is worthwhile. Any command that you choose on a menu is repeated on the command line, and a prompt or list of options may appear. If you have Dynamic Input on, the tooltip displays the prompt. (Click the DYN button on the status bar to turn it on — and off.) See the section "Responding to commands" later in this chapter for more information on what to do next.

Using shortcut menus

Shortcut menus appear when you right-click your mouse. The purpose of shortcut menus is to speed up your work; they can be faster than using the command line because you don't have to take your eyes off the screen. The shortcut menus try to anticipate the most common tasks you might want to complete. As a result, the menu that appears when you right-click depends on the situation:

- If you have neither started a command nor selected any objects, you get the default menu when you right-click in the drawing area. Here you can cut, copy, paste, undo, pan, zoom, and so on.
- If you've selected any objects, you see the edit-mode menu, which lists the most common editing commands.
- If you've started a command, the command-mode menu opens, letting you choose an option for that command. I explain this in more detail later in this chapter.
- When a dialog box is open, you can right-click active sections to see the dialog-mode menu, which varies with the dialog box.
- Other menus include the toolbar list you get when you right-click a toolbar and the command-line history you see when you right-click the command line and choose Recent Commands.

These menus are explained as appropriate throughout this book. You also have an opportunity to use many of them in the exercises.

In earlier releases, right-clicking was equivalent to pressing Enter. You can customize how right-clicking works — and that includes changing it back to the way it worked in earlier releases. Choose Tools ⇨ Options and choose the User Preferences tab. Then click the Right-click Customization button. For more information, see Appendix A.

TIP   When you set right-click customization, you can turn on time-sensitive right-clicking. Time-sensitive right-click is a great feature that gives you the best of two worlds — the right mouse button can be used both as an equivalent to pressing Enter and to open the shortcut menus. If you turn on time-sensitive right-clicking, a quick right-click is equivalent to pressing Enter and will repeat the last command or end any commands that require Enter to end. A longer right-click (hold your finger on the mouse button slightly longer) opens the shortcut menu. You can specify the length of time required for the longer right-click, which is 250 milliseconds by default.

Using dialog boxes

Dialog boxes offer the user a simple way to control AutoCAD or AutoCAD LT without memorizing a lot of technical commands and option names. They guide you through a task by clearly laying out all the choices.

If you're familiar with any other Windows program, you're familiar with dialog boxes. As a brief example, look at the Hatch and Gradient dialog box (choose Hatch from the Draw toolbar), which enables you to specify how you fill enclosed areas. This dialog box has most of the common features of a dialog box and is shown in Figure 3.1. (The AutoCAD LT version of this dialog box doesn't include the Gradient tab.) I cover this dialog box in detail in Chapter 16.

FIGURE 3.1

The Hatch and Gradient dialog box is typical of many AutoCAD and AutoCAD LT dialog boxes.

Drop-down list   Tab   Button   Help on dialog box

Option button   Text box   Check box   Expand arrow

TIP   By default, you can enter mathematical expressions for values in dialog box text boxes, starting with an equal sign (=). For example, in the Angle box in Figure 3.1, you can enter =20+10. Press Alt+Enter to complete the process. You can also enter mathematical expressions in palette text boxes.

TIP   If a dialog box has a question mark (?) icon in the top-right corner, click it to change the cursor to a question mark. Then click an item in the dialog box to display a brief explanation of that item. Also, many drop-down lists let you enter text as well as choose an item from the list. For example, in the text box of the Angle drop-down list in Figure 3.1, you can type an angle, such as 32, that is not on the drop-down list.

When you've finished using a dialog box, click OK to accept any settings you specified or click Cancel to discard any changes.

Using toolbars

Toolbars provide a quick way to execute a command with one click of the mouse. On the other hand, those little pictures on the toolbar buttons are not always self-explanatory. Until you get used to the location of the buttons, you may find yourself wandering (with the mouse cursor) from button to button, reading tooltips. However, once you are familiar with the location of frequently used toolbar buttons, toolbars usually become a favorite way to execute commands.

In the default AutoCAD (LT) Classic workspace, you have the Standard, Styles, Layers, Properties, Draw, and Modify toolbars showing. You can open other toolbars as you need them.

CROSS-REF   You can customize toolbars to suit your needs. Toolbar customization is covered in Chapter 29.

When you click a toolbar button, in order to complete the command, you usually need to look at the Dynamic Input tooltip, or on the command line, to follow the prompts there. I explain the command line and Dynamic Input later in this chapter.

A few of the toolbars have *flyouts,* attached toolbars containing additional buttons. For example, on the Standard toolbar, the Zoom button has a tiny arrow on its lower-right corner. Click and hold a second and the flyout flies out, revealing several other buttons, all related to zooming in and out. Drag down and choose any one of the options.

To display a toolbar, right-click any toolbar and choose the toolbar you want to display. Displayed toolbars have a checkmark next to their name. To hide a toolbar, follow the same procedure — choose the toolbar to deselect it.

TIP   To display the Express Tools (AutoCAD only) or Autodesk Impression toolbars, right-click in the gray space *outside* any toolbar. For example, you can right-click to the right side of the Properties toolbar or below the Draw toolbar. From the shortcut menu, choose EXPRESS and then the toolbar that you want to display. (Autodesk impression is another Autodesk product that works together with AutoCAD to create models that look hand-drawn.)

As soon as a toolbar is open, you can close it by clicking the Close button at the upper-right corner, as long as it is not *docked* — that is, parked at one edge of the screen. Toolbars can *float* within the drawing area or even outside the application window (when it is not maximized). You can move them by dragging them and reshape them by dragging any edge. To dock a floating toolbar, drag it by its title bar to any edge of the application window. Docked toolbars have *grab bars* (which look like a double line) at one end; grab bars enable you to easily undock and move the toolbars.

TIP   To prevent a toolbar from docking as you move it to the edge of the screen, press and hold Ctrl as you drag. To close all the toolbars and palettes, press Ctrl+0. You now have more space to draw. To get back your toolbars and palettes, press Ctrl+0 again.

Learning how to move, dock, display, and hide toolbars is worth your time. This small effort can greatly increase your comfort level as you draw.

Using palettes

A palette is a window that you can dock or float (like a toolbar). Palettes combine related functions in one place. AutoCAD and AutoCAD LT have several palettes that are covered throughout this book. Two palettes, the Tool Palettes window (which has several tabs) and the Dashboard, offer a wide range of commands.

To see palettes only when you need them, you can auto-hide them. Right-click the palette's title bar and choose Auto-hide from the shortcut menu. To dock a palette, choose Allow Docking from the same shortcut menu.

NOTE   You can dock and auto-hide a palette. Right-click the palette's title bar and choose Anchor Right or Anchor Left. The palette collapses to a thin vertical strip and opens only when you hover the mouse cursor over it. You can also anchor more than one palette on a site. They fit together on the right or left side and unroll to their full length when you hover the cursor over them.

Tool palettes

Tool palettes are another way to give AutoCAD and AutoCAD LT commands. To open the Tool Palettes window, choose Tool Palettes Window from the Standard or Standard Annotation toolbar or choose Tools ⇨ Palettes ⇨ Tool Palettes. The palettes are actually a collection of tabs that are used to organize tools with similar functionality. Click the Command Tool Samples tab, shown in Figure 3.2. Because of the number of tabs, some of the tabs are bunched up at the bottom. To choose these tabs, right-click those bottom tabs and choose a tab from the list that appears. The AutoCAD LT Tool Palettes window contains fewer tabs, and some of the tabs are slightly different.

FIGURE 3.2
_____

The Command Tool Samples tab of the Tool Palettes window, shown in AutoCAD. (The AutoCAD LT tab doesn't include the VisualLisp Expression item.)

Each of the items on a Tool palette is a tool. The tools on the Command Tool Samples tab contain commands that you can use. For example, you can draw a line by clicking the Line tool. The effect is the same as clicking the Line button on the Draw toolbar.

The first two tools have *flyouts*, which are like toolbar flyouts. Click the small arrow and the flyout appears, containing other command buttons. Click the command button that you want in order to start that command.

CROSS-REF   You can use tool palettes to insert objects, fill in closed areas, and add other content. For more information, see Chapter 26. I also explain how to customize tool palettes in Chapter 29. For example, you can put custom commands on a tool palette.

The Dashboard

The Dashboard is a palette that contains commands and settings. Common tools are grouped together in sections called control panels. AutoCAD 2008 has expanded the content of this feature by adding new control panels for 2D drafting tools such as text, layers, dimensions, tables, and object properties; these tools are covered in other parts of this book.

To open the Dashboard, choose Tools ⇨ Palettes ⇨ Dashboard or type **dashboard** on the command line. The full Dashboard used in 2D drawing is shown in Figure 3.3.

FIGURE 3.3

The Dashboard combines many commands and settings in one place.

You can control which sections of the Dashboard appear. Right-click the palette's title bar or grab bars (the horizontal bars at the top) and choose Control Panels. Then choose the section that you want to display or hide. A checkmark appears next to items that are currently displayed. You can further customize what appears in each control panel. For more information, see Chapter 33.

Most of the items on the Dashboard are buttons that you use just like toolbar buttons — you click a button to execute a command. Some controls are settings, and you can enter a value, check a check box, drag a slider, or choose an item from a drop-down list.

The Command Line and Dynamic Input

You can execute a command by typing it directly on the command line, directly to the right of the Command: prompt. The command line is a place to enter commands as well as coordinates and values, as shown in Figure 3.4.

FIGURE 3.4

The command line.

The command line is actually a window that you can move like a palette. By default, it is docked at the bottom of the drawing area. The window usually shows three lines of text, the Command: prompt, where you type, and two lines of text from the previous command. You can drag the top edge of the window to display more than three lines.

TIP By default, AutoCAD and AutoCAD LT display the command line. You can hide the command-line window using the COMMANDLINEHIDE command, and display it with the COMMANDLINE command. An easier way is to press Ctrl+9, which toggles the Command window on and off. Another option for the command line is to undock the Command window, right-click the window's title bar on the left, and choose Auto-hide. The Command window collapses to its title bar until you place the cursor over it.

Commands that you choose from a toolbar button, menu, or tool palette are all echoed on the command line.

Using Dynamic Input

You can also use the Dynamic Input feature to execute commands that you type. Dynamic Input displays whatever you type in a tooltip box near the cursor. Dynamic Input also displays prompts at the cursor, so that you don't have to look down at the command line. Note that Dynamic Input does not completely replace the command line; in some situations the command line displays necessary prompts that the Dynamic Input tooltip omits. For more information about Dynamic Input settings, see Chapter 4.

You can turn Dynamic Input on and off using the DYN button on the status bar. When Dynamic Input is on, a tooltip box echoes what you type, displays prompts, and then displays your responses at the cursor as you type, as shown in Figure 3.5. This input is echoed on the command line after you press Enter. When Dynamic Input is off, commands and other input that you type appear on the command line as you type them.

FIGURE 3.5

The Dynamic Input tooltip prompts you for input and then displays your input as you type.

Understanding command names

All commands have a special one-word command name. This may or may not be the same as the wording that appears on the toolbar's tooltip or on the menu. However, you can be sure of one thing: every command can be executed by typing its name on the command line or in the Dynamic Input tooltip. Fast typists often prefer to type the command because they find it faster than searching for a command on a menu, toolbar, palette, or the Dashboard. Most users use a combination of the command line and other user interface options.

Some of the commands are easy to type, such as LINE or ARC. Others are long and harder to remember, such as HATCHEDIT, DDPTYPE, or EXTERNALREFERENCES. Command names such as these can quickly drive you to use a menu or toolbar.

CROSS-REF If you like typing commands, you can create short versions of the command names, called *aliases.* Many are already included with AutoCAD and AutoCAD LT. Aliases are covered in Chapter 29.

You can edit what you have typed on the command line. If you type a long command or a difficult coordinate, and make a mistake, you can backspace up to the mistake and retype the last part correctly. Table 3-1 shows how to use the keyboard edit keys to edit the command line.

TIP When you start to type a command, and you aren't sure of the exact spelling, you can start typing what you know and then press the Tab key to cycle through all the possibilities in the Dynamic Input tooltip or on the command line. Press Enter when you see the command that you want. This AutoComplete feature works for system variables (which I cover in Chapter 5) and command aliases as well. For example, several commands start with "COPY". You can type copy and then repeatedly press Tab to see these commands.

TABLE 3.1

Command-Line Editing Keys

Key	Function
Backspace	Backspaces through the text on the command line, erasing each letter as it backspaces.
Left arrow	Moves backward through the text of the command, without erasing.
Right arrow	Moves forward through the text of the command, without erasing.

Key	Function
Home	Moves the command-line cursor to the beginning of the text.
End	Moves the command-line cursor to the end of the text.
Insert	Toggles between Insert/Overwrite modes. Insert mode inserts text. Overwrite mode types over existing text. Note that there is no visual confirmation of which mode you are in.
Delete	Deletes the character to the right of the cursor on the command line.
Ctrl+V	Pastes text from the Windows Clipboard.

You can scroll through and reuse previous command-line entries. To repeat the last line you entered, press the up arrow. Press Enter to execute it. To see more of the command-line entries, press F2 on your keyboard to open the Text Window. Scroll until you find the entry you want, highlight it, and then right-click and choose Paste To CmdLine from the shortcut menu. You now see the highlighted text on the current command line. You can copy selected text from the command-line history or the entire history to the Clipboard. You can also choose Recent Commands from the Text Window's shortcut menu and choose one of the commands from the submenu that appears.

TIP Switching from the mouse to the keyboard and back is time-consuming. In general, if you're picking points using the mouse (covered in Chapter 4), using menus, toolbars, and so on to give commands is faster. If you're typing coordinates as you did in Chapter 1, your hands are already at the keyboard, so typing commands at the keyboard is easier.

Responding to commands

When you execute a command by any method, you usually need to respond to the command. AutoCAD displays a prompt that tells you what you need to do next.

The format for command prompts on the command line is as follows:

```
current instruction or [options] <current value>:
```

The current instruction explains what you need to do. For example, if you choose an editing command, the prompt usually instructs you to "Select objects." The text in the square brackets lists the various options available for the command. The angled brackets tell you the current value or default option for the command, if any.

In the Dynamic Input tooltip, you first see the following:

```
current instruction or ↓
```

If the current instruction is to specify a point, you also see the cursor's X and Y coordinates. Figure 3.6 shows a prompt for the CIRCLE command. After specifying the center of the circle, this command has a current instruction to specify the radius, an option to specify the diameter, and a current value of 1.0000, the radius of the previously drawn circle.

NOTE Throughout this book, I show the prompt as it appears on the command line, because this prompt includes the options. If you are looking at the Dynamic Input tooltip, you can press the down arrow to display the options at the tooltip or right-click to display the shortcut menu.

FIGURE 3.6

To see the options and a current value (if any) in the Dynamic Input tooltip, press the down arrow on your keyboard.

When you see a prompt, the possible types of responses are as follows:

- **Specify a point:** You can pick a point by clicking with the mouse. You can also enter an X,Y coordinate or displacement — whatever you type appears both in the Dynamic Input tooltip and on the command line. Chapter 4 explains how to specify points.
- **Enter a value or text:** You type the value or the text and press Enter. If Dynamic Input is on, you see your input as you type in the tooltip but you don't see the value on the command line until you press Enter. If Dynamic Input is off, you see your input as you type on the command line.
- **Select an object:** Most editing commands require that you select one or more objects. You can click an object to select it. I explain all the other methods to select objects in Chapters 9 and 10.
- **Choose an option.** Many commands have options that you need to choose before continuing to use the command. To choose an option using the command line, do one of the following:
  - Type the one or two letters that are capitalized in the option name — usually (but not always) the first letter(s) of the option. You can type the letter(s) in lowercase. Press Enter.
  - Press Enter to choose a default option or current value.
  - Right-click in the drawing area and choose one of the options from the shortcut menu. This works best for options that won't need any numerical input on the command line.

  To choose an option using the Dynamic Input tooltip, press the down arrow on your keyboard to display the options. If there is a default value, you see a mark next to it. Then click one of the options.

At this point, additional options and prompts may appear; you respond in the same way that I have just described, depending on the type of information that the command needs.

In the following exercise, you practice using command options and picking points on the screen with the mouse.

STEPS: Using Command Options

1. Open a new drawing using the `acad.dwt` or `acadlt.dwt` template. Make sure that the AutoCAD or AutoCAD LT Classic workspace is chosen in the Workspaces toolbar. Close any palettes that may be open.

 2. Choose Polyline on the Draw toolbar. (A polyline can contain both line and arc segments. I discuss polylines in Chapter 16.)

3. Look at the command line and the Dynamic Input tooltip. (If you don't see the Dynamic Input tooltip near the cursor, click the DYN button on the status bar.) You see the following prompt:

```
Specify start point:
```

You also see the current coordinate location of the cursor in the Dynamic Input tooltip. Move the mouse cursor anywhere in the middle of the screen, and click to specify the start point. This is called *picking a point*.

4. Now see the following prompts, the first on the command line and the second in the Dynamic Input tooltip:

```
Specify next point or [Arc/Halfwidth/Length/Undo/Width]:
Specify next point or ↓
```

Suppose that you want to specify the width of the polyline. Because specifying the next point is the main instruction, right-click to display the shortcut menu and choose Width, which is one of the options. The program responds with the `Specify starting width:` prompt. Follow the prompts:

```
Specify starting width <0.0000>: .5 ↵
Specify ending width <0.5000>: .25 ↵
```

5. The prompt to specify the next point returns. Move the mouse so that your cursor is away from the first point that you picked and pick another point. You now see the same prompt repeated.

6. This time, you want to change the width. To specify the width this time, type **w** ↵. Follow the prompts:

```
Specify starting width <0.2500>: ↵ to accept the default value.
Specify ending width <0.2500>: ↵ to accept the default value again.
```

7. Move your mouse so that the new segment is at a different angle than the first one. Pick any point on the screen. The same prompt appears again.

8. Press the down arrow to display the Dynamic Input shortcut menu. Choose `Close` from the menu. AutoCAD closes the polyline so that you now have a triangle, and ends the command.

Do not save this drawing.

 You may have noticed an underscore (_) before commands. This mark allows translation to foreign languages and can be ignored.

Command Techniques

To make working with commands easier, AutoCAD and AutoCAD LT offer shortcuts for repeating and canceling commands as well as sophisticated undo and redo options. You can also use certain commands in the middle of another command.

You can have more than one command in process concurrently, one in each open drawing. You can switch from one open drawing to another without interrupting your commands. For example, if you're in the middle of drawing a circle in one drawing, you can open a new drawing and start another command to get some information you need for the circle. Then you can return to the first drawing and complete the circle.

Repeating commands

The most common way to repeat a command you have just used is to press Enter. The most recent command appears again.

> **TIP** You can also press the Spacebar at the `Command:` prompt to repeat a command you just used. This technique works well if you want to keep one hand on the mouse and use the other hand to press the Spacebar.

If you know in advance that you'll be using a command several times, you can use another technique — type **multiple** ↵. At the `Enter command name to repeat:` prompt, type the command name on the command line. The command automatically reappears on the command line. For example, you could type **multiple** and then **arc** if you knew you were going to draw several arcs in a row. To stop repeating the command, press Esc.

> **TIP** If you create a toolbar button that executes a customized set of actions (as I explain in Chapter 29), right-click and choose the top option of the shortcut menu to repeat the action of the toolbar button. You cannot press Enter to get this effect.

Using recent input

You may need to use the same input again and again. For example, you may want to draw several circles with the same radius. You can use the recent input list to choose a recently used radius instead of typing it again. You can access recent points, values (such as distances and angles), and text strings.

When you see a prompt for input, right-click and choose Recent Input from the shortcut menu. (In a few instances, no shortcut menu is available, so you can't use this feature.) You can then choose one of the recent input items from the list. You can also press the up or down arrows to cycle through the recent input in the Dynamic Input tooltip.

The Recent Input feature displays items that are appropriate for the current prompt. For example, if the prompt asks for a radius, you don't see angles or X,Y coordinates; you see only lengths.

Canceling commands

Sometimes you start a command and then realize you don't need it. In this situation, you can cancel the command and then choose a different command. Press the Esc key to cancel a command that you've already started. The `Command:` prompt reappears.

In the following exercise, you practice the techniques for repeating and canceling commands, as well as using recent input.

STEPS: Repeating and Canceling Commands

1. Start a new drawing using the `acad.dwt` or `acadlt.dwt` template. Make sure that the AutoCAD Classic or AutoCAD LT Classic workspace is chosen in the Workspaces toolbar. Close any palettes that may be open.
2. Choose Circle on the Draw toolbar.
3. At the `Specify center point for circle or [3P/2P/Ttr (tan tan radius)]:` prompt, pick a center point anywhere near the center of the screen.
4. At the `Specify radius of circle or [Diameter]:` prompt, type **2** ↵. The circle appears in the drawing area.

5. Press Enter. The CIRCLE command's first prompt appears again.

6. Follow these prompts:

```
Specify center point for circle or [3P/2P/Ttr (tan tan radius)]:
Right-click and choose 2P from the shortcut menu.
Specify first end point of circle's diameter: Pick any point on the
screen.
Specify second end point of circle's diameter: Press Esc.
```

The prompts disappear.

7. Press the Spacebar. Looking at the Dynamic Input tooltip, you see the `Specify center point for circle or ↓` prompt. Pick any point on the screen.

8. At the `Specify radius of circle or ↓` prompt, right-click and choose Recent Input ⇨ 2.0000 from the shortcut menu to create another circle with a radius of 2.

Do not save this drawing.

Undoing a command

Most Windows applications offer Undo and Redo commands on the Standard toolbar. AutoCAD and AutoCAD LT are no different. Some applications remember a list of your last few actions so that you can undo them one by one. AutoCAD and AutoCAD LT remember every command you execute starting from the time you open a drawing. You can therefore undo every action and return your drawing to its condition when you opened it.

Actually, there are a few obvious exceptions. For example, if you print a drawing, you can't unprint it, and you can't unsave a drawing, either. Similarly, commands that provide you with information, such as the coordinates of a point, cannot be undone.

 Some commands have their own undo options. I explain these undo options when I discuss these commands throughout the book.

 Each time you click Undo on the Standard or Standard Annotation toolbar, you undo one command. If you click the down arrow to the right of the Undo button, you can see all the commands that you've executed. To undo several commands, click the earliest command that you want to undo. If you choose the bottom-most command, you undo all the commands and get the message:

```
Everything has been undone
```

When you start the UNDO command, you see the following options on the command line:

```
Enter the number of operations to undo or
[Auto/Control/BEgin/End/Mark/Back] <1>:
```

`Enter the number of operations to undo` is the default instruction. If you type a number, such as **3**, you undo your last three commands. This action is equivalent to choosing the third command on the Undo button's drop-down list. Table 3-2 explains the other options.

TABLE 3.2

Options of the UNDO Command

Option	What It Does
Auto	Can be On or Off. Applies to a menu item that executes more than one command at a time. When Auto is On (the default), the entire menu item is undone in one step. When Auto is Off, UNDO undoes each step one at a time.
Control	Offers three sub-options. All, the default, gives you the full UNDO capability. None disables the UNDO command. One enables you to undo only one step at a time, effectively turning the UNDO command into the U command.
Begin	Works with the End option. This starts a group at the current point of the list of commands. Then, when you use the End option, UNDO undoes all the commands in the group. The U command also undoes everything within a group.
End	Marks the end of all commands in the group created by using the Begin option.
Mark	This option works with the Back option. It is somewhat similar to the Begin option, but you can place several marks as you work.
Back	When you use this option, AutoCAD or AutoCAD LT undoes only to the most recent Mark point. The next Back option you use undoes to the Mark point before that.

As you undo commands, the command line lists the commands that are being undone. Sometimes, you see the word *Group,* which means that a group of commands is being undone. However, sometimes the word *Group* is used even for a single command. This use of the word *Group* is not significant and can be ignored.

TIP You can tell AutoCAD or AutoCAD LT to combine consecutive zooms and pans when you undo commands to help you quickly get back to your previous situation. Choose Tools ➪ Options and click the User Preferences tab. Then check the Combine Zoom and Pan Commands check box in the Undo/Redo section.

Using the Back option when no Mark has been created undoes everything you have done in a drawing session! Luckily, you get the following warning message:

```
This will undo everything. OK? <Y>
```

Type **n** ↵ if you do not want to undo everything.

Redoing a command

If you undo a command, you might realize that you want to undo the undo. This is called redoing a command. Don't confuse redoing a command with repeating a command. Redoing only applies when you have just undone a command.

The MREDO command on the Standard or Standard Annotation toolbar redoes the effect of the previous UNDO commands. You can redo multiple UNDO commands. You can choose recently undone commands from the Redo drop-down list.

NOTE The old REDO command that only redoes one command still exists, but the Redo button on the Standard toolbar executes the MREDO command that redoes multiple UNDO commands.

In the following exercise, you practice using the UNDO and MREDO commands.

STEPS: Undoing and Redoing Commands

1. Start a new drawing using acad.dwt or acadlt.dwt as the template. If you're using AutoCAD, make sure that the AutoCAD Classic or AutoCAD LT Classic workspace is chosen in the Workspaces toolbar. Close any palettes (except the Tool Palettes window) that may be open.

2. Choose Line on the Command Tool Samples tab of the tool palette. (If necessary, press Ctrl+3 to display the Tool Palettes window and click the Command Tool Samples tab. If you can't find the Command Tool Samples tab, right-click at the bottom of the tabs, where they overlap and choose Command Tool Samples from the list of tabs.)

3. Follow the prompts to draw one line, and press Enter to end the command.

4. On the Command Tool Samples tab of the Tool Palettes window, click the right arrow to the right of the Line button to open the flyout. Choose Arc.

5. Using the default options, pick any three points to draw an arc.

6. On the Command Tool Samples tab of the Tool Palettes window, click the right arrow to the right of the Arc button to open the flyout. Choose Circle.

7. Pick one point to be the center of the circle and another nearby point to specify the radius. Your drawing now contains a line, an arc, and a circle, and looks something like Figure 3.7. Of course, your objects will look different because you picked different points.

8. Click the Undo button on the Standard toolbar. The circle disappears.

9. Click the down arrow to the right of the Undo button on the Standard toolbar. Choose Line. The arc and the line disappear.

10. Click the down arrow to the right of the Redo button on the Standard toolbar. Choose Circle. All three objects reappear because they were undone by the previous UNDO commands.

Do not save this drawing. If you are continuing, keep the drawing on the screen for the next exercise.

FIGURE 3.7

Your drawing should contain a line, an arc, and a circle.

CROSS-REF The OOPS command restores the most recently erased object or set of objects, even if you have used other commands in the meantime. See Chapter 18 for further information.

Using one command within another command

Certain commands can be used within another command. These are called *transparent commands*. After a transparent command is completed, the original command continues its regular operation. Many transparent commands help you display the drawing differently so that you can complete the original command easily. Other transparent commands change settings. In fact, almost any command that doesn't select objects, create new objects, cause regeneration, or end the drawing session can be used transparently. When you start transparent commands from toolbars or menus, they are automatically transparent. If you want to type a transparent command on the command line or in the Dynamic Input tooltip, you need to type an apostrophe (') before the command name.

In this exercise, you practice using transparent commands and two commands concurrently.

 The drawing used in the following exercise on using transparent commands and two commands concurrently, abqs-01.dwg, is in the Results folder on the DVD.

STEPS: Using Transparent Commands and Two Commands Concurrently

1. From the previous exercise, you have a line, an arc, and a circle on the screen. If not, begin a new drawing using acad.dwt or acadlt.dwt as the template and draw a line and an arc anywhere on the screen. (You don't need the circle.) Because you haven't saved this drawing, it is called drawing1.dwg.

NOTE   If you start a new drawing, make sure that the AutoCAD Classic or AutoCAD LT Classic workspace is chosen in the Workspaces toolbar. Close any palettes that may be open.

2. Choose View ➪ Zoom ➪ Out. The drawing zooms out, appearing smaller.

3. Choose Open from the Standard toolbar and open abqs-01.dwg from the Results folder on the DVD. This is a drawing of a window from the Quick Start chapter.

4. Choose Window ➪ drawing1.dwg to display your original drawing.

5. Choose Circle from the Draw toolbar. The following prompt appears:

   ```
   Command: Specify center point for circle or [3P/2P/Ttr (tan tan
   radius)]: Pick any point at the center of your screen.
   Specify radius of circle or [Diameter]:
   ```

6. At this point, say that you want to see the drawing closer up to properly decide where to place the radius of the circle. Type **'zoom** ↵. The following appears on the command line. (You may need to press F2 to see the entire prompt. Press F2 again to close the Text Window.) Follow the prompts.

   ```
   >>Specify corner of window, enter a scale factor (nX or nXP), or
   [All/Center/Dynamic/Extents/Previous/Scale/Window/Object] <real
   time>: 2x ↵
   Resuming CIRCLE command.
   Specify radius of circle or [Diameter]:
   ```

7. Let's say that you want the radius to be equal to the width of the window in your other drawing. Choose Window ➪ abqs-01.dwg.

8. The dimension text clearly states that the window is 3'8" wide, which is 44 inches.

9. Choose Window ➪ drawing1.dwg.

10. Type 44 ↵ to create the circle. Choose View ➪ Zoom ➪ Out until you can see the entire drawing, including the circle that you just drew.

11. Close abqs-01.dwg. Do not save drawing1.dwg.

Looking at the prompts for the transparent use of the ZOOM command carefully, note three features:

- The ZOOM command is preceded by an apostrophe. This is the sign of a transparent command.
- The prompt for the transparent command is preceded by >>. This helps you distinguish between the prompts of the original command and the transparent command that is embedded in it.
- When the transparent command is complete, the prompt tells you. In this case, you see `Resuming CIRCLE command`.

Experiment using transparent commands, and you'll soon find them indispensable.

Of Mice and Pucks

For the sake of simplicity, this book assumes that you're using a mouse, but some people use a digitizing tablet and a *puck* (or a stylus). A typical digitizing tablet and puck are shown in Figure 3.8. A puck often has more buttons than a mouse and also has crosshairs on a transparent area that you can use for accurately picking points from a paper drawing.

FIGURE 3.8

A digitizer and puck.

The digitizing tablet is generally configured to include an area that represents the screen you draw on as well as a customizable command area that you use for commands. This command area of the tablet functions as another menu. Figure 3.9 shows the default tablet provided with AutoCAD. (AutoCAD LT has a similar one.) Usually, you would customize the tablet to suit individual needs. Each square is equivalent to a toolbar button and executes a command when you click it. The top area is left blank for you to include your own commands. This area is often used to insert parts from a library of standardized parts. Examples would be gaskets and valves in a mechanical drawing environment or doors and windows in an architectural environment.

FIGURE 3.9

The standard tablet menu.

The square area in the right-center represents the drawing area. In this area, the puck functions like a mouse to draw, as well as to access menus and dialog box options. The tablet can also be used for a process called *digitizing,* which means transferring data from paper into AutoCAD or AutoCAD LT. This transference is often done by putting a paper document directly on the tablet and using the entire tablet as a drawing area. Because the puck has crosshairs on a transparent surface, you can pick points on the drawing, which then become endpoints of lines, for example.

Getting Help

AutoCAD and AutoCAD LT have so many commands with so many options that every user needs help at some time. AutoCAD and AutoCAD LT come with a very complete Help system. A complete set of links and tabs makes navigating through the topics and finding related material easy.

CROSS-REF See Appendix B for help that is available on the Internet and other resources for AutoCAD and AutoCAD LT.

Getting help on a command

The easiest way to get help on a command is to start the command and press F1. The help screen for that command opens up. Figure 3.10 shows the screen that opens when you type **zoom** ⏎ and then press F1.

FIGURE 3.10

The help screen for the ZOOM command.

NOTE After you have opened the Help window one time, when you press F1 it may only cause the window to blink on the Windows taskbar. Go to the taskbar and click the blinking button to open the Help window.

Finding help with Quickstart links

Quickstart links are hyperlinks that you find at selected locations to help you understand a feature or concept. For example, if you choose Plot from the Standard or Standard Annotation toolbar, the Plot dialog box opens with a link to more help on plotting, as shown in Figure 3.11. Some other locations for these links are on a new tool palette and on the Sheet Set Manager (both discussed in Chapter 26). If the feature is new, the link goes to the New Features Workshop, which I cover later in this chapter.

FIGURE 3.11

Click the Learn about Plotting hyperlink to go to a Help page on plotting.

Using the main Help system

When you have a question, try the Help system. AutoCAD and AutoCAD LT come with the most complete Help documentation I have ever seen in a program.

Pressing F1 (with no command active) or choosing Help ➪ Help opens the User Documentation window, shown in Figure 3.12. Click the Show button to display four tabs to the left.

FIGURE 3.12

The main Help window in AutoCAD.

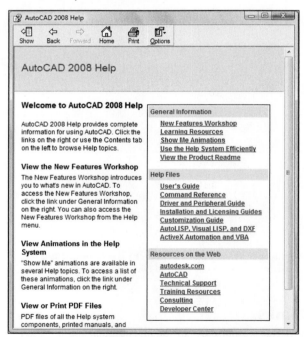

The Help system has three tabs that offer different ways of finding the help you need. You might need to drag the border between the tabs and the right panel to see the rightmost tab.

The Contents tab

The Contents tab displays help organized by topic. It's like the table of contents of a book. Double-click the icon of a book to open that topic and see subtopics. Click a topic to see it displayed in the right panel. Double-click Command Reference on the Contents tab to get help on commands and system variables. Double-click User's Guide for the "how-to" manual.

The Index tab

If you have an idea in your head but don't know the command name, you may want to use the index. The index is an alphabetical listing of topics. In the text box, type the first few letters of the word or words for which you want help. As you type, the list jumps to the closest match. When you've found the topic you want, highlight it and click Display (or double-click it). Sometimes subtopics appear from which you can choose.

The Search tab

The Search tab enables you to ask a question. Type a question or phrase in the text box and click the Ask button. Choose a topic to display it on the right.

Working with Help screens

The Help screens have several features that you should know so you can make the best use of them. Many of the topics displayed on the right have three tabs:

- **Concept:** The overall description
- **Procedure:** How to do it
- **Quick Reference:** Related commands and system variables or the documentation of a command, for example, depending on the topic

After you arrive at the Help screen you want, look for links to related topics.

At the top of most screens are several buttons. The selection of buttons depends on which aspect of Help you're accessing. These buttons help you navigate the Help system quickly and easily:

- **Hide/Show:** Hides the left pane so that you can work and look at a Help screen at the same time. When hidden, the button becomes a Show button that displays the left pane.
- **Back:** Returns you to the previous Help screen you viewed.
- **Forward:** Returns you to the Help screen you viewed before you clicked the Back button.
- **Home:** Displays the main Help window.
- **Print:** Prints the topic.
- **Options:** Offers further options such as going to the Home Help page and refreshing the screen.

Using the InfoCenter

The InfoCenter is a simple new way to access Help, the Communication Center, and Favorite resources. This tool is located right out in the open, in the upper right-hand corner of the AutoCAD or AutoCAD LT window shown in Figure 3.13.

FIGURE 3.13

The Info Center gives you easy access to Help, the Communication Center, and your Favorite resources.

Communication Center

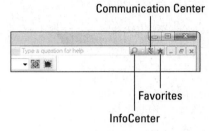

Favorites

InfoCenter

Search Help

The Search field enables you to enter a search term and get results from the Help files and the New Features Workshop. Enter one or more terms and press Enter. The results drop-down, and you can choose the item you want to open it in the Help window.

> **TIP** You can add your own resources to search through those, as well. Click the InfoCenter button and click the Settings button to open the InfoCenter Settings dialog box. Click the New button to add resources. You can add resources from the following file types: TXT, DOC, CHM, HLP, HTML, HTM, PDF, and XML. This is a great place to reference your CAD Standards Manual and/or those of your clients. You can also choose which of the standard resources you want to search, depending on your needs.

The Communication Center

The Communication Center tool in the InfoCenter shows Live Updates (software updates), subscription announcements and lessons (for subscription members), articles, and tips. It now also displays RSS feeds of the knowledge base, blogs, and the discussion group. You can customize the settings, as well. For more information, see Chapter 26.

Favorites

These are quick links to items that you have tagged as useful. You can tag these items from your Search results or in the Communication Center drop-down list. To the right of each item is a white star. Click the star to turn it yellow and add it to the Favorites list.

Getting more help

The Help menu has some additional options that provide assistance that is more specialized. When you choose Help from the menu bar, choose one of these three other items:

- **New Features Workshop:** Provides a combination of explanation, tutorials, and animated demos on new AutoCAD 2008 and AutoCAD LT 2008 features.
- **Support for Subscribers:** If you are a member of Autodesk's Subscription program, you see items that are especially for subscribers. These items connect you to online e-learning resources, as well as access to support services, but are not available for AutoCAD LT.

■ **Additional Resources:** Connects you to various support and training options on Autodesk's Web site, Developer Help (the Help system for topics relating to programming AutoCAD (AutoCAD only), and Autodesk User Group International (AUGI, the Autodesk user group organization).

■ **Customer Involvement Program:** Lets you participate in a program that collects and transmits usage (but no personal) data as you work in AutoCAD. Autodesk uses this data to improve future releases of AutoCAD.

In this exercise, you practice using the Help system.

STEPS: Using AutoCAD Help

1. If AutoCAD or AutoCAD LT is not open, start the program with the `acad.dwt` or `acadlt.dwt` template. If the program is already open, you can do this exercise with any drawing on the screen. Make sure that the AutoCAD Classic or AutoCAD LT Classic workspace is chosen in the Workspaces toolbar. For both AutoCAD and AutoCAD LT, close any palettes that may be open

2. Choose Circle from the Draw toolbar. At the prompt, press F1 on the keyboard. The Circle Help screen opens. (If it doesn't open, click the Help window's button on the Windows taskbar.)

3. Click 2P (Two Points), which appears underlined. The 2P description appears. Read the description of the 2P option.

4. Click the Close button at the top-right corner of the Help screen. Press Esc to exit the CIRCLE command.

5. Choose Help ⇨ Help. Click the Help window's button on the Windows taskbar. If the left, tabbed pane does not appear, click the Show button in the Help window.

6. Click the Contents tab if it is not on top. Double-click User's Guide. From the list, double-click The User Interface and then click the plus sign next to Toolbars, Menus, and the Dashboard.

7. Click Shortcut Menus. Read the text in the right pane.

8. Click the Procedures tab in the right pane of the Help window. Click the To Display a Shortcut Menu link and read the text.

9. On the left side of the Help window, click the Index tab.

10. In the text box at the top, type **transparent commands**. (Don't press Enter.)

11. From the two subtopics shown below, double-click the Commands that Can Be Used As entry.

12. In the right pane, scroll down until you see the heading Interrupt a Command with Another Command or System Variable. Read the text.

13. In the left pane, click the Contents pane again. Scroll down and double-click Command Reference, then double-click Commands.

14. Double-click C Commands, then click CIRCLE. You see the Circle Help screen again. You can find help on any command from the Command Reference.

15. In the AutoCAD InfoCenter window, type **transparent commands** in the Search text box and press Enter. Choose Enter Commands on the Command Line (Quick Reference). If necessary, click the Help button on the Windows taskbar. You should see the Quick Reference tab of the topic. Click the Concept tab to view the same content that you saw in Step 11.

16. Click the Close button of the Help window.

Summary

In this chapter, you read all you need to know about how to use AutoCAD and AutoCAD LT commands. Specifically, you read about:

■ Using the menus

■ Using shortcut menus

■ Using a dialog box

■ Working with toolbars

■ Using tool palettes and the Dashboard

■ Understanding command names

■ Using and editing the command line

■ Using the Dynamic Input tooltip to enter and respond to commands

■ Responding to command options and using the command line and shortcut menus

■ Repeating commands

■ Canceling commands

■ Undoing and redoing commands

■ Using transparent commands

■ Using a puck and digitizing tablet to enter commands

■ Getting help

In the next chapter, I explain how to specify coordinates, an essential skill before you start to draw.

Chapter 4

Specifying Coordinates

S pecifying points in a drawing is one of the most fundamental tasks you do in AutoCAD and AutoCAD LT. Unless you know how to specify a point, you can't draw anything real, whether a house or a gasket. Most objects you draw have a specific size, and you need to specify that information. You draw lines, arcs, and circles by specifying the coordinates of points on the screen. As with most tasks, AutoCAD and AutoCAD LT offer many ways to accomplish this.

Understanding the X,Y Coordinate System

Remember when you studied geometry and trigonometry in high school? You created graphs by drawing X and Y axes. Then you plotted coordinates on graph paper. AutoCAD and AutoCAD LT work the same way.

Look at two displays of the User Coordinate System (UCS) icon, as shown in Figure 4.1. The UCS icon on the left is the default for 2D drawing; the one on the right is the default for 3D drawing and includes the Z axis. In this chapter, I focus on the X and Y axes.

CROSS-REF The UCS icon can take on different appearances. See Chapter 8 for details. For information on the UCS icon in 3D work, see Chapter 21.

IN THIS CHAPTER

Working with absolute, relative, and polar coordinates

Using direct distance entry, orthogonal mode, and polar tracking

Using snap settings

Working with object snaps (OSNAPS)

Locating points

FIGURE 4.1

The UCS icon shows the direction of the X and Y axes. If you're in a 3D display, you also see the Z axis.

The X arrow points along the X axis in the positive direction. This means that as you go in the direction of the arrow, the X coordinates increase. The Y arrow points along the Y axis in the positive direction.

Using this system, every 2D point on the screen can be specified using X and Y coordinates. This is called a *Cartesian* coordinate system. The universal convention is to place the X coordinate first, then a comma (but no space), and then the Y coordinate. By default, the intersection of the X,Y axes is 0,0. Use negative numbers for points to the left of the X axis or below the Y axis.

Drawing units

What do the coordinates measure? When you draw in AutoCAD or AutoCAD LT, you draw in undefined units. A line from point 3,0 to point 6,0 is three units long. While you're drawing, these units can be anything — a millimeter, a centimeter, a meter, an inch, a foot, or a mile. In reality, you should know exactly what the units represent. After all, you don't want your 36-foot-wide house to end up 36 inches wide!

When you set up a drawing, you specify how units are displayed — for example, whether partial units show as decimal points or fractions. (I cover units in Chapter 5.) However, you don't actually specify what the units represent until you print or plot your drawing — covered in Chapter 17.

To ensure accuracy, you should draw full size. If you're drawing a plan for a factory that will be 120 feet long, for example, you create lines with those measurements. On the screen, you can zoom in to see small details or zoom out to see the whole factory, so that you have no reason not to use the actual line lengths. It's only when you need to print those 120-foot-long lines on a real sheet of paper that you have to specify how to plot out your drawing at a reduced scale.

Types of measurement notation

Users are typically familiar only with the type of notation used in their own field of specialty, whether scientific, architectural, engineering, or whatever. However, you should be at least somewhat familiar with all the major forms of measurement notation.

NOTE   **If you are using engineering or architectural units, AutoCAD and AutoCAD LT display parts of inches (fractions) differently than the format you must use to type them in. You must type in coordinates without any spaces because in AutoCAD a space is equivalent to pressing Enter, and that ends your input. Use a hyphen between whole and partial inches — for example, 3'2-1/2". (You can omit the " after the inches because inches are assumed in engineering and architectural units if no symbol follows a number.) However, this appears on the status bar as 3'-2 1/2". This can be confusing because the hyphen is in a different place, and you see a space between the whole and partial inches.**

Typing Coordinates

One of the more basic ways to specify the location of an object is to type its coordinates using the keyboard. You can enter several types of coordinates. Use the type of coordinates that suit your specific situation.

TIP   If you need to enter a coordinate that you've typed recently, use the Recent Input feature. Right-click and choose Recent Input from the shortcut menu. Then choose the coordinate that you want from the list that appears.

Using the Dynamic Input tooltip to enter coordinates

Dynamic Input enables you to enter text input near the cursor. In Chapter 3, I explained how to use the Dynamic Input tooltip for commands and command options. Here I explain how to use it to enter coordinates.

The DYN button on the status bar turns Dynamic Input on and off. Because you can look at the tooltip near the cursor when you enter text, you can keep your attention on the drawing area, rather than looking down at the command line. Dynamic Input applies to commands that you type, responses to prompts, and coordinates.

Typing coordinates in the Dynamic Input tooltip

You can type 2D coordinates in the Dynamic Input tooltip in the same way you type them on the command line — in the format **x,y**. You can press Tab between the X and Y coordinates instead of typing a comma, but typing the comma is probably easier and therefore more accurate.

When you draw a line, after you specify the first point, you see only one tooltip box because AutoCAD assumes that you want to enter only the distance, using the current angle of the temporary line shown on the screen. However, as soon as you type a comma or press the Tab key, a second box appears so that you can enter the Y coordinate, as shown in Figure 4.2. The same situation applies when you want to move or copy an object and want to specify an X,Y displacement.

In Figure 4.2, note the lock next to the X coordinate. Before you type any part of the coordinate, both the X and Y values vary as you move the mouse. When you enter a value for the X coordinate, you fix this value, as the lock indicates. However, the Y coordinate is still unlocked until you type a value.

CROSS-REF   If you need to enter a three-dimensional coordinate, type a comma after the Y coordinate. A third tooltip box appears so that you can enter a Z value. For more information on 3D coordinates, see Chapter 21.

FIGURE 4.2

As you enter an X,Y coordinate, two boxes appear, one for each part of the coordinate.

Specifying Dynamic Input settings

You can specify how Dynamic Input works for coordinates that you type. Changing the settings gives you very different results when you type coordinates, so you should familiarize yourself with the settings options.

To specify settings for the Dynamic Input feature, right-click the DYN button on the status bar and choose Settings to display the Dynamic Input tab of the Drafting Settings dialog box, as shown in Figure 4.3.

Use the Dynamic Input tab of the Drafting Settings dialog box to specify how your Dynamic Input works when you type coordinates.

Pointer Input section. The Enable Pointer Input check box is selected by default, which means that the Dynamic Input tooltip includes an input box where you can type coordinates at the start of any command. If you uncheck this check box, you see these first coordinates only on the command line as you enter them. However, whether the check box is checked or not, as long as the DYN button is selected on the status bar, you see the input box for subsequent coordinates in a command. For example, if you are drawing a line, and the Enable Pointer Input check box is not checked, you don't see coordinates that you type for the start point in the Dynamic Input tooltip, but for the next point, you see the input box and coordinates that you type appear in that box.

Click the Settings button to open the Pointer Input Settings dialog box. Here you can make the following choices:

■ **Default format for second or next points.** You can choose to default to polar or Cartesian format. The default is polar format, which shows distances. I explain polar format in the "Polar coordinates" section later in this chapter. You can also choose between relative and absolute coordinates, as shown in Figure 4.4. The default is relative coordinates, which indicate a distance and direction from a previously specified point. I explain both absolute and relative formats in the next few sections of this chapter.

- **Tooltip visibility.** You can specify that you see the tooltip only when you start typing a point in response to a prompt, automatically at a prompt for a point (the default), or always.

FIGURE 4.4

The Pointer Input Settings dialog box sets important options for Dynamic Input.

WARNING The settings in this dialog box are very important for determining how all your coordinate entry works when Dynamic Entry is turned on. If you are upgrading from an earlier version of AutoCAD, you are used to the entry of X,Y coordinates denoting absolute, not relative coordinates. However, with Dynamic Input turned on, the default is relative coordinates. This is a great default and will speed up your coordinate entry, but could be very confusing if you are unaware of this setting or where to change it.

Dimension Input section. The Enable Dimension Input Where Possible check box is selected by default. This section has nothing to do with dimensions! Instead, it refers to distances or lengths as well as angles, as opposed to points or coordinates. With this check box selected, after you indicate a first point, such as the start of a line or the center of a circle, you see a dimension tooltip that shows the length of the line segment or radius of the circle, as shown in Figure 4.5. You specify the length by typing in this tooltip. If you uncheck the check box, you don't see this dimension tooltip.

FIGURE 4.5

The so-called dimension input tooltip shows distances and angles.

Click the Settings button in this section of the dialog box to open the Dimension Input Settings dialog box. Here you can change settings relating to dimension input during grip editing. I discuss grip editing in Chapter 10.

NOTE If you uncheck both the Enable Pointer Input and the Enable Dimension Input Where Possible check boxes, you turn off Dynamic Input.

Dynamic prompts section. The Show Command Prompting and Command Input Near the Crosshairs check box enables the display of command prompts and your input in response to these prompts in the Dynamic Input tooltip. This part of Dynamic Input is supposed to take the place of the command line. However, the prompts are not an exact echo of what you see on the command line, and certain prompts do not appear in the tooltip.

NOTE If you like Dynamic Input, try turning off the command line, using the COMMANDLINEHIDE command or by pressing Ctrl+9. If this works for you, you'll have more room for your drawing area. You can always get the command-line window back with the COMMANDLINE command or by pressing Ctrl+9 again. You can also undock the Command window, right-click its title bar, and choose Auto-hide. Then, the Command window collapses to just its title bar; when you place the cursor over it, it automatically expands again.

Click the Drafting Tooltip Appearance button to open the Tooltip Appearance dialog box. Here you can change the color of the tooltip, change its size and transparency, and apply the settings to all drafting tooltips in AutoCAD.

Overriding Dynamic Input settings

The default Dynamic Input settings ensure that your input in the tooltip is always interpreted as polar, relative coordinates. However, you may want to override this setting for an individual coordinate. You can override this setting by using a symbol before your X coordinate as you type it. AutoCAD provides three overrides that you can use:

- **Absolute:** To override the default setting of relative coordinates and enter an absolute coordinate, type **#**. For example, you could type **#0,0** to specify the 0,0 coordinate. See the next section of this chapter for more information on absolute coordinates.

- **Relative:** If you have set your Dynamic Input for absolute coordinates, you can enter **@** to override the setting and type a relative coordinate. For example, you could type **@3,4**. See the "Relative Cartesian coordinates" and "Polar coordinates" sections for a detailed explanation of relative coordinates.

- **World:** Normally, coordinates that you type are interpreted in the current User Coordinate System. The default coordinate system is called the World Coordinate System. If you have created a custom coordinate system but want to enter a World Coordinate System coordinate, type *** before the X coordinate. For more information, see the "Understanding User Coordinate Systems" section in Chapter 8 (for two-dimensional drawings) and the "Working with the User Coordinate System" section in Chapter 21 (for three-dimensional drawings).

TIP To temporarily turn off Dynamic Input, press and hold the F12 key. You might do this while you are picking points if you find that the tooltip obscures objects that you need to see. As soon as you release the F12 key, Dynamic Input returns.

Absolute Cartesian coordinates

When you type a line and enter the actual coordinates, such as a line from point 3,2 to 6,9, you are using absolute Cartesian coordinates. Absolute coordinates are measured from 0,0. These coordinates are probably familiar to you from high-school geometry class.

If you have Dynamic Input on with the default setting of relative units, you must enter the # symbol before entering the X portion of an absolute Cartesian coordinate when specifying the second or next point, as explained in the previous section.

In this exercise, you practice entering absolute Cartesian coordinates.

STEPS: Entering Absolute Cartesian Coordinates

1. Start a new drawing using the `acad.dwt` or `acadlt.dwt` template. If you're using AutoCAD, make sure that the AutoCAD Classic workspace is chosen in the Workspaces toolbar or the AutoCAD LT Classic workspace if you are using AutoCAD LT. Close any palettes that may be open.

2. If you have Dynamic Input on, right-click the DYN button on the status bar and choose Settings. In the Pointer Input section, click the Settings button. In the Pointer Input Settings dialog box, click the Absolute Coordinates option (unless this option is already selected). Click OK twice to return to your drawing.

3. Choose Line from the Draw toolbar. Follow these prompts:

```
Specify first point: -10,-5 ↵
Specify next point or [Undo]: 21,-5 ↵
Specify next point or [Undo]: 21,49 ↵
Specify next point or [Close/Undo]: -10,49 ↵
Specify next point or [Close/Undo]: c ↵ (to close the rectangle)
```

Most of the lines are off the screen. By default, a new drawing starts with 0,0 at the lower-left corner of your screen; therefore, negative coordinates do not show.

4. Choose View ➪ Zoom ➪ Zoom Out from the menu. If you still can't see the entire rectangle, choose Zoom Out again until you can see it. Your picture should look like Figure 4.6.

FIGURE 4.6

A rectangle drawn by using absolute coordinates.

If the prompt responds with `Invalid Point` or `Point or option keyword required`, you have entered a coordinate incorrectly. Try typing the coordinate again. Also, don't forget that you can undo a command if you make a mistake. (See Chapter 3 for details.)

5. Start the LINE command again and follow these prompts:

    ```
    Specify first point: -8,-2 ↵
    Specify next point or [Undo]: 19,-2 ↵
    Specify next point or [Undo]: 19,21.5 ↵
    Specify next point or [Close/Undo]: -8,21.5 ↵
    Specify next point or [Close/Undo]: c ↵
    ```

6. Once more, start the LINE command and follow these prompts:

    ```
    Specify first point: -8,22.5 ↵
    Specify next point or [Undo]: 19,22.5 ↵
    Specify next point or [Undo]: 19,46 ↵
    Specify next point or [Close/Undo]: -8,46 ↵
    Specify next point or [Close/Undo]: c ↵
    ```

7. If you changed the Dynamic Input settings in Step 1, you should change them back. Right-click the DYN button on the status bar and choose Settings. In the Pointer Input section, click the Settings button. In the Pointer Input Settings dialog box, click the Relative Coordinates option. Click OK twice to return to your drawing.

8. Save this drawing in your `AutoCAD Bible` folder as `ab04-01.dwg`.

You can now see that you've drawn a simple window, as shown in Figure 4.7.

FIGURE 4.7

A window drawn with absolute coordinates.

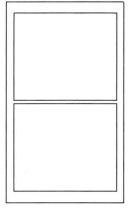

Two questions may have occurred to you during this exercise. First, isn't there a better way of entering absolute coordinates? Typing them in is slow and prone to error. Second, how do you know the absolute coordinates for what you're drawing? Read on for the answers.

Relative Cartesian coordinates

In practice, you usually don't know the absolute coordinates of the points you need to specify in order to draw an object. Whether you're drawing an architectural layout, a physical object (as in mechanical drawing), or an electrical schematic, you don't have X,Y coordinates from which you can work. However, you often do have the measurements of what you're drawing. Usually, you start from any suitable point and work from there. In this situation, you know only the length of the lines you're drawing (if you're drawing lines). Real life doesn't have a 0,0 point. Relative coordinates were developed for these situations.

Relative coordinates specify the X and Y distance from a previous point. They are called *relative coordinates* because they have meaning relative only to a point previously specified. Suppose that you need to draw a window. You can start the window from any point. From there, you have the measurements you need. (The measurements may be shown on a piece of paper you're working from, or you may have the actual window sitting next to you so you can measure it.)

If you have Dynamic Input on — set to the default option of relative units — X,Y coordinates are automatically relative. If you have Dynamic Input off or have set Dynamic Input to absolute coordinates, as described earlier in this chapter, you specify that the coordinates are relative by using the @ symbol. For example, if you start a line by picking any point with the mouse, and you know it should be two units long, you can specify the next point as @2,0. The result is a line starting with the first point you picked and ending two units along the X axis, as shown in Figure 4.8. The line is horizontal because the Y coordinate is 0. In a relative coordinate, this means that the Y distance does not change.

FIGURE 4.8

A line whose start point could be anywhere and whose endpoint is specified with the relative point @2,0 is a horizontal line two units long.

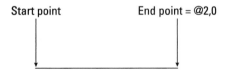

Start point   End point = @2,0

Relative Cartesian coordinates are often used for lines drawn at 90-degree angles (that is, they are either horizontal or vertical). These are called *orthogonal lines*. However, when you create a diagonal line from point 3,3 to point @2,5, the length of the line is not immediately obvious.

When you specify a positive number, such as the 2 in @2,0, the direction is positive. If you want to draw a line in the negative direction of an axis, type a minus sign before the number. Figure 4.9 shows how to draw lines in four directions using relative coordinates.

FIGURE 4.9

Drawing lines in the four orthogonal directions with relative coordinates. The arrow on each line shows the direction of the line.

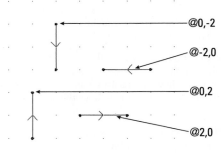

Polar coordinates

Another common situation is to know the distance and angle of a point from either 0,0 or a previous point. In this case, you can use *polar coordinates,* which can be either absolute or relative. Most commonly, you use relative polar coordinates.

Polar coordinates take the form distance<angle. (To type the angle symbol, use the less-than symbol on your keyboard.) If you have Dynamic Input on, set to the default options of relative coordinates, polar coordinates are automatically relative. If you have Dynamic Input off or have set Dynamic Input to absolute coordinates, as described earlier in this chapter, you need to add the @ sign before a relative polar coordinate. If you also have the default option of polar format, you first see coordinates in polar format. Enter the distance, press the Tab key, and then enter the angle. You can also type the angle (<) symbol instead of using the Tab key. To switch to Cartesian format, just type a comma between the X and Y coordinates.

With Dynamic Input on, angles are measured from 0 to 180, with 0 to the right, going either clockwise or counterclockwise. Watch the dotted lines near the angle tooltip to see exactly what the angle shown in the tooltip is measuring. You can use negative angles. With Dynamic Input off, angles are measured counterclockwise, with 0 to the right, ranging from 0 to 360.

In the following series of steps, you draw part of a portico, the decorative molding above a door or window. Because it is an architectural design, you use architectural units. In this case, only inches are used, which don't need to be specified. You can specify feet by using an apostrophe (also called a *prime*) after any number.

When typing architectural units, partial inches are indicated by fractions in the form a/b. You need to separate the fraction from the whole inches by a hyphen. This can be a little confusing because the hyphen is also used for negative numbers. For example, to draw a horizontal line of 5¼ inches in the negative direction of the X axis, you would type **-5-1/4,0**. (The 0 indicates no change in the Y axis because it is a horizontal line.)

ON the DVD-ROM The drawing used in this exercise on using relative and polar coordinates, ab04-a.dwg, is in the Drawings folder on the DVD.

STEPS: Using Relative and Polar Coordinates

1. Open `ab04-a.dwg` from the DVD. Make sure that the AutoCAD Classic or AutoCAD LT Classic workspace is chosen in the Workspaces toolbar. Close any palettes that may be open.

2. As you move your mouse around, notice that the coordinates displayed on the status bar are in architectural units (that is, in feet and inches). If the coordinates are grayed out, click them to turn them on.

3. Choose File ➪ Save As and save the drawing in your `AutoCAD Bible` folder as `ab04-02.dwg`.

NOTE The next steps involve some complex typing. If you get an error message, try typing the coordinate again. If you realize you made a mistake after ending the command, click Undo on the Standard toolbar. This exercise assumes that you are using the default Dynamic Input settings of polar format and relative coordinates and that Dynamic Input is on. See the section "Using the Dynamic Input tooltip to enter coordinates" earlier in this chapter for details.

4. Start the LINE command. Follow these prompts:

   ```
   Specify first point: Pick any point at the lower-left corner of your
   screen.
   Specify next point or [Undo]: 0,-3/4 ↵
   Specify next point or [Undo]: 75-1/4,0 ↵
   Specify next point or [Close/Undo]: 0,3/4 ↵
   Specify next point or [Close/Undo]: c ↵
   ```

5. Start the LINE command again. Follow the prompts:

   ```
   Specify first point: ↵. This starts the line at the last endpoint you
   specified.
   Specify next point or [Undo]: 4-3/4,0 ↵
   Specify next point or [Undo]: 43<40 ↵
   Specify next point or [Close/Undo]: 43<-40 ↵
   Specify next point or [Close/Undo]: -2-1/4,0 ↵
   Specify next point or [Close/Undo]: 39-7/8<140 ↵
   Specify next point or [Close/Undo]: 39-7/8<-140 ↵
   Specify next point or [Close/Undo]: ↵ to end the command.
   ```

NOTE In this exercise, you draw a line on top of a line, which is not good drawing practice. Later in this chapter and in coming chapters, you learn techniques to avoid this.

6. Save your drawing. You have created a portion of a portico, which goes over a window of a house, as shown in Figure 4.10.

FIGURE 4.10

Part of a portico over a window, drawn using relative Cartesian and polar coordinates in architectural notation.

You can type @ ↵ at the first prompt of any drawing command to indicate the most recent coordinate specified.

Notice that using relative coordinates, both Cartesian and polar, is much more realistic than using absolute coordinates. However, typing in all those coordinates is still awkward. Typing in coordinates is often the only way to get exactly what you want. Nevertheless, several other techniques for specifying coordinates are easier in many circumstances. I discuss these techniques in the next few sections.

Direct distance entry

One shortcut for entering coordinates is direct distance entry. After you specify the start point of a line, at the `Specify next point or [Undo]:` prompt, simply move the mouse cursor in the direction you want the line to go and type in the line's length. It works best in orthogonal mode or with polar tracking (discussed in the following section), which makes specifying exact angles easy.

 You can use direct distance entry for any command that requires you to specify a distance and a direction, including both drawing and editing commands.

Orthogonal mode

Lines drawn at 0, 90, 180, and 270 degrees are called *orthogonal lines*. When in orthogonal mode — *ortho* for short — you can only draw orthogonal lines with the mouse. Ortho mode also affects editing. For example, with ortho mode on, you can only move objects vertically or horizontally. Combined with snap and grid, ortho mode makes drawing easier and more efficient. Ortho mode is also great for direct distance entry.

Click ORTHO on the status bar to toggle ortho mode on and off. You cannot have polar tracking on at the same time that ortho mode is on. Polar tracking is discussed next.

NOTE Orthogonal mode only affects points picked directly on the screen by using your mouse. Any relative or absolute coordinates that you type in the Dynamic Input tooltip or on the command line override orthogonal mode. For example, if you use a polar coordinate of 5<45 in the Dynamic tooltip, you'll get a line at an angle of 45 degrees, even when ortho mode is on.

Polar tracking

Polar tracking guides you, using a tooltip and vector line, when you want to draw (or edit) at an angle other than the four orthogonal angles, as shown in Figure 4.11. You can use polar tracking for orthogonal angles as well. If you have Dynamic Input on, just look for the word "Polar" to distinguish between the Dynamic Input and the polar tooltips.

Polar tracking makes it easy to use direct distance entry to specify distances for many angles. To use polar tracking, you first set the angles that you want to use.

FIGURE 4.11

When polar tracking is on, a tooltip appears when you move the cursor close to one of the polar angles. Here you see a tooltip indicating an angle of 45 degrees.

Polar tracking vector

Polar: 3'-0 3/8" < 45d — Polar tracking tooltip

Setting polar tracking angles

To set the angles, choose Tools ➪ Drafting Settings or right-click the POLAR button on the status bar and choose Settings. The Drafting Settings dialog box opens. If necessary, click the Polar Tracking tab, which you can see in Figure 4.12.

FIGURE 4.12

The Polar Tracking tab of the Drafting Settings dialog box.

To set polar tracking, you can define two types of angles:

- **Increment angle:** To set the increment angle, click the Increment Angle drop-down arrow, where you can pick from angles that range from every 90 degrees to every 5 degrees. You can also type your own incremental angle in the text box. Polar tracking will then apply to that angle and its multiples.

- **Additional angles:** If you think that you'll need other angles, check Additional Angles, click New, and then type in an angle. You can add up to 10 additional angles. Note that additional angles that you add are not incremental angles — if you type 35, only 35 degrees will be marked, not 70 degrees or other multiples of 35. To delete an additional angle, select it and click Delete.

On the right side of the dialog box, you can choose how polar tracking works with object snap tracking (covered later in this chapter). You can set object snap tracking to use all the polar angle settings or limit it to orthogonal angles only. You can also set whether polar angles are measured absolutely (relative to 0 degrees) or relative to the segment drawn most recently. By default, absolute angles are used. To turn on polar tracking, check the Polar Tracking On check box on the Polar Tracking tab of the Drafting Settings dialog box. If you are not in the dialog box, press F10 or click the POLAR button on the status bar.

To customize how polar tracking works, click Options in the Drafting Settings dialog box to open the Options dialog box with the Drafting tab on top. The following settings in the AutoTracking Settings section apply to polar tracking:

- **Display polar tracking vector** turns on and off the polar tracking vector, which is the faint dotted line that extends to the end of the screen.

- **Display AutoTrack tooltip** turns on and off the tooltip that tells you the distance and angle.

Using polar tracking

To use polar tracking, you need to move the cursor slowly through the angles to allow time for the calculation and display of the vector and tooltip. Suppose that you're drawing a line. Specify the start point. To specify the second point, move the cursor in the approximate angle of the line you want to draw. When you see the polar tracking vector and tooltip, leave the mouse where it is and type the length of the line. Then press Enter to create the line with the proper length and angle. You'll find this method easier than typing polar coordinates for lines with angles specified in your polar tracking settings.

> **TIP** Turn on NumLock on your keyboard and use the numerical pad for typing lengths. Use the Enter key on the numerical pad as well.

You can specify a polar angle for just one command. If you're drawing a line, after specifying the first point, for example, type the angle preceded by the angle symbol (<). The next segment is then locked to that angle while you type its length. A polar angle specified in this way is called a *polar override angle* because it overrides the current polar angles in effect. Of course, a polar override is not faster than simply typing a polar coordinate, but it does let you see the angle of the line segment before you type its length.

In the following exercise, you practice using direct distance entry with ortho mode and polar tracking.

> **ON the DVD-ROM** The drawing (ab04-b.dwg) used in the following exercise on using direct distance entry with ortho mode and polar tracking is in the Drawings folder on the DVD.

STEPS: Using Direct Distance Entry with Ortho Mode and Polar Tracking

1. Open the drawing ab04-b.dwg from the DVD. Make sure that the AutoCAD Classic or AutoCAD LT Classic workspace is chosen in the Workspaces toolbar. Close any palettes that may be open. Check that polar tracking is set for 45 degrees, as described previously in this chapter.

2. Choose File ⇨ Save As to save the drawing in your AutoCAD Bible folder as ab04-03.dwg. If ORTHO is not on (that is, if the ORTHO button on the status bar doesn't look pushed in), click ORTHO.

3. Start the LINE command and, at the Specify first point: prompt, type **2,2** ↵.

4. Move the mouse horizontally to the right and then type **.5** ↵.

5. Move the mouse up vertically (in the 90-degree direction) and then type **.5** ↵.

6. Move the mouse horizontally to the right and then type **2** ↵. Your drawing should look like Figure 4.13.

FIGURE 4.13

Drawing with direct distance entry enables you to specify coordinates by typing in a length after you move the pointer in the desired direction.

7. Move the mouse up in the 90-degree direction and then type **.5** ↵.

8. Move the mouse to the left in the 180-degree direction and then type **2** ↵.

9. Move the mouse up in the 90-degree direction and then type **.5** ↵.

10. Move the mouse to the left in the 180-degree direction and then type **.5** ↵.

11. Type **c** ↵ to close the figure. Press Enter again to end the command.

12. Click POLAR on the status bar. The ORTHO button pops out.

13. Start the LINE command again. Press Enter to start the new line from the most recent point. At the Specify next point or [Undo]: prompt, move the cursor diagonally up and to the left so the line is approximately in the 135-degree direction. When you see the tooltip confirming the angle, release the mouse button and type **.7071** ↵.

14. Move the cursor up until you see the polar tracking tooltip confirming a 90-degree angle. Type **.5** ↵.

15. Move the cursor diagonally in the 45-degree direction until you see the tooltip. Type **.7071** ↵. Press Enter again to end the LINE command.

16. Save your drawing. It should look like Figure 4.14.

FIGURE 4.14

The completed drawing of a bolt.

Displaying Coordinates

As you work, you can refer to the coordinate display on the status bar. This display helps you know where your cursor and objects are when you draw and is also helpful when editing, by informing you how far and in what direction you are moving or copying objects.

NOTE You can set the Dynamic Input tooltip to show coordinates all the time, even when you're not in a command. See the section, "Specifying Dynamic Input settings" earlier in this chapter.

AutoCAD and AutoCAD LT have three coordinate display modes:

- **Dynamic absolute coordinates (absolute):** Absolute coordinates that change as you move the mouse, as shown in Figure 4.15.

FIGURE 4.15

Dynamic absolute coordinates.

| 0.7409, 2.1450 , 0.0000 |

- **Static absolute coordinates (off):** Absolute coordinates that change only when you specify a point, as shown in Figure 4.16. The coordinate display is dimmed.

FIGURE 4.16

Static absolute coordinates.

| 0.3485, 3.0654 , 0.0000 |

- **Dynamic polar coordinates (relative):** Polar coordinates that change continuously as you move the mouse, as shown in Figure 4.17. They appear after you've already specified a point and are ready to specify the next point, as when you're in the process of drawing a line.

FIGURE 4.17

Dynamic polar coordinates.

| 1.4580< 29   , 0.0000 |

The easiest way to change the coordinate display is to click the coordinates area on the status bar. You can also right-click the coordinate display and choose Relative, Absolute, or Off from the shortcut menu.

For purposes of this chapter, I ignore the Z coordinate that follows the X and Y coordinates (in AutoCAD only). In two-dimensional drawings, the Z coordinate is always zero.

In the following exercise, you practice using the coordinate display options. You can do this exercise with any new or existing drawing open on the screen. If you have Dynamic Input on, compare the display in the Dynamic Input tooltip and the display on the status bar.

STEPS: Using Coordinate Display Options

1. Look at the coordinate display on the status bar. It should be shown in black. If the coordinates are shown in gray, click the coordinates.

2. Move the mouse around in a few directions. Notice how the coordinates constantly change with the mouse movement.

3. Right-click the coordinates and choose Off. The coordinate display is grayed out.

4. Move the mouse around again. The coordinate display does not change with the movement of the mouse.

5. Start the LINE command and pick any point on the screen.

6. Watch the coordinate display as you pick any point at the Specify next point or [Undo]: prompt.

7. Pick several other points and watch as the coordinate display changes only when you pick a point. This is the static coordinate display.

8. Click the coordinates again without ending the LINE command.

9. Move the mouse to another point that you would like to pick, but watch the coordinate display before you pick the point. This time, the length and angle of the new line segment are shown. These are dynamic polar coordinates.

10. Pick a few more points, watching the polar coordinates.

11. Right-click the coordinates and choose Absolute to return to dynamic absolute coordinates.

12. Press Enter to end the LINE command. Do not save your drawing.

Picking Coordinates on the Screen

The easiest and quickest way to specify coordinates is to pick them directly on the screen with the mouse. Several techniques are available to help you do so accurately.

You can adjust the size of the crosshairs that cross the cursor. By default, they are 5 percent of screen size. To change the crosshair size, choose Tools ➪ Options and click the Display tab. In the Crosshair size text box, you can type a new percentage or drag the bar to increase or decrease the percentage. Choose OK.

Snap settings

The SNAP command is often an alternative to tedious entry of coordinates. This command restricts the cursor to an incremental distance that you choose, such as 0.5 units. You can set the snap size to anything you want. For example, if all your measurements are rounded off to the nearest 0.25 units, you can set your snap to 0.25.

The snap technique is not very useful when you need to draw to three or more decimal places of accuracy. And when you're zoomed out in a large drawing, the snap points may be so close together that you cannot easily find the one you want. But in the right situation, snap is one of the quickest, most accurate drawing techniques available.

AutoCAD and AutoCAD LT provide two types of snap settings, grid snap and polar snap.

Snapping to a grid

When you snap to a grid, an invisible grid becomes active (which you can make visible using the GRID command, discussed in the next section). As soon as you turn on snap, the mouse cursor can move only to the snap grid points.

To set the snap size, choose Tools ➪ Drafting Settings or right-click the SNAP button on the status bar and choose Settings. The Drafting Settings dialog box opens, as shown in Figure 4.18. (If necessary, click the Snap and Grid tab.) In the Snap X Spacing text box of the Snap Spacing section, type the spacing you want between snap points. Make sure that Grid snap and Rectangular snap are checked in the Snap Type section of the dialog box. Click OK.

FIGURE 4.18

The Snap and Grid tab of the Drafting Settings dialog box. (The AutoCAD LT dialog box is slightly different.)

CROSS-REF   Note that you can change the angle of the snap spacing. In Chapter 8, I discuss rotating the angle of the snap and grid. Chapter 8 also discusses Isometric snap, used for isometric drawing.

Usually you want the X spacing (going across) to be the same as the Y spacing (going up and down). By default, the Equal X and Y Spacing check box is selected so you need to specify only the X spacing, and the Y spacing changes automatically to equal the X spacing. X and Y spacing will be different only if you type a different number in the Snap Y spacing box.

You can also turn snap on in this dialog box by clicking the On check box. However, the most common way to turn snap on, after you've set the spacing, is to click SNAP on the status bar (or press the F9 key). Click it again to turn snap off.

Snapping at polar angles

After you set polar tracking settings, discussed earlier in this chapter in the "Polar tracking" section, you can snap to increments along the polar angles you have set. When PolarSnap is on, the polar tooltip only shows distances in increments of the snap setting. When you see the distance you want, just click. PolarSnap makes it easy to draw accurately without having to type coordinates.

To use PolarSnap, follow these steps:

1. Right-click the SNAP button on the status bar and click Settings to open the Drafting Settings dialog box with the Snap and Grid tab displayed, as just explained.
2. Check PolarSnap in the Snap Type section of the dialog box (refer to Figure 4.18).
3. Type a number in the Polar Distance text box.
4. Click OK to close the dialog box.
5. Click SNAP on the status bar.

Note that PolarSnap and Grid snap are mutually exclusive. If PolarSnap is on, the cursor will not snap to the grid. Used with polar tracking, PolarSnap is a powerful tool. Remember that you can polar track along orthogonal as well as other angles.

 You can choose either PolarSnap or Grid snap (switch between them) by right-clicking SNAP on the status bar. A shortcut menu lets you choose the type of snap you want, or turn both off.

The grid

Sometimes you may find it helpful to see a grid of dots to help get your bearings while you draw, as shown in Figure 4.19. If the dot grid is not visible, click GRID on the status bar or press the F7 key. Notice how you can quickly judge the approximate width of a windowpane, knowing that the grid dots are half a foot apart. If you turn on snap, the grid helps you visualize the snap points. However, the grid dots do not have to be set to the same spacing as the snap points.

FIGURE 4.19

A portion of a drawing with the grid turned on and set to 6 inches.

Thanks to Henry Dearborn, AIA, Fairfield, Iowa, for this drawing.

Some users find the grid annoying, but when you first start to use AutoCAD or AutoCAD LT, you may find it helpful. Even accomplished users can take advantage of the grid, especially when starting a new drawing.

 If you're working with a small snap spacing and the dot grid is too dense, set the dot grid to two or more times the size of the snap spacing.

To set the grid size, choose Tools ➪ Drafting Settings to open the Drafting Settings dialog box (refer to Figure 4.18). If necessary, click the Snap and Grid tab. In the X Spacing text box of the Grid Spacing section, type the spacing you want between grid points. Click OK.

As with the snap feature, you usually want the X spacing (going across) to be the same as the Y spacing (going up and down). You only need to specify the X spacing; the Y spacing automatically changes to be the same, as long as the Equal X and Y Spacing check box is selected in the Drafting Settings dialog box. X and Y spacing will only be different if you type a different number in the Y Spacing box.

You can turn on the Grid in this dialog box by clicking the On check box, but it's easier to click GRID on the status bar (or press F7).

In the following exercise, you practice using polar and grid snap points as well as grid dots.

 The drawing used in the following exercise on using snap points and grid dots, ab04-b.dwg, **is in the** Drawings **folder on the DVD.**

STEPS: Using Snap Points and Grid Dots

1. Open ab04-b.dwg from the DVD. Make sure that the AutoCAD Classic or AutoCAD LT Classic workspace is chosen in the Workspaces toolbar. Close any palettes that may be open.

2. Choose File ➪ Save As to save the drawing in your AutoCAD Bible folder as ab04-04.dwg.

3. Choose Tools ➪ Drafting Settings. The Drafting Settings dialog box opens. Click the Snap and Grid tab if it is not displayed. In the Snap Type section, make sure that you check Grid snap and Rectangular snap.

4. In the Snap Spacing section, change the Snap X Spacing to 0.5.

5. In the Grid Spacing section, make sure that the Equal X and Y Spacing check box is selected. Click in the Grid X spacing text box. Change the Grid X spacing to 0.5. Click OK. The Grid Y spacing automatically changes to match the Grid X spacing of 0.5.

6. On the status bar, click SNAP, GRID, and ORTHO. The grid appears. Make sure that the OSNAP and OTRACK buttons on the status bar are off. (AutoCAD LT doesn't have the OTRACK button.)

7. Choose View ➪ Zoom ➪ All.

8. Move the mouse around and watch the coordinates on the status bar. (Right-click the coordinate and choose Absolute if they are in static mode.) They show halves of units because you have set the snap to 0.5.

9. Start the LINE command. At the Specify first point: prompt, click when the coordinates on the status bar show 2.0000,2.0000. (AutoCAD users can ignore the third Z coordinate, which is always 0.0000 in 2D drawings.) If you have Dynamic Input on, you'll find the coordinates in the Dynamic Input tooltip easier to read.

10. Move the mouse around and watch the coordinates. If you don't see polar coordinates (for example 3.0000<0), right-click the coordinates and choose Relative.

11. Move the mouse to the right until the coordinates read 8.5000<0 and click the pick (left) button. You have drawn a horizontal line with a length of 8.5 units.

12. Click the right mouse button and choose Enter to end the LINE command.

13. Move the mouse cursor away from the end of the new line and back to it again, and the absolute coordinates appear. They should be 10.5000,2.0000.

14. Right-click and choose Repeat Line to start the LINE command again. Use the coordinate display to start the line at 1.5000,1.5000. (For the rest of this exercise, ignore the Dynamic Input tooltip.) Continue to pick points (rather than type them) and draw the following line segments, as shown in the coordinate display:

        0.5000<0
        3.0000<90
        0.5000<180
        3.0000<270

15. End the LINE command.

16. Start the LINE command and pick points, drawing the following line segments (as shown in the coordinate display) starting from 10.5000,1.50. Then end the LINE command:

        0.5000<0
        3.0000<90
        0.5000<180
        3.0000<270

17. Starting from 2.0000, 4.0000 draw an 8.5-unit line at 0 degrees. End the LINE command.

18. Start the LINE command again. At the first prompt, pick 11.0000,2.0000. Right-click SNAP on the status bar and choose Settings. In the Snap Type section, choose PolarSnap. (This is equivalent to choosing the PolarSnap On feature on the SNAP button shortcut menu.) In the Polar Spacing section, change the Polar Distance to 0.5. Choose the Polar Tracking tab and (if necessary) set the Increment Angle to 45 degrees. Click OK. Click POLAR on the status bar.

19. Move the cursor in a 45-degree direction from 11.0000,2.0000 until you see the tooltip. Move along the polar tracking vector until the tooltip says 3.5000 < 45° and click. End the LINE command.

20. Right-click the SNAP button and choose Grid Snap On. Start the LINE command and, at the `Specify first point:` prompt, choose 11.0000,4.0000.

21. Right-click the SNAP button and choose PolarSnap On. Move the cursor in a 45-degree direction until the tooltip says 3.5000 < 45° and click. End the LINE command.

22. Save your drawing. Your drawing should look like Figure 4.20.

As you no doubt experienced, this is a much easier way to draw compared to typing in coordinates. Note that drawing with snap on works better when you're drawing small objects. However, even when drawing an office building, you spend a great deal of time working on small details that may be easier to draw with snap on.

FIGURE 4.20

The completed pipe section.

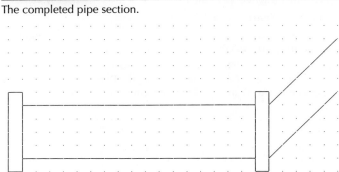

Object snaps

Often you need to draw relative to an existing object. For example, you may need to start a line from the endpoint or midpoint of an existing line. *Object snaps* (OSNAPS for short) enable you to precisely specify a point by snapping to a geometrically defined coordinate on an existing object. OSNAPS provide a very precise and efficient way to draw.

You can start an object snap in one of four ways:

- Display the Object Snap toolbar and choose the object snap that you want.
- Right-click, choose Snap Overrides from the shortcut menu, and then choose the object snap that you want from the menu.
- Access the object snap shortcut menu by holding down the Shift key and right-clicking. Choose the object snap that you want from the shortcut menu.
- Type the object snap's abbreviation on the command line.

CROSS-REF On multibutton mice, you can customize one of the buttons to show the Object Snap menu. Displaying the Object Snap menu with the click of a mouse button is very convenient. Customizing the mouse is discussed in Chapter 33.

When you specify an object snap, a prompt for that object snap appears on the command line. For example, if you choose a midpoint object snap, you see mid of on the command line. Unfortunately, the Dynamic Input tooltip does not show this prompt.

TIP When you use Dynamic Input and object snaps together, the tooltip alternates between showing the Dynamic Input tooltip and the object snap tooltip, or displays them as separate tooltips. To keep all the tooltips together, set the TOOLTIPMERGE system variable to 1.

Table 4.1 lists the object snaps. Use the abbreviation to type the object snap from the keyboard.

TABLE 4.1

Object Snaps

Object Snap	Abbreviation	Uses
Endpoint	End	Lines, arcs, and so on.
Midpoint	mid	Lines, arcs, and so on.
Intersection	Int	Intersection of lines, circles, arcs.
Apparent Intersection*	App	The intersection that would be created if two objects were extended until they met.
Extension	Ext	Extends lines, arcs, and so on past their endpoints but in the same direction. After choosing this object snap, pause over the endpoint of a line or arc until you see a small plus sign. As you move the mouse cursor along the extension path, a temporary extension path appears so that you can draw to or from points on the extension path.
Center	Cen	Circles, arcs, ellipses.
Quadrant	Qua	Nearest quadrant (0-, 90-, 180-, or 270-degree point) of a circle, arc, or ellipse.
Perpendicular	Per	Arc, circles, ellipses, lines, multilines, polylines, rays, splines, or construction lines. The Deferred Perpendicular mode lets you draw a line perpendicular *from* one of these objects. Start the line command and choose the Perpendicular object snap. Click the object that you want to draw perpendicular from and then move the cursor away from that object. You see the Deferred Perpendicular tooltip and a temporary perpendicular line that follows your cursor along the original object. You can then complete the perpendicular line.
Parallel	Par	Continues a line, polyline, and so on so that it's parallel to an existing line or other straight-line segment. After you choose this object snap, pause over the line you want to draw parallel to until you see a small parallel line symbol. As you move the mouse cursor parallel to the object, a temporary parallel path appears to help you create the parallel segment.
Tangent	Tan	Starts or continues a line from or to a point tangent with an arc, circle, or ellipse (see Figure 4.21).
Node	Nod	Point objects (discussed in Chapter 7).
Insertion	Ins	Insertion point of text (see Chapter 13) or a block (see Chapter 18).
Nearest	Nea	Nearest point on any object.
None	Non	Turns off any object snap modes.

* Apparent Intersection also applies to 3D objects that appear to intersect because of the angle of view.

FIGURE 4.21

A line drawn tangent to an arc.

When drawing a line, think of it as having a starting point and an ending point. After the line is drawn, however, both of these points are considered endpoints in terms of object snaps. When picking the end-point of a line for the endpoint object snap, pick a point on the line closer to the endpoint that you want. The same applies to arcs. Although the arc prompts read Start point and End, both are considered end-points for purposes of object snaps.

AutoSnap is a feature that helps you work with object snaps. When you move the cursor near the geometric point you have specified, such as an endpoint, you are notified in three ways:

- **Marker:** An object snap shape appears. Each object snap has a differently shaped marker.
- **AutoSnap tooltip:** A label displays the name of the object snap.
- **Magnet:** A pull gently moves the cursor toward the geometric point.

Figure 4.22 shows an endpoint marker and AutoSnap tooltip.

FIGURE 4.22

AutoSnap shows you the endpoint of the line.

You can customize the AutoSnap feature to suit your needs or make it go away completely if you want. Choose Tools ➪ Options and click the Drafting tab. Here you can individually turn on and off the marker, AutoSnap tooltip, and the magnet. You can also change the marker size and color. For more information, see "The Drafting tab" section in Appendix A.

In the following exercise, you practice using object snaps.

STEPS: Using Object Snaps

1. Start a new drawing using the acad.dwt or acadlt.dwt template. Make sure that the AutoCAD Classic or AutoCAD LT Classic workspace is chosen in the Workspaces toolbar. Close any palettes that may be open.

2. Save the drawing in your AutoCAD Bible folder as ab04-05.dwg.

3. Click ORTHO on the status bar to turn on ortho mode. If the OSNAP button is on, click OSNAP on the status bar to turn off running object snaps (covered in the next section).

4. Start the LINE command. Follow the prompts:

```
Specify first point: 2,7 ↵. Move the cursor downward.
Specify next point or [Undo]: 4 ↵. Move the cursor to the right.
Specify next point or [Undo]: 4 ↵. Move the cursor up.
Specify next point or [Close/Undo]: 4 ↵
Specify next point or [Close/Undo]: Press Enter to end the command.
```

Your drawing should look like Figure 4.23. The circled numbers are reference points for this exercise.

FIGURE 4.23

These three lines are the start of a mounting bracket.

5. Choose Arc from the Draw toolbar. Follow these prompts:

```
Specify start point of arc or [Center]: Right-click. From the
shortcut menu, choose Snap Overrides ⇨ Endpoint.
_endp of Move the cursor to ❶ in Figure 4.23. When you see the
endpoint marker and AutoSnap tooltip, click.
Specify second point of arc or [Center/End]: Right-click and choose
Center.
Specify center point of arc: Press Shift and right-click. Choose
Midpoint from the shortcut menu.
```

_mid of *Move the cursor to ❷ and pick.*
Specify end point of arc or [Angle/chord Length]: **end** ↵. *Move the cursor to ❸ and pick.*

6. Choose Circle from the Draw menu. Follow the prompts:

Specify center point for circle or [3P/2P/Ttr (tan tan radius)]: *Choose Center from the Object Snap shortcut menu.*
cen of *Move the cursor over the arc until you see the Center marker and tooltip, and then click.*
Specify radius of circle or [Diameter]: **.75** ↵

7. Start the LINE command and use any method you want to draw a line from the endpoint at ❸ to the endpoint at ❹. End the LINE command.

NOTE When you press Shift and right-click to get the object snap menu, the mouse pointer must be in the drawing area. If it is on a toolbar, you get the Toolbars list. If that happens, press the Esc key, or hold down the Shift button and right-click again in the drawing area.

8. Save your drawing. It should look like Figure 4.24.

FIGURE 4.24

The start of a drawing of a mounting bracket (including a construction line that would later be erased). It was created by using the endpoint, midpoint, and center object snaps.

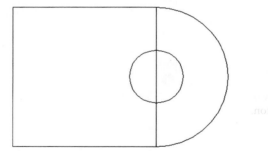

Running object snaps and OSNAP mode

The endpoint object snap is probably the most commonly used of all the object snaps. It would be nice to have a method of using object snaps that you use often without resorting to a menu, toolbar, or keyboard entry. The solution is to set a *running object snap*, which keeps one or more object snaps on until you turn them off.

TIP Many users like to work with three or four running object snaps on at once, such as endpoint, midpoint, center, and intersection. If you can't find the object snap you want because you have several object snaps near each other, press the Tab key to cycle through the object snaps, one by one, until you find the one that you want.

To set running object snaps, choose Tools ➪ Drafting Settings (or right-click the OSNAP button on the status bar and choose Settings) to open the Drafting Settings dialog box, as shown in Figure 4.25. (If necessary, click the Object Snap tab.) Choose the object snaps that you want and click OK. To clear a checked object snap, click it. Click Clear All to clear all running snaps.

FIGURE 4.25

Use the Object Snap tab of the Drafting Settings dialog box to set running object snaps.

You use the OSNAP button on the status bar to turn on your running object snaps. If you want to turn them off temporarily, just click the OSNAP button or press F3. This capability to toggle running object snaps on and off makes it easy to work with running object snaps on almost all the time because you can turn them off at the click of a button.

Overriding Coordinate Settings

Sometimes you're in the middle of a command and want to turn off an object snap just for a second. You're trying to pick a point and that pesky object snap marker keeps appearing just when you don't want it. Or you may want to turn Snap mode on or off for part of a command. The temporary overrides exist for this purpose. There are two kinds of temporary overrides:

■ **Toggles:** You press a key or combination of keys. The setting switches on or off. You then press the same keyboard shortcut to reverse the setting. For example, if you have ortho mode on, you can press F8 to turn it off. To turn ortho back on, press F8 again.

■ **Temporary overrides:** You press and hold a key or key combination. The setting switches on or off only while you're holding down the keyboard shortcut. The setting reverts to its original setting when you release the key or key combination. For example, if you have ortho on, you can press Shift to temporarily turn it off. As soon as you release the Shift key, ortho comes back on.

Table 4.2 lists these overrides. Note that each setting has two shortcuts, one for your left hand and one for your right hand. Use whichever one you like. You can customize the keys for these overrides. (For more information, see Chapter 33.)

TABLE 4.2

Coordinate Setting Overrides

Setting	Toggle	Temporary Override	Description
Toggle object snap mode	F3	Shift+A; Shift+'	Equivalent to clicking the OSNAP button on the status bar.
Turn on object snap mode		Shift+S; Shift+;	Use when object snap mode is off and you want to briefly turn it on.
Endpoint object snap		Shift+E; Shift+P	Temporarily turns on an endpoint object snap when OSNAP mode is off.
Midpoint object snap		Shift+V; Shift+M	Temporarily turns on a midpoint object snap when OSNAP mode is off.
Center object snap		Shift+C; Shift+,	Temporarily turns on a center object snap when OSNAP mode is off.
Turn off object snap and object tracking (OTRACK) modes		Shift+D; Shift+L	Equivalent to deselecting both the OSNAP and the OTRACK buttons on the status bar. (I explain object tracking in the next section.)
Ortho mode	F8	Shift	Equivalent to clicking the ORTHO button on the status bar.
Snap mode	F9		Equivalent to clicking the SNAP button on the status bar.
Polar mode	F10	Shift+X; Shift+.	Equivalent to clicking the POLAR button on the status bar.
Object snap tracking mode	F11	Shift+Q; Shift+]	Equivalent to clicking the OTRACK button on the status bar (I explain this in the next section).
Dynamic Input	F12		Equivalent to clicking the DYN button on the status bar.

> **TIP** To customize the hold-down time for temporary overrides, go to the Windows Control Panel (Start ➪ Control Panel) and double-click the Keyboard item. In the Character Repeat section, adjust the Repeat Rate control.

In the following exercise, you practice using running object snaps with OSNAP mode.

STEPS: Using Running Object Snaps with OSNAP Mode

1. Start a new drawing using the `acad.dwt` or `acadlt.dwt` template. Make sure that the AutoCAD Classic or AutoCAD LT Classic workspace is chosen in the Workspaces toolbar. Close any palettes that may be open.

2. Save the file in your `AutoCAD Bible` folder as `ab04-06.dwg`.

3. Choose Tools ⇨ Drafting Settings and click the Object Snap tab. Choose Endpoint. Uncheck all other object snaps and click OK.

4. Start the LINE command and start the line at 2,2.

5. Turn on ortho mode by clicking the ORTHO button on the status bar. If OSNAP is not on, click it on the status bar.

6. Move the mouse in the 0-degree direction and type **6** ↵.

7. Move the mouse up in the 90-degree direction, type **3** ↵, and end the LINE command.

8. Start the ARC command. At the `Specify start point of arc or [Center]:` prompt, pick the endpoint at ❶, shown in Figure 4.26. (Look for the marker and AutoSnap tooltip.)

FIGURE 4.26

Drawing a steam boiler with an endpoint running object snap.

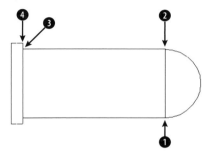

9. At the `Specify second point of arc or [Center/End]:` prompt, right-click (or press the down arrow if Dynamic Input is on) and choose End. Pick the endpoint at ❷, shown in Figure 4.26.

10. At the `Specify center point of arc or [Angle/Direction/Radius]:` prompt, right-click (or press the down arrow if Dynamic Input is on) and choose Angle, and then type **180** ↵.

11. Start the LINE command and at the `Specify first point:` prompt, pick the endpoint at ❷ in Figure 4.26.

12. Move the mouse to the left in the 180-degree direction, type **6** ↵, and end the LINE command.

13. Right-click the SNAP button on the status bar and choose Settings. Make sure that the Equal X and Y Spacing check box is selected. Click Grid Snap in the Snap type section. Set the Snap X spacing to 0.25. Check the Snap On check box. Click OK.

NOTE If the boiler is too small, choose View ⇨ Zoom ⇨ All.

14. Start the LINE command. At the `Specify first point:` prompt, place the cursor 0.25 units above ❸ in Figure 4.26 (at 2,5.25). If you see the endpoint marker for the nearby line, press F3 to turn off the running OSNAP temporarily. Pick point 2,5.25.

15. At the `Specify next point or [Undo]:` prompt, pick point 2,1.75. (If necessary, right-click the coordinates and choose Absolute to get absolute coordinates.)

16. If Dynamic Input is not on, click the DYN button on the status bar. Follow the prompts:

```
Specify next point or [Undo]: Pick .5<180. (This means that you see a
length tooltip of .5 and an angle tooltip of 180°.)
Specify next point or [Close/Undo]: Pick 3.5<90.
Specify next point or [Close/Undo]: (If you turned off OSNAP in Step
13, press F3 to turn it on again.) Pick the endpoint at ❹ in Figure
4.26.
Specify next point or [Close/Undo]: ↵
```

17. Save your drawing.

> **NOTE** Even if you have running object snaps, if you specify an object snap during a command, it overrides the running object snap. For example, having a running endpoint object snap does not mean you can't use a midpoint object snap for any specific drawing command.

By default, if you type absolute or relative coordinates, they take precedence over any running object snaps. This lets you leave running object snaps on but override them with keyboard entry of typed coordinates whenever you want. In general, the default gives you the most control and flexibility. However, you can change this default to give running object snaps precedence. To change the default, choose Tools ➪ Options, click the User Preferences tab, and use the Priority for Coordinate Data Entry section of the dialog box.

Locating Points

Sometimes you need to locate a point that is not on an existing object. For example, you may need a point a certain distance and angle from an existing object. This section explains three techniques that enable you to locate points that are not on objects—object snap tracking, point filters, and the From feature.

Object snap tracking

The purpose of tracking is to let you specify a point based on the object snaps of existing objects. Temporary tracking lines are drawn from points you specify, and guide you so that you can easily specify the point that you want. Use the OTRACK button on the status bar to turn object snap tracking on and off. Object snap tracking can easily handle all of the following tasks and many more:

■ You're drawing a line and have specified the start point. You want the endpoint to be exactly vertical to the endpoint of an existing line.

■ You're drawing a circle inside a rectangle (which could be a hole inside a sheet-metal plate). You want the center of the circle to be exactly centered inside the rectangle, at the intersection of the midpoints of the rectangle's two sides.

■ You want to start a line at the point where two existing lines would intersect if they were extended.

To start using object snap tracking, at least one object snap must be active. Turn on a running object snap, as explained in the previous sections. Then click OTRACK on the status bar.

With object snap tracking on, follow these steps:

1. Start a command that requires you to specify a point.

2. Place the cursor briefly over an object snap, such as the endpoint of a line, to temporarily *acquire* it. You can acquire more than one point. These acquired points are used to calculate the tracking paths. You see a small plus sign (+) over the object snap as confirmation, as shown in Figure 4.27.

FIGURE 4.27

When you pause over an object snap and then move the cursor slightly, you see a plus sign (+) at the acquired point to show that the point has been acquired and can now be used for object snap tracking.

Acquired point

Cursor

3. Move the cursor away from the object snap toward your desired point. You see the temporary alignment paths as you move the cursor over available drawing paths, as shown in Figure 4.28. If ORTHO is on, you see only horizontal and vertical paths. If POLAR is on, you see polar paths based on the polar angle settings, as explained earlier in this chapter.

FIGURE 4.28

With the endpoint object snap active and ORTHO on, AutoCAD displays temporary alignment paths based on the acquired point.

Acquired endpoint of existing arc

Temporary alignment path

Desired endpoint of new line (at the "X")

Endpoint: 3'-9 15/16" < 270°

Cursor
Start point of new line
Tooltip

4. When you see a tooltip and a small x, click. You can now continue or complete the command using this point.

After you acquire a point, you can clear it in any one of three ways:

- Move the cursor back over the point's plus sign.
- Click OTRACK off using the status bar.
- Start any new command.

You can customize the following features of object snap tracking on the Drafting tab of the Options dialog box (choose Tools ⇨ Options):

- Uncheck Display Polar Tracking Vector to eliminate the tracking paths.
- Uncheck Display Full-Screen Tracking Vector to display the tracking paths only from the cursor to the object snap point.
- Uncheck Display AutoTrack Tooltip to eliminate the tooltips.
- In the Alignment Point Acquisition section, choose Shift to Acquire, which will require you to press Shift to acquire a point when the cursor is over an object snap point.

In the following exercise, you practice locating points with object snap tracking.

 The drawing used in the following exercise on locating points with object snap tracking, `ab04-c.dwg`, is in the `Drawings` folder on the DVD.

STEPS: Locating Points with Object Snap Tracking

1. Open `ab04-c.dwg` from the DVD. Make sure that the AutoCAD Classic or AutoCAD LT Classic workspace is chosen in the Workspaces toolbar. Close any palettes that may be open.

2. Save the drawing as `ab04-07.dwg` in your `AutoCAD Bible` folder. This drawing is a section of a simple plan layout of an apartment. Set endpoint and midpoint running object snaps only. Make sure that OSNAP and OTRACK are on and that POLAR and ORTHO are off.

3. Start the LINE command. At the `Specify first point:` prompt, pick the endpoint at **1** in Figure 4.29. Be sure to pick on the endpoint itself, in order to acquire it.

4. At the `Specify next point or [Undo]:` prompt, pass the cursor over **2**. Move the cursor down a little, and you see the small plus sign showing that this endpoint has been acquired.

5. Move the cursor down until it is to the left of **1** and vertical to **2**. When you see the tooltip (reading Endpoint: < 270°, Endpoint: < 180°) and the small x marking the intersection of the two points, click to end the line segment.

6. At the `Specify next point or [Undo]:` prompt, click at **2** and end the LINE command.

7. Start the LINE command again. At the `Specify first point:` prompt, pick the endpoint of the arc at **3** in Figure 4.29. If you're not sure that you found the right endpoint, press Tab until the arc is highlighted. Make sure that you've acquired the endpoint by clicking the endpoint itself or passing the crosshairs over it.

8. At the `Specify next point or [Undo]:` prompt, pass the cursor over **4** until you see the small plus sign. Move the cursor slightly to the left until you see the tooltip (reading Endpoint: < 90°, Endpoint: < 180°) and click.

9. At the `Specify next point or [Undo]:` prompt, pick the endpoint at **4** and end the LINE command.

10. Start the CIRCLE command. At the `Specify center point for circle or [3P/2P/Ttr (tan tan radius)]:` prompt, pass the cursor over **5** and then over **6** to acquire both midpoints.

FIGURE 4.29

The tub, door, and sink to be completed in this plan layout.

11. Move the cursor to the middle of the sink, where lines from both midpoints would intersect until you see the tooltip (reading Midpoint: < 270°, Midpoint: < 180°) and click.

12. At the `Specify radius of circle or [Diameter]:` prompt, type **7.5** ↵ to complete the sink.

13. Save your drawing. It should look like Figure 4.30.

FIGURE 4.30

The completed drawing.

Using the temporary tracking feature

The temporary tracking feature is similar to object snap tracking, but limits you to horizontal and vertical directions. Follow these steps:

1. Start a command.
2. At a prompt to specify a point, enter **tracking** ↵ (or **tk**) at the command prompt.
3. At the `First tracking point:` prompt, specify a point (usually using object snaps) that is horizontal or vertical to the final point you want to specify.
4. Immediately move the cursor horizontally or vertically toward the final point that you want to specify. You see a rubber-band line.
5. At the `Next point:` prompt, move the cursor from the rubber-band line to specify a second point that is also vertical or horizontal to the final point.
6. Press Enter to end tracking and continue the command.

The cursor moves to the intersection of the vertical and horizontal rubber-band lines. You can now continue your command.

Point filters

Point filters enable you to specify a coordinate using the X coordinate of one existing object snap and the Y coordinate of another. You construct an X,Y coordinate based on coordinates of existing objects. If this sounds complicated, it is. Object snap tracking should mostly eliminate the need to go back to the old point filter way of doing things. (Point filters have been around for a long time.)

Here's how to use point filters:

1. Start a command to draw an object.
2. To specify a coordinate, type **.x** or **.y** on the command line. You can also find point filters on the object snap shortcut menu (Shift+right-click).
3. The prompt requests a point. Generally, you specify the point by using an object snap.
4. The prompt requests the other coordinate value, which you generally provide by using an object snap. (If you're working in 2D, ignore the request for a Z coordinate.)
5. Continue your command.

 You don't need to use existing coordinates for both the X and Y portions of the coordinate. For example, you can construct an X,Y coordinate by using the Y coordinate of an existing line and picking the X coordinate anywhere on the screen.

From feature

The From feature enables you to create a new object starting at a known distance and direction from an existing object. It's like creating one or more invisible lines between the existing object and the new object, helping you to start the new object in the proper place. Use the From feature when the point you need to specify is a known X,Y distance from an object snap but not on any object snap itself. Here's how to use the From feature:

1. Start a command to draw an object, such as LINE.
2. Press Shift+right-click, and choose From on the shortcut menu. You can also type **from** on the command line or in the Dynamic Input tooltip.

3. The prompt requests a base point, which you usually provide by using an object snap, such as an endpoint.

4. The prompt requests an Offset, which you provide by using relative or polar coordinates. You can type coordinates or look at the coordinates in the Dynamic Input tooltip or on the status bar and click when you see what you want.

NOTE When you specify the offset for the From feature, you need to use the @ symbol to indicate relative coordinates, even if Dynamic Input is set to the default of relative coordinates. The Dynamic Input relative coordinates setting only applies to the second coordinate that you enter. For example, if you are drawing a line, the first coordinate you enter is considered absolute, and subsequent coordinates are considered relative.

5. Continue the command you started (in Step 1).

In the following exercise, you practice using the From feature.

ON the DVD-ROM The drawing used in the following exercise on using the From feature, ab04-06.dwg, is in the Results folder on the DVD.

STEPS: Using the From Feature

1. Open ab04-06.dwg, which you created in an earlier exercise. If you did not do the previous exercise, open the drawing from the Results folder of the DVD. If you're using AutoCAD, make sure that the AutoCAD Classic or AutoCAD LT Classic workspace is chosen in the Workspaces toolbar. Close any palettes that may be open. Make sure ortho mode is on and SNAP is off. OSNAP should be on. Set a running object snap for endpoint.

2. Save the drawing as ab04-08.dwg in your AutoCAD Bible folder.

3. Start the LINE command.

4. From the Object Snap shortcut menu, choose From.

5. The prompt asks you for a base point. Pick the endpoint at ❶ in Figure 4.31.

FIGURE 4.31

Using the From feature to complete the steam boiler.

6. At the <Offset>: prompt, type **@-1,0.5**↵.

7. You are now ready to continue the line at the Specify next point or [Undo]: prompt. Press F3 to turn off OSNAP. Move the cursor in the 90-degree direction and type **2** ↵.

8. Move the mouse in the 180-degree direction and type **1** ↵.

9. Move the mouse in the 270-degree direction and type **2** ↵.

10. Right-click and choose Close from the shortcut menu to close the rectangle and end the LINE command.

11. Save your drawing. It should look like Figure 4.32.

FIGURE 4.32

The completed steam boiler.

Summary

This chapter covered a great deal about specifying coordinates. These skills form the basis for all your future work with AutoCAD and AutoCAD LT. You read about:

- The X,Y coordinate system
- Using Dynamic Input
- Using absolute Cartesian coordinates
- When and how to use relative Cartesian coordinates
- Absolute and relative polar coordinates
- Direct distance entry
- The orthogonal (ORTHO) mode
- Using polar tracking
- Controlling the display of coordinates on the status bar
- Grid and PolarSnap settings
- Using the visible grid
- Using object snaps (OSNAPS) to specify geometric points on objects
- Running object snaps and turning OSNAP on and off
- Temporarily overriding coordinate settings
- Using object snap tracking to locate points
- Using point filters to locate points
- The From feature for locating points not on an object

The next chapter introduces you to the basics of setting up a drawing.

Chapter 5

Setting Up a Drawing

Often, the first step after you start a new drawing is to set its size and unit type. These and other setup options are discussed in this chapter. The entire process of setting up a drawing is essential for ensuring accurate results. You can save most of these settings in a template to avoid having to recreate them each time you start a new drawing.

Choosing Unit Types

One of the first tasks in setting up a drawing is to choose the unit type. Units define how objects are measured. You can save the unit type in a template.

The coordinates you use in AutoCAD or AutoCAD LT are measured in units that can represent any real-world measurement, such as inches or millimeters. A surveyor or city planner might even use miles or kilometers as the base unit. However, different disciplines have customs that express units differently, and you should use the unit type appropriate for the type of drawing you're creating. This ensures that everyone involved understands the drawing. AutoCAD and AutoCAD LT offer five types of units, as shown in Table 5.1. The sample measurement column shows how a line 32.5 units long would be displayed in the various unit types.

TABLE 5.1

Unit Types

Unit Type	Sample Measurement	Description
Decimal	32.50	Number of units, partial units in decimals
Engineering	2'–8.50"	Feet and inches, partial inches in decimals
Architectural	2'–8 1/2"	Feet and inches, partial inches in fractions
Fractional	32 1/2	Number of units, partial units in fractions
Scientific	3.25E+01	Base number + exponent

Notice how the engineering and architectural units translate a line of 32.5 units into feet and inches. Engineering and architectural units assume a unit of 1 inch, unlike the other unit types, which can represent any measurement.

The unit type affects how coordinates are shown on the status bar and how information about objects is listed. You generally input coordinates by using the type of units you've chosen, although in some cases you can input coordinates in another unit type.

NOTE   If you're using engineering or architectural units, AutoCAD and AutoCAD LT display partial inches differently than the format you must use to type them in. You must type coordinates without any spaces, because a space is equivalent to pressing Enter, and that ends your input. Use a hyphen between whole and partial inches, for example, 3'2-1/2". (You can omit the " after the inches because inches are assumed in engineering and architectural units if no symbol follows a number.) However, this appears on the status line as 3'-2 1/2". This can be confusing because the hyphen is in a different place, and you see a space between the whole and partial inches.

Setting the drawing units

When you know the units you want to use, you set them in the Drawing Units dialog box. To set the units, choose Format ➪ Units to open the Drawing Units dialog box, shown in Figure 5.1. The left side of the Drawing Units dialog box enables you to choose which unit type you want to use. In the Precision box in the Length section, click the arrow and a list of precision options drops down. Click the one you want.

CAUTION   AutoCAD and AutoCAD LT round off measurements to the nearest precision value you choose. Say that you choose a precision of two decimal places, using decimal units. You want to draw a line so that it is 3.25 units long, but when you type the coordinate, by accident you press the 4 key at the end, resulting in a line 3.254 units long. This line is displayed as 3.25 units long, making it difficult for you to spot the error. Therefore, setting a higher precision than you need to show is a good idea.

FIGURE 5.1

The Drawing Units dialog box.

Setting the angle type

As with units, your choice of angle type depends on your profession and work environment. Decimal Degrees is the default. Table 5.2 lists the types of angles.

TABLE 5.2

Angle Types

Angle Type Name	Sample Measurement	Description
Decimal Degrees	32.5	Degrees, partial degrees in decimals
Deg/Min/Sec	32°30'0"	Degrees, minutes, and seconds
Grads (gradians)	36.1111g	Gradians
Radians	0.5672r	Radians
Surveyor	N 57d30' E	Surveyor (directional) units

NOTE A minute is $\frac{1}{60}$ degree and a second is $\frac{1}{60}$ minute. Gradians and radians are simply alternate ways of measuring angles. A gradian is a metric measurement equal to $\frac{1}{100}$ of a right angle. Radians measure an angle by placing a length, equal to the radius, along the circle's circumference. Radians range from 0 to $2 \times \pi$ instead of from 0 to 360 as degrees do. A radian is approximately 57.30 degrees. Surveyor units measure angles in directions, starting with north or south and adding an angle in degrees, minutes, seconds format that shows how far the angle is from north or south and in which direction (east or west).

To set the angle type, choose the option you want from the Type drop-down list of the Angle section of the Drawing Units dialog box (shown in Figure 5.1).

CROSS-REF   Changing these angle settings does not automatically change the way your dimensions appear. Use the Dimension Style Manager, which is discussed in Chapter 15, to change dimensions.

Setting the angle measure and direction

By convention, degrees increase in a counterclockwise direction, and you measure angles so that 0 degrees starts to the right, also called the East direction. To change the angle direction, click Clockwise in the Drawing Units dialog box.

To change the direction of 0 degrees, click Direction to open the Direction Control dialog box, shown in Figure 5.2.

FIGURE 5.2

The Direction Control dialog box.

Here you can choose to have 0 degrees start in a direction other than East. You can also choose Other and type any other angle or click the Pick an Angle button to pick two points on your screen that specify an angle. Choose OK to close the Direction Control dialog box. Click OK to close the Drawing Units dialog box.

NOTE   Changing the angle direction affects what happens when you input angles and what you see in the coordinate display. It does not change the absolute coordinates, which are set according to the User Coordinate System (UCS). Chapter 8 covers using and customizing UCSs.

If you are using Dynamic Input, the angle that you see in the Dynamic Input tooltip never goes above 180°. This angle in the tooltip represents the angle to your current point and goes from 0° to 180° in both the clockwise and counterclockwise directions.

CROSS-REF   At the bottom of the Units dialog box, you can choose units for lighting. See my discussion of lighting in Chapter 25 for more information.

STEPS: Setting Drawing Units

1. Begin a new drawing using the `acad.dwt` or `acadlt.dwt` template. Make sure that the AutoCAD Classic or AutoCAD LT Classic workspace is chosen in the Workspaces toolbar. Close any palettes that may be open. If Dynamic Input isn't on, click the DYN button on the Status bar.

2. Save the drawing as `ab05-01.dwg` in your `AutoCAD Bible` folder.

3. Choose Format ➪ Units to open the Drawing Units dialog box.

4. In the Length section, choose Architectural.

5. Click the arrow to the right of the Precision drop-down list box in the Length section. Choose 0'-0 1/8".

6. In the Angle section, choose Deg/Min/Sec.

7. In the Precision box, choose 0d00'.

8. In the Units to Scale Inserted Content drop-down list, set the units to Inches.

9. Click OK.

10. Start the LINE command. Follow the prompts:

```
Specify first point: 2,2 ↵
Specify next point or [Undo]: 1'<0 ↵
Specify next point or [Undo]: 6-3/4<153 ↵
Specify next point or [Close/Undo]: Right-click and choose Close.
```

11. Choose View ➪ Zoom ➪ All to zoom to the entire drawing. Save your drawing. If you're continuing through the chapter, keep it open.

> **NOTE** You would not actually use Deg/Min/Sec for angles in an architectural drawing, but the exercise gives you the opportunity to set the angular units.

Drawing Limits

You can specify the area of your drawing, also called the *limits*. The drawing limits are the outer edges of the drawing, specified in X,Y units. You need to set only the width and length of the drawing. Together, these two measurements create an invisible bounding rectangle for your drawing.

Almost universally, the lower-left limit is 0,0, which is the default. Therefore, the upper-right corner really defines the drawing size. Remember that you typically draw at life size (full scale). Therefore, the size of your drawing should be equal to the size of the outer extents of what you're drawing, plus a margin for a title block (if you plan to add one), annotation, and dimensioning. If you want to show more than one view of an object, as is common in both architectural and mechanical drawings, you need to take this into account.

To decide on the upper-right corner of your drawing *limits* (the width and length of your drawing), you need to consider what the drawing units mean for you. Generally, the smallest commonly used unit is used, often inches or millimeters. Therefore, if you're drawing a plan view of a house that is approximately 40 feet across (in the X direction) by 30 feet deep (in the Y direction), this translates to a top-right corner of 480,360. Adding room for a title block brings you to about 500,380.

> **CROSS-REF** In Chapter 17, I explain how you can put the title block on a *layout*. A layout simulates the sheet of paper that you will use to plot the drawing. If you use a layout, you don't need to leave room for the title block when you set the limits.

The limits define an artificial and invisible boundary to your drawing. However, you can draw outside the limits. The limits affect the size of the grid, when displayed. (See Chapter 4 for a discussion of the grid.) The ZOOM command with the All option also uses the limits, but only if no objects are outside the limits. (See Chapter 8 for a discussion of the ZOOM command.)

To set the drawing limits, choose Format ⇨ Drawing Limits to start the LIMITS command. Press Enter to accept the lower-left corner default of 0,0 that appears on the command line. Then type the upper-right corner coordinate that you want and press Enter.

ON the DVD-ROM The drawing used in the following exercise on setting the drawing limits, ab05-01.dwg, is in the Results folder on the DVD.

STEPS: Setting the Drawing Limits

1. If you did the previous exercise, continue to use ab05-01.dwg. Otherwise, open ab05-01.dwg from the Results folder of the DVD. Make sure that the AutoCAD Classic or AutoCAD LT Classic workspace is chosen in the Workspaces toolbar. Close any palettes that may be open. If Dynamic Input isn't on, click the DYN button on the Status bar.

2. Save the drawing as ab05-02.dwg in your AutoCAD Bible folder.

3. Choose Format ⇨ Drawing Limits.

4. Press Enter to accept the lower-left default of 0,0.

5. Type **16,10** ↵.

6. To create a border at the limits of the drawing, start the LINE command. Follow the prompts:
   ```
   Specify first point: 0,0 ↵
   Specify next point or [Undo]: 16<0 ↵
   Specify next point or [Undo]: 10<90 ↵
   Specify next point or [Close/Undo]: 16<180 ↵
   Specify next point or [Close/Undo]: Right-click and choose Close.
   ```

7. Choose View ⇨ Zoom ⇨ All.

8. Save your drawing. If you're continuing through the chapter, keep it open.

Understanding Scales

You need to consider the fact that your drawing will most likely be plotted onto a standard paper (sheet) size. The standard orientation for drafting (and the default for most plotters) is *landscape* orientation, meaning that as you look at the drawing, the paper is wider than it is tall. Figure 5.3 shows an example. These conventions have carried over from the days of hand drafting. (In a computer program, this is not really necessary, because you can rotate the drawing when you plot it.) To scale a drawing onto a piece of paper in a pleasing manner requires a rectangular shape that somewhat resembles the proportions of standard paper sizes.

Drawings are usually oriented horizontally, as in this example.

Thanks to Henry Dearborn, AIA, Fairfield, Iowa, for this drawing, which I have altered somewhat.

In addition, although you specify the scale at plotting time, it helps to be aware of the scale you'll use when plotting your drawing at the outset. The scales used for Geographic Information Systems (GIS), where you might be drawing an entire county, will be different from those used when drawing a house. The scales used in mechanical drafting are again totally different. In fact, in mechanical drafting, if you're drawing a very small object, such as a 2-inch screw-plate, you might scale *up* (that is, enlarge the drawing when plotting).

One important reason for establishing the scale at the beginning is to ensure that text, whether annotations or dimensions, is readable in its final plotted form. Applying a scale ensures that text remains a reasonable size even as the rest of the drawing is scaled up or down. Scale also affects linetypes that contain dots or dashes.

Some drawings are not scaled. Examples are electrical or electronic schematics, piping diagrams, and railroad schematics. These drawings are representations of electrical or electronic connections but do not resemble the actual physical object that will eventually be created from the drawing. These drawings can be any size as long as they are clear and organized.

CROSS-REF You can lay out various views of your drawing on an imaginary piece of paper, called a *paper space layout,* to prepare it for plotting. You can annotate on a paper space layout to avoid having to adjust the size of these components to the scale of the drawing. See Chapter 17 for more information on layouts and plotting.

When determining your scale to fit a drawing on a sheet of paper, be aware that a plotter cannot print on the entire sheet. A certain amount of the margin around the edge is not available for drawing. Plotters differ in this respect. The plotter's manual can let you know the width of this unprintable margin. On average, you can assume a half-inch margin on each side; thus you should subtract 1 inch from both the length and width sheet measurements to determine the actual drawing space. Table 5.3 shows standard U.S. sheet sizes.

TABLE 5.3

Standard Paper Sheet Sizes in the United States (in inches)

Size	Width	Height	Size	Width	Height
A	11	8½	D	34	22
B	17	11	E	44	34
C	22	17			

Table 5.4 lists standard metric sheet sizes.

TABLE 5.4

Standard Metric Paper Sheet Sizes (in millimeters)

Size	Width	Height	Size	Width	Height
A4	297	210	A1	841	594
A3	420	297	A0	1,189	841
A2	594	420			

Working with scale formats

A scale is often indicated in the format *plotted size=actual size* or *plotted size:actual size*. Because you draw at actual size, the actual size is also the drawing size. For example, a scale of ¼"=1' means that ¼ inch on the drawing, when plotted out on a sheet of paper, represents 1 foot in actual life — and in the drawing. This is a typical architectural scale. A windowpane 1 foot wide would appear ¼-inch wide on paper.

From the scale, you can calculate the scale *factor.* You use the factor when you set the size for text (see Chapter 13) or for dimensions (see Chapter 15). To do this, the left side of the scale equation must equal 1, and the two numbers must be in the same measurement (for example, both in inches). This requires some simple math. For ¼"=1', you would calculate as follows:

¼"=1'

1"=4'   Both sides of the equation multiplied by 4

1"=48"   4' converted to 48"

Therefore, the scale factor is 48. This means that the paper plot is ¹⁄₄₈ of real size.

In mechanical drawing, you might draw a metal joint that is actually 4 inches long. To fit it on an 8½-x-11-inch sheet of paper, you could use a 2"=1" scale, which means that 2" on the paper drawing equals 1" in actual life and the drawing. Calculate the scale factor:

2"=1"

1"=½"

The scale factor is ½. This means that the paper plot is twice the real size.

Most professions use certain standard scales. Therefore, you do not usually have a choice to pick any scale you want, such as 1":27'. Instead, the conventions of your profession, client, or office dictate a choice of only a few scales. Some typical architectural scale factors are:

- 192: 1/16" = 1'
- 96: 1/8" = 1'
- 48: 1/4" = 1'
- 24: 1/2" = 1'
- 12: 1" = 1'

Civil engineering scales are somewhat different and range to larger sizes — a bridge is bigger than a house. Some typical scale factors are:

- 120: 1" =10'
- 240: 1" =20'

Metric scales can be used for any purpose. You would most typically work in millimeters, but these could represent any metric measurement:

- 1000: 1mm = 10 meters
- 500: 1mm = 5 meters
- 100: 1 mm = 1 meter

Using annotative scales

AutoCAD 2008 and AutoCAD LT 2008 allow you to assign an *annotative property* to certain objects so that they automatically resize to the proper scale when you lay out the drawing for plotting. The following types of objects can be annotative:

- Text (see Chapter 13)
- Dimensions and leaders (see Chapters 14 and 15)
- Hatches (see Chapter 16)
- Blocks and attributes (see Chapter 18)

NEW FEATURE AutoCAD 2008/AutoCAD LT 2008 introduces annotative scaling, which allows you to display and plot certain *annotative objects* at various scales. This feature allows you to automate the process of scaling these annotative objects when you lay them out for plotting. You would especially use annotative scaling when you need to display your drawing at more than one scale. For example, you might display the entire drawing at one scale and a detail at another scale. (See Chapters 13, 14, 15, 16, 17, and 18 for more detailed information on annotative styles and objects.)

Using annotative objects avoids the necessity to manually figure out how large these objects need to be; when you scale them, they will be the proper size. For example, if your drawing scale will be 1:48, as in the example in the previous section, and you want your text to be ¼" high, then you would need to multiply the desired height of the text (¼") by the scale factor to get a text height of 12. However, by setting the annotative scale for the text to 1/4" = 1'-0", you can simply set the height of the text to ¼" and not worry about the calculations.

The procedure for creating annotative objects differs somewhat for each type of object, but the overall process is the same:

1. If necessary, create an annotative style and make it current. Annotative text, dimensions, and multileaders require an annotative style.

2. Decide on the scales that you will use for each object. For example, you might have two text objects each at a different scale, or one text object that you need to display at two different scales.

3. If you want each text object to have a different scale, turn off the ANNOAUTOSCALE system variable. This system variable, when on, automatically adds scales to annotative objects as you add annotative scales; the result is that each object has more than one scale. To turn ANNOAUTOSCALE off, click the icon on the right side of the status bar to the left of the Annotation Scale pop-up list. When on, there's a yellow lightning bolt; when off, the lightning bolt is gray.

4. Set the annotation scale for the first object. To do so, click the Annotation Scale button at the right side of the status bar to display the scale list and choose the scale you want. For example, choose 1/4" = 1'-0" if you plan to display the text at the 1/4" = 1'-0" scale. (In the next section, I explain how to customize this scale list.)

5. Create the object.

6. When you're ready to plot, you can set the desired annotative scale, and plot. You can also create viewports and set their scale. See Chapter 17 for details and an exercise using annotative objects.

If you want one object to have more than one scale, you can add an annotative scale to it. Follow these steps:

1. Select the object and right-click in the drawing area.

2. Choose Annotative Object Scale ⇨ Add/Delete Scales to open the Annotation Object Scale dialog box, as shown in Figure 5.4.

The Annotation Object Scale dialog box enables you to add an annotation scale to an annotation object.

3. Click Add to display the Add Scales to Object dialog box, where you can choose one or more scales.

4. Click OK twice to close both dialog boxes.

You can also open the dialog box by clicking the Add/Delete Scales button in the Annotation Scaling control panel of the Dashboard. Another way is to display the Properties palette, click the Annotative Scale item, and click the Ellipsis button that appears.

For each scale that you assign to an object, AutoCAD or AutoCAD LT automatically creates a representation of that object in an appropriate size. Therefore, you may have a text object shown at three sizes. At any time, you can view any single scale for an annotative object, or view all of its scales. Remember that you may have one or more scales for any one annotative object. If you don't see all scales of an annotative object, click the Annotation Visibility button on the right side of the status bar. This button controls the ANNOALLVISIBLE system variable. By default, it is on, displaying all scales. When you turn it off, you see only the text for the current annotative scale. To immediately plot, you would turn off this system variable so that you plot only the text for the current annotative scale.

Customizing the scale list

You generally choose a scale during the process of laying out a drawing. AutoCAD and AutoCAD LT have a list of scales from which you can choose. You can find this list in several places (which I discuss throughout the book):

- On the Annotation Scale list on the status bar, as mentioned in the previous section
- In the Add Scales to Object dialog box, also mentioned in the previous section
- In the VP Scale list of the status bar, when you select a viewport (see Chapter 17)
- In the Plot Scale section of the Plot dialog box (see Chapter 17)
- In the Plot Scale section of the Page Setup dialog box (see Chapter 17)
- In the Viewports toolbar drop-down list
- In the Standard scale item of the Properties palette when a Viewport is selected (see Chapter 17)
- In the Sheet Set Manager (AutoCAD only), when placing a view on a layout (see Chapter 26)
- In the Layout wizard (see Chapter 17)

You might use unusual scales in your office or want a list that includes only the scales that you use. You can customize the scale list for this purpose.

To customize the scale list, choose Format ⇨ Scale List. The Edit Scale List dialog box opens, shown in Figure 5.5.

FIGURE 5.5

Use the Edit Scale List dialog box to create your own custom scales.

To add a new scale, click Add. In the Add Scale dialog box, name the scale. The name is what will show on the list. You can use existing scales as a guide. Then define the scale by completing the Paper Units and Drawing Units text boxes. For example, to add a 1:12 scale, you would name the scale 1:12, set the Paper Units to 1 and the Drawing Units to 12.

To delete scales that you don't use, select the scale and click Delete. You can also edit existing scales (select the scale and click Edit), move them up or down in the order of the list, and reset the list (click Reset) to its original status. Click OK when you're done.

NEW FEATURE AutoCAD 2008 now stores the scales list within the drawing file, and so this list can vary. Scales used in any externally referenced files will also show up in this list, even if they weren't originally set in your host file.

Deciding on a scale and sheet size

As soon as you know the size of your drawing and the scale appropriate for your situation, you need to consider the sheet size of the paper on which you want to plot. Again, you often find that certain factors limit your choices. Your plotter or printer may be limited to certain sheet sizes. The conventions used in your discipline or working environment also affect your decision. You may be working on a series of drawings that are all to be plotted on the same size sheet of paper.

As an example, the architectural drawing in Figure 5.3 is 175 feet wide by 120 feet high. The two most typical scales for a drawing of a house are ¼"=1' and ⅛"=1'. On a small plotter, you might have a choice of sheet sizes A, B, or C. The following steps show the calculations you need to do in order to decide on a scale, obtain the scale factor, and determine the appropriate sheet size.

In this exercise, you practice determining the scale and sheet size. You need only a sheet of paper and a pencil. Use Figure 5.3 as a reference.

STEPS: Determining the Scale and Sheet Size

1. To calculate the plotted size of the drawing at ¼"=1', you can start with the width, which is 175'. Take one-quarter of 175 to get the width of the drawing in inches, which is 43¾".

2. Take one-quarter of the height, 120', to get the height of the drawing in inches, which is 30".

3. A C-size sheet (see Table 5.3) is 22"×17", which is too small for a 43¾"×30" drawing.

4. Recalculate the drawing at ⅛"=1'. Take one-eighth of 175 to get 21⅞. Take one-eighth of 120 to get 15".

5. The actual drawing space (minus the margins the printer requires) on a C-size sheet is about 21"×16". The height of the drawing at this scale is adequate, but the width is ⅞" too long. Therefore, the best option is to simply make the drawing ⅞" narrower because the drawing has some extra room. This lets you fit the drawing on a C-size sheet.

6. To calculate the scale factor of a ⅛"=1' scale, multiply 1' by 8 to get 8' and convert it to inches, which is 96 (8×12).

Rearranging the views, dimensions, and text on a drawing to fit a standard scale factor and sheet size is a typical task. There is no actual setup step for setting the drawing scale, but you use it when you insert text or dimensions and when you plot the drawing.

Creating a Title Block

A *title block* is a rectangle that includes spaces for the drawing title, company name, drafter name, and so on. It generally comes with a border that bounds your drawing. Many drawings require title blocks. You can insert an existing title block in two ways:

- When creating a new drawing, choose File ⇨ New to open the Select Template dialog box. Choose one of the templates that include a title block, either one that comes with AutoCAD or a custom template that you created. For example, acad –Named Plot Styles.dwt includes a title block and border that fit on an A-size sheet. The title block and border appear on a layout tab. (Chapter 17 covers layouts.)

- After you open a drawing, you can insert a drawing of a title block into it. Choose Insert ⇨ Block. (Chapter 18 covers blocks.) In the Insert dialog box, type the name of the drawing or block, or click Browse to find it. Some of the templates have a corresponding drawing that you can insert. To insert the file or block at 0,0 with no scaling or rotation, uncheck all of the Specify On-Screen check boxes. Check Explode if you expect to edit the inserted title block after it's in your drawing. Click OK.

To find the location of the templates and their corresponding drawings, choose Tools ⇨ Options and click the Files tab. Double-click Template Settings and then double-click Drawing Template File Location. You see the path to the location displayed. (The path is very long!) This folder may be hidden in Windows Explorer. For instructions on displaying hidden folders, go to Windows Help and type **hidden folders** in the search box.

| CROSS-REF | As explained in Chapter 2, you can create your own title block, make a template from it, and then start a drawing based on that template. |

Specifying Common Setup Options

A few other items are generally set up in advance and are included in a template. Other chapters of this book cover the following:

- **Layers** (covered in Chapter 11) enable you to organize your drawing into meaningful groups. In an architectural drawing, for example, you might create a layer for walls, another for doors, and one for electrical fixtures.
- **Text styles** (covered in Chapter 13) enable you to format the font and other text characteristics.
- **Table styles** (covered in Chapter 13) format tables.
- **Multileader styles** (covered in Chapter 14) create styles for multileaders (leaders that can contain more than one arrow).
- **Dimension styles** (covered in Chapter 15) format the dimensions that measure your objects.

If you know you'll be using snap, grid, and Ortho modes (covered in Chapter 4) a lot in certain drawings, and you know the suitable settings for snap and grid, you can set these and save them in a template because these settings are saved with the drawing. In other cases, you might want to leave them off and turn them on only when you need them.

System Variables

When you change settings in AutoCAD or AutoCAD LT, such as the unit type, angle type, drawing limits, blip marks, snap mode (on or off), grid mode, or ortho mode, you're actually changing *system variables*. These are simply settings that are stored in each drawing or in the Windows registry (which stores settings that apply to all drawings). Usually, you don't need to pay any direct attention to them, but they're the nuts and bolts behind the dialog boxes that you use to change the settings. When you start customizing AutoCAD, you need to learn about them because programming code and script files (macros) cannot access dialog boxes. Also, a few system variables are accessible only by typing them directly on the command line. Appendix B provides more information on system variables. Throughout this book, I occasionally mention system variables when using them directly is useful. Some system variables store information about a drawing or the drawing environment, such as the drawing name and path. These are *read-only,* meaning that you cannot change them. They exist to provide information and are often used in AutoLISP programs. (AutoLISP works in AutoCAD only.)

Information about each system variable, where it is stored, its default, and whether it is read-only is in the Help system. Choose Help ➪ Help and double-click Command Reference on the Contents tab. Then double-click System Variables. In the Options dialog box (Tools ➪ Options), system variables that are stored in a drawing have a drawing file icon next to them.

You can type system variables on the command line, just like regular commands. The Express Tools (AutoCAD only) contain an editor (choose Express ➪ Tools ➪ System Variable Editor) that enables you to edit system variable values in a dialog box; it also provides helpful supporting information.

Many settings, such as running object snaps, the type of snap (grid or polar), and the polar distance when you're using PolarSnap, are saved in the Windows registry, not in your drawing. As a result, when you open AutoCAD or AutoCAD LT, they're automatically set to the same setting that you had when you last closed the program, regardless of the setting in the drawing. Therefore, you cannot save these settings in a template.

In this exercise, you practice specifying the drafting settings and creating a template.

  The drawing used in the following exercise on setting drawing aids and creating a template, ab05-02.dwg, is in the Results folder on the DVD.

STEPS: Setting Drawing Aids and Creating a Template

1. If you did the exercise on drawing limits, use that drawing or open ab05-02.dwg from the Results folder of the DVD.

2. Save the drawing as ab05-03.dwg in your AutoCAD Bible folder.

3. Choose Tools ➪ Drafting Settings.

4. On the Snap and Grid tab, the snap spacing is set to ½". In the Grid Spacing section, change the X and Y spacing to 1". Make sure the Snap Type is set to Grid Snap and Rectangular Snap. Click OK.

5. Click SNAP and GRID on the status bar to turn them on. Make sure OSNAP is turned off.

6. Choose Format ➪ Units. Change the Angle Type back to Decimal Degrees. Click OK.

7. Using the coordinate display as your guide, start the LINE command and draw line segments from 2.5, 1.5 to .5<270 to 11<0 to .5<90. End the LINE command.

8. Restart the LINE command. Again use the coordinate display to draw line segments from 2,2 to .5<270 to 12<0 to .5<90. End the LINE command.

9. Save your drawing. It should look like Figure 5.6. Notice how the grid and snap settings facilitate the drawing process.

   The architectural units create a different drawing experience than decimal units would. Setting up a drawing creates a drawing environment suited to your work needs.

FIGURE 5.6

The final architectural drawing.

10. Choose File ⇨ Save As. In the Save Drawing As dialog box, click the Files of Type drop-down list box and choose AutoCAD Drawing Template (*.dwt) or AutoCAD LT Drawing Template (*.dwt). Notice that you're automatically in the Template folder.

11. In the File Name text box, change the name to archroof.dwt. Click Save.

12. In the Template Options dialog box, type **Arch units, 16,10 limits, snap & grid** and click OK. The Measurement drop-down list should be set to English.

13. Choose File ⇨ New. Choose the archroof template and click Open. A new drawing is created based on the template.

14. Move the cursor around and look at the coordinate display to confirm that the grid is set to 1", although the snap is set to ½".

    Do not save this new drawing.

Customizing with the MVSETUP Command

The MVSETUP command is used in two different ways: to set up a drawing and to create viewports for paper space layouts (covered in Chapter 17). This command does not exist in AutoCAD LT.

MVSETUP provides a command-line routine to walk you through some of the basic setup functions discussed in this chapter. You can use MVSETUP when you start to customize AutoCAD to set up a drawing from a script file or AutoLISP program (topics covered in Parts VI and VII of this book). To use MVSETUP, type **mvsetup** ↵ on the command line. AutoCAD responds with the following prompt:

```
Enable paper space? [No/Yes] <Y>:
```

Type **n** ↵ to use MVSETUP without entering paper space.

The next prompt lets you enter the units type:

```
Enter units type [Scientific/Decimal/Engineering/Architectural/Metric]:
```

Choose the option you want. Then AutoCAD displays a list of scale factors appropriate to the units option you chose. At the `Enter the scale factor:` prompt, type in a numeric scale factor.

Finally, AutoCAD prompts you to set the drawing limits with the following two prompts:

```
Enter the paper width:
Enter the paper height:
```

After each prompt, enter a number based on the size of the paper on which you plan to plot. AutoCAD draws a rectangle of the size that you indicated for the drawing limits.

Using the Setup Wizards

There are two wizards to help you set up a drawing. You need to activate the Startup dialog box to find them:

1. On the command line, or in the Dynamic Input tooltip, enter **startup** ↵, and then enter **1** ↵.
2. Choose File ➪ New. You see the Startup dialog box.
3. Click the Use a Wizard button. Choose Quick Setup for fewer options or Advanced Setup for more options.
4. Click OK and follow the prompts of the wizard.

Summary

This chapter explained setting up a drawing so that it behaves the way you want it to. You read about:

- Setting the unit type
- Setting the angle type, measure, and direction
- Drawing limits
- Using scales and calculating a scale factor
- Setting drawing aids and creating a template that includes the settings that you want
- Using MVSETUP (AutoCAD only) or the setup wizards to set up your drawing

This chapter ends Part I, "AutoCAD and AutoCAD LT Basics." Now that you know the basics, you can go on to Part II, "Drawing in Two Dimensions." The next chapter covers drawing simple lines, polygons, rectangles, and infinite construction lines.

Part II

Drawing in Two Dimensions

Now that you have the basics under your belt, it's time to draw! This part contains all the basic information you need for two-dimensional drawing and design — which is quite a lot of content!

In Part II, you learn techniques for basic two-dimensional drawing and editing in AutoCAD and AutoCAD LT. After I discuss drawing simple lines and curves, I explain how you can control the display of your drawings. You can also find chapters on creating text, drawing dimensions, and creating dimension styles. Separate chapters cover how you can obtain information from your drawing, and how to draw complex objects. Part II winds down with a chapter on plotting and printing.

Chapter 6

Drawing Simple Lines

Lines are the most commonly drawn object in 2D AutoCAD drawings — you'll use the LINE command a lot! Straight edges just happen to be very common in the real world. Related commands for drawing rectangles, polygons, and construction lines are also important, so you should have all of these commands in your arsenal. This chapter explains how to draw all these types of objects.

Using the LINE Command

The LINE command draws straight line segments. Part I included several exercises in which you drew lines. However, the LINE command has several options, and you can still learn a few tricks of the trade by focusing on the actual LINE command.

To draw a line, choose Line from the Draw toolbar. At the `Specify first point:` prompt, specify any point. Continue to specify points until you're finished. Press Enter to end the command. You can also right-click and choose Enter from the shortcut menu. The LINE command assumes that you will continue to use it over and over. For this reason, the command continues to prompt you until you press Enter.

If you continue to draw line segments, the subsequent prompts are different. Here's how to use them:

- The command displays the `Specify next point or [Undo]:` prompt for the next two segments. Right-click (or press the down-arrow key if you have Dynamic Input on) and choose Undo (or type **u ↵**) to undo only the last line segment that you created — without exiting the LINE command.

- After creating at least two line segments, the command displays the `Specify next point or [Close/Undo]:` prompt. Right-click (or press the down-arrow key if you have Dynamic Input on) and choose Close (or type **c** ↵) to automatically draw a line from the endpoint of the last segment to the original start point, thereby creating a closed figure. You can continue to use the Undo option as well.

If you previously drew a line, press Enter at the `Specify first point:` prompt to start the line at the endpoint of the last line. If you most recently drew an arc, press Enter to start the line at the endpoint of the arc and draw it tangent to the arc.

STEPS: Using the LINE Command

1. Start a new drawing by using the `acad.dwt` or `acadlt.dwt` template.

NOTE   This exercise assumes that you have Dynamic Input on (click the DYN button on the status bar to turn it on, if necessary) and that you are using the default settings of polar format and relative coordinates. Make sure that the AutoCAD Classic or AutoCAD LT Classic workspace is chosen in the Workspaces toolbar. For both AutoCAD and AutoCAD LT, close any palettes that may be open.

2. Save the drawing in your `AutoCAD Bible` folder as `ab06-01.dwg`.

3. Start the LINE command. At the `Specify first point:` prompt, choose any point in the center of your drawing.

4. Click ORTHO on the status bar.

5. Move the cursor to the right in the 0-degree direction and type **.4667** ↵.

6. Type **.7341<129** ↵. (Instead of typing the < symbol, you can press the Tab button to move to the Dynamic Input angle tooltip.)

7. Move the cursor to the right in the 0-degree direction and type **.4668** ↵.

8. Assume that this was a mistake. Type **u** ↵.

9. The `Specify next point or [Close/Undo]:` prompt reappears. With the cursor still in the 0-degree direction, type **.4667** ↵.

10. Type **c** ↵ to close the figure. This ends the LINE command.

11. Start the LINE command again.

12. At the `Specify first point:` prompt, press Enter. The line starts at the previous endpoint.

13. Type **.8071<270** ↵ and press Enter to end the LINE command.

14. Save your drawing. It should look like Figure 6.1.

FIGURE 6.1

The completed gate valve symbol.

CROSS-REF Other aspects of lines are covered elsewhere in this book. Chapter 11 explains how to draw dashed and dotted lines. Chapter 16 explains how to create *polylines*, which combine line segments and curves into one object. Chapter 16 also covers *multilines* and *dlines* — sets of parallel lines that you draw all at once. Chapter 21 discusses how to draw 3D lines and polylines.

Drawing Rectangles

The RECTANG command draws rectangles. Rectangles are used in all disciplines. The RECTANG command has a number of options that specify how the rectangle appears and how you define the rectangle's dimensions.

Choose Rectangle from the Draw toolbar. The first prompt is as follows:

```
Specify first corner point or [Chamfer/Elevation/Fillet/
Thickness/Width]:
```

Select one of the options. If you don't want to use any of the options, just specify one corner of the rectangle, using any method of specifying a coordinate.

CROSS-REF You can chamfer and fillet the corners as you create the rectangle. (Chapter 10 covers chamfering and filleting.) You can specify a width for the rectangle's line (see Chapter 16). You can also create a 3D box by using the elevation and thickness options (see Chapter 21). The RECTANG command creates a *polyline*, meaning that all four sides of the rectangle are one object, instead of four separate line objects. Chapter 16 covers polylines.

If you use one of the options, the first prompt returns so that you can specify the first corner point or use another option. After you specify the first point, you see the `Specify other corner point or [Area/Dimensions/Rotation]:` prompt.

To immediately create the rectangle, specify the corner diagonally opposite the first corner that you specified. You can use any method of specifying coordinates. For example, if you know that the rectangle should be 6 inches wide and 3 inches high, you can specify the second point as 6,3. (If Dynamic Input is off or set to absolute coordinates, add the @ symbol before the X,Y coordinates.) You can also use one of the options below:

- **Area:** If you know the area of the rectangle, and only its length or width, then use this option. First you enter the area. Then you specify either the length or the width, and AutoCAD calculates the side that you didn't specify, based on the area you entered.

- **Dimensions:** If you know the length and width of the rectangle, then use this option (although it may be simpler to specify the opposite corner, as I described earlier). You are prompted for the length and width. You then need to move the mouse to specify if you want the second corner to be above and to the right, or in any other direction from the first corner. When you see the rectangle you want, click it.

- **Rotation:** If you want to rotate the rectangle as you create it, then simply enter a rotation angle and pick the opposite corner. Alternatively, instead of entering a rotation angle, you can pick two points to specify a rotation angle and then pick the opposite corner. This last option is great if you want to align the rectangle with an existing object.

NOTE All of the options for rectangles, except for Area, remain as defaults for future rectangles that you draw. As a result, you can use the Dimensions option to quickly draw a number of identical rectangles.

Drawing Polygons

 The POLYGON command enables you to draw multi-sided, closed figures with equal side lengths. You can draw polygons that have from 3 to 1,024 sides. To draw a polygon, choose Polygon from the Draw toolbar.

First specify the number of sides. Then choose one of three methods of defining the polygon, as described in Table 6.1.

TABLE 6.1

POLYGON Command Options

Option	Description
Edge	Right-click and choose the Edge option. Specify the two endpoints of any edge of the polygon to complete the polygon.
Inscribed in circle	After specifying the center, right-click and choose Inscribed in Circle. Then specify the radius from the center to a vertex (point). This defines the polygon with reference to an imaginary circle whose circumference touches all the vertices of the polygon.
Circumscribed about circle	After specifying the center, right-click and choose Circumscribed about Circle. Then specify the radius from the center to the midpoint of a side. This defines the polygon with reference to an imaginary circle whose circumference touches all the midpoints of the polygon's sides.

If you type a number for the radius, then the bottom edge of the polygon is horizontal. However, if you pick a point for the radius with your mouse, you can specify the orientation of the polygon. As you rotate the mouse cursor around the center, you see the polygon rotate. Click when you like what you see.

 When you type a number for the radius, the bottom edge actually aligns with the snap rotation angle, which is usually 0. Chapter 8 explains how to change this angle.

The POLYGON command creates a polyline, meaning that the entire polygon is one object, rather than a series of line segments.

In the exercise that follows, I indicate inches with a double prime (") and feet with a single prime ('). You may find this notation clearer when a measurement has both feet and inches, but you do not actually need to type the double prime for inches. When you have a measurement that is only in inches, it saves time to leave out the double prime.

 The drawing used in this exercise on drawing rectangles and polygons, ab06-a.dwg, is in the Drawings folder on the DVD.

STEPS: Drawing Rectangles and Polygons

1. Open ab06-a.dwg from the DVD.
2. Save the drawing in your AutoCAD Bible folder as ab06-02.dwg. Verify that snap and grid are on, set at 1". OSNAP should be off.

This exercise assumes that you have Dynamic Input on (click the DYN button on the status bar to turn it on, if necessary) and that you use the default settings for the polar format and relative coordinates. Make sure that the AutoCAD Classic or AutoCAD LT Classic workspace is chosen in the Workspaces toolbar.

3. Choose Rectangle from the Draw toolbar.

4. At the `Specify first corner point or [Chamfer/Elevation/Fillet/Thickness/Width]:` prompt, move the cursor to 0'-1",0'-1" and click. At the `Specify other corner point or [Area/Dimensions/Rotation]:` prompt, type **2'1",1'9"** ↵.

5. Start the RECTANG command again. At the `Specify first corner point or [Chamfer/Elevation/Fillet/Thickness/Width]:` prompt, Shift+right-click and choose the From object snap. Pick the bottom-left corner of the rectangle. At the `<Offset>:` prompt, type **@2,2** ↵ to start the second rectangle 2 inches up and 2 inches to the right of the first rectangle.

6. At the `Specify other corner point or [Area/Dimensions/Rotation]:` prompt, type **1'9",1'3"** ↵.

7. Right-click and choose Repeat Rectangle to start the RECTANG command again. At the prompt, find 0'8",1'7" (on a snap point) and click. At the `Specify other corner point or [Area/Dimensions/Rotation]:` prompt, type **11,2** ↵. (You don't need to type the double-prime for inches.)

8. Again, start the RECTANG command. At the prompt, find 1'1",1'8" and click. At the `Specify other corner point or [Area/Dimensions/Rotation]:` prompt, type **1,-5** ↵.

9. Start the POLYGON command. At the `Enter number of sides <4>:` prompt, type **5** ↵. At the `Specify center of polygon or [Edge]:` prompt, type **10,1'8** ↵ to indicate the center.

10. At the `Enter an option [Inscribed in circle/Circumscribed about circle] <I>:` prompt, press Enter to accept the default. This means that you indicate the radius from the center to the vertices. (If your prompt shows `<C>` as the default, type **i** ↵.)

11. At the `Specify radius of circle:` prompt, type **1/2** ↵. AutoCAD or AutoCAD LT draws the pentagon.

12. Repeat Steps 9 through 11 using a center of 1'5,1'8.

13. Start the POLYGON command again. At the `Enter number of sides <5>:` prompt, type **3** ↵.

14. At the `Specify center of polygon or [Edge]:` prompt, right-click and choose the Edge option.

15. At the `Specify first endpoint of edge:` prompt, choose the top-left corner of the faucet rectangle (1'1",1'8"), which is on a snap point.

16. At the `Specify second endpoint of edge:` prompt, choose the top-right corner of the faucet rectangle to complete the triangle.

17. Turn off the grid to get a better look at the drawing. You have completed the sink, which should look like Figure 6.2. Save your drawing.

FIGURE 6.2

The completed sink, drawn with rectangles and polygons.

Thanks to Bill Wynn of New Windsor, Maryland, for this drawing, which he created in his AutoCAD class as part of a plan drawing of an entire house.

Creating Construction Lines

Sometimes you want to create a line that is used solely for the purpose of reference. A construction line is a temporary or reference line used to help you draw or to show a relationship between objects. For example, you might want to do the following:

- Draw two lines from the midpoints of two perpendicular lines so that you can use their intersection as the center for a circle.
- Draw a line from one object to another to visually indicate the relationship between the two objects.
- Show the relationship between equivalent parts of a model shown in front and right-side views.
- Draw a line through the center of an object shown in cross-section so that you can show dimensions from the centerline to the edge of the object.

You could use regular lines for these purposes. However, construction lines (also known as *xlines*) are unique in that they extend infinitely in both directions. This makes them especially useful for seeing the relationships among various objects in your drawing.

Of course, construction lines are not actually infinite. However, they extend to the edge of the drawing area on your screen, and if you zoom out to see more of your drawing, they expand so that they always extend to the edge of the screen. The object snap tracking feature sometimes eliminates the need for construction lines; nevertheless, sometimes you can work more easily having a line visible for several commands and then erasing it.

If you zoom to show the extents of your drawing, AutoCAD or AutoCAD LT ignores the xlines and shows you just the extents of the regular objects in your drawing. Chapter 8 covers the ZOOM command.

 The XLINE command offers several ways to create construction lines. Start the command by choosing Construction Line from the Draw toolbar. You see the following prompt:

```
Specify a point or [Hor/Ver/Ang/Bisect/Offset]:
```

Table 6.2 lists the possible options. AutoCAD or AutoCAD LT continues to prompt you for more points so that you can continue to draw construction lines — much like the LINE command. Press Enter to end the command.

TABLE 6.2

XLINE Command Options

Option	Description
Specify a point	This option enables you to define the construction line with two points. At the first prompt, specify a point. At the `Specify through point:` prompt, specify another point. The first point becomes the base point for subsequent construction lines that you can draw by specifying other through points.
Hor	To draw a construction line parallel to the X axis, type **h** ↵ to specify the Horizontal option. The command responds with the `Specify through point:` prompt. Specify one point. This is useful for drawing a series of horizontal construction lines.
Ver	To draw a construction line parallel to the Y axis, type **v** ↵ to specify the Vertical option. The command responds with the `Specify through point:` prompt. Specify one point.
Ang	Type **a** ↵ (for Angle). The command responds with the `Enter angle of xline (0) or [Reference]:` prompt. If you enter an angle, the command asks for a through point. You can also type **r** ↵ and select a line as a reference, and then provide an angle and a through point. AutoCAD or AutoCAD LT then calculates the angle of the construction line from the angle of the reference line. This is useful for drawing a series of construction lines at a specified angle.
Bisect	To draw a construction line that bisects an angle (divides the angle in half), type **b** ↵. The command responds with the `Specify angle vertex point:` prompt. Choose any point that you want the construction line to pass through. Then, at the `Specify angle start point:` prompt, choose a point that defines the base of the angle. At the `Specify angle end point:` prompt, choose a point that defines the end of the angle.
Offset	To draw a construction line parallel to a line, type **o** ↵. You can specify the offset distance by typing in the number or using the Through option to pick a point through which the construction line should pass. Either way, the next step is to select a line. If you specified an offset distance, the command displays the `Specify side to offset:` prompt. Respond by picking a point on the side of the selected line on which you want the construction line to appear.

Creating Rays

Rays are similar to construction lines, except that they start at a specific point and extend to infinity in one direction only. If you need a line to extend only in one direction, using a ray may be less confusing.

NOTE You can use most object snaps with construction lines and rays. (You can't use an endpoint for construction lines or a midpoint for rays.) You can edit construction lines and rays like any other object.

To draw a ray, choose Draw ⇨ Ray. At the `Specify start point:` prompt, specify the start point for the ray. At the `Specify through point:` prompt, specify another point. AutoCAD or AutoCAD LT continues to ask for through points. Press Enter to end the command.

ON the DVD-ROM The drawing used in this exercise on drawing construction lines and rays, ab06-b.dwg, is in the Drawings folder on the DVD.

STEPS: Drawing Construction Lines and Rays

1. Open `ab06-b.dwg` from the DVD.
2. Save the drawing as `ab06-03.dwg` in your `AutoCAD Bible` folder. Make sure that the AutoCAD Classic or AutoCAD LT Classic workspace is chosen in the Workspaces toolbar.

3. Choose Construction Line from the Draw toolbar.
4. At the `Specify a point or [Hor/Ver/Ang/Bisect/Offset]:` prompt, choose point ❶, shown in Figure 6.3.
5. At the `Specify through point:` prompt, choose point ❷, shown in Figure 6.3.

FIGURE 6.3

A pipe with cross-section.

6. Press Enter to end the command. Notice that the drawing has been set up so that the construction line is drawn in green and with a noncontinuous linetype. This is to distinguish it from the main drawing. (See Chapter 11 for details on how to set up a drawing in this way.)
7. Choose Draw ➪ Ray.
8. At the `Specify start point:` prompt, choose point ❸, shown in Figure 6.3.
9. At the `Specify through point:` prompt, choose point ❹, shown in Figure 6.3. Press Enter to end the command.
10. Save your drawing.

Summary

This chapter covered the ins and outs of lines. You read about:

- Using the LINE command
- Drawing rectangles
- Drawing polygons
- Creating construction lines, including xlines that extend infinitely in both directions and rays that extend infinitely in one direction

The next chapter explains how to draw curves and point objects. Curves include circles, arcs, ellipses, and donuts.

Chapter 7

Drawing Curves and Points

AutoCAD and AutoCAD LT offer a number of ways to create curved objects. You can draw circles, arcs, ellipses, and donuts (also spelled as doughnuts). In this chapter, I also cover point objects, which are neither curves nor lines but don't deserve their own chapter.

CROSS-REF Several complex objects — such as polylines, splines, regions, and boundaries — involve curves. These are covered in Chapter 16.

Drawing Circles

Circles are common objects in drawings. In mechanical drawings, they often represent holes or wheels. In architectural drawings, they may be used for doorknobs, trash baskets, or trees. In electrical and piping schematics, they are used for various kinds of symbols.

Understanding the circle options

The CIRCLE command provides five ways to draw a circle. To draw a circle, choose Circle from the Draw toolbar. The command responds with the `Specify center point for circle or [3P/2P/Ttr (tan tan radius)]:` prompt. Table 7.1 describes how to use these options.

IN THIS CHAPTER

Drawing circles

Drawing arcs

Creating ellipses

Drawing donuts

Creating points

121

TABLE 7.1

Five Ways to Draw a Circle

Option	Description
Center Radius	This option is the default. Specify the center and then the radius. You can type the radius as a distance, or pick a point where you want the circumference to be.
Center Diameter	Specify the center. Choose the `Diameter` option and type the length of the diameter, or pick a point to specify the diameter.
2P	2P stands for two points. Choose the `2p` option. Specify one point on the circumference, and then an opposite point on the circumference. These two points define the diameter of the circle.
3P	3P stands for three points. Choose the `3p` option. Specify three points on the circumference.
Tangent, Tangent, Radius	Choose the `Ttr` option. The CIRCLE command prompts `Specify point on object for first tangent of circle:` and provides an aperture to let you pick a point. Then the command prompts `Specify point on object for second tangent of circle:` and you pick a second point. These points can be any points on the object(s) to which you want your circle to be tangent. Finally, type a radius.

> **TIP** You can also create a circle tangent to other objects by using the two-point (2P) method or three-point (3P) method, and picking those points with the Tangent object snap. Also, when you choose Draw ➪ Circle (from the menu), AutoCAD and AutoCAD LT include a tan tan tan option, enabling you to specify a circle tangent to three objects.

Drawing circles

Drawing circles is fairly straightforward. Often, you can use object snaps to define part of the circle. In the following exercise, you practice using the most common methods of creating a circle.

 The drawing used in the following exercise on drawing circles, ab07-a.dwg, is in the Drawings folder on the DVD.

STEPS: Drawing Circles

1. Open ab07-a.dwg from the DVD.

2. Save the file as ab07-01.dwg in your AutoCAD Bible folder. This is a drawing of an air compressor from which all the circles have been removed. Make sure that OSNAP is on. Set a running object snap for endpoints only. Make sure that the AutoCAD Classic or AutoCAD LT Classic workspace is chosen in the Workspaces toolbar.

 3. Choose Circle from the Draw toolbar. Right-click and choose 2P from the shortcut menu. At the `Specify first end point of circle's diameter:` prompt, pick the endpoint at ❶ in Figure 7.1. At the `Specify second end point of circle's diameter:` prompt, pick the endpoint at ❷.

4. Repeat the CIRCLE command by right-clicking and choosing Repeat Circle. Right-click and choose 2P from the shortcut menu. Pick the endpoints at ❸ and ❹ in Figure 7.1.

FIGURE 7.1

The air compressor without its circles.

5. Repeat the CIRCLE command by pressing Enter. At the `Specify center point for circle or [3P/2P/Ttr (tan tan radius)]:` prompt, pick the endpoint at **5**. At the `Specify radius of circle or [Diameter]:` prompt, pick the endpoint at **6**.

6. Repeat the CIRCLE command. At the `Specify center point for circle or [3P/2P/Ttr (tan tan radius)]:` prompt, pick the endpoint at **7**. At the `Specify radius of circle or [Diameter]:` prompt, right-click and choose Diameter; then type **.25** ↵.

7. Repeat the CIRCLE command by right-clicking and choosing Repeat Circle. At the `Specify center point for circle or [3P/2P/Ttr (tan tan radius)]:` prompt, right-click and choose 3P. At the `Specify first point on circle:` prompt, pick the endpoint at **8** in Figure 7.1. At the `Specify second point on circle:` prompt, pick the endpoint at **9**. At the `Specify third point on circle:` prompt, choose a midpoint object snap and pick the midpoint at **10**.

8. For the last circle on the right, choose any method that you want to use to draw a circle. The circle should be the same size and placement as the second circle from the left.

9. Repeat the CIRCLE command. At the `Specify center point for circle or [3P/2P/Ttr (tan tan radius)]:` prompt, choose the Center object snap ↵ and pick **7**. At the `Specify radius of circle or [Diameter]:` prompt, type **.05** ↵.

10. Repeat Step 9 to create a circle inside the circle whose center is at **5** and whose radius is 0.05.

11. Repeat the CIRCLE command. At the `Specify center point for circle or [3P/2P/Ttr (tan tan radius)]:` prompt, pick the endpoint at **11**. At the `Specify radius of circle or [Diameter]:` prompt, pick the endpoint at **12**.

12. Repeat Step 11, choosing the endpoint at **13** for the center of the circle and the endpoint at **14** for its radius, as shown in Figure 7.1.

13. Save your drawing. It should look like Figure 7.2.

FIGURE 7.2

The completed air compressor.

Thanks to the U.S. Army Corps of Engineers at Vicksburg, Mississippi, for this drawing. They maintain a Web site of drawings at http://cadlib.wes.army.mil.

CROSS-REF　It may have occurred to you that this task would have been easier if you could simply have copied one circle to another location instead of creating each circle from scratch. I cover copying in Chapter 9.

Drawing Arcs

An arc is a portion of a circle. Therefore, to define an arc, you have to define not only a circle — for example, by specifying a center and a radius — but also the start and endpoints of the arc. The ARC command offers several methods for defining an arc. The method you pick depends on the information that you have about the arc that you want to draw.

CROSS-REF　You can close an arc to create a circle using the JOIN command. For more information, see the section "Joining objects" in Chapter 10.

Understanding arc options

Making sense of all of the arc options may seem overwhelming, but after you understand the parts of an arc you can choose the options that suit your needs. Figure 7.3 shows the parts of an arc that you can use to draw an arc. Refer to this figure as you read through the arc options.

The parts of an arc.

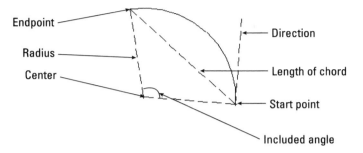

Figure 7.4 shows the flow of the arc options. When you start the ARC command, you have two options, Start Point and Center. Depending on how you start, more options become available.

You can also press Enter at the first arc prompt to draw a second arc starting from the endpoint of the most recently drawn arc, line, polyline, or other object. The new arc continues in the same direction as the end of the first object. The only other prompt is the endpoint.

The ARC command options.

Drawing arcs

 To draw an arc, choose Arc from the Draw toolbar or the 2D Draw control panel of the Dashboard. Object snaps are often helpful when drawing arcs.

When drawing an arc by using the Start, End, and Radius options, the three specifications actually define two possible arcs, one minor and one major. The ARC command draws the minor arc by default, in the counterclockwise direction. (A minor arc is less than half a circle.) If you enter a negative number for the radius, the command draws the major arc. The options requiring an angle also define two possible arcs, one drawn counterclockwise and one drawn clockwise. AutoCAD and AutoCAD LT draw the counterclockwise arc by default. If you type a negative number for the angle, the arc is drawn clockwise.

ON the DVD-ROM The drawing used in the following exercise on drawing arcs, ab07-b.dwg, is in the Drawings folder on the DVD.

STEPS: Drawing Arcs

1. Open ab07-b.dwg from the DVD.

2. Save the file as ab07-02.dwg in your AutoCAD Bible folder. ORTHO is on, and units are set to Fractional. Choose Tools ⇨ Drafting Settings (clicking the Object Snap tab, if necessary) and set running object snaps for intersection, center, and endpoint. Make sure OSNAP is on. In this exercise, you draw part of the sealing plate shown in Figure 7.5.

3. For a change of pace, start the LINE command by choosing Line from the 2D Draw control panel of the Dashboard. (Choose Tools ⇨ Palettes ⇨ Dashboard to open the Dashboard.) Start at 2,3 and use Direct Distance Entry to create a 7-unit horizontal line to the right. End the LINE command. (See Chapter 4 for a full explanation of how to use Direct Distance Entry.)

4. Draw another line starting at 5-1/2,1-5/8 and draw it 2-3/4 units long in the 90-degree direction. These two lines are center lines and would ordinarily appear in a different color and linetype than the object you're drawing. (You can read about colors and linetypes in Chapter 11.)

5. Draw a circle with its center at the intersection of the two lines (use the Intersection object snap) and a radius of 11/16.

6. Use the Center object snap to draw another circle with the same center as the first circle and a radius of 1.

7. Draw a third circle, using the From object snap (Shift+right-click to open the object snap menu, and then choose From). For the base point, use the Center object snap and pick either of the first two circles that you drew. The offset is @-1-15/16,0 (this means 1-15/16 units to the left of the center of the first two circles). Its radius is ⅜.

8. Draw a fourth circle. Use the From object snap again. For the base point, use the Center object snap and pick either of the first two circles. The offset is @1-15/16,0. The radius is ⅜.

FIGURE 7.5
_____

The dimensioned sealing plate for a valve.

Thanks to Jerry Bottenfield of Clow Valve Company in Oskaloosa, Iowa, for this drawing.

9. Choose Arc from the 2D Draw control panel of the Dashboard. Follow the prompts:

   Specify start point of arc or [Center]: *Choose the From object snap.*
   Base point: *Use the Center object snap to pick the center of the leftmost circle.*
   <Offset>: **@-5/8,0** ↵
   Specify second point of arc or [Center/End]: *Right-click and choose Center. Use the Center object snap to pick the center of the leftmost circle.*
   Specify end point of arc or [Angle/chord Length]: *Right-click and choose Angle.*
   Specify included angle: **67.23** ↵

10. Start the LINE command. At the Specify first point: prompt, press Enter to continue the line in the same direction as the end of the arc. At the Length of line: prompt, type **1-13/16** ↵. End the LINE command.

11. Start the ARC command again. Follow the prompts:

    Specify start point of arc or [Center]: *Use the Endpoint object snap to pick the end of the line that you just drew.*
    Specify second point of arc or [Center/End]: *Right-click and choose Center. Use the Center object snap and pick any point on one of the large central circles.*
    Specify end point of arc or [Angle/chord Length]: *Use Endpoint object snap to pick the lower end of the vertical construction line.*

12. Repeat the ARC command. Follow the prompts:

    ```
    Specify start point of arc or [Center]: Right-click and choose
    Center. Use the Center object snap and pick any point on one of the
    large central circles.
    Specify start point of arc: Use the Endpoint object snap to pick the
    endpoint of the arc that you just completed.
    Specify end point of arc or [Angle/chord Length]: Right-click and
    choose Angle.
    Specify included angle: 22.77 ↵
    ```

13. Start the LINE command. At the `Specify first point:` prompt, press Enter to continue the line in the same direction as the end of the arc. At the `Length of line:` prompt, type **1-13/16** ↵. End the LINE command.

14. Start the ARC command. Follow the prompts:

    ```
    Specify start point of arc or [Center]: Use the Endpoint object snap
    to pick the endpoint of the line that you just drew.
    Specify second point of arc or [Center/End]: Right-click and choose
    End.
    Specify end point of arc: Choose the From object snap.
    _from Base point: Use the Center object snap to pick the center of
    the rightmost circle.
    <Offset>: @5/8,0 ↵
    Specify center point of arc or [Angle/Direction/Radius]: r ↵
    Specify radius of arc: 5/8 ↵
    ```

15. Save your drawing. Your drawing should look like Figure 7.6. You can complete this drawing in Chapter 10 by creating a mirror image.

FIGURE 7.6

The partially completed sealing plate, created by using lines, circles, and arcs.

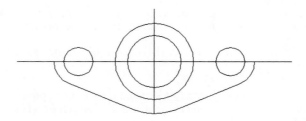

Creating Ellipses and Elliptical Arcs

You can create ellipses (ovals) as well as elliptical arcs, which are partial ellipses. Like a circle, an ellipse has a center. The difference, of course, is that an ellipse has a longer radius along its major axis and a shorter radius along its minor axis.

Understanding ellipse options

You can draw an ellipse by defining the center first. Another option is to define the axis endpoints first. If you want to draw an elliptical arc, you must specify the start and end angle.

Creating ellipses

The default option is to specify endpoints 1 and 2 of the first axis. Then you specify the second axis distance, which is the distance from the first axis line to the circumference along the second axis.

Instead of specifying a second axis distance, you can choose the Rotation option. The Rotation option defines the minor axis by specifying an angle from 0 degrees to 90 degrees, which is the ratio of the major axis to the minor axis. (Actually, the command only accepts up to 89.4 degrees.) When the angle is 0, you get a circle. As the angle increases, the ellipse gets flatter and flatter until you reach 89.4 degrees. A 45-degree angle results in a minor axis whose length is the square root of the major-axis length.

Instead of specifying endpoints, you can use the Center option to specify the center of the ellipse. Then specify the endpoint of the first axis, which can be either the major or the minor axis. Finally, specify the other axis distance, which is the radius from the center to the circumference along the second axis. Again, instead of specifying the second axis distance, you can define the ellipse by using the Rotation option.

Creating elliptical arcs

To draw an elliptical arc, use the Arc option of the ELLIPSE command. In AutoCAD only, there is an Ellipse Arc button on the Draw toolbar. (This button is equivalent to choosing the Arc option of the ELLIPSE command and offers no additional functionality.) The first prompts are the same as for an ellipse. Then the command continues with the `Specify start angle or [Parameter]:` prompt, offering the following options:

- **Start angle:** This option is the default. Specify the start angle, which the command redefines to start along the major axis. The command responds with the `Specify end angle or [Parameter/Included angle]:` prompt.

- **End angle:** Specify the end angle to complete the ellipse arc.

- **Included angle:** After specifying the start angle, you can complete the arc by specifying the included angle from the start point to the endpoint, going counterclockwise.

- **Parameter:** Choose this option to define the arc portion by the ellipse's area rather than its included angle (which defines the arc portion by its circumference). The command responds with the `Specify start parameter or [Angle]:` and `Specify end parameter or [Angle/Included angle]:` prompts. By typing in angles, you define the percent of the full ellipse's area that you want to include. (For example, starting at 15 degrees and ending at 105 degrees includes 90 degrees and therefore draws one-quarter of an ellipse.) The options in brackets let you return to regular angle specification.

Drawing ellipses

To draw an ellipse, choose Ellipse from the Draw toolbar. In addition to the information that the command explicitly requests in the prompts, you need to know the angle of the first axis that you define. Not all ellipses are horizontal or vertical. You control the orientation when you stipulate the second point of the first axis. The second axis is automatically perpendicular to the first axis.

To draw an elliptical arc, choose Ellipse Arc from the Draw toolbar (in AutoCAD) or use the Arc option of the ELLIPSE command. When you draw an elliptical arc, the command introduces a helpful but sometimes confusing feature: while you're defining the arc angles, the command redefines 0 degrees along the major axis. This helps you to define the included angle in an orientation that relates to the ellipse, rather than the usual orientation where 0 degrees is to the right.

In this exercise, you practice drawing ellipses and elliptical arcs.

 The drawing used in the following exercise on drawing ellipses and elliptical arcs, ab07-c.dwg, is in the Drawings folder on the DVD.

STEPS: Drawing Ellipses and Elliptical Arcs

1. Open ab07-c.dwg from the DVD.

2. Save the file as ab07-03.dwg in your AutoCAD Bible folder. The drawing shows an empty conference room. Snap is on, set to 6". ORTHO and OSNAP should be on, with a running object snap set for endpoint only.

3. Choose Ellipse from the Draw toolbar or the 2D Draw control panel of the Dashboard. At the Specify axis endpoint of ellipse or [Arc/Center]: prompt, right-click and choose Center. At the Specify center of ellipse: prompt, choose 8',10', which is a snap point. At the Specify endpoint of axis: prompt, move the cursor to the right until the coordinates read 3'<0 and click. (If necessary, right-click the coordinates on the status bar and choose Relative, or look at the Dynamic Input tooltips.) At the Specify distance to other axis or [Rotation]: prompt, move the cursor up until the coordinates read 6'6"<90 and click. This completes the conference table.

4. Start the ELLIPSE command again. Follow the prompts:

   Specify axis endpoint of ellipse or [Arc/Center]: *Right-click and choose Arc.*
   Specify axis endpoint of elliptical arc or [Center]: *Right-click and choose Center.*
   Specify center of elliptical arc: *Pick 8',3', a snap point.*
   Specify endpoint of axis: *Move the cursor to the right until the coordinates read 1'<0 and pick. (You can also look at the Dynamic Input tooltips.)*
   Specify distance to other axis or [Rotation]: *Move the cursor up until the coordinates read 6"<90 and pick.*
   Specify start angle or [Parameter]: **162** ↵
   Specify end angle or [Parameter/Included angle]: **18** ↵

5. Turn off ORTHO. Start the LINE command. At the Specify first point: prompt, use the Endpoint running object snap and pick the right side of the elliptical arc. At the Specify next point or [Undo]: prompt, right-click the coordinates and choose Absolute (if necessary), and press and hold Shift+A to temporarily override OSNAP mode while you pick the snap point 8'6",3'. End the LINE command.

6. Start the LINE command. At the Specify first point: prompt, use the Endpoint object snap to pick the left side of the ellipse arc. At the Specify next point or [Undo]: prompt, press and hold Shift+A while you pick the snap point 7'6",3'. End the LINE command.

7. Choose Ellipse again. Follow the prompts:

```
Specify axis endpoint of ellipse or [Arc/Center]: Right-click and
choose Arc.
Specify axis endpoint of elliptical arc or [Center]: Use the Endpoint
object snap to pick the free endpoint of the line on the right.
Specify other endpoint of axis: Use the Endpoint object snap to pick
the free endpoint of the line on the left.
Specify distance to other axis or [Rotation]: 3<90 ↵ (If you don't
have Dynamic Input on and set to the default of relative coordinates,
then type @ before the distance.)
Specify start angle or [Parameter]: Use the Endpoint object snap to
pick the free endpoint of the line on the right.
Specify end angle or [Parameter/Included angle]: Use Endpoint object
snap to pick the free endpoint of the line on the left.
```

8. Start the ELLIPSE command again. At the Specify axis endpoint of ellipse or [Arc/Center]: prompt, pick point 2',18', a snap point. At the Specify other endpoint of axis: prompt, pick point 2',16', also a snap point. (The coordinates on the status bar display this point in absolute coordinate mode. The Dynamic Input tooltips show 2' and 90°.) At the Specify distance to other axis or [Rotation]: prompt, move the cursor to the right until the coordinates read 6"<0. (Right-click the coordinates and choose Relative, if necessary.) This is also a snap point. Click the mouse button to complete the small side table.

9. Save your drawing. It should look like Figure 7.7.

FIGURE 7.7

The conference room with a conference table, a chair, and a side table.

Making Donuts

A donut is a wide polyline that looks like two concentric circles, with the area between the circles filled in. You define a diameter for the inner and outer circles. AutoCAD and AutoCAD LT accept both DONUT and DOUGHNUT if you type in the command. Donuts are often used in electrical drawings to create symbols. If the inner circle's radius is zero, you create a filled-in circle.

The setting of the FILL command determines whether the donut is filled. Type **fill** ↵ and type **on** ↵ or **off** ↵. FILL is on by default. Turning FILL off displays a radial pattern of lines, as shown in Figure 7.8. Type **regen** ↵ or choose View ➪ Regen to update existing donuts to the new FILL setting. If you have many filled objects in your drawing, then your drawing may take some time to display. You can save time by turning FILL off while you draw. Then turn FILL on just before you need to print or plot the drawing.

FIGURE 7.8

The parts of a donut, shown with FILL off.

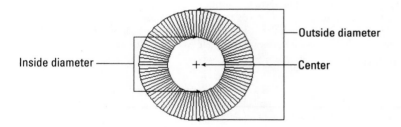

Inside diameter —

— Outside diameter

— Center

Understanding DONUT options

The DONUT command has the following prompts:

- `Specify inside diameter of donut <0.5000>`: Type the diameter of the inside circle or pick two points to specify the inside diameter. The number in brackets is the last inside diameter that you defined, or 0.5 if you haven't previously used the DONUT command in this drawing session.

- `Specify outside diameter of donut <1.0000>`: Type the diameter of the outside circle or pick two points to specify the outside diameter. The outside diameter must be larger than the inside diameter. The number in brackets is the last outside diameter that you defined, or 1.0 if you haven't previously used the DONUT command in this drawing session.

- `Specify second point`: If you define the inside or outside diameter by picking a point, the command asks for a second point. Use this technique if you're using object snaps to define the diameters.

- `Specify center of donut or <exit>`: Specify the center of the donut. Pressing Enter ends the command.

Drawing donuts

Drawing donuts is relatively easy. Choose Draw ⇨ Donut. Then specify the inner and outer diameters and the center. The DONUT command continues to prompt for centers so that you can place additional donuts. Press Enter to end the command.

 You can use the hatch feature to fill in any object with a solid fill, with a great deal more flexibility in the shape of your objects. (Chapter 16 discusses hatching.) As a result, the DONUT command is not as essential as it once was.

You draw some donuts in the next exercise.

Placing Points

A point simply marks a coordinate. Points are generally used for reference. It is sometimes helpful to mark a point that you will use later as a guide to place an object or to help you return an object to its original position. When it's no longer needed, you may erase the point. This is a typical construction method. In some cases, the From object snap or object snap tracking can be used instead of a point.

CROSS-REF **The DIVIDE and MEASURE commands place point objects along an object. Chapter 12 covers these commands.**

Changing the point style

Because points can be hard to see, and because various disciplines have different conventions for drawing point objects, AutoCAD and AutoCAD LT provide 20 types of point styles that you can use in your drawing. Before you draw a point, you should set the point style. You can save this setting in your template.

Choose Format ⇨ Point Style to open the Point Style dialog box, shown in Figure 7.9.

To set the point style, click the box showing the style that you want. Then set the point size, which has the following options:

- **Set Size Relative to Screen:** Use this option if you want the point to always appear the same size, no matter how much you zoom in and out — for example, when you're using the point as a reference. The size is set as a percentage of the screen. This option is the default, with the size set to 5 percent of the screen.

- **Set Size in Absolute Units:** Use this option if you want the point to have a real size, just like any other object. The size is set in units. Use this option when you want the point to stay the same size relative to other objects in your drawing.

Click OK to close the dialog box.

 When you change the point style, previously drawn points automatically and immediately change to the new style.

FIGURE 7.9

Choosing a point style.

Creating points

After you determine the point style, you're ready to create points. Choose Point from the Draw toolbar or from the 2D Draw control panel of the Dashboard. You see the following on the command line:

```
Current point modes:  PDMODE=0  PDSIZE=0.0000
Specify a point:
```

Specify the point that you want, either by picking a point on the screen or by typing coordinates. (You can specify a Z coordinate to create a point in 3D space. For more information, see Chapter 21.) You can use object snaps to specify the point. When you start the POINT command from the Draw toolbar or the Dashboard, the command automatically repeats the prompt so that you can continue to specify points. To end the command, press Esc. When you choose Draw ➪ Point, you can choose Single Point or Multiple Point from the submenu. The command-line version draws single points.

If BLIPMODE is on and you're using the first point style — a small dot — you cannot see the point until you use the REDRAW command to remove the blips.

TIP If you're using the points for temporary reference, instead of erasing them, you can set the point style to the second style in the Point Style dialog box (no dot) before plotting. As a result, the points do not appear on your plot. You can also put your points on a layer with a Not Plottable property. (See Chapter 11 for more on layers.)

After you create a point, use the Node object snap to snap to the point.

ON the DVD-ROM The drawing used in the following exercise on drawing donuts and points, ab07-d.dwg, is in the Drawings folder on the DVD.

STEPS: Drawing Donuts and Points

1. Open ab07-d.dwg from the DVD.
2. Save the file as ab07-04.dwg in your AutoCAD Bible folder. The drawing contains a rectangle and connecting wires for an electrical switch. Make sure that OSNAP is on. Set running object

snaps for endpoint, center, node, and quadrant. This exercise assumes that you have Dynamic Input on, with the default setting of relative coordinates.

3. Choose Format ➪ Point Style. The Point Style dialog box opens. Choose the third point type, which is the plus sign. The Set Size Relative to Screen option button should be checkmarked. The Point Size should be 5.0000%. Choose OK.

4. Choose Point from the Draw toolbar or the 2D Draw control panel of the Dashboard. Follow the prompts:

   ```
   Specify a point: Use the From object snap. (Shift+right-click to open
   the Object Snap shortcut menu.)
   Base point: Use the Endpoint object snap to pick the top-left corner
   of the rectangle.
   <Offset>: @.08,-.09 ↵
   Specify a point: Press Esc to complete the command.
   ```

5. Choose Draw ➪ Donut. Follow these prompts:

   ```
   Specify inside diameter of donut <0.5000>: .04 ↵
   Specify outside diameter of donut <1.0000>: .06 ↵
   Specify center of donut or <exit>: Use the Node object snap to pick
   the point that you drew.
   Specify center of donut or <exit>: @.19,0 ↵
   Specify center of donut or <exit>: ↵
   ```

6. Start the POINT command again. Follow the prompts:

   ```
   Specify a point: Press Shift+right-click and choose Mid Between 2
   Points from the shortcut menu.
   First point of mid: Use the Center object snap to pick the center of
   the right-hand donut. (You may have to press Tab until you get the
   center object snap, and not a quadrant object snap.)
   Second point of mid: Press and hold Shift to temporarily turn on
   ORTHO. Right-click and choose Snap Overrides➪Perpendicular and pick
   the lower horizontal line of the rectangle. Release the Shift key.

   Specify a point: Press Esc.
   ```

7. Start the LINE command. Follow the prompts:

   ```
   Specify first point: Use the Quadrant object snap to pick the right
   (0 degrees) quadrant of the left donut. If you don't see the Quadrant
   SnapTip, press Tab until it appears.
   Specify next point or [Undo]: Use the Node object snap to pick the
   point that you just drew. End the LINE command.
   ```

8. Save your drawing. It should look like Figure 7.10.

FIGURE 7.10

The completed electrical switch. The points show as plus signs.

Summary

In this chapter, you learned how to draw curved objects and points in AutoCAD and AutoCAD LT. You discovered:

- All the ways to draw circles
- How to define and draw an arc
- How to define an ellipse and an elliptical arc
- How to draw a donut
- How to set the point style and draw points

In the next chapter, you will learn how to display your drawing for the greatest ease and comfort.

Chapter 8

Viewing Your Drawing

Often you may wish that you could zoom in to see a particular part of a drawing more closely or move the display in a certain direction to reveal an area that is hidden. You may also want to save a view so that you can return to it at some other time. In this chapter, you read about controlling the display of your drawing to meet all of your drawing needs and increase your productivity. This chapter covers viewing a 2D drawing.

IN THIS CHAPTER

Panning and zooming

Working with views

Using Aerial View to pan and zoom

Creating tiled viewports

Rotating the snap angle

Creating User Coordinate Systems

Drawing isometrically

> **NOTE** This entire chapter assumes that you're using the AutoCAD Classic or AutoCAD LT Classic workspace and the 2D Wireframe visual style. To do so, choose AutoCAD Classic or AutoCAD LT Classic from the Workspace toolbar. (If the Workspace toolbar is not visible, right-click any toolbar button and choose Workspace from the list of toolbars.) To set the visual style to 2D Wireframe, choose View Í Visual Styles Í 2D Wireframe. Visual styles are mostly used for 3D drawings. I cover viewing 3D drawings in Chapter 22.

Regenerating and Redrawing the Display

AutoCAD and AutoCAD LT are *vector programs,* which means that they store information about objects in your drawing in terms of coordinates and equations. To display your drawing on your computer screen, the programs convert the vector information to pixels. Occasionally, you may need to redisplay the objects on your screen. One way is to recalculate the entire drawing, in a process called *regenerating* (the REGEN command). Another way is to quickly access a *virtual screen* from your computer's memory; this is called *redrawing* (the REDRAW command). Keep in mind that redrawing is quicker than regenerating.

When should you use the REDRAW and REGEN commands?

137

- Use the REDRAW command to remove blips or to quickly refresh the screen. (In AutoCAD only, the REDRAWALL command redraws the display in all viewports. Viewports are covered later in this chapter.) To redraw the screen, choose View ➪ Redraw (which executes the REDRAWALL command in AutoCAD or the REDRAW command in AutoCAD LT).

- Use the REGEN command whenever you want to recalculate and redisplay the entire drawing. In common usage, the word *regen* refers to the REGEN command as well as *regenerate* or *regeneration*. To regenerate the entire drawing, type **regen** ↵ at the command line. (The REGENALL command regenerates all viewports.)

Certain zooms and pans may require a regeneration, which AutoCAD does automatically. In recent releases, the mechanics behind the display of drawings have significantly improved. It is now rarely necessary to regenerate a drawing.

Panning

Often you cannot see the entire drawing on your screen. You therefore need a way to see the parts of your drawing that are not currently visible.

To *pan* means to move the display without changing the magnification. The word *pan* refers to the expression of panning a camera across a scene or view. You pan to view a different part of your drawing.

Using the PAN command

The PAN command moves the display in the direction and distance that you indicate without changing the magnification. *Real-time* panning moves the drawing as you move the cursor.

 To pan the drawing, choose Pan Realtime from the Standard toolbar or the 2D Navigate control panel of the Dashboard. (If the Dashboard is not displayed, choose Tools ➪ Palettes ➪ Dashboard.) The cursor changes to a hand. Place the cursor anywhere in your drawing, then click and drag in the direction that you want the objects to go. Press Shift as you pan to constrain panning to vertical or horizontal directions. Pan can be used transparently, while you're in the middle of another command. You can use Microsoft IntelliMouse pointing devices for panning. To pan, click and hold down the wheel, and move your mouse. You see the same panning cursor, the hand, as you do when you pan by clicking the Pan Realtime button on the Standard toolbar.

> **TIP** You can pan past the edge of the screen (actually the viewport) in Windows XP and Vista. This means that when the cursor reaches the edge of the screen, you can continue moving your mouse in the same direction to continue the pan.

To leave Pan mode, press Esc or Enter, or start any command using a menu or toolbar. You can also right-click to open the shortcut menu and choose Exit or one of the other display options. If you pan using the mouse wheel, you don't need to press Esc or Enter to leave Pan mode.

Using the scroll bars

You can use the scroll bars to pan vertically and horizontally as you would with any Windows program. However, you can't easily predict just how much the drawing view will move. Therefore, the scroll bars are less useful than the PAN command.

You can use the scroll bars in three ways:

■ Drag the scroll box in the desired direction and in the desired amount.

■ Click the scroll bar between the scroll box and the up or down arrow.

■ Click the up or down arrow to move the drawing view slightly.

 You can turn the display of the scroll bars on and off. Choose Tools ⇨ Options to open the Options dialog box. On the Display tab, check or uncheck the Display Scroll Bars in Drawing Window check box.

ON the DVD-ROM The drawing used in the following exercise on panning and scrolling, ab08-a.dwg, is in the Drawings folder on the DVD.

STEPS: Panning and Scrolling

1. Open ab08-a.dwg from the DVD. This is an air compressor, as shown in Figure 8.1.

FIGURE 8.1

The air compressor is zoomed in so that you can see only part of the drawing.

 2. Choose Pan Realtime from the Standard toolbar. Move the cursor to ❶ in Figure 8.1, then click and drag to ❷. The air compressor moves up and to the right. (Note that by the time you get to ❷, the display of the air compressor has moved — however, you should drag to where ❷ was on the screen.) Press Esc.

3. The scroll box of the horizontal scroll bar is all the way to the left. Click anywhere in the scroll bar to the right of the scroll box. The air compressor moves to the left.

4. Click anywhere in the vertical scroll bar between the scroll box and the down arrow at the bottom of the scroll bar. The air compressor moves up as you scroll down.

5. Click the right arrow on the horizontal scroll bar three times. The drawing moves slightly to the left each time. Your drawing should look something like Figure 8.2. You may have a different view if you chose slightly different pan points.

Do not save this drawing.

FIGURE 8.2

The final view. Your view may be somewhat different.

Using the ZOOM Command

The ZOOM command enables you to zoom in and out of your drawing, like the zoom lens of a camera. When you zoom in, everything is magnified so that you can see it more easily, but you see less of the entire drawing. When you zoom out, objects look smaller, but you can see more of the drawing. The ZOOM command has several options that make it easy to see just what you need at an appropriate size.

CROSS-REF Zooming does not affect the actual size of objects, just as zooming with a camera lens does not affect the size of the scene you're viewing. Chapter 9 covers changing the actual size of objects, known as *scaling*.

 When you use *real-time* zoom, the drawing zooms in and out as you move the cursor. To use real-time zoom, choose Zoom Realtime from the Standard toolbar or the 2D Navigate control panel of the Dashboard. (If the Dashboard is not displayed, choose Tools ➪ Palettes ➪ Dashboard.) The cursor changes to a magnifying glass with a plus sign on one side and a minus sign on the other side. You determine whether you zoom in or out, depending on the movement of the cursor:

- To zoom in, click and drag up in the direction of the plus sign.
- To zoom out, click and drag down in the direction of the minus sign.

A movement from the middle of the screen to the top edge zooms in 100 percent. A movement from the middle of the screen to the bottom edge zooms out 100 percent.

TIP You can zoom past the edge of the screen (actually the viewport) in Windows XP and Vista. As you move the mouse up or down to zoom, when you reach the edge of the viewport, continue to move the mouse in the same direction to continue the zoom in or out.

You can zoom with Microsoft IntelliMouse pointing devices. Rotate the wheel up to zoom in and down to zoom out. There is no Zoom Realtime cursor, and you don't need to press Esc or Enter to leave Zoom mode. You can also double-click the wheel to do a zoom to the extents of the drawing.

 To control how much you zoom for each incremental movement of the wheel, change the ZOOMFACTOR system variable.

Right-click to open the shortcut menu to exit Zoom mode or to choose one of the display options listed. To end real-time zoom, you can also press Esc or Enter or start any command using a menu or toolbar.

Understanding ZOOM options

The Zoom flyout on the Standard toolbar has nine options. The Standard toolbar also has a separate Zoom Previous button. Table 8.1 outlines the Zoom options.

 The new Standard Annotation toolbar does not contain the ZOOM option buttons. You can open the Zoom toolbar by right-clicking any toolbar and choosing Zoom. The 2D Navigate control panel of the Dashboard contains buttons for the Window and Extents options.

TABLE 8.1

Zoom Options

Button	Option	Description
	Window	Lets you define a rectangular window as the boundaries of the new display. The command prompts you for the two diagonally opposite corners of the window. Use the Window option to zoom in on any area already displayed in your drawing. When you use Zoom Window, the command displays everything in the window that you specify but reshapes the display to fit your screen. As a result, you may see objects that were outside the specified window. You can move the mouse past the drawing area to define the window past the edge of the screen — the display moves to allow you to pick a corner.
	Dynamic	Enables you to zoom and pan in one operation. This option is covered in the next section of this chapter.
	Scale	Enter a number to scale the display relative to the drawing limits (a kind of absolute scaling). Enter a number followed by **x** to scale the display relative to the current view (relative scaling). Enter a number followed by **xp** to scale the display relative to paper space units (discussed in Chapter 17). A number less than 1 (such as 0.5) reduces the size of the objects on the screen (by half when you use 0.5). A number greater than 1 (such as 2) increases the size of the objects on the screen (to twice the size when you use 2).
	Center	Lets you specify a new center for the display, and then a new magnification/height. The current magnification/height is shown in brackets for your reference. Type a smaller number to increase the magnification, making the objects larger. Type a larger value to decrease the magnification, making the objects smaller.
	Object	Lets you zoom in to selected objects.

continued

TABLE 8.1   *(continued)*

Button	Option	Description
	In	Uses the Scale option with a value of 2x. See the Scale option.
	Out	Uses the Scale option with a value of 0.5x. See the Scale option.
	All	Zooms the display to the greater of the drawing extents or the drawing limits.
	Extents	Zooms to the outer extents of the drawing. You can also double-click the wheel of an IntelliMouse pointing device.
	Previous	Redisplays the most recent display of your drawing. This option has its own button on the Standard toolbar.

When you use one of the Zoom options, you see the objects in your drawing become larger or smaller in a smooth transition. The smooth transition helps you to orient yourself to the new display. To turn off this feature, use the VTOPTIONS command. In the View Transitions dialog box that opens, uncheck the Enable Animation for Pan & Zoom check box.

NOTE   When you undo consecutive ZOOM and PAN commands, they count as one operation. Because people often use several ZOOM or PAN operations together, combining them helps you to get back to your previous state more quickly. To disable this feature, choose Tools ⬦ Options. On the User Preferences tab, uncheck the Combine Zoom and Pan Commands check box in the Undo/Redo section.

Using ZOOM Dynamic

The Dynamic option of ZOOM enables you to pan and zoom in one operation. The Aerial View (discussed in the next section) offers more sophisticated options, but the simplicity of ZOOM Dynamic is sometimes just what you need.

When you start ZOOM Dynamic, you see the virtual screen area of the drawing in a blue dashed rectangle; this view box represents the drawing extents or limits, whichever is greater. Your current view is bounded in a green, dashed rectangle. Your mouse cursor changes, based on the two modes of ZOOM Dynamic. Each time you click the left mouse button, you switch modes. Here's how the two modes work:

- **Pan mode:** The view box contains an X and can move freely around any displayed area of the drawing.
- **Zoom mode:** The view box contains an arrow. The left side of the box is fixed at the point where you changed to Zoom mode. As you move the cursor, the box expands or shrinks, letting you zoom to any magnification.

When the view box displays the view that you want, click the right mouse button and choose Enter (or press Enter). The command pans and zooms to show that view. Figure 8.3 shows the screen during a ZOOM Dynamic operation.

FIGURE 8.3

Using ZOOM Dynamic.

← Generated area of drawing

View box in Zoom mode

AIR COMPRESSOR

←Current view

STEPS: Using ZOOM Options

1. Open ab08-b.dwg from the DVD. This is a drawing of a warehouse, as shown in Figure 8.4.

2. To read the text in the lower-right corner, choose Zoom Window from the Zoom flyout of the Standard toolbar.

3. At the Specify first corner: prompt, pick ❶, as shown in Figure 8.4. At the Specify opposite corner: prompt, pick ❷. AutoCAD or AutoCAD LT zooms in to display the window that you specified, as shown in Figure 8.5.

4. Choose Zoom All from the Zoom flyout of the Standard toolbar.

5. Choose Zoom Previous from the Standard toolbar. You return to the previous display.

6. Choose Zoom Extents from the Zoom flyout of the Standard toolbar. The drawing fills the screen. In this drawing, the drawing extents are similar to the drawing limits, so that you see little difference between using Zoom All and Zoom Extents.

FIGURE 8.4

A drawing of a large warehouse, with shelving and conveyor belts.

Thanks to Bryan Kelly of ATI Corporation, Fairfield, Iowa, for this drawing.

 7. Choose Zoom Center from the Zoom flyout. At the `Specify center point:` prompt, pick ❸ in Figure 8.4. At the `Enter magnification or height <5315.176>:` prompt, type **500** ↵. You zoom in on the office.

 8. Choose Zoom Realtime from the Standard toolbar. Place the cursor at the top of the drawing, then click and drag to the bottom of the screen. The display zooms out about 200 percent.

FIGURE 8.5

Your display should look approximately like this figure after using ZOOM Window.

 9. Choose Zoom Scale from the Zoom flyout of the Standard toolbar. Type **2x** ↵. The display zooms in, doubling the scale of the view and returning you approximately to the previous view of the office.

10. Choose Zoom Dynamic from the Zoom flyout. You now see the entire drawing. The current view is shown with a green dashed line. The mouse cursor is a box with an X in it. You are now in Pan mode. To zoom in on the right side of the warehouse, move the Pan box to the lower-right corner of the warehouse and click with the pick (left) button.

11. You are now in Zoom mode. The Zoom box contains an arrow. Move the mouse to the left to shrink the Zoom box. Notice that the Zoom box is fixed at its left side. When the Zoom box is about half of its original size, left-click again.

12. You are back in Pan mode again. Move the Pan box to the bottom-right corner of the warehouse. Right-click and choose Enter to zoom in on this new view. Your display should look approximately like Figure 8.6.

FIGURE 8.6

The new view of the drawing after using Zoom Dynamic.

13. Choose Zoom All from the Zoom flyout. Do not save your drawing. If you're continuing to the next exercise, leave the drawing open.

Using Aerial View

Aerial View functions like a souped-up version of ZOOM Dynamic. You can use Aerial View to pan and zoom. If you need to pan and zoom often, you can leave the Aerial View window open and use it whenever you need to. Aerial View is most useful with large maps or floor plans, or any drawing with a lot of detail. You can use it transparently.

To open Aerial View, choose View ⇨ Aerial View. The Aerial View window opens, as shown in Figure 8.7. The Aerial View window can be active or inactive. When active, its title bar is shown in color (usually blue). When inactive, the title bar is gray. Inside the window, you see your entire drawing. To close Aerial View, click the Aerial View window's Close button. Aerial View has its own toolbar and menu.

FIGURE 8.7

The Aerial View window.

Zoom Out

Zoom In   Global

While you work in your drawing, the drawing window is active and the Aerial View window is inactive. To pan and zoom using Aerial View:

1. Click anywhere inside the Aerial View window to activate Aerial View. You see a pan/zoom box that looks like the box that you see when you use ZOOM Dynamic. It has an X in it, indicating that you can pan.

2. Move the pan/zoom box over the part of the drawing on which you want to zoom in. The display in the main screen pans as you move your mouse.

3. Click to switch to Zoom mode. You see the arrow in the box, indicating that you can zoom. Move your mouse to resize the window so that it covers the area that you want to see. In the main drawing window, you immediately see the new zoomed view.

4. Continue to click to switch between Zoom and Pan modes as necessary.

5. Right-click or press Esc to fix the new view.

To quickly zoom out in the Aerial View display, click Zoom Out on the Aerial View toolbar. To quickly zoom in, click Zoom In on the toolbar. To see your entire drawing in the Aerial View display only, click Global on the toolbar.

The Aerial View Options menu contains two options that affect how Aerial View works. Both features are also available by right-clicking the Aerial View window shortcut menu.

■ Auto Viewport applies only when you have more than one viewport. I discuss viewports later in this chapter. If this option is checked, the view in the Aerial View window changes as you change the active viewport in the main drawing area.

■ Dynamic Update determines whether the view in the Aerial View window is continually (dynamically) updated as you edit your drawing. If you find that Aerial View slows down your computer (but you don't want to close it entirely), choose this option to turn Dynamic Update off. Choose the option again to turn it on.

Creating Named Views

After you've done a lot of panning and zooming in a drawing, you may find that you return to the same part of your drawing again and again, especially if the drawing undergoes a lot of changes. In a large drawing, it can take some time to display the part of the drawing that you want, especially if AutoCAD or AutoCAD LT needs to regenerate the drawing. You can speed up the process by saving views.

A *view* is simply a display of a drawing on your screen. A view can show any part of your drawing at any magnification. After you have the display that you want, you give the view a name and then save it. AutoCAD or AutoCAD LT then lets you retrieve that view at any time, without zooming or panning.

> **NOTE** You can also turn a view into a *floating viewport,* which you use to lay out your drawing for plotting. For example, if you have a top view, a side view, and a section view, you can easily use these views for your final plot. You turn a view into a viewport using the Sheet Set Manager, which I cover in Chapter 26. For now, you should be aware that you can use views both for the purpose of facilitating drawing and editing as well as for the final layout of your design for plotting. (AutoCAD only.)

Saving a view

 First display the view that you want to save on the screen. You can use the ZOOM and PAN commands. Then choose View ➪ Named Views to start the VIEW command and open the View Manager. (You can also choose Named Views from the View toolbar.) The View Manager opens, as shown in Figure 8.8.

FIGURE 8.8

The View Manager dialog box.

The Views pane lists the following types of views:

- **Current:** The current display.

- **Model views:** All named views, including cameras, in model space. *Model space* is where you draw. I cover the concept of model space in Chapter 17. Cameras are a way to define 3D views (they are not available in AutoCAD LT); I explain cameras in Chapter 22.

■ **Layout views:** All named views created in a layout (paper space). A layout is a mechanism for laying out your drawing in preparation for plotting or printing. I explain layouts in Chapter 17.

■ **Preset views:** Preset views that come with AutoCAD and AutoCAD LT. These are the same views that you see by choosing View ➪ 3D Views.

When you choose a view in the Views panel, you see its properties in the central panel of the View Manager. The available properties depend on the type of view. You can use the properties panel to change most of a view's properties; some are for information only and are not editable. Some of the properties only apply to 3D views, and some are not available in AutoCAD LT. Table 8.2 lists the properties that may appear in the View Manager.

TABLE 8.2

View Properties

Property	Description
Name	Named Views, Cameras, and Layout Views
Category	The category that you specify when you create a new named view. A category is optional and applies only to model and layout views. If you specify a category, it appears on the Sheet Views tab of the Sheet Set Manager (covered in Chapter 26).
Viewport association	Specifies whether the view is associated with a viewport on a sheet in a sheet set. This applies only to layout views.
UCS	The name of the User Coordinate System (UCS) saved with the view. When you create a named view, you can save a UCS with that view.
Layer snapshot	Specifies whether the current layer states are saved with the view. You can save this *layer snapshot* with a model or layout view. I cover layer snapshots and layer states in Chapter 11.
Location	Specifies the layout tab name when you define a named view on a layout tab. See Chapter 17 for a discussion of layout tabs.
Annotation Scale	Stores the annotation scale that was current when you defined the view. See Chapter 17 for more on annotation scales.
Visual style	Specifies a visual style for the view. This applies only to model views. I explain visual styles in Chapter 22; they apply mostly to 3D drawings. For 2D drawings, the visual style is 2D Wireframe.
Background	Specifies a background for the view. Backgrounds apply only to 3D model views (AutoCAD LT does not offer backgrounds). Choose Solid, Gradient, Image, or Sun & Sky to open the Background dialog box. I cover backgrounds more in the "Adding a Background to a Named View" section of Chapter 22.
Live section	Specifies a live section object applied to the view. See the "Creating an interactive section object" section in Chapter 24 for more on live sections.
Camera X	Displays the X coordinate of the view's camera. This is for information only and does not apply to layout views.
Camera Y	Displays the Y coordinate of the view's camera. This is for information only and does not apply to layout views.
Camera Z	Displays the Z coordinate of the view's camera. This is for information only and does not apply to layout views.
Target X	Displays the X coordinate of the view's target. This is for information only and does not apply to layout views.

Property	Description
Target Y	Displays the Y coordinate of the view's target. This is for information only and does not apply to layout views.
Target Z	Displays the Z coordinate of the view's target. This is for information only and does not apply to layout views.
Roll angle	Specifies the angle that the view is tilted around the line of site. This is for information only and does not apply to layout views.
Height	Specifies the height of the view. This is for information only and does not apply to camera views.
Width	Specifies the width of the view. This is for information only and does not apply to camera views.
Perspective	Specifies whether a view is a perspective view. This applies to model views. I discuss perspective views in Chapter 22.
Lens length (mm)	Specifies the lens length in millimeters. This applies to perspective views only. The LENSLENGTH system variable controls the default value for this setting. Changing this value also changes the Field of View setting, which is another way of expressing this setting.
Field of view	Specifies the field of view of a perspective view. Changing this value also changes the Lens Length setting. This does not apply to layout views.
Front plane	Specifies the offset for the front clipping plane if you enabled front clipping. I cover clipping in Chapter 22; it applies to 3D views only.
Back plane	Specifies the offset for the back clipping plane if you enabled back clipping.
Clipping	Turns clipping on or off.

To create a new named view, click New to open the New View dialog box, shown in Figure 8.9. Type a name for your view in the View Name text box.

FIGURE 8.9

The New View dialog box.

View names can be up to 255 characters and can include spaces. As I explained in Table 8.2, you can save a category, a layer snapshot, a User Coordinate System, a live section, and a visual style with a view. Select the Current Display option button to use the current display as the view. Otherwise, click the Define View Window button, and specify a window around the view that you want.

Choose OK to return to the View Manager dialog box, where you see your new view listed. Click OK to return to your drawing.

> **TIP** In a very large drawing, you might create views as soon as you create the title block — for example, one for each quadrant of the drawing and another for the title block lettering. This helps you move quickly from one section of the drawing to another. As you determine the need for more specific views, you can add them.

You can use the New View dialog box to define several views at once. Here's how:

1. Choose View ⇨ Named Views.
2. Click New.
3. Type the name of the first view in the View Name text box.
4. Click the Define View Window button to return to your drawing.
5. If necessary, adjust the display by zooming and panning. The display change is made transparently.
6. At the prompts, pick two diagonally opposite corners of a rectangular window.
7. Press Enter to return to the New View dialog box.
8. Click OK to return to the View Manager.
9. Repeat Steps 2 through 8 for all additional views. Then click OK to return to your drawing.

Displaying a view

The View Manager enables you to easily display any view that you have saved. Follow these steps:

1. Choose View ⇨ Named Views.
2. Choose the view that you want to restore.
3. Click Set Current.
4. Click OK.

For quick access to named views, display the View toolbar and choose a named view from the drop-down list. You can also use the drop-down list in the 2D Navigate control panel of the Dashboard.

Managing named views

You can use the View Manager to manage named views. You can also find these features by right-clicking inside the View Manager.

- To delete a view, choose the view that you want to delete and click the Delete button or press the Delete key on your keyboard.
- To rename a view, select it, type a new name in the Properties pane (next to the Name property), and press Enter.
- To change the layer states that you saved with the view, change the states of any layers before opening the dialog box. Then open the View Manager dialog box, choose a named view, and click Update Layers. The view now uses the current layer states. (I explain layers in Chapter 11.)

■ To edit the boundaries of a view, choose the Edit Boundaries button. You are now back in your drawing and the current view boundaries are shown in black or white (depending on the color of your background). At the prompts, specify the two opposite corners that you want to serves as boundaries for the view and press Enter.

 The drawing used in the following exercise on working with views, ab08-b.dwg, is in the Drawings folder on the DVD.

STEPS: Working with Views

1. Open ab08-b.dwg from the DVD if it is not already open from the previous exercise.

2. Save the file as ab08-01.dwg in your AutoCAD Bible folder.

3. Choose View ⇨ Named Views to open the View Manager.

4. Click New to open the New View dialog box.

5. In the View Name text box, type **top left**.

6. In the Category text box, type **quarter-sections** if you are using AutoCAD. If you use the Sheet Set Manager to define sheets (as explained in Chapter 26), this category could be used for a series of layout sheets that display quarters of the building.

7. Click the Define Window option button or the Define View Window button. This action returns you to your drawing temporarily.

8. At the Specify first corner: prompt, pick the top-left corner of the drawing. At the Specify opposite corner: prompt, pick somewhere around the center of the warehouse. Press Enter to return to the New View dialog box.

9. Click OK once.

10. Click New. Type **bottom left** in the text box of the New View dialog box and again enter **quarter-sections** as the category.

11. Click the Define View Window button. At the Specify first corner: prompt, pick the bottom-left corner of the drawing. At the Specify Opposite corner: prompt, again pick around the center of the warehouse. Press Enter. Back in the New View dialog box, click OK. The View Manager dialog box should list both of your views. Click OK to close the View Manager.

12. If the Dashboard is not displayed, choose Tools ⇨ Palettes ⇨ Dashboard. If the 2D Navigate control panel is not displayed, right-click anywhere in the Dashboard and choose Control panels ⇨ 2D Navigate. Choose bottom left from the drop-down list in the 2D Navigate control panel of the Dashboard. AutoCAD or AutoCAD LT displays the view.

13. Save your drawing. The views that you created are now part of the drawing database.

Using named views to manage a drawing

Using named views provides three additional advantages:

■ You can use named views when you open a drawing so that one of its views is immediately displayed.

■ You can open only the part of a drawing contained in a view.

■ You can turn a named view into a floating viewport for plotting purposes. (AutoCAD only.)

I explain these techniques in the next three sections.

A drawing with a view

After you've saved views, you can use them to open a drawing so that a view is immediately displayed. Click Open on the Standard toolbar. In the Select File dialog box, choose the file that you want to open and check the Select Initial View check box. Then click Open. In the Select Initial View dialog box, choose the view that you want to display, and click OK.

Partially opening a drawing

You may have a very large drawing that is slow and cumbersome to work with when it is completely loaded. For example, if you have a surveyor's drawing of an entire county, but you need to work only with one plat, you can open a named view containing only that plat. This feature is not available in AutoCAD LT.

To partially open a drawing from within AutoCAD, follow these steps:

1. Choose File ➪ Open to open the Select File dialog box.
2. Choose a drawing and then click the Open button's drop-down box. Choose Partial Open to open the Partial Open dialog box, shown in Figure 8.10.

FIGURE 8.10

Use the Partial Open dialog box to open only the part of a drawing contained in a named view.

3. Choose a view from the list of named views.
4. Choose one or more layers. To include all of the layers, click Load All. If you don't include at least one layer, no objects are loaded. (Chapter 11 covers layers.) Click Open.

After you've partially opened a drawing, you can load more of the drawing. Choose File ➪ Partial Load. This item is available only if the current drawing has been partially opened. AutoCAD opens the Partial Open dialog box. You can change the view. To display the entire drawing (from whatever is loaded), choose the default view, *Extents*. To define a new view on the fly, click the Pick a Window button and define the two diagonal corners of the view that you want to see. Check the layers that you want to include or click Load All. Click OK to load the newly specified view and layers.

Using named views with sheet sets

You can combine layouts from more than one drawing into a sheet set. (AutoCAD LT doesn't include this feature.) Sheet sets are a powerful way to organize many layouts. I cover them in detail in Chapter 26. However, at this point you should know that named views have a value beyond helping you display an area of your drawing. They can also turn into your final layout for plotting.

Suppose that you're drawing a mechanical model with a top view, a side view, and a section view. In the final plot, you want to display these three views on one sheet of paper. Without sheet sets, you would create three floating viewports and individually pan and zoom to get the three views. (For more information on floating viewports, see the "Floating Viewports" sidebar in this chapter, as well as Chapter 17.) Using the sheet-set feature, as you work you can create named views of the three parts of the drawing. Then you can use those same views to create the floating viewports for plotting.

Working with Tiled Viewports

Tiled viewports enable you to divide up the screen into rectangular bounding boxes. You can then show different views of your drawing in each viewport — at one time. The purpose of tiled viewports is to help you draw. For example:

- You can see the whole drawing in one viewport and a zoomed-in portion of that drawing in another viewport.
- You can see widely separated views of a large drawing at one time.

CROSS-REF There are two types of viewports — *tiled* and *floating*. For more information on floating viewports, see the "Floating Viewports" sidebar in this chapter. For a detailed discussion, turn to Chapter 17.

Actually, you're already using a tiled viewport because the regular single view of your drawing that you've been working with represents the default of a one-tile viewport.

Tiled viewports have the following characteristics:

- No matter how many viewports you have, they always collectively take up the entire screen. They are not separate entities but a way of dividing up the screen.
- Only one viewport can be active at a time. The active viewport has a bold border.
- The crosshairs appear only in the active viewport.
- The UCS (User Coordinate System) icon (if set to On) appears in each viewport.
- Any change that you make to your drawing in one viewport automatically appears in every other viewport (or in viewports that show the part of the drawing where you made the change).
- You can create up to 64 viewports — but you'll never want to create that many!
- You can begin a command in one viewport and finish it in another. For example, you can start a line in one viewport, switch to a second viewport, and end the line there.
- You can save and restore viewport configurations.

Figure 8.11 shows a drawing divided into three tiled viewports. Each viewport shows a different view of the same drawing.

FIGURE 8.11

A drawing showing three tiled viewports with a different view in each viewport.

Thanks to Jerry Bottenfield of Clow Valve Company, Oskaloosa, Iowa, for this drawing.

Configuring tiled viewports

Creating tiled viewports involves deciding how you want to divide up the screen. A set of tiled viewports is called a *configuration*. A few simple configurations come with AutoCAD and AutoCAD LT, but you can create your own by further dividing up any of the viewports. You can also join two viewports. Finally, you can always return to the default of one viewport.

Creating tiled viewports

To add viewports, choose View ➪ Viewports. This opens a submenu from which you can choose from the preset configurations.

You can choose to create up to four tiled viewports from the submenu, at which point you respond to the options that appear on the command line. For example, if you choose 2 Viewports, the command responds with the `Enter a configuration option [Horizontal/Vertical] <Vertical>:` prompt. Right-click and choose Horizontal or Vertical to create two horizontal or vertical viewports. If you choose 4 Viewports, you get four equal viewports, one in each corner. However, if you choose 3 Viewports, you can choose from several options to configure the three viewports.

An easier way to configure viewports is to choose New Viewports from the submenu. The Viewports dialog box opens with the New Viewports tab on top, as shown in Figure 8.12. You choose the configuration that you want here. You see a preview of the configuration.

FIGURE 8.12

The Viewports dialog box makes it easy to choose a configuration.

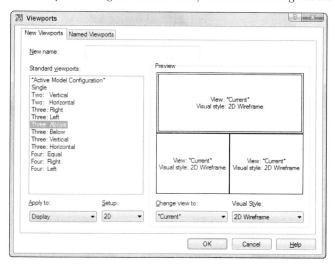

If you have named views in your drawing, you can specify a view for each viewport to display. Click a viewport in the Preview pane and choose a named view from the Change View To drop-down list box at the bottom of the dialog box. You can also choose a visual style from the Visual Style drop-down list if you are using AutoCAD. If your drawing is in 3D, you can choose 3D from the Setup drop-down list box, and AutoCAD creates standard orthogonal views in the viewports. When you've specified your viewport configuration, click OK to return to your drawing.

The Viewports dialog box is usually the best place to start creating viewports. However, if the standard configurations do not meet your needs, you can use one of them as a starting point and then use the other options.

Notice the Apply To drop-down list at the bottom-left corner of the Viewports dialog box in Figure 8.12. By default, the tiled viewport configurations apply to the entire display, meaning that they replace your current configuration. You can also choose to apply the configuration to the current viewport. The active viewport has a bold border and crosshairs. To make a viewport active, click anywhere inside that viewport. Then choose View ➪ Viewports ➪ New Viewports, choose Current Viewport from the Apply To drop-down list, and choose the configuration that you want for that viewport.

Let's say that you have four equal viewports, and the top-left viewport is active. If you choose the Four: Equal configuration from the Viewports dialog box while the top-left viewport is active and apply it to the current viewport, the top-left viewport is divided into four viewports. Now you have seven viewports in the drawing.

Removing tiled viewports

One way to remove a tiled viewport is to join it to another viewport. To join one viewport to another, choose View ➪ Viewports ➪ Join. At the `Select dominant viewport <current viewport>:` prompt, click the viewport that you want to retain or press Enter if you want to retain the current viewport.

At the Select viewport to join: prompt, click the adjacent viewport that you want to join into the dominant viewport. When the two viewports merge, you lose the display in this second viewport. Together, the adjacent viewports must form a rectangle.

The only other way to remove all tiled viewports in one step is to return to the single viewport configuration. Choose View ⇨ Viewports ⇨ 1 Viewport. The display in the current viewport remains.

Using tiled viewports

After you've created the viewport configuration that you want, you're ready to use it. The first step is to create the views that you need in each viewport.

Creating viewport views

Creating views in each viewport involves two steps:

1. Make a viewport current by clicking anywhere inside it.
2. Zoom and pan until you have the view that you want.

 Many users choose one viewport to display the entire drawing and the other viewports to display zoomed-in views of smaller sections.

Drawing from viewport to viewport

After you have the viewport configuration and views that you need, you can start to draw. One of the great advantages of viewports is that you can draw from one viewport to another. In a large drawing, you may need to draw a line from one end of the drawing to another, but when you display the entire drawing you can't see the detail well enough to specify where to start and end the line. The basic steps to draw from one viewport to another are as follows:

1. Click the viewport where you want to start. This might be a small detail of one corner of your drawing.
2. Start the command and specify any options that you need. Specify any necessary coordinates as you usually would.
3. To continue the command in a second viewport, click to activate that viewport. Continue the command, specifying coordinates as necessary.
4. You can continue the command in a third viewport by clicking it. Do this until you've completed the command. If you have a viewport displaying the entire drawing, you immediately see the results in that viewport as well.

You can also use viewports to edit your drawing. All commands except those that change the display — such as zooming, panning, and creating views — can be started in one viewport and continued in another.

Saving and restoring viewport configurations

You can save a tiled viewport configuration. If you find yourself creating a particular configuration over and over, you should save it. Saving a configuration is just a matter of giving it a name. You can then restore it when needed. Viewport configuration names can be up to 255 characters and can include spaces.

Saving a viewport configuration

After you create a viewport configuration that you like, follow these steps to save it:

1. Choose View ⇨ Viewports ⇨ New Viewports if you aren't already in the Viewports dialog box.
2. Type a name in the New Name text box.
3. Click OK.

Restoring a viewport configuration

After returning to one viewport or using a different configuration, you can restore a named viewport configuration, as follows:

1. Choose View ⇨ Viewports ⇨ Named Viewports to open the Viewports dialog box with the Named Viewports tab on top, shown in Figure 8.13.

FIGURE 8.13

The Named Viewports tab lists saved viewport configurations.

2. Choose the viewport that you want to restore.
3. Click OK.

Floating Viewports

AutoCAD and AutoCAD LT have two types of viewports: *tiled viewports,* which are discussed here, and *floating viewports,* which I cover in Chapter 17. These two types of viewports have many similarities, but they have different purposes. Whereas the purpose of tiled viewports is to help you draw and edit your drawing, floating viewports are used to lay out your drawing for plotting.

Floating viewports create layouts, which enable you to treat your screen like a sheet of paper. You create floating viewports and perhaps a title block on this electronic sheet of paper. You can create one or more layouts. Each floating viewport can show a different view of your drawing — just like tiled viewports. But floating viewports then let you plot all of those views on one sheet of paper. You can't do that with tiled viewports, which are just devices to let you temporarily display your drawing in a way that helps you draw and edit. However, you can also draw and edit using floating viewports.

Tiled viewports are covered here because they are appropriate for learning how to draw and edit your drawing. Floating viewports are covered in Chapter 17 because you use them to lay out your drawing for plotting.

ON the DVD-ROM The drawing used in the following exercise on creating, naming, and restoring tiled viewport configurations, `ab08-c.dwg`, is in the `Drawings` folder on the DVD.

STEPS: Creating, Naming, and Restoring Tiled Viewport Configurations

1. Open `ab08-c.dwg` from the DVD.
2. Save the file as `ab08-02.dwg` in your `AutoCAD Bible` folder.
3. Choose View ➪ Viewports ➪ New Viewports to open the Viewports dialog box.
4. In the listing at the left of the dialog box, choose Three: Above. Click OK. You see three tiled viewports.
5. Click the bottom-right viewport. Choose Zoom Window on the Zoom flyout of the Standard toolbar and choose a window around the left portion of the threaded model (the upper part of the drawing).
6. Click the bottom-left viewport. Choose Zoom Window on the Zoom flyout of the Standard toolbar and choose a window around the bottom-left portion of the drawing (not including the title block).
7. Click the top viewport. Choose Zoom Extents from the Zoom flyout of the Standard toolbar. Figure 8.14 shows the results.
8. Choose View ➪ Viewports ➪ New Viewports. In the New Name text box, type **3 view O Ring** and click OK.
9. With the top viewport still active, choose View ➪ Viewports ➪ 1 Viewport to display the view shown in the last active viewport.
10. Choose View ➪ Viewports ➪ Named Viewports.

FIGURE 8.14

The three tiled viewports now display three different views.

11. Choose 3 view O Ring and click OK to restore the viewport configuration, including the views in each viewport.

12. Save your drawing.

Using Snap Rotation

Not all 2D drawings are vertical and horizontal. In some drawings, significant portions of your objects are drawn at nonorthogonal angles. One example is an auxiliary view to show the "true size" of an inclined surface. Sometimes it helps to rotate the crosshairs to match the major angles of the drawing.

Consider Figure 8.15. A great deal of this drawing is at an angle. You could handle this in four ways:

- Draw as normal, specifying the necessary angles.
- Rotate the snap, which also rotates the grid and crosshairs.
- Create a new UCS (User Coordinate System). (Creating a new UCS is covered later in this chapter.)
- Draw the entire model vertically and rotate it afterward.

FIGURE 8.15

In 2D drawings such as this, you should consider various options, such as rotating the snap or creating a new UCS.

Thanks to Robert Mack of The Dexter Company, Fairfield, Iowa, for this drawing.

If you need to draw several objects at a certain angle, such as 45 degrees, you can rotate the snap to that angle. The grid and crosshairs rotate to follow suit. This technique works best when the decimal point accuracy required lets you draw using snap points. You can also use this technique to guide the cursor at an appropriate angle for direct distance entry, although polar tracking is another way to accomplish the same task.

To change the snap rotation angle, you use the SNAPANG system variable. Enter **snapang** ↵ on the command line. At the Enter new value for SNAPANG <0>: prompt, enter an angle. For example, if you enter **45** ↵, the crosshairs, snap, and grid rotate 45 degrees.

Note that you can also set an X base and a Y base. This simply ensures that the grid goes through a point of your choice, which is very important if you're using Snap mode to draw. If you're just starting to draw an object, use the 0,0 base and draw to the existing snap points. However, if you have an existing object and need to add to it, changing the base can be very helpful. Setting X and Y bases does not change the coordinates, which are tied to the UCS. (The UCS is discussed in the next section.) To set the base, use the SNAP-BASE system variable on the command line and specify a coordinate for the base. You can use an object snap.

CROSS-REF You can use the ID command to get the coordinates of a point. Then use these coordinates as the X and Y bases. Chapter 12 covers the ID command.

After setting the snap angle, you may want to turn the grid on to help you get your bearings. The crosshairs and grid now reflect the new snap angle. Figure 8.16 shows the same drawing with a snap angle of 45 degrees. Notice how the crosshairs now match the angle of the drawing. The crosshairs have been set to 100 percent of screen size, which is useful when rotating the snap angle. (To reset the crosshairs size, choose Tools ➪ Options and use the Crosshair Size section of the Display tab.)

FIGURE 8.16

The snap angle in this drawing has been changed to 45 degrees. Note that the grid follows the snap.

Understanding User Coordinate Systems

You can create a new UCS (User Coordinate System) rather than rotate the snap angle. The results are similar, except that when you create a UCS you also affect the X,Y coordinates. The UCS is much more flexible when you start drawing in three dimensions.

By default, a drawing is set up by using a *World Coordinate System*. This sets the origin of the X,Y points at 0,0 and the angles using the familiar East (right-facing) equals 0 degrees system. Figure 8.17 shows the UCS icon in its default display.

FIGURE 8.17

The UCS icon in its default display.

You can easily create your own UCS and even save it for future use in the drawing. To define a UCS in a 2D drawing, you indicate the angle of the X and Y axes and an origin point. The origin point then becomes the new 0,0 coordinate. You have several options for specifying the UCS.

Understanding UCS options

Understanding the UCS options will help you create a new UCS more easily, based on the information that you have available. To create a UCS, choose Tools ➪ New UCS. A submenu opens, offering the options listed in Table 8.3.

TABLE 8.3

UCS Options

Option	Meaning
World	Specifies the default UCS, with the X axis horizontal, the Y axis vertical, and the origin at the initial 0,0 location.
Previous	Switches you to the previous UCS you were using.
Face	Aligns the UCS with the face of a 3D solid.
Object	Enables you to align the UCS with an object. In general, this option uses the most obvious object snap as the origin and aligns the X axis with the object. For example, when you choose a line, the endpoint nearest your pick point becomes the origin and the X axis aligns with the angle of the line. When you choose a circle, the X axis points toward the point that you pick on the circumference.
View	Aligns the X and Y axes with the current view. Used in 3D drawing. This option arbitrarily sets the origin.
Origin	Specifies a new 0,0 point of your choice, relative to the current origin.
Z Axis Vector	Specifies which way the Z axis points. This option is not used in 2D drawing.
3 Point	Enables you to specify three points. The first point is the origin, the second point indicates the positive direction of the X axis, and the third point indicates the positive direction of the Y axis.
X	Keeps the current origin and rotates the Y and Z axes around the current X axis. You specify the angle. This is used in 3D drawing.
Y	Keeps the current origin and rotates the X and Z axes around the current Y axis. You specify the angle. This is used in 3D drawing.
Z	Keeps the current origin and rotates the X and Y axes around the current Z axis. You specify the angle. This option can be used in 2D drawing.
Apply	Applies the current UCS to a specified viewport. (AutoCAD only.)

Saving and restoring a custom UCS

After you create a UCS, you can save it so that you can easily switch back and forth between the World Coordinate System and your UCS. To save a UCS, follow these steps:

1. Specify the UCS as described in the previous section.
2. Choose Tools ➪ Named UCS to open the UCS dialog box with the Named UCSs tab on top, as shown in Figure 8.18. If your current UCS is not named, it is listed as Unnamed and highlighted. Previously named UCSs are also listed. You can also use this dialog box to return to the previous UCS or the World Coordinate System (WCS).
3. Click Unnamed. Type a name for the UCS and press Enter. The name can be up to 255 characters and can include spaces.
4. Click OK.

To restore a saved UCS, choose Tools ⇨ Named UCS. Choose the UCS that you want to use and click Set Current. Then click OK (or display the UCS II toolbar and choose the UCS from the drop-down list). You can use the UCS dialog box to return to the previous UCS that you used; choose Previous and click Set Current. You can also choose UCS Previous from the UCS toolbar. Using this button, you can quickly switch back and forth between two UCSs. To delete a saved UCS, select it in the UCS dialog box and press the Del key. You can also select a UCS, right-click, and choose one of the options from the shortcut menu.

FIGURE 8.18

Use the UCS dialog box to save and restore a UCS.

Controlling the UCS icon

When you start a new drawing, the UCS icon is at the bottom-left of your drawing at 0,0. By default, the icon remains at 0,0 even if you pan around the drawing. The icon may, therefore, end up in the middle of your drawing. If 0,0 is not displayed, then the icon reverts to the bottom-left of your drawing.

You can turn off the UCS icon completely. If you aren't working with customized UCSs, you often have no reason to see the UCS in a 2D drawing. If you want the UCS icon on, you can also display it only at the bottom-left of your drawing. This keeps the icon out of the way so that it does not obstruct your drawing.

If you create a new UCS, keeping the UCS icon at the 0,0 point (the origin) of your new UCS helps you to get your bearings. A plus sign appears in the icon to indicate the origin. However, if the origin is out of the current display or so close to the edge that the icon won't fit, the UCS icon appears at the lower-left corner of your drawing anyway.

To control the UCS icon, choose View ⇨ Display ⇨ UCS Icon. (Don't confuse this with Tools ⇨ New UCS, which creates a custom UCS.) A submenu opens with the following items:

- **On:** Toggles the display of the UCS icon on and off.
- **Origin:** Toggles the placement of the UCS icon at the origin on and off.

You can customize the look of the UCS icon. To do this, choose View ⇨ Display ⇨ UCS Icon ⇨ Properties to open the UCS Icon dialog box, shown in Figure 8.19. As you make changes, you can see the result in the preview box.

FIGURE 8.19

Use the UCS Icon dialog box to customize the look of the UCS icon.

Choose between 2D and 3D styles. The 3D style shows the Z axis, but you won't see it when you're looking at your model from the top (called *Plan view*). If you choose the 3D style, you can check the Cone box to display a cone effect for the arrows of the X and Y axes. Either way, the Z axis has no arrow, which enables you to distinguish it from the X and Y axes. You can also choose a line width from 1 to 3, 1 being the default.

You can change the size of the icon. Just drag the slider up and down to get the result you like. Finally, you can change the color of the icon, both in model space and in paper space layouts. Click OK to close the dialog box.

Using a custom UCS

Although it seems confusing at first, after you try creating your own UCS, it's easier to understand how the process works.

In this exercise, you practice drawing with a custom UCS to create the basic framework for the drawing shown previously in Figures 8-15 and 8-16, a bearing housing for a commercial dryer.

ON the DVD-ROM The drawing used in the following exercise on drawing with a custom UCS, ab08-d.dwg, is in the Drawings folder on the DVD.

STEPS: Drawing with a Custom UCS

1. Open ab08-d.dwg from the DVD. This exercise assumes that you have Dynamic Input on, with the default relative coordinates setting.

2. Save the file as ab08-03.dwg in your AutoCAD Bible folder. ORTHO should be on. If necessary, turn on OSNAP. Set a running object snap for endpoints only.

3. Choose Tools ➪ New UCS ➪ Z. Because no objects exist in the drawing, you cannot easily use the 3 Point or Object options that might otherwise be useful.

4. At the Specify rotation angle about Z axis <90>: prompt, type **45** ↵. The UCS icon and crosshairs are displayed at a 45-degree angle.

5. Choose Line from the Draw toolbar. At the prompt, pick a point in the middle of your screen. At the Specify next point or [Undo]: prompt, type **1.25<90** ↵. End the LINE command.

6. Choose Rectangle from the Draw toolbar. Choose the From object snap. At the `Base point:` prompt, use the Endpoint object snap to pick the endpoint of the line that you just drew. At the `<Offset>:` prompt, type **@.875,0** ↵. At the `Specify other corner point or [Dimensions]:` prompt, type **-5.5,1.5** ↵. The command creates the rectangle at the proper angle.

7. Start the LINE command. Follow the prompts:

   Specify first point: *Choose the From object snap.*
   Base point: *Use the Endpoint object snap to pick point* ❶ *in Figure 8.20.*

   <Offset>: *Type* **@-.875,0** ↵

   Specify next point or [Undo]: *Move the cursor in the 90° direction (which looks like the 135° direction because of the rotated UCS).* **.625** ↵
   Specify next point or [Undo]: *Move the cursor in the 180° direction.* **3.75** ↵
   Specify next point or [Close/Undo]: *Move the cursor in the 270° direction.* **.625** ↵
   Specify next point or [Close/Undo]: ↵

8. Start the LINE command again.

   Turn on OTRACK on the status bar and follow the prompts:

   Specify first point: *Pass the cursor over* ❷ *and then over* ❸ *to acquire these points. Move the cursor to* ❹ *at the intersection of the two temporary tracking lines and click.*
   Specify next point or [Undo]: *Move the cursor in the 270° direction relative to the UCS.* **1.25** ↵.

   Specify next point or [Undo]: ↵

FIGURE 8.20

Using a customized UCS to start to draw a detail for a drill.

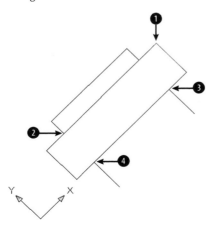

9. Because you would normally continue working on this drawing, you should save the UCS. Choose Tools ⇨ Named UCS. In the UCS dialog box, click Unnamed. Type **Rotated 45** and press Enter.

10. Still in the dialog box, choose World, click Set Current, and click OK to return to your drawing. The UCS icon and crosshairs return to their familiar angle.

11. To return to the Rotated 45 UCS, choose Tools ⇨ Named UCS to open the UCS dialog box. Choose Rotated 45 and click Set Current. Click OK to restore the Rotated 45 UCS.

12. Save your drawing.

> **TIP** After creating a new, rotated UCS such as the one in the previous exercise, type **plan** (to start the PLAN command) and use the Current UCS option to remove the rotation. Now you aren't working at an angle in your UCS. To return to the World UCS, type **plan** again and choose the World option to return to your drawing's previous state.

Creating Isometric Drawings

An *isometric* drawing is a 2D drawing made to look like a 3D drawing. Every child learns how to draw a box that looks three-dimensional. By drawing parallelograms instead of squares, the drawing gives the impression of being in three dimensions. AutoCAD and AutoCAD LT enable you to do the same thing.

Understanding isometric planes

The ISOPLANE (short for isometric plane) command rotates the crosshairs to the special angles required for isometric drawing. You then toggle the ISOPLANE setting from left to right to top, to draw on each of the three "planes." As you do so, the angles of the crosshairs, snap, and grid change to the appropriate angles.

These angles are 30 degrees for the X axis, 90 degrees for the Z axis, and 150 degrees for the Y axis. As you toggle among the planes, you see the crosshairs take on various configurations of these angles. Figure 8.21 shows the standard isometric cube. You can see three sides — left, right, and top. In the figure, the crosshairs are set to the right isometric plane.

FIGURE 8.21

The isometric cube.

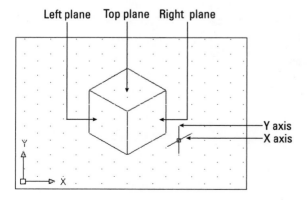

Isometric drawing is not often used for precise drawing because specifying the exact points that you need, can be difficult. Also, true 3D drawing has mostly supplanted isometric drawing. It is, however, used for piping work as well as for illustrations.

TIP Use snap points and object snaps as much as possible in an isometric drawing. Also, you can enlarge crosshairs to better visualize the isometric planes. (Choose Tools ➪ Options and click the Display tab. Set the Crosshair Size value to 100.) The grid is also a helpful aid.

Drawing in Isometric mode

To start Isometric mode, choose Tools ➪ Drafting Settings to open the Drafting Settings dialog box. On the Snap and Grid tab, in the Snap Type section, choose Grid Snap (if it is not already selected), and then Isometric Snap to enter Isometric mode. While you're there, turn on Snap and Grid if you want them on. Click OK. After you're in Isometric mode, press F5 to toggle from plane to plane.

Drawing lines in Isometric mode is fairly straightforward if the lines are parallel to one of the isometric plane angles. Circles and arcs in Isometric mode must be drawn as ellipses and elliptical arcs. When you're in Isometric mode, the ELLIPSE command has an Isocircle option.

STEPS: Drawing in Isometric Mode

1. Start a new drawing by using the `acad.dwt` or `acadlt.dwt` template.

2. Save the drawing in your `AutoCAD Bible` folder as `ab08-04.dwg`.

3. Right-click the SNAP button on the status bar and choose Settings. On the Snap and Grid tab, in the Snap Type section, choose Grid Snap (if it is not already selected), and then Isometric Snap.

4. In the Snap Spacing section, ensure that the Snap Y spacing is set to 0.5 and click Snap On. In the Grid Spacing section, ensure that the Grid Y spacing is set to 0.5 and click Grid On. Click OK to return to your drawing.

5. Choose Tools ➪ Options and click the Display tab. In the Crosshair Size text box, change the crosshair size to 100. This enlarges the crosshairs. Click OK.

6. Press F5 until you see the `<Isoplane Left>` prompt.

7. Do a Zoom All to zoom into the area covered by the grid.

8. Start the LINE command. Follow the prompts:

   ```
   Specify first point: Use the coordinate display to choose 3.4641,2,
   which is a snap point. (It may take you a while to find the point.)
   Specify next point or [Undo]: Choose 6.4952,0.25. (Right-click the
   coordinates and choose Absolute to get dynamic absolute coordinates.)
   Specify next point or [Undo]: Choose 6.4952,1.25.
   Specify next point or [Close/Undo]: Choose 3.4641,3.
   Specify next point or [Close/Undo]: Right-click and choose Close to
   close the left side of the model. All of these points are snap
   points.
   ```

   The results are shown in Figure 8.22.

FIGURE 8.22

The left side of the iron plate. The cursor has been changed to extend to 100 percent of the screen.

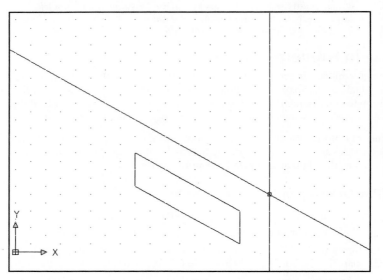

9. Press F5 twice until you see <Isoplane Right> on the command line.

10. Start the LINE command again. Follow the prompts:

    Specify first point: *Pick 6.4952,1.25. Right-click the coordinates and choose Relative to get dynamic polar coordinates.*

    Specify next point or [Undo]: *Pick when the coordinates show 2.0000<30.*
    Specify next point or [Undo]: *Use the polar coordinate display to draw a line of 1.0000<270.*

    Specify next point or [Close/Undo]:Draw a line of 2.0000<210. Specify next point or [Close/Undo]: ↵

11. Press F5 twice until you see <Isoplane Top> on the command line.

12. Start the LINE command. Start the line at 8.2272,2.25, which is a snap point. Draw a line of 3.500<150 and continue another line of 2.000<210. End the LINE command. This completes the box.

13. Choose Ellipse from the Draw toolbar. Right-click and choose Isocircle from the shortcut menu. At the Specify center of isocircle: prompt, choose 5.1962,3. At the Specify radius of isocircle or [Diameter]: prompt, type .5 ↵ to draw the ellipse. Your drawing should look like Figure 8.23.

14. Change the cursor size back to 5 (%). Save your drawing.

FIGURE 8.23

The completed iron plate with a hole in it, drawn isometrically.

TIP Polar coordinate display is very helpful while drawing isometrically. The coordinates are easier to understand than the unusual absolute snap point coordinates created by ISOPLANE.

Summary

In this chapter, you read how to control the display of your drawing. You learned about:

- The PAN and ZOOM commands, including real-time pan and zoom and the many ZOOM options
- Using Aerial View to pan and zoom
- Saving several views of your drawing so that you can retrieve them quickly
- Creating tiled viewports for drawing and editing, as well as learning how to name and display useful viewport configurations
- Rotating the snap and grid
- Creating a User Coordinate System, saving a useful UCS, and then setting it as current at any time
- Setting the snap style to isometric to create isometric drawings

In the next chapter, you discover how to start editing your drawings.

Chapter 9

Editing Your Drawing with Basic Tools

No drawing project is ever completed without changes. You make changes in a drawing for many reasons. Some editing processes are simply part of the drawing process, such as copying an object instead of drawing it a second time from scratch. Other types of editing involve making changes to many objects at once, such as moving an entire section of a drawing to make room for additional objects. You often also need to erase, move, rotate, and resize objects.

Editing a Drawing

Making changes to a drawing is called *editing*. In order to edit an object, you need to select it. AutoCAD and AutoCAD LT offer numerous techniques for selecting objects. In this chapter, I cover basic editing commands as well as most of the ways to select objects. The rest of the 2D editing commands, as well as additional selection and editing methods — grips, the Properties palette, selection filters, and groups — are covered in the next chapter.

Most of the editing commands are on the Modify toolbar or in the 2D Draw control panel of the Dashboard. (If the Modify toolbar is not displayed, right-click any toolbar button and choose Modify from the toolbar list. To display the Dashboard, choose Tools ➪ Palettes ➪ Dashboard.) In most cases, you can do one of the following:

- Start the command first and then select the objects to which the command applies.
- Select the objects first and then start the command.

The question of which comes first, the command or the object, is fully covered later in this chapter.

AUTOCAD ONLY Although you can use the editing tools that I describe in this chapter in a 3D environment, this chapter assumes that you are working in a 2D environment. (AutoCAD LT doesn't offer a 3D environment.) To make sure you're in a 2D environment, set the workspace to AutoCAD Classic or 2D Drafting & Annotation (choose it from the Workspaces toolbar drop-down list) and set the visual style to 2D Wireframe (View ➪ Visual Styles ➪ 2D Wireframe). If you still see the Z axis on the UCS icon, choose View ➪ 3D Views ➪ Top. Another method is to set the workspace to AutoCAD Classic or 2D Drafting & Annotation, and then start a new drawing based on the default `acad.dwt` template.

Understanding object-selection basics

When you start to edit drawings, it is important to first learn how to select objects. The simplest selection technique is to place the *pickbox* — the box at the intersection of the crosshairs — over the object and click with the pick button on the mouse. This is known as *picking* an object.

When you pass the cursor over an object before choosing any editing command, the object becomes thicker and dashed. This *rollover highlighting* helps you to know which object you will select when you click. This feature is helpful in a busy drawing with many objects close together or overlapping. I explain how to fine-tune this effect in the next chapter.

If you start an editing command before selecting an object, the command responds with the `Select objects:` prompt. When you then pick an object to select it, AutoCAD or AutoCAD LT highlights it, usually by making the object dashed, as shown in Figure 9.1. The command continues to provide `Select objects:` prompts so that you can select other objects.

FIGURE 9.1

The selected line is dashed.

The command continues to provide `Select objects:` prompts so that you can select other objects. Continue to select objects until you have selected all of the objects that you want to edit. Then press Enter to end the `Select objects:` prompt.

When you select an object before choosing an editing command, the lines of the selected object become dashed and you also see one or more small boxes, called *grips,* as shown in Figure 9.2. Chapter 10 covers grips. In the next few exercises, you use this picking technique to select objects. Other selection methods are covered later in this chapter.

FIGURE 9.2

The selected line is dashed and also displays grips.

Erasing objects

 Somehow, no drawing is ever completed without erasing an object. The ERASE command is very simple — it has no options. To erase an object, select the object and choose Erase on the Modify toolbar (or from the 2D Draw control panel of the Dashboard). or press Del on the keyboard. Alternatively, choose Erase and then select the object.

ON the CD-ROM The drawing used in the following exercise on picking and erasing objects, ab09-a.dwg, is in the Drawings folder on the CD-ROM.

STEPS: Picking and Erasing Objects

1. Open ab09-a.dwg from the CD-ROM.
2. Save the file as ab09-01.dwg in your AutoCAD Bible folder. This drawing is a schematic of a gas extraction well, shown in Figure 9.3.
3. To erase the line at point ❶ of Figure 9.3, move the mouse until the pickbox at the intersection of the crosshairs is anywhere over the line. The line thickens and is dashed. Click the line. Now the line is dashed and displays grips.

FIGURE 9.3

The gas extraction well schematic.

Thanks to the Army Corps of Engineers for this drawing. The COE maintains a Web site of drawings at http://cadlib.wes.army.mil.

4. Choose Erase from the Modify toolbar or the 2D Draw control panel of the Dashboard. The line is erased.

5. Right-click and choose Repeat Erase.

6. At the `Select objects:` prompt, pick the line at point **2** in Figure 9.3.

7. The command responds with `1 found` and repeats the `Select objects:` prompt. Right-click to end the `Select objects:` prompt. The line is erased.

8. Save your drawing.

 The OOPS command restores the most recently erased object and is covered in Chapter 18.

Moving objects

Use the MOVE command to move objects in your drawing. You need to specify the distance and direction that you want the object to move.

 To move an object, select it and choose Move on the Modify toolbar or in the 2D Draw control panel of the Dashboard. Alternatively, choose Move and then select the object.

When you choose the MOVE command and then select an object, the command responds with the following prompt:

```
Specify base point or [displacement] <Displacement>:
```

You now have two ways of specifying how to move the object or objects:

■ **Displacement method:** At the prompt, state the entire displacement as an X,Y coordinate such as 2,3 or a polar coordinate such as 2<60. Because the word *displacement* already implies the relative distance from the object, you do not use @. The command responds with the `Specify second point of displacement or <use first point as displacement>:` prompt. Because you've already specified all the necessary information, press Enter. AutoCAD or AutoCAD LT uses the first point you indicated as the displacement (the default) and moves the object.

TIP The MOVE command remembers the most recent displacement throughout a session. To move an object the same displacement as you just moved another object, press Enter at the `Specify base point or [Displacement] <Displacement>:` prompt. At the `Specify displacement <2.0000, 3.0000, 0.0000>:` prompt, you see in angled brackets the last displacement that you used. Press Enter to move the object using this displacement.

■ **Base point/second point method:** At the `Specify base point or [Displacement] <Displacement>:` prompt, pick a base point. This can be anywhere in your drawing but is usually on or near the object that you want to move. At the `Specify second point of displacement or <use first point as displacement>:` prompt, specify the distance and angle of movement either by picking a second point on the screen or by typing a relative coordinate. If you have Dynamic Input on, set to the default of relative coordinates, you don't need to add the @ symbol before the coordinates.

The displacement method requires less input and is simpler when you know the exact displacement so that you can type it in. The only disadvantage is that, as soon as you type in the displacement, you sometimes see a confusing temporary drag line and copy of your object or objects. Ignore this display and press Enter. Your object or objects move as you specified. The base point/second point method works best when you want to move an object relative to another object on the screen.

When you specify a base point, choose an object snap on the object or a nearby related object for exact results.

You can use PolarSnap with the base point/second point method to move an object. Turn on PolarSnap and, if necessary, use the Drafting Settings dialog box to set the increment. If the polar distance is 0, you can set it to a new value. AutoCAD and AutoCAD LT use the Snap X spacing value that you specified in the Drafting Settings dialog box. At the first prompt, pick a point such as an object snap on the object. At the second prompt, drag the object in the desired direction. Use the tooltip to guide you and then click.

You can use drag-and-drop to move objects if you aren't too particular about where they end up. Here's how it works:

1. Pick an object.
2. Continue to pick as many objects as you want to move. They all show grips.
3. Pick any of the objects, but not on a grip. Keep the mouse button pressed until the cursor changes to an arrow with a small rectangle.
4. Drag the object(s) to any other location in your drawing.

For a little more control over the placement of your objects, you can use the Windows Clipboard. Pick the object(s) that you want to move. Right-click and choose Cut from the shortcut menu. Right-click a second time and choose Paste. At the prompt for an insertion point, you can pick with an object snap or by typing coordinates. However, you can't control the base point (which is 0,0) as you can with the MOVE command, because it's always the lower-left corner of the object or of a bounding box around the object.

 The drawing used in the following exercise on moving objects, ab09-b.dwg, is in the Drawings folder on the CD-ROM.

STEPS: Moving Objects

1. Open ab09-b.dwg from the CD-ROM.
2. Save the file as ab09-02.dwg in your AutoCAD Bible folder. This drawing shows the plan of a bathroom. Each object is a *block,* a set of objects that you can select as one object. (Chapter 18 covers blocks.) Make sure that OSNAP is turned on. Set a running object snap for intersection only.

3. Pick anywhere on the tub to select it. Notice the rollover highlighting before you click and the grip and dashed lines that appear after you click. Choose Move on the Modify toolbar or in the 2D Draw control panel of the Dashboard. Follow the prompts:

   ```
   Specify base point or [Displacement] <Displacement>: Move the cursor
   to the Intersection at ❶ in Figure 9.4 and click.
   Specify second point of displacement or <use first point as
   displacement>: Move the cursor to the Intersection at ❷ in Figure
   9.4 and click.
   ```

   The tub moves to the bottom-right corner of the bathroom.
4. Choose Move on the Modify toolbar or in the 2D Draw control panel of the Dashboard. Follow the prompts:

   ```
   Select objects: Pick the sink.
   Select objects: ↵
   Specify base point or [Displacement] <Displacement>: 4'<0 ↵
   Specify second point of displacement or <use first point as
   displacement>: ↵
   ```

The sink moves 4 feet to the right.

The bathroom plan.

Thanks to Bill Wynn of New Windsor, Maryland, for this drawing.

5. Click SNAP on the status bar to turn it on. Now, right-click SNAP. Choose PolarSnap On (unless it is already on, in which case it is unavailable). Click POLAR on the status bar.

6. Pick the toilet and choose Move on the Modify toolbar or in the 2D Draw control panel of the Dashboard. At the `Specify base point or [Displacement] <Displacement>:` prompt, pick the intersection at the bottom-left corner of the toilet tank. At the `Specify second point of displacement or <use first point as displacement>:` prompt, move the toilet to the left until you see `0'-6"<180°` on the tooltip and click. The toilet moves 6 inches to the left. (If you can't get a 180° tooltip, check your polar angle settings.)

7. Save your drawing.

Copying objects

Copying is very similar to moving. In fact, the only difference is that AutoCAD or AutoCAD LT does not remove the object from its original spot, so you end up with two objects instead of one.

 To copy an object, select it and choose Copy on the Modify toolbar or in the 2D Draw control panel of the Dashboard. Alternatively, choose Copy and then select the object.

When you choose the COPY command and have selected an object, the command responds with the following prompt:

```
Specify base point or [Displacement/mOde] <Displacement>:
```

You now have two ways of specifying where to copy the object or objects:

■ **Displacement method:** At the `Specify base point or [Displacement/mOde] <Displacement>:` prompt, state the entire displacement as an X,Y coordinate such as 2,3 or a polar coordinate such as 2<60. Because the word *displacement* already implies the relative distance from the object, you do not use @. The command responds with the `Specify second point of displacement or <use first point as displacement>:` prompt. Because you've already specified all of the necessary information, press Enter. The command uses the first point that you indicated as the displacement (the default), copies the object, and ends the command.

TIP The COPY command remembers the most recent displacement throughout a session. To copy an object the same displacement as you just copied any object, press Enter at the `Specify base point or [Displacement/mOde] <Displacement>:` prompt. At the `Specify displacement <2.0000, 3.0000, 0.0000>:` prompt, you see in angled brackets the last displacement that you used. Press Enter to copy the object using this displacement.

- **Base point/second point method:** At the `Specify base point or [Displacement/mOde] <Displacement>:` prompt, pick a base point. This can be anywhere in your drawing. At the `Specify second point of displacement or <use first point as displacement>:` prompt, specify the distance and angle of movement either by picking a second point on the screen or by typing in a relative coordinate. If you have Dynamic Input on and set to the default of relative coordinates, you don't need to add the @ symbol before the coordinates.

If you use the base point/second point method, the COPY command continues to prompt you for additional copies. However, scripts and other routines use the earlier functioning, in which the command ends after creating one copy. After you make one copy, you see the `Specify second point or [Exit/Undo] <Exit>:` prompt. Press Enter to use the Exit option and end the command.

NOTE The COPYMODE system variable lets you specify if you want the COPY command to repeat or not. By default, as I just described, COPY repeats. Set the system variables value to 1 to end the COPY command after one copy. You can also change how the COPY command works as you use it, with the Mode option. Choose either the Single or Multiple (the default) suboption.

If you've created more than one copy, the Undo option enables you to undo the last copy that you've created. You can then continue to make more copies or end the command.

You can use PolarSnap to copy objects in the same way that you use it to move objects. For details, see the previous section.

You can also use drag-and-drop to copy objects. Follow the steps in the previous section on moving objects, but press and hold the Ctrl key as you drag the object. Notice the plus sign in the cursor's rectangle. In the same way, you can use the Clipboard to copy and paste objects from one location in a drawing to another.

 The drawing used in the following exercise on copying objects, ab09-c.dwg, is in the Drawings folder on the CD-ROM.

STEPS: Copying Objects

1. Open ab09-c.dwg from the CD-ROM.
2. Save the file as ab09-03.dwg in your AutoCAD Bible folder. This drawing shows part of an electrical schematic. Make sure that OSNAP is turned on. Set a running object snap for endpoint only.
3. Use ZOOM Window to zoom into the area of the drawing marked ❶ in Figure 9.5. This shows a 24-volt transformer.

FIGURE 9.5

The electrical schematic.

Thanks to Robert Mack of the Dexter Company, Fairfield, Iowa, for this drawing.

4. Note that three of the arcs that make up the right side of the transformer are missing. Pick the arc at ❶ in Figure 9.6. Choose Copy from the Modify toolbar or in the 2D Draw control panel of the Dashboard. Follow the prompts:

   ```
   Specify base point or [Displacement/mOde] <Displacement>: Pick the
   endpoint at the top of the arc at ❷ (see Figure 9.6).
   Specify second point of displacement or <use first point as
   displacement>: Pick the endpoint at the bottom of the first arc at ❸.
   Specify second point or [Exit/Undo] <Exit>: Pick the endpoint at the
   bottom of the second arc at ❹.
   Specify second point or [Exit/Undo] <Exit>: Pick the endpoint at the
   bottom of the third arc at ❺.
   Specify second point or [Exit/Undo] <Exit>: ↵
   ```

5. Choose ZOOM Previous from the Standard toolbar to return to your previous view.

6. Pick the circle at ❷ in Figure 9.5 (which shows the entire schematic section). Note the grips. You also want to select the text inside the circles, but it's hard to see because of the grips. Press Esc to remove the grips.

7. Choose Copy from the Modify toolbar or in the 2D Draw control panel of the Dashboard. Now select the circle at ❷ in Figure 9.5 again. This time no grips obscure the text. Separately pick both lines of text inside the circle.

FIGURE 9.6

Close-up of the transformer.

8. Continuing to select objects to copy, select the circle at ❸ in Figure 9.5. Also select the two lines of text inside the circle. Right-click to end the `Select objects:` prompt.

9. At the `Specify base point or [Displacement/mOde] <Displacement>:` prompt, pick the endpoint at ❹ in Figure 9.5. At the `Specify second point of displacement or <use first point as displacement>:` prompt, pick the endpoint at ❺ in Figure 9.5. Press Enter to end the COPY command. This action copies the two circles with the text.

10. Save your drawing.

Copying and moving objects from one drawing to another

If you use other Windows programs, you often use the CUT command to move and the COPY command to copy objects. Then you use the PASTE command to specify a new location. In AutoCAD and AutoCAD LT, these commands are called CUTCLIP, COPYCLIP, and PASTECLIP. (The CLIP refers to the Windows Clipboard.) Although the MOVE and COPY commands provide more accuracy within one drawing, you can use the Clipboard to move and copy objects from one drawing to another.

You can copy objects from one drawing to another by using the drag-and-drop technique. The easiest way is to open both drawings and then choose Window ➪ Tile Vertically. Select the object(s) that you want to copy, point to one of them, and drag them to the second drawing. However, you don't have much control over the exact placement of the new objects. From drawing to drawing, AutoCAD or AutoCAD LT copies the objects, instead of moving them.

For more control over the placement of your objects, use the Windows Clipboard. A special feature, Copy with Base Point, gives you control over the placement of your objects. Follow these steps:

1. Pick the object(s) that you want to copy.

2. Right-click and choose Copy with Base Point from the shortcut menu.

3. At the `Specify base point:` prompt, specify a base point. An object snap is a good idea here. This action copies the object(s) to the Clipboard, including the base point.

4. Switch to the second drawing.

5. Right-click in the drawing area and choose Paste (or click Paste on the Standard toolbar). At the prompt for an insertion point, specify the insertion point by picking, using an object snap, or typing coordinates. This action pastes the object.

To copy the object(s) to the same coordinates as the original drawing, in Step 5 choose Paste to Original Coordinates from the shortcut menu. AutoCAD or AutoCAD LT pastes the object(s) in the second drawing, matching the coordinates. Depending on your drawing, you may need to ZOOM and PAN to see the pasted copy.

You cannot specify a base point for moving (cutting) an object, but you can specify the insertion point when you paste it. The lower-left extent of the selected object(s) is the base point.

CROSS-REF You can drag objects from a drawing into another application, such as a word-processing document. For more information on working with AutoCAD or AutoCAD LT and other applications, see Chapter 27.

In the following exercise, you practice copying objects from one drawing to another.

ON the CD-ROM The drawing used in the following exercise on copying objects from one drawing to another, ab09-c.dwg, is in the Drawings folder on the CD-ROM.

STEPS: Copying Objects from One Drawing to Another

1. Close any open drawings. Open ab09-c.dwg from the CD-ROM. Save the file as ab09-04.dwg in your AutoCAD Bible folder. Then choose Open from the Standard toolbar and open ab09-03.dwg from your AutoCAD Bible folder. If you didn't do the previous exercise, open ab09-03.dwg from the Results folder on the CD-ROM.

2. Choose Window ➪ Tile Vertically. This displays the drawings side by side, as shown in Figure 9.7.

3. In ab09-03.dwg, which should be active, make sure that OSNAP is turned on. Set a running object snap set for endpoint only.

4. Pick the circle at ❶ and the two lines of text inside it.

5. Move the cursor off the selected objects and right-click. Choose Copy with Base Point from the shortcut menu.

6. At the Specify base point: prompt, pick the endpoint at ❷ in Figure 9.7.

7. Click anywhere in ab09-04.dwg to make it the current drawing. Right-click and choose Paste from the shortcut menu. At the Specify insertion point: prompt, pick the endpoint at ❸ in Figure 9.7 to paste the objects.

8. Click in ab09-03.dwg. Press Esc to clear any grips. Pick the circle at ❹ in Figure 9.7. (Don't include the text this time.) Click again and hold the mouse button on the circle, but not on the grips, until you see the pointer arrow with the rectangle. Drag the circle to ❺ in Figure 9.7. As you can see, you have no way to precisely place the circle.

FIGURE 9.7

To copy objects from one drawing to another, display them both on the screen together. (The drawings may appear reversed on your screen.)

9. Click in ab09-03.dwg again. This time pick both lines of text inside the circle at ④. Right-click and choose Copy with Base Point. At the Specify base point: prompt, pick the endpoint at the left quadrant of the circle.

10. Click in ab09-04.dwg. Right-click and choose Paste to Original Coordinates to paste the two lines of text inside the circle (depending on how accurately you dragged the circle).

11. Save ab09-04.dwg. Click in ab09-03.dwg and click its Close box. Don't save changes to ab09-03.dwg.

Rotating objects

If your design changes or you drew at an incorrect angle, you may need to rotate one or more objects. You can easily rotate an object or objects around a base point that you specify. The base point is usually an object snap point on the object. To indicate the rotation, specify an angle of rotation. As explained in Chapter 5, by default, zero degrees is to the right, and degrees increase counterclockwise. (To change the default, choose Format ➪ Units.) By specifying a negative angle, you can turn objects clockwise.

To rotate an object, choose Rotate from the Modify toolbar or in the 2D Draw control panel of the Dashboard and select an object. Alternatively, select an object and then choose Rotate from the Modify toolbar or in the 2D Draw control panel of the Dashboard. At the Specify base point: prompt, indicate the point around which you want to rotate. At the Specify rotation angle or [Copy/Reference]: prompt, type an angle at the command line.

TIP Use the Copy option to create a copy of the original object. After you use this option, the same prompt returns so that you can specify a rotation angle. You end up with two objects, one at the original rotation angle and one at the new rotation angle.

181

The most recent rotation angle that you specify becomes the default for other rotations during the same session. For example, if you rotate an object 330°, the next time you rotate an object, the prompt appears as Specify rotation angle or [Copy/Reference] <330>:. Press Enter to rotate the object using the default rotation.

The purpose of the Reference option is to let you specify an absolute rotation angle for an object. For example, let's say you want to rotate a line, whose angle you don't know, to 45°. At the Specify the reference angle <0>: prompt, you type in an angle or specify an angle by picking two points. These can be object snap points on the object that specify the object's current angle; in the example, you would use the endpoints of the line. At the Specify the new angle or [Points] <0>: prompt, type or pick a new angle or specify two points to determine the new angle. You can also pick an object snap on another object in the drawing to indicate this new angle. In the example, you would enter **45** to rotate the line to 45°. You can use the Reference option to align the object with the X or Y axis or with another object in your drawing.

ON the CD-ROM The drawing used in the following exercise on rotating objects, ab07-03.dwg, is in the Results folder on the CD-ROM.

STEPS: Rotating Objects

1. Open ab07-03.dwg from the Results folder of the CD-ROM. If you did the exercise on ellipses in Chapter 7, you can open this drawing from your AutoCAD Bible folder.

2. Save the file as ab09-05.dwg in your AutoCAD Bible folder. This drawing shows a conference room, as shown in Figure 9.8.

3. Set center, quadrant, and perpendicular running object snaps. OSNAP should be on. Polar Tracking should be off.

4. Pick the small elliptical table at the top-left corner of the conference room. Choose Rotate from the Modify toolbar or in the 2D Draw control panel of the Dashboard.

FIGURE 9.8

The conference room.

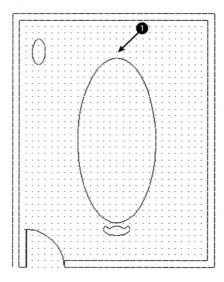

5. At the Specify base point: prompt, pick the top quadrant of the ellipse. At the Specify rotation angle or [Copy/Reference]: prompt, type **90** ↵. This action rotates the small table 90 degrees around the base point.

6. Click SNAP on the status bar to turn off snap.

7. To make a copy of the chair and rotate it at the same time, start the ROTATE command. At the Select objects: prompt, pick the arc that makes the back of the chair at the bottom of the drawing. The command responds 1 found. Continue to pick the two lines that make the arm-rests and the arc that makes the front of the chair, making sure that each time you see the response 1 found. Press Enter to end the Select objects: prompt.

8. To copy and rotate the selected chair, follow the prompts:

   Specify base point: *Use the Center object snap to select the center of the large table.*
   Specify rotation angle or [Copy/Reference] <90>: *Right-click and choose Copy.*
   Specify rotation angle or [Copy/Reference] <90>: **180** ↵.

9. Start the COPY command and select the four objects in the new chair. Press Enter to end object selection. Follow the prompts:

   Specify base point or [Displacement/mOde] <Displacement>: *Use the Center object snap to select the center of the arc that makes up the back of the chair.*
   Specify second point of displacement or <use first point as displacement>: *Pick a point about a third of the way around the right side of the conference table.*
   Specify second point or [Exit/Undo] <Exit>: *Pick a point about halfway around the right side of the conference table.*
   Specify second point or [Exit/Undo] <Exit>: *Pick a point about two-thirds of the way around the right side of the conference table.*
   Specify second point or [Exit/Undo] <Exit>: ↵

10. Start the ROTATE command and select the four objects in the first of the three chairs (the top one) that you just created. Right-click to end object selection. At the Specify base point: prompt, pick the center object snap of either arc of the chair. At the Specify rotation angle or [Copy/Reference]: prompt, move the cursor around, watch the image of the chair rotate, and click when the chair faces the angle of the table.

11. Repeat Step 10 for the second chair.

12. Start the ROTATE command and select the four objects in the last chair that you created by using the COPY command. Follow the prompts:

   Specify base point: *Choose the Center object snap of either of the chair arcs.*
   Specify rotation angle or [Copy/Reference]: *Right-click and choose Reference from the shortcut menu.*
   Specify the reference angle <0>: *Use the Quadrant object snap to pick the back arc of the chair.*
   Specify second point: *Use the Quadrant object snap to pick the front arc of the chair.*
   Specify the new angle or [Points] <0>: *Use the Perpendicular object snap to choose the conference table next to the chair.*

13. Save your drawing.

Scaling objects

Scaling, or resizing, objects is another common editing task in AutoCAD or AutoCAD LT. As with rotating objects, you specify a base point, usually an object snap on the object. The base point is the one point on the object that does not move or change as you scale the object. The most common way to resize an object is to specify a scale factor. The current object has a scale factor of 1. Therefore, to increase the size of the object, type in a number greater than 1. For example, a scale factor of 2 doubles the size of the object. To decrease the size of the object, type in a number less than 1. A scale factor of 0.25 creates an object one-quarter of its previous size. The most recent scale factor that you specify becomes the default for other scaling operations during the same session.

Use the Copy option to create a copy of the original object. After you use this option, the same prompt returns so that you can specify a scale factor. You end up with two objects, one at the original scale and one at the new scale.

As with the ROTATE command, you can scale by using the Reference option to specify an absolute length. You specify the reference length, usually the current length of the object, by typing it in or using object snaps on the object. At the `Specify new length or [Points] <0'-1">` prompt, you can type a new length or pick two points. You can use the Points option to match the size of another existing object.

 To scale an object, choose Scale from the Modify toolbar or in the 2D Draw control panel of the Dashboard and select the object. Alternatively, you can select the object and choose Scale from the Modify toolbar or in the 2D Draw control panel of the Dashboard.

ON the CD-ROM The drawing used in the following exercise on scaling objects, ab09-d.dwg, is in the Drawings folder on the CD-ROM.

STEPS: Scaling Objects

1. Open ab09-d.dwg from the CD-ROM.
2. Save the file as ab09-06.dwg in your AutoCAD Bible folder. This drawing, shown in Figure 9.9, shows part of a valve that is manufactured in several sizes. In this exercise, you scale both views to represent a different-sized valve piece. Ensure that OSNAP is on. Set running object snaps for quadrant and endpoint.

FIGURE 9.9

The valve piece in two views.

Thanks to Jerry Bottenfield of Clow Valve Company, Oskaloosa, Iowa, for this drawing.

3. Choose Scale from the Modify toolbar or in the 2D Draw control panel of the Dashboard. At the `Select objects:` prompt, pick both circles in the top view (they're actually arcs because they're broken at the bottom) and the two short lines at the bottom of the circles. Press Enter to end object selection. Follow the prompts:

    ```
    Specify base point: Use the Quadrant object snap to pick the left
    quadrant of the inner circle.
    Specify scale factor or [Copy/Reference]: Right-click and choose
    Reference.
    Specify reference length <1>: Use the Quadrant object snap to pick
    the left quadrant of the inner circle again.
    Specify second point: Use the Quadrant object snap to pick the right
    quadrant of the inner circle.
    Specify new length or [Points] <1.000>: 1 ↵
    ```

    Because the distance between the two quadrants that you chose is 2.5 units, the SCALE command scales the objects to 40 percent (1 divided by 2.5).

4. Right-click and choose Repeat Scale. Select all eight lines in the bottom view, including the green dashed lines. Be sure that you see 1 found each time. If necessary, use ZOOM Window to zoom in. Right-click to end object selection after you finish selecting the lines. Follow the prompts:

    ```
    Specify base point: Use the Endpoint object snap at point ❶ in
    Figure 9.9.
    Specify scale factor or [Copy/Reference]: .4 ↵
    ```

5. Save your drawing. It should look like Figure 9.10.

FIGURE 9.10

The valve piece has now been scaled down.

Using the CHANGE command

The CHANGE command changes the endpoint of a line and the radius of a circle. Note that you can also use grips and the Properties palette, both of which are covered in the next chapter, to change line endpoints and circle radii (among other object properties).

> **NOTE** You can use the CHANGE command to change text (which I cover in Chapter 13), the text and text properties of block attributes (not yet contained in a block), as well as the location and rotation of blocks (Chapter 18), but other newer commands do those jobs better. The Properties option of this command can change many object properties, but it's generally easier to use the Properties palette. However, these features of the CHANGE command can be useful when writing scripts or AutoLISP code, covered in Parts VI and VII of this book.

To change an object, select it and type **change** ↵ on the command line. Alternatively, you can type **change** ↵ on the command line and select the object.

> **CAUTION** The CHANGE command works differently, depending on whether you select lines or circles. For this reason, it can give unexpected results if you choose lines and circles at the same time. Use the command for either lines or circles but not for both at once.

Changing lines

If you select one line, the CHANGE command changes the endpoint closest to where you picked the line. The command prompts you for a change point. When you pick the point, the command brings the endpoint of the line to that change point, as shown in Figure 9.11. You can use an object snap to specify the change point. If ORTHO is on, the line becomes orthogonal, bringing the endpoint of the line as close as possible to the change point that you specify, as shown in Figure 9.11.

FIGURE 9.11

Using the CHANGE command on one line.

If you select more than one line, CHANGE works differently: it moves the nearest endpoints of all of the lines to the change point so that all of the lines meet at one point, as shown in Figure 9.12.

FIGURE 9.12

Using the CHANGE command on several lines. The original lines are shown as continuous. The new lines, after using the CHANGE command, are dashed.

Changing circles

Changing the radius of a circle has the same result as scaling it. When you select a circle, the command prompts you for a change point. If you pick one, AutoCAD or AutoCAD LT resizes the circle so that it passes through the new point. You can also press Enter. You then get a prompt to enter a new radius.

If you select more than one circle, the command moves from circle to circle, letting you specify a new radius for each, one at a time. You can tell which circle is current because of its drag image, which lets you drag the size of the circle.

If you select more than one circle and try to pick a change point, the command responds with Change point ignored. At that point, one circle becomes active, and you can then pick a change point.

Selecting Objects

If you've been following through this chapter's exercises, you've probably thought it tedious to pick several objects one at a time. Imagine trying to individually pick every object in a drawing just to move all of the objects one-half unit to the left! Of course, there is a better way. In fact, AutoCAD and AutoCAD LT offer many ways of selecting objects. Selected objects are also called the *selection set* of objects.

Selecting objects after choosing a command

When you choose an editing command, you see the Select objects: prompt. This prompt has 16 options — all you could ever want for selecting objects — but these options are not shown on the command line or in the Dynamic Input prompt. To specify an option, type the option abbreviation. Because the Select objects: prompt repeats until you press Enter, you can combine options to select objects for any command. In the following list of options, the capitalized letters of the option are the abbreviation that you type (uppercase or lowercase letters work) at the Select objects: prompt.

- **Window:** The Window option lets you pick two diagonal corners that define a window. All objects entirely within the window are selected. Figure 9.13 shows the process of picking the window. Figure 9.14 shows the result — to indicate that the selected objects are highlighted, they display dashed instead of continuous lines. As you move your mouse to specify the second diagonal corner, a blue transparent rectangle appears to help you preview which objects will be selected.

> **TIP** You can drag past the edge of the screen (actually the viewport) to specify a window. Hold down the mouse button and continue to move the mouse in the same direction. The display automatically pans so that you can see objects that were off the screen. When you see all of the objects that you need to select, pick the second corner of the window.

- **Last:** The Last option selects the last object that was created and is visible within the current view. Often you create an object and then want to move or copy it. In this situation, the Last option is an easy way to select the object that you just created.

FIGURE 9.13

Selecting objects with a window. The window selects only objects that lie entirely within the window.

FIGURE 9.14

The selected object is highlighted.

■ **Crossing:** Crossing enables you to pick two diagonal corners that define a window. All objects entirely or partly within the window are selected. As you move your mouse to specify the second diagonal corner, a green transparent rectangle appears to help you preview which objects will be selected. Figure 9.15 shows the process of picking the window. Figure 9.16 shows the result — the selected objects are highlighted.

TIP   You can drag past the edge of the screen (actually the viewport) to specify a crossing window. Hold down the mouse button and continue to move the mouse in the same direction. The display automatically pans so that you can see objects that were off the screen. After you see all of the objects that you need to select, pick the second corner of the crossing window.

FIGURE 9.15

Selecting objects with a crossing window. The crossing window selects any objects that lie within or partly within the window.

FIGURE 9.16

The selected objects are highlighted.

- **BOX:** The BOX option is a combination of the Window and Crossing options. If you pick the two window corners from left to right, the selection functions as if you used the Window option. If you pick the two points from right to left, the selection functions as if you used the Crossing option. By default, you can select objects this way without specifying the BOX option. See the description of implied windowing later in this chapter.

- **ALL:** The ALL option selects all objects on thawed and unlocked layers in the drawing. (I discuss layers in Chapter 11.) Use the ALL option when you want to select everything, including objects that you can't currently see on the screen.

■ **Fence:** The Fence option enables you to specify a series of temporary lines to select any object crossing the lines. Figure 9.17 shows the process of defining a selection fence. Figure 9.18 shows the result — the selected objects are highlighted.

FIGURE 9.17

Using a fence to select objects.

FIGURE 9.18

The selected objects are highlighted.

■ **WPolygon:** The Window Polygon option (WPolygon) is like the Window option, except that you create a polygon instead of a rectangular window. This option selects all objects that lie entirely within the polygon.

■ **CPolygon:** The Crossing Polygon option (CPolygon) is like the Crossing option, except that you create a polygon instead of a rectangular window. This option selects all objects that lie entirely or partly within the window.

- **Group:** The Group option selects a named group of objects. (Chapter 10 covers groups.) If you need to work regularly with a certain set of objects, you can place them in a group and then easily select them with one click.

- **Remove:** The Remove option enables you to deselect objects. After you use this option, all objects that you select are deselected and are therefore removed from the selection set. Use the Add option to once again select objects.

> **TIP** An alternative to using Remove to deselect objects is to press Shift and deselect objects by picking or implied windowing. Implied windowing is discussed later in this chapter.

- **Add:** The Add option sets the selection mode to add objects to the selection set. Use the Add option after using the Remove option to start selecting objects again.

- **Multiple:** The Multiple option turns off highlighting as you select objects. However, you cannot preview which objects are in the selection set.

- **Previous:** The Previous option automatically selects all objects that you selected for the previous command. Objects selected and edited by using grips are not remembered for this option. (The next chapter covers grips.)

- **Undo:** The Undo option deselects the object(s) selected at the last `Select objects:` prompt. (If you removed objects from the selection set at the last `Select objects:` prompt, Undo reselects them.)

- **AUto:** The AUto option combines picking with the BOX option. By default, you can select objects this way without specifying this option. See the description of implied windowing later in this chapter.

- **SIngle:** When you specify this option, you get another `Select objects:` prompt. You select objects by using any option, and then AutoCAD immediately ends the selection process. You don't have to press Enter.

- **SUbobject:** The SUbobject option is used only for 3D solids and allows you to select vertices, edges, and faces. For more information, see Chapter 24.

- **Object:** Ends the selection of subobjects so that you can select other objects.

- **CLass:** The CLass option allows you to select certain objects that were created in another application. Certain applications, such as Autodesk Map, can add a feature classification to an object. Doing so creates an associated classification (XML) file. If you have such an object and the XML file is present, you can select objects by classification property. (AutoCAD only.)

Cycling through objects

It may happen that you have many objects close together in a drawing, making it hard to select the object or point that you want. You could always zoom in, but in a complex drawing this can take quite a bit of time. Another trick is to use *object cycling*. At the `Select objects:` prompt, place the cursor over the area where more than one object overlaps. Then hold down the Shift key and press the Spacebar. One object is highlighted. If it is not the one you want, with the Shift key still down, press the Spacebar again. AutoCAD or AutoCAD LT cycles through the objects. When the object that you want is highlighted, pick the object. You can continue to select other objects or end object selection by pressing Enter.

Selecting objects before choosing a command

If you select objects before choosing a command, your options are more limited than if you choose a command first. Nevertheless, you have enough flexibility for most situations. The reason for the limitation is that the Command: prompt is active, and anything that you might type at the keyboard to indicate a selection option could be confused with a command. You can pick the object to highlight it, use implied windowing, or use the SELECT command to select objects in advance.

The purpose of the SELECT command is simply to select objects. This command then saves these objects for use with the Previous selection option. Choose an editing command and type **p** ↵ at the Select objects: prompt to select the objects that you selected with the SELECT command.

Implied windowing

Implied windowing is equivalent to the Auto selection option listed earlier in this chapter. By default, implied windowing is always active. As a result, implied windowing is useful for selecting objects before or after choosing a command. By carefully choosing which way you create a selection window, you determine how you select objects:

- **From right to left:** If the first window corner is to the right of the second one, you create a crossing window. The crossing window selects all objects that lie entirely or partially within the window.

- **From left to right:** If the first window corner is to the left of the second one, you create a regular selection window. The window selects all objects entirely within the window.

 The drawing used in the following exercise on selecting objects, ab09-e.dwg, is in the Drawings folder on the CD-ROM.

STEPS: Selecting Objects

1. Open ab09-e.dwg from the CD-ROM, as shown in Figure 9.19.

2. Save the file as ab09-07.dwg in your AutoCAD Bible folder. Make sure that OSNAP is on. Set running object snaps for endpoint and perpendicular.

3. Draw a line from ❶ to ❷ in Figure 9.19. You will use this later to illustrate the Last selection option.

4. Type **select** ↵.

5. To select the six-burner stovetop, pick a point near ❸, being careful that the pickbox at the intersection of the crosshairs doesn't touch any object. Transparently zoom in and back out, if necessary. Then move the mouse to ❹ and pick again. The objects that you have chosen appear dashed to indicate that they have been selected.

6. To select the last object that was created — the line drawn in Step 1 — type **l** ↵. It now appears dashed.

7. Turn off OSNAP. To select the interior lines on the kitchen's island by using a fence, type **f** ↵. Then pick points ❺, ❻, and ❼. Press Enter to end the fence.

8. Type **r** ↵ at the Select objects: prompt (the prompt changes to Remove objects:) and pick the line at ❽ to remove the external island line picked in Step 7. At this point, all of the selected items should be dashed, as shown in Figure 9.20.

9. Press Enter to complete the command.

FIGURE 9.19

A kitchen floor plan.

FIGURE 9.20

Kitchen floor plan with all selected items shown with dashed lines.

10. Turn on OSNAP. Start the MOVE command. At the Select objects: prompt, type **p** ↵ and then press Enter again to end object selection. At the Specify base point or [Displacement] <Displacement>: prompt, pick the endpoint at ❾ in Figure 9.19. At the Specify second point of displacement or <use first point as displacement>: prompt, pick the endpoint at ❿. All of the objects move.

11. Save your drawing.

Customizing the selection process

You can customize the way that you select objects. To do so, choose Tools ➪ Options and click the Selection tab, as shown in Figure 9.21.

The Selection tab of the Options dialog box.

Selection preview

The Selection Preview section applies to rollover highlighting and the transparent selection rectangle. You can specify whether you want these effects to appear only if a command is active or even when no command is active (when you are selecting objects before choosing a command).

Click the Visual Effect Settings button to open the Visual Effect Settings dialog box, where you can specify the following settings:

■ **Rollover highlighting:** In the Selection Preview Effect section, you can choose the thicken effect, the dash effect, or both. The default is to show both. Click the Advanced Options button to exclude certain types of objects from the rollover highlighting effect. Some people find this effect distracting, but by customizing these settings, you may find a solution that works for you (other than turning it off).

■ **Selection rectangle:** In the Area Selection Effect section, you can turn the effect off, change the colors for the window and crossing rectangles, and change the opacity percentage.

Noun/verb selection

As you already know, the editing process consists of two parts: using a command, such as COPY or MOVE, and selecting objects. In AutoCAD/AutoCAD LT lingo, *noun* means an object in your drawing. *Verb* refers to a command because a command acts on an object. This option lets you decide whether you want to be able to select objects before starting a command.

In Windows programs, you typically select objects before starting a command. For example, if you're using Microsoft Word and want to erase a sentence, you select the sentence first, and then press Del.

By default, noun/verb selection is available, as shown in the first option in the Selection Modes section of the Selection tab in Figure 9.21. With this option enabled, you can select objects first, without giving up the ability to choose commands first. This gives you maximum flexibility.

The advantage of selecting objects first is that, when you switch between Windows programs, you don't have to change habitual ways of selecting objects. The disadvantage of selecting objects first is that some AutoCAD and AutoCAD LT commands don't let you select objects first, which can be confusing. Also, when you select objects first, grips appear — sometimes obscuring the objects that you need to select.

Commands and Object Selection

Certain commands require you to choose objects in a specific order or require objects that have a certain relationship to each other. For example, the TRIM command (covered in the next chapter) requires that you first select an object to trim to (the cutting edge), and then the object to trim. If you selected the objects in advance, the program wouldn't know which object to trim. Only after you start the TRIM command does AutoCAD or AutoCAD LT know to prompt you exactly for the objects that it needs to complete the command. Other commands require that you select objects that are related in some way. The FILLET command (also covered in the next chapter) joins objects that meet — or would meet if extended — by drawing an arc to create a rounded corner. Here again, the command would be meaningless if, say, you selected three or more objects, so the command requires that you use the command first and then specifically prompts you to select the first object and then the second object.

Many commands allow you to select objects first, but the following are some of the most common:

■ ARRAY	■ ERASE	■ OFFSET
■ BLOCK	■ EXPLODE	■ ROTATE
■ CHANGE	■ HATCH	■ SCALE
■ CHPROP	■ LIST	■ STRETCH
■ COPY	■ MIRROR	■ WBLOCK
■ DVIEW	■ MOVE	

These commands enable you to select any number of objects without restriction, so that selecting the objects first and the command second works well.

Use Shift to add to selection

Use Shift to Add to Selection is the second option in the Selection Modes section of the Selection tab of the Options dialog box. By default, this option is not checked. In AutoCAD and AutoCAD LT, you often select more than one object at a time for editing. Therefore, the default is to simply let you select object after object — when you select a second object, the first object stays selected — so that you can easily select any number of objects you want.

However, Windows programs typically enable you to select only one object at a time. To select multiple objects, you need to hold down Shift as you select. Similarly, if you check the Use Shift to Add to Selection option, then after selecting one object, you must hold down Shift to select any additional objects.

Press and drag

One of the ways to select objects is to create a window that includes a number of objects. You're already familiar with creating a similar window from using ZOOM with the Window option. If the Press and Drag option is checked, you need to pick at one corner of the window and, without releasing the pick button, drag the cursor to the diagonally opposite corner. This type of action is typical of Windows programs.

By default, this option is not checked, which means that to create a window, you pick at one corner of the window, release the mouse button, and pick again at the diagonally opposite corner.

 This setting does not affect the ZOOM Window operation, which always requires two separate picks, one for each corner.

Implied windowing

By default, this option is on. Implied windowing means that, if you pick any point not on an object, AutoCAD or AutoCAD LT assumes that you want to create a selection window. You can then pick the opposite corner to select objects. If you pick the corners from right to left, you get a crossing window. If you pick the corners from left to right, you get a standard selection window. If implied windowing is not on when you pick a point not on an object, the program assumes that you missed some object and gives you this message on the command line:

    0 found

This option applies only when you have started a command and see the Select objects: prompt. If you turn this option off, you can still enter the Crossing or Window selection options manually (by typing c ↵ or w ↵). When selecting objects before starting the command, implied windowing is always on.

Object grouping

Creating groups of objects is discussed in the next chapter. Groups are sets of objects that you name. If object grouping is on (the default) when you select one object in a group, all of the objects in the group are automatically selected. Object grouping is a global setting; you can also set object grouping on or off for individual groups.

Associative hatch

If checked, the Associative Hatch option selects boundary objects when you select a hatch within the boundary. This option is off by default. Checking this option is equivalent to setting the PICKSTYLE system variable to 2. Chapter 16 covers hatches.

Pickbox size

The pickbox is the box that you see at the intersection of the crosshairs when selecting (or picking) objects. The Pickbox Size area lets you set the size of the pickbox.

NOTE If Noun/Verb Selection is off and grips are disabled, no pickbox appears at the intersection of the crosshairs until you start an editing command and the command line displays the `Select objects:` prompt. However, if either Noun/Verb Selection or grips are on, the pickbox is always at the crosshairs, letting you select objects at any time.

Summary

All drawings need to be edited, either as part of the drawing process or to make corrections. In this chapter, you read about:

- Erasing objects
- Moving objects
- Copying objects
- Rotating objects
- Scaling objects
- Using the CHANGE command on lines and circles
- The many ways of selecting objects
- Customizing the object-selection features

The next chapter covers the more-advanced editing commands and options.

Chapter 10

Editing Your Drawing with Advanced Tools

This chapter completes the discussion of geometric editing commands — covering the more complex commands used to refine the details of your drawing. These commands enable you to copy, move, resize, break, and cover objects, as well as construct corners. I also discuss grips, which make it easy to move, mirror, rotate, scale, and stretch objects, and I explain how to double-click and use the Properties palette to edit objects. I end the chapter with a discussion of three ways to control the selection of objects — groups, filters, and the Quick Select feature.

Many of the instructions in this chapter use the Modify toolbar; if it is not displayed, right-click any toolbar button and choose Modify from the list of toolbars.

AUTOCAD ONLY Although you can use the editing tools that I describe in this chapter in a 3D environment, this chapter assumes that you are working in a 2D environment. (AutoCAD LT doesn't offer a 3D environment.) To make sure you're in a 2D environment, set the workspace to AutoCAD Classic or 2D Drafting & Annotation (from the Workspaces toolbar drop-down list) and set the visual style to 2D Wireframe (View ⌐ Visual Styles ⌐ 2D Wireframe). If you still see the Z axis on the UCS icon, choose View ⌐ 3D Views ⌐ Top. Another method is to set the workspace to AutoCAD Classic or 2D Drafting & Annotation, and then start a new drawing based on the default `acad.dwt` template.

Copying and Moving Objects

Three commands enable you to copy objects in very specific ways. MIRROR creates a mirror image. ARRAY copies objects in a rectangular or circular pattern. OFFSET creates parallel objects. Although these commands make copies of objects, they produce a result that would be difficult or impossible to produce simply by using the COPY command. The ALIGN and 3DALIGN commands move objects by aligning them with other objects in the drawing.

Using the MIRROR command

Many drawings have symmetrical elements. Often, especially in mechanical drawings, you can create one-half or one-quarter of a model and complete it simply by mirroring what you have drawn.

 To mirror, select an object or objects and then choose Mirror from the Modify toolbar or from the 2D Draw control panel of the Dashboard. Alternatively, choose Mirror from the Modify toolbar or from the 2D Draw control panel of the Dashboard and then select an object or objects.

The command prompts you for the first and second points of the mirror line. This is an imaginary line across which the command creates the mirrored object. The length of the line is irrelevant — only its start point and direction are important.

 Most mirror lines are orthogonal. Therefore, after you specify the first mirror point, you can turn on ORTHO and move the mouse in the direction of the second point. You can then quickly pick the second point. Polar tracking can also easily guide you to specify an orthogonal mirror line.

The command then asks if you want to erase the source objects. The source objects are the objects you have selected to mirror. If you want to keep them, type **n** ↵ or press Enter. You keep the source objects when you're building a symmetrical model and want the mirror image to be added to the original object(s). Type **y** ↵ when you want to edit an object (change its orientation) so that only the mirror image is retained in the drawing.

The drawing used in the following exercise on mirroring objects, ab07-02.dwg, is in the Results folder on the DVD.

STEPS: Mirroring Objects

1. Open ab07-02.dwg from the Results folder of the DVD. If you completed the exercise on arcs in Chapter 7, you can open this drawing from your AutoCAD Bible folder.

2. Save the file as ab10-01.dwg in your AutoCAD Bible folder. Make sure OSNAP is on. Set a running object snap for intersections only.

3. Choose Erase on the Modify toolbar or from the 2D Draw control panel of the Dashboard. At the Select objects: prompt, pick the line and two arcs to the bottom-right of the two centerlines and then press Enter. The resulting model should look like Figure 10.1.

 4. Choose Mirror from the Modify toolbar or from the 2D Draw control panel of the Dashboard. At the Select objects: prompt, pick the remaining exterior line and two arcs, and press Enter.

5. At the Specify first point of mirror line: prompt, pick intersection ❶ in Figure 10.1. At the Specify second point of mirror line: prompt, pick intersection ❷.

6. The command prompts: Erase source objects? [Yes/No] <N>: Press Enter to accept the default, No.

7. Again choose Mirror from the Modify toolbar or from the 2D Draw control panel of the Dashboard. At the Select objects: prompt, type **p** ↵ to pick the original lines. Then pick the new exterior line and two arcs, and then press Enter.

8. At the Specify first point of mirror line: prompt, pick intersection ❷. At the Specify second point of mirror line: prompt, pick intersection ❸. Press Enter again at the Erase source objects? [Yes/No] <N>: prompt.

9. The command completes the mounting plate. Save your drawing. It should look like Figure 10.2.

FIGURE 10.1

A partially completed mounting plate.

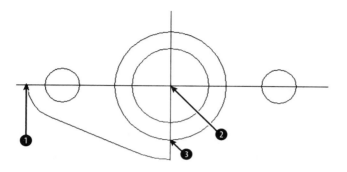

FIGURE 10.2

The completed mounting plate.

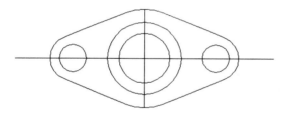

Using the ARRAY command

The ARRAY command creates a rectangular or polar (circular) pattern by copying the object(s) you select as many times as you specify. The ARRAY command is a powerful drawing tool. It can quickly create large numbers of objects, thus saving a huge amount of time and effort.

Rectangular arrays

A rectangular array creates a grid of rows and columns of one or more objects. Figure 10.3 shows an example of a rectangular array. To create a rectangular array, follow these steps:

FIGURE 10.3

The garage door was drawn with one panel, as shown on the left side. A rectangular array created the rest of the door panels, as shown on the right.

Thanks to Henry Dearborn, AIA, Fairfield, Iowa, for this drawing.

1. Select the object or objects and choose Array from the Modify toolbar or from the 2D Draw control panel of the Dashboard. Alternatively, choose Array from the Modify toolbar or from the 2D Draw control panel of the Dashboard and select the object or objects. The Array dialog box opens, as shown in Figure 10.4.

FIGURE 10.4

The Array dialog box.

2. Click Rectangular Array at the upper-left corner of the dialog box (if it is not already selected).

3. If you've already selected one or more objects, the dialog box indicates the number of selected objects. If you haven't selected any object, click Select Objects to return to your drawing and select objects. Press Enter to end object selection and return to the dialog box.

4. In the Rows and Columns text boxes, type the total number of rows and columns that you want.

5. Type the distance you want between the rows in the Row Offset text box. The preview panel doesn't display any change when you change the row or column offsets.

6. Type the distance you want between the columns in the Column Offset text box.

7. If you want to specify the offsets by picking points on your screen, click one of the following buttons:

   ▪ Pick Both Offsets

 ▪ Pick Row Offset

 ▪ Pick Column Offset

 8. If you want to change the angle of the array, type an angle in the Angle of Array text box. The preview panel displays the results of this value. To specify the angle by picking, click the Pick Angle of Array button.

9. To preview the array, click Preview. Then choose Accept to create the array, Modify to return to the Array dialog box, or Cancel to end the command.

10. To create the array, click OK.

If you change the Snap angle or the UCS (as explained in Chapter 8), AutoCAD and AutoCAD LT create the rectangular array at the angle of the snap or UCS.

 If you need to create a number of copies of an object along a straight path, use a one-column or one-row array instead of the COPY command. It's faster and easier.

Polar (circular) arrays

A polar array creates copies of one or more objects arrayed in a circle around a center point. An example of a polar array is shown in Figure 10.5.

FIGURE 10.5

The pulley was drawn with one spoke, as shown on the left. A polar array created the additional spokes.

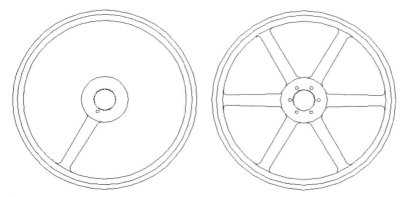

Thanks to Robert Mack of the Dexter Company, Fairfield, Iowa, for this drawing.

To create a polar array, follow these steps:

1. Select the object or objects and choose Array from the Modify toolbar or from the 2D Draw control panel of the Dashboard. Alternatively, choose Array from the Modify toolbar or from the 2D Draw control panel of the Dashboard and select the object or objects. The Array dialog box opens.

2. Click Polar Array at the top of the dialog box (if it is not already selected).

3. If you've already selected one or more objects, the dialog box indicates the number of selected objects. If you haven't selected any objects, click Select objects to return to your drawing and select objects. Press Enter to end object selection and return to the dialog box.

4. Specify the center point by typing X and Y coordinates, or click the Pick Center Point button. If you selected an object first, check that the center point displayed is what you want.

5. Select the two items that you want to specify from the Method drop-down box. You can choose any two from the three choices:

    *   **Total Number of Items:** Sets the total number of items in the resulting array, including the one that you are arraying.

    *   **Angle to Fill:** Sets the number of degrees that the polar array covers. For example, to array around half of a circle, specify 180°.

    *   **Angle Between Items:** Specifies the number of degrees between each item in the polar array.

6. Complete the values of the two items that you specified. You can click the buttons to pick the angle to fill or the angle between items on the screen.

7. Check the Rotate Items as Copied check box to rotate the objects that you are arraying. Uncheck the box to leave them unrotated.

8. Click Preview to preview the array. Then choose Accept to create the array, Modify to return to the dialog box, or Cancel to cancel the command.

9. Click OK to create the array.

You can specify which point on the last object selected that AutoCAD and AutoCAD LT uses to array the objects. The command makes a calculation of the distance from the center point of the array to a base point on the last object selected. Otherwise, the command uses a default point based on the type of object selected. Table 10.1 lists the default base points. If you are arraying more than one object, you may not obtain the result you want without specifying the base point. Even for one object, you may want to change the base point that is used.

To specify the base point, click the More button at the bottom of the dialog box. The dialog box opens up to display the Object Base Point section. Uncheck Set to Object's Default. You can then either type in coordinates or, more likely, click the Pick Base Point button and use an object snap to pick the desired point on an object. The preview box adjusts according to your choice but, because the preview only shows rectangles in the place of your object, the display may not be very helpful.

AUTOCAD ONLY You can use the Express Tools COPYM command to enhance your copying options. Choose Express ➪ Modify ➪ Multiple Copy. You can create evenly spaced copies between two points, copy objects according to a specified measurement, and create arrays. For information on installing the Express Tools, see Appendix A.

TABLE 10.1

Object Base Points for Arrays

Type of Object	Default Base Point
Arc, circle, or ellipse	Center point
Polygon or rectangle	First corner
Line, polyline (2D or 3D), ray, spline, or donut	Starting point
Text (single-line or paragraph), block	Insertion point
Construction line (xline)	Midpoint
Region	Grip point

ON the DVD-ROM The drawing used in the following exercise on arraying objects, `ab10-a.dwg`, is in the `Drawings` folder on the DVD.

STEPS: Arraying Objects

1. Open `ab10-a.dwg` from the DVD.
2. Save the file as `ab10-02.dwg` in your `AutoCAD Bible` folder. It looks like Figure 10.6. OSNAP should be on. Set center and intersection running object snaps.

FIGURE 10.6

A partially completed mounting bracket.

3. Choose Array on the Modify toolbar or from the 2D Draw control panel of the Dashboard. The Array dialog box opens.
4. Click the Select Objects button of the Array dialog box. In the drawing, pick the horizontal centerline ❶ in Figure 10.6 and then press Enter. You return to the dialog box.
5. Make sure that Rectangular Array is selected at the top of the dialog box.
6. In the Rows text box, type **4**. In the Columns text box, type **1**.

7. In the Row Offset text box, type **1**. (You don't need to specify the column offset because you are creating only one column.)

8. Click Preview. You should see a total of four horizontal lines, as shown in Figure 10.7. Click Accept in the small dialog box that appears. (If you don't see the four lines, click Modify and recheck the settings in the Array dialog box.)

9. To add the holes to the pattern, again choose Array from the Modify toolbar or from the 2D Draw control panel of the Dashboard.

10. Click the Select Objects button in the Array dialog box. In the drawing, pick circle ❷ in Figure 10.6 and then press Enter.

11. Back in the Array dialog box, type **4** in the Rows text box and type **2** in the Columns text box.

12. Click the Pick Both Offsets button. In the drawing, pick the center of circle ❷ and the intersection of centerlines near ❸ in Figure 10.6. (You can also pick the intersection of centerlines at the center of circle ❷. If necessary, press Tab until you see the object snap that you want.)

13. Click Preview to preview the array. If the circles look like Figure 10.7, click Accept. Otherwise, click Modify and check your settings. After you're done, the command arrays the holes to fit the centerlines.

14. To create a six-hole bolt circle, pick hole ❹ in Figure 10.6.

15. Choose Array from the Modify toolbar or from the 2D Draw control panel of the Dashboard.

16. In the Array dialog box, choose Polar Array.

17. Next to the Center Point text boxes, click the Pick Center Point button. In the drawing, pick the center of the large circle at ❺ in Figure 10.6.

18. The Method should read "Total number of items & Angle to fill." In the Total Number of Items text box, type **6**. In the Angle to Fill text box, type **360**.

19. Click Preview to see the array. It should look like Figure 10.7. If it does, click Accept. Otherwise, click Modify and recheck the settings in the Array dialog box. AutoCAD or AutoCAD LT completes the mounting bracket.

20. Save your drawing. It should look like Figure 10.7.

FIGURE 10.7

The completed mounting bracket.

Offsetting objects

The OFFSET command creates lines or curves parallel to one existing object. The beauty of this command is apparent when you start to create complex objects, such as polylines, which are covered in Chapter 16. Polygons and rectangles are *polylines,* which means that all of the line segments are one object. For example, using OFFSET, you can create concentric polygons in one step. Figure 10.8 shows two concentric polygons. The outside polygon was created with the POLYGON command, and the inside polygon was created by using OFFSET.

FIGURE 10.8

Use OFFSET to create concentric polygons.

 To offset an object, choose Offset from the Modify toolbar or from the 2D Draw control panel of the Dashboard.

The command responds with the following list of settings and prompt:

```
Current settings: Erase source=No  Layer=Source  OFFSETGAPTYPE=0
Specify offset distance or [Through/Erase/Layer] <Through>:
```

The settings show how the OFFSET command's options will function. Set the Erase option to Yes to erase the selected object and leave only the offset. Use the Layer option to specify if you want the new object to be on the same layer as the source object or on the current layer.

NOTE The OFFSETGAPTYPE system variable determines what the command does to close gaps when you offset closed polylines. By default (a value of 0), AutoCAD extends the polyline segments. A value of 1 fills the gaps with arcs, and a value of 2 fills the gaps with chamfered corners. (I cover chamfers later in this chapter.)

The OFFSET command offers two ways to specify the offset:

- If you type an offset distance, the command responds with the Select object to offset or [Exit/Undo] <Exit>: prompt. You can select one object. Then the Specify point on side to offset or [Exit/Multiple/Undo] <Exit>: prompt appears. Pick a point to indicate on which side of the object you want to create the offset copy. The command creates the offset and continues to show the Select object to offset or [Exit/Undo] <Exit>: prompt so that you can offset other objects by using the same offset distance. Press Enter to exit the command.

- If you want to indicate a *through point* (a point that the offset passes through, such as an object snap on another object), type **t** ↵ or right-click and choose Through from the shortcut menu. The command displays the `Select object to offset or [Exit/Undo] <Exit>:` prompt. Pick one object. At the `Specify through point or [Exit/Multiple/Undo] <Exit>:` prompt, pick a point through which you want the offset to go to create the offset.

Use the new Undo option if you don't like the result of the offset. After you offset an object, the prompt repeats so that you can offset additional objects. Press Enter to end the command.

 The drawing used in the following exercise on using the OFFSET command, `ab10-b.dwg`, is in the `Drawings` folder on the DVD.

STEPS: Using the OFFSET Command

1. Open `ab10-b.dwg` from the DVD.
2. Save the file as `ab10-03.dwg` in your `AutoCAD Bible` folder. It looks like Figure 10.9. Set a running object snap for center, and turn on OSNAP.

FIGURE 10.9

A tension arm for a commercial dryer.

Thanks to Robert Mack of the Dexter Company, Fairfield, IA for this drawing.

3. Choose Offset on the Modify toolbar or from the 2D Draw control panel of the Dashboard. Follow the prompts:

```
Specify offset distance or [Through/Erase/Layer] <Through>: ↵ or
specify the Through option if it does not appear as the default.
Select object to offset or [Exit/Undo] <Exit>:
Pick ❶ in Figure 10.9.
Specify through point or [Exit/Multiple/Undo] <Exit>: Pick the center
of ❷.
        Select object to offset or [Exit/Undo] <Exit>: ↵
```

This action copies the centerline through the upper circles.

4. Again choose Offset from the Modify toolbar or from the 2D Draw control panel of the Dashboard. At the `Specify offset distance or [Through/Erase/Layer]` `<Through>:` prompt, type **4-19/64** ↵. Pick the centerline ❸ at the `Select object to` `offset or [Exit/Undo] <Exit>:` prompt, and then click near ❹ at the `Specify point` `on side to offset or [Exit/Multiple/Undo] <Exit>:` prompt. Press Enter to end the command. The vertical centerline appears 4-19/64 units to the right of the original.

5. Save your drawing. It should look like Figure 10.10.

FIGURE 10.10

The completed tension arm.

Aligning objects

The ALIGN and 3DALIGN commands let you move and rotate an object or objects in one procedure. They are useful in both 2D and 3D environments. By specifying where selected points on an object move, you can align the object with other objects in your drawing, as shown in Figure 10.11. You can align in two ways:

- **ALIGN command:** This command prompts you by point. You specify the first source point (on the object you're aligning), then the first destination point (where that source point will end up). Then you specify the second set of source and destination points. For 3D, you go on to a third set. Finally, you can scale the selected object to match the destination points.

- **3DALIGN command:** This command prompts you by object. You specify two or three points on the source object, then the points at the destination location. As you specify destination points, you see the object move and align in real time. You cannot scale the object. See Chapter 24 for an exercise that uses the 3DALIGN command in 3D editing.

Aligning requires several steps. Even so, it can save time when you need to move and rotate at the same time, especially if you don't know the rotation angle that you need.

AUTOCAD ONLY AutoCAD LT doesn't include the ALIGN or the 3DALIGN command. Instead, you would need to use a combination of the MOVE and ROTATE commands. The Reference option of the ROTATE command would be helpful to align objects. I discuss the MOVE and ROTATE commands in Chapter 9.

FIGURE 10.11

Aligning a door with a wall.

Before   After

Using the ALIGN command

If you prefer to think, "This point will go here and that point will go there," use the ALIGN command. You can also scale the object that you're aligning. Choose Modify ⇨ 3D Operations ⇨ Align and select an object or objects. You can also select the object or objects first. Then follow these steps:

1. The prompt asks for the first source point. Specify a point, usually an object snap on the object that you want to move.

2. The prompt asks for the first destination point. Specify the point where you want the first source point to end up.

3. The prompt asks for the second source point. If you press Enter, AutoCAD simply moves the selected objects. To continue to align, specify another point, usually another object snap on the object that you want to move.

4. The prompt asks for the second destination point. Specify the point where you want the second source point to end up.

5. The prompt asks for the third source point. You use this for 3D alignment, to specify how you want to rotate the object in the third dimension. For 2D alignment, press Enter to continue the command.

6. The prompt displays the `Scale objects based on alignment points? [Yes/No] <N>:` prompt. If the distances between the source and destination points are not the same, type **y** if you want to scale the original object so that the source and destination points match exactly.

Using the 3DALIGN command

If you like to think, "These are the points on the source object that I want to align and then these are the destination points that I want to align them to," and if you don't need to scale your object, use the 3DALIGN command. To align an object using the 3DALIGN command, choose 3D Align on the Modeling toolbar or choose Modify ➪ 3D Operations ➪ 3DAlign and select an object or objects. You can also select the object or objects first.

Then follow these steps:

1. The message, `Specify source plane and orientation`, explains that you now need to specify the source points, which define the plane and orientation of the source object. The first prompt asks for the base point. Specify a point, usually an object snap on the object that you want to move. This point will match the first destination point. You can use the Copy option to make a copy of the object rather than move it. If you use the Continue option here, you only move the object.

2. The prompt asks for the second point. Specify another point on the *source* object. This point will match the second destination point. Use the Continue option to start specifying destination points.

3. The prompt asks for the third point. In 3D work, you need the third point to specify the plane.

4. The message, `Specify destination plane and orientation`, explains that you now need to specify the destination points for the base points you just specified. The prompt asks for the first destination point. Specify the point where you want the first base point to end up. As soon as you do this, the object moves to match the first base and destination points so that you can see how the object will look.

5. The prompt asks for the second destination point. The second base point will match this point. If you press Enter at this point, the command aligns the object with the X axis of the current UCS.

6. The prompt asks for the third destination point. You use this for 3D alignment, to specify how you want to rotate the object in the third dimension. For 2D alignment, you can place the cursor on either side of the aligning line you specified, to mirror the object in either direction. When you see the direction that you want, press Enter to end the command and align the object.

The following exercise uses the 3DALIGN command to align objects.

 The drawing used in the following exercise on aligning objects in two dimensions, `ab10-c.dwg`, is in the `Drawings` folder on the DVD.

STEPS: Aligning Objects in Two Dimensions

1. Open `ab10-c.dwg` from the DVD.
2. Save the file as `ab10-04.dwg` in your `AutoCAD Bible` folder. It looks like Figure 10.12.

FIGURE 10.12

A base assembly for a commercial washing machine.

Thanks to Robert Mack of the Dexter Company, Fairfield, Iowa, for this drawing.

3. Choose Modify ⇨ 3D Operation ⇨ 3D Align and follow the prompts:

```
Select objects: Select the horizontal angle by using a window,
picking near ❶ and then ❷. Press Enter to end object selection. This
angle needs to be aligned with the long, diagonal support angle.
Specify base point or [Copy]: Pick the endpoint at ❸ in Figure
10.12.
Specify second point or [Continue] <C>: Pick the endpoint at ❺.
Specify third point or [Continue] <C>: ↵
Specify destination plane and orientation ... Specify first
destination point: Pick the endpoint at ❹.
Specify second destination point or [eXit] <X>: Pick the endpoint at ❻.
Specify third destination point or [eXit] <X>: Place the cursor to
the right of the new location of the horizontal angle so that it is
aligned as shown in Figure 10.13, and press Enter.
```

4. Save your drawing. It should look like Figure 10.13.

FIGURE 10.13

The washing machine base.

Resizing commands

Four editing commands resize objects in specific ways. The TRIM and EXTEND commands change the endpoint of an object to meet another object. LENGTHEN lets you lengthen or shorten a line, polyline, arc, or elliptical arc. STRETCH is used to stretch (longer or shorter) a group of objects, letting you change their direction at the same time.

Trimming objects

As you edit a drawing, you may find that lines or arcs that once perfectly met other objects now hang over. To trim an object, you must first specify the *cutting edge,* which defines the point at which to cut the object you want to trim. You define the cutting edge by selecting an object. You can select several cutting edges and several objects to trim at one time, as shown in Figure 10.14. When you select an object to trim, you must pick the object on the side that you want trimmed (not on the side that you want to remain). A common use for the TRIM command is to create intersections of walls in architectural floor plans.

TIP While using the TRIM command, you can switch to extending objects by pressing the Shift key as you select objects to trim.

The object you want to trim does not have to actually intersect the cutting edge. You can trim an object to a cutting edge that would intersect the object if extended. This is called *trimming to an implied intersection,* an example of which is shown in Figure 10.15.

213

FIGURE 10.14

Trimming two objects by using two cutting edges.

Before trimming   After trimming

FIGURE 10.15

Trimming two arcs to an implied intersection.

Before trimming   After trimming

You can trim arcs, circles, ellipses, elliptical arcs, lines, polylines, xlines, rays, and splines. You can use polylines, arcs, circles, ellipses, elliptical arcs, lines, rays, regions, splines, text, or xlines as cutting edges. An object can be used as both a cutting edge and an object to be trimmed in the same trimming process. You can also trim to objects within blocks. (Chapter 18 covers blocks.)

 To trim an object, choose Trim from the Modify toolbar or from the 2D Draw control panel of the Dashboard. The command displays the Current settings: Projection=UCS, Edge=None Select cutting edges . . . Select objects or <select all>: prompt. The prompt lets you know the values of the two system variables that affect trimming. The Projection setting is used only for 3D models and can trim based on either the current UCS or the current view. The Edge setting is used for implied intersections. When Edge is set to Extend, the command trims to the implied intersection of the cutting edge and the object to be trimmed. At this prompt, pick the object(s) that you want to use as a cutting edge or press Enter to select all objects as edges. Press Enter to end object selection.

You can trim to an actual or an *implied* intersection (an intersection that would exist if objects were extended):

- If you want to trim to an actual intersection, at the `Select object to trim or shift-select to extend or [Fence/Crossing/Project/Edge/eRase/Undo]:` prompt, select the objects that you want to trim. You can use the Fence option to draw lines that criss-cross the objects that you want to trim. Use the Crossing option to select the objects with a crossing window. Be sure to pick each object between the cutting edge and the end you want to trim off. Press Enter to end object selection. This action trims the object(s).

- If you want to trim to an implied intersection, at the `Select object to trim or shift-select to extend or [Fence/Crossing/Project/Edge/eRase/Undo]:` prompt, type **e** ↵. The Extend option responds with the `Enter an implied edge extension mode [Extend/No extend] <No extend>:` prompt. Type **e** ↵. Then select the objects that you want to trim at the `Select object to trim or shift-select to extend or [Fence/Crossing/Project/Edge/eRase/Undo]:` prompt. Be sure to pick each object at or near the end that you want to trim. Press Enter to end object selection and trim the object(s).

Use the Undo option if the results of the trim are not what you want. You can then continue to select objects to trim. The new eRase option lets you erase an object instead of trimming it, without leaving the TRIM command.

 The drawing used in the following exercise on trimming objects, ab10-d.dwg, is in the Drawings folder on the DVD.

STEPS: Trimming Objects

1. Open ab10-d.dwg from the DVD.

2. Save the file as ab10-05.dwg in your AutoCAD Bible folder. It looks like Figure 10.16.

3. Start the TRIM command. At the `Select objects or <select all>:` prompt, pick lines at ❶ and ❷ in Figure 10.16, and then press Enter.

4. At the `Select object to trim or shift-select to extend or [Fence/Crossing/Project/Edge/eRase/Undo]:` prompt, again pick lines at ❶ and ❷ in Figure 10.16. Be sure to pick them outside the intersection, as shown. Press Enter to end the command.

   The command trims the lines. Each line is used as the cutting edge for the other line.

5. Again choose Trim on the Modify toolbar or from the 2D Draw control panel of the Dashboard. At the `Select objects or <select all>:` prompt, pick the line at ❸ in Figure 10.16 and press Enter.

6. At the `Select object to trim or shift-select to extend or [Fence/Crossing/Project/Edge/eRase/Undo]:` prompt, right-click and choose Edge. Then right-click and choose Extend at the `Enter an implied edge extension mode [Extend/No extend] <Extend>:` prompt.

7. Pick the line at ❹ in Figure 10.16 to trim the line. Press Enter to end the command.

8. Start the TRIM command again. At the `Select objects or <select all>:` prompt, pick ❺ and press Enter. At the `Select object to trim or shift-select to extend or [Fence/Crossing/Project/Edge/eRase/Undo]:` prompt, pick the lines at ❻ and ❼. Press Enter to end the command.

9. Save your drawing. It should look like Figure 10.17.

FIGURE 10.16

A schematic of an air compressor.

FIGURE 10.17

The completed clamp in two views.

AUTOCAD ONLY Express Tools contains a command, EXTRIM, which is available on the command line. EXTRIM can use a polyline, line, circle, arc, ellipse, image, or text as the cutting line. You specify one side of the cutting object, and EXTRIM trims everything on that side. For example, if you choose a closed polyline and pick inside it, every object inside the polyline is trimmed.

Extending objects

The EXTEND command has similar prompts to the TRIM command, but instead of trimming objects to a cutting edge, it extends them to a *boundary edge* (see Figure 10.18). As with TRIM, when you select an object to extend, you must pick the object on the side that you want extended (not on the side that you want left as is).

The object you want to extend does not have to actually intersect the boundary edge after its extension. You can extend an object to a boundary edge that would intersect the extended object if it were longer. This is called extending to an implied intersection, an example of which is shown in Figure 10.19.

FIGURE 10.18

Extending two lines by using an arc as the boundary edge.

Pick points
on lines

Boundary edge →

FIGURE 10.19

Extending a line to an implied intersection.

Boundary edge   Pick point on line

You can extend arcs, elliptical arcs, lines, open polylines, and rays. You can use polylines, arcs, circles, ellipses, elliptical arcs, lines, rays, regions, splines, text, or xlines as boundary edges. An object can be used as both a boundary edge and an object to be extended in the same extending process.

217

While using the EXTEND command, you can switch to trimming objects by pressing the Shift key as you select objects to trim.

To extend an object, choose Extend from the Modify toolbar or from the 2D Draw control panel of the Dashboard. The command displays the `Current settings: Projection=UCS, Edge=Extend Select boundary edges ... Select objects or <select all>:` prompt. The prompt lets you know the values of the two settings that affect how the object is extended. Projection is used only for 3D models and can extend based on either the current UCS or the current view. Edge is used for implied intersections. When Edge is set to Extend, the command extends to the implied intersection of the boundary edge and the object to be extended. At this prompt, pick the object(s) that you want to use as the boundary edge(s) or press Enter to select all objects. Press Enter to end object selection. You can extend to an actual or implied intersection:

- If the extension will result in an actual intersection, at the `Select object to extend or shift-select to trim or [Fence/Crossing/Project/Edge/Undo]:` prompt, select objects to extend. You can use the Fence option to draw lines that criss-cross the objects you want to extend. Use the Crossing option to select the objects with a crossing window. Be sure to pick each object at the end that you want to extend. Press Enter to end object selection and extend the object(s).

- If you want to extend to an implied intersection, at the prompt, right-click and choose Edge. The option responds with the `Enter an implied edge extension mode [Extend/No extend] <Extend>:` prompt. Right-click and choose Extend. Then select the objects that you want to extend at the `Select object to extend or shift-select to trim or [Fence/Crossing/Project/Edge/Undo]:` prompt. Be sure to pick each object at the end that you want to extend. Press Enter to end object selection and extend the object(s).

Use the Undo option if the results of the extension are not what you want. You can then continue to select objects to extend. You can use the Fence object selection method to select objects to extend the side of the object that the fence line crosses.

The drawing used in the following exercise on extending objects, `ab10-e.dwg`, is in the `Drawings` folder on the DVD.

STEPS: Extending Objects

1. Open `ab10-e.dwg` from the DVD.

2. Save the file as `ab10-06.dwg` in your `AutoCAD Bible` folder. It looks like Figure 10.20.

3. Choose Extend on the Modify toolbar or from the 2D Draw control panel of the Dashboard. At the `Select objects or <select all>:` prompt, pick the line at ❶ in Figure 10.20 and then press Enter.

4. At the `Select object to extend or shift-select to trim or [Fence/Crossing/Project/Edge/Undo]:` prompt, pick the line at ❷ in Figure 10.20. Press Enter to finish selecting objects. The command extends the line.

5. Repeat the EXTEND command. At the `Select objects or <select all>:` prompt, pick the lines at ❸ and ❹ in Figure 10.20 and then press Enter.

6. At the `Select object to extend or shift-select to trim or [Fence/Crossing/Project/Edge/Undo]:` prompt, right-click and choose Edge. Right-click and choose Extend at the `Extend/No extend <No extend>:` prompt.

FIGURE 10.20

An electrical schematic.

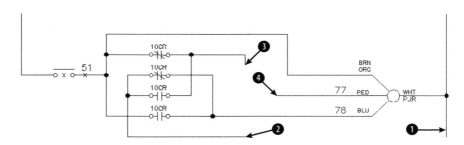

7. Pick lines ❸ and ❹ in Figure 10.20 again at the points shown. The lines extend to meet. Press Enter to end the command.

8. Save your drawing. It should look like Figure 10.21.

FIGURE 10.21

The completed electrical schematic.

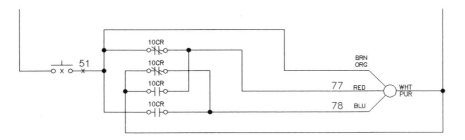

Lengthening objects

The LENGTHEN command both lengthens and shortens. It works on open objects, such as lines, arcs, and polylines, and also increases or decreases the included angle of arcs. (You can change the length of an arc as well as its included angle by using LENGTHEN.) AutoCAD and AutoCAD LT offer several ways of defining the new length or included angle. Use LENGTHEN if you want to lengthen or shorten an object when there is no available intersecting edge or boundary to use with TRIM or EXTEND.

In the LENGTHEN command, the length of an arc is measured along its circumference. Don't confuse this with the Length of Chord option of the ARC command, which refers to the length of a line stretched from one endpoint of the arc to the other endpoint.

To lengthen (or shorten) an object, choose Modify ⇨ Lengthen. You cannot select objects before the LENGTHEN command. The command responds with the `Select an object or [DElta/Percent/Total/DYnamic]:` prompt. Choose one of the following options:

- **Select object:** This is the default. However, its purpose is to display the current measurements of the object. This can help you to decide how to define the final length or angle of the object. The current length is displayed at the command line, and the previous prompt is repeated.

- **DElta:** Right-click and choose DElta. *Delta* means the change, or difference, between the current and new length or included angle. The option responds with the `Enter delta length or [Angle] <0.0000>:` prompt. If you want to change an included angle, right-click and choose Angle. Then type the change in the included angle. Otherwise, simply type the change in the length of the object. A positive number increases the length or included angle. A negative number decreases the length or included angle.

- **Percent:** Right-click and choose Percent. At the `Enter percentage length <100.0000>:` prompt, type in what percent of the original object you want the final object to be. Amounts over 100 lengthen the object. Amounts under 100 shorten the object. You cannot change an included angle using this option.

- **Total:** Right-click and choose Total. At the `Specify total length or [Angle] <1.0000)>:` prompt, you can either choose the Angle suboption, as described for the DElta option, or use the default total-length option. Either way, you enter the total angle or length you want.

- **DYnamic:** Right-click and choose DYnamic. This option lets you drag the endpoint of the object closest to where you picked it. You can use an object snap to specify the new endpoint.

After you've used an option to specify the length you want, you see the `Select an object to change or [Undo]:` prompt. Here you select the object you want to change. Be sure to pick the endpoint of the object for which you want to make the change.

The same prompt continues so that you can pick other objects by using the same length specifications. Choose Undo to undo the last change. Press Enter to end the command.

The drawing used in the following exercise on lengthening and shortening objects, `ab10-f.dwg`, is in the `Drawings` folder on the DVD.

STEPS: Lengthening and Shortening Objects

1. Open `ab10-f.dwg` from the DVD.

2. Save the file as `ab10-07.dwg` in your `AutoCAD Bible` folder. It is a capacitor symbol from an electrical schematic, as shown in Figure 10.22.

3. Choose Modify ⇨ Lengthen and follow the prompts:

```
Select an object or [DElta/Percent/Total/DYnamic]: Pick the line at
❶ in Figure 10.22.
Current length: 0.200
Select an object or [DElta/Percent/Total/DYnamic]: Right-click and
choose Delta.
Enter delta length or [Angle] <0.000>: .07 ↵
Select an object to change or [Undo]: Pick the line at ❶ in Figure
10.22.
Select an object to change or [Undo]: ↵
```

This action lengthens the line.

FIGURE 10.22

A poorly drawn capacitor symbol.

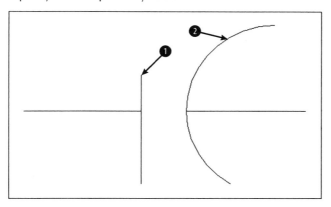

4. Start the LENGTHEN command again and follow the prompts:

```
Select an object or [DElta/Percent/Total/DYnamic]: Pick the arc at ❷
in Figure 10.22.
Current length: 0.407, included angle: 150
Select an object or [DElta/Percent/Total/DYnamic]: Right-click and
choose Total.
Specify total length or [Angle] <1.000)>:)>: Right-click and choose
Angle.

Specify total angle <57>: 120 ↵
Select an object to change or [Undo]: Pick the arc at ❷ in Figure
10.22.
Select an object to change or [Undo]: ↵
```

This action shortens the arc.

5. Save your drawing. It should look like Figure 10.23.

FIGURE 10.23

The completed capacitor symbol.

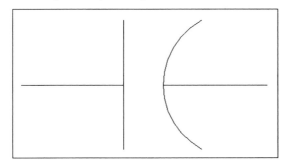

Stretching objects

The STRETCH command is generally used to stretch groups of objects. For example, you can use this command to enlarge a room in a floor plan. You can also shrink objects. You can change not only the length of the objects but the angle as well. You use a crossing window to choose the objects to be stretched. All objects that cross the boundaries of the crossing window are stretched. All objects that lie entirely within the crossing window are merely moved. Successful stretching involves precise placement of the crossing window. Figure 10.24 shows the process of stretching a garage. Note that the walls that cross the boundaries of the crossing window are stretched. However, the dormer that is entirely within the crossing window is just moved. This maintains the integrity of the model.

You cannot stretch circles, text, or blocks. You can stretch arcs, although the results may not be what you expect.

The real power of the STRETCH command is in stretching a number of objects at once. However, you can also stretch one line. The results are similar to using the CHANGE command to change the endpoint of a line or to editing with grips (discussed later in this chapter).

FIGURE 10.24

Stretching a garage.

Before stretching   After stretching

 To stretch objects, choose Stretch from the Modify toolbar or from the 2D Draw control panel of the Dashboard. The command responds with the `Select objects to stretch by crossing-window or crossing-polygon . . .` instruction and then the `Select objects:` prompt. Create the crossing window and select the objects that you want to stretch. (You can also use a crossing polygon — type **cp** at the `Select objects:` prompt.) After completing the crossing window, check to see which objects are highlighted. This helps you avoid unwanted results. You can use the object selection Remove option (type **r** ↵ at the command prompt) to remove objects by picking the objects that you don't want to stretch or move. (Then use the Add option [type **a** ↵] to continue selecting objects if necessary.)

The STRETCH command remembers the most recent displacement throughout a session. To stretch an object by the same displacement that you most recently used, press Enter at the `Specify base point or [Displacement] <Displacement>:` prompt. At the `Specify displacement <2.0000, 3.0000, 0.0000>:` prompt, you see in angled brackets the last displacement that you used. Press Enter to stretch the object using this displacement.

 You can use multiple crossing windows to select the objects that you want to stretch. You can also pick to select objects, although these objects are simply moved.

When you've finished selecting objects, you see the `Specify base point or Displacement <Displacement>:` prompt. This step is just like moving objects, and you can respond in two ways.

- Pick a base point. At the `Specify second point or <use first point as displacement>:` prompt, pick a second point. Object snap and PolarSnap are helpful for picking these points.
- Type a displacement without using the @ sign. For example, to lengthen the objects by 6 feet in the 0-degree direction, type **6'<0** ↵. Then press Enter at the `Specify second point or <use first point as displacement>:` prompt.

 Usually, you want to stretch at an orthogonal angle. If you're going to stretch by picking, turn ORTHO on. Object snaps, polar tracking, and Snap mode are other helpful drawing aids for stretching.

When specifying a displacement by typing at the keyboard, you can use both positive and negative distances. For example, 6'<180 is the same as –6'<0. Both would stretch the objects 6 feet to the left.

 The drawing used in the following exercise on stretching objects, ab10-g.dwg, is in the Drawings folder on the DVD.

STEPS: Stretching Objects

1. Open ab10-g.dwg from your DVD.
2. Save the file as ab10-08.dwg in your AutoCAD Bible folder. This drawing is the plan view of a garage, as shown in Figure 10.25. Turn on polar tracking by clicking POLAR on the status bar. Click SNAP on the status bar and then right-click SNAP to make sure that PolarSnap is on (the PolarSnap item will be unavailable if it is already on); otherwise, choose PolarSnap. Turn on OSNAP and set a running object snap for endpoints.
3. Choose Stretch from the Modify toolbar or from the 2D Draw control panel of the Dashboard. At the `Select objects:` prompt, pick ❶ in Figure 10.25. At the `Specify opposite corner:` prompt, pick ❷. The prompt notifies you that it found 32 objects. Press Enter to end object selection.
4. At the `Specify base point or [Displacement] <Displacement>:` prompt, pick the endpoint at the bottom-right corner of the garage. At the `Specify second point or <use first point as displacement>:` prompt, move the cursor to the right until you see the polar tracking tooltip. Click when the tooltip says 6'-0"<0. (If you can't find it, type **6',0** ↵. If you're not using Dynamic Input or have Dynamic Input set to absolute coordinates, add the @ symbol first.) This action stretches the garage by 6 feet.
5. Save your drawing. It should look like Figure 10.26.

FIGURE 10.25

A plan view of a garage.

FIGURE 10.26

The longer garage.

Using Construction Commands

Four additional commands are commonly used in the process of constructing models. The BREAK command removes sections of objects at points that you specify. JOIN, a new command, joins co-linear lines, polylines, arcs, elliptical arcs, or splines. CHAMFER creates corners, and FILLET creates rounded corners.

Breaking objects

Drawing a long line and then breaking it into two or more shorter lines is often much easier than drawing two separate lines. A common use for BREAK is to break a wall at a door or a window in an architectural floor plan. You specify two points on the object, and the command erases whatever is between those two points. Typically, you use object snaps to specify the points. Sometimes, you can use TRIM to break an object, but if you have no convenient cutting edge, you may find BREAK more efficient.

You can break lines, polylines, splines, xlines, rays, circles, arcs, elliptical arcs, and ellipses.

To break a line, choose Break from the Modify toolbar or from the 2D Draw control panel of the Dashboard. You cannot select the object first. The command responds with the Select object: prompt. (Notice that you can only select one object to break.) At this prompt, you have two choices:

- Select the object at one of the break points that you want to create. You then see the Specify second break point or [First point]: prompt. Because you have already specified the first point, you can now specify the second point. The command breaks the object between the two points.

- Select the object by using any method of object selection. You then see the Specify second break point or [First point]: prompt. Right-click and choose First point. At the Specify first break point: prompt, pick the first break point. At the Specify second break point: prompt, pick the second break point. The command breaks the object between the two points.

> **TIP** Sometimes you may want to break an object into two pieces at a point, without erasing any part of the object. Use the Break at Point button on the Modify toolbar or from the 2D Draw control panel of the Dashboard to help you easily break an object at a point. After selecting the object, pick where you want to break the object at the Specify second break point or [First point]: prompt. The two new objects look the same as before on the screen — until you select one of the objects. To break objects at a point, AutoCAD and AutoCAD LT use @, which always signifies the last point entered, to specify the second break point. Thus, the first and second break points are the same.

You can use BREAK to shorten an object. Pick one point on the object where you want the new endpoint to be. Pick the other point past its current endpoint to cut off the object at the point you picked on the object.

Joining objects

The opposite of breaking objects is joining them. The JOIN command lets you join lines, polylines, arcs, elliptical arcs, and splines. The objects must be along the same linear, circular, or elliptical path. The objects can overlap, have a gap between them, or touch end-to-end.

To join objects, choose Join from the Modify toolbar or from the 2D Draw control panel of the Dashboard. Follow these prompts:

```
Select source object: Select the first object that you want to join.
Select lines to join to source: Select the second object. (AutoCAD
knows which type of object you've selected for the first prompt and
inserts it into the second prompt.) You can continue to select other
objects. Press Enter to end selection.
```

AutoCAD joins the objects.

A very nice touch is the ability to close arcs (to circles) and elliptical arcs (to ellipses). If your first object is either type of arc, you see the Select arcs to join to source or [cLose]: prompt. Use the cLose option to close the arc.

 The drawing used in the following exercise on breaking and joining objects, ab10-h.dwg, is in the Drawings folder on the DVD.

STEPS: Breaking and Joining Objects

1. Open ab10-h.dwg from your DVD.

2. Save the file as ab10-09.dwg in your AutoCAD Bible folder. This is a site plan, as shown in Figure 10.27. Turn on OSNAP and set running object snaps for endpoint and intersection.

 3. Choose Break from the Modify toolbar or from the 2D Draw control panel of the Dashboard. At the Select object: prompt, pick the line at ❶. At the Specify second break point or [First point]: prompt, pick ❷. This action shortens the line.

4. Repeat the BREAK command. At the Select object: prompt, pick the circle (it's a maple tree) anywhere along its circumference. At the Specify second break point or [First point]: prompt, right-click and choose First point. At the Specify first break point: prompt, pick the intersection at ❸. At the Specify second break point: prompt, pick the intersection at ❹ to break the circle.

NOTE AutoCAD and AutoCAD LT break circles counterclockwise. If you had picked ❹, and then ❸, only the smaller arc would have remained.

 5. Let's say that you decide this is a mistake. Choose Join from the Modify toolbar or from the 2D Draw control panel of the Dashboard. At the Select source object: prompt, select the circle (tree) that you just broke into an arc. At the Select arcs to join to source or [cLose]: prompt, right-click and choose cLose. The arc becomes a full circle again.

6. To break the line at ❺, Turn on Object Snap Tracking by clicking OTRACK on the status bar. Start the BREAK command again. Follow the prompts:

Select object: *Pick the line at ❺.*
Specify second break point or [First point]: *Right-click and choose First point.*
Specify first break point: *Move the cursor to ❻ to acquire it as a tracking point. Then move the cursor to the right onto the line you are breaking. When you see the Endpoint: Intersection tooltip, click. (You have no visual confirmation yet that you picked the right point.)*
Specify second break point: *Move the cursor to ❼ to acquire it as a tracking point. Then move the cursor onto the line you are breaking. At the Endpoint: 4'-2 3/4"<0.0000 tooltip, click.*

7. Start the JOIN command. At the Select source object: prompt, select the line at ❽. At the Select lines to join to source: prompt, select the line at ❾. Press Enter to end selection and join the lines into one.

8. Save your drawing. It should look like Figure 10.28.

FIGURE 10.27

A site plan.

FIGURE 10.28

The edited site plan.

For AutoCAD only: Two AutoLISP programs on the DVD can help you with breaking and unbreaking objects. `Pend` puts a break line at the end of a pipe. See `\Software\Chapter 10\Pend`. `Br` draws a line with a break symbol. See `\Software\Chapter 10\Br`.

The Express Tools contain a command, BREAKLINE, to create a break symbol. Choose Express ➪ Draw ➪ Break-Line Symbol. Another Express Tools command, OVERKILL (available on the command line), deletes objects that are on top of other objects.

Creating chamfered corners

The CHAMFER command creates corners from two nonparallel lines. You can also chamfer xlines, rays, and polylines. You can simply extend the lines to meet at an intersection (a square corner), or create a beveled edge. If you create a beveled edge, you define the edge by either two distances or one distance and an angle relative to the first line that you're chamfering. Figure 10.29 shows the elements of a chamfered corner.

FIGURE 10.29

A chamfered corner.

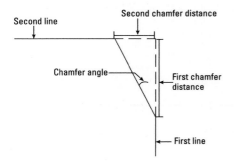

Chamfering is a two-step process. First you define how you want to chamfer the corner, specifying either two distances from the corner or a distance and an angle. Then you select the two lines that you want to chamfer.

To chamfer, choose Chamfer from the Modify toolbar or from the 2D Draw control panel of the Dashboard. You cannot select objects before the CHAMFER command. The command responds with the `(TRIM mode) Current chamfer Dist1 = 0.0000, Dist2 = 0.0000 Select first line or [Undo/Polyline/Distance/Angle/Trim/mEthod/Multiple]:` prompt. The command starts by listing the current settings. (The CHAMFER command remembers the last-used chamfer data.) You can define two distances from a corner or one distance and an angle:

- To define two distances from the corner, right-click and choose Distance. At the `Specify first chamfer distance <0.0000>:` prompt, type the first chamfer distance or press Enter to accept the default (which is the last distance that you defined). At the `Specify second chamfer distance <0.0000>:` prompt, type the second distance. The default for this is always the first chamfer distance because equal chamfer distances are so common.

- To define a distance (from the corner) and an angle, right-click and choose Angle. At the `Specify chamfer length on the first line <1.0000>:` prompt, enter a distance. This is the same as the first chamfer distance. At the `Specify chamfer angle from the first line <0.0000>:` prompt, type the angle between the first line and the chamfer line.

Now that you have specified the settings that you want, you're ready to chamfer. Your distances or distance and angle are displayed as you just specified them. The command repeats the `Select first line or [Undo/Polyline/Distance/Angle/Trim/mEthod/Multiple]:` prompt. Select the first line. If you aren't creating a chamfer with equal distances, the order in which you select the lines is important. The command trims the first line selected by the first distance, and the second line selected based on either the second distance or the angle. At the `Select second line or shift-select to apply corner:` prompt, select the second line to chamfer the lines.

If the lines already intersect, the command trims them to create a corner. The pick points on intersecting lines should be on the part of the lines that you want to keep, not on the part of the lines that you want to trim off.

 To quickly create a square corner if you have non-zero settings, press Shift as you select the second line. Of course, you can still set each distance to zero.

 Choose the Polyline option to chamfer an entire polyline at once. Chapter 16 covers polylines, and Chapter 24 discusses chamfering 3D models.

By default, CHAMFER trims the original lines that it chamfers. If you want to keep the full original lines when you add the chamfer line, choose the Trim option and choose No Trim. Use the Multiple option to continue the prompts and chamfer several corners in one command. The new Undo option lets you undo your last chamfer and try again.

The drawing used in the following exercise on chamfering lines, ab10-i.dwg, is in the Drawings folder on the DVD.

STEPS: Chamfering Lines

1. Open ab10-i.dwg from your DVD.
2. Save the file as ab10-10.dwg in your AutoCAD Bible folder. This drawing is a very small section of a "porcupine" mixer, as shown in Figure 10.30.

FIGURE 10.30

A mechanical drawing showing a small section of a "porcupine" mixer.

3. Choose Chamfer from the Modify toolbar or from the 2D Draw control panel of the Dashboard. CHAMFER states the current mode and distances. At the `Select first line or [Undo/Polyline/Distance/Angle/Trim/mEthod/Multiple]`: prompt, pick ❶ in Figure 10.30. At the `Select second line`: prompt, pick ❷. (If the current distances are not zero, press Shift as you pick ❷.) The command chamfers the two lines to make a corner. (If this doesn't work, you may have the Trim option set to No Trim. Change the setting to Trim and try again.)

4. Repeat the CHAMFER command. Follow the prompts:

```
Select first line or [Undo/Polyline/Distance/Angle/Trim/mEthod/
Multiple]: Right-click and choose Angle.
Specify chamfer length on the first line <1>: 9/16 ⏎
Specify chamfer angle from the first line <0>: 45 ⏎
```

5. At the `Select first line or [Undo/Polyline/Distance/Angle/Trim/mEthod/Multiple]`: prompt, pick ❸ in Figure 10.30. At the `Select second line`: prompt, pick ❹. The command chamfers the two lines, as shown in Figure 10.31.

6. Save your drawing.

FIGURE 10.31

The edited drawing after using the CHAMFER command.

Creating rounded corners

The FILLET command creates rounded corners, replacing part of two lines with an arc. Fillets are often used in mechanical drawings. In certain cases, you can use FILLET instead of the ARC command to create arcs. As with CHAMFER, you can fillet lines, xlines, rays, and polylines — they can even be parallel. You can also fillet circles, arcs, elliptical arcs, and ellipses.

The FILLET command defines the fillet arc by its radius, as shown in Figure 10.32.

FIGURE 10.32

A fillet consisting of two lines and an arc.

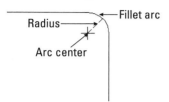

Like chamfering, filleting is a two-step process. First you define the radius of the fillet arc. Then you select the two lines that you want to fillet. You cannot select objects before the FILLET command.

To fillet, follow these steps:

1. Choose Fillet from the Modify toolbar or from the 2D Draw control panel of the Dashboard. The command responds with the `Current settings: Mode = TRIM, Radius = 0.0000 Select first object or [Undo/Polyline/Radius/Trim/Multiple]:` prompt.
2. Right-click and choose Radius.
3. At the `Specify fillet radius <0.0000>:` prompt, type the radius you want. The default is either 0.0000 or the last radius that you specified.
4. The command repeats the `Select first object or [Undo/Polyline/Radius/Trim/Multiple]:` prompt. Select the first object that you want to fillet.
5. At the `Select second object or shift-select to apply corner:` prompt, select the second object that you want to fillet. This action creates the fillet.

By default, FILLET trims the original lines that it fillets, but the FILLET command recalls the last setting you used. If you want to keep the full original lines when you create a fillet, right-click and choose the Trim option, and then choose No Trim.

CROSS-REF Choose the Polyline option to fillet an entire polyline at once. Chapter 16 covers polylines, and Chapter 24 discusses filleting 3D models.

Filleting with a zero radius gives the same results as chamfering with distances set to zero. (See the previous section on chamfering.) If your existing settings are non-zero, you can press Shift as you select the second object to create a square corner.

The order in which you select the two objects to be filleted is not important. However, *where* you pick the objects is quite important. If two objects intersect, the command keeps the objects on the same side of the intersection as your pick point and fillets them. Those parts of the objects on the far side of the intersection are erased.

When you fillet arcs and lines, if more than one fillet is possible, FILLET connects the endpoints closest to your pick points. Filleting circles and lines can produce unexpected results. Sometimes you need to experiment to find the proper pick points.

TIP Use the Multiple option to continue the prompts and fillet several corners in one command.

The drawing used in the following exercise on filleting objects, `ab10-i.dwg`, is in the `Drawings` folder on the DVD.

STEPS: Filleting Objects

1. Open `ab10-i.dwg` from your DVD.

2. Save the file as `ab10-11.dwg` in your `AutoCAD Bible` folder. This is the same drawing used in the previous exercise. It is shown in Figure 10.33.

A mechanical drawing showing a small section of a "porcupine" mixer.

3. Choose Fillet from the Modify toolbar or from the 2D Draw control panel of the Dashboard. At the `Select first object or [Undo/Polyline/Radius/Trim/Multiple]:` prompt, right-click and choose Radius. At the `Specify fillet radius <1/2>:` prompt, type **5/8** ↵.

4. At the `Select first object or [Undo/Polyline/Radius/Trim/Multiple]:` prompt, pick the line at ❶ in Figure 10.33. At the `Select second object or shift-select to apply corner:` prompt, pick the line at ❷ to fillet the two lines.

5. Repeat the FILLET command. At the `Select first object or [Undo/Polyline/Radius/Trim/ Multiple]:` prompt, right-click and choose Radius. At the `Enter fillet radius <5/8>:` prompt, type **1/4** ↵.

6. At the `Select first object or [Undo/Polyline/Radius/Trim/Multiple]:` prompt, right-click and choose Multiple. Pick the line at ❸ in Figure 10.33. At the `Select second object or shift-select to apply corner:` prompt, pick the line at ❹ to fillet the two lines. The prompts continue. This time pick at ❺ and ❻.

7. If you want, you can connect the two loose lines that the fillets created and create some more fillets in the drawing.

8. Save your drawing. It should look like Figure 10.34.

The filleted drawing.

Creating a Revision Cloud

You may need to mark areas of your drawings that contain revisions in order to draw attention to these revisions. A common method is to draw a *revision cloud* around the revised objects. Figure 10.35 shows a drawing with a revision cloud, which is a series of arcs that indicate that an area of the drawing has been revised.

The revision cloud shows where the drawing has been modified.

To create a revision cloud, follow these steps:

1. Choose Revcloud from the Draw toolbar.

2. At the `Specify start point or [Arc length/Object/Style] <Object>:` prompt, you can choose three options:

   ▪ To change the length of the arc, right-click and choose Arc Length. Then specify a new arc length. For a variable, hand-drawn look, you can specify a minimum arc length and a maximum arc length that is up to three times the length of the minimum.

   ▪ To change a closed object into a revision cloud, right-click and choose Object. Then pick a circle, ellipse, closed polyline, or closed spline. You can choose to reverse the direction of the revision cloud. The object is converted to a revision cloud, and the command ends.

   ▪ To choose from two available cloud styles, right-click and choose Style. At the next prompt, choose either the Normal or Calligraphy option. A calligraphy revision cloud has a variable line width so that it looks as if you drew it with a calligraphy pen.

3. Click where you want the revision cloud to start. You also see an instruction, `Guide crosshairs along cloud path. . .`, which means that you don't have to pick to create the arcs. You just have to move the crosshairs along the path of the desired cloud.

4. Move the crosshairs counterclockwise to create a circular or elliptical shape. When you approach the start point, the command ends automatically. (You can end the cloud at any time by pressing Enter.)

> **NOTE** If you want, you can pick each arc endpoint to control the size of the arcs. However, if you move the crosshairs farther than the arc length, an arc is created automatically. REVCLOUD multiplies the arc length by the Overall Scale factor (see Chapter 15) to adjust for different scale factors.

Hiding Objects with a Wipeout

A *wipeout* covers existing objects in order to clear space for some annotation or to indicate that the covered objects will be changed and should therefore be ignored. A wipeout is a polygonal area with a background that matches the background of the drawing area. The WIPEOUT command creates a polygon of the same color as the background of your drawing area.

To create a wipeout, follow these steps:

1. Choose Draw ➪ Wipeout.

2. At the `Specify first point or [Frames/Polyline] <Polyline>:` prompt, specify the first point of a shape that will cover existing objects. To use a polyline as the shape, right-click and choose Polyline. (The polyline can't contain any arcs when you use it for this purpose.) Then select the polyline and choose whether or not to erase the polyline.

3. At the `Specify next point or [Undo]:` prompt, if you specified a point, specify the next point.

4. At the `Specify next point or [Close/Undo]:` prompt, specify another point or use the Close option to close the wipeout shape. You can also press Enter to end the command and use the shape that you specified.

By default, the wipeout has a frame around it, using the current layer's color. You can hide the frames of all wipeouts by starting the WIPEOUT command, choosing the Frames option, and then choosing Off.

You can create a background mask especially for text. This mask covers a rectangle around your text so that you can read the text more easily. For more information, see Chapter 13.

Double-Clicking to Edit Objects

You can double-click objects to edit them. What happens after you double-click depends on the type of object. In most cases, double-clicking an object just opens the Properties palette where you can change the object's properties. For more information about using the Properties palette, see the section "Editing with the Properties Palette" later in this chapter.

When you double-click certain types of objects in a drawing, you see a dialog box that is specific to these objects:

- **Attribute definition:** Opens the Edit Attribute Definition dialog box (the DDEDIT command). See Chapter 18 for more information.

- **Attribute within a block:** Opens the Enhanced Attribute Editor dialog box (the EATTEDIT command) in AutoCAD and the Edit Attributes dialog box (the ATTEDIT command) in AutoCAD LT. See Chapter 18 for more information.

- **Block:** Opens the Edit Block Definition dialog box. You can choose the block from a list and click OK to enter the Block Editor. (See Chapter 18 for more information.)

- **Hatch:** Opens the Hatch Edit dialog box (the HATCHEDIT command). See Chapter 16 for more information.

- **Mline:** Opens the Multilines Edit Tools dialog box (the MLEDIT command). Mlines are not available in AutoCAD LT, which has a similar feature, called Dlines. See Chapter 16 for more information.

- **Mtext or leader text:** Opens the In-Place Text Editor (the MTEDIT command). See Chapter 13 for more information.

- **Polyline:** Starts the PEDIT command.

- **Text (TEXT or DTEXT commands):** Opens the In-Place Text Editor (the DDEDIT command). See Chapter 13 for more information.

- **Xref:** Opens the Reference Edit dialog box (the REFEDIT command) in AutoCAD. In AutoCAD LT, displays the Properties palette. See Chapter 19 for more information.

 You can customize what happens when you double-click an object. For example, you could choose to display the Properties palette instead of the Reference Edit dialog box when you double-click an xref. See Chapter 33 for details.

The DBLCLKEDIT system variable specifies whether double-clicking opens a dialog box in these instances. To turn off double-clicking to edit objects, choose Tools ➪ Options and click the User Preferences tab. Uncheck the Double Click Editing check box in the Windows Standard Behavior section of the dialog box.

Grips

Grips offer a way to edit objects without choosing commands. By using grips, you can quickly stretch, move, rotate, scale, copy, and mirror objects.

When you select an object without first choosing a command, the object appears highlighted with *grips* — small boxes at preset object snap points. (If you don't see grips, they may be turned off. See the "Customizing grips" section later in this chapter to find out how to turn them back on.) You can continue to select more objects in this way.

You then click to activate a grip and use the grip to manipulate the object. When the grip is activated, it turns red (by default). An activated grip is also called a *hot grip,* as shown in Figure 10.36. In some cases, you activate more than one grip at a time. To activate more than one grip, hold down Shift and then click the grips. If you activate a grip in error, click it again to deactivate it. Grips are so called because you can "hold on to" the object by dragging the grips with the mouse.

After you activate a grip, right-click with the mouse to open the Grip shortcut menu, which lists all of the grip options.

FIGURE 10.36

Moving a line. Grips appear at preset object snaps. You use the hot grip to manipulate an object.

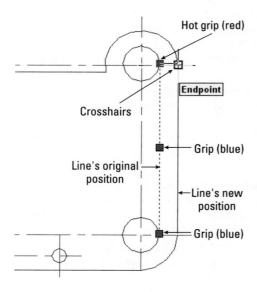

You can also press the Spacebar or Enter to cycle through five possible commands on the command line. As long as you're familiar with the STRETCH, MOVE, ROTATE, SCALE, and MIRROR commands, you can easily learn how to accomplish the same edits by using grips because the prompts are so similar. After you complete the edit, the object remains highlighted and the grips remain, so that you can further edit the object. If you want to edit another object, press Esc once to remove the grips. Then select another object or objects or choose another command.

NOTE If you use Dynamic Input, you can customize how many and which tooltips appear when you grip edit. Right-click the DYN button on the status bar and choose Settings to open the Drafting Settings dialog box with the Dynamic Input tab on top (I explain this dialog box in the "Specifying Dynamic Input settings" section of Chapter 4). Click the Settings button in the Dimension Input section to open the Dimension Input Settings dialog box. The settings here apply to grip editing. By default, the Show Two Dimension Input Fields at a Time option is selected. Although this setting usually works well, you can go down to one input field or specify additional fields. When you select multiple grips to edit an object, no Dynamic Input field appears.

Stretching with grips

Stretching with grips involves understanding how the grip points relate to the object. For example, you cannot stretch a line from its midpoint — if you think about it, there's no way to define in which direction to stretch the line. Also, you cannot stretch a circle, you can only scale it. Aside from these types of limitations, anything goes.

Stretching one line

You can stretch one line. The result is similar to using the CHANGE command to change a line's endpoint. To stretch a line, select it, and click the grip at the endpoint that you want to stretch. The prompt on the command line responds with

```
** STRETCH **
Specify stretch point or [Base point/Copy/Undo/eXit]:
```

STRETCH is the first grip-editing command on the command line. Simply specify the new endpoint for the line, using any method of specifying a coordinate, to stretch the line. The other options work as follows:

- Base point lets you define a base point — other than the activated grip — and a second point. Right-click to open the Grip shortcut menu and choose Base Point. The option displays the `Specify base point:` prompt. Define a base point. Again you see the original `Specify stretch point or [Base point/Copy/Undo/eXit]:` prompt. Define the second stretch point to stretch the line.

- Copy puts you in Multiple mode. Right-click to open the Grip shortcut menu and choose Copy. Again you see the original `Specify stretch point or [Base point/Copy/Undo/eXit]:` prompt. Specify a new point to keep the original line, and create a new line stretched to the new point. You can continue to create new stretched lines.

- Undo undoes the last edit. Right-click to open the Grip shortcut menu and choose Undo.

- eXit returns you to the Command prompt. Right-click to open the Grip shortcut menu and choose Exit. Esc also returns you to the Command prompt.

Stretching multiple lines

Stretching more than one line at a time is similar to the most common use of the STRETCH command. However, it can also be somewhat confusing.

As explained earlier in this chapter, when you use the STRETCH command, objects that cross the crossing window are stretched, while objects entirely within the crossing window are moved. When you stretch multiple lines, you should activate endpoint grips to stretch lines, and activate midpoint grips to move lines. Picking all of those grips accurately can be difficult and time-consuming. Also, small objects that are close together create a lot of overlapping grips that are hard to select. For this reason, stretching multiple lines works best with simple models.

To stretch multiple lines, follow these steps:

1. Choose the objects that you want to stretch. The objects are highlighted and display grips. You can use any method of choosing objects—you are not limited to crossing windows.

2. Hold down Shift and pick each grip that you want to stretch. If there are internal objects that you want to move with the stretch, select their grips, too; these include the midpoints of the lines and arcs, and the centers of the circles.

3. Release Shift and pick a grip to use as a base point. You see the prompt:

   ```
   ** STRETCH **
   Specify stretch point or [Base point/Copy/Undo/eXit]:
   ```

4. Specify a new stretch point. You can also use any of the other options.

At the end of this section on grips, you have the opportunity to try them out in an exercise.

Moving with grips

It's easy to move objects with grips. First, choose all of the objects that you want to move. Then click any grip to activate it. This becomes the base point. Right-click to open the Grip shortcut menu and choose Move.

 You can also press the Spacebar to cycle through the grip editing modes. For example, to move an object, press the Spacebar once.

After you choose Move editing mode, you see the prompt:

```
** MOVE **
Specify move point or [Base point/Copy/Undo/eXit]:
```

Use any method to specify the second point. Be sure to use @ if you're typing in relative coordinates. The selected objects move. The other options work as follows:

- Base point lets you define a base point, other than the activated grip. Right-click to open the Grip shortcut menu and choose Base Point. You see the `Specify base point:` prompt. Define a base point. The original `Specify move point or [Base point/Copy/Undo/eXit]:` prompt returns. Define the second move point to move the objects.

- Copy puts you in Multiple mode and lets you copy objects. Right-click to open the Grip shortcut menu and choose Copy (or type **c** ↵). You see the original `Specify move point or [Base point/Copy/Undo/eXit]:` prompt. Specify a new point to keep the original object and create a new object where you specify. You can continue to create new objects.

- Undo undoes the last edit. Right-click to open the Grip shortcut menu and choose Undo.

- eXit returns you to the Command prompt. Right-click to open the Grip shortcut menu and choose Exit. Esc also returns you to the Command prompt.

Rotating with grips

Rotating with grips is very similar to using the ROTATE command. First, choose all of the objects that you want to rotate. Then click any grip to activate it. This becomes the base point. Right-click to open the Grip shortcut menu and choose Rotate. You see the prompt:

```
** ROTATE **
Specify rotation angle or [Base point/Copy/Undo/Reference/eXit]:
```

Type in a rotation angle or pick a point to rotate the objects. The other options work as follows:

- Base point lets you define a base point, other than the activated grip. Right-click to open the Grip shortcut menu and choose Base Point. You see the `Specify base point:` prompt. Define a base point. The original `Specify rotation angle or [Base point/Copy/Undo/ Reference/eXit]:` prompt returns. Specify the rotation angle to rotate the objects.

- Copy puts you in Multiple mode and lets you copy objects. Right-click to open the Grip shortcut menu and choose Copy. Again, you see the original `Specify rotation angle or [Base point/Copy/Undo/Reference/eXit]:` prompt. Specify a rotation angle to keep the original object and create a new rotated object where you specified. You can continue to create new objects.

- Undo undoes the last edit. Right-click to open the Grip shortcut menu and choose Undo.

- Reference lets you specify both a reference angle and a new angle. Right-click to open the Grip shortcut menu and choose Reference. You see the `Specify a Reference angle <0>:` prompt. Type an angle or pick two points to specify an angle. The `Specify new angle or [Base point/Copy/Undo/Reference/eXit]:` prompt appears. Type an angle or pick a point. This works like the Reference option for the ROTATE command. (See Chapter 9.)

- eXit returns you to the Command prompt. Right-click to open the Grip shortcut menu and choose Exit. Esc also returns you to the Command prompt.

Scaling with grips

Scaling with grips is very similar to using the SCALE command. First, choose all of the objects that you want to scale. Then click any grip to activate it. This becomes the base point. Right-click to open the Grip shortcut menu and choose Scale. You see the prompt:

```
** SCALE **
Specify scale factor or [Base point/Copy/Undo/Reference/eXit]:
```

Type a scale factor to scale the objects. The other options work as follows:

- Base point lets you define a base point, other than the activated grip. Right-click to open the Grip shortcut menu and choose Base Point. You see the `Specify base point:` prompt. Define a base point. The original `Specify scale factor or [Base point/Copy/Undo/ Reference/eXit]:` prompt appears. Define the scale factor to scale the objects.

- Copy puts you in Multiple mode and lets you copy objects. Right-click to open the Grip shortcut menu and choose Copy. You see the original `Specify scale factor or [Base point/Copy/Undo/Reference/eXit]:` prompt. Specify a scale factor to keep the original object and create a new scaled object. You can continue to create new scaled objects.

- Undo undoes the last edit. Right-click to open the Grip shortcut menu and choose Undo.

- Reference lets you specify a reference length and a new scale. Right-click to open the Grip shortcut menu and choose Reference. You see the `Specify reference length <1>:` prompt. Type a length or pick two points to specify a length. You see the `Specify new length or [Base point/Copy/Undo/Reference/eXit]:` prompt. Type a length or pick a point. This works like the Reference option for the SCALE command. (See Chapter 9.)

- eXit returns you to the Command prompt. Right-click to open the Grip shortcut menu and choose Exit. Esc also returns you to the Command prompt.

Mirroring with grips

Mirroring with grips is similar to using the MIRROR command. First, choose all of the objects that you want to mirror. Then click any grip to activate it. This becomes the first point of the mirror line. Right-click to open the Grip shortcut menu. Choose Mirror. You see the prompt:

```
** MIRROR **
Specify second point or [Base point/Copy/Undo/eXit]:
```

Specify the second point of the mirror line to mirror the objects.

> **CAUTION** By default, AutoCAD and AutoCAD LT erase the original objects. To keep the original objects, you must use the Copy option. This feature is the opposite of the MIRROR command, where the default is to keep the original objects.

The other options work as follows:

- Base point lets you define a base point, other than the activated grip, as well as a second point. Right-click to open the Grip shortcut menu and choose Base Point. You see the `Specify base point:` prompt. Define a base point — that is, the first point of the mirror line. The original `Specify second point or [Base point/Copy/Undo/eXit]:` prompt appears. Define the second point of the mirror line to mirror the objects.

- Copy puts you in Multiple mode and lets you keep the original objects. Right-click to open the Grip shortcut menu and choose Copy. You see with the original `Specify second point or [Base point/Copy /Undo/eXit]:` prompt. Specify the second point to keep the original objects and create new mirrored objects. You can continue to create new mirrored objects.

- Undo undoes the last edit. Right-click to open the Grip shortcut menu and choose Undo.

- eXit returns you to the Command prompt. Right-click to open the Grip shortcut menu and choose Exit. Esc also returns you to the Command prompt.

> **ON the DVD-ROM** The drawing used in the following exercise on editing with grips, ab10-j.dwg, is in the Drawings folder on the DVD.

STEPS: Editing with Grips

1. Open ab10-j.dwg from the DVD.

2. Save the file as ab10-12.dwg in your AutoCAD Bible folder. This is a small section of a drive block, seen from above, as shown in Figure 10.37. Make sure that ORTHO and OSNAP are on.

3. Use a selection window to select the entire model. Now hold down Shift and place a selection window around the small circles and rectangle at the center of the model to deselect them.

4. Pick the grip at ❶ in Figure 10.37 to activate it. You see the following prompt:
```
** STRETCH **
Specify stretch point or [Base point/Copy/Undo/eXit]:
```

5. Right-click and choose Mirror from the shortcut menu. You see the following prompt:
```
** MIRROR **
Specify second point or [Base point/Copy/Undo/eXit]:
```

6. Right-click and choose Copy so that the original objects that you mirror are not deleted.

7. At the `Specify second point or [Base point/Copy/Undo/eXit]:` prompt, move the cursor to the right. You can see the mirror image of the model. Pick any point to the right (in the 0-degree direction) of the activated grip.

FIGURE 10.37

This small section of a drive block, seen from above, can be edited with grips.

8. Right-click and choose Exit to return to the command line. The original objects are still highlighted.

9. Use a large selection window to select all of the new objects, including the small rectangle and circles in the middle. Everything (old and new) should be highlighted and display grips.

10. Pick the grip at ❷ in Figure 10.37 to activate it. Right-click and choose Rotate from the shortcut menu. At the `Specify rotation angle or [Base point/Copy/Undo/Reference/ eXit]:` prompt, type **90** ↵. This action rotates the model.

11. Pick the bottom-right grip to activate it. Right-click and choose Scale from the shortcut menu. At the `Specify scale factor or [Base point/Copy/Undo/Reference/eXit]:` prompt, type **.5** ↵. This action scales the model.

12. Pick the grip at the midpoint of the bottom line. Right-click and choose Move from the shortcut menu. At the `Specify move point or [Base point/Copy/Undo/eXit]:` prompt, type **0,–3** ↵. The model should look like Figure 10.38.

FIGURE 10.38

The drive block section, after several grip edits, looks a little like a cookie jar.

13. Press Esc to remove all grips. Define a crossing window by picking first at ❶, and then at ❷ (see Figure 10.38).

14. Hold down Shift and pick all of the grips along the bottom three lines. Release Shift and pick the grip at the middle of the bottom line. At the `Specify stretch point or [Base point/Copy/ Undo/eXit]:` prompt, type **0,1** ↵ to shrink the model.

   If the stretch does not come out right (it might be hard to see and activate all of the grips), choose Undo from the Standard toolbar to undo the stretch and try again.

15. Save your drawing.

Customizing grips

You can turn grips on and off and customize their size and color. Choose Tools ➪ Options and click the Selection tab to open the dialog box shown in Figure 10.39.

FIGURE 10.39

Use the Selection tab of the Options dialog box to customize grips.

By default, grips are enabled. Also by default, grips are turned off for blocks. (Chapter 18 covers blocks.) When grips are off for blocks, you see only one grip when you select a block; this is its insertion point. When grips for blocks are on, you see all of the grips you would normally see for objects.

In the Grips section, you can choose the colors that you want for unselected and selected (hot) grips. Click the drop-down lists to choose a color.

The Grip Size section lets you drag the slider bar to set the size of the grips. Click OK after you have made the desired changes.

Editing with the Properties Palette

The Properties palette displays the properties of selected objects. You can also use the Properties palette to change the properties of objects.

 To open the Properties palette, click Properties on the Standard or Standard Annotation toolbar, choose Tools ⇨ Palettes ⇨ Properties, or press Ctrl+1. The Properties palette, shown in Figure 10.40, opens on your screen.

FIGURE 10.40

Use the Properties palette to edit objects and their properties.

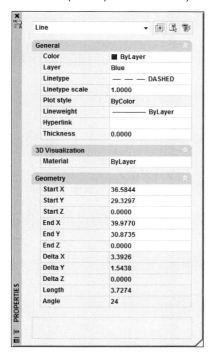

Managing the Properties palette

The auto-hide feature of the Properties palette makes it easy to work with the palette open all the time. Whenever the cursor moves off the palette, it collapses to just display the title bar. To auto-hide the palette, right-click the title bar and choose Auto-hide. You can also dock it; choose Anchor Left or Anchor Right from the title bar's shortcut menu. The Allow Docking item there should also be checked; if it isn't, choose it from the same shortcut menu.

The Properties palette has its own undo function. Right-click the palette (but not on the item that you changed) in the Properties palette and choose Undo. Multiple levels of undo are available. For more information about palettes, see Chapter 26.

To resize the window, point to its edge until you see the double-headed arrow cursor, and then click and drag. You can also resize the two columns by pointing to the column dividing line until you see the double-headed arrow and then clicking and dragging. If the Properties palette has too many rows for its size, use the scroll bar to see the undisplayed rows.

Using the Properties palette

The Properties palette can be used to directly edit objects and to edit other object properties as well:

- You can change the layer, color, linetype, linetype scale, and lineweight of objects (see Chapter 11).
- You can edit text and text properties (see Chapter 13).
- You can edit plot styles (see Chapter 17).
- You can edit blocks (see Chapter 18).
- You can edit hyperlinks (see Chapter 28).

To change values in the Properties palette, do one of the following:

- Click a value, select the text, type a new value, and press Enter.
- Click a value, click the down arrow to the right of the value, and choose from the drop-down list.
 - Click a value, click the Pick a Point button, and specify a new point by picking on the screen.

In Figure 10.40, you see the result of opening the Properties palette with one line selected. To change either endpoint of the selected line, type new coordinates in the Properties palette and press Enter. Of course, this method of editing a line is useful only when you know the absolute coordinates that you want. When you select a geometric property, such as Start X, which is the X coordinate of the line's start point, you can also use the Pick a Point button that appears. You can click this button and then pick a new start point directly on your screen. The new point becomes the new start point of the line, changing both the X and Y coordinates of the start point if your pick point requires it.

The information that you see in the Properties palette depends on the objects selected:

- If no object is selected, you see only properties that apply to the entire drawing, such as UCS, current layer, and viewport data. You can select an object while the window is open to display data on that object.
- If one object or one type of object (such as all lines) is selected, you see both general information and geometrical information on that object or object type.
- If more than one type of object is selected, you see general information, such as layer, color, and linetype data, but no geometry data.
- If more than one object is selected and you choose one type of object from the drop-down list at the top of the palette, you see information applying only to that type of object. This drop-down list provides a quick way to filter the type of objects that you can edit.

The Properties palette has three buttons in its upper-right corner.

The Toggle Value of PICKADD Sysvar button turns PICKADD on and off. PICKADD changes how you select more than one object. When it's on (set to 1), which is the default, you can continue to select objects and they're added to the selection set. When it's off (set to 0), you need to press Shift to add objects to the selection set; otherwise, selecting an object deselects previously selected objects.

Here's how to change the PICKADD variable:

- When you see the 1, PICKADD is off. Click the button to turn PICKADD on.

- When you see the plus, PICKADD is on. Click the button to turn PICKADD off.

The Select Objects button enables you to select objects for editing in the Properties palette. After you select the objects you want, you can change their properties. If you're going to pick objects or use implied windowing, the Select Objects button offers no advantage. You can just select the objects and apply changes in the Properties palette. However, if you want to use a fence or polygon method of selection, the Select Objects button is helpful. Follow these steps:

1. Click the Select Objects button.
2. On the command line, type the selection method that you want (such as **f** for fence) as you would if a command were active or you had started the SELECT command.
3. Select the objects that you want.
4. Press Enter to end object selection.
5. Use the Properties palette to make the desired changes. (You can also start an editing command to use with the selected objects.)

The Quick Select button opens the Quick Select dialog box, which is covered in the next section. The Quick Select dialog box lets you create a selection set according to specified criteria (for example, all green lines). You can then change the properties of these green lines.

Click the Properties palette's close box to close the window. I cover the Properties palette further in the next chapter and in later chapters as appropriate.

Selection Filters

Sometimes you need a more powerful way to select objects. For example, you may want to:

- Select all the lines in your drawing to change their color
- Check the arc radii of all your fillets
- Find short line segments that should be erased

Before selection filters, you had to write an AutoLISP program to accomplish these functions. (Sometimes an AutoLISP program is still the easiest way to go. See Chapters 34 through 36.) Now you can create fairly complex filters that select only the objects you want.

Using Quick Select to select objects

As its name suggests, Quick Select is a quick, flexible, and simple way to create object selection filters. Use the FILTER command, which is covered in the following sections, to create more-complex filters or when you want to save filtering criteria for future use.

Start Quick Select in one of these ways:

- Choose Tools ⇨ Quick Select.
- With no command active, right-click in the drawing area and choose Quick Select.
- Click the Quick Select button in the Properties palette.
- Type **qselect** ↵ on the command line.

The Quick Select dialog box opens, as shown in Figure 10.41.

FIGURE 10.41

Use the Quick Select dialog box to quickly create a selection set of objects based on specified criteria.

To create a filter, start at the top of the dialog box and work your way down. Here's how it works:

- **Apply to:** By default, the filter applies to the entire drawing, but you can use the Select Objects button to return to your drawing and select objects. The rest of the filter will then apply only to selected objects, which is called Current Selection in the drop-down list. If you use this feature at all, you would usually use a window to select an area of your drawing. (The Select Objects button is unavailable if Append to Current Selection Set is checked at the bottom of the dialog box.)

- **Object type:** By default, the filter lists Multiple as the object type. Click the drop-down list to choose from the object types available in your drawing (or in your selection set if you created one), such as line, circle, ellipse, polyline, and so on. You can choose only one type of object. To create a filter that includes more than one type of object (but not all types), use the FILTER command, which I describe in the next section.

■ **Properties:** Here you choose the properties that you want to filter. (Most of these properties are covered in the next chapter.) The drop-down list includes all properties in the drawing's database; these properties depend on the object type you chose. You can choose only one property. The values in the next two sections depend on your choice in the Properties section. If you want to create a filter that specifies criteria for more than one property, use the FILTER command.

■ **Operator:** After you've chosen a property, you can set it equal to or not equal to a certain value. You can set certain properties as greater than or less than a value. You can use wildcard matching characters (such as * and ?) for editable text. You can also select all objects that fit the previous criteria. Choose the desired operator from the drop-down list.

■ **Value:** Here you finally choose the value for your property. For example, you can set the color equal (or not equal) to green or the linetype equal to DASHED. Choose the desired value from the drop-down list or enter a value in the text box.

> **TIP** You can choose Block Reference as the object type, Name as the property, and the name of a block as the Value to select all instances of that block.

■ **How to apply:** As soon as you create a filter, you can use it to create a selection set. To do this, check Include In New Selection Set. To use Quick Select to select everything except objects that meet your selection criteria, choose Exclude from New Selection Set.

■ **Append to current selection set:** Check this box to add objects that meet your criteria to an existing selection set.

Click OK to select the objects that meet your criteria, and close the dialog box. You can start a command and use the selection set. If the command must be started before selecting objects, you can use the Previous option (type **p** ↵) at the `Select objects:` prompt to select the objects that you selected using Quick Select.

> **AUTOCAD ONLY** The Express Tools include two commands to create filtered selection sets. FASTSELECT creates a selection set of objects that touch the object that you pick. You can create chains of objects to include objects that touch other touching objects. Choose Express ⌐ Selection Tools ⇨ Fast Select. GETSEL creates a selection of objects of the layer and object type that you select. Choose Express ⌐ Selection Tools ⇨ Get Selection Set.

Using the FILTER command

The advantage of using the FILTER command over Quick Select is that you can create more-complex filters and save them.

To create a filter, type **filter** ↵ on the command line to open the Object Selection Filters dialog box, as shown in Figure 10.42. If you've already chosen a command, type **'filter** at the `Select objects:` prompt to create the selection filter transparently. The box at the top of the dialog box lists the filters that you specified.

> **NOTE** The selection filter finds only colors and linetypes of objects that have been specifically set as such, rather than as part of a layer definition. Chapter 11 covers layers, colors, and linetypes.

Creating a single filter

Use the Select Filter section of the dialog box to specify a filter. The drop-down box lists all of the possible filters. Click the arrow to display the drop-down list. You can choose from several types of items:

- Objects
- Object properties such as color or layer
- Object snaps such as arc center or circle radius
- Logical operators such as AND, OR, and NOT (these logical operators combine filter specifications in various ways)

The first step is to choose a filter. In Figure 10.42, Line was chosen from the drop-down list. If the item chosen does not need any further clarification, click Add to List. The filter appears in the box at the top of the dialog box. Notice that the filter appears as Object = Line.

FIGURE 10.42

A filter that chooses all lines.

Many filters require a value. You have two ways to enter a value:

- If you choose an object that can be listed, the Select button becomes active. Click it and choose the value that you want. For example, if you choose Color or Layer, you can choose from a list of colors or layers.
- If you choose an object that can have any value, the boxes below the drop-down list box become active. They are labeled X, Y, and Z, but this is misleading. These boxes are used for X, Y, and Z coordinates only when you choose a filter requiring coordinates, such as Viewport Center. In most cases, you use the X box to give the filter a value. In this situation, the Y and Z boxes are not used. For example, if you choose Text Height, you type the height in the X box.

Keep in mind that you don't always want to specify that a filter *equals* a value. For example, if you want to create a filter that selects all circles with a radius less than 0.75, then when you choose Circle Radius, the X box becomes active. Click the arrow to display the drop-down list of relational operators and choose one. Table 10.2 lists the relational operators.

TABLE 10.2

Relational Operators in the Object Selection Filters Dialog Box

Operator	Definition
=	Equal to
! =	Not equal to
<	Less than
<=	Less than or equal to
>	Greater than
>=	Greater than or equal to
*	Equal to any value

Adding a second filter

To add a second filter, you first decide on the relationship between the first and the second filter and then assign a logical operator. Logical operators always come in pairs — when you begin one operator, you must also end it. The logical operators are at the end of the drop-down list of filter objects.

NOTE When two or more filters are listed without logical operators, the filter calculates them as if they were grouped with the AND operator. This means that the filter selects only objects that meet all of the criteria specified.

Table 10.3 explains the four logical operators, which are called *grouping operators* because they group filter specifications together. The Example column explains the results of two filter specifications: Color = 1-Red and Object = Circle.

TABLE 10.3

Logical (or Grouping) Operators Used for Selection Filters

Operator	Explanation	Example
AND	Finds all objects that meet all criteria.	Finds red circles.
OR	Finds objects that meet any of the criteria.	Finds all red objects and all circles.
XOR	Finds objects that meet one criterion or the other but not both. Requires two criteria between Begin XOR and End XOR.	Finds red objects that are not circles and circles that are not red.
NOT	Excludes objects that meet the criteria. May have only one criterion between Begin NOT and End NOT.	If the NOT operator groups the Object = Circle filter, then it finds all red objects that are not circles.

Click Substitute and choose a saved filter to insert a saved filter into the filter you're currently defining. To add filters based on existing objects, choose Add Selected Object. This action adds all the properties of the object to the filter definition, which is often more than you want.

Figure 10.43 shows a filter that selects all lines and all polylines. The XOR operator was used because it finds objects that meet one criterion or the other but not both. Obviously, no object can be both a line and a polyline. This is a good example of a filter that you cannot create using Quick Select.

FIGURE 10.43

A filter that selects all lines and all polylines.

Naming and editing filters

After you've completed the filter, you should save it. Even if you don't think you'll use it again, you may make an editing error in the drawing while using it and have to go back to it. To save a filter, type a name in the Save As text box and click Save As.

You edit a listed filter by using three buttons:

- **Edit Item:** Choose the line containing the item and click this button to edit the item. The object name now appears in the drop-down box, and you can specify new values for it.
- **Delete:** Choose Delete to delete a chosen item in a filter.
- **Clear List:** Choose Clear List to clear all of the items in a filter and start over.

To choose a named filter to edit, choose it from the Current drop-down list.

Using filters

You can use filters in two ways. Most often, you choose a command first and then realize that you need a filter to select the objects. In this situation, follow these prompts:

```
Select objects: 'filter ⏎
Define the filter in the Object Selection Filters dialog box. Click
Apply.
Applying filter to selection.
Select objects: Type all ⏎ or use a large selection window to select
all of the objects that you want to consider in the filter.
x found
Select objects: ⏎
```

```
Exiting filtered selection. x found
Select objects: ↵
```

The command's usual prompts then continue.

Alternatively, you can start the FILTER command and define the filter. Click Apply. At the `Select objects:` prompt, type **all** or use a selection window. Press Enter to end object selection. Then start the editing command and use the Previous selection option to select the filtered objects.

STEPS: Using Selection Filters

1. Open `ab10-k.dwg` from the DVD.
2. Save the file as `ab10-13.dwg` in your `AutoCAD Bible` folder. Notice that two lines of text appearing in the middle of the drawing plus the text at the bottom of the drawing are black/white rather than blue like all of the other text. You want to check the color of all of the text and correct it if necessary.
3. Right-click the drawing area and choose Quick Select. In the Quick Select dialog box, click the Object Type drop-down list and scroll down until you see Text. Choose it.
4. In the Properties section, Color should be selected. If not, select it. In the Operator section, choose <> Not Equal. In the Value section, choose ByLayer. Include In New Selection Set should be chosen. Append to Current Selection Set should not be checked. Click OK to select three items of black/white text.
5. Press Esc to deselect the objects and remove the grips. Now you'll try the same thing using the FILTER command, but adding a level of complexity.
6. Type **filter** ↵. The Object Selection Filters dialog box opens.
7. In the Select Filter drop-down list, choose Text. Click Add to List. At the top, the filter reads `Object = Text`.
8. From the Select Filter drop-down list, choose `**Begin AND` (this is toward the bottom of the list) and click Add to List.
9. From the Select Filter drop-down list, choose Color. In the drop-down list next to X: choose ! = (not equal). Then choose Select. In the Select Color dialog box, choose BYLAYER. Click OK. In the Object Selection Filters dialog box, choose Add to List. The BYLAYER color number displays as 256. (Layers and colors are covered in the next chapter.)
10. You may want to select only the smaller text, and not the heading at the bottom of the drawing, where you know that the larger text's height is greater than .1 and the smaller text's height is smaller than .1. From the Select Filter drop-down list, choose Text Height. From the X: drop-down list, choose < (less than). In the text box to the right of X:, type **.1.** Choose Add to List.
11. From the Select Filter drop-down list, choose `**End AND` and click Add to List.
12. In the Save As text box, type **bad text.** Click Save As. The Object Selection Filters dialog box should look like the following:

```
Object = Text
**Begin AND
Color !=256 - ByLayer
Text Height < 0.100000
**End AND
```

13. Click Apply.

14. At the Select objects: prompt, type **all** ↵. The prompt tells you that 2 were found. Press Enter until you see the Command prompt.

15. Choose Color Control from the Object Properties toolbar. Choose ByLayer from the drop-down list. The two text objects change to the BYLAYER layer, where they change to a blue color like all of the other text.

16. Save your drawing.

As you can see, although Quick Select is much easier to use than the FILTER command for all but very complex filters, the FILTER command offers more control.

Groups

Groups let you save a selection set of objects so that you can easily select them whenever you need to edit them. If you have a certain set of objects that you need to edit as a group, and a busy drawing that makes their selection time-consuming, then groups are for you. After you set up the group, you can pick any object in the group to automatically select all of the objects in the group. An object can belong to more than one group.

NOTE Although both AutoCAD and AutoCAD LT include the group feature, the dialog box for creating and managing groups is different for AutoCAD and AutoCAD LT. Over the next few sections, be sure to note which program I'm discussing.

Creating and modifying groups in AutoCAD

To create or modify a group, type **group** ↵ on the command line to open the Object Grouping dialog box, as shown in Figure 10.44.

FIGURE 10.44

The Object Grouping dialog box.

Creating a new group

To create a new group in AutoCAD, follow these steps.

1. Type a name in the Group Name text box. You can use a maximum of 31 characters with no spaces. You can use the hyphen (-) and underscore (_) anywhere in the name.

2. If you want, you can type a description of up to 448 characters. The description can include spaces.

3. Click New. AutoCAD returns you to your drawing with the Select objects: prompt. Select the objects that you want to be in the group. Press Enter to end object selection. AutoCAD returns you to the dialog box.

4. Click OK.

You can now use your group.

The Group Identification section of the Object Grouping dialog box also has a Find Name button. Use this feature to find the name of the group to which an object belongs. AutoCAD lets you select an object and then lists the group's name or names.

The Highlight button highlights a group. First choose a group from the list in the Object Grouping dialog box. Click Highlight and AutoCAD returns to your drawing and highlights all of the objects in your group. Click Continue to return to the dialog box. Use this feature when you aren't sure which group you want to work with.

Changing a group

The Change Group section of the Object Grouping dialog box gives you a great deal of flexibility in managing groups. To change a group in AutoCAD, click any existing group in the Group Name list at the top of the dialog box. The buttons in the Change Group section all become active. You can then do the following:

- **Remove:** AutoCAD switches to the drawing area with the Select objects to remove from group . . . prompt. Select objects to remove and press Enter to end object removal. AutoCAD returns you to the dialog box. Click OK.

- **Add:** AutoCAD switches to the drawing area with the Select objects to add to group . . . prompt. Select objects to add and press Enter to end object selection. AutoCAD returns you to the dialog box. Click OK.

- **Rename:** Choose the group that you want to rename. Change the name in the Group Name text box. Click Rename. The name changes in the Group Name list at the top of the dialog box. Click OK.

- **Re-Order:** Each object in the group has a number, starting from zero. In rare cases, the order may be important to you. For example, you may be running a program that processes the members of a group. Choose the group that you want to reorder. Click Re-Order. AutoCAD opens the Order Group dialog box. If you simply want to reverse the order of all of the objects, click Reverse Order. Otherwise, click Highlight. AutoCAD opens a small Object Grouping message box with Next and Previous buttons. At the bottom-right corner, the box displays Object: 0, and one of the objects in the group is highlighted. Click Next to move from object to object. If you're going to reorder the objects, you probably need to write down the number of each object. Click OK to return to the Order Group dialog box. Complete the following text boxes:

  - **Remove from position:** This text box is the position number of the object that you want to move.

  - **Replace at position:** This text box is the new position number that you want for the object.

  - **Number of objects:** This text box is the object number or range of numbers that you want to reorder.

- **Description:** Updates a description for the group. Type a new description in the Group Identification section of the dialog box. Then click Description.

- **Explode:** Removes the group entirely. All of the objects remain in your drawing, but they are no longer grouped.

- **Selectable:** Toggles the selectability of the group. If a group is selectable, then selecting one object of the group selects the entire group. If a group is not selectable, then selecting one object of the group does not select the entire group. This option lets you temporarily work with one object in the group without having to explode the group. You can also press Ctrl+Shift+A to toggle the selectability of the group.

TIP   When you choose Highlight from the Order Group dialog box, the Object Grouping message box opens in the middle of the screen, covering your objects. Drag it to one corner of the screen so that you can see which objects are being highlighted.

Creating and modifying groups in AutoCAD LT

To create or modify a group in AutoCAD LT, choose Tools ➪ Group Manager to open the Group Manager window, as shown in Figure 10.45. You can dock this window by dragging it to the top or bottom of the drawing area.

FIGURE 10.45

Use the Group Manager window to create and manage groups in AutoCAD LT.

Creating a new group

To create a new group in AutoCAD LT, follow these steps.

1. With the Group Manager open, select the objects that you want to include in the group. (An object can belong to more than one group.)

2. Click the Create Group button. An empty box appears under the Group column of the Group Manager.

3. Type a name for your group and press Enter. You can use a maximum of 31 characters with no spaces. You can use the hyphen (-) and underscore (_) anywhere in the name.

4. If you want, click in the Description column and add a description for your group.

A light bulb appears in the Selectable column to indicate that the group is selectable (that is, functioning as a group). To close the Group Manager, click its Close button at the upper-right corner of the window. You can now use your group.

Changing a group in AutoCAD LT

Use the Group Manager toolbar to manage your groups. To work with your groups, click any existing group. You can then do the following:

- **Ungroup:** Deletes the group. All of the group's objects become individual objects again.
- **Add to Group:** Select an object or objects not in the group and click this button to add the selected object or objects to the group.
- **Remove from Group:** To remove an object from a group, click the Selectable icon. You can now choose individual objects in the group without selecting the entire group. Click in your drawing and pick the object that you want to remove. Then click the Remove from Group button.
- **Details:** Opens a window with more information about the group and its objects.
- **Select Group:** To select the group from the Group Manager, select the group name and click the Select Group button.
- **Deselect Group:** Deselects the group.

To toggle a group from selectable to not selectable, click the group's icon in the Selectable column. When a group is not selectable, you can individually select its objects.

Using groups

Using a group is very simple. If a group is selectable, just pick any object in the group to select all of the objects in the group. You can then edit the objects in the group as a whole. If you need to temporarily edit one object in a group, then turn off the group's selectability, as described in the previous sections.

You can change the selectable status of all groups in your drawing by choosing Tools ⇨ Options and clicking the Selection tab. Deselect Object Grouping in the Selection Modes section to disable object grouping entirely.

Summary

This chapter covered all of the more advanced editing commands. You read about:

- Mirroring objects
- Creating rectangular and polar arrays
- Creating an offset of an object
- Aligning objects
- Trimming and extending objects
- Stretching objects
- Lengthening (and shortening) objects
- Breaking and joining objects
- Creating chamfered corners and fillets for square, beveled, and rounded corners
- Using grips to stretch, move, mirror, rotate, and scale objects
- Double-clicking objects to edit them
- Using the Properties palette to see the properties of objects and to edit objects
- Creating filtered sets of selected objects with the Quick Select feature and the FILTER command
- Creating and using named groups of objects

In the next chapter, I cover layers, colors, linetypes, and lineweights.

Chapter 11

Organizing Drawings with Layers, Colors, Linetypes, and Lineweights

Until you learn about layers, you draw everything in black or white. Drawing everything in one color is not a very good way to draw — besides, it's boring! If everything is the same color, it's hard to distinguish the various elements of a drawing. If you've followed the exercises throughout this book, you've opened some drawings from the DVD that used various colors and linetypes (such as dashed lines). For example, in some of the architectural drawings, you may have noticed that the walls are a different color than the fixtures (refrigerator, sink, and so on) in the kitchen. When you create text and dimensions, covered in Chapters 13, 14, and 15, you almost always use a color that stands out from the main model that you're drawing. You can also create objects with varying line widths, called *lineweights*. This use of color, linetype, and lineweight helps to organize your drawings, making them easier to understand.

Most often, you assign color, linetype, and lineweight to a layer. A layer is simply an organizational tool that lets you organize the display of objects in your drawing. Every object must be on a layer, and every layer must have a color, a linetype, and a lineweight. You define layers to meet your drawing needs. Layers, colors, linetypes, and lineweights are called *object properties*. You can easily change any object's properties. This chapter explains how to create and change these object properties to organize your drawing.

Working with Layers

The best way to organize your drawing into colors, linetypes, and lineweights is to use layers. Layers offer powerful features that enable you to distinguish all of the various elements of your drawing. In an architectural drawing, for example, common layers are walls, doors, windows, plumbing, electrical, fixtures, structural elements, notes (text), dimensions, and so on. Mechanical drawings might use center, hidden, hatch, object, and title block layers. Each discipline has its own conventions, and you might have specific conventions to follow where you work.

Creating layers is an important part of setting up a drawing, in addition to the setup features covered in Chapter 5. You should create and save layers in your templates so that they're available to you when you start to draw. Layers give you many ways to organize your drawing. For example, you can:

- Assign different colors, linetypes, and lineweights to layers.
- Assign the various colors to different pens in a pen plotter, resulting in a paper drawing with varying colors or line widths.
- Control the visibility of layers. Making a layer invisible lets you focus on just the objects that you need to draw or edit.
- Control which objects are plotted.
- Lock a layer so that objects on that layer cannot be edited.

 You can also assign a plot style to a layer. A *plot style* is a group of settings that affects how your drawing is plotted. Chapter 17 covers plot styles.

Understanding layers

Besides having a color, linetype, and lineweight, every layer must have a name. All drawings come with a default layer, called layer 0 (zero). Its color is black/white, its linetype is Continuous, and its lineweight is Default. (The lineweight for Default is 0.010 inch or 0.25 mm.) Most of the exercises in this book up to this point have used layer 0. To create a new layer, you must give it a name, a color, a linetype, and a lineweight. You can then start drawing on that layer.

Layers have four *states*. These states control visibility, regeneration, editability, and plottability of layers:

- **On/Off:** On layers (the default) are visible. Off layers are invisible and are regenerated with the drawing. Off layers are not plotted.
- **Thawed/Frozen:** Thawed layers (the default) are visible. Frozen layers are invisible and are *not* regenerated with the drawing. However, when you thaw a frozen layer, the drawing regenerates. If you have floating viewports (covered in Chapter 17), you can also freeze a layer just in the current viewport, or only for new viewports that you create. You can also create a layer that is frozen in all viewports. Frozen layers are not plotted.
- **Unlocked/Locked:** Unlocked layers (the default) are visible and editable. Locked layers are visible but cannot be edited.
- **Plottable/Not Plottable:** Plottable layers are plotted. Not plottable layers are not plotted. This setting affects only layers that are on or thawed, because off and frozen layers are not plotted anyway.

Creating new layers

 To create a new layer, choose Layer Properties Manager from the Layers toolbar or from the Layers control panel of the Dashboard. (To display the Layers toolbar, right-click any toolbar button and choose Layers from the list of toolbars. To display the Dashboard, choose Tools ➪ Palettes ➪ Dashboard.) The Layer Properties Manager dialog box opens, as shown in Figure 11.1. This dialog box lists all current layers and their properties. You can also create new layers and modify existing ones. The left panel allows you to filter the list of layers. For more information on layer filtering, see the section "Filtering the layer list" later in this chapter.

FIGURE 11.1

The Layer Properties Manager is the place to manage all of your layers.

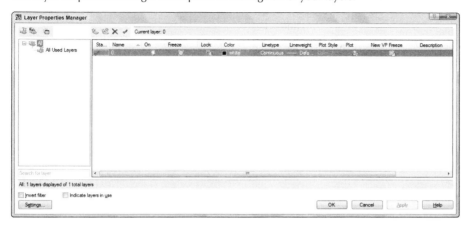

Table 11.1 explains the columns in the dialog box. For a description of the icons in most of the columns, see Table 11.2 later in this chapter.

TABLE 11.1

Columns in the Layer Properties Manager

Column Name	Description
Status	Shows the status of each layer. Used layer. Unused layer. Current layer.
Name	Shows the name of the layer. To change the layer, click once to display a border and click again to type a new name.
On	Shows the current on/off state of a layer. Click to turn the layer on or off.
Freeze	Shows the current freeze/thaw state of a layer. Click to freeze or thaw a layer.
Lock	Shows the current locked/unlocked state of a layer. Click to lock or unlock a layer.
Color	Shows the current color of the layer. Click to change the color.
Linetype	Shows the current linetype of the layer. Click to change the linetype.
Lineweight	Shows the current lineweight of the layer. Click to choose a new lineweight.

continued

TABLE 11.1   *(continued)*

Column Name	Description
Plot Style	Shows the current plot style of the layer. Click to select a new plot style. (Chapter 17 covers plot styles.)
Plot	Shows the current plottable/not plottable state of the layer. Click to make the layer plottable or not plottable.
Current VP Freeze	Shows the freeze/thaw state of the layer in the current floating viewport. Click to freeze or thaw the layer in active floating viewports. This column is displayed only if you have floating viewports and a layout tab is active. (Chapter 17 covers floating viewports.)
New VP Freeze	Shows the current freeze/thaw state of the layer in new floating viewports that you create. Click to freeze or thaw the layer in new viewports. This column is displayed only if you have floating viewports and a plot layout is active. (Chapter 17 covers floating viewports.)
Description	Provides a place to enter a description of a layer.

> **NOTE** When you open the Layer Properties Manager with a layout active, four additional columns appear that let you override layer properties for specific viewports. I explain this feature in more detail in Chapter 17.

To adjust the display in the Layer Properties Manager, you can do the following:

- Change the width of any column in the Layer Properties Manager by placing the cursor over the line dividing two column headings, and dragging.
- Double-click the line dividing two columns to minimize/maximize the column width.
- Click any column head to sort the layers by that column. Click again to sort in the opposite order.
- Right-click any heading and display a shortcut menu where you can choose which columns you want to see.
- Drag any column to any location to specify the order of the columns.
- Resize the entire dialog box by dragging on any side.

Naming the layer

 Click the New Layer icon. A new layer appears, named `Layer1`, as shown in Figure 11.2. The name is highlighted so that you can immediately type in a new name for the layer. Press Enter after you type the name.

> **NOTE** Next to the New Layer button is the New Layer VP Frozen in All Viewports button for creating a layer that is frozen in all viewports. I discuss freezing layers in viewports in Chapter 17, where I discuss viewports.

> **TIP** To create several new layers at once, click New and type all of the layer names that you want, separated by commas. Press Enter after the last layer that you want. If you want a new layer to have the same color and/or linetype as an existing layer — which is very common — choose that existing layer and click New. The new layer inherits the properties of the selected layer. You can then make any changes that you want.

Layer names can be up to 255 characters long and may include spaces. Layer names retain the uppercase/lowercase characters that you type. Layer names may not include the following symbols: < > / \ " ; ? * | , = `.

FIGURE 11.2

The new layer appears as Layer1 and is highlighted so that you can enter the new layer name.

Assigning a color

To change the default color, move the cursor to the color box in the same row as the new layer. Click to open the Select Color dialog box, as shown in Figure 11.3, with the Index Color tab displayed. (The AutoCAD LT Select Color dialog box doesn't have any other tabs.)

FIGURE 11.3

The Select Color dialog box.

Click the color that you want. At the bottom of the dialog box, the color's name or number appears along with a sample of the color. Click OK to close the dialog box and return to the Layer Properties Manager.

Note that the Index Color tab offers you a choice of standard colors, gray shades, and a fuller palette of colors. The standard colors are the original colors that AutoCAD (and then AutoCAD LT) offered, and they're the ones most often used, even today. Their advantage is that each color is easily distinguishable from the others. These colors have both a name and a number, whereas other colors have only a number (an *index*). The standard colors are red (1), yellow (2), green (3), cyan (4), blue (5), magenta (6), and white (7).

NOTE You have the choice of using many different colors for the background color of a drawing, but commonly it is a black or a white screen. The default screen is black and the default color for 7 is white. When you work on a white screen, objects using the color of 7 appear black (or else they would be invisible), but the color is still called white. Therefore, if you choose the black color tile in the Select Color dialog box, the color is listed as white. To change the screen color, choose Tools ➪ Options and click the Display tab. Then click the Colors button. For a 2D drawing, choose 2D model space from the Context box and choose Background from the Interface Element box. Then use the Color drop-down list to specify a color.

AUTOCAD ONLY AutoCAD offers two other tabs in the Select Color dialog box. The True Color tab lets you define any color, and the Color Books tab lets you use special files that define colors.

For more color choices, click the True Color tab (AutoCAD only), shown in Figure 11.4.

FIGURE 11.4

The True Color tab of the Select Color dialog box offers a more precise way to define color.

To define a color, first choose the color model from the Color Model drop-down list. You have two choices:

- **HSL (Hue, Saturation, Luminance):** Hue is the actual wavelength of light that defines the color. Saturation is the purity or intensity of the color. Luminance is the brightness of the color.
- **RGB (Red, Green, Blue):** Defines a color according to the intensity of red, green, and blue in the color.

If you choose the HSL color model, specify the color as follows:

1. Specify the hue by dragging the crosshairs horizontally across the colors, or type a value from 0° to 360° in the Hue text box.
2. Specify the saturation by dragging the crosshairs vertically over the colors, or type a value from 0% to 100% in the Saturation text box.
3. Specify the luminance by dragging the bar on the color slider, or type a value from 0% to 100% in the Luminance text box.

When you define a color using the HSL color model, you also see the RGB values displayed in the Select Color dialog box.

If you choose the RGB color model, specify the red color by dragging the color bar, or type a value from 1 to 255 in the Red text box. Do the same for the green and blue color values.

You can also choose a color using the Color Books tab (AutoCAD only), shown in Figure 11.5.

FIGURE 11.5

The Color Books tab of the Select Color dialog box.

The Color Books tab of the Select Color dialog box displays colors in *color books*. Color books are files that define colors. AutoCAD includes several Pantone color books. Pantone is a commonly used system of matching colors that is often used for printing on paper and fabric.

To use a color from a color book, follow these steps:

1. On the Color Books tab of the Select Color dialog box, choose a color book from the Color Book drop-down list.
2. Drag the color slider or use the up and down arrows to choose a "page" of the color book. On the left, you see the colors for that page. A page can hold up to 10 colors.
3. Choose one of the colors on the left side of the dialog box.
4. Click OK.

Assigning a linetype

The default linetype is a continuous line, but you can also use many other linetypes. These linetypes are repeating patterns of dashes and/or dots and spaces, although they can also include text and shapes. Linetypes are covered more fully later in this chapter.

To change the default linetype, move the cursor to the linetype in the new layer's row. Click to open the Select Linetype dialog box, as shown in Figure 11.6.

Installing Color Books

You can install additional color books. Color book files must have an `.acb` file extension. In addition to Pantone color books, you may be able to find DIC or RAL color specification files.

The default location for color books is in the `Support\Color` subfolder of your `AutoCAD 2008` program folder. If you copy color-book files there, you can find them on the Color Books tab of the Select Color dialog box. Another default location is in the `Documents and Settings\username\Application Data\Autodesk\AutoCAD 2008\R17.1\enu\Support\Color` folder. You use this folder for color books that you install. To use color books from another location, follow these steps:

1. Choose Tools ⇨ Options to open the Options dialog box.
2. Choose the Files tab.
3. Double-click the Color Book Locations item.
4. Click Add and then click Browse. Locate the color book file and click OK.

If you have the Select Color dialog box open while you copy a new color book file to a location, close the dialog box and re-open it to access the new colors.

FIGURE 11.6

The Select Linetype dialog box as it appears before you have loaded any linetypes.

If the linetype that you want appears on the list, click the linetype and choose OK to close the dialog box. If the linetype does not appear, you need to load the linetype. Click Load to open the Load or Reload Linetypes dialog box, shown in Figure 11.7.

Linetypes are stored in text (or ASCII) files with the filename extension .lin. The standard linetypes are stored in acad.lin in AutoCAD and in acadlt.lin in AutoCAD LT. You can create your own linetypes and store them in acad.lin or acadlt.lin. You can also store them in another file that you create with the extension .lin. Click File at the top of the dialog box if you want to load a linetype from a file that you created. Choose the linetype file that you want to load and click Open.

FIGURE 11.7

The Load or Reload Linetypes dialog box.

CROSS-REF See Chapter 31 for a full discussion of creating your own linetypes.

To choose a range of linetypes to load, click the first linetype in the range, press Shift, and click the last linetype in the range. To choose more than one noncontiguous linetype, press Ctrl for each additional linetype that you choose. To select all or clear all of the linetypes, right-click in the dialog box and choose the desired option from the shortcut menu.

As soon as you load a linetype and click OK, you return to the Select Linetype dialog box. The loaded linetype now appears on the list. Choose it and click OK. You're now back in the Layer Properties Manager dialog box.

Assigning a lineweight

A lineweight assigns a width to a line. When you give a layer a lineweight, every object on that layer has the same lineweight. A lineweight can help to distinguish various elements of your drawing, both on-screen and on paper. For example, you could use a thicker lineweight to indicate planned construction changes, for dimension lines, or to represent the true width of an object. The LWT button on the status bar toggles the display of lineweights on and off. By default, LWT is off.

To set a lineweight for a layer, click the Lineweight column of that layer to open the Lineweight dialog box, shown in Figure 11.8. Choose a lineweight and click OK.

FIGURE 11.8

When you click the Lineweight column of the Layer Properties Manager, the Lineweight dialog box opens so that you can choose a lineweight.

Lineweights have the following features:

- The default lineweight value for layers and objects is called DEFAULT, which has a value of 0.010 inch or 0.25 mm.

- On the Model tab, where you draw, lineweights are displayed in relation to pixels, the unit of measurement for computer screens. A lineweight of 0 is displayed with a width of 1 pixel. Wider lineweights are calculated proportionally to the actual width of the lineweight. The lineweight display on the Model tab does not change as you zoom in or out.

- On Layout tabs (covered in Chapter 17), lineweights are displayed in real-world units as they will be plotted. Lineweights act like other objects in your drawing and look bigger or smaller as you zoom in and out.

- By default, lineweights are measured in millimeters. You can format lineweights by choosing Format ⇨ Lineweight. The Lineweight Settings dialog box opens, as shown in Figure 11.9. The Lineweights section lists available lineweights. Choose a default lineweight from the Default drop-down list. The default is 0.01 inch or 0.25 mm. The Adjust Display Scale slider determines how lineweights are displayed on the Model tab. Adjust this setting if you use several closely related lineweights but can't distinguish them on your screen. The Display Lineweight check box turns the display of lineweights on and off. (See the next bullet for an easier way to do this.)

- To turn the display of lineweights on and off, just click the LWT button on the status bar.

If you don't want to use lineweights, you can just ignore them and display every object using the default lineweight.

After you've set your new layer's color, linetype, and lineweight in the Layer Properties Manager, you're ready to use the layer. You can click Apply after any change to apply the change without closing the dialog box. Click OK to close the Layer Properties Manager.

FIGURE 11.9

The Lineweight Settings dialog box lets you format how lineweights are measured and displayed.

NOTE Many people have CAD standards that restrict which layers should be in a drawing. You can specify that you want to receive a notification whenever a new layer is added to a drawing. Then you can decide if the layer meets your CAD standards. For more information, see Chapter 26, where I cover CAD standards.

ON the DVD-ROM The drawing used in the following exercise on creating layers, ab11-a.dwg, is in the Drawings folder on the DVD.

STEPS: Creating a New Layer

1. Open ab11-a.dwg from the DVD.

2. Save the file as ab11-01.dwg in your AutoCAD Bible folder.

3. Choose Layer Properties Manager from the Layers toolbar or the Layers control panel of the Dashboard to open the Layer Properties Manager.

4. Click the New Layer icon. A new layer named Layer1 appears, highlighted. Type **Walls** ↵ as the name for the new layer.

5. Click the color square in the Color column to open the Select Color dialog box. Choose the blue square from the Standard Colors and click OK.

6. Choose the New Layer icon again to create another new layer. Type **Hidden** ↵.

7. Click the color square in the Color column to open the Select Color dialog box.

8. If you have AutoCAD, do the following:

   In the Select Color dialog box, click the True Color tab. From the Color Model drop-down list, choose RGB. In the Color text box, type **141, 218, 189**. (In some instances, you may have to re-choose RGB from the Color Model drop-down list to make the Color text box active.) Press Tab. You should see a teal (blue-green) color. Click OK.

   If you have AutoCAD LT, do the following:

   Find Index Color 121 (a teal color) and click. Then click OK.

9. In the main layer listing, click Continuous in the same row as the Hidden layer to open the Select Linetype dialog box. Click Load to open the Load or Reload Linetypes dialog box. Scroll down until you see the HIDDEN linetype. Choose it and click OK. In the Select Linetype dialog box, choose HIDDEN and click OK.

10. Click the Description column for the Hidden layer. Click again so that a text cursor appears. Type **teal, hidden lines** ↵.

11. Click OK to close the Layer Properties Manager.

12. Click the Layer Control drop-down list on the Layers toolbar or the Layers control panel of the Dashboard to see the two layers that you just created listed there. Click again to close the box.

13. Save your drawing.

Using layers

To use a layer that you have just created, click the Set Current icon in the Layer Properties Manager or double-click the layer's name. Then click OK to return to your drawing. Objects that you create now are drawn on that layer and display with the layer's color, linetype, and lineweight. (The lineweight shows only if the LWT button on the status bar is on.)

All objects that you draw go on the current layer. After you have the layers you need, you need to switch from layer to layer as you draw. You can continue to choose Layers in the Layer Properties Manager, click the name of a layer, click Set Current, and then click OK. However, there is an easier way — through the Layer Control drop-down list on the Layers toolbar, shown in Figure 11.10, or the Layers control panel of the Dashboard. (If the Layers toolbar is not displayed, right-click any toolbar button and choose Layers from the list of toolbars. To display the Dashboard, choose Tools ➪ Palettes ➪ Dashboard.)

FIGURE 11.10

The Layer Control drop-down list.

The Layer Control window has three display modes:

- If no object is selected, it displays the current layer.
- If one or more objects are selected, it displays the layer of the selected object(s).
- When objects on varying layers are selected, the Layer Control list goes blank, indicating that more than one layer is included in the selection.

To check the current layer, make sure that no object is selected. If necessary, press Esc to deselect any objects.

To open the Layer Control drop-down list, click its down arrow. You see a list of all of your layers, including their states and colors. When you pass the mouse over the items, a tooltip tells you what they mean. The Layer Control drop-down list has three functions:

- It switches the current layer so that you can draw on a new layer.
- It changes the following states of any specific layer on the list:
  - On/Off
  - Frozen/Thawed
  - Frozen in Current Viewport/Thawed in Current Viewport
  - Locked/Unlocked
- It changes the layer of a selected object.

Take the time to learn how to use this drop-down list; it can save you a great deal of time. To change other states of a layer (such as plottable/not plottable), open the Layer Properties Manager.

Switching the current layer

To switch the current layer, make sure that no object is currently selected, click the Layer Control drop-down list arrow, and click the name of the layer that you want to be current. Be careful to click only the name — otherwise, you may change the layer's state. You may need to press Esc first to deselect all objects. After you click a new layer name, the drop-down list automatically closes.

 The Layer Previous button on the Layers toolbar, or in the Dashboard's Layers control panel, switches you to the last layer that you used. If you click it again, you're in the layer before that. Use Layer Previous as a shortcut to finding and choosing the last layer that you used on the Layer Control drop-down list. (Layer Previous is not available in AutoCAD LT.)

Changing a layer's state

After you create a layer, you can manage that layer — and all of the objects on that layer — by changing its states. You can change some layer states through the Layer Control drop-down list; others must be changed in the Layer Properties Manager. Each layer state has different properties and uses:

- **On/Off:** Turn layers off when objects on those layers interfere with the drawing process. For example, if you want to edit only objects on your Object layer, but objects exist on other layers nearby, you can turn off the other layers and easily select the objects on the Object layer with a window. Then turn the other layers back on. The on/off state is available on the Layer Control drop-down list.
- **Thaw/Freeze:** You can freeze layers for reasons similar to those that lead you to turn off layers. In general, freeze layers when you want to work without those layers for a longer period of time. The thawed/frozen state is available on the Layer Control drop-down list.
- **Thaw/Freeze in Current Viewport:** You may want to freeze or thaw layers in some floating viewports but not in others. For example, if you want to display dimensions in one viewport but not in others, freeze your dimensions layer in all of the viewports except one. You can change this state on the Layer Control drop-down list if you're working on a layout. You can also click the Current Viewport Freeze icon in the Layer Properties Manager.
- **Thaw/Freeze in New Viewports:** You can also freeze or thaw layers in future viewports that you create. For example, after you display dimensions or text in one viewport, you may want to make sure that they won't appear in any new viewports that you create. This state is available in the New Viewport Freeze column of the Layer Properties Manager.

CROSS-REF See Chapter 17 for an explanation of floating viewports and layouts.

- **Unlock/Lock:** Lock a layer when you want to ensure that objects on that layer are not changed. You can still use objects on locked layers for reference (for example, you can use their object snaps). Click the lock/unlock icon on the Layer Control drop-down list.

NEW FEATURE When you select an object on a locked layer, it doesn't display grips, because you can't edit it.

- **Plot/No Plot:** Make a layer not plottable when you want to create reference text or revision marks on your drawing but don't want to plot them. You may also have a drawing that contains both actual and planned structures; this feature enables you to plot showing only the actual structures. Being able to change a layer's plottable state makes it possible for you to create variations on your drawing, perhaps for different users, such as electricians, plumbers, and roofers. The plot/no plot state is available in the Plot column of the Layer Properties Manager.

TIP Both the off and frozen states make layers invisible. The purpose of frozen and thawed layer states is to reduce regeneration time — this is the main difference between On/Off and Thawed/Frozen layer visibility options. However, today's computers are faster, and recent releases of the software have reduced the need for regeneration. Also, remember that thawing a layer causes a regeneration, whereas turning a layer back on only causes a redraw. As a result, you might actually save a regeneration by using On/Off instead of Thawed/Frozen.

Click any of the state icons to toggle a layer's state. For example, if you want to freeze a layer, click its sun icon; it switches to a snowflake icon. Table 11.2 shows the icons for each state.

TABLE 11.2

Layer State Icons

State	Icon	State	Icon
On		Off	
Thawed (in all viewports)		Frozen (in all viewports)	
Thawed (in current viewport)		Frozen (in current viewport)	
Thawed (in new viewports)		Frozen (in new viewports)	
Unlocked		Locked	
Plottable		Not plottable	

When you change a layer's state, the drop-down list stays open so that you can change the state of more than one layer at a time. Click the top of the list to close it.

CAUTION Be careful when editing a drawing with frozen or off layers — it's easy to forget about them. For example, you could move a whole section of your drawing and inadvertently leave the frozen objects in that section behind.

Saving layer states

Often you work with sets of layer states. For example, you may lock certain layers during part of the editing process to avoid changing objects on those layers. You may also set some layers as not plottable just before final plotting, but want them plotted for a draft plot. You may also want to temporarily change the properties of certain layers — color, linetype, lineweight, and plot style — and then change them back.

You could spend a lot of time adjusting all of these layer states and properties. Instead, you can save and restore sets of layer states — the properties and states of all of the layers in a drawing. You can save layer states to automate the process of restoring layer states and properties by saving the set of all layer states and properties. After you save this set, you can restore it at any time. The term *layer states* includes the set of all layer states as well as their properties.

You can also export layer-state settings to a file. You can then use the layer-state settings in another drawing with the same or similar layers.

To save a layer state, follow these steps:

1. Set all of the layer states and properties the way you want them. Usually, you've already done this and should save the state before making changes that you plan to reverse later on.

2. Choose Layer Properties Manager from the Layers toolbar of the Layers control panel of the Dashboard. In the Layer Properties Manager, click the Layer States Manager icon to open the Layer States Manager dialog box, shown in Figure 11.11. Alternatively, you can click the Layer States Manager icon on the Layers toolbar or in the Dashboard's Layers control panel (the LAYERSTATE command) to go directly to the Layer States Manager.

FIGURE 11.11

The Layer States Manager dialog box.

3. Click New and type a name for your layer state in the New Layer State Name text box of the New Layer State to Save dialog box. If you want, type a description. Click OK.

4. Back in the Layer States Manager, choose the layer states and properties that you want to save in the Layer Properties to Restore section. (If you don't see this section, click the More Restore Options arrow button at the lower-right corner of the dialog box.)

CAUTION   States and properties that you do not save are not affected later when you restore the layer state. For example, if you save only the on/off state and then change both a layer's on/off state and its color, when you restore the layer state, only the on/off state is returned to its original setting; the layer retains its new color.

5. If you want your drawing to look exactly as it did when you saved the layer state (in terms of layers), check the Turn Off Layers Not Found in Layer State check box. Any new layers that you create after saving the layer state are then turned off when you restore your layer state.

6. Click Close.

 To restore a layer state, open the Layer States Manager. Choose the layer state and click Restore. If the Layer Properties Manager is open, click OK to close it.

The Layer States Manager enables you to manage layer states in the following ways:

- **Restore:** Restores a saved layer state.
- **Delete:** Deletes a layer state.
- **Import:** Imports a layer state that has been previously exported as a `.las` file. Importing a layer state gives you access to layer states that others have saved. Click Import to open the Import Layer States dialog box.

NEW FEATURE   You can now import a layer state from a DWG (drawing), DWT (template), or DWS (standards) file. (Standards files are covered in Chapter 26.) In the Import Layer States dialog box, choose the type of file you want from the Files of Type drop-down list. Also, the Layer States Manager now includes layer states from xrefs. (See Chapter 19 for information about xrefs.)

- **Export:** Saves the settings of a layer state in a `.las` file. Exporting a layer state gives others access to your layer state settings.

You can choose which properties and states you want to restore. If necessary, click the More Restore Options arrow button to expand the Layer States Manager. Then check or uncheck any of the property and states check boxes. To rename a layer state, click its name, type a new name, and press Enter. After you finish using the Layer States Manager, click Close to close the dialog box.

Changing an existing object's layer

Sometimes you need to change the layer of an object or objects that you've already drawn. You can do this easily by selecting one or more objects and clicking the layer name that you want for the object in the Layer Control drop-down list (from the Layers toolbar or the Dashboard's Layers control panel). The list automatically closes.

NOTE   If you turn off Noun/verb selection, as I explain in "Customizing the selection process" in Chapter 9, you cannot select an object and change its layer from the Layer Control drop-down list. Instead, you can change the layer in the Properties palette.

You can also change an object's layer in the Properties palette. Choose Properties on the Standard or the Standard Annotation toolbar or press Ctrl+1. Use the Properties palette if you want to change more than one property of an object at one time.

It's easy to inadvertently change an object's layer. Make sure that objects are not selected (press Esc) if you're about to use the Layer Control drop-down list just to change the current layer.

Making an object's layer current

 If you're adding an object, you usually want to draw on the same layer as an existing object. You could select the object to see what layer it's on, press Esc to deselect the object, and then choose that layer from the Layer Control drop-down list to make it current. However, this process is easier with the Make Object's Layer Current button on the Layers toolbar or in the Layers control panel of the Dashboard. Simply select an object and click the button. That object's layer is now current.

Using special layer tools

A set of layer tools that were once in the Express Tools collection are very helpful for working with layers. You can now find them by choosing Format ⇨ Layer Tools and choosing one of the tools from the sub-menu. Table 11.3 lists the Layer tools and what they do.

TABLE 11.3

Layer Tools

Layer Tool Name	Menu	Description
LAYMCUR	Format ⇨ Layer Tools ⇨ Make Object's Layer Current	Makes the layer of the selected object the current layer.
LAYERP	Format ⇨ Layer Tools ⇨ Layer Previous	Makes the previous layer that you used the current layer. (AutoCAD only)
LAYWALK	Format ⇨ Layer Tools ⇨ Layer Walk	A full-featured command that helps you to see which objects are on which layers. Using the dialog box and the shortcut menu, you can list the number of objects on each layer, count the total number of layers, save layer states, and purge unused layers.
LAYMCH	Format ⇨ Layer Tools ⇨ Layer Match	Changes the layer of selected objects to match that of another selected object.
LAYCUR	Format ⇨ Layer Tools ⇨ Change to Current Layer	Changes the selected object's layer to the current layer.
COPYTOLAYER	Format ⇨ Layer Tools ⇨ Copy Objects to New Layer	Copies objects while changing the copy to the layer that you specify.
LAYISO	Format ⇨ Layer Tools ⇨ Layer Isolate	Turns off all layers except the layer of an object that you select, to isolate a specific layer. You can now lock and fade layers. (I explain this command further after this table.)
LAYVPI	Format ⇨ Layer Tools ⇨ Isolate Layer to Current Viewport	Freezes all layers except the layer of an object that you select in all viewports except the current one, isolating the selected layer in the current viewport. (See Chapter 17 for information on viewports.)

continued

TABLE 11.3	*(continued)*	
Layer Tool Name	**Menu**	**Description**
LAYUNISO	Format ⇨ Layer Tools ⇨ Layer Unisolate	Restores the state of layers that existed before you used LAYISO. (I explain this command further after this table.)
LAYOFF	Format ⇨ Layer Tools ⇨ Layer Off	Turns the layer of the selected object(s) off.
LAYON	Format ⇨ Layer Tools ⇨ Turn All Layers On	Turns all layers on.
LAYFRZ	Format ⇨ Layer Tools ⇨ Layer Freeze	Freezes the layer of the selected object(s).
LAYTHW	Format ⇨ Layer Tools ⇨ Thaw All Layers	Thaws all layers.
LAYLCK	Format ⇨ Layer Tools ⇨ Layer Lock	Locks the layer of the selected object(s).
LAYULK	Format ⇨ Layer Tools ⇨ Layer Unlock	Unlocks all layers.
LAYMRG	Format ⇨ Layer Tools ⇨ Layer Merge	Changes the layer of all objects on the first layer selected to the second layer selected. The first layer is purged.
LAYDEL	Format ⇨ Layer Tools ⇨ Layer Delete	Deletes objects from the specified layer and purges that layer.

NEW FEATURE The LAYISO command has been updated to include the ability to lock layers (other than the one you're isolating) and to fade those layers instead of turning them off. The default is to lock layers and fade them by 50 percent. You can change the default using the Settings option. For example, you can choose to turn off the layers or change the fade percentage. Use the LAYUNISO command to unisolate layers. These commands are now in the expanded section of the Layers control panel of the Dashboard. In the Layers control panel, click the double-down arrow at the lower-left corner. (The arrow doesn't appear until you pass your cursor over that area.) Then drag the Locked Layer Fading slider to the left or right to decrease or increase fading.

ON the DVD-ROM The drawing used in the following exercise on working with layers, ab11-b.dwg, is in the Drawings folder on the DVD.

STEPS: Working with Layers

1. Open ab11-b.dwg from the DVD.
2. Save the file as ab11-02.dwg in your AutoCAD Bible folder. This drawing is shown in Figure 11.12. The current layer is 0. Make sure that OSNAP is on. Set running object snaps for endpoint and quadrant. Display either the Layers toolbar or the Layers control panel of the Dashboard.
3. Click the Layer Control drop-down list and click Pipes to change the current layer to Pipes.
4. Start the LINE command. Draw a line from ❶ to ❷ in Figure 11.12, using the Quadrant running object snap.
5. Click the Layer Control drop-down list and click Object to change the current layer to Object.

FIGURE 11.12

This gas extraction well plan drawing needs to be completed.

GAS EXTRACTION WELL PLAN
N.T.S.

Thanks to the Army Corps of Engineers for this drawing.

6. Click the Layer Control drop-down list and click the On/Off icon of the Dim layer. Click again at the top of the list to close it.

7. Start the CIRCLE command. Right-click and choose 2p to use the two-point option. Draw a circle from the endpoint of ❸ to ❹ in Figure 11.12 using the Endpoint running object snap.

8. Without changing the layer, start the CIRCLE command and again use the 2p option. Draw a circle between the endpoints at ❺ and ❻.

9. The last circle was drawn on the wrong layer. To change its layer, select the circle. Then click the Layer Control drop-down list and choose Pipes. Press Esc to remove the grips and see the result. The circle is now on the Pipes layer. Notice that the current layer is still Object in the Layer Control display.

10. Pick any red object (the Pipes layer). Choose Make Object's Layer Current from the Layers toolbar or choose Format ▷ Layer Tools ▷ Make Object's Layer Current. The Pipes layer is now the current layer. Draw a line from the right quadrant of the circle at ❶ to the left quadrant of the circle at ❺ and ❻ in Figure 11.12.

11. You want to draw a line on the Object layer. This is the previous layer that you used.

   ▪ **If you have AutoCAD:** Click Layer Previous on the Layers toolbar or in the Layers control panel of the Dashboard. The Object layer is now the current layer.

   ▪ **If you have AutoCAD LT:** Click the Layer Control drop-down list and click Object.

12. Draw a line from the endpoint at ❼ to the endpoint at ❽.

13. Pick any text to see what layer it is on. The Layer Control drop-down list changes to show the Text layer. Press Esc to deselect the text. Now choose the words GAS EXTRACTION WELL PLAN at the bottom of the drawing. Click the Layer Control drop-down list and choose Text. Press Esc to remove the grips.

14. Save your drawing. It should look like Figure 11.13.

FIGURE 11.13

The completed drawing.

Later in this chapter, I explain how to import layers from other drawings.

Modifying layers

Sometimes you need to change the properties of a layer, such as its color or linetype. Changing a layer's properties is a powerful tool because every object on that layer is automatically regenerated with the new properties. Other layer housekeeping tasks are renaming and deleting layers. You use the Layer Properties Manager for these functions.

Managing columns

If you have many layers in a drawing, sorting can help you find the layers on which you need to work. You can sort the layer listing in a drawing by any column, by clicking once on the column title. Click again to see the list in reverse order. Long layer names display a tooltip with the entire layer name.

TIP If sorting by layer name does not appear to be working, increase the value for the MAXSORT system variable, which determines the maximum number of symbols that AutoCAD or AutoCAD LT sorts. Type maxsort ↵ on the command line and enter a larger number. Press Enter.

NEW FEATURE You can change the order of the columns by dragging them. For example, you may want to place the Color column next to the Name column. You can also choose which columns appear in the Layer Properties Manager. Right-click any column name and uncheck any column that you don't want to see. This choice remains until you change it. If you want to see a column again, right-click a column name again and check that column.

Filtering the layer list

Some complex drawings may have dozens of layers, and you may have a hard time finding the layer that you want to change in the Layer Properties Manager. You can filter the layer list so that you only see the layers that you want. This makes it easy to change a group of layers at once. The filter tree panel on the left side of the Layer Properties Manager contains one filter, All Used Layers, as well as the default that displays all layers. To display only used layers, click the All Used Layers filter in the filter tree panel.

 NOTE If you don't see the filter tree panel, right-click in the Layer Properties Manager and choose Show Filter Tree.

You can create your own filters. There are two types of filters:

- **Properties filter:** Defines a filter by the properties of the layer. For example, you can create a filter that displays only green layers or layers that start with the letter *A*.

- **Group filter:** Defines a filter by selecting layers that go into a filter. A group filter offers complete flexibility to filter layers. For example, you might want to create a group filter that contains all of your text, annotation, and dimension layers.

To create a properties filter, click the New Property Filter button to open the Layer Filter Properties, shown in Figure 11.14. Notice that the Filter Definition pane at the top has the same columns as the Layer Properties Manager.

Name the filter in the Filter Name text box. To choose a property, click in that property's column. Then do one of the following:

- If a drop-down arrow appears, click the arrow and choose one of the options from the drop-down list. (To remove a property, choose the blank line at the top of the drop-down list.)

- If an ellipsis button appears, click the button and choose a property from the dialog box that opens. For example, you can choose a layer color from the Select Color dialog box. (To remove a property, select the text, press Del, and click anywhere outside the column.)

- To specify a filter for a named property, such as the name or linetype of a layer, you can use wildcards. The two most common wildcard characters are * (asterisk), which replaces any number of characters, and ?, which replaces any single character. Figure 11.14 shows the layer name filter set to h*. The color is also specified as magenta. Therefore, the filter includes only layers whose names start with the letter *H* and are magenta.

As you work, the Filter Preview pane shows the results of your filter. When you're done, click OK. The Layer Properties Manager now shows only the layers that match your filter specifications.

 To create a group filter, open the Layer Properties Manager and click the New Group Filter button. Enter a name for the filter in place of the default name that appear In the filter tree panel, choose a filter that displays the layers you need, such as All. Then simply drag the layers that you want onto the group filter's name.

TIP To add layers by selecting objects that are on the layers you want, right-click the filter and choose Select Layers ⇨ Add. You return to your drawing where you can select objects. Press Enter to end object selection.

To display all layers except the ones specified by any filter, click Invert Filter. If you want to filter the Layer Control listing in the same way, click the Settings button. In the Layer Settings dialog box that opens, check Apply Layer Filter to Layer Toolbar. Click OK.

Click OK to close the Layer Properties Manager and return to your drawing.

FIGURE 11.14

The Layer Filter Properties dialog box.

TIP   When you work with a large number of layers, think carefully about how you name them. Naming layers in groups is common. For example, if you have several text layers, you could name them Text Title, Text Notes, and Text Schedule. A systematic layer-naming scheme makes it easy to filter the layers that you need, which in turn makes it easy to make changes to groups of layers.

ON the DVD-ROM   Layerhtm displays a copy of the Layer Properties Manager in your browser, so that you can print it. Look in Software\Chapter 11.

Changing a layer's color, linetype, and lineweight

To change a layer's color, choose Layer Properties Manager from the Layers toolbar or the Dashboard's Layers control panel to open the Layer Properties Manager. Choose the color swatch of the layer that you want to modify. The Select Color dialog box opens. Choose a color and click OK twice to return to your drawing. For more information about choosing colors, see the section "Assigning a color" earlier in this chapter.

To change a layer's linetype, follow the same procedure as for changing the color. If you need to choose a linetype that is not on the list, click the linetype of the layer to open the Select Linetype dialog box. There you can either choose a loaded linetype or load a linetype if necessary.

To change a layer's lineweight, open the Layer Properties Manager and click the lineweight for any layer. Choose a new lineweight from the Lineweight dialog box.

TIP   You can modify more than one layer at a time. In the Layer Properties Manager, right-click and choose Select All to choose all of the layers. Choose Clear All to deselect all of the layers. You can choose a range of layers by clicking the first layer in the range, pressing Shift, and clicking the last layer in the range. Finally, you can choose individual layers by pressing Ctrl for each additional layer. Changes that you make to color, linetype, or lineweight affect all of the selected layers.

CROSS-REF   When you're ready to lay out a drawing for plotting, you generally work on a layout and create floating viewports. You can change the properties of a layer in a viewport. For example, you might want a layer to appear in a different color when you display it in a small detail view from the color that you want in a larger context. For more information, see Chapter 17 where I cover layouts and viewports.

Renaming layers

Thinking out your layer-naming scheme in advance is best. Many disciplines and organizations have layer-naming standards. However, sometimes you simply need to rename a layer.

To rename a layer, choose Layer Properties Manager from the Layers toolbar or the Dashboard's Layers control panel to open the Layer Properties Manager. Click the name of the layer, and then click a second time. A border appears, and the name is highlighted. Type the new name and press Enter. Alternatively, you can right-click the layer name and choose Rename Layer from the shortcut menu or just press F2.

 NOTE You cannot rename layer 0. Layer 0 is the default layer and always remains the same. You can set CAD standards that allow you to check for non-standard layer names. For more information, see Chapter 26.

Deleting layers

To delete a layer, open the Layer Properties Manager. Click the name of the layer. Press Delete and then click OK.

NOTE You cannot delete the current layer or any layer that has objects on it. (Where would those objects go?) You also cannot delete layer 0, which is the default layer. Finally, you cannot delete layers from external references (covered in Chapter 19).

Purging layers and linetypes

Layer and linetype definitions add to the size of your drawing because they're kept in the drawing's database. Therefore, eliminating layers and linetypes that you aren't using is worthwhile. You can delete them, but sometimes it's hard to know which layers contain no objects. The PURGE command lets you delete many types of unused definitions, including layers and linetypes.

To purge layers and linetypes, choose File ⇨ Drawing Utilities ⇨ Purge. The Purge dialog box opens, as shown in Figure 11.15.

FIGURE 11.15

The Purge dialog box.

NOTE The Incremental Save Percentage option may prevent a purge during a drawing session from removing all unreferenced layers or linetypes from the drawing. To avoid this, you can either set incremental save to zero, or save the drawing and reopen it and then immediately use the PURGE command. To set this option, choose Tools ⇨ Options ⇨ Open and Save tab.

At the top of the dialog box, you can choose to view objects that you can purge or objects that you cannot purge. Why would you want to view objects that you cannot purge? Sometimes it's hard to figure out why you can't purge a certain object, and the dialog box has a handy feature that lets you select an object and view possible reasons why it cannot be purged.

To start purging, choose View Items You Can Purge. A plus sign (+) next to each type of object indicates that it contains purgeable objects. For example, Figure 11.15 indicates that you can purge blocks, dimension styles, and shapes. Click the plus sign to display the specific items.

To purge an individual item, select it and click Purge. Check the Confirm Each Item to Be Purged option if you want to see a dialog box asking you to confirm each purge. Click Purge All to purge all possible items. Check the Purge Nested Items option to purge items within other named objects. Usually, these are layers, linetypes, and so on inside blocks.

TIP You can select more than one item at a time to purge. To select an additional item, press Ctrl as you click. To select a contiguous group of items, click the first item in the group, press and hold Shift, and then select the last item in the group.

After you're done purging, click Close to close the Purge dialog box.

ON the DVD-ROM The drawing used in the following exercise on modifying layers, ab11-c.dwg, is in the Drawings folder on the DVD. *(Thanks to Michael J. Lemmons of Winston Products Company in Louisville, Kentucky, for this drawing.)*

STEPS: Modifying Layers

1. Open ab11-c.dwg from the DVD.

2. Save the file as ab11-03.dwg in your AutoCAD Bible folder.

3. Choose Layer Properties Manager from the Layers toolbar or from the Layers control panel of the Dashboard.

4. Click the New Property Filter button. In the Filter Name text box, type **M layers.** In the Name column, type **m*** to list all layers starting with the letter M. Click OK. The layer list now looks like Figure 11.16.

5. In the Layer Properties Manager, click the top layer. Press Shift and click the next-to-last layer. All of the layers except for Mydims are selected. Click anywhere in the Linetype column to open the Select Linetype dialog box and choose Dashed. Click OK. Notice that all of the selected layers now have a dashed linetype. Click OK to return to the drawing. The layers that you selected now have the dashed linetype.

6. Open the Layer Properties Manager again. Choose Mydims. Click it a second time so that the name of the layer is highlighted. Type **Titles ⏎**. The name of the layer is changed. Click OK.

7. Start the ERASE command and pick anywhere on the title block (it is all one object) and the three labels FRONT, TOP, and RIGHT SIDE. Press Enter to end the command.

FIGURE 11.16

FIGURE 11.16

The Layer Properties Manager now shows only layers starting with the letter *M*.

8. Choose Layer Properties Manager from the Layers toolbar again. Notice that the Titles layer is not on the list because this layer no longer starts with the letter M. In the Filter Tree panel, click All to display all of the layers.

9. Scroll down the list of layers and choose Titles. Check the Indicate Layers in Use check box at the bottom of the dialog box. You can see that its Status icon is off, indicating that the layer contains no objects. Click the Delete button. Click OK to close the dialog box.

10. Save your drawing.

Changing Object Color, Linetype, and Lineweight

The properties of layers — color, linetype, lineweight — can also apply directly to objects. You can assign a color, linetype, and lineweight to an object. You can also set a current color, linetype, and lineweight so that all of the future objects that you draw have those properties, regardless of the properties assigned to their layer. In most cases, you should avoid assigning properties directly to objects because the organizational value of layers is lost.

CROSS-REF You can also assign plot styles to objects. See Chapter 17 for more information.

When you create a layer, and assign it a color, linetype, and lineweight, those properties of the object are *ByLayer*. This means that the object picks up those properties from the properties of its layer.

CROSS-REF When you create a block with objects whose properties are ByBlock and you insert the block, it takes on the current color (or the color of the current layer). (For more information about blocks and layers, see Chapter 18.)

NEW FEATURE A new command, SETBYLAYER, changes the individual properties of an object to BYLAYER.

Because it's so helpful to organize object properties by layer, you can use the SETBYLAYER command to return objects' properties to ByLayer. Choose Modify ➪ Change to ByLayer. At the Select objects or [Settings]: prompt, select objects. At the Change ByBlock to ByLayer? [Yes/No] <Yes>: prompt, choose Yes if you want to change the properties of objects in blocks to ByLayer. At the Include blocks? [Yes/No] <Yes>: prompt, choose Yes if you want to include blocks that are in the selection set. (Chapter 18 covers blocks.) All objects that you selected become ByLayer and therefore pick up the color of their layer (unless you chose objects that were set to ByBlock and chose No at the first prompt).

If you choose the Settings option at the first prompt, the SetByLayer Settings dialog box opens, where you can choose which properties you want to set to ByLayer. For example, if you had an object whose color was set to green and whose linetype was set to dashed, you could uncheck the Linetype check box to change the color to ByLayer, but leave the linetype set to dashed.

Changing an object's color

You can control an object's color by using the Color Control drop-down list, which you can find on the Properties toolbar, as shown in Figure 11.17, or in the Object Properties control panel of the Dashboard. (If the Properties toolbar is not displayed, right-click any toolbar button and choose Properties from the list of toolbars. To display the Dashboard, choose Tools ➪ Palettes ➪ Dashboard; right-click the Dashboard and choose Control Panels ➪ Object Properties.) For more information about choosing colors, see the section "Assigning a color" earlier in this chapter. As with the Layer Control drop-down list, the Color Control drop-down list shows the color of any selected object. When you create a layer, assign it a color, and draw with that layer, the color is displayed as ByLayer.

FIGURE 11.17

The Color Control drop-down list on the Properties toolbar.

As I explained earlier in this chapter, the ByLayer color means that the color of the object is taken from the color of the object's layer. At the same time that you see the selected object's color in the Color Control drop-down list, you can look over to the Layer Control drop-down list and confirm the color assignment of the object's layer.

The ByBlock color creates objects by using color 7 (white or black, depending on the screen color), but if the objects are placed in a block, the block takes on the current color when inserted. (For information about blocks, see Chapter 18.)

The best way to organize a drawing is to assign colors by layer. It can be confusing if related elements, such as centerlines in a mechanical drawing, appear in different colors. Also, if you see another line with the same color and linetype as most centerlines, you may assume that it's a centerline in the wrong place. It is standard practice to organize colors by layer.

Colors have a special significance because when you plot, you can assign colors to pens — although you can also use plot styles (see Chapter 17). If you use a color-based system, color is the basis that you use for plotting with various width pens or colors. You may want to temporarily change the color of an object to emphasize it in a plot or for some other reason. However, you should generally refrain from directly changing the color of objects.

If you need to change the color of an object, here are two ways to do it:

- To change just an object's color, select the object. Click the Color Control drop-down list and choose the color that you want.
- If you want to change other properties at the same time, select the object and choose Properties from the Standard or Standard Annotation toolbar (or press Ctrl+1). In the Properties palette that opens, you can change all of the properties of the object. To change the color, choose Color and click the drop-down arrow that appears. Choose the color that you want.

You can always change an object's color back to ByLayer, using the same technique. The new SETBYLAYER command, described in the previous section, is another way to change objects back to ByLayer.

Changing the current color

When you change the current color, all future objects are drawn using that color, regardless of their layer. In general, you should do this only when you have a special need for two objects to be on one layer but have different colors. An example might be text in a title block. You might want the text to have the same layer so that you can freeze it and thaw it (or turn it on and off) easily without having to remember that the text and title block are on two separate layers. If you also want part of the text to have a different color, change the current color before typing in that part of the text. Remember to change the current color back to ByLayer before drawing anything else.

To change the current color, make sure that no object is selected. Then click the Color drop-down list of the Properties toolbar or in the Object Properties control panel of the Dashboard. You can also open the Properties palette and choose the color that you want. To use a color not on the list, choose Select color to open the Select Color dialog box. (See the section "Assigning a color" earlier in this chapter for more information on assigning colors.) To change the current color back to ByLayer, use the same techniques and choose ByLayer or use the SETBYLAYER command discussed earlier in this chapter. You have an opportunity to do an exercise on changing colors after the "Changing the current lineweight" section.

Changing an object's linetype

Linetypes work according to the same principles as colors. You can change the linetype of an existing object or objects. You can control an object's linetype by using the Linetype Control drop-down list on the Properties toolbar, shown in Figure 11.18, or in the Object Properties control panel of the Dashboard. The Linetype Control drop-down list shows the linetype of any selected object. When you create a layer, assign it a linetype, and draw with that layer, the linetype is displayed as ByLayer.

FIGURE 11.18

The Linetype Control drop-down list on the Properties toolbar.

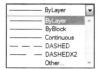

The ByLayer linetype simply means that the linetype of the object is taken from the linetype of the object's layer.

The best way to organize a drawing is to assign linetypes by layer. It can be confusing if similar elements, such as plat borders in a surveyor's drawing, appear in different linetypes. Also, if you see another line with the same color and linetype as most plat borders, you may assume that it's a plat border in the wrong place.

If you need to change the linetype of an object, you have two options:

- To change an object's linetype, select the object. Click the Linetype Control drop-down list and choose the linetype that you want.
- Select the object and open the Properties palette. Click the Linetype item, and then click the drop-down arrow that appears. Choose from one of the linetypes.

You can always change an object's linetype back to ByLayer, using the same methods or with the SETBYLAYER command, discussed earlier in this chapter.

As discussed in the "Assigning a linetype" section earlier in this chapter, you need to load a linetype before you can use it for the first time. To load a linetype, choose Linetype Control from the Properties toolbar. Scroll down to the bottom of the list and choose Other to open the Linetype Manager. Choose Load to open the Load or Reload Linetypes dialog box, choose the linetype file (if not the default), and choose the linetype that you want to load. Click OK. Choose the linetype again in the Linetype Manager and click OK to return to your drawing.

To filter the list of linetypes, choose from the Linetype Filters drop-down list box in the Linetype Manager.

Changing the current linetype

You can also change the current linetype. When you change the current linetype, all future objects that you draw have that linetype and are not drawn according to their layer's assigned linetype. In general, you should do this only when you have a special need for two objects to be on one layer but have different linetypes. An example might be a table containing notes in one corner of a drawing. You might want the lines that make up the table to have the same layer so that you can freeze it and thaw it (or turn it on and off) easily without having to remember that the table is on two separate layers. If you also want some of the lines to have a different linetype, change the current linetype before adding those lines. Remember to change the current linetype back to ByLayer before drawing anything else.

To change the current linetype, click the Linetype Control drop-down list and choose the linetype that you want, first making sure that no objects are currently selected. You can also use the Properties palette. To change the current linetype back to ByLayer, choose ByLayer for the linetype or use the SETBYLAYER command, discussed earlier in this chapter.

Changing an object's lineweight

Lineweights let you represent objects with varying line widths. The widths can represent the width of a pen in a pen plotter that will be used to plot that object. Lineweights can also be used as an organizational tool, to distinguish certain types of objects just as colors and linetypes do. Finally, you can use lineweights to represent the actual properties of objects, such as the width of wires in an electrical schematic.

Lineweights work according to the same principles as colors and linetypes. You can control an object's lineweight by using the Lineweight Control drop-down list on the Properties toolbar, as shown in Figure 11.19, or in the Object Properties control panel of the Dashboard. The Lineweight Control drop-down list shows the lineweight of any selected object. When you create a layer, assign it a lineweight, and draw with that layer, the lineweight is displayed as ByLayer.

FIGURE 11.19

The Lineweight drop-down list on the Properties toolbar.

As with colors and linetypes, the best way to organize a drawing is to assign lineweights by layer. If you need to change the lineweight of an object, do one of the following:

- Select the object. Click the Lineweight Control drop-down list and choose the lineweight that you want.

- Select the object and open the Properties palette. To change an object's lineweight, click Lineweight, and then click the drop-down arrow that appears. Choose from one of the lineweights.

Changing the current lineweight

You can also change the current lineweight. When you change the current lineweight, all future objects that you draw have that lineweight and are not drawn according to their layer's assigned lineweight.

To change the current lineweight, click the Lineweight Control drop-down list and choose the lineweight that you want, first making sure that no objects are currently selected. You can also use the Properties palette. To change the current lineweight back to ByLayer, choose ByLayer as the lineweight or use the SETBYLAYER command, discussed earlier in this chapter.

ON the DVD-ROM The drawing used in the following exercise on changing colors, linetypes, and lineweights, ab11-d.dwg, is in the Drawings folder on the DVD.

STEPS: Changing Colors, Linetypes, and Lineweights

1. Open ab11-d.dwg from the DVD.

2. Save the file as ab11-04.dwg in your AutoCAD Bible folder. This is an elevation view of a lavatory cabinet, shown in Figure 11.20. Display either the Properties toolbar or the Dashboard's Object Properties control panel.

A lavatory cabinet.

ELEVATION
SCALE : 1"=1'-0"

Thanks to the Army Corps of Engineers for this drawing.

3. Pick one of the reflection lines in the mirror. Notice that the color is red but the layer's color, as shown in the Layer Control drop-down list, is Magenta. Select all of the reflection lines. Click the Color Control drop-down list and choose ByLayer from the top of the list. Press Esc to remove the grips.

4. Select the green dimension at the bottom of the cabinet. (The dimension is all one object.) To make it more visible, click the Color Control drop-down list and choose Red. Press Esc to see the result.

5. Pick the lines at ❶ and ❷ in Figure 11.21. Click the Linetype Control drop-down list and choose the Hidden linetype. Press Esc so that the hidden lines are no longer selected.

6. Select the dashed arc that represents the bottom curvature of the sink. Click the Lineweight Control drop-down list and choose 0.30 mm. Press Esc. Click LWT on the status bar to turn on the display of lineweights and see the result.

7. Click the Color Control drop-down list box and choose Cyan to make it the current color.

8. Start the RECTANG command. Draw a rectangle inside the left cabinet. Use the COPY command to copy the rectangle to the right cabinet. (To copy, use an intersection object snap at point ❸ as the base point and ❹ as the second point of displacement.) The rectangles are drawn in cyan.

9. Save your drawing. It should look like Figure 11.21.

FIGURE 11.21

The finished cabinet.

Working with Linetype Scales

A noncontinuous linetype is a repeating pattern of dots, dashes, and spaces. Linetypes can also include repeating text or shapes. You may find that the linetype patterns in your drawing are too long or short for clarity. The linetype scale may even be so big or so small that the line looks continuous. How often the pattern is repeated is affected by three factors:

- The linetype definition
- The global linetype scale
- The individual object's linetype scale

Changing linetype spacing by using a different linetype

One choice is to change the linetype. A number of linetypes come in short, medium, and long variations, such as Dashedx2, Dashed, and Dashed2, as shown in Figure 11.22.

FIGURE 11.22

A number of the standard linetypes come in three variations, such as Dashedx2, Dashed, and Dashed2.

AutoCAD's `acad.lin` and AutoCAD LT's `acadlt.lin` contain a number of ISO linetypes that meet the specifications of the International Standards Organization. Your organization or field of specialty may require the use of these linetypes. If so, you should know that the ISO linetype pattern definitions are much longer than the other linetype definitions. Figure 11.23 shows the ISO dash linetype and the regular dashed linetype. You may need to make adjustments to the linetype scale as a result.

FIGURE 11.23

A comparison of the regular dashed linetype and the ISO dash linetype.

Changing linetype spacing by changing the global linetype scale

Another choice is to change the global linetype scale, which affects all noncontinuous linetypes in your drawing. AutoCAD and AutoCAD LT multiply the linetype definition by the global linetype scale to calculate the length of each repetition of the linetype:

- Linetype scales larger than 1 result in longer sections — and fewer repetitions of the linetype definition per unit.

- Linetype scales smaller than 1 result in shorter sections — and more repetitions of the linetype definition per unit.

CROSS-REF You can also change the scale of a linetype that appears in a viewport on a layout. For more information, see Chapter 17.

When you change the linetype scale, the drawing regenerates to change all of the linetypes. Figure 11.24 shows three versions of a drawing with linetypes at linetype scales of 0.5, 1, and 2. As you can see, a scale of 2 is too large and a scale of 0.5 is too small. A scale of 1 is just right. (Goldilocks would have been happy with it.)

For purposes of drawing, you simply want to make sure that you can distinguish the linetype both when you can see the entire drawing on the screen and when you zoom in close. The main reason to scale linetypes is for plotting. A linetype scale that works for a drawing of a house on-screen may appear continuous when you plot it at a scale factor of 1=96.

FIGURE 11.24

Three versions of a drawing, using linetype scales of 0.5, 1, and 2.

Linetype scale = 0.5   Linetype scale = 1   Linetype scale = 2

If you want the linetype to appear exactly according to its definition, use the scale factor for the linetype scale. Chapter 5 covers scale factors. If the scale factor doesn't give you the results that you want, try a linetype scale of one-quarter to one-half of the scale factor — in the 1=96 example, you might use a linetype scale of 24 or 48.

To change the linetype scale, choose Format ⇨ Linetype to open the Linetype Manager, shown in Figure 11.25. Alternatively, you can open the Linetype Manager by clicking Other from the Linetype Control drop-down list on the Properties toolbar or the Dashboard's Object Properties control panel. Click Show Details if the lower portion of the dialog box is not displayed.

FIGURE 11.25

The Linetype Manager dialog box.

In the Global scale factor text box, type the scale factor that you want. Click OK. The drawing regenerates, changing the scale of every noncontinuous linetype in the drawing.

The global linetype scale is held in the LTSCALE system variable. You can change the linetype scale by typing LTSCALE at the command line and typing a scale.

Changing linetype spacing by changing the object linetype scale

On occasion, you may want the linetype spacing to be different for one object — or a small group of objects — only. Perhaps the object is too small to show the linetype pattern or you want to set it off visually. The *current object linetype scale* works like setting a current color or linetype — all objects drawn after you set the object linetype scale are drawn with the new linetype scale. In most cases, you want to make sure that you change the current object linetype scale back to its default of 1 after using it for that one object or group of objects.

Changing the current object linetype scale

To change the linetype scale, choose Format ➪ Linetype to open the Linetype Manager, as shown in Figure 11.25. Click Show Details if the lower portion of the dialog box is not displayed. In the Current Object Scale text box, type the scale factor that you want. Click OK. Now all objects that you draw use the current object linetype scale. When you're done drawing objects at that linetype scale, remember to change the linetype scale back to 1.

The current object linetype scale is held in the CELTSCALE system variable. You can also change the current object linetype scale by typing **celtscale** at the command line and typing in a scale.

If you have also set the global linetype scale to a value other than 1, AutoCAD and AutoCAD LT multiply the two linetype scales to calculate the final result. For example, if you have a global linetype scale of 12 and a current object linetype scale of 0.5, objects you draw will have a resulting linetype scale of 6.

Changing an existing object's linetype scale

You will often draw an object without setting a special object linetype scale and then decide that you want to change its linetype scale. To change an object's linetype scale, select the object and open the Properties palette. Click Linetype Scale and then type the new linetype scale. This linetype scale affects only the selected object. It does not affect the global linetype scale.

The drawing used in the following exercise on changing linetype scales, ab11-e.dwg, is in the Drawings folder on the DVD.

STEPS: Changing Linetype Scales

1. Open ab11-e.dwg from the DVD.

2. Save the file as ab11-05.dwg in your AutoCAD Bible folder. This drawing is of a bushing, as shown in Figure 11.26. Notice that the linetype doesn't show clearly on the short line at ❶ and in the small circle at ❷.

3. Choose Format ➪ Linetype. Click Show Details to open the Details section of the Linetype Manager, if necessary. Change the Global scale factor to 0.5. Click OK. The drawing regenerates. Note that the circles are better, but the short line at ❶ still looks like a continuous line.

4. Choose the line at ❶. Choose Tools ⇨ Palettes ⇨ Properties to open the Properties palette (if it isn't already open). Click Linetype scale and change it to 0.5. Press Enter. Press Esc to remove the grips and see the result. Notice the difference in the line, which now has a linetype scale of 0.5 (global) times 0.5 (object) = 0.25.

5. Save your drawing. It should look like Figure 11.27.

FIGURE 11.26

This drawing of a bushing has two noncontinuous linetypes.

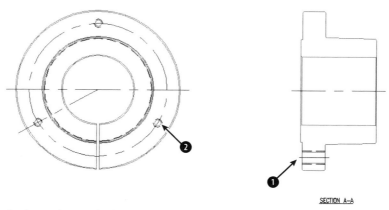

Thanks to Robert Mack of the Dexter Company, Fairfield, Iowa, for this drawing.

FIGURE 11.27

The drawing's noncontinuous lines are now more appropriate.

Importing Layers and Linetypes from Other Drawings

The DesignCenter gives you access to drawing content and definitions, such as layers, linetypes, blocks (see Chapter 18), plot layouts (see Chapter 17), and so on that exist in other drawings. I cover the DesignCenter in more detail in Chapter 26, but here I explain how to import layers and linetypes from another drawing. Autodesk calls this *mining your design*. In other words, after you've created a layer or a linetype, you can easily use it in any new or existing drawing.

 To open the DesignCenter, shown in Figure 11.28, choose DesignCenter from the Standard or Standard Annotation toolbar, press Ctrl+2, or choose Tools ⇨ Palettes ⇨ DesignCenter. The DesignCenter's left pane works like the Windows Explorer left pane, letting you navigate throughout your hard drive or your network. (If you don't see the left pane, click the Tree View Toggle button on the DesignCenter's toolbar.) If the DesignCenter opens, showing only open drawings, click Desktop on the toolbar and navigate to the desired folder. After you click a folder, the drawings in that folder are listed on the right side. Choose Large Icons from the Views drop-down list to see a small preview of each item. To access layers and linetypes, either double-click a drawing icon or click its plus sign. Now you see the various definition categories in the right pane. To see the list of the layers or linetypes, double-click the layers or linetypes icon in either the left or right pane. To import a layer or linetype, double-click the layer or linetype's icon to bring the layer or linetype definition into your drawing. Click the Layer Control or Linetype Control drop-down list to check it out!

FIGURE 11.28

The DesignCenter lets you locate definitions that are contained in other drawings and import them into your current drawing.

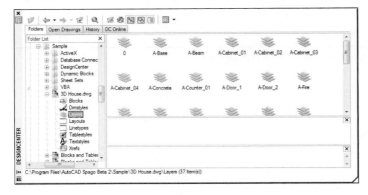

Click the DesignCenter's Close button to close the DesignCenter.

CROSS-REF   AutoCAD enables you to *translate* layers. For example, you can specify that all objects on layer `dashed` be changed to the layer `hidden`. Use this feature to maintain layer standards that you have set up. Chapter 26 fully covers layer translating. This feature is not available in AutoCAD LT.

Matching Properties

You may be familiar with the Format Painter button available on the toolbars of many Windows applications. AutoCAD and AutoCAD LT offer something similar that at the same time enables you to specify which properties you want to match. AutoCAD calls this process *matching properties*. It is similar to Excel's Paste Special command.

An object can have so many properties that this can be a useful tool. To match properties, you need two objects, a source object and a destination object (or objects). Follow these steps to match properties:

1. Choose the object whose properties you want to match (the source object).

2. Choose Match Properties from the Standard or Standard Annotation toolbar. You see a Format Painter cursor with a pickbox. On the command line, you see the Select destination object(s) or [Settings]: prompt.

> **NOTE** You can choose Match Properties from the Standard toolbar first and then choose the source object.

3. If you want to match all of the object's properties, select the object(s) that you want to receive the matching properties, that is, the destination object(s).

4. If you want to match only some of the object's properties, right-click and choose Settings to open the Property Settings dialog box, shown in Figure 11.29. Uncheck all of the properties that you don't want to match and click OK. The previous prompt returns. Select the object(s) that you want to receive the matching properties, that is, the destination objects(s).

FIGURE 11.29

The Property Settings dialog box.

5. Press Enter to end object selection and match the properties.

> **ON the DVD-ROM** The drawing used in the following exercise on matching properties, ab11-f.dwg, is in the Drawings folder on the DVD.

STEPS: Matching Properties

1. Open ab11-f.dwg from the DVD.

2. Save the file as ab11-06.dwg in your AutoCAD Bible folder. This is a drawing of a master-bedroom-suite plan, as shown in Figure 11.30.

3. Pick the wall at ❶ in Figure 11.30. Click Match Properties from the Standard toolbar. At the Select destination object(s) or [Settings]: prompt, use a crossing window to select all of the folding closet doors on both sides of the line that you just selected. Press Enter to end object selection. This action matches the properties of the doors to the properties of the wall. (The doors turn from gray to black/white.)

4. Pick the text MASTER SUITE. Choose Match Properties from the Standard (or Standard Annotation) toolbar. At the Select destination object(s) or [Settings]: prompt, right-click and choose Settings. In the Property Settings dialog box, deselect all of the boxes except for Text in the Special Properties section. Click OK.

5. At the Select destination object(s) or [Settings]: prompt, choose the text CL. in both closets and press Enter to end the command. This action matches the text properties of the text. Notice that the CL. text becomes bold.

6. Save your drawing.

FIGURE 11.30

The master-bedroom-suite plan.

Summary

In this chapter, you read all about layers, colors, linetypes, and lineweights. You learned about:

- Using layers to help you organize your drawings by assigning the same properties to related objects
- Creating a layer by giving it a name, color, linetype, and lineweight
- Changing the layer of existing objects, using the Layer Control drop-down list or the Properties palette
- Layer states — On/Off, Thawed/Frozen, Unlocked/Locked, and Plottable/Not Plottable
- Changing the properties of existing layers
- Saving sets of layer states and properties and later restoring them
- Filtering the layer listing
- Purging unused layers and linetypes
- Altering the color, linetype, and lineweight of any object
- Globally changing the linetype scale, changing the current linetype scale, and changing the object linetype scale of existing objects
- Using the DesignCenter to import layers and linetypes from other drawings
- Utilizing the Match Properties command to copy properties from one object to one or more destination objects

The next chapter explains how to get detailed information from your drawing.

Chapter 12

Obtaining Information from Your Drawing

Your drawing is intelligent in many ways. For example, several commands can give you the details of each object. In addition, you can view listings that provide information about your drawing as a whole. You can also list system variables, which I've mentioned previously in this book, along with their current settings.

You can perform calculations on objects that may assist you in certain drawing tasks. For example, you can divide an object into any number of segments by placing point objects along the object, or you can place point objects at a specified distance along the object. You can use AutoCAD's calculator, which not only does regular numerical calculations but also works with coordinates and geometric points on objects. This chapter shows you how to discover the hidden data in your drawing.

> ## IN THIS CHAPTER
>
> Obtaining drawing-wide information
>
> Obtaining information about objects
>
> Measuring and segmenting objects
>
> Using AutoCAD's calculator

Drawing-Level Information

Some information applies to the drawing as a whole or even to your computer system as a whole, rather than to individual objects. This information can be important when there is a problem or when you simply need to find the status of system variables.

Listing the status of your drawing

The STATUS command is available only in AutoCAD and provides a standard list of information that can be very helpful. To use the STATUS command, choose Tools ➪ Inquiry ➪ Status. Figure 12.1 shows a sample status listing.

FIGURE 12.1

A sample listing from the STATUS command.

The command lists the number of objects in your drawing, followed by the limits and extents of the drawing, and the extents of the current display on your screen. Other items are the snap and grid spacing as well as the current layer, color, linetype, and lineweight. You can see that Fill is on but that the other drawing aid settings are off. Endpoint and intersection running object snaps are on. Finally, information also appears about free disk space and free memory.

Obviously, much of this information is available without using the STATUS command. The easiest items to find are the current layer, color, linetype, and lineweight, which are visible on the Layers and Properties toolbars. (If those toolbars aren't displayed, right-click any toolbar and choose them from the list.) However, you would have to use a number of commands to obtain other information such as the snap and grid spacing and the drawing limits. The free disk and memory statistics provide valuable information not otherwise obtainable from within your drawing. STATUS puts it all together in one listing.

The most common use for STATUS is to troubleshoot problems. For example, you can send the listing to a colleague in another office who needs to work on the same drawing. Your colleague can then work more easily by using the same settings that you have used.

Listing system variables

In the previous chapter, I mentioned that the global linetype scale is stored in the LTSCALE system variable, and that the object linetype scale is stored in the CELTSCALE system variable. You may want to know the settings of a group of related system variables. The SETVAR command provides a listing of all the system variables and their settings. It may be quicker to view system-variable settings by using the SETVAR command than by typing each individual system variable on the command line. For more information about how AutoCAD and AutoCAD LT store settings in system variables, see Chapter 5.

Too many system variables exist to show the entire listing here, but a few can convey the wealth of information that is available, as shown in Figure 12.2.

FIGURE 12.2

A partial SETVAR listing.

> **NOTE** Read-only system variables are for information only and cannot be changed. An example is LOGINNAME (AutoCAD only), which shows the name of the current user who is registered on the system. Other system variables can be changed.

Although some system variables allow a variety of values, many are either on or off. In general, a setting of 1 means on and 0 means off.

You can set most system variables in a dialog box. For example, in Chapter 11 you set the LTSCALE system variable by using the Linetype Manager. However, a few system variables can be accessed only by typing them on the command line.

You can use SETVAR to set system variables that are not read-only, as well as to list them. To list the system variables, choose Tools ➪ Inquiry ➪ Set Variable. If you are using AutoCAD LT, it can be accessed only at the command line by typing **SETVAR**. At the `Enter variable name or [?]:` prompt, type **?** ↵. At the `Enter variable(s) to list <*>:` prompt, press Enter to list all of the system variables, or type the name of a variable. (You can use the * and ? wildcards in the name.) The command either lists all of the system variables or just the variable you typed.

If you type a variable, the command prompts you for a new value so that you can change it. For example, if you type **celtscale**, you see the `Enter new value for CELTSCALE <1.0000>:` prompt. You can then change the system variable by typing in a new value. You can also press Enter to accept the current setting.

Tracking drawing time

You can track the time you spend working on a drawing. This feature is most often used for billing time to clients, or when your boss wants to see how much you're accomplishing.

> **CROSS-REF** Chapter 17 covers the PLOTSTAMP command, which can optionally make a log file of plotting activity. Chapter 26 explains how to keep a log file of your overall drawing activity.

To use the TIME command, choose Tools ➪ Inquiry ➪ Time. A typical listing is shown in Figure 12.3.

FIGURE 12.3

A typical TIME listing.

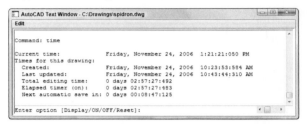

```
AutoCAD Text Window - C:\Drawings\spidron.dwg

Edit

Command: time

Current time:              Friday, November 24, 2006  1:21:21:050 PM
Times for this drawing:
  Created:                 Friday, November 24, 2006  10:23:53:584 AM
  Last updated:            Friday, November 24, 2006  10:43:44:310 AM
  Total editing time:      0 days 02:57:27:492
  Elapsed timer (on):      0 days 02:57:27:483
  Next automatic save in:  0 days 00:08:47:125

Enter option [Display/ON/OFF/Reset]:
```

Table 12.1 explains the listing that you see when using the TIME command.

TABLE 12.1

TIME Command Information

Listing	Comments
Current time	The current date and time. The time is displayed to the nearest millisecond.
Created	The date and time when the drawing was created.
Last updated	The date and time of the last save of the drawing.
Total editing time	Accumulates the time spent in the drawing from session to session, not including plotting time or time that you worked on the drawing and quit without saving your changes.
Elapsed timer	Also accumulates time spent in the drawing, although you can turn this feature on and off and reset it.
Next automatic save in	Shows when your drawing will automatically be saved. Choose Tools ➪ Options and click the Open and Save tab to set how often you want to automatically save your drawing.

You can think of total editing time as your car's odometer, and elapsed time as a timer that is similar to a trip meter that some cars have to enable you to time a specific trip.

At the end of the listing, you see the `Enter option [Display/ON/OFF/Reset]:` prompt. The Display option redisplays the listing with updated times. ON and OFF turn the elapsed time on and off. The Reset option resets the elapsed time to zero.

AUTOCAD ONLY The Express Tools contain a tool called EDITTIME (choose Express ➪ Tools ➪ Dwg Editing Time) that tracks active editing time.

ON the DVD-ROM The drawing used in the following exercise on obtaining drawing information, `ab12-a.dwg`, is in the `Drawings` folder on the DVD.

STEPS: Obtaining Drawing Information

1. Open ab12-a.dwg from the DVD.

2. Skip to Step 3 if you are using AutoCAD LT. Choose Tools ➪ Inquiry ➪ Status. Look at the listing to see how many objects it contains. Check the limits of the drawing. Look at the grid spacing. Read through any other items that interest you.

3. Choose Tools ➪ Inquiry ➪ Set Variable, or type **SETVAR** at the command line if you are using AutoCAD LT. At the Enter variable name or [?]: prompt, type ? ↵. At the Enter variable(s) to list <*>: prompt, press Enter to accept the default. Look for the BLIPMODE setting. Check the location of the drawing (DWGPREFIX). Look for the global linetype scale (LTSCALE). Press Enter until you see the Command: prompt again.

4. Press Enter to start the SETVAR command again. At the Enter variable name or [?]: prompt, type **ltscale** ↵. Type **50** ↵ to change the linetype scale. Type **regen** ↵. The noncontinuous linetypes should now show up more clearly.

5. Choose Tools ➪ Inquiry ➪ Time. Check the current time against your watch. The command takes the time from your computer's clock. Look at the total editing time to see the total time during which you have worked on the drawing. Press Enter to end the command.

6. Do not save this drawing. Leave the drawing open if you're going on to the next exercise.

Object-Level Information

Several commands and features exist solely to provide information about the objects in your drawing.

Listing objects

The LIST command displays information about selected objects. The information displayed depends on the object. For example, the LIST command gives you the radius of a circle and the length of a line.

To list an object, choose Tools ➪ Inquiry ➪ List. Figure 12.4 shows a typical listing for a line.

FIGURE 12.4

A typical listing for a horizontal line.

```
        LINE      Layer: "objects"
                  Space: Model space
        Handle = 3AD
   from point, X=0'-4 9/64"  Y=0'-1 3/64"  Z=    0'-0"
     to point, X=0'-5 41/64" Y=0'-1 3/64"  Z=    0'-0"
Length =0'-1 1/2",   Angle in XY Plane =       0
        Delta X =0'-1 1/2", Delta Y =    0'-0", Delta Z =    0'-0"
```

Table 12.2 explains the information that you see when you list an object.

TABLE 12.2

LIST Command Information

Data	Comments
Layer	Lists the object's layer. If the color and linetype are not ByLayer or ByBlock, then AutoCAD lists these as well.
Space	Tells you whether the object is in model space or paper space. (Chapter 17 covers paper space.)
Handle	Every object in your drawing has a handle. Your drawing's internal database uses handles to keep track of objects.
From point	Because the example in Figure 12.4 lists a line, it shows the start point.
To point	The endpoint of the line.
Length	The line's length.
Angle in XY Plane	The line's angle. This line is horizontal, and so its angle is zero.
Delta X	The change in the X coordinate from the start point to the endpoint.
Delta Y	The change in the Y coordinate from the start point to the endpoint.

The Layers and Properties toolbars make it easy to tell an object's layer, linetype, and color. Remember that when you select an object, its layer, linetype, lineweight, color, and plot style appear in these toolbars.

Calculating distances

You can easily calculate the distance between any two points by using the DIST command. Choose Tools ➪ Inquiry ➪ Distance. The command prompts you for two points. You can use any means of specifying a point, although object snaps or snap mode are useful if you want to be sure of which point you're specifying. Here is a typical display for a vertical line:

```
Distance = 19'-0", Angle in XY Plane = 270, Angle from XY Plane = 0
Delta X = 0'-0", Delta Y = -19'-0", Delta Z = 0'-0"
```

You can use this information to check dimensions (covered in Chapter 14) or to make calculations that you need for drawing.

Finding coordinates

Finding a coordinate is even easier than calculating a distance. Choose Tools ➪ Inquiry ➪ ID Point (or just type **id** ↵). The ID command prompts you for a point. You can use any means of specifying a point, although object snaps or snap mode are useful. Here is a typical listing:

```
X = 61'-5 1/8" Y = 32'-4 5/8" Z = 0'-0"
```

You can use this information to find an absolute coordinate.

> **CAUTION**   If you're working in 3D, be aware that if you check the Replace Z Value with Current Elevation check box on the Drafting tab of the Options dialog box, you may get inaccurate results when you pick points for the ID and DIST commands. For more information on this option, see Chapter 21, where I discuss 3D coordinates.

The drawing used in the following exercise on obtaining object information, `ab12-a.dwg`, is in the `Drawings` folder on the DVD.

STEPS: Obtaining Object Information

1. Open `ab12-a.dwg` from the DVD if it isn't already open from the previous exercise. This is a civil engineering drawing that shows several plots of land, as shown in Figure 12.5. OSNAP should be on. Set a running object snap for the endpoint.

FIGURE 12.5

A civil engineering drawing of several plots of land.

2. Choose Tools ➪ Inquiry ➪ List. At the `Select objects:` prompt, pick ❶ in Figure 12.5. Press Enter to end object selection. The result is shown in Figure 12.6. Note the surveyor's units.

FIGURE 12.6

The result of using the LIST command on an arc.

```
        ARC       Layer: "0"
                  Space: Model space
        Handle = 7D3951
center point,  X=  7249.24  Y=  3753.29  Z=    0.00
radius    1937.35
 start angle S 89d28'56" W
   end angle S 76d38'19" W
length    434.28
```

3. Choose Tools ➪ Inquiry ➪ Distance. At the `Specify first point:` prompt, choose the endpoint at ❷ in Figure 12.5, using the endpoint running object snap. At the `Specify second point:` prompt, choose the endpoint at ❸. Here's the result:
```
Distance = 2740.90, Angle in XY Plane = N 89d23'34" E, Angle from XY
Plane = E
Delta X = 2740.75, Delta Y = 29.05, Delta Z = 0.00
```

4. Choose Tools ⇨ Inquiry ⇨ ID Point. At the `Specify point:` prompt, pick the endpoint at ❹ in Figure 12.5. Here is the result:

   `X = 6065.67 Y = 3450.58 Z = 0.00`

5. Do not save this drawing. Leave the drawing open if you're going on to the next exercise.

> **NOTE** The precision set in the Units dialog box (Format ⇨ Units) affects the results of the LIST, DIST, and ID commands. See Chapter 5 for more information on the Units dialog box.

Calculating area and perimeter

You can also calculate the area and perimeter of any area. To start the AREA command, choose Tools ⇨ Inquiry ⇨ Area.

You can specify points bounding the area that you want to calculate. The points don't have to be on an object. The command calculates the area and perimeter as if you had drawn lines between all of the points. The command automatically closes the area if you don't close the area by assuming that the last point is the same as the first point. This option is limited to areas with straight sides.

Instead of picking points, you can use the Object option to calculate the area of objects, which gives you the flexibility to use areas that include curves. Acceptable objects are circles, ellipses, splines, polylines, polygons, regions, and objects created with the 2D SOLID command. (Chapter 16 covers splines, polylines, regions, and solids.) This option calculates an area but adds a length instead of a perimeter. For a circle, you get a circumference. Although a polyline may have the exact same shape as an arc, you cannot calculate the area of an arc. Polylines and splines can be open. In this case the area is calculated as if you had drawn a line from the endpoint to the start point, but it does not include that last imaginary line when calculating the length.

> **CROSS-REF** You can create a label that displays the area of a closed object using a field. See the section "Inserting Fields" in Chapter 13.

To calculate the area of irregular shapes, you can keep a running total by using the Add option. Start by specifying the first area. Then use the Add option and specify a second area. The result is the sum of the two areas. You can continue to add areas. You can also use the Subtract option to subtract areas.

Figure 12.7 shows an example of calculating the open area in an office floor plan by picking points. The point objects show the points that were used to calculate the area and perimeter.

You can also use the BOUNDARY command to create one polyline or region from a complex area. (Chapter 16 covers boundaries and polylines.) You can then use the Object option of the AREA command instead of picking points. However, notice that BOUNDARY included the open doors in the area selected for the office floor plan, as shown in Figure 12.8.

> **ON the DVD-ROM** The drawing used in the following exercise on using the AREA command, ab12-a.dwg, is in the Drawings folder on the DVD.

FIGURE 12.7

Calculating the area and perimeter for an office floor plan.

FIGURE 12.8

Using the BOUNDARY command to create an object for use with the AREA command. The boundary is indicated with a dashed line.

STEPS: Using the AREA Command

1. Open `ab12-a.dwg` from the DVD if it isn't already open from the previous exercise.

2. Use ZOOM Window to zoom in on the parcels of land labeled D and E, as shown in Figure 12.9. OSNAP should be on with a running object snap for the endpoint.

FIGURE 12.9

The AREA command can calculate the area of parcels D and E.

---

3. Choose Tools ➪ Inquiry ➪ Area.

4. At the `Specify first corner point or [Object/Add/Subtract]:` prompt, right-click and choose Add to start Add mode. At the `Specify first corner point or [Object/Subtract]:` prompt, pick ❶ in Figure 12.9 by using the Endpoint running object snap. At the `Specify next corner point or press ENTER for total (ADD mode):` prompt, continue to pick ❷, ❸, ❹, and ❺. Press Enter. The command line lists the area and perimeter. (Your figures may be different if you picked different points.)

```
Area = 123575.16, Perimeter = 1480.17
Total area = 123575.16
```

5. At the `Specify first corner point or [Object/Subtract]:` prompt, pick ❻ in Figure 12.9. At the `Specify next corner point or press ENTER for total (ADD mode):` prompt, pick ❼, ❽, and ❾. Press Enter to complete point selection. The command line reports the area and perimeter of the second area and adds the two areas together to give you the total area. Press Enter again to end the command.

```
Area = 183399.88, Perimeter = 1884.62
Total area = 306975.04
```

6. Do not save the drawing. Keep it open if you're continuing to the next exercise.

NOTE   The MASSPROP command is mostly used for 3D drawings, but it can also be used on *regions*, which are 2D solid surfaces, such as a shape cut from sheet metal. This command provides area and perimeter but also other engineering calculations, such as centroids, moments of inertia, the product of inertia, and so on. Chapter 24 covers this command further.

Getting information from the Properties palette

You can also obtain information about an object by selecting it and opening the Properties palette. (Click Properties on the Standard toolbar or choose Tools ⇨ Palettes ⇨ Properties.) In Chapter 11, I discuss using this Properties palette to change layer, color, linetype, and lineweight properties. As you can see in Figure 12.10, the window also lists the line's start and endpoints; delta (change) in X, Y, and Z; length; and angle — much like the LIST command. However, you can change the start and endpoints directly in the palette.

FIGURE 12.10

The Properties palette lists information about a selected object.

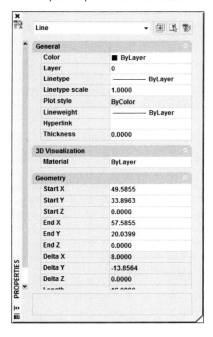

The DVD contains three routines that provide information about your objects. Linesum provides the total length of selected lines. Arcsum adds the lengths of selected arcs. Polydis provides the length of a selected polyline. Look in the Software\Chapter 12 folder.

Measurement Commands

The DIVIDE command divides an object into equally spaced sections. The MEASURE command divides an object into sections of a specified length. These commands are useful in many fields. For example, you may need to space bolt holes evenly around the edge of a bushing, or place fence studs along the edge of a plot every 5 feet.

Dividing objects

The DIVIDE command divides an object into equal sections. DIVIDE does not break the object — it simply places point objects along the selected object. You can then use the Node object snap if you want to draw from those points.

To divide an object, choose Draw ➪ Point ➪ Divide. Select the object that you want to divide. The command responds with the `Enter the number of segments or [Block]:` prompt. Enter the number of segments that you want to create. AutoCAD places the point objects and ends the command.

> **NOTE** Remember that you can set the point display by choosing Format ➪ Point Style. An easy-to-see point style is especially useful for the DIVIDE command. Specify the point style *before* using the command.

For example, to create eight segments, you need to place seven point objects. If you have in your mind the number of point objects that you want, simply add one when specifying the number of segments.

You can use the Block option to place a block of your choice along the object instead of a point object. The block must exist in your drawing. (Chapter 18 covers blocks.) If you choose the Block option (right-click and choose Block), the option responds with the `Enter name of block to insert:` prompt. Type the name of the block. The prompt asks, `Align block with object? [Yes/No] <Y>`. Answer Y or N, depending on whether you want to align the block with the object.

> **NOTE** Aligning a block is appropriate for curved objects and blocks that are not completely symmetrical.

The prompt asks for the number of segments that you want, and you type that number, as described earlier. Figure 12.11 shows an electrical schematic. Here you want to divide a line so that you can evenly space wires entering the ignition module. Four wires need to come in so that the line is divided into five segments by an easy-to-see point object.

FIGURE 12.11

Dividing a line into five segments by using point objects.

Thanks to Robert Mack of the Dexter Company, Fairfield, Iowa, for this drawing.

You can practice using the DIVIDE command after the next section.

Measuring objects

The MEASURE command is similar to the DIVIDE command, except that you specify the distance between point objects instead of the total number of segments. The command starts measuring from the endpoint closest to where you pick the object. MEASURE does not break the object — it simply places point objects along the object. You can then use the Node object snap if you want to draw from those points.

To measure an object, choose Draw ⇨ Point ⇨ Measure. Select the object that you want to measure. The command responds with the `Specify length of segment or [Block]:` prompt. Type the segment length where you want to place the point objects and end the command.

Remember that you can set the point display by choosing Format ⇨ Point Style. An easy-to-see point style is especially useful for the MEASURE command. Specify the point style *before* using the command.

As with the DIVIDE command, you can place a block along the object using the Block option, as long as the block exists in your drawing. The option prompts you for the name of the block and lets you choose whether you want to align the block with the object. The prompt asks for the segment length, and you type in the lengths between the points, as described earlier. Figure 12.12 shows a plat drawing with one side of a lot measured into 20-foot segments.

FIGURE 12.12

Measuring a line into 20-foot segments by using point objects.

Thanks to Bill Maidment of Caltech, Inc. Fairfield, Iowa, for this drawing.

 The drawing in the following exercise on using the DIVIDE and MEASURE commands, `ab12-a.dwg`, is in the `Drawings` folder on the DVD.

STEPS: Using the DIVIDE and MEASURE Commands

1. Open `ab12-a.dwg` from the DVD if it isn't already open from the previous exercise.
2. If you didn't do the previous exercise, use ZOOM Window to zoom in to the parcels labeled D and E, as shown in Figure 12.13.
3. Choose Format ⇨ Point Style and choose the fourth style in the first row. Choose Set Size Relative to Screen and set the size to 5%. Click OK.

4. Choose Draw ➪ Point ➪ Divide. At the `Select object to divide:` prompt, choose ❶ in Figure 12.13. At the `Enter the number of segments or [Block]:` prompt, type **3** ↵. The command places two points along the line, dividing it into three segments. (If you want, draw lines from the points perpendicular to the opposite side of the parcel to divide it into three parcels.)

5. Choose Draw ➪ Point ➪ Measure. At the `Select object to measure:` prompt, choose ❷ in Figure 12.13. At the `Specify length of segment or [Block]:` prompt, type **120** ↵ (10 feet). The command places two points along the line.

6. Do not save your drawing. Keep it open if you're continuing to the next exercise.

FIGURE 12.13

The site plan zoomed in to parcels D and E.

AutoCAD's Calculator

To start the calculator, choose Tools ➪ Palettes ➪ QuickCalc or press Ctrl+8 to start the QUICKCALC command. The calculator opens as a palette. Use the palette for stand-alone calculations, as you would use a physical hand-held calculator. To start the calculator within a command, type **'quickcalc** or **'qc** on the command line. When you start the calculator transparently, it appears as a window, rather than as a palette, as shown in Figure 12.14. Note that if you have the palette version of QuickCalc open when you use QuickCalc transparently, the palette temporarily closes until you finish the calculation. In other words, you can only use one format of QuickCalc at a time.

NOTE   The CAL command, which is the command-line calculator available in earlier releases of AutoCAD only, still exists. In fact, it's now available in AutoCAD LT as well.

FIGURE 12.14

The graphical calculator looks similar to a hand-held calculator.

Distance Between Two Points

Get Coordinates

Clear History | Angle of Line Defined by Two Points

Clear | Intersection of Two Lines Defined by Four Points

History Area

Input Box

Apply Button

The History area stores previous calculations. You can reuse History area data by double-clicking the expression or the result that you want. This places the data in the input area. First be sure to clear the input area of current data, if you don't want to keep it.

Calculating numbers

Calculating numbers is straightforward and uses the standard rules of precedence. For example, if you type **3*(2+3)/5-1** ↵, the calculator displays the answer, 2, as shown in Figure 12.15. After any calculation, you can either press Enter or click QuickCalc's = button.

FIGURE 12.15

You can use the calculator just like a hand-held one. The calculator stores earlier calculations for easy reference in the History area.

Because the 2+3 sum is in parentheses, it is calculated first so that the expression multiplies 3 by 5 (which is 15), divides it by 5 (which is 3), and subtracts 1 (which is 2).

Let's say you want to draw a horizontal line. You know it has to be the total of two other lines whose length you know. Follow these steps:

1. Start the LINE command.

   Specify first point: Pick the start point for the line.
   Specify next point or [Undo]: *Type* **'quickcalc** ↵ (The QuickCalc window opens.)

2. Press the Num Lock key.

3. In the Input area of the QuickCalc window, delete the 0.

4. Type **3.953+6.8725** ↵.

5. Click the Apply button at the bottom of the calculator. The QuickCalc window disappears and the sum appears on the command line.

6. Move the cursor to the right so that you can use Direct Distance Entry to draw at a zero-degree angle.

7. Press Enter to draw the line segment.

8. Continue the LINE command or press Enter to end the command.

You can use feet and inches as well. Use the format 6'5" or 6'-5". Don't put any spaces between the feet and inches. With the calculator, all inches must be marked with a double prime ("), unlike regular AutoCAD command-line usage. Note that your drawing must be using architectural units for this technique to work properly. (For more information on using feet and inches, see the sidebar "Subtracting Feet and Inches in QuickCalc.")

The QuickCalc toolbar has several buttons that are shortcuts for often-used tasks. These buttons are:

- Get Coordinates
- Distance Between Two Points
- Angle of Line Defined by Two Points
- Intersection of Two Lines Defined by Four Points

In each case, you are returned to the drawing area to specify the point or points that you need. For example, to draw a line the same length as another line, follow these steps:

1. Start the line.
2. Start QuickCalc transparently.
3. Click the Distance Between Two Points button on the QuickCalc toolbar.
4. You then return to your drawing where you can specify two points using any method, such as object snaps.
5. Back in QuickCalc, you see the distance in the Input area. Click Apply to paste this number into the command line.
6. Move the cursor in the direction that you want to draw, and press Enter to draw the line.

Using coordinates

You can use coordinates in QuickCalc expressions. Coordinates are enclosed in square brackets. For example, if you want to draw a line that is equal to the length of two other objects in your drawing that you happen to know are 3.953 and 6.8725 units long, and you want the line to be at a 20-degree angle, then you can follow these steps:

1. Start the LINE command.
2. At the `Specify first point:` prompt, specify your first point.
3. At the `Specify next point or [Undo]:` prompt, type **'quickcalc**.
4. In the calculator input box, type **[@(3.953+6.8725)<20]** ⏎. Note that the calculator converts your expression to absolute coordinates.
5. Click the Apply button at the bottom of the calculator. AutoCAD draws the line segment.

Subtracting Feet and Inches in QuickCalc

If you type the expression **3'2-1/2"**, AutoCAD converts it to 3'-2-1/2", adding a hyphen between the feet and inches.

However, if 3'2" is the same as 3'–2", then how do you subtract 2" from 3'?

The solution is to put parentheses around the 3 feet so that AutoCAD doesn't assume that the next expression is part of the same feet-inches expression, as shown here:

```
(3')–2"
```

The result is 2'-10". In this expression, AutoCAD subtracts 2" from 36" (3 feet).

Using object snaps

You can use the object snaps as part of a QuickCalc expression, when you use it transparently. When you press Enter after completing the expression, AutoCAD prompts you for the objects for each object snap in the expression, one after another.

For example, you could draw a line to the center of a triangle in this way. Figure 12.16 shows the process of drawing a line to the center of a triangle.

FIGURE 12.16

In this drawing, you can use QuickCalc to draw a line to the center of the triangle.

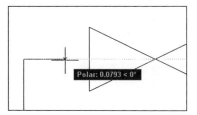

To draw a line to the center of the triangle, follow these steps:

1. Start the LINE command.
2. At the `Specify first point:` prompt, pick any start point.
3. At the `Specify next point or [Undo]:` prompt, type **'quickcalc** ↵.
4. In the QuickCalc input box, type **(end+end+end)/3** ↵. The QuickCalc window disappears, and you see a pickbox.
5. Pick the three corners of the triangle in succession. The QuickCalc window reappears with a coordinate in the Input box.
6. Click Apply to draw the line.

You can use QuickCalc as a substitute for the From object snap. For example, at the `Specify first point:` prompt, you can start QuickCalc transparently and type **mid+[3,–2.5]** ↵ in the Input box. AutoCAD prompts you for the object for which you want the midpoint. Click Apply to start the line (3,–2.5) units from there.

Using the scientific calculator

QuickCalc has its own scientific calculator, which you can use to calculate advanced formulas. Table 12.3 lists these functions.

TABLE 12.3

CAL Mathematical Functions

Function	What It Does
sin(angle)	Calculates the sine of the angle
Cos(angle)	Calculates the cosine of the angle
Tan(angle)	Calculates the tangent of the angle
asin(real)	Calculates the arc sine of the real number
acos(real)	Calculates the arc cosine of the real number
atan(real)	Calculates the arc tangent of the real number
ln(real)	Calculates the natural log of the real number
Log(real)	Calculates the base-10 log of the number
Exp(real)	Calculates the natural exponent of the real number
Exp10(real)	Calculates the base-10 exponent of the real number
Abs(real)	Calculates the absolute value of the real number (the number not including its + or – sign); this function is also used to calculate lengths
Rnd(real)	Rounds the number to its nearest integer
trunc(real)	Truncates any decimal value leaving only the integer
r2d(angle)	Converts radian angles to degrees
d2r(angle)	Converts degree angles to radians

Converting units

You can use the Units Conversion section of QuickCalc to convert units of length, area, volume, and angular measurements. For example, you can convert acres to square feet or meters to inches. Follow these steps:

1. If necessary, click the double down arrow to expand the Units Conversion section of QuickCalc.
2. From the Units Type drop-down list, choose the type of units that you want to convert.
3. From the Convert From drop-down list, choose the unit with which you want to start.
4. From the Convert To drop-down list, choose the unit to which you want to convert.
5. In the Value to Convert text box, type the value that you want to convert, and press Enter.

 6. To use this value on the command line, click the value that you entered, and then click the Return Conversion to Calculator Input Area button. Then click the Paste Value to Command Line button on the calculator's toolbar.

Working with QuickCalc variables

QuickCalc comes with some variables that you can use as part of calculated expressions. These include functions and one constant — the so-called Golden Ratio or Golden Number, Phi. Table 12.4 lists the functions and what they do.

TABLE 12.4

Special CAL Functions

Function Name	Full Function	What It Does
Rad		Gets the radius of the selected object.
Dee	dist(end,end)	Calculates the distance between two points; you can also use the Distance Between Two Points button on the QuickCalc toolbar.
Ille	ill(end,end,end,end)	Calculates the intersection of two lines based on their four endpoints; you can also use the Intersection of Two Lines Defined by Four Points button on the QuickCalc toolbar.
mee	(end+end)/2	Calculates the midpoint between two endpoints.
Nee	nor(end,end)	Calculates a one-unit vector in the XY plane that is normal (perpendicular) to two endpoints.
Vee	vec(end,end)	Calculates a vector from two endpoints.
Vee1	vec1(end,end)	Calculates a one-unit vector from two endpoints.

To use these functions, follow these steps:

1. Start a command.
2. At the prompt where you need the function, type '**quickcalc.** The QuickCalc window opens.
3. From the Variables list, double-click the function that you want to place in the Input box of the QuickCalc window.
4. Press Enter. You return to your drawing and see a pickbox cursor.
5. Pick the required points. The QuickCalc window returns, and you see an absolute coordinate in the Input box.
6. Click the Apply button.
7. Continue the command.

 A vector is a direction that is expressed as delta X, delta Y, delta Z. For example, using the vee function on a horizontal line that is 4 units long results in a vector direction of 4,0,0.

Remember that you can specify the points for the functions in many ways, most commonly by object snaps.

Using QuickCalc in the Properties palette

QuickCalc is also available in the Properties palette, where you can use it to calculate values that represent properties of objects, such as the X coordinate of the start point of a line. You can even use QuickCalc like the CHANGE command to specify a new start point for a line, using the Get Coordinate button.

To change an object's property in the Properties palette, follow these steps:

1. Select the object.

2. Display the Properties palette. (Press Ctrl+1 or click the Properties button on the Standard or Standard Annotation toolbar.)

3. Click any value in a white text box. (Gray boxes are not editable.)

 4. Click the QuickCalc icon that appears. QuickCalc opens with the current value in the Input box.

5. Delete the value and enter any mathematical expression. Press Enter or click QuickCalc's equal sign (=) button.

6. Click Apply to change the object. The new value also appears in the Properties palette.

TIP For simple calculations, you don't need to use QuickCalc. When set to 1 (the default), the CALCINPUT system variable allows you to type expressions into any text box that can take a value, including the Properties palette. Start the expression with the equal sign (=) and press Alt+Enter on your keyboard at the end of the expression. For example, you could enter =1/16+1/8 to change the thickness of an object. You can even enter =sqrt(8) to obtain the square root of 8, or enter =2^3 to obtain the cube of 2! Don't forget to press Alt+Enter after you enter the expression.

ON the DVD-ROM The drawing used in the following exercise on using the QuickCalc command, ab12-a.dwg, is in the Drawings folder on the DVD.

STEPS: Using the QUICKCALC Command

1. Open ab12-a.dwg from the DVD if you don't have it open from the previous exercise.

2. Save the drawing as ab12-01.dwg in your AutoCAD Bible folder.

3. If you did not do the previous exercise, use ZOOM Window to zoom in on the parcels labeled D and E, as shown in Figure 12.17.

FIGURE 12.17

Parcels D and E in the civil engineering drawing.

4. In the exercise on calculating area earlier in this chapter, you calculated a total area of 306975.04, in square inches. To calculate this area in square feet, type **quickcalc** ↵. In the Units Conversion section, choose Area from the Units Type drop-down list. In the Convert From drop-down list, choose Square Inches. In The Convert To drop-down list, choose Square Feet. In the Value to Convert text box, type **306975.04** ↵. AutoCAD calculates 2131.77111.

5. In the exercise on the DIVIDE command earlier in this chapter, you divided a line into three segments by placing two points on the line. To calculate the length of those segments, open QuickCalc. From the Variables section, choose the dee function and click the Return Variable to Input Area button. You see the expression dist(end,end) in the Input area. Click at the end of the expression and type **/3** ↵. In your drawing, the command line prompts you for the two endpoints. Pick the two ends of the line at **A** in Figure 12.17. QuickCalc calculates 262.37.

6. Close the QuickCalc palette.

7. You may want to draw a line starting from the intersection of two intersecting lines, going from corner to diagonally opposite corner and ending perpendicular to the top line of the land parcel. To do this, start the LINE command. At the Specify first point: prompt, type **'quickcalc** ↵.

8. Click the Intersection of Two Lines Defined by Four Points button. Pick the endpoints in Figure 12.17 at **1** and **2** to define the first line, and then at **3** and **4** to define the second line. Click the Apply button. AutoCAD starts the line at the intersection of the two lines. At the Specify next point or [Undo]: prompt, choose the Perpendicular object snap and pick **5**. End the LINE command. Figure 12.18 shows the result.

FIGURE 12.18

You can use the QUICKCALC command to calculate the intersection of two lines without drawing the lines.

9. Save your drawing.

Summary

A great deal of information is available to you in each drawing. In this chapter you read about:

- Getting a general status listing
- Listing system variable settings
- Tracking drawing time
- Getting information about individual objects by using the LIST, DIST, and ID commands
- Calculating area and perimeters
- Using the Properties palette to display all of an object's properties
- Dividing and measuring objects by placing point objects along them
- Using AutoCAD's QuickCalc calculator to use calculated results as part of your command input

In the next chapter, I explain how to create and edit text.

Chapter 13

Creating Text

Every drawing includes text that labels or explains the objects in the drawing; this text is often called *annotation*. In each release, the capabilities of the text feature have improved so that you can now easily format and edit text to provide a professional appearance to your drawing. A wide range of font, alignment, and spacing options is available. You can also import text from a word processor. This chapter tells you all that you need to know about creating text in AutoCAD and AutoCAD LT.

Creating Single-Line Text

A great deal of text in a drawing consists of short labels or comments. Use single-line text when you want each line of text to be a separate object or when you're creating a small amount of text. Single-line text has fewer options than the multi-line text that I explain later in this chapter, but it's easy to create and to accurately place in a drawing.

It is very easy to create a single line of text using the defaults, such as font and height. Choose Draw ⇨ Text ⇨ Single Line Text. Alternatively, choose Single Line Text from the Text control panel of the Dashboard. This starts the DTEXT command (which is the same as the TEXT command).

Follow the prompts:

```
Current text style: "Standard" Text height:
0.2000 Annotative: No
Specify start point of text or [Justify/Style]: Pick
a start point for the text.
Specify height <0.2000>: Type a height, or press
Enter to accept the default.
Specify rotation angle of text <0>: Type a rotation
angle, or press Enter to accept the default.
```

> *You see a cursor at the insertion point. Type one line of text. Press*
> *Enter. You can continue to type more lines of text.*
> *Press Enter to end the command.* You can also click another location on
> the screen to start a new text object.

You cannot use the Return button of the mouse or the Spacebar to end the command.
You can type -text on the command line to use the original TEXT behavior, which ends the
command after one line of text. You must use the TEXT command (rather than the DTEXT command) for
script files, menus, or AutoLISP routines. (See Parts VI and VII of this book for more information.)

The next section covers the Justify option. The Style option and the Annotative property are discussed later
in this chapter.

One advantage of DTEXT is that each line of text is a separate object, making it easy to move or copy individual lines of text. Unfortunately, you cannot control the spacing between the lines.

It (for the TEXT command) and Idt (for DTEXT) allow you to specify the spacing between
lines of text as you create them. Look in \Software\Chapter 13\It. Txtstack, in
\Software\Chapter 13\txtstack, adjusts spacing between lines of single-line text. You can use
txt2mtxt to convert single-line text to multiline text. Look in \Software\Chapter 13\txt2mtxt. These
programs work only in AutoCAD. (*Thanks to Leonid Nemirovsky,* http://home.pacifier.com/~nemi,
for creating It.lsp *and* Idt.lsp *at my request.)*

DTEXT remembers the location of the previous line of text even if you've used other commands in the
meantime. To continue text below the last line of text that you have created, press Enter at the Specify
start point of text or [Justify/Style]: prompt.

You can also create text connected to arrows that point to objects, called leaders. Chapter 14
covers leaders.

Justifying single-line text

When you pick a start point for text, the relationship between the start point and the actual letters is determined by the justification. The start point is also called the *insertion point*. When you want to refer to text by
using object snaps, you use the Insertion object snap. If you select text without first choosing a command,
grips appear at the insertion point as well as the bottom-left corner.

By default, text is left-justified. To change the text's justification, right-click and choose Justify at the
Specify start point of text or [Justify/Style]: prompt. The command responds with this
bewildering prompt:

    Enter an option [Align/Fit/Center/Middle/Right/TL/TC/TR/ML/MC/
    MR/BL/BC/BR]:

Align and Fit offer two ways to fit text into a specified space. Both respond with the same two prompts:

    Specify first endpoint of text baseline:
    Specify second endpoint of text baseline:

Specify the beginning and the end of the text line. Align then prompts you for the text and squeezes or
stretches the text to fit within the text line. The height of the text changes accordingly, to maintain the proportions of the font.

The Fit option adds the `Specify height <0.2000>:` prompt. Type the height that you want and then type the text. Fit also squeezes or stretches the text to fit within the text line, but maintains the text height that you specified, distorting the font letters to fit the space. Figure 13.1 shows an example of normal, aligned, and fitted single-line text.

FIGURE 13.1

Normal (left-justified), aligned, and fitted text.

The other justification options are listed in Table 13.1. They specify the placement of the text's insertion point in relation to the text line. Each insertion point is marked with a small *x*.

TABLE 13.1

Text Justification Options

Example	Option	Description
Garage	Left	Because this is the default justification, there is no sub-option for left-justification when you choose the Justify option. The insertion point is on the baseline.
Garage	Center	Text is centered around the insertion point. The insertion point is on the baseline.
Garage	Right	Text is right-justified from the insertion point. The insertion point is on the baseline.
Garage	Middle	Text is centered both vertically and horizontally. The vertical center point is measured from the bottom of the lowest to the top of the tallest possible letter.
Garage	Top Left	Text is left-justified, and the insertion point is at the top of the highest possible letter. For some fonts, the insertion point appears slightly above the highest letter; for others, it appears exactly at the top.
Garage	Top Center	Text is centered, and the insertion point is at the top of the highest possible letter.
Garage	Top Right	Text is right-justified, and the insertion point is at the top of the highest possible letter.
Garage	Middle Left	Text is left-justified and centered vertically. The vertical center point is measured from the bottom of the lowest to the top of the tallest possible letter.

continued

TABLE 13.1	(continued)	
Example	Option	Description
Garage	Middle Center	Text is centered both horizontally and vertically. The vertical center point is measured from the bottom of the lowest to the top of the tallest possible letter.
Garage	Middle Right	Text is right-justified and centered vertically. The vertical center point is measured from the bottom of the lowest to the top of the tallest possible letter.
Garage	Bottom Left	Text is left-justified. The insertion point is below the lowest descending letter. For some fonts, the insertion point appears slightly below the lowest letter; for others, it appears exactly at the bottom.
Garage	Bottom Center	Text is centered. The insertion point is below the lowest descending letter.
Garage	Bottom Right	Text is right-justified. The insertion point is below the lowest descending letter.

> **TIP** If you know the option abbreviation of the justification that you want, you can use it at the `Specify start point of text or [Justify/Style]:` **prompt.**

Setting the height

Setting the height of text is fairly straightforward. The default is 0.2 units, although this is not suitable for all applications. The main point to consider is the scale factor. If you're drawing a house and plan to plot it at 1"=8' (1=96), you need to figure out how big to make the text so that you can still read it when it is scaled down.

For example, if you want the text to be 0.2 units high and your scale factor is 96, your text needs to be 19.2 inches high (0.2×96). On the other hand, if you're drawing a very small object, such as a computer chip, and your scale is 0.10, then your text needs to be 0.02 inches high. The dimension text in Figure 13.2 is 5 inches high, but at a scale factor of 64, it plots at 5/64 inches high.

FIGURE 13.2

The dimension text in this drawing is 5 inches high.

AutoCAD and AutoCAD LT calculate text height in units. Most word processors calculate text height in points. A point is $\frac{1}{72}$ of an inch. Therefore, 12-point text, a standard for most business letters, is about 0.17 inches high. The default of 0.2 units, if you're using inches as your unit, is just over 14 points, which is usually appropriate for annotating a drawing. (You don't usually hold a drawing as close as you would a letter, so a larger point size is appropriate.)

NEW FEATURE You can create *annotative* single-line text, using an annotative text style. This feature automatically scales text according to your scale. For more information, see the section "Understanding Text Styles" later in this chapter. To make existing single-line text annotative, select the text and change the Annotative property in the Properties palette from No to Yes.

For more information about changing the scale of text, see the section "Editing single-line text" later in this chapter.

Setting the rotation angle

The final prompt in DTEXT is the rotation angle. This angle applies to the entire line of text, not to individual characters. (You can specify slanted text, called *oblique text*, using the STYLE command covered later in this chapter.) Figure 13.3 shows text rotated to 315 degrees.

FIGURE 13.3

Text rotated to 315 degrees.

Adding special characters and formatting

The DTEXT command does not offer the same type of formatting options that are available for paragraph (multiline) text (covered later in this chapter). Therefore, you have to use codes to create special characters and formats. These codes are shown in Table 13.2.

TABLE 13.2

Special Character Codes for Text Fonts

Code	Results
%%o	Toggles the overscore mode on/off
%%u	Toggles the underscore mode on/off
%%d	Draws a degree symbol (°)
%%p	Draws a plus/minus tolerance symbol (±)
%%c	Draws a circle-diameter dimensioning symbol (ø)

Figure 13.4 displays text using some of these codes, along with the entries that created them.

FIGURE 13.4

Using special characters and formatting with text fonts.

35.3 not 35.8   %%u35.3%%u not 35.8

ø1.5   %%c1.5

±.002   %%p.002

ON the DVD-ROM   **The drawing used in the following exercise on creating text with DTEXT,** 13-a.dwg, **is in the** Drawings **folder on the DVD.**

STEPS: Creating Text with DTEXT

1. Open ab13-a.dwg from your DVD.

2. Save the file as ab13-01.dwg in your AutoCAD Bible folder. This is a master-bathroom plan drawing, as shown in Figure 13.5. Make sure that OSNAP is on. Set running object snaps for endpoint, midpoint, and intersection.

FIGURE 13.5

FIGURE 13.5

The master bathroom.

3. If the Dashboard isn't open, enter **dashboard** on the command line. If you don't see the Text control panel, right-click the top or right border and choose Control Panels ➪ Text. Choose Single Line Text from the Text control panel. Follow the prompts:

```
Current text style: "ROMANS" Text height: 0'-4 1/2" Annotative:  No
Specify start point of text or [Justify/Style]: Right-click and
choose Justify.
Enter an option
[Align/Fit/Center/Middle/Right/TL/TC/TR/ML/MC/MR/BL/BC/BR]: Right-
click and choose BC.
Specify bottom-center point of text: Use the Midpoint running object
snap to pick ❶ in Figure 13.5.
Specify rotation angle of text <0>: Pick the endpoint at ❷.
Enter text: 2-0 ↵
Enter text: ↵
```

4. Start the DTEXT command again. Follow the prompts:

```
Specify start point of text or [Justify/Style]: Right-click and
choose Justify.
Enter an option
[Align/Fit/Center/Middle/Right/TL/TC/TR/ML/MC/MR/BL/BC/BR]: Right-
click and choose Middle.
Specify middle point of text: Pick ❸ in Figure 13.5. (This point
doesn't have to be exact.)
Specify rotation angle of text <45>: 0 ↵
Enter text: %%UMASTER BATH ↵
Enter text: ↵
```

5. Save your drawing. It should look like Figure 13.6.

The master-bathroom plan drawing with added single-line text.

Editing single-line text

As with any drawing object, the need often arises to edit your text. You can edit single-line text in two ways.

The most common way to edit single-line text is to use the DDEDIT command. Double-click the text to start the command. Remember that each line of text created with DTEXT or TEXT is a separate object.

The text appears in a border with your text highlighted in an edit box, as shown in Figure 13.7. You can start typing to completely replace the text or click where you want to change part of the text and use standard Windows techniques to edit the text. Press Enter or click anywhere outside the border. DDEDIT prompts you to select another annotation object. Press Enter to end the command.

 If the text is rotated, the text remains at its current rotation angle during editing instead of reverting to horizontal.

Editing single-line text in place in the drawing.

If you find other nearby or overlapping objects to be distracting, right-click and choose Editor Settings ⇨ Opaque Background to create an opaque background inside the editing border while you edit. Alternatively, you can right-click, choose Editor Settings ⇨ Text Highlight Color, and specify any color you want in the Select Color dialog box.

You can also change text using the Properties palette. Select any text object and open the Properties palette (Ctrl+1). Here you can edit the text content as well as every other conceivable property, including layer, linetype, lineweight, color, insertion point, justification, rotation angle, and others that I cover in the next section on text styles.

Scaling text

If you want to scale text and use the SCALE command, the text may move, depending on the base point you use. Instead, you can use the SCALETEXT command to change the scale of selected text without moving the text insertion point. This command works with either one text object or several at once. All of the text objects stay in their original location.

To use SCALETEXT, follow these steps:

1. Choose Modify ⇨ Object ⇨ Text ⇨ Scale.

2. Select the text objects that you want to scale.

3. At the `Enter a base point option for scaling [Existing/Left/Center/ Middle/Right/TL/TC/TR/ML/MC/MR/BL/BC/BR] <Existing>:` prompt, press Enter to use the existing insertion point of the selected text, or choose a new base point. (Your last choice for this prompt becomes the new default, so if you used another option, type **e ↵**.) These options are the same as the Justify options described earlier in this chapter.

4. At the `Specify new model height or [Paper height/Match object/Scale factor] <3/32>:` prompt, right-click and choose Scale factor to specify a scale factor, just as you would for the SCALE command (see Chapter 9). You can also type a new height or use the Match Object option to match the height of the selected text objects to another existing text object. The prompt asks you to select an object with the desired height.

For annotative text only, you can specify a paper height, which means the height you want the text to appear when plotted.

5. If you have chosen the Scale Factor option, then type the factor that you want at the `Specify scale factor or [Reference] <2>:` prompt.

6. If you want to specify the scale factor with reference to existing text or a value, use the Reference option. At the `Specify reference length <1>:` prompt, type a length or specify two points that measure the reference length. At the `Specify new length:` prompt, type a value or pick two points to indicate the new length.

If you want to scale text to automatically fit a drawing scale, you can use annotative text. For more information, see the upcoming section "Understanding Text Styles."

Justifying text

The JUSTIFYTEXT command lets you change the justification of selected text objects without moving the text. To use JUSTIFYTEXT, choose Modify ⇨ Object ⇨ Text ⇨ Justify. Then select the text objects that you want to modify. At the `Enter a justification option [Left/Align/Fit/Center/Middle/ Right/TL/TC/TR/ML/MC/MR/BL/BC/BR] <Left>:` prompt, right-click and choose the justification that you want.

The drawing used in the following exercise on editing text, ab13-b.dwg, is in the Drawings folder on the DVD.

STEPS: Editing Text

1. Open ab13-b.dwg from your DVD.

2. Save the file as ab13-02.dwg in your AutoCAD Bible folder. This is an air and vacuum release valve, as shown in Figure 13.8.

3. Double-click the text 1/2" piping. A highlighted border appears around the text. Select only the text 1/2 and type **3/8**. Press Enter or click anywhere outside the text border. The DDEDIT prompt continues to prompt you to select another annotation object. Press Enter to end the command.

4. Display the Properties palette (Ctrl+1). Click Quick Select in the Properties palette. In the Quick Select dialog box, choose Text from the Object Type drop-down list. In the Operator drop-down list, choose Select All. Click OK to select all of the text objects in the drawing.

FIGURE 13.8

An air and vacuum release valve.

Thanks to the Army Corps of Engineers for this drawing.

---

5. Choose Layer. From the Layer drop-down list, choose TEXT. Choose Color. From the Color drop-down list, choose ByLayer. All text is now on the TEXT layer using the ByLayer color. Press Esc to remove the grips and see the result.

6. Select the text at the bottom of the drawing that reads N.T.S. From the grips you can tell that it has a middle-left justification. Choose Modify ⇨ Object ⇨ Text ⇨ Justify, or type **justifytext** ↵ on the command line. At the prompt, type **bc** ↵.

   The command ends. You can select the text again to see that the insertion point grip is now at the bottom-center of the text.

7. Choose Modify ➪ Object ➪ Text ➪ Scale, or type **scaletext** ↵ on the command line. Follow the prompts:

```
Select objects: Select the two lines of text at the bottom of the
drawing.
Select objects: ↵
Enter a base point option for scaling
[Existing/Left/Center/Middle/Right/TL/TC/TR/ML/MC/MR/BL/BC/BR] <BC>:
Type e ↵ to use the existing base point.
Specify new model height or [Paper height/Match object/Scale factor]
<1/8">: Right-click and choose Scale factor.
Specify scale factor or [Reference] <2">: Type 1.5 ↵.
```

8. You can click the Properties palette's Close button to close it. Save your drawing.

Understanding Text Styles

You may not always want to use the default font. You can create text styles that give you full creative control over the font, font style (bold, italic, or both), character width, obliquing angle, and text height. You can even design backward, upside-down, and vertical text. (Vertical text is like the text that you occasionally see on the spine of a book. It goes down instead of to the right.)

Text styles are similar to layers, which I discuss in Chapter 11. Like a layer, each text style:

- Has a name and several properties
- Is saved with the drawing
- Can be made current when you want to use it
- Can be renamed and deleted

Creating text styles is part of the typical drawing setup procedure. You should include text styles in your drawing templates. AutoCAD and AutoCAD LT come with two types of fonts: the original .shx fonts, which are created using *shape* files; and TrueType fonts, which are used by most Windows applications.

 See Chapter 32 for instructions on creating shape files and your own fonts.

Creating a new text style

To create a new text style, choose Format ➪ Text Style. This starts the STYLE command and opens the Text Style dialog box, as shown in Figure 13.9.

Choose New to open the New Text Style dialog box, as shown in Figure 13.10. Type the name of your new text style and click OK. Text style names can be up to 255 characters and can include spaces. You return to the Text Style dialog box where you can define the new text style.

At the top-left of the Text Style dialog box is the list of currently defined styles in the drawing. At the lower-left corner is a preview of the style that is selected in the Styles list.

FIGURE 13.9

The Text Style dialog box.

FIGURE 13.10

The New Text Style dialog box.

Font

In the Font section of the Text Style dialog box, you specify the font name and font style. Click the Font Name drop-down list arrow to see the list of fonts. Fonts with the double-T icon are TrueType fonts. The other fonts are defined in a shape file that has the `.shp` filename extension. They are compiled into a file with the `.shx` filename extension for faster access. For more information on working with fonts, see Chapter 32.

Click a font to choose it. You can see a preview of the font in the Preview at the lower-left corner of the dialog box.

If the font that you've chosen supports different styles, such as bold or italic, you can choose one of them in the Font Style drop-down box. None of the AutoCAD or AutoCAD LT fonts supports font styles, but many of the TrueType fonts do.

> **NOTE** AutoCAD supports fonts with many characters (called *big fonts*), such as Japanese and Chinese. To use these fonts, check the Use Big Font check box. The Font Style drop-down list changes to become the Big Font drop-down list, where you can choose from a list of big fonts.

Size

The Size section of the dialog box lets you specify the height of the text. There are two types of height: one for model space and one for layouts. (I discuss layouts in Chapter 17.)

- **Height in the drawing:** If you are going to use the text style in the main drawing area (model space, where you draw and edit), use the Height text box to enter the height of the text. Remember to take into account the scale factor, if necessary.

- **Height in a viewport:** If you are going to use the text style for text that you will display in a scaled viewport on a layout (which I cover in Chapter 17), check the Annotative check box. Then use the Paper Text Height text box to enter the height of the text. You don't need to adjust for the scale factor when you enter a height, because annotative objects facilitate that process for you.

> **NOTE** If you check the Annotative check box, you can also check the Match Text Orientation to Layout check box. If you rotate the viewport using the MVSETUP command, with the Align ⇨ Rotate view options, the text remains horizontal and does not rotate.

> **NEW FEATURE** AutoCAD 2008 introduces *annotative* objects, which automatically scale according to the scale of a viewport on a layout. You use a layout to arrange a drawing for plotting, and viewports display various views of the drawing. Each viewport can have a different scale, and annotative objects automatically adjust in size accordingly. I discuss annotative objects more in Chapter 17.

In both types of height, you can leave the height at zero if you want to be able to vary the text height within that one style. If the height is zero, the DTEXT and TEXT commands prompt you for a height when you use these commands to place text.

> **CAUTION** If you create a text style using a height other than zero and then use that text style when you define a dimension style, the text style height overrides the text height that you specify separately in the dimension style. See Chapter 15 for more information on dimension styles.

Effects

In the Effects section, you specify the orientation, width factor, and oblique angle of the text style.

The default width factor of characters is set to 1. You can specify a smaller number to compress text and a larger number to expand it, as shown in Figure 13.11.

FIGURE 13.11

Text using different width factors.

Width = 1.5 Bearing Housing
Width = .8 Bearing Housing

The term *oblique angle* refers to the angle of the individual letters. It is generally used to create an effect, such as italic text. You don't need to use an oblique angle if you're using a TrueType font that supports italic text.

The angle definition used to define oblique text is different from the angle definition used for other objects. Up and down text, which is normal text, has a zero oblique angle. A positive angle slants the text to the right; this is typical for italic text. A negative angle slants the text to the left. Figure 13.12 shows text with a positive and negative oblique angle.

FIGURE 13.12

Text using different oblique angles.

Oblique angle = –10   Bearing Housing

Oblique angle = 10   *Bearing Housing*

You can create text that is backward (like a mirror image) or upside down. Some fonts also let you create vertical text. Figure 13.13 shows an example of each kind of text. Check the appropriate check box to create the effect that you want.

FIGURE 13.13

Upside-down, backward, and vertical text.

After you finish defining your text style, click Apply to make it current. Click Close to return to your drawing.

Renaming and deleting text styles

You can rename and delete text styles easily. To rename a text style, start the STYLE command to open the Text Style dialog box. Select the text style, click the text style's name again, enter a new name, and press Enter.

To delete a text style, choose it from the Styles box of the Text Style dialog box and click Delete. A message box asks you to confirm the deletion. Click OK to delete the text style. You cannot delete a text style that is being used.

ON the DVD-ROM The drawing used in the following exercise on creating text styles, ab13-b.dwg, is in the Drawings folder on the DVD.

STEPS: Creating Text Styles

1. Open ab13-b.dwg from your DVD.
2. Save the file as ab13-03.dwg in your AutoCAD Bible folder.
3. Choose Format ⇨ Text Style to open the Text Style dialog box. Click New. In the New Text Style dialog box, type **Notes** and click OK.

4. From the Font Name drop-down list, choose `romans.shx`. In the Height text box, enter a height of **1/16"**. In the Width Factor text box, enter a width factor of **.95**. In the Oblique Angle text box, type **10**. Click Apply to make the new style current. Click Close.

5. Start the DTEXT command. At the `Specify start point of text or [Justify/Style]:` prompt, pick a start point at the lower-left corner of the drawing. At the `Specify rotation angle of text <0>:` prompt, press Enter. At the prompt, type **Note: Not drawn to scale.** ↵. Press Enter again to end the command.

6. Save your drawing. It should look like Figure 13.14. If you're going on to the next exercise, keep this drawing open.

FIGURE 13.14

The addition of text using a new text style.

Modifying a text style

To change a style, choose Format ➪ Text Style. From the Styles list, choose the text style that you want to change. Make changes in the same way that you did when creating the style. Choose Apply and then Close. The drawing regenerates, and the text that uses the style that you changed is modified accordingly. This is a powerful way to control the look of text in your drawing.

NOTE Unfortunately, only changes to the font and text style affect current text. Other changes, such as width factor, oblique angle, orientation, and height, are ignored. However, new text takes on these other changes.

Making a style current or changing a text object's style

You can choose the current style when you use one of the text commands. If you use DTEXT or TEXT, the command displays the `Specify start point of text or [Justify/Style]:` prompt. Right-click and choose Style. (The prompt also displays the current style and height.) If you know the name of the style that you want to use, type it and press Enter. The `Specify start point of text or [Justify/Style]:` prompt repeats. You can choose the Justify option or pick a start point to continue the command.

If you use MTEXT, the In-Place Text Editor opens, as explained in the next section. Choose the text style that you want from the Style drop-down list.

The Styles toolbar and the Text control panel of the Dashboard offer an easy way to make a style current or to change the text style of existing text. To make a style current, choose the style from the Text Style Control drop-down list with no text selected. To change the text style of existing text, select the text and choose a new style from the list. You can also change the style of selected text in the Properties palette.

Importing a text style

As explained in Chapter 11, you can use the DesignCenter to import features from other drawings. To import a text style, follow these steps:

1. Open the DesignCenter (Ctrl+2).
2. In the left pane, navigate to the drawing that has the text style that you want.
3. Double-click the drawing icon or click its plus sign.
4. To see the list of the text styles, double-click the text style's icon in either the left or right pane.
5. Double-click the text style's icon to import it into your drawing.
6. Click the DesignCenter's Close button to close the DesignCenter.

 The drawing used in the following exercise on modifying text styles, ab13-03.dwg, is in the Results folder on the DVD.

STEPS: Modifying Text Styles

1. If you have ab13-03.dwg open from the previous exercise, continue to use it for this exercise. Otherwise, open ab13-03.dwg from the Results folder of your DVD.
2. Save the file as ab13-04.dwg in your AutoCAD Bible folder.
3. The note at the bottom-left corner of the drawing uses the Notes text style. Choose Format ⇨ Text Style. In the Text Style dialog box, make sure that the NOTES style name is listed, and then choose italic.shx from the Font Name drop-down list. Choose Apply and then Close.
4. The drawing regenerates, and the font of the text changes.
5. Save your drawing.

Creating Multiline Text

Single-line text is awkward when you want to type quite a bit of text. The main disadvantage is that single-line text does not wrap text to the next line to keep a neat right margin. Multiline text solves this problem and also offers many more formatting options compared to single-line text. The entire paragraph of multi-line text is one object. Don't confuse multiline text, which is also called *paragraph text,* with *multilines* (which I cover in Chapter 16).

Using the In-Place Text Editor

 To create paragraph text, choose Multiline Text from the Draw toolbar or the Text control panel of the Dashboard. (If the Draw toolbar isn't displayed, right-click any toolbar button and choose Draw from the list of toolbars. To display the Dashboard, choose Tools ⇨ Palettes ⇨ Dashboard.)

This starts the MTEXT command. The prompt tells you the current style, text height, and whether or not the style is annotative. For example:

```
Current text style: "ROMANS" Text height: 4 1/2" Annotative: No
```

The command continues with the `Specify first corner:` prompt. Specify one corner of a bounding box to indicate where to place the text. At the `Specify opposite corner or [Height/Justify/Line spacing/Rotation/Style/Width/Columns]:` prompt, specify the diagonally opposite corner of the bounding box. You can also choose one of the other options to specify the text properties before you type the text. Some of these options are also available in the In-Place Text Editor, which opens after you specify the bounding box. Figure 13.15 shows the In-Place Text Editor.

TIP When you specify the corners of the Mtext box, you see sample text at the cursor to give you an idea of the actual current height of the text. You can change the sample text with the MTJIGSTRING system variable.

FIGURE 13.15

The In-Place Text Editor.

Type your text in the boundary. The In-Place Text Editor wraps the text to the next line when the text meets the right side of the bounding box that you specified. Although you've created a bounding box with four sides, only the *paragraph width* (that is, the left and right margins) limits the text. If you type too much text for the bounding box, the bounding box expands vertically. (This feature functions differently if you use columns, which I explain in the discussion of the Options toolbar.)

To format selected or new text, use the buttons on the In-Place Text Editor toolbar:

- **Style:** Choose any text style from the Style drop-down list.
- **Font:** Choose any font from the Font drop-down list.
- **Annotative:** Click to turn the annotative feature on or off.
- **Text Height:** Choose a height from the drop-down list or type a new height in the Text Height box.
- **Bold:** If Bold style is supported for the font, select text and click Bold.
- **Italic:** If Italic style is supported for the font, select text and click Italic.
- **Underline:** Select text and click Underline.
- **Overline:** Overscores selected text.
- **Undo:** Undoes the last Mtext edit.
- **Redo:** Redoes the last undo operation.
- **Stack/Unstack:** Toggles stacking and unstacking fractions. Use this option to stack characters that are neither numerals nor immediately before or after the three AutoStack symbols (slash, pound sign, and carat). Select the text and click Stack/Unstack. See the next section for more details.

- **Color:** Choose ByLayer or any color from the Color drop-down list. To choose from additional colors, choose Select Color to open the Select Color dialog box. (See Chapter 11 for details on using this dialog box.)
- **Ruler:** Turns off the ruler.
- **OK:** Click to close the editor. You can also close the editor by clicking anywhere outside the editor or by pressing Ctrl+Enter.
- **Options:** Click to display a menu of options for the editor. You can access the same options by right-clicking in the text-editing area to display the shortcut menu. I discuss these options later in this section.

> **TIP** To create an exponent (or superscript), type a number and then a carat, as in 2^. Select the number and the carat and then click the Stack/Unstack button. To create a subscript, type a carat, and then the number, as in ^2, and then stack it.

The Options toolbar on the second row offers easy access to formatting tools. It displays the following buttons:

- **Columns:** Creates multiple column text. Click the down arrow to display the options:
  - **No Columns:** The default option, which creates one column of text.
  - **Dynamic Columns:** Creates columns based on the amount of text. Text automatically flows from one column to the next. The vertical height of the bounding box does not change as you add text; if you enter more text than can fit in the box, another column automatically starts, with no limit.
  - **Static Columns:** Creates a set number of columns of a specified height and width. Text automatically flows from one column to the next, but you can specify the number of columns.
  - **Insert Column Break:** Forces a column break. Place the cursor at the desired location and press Alt+Enter.
  - **Column Settings:** Opens the Column Settings dialog box, shown in Figure 13.16. Here you can specify the type of columns, their width, height, and gutter (the spacing between columns).

> **NEW FEATURE** Columns are new for AutoCAD 2008 and AutoCAD LT 2008.

FIGURE 13.16

You can specify exact column settings in the Column Settings dialog box.

> **TIP** You can grip-edit column text. Use one of the lower grips to change the vertical height. Use the right-facing arrow to change the column width.

- **MText Justification:** Choose a justification from the submenu. The justifications are discussed in the "Justifying single-line text" section earlier in this chapter.

- **Paragraph:** Opens the new Paragraph dialog box, shown in Figure 13.17, where you can specify the following settings:

  - **Tabs:** You can choose left, center, right, and decimal tabs, as well as their position. Click Add to add the tab. A decimal tab centers text around a decimal point. (If you choose a decimal tab, you can choose a decimal style from the Specify Decimal Style drop-down list — period, comma, or space.)

  - **Paragraph Alignment:** Check the Paragraph Alignment check box and choose Left, Center, Right, Justified, or Distributed. Justified text has even margins on either side. Distributed text also has even margins, but if necessary, text is stretched out (adding space between the letters) to meet the margin.

  - **Paragraph Spacing:** Sets spacing between paragraphs. You can set spacing both before and after, but if you set both, the two values are added.

  - **Left Indent:** Sets the left margin for the first line of a paragraph and the rest of the paragraph. Use this indentation for creating bulleted and numbered lists. To indent an entire paragraph, use both first-line and paragraph indentation.

TIP It's easier to set indentation and tabs on the In-Place Text Editor's ruler than in the dialog box. Drag the first-line indent marker (the top triangle at the left of the ruler) or the paragraph indent marker (the bottom triangle) to the left or right. To set a tab, click on the ruler where you want the tab. To delete a tab, drag a tab marker off the ruler. Note that the bullets and numbering feature makes these settings less important than previously.

  - **Paragraph Line Spacing:** You can set the spacing of lines of text within a paragraph. For example, from the Line Spacing drop-down list, you can choose Multiple to Single or Double-space lines. Choose Exactly to specify the distance between lines in units. Choose At Least to set a minimum spacing (this is good for situations when you have text or symbols of varying heights and want to leave room for the larger items.

FIGURE 13.17

The Paragraph dialog box offers one place where you can specify many settings relating to paragraphs.

- **Left:** Left-justifies the text in the editor and sets the insertion point to the left of the text.
- **Center:** Centers the text in the editor and sets the insertion point to the center of the text.
- **Right:** Right-justifies the text in the editor and sets the insertion point to the right of the text.
- **Justify:** Justifies both the left and right margins.
- **Distribute:** Justifies both the left and right margins, even for short lines of text, stretching the spacing between the letters as necessary.
- **Line Spacing:** Sets line spacing in multiples of single-line spacing. You can choose More to open the Paragraph dialog box, which was discussed previously.
- **Numbering:** Displays a submenu that lets you manage bullets and numbering:
  - **Off:** Removes bullets and numbering from the selected text.
  - **Lettered:** Lets you create lettered lists. You can choose uppercase or lowercase letters.
  - **Numbered:** Creates a numbered list.
  - **Bulleted:** Creates a bulleted list.
  - **Restart:** Restarts numbering (or lettering) from the beginning.
  - **Continue:** Continues numbering (or lettering) from the last list.
  - **Allow Auto-list:** Automatically starts a numbered list if you type **1.**, a lettered list if you type **A.**, or a bulleted list if you type a dash (-) or an asterisk (*).
  - **Use Tab Delimiter Only:** Creates a list only if you use a tab after some text, and not when you use a space. On by default.
  - **Allow Bullets and Lists:** Turns on the feature that automatically numbers (or letters) items that are in a list. For example, if you delete an item, the rest of the items are automatically adjusted.
- **Insert Field:** Inserts a field into the text. For more information, see the section "Inserting Fields" later in this chapter. (Fields are not available in AutoCAD LT.)
- **UPPERCASE:** Converts selected text from lowercase to uppercase.
- **Lowercase:** Converts selected text from uppercase to lowercase.
- **Symbol:** Inserts the degree, plus/minus, or diameter symbol, a non-breaking space, and a number of other symbols. You can also choose Other to open the Windows Character Map to select any of the available symbols. Click a symbol, and then click Select. Click Copy and then click the Close button to close the Windows Character Map. In the In-Place Text Editor, press Ctrl+V to paste in the symbol.
- **Oblique Angle:** Specifies the angle for the letters in selected text. For example, you can use the oblique angle to create italicized text. Enter a number that represents an angle from upright. A negative value angles text to the left.
- **Tracking:** Specifies the spacing between letters of selected text. Enter a number in the text box; the number works like a scale factor.
- **Width Factor:** Specifies the width of selected letters. Enter a number in the text box; the number works like a scale factor.

Right-click in the editor to display the shortcut menu. The shortcut menu contains many important controls. These controls are also available from the Options button on the In-Place Text Editor main toolbar. Here I discuss the options that are not available on the two Text Editor toolbars:

- **Cut:** Places selected text in the Windows Clipboard and removes it from the editor.
- **Copy:** Places selected text in the Windows Clipboard without removing it from the editor.

- **Paste:** Places text from the Windows Clipboard.

- **Editor Settings:** Opens a submenu that lets you toggles the display of the main toolbar, the Options toolbar, and the ruler. You can also create a temporary opaque background for the In-Place Text Editor that may help you to edit text more easily if the text overlaps other objects. This background disappears when you close the editor. Finally, you can choose the color of the high-light when you select text.

- **Import Text:** Opens the Select File dialog box, which lets you choose a text (.txt) or Rich Text Format (.rtf) file to import. (Rich Text Format preserves formatting from application to application, while text-only documents do not retain formatting.) Find the file, choose it, and click Open to place the text in the In-Place Text Editor. The maximum file size is 32K. Other techniques for importing text are covered later in this chapter.

- **Background Mask:** Opens the Background Mask dialog box, shown in Figure 13.18. This feature creates a background around your text that covers other objects so that you can easily read the text. Check the Use Background Mask check box. Specify a border offset factor to create a margin around the text. The default margin setting of 1 does not create any margin. Then check the Use Drawing Background Color check box to use the color of your drawing screen, or choose another color from the drop-down list. Click OK.

FIGURE 13.18

Use the Background Mask dialog box to create a background around your text so that other objects do not obscure the text.

- **Find and Replace:** Opens the Find and Replace dialog box so that you can find or replace specified text. If you want the search to match the case of the specified text, choose Match Case. If you want to restrict the search to whole words that match the specified text, choose Whole Words. If you only want to find text, ignore the Replace text box. To both find and replace text, enter text in both boxes. Make sure that the cursor is at the beginning of the text if you want to search the entire Mtext object.

- **Select All:** Selects all of the text.

- **AutoCAPS:** Automatically changes newly typed and imported text to uppercase, even if the Caps Lock key is not on. (And it's a cute pun on AutoCAD.)

- **Remove Formatting:** Removes character formatting, such as bold and italic, paragraph formatting (such as indenting), or all formatting.

- **Combine Paragraphs:** Combines separate paragraphs into one. Select the paragraphs that you want to combine before applying this command.

- **Character Set:** Lets you choose the language that you want to work with, so that you have the characters that you need for that language.

> **TIP**   The TEXTTOFRONT command moves all text in your drawing to the front (top) of the drawing order. For the background mask to work, your text needs to be on top, so you can use this command when you are creating text with background masks. The display order of objects is controlled by the DRAWORDER command, which I discuss in Chapter 27, at the end of the "Controlling image display" section.

After you finish creating multiline text, close the editor in one of three ways:

- Click OK on the Text Formatting bar.
- Click anywhere outside the In-Place Text Editor (but inside the drawing area).
- Press Ctrl+Enter.

> **TIP**   You can snap to the corners of the Mtext bounding box using the node object snap. (See Chapter 4 for an explanation of object snaps.) To turn this feature off, change the OSNAPNODELEGACY system variable to 1.

Creating Stacked Fractions Automatically

You can create automatic stacked fractions and tolerances as you type, by using a system similar to those described earlier for creating special characters with DTEXT/TEXT.

You can also type unstacked fractions (as in 1/2), select the fraction text, and then click Stack/Unstack on the Character tab. To create stacked fractions as you type, open the In-Place Text Editor and follow these steps:

1. Type the numerator, which is the character that you want on top.
2. Type the character that defines the fraction format that you want (see the example):
   - Type a slash (/) to create a fraction separated by a horizontal line.
   - Type a pound symbol (#) to create a fraction separated by a diagonal line.
   - Type a carat (^) to create a tolerance stack, which is like a fraction separated by a horizontal line, except that there is no horizontal line.

$\frac{3}{5}$ ←——— Typed as 3/5

$\tfrac{3}{5}$ ←——— Typed as 3#5

$\genfrac{}{}{0pt}{}{3}{5}$ ←——— Typed as 3^5

3. Type the denominator.
4. Type a space (or other nonnumeric character). The AutoStack Properties dialog box opens.
5. Change any settings that you want to change, and click OK to create the stacked fraction.

To use the settings in the AutoStack Properties dialog box:

- Uncheck Enable AutoStacking to disable the automatic stacked fraction feature.
- Uncheck Remove Leading Blank if you want to retain a space between whole numbers and fractions.
- Choose whether you want the slash to result in a fraction with a horizontal line or a fraction with a slash. This choice does not affect how the pound sign and carat work. If you want the slash to result in a fraction with a slash (which would seem to make more sense), then you do not have an automatic way to create a fraction with a horizontal line.
- Check Don't Show This Dialog Again; Always Use These Settings to stop the dialog box from opening when you create automatic stacked fractions.
- Click OK to create the stacked fraction, or Cancel to leave the numbers as you typed them.

AutoStack works only with numerals immediately before and after the slash, pound sign, and carat.

You can also set the properties of individual stacked fractions. Right-click the fraction in the In-Place Text Editor and choose Stack Properties from the menu. In the Stack Properties dialog box, you can change the following properties:

- **Text:** Edit the upper and lower text.
- **Style:** Change the fraction style. (Refer to the example under Step 2 for the three possible styles.)
- **Position:** Position the fraction so that the top, center, or bottom is aligned with other text.
- **Size:** Change the size of the numbers that make up the fraction. Fraction numbers are usually smaller than regular numbers.

Specifying and changing line spacing

You can specify the spacing between lines in multiline text before you open the Multiline Text Editor. (You can also use the Paragraph dialog box once you're in the editor, as described previously.) Line spacing is useful for fitting text into a schedule or table in your drawing. Of course, you can also use the table feature, which I discuss in the "Creating Tables" section later in this chapter. To set line spacing to an exact unit distance, follow these steps:

1. Start the Mtext command.
2. At the `Specify first corner:` prompt, pick the first corner of your Mtext box.
3. At the `Specify opposite corner or [Height/Justify/Line spacing/Rotation/ Style/Width/Columns]:` prompt, choose Line spacing.
4. At the `Enter line spacing type [At least/Exactly] <Exactly>:` prompt, choose Exactly.
5. At the `Enter line spacing factor or distance <1x>:` prompt, type a number, such as **1**, to specify a one-unit space between lines of text. (If you type **1x**, you get single line spacing, which varies according to the size of the text.)
6. Continue with the command.

This setting persists for future Mtext objects. To change existing line spacing, select (but do not double-click) the multiline text object. Open the Properties palette and set one or more of the following:

- **Line space factor:** Specifies line spacing as a multiple of lines. Single line spacing is 1.0000, and double line spacing is 2.0000.
- **Line space distance:** Specifies line spacing in units. Use this measurement (along with a line space style of Exactly) to fit text into an existing table or schedule.
- **Line space style:** Choose At Least (the default) to adjust line spacing based on the height of the largest character in the line of text. Choose Exactly to specify line spacing that is the same, regardless of differences in character height.

Specifying width and rotation

To change the width of an Mtext object, you can use its grips:

1. Select the Mtext object.
2. Click one of the grips that you want to stretch to make it "hot." (For instructions on using grips to edit objects, see Chapter 10.)
3. At the `Specify stretch point or [Base point/Copy/Undo/eXit]:` prompt, pick a new location for the grip, in order to make the multiline text wider or narrower.

You can use the Properties palette to change the width and height. You can specify the exact width when creating the Mtext object by using the Width option after you specify the first corner of the Mtext box. Otherwise, you generally specify the width by picking the two corners of the Mtext box.

 When the In-Place Text Editor is open, you can change the width of the Mtext object by dragging on the right edge of the ruler.

To rotate an existing Mtext object, use the Properties palette or use the grips:

1. Select the Mtext object.
2. Click one of the grips to make it "hot."
3. Right-click and choose Rotate.
4. At the `Specify rotation angle or [Base point/Copy/Undo/Reference/eXit]:` prompt, pick a new location for the grip or type a rotation angle.

You can also specify the rotation while creating the Mtext object. Use the Rotate option that appears on the command line after you specify the first corner.

Creating text for different scales

You may plan to display certain sections of your drawing at more than one scale. For example, you may want to show the entire model at a 1:4 scale, but a detail of the model at a 1:1 scale. If you have some text next to the model and want that text to appear at both scales, you have a problem — how do you get the text to appear the same size in both places? Without addressing this problem, your text will be either too big or too small at one of the scales. Another situation may be that you want one text object to appear at one scale, but another to appear at a different scale.

You create displays of various scales by using floating viewports on a layout. I cover viewports and layouts in Chapter 17, and you'll find further coverage of this topic there. However, if you know the scales you want to use, you can plan for this situation while you're in the drawing and editing stage by using *annotative* text.

Annotative objects, including annotative text, are new for AutoCAD 2008. Annotative objects create representations at various scales that you can automatically display at those scales when you lay out your drawing for plotting. The following objects can be annotative: text, tables, dimensions, tolerances, multileaders, blocks, and attributes. Text styles, dimension styles, and table styles can also be annotative; if you create an object using an annotative style, then the object is annotative. See the chapters that cover each of these objects for more information on their annotative property.

Previously, to create text that appeared in viewports of different scales, you needed to create a separate layer for each scale. You could then put the text on different layers and turn off the layers that you didn't want in each viewport. You might also have created separate text styles for each text object. This was a complicated and time-demanding task. Annotative text can eliminate the need for separate layers and text styles when you need to display text at more than one scale.

To create annotative text, follow these steps:

1. Create an annotative text style and make it current. To create an annotative text style, see the "Understanding Text Styles" section earlier in this chapter. AutoCAD also comes with a text style named Annotative that you can use.

2. Decide on the scales that you will use for each text object. For example, you might have two text objects each at a different scale, or one text object that you need to display at two different scales.

3. If you want each text object to have a different scale, turn off the ANNOAUTOSCALE system variable. When this system variable is on, it automatically adds scales to annotative objects as you add annotative scales; the result is that each object has more than one scale. To turn ANNOAUTOSCALE off, click the icon on the right side of the status bar to the right of the Toolbar/Window Positions Locked/Unlocked icon. When on, there's a yellow lightning bolt; when off, the lightning bolt is gray.

4. Set the annotation scale for the first text object. To do so, click the Annotation Scale button at the right side of the status bar to display the scale list and choose the scale you want. For example, choose 1:4 if you plan to display the text in a viewport at the 1:4 scale.

In Chapter 5, I explain scales in general and how to edit the scale list.

5. Start the DTEXT or MTEXT command and enter the text.

6. Repeat Steps 4 and 5 for each separate scale and text item.

7. When you're ready to plot, you can set the desired annotative scale, and plot. You can also create viewports and set their scale. See Chapter 17 for details and an exercise using annotative objects.

If you want one text object to have more than one scale, you can add an annotative scale to it. Follow these steps:

1. Select the text and right-click in the drawing area.

2. Choose Annotative Object Scale ➪ Add/Delete Scales to open the Annotation Object Scale dialog box, shown in Figure 13.19.

3. Click Add to display the Add Scales to Object dialog box, where you can choose one or more scales.

4. Click OK twice to close both dialog boxes.

FIGURE 13.19

You can add or delete scales for annotative objects in the Annotation Object Scale dialog box.

You can also open the dialog box by clicking the Add/Delete Scales button in the Annotation Scaling control panel of the Dashboard. Another way is to display the Properties palette, click the Annotative Scale item, and click the Ellipsis button that appears.

At any time, you can view the text for any single scale or view the text for all scales. (This applies to all types of annotative objects, not just text.) Remember that you may have one or more scales for any one text item. If you don't see all scales of an annotative object, click the Annotation Visibility button on the right side of the status bar. This button controls the ANNOALLVISIBLE system variable. By default, it is on, displaying all scales. When you turn it off, you see only the text for the current annotative scale. To immediately plot, you would turn off this system variable so that you plot only the text for the current annotative scale.

If you want to change a text object that is not annotative to one that is annotative, you can use the Properties palette. Follow these steps:

1. Select the text.

2. Display the Properties palette.

3. In the Properties palette, select the Annotative property and choose Yes from the drop-down list. The Annotative Scale property is displayed in the Properties palette once the Annotative property is set to Yes.

4. Select the Annotative Scale property and click the Ellipsis button that is displayed to open the Annotation Object Scale dialog box, shown in Figure 13.19.

5. Click Add to display the Add Scales to Object dialog box, where you can choose one or more scales.

6. Click OK twice to close both dialog boxes.

Editing paragraph text

To edit paragraph text, double-click the text to start the In-Place Text Editor.

Make your changes in the editor. The techniques are similar to those in any word processor. You can:

- Select text and press the Delete key to delete the text, or type to replace the selected text.

- Click to move the insertion point to where you want to insert text and start typing. (To type over text, press Insert to enter overtype mode.)

- Use the toolbar or shortcut menu (right-click) to change formatting.

To change characters, you must first highlight the characters. This lets you make height or font changes to individual words or even letters. When changing properties that affect the entire paragraph, such as justification, you do not first highlight the characters.

 Rotated text remains rotated when you edit it in the In-Place Text Editor, rather than reverting to horizontal.

If you right-click in the In-Place Text Editor with the cursor on a field, you have options to edit the field, update it, or convert it to regular text. For more information about fields (for AutoCAD only), see the section "Inserting Fields" later in this chapter.

 Mmt combines two MText objects into one MText paragraph. Look in \Software\Ch13\Mmt on the DVD. Txtexport exports text to a text file. It's in \Software\Chapter 13\ txtexport. These features work with AutoCAD only.

Importing text

As mentioned earlier, you can import text using the In-Place Text Editor. You can also import text in three other ways:

- You can use drag-and-drop to insert text from a .txt file into a drawing. Open Windows Explorer and locate the file. Position the Explorer window so that you can see the file name and your drawing at the same time. Click the file and drag it to your drawing. Close Windows Explorer and move the text to the desired location. The new text becomes multiline text in the drawing.

- You can copy text from another file to the Windows Clipboard. Open the other file, select the text, and choose Copy from the Standard toolbar. Return to your drawing by clicking the AutoCAD or AutoCAD LT button on the Windows Taskbar. Choose Paste from the Standard toolbar. The OLE Properties dialog box opens, by default. Specify the properties of the object and click OK.

- If you have the In-Place Text Editor open, you can paste the text directly into the editor. Right-click in the editor and choose Paste (or press Ctrl+V). You can then format the text.

CROSS-REF For more information on importing text, see Chapter 27.

ON the DVD-ROM The files used in the following exercise on creating multiline text, ab13-c.dwg and ab13-c.txt, are in the Drawings folder on the DVD.

STEPS: Creating Multiline Text

1. Open ab13-c.dwg from your DVD.
2. Save the file as ab13-05.dwg in your AutoCAD Bible folder. This is a plat drawing, as shown in Figure 13.20.
3. Choose Multiline Text from the Text control panel of the Dashboard. At the prompts, pick points ❶ and ❷ in Figure 13.20. The In-Place Text Editor opens. In the Text Height box, type a height of **12.5**. In the main editing box, type the following:

   ```
   Containing 108.33 acres including 5.97 acres existing R.O.W. and 4.56
   acres proposed R.O.W.
   ```
4. Highlight the text 108.33 and click Underline. Right-click in the text window and choose Justification ➪ Middle Left. Click OK to place the text.

FIGURE 13.20

The plat drawing.

Thanks to Bill Maidment of Cantech, Inc., Fairfield, Iowa, for this drawing.

5. Open Windows Explorer (Start ➪ Programs ➪ Windows Explorer). Find `ab13-c.txt` on your DVD. Move the Windows Explorer window so that you can see both `ab13.txt` and your drawing screen. Drag `ab13-c.txt` from the Windows Explorer window to ❸ in Figure 13.20. If necessary, pick a grip, press the Spacebar once to choose the Move option, and click at the proper location.

6. Select the text and open the Properties palette (Ctrl+1). Next to the Defined Width item, type **500** ↵. Next to the Defined Height item, type **12.5** ↵.

7. Use ZOOM Window to zoom in on the new text. This text was originally single-line text in an older drawing. You can see why you wouldn't want to retype it!

8. Choose View ➪ Zoom ➪ Previous to return to your original view. Use Zoom Window to zoom in to the area bounded by ❹ and ❺. Set the current layer to 0, which is a gray color.

9. Above the text about the proposed R.O.W. (right of way) is a yellow centerline. You want to place text on that line with a background mask so that the line doesn't make the text hard to read. Choose Multiline Text from the Draw toolbar.

10. At the prompt, pick ❹ and ❺, centering the boundary box around the yellow centerline. In the Text Height box of the Text Formatting toolbar, change the text to 12.5. The text style should be ROMANS. Type the following text:

    64TH AVE N.W. EXISTING R.O.W. 66' – CURRENT

11. Press the Spacebar to add a space after CURRENT, and right-click to open the shortcut menu. Choose Symbol ➪ Center Line to add the centerline symbol to the end of the text.

12. Right-click and choose Background Mask. In the Background Mask dialog box, select the Use Background Mask check box. Choose Red as the background color and click OK. Click anywhere outside the In-Place Text Editor to place the text. You can see that it uses the centerline symbol and has a red background that hides the yellow centerline behind the text.

13. Start the MTEXT command. At the prompts, define a border somewhere in the middle of the drawing. The width should be equal to about three of the plats that you see at the top. Type **Plat Acreage** ↵.

14. Type **1.**, press Tab, **22.93** ↵. Be sure to insert a tab after the period. AutoCAD and AutoCAD LT automatically create a numbered list when you use this format. You should now see the number two with a period after it (2.).

15. Finish the rest of the numbered list as follows:

```
2. 2.85 ↵
3. 1.51 ↵
4. 1.38
```

16. Click anywhere outside the In-Place Text Editor area to end the MTEXT command.

17. Choose Zoom Previous to return to your original view. Save your drawing.

Creating Tables

Tables, which are often called schedules, are very common in drawings. You can save your formatting in table styles for consistency among drawings. You should save table styles in your templates.

Inserting a table

To insert a table, choose Table from the Draw toolbar to start the TABLE command. (If the Draw toolbar is not displayed, right-click any toolbar and choose Draw from the list of toolbars.) Alternatively, choose Table from the Tables control panel of the Dashboard. (If the Draw toolbar is not displayed, right-click any toolbar and choose Draw from the list of toolbars. To display the Dashboard, choose Tools ➪ Palettes ➪ Dashboard.)

The Insert Table dialog box opens, as shown in Figure 13.21.

FIGURE 13.21

Use the Insert Table dialog box to create a table in your drawing.

On the left side of the Insert Table dialog box, you see a preview of how the table will look. By default, you see either the Standard table style or the last table style that you used. Choose the table style that you want from the Table Style name drop-down list. In the next section, I explain how to define a table style.

In the Insert Options section, you can choose from three options for getting data into the table:

- **Start from empty table:** Use this option when you want to manually enter (type) the data.
- **From a data link:** This option creates a table from Microsoft Excel spreadsheet data or a comma delimited (CSV) file. When you choose this option, most of the rest of the Insert Table dialog box is unavailable.
- **From object data in the drawing (Data Extraction):** This option creates a table from properties of existing objects in the drawing (AutoCAD only).

If you choose to start from an empty table, you can choose from one of the following options in the Insertion Behavior section of the dialog box:

- **Specify insertion point:** You place the table in your drawing by specifying an insertion point. You use the Column & Row Settings section to specify the number of columns and their width, as well as the number of rows and their height (in terms of lines of text).
- **Specify window:** You pick a point at the upper-left corner of the table and then move the mouse to specify the lower-right corner. You use the Column & Row Settings section to specify the number of columns and the line height of the rows. As you move the mouse to the right, the columns widen, and as you move the mouse downward, additional rows are added. Click when you see the size that you want.

In the Set Cell Styles section, you specify which cell styles go where. See the next section for an explanation of cell styles. By default, the First Row Cell Style uses the Title cell style, the Second Row Cell Style uses the Header cell style, and All Other Row Cell Styles use the Data cell style. If you create your own cell styles, you can choose them from the drop-down lists here.

If the table style shown is what you want, click OK. Then specify an insertion point or a window to place the table.

CROSS-REF You can also add a table to a tool palette and insert a table from the tool palette. For more information on tool palettes, see "Adding command tools" in Chapter 26.

Specifying a table style

You have a great deal of control over how your table looks. You can make it plain or fancy. To design your table, you create a table style by choosing Format ⇨ Table Style to open the Table Style dialog box, shown in Figure 13.22. Alternatively, you can choose Table Style from the Tables control panel of the Dashboard or by clicking the Launch the Table Style Dialog button in the Table Style section of the Insert Table dialog box.

On the left side of the Table Style dialog box is a list of styles. From the List drop-down menu at the bottom, you can choose to display all styles or only styles that are in use in your drawing. To make a table style current, choose the style that you want and click Set Current.

TIP An easier way to make a table style current is to choose the table style from the Table Style drop-down list on the Styles toolbar or from the Tables control panel of the Dashboard. Choose your table style before you start to create a table. You can also import table styles from the DesignCenter. (For more information on the DesignCenter, see Chapter 26.)

FIGURE 13.22

The Table Style dialog box gives you the tools to create tables with style.

To create a new style, click the New button. In the Create New Table Style dialog box, enter a Name in the New Style Name text box. From the Start With drop-down list, choose an existing table style as a basis for your new style. The new table style inherits the properties of this existing style so that you have to specify only the differences that you want. Then click Continue to open the New Table Style dialog box, as shown in Figure 13.23.

NEW FEATURE You can select an existing table in the drawing as a starting point. In the Starting Table section, click the button to select a table in your drawing.

FIGURE 13.23

The New Table Style dialog box is the place to define a new table style.

As you define your new table style, the preview panel shows you the results. In this dialog box, you use the Cell Styles drop-down list to format data in the cells of the table, column headers, and the table's main title. Each category is one of the pre-existing *cell styles* (data, header, and title (but you can create your own.

NEW FEATURE Cell styles are new. You can format a cell and save it as a style so that you can easily use it again.

You use the three tabs to define general, text, and border formatting for each cell style. In this way, you format the entire table. The three cell styles are very similar, but have slightly different defaults. For example, the Title cell style has centered text and a larger height than the headers and data cells.

 To create a cell style as you work, first click the Create a New Cell Style button in the Cell Styles section of the dialog box. In the Create New Cell Style dialog box, enter a name and choose an existing cell style to start from. Click Continue. You return to the New Table Style dialog box, where you can now specify formatting.

 At any time, you can manage cell styles by clicking the Manage Cell Styles button. In the Manage Cell Styles dialog box, you can rename and delete existing cell styles.

General properties

The General tab lets you define the following properties:

- **Fill color:** Click the drop-down list to choose a color, or choose Select Color to open the Select Color dialog box. The default is None, which shows the background color of your drawing area.

- **Alignment:** Use the Alignment drop-down list to specify the text alignment within each cell. For example, you might want to use Middle Center for the title and column headings, and Middle Left for the data cells.

- **Format:** Click the Ellipsis button to open the Table Cell Format dialog box, where you can specify the data format. The default is general, which is good for text, but you can also format data for angles, currency, dates, decimal numbers, percentages, points, text, and whole numbers. Click the Additional Format button to open the Additional Format dialog box, where you can add a prefix or suffix, specify the number separator, and format zero suppression.

- **Type:** Choose Data or Label. Use a label cell for a header or title. If you break a table into sections, then you can repeat label cells for each section. It's common to repeat headers when breaking a table.

- **Margins:** The cell margins are the space between the text and the cell borders. The horizontal margins affect the left and right sides of the text, while the vertical margins affect the top and bottom of the text. Enter a value in the Horizontal and Vertical text boxes.

Check the Merge Cells on Row/Column Creation check box for titles that you want to span across an entire table.

Text properties

The Text tab lets you specify properties for cells. You can choose a text style from the Text Style drop-down list or click the Ellipsis button to open the Text Style dialog box. (See the "Understanding Text Styles" section earlier in this chapter for a discussion of text styles.)

You can also specify the text height (if the text style has a height of 0), a text color, and a text angle. The default text color is ByBlock, which means that the text color is the same as the actual table (which is a block. (I explain blocks and the ByBlock attribute in Chapter 18.) You can also choose ByLayer, which gives the text the properties of the current layer.

Border properties

Use the Borders tab to specify the properties of the lines around the cells. Choose one of the border buttons to specify which borders you want to see. For example, for the data cells, if you choose Outside Borders, the data area of the table will not have any grid lines between the data cells, only around the outside of the cells.

CAUTION If you inadvertently create a table style with only outside borders, you may not notice the absence of borders in your drawing, where grid lines show between the cells so that you can more easily fill in the table. Choose Plot Preview on the Standard (or Standard Annotation) toolbar to see the final result more accurately.

Choose a border lineweight from the Lineweight drop-down list. For example, you may want a slightly thicker lineweight for the title cell. If you don't want to use continuous lines, then choose a linetype from the Linetype drop-down list. Then choose a color from the Color drop-down list. If you leave the ByBlock defaults, the lineweight, linetype, and color will match the layer of the table.

Completing the table style

Repeat the process of specifying general, text, and border properties for each of the three cell styles or your own styles. You access the styles from the Cell Styles drop-down list.

If you're creating your own cell styles, you specify which cell style goes where when you insert the table. (See Figure 13.21 earlier in this chapter.) Remember that you choose a cell style for the first row (usually the title), second row (usually the headers), and for all other rows (usually the data cells). Therefore, you would usually create three cell styles, one for each of these categories.

When you're done, click OK to return to the Table Style dialog box. Click Close. If you opened the Table Style dialog box from the Insert Table dialog box, then you're back in the Insert Table dialog box. If you opened the Table Style dialog box separately, open the Insert Table dialog box as described earlier in this chapter and choose the table style you want from the Table Style drop-down list. Either way, specify any other settings you want and insert the table.

Adding data to a table

You can add data to a table from three sources:

- You can enter data by typing it.
- You can link to external data, such as a Microsoft Office Excel worksheet or comma delimited (CVS) file.
- You can extract data from existing objects in the drawing. (AutoCAD only)

You choose which method you want to use in the Insert Options section of the Insert Table dialog box.

NEW FEATURE Creating tables from external data or object data is new for AutoCAD 2008. AutoCAD LT includes the ability to create a table from external data, but not from object data.

Entering data into a table

After you've placed a table, you can then enter data into the table. The cursor is automatically placed in the first cell, and you can just start typing. Press Tab to move to the next cell. Continue in this way until you have completed the table. Figure 13.24 shows an example of a table.

FIGURE 13.24

A nicely styled schedule of parts.

Parts Schedule		
Tag	Part No.	Description
11	9075-052-002	Collar-Shaft
17	9029-072-001	Bracket-Tube Assembly
19	9081-114-001	Channel Motor Mtg. Rod

TIP You can create a complete table on the fly by importing data from Microsoft Excel. Select the data in Excel and copy it to the Windows Clipboard. In AutoCAD, choose Edit ➪ Paste Special. In the Paste Special dialog box, choose AutoCAD Entities and click OK. At the prompt, pick an insertion point.

If you are using AutoCAD, you can insert a field into any cell in a table. Click a blank cell, right-click, and choose Insert ➪ Field. For more about fields, see the "Inserting Fields" section, later in this chapter. You can also insert blocks into a table. (I explain blocks in Chapter 18.) To do so, click a blank cell, right-click, and choose Insert ➪ Block.

You can create tables that function like a spreadsheet. To enter a formula into a cell, follow these steps:

1. Select the cell.
2. Right-click and choose Insert ➪ Formula.
3. Choose one of the sub-options.

  - **Sum:** Adds rows or columns. At the Select first corner of table cell range: prompt, pick inside the first cell. At the Select second corner of table cell range: prompt, pick inside the last cell. You see the formula listed in the cell, for example, =Sum(C3:C5).

  - **Average:** Averages rows or columns. At the Select first corner of table cell range: prompt, pick inside the first cell. At the Select second corner of table cell range: prompt, pick inside the last cell. You see the formula listed in the cell, for example, =Average(C3:C5).

  - **Count:** Counts the number of cells in a row or column. At the Select first corner of table cell range: prompt, pick inside the first cell. At the Select second corner of table cell range: prompt, pick inside the last cell. You see the formula listed in the cell, for example, =Count(C3:C5).

  - **Cell:** Displays the value of another cell. At the Select table cell: prompt, select the cell that you want to display. You see the formula listed in the cell, for example, =C3.

  - **Equation:** Lets you write your own equation. You just see an equal sign (=) in the cell. Enter the equation, for example =a3+b4.

NOTE To create equations, you use the same conventions as for spreadsheets. For example, you use an asterisk (*) for multiplication, a slash (/) for division, a caret (^) for powers, and sqrt for a square root.

You also see row headings (1,2,3, and so on) and column headings (A, B, C, and so on), so that you can easily figure out any cell's address.

4. Press Enter to place the value of the formula.

You can auto-fill data like you can in Excel. This makes it easy to copy data along a row or column and to automatically create incremental data, such as consecutive numbers.

To auto-fill cell data, click in a cell that you've already filled with a value. Click and drag the cyan (turquoise) diamond to the desired cell and click. To auto-fill incremental data, such as consecutive numbers, drag across two cells that already have incremental data. For example, if you typed 1 and 2, drag across those cells. Then click-and-drag the cyan diamond to the desired cell and click. Before the final click, a tooltip shows you what results to expect.

Linking to external data

You can create a table that links to external data that was created in Microsoft Excel or that is in comma-delimited (CSV) format. The link maintains its connection, so that if you change the spreadsheet, the table in your drawing also changes. You also have the option to change the external data from within AutoCAD.

In Chapter 20, I cover the external database connectivity feature. While this feature also allows you to connect to Microsoft Access databases, and several other types of database, it's more complicated to use.

To create a linked table, you first need an Excel or CSV file. Make sure that you know the file's name and location. Then choose Table from the Draw toolbar or the Tables control panel of the Dashboard. From the Insert Options section of the Insert Table dialog box, choose From a Data Link. For the rest of the dialog box, see the section "Creating Tables" earlier in this chapter.

 To connect to a link you've already created, choose it from the drop-down list. To create a new link to a spreadsheet, click the Launch the Data Link Manager Dialog button to open the Select a Data Link dialog box. Choose Create a New Excel Data Link. In the Enter Data Link Name dialog box, enter a meaningful name and click OK.

The New Excel Data Link dialog box opens. Click the Ellipsis button at the right to choose an Excel file. When you click Open, you return to the New Excel Data Link dialog box, with your data link listed, as shown in Figure 13.25.

In the Link Options section, you can choose which sheet you want to use, and you can link to a named range (you can name ranges of cells in Excel) or you can specify a range, such as A1:H20. Click OK to return to the Select a Data Link dialog box, where your data link is now listed and highlighted. Click OK to return to the Insert Table dialog box. You should see your table in the Preview box.

You can click the More Options arrow at the lower-right corner of the dialog box to convert cell data to text, to turn off the ability to save changes that you make in AutoCAD back to the source spreadsheet, and to control cell formatting. You can choose whether or not to use Excel formatting and keep the table updated to the formatting in the Excel file.

Click OK one more time and specify an insertion point to insert the table into your drawing. You may have to resize the table to avoid unwanted word wrapping in the cells. (See the upcoming section "Modifying a table" for instructions.) Figure 13.26 shows the result.

FIGURE 13.25

You can create a table that links to Excel data.

FIGURE 13.26

A table created from, and linked to, an Excel worksheet.

Code	Style	Exterior	Interior	Rough Opening
A	Casement	Ultrex	Wood	2'5" x 3'11 5/8"
B	Casement	Ultrex	Wood	2'5" x 4'11 5/8"
C	Casement	Ultrex	Wood	2'5" x 4'11 5/8"
D	Awning	Ultrex	Wood	2'5" x 1'-11 5/8"
E	Transom	Wood	Wood	N/A

When you create a linked table, it's locked to prevent changes; this makes sense, because the content should come from the Excel spreadsheet. However, you can unlock it and make changes; you can save these changes back to the spreadsheet to keep the two data sources the same. To unlock data (both content and formatting), select one or more cells, right-click, and choose Locking ➪ Unlocked.

After changing the data, right-click and then choose Data Links ➪ Upload User Changes to Source File.

Extracting data from drawing objects

You can create a table that contains information about the objects in your drawing. For example, you might want to display the number of window blocks and their location. If a circle represents trees and bushes in a landscaping plan, you could list the number of circles and their layer; perhaps you have a tree and a bush layer.

NEW FEATURE Extracting data from drawing objects is new for AutoCAD 2008. (This feature is not available in AutoCAD LT.) You can extract data from all objects, not just blocks. For information about extracting data from blocks using attributes, see Chapter 18.

To create a table from object data, choose Table from the Draw toolbar or the Tables control panel of the Dashboard. In the Insert Table dialog box (see Figure 13.21 earlier in this chapter), choose From Object Data in the Drawing (Data Extraction) in the Insert Options section and click OK. Page 1 of the Data Extraction Wizard opens, as shown in Figure 13.27.

FIGURE 13.27

The Data Extraction Wizard guides you through the process of creating a table from object data.

Choose to create a new extraction or edit an existing one. If you want to create a new extraction, you can use one of two types of files as a template, to use settings you've specified previously:

- **DXE:** When you create a data extraction table, AutoCAD creates a DXE file that contains settings for the extraction.

- **BLK:** When you extract attribute information from blocks, you can save a BLK file, which is a template that defines the settings for the extraction.

The following explains how to create a new data extraction without a template. Choose Create a New Data Extraction and click Next. The Save Data Extraction As dialog box opens, so you can save a DXE file; this is the file that you can use in the future as a template. Choose a name and location and click Save.

On the Define Data Source (Page 2 of 8) page of the wizard, you define which objects you want to include and where they come from. You can use a Sheet Set, which is a collection of drawings (covered in Chapter 26) or choose any drawings that you want. The Drawing Files and Folders box lists the drawings and their locations. If you want to use objects from other drawings, click Add Drawings. To add all the drawings in a folder, click Add Folder.

If you choose multiple drawings, you create a table from all the objects in those drawings. If you want to select specific objects, you can do so only in the current drawing. In that case, choose the Select Objects in the Current Drawing option. The following assumes that you are selecting objects in the current drawing.

Click the Settings button to open the Additional Settings dialog box, shown in Figure 13.28, where you define which types of objects you want to include. These settings are particularly important if you are extracting data from entire drawings (rather than selecting objects) and you have blocks or xrefs in those drawings. (I cover blocks in Chapter 18 and xrefs in Chapter 19.) Choose whether you want to extract data from blocks and xrefs and whether to include xrefs in the block count. You can also choose whether to include objects only in model space or all objects in the drawing, meaning also objects in layouts. (See Chapter 17 for coverage of layouts.)

FIGURE 13.28

You can specify what kinds of objects you want to include in your data extraction.

 You're now ready to select objects. Click the Select Objects in the Current Drawing button. You return to your drawing, where you select objects. End selection to return to the wizard. Click Next.

The Select Objects page shows the objects you've selected. You can choose to display only blocks or only non-blocks, instead of the default, which is to display all object types. If you're interested in blocks, you can choose to include only blocks with attributes. Finally, you can choose to display objects that are currently in use because some blocks may be defined but not inserted into the drawing. (See Chapter 18 for information about attributes.) Then click Next.

On the Select Properties page, you specify which properties of the objects you want to include. The properties come in 10 categories:

- **3D Visualization:** Includes materials assigned to objects. (See Chapter 22.)
- **Attribute:** Includes blocks and dynamic blocks with attributes. (See Chapter 18.)
- **Drawing:** File-related information including the author, date created, dated accessed, location, name, size, total editing time, and so on.
- **Dynamic blocks:** Properties of dynamic blocks. (See Chapter 18.)
- **General:** Includes color, layer, linetype, linetype scale, plot style, thickness, and hyperlink.
- **Geometry:** Depending on the type of object, can include area; center; circumference; diameter; length; radius; start angle; total angle; delta (change) in X, Y, and Z; start of X, Y, and Z coordinates; and so on.

- **Misc:** Includes closed (or open).
- **Pattern:** Includes hatch pattern properties, which I cover in Chapter 16.
- **Table:** Includes table properties.
- **Text:** Includes single or multiline text properties.

For each category, you can choose which property you want to include by checking the check boxes. As you can see, your choices depend on why you're extracting the data. In some cases, you may want drawing information for archiving purposes; in other cases, you may be interested only in geometry data. When you're done, click Next.

On the Refine Data page, you can reorder and sort columns, filter the results, combine identical rows, specify if you want a count or a name column, add formulas, and include external data. Click on a column and right-click for numerous options, including the ability to rename and hide columns. Click on any column to sort by that column and click again to reverse the sorting order. Right-click and choose Filter Options to open the Filter Name dialog box, which is similar to the Quick Select feature (described in Chapter 10), but has fewer options.

> **TIP** To add formulas such as totals to a column, right-click the column and choose Insert Totals Footer. You can choose Sum, Max, Min, or Average. You can also create a new column from data in other columns. Right-click any column and choose Insert Formula Column. Use the Insert Formula Column dialog box to specify the formula. Click OK.

Click the Full Preview button to see what the table will look like in a new window; then click the window's Close button to return to the wizard and click Next.

On the Choose Output page, you can choose to create a table and insert it into a drawing, output the data to an external file (XLS, CSV, MDB, or TXT), or both. If you choose to create an external file, click the Ellipsis button to browse to a location and give the file a name. Then click Next.

If you chose to create a table, you now choose a table style or manually set up the table. Then click Next. The Finish page explains that you need to specify an insertion point for the table and that the external file you requested (if any) will be created when you click the Finish button. Click the Finish button and you're done.

Modifying a table

You may need to change the data in a table, or you may want to change the way the table looks. Either way, you can modify a table easily. However, you need to know some of the techniques involved, because tables in AutoCAD and AutoCAD LT are a little different from tables in your word processor.

Changing the text

Changing the text of a table is like changing any multiline text. Double-click the text inside a table, being careful not to double-click the grid lines. The In-Place Text Editor opens. You can use any of the techniques for editing text that I discuss in the "Editing paragraph text" section earlier in this chapter. You can change the properties of the text so that they don't match the table style. For example, you can change the height or font of the text.

Changing table properties

You can also change properties of the actual table. If you double-click the table itself — that is, any of the grid lines — the Properties palette opens. Here, you can modify any conceivable table property, including its layer, its color, the number of rows or columns, or any of its style properties. If you want to revert to old-fashioned lines, you can explode the table. Of course, you can no longer edit the table as a table anymore; you just have lines and text.

To select the entire table, click any gridline of the table. You see grips at the corners of the table and at several other cell junctions. To understand editing tables with grips, imagine that the left side of the table is the stable side, while the right side of the table is the flexible side. The top-left grip is the base point for the entire table. You can do the following edits with grips:

- **Upper-left grip:** Moves the entire table.
- **Upper-right grip:** Stretches the table horizontally. As you change the width of the table, the columns also stretch proportionally.
- **Lower-left grip:** Stretches the table vertically. As you change the height of the table, the rows also stretch proportionally.
- **Lower-right grip:** Stretches the table both vertically and horizontally. The columns and rows adjust proportionally.
- **Top-of-column grip:** Adjusts the width of the column to the left or right of the grip. The entire table adjusts accordingly. If you press Ctrl while moving a column grip, the adjacent columns adjust, but the width of the table remains unchanged.

If you select the table and right-click, then you can use the shortcut menu to make additional changes to the table. For example, you can size columns or rows equally or remove property overrides. If you make a change to a cell, such as the cell's alignment or color, you can use the Remove All Property Overrides item on the shortcut menu to change the cell's properties back to match the rest of the table.

Changing cell properties

To select a cell, click inside that cell. You can also click a column or row header, or drag across several cells to select them. The Table toolbar appears, displaying the following items:

- **Insert Row Above:** Inserts a row above the selected cell or row.
- **Insert Row Below:** Inserts a row below the selected cell or row.
- **Delete Row(s):** Deletes the selected row or the row of the selected cell.
- **Insert Column to the Left:** Inserts a column to the left of the selected cell or row.
- **Insert Column to the Right:** Inserts a column to the right of the selected cell or row.
- **Delete Column(s):** Deletes the selected column or the column of the selected cell.
- **Merge Cells:** Merges selected cells.
- **Unmerge Cells:** Unmerges selected cells that you previously merged.
- **Cell Borders:** Opens the Cell Border Properties dialog box, where you can specify border properties for that individual cell.
- **Cell Alignment:** Changes the alignment of the text in the cell, using the standard text-alignment options available for multiline text.
- **Locking:** Locks or unlocks the format and/or the data of the selection. Text from external links or data extraction is locked by default.
- **Data Format:** Allows you to choose a format from a drop-down list. Choose Custom Table Cell Format to open the Table Cell Format dialog box, where you can change the data type and format.

- **Insert Block:** Opens the Insert a Block in a Table Cell dialog box, where you can select the block that you want to insert, specify the block's alignment in the cell, and set its scale and rotation angle. If you select the Autofit check box, the block is automatically scaled to fit the table cell.

- **Insert/Edit Field:** Lets you insert or edit a field. I discuss fields in the next section of this chapter. (AutoCAD only)

- **Insert Formula:** Lets you insert a formula, as explained in the "Entering data into a table" section earlier in this chapter.

- **Manage Cell Content:** Applies when you have more than one block in a cell. The Manage Cell Content dialog box opens, where you can change the order of the blocks and change the way they're laid out.

- **Match Cell:** Matches cell properties. At the Select destination cell: prompt on the command line, pick another cell that you want to have the same properties. The prompt repeats until you press Enter.

- **Cell Styles:** Enables you to choose a cell style for the selected cell.

- **Link Cell:** Enables you to link the selected cell to an Excel spreadsheet. For more information, see the section "Linking to an external spreadsheet" earlier in this chapter.

- **Update Data Links:** Updates links to an external spreadsheet, in case that spreadsheet has changed.

You can access some additional options by right-clicking with a cell or cells selected:

- **Remove All Property Overrides:** Removes any formatting that you applied to the selected cell.

- **Edit Text:** Opens the In-Place Text Editor so that you can edit text.

- **Delete All Contents:** Deletes any text or block in the current cell.

- **Columns ⇨ Size Equally:** Makes two or more columns that you select equally wide.

- **Rows ⇨ Size Equally:** Makes all of your rows an equal height.

- **Merge Cells:** Merges two or more cells together. You can choose to merge all of the selected cells into one cell, to merge them by row, or to merge them by column.

- **Unmerge Cells:** Unmerges merged cells and recreates all of the original cells.

- **Properties:** Opens the Properties palette so that you can change the cell's properties.

When you edit a table, column and row headers appear so that you can easily refer to cells in your formulas. You can change the background color of these headers to make the text clearer. Select a table, right-click and choose Table Indicator Color. You can then choose a color in the Select Color dialog box.

You can select multiple cells and apply changes to those cells. To select multiple cells, use one of the following techniques:

- Click a row or column header to select an entire row or column.

- Click inside one cell and drag over the other cells that you want to select. Release the mouse button at the last cell.

- Click inside one cell, hold down Shift, and click inside the last cell that you want to select.

TIP To enter the same text in multiple cells, select the cells. Then open the Properties palette and enter the text in the Contents item. The text appears in all of the selected cells.

When you select multiple cells, you can also merge the cells. Right-click and choose Merge Cells from the shortcut menu. By merging cells, you can create fairly complex table structures.

You can export a table to comma-delimited (`.csv`) format. You can then open the table data with a database or spreadsheet program. To export a table, follow these steps:

1. Select the table.
2. Right-click and choose Export.
3. In the Export Data dialog box, choose a name and location for the file.
4. Click Save.

Breaking a table into sections

Sometimes you need to fit a table into a tight space; to do so, you might want to break up the table into two or more sections.

NEW FEATURE   The ability to break a table is new for AutoCAD 2008 and AutoCAD LT 2008.

Breaking a table is easy, but you can also access a number of settings to fine-tune how it works. To break a table, click it once to select it. Then drag the cyan down arrow, located at the bottom of the table, upwards to the point where you want the table to break (as shown in Figure 13.29), and click.

FIGURE 13.29

You can break a table by dragging upward on the Table Breaking arrow.

To adjust breaking settings, open the Properties palette. In the Table Breaks section, you can set the direction of subsequent sections, repeat top labels, and repeat bottom labels. You can also manually set the position of sections, individually set the height of subsequent sections (otherwise, they're all the same size as the first section), and set the spacing between the sections. In this example, I chose to repeat top labels; you can see the result in Figure 13.30.

FIGURE 13.30

After breaking, the table appears in two sections with top labels on each section.

Trees and Bushes—Jones				Trees and Bushes—Jones			
Trees or Bushes	Diameter	Area	Circumference	Trees or Bushes	Diameter	Area	Circumference
1	10'–0"	942'–5 3/4"	31'–5"	1	6'–0"	339'–3 1/2"	18'–10 3/16"
1	8'–0"	603'–2 1/4"	25'–1 9/16"	1	15'–0"	2120'–6 7/8"	47'–1 1/2"
1	2'–0"	37'–8 3/8"	6'–3 3/8"	1	20'–0"	3769'–10 15/16"	62'–10"
1	4'–0"	150'–9 9/16"	12'–6 13/16"	8			
1	5'–0"	235'–7 7/16"	15'–8 1/2"				

The drawing used in the following exercise on creating tables, `ab13-c.dwg`, is in the `Results` folder on the DVD.

STEPS: Creating Tables

1. Open `ab13-c.dwg` from the DVD. This is the same drawing used in the previous exercise.

2. Save the file as `ab13-06.dwg` in your `AutoCAD Bible` folder.

 3. Choose Table from the Draw toolbar or the Tables control panel of the Dashboard. (If the Draw toolbar is not displayed, right-click any toolbar and choose Draw from the list of toolbars. To display the Dashboard, choose Tools ➪ Palettes ➪ Dashboard.) You'll create a table showing some of the plat numbers and their acreage.

 4. In the Insert Table dialog box, click the Launch the Table Style Dialog button to the right of the Table Style Name drop-down list.

5. In the Table Style dialog box, click New. In the Create New Table Style dialog box, enter **Acreage Schedule** in the New Style Name text box. The Start With text box should read `Standard`. Click Continue. The New Table Style dialog box opens.

 6. Make sure that the Data cell style appears in the Cell Styles drop-down list. To the right, click the Create a New Cell Style button, so that you can save the formatting that you will specify. In the Create New Cell Style dialog box, enter **Plat Data** and click Continue.

7. On the General tab, you want the numbers in the table to be right-aligned, and so you need to choose Middle Right from the Alignment drop-down list. In the Cell Margins section, change both the Horizontal and Vertical text box values to **5**.

8. Click the Text tab. From the Text Style drop-down list, choose ROMANS. In the Text Height text box, enter **12.5**.

9. To format the column headers, choose Header from the Cell Style drop-down list. Again, click the Create a New Cell Style button and name the cell style **Plat Header** and click Continue. On the General tab, leave the alignment as Middle Center, but change the cell margins to **5**. On the Text tab, again set the Text Style to ROMANS and the Text Height to **12.5**.

10. Choose Title from the Cell Style drop-down list. Create a new cell style named **Plat Title**. Make the following changes:

    - **General tab:** Change the cell margins to **5**. From the Fill Color drop-down list, choose Blue.
    - **Text tab:** Choose ROMANT (for a different look). Change the Text Height to **13.5** to make the title text bigger than the rest of the table text. Click the Text Color drop-down list and choose Select Color. From the Select Color dialog box, choose the light gray color (254) on the Index Color tab. Click OK to return to the New Table Style dialog box.
    - **Borders tab:** From the Color drop-down list, choose Blue to match the fill. Click the All Borders button.

11. Click OK to return to the Table Style dialog box and click Set Current. Then click Close to return to the Insert Table dialog box.

12. In the Insertion Behavior section of the dialog box, make sure that the insertion behavior is set to `Specify insertion point`. In the Columns & Row Settings section, set the number of columns to 2 and the column width to 100. Set the number of data rows to 5. The row height should be 1 (which means one row high).

13. In the Set Cell Styles section, set the First Row Cell Style to Plat Titles, set Second Row Cell Style to Plat Header, and set All Other Row Cell Styles to Plat Data. Then click OK.

14. In your drawing, pick an insertion point anywhere in the lower-right area of the drawing. The In-Place Text Editor opens. Because you need to zoom in first, click anywhere outside the editor and do a ZOOM Window around the table. Then double-click the table to open the In-Place Text Editor again, with the cursor in the title cell.

> **TIP**   To zoom in without exiting the In-Place Text Editor, you can use the wheel of your mouse (if you have one). I explain how to zoom using the mouse wheel in the section "Using the ZOOM Command" in Chapter 8.

15. Complete the data for the four plats as shown in Figure 13.31, pressing Tab to go from cell to cell.

16. Type **Total** in the last row. Right-click the cell and choose Alignment ⇨ Middle Left from the shortcut menu.

17. Click anywhere outside the In-Place Text Editor and then click the lower-right cell to select it. Right-click the cell and choose Insert ⇨ Formula ⇨ Sum from the shortcut menu.

18. At the `Select first corner of table cell range:` prompt, click anywhere inside cell B3. At the `Select second corner of table cell range:` prompt, click anywhere inside cell B6. Press Enter. Your table should look like Figure 13.31.

FIGURE 13.31

The plat acreage table.

Plat Acreage	
Plat	Acreage
1	22.93
2	2.85
3	1.51
4	1.38
Total	28.67

19. Save your drawing.

Inserting Fields

Most drawings contain information about the drawing, such as the last date it was revised, the person who saved the drawing, or the sheet number in a sheet set. Draft plots often contain additional information such as the time and drawing name. You may also want to insert information about drawing objects, such as the area or circumference of a circle. Fields store information and allow you to insert it into a drawing. You can also place fields in block attributes, which I discuss in Chapter 18. When your drawing changes, you can update the fields to keep them current.

> **AUTOCAD ONLY**   Fields are not available in AutoCAD LT. If you open an AutoCAD drawing with fields in AutoCAD LT, the fields display and update properly, unless you have changed the value of the FIELDEVAL system variable to disable updating in certain situations.

You can insert fields anywhere that you might normally use text. As you start using fields, you'll think of many uses for them. You can format the text of a field in the same way that you format any multiline text.

Sfld **creates custom fields. Look in** \Software\Chapter 13\sfld**.**

Creating fields

To create a new field as a multiline text object, you can use two methods:

- Choose Insert ➪ Field (the FIELD command).
- Open the In-Place Text Editor or any other text box where you can enter text, right-click in the editor or text box, and choose Insert Field from the shortcut menu.

Whichever method you use, the Field dialog box opens, as shown in Figure 13.32.

FIGURE 13.32

Use the Field dialog box to choose, format, and insert a field into your drawing. Here you see the options for the Date field.

The Field dialog box offers a huge variety of fields. To give you an idea of the possibilities, here are the available categories of fields:

Date & Time: Offers various formats for inserting dates and times.

Document: Relates to data that you complete in the Properties dialog box. (Choose File ➪ Drawing Properties.)

Linked: Creates a field from a hyperlink.

Objects: Offers properties relating to block attributes (that you insert from the Block Editor), formulas in tables, named objects (such as named views, layers, blocks, and so on), and objects (any object that you select).

Other: Displays values of AutoLISP variables and system variables.

Plot: Displays plot-related information such as scale, sheet size, and orientation.

SheetSet: Displays values relating to sheet sets. (I cover sheet sets in Chapter 26.)

Note that there are two date-related fields. The `CreateDate` field creates a date based on the current date. This field does not change if you open the drawing on a future date. For example, you can use this field to show the last time a drawing was updated. The `Date` field always shows the current date.

To insert a field, follow these steps:

1. Choose a field category from the Field Category drop-down list. You can use the All category to display all of the fields. The other categories help you to filter the fields, so that you can more easily find the field that you want.
2. From the Field Names list, choose the field that you want to use.
3. Depending on the field that you choose, you can usually select a format or example for the field. For example, you can choose a date format (such as m/d/yyyy) or a text format (such as title case).
4. Click OK.

   - If you opened the Field dialog box by choosing Insert ➪ Field, the MTEXT command starts, and you see the `Specify start point or [Height/Justify]:` prompt. Pick a start point or use one of the options.
   - If you started the MTEXT command first, the value of the field appears in the In-Place Text Editor. Click OK on the editor's main toolbar to place the text.

By default, fields appear in your drawing with a gray background. This background doesn't plot. If you want, you can remove the background by choosing Tools ➪ Options and clicking the User Preferences tab. In the Fields section, uncheck the Display Background of Fields check box. Click OK to close the Options dialog box.

CROSS-REF I cover the Properties dialog box and sheet sets in Chapter 26. For more information about hyperlinks, see Chapter 28.

Figure 13.33 shows an example of a title block that uses fields.

FIGURE 13.33

Filling in a title block is easier when you use fields.

Editing and updating fields

To edit a field, double-click the field's text to open the In-Place Text Editor. Select the text, right-click, and choose Edit field. The Field dialog box opens. You edit a field in the same way that you define the field originally. When you're done, click OK. The field is reevaluated immediately. Close the In-Place Text Editor to place the edited field.

By default, a field is evaluated and updated, if necessary, whenever you open, save, plot, eTransmit, or regenerate a drawing. (See Chapter 28 for information on eTransmitting a drawing.) You can change when AutoCAD updates a field by choosing Tools ➪ Options and clicking the User Preferences tab. In the Fields section, click Field Update Settings. Check or uncheck the items that you want, and then click Apply & Close. Click OK to close the Options dialog box.

You can manually update a field if you want. For example, you may have an object field that displays the radius of a circle. If you resize the circle, you probably want to update the field.

To update a field, double-click the field to open the In-Place Text Editor. Select the text, right-click, and choose Update Field. Close the In-Place Text Editor to return to your drawing. Another method is to select the field and choose Tools ➪ Update Fields. You can select as many fields as you want.

 To update all of the fields in a drawing, press Ctrl+A to select all of the objects in your drawing and choose Tools ➪ Update Fields.

You can convert a field to text. Double-click the field to open the In-Place Text Editor. Select the text in the field, right-click and choose Convert Field to Text.

What happens to fields when you save a 2005 or later drawing to an earlier release of AutoCAD? The fields display as their last value in the newer drawing but are not updated.

ON the DVD-ROM The drawing used in the following exercise on using fields, `ab13-d.dwg`, is in the `Drawing` folder on the DVD.

STEPS: Using Fields

1. Open `ab13-d.dwg` from your DVD. Save the file as `ab13-07.dwg` in your `AutoCAD Bible` folder. This drawing is zoomed in on the title block.

2. To set some of the drawing properties, choose File ➪ Drawing Properties. (I cover the Properties dialog box in Chapter 26.) On the Summary tab, type the following in the Title field: **6" thru 12" 2727 EPV Valves**.

3. On the Custom tab, click Add. Enter the following two fields and values:

   ```
   Drafter     Enter your initials
   Dwg No      SK-1972
   ```

4. Click OK to return to your drawing.

5. Choose Multiline Text from the Draw toolbar. Pick two boundary points within the Title box of the title block. The In-Place Text Editor opens. Right-click and choose Insert Field to open the Field dialog box.

6. From the Field Category drop-down list, choose Document. From the Field Names list, choose Title. From the Format list, choose Title Case. Click OK. Click anywhere outside the In-Place Text Editor to place the field.

7. Again choose Multiline Text from the Draw toolbar. Pick two boundary points within the Dwg No box of the title block. In the In-Place Text Editor, right-click and choose Insert Field to open the Field dialog box.

8. From the Field Names list, choose Dwg No. Click OK. Click anywhere outside the In-Place Text Editor to place the field.

9. Again choose Multiline Text from the Draw toolbar. Pick two boundary points within the Date box of the title block. In the In-Place Text Editor, right-click and choose Insert Field.

10. From the Field Category drop-down list, choose Date & Time. From the Field Names list, choose CreateDate. From the Format list, choose M/d/yy. Click OK. Click anywhere outside the In-Place Text Editor to place the field.

11. If necessary, move the text so that it fits better in the title block. Save your drawing. The title block should look like Figure 13.34.

FIGURE 13.34

The title block after adding some fields.

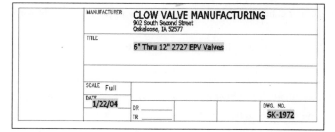

Managing Text

Text is a complex object type that increases your drawing size and adds redraw and regeneration time. The more-complex fonts, such as the TrueType fonts, can have a significant impact on how long it takes to open and save a file. The techniques described in this section help you to manage text and improve performance while editing your drawing.

Using Quicktext

The QTEXT command replaces all text with rectangles that approximate the placement of the original text, as shown in Figure 13.35. All text objects, including dimensions, attributes, and tolerances, are affected. To use QTEXT, type **qtext** ↵ on the command line. Type **on** ↵ to display the rectangles; type **off** ↵ to return to regular text. Then type **regen** ↵ at the command line. Quicktext takes effect only after a regeneration; it does not apply to OLE objects that you have pasted into a drawing from the Windows Clipboard (see Chapter 27).

FIGURE 13.35

A drawing with QTEXT on. Rectangles have replaced all of the text.

Thanks to Rod Greer of R. G. Greer Design, Inc., Fergus, Ontario, for this drawing.

Using AutoCAD and AutoCAD LT fonts

AutoCAD and AutoCAD LT fonts are simpler than TrueType fonts, and AutoCAD fonts also have a range of complexity. The simplest font is txt.shx, which is the font used by the default Standard text style. You can easily define a text style using an AutoCAD or AutoCAD LT font and then change the font to something nicer just before plotting. Be aware that the text may take up more or less space than before.

When your drawing cannot find the specified font, it uses an alternate font. This may happen if you receive a drawing from someone else that uses a custom or third-party font that you don't have. You can specify the alternate font by choosing Tools ➪ Options and clicking the plus sign next to Text Editor, Dictionary, and Font File Names on the Files tab. Choose Alternate Font File to specify the alternate font, which is simplex.shx by default.

You can further control the fonts used in your drawing by customizing the Font Mapping File, \acad.fmp (or \acadlt.fmp). The format is current_font; font_to_substitute. (You need to use the actual filenames of the fonts.) To substitute a simpler font for the Arial Black font, you can add the following line:

```
Ariblk.ttf;simplex.shx
```

To find the Windows TrueType fonts, look in the Fonts subfolder of your Windows folder.

> **NOTE** To find acad.fmp (or acadlt.fmp), choose Tools ➪ Options and click the File tab. Double-click Text Editor, Dictionary, and Font File Names. Double-click Font Mapping File. Click the path list to view the location of acad.fmp (or acadlt.fmp). AutoCAD and AutoCAD LT only read the font-mapping file when you open a new drawing, so that any changes that you make are effective only after you start a new drawing.

Freezing text layers

Freezing text layers can reduce regeneration time dramatically; this is a good reason to give text its own layer. Don't forget to freeze dimension text, as well. Dimensions (see Chapter 14) are usually placed on a separate layer.

Using MIRRTEXT

When you mirror sections of your drawing that include text, you usually don't want any backward text (unless you're Alice going through the looking glass). The MIRRTEXT system variable controls whether text is mirrored or retains its normal orientation. The default value for MIRRTEXT is off, so that mirrored text is not backward. The text is copied to the mirrored location, but reads from left to right (if that's the direction of the language that you're using).

If you do want to mirror the text, type **mirrtext** ↵. At the Enter new value for MIRRTEXT <0>: prompt, type **1** ↵ to turn MIRRTEXT on. This system variable is saved with the drawing, and so you may still need to change it when you open older drawings.

ON the DVD-ROM The drawing used in the following exercise on managing text, ab13-e.dwg, is in the Drawings folder on the DVD.

STEPS: Managing Text

1. Open ab13-e.dwg from your DVD.
2. Save the file as ab13-08.dwg in your AutoCAD Bible folder. This is a small section of an electrical schematic, as shown in Figure 13.36. Make sure that ORTHO and OSNAP are on, and set running snaps for endpoint, midpoint, and intersection.

FIGURE 13.36

A section of an electrical schematic.

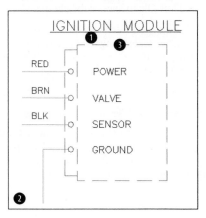

3. Type **qtext** ↵. At the Enter mode [ON/OFF] <OFF>: prompt, type **on** ↵. Type **regen** ↵. The command replaces the text with rectangles.

4. Type **qtext** ↵. At the Enter mode [ON/OFF] <ON>: prompt, type **off** ↵. Type **regen** ↵. Your original text reappears.

5. Start the MIRROR command. Follow the prompts:

   Select objects: *Start a window by picking* ❷ *in Figure 13.36.*
   Specify opposite corner: *Pick* ❶*. Press Enter to end object*
   selection.
   Specify first point of mirror line: *Use the Midpoint running object*
   snap to pick the midpoint at ❸*.*
   Specify second point of mirror line: *Pick any point vertical to the*
   first point.
   Erase source objects? [Yes/No] <N>: ↵

   The command mirrors the objects and the text, because the MIRRTEXT system variable was set to 1. The text is backward.

6. Choose Undo from the Standard (or Standard Annotation) toolbar.

7. Type **mirrtext** ↵. At the Enter new value for MIRRTEXT <1>: prompt, type **0** ↵.

8. Repeat the mirror operation using the same instructions as in Step 5. This time the command mirrors the objects, but the text reads properly, as shown in Figure 13.37

FIGURE 13.37

The text on the right was mirrored with MIRRTEXT set to 0.

9. Save your drawing.

Express Tools has a number of text routines that you may find very helpful. Table 13.3 lists these tools.

TABLE 13.3

Express Tools for Text

Command	Menu	Description
RTEXT	Express ⇨ Text ⇨ Remote Text	Displays text from an outside file. You can specify the text style, height, and rotation. Use RTEDIT on the command line to edit remote text.
TEXTFIT	Express ⇨ Text ⇨ Text Fit	Stretches or shrinks Text objects (but not MText) to fit between two points.
TEXTMASK	Express ⇨ Text ⇨ Text Mask	Creates a wipeout, 3D face, or 2D solid object behind the text, with a little extra space around the text. You can use this to make text on top of a hatch more legible.
TEXTUNMASK	Express ⇨ Text ⇨ Text Unmask	Removes a text mask.
TXTEXP	Express ⇨ Text ⇨ Explode Text	Transforms Text or Mtext into geometrical shapes.
TXT2MTXT	Express ⇨ Text ⇨ Convert Text to MText	Converts Text objects to Mtext objects.
ARCTEXT	Express ⇨ Text ⇨ Arc-Aligned Text	Aligns text along an arc.
TORIENT	Express ⇨ Text ⇨ Rotate Text	Rotates multiple text, Mtext, and attribute definitions to a specified angle without moving them, or aligns them so that they're horizontal or right-side up for easy reading.
TCIRCLE	Express ⇨ Text ⇨ Enclose Text with Object	Encloses selected Text or Mtext inside a circle, a *slot* (a rectangle, but with arcs at each end), or a rectangle.
TCOUNT	Express ⇨ Text ⇨ Automatic Text Numbering	Numbers lines of text by adding a prefix or suffix, or by overwriting the text.
TCASE	Express ⇨ Text ⇨ Change Text Case	Offers the following ways to change the case of text: uppercase, lowercase, sentence case, title case, and toggle case.

Finding Text in Your Drawing

In a large, complex drawing with a lot of text, you may have difficulty finding specific text that you need to edit. The FIND command lets you find and replace text anywhere in your drawing — not only single-line text and multiline text but also text in tables, block attributes, dimensions, hyperlink descriptions, and hyperlinks.

To use the FIND command, choose Edit ⇨ Find to open the Find and Replace dialog box, as shown in Figure 13.38.

FIGURE 13.38

The Find and Replace dialog box finds text anywhere in your drawing.

Here's how to use the Find and Replace dialog box:

1. Type the text that you want to find in the Find Text String text box. Use the drop-down list to choose recently used text strings.

 When finding text, you can use wildcard characters such as * (for any number of characters), ? (for any single character), and # (for any numeric character) in the Find Text String text box.

2. If you want to replace the text that you find with new text, type it in the Replace With text box. This box also includes a drop-down list of recently used text strings.

3. If you want to limit or expand the scope of your search, use the Search in drop-down box. If you selected objects before starting the FIND command, this drop-down list displays Current Selection. You can choose Entire Drawing from this list. You can also click the Select Objects button to return to your drawing and select objects. The FIND command then limits its search to selected objects.

4. Choose Options to specify the type of text that FIND will search. By default, it searches all types of text, including attributes (see Chapter 18), dimensions (see Chapter 14), tables, and hyperlinks (see Chapter 28). The command can find text in fields, as well. You can also choose the Match Case and Find Whole Words Only options.

5. Click Find or Find Next to find the next instance of the text string. The dialog box displays the text in the context of the text around it.

6. Click Replace to replace the text string with the replacement text. Click Replace All to replace all instances of the text string with the replacement text.

7. If the Search In drop-down list is set to Current Selection, you can click Select All to return to your drawing with all instances of the text string that you've searched for selected. The prompt on the command line tells you how many objects it has selected. For example, you can use this feature to delete all of these objects. Also, because the objects have grips, it is easy to locate them in your drawing; this is useful when a drawing is so large that you can't read the text when you have the entire drawing displayed on your screen.

8. Use the Zoom To button to zoom in to a selection that the FIND command has found. You can then edit the text. As with the Select All button, this feature is useful for large drawings where the text is not legible unless you zoom in.

9. After you're finished, click Close to close the dialog box.

Checking Your Spelling

If you take pride in the accuracy of your drawings, you might as well make sure that the text is spelled correctly. You can use the SPELL command to check your spelling. The spelling checker acts just like the one in your word processor.

NEW FEATURE   Spelling has been enhanced. You don't have to select objects first; you can specify whether to check the entire drawing, current space/layout or selected objects, and when a word is misspelled, the feature highlights and zooms in to the word. You can also specify which types of text to check or ignore.

   If you want, you can select some objects first. Choose Tools ➪ Spelling or choose Spell Check in the Text control panel of the Dashboard to open the Check Spelling dialog box, as shown in Figure 13.39.

FIGURE 13.39

The Check Spelling dialog box.

From the Where to Check drop-down list, choose Entire Drawing, Current Space/Layout, or Selected Objects. (I cover layouts in Chapter 17.) Click the Settings button to open the Check Spelling Settings dialog box, where you can choose if you want to include dimension text (see Chapter 14), block attributes (see Chapter 18), or external references (see Chapter 19). You can also ignore capitalized words (proper names), words that include numbers, uppercase words, words with mixed cases, such as EllenFinkelstein.com, and words containing punctuation. Click OK when you're done.

In the Check Spelling dialog box, click Start. When the first misspelled word appears in the Not in Dictionary text box, you have the following options:

- **Add to Dictionary:** Choose Add to add the word to the dictionary. The word will not appear again as misspelled.

- **Ignore:** Choose Ignore to ignore the current instance of this word only.

- **Ignore All:** Choose Ignore All to ignore all instances of this word.

- **Change:** Select the suggested word that you want, and choose Change to change the current instance of the word to the suggested word that you selected.

- **Change All:** Select the suggested word that you want, and choose Change All to change all instances of the word to the suggested word that you selected.

Notice that the drawing zooms in and highlights each word. The command automatically moves from word to word until you see the message `Spelling Check Complete`. Click OK and click Close to close the Check Spelling dialog box.

Customizing the Spelling Dictionary

You can change the main and custom spelling dictionaries. To change the main dictionary, choose one from the Main Dictionary drop-down list; these are dictionaries in different languages. Choose Dictionaries from the Check Spelling dialog box to open the Dictionaries dialog box, as shown in Figure 13.40.

FIGURE 13.40

The Dictionaries dialog box.

The custom dictionary is the dictionary that you add to when you click Add in the Dictionaries dialog box. It is a simple text file that includes words that you have added during spelling checks, as well as a list of drawing-related words that come with the file. You can add words to the custom dictionary by typing them in the Content text box and clicking Add.

TIP Another way to edit the custom dictionary is to open the file directly with a text editor. The custom dictionary is called `sample.cus`. To find `sample.cus`, choose Tools ⇨ Options and click the File tab. Double-click Text Editor, Dictionary, and Font File Names. Then double-click Custom Dictionary File. Click the path list to view the location of `sample.cus`.

You can use a different custom dictionary. For example, it can be useful to use the same dictionary in your drawing as you use in your word processor. Here's how to use the Microsoft Word dictionary:

1. Find Word's custom dictionary. If necessary, choose Start ⇨ Find (or Search) and use the Windows Find dialog box to find the file. It is called `custom.dic`. You can open this file with Notepad and edit it directly.

2. As explained in the previous Tip, find the location of `sample.cus`. Use Windows Explorer to copy `custom.dic` to that folder. You can hold down Ctrl as you drag it from one folder to another or use the right mouse button to click the file, choose Copy, and then paste it in its new location.

3. Click `custom.dic` to highlight it. Click it again and change its filename extension to `.cus`. Press Enter. Windows asks you whether you are sure you want to do this. Click Yes.

4. Click Dictionaries in the Check Spelling dialog box to open the Dictionaries dialog box. From the Current Custom Dictionary drop-down list, choose Manage Custom Dictionaries, and click Add. Find the file, and click Open.

5. Click Close three times to return to your drawing.

Summary

In this chapter, you learned how to create, edit, and manage text. You read about:

- Using DTEXT and TEXT to create single-line text
- Editing single-line text
- Creating text styles to control the formatting of your text, including creating annotative text styles
- Utilizing MTEXT for creating and editing paragraph text, including using the In-Place Text Editor
- Importing text
- Creating tables to clearly display data, including linking to external data and extracting object data
- Using fields to automate the insertion of text
- Managing text for the fastest display
- Finding and replacing text and checking spelling in your drawing

In the next chapter, you read about how to create dimensions.

Chapter 14

Drawing Dimensions

D imensions are an important part of most drawings. Dimensions indicate the measurement of the models that you've created and are used in the manufacturing process. The dimensions in AutoCAD and AutoCAD LT offer a great deal of flexibility. In this chapter, I cover the process of drawing dimensions. In the next chapter, I explain how to customize the format of your dimensions by using dimension styles. (Even though you should create a dimension style before you dimension, you need to understand dimensions before you can create a style; therefore, I cover dimensions first.)

Working with Dimensions

You usually add dimensions after you complete all or most of a drawing. When you dimension a drawing all at once, you can create a unified, organized look for your dimensions. Before you can dimension a drawing, you need to understand the elements of a dimension and how to prepare for dimensioning.

CROSS-REF In Chapter 17, I explain how to dimension a drawing on a paper space layout and also how to work with *annotative* dimensions that automatically scale according to the scale of the drawing. In Chapter 15, I explain how to create a dimension style, including one that is annotative.

The elements of a dimension

A dimension is a complex object, containing many parts. Understanding these parts and how they relate to the object you're dimensioning is an important first step. Figure 14.1 shows a typical linear dimension.

FIGURE 14.1

The parts of a dimension.

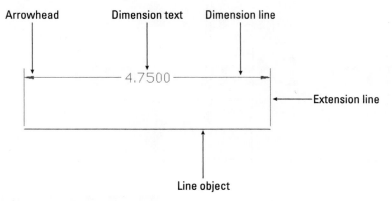

The parts of a dimension are:

- **Extension lines:** These extend from the dimensioned object to the dimension line and arrowheads. A small gap usually separates the dimensioned object and the start of the extension lines. Extension lines visually clarify the extents of the object being dimensioned.

> **NOTE** Relative to dimensions, the word *extension* (or *extend*) is used in two other ways besides referring to extension lines. First, the extension line itself usually extends from the object being dimensioned past the dimension line. You can specify the amount of this extension. Second, in architectural dimensions, the dimension line extends past the extension lines. You can specify this extension as well.

- **Dimension text:** This tells you the actual measurement of the dimensioned object. You can format this text in decimals, fractions, scientific units, and so on.
- **Dimension line:** This extends between the extension lines.
- **Arrowheads:** These mark the intersection of the dimension line and the extension lines. They can take several forms, such as tick marks, open arrows, or dots.

Dimensions have two interesting properties that you need to understand before you can successfully work with them:

- **Dimensions are blocks.** I have mentioned blocks earlier in this book, and they are fully covered in Chapter 18. Blocks are groups of objects that you can manipulate as one object. As a result, if you pick a dimension, all parts of the dimension are selected.
- **Dimensions are associative.** This means that an association connects the dimension and the object it dimensions. If you change the size of the object, the dimension automatically adjusts appropriately.

All parts of a dimension can be formatted individually. You generally format a dimension by creating a *dimension style,* which is a named set of formats for dimensions — just as a text style is a named set of formats for text. (Dimension styles are the topic of the next chapter.)

Preparing to dimension

Dimensioning requires some preparation to get the result that you want. Before starting to create dimensions, you should prepare as follows:

1. Create a layer for your dimensions. It's important that dimensions be easily distinguishable from the rest of your drawing. The color is usually a contrast to that of your models. For example, if your models are black (and you're working on a white screen), you might want your dimensions to be green, magenta, or cyan.

TIP If you often turn layers on and off (or freeze and thaw them), you may want to create a separate dimension layer for each layer of drawing data. For example, if you dimension an electrical layer that you turn off regularly, you can have a special Dim-elec dimension layer that you can turn off with the electrical layer.

2. If you're dimensioning an existing drawing that was created in a pre-2002 version of AutoCAD or AutoCAD LT, turn on associative dimensioning with the DIMASSOC system variable. Type **dimassoc** on the command line and type **2** ↵ at the prompt. (You can also choose Tools ⇨ Options, click the User Preferences tab, and check the check box in the Associative Dimensioning section of the dialog box. Then click OK.)

3. Create a text style for your dimensions. If you want your dimensions to be annotative, make sure that the text style is annotative. For more information, see Chapter 13.

TIP Set the height of the text style to zero. You can then set the text height when you create the dimension style. If you do specify a fixed height in your text style, that height overrides any height that you specify in the dimension style.

4. Choose Tools ⇨ Drafting Settings, click the Object Snap tab, and set the running object snaps that you want. Endpoint and intersection are a necessity. Add center and quadrant if you need to dimension arcs and circles. Click OSNAP on the status bar to turn it on.

5. Create a dimension style. If you want your dimensions to be annotative, make sure that the dimension style is annotative. The next chapter covers dimension styles. Annotative dimensions are valuable when you will be displaying your model at more than one scale, in separate viewports.

6. Save your dimension layer, dimension text style, and dimension style in your drawing templates.

7. If you want your dimensions to be annotative, change to the desired annotation scale, using the Annotation Scale list on the status bar. (You can add or delete annotation scales later if you need to.)

The Dimension toolbar makes it easy to find the dimension commands quickly. The Dimension menu offers most of the same commands as the toolbar. To display the Dimension toolbar, right-click any toolbar and choose Dimension from the list.

NEW FEATURE The Dashboard now has a Dimensions control panel that contains the same tools as the Dimension toolbar. However, because there are so many dimension buttons, not all of them are visible at once. Use the down arrow to the right of the buttons in the top row to display the rest of the buttons.

Drawing Linear Dimensions

Just as the most common objects are lines, the most common dimensions are linear dimensions. Use linear dimensions for lines, or a straight segment of a polyline, rectangle, or block. You can also use a linear dimension for arcs and circles — you get the linear length of the arc (not its perimeter length) and the diameter of the circle.

Specifying the dimensioned object

To dimension a line, choose Linear from the Dimension toolbar or the Dimensions control panel of the Dashboard. The command responds with the `Specify first extension line origin or <select object>:` prompt. You can now either pick two extension line origin points or press Enter and select an object for dimensioning.

If you're dimensioning more than one object, such as the distance from the endpoint of one line to the endpoint of another line, pick the first extension line origin. At the `Specify second extension line origin:` prompt, pick the second extension line origin. The two points on the objects that you pick define the length of the dimension.

If you're dimensioning one object, press Enter at the `Specify first extension line origin or <select object>:` prompt. The `Select object to dimension:` prompt appears. Pick the object.

> **CAUTION** Always use the Select Object option if possible for the most reliable results. Proper association of dimensions with their objects depends on the points that you specify. If you can't select an object and the point you need to specify is an intersection, don't click on the intersection. Instead, click on the object that you want to measure near the intersection and let the object snap specify the intersection for you. If you're not using the Select Object option, always use an object snap for accuracy.

At the `Specify dimension line location or [Mtext/Text/Angle/Horizontal/Vertical/Rotated]:` prompt, pick a point for the location of the dimension line. As you move the mouse, you can see the results on your screen, as shown in Figure 14.2. If you want an exact location, you can type in a relative coordinate, such as **@0,.5** to specify that the dimension line should be 0.5 units from the object. Snap mode may also work well for you, depending on the drawing environment.

Object snap tracking makes it a snap to pick points for dimensioning. For example, if you're dimensioning a house, your first extension line origin may be the outside corner of the house, but the second extension line origin may be an inner wall. At the `Specify first extension line origin or <select object>:` prompt, move the cursor over the inner wall endpoint to acquire it. Move the cursor back to the line you're dimensioning and click when you see the tooltip showing the snap point you chose. The dimension goes just where you need it.

> **ON the DVD-ROM** The drawing used in the following exercise on drawing linear dimensions, `ab14-a.dwg`, is in the `Drawings` folder on the DVD.

FIGURE 14.2

Picking a dimension line location for a linear dimension.

Pick point

Dimensioned object

STEPS: Drawing Linear Dimensions

1. Open ab14-a.dwg from your DVD.

2. Save the file as ab14-01.dwg in your AutoCAD Bible folder. This is a plan of a bedroom, as shown in Figure 14.3. ORTHO and OSNAP should be on. Set a running object snap for endpoint only. OTRACK should be off. The current layer should be set to Dim.

3. To display the Dimension toolbar, right-click any toolbar. Click Dimension. If you want, drag the toolbar to the top or bottom of your screen until it docks. If you want to use the Dashboard, display it (Tools ⇨ Palettes ⇨ Dashboard). If the Dimension control panel is not displayed, right-click the Dashboard and choose Control Panels ⇨ Dimensions.

4. Choose Linear from the Dimension toolbar or Dimensions control panel of the Dashboard. Because you are dimensioning the vertical length of the room, you really want the dimension to be attached to the bottom and top horizontal lines, so that if you move those lines to make the room longer or shorter, the dimension changes. At the Specify first extension line origin or <select object>: prompt, pick ❶ in Figure 14.3, close enough to the corner to get the endpoint object snap marker. At the Specify second extension line origin: prompt, pick ❷ in the same way. At the Specify dimension line location or [Mtext/Text/Angle/Horizontal/Vertical/Rotated]: prompt, move the cursor to the right until you have sufficient space for the dimension text and click.

FIGURE 14.3

A bedroom plan.

5. Repeat the DIMLINEAR command. At the `Specify first extension line origin or <select object>:` prompt, press Enter. At the `Select object to dimension:` prompt, pick ❸ (the window) in Figure 14.3. At the `Specify dimension line location or [Mtext/Text/Angle/Horizontal/Vertical/ Rotated]:` prompt, move the cursor down until you have sufficient space for the dimension text and click.

6. Save your drawing. It should look like Figure 14.4.

FIGURE 14.4

The bedroom with two linear dimensions.

Using dimension options

You can also use one of the options offered at the command prompt to further control the final dimension. Dimension options control the text and the angle of the dimension.

MText

The MText option lets you replace the calculated dimension text or add a prefix or suffix to it. When you right-click and choose MText at the `Specify dimension line location or [Mtext/Text/Angle/Horizontal/Vertical/Rotated]:` prompt, the In-Place Text Editor opens, as shown in Figure 14.5.

FIGURE 14.5

Changing the dimension text with the In-Place Text Editor.

The best use of the MText option is to add some text before or after the measurement, such as **TYP** "typical" (used when one dimension applies to several objects) or **subject to final approval.** To add text before the measurement, simply start typing. To add text after the measurement, press the End or Right Arrow key and then type. To replace the existing text, click the text to select it and enter the replacement text. Then click OK to close the In-Place Text Editor.

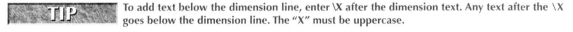 **Typing your own dimension text is most commonly used where a dimension represents several sizes and refers to a size chart elsewhere in the drawing. For example, the text "Dim A" might be used for this purpose. If you replace the existing text, you can obtain the original text again by editing the dimension (double-click the dimension) and changing the Text Override item in the Properties palette to <>.**

If the measurement text itself does not appear the way you want it, you should change the annotation specifications in the dimension style. You can also specify a prefix or suffix (such as *mm*) for all dimensions, as I explain in the next chapter. When you delete the text and type your own dimension text, you lose the ability of the dimension's measurement to automatically adjust to any change in the object's size.

TIP **To add text below the dimension line, enter \X after the dimension text. Any text after the \X goes below the dimension line. The "X" must be uppercase.**

Text

The Text option also lets you change dimension text but does not open the In-Place Text Editor. Instead, you can quickly retype the entire dimension text as you want it on the command line.

Angle

The angle of the text (horizontal, vertical, or aligned) is specified in your dimension style. However, you can use this option to change the angle of the dimension text for a particular circumstance. Right-click and choose Angle to get the `Specify angle of dimension text:` prompt. Type in an angle or pick two points to align the text with an existing object.

Horizontal/vertical

The DIMLINEAR command assumes that you want a horizontal dimension if you select a horizontal object or two definition points running horizontally — ditto for a vertical dimension. Also, if you want to draw a vertical dimension of an object at an angle, you can specify this simply by moving the mouse cursor horizontally when specifying the dimension line location, as shown in Figure 14.6. If for some reason you need to force either a horizontal or vertical dimension, you can use the vertical or horizontal options.

FIGURE 14.6

By dragging the mouse cursor to the right, you can create a vertical dimension for this angled line. The vertical dimension measures the change in the Y coordinates of the line, not the length of the line.

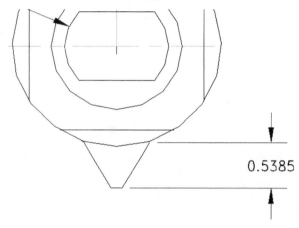

0.5385

Rotated

Use a rotated linear dimension when the length that you want to dimension is not parallel to the extension line origins. Just as the vertical dimension in Figure 14.6 does not measure the length of the line to which its extension lines extend, a rotated linear dimension does not measure a specific object, but the distance of an imaginary line parallel to the dimension line. Rotated dimensions are not very common, but when you need them, they're the only way to get the dimension measurement that you need.

To use a rotated dimension, start a linear dimension, pick the two extension line origins, and choose the Rotated option. At the Specify angle of dimension line <0>: prompt, type the angle (or pick two points) to draw the dimension.

Figure 14.7 shows a hexagonal stepping-stone with a rotated linear angle. The extension lines of the dimension extend to a line at 104.5 degrees, but in this case you want to measure a length at an angle of 135 degrees. Note that the dimension really measures an imaginary line parallel to the dimension line, shown in the figure as a dashed line, rather than the side of the hexagon.

FIGURE 14.7

Drawing a rotated linear dimension for a hexagonal stepping-stone.

Creating jogged dimension lines

A jog line is a zigzag used to indicate that the displayed measurement doesn't match the length of an object. For example, you might shorten an object to display it within a certain area, but manually override the dimension text to show the proper length. In this case, the jog line indicates that the visual length of the line is not to scale (NTS).

NEW FEATURE Jog lines for linear and aligned dimensions are new for AutoCAD 2008 and AutoCAD LT 2008. I discuss aligned dimensions in the next section. The new command is DIMJOGLINE.

 First you create a linear or aligned dimension. (You may have modified the measurement text, as explained previously in this chapter in the discussion of the MText option.) Then you add the jog line, using the DIMJOGLINE command. Choose Dimension ➪ Jogged Linear, or click the Jogged Linear button on the Dimension toolbar or in the Dimensions control panel of the Dashboard.

At the `Select dimension to add jog or [Remove]:` prompt, select a dimension. At the `Specify jog location (or press ENTER):` prompt, press Enter to place the jog line midway between the dimension text and the first extension line, as shown in Figure 14.8. Alternatively, you can pick a location for the jog line.

You can move the jog line by stretching its grip. Select the dimension, select the jog line's grip, and move it to another location.

FIGURE 14.8

You can add a jog line to a dimension to indicate that the displayed measurement is different from the length of the dimensioned object.

24' NTS

Drawing Aligned Dimensions

When you want to dimension a linear object that is not orthogonal, use an aligned dimension. The dimension lines of an aligned dimension are always parallel to the object, unlike rotated dimensions. An aligned dimension measures the actual length of the object, not a vertical or horizontal distance that you dimension with a linear dimension. Therefore, your choice of linear, linear rotated, or aligned dimension depends on the distance that you want to measure. Figure 14.9 shows several aligned dimensions.

FIGURE 14.9

Three aligned dimensions.

Specifying the dimensioned object

 To create an aligned dimension, choose Aligned from the Dimension toolbar or the Dimension control panel of the Dashboard. This starts the DIMALIGNED command. The command responds with the Specify first extension line origin or <select object>: prompt. As with linear dimensions, you can now either pick two extension line origins or press Enter to select an object.

You then see the Specify dimension line location or [Mtext/Text/Angle]: prompt. Pick a point for the location of the dimension line. If you want an exact location, you can type in a relative coordinate, such as @2<45. This specifies that the dimension line should be 2 units in a 45-degree direction from the extension line origins that you specified.

Using the options

After you've chosen what you want to dimension, you have three options: MText, Text, and Angle. The previous section discusses these options in detail.

 The drawing used in the following exercise on drawing aligned dimensions, ab14-b.dwg, **is in the** Drawings **folder on the DVD.**

STEPS: Drawing Aligned Dimensions

1. Open ab14-b.dwg from your DVD.

2. Save the file as ab14-02.dwg in your AutoCAD Bible folder. This is part of a floor plan of a house, as shown in Figure 14.10. OSNAP should be on. Set running object snaps to endpoint and intersection. If the Dimension toolbar isn't visible, right-click any toolbar and choose Dimension, or display the Dashboard with its Dimensions control panel.

FIGURE 14.10

A section of a floor plan of a house.

3. Choose Aligned from the Dimension toolbar or from the Dimensions control panel of the Dashboard. Follow the prompts:

```
Specify first extension line origin or <select object>: Choose ❶ in
Figure 14.10.
Specify second extension line origin: Choose ❷ in Figure 14.10.
Specify dimension line location or
[Mtext/Text/Angle]: Right-click and choose Mtext. In the In-Place
Text Editor, press the End key on the keyboard and type a space, then
type Typ. Click OK.
Specify dimension line location or
[Mtext/Text/Angle]: Pick a location for the dimension line.
```

4. Save your drawing. It should look like Figure 14.11.

FIGURE 14.11

The house plan with an aligned dimension.

Creating Baseline and Continued Dimensions

Often, you want to create a whole series of attached, connected dimensions. You can accomplish this in two ways:

- *Baseline* dimensions are a series of dimensions that all start from one point. The first extension line is the same for all of the dimensions. The second dimension includes the first dimension plus an additional distance and so on.

- *Continued* dimensions are a series of dimensions that are all attached. The second dimension starts where the first dimension ends and so on. Each dimension measures a different object or distance.

Figure 14.12 shows both baseline and continued linear dimensions. You can also create baseline and continued angular and ordinate dimensions. Quick Dimension, covered later in this chapter, can quickly create baseline and continued linear dimensions. Here I cover the traditional method.

Drawing baseline dimensions

To draw a baseline dimension, first create one linear, angular, or ordinate dimension in the regular way. (Angular and ordinate dimensions are covered later in this chapter.) Then choose Baseline from the Dimension toolbar or from the Dimensions control panel of the Dashboard. The command responds with the `Specify a second extension line origin or [Undo/Select] <Select>:` prompt.

If the previous dimension was a linear, angular, or ordinate dimension, the command uses the first extension line as the base for the new baseline dimension. Specify a new second extension line origin, and the command creates the baseline dimension with the same first extension origin as the original dimension and the new second extension origin that you just specified.

FIGURE 14.12

A floor plan of a house using both baseline and continued dimensions.

Baseline dimensions   Continued dimensions

If you don't want to work with the previous dimension in the drawing, press Enter. The command responds with the `Select base dimension:` prompt. Be careful to pick the dimension closer to the side you want to use as the baseline. The command then prompts you to specify a second extension line origin. Doing so creates the dimension.

The command continues to prompt you for second extension line origins so that you can quickly create a chain of baseline dimensions. At each prompt, you can right-click and choose Undo to undo the previous dimension. You can also press Enter at any time and select a different dimension from which to work. Press Esc to end the command (or press Enter twice).

Drawing continued dimensions

Continued dimensions work similarly to baseline dimensions. To continue a dimension, first create one linear, angular, or ordinate dimension in the regular way. Then choose Continue from the Dimension toolbar or from the Dimensions control panel of the Dashboard. The command responds with the `Specify a second extension line origin or [Undo/ Select] <Select>:` prompt.

If the previous dimension was a linear, angular, or ordinate dimension, the command uses the second extension line as the beginning of the new continued dimension. Specify a new second extension line origin to create the continued dimension.

If you don't want to continue from the previous dimension in the drawing, press Enter. The command responds with the `Select continued dimension:` prompt. Be careful to pick the dimension closer to the side from which you want to continue. You then get a prompt to specify a second extension line origin. Doing so creates the dimension.

The command continues to prompt you for second extension line origins so that you can quickly create a chain of continued dimensions. At each prompt, you can right-click and choose Undo to undo the previous dimension. You can also press Enter at any time and select a different dimension from which to work. Press Esc to end the command (or press Enter twice).

The drawing used in the following exercise on drawing baseline and continued dimensions, `ab14-b.dwg`, is in the `Drawings` folder on the DVD.

STEPS: Drawing Baseline and Continued Dimensions

1. Open `ab14-b.dwg` from your DVD.

2. Save the file as `ab14-03.dwg` in your `AutoCAD Bible` folder. This is the same drawing used in the previous two exercises, as shown in Figure 14.13. OSNAP should be on with running object snaps for endpoint and intersection. If the Dimension toolbar isn't visible, right-click any toolbar and choose Dimension. Alternatively, you can display the Dashboard with its Dimensions control panel.

FIGURE 14.13

A house plan with an octagonal ceiling.

3. Turn on ORTHO and OTRACK on the status bar.

4. Choose Linear from the Dimension toolbar or from the Dimensions control panel of the Dashboard. Follow the prompts:

    ```
    Specify first extension line origin or <select object>: Pick the
    endpoint at ❶ in Figure 14.13.
    Specify second extension line origin: Pass the cursor over ❸ to
    acquire it for object snap tracking. Move the cursor to the right so
    that it's vertically under ❶, and click when you see the 1'-6"<0°
    tooltip.
    Specify dimension line location or
    [Mtext/Text/Angle/Horizontal/Vertical/Rotated]: Pick a dimension line
    location to the right of the model.
    ```

5. Choose Continue from the Dimension toolbar or from the Dimensions control panel of the Dashboard.

At the Specify a second extension line origin or [Undo/Select] <Select>: prompt, move the cursor over the endpoint or intersection at ❹ to acquire it for object snap tracking. Move the cursor to the right, vertically below ❶, and click when you see the tooltip.

This action places the continued dimension. Notice that the dimension uses a leader to place the text because there is not enough room between the extension lines. (If the leader is placed to the left, select it and pick the grip on the text. Pick a point to the right of the model and click to move the leader to the right.)

6. The command repeats the Specify a second extension line origin or [Undo/Select] <Select>: prompt. Pick the endpoint at ❷ in Figure 14.13 to place the dimension. Press Enter twice to end the command.

7. Choose Linear from the Dimension toolbar or from the Dimensions control panel of the Dashboard. Follow the prompts:

   Specify first extension line origin or <select object>: *Choose the endpoint at ❺ in Figure 14.13.*

   Follow these prompts:

   Specify second extension line origin: *Move the cursor over ❼ to acquire it. Move the cursor down so that it's horizontal to ❺. When you see the 4'0"<270° tooltip, click.*
   Specify dimension line location or [Mtext/Text/Angle/Horizontal/Vertical/Rotated]: *Pick a dimension line location fairly close to the line you dimensioned, leaving just enough room for the dimension text.*

8. Choose Baseline from the Dimension toolbar or from the Dimensions control panel of the Dashboard. At the Specify a second extension line origin or [Undo/Select] <Select>: prompt, pick the endpoint or intersection at ❻ in Figure 14.13. Press Enter twice to end the command.

9. Save your drawing. It should look like Figure 14.14.

FIGURE 14.14

The floor plan with baseline and continued dimensions.

Dimensioning Arcs and Circles

When you dimension an arc or a circle, you measure its radius or diameter. It's also common to mark arc and circle centers to clarify what you're measuring. Arc and circle dimensions are most commonly used in mechanical drawings.

Marking arc and circle centers

Circle and arc centers are often marked in mechanical drawings because the center is an important aspect of a circle or arc but is not obvious without a mark. You set the size and type of mark when you create a dimension style, as explained in the next chapter. You can use a center mark (a small cross) or centerlines, as shown in Figure 14.15.

Choose Center Mark from the Dimension toolbar or from the Dimensions control panel of the Dashboard. At the `Select arc or circle:` prompt, pick the arc or circle you want to mark. The command draws the mark or lines.

FIGURE 14.15

Circles — one with a center mark and the other with centerlines.

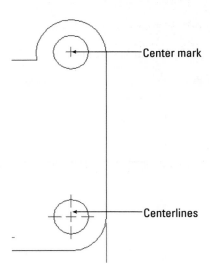

Center mark

Centerlines

Dimensioning arc lengths

To dimension the length of an arc, choose Arc Length from the Dimension toolbar or from the Dimensions control panel of the Dashboard. You can dimension the length of an arc or an arc segment in a polyline. At the `Select arc or polyline arc segment:` prompt, select an arc. At the `Specify arc length dimension location, or [Mtext/Text/Angle/Partial/Leader]:` prompt, pick where you want the dimension line (which is an arc) to appear. The command automatically adds an arc symbol before the measurement. You can specify the arc symbol above the measurement or choose to display no symbol — you set this in your dimension style. Figure 14.16 shows an example of an arc length dimension.

You can also choose the MText, Text, or Angle option, as described in the section "Drawing Linear Dimensions." The Partial option lets you dimension part of an arc. At the prompts, you specify where you want to start and end the dimension. The Leader option inserts an arrow pointing to the arc.

Creating radial dimensions

To dimension the radius of a circle or arc, choose Radius from the Dimension toolbar or from the Dimensions control panel of the Dashboard. The command responds with the Select arc or circle: prompt. Select an arc or circle. At the Specify dimension line location or [Mtext/Text/Angle]: prompt, pick where you want the dimension line to appear. The command automatically adds an R before the measurement to indicate the radius, as shown in Figure 14.16.

FIGURE 14.16

The circle's radius dimension uses a leader (a line and arrow pointing to the object) because the circle is too small to place the dimension inside it. The arc displays an arc length dimension.

You can also choose the MText, Text, or Angle option, as described in the "Drawing Linear Dimensions" section earlier in this chapter.

A radius dimension usually passes through the center of the arc or circle. If you are dimensioning a large arc or circle, you may find that you can't see the center at the same time as you see the circumference without zooming out too far. In this instance, you can use the jogged radial dimension, which lets you specify an arbitrary center for the arc or circle. Choose Dimension ➪ Jogged. You can also choose Jogged from the Dimension toolbar or the Dimensions control panel of the Dashboard.

NEW FEATURE You can now create an extension arc (similar to an extension line) for a radius dimension that extends beyond the end of an arc. This allows you to place the dimension anywhere in the circle of which the arc is a part. When you specify the location of the dimension, just move the cursor past the arc's endpoint and continue around to the desired point.

Creating diameter dimensions

To dimension the diameter of an arc or circle, choose Diameter from the Dimension toolbar or from the Dimensions control panel of the Dashboard. The command responds with the Select arc or circle: prompt. Select an arc or circle. At the Specify dimension line location or [Mtext/Text/Angle]: prompt, pick where you want the dimension line to appear. The command automatically adds the diameter symbol before the measurement to indicate the dimension, as shown in Figure 14.17.

FIGURE 14.17

A diameter dimension.

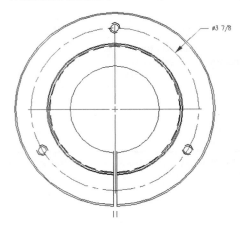

You can also choose the MText, Text, or Angle option, as described in the section "Drawing Linear Dimensions."

NEW FEATURE You can now create an extension arc (similar to an extension line) for a diameter dimension that extends beyond the end of an arc. This allows you to place the dimension anywhere in the circle of which the arc is a part. When you specify the location of the dimension, just move the cursor past the arc's endpoint and continue around to the desired point.

Dimensioning Angles

You have several options for dimensioning angles. You may want to dimension the angular relationship between two lines, but the lines may intersect at their midpoints or may not intersect at all. Therefore, you need to be able to specify the vertex of the angle you want to dimension. Figure 14.18 shows an angular dimension with the points used to define it.

 To create an angular dimension, choose Angular from the Dimension toolbar or from the Dimensions control panel of the Dashboard. This starts the DIMANGULAR command. The command displays the `Select arc, circle, line, or <specify vertex>:` prompt, and responds differently, depending on what you select:

- If you press Enter, the command asks for the angle vertex, the first angle endpoint, and the second angle endpoint. These three points define the angle.
- If you select an arc, the command dimensions the entire arc, using the arc's center as the angle vertex.

- If you select a circle, the command uses the pick point as the first angle endpoint and the circle's center as the angle vertex. You then see the `Specify second angle endpoint:` prompt. Pick a point on the circle.
- If you select a line, the command asks for a second line. The command measures the angle between the two lines. If the lines don't intersect, the command uses their implied intersection as the angle vertex.

FIGURE 14.18

An angular dimension.

Thanks to Mary Redfern of the Bethlehem Corporation, Easton, Pennsylvania, for this drawing.

After you define the angle, the command responds with the `Specify dimension arc line location or [Mtext/Text/Angle/Quadrant]:` prompt. Pick a point for the dimension arc line — which is the same thing as a dimension line, except that the command uses an arc for angular dimensions.

NEW FEATURE The new Quadrant option lets you lock the location of the dimension line to a specified quadrant of the circle in which the angle lies. For example, you can fix the dimension line outside two lines forming an angle while placing the text within those two lines. After choosing the Quadrant option, at the `Specify quadrant:` prompt, click where you want the dimensions line to appear. You can then specify any location for the text of the dimension.

You can also choose the MText, Text, or Angle option, as covered in the section "Drawing Linear Dimensions."

In the following exercise, you get to practice drawing radial, diameter, and angular dimensions.

Dimensioning Minor, Major, and Supplemental Angles

When two lines meet at an angle, they create two angles, the *minor angle* and the *major angle*. The angle that is less than 180 degrees is the minor angle. The major angle is always more than 180 degrees. You can also measure the *supplemental angle,* which is the difference between 180 degrees and the minor angle. These angles are shown here.

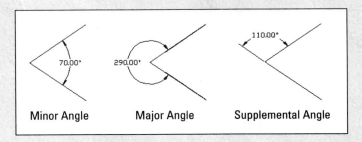

Minor Angle   Major Angle   Supplemental Angle

Here's how you create each type of dimension. Start the DIMANGULAR command. The command responds with the `Select arc, circle, line, or <specify vertex>:` prompt.

To dimension the minor angle, select both lines. Then at the `Specify dimension arc line location or [Mtext/Text/Angle/Quadrant]:` prompt, place the dimension arc line inside the angle, as shown in the figure. (You can also press Enter, specify the angle vertex and the two lines, and place the dimension arc line inside the angle.)

To dimension the major angle, press Enter. Do not select the lines. At the prompts, specify the angle vertex and the two lines. At the `Specify dimension arc line location or [Mtext/Text/Angle/Quadrant]:` prompt, place the dimension arc line outside the angle, as shown in the figure.

To dimension the supplemental angle, select both lines. At the `Specify dimension arc line location or [Mtext/Text/Angle/Quadrant]:` prompt, place the dimension arc line outside the angle, as shown in the figure.

As you can see, how you specify the angle and where you place the dimension arc line determine which angle you measure.

ON the DVD-ROM The drawing used in the following exercise on drawing radial, diameter, and angular dimensions, `ab14-c.dwg`, is in the `Drawings` folder on the DVD.

STEPS: Drawing Radial, Diameter, and Angular Dimensions

1. Open `ab14-c.dwg` from your DVD.
2. Save the file as `ab14-04.dwg` in your `AutoCAD Bible` folder. This is a view of a bearing housing for an industrial washing machine, as shown in Figure 14.19. OSNAP should be on. Set running object snaps to endpoint, intersection, and center. If the Dimension toolbar isn't visible, right-click any toolbar and choose Dimension. Alternatively, display the Dashboard with its Dimensions control panel.

FIGURE 14.19

A bearing housing for an industrial washing machine.

Thanks to Robert Mack of the Dexter Company, Fairfield, Iowa, for this drawing.

3. Choose Center Mark from the Dimension toolbar or from the Dimensions control panel of the Dashboard. At the `Select arc or circle:` prompt, pick one of the four small circles at the corners of the model. Repeat the command for the other three circles.

4. Choose Diameter from the Dimension toolbar or from the Dimensions control panel of the Dashboard. At the `Select arc or circle:` prompt, choose the outer of the two circles at ❶ in Figure 14.19. At the `Specify dimension line location or [Mtext/Text/Angle]:` prompt, pick a location for the dimension line.

5. Choose Radius from the Dimension toolbar or from the Dimensions control panel of the Dashboard. At the `Select arc or circle:` prompt, choose ❷ from Figure 14.19. At the `Specify dimension line location or [Mtext/Text/Angle]:` prompt, pick a location for the dimension line to the left of the ar To move the text outside the figure, select it, right-click and choose Dim Text Position ⇨ Move with Leader. Then specify a location to the right of the arc.

6. Choose Angular from the Dimension toolbar or from the Dimensions control panel of the Dashboard. Follow the prompts:

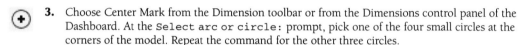

```
Select arc, circle, line, or <specify vertex>: ↵
Specify angle vertex: Pick ❸ in Figure 14.19.
Specify first angle endpoint: Pick the endpoint at ❹. (Press Tab if
necessary until you see the endpoint tooltip.)
Specify second angle endpoint: Pick the endpoint at ❺.
Specify dimension arc line location or [Mtext/Text/Angle/Quadrant]:
Choose a location for the dimension line.
```

7. Repeat the DIMANGULAR command. At the `Select arc, circle, line, or <specify vertex>:` prompt, pick the arc at ❻. At the `Specify dimension arc line location or [Mtext/Text/Angle/Quadrant]:` prompt, pick a location for the dimension line.

8. Choose Arc Length from the Dimension toolbar or from the Dimensions control panel of the Dashboard. At the Select arc or polyline arc segment: prompt, again pick the arc at ❻. At the Specify arc length dimension location, or [Mtext/Text/Angle/Partial]: prompt, pick a location for the dimension line farther out than the previous dimension that you drew.

9. Start the DIMANGULAR command. At the Select arc, circle, line, or <specify vertex>: prompt, pick ❼ in Figure 14.19. At the Second line: prompt, pick ❽. At the Dimension arc line location [Mtext/Text/Angle/Quadrant]: prompt, pick a location for the dimension line to the left of the model.

10. Save your drawing. It should look like Figure 14.20.

FIGURE 14.20

The bearing housing with center marks, radial and diameter dimensions, arc length, and angular dimensions.

Creating Ordinate Dimensions

Ordinate dimensions are used in mechanical drawing. They dimension an object by labeling X or Y coordinates based on a 0,0 coordinate placed somewhere on the model. Figure 14.21 shows a drawing with some ordinate dimensions.

To place the 0,0 coordinate on the model, choose Tools ➪ New UCS ➪ Origin. At the prompt, pick a point on the model, using object snaps for an exact measurement. If you want to check the UCS, choose View ➪ Display ➪ UCS Icon ➪ Origin. Also make sure that On is checked. As long as there is room, the UCS icon moves to the new 0,0 coordinate.

FIGURE 14.21

Ordinate dimensions in a mechanical drawing of a tension arm for a commercial dryer.

FLAT BLANK LAYOUT

 To create an ordinate dimension, choose Ordinate from the Dimension toolbar or from the Dimensions control panel of the Dashboard. At the `Specify feature location:` prompt, pick the part of the model that you want to dimension. Running object snaps with OSNAP turned on makes this an easy task.

At the `Specify leader endpoint or [Xdatum/Ydatum/Mtext/Text/Angle]:` prompt, pick the endpoint for the leader. The location where you pick the leader endpoint determines which coordinate to dimension — the X coordinate (Xdatum) or Y coordinate (Ydatum). Pick the leader endpoint perpendicular from the coordinate's axis that you want to measure. To measure an X coordinate, move up or down from the feature you selected. To measure a Y coordinate, move left or right to pick the leader endpoint.

Usually you work with ORTHO on to create straight lines. If you need to create bent lines to avoid previously drawn dimensions, turn ORTHO off. If you pick a leader endpoint at a nonorthogonal angle from the feature, you may need to force the measurement of the coordinate that you want using either the Xdatum or Ydatum option. Use the MText option to open the In-Place Text Editor and edit the dimension text. Use the Text option to change all of the text on the command line.

To perfectly line up the dimensions, when specifying the leader endpoint, use object tracking to track the endpoint of the previous leader. You can also turn on SNAP.

ON the DVD-ROM The drawing used in the following exercise on drawing ordinate dimensions, `ab14-d.dwg`, is in the `Drawings` folder on the DVD.

STEPS: Drawing Ordinate Dimensions

1. Open `ab14-d.dwg` from your DVD.
2. Save the file as `ab14-05.dwg` in your `AutoCAD Bible` folder. This drawing shows a simple sheet-metal template, as shown in Figure 14.22. Snap should be on. Set a snap distance of 0.25 units. Right-click the SNAP button on the status bar and make sure that grid snap is on. If the Dimension toolbar isn't visible, right-click any toolbar and choose Dimension. Alternatively, display the Dashboard with its Dimensions control panel.

FIGURE 14.22

A sheet-metal template.

3. Choose Tools ➪ New UCS ➪ Origin. At the `Specify new origin point <0,0,0>:` prompt, pick ❶ in Figure 14.22.

4. Choose Ordinate from the Dimension toolbar or from the Dimensions control panel of the Dashboard. At the `Specify feature location:` prompt, choose ❶ in Figure 14.22. At the `Specify leader endpoint or [Xdatum/Ydatum/Mtext/Text/Angle]:` prompt, pick a point 0.5 units to the left of ❶, as shown in Figure 14.23. (Because Snap is on, this is easy. If necessary, click the coordinates at the lower-left corner of the screen until you get polar coordinates to display in the lower-left area of the drawing screen.)

FIGURE 14.23

The dimensioned template.

5. Repeat the DIMORDINATE command. At the `Specify feature location:` prompt, choose ❶ in Figure 14.22. At the `Specify leader endpoint or [Xdatum/Ydatum/Mtext/ Text/Angle]:` prompt, pick a point 0.5 units below ❶.

6. Continue to dimension the drawing, using Figure 14.23 as a guide.

 TIP   Type multiple ↵ dimordinate ↵ to automatically repeat the command. Press Esc when you no longer need the command.

7. Save your drawing.

Drawing Leaders

Leaders are lines pointing to objects. At the end of a leader, you place any text that you want. Use leaders to label objects or provide explanatory text. Leaders do not calculate dimension text, but if you use an object snap to place the arrow point, they follow along if you move the object. Figure 14.24 shows two leaders.

FIGURE 14.24

Use leaders to point to objects and add explanatory text.

BURR THIS SIDE

.125 R. TYP.

 NEW FEATURE   AutoCAD 2008 and AutoCAD LT 2008 introduce *multileaders,* which are leaders that support multiple lines. These leaders introduce several other enhancements as well, including multi-leader styles. Multileader styles can be annotative, which allows them to scale automatically to the current annotative/viewport scale. A new Multileader toolbar and a control panel on the Dashboard contain tools for the multileader feature. The earlier QLEADER and LEADER commands still exist, but they offer fewer options.

Creating a multileader

To create a multileader using the default style and settings, choose Multileader from the Multileader toolbar or from the Multileaders control panel of the Dashboard. (To display the toolbar, right-click any toolbar and choose Multileader. To display the control panel, choose Tools ➪ Palettes ➪ Dashboard. Then right-click the Dashboard and choose Control Panels ➪ Multileaders.) At the `Specify leader arrowhead loca-tion or [leader Landing first/Content first/Options] <Options>:` prompt, specify where you want the tip of the arrow (the *head* of the leader) to go. If you want a precise point, you may want to use an object snap. At the `Specify leader landing location:` prompt, specify where you want the end of the line to go. This line will be next to the text or block.

The In-Place Text Editor opens, where you can enter the text for the leader. (See Chapter 13 for a discussion of the text editor.) You can use the editor's toolbar to format the text at this time. For example, you can choose an existing text style, a font, or a font size. Click OK in the editor's toolbar or click anywhere outside of the editor to close the editor and place the leader. Notice that the command adds a short horizontal *landing line* that connects a diagonal arrow to the text.

When you start the MLEADER command, you have the following options at the first prompt:

- **leader Landing first:** Lets you first specify the point where the line meets the text. If you choose this option, AutoCAD continues to prompt you for the leader landing first.

- **Content first:** Lets you specify a location for the text label, and then enter the text.

- **Options:** Displays the following sub-options:

  - **Leader type:** Offers you options relating to the leader. You can use the Type sub-option to choose a straight line (the default), a spline, or no line at all. Choose the Landing sub-option to choose whether or not you want a landing, and if so, its length.

  - **leader lAnding:** Lets you choose whether you want a landing (Yes) or not (No).

  - **Content type:** Lets you choose whether you want the leader to end with Mtext (the default), a block, or nothing. If you choose the Block sub-option, you enter the name of the block. (Blocks are covered in Chapter 18.)

  - **Maxpoints:** Lets you specify the maximum number of points of the line. A three-point line will have three vertices.

  - **First angle:** Lets you enter an angle to constrain the first angle after the arrowhead segment. For example, you could constrain the angle to 90°.

  - **Second angle:** If you specified more than two points, you can constrain a second angle.

  - **eXit options:** Exits the Options prompts and returns you to the main prompts for the MLEADER command.

To add or remove a leader, you use the MLEADEREDIT command. On the Multileader toolbar or the Multileaders control panel of the Dashboard, choose Add Leader to add a leader, and then select the multileader and specify the endpoint of the new arrowhead(s). Choose Remove Leader to remove a leader on a multileader that has more than one; select the multileader, specify which leader line to remove, and press Enter to end the command.

Creating a multileader style

Although you have a lot of settings available when you create a multileader, you can best define its look by using a multileader style. Just as a text style defines how text looks, a multileader style controls the look of multileaders. Once you have your multileader style, you don't need to fuss with all of the options; you can just choose a style and create your leaders. While the settings are similar, because you save a style, you can easily use it again and again.

To create a multileader style, choose Multileader Style from the Multileader toolbar or from the Multileaders control panel of the Dashboard to open the Multileader Style Manager, shown in Figure 14.25.

FIGURE 14.25

The Multileader Style Manager.

To create a new style, click the New button to open the Create New Multileader Style dialog box, shown in Figure 14.26. Here you name your style and choose an existing style as a basis for the style. You can also specify that the style should be annotative by checking the Annotative check box. Note that if you want the multileaders to be annotative, then any blocks and text styles that they use need to be annotative, as well.

CROSS-REF **Annotative objects scale automatically to the current annotative/viewport scale when you plot them. For more information, see Chapter 17. For information about annotative text styles, see Chapter 13. I cover blocks in Chapter 18.**

FIGURE 14.26

Name your multileader style in the Create New Multileader Style dialog box.

When you've named your style, click Continue to open the Modify Multileader Style dialog box, shown in Figure 14.27 with the Leader Format tab displayed. If you choose an existing multileader style from the Multileader Style Manager and click Modify, you get to this same dialog box.

FIGURE 14.27

Define a multileader style in the Modify Multileader Style dialog box.

On the Leader Format tab, you can format the line and the arrow as follows:

- **Type:** Choose Straight, Spline (curved), or None from the drop-down list.
- **Color:** Choose a color from the drop-down list. These are the same colors that you can choose for any object. For more information, see Chapter 11. The default is ByBlock, which means that the leader takes on the color of the current layer (or the current color).
- **Linetype:** Choose a linetype from the drop-down list. Choose Other to open the Select Linetype dialog box, where you can choose a loaded linetype, or load another linetype. (I explain linetypes in Chapter 11.)
- **Lineweight:** Choose a lineweight from the drop-down list. (Chapter 11 discusses lineweights.)
- **Symbol:** In the Arrowhead section, you can choose the type of arrow you want to use from the drop-down list.
- **Size:** Enter an arrowhead size, or use the up and down arrows to change the current size.
- **Break size:** Enter a value for a break to use with the DIMBREAK command. (I explain the DIMBREAK command later in this chapter.)

On the Leader Structure tab, shown in Figure 14.28, you specify some more detailed information about the leader's line:

- **Maximum Leader Points:** By default, a leader line has two points. You can allow for more vertices by adding points.
- **First Segment Angle:** You can constrain the angle of the first segment, which is horizontal by default. Choose from 15° increments up to 90°.
- **Second Segment Angle:** You can constrain the angle of the second segment, which is horizontal by default. Choose from 15° increments up to 90°.

- **Automatically Include Landing:** In the Landing Settings section, you can decide whether you want a horizontal landing (the short line next to the text). Uncheck the check box if you don't want one.

- **Set Landing Distance:** To specify the length of the landing line, check this check box and enter a value in units.

- **Annotative:** In the Scale section, check this check box to make the multileaders annotative, as explained earlier in this section. If the multileaders are not annotative, you can automatically scale them to the scale of the viewport or specify a scale for all multileaders.

FIGURE 14.28

The Leader Structure tab of the Modify Multileader Style dialog box lets you specify detailed information about the leader line.

The Content tab offers settings related to text and the label part of the leader. First, you specify the Multileader Type, which can be Mtext, a block, or nothing at the end of a leader.

- **Mtext:** If you choose Mtext (multiline text), you specify default text content (if any), the text style, text angle, and text color. You specify the text height (which is the paper height if the style is annotative). You can force the text to be left justified in all situations. Check the Frame Text check box to put a box around the text. Finally, you specify how the landing line attaches to the text and the gap between the landing line and the text.

- **Block:** If you choose a block, you either specify one of several standard blocks or your own block (User Block). The standard blocks are detail callout, slot, circle, box, hexagon, and triangle. The blocks contain attributes (discussed in Chapter 18) that allow you to add a number (or a letter) inside each shape. For example, you might label various parts of the drawing A, B, and C. Usually, you would then have some annotation elsewhere to provide further information about these objects. You also choose how the landing line attaches to the block and the block's color.

Throughout this process, the preview window displays a representation of how the multileader will look. Note, however, that several features depend on how you insert the leader. For example, you don't see any difference in the preview when you constrain the leader line's angles. When you're done, click OK and then Close to return to your drawing.

Your multileader style is now current, and you can use it to draw multileaders. To change a current style, choose it from the Multileader Style Control drop-down list on the Multileader toolbar or the Multileaders control panel of the Dashboard. To change the style of an existing multileader, select it and choose the desired style.

Aligning and combining leaders

Two commands allow you to align multileaders and combine them. You align leaders to make them look more orderly, using the MLEADERALIGN command. There are several options that you can use, depending on the desired result.

 To start the command, choose Align Multileaders from the Multileader toolbar or the Multileaders control panel of the Dashboard. At the `Select multileaders:` prompt, select the multileaders that you want to align.

At the `Select multileader to align to or [Options]:` prompt, you specify the multileader that you want to act as a basis for the others. The command then aligns the other multileaders with this one. At the `Specify direction:` prompt, you can specify a direction for the alignment. This default use of the command does not align the multileader lines or the arrows, just the end of the landing line nearest the Mtext or block. In most cases, you'll probably want to use a vertical alignment; in this case, the ends of the landing lines align, all in a row. However, you can use any direction. As you move the cursor, you see a preview of the results. When you like what you see, click.

> **TIP** When you select multileaders for the MLEADERALIGN command, you can include other objects, and the command filters them out. This makes it easy to use a window to select a number of multileaders that are interspersed among other objects.

Instead of selecting the multileader to align to, you can select the Options option and choose one of the following sub-options:

- **Distribute:** Lets you specify the two points between which the landing lines of all the selected multileaders fit, evenly spaced. For example, you can evenly space four multileaders between two points in this way. After you use this option, the command continues to default to this mode so that you can distribute other sets of multileaders. Use Options to switch to another mode.
- **Make leader segments parallel:** Makes the leader lines parallel, without changing their endpoints. Select the multileader that you want to align the others to. After you use this option, the command continues to default to this mode. Use Options to switch to another mode.
- **Specify spacing:** You specify a spacing, in units, between each of the multileaders. Then you specify which multileader to align the others to and the direction; all of them line up (according to the ends of their landing lines), spaced according to the spacing you specified. After you use this option, the command continues to default to this mode. Use Options to switch to another mode.
- **Use current spacing:** Uses the current spacing between the ends of the landing lines. This is the default mode; as described previously, you specify which multileader to align the others to and the direction.

The MLEADERCOLLECT command works only with multileaders that use blocks as their content. The purpose of this command is to group separate leaders into one leader with all of the blocks connected. For example, if you are using multileaders to point out objects that need additional annotation, multiple comments might apply to one object. You would then need a multileader that ended with more than one letter or number. Figure 14.29 shows three individual multileaders before and after being collected, using a vertical arrangement.

FIGURE 14.29

You can collect several multileaders that end in blocks into one multileader.

To collect a multileader, remember that you need a style that uses blocks rather than Mtext. To collect them, choose Collect Multileaders from the Multileader toolbar or the Multileaders control panel of the Dashboard. At the Select multileaders: prompt, select the multileaders in the order you want them to appear. This is important, because the command groups them according to how you select them.

However, the command also uses the last multileader you choose for its final location. For example, if you first choose a block labeled 1 and then choose a block labeled 2, the final multileader will point to the location of label 2. If necessary, you can easily move the multileader using its grips.

At the Select multileaders: prompt, choose the multileaders, taking into account the final order and location you want, as I just described. At the Specify collected multileader location or [Vertical/Horizontal/Wrap]: prompt, specify where the blocks will now appear. You can see a preview as you move the cursor. You can also choose one of the following options:

- **Vertical:** Places the blocks in a vertical line.
- **Horizontal:** Places the blocks in a horizontal line.
- **Wrap:** Lets you specify either a width or a number of blocks. After that, the blocks wrap to the next line.

After you choose an option, the previous prompt repeats. Specify a location for the collected multileader.

AUTOCAD ONLY The Express Tools include the QLDETACHSET command, which detaches a leader's annotation from the leader line, to create two separate objects. Choose Express ➪ Dimension ➪ Leader Tools ➪ Detach Leaders from Annotation. QLATTACH attaches leaders and MText objects. Choose Express ➪ Dimension ➪ Leader Tools ➪ Attach Leader to Annotation. These tools work with leaders that you create with the QLEADER command; they don't apply to the new multileaders.

The drawing used in the following exercise on drawing multileaders, ab14-e.dwg, is in the Drawings folder on the DVD.

STEPS: Drawing Multileaders

1. Open ab14-e.dwg from your DVD.

2. Save the file as ab14-06.dwg in your AutoCAD Bible folder. This is a drawing of a set of pulleys, as shown in Figure 14.30. Display either the Multileader toolbar (right-click any toolbar and choose Multileader) or the Multileaders control panel of the Dashboard (choose Tools ➪ Palettes ➪ Dashboard and, if necessary, right-click the Dashboard and choose Control Panels ➪ Multileaders). OSNAP should be turned off. Click the LWT button on the status bar to turn it on (if necessary).

FIGURE 14.30

A set of pulleys.

3. Choose Multileader Style from the Multileader toolbar or from the Multileaders control panel of the Dashboard to open the Multileader Style Manager. Click New, enter **Bold** in the New Style Name text box, make sure that the Annotative check box is checked, and click Continue. You'll create a multileader style that stands out by its color and width.

4. On the Leader Format tab, choose Green from the Color drop-down list. Choose 0.40 mm from the Lineweight drop-down list.

5. On the Leader Structure tab, check the Set Landing Distance check box (if necessary) and change the value to 1/2.

6. On the Content tab, change the Text Style to DIMTXT. Check the Frame Text check box. Click OK to return to the Multileader Style Manager. The Bold style should be selected. Click Close to return to your drawing. You should see the Bold style displayed in the Multileader Style Control drop-down list of the Multileader toolbar or the Multileaders control panel of the Dashboard.

7. Choose Multileader from the Multileader toolbar or the Multileaders control panel of the Dashboard. The Select Annotation Scale dialog box may open to remind you to set the annotation scale. Leave the default of 1:1 and click OK.

Follow the prompts:

```
Specify leader arrowhead location or [leader Landing first/Content
first/Options] <Options>: Pick ❶ in Figure 14.30 (near but not on
the drawing object).
Specify leader landing location: Pick ❷.
The In-Place Text Editor opens. Enter BREAK EDGES ↵. Enter TYP (8)
PLACES. Click anywhere outside the editor.
```

8. Repeat the MULTILEADER command. Pick points ❸ and then ❹ in Figure 14.30. This time, type **DRILL 'F' HOLE**. Again, click anywhere outside the editor to place the multileader.

9. Repeat the MULTILEADER command. Pick points ❺ and ❻. The text should be **1/16 R**. If the AutoStack Properties dialog box appears after you type 1/16, uncheck the Enable AutoStacking check box and click OK. Click outside the editor to place the multileader.

10. To add a leader to the last multileader, click Add Leader from the Multileader toolbar or the Multileaders control panel of the Dashboard. Select the last leader that you drew. Specify ❼ and then press Enter.

11. Save your drawing. It should look like Figure 14.31.

FIGURE 14.31

The pulleys with three multileaders.

Using Quick Dimension

Quick Dimension enables you to dimension several objects at one time. You can use Quick Dimension for baseline, continued, and ordinate dimensions. You can also dimension multiple circles and arcs. Later in this chapter, I explain how you can use Quick Dimension to edit dimensions as well. Although Quick Dimension may seem like the answer to all of your dimension-related prayers, you can't use it in every case. However, it works well in "mass-production" situations. Dimensions created with the QDIM command are fully associative, so that any changes that you make to objects automatically update their associated dimensions.

AUTOCAD ONLY The Quick Dimension feature is not available in AutoCAD LT.

Here's how it works, in three easy steps:

1. Choose Quick Dimension from the Dimension toolbar or the Dimensions control panel of the Dashboard.

2. At the `Select geometry to dimension:` prompt, select all of the objects that you want to dimension. You can't use object snaps; you need to select objects. If you select an object in error, type **r** ↵ and then pick the object again to remove it. Then type **a** ↵ to start adding objects again.

3. At the `Specify dimension line position, or [Continuous/Staggered/Baseline/Ordinate/Radius/Diameter/datumPoint/Edit/seTtings]` `<Continuous>:` prompt, right-click and choose the type of dimension that you want to create. Figure 14.32 shows a set of continuous dimensions. The Datum Point option sets a new base point for baseline and ordinate dimensions. You can press Enter to use the type of dimension that you just used previously because that shows as the default. The command immediately creates the dimensions for you.

FIGURE 14.32

A set of continuous dimensions created with Quick Dimension.

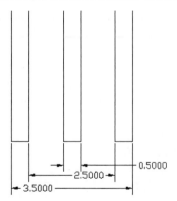

ON the DVD-ROM The drawing used in the following exercise on using Quick Dimension to create dimensions, ab14-f.dwg, is in the Drawings folder on the DVD.

STEPS: Using Quick Dimension to Create Dimensions

1. Open ab14-f.dwg from your DVD.

2. Save the file as ab14-07.dwg in your AutoCAD Bible folder. This is the same drawing that you used in the previous exercise, except that some of the dimensions have been removed (see Figure 14.33). OSNAP should be turned off. If the Dimension toolbar isn't displayed, right-click any toolbar and choose Dimension. Alternatively, display the Dashboard with its Dimensions control panel. (Choose Tools ⇨ Palettes ⇨ Dashboard and, if necessary, right-click the Dashboard and choose Control Panels ⇨ Dimensions.)

FIGURE 14.33

You can use Quick Dimension to dimension the circles and create continuous dimensions.

3. Choose Quick Dimension from the Dimension toolbar or the Dimensions control panel of the Dashboard. Follow the prompts:

```
Select geometry to dimension: Pick the circle at ❶ in Figure 14.33.
Select geometry to dimension: Pick the circle at ❷.
Select geometry to dimension: ↵
Specify dimension line position, or
[Continuous/Staggered/Baseline/Ordinate/Radius/Diameter/datum
Point/Edit/seTtings]
<Staggered>: Right-click and choose Radius.
Specify dimension line position, or
[Continuous/Staggered/Baseline/Ordinate/Radius/Diameter/datum
Point/Edit/seTtings]
<Radius>: Pick a point on the left circle at about 80 degrees from
the right quadrant.
```

Quick Dimension places the radius dimensions.

4. Repeat the QDIM command. Follow the prompts:

```
Select geometry to dimension: Pick the line at ❸ in Figure 14.33.
Select geometry to dimension: Pick the line at ❹.
Select geometry to dimension: Pick the vertical centerline at ❺.
Select geometry to dimension: Pick the vertical centerline at ❻.
Select geometry to dimension: Pick the line at ❼.
Select geometry to dimension: ↵
Specify dimension line position, or
[Continuous/Staggered/Baseline/Ordinate/Radius/Diameter/datumPoint/Ed
it/seTtings]
<Staggered>: Right-click and choose Baseline.
```

```
Specify dimension line position, or
[Continuous/Staggered/Baseline/Ordinate/Radius/Diameter/datumPoint/Ed
it/seTtings]
<Baseline>: Pick a point below the model.
```

Quick Dimension places the baseline dimensions.

5. Save your drawing. It should look approximately like Figure 14.34.

FIGURE 14.34

The model with added radius and baseline dimensions.

Creating Inspection Dimensions

Inspection dimensions specify how often you want the manufacturer of a part to check its measurements, and sometimes to what tolerance. For example, you may want 50 percent of the parts to be checked and require that they be accurate to within 1/16 of an inch. Inspection dimensions allow you to add a label and inspection percentage to an existing dimension. Figure 14.35 shows an inspection dimension, using a rounded frame.

NEW FEATURE   Inspection dimensions are new for AutoCAD and AutoCAD LT 2008. You create inspection dimensions by selecting an existing dimension.

FIGURE 14.35

An inspection dimension adds a label and an inspection percentage to a dimension for the purpose of quality control.

 To create an inspection dimension, first select an existing dimension. Then choose Inspection from the Dimension toolbar, or Diminspect from the Dimensions control panel of the Dashboard, to open the Inspection Dimension dialog box, shown in Figure 14.36.

FIGURE 14.36

Use the Inspection Dimension dialog box to format inspection dimensions.

If you haven't already selected a dimension, you can click the Select Dimensions button and do so at this point. In the Shape section, choose the Round, Angular, or None option. In the Label/Inspection Rate section, check the Label check box if you want to add a text label. Then enter the text of the label. The Inspection Rate check box is checked by default. Enter an inspection rate and click OK.

To change the values of an inspection dimension, select it and use the Misc section of the Properties palette.

Creating Geometric Tolerances

You can use the TOLERANCE command to create geometric tolerances. (For another way to specify tolerances, see the "Formatting tolerances" section in Chapter 15.) This command creates feature control frames, which define tolerances. This method of denoting tolerances conforms to international standards such as ISO (International Standards Organization), ANSI (American National Standards Institute), or JIS (Japanese Industrial Standards). Figure 14.37 shows a drawing that uses tolerance feature-control frames.

FIGURE 14.37

An example of tolerance feature-control frames.

Thanks to Jerry Butterfield of Clow Value Company, Oskaloosa, Iowa, for this drawing.

Starting the tolerance frame

Creating a tolerance frame is a step-by-step process that depends on what information you want to include. To start the frame, choose Tolerance from the Dimension toolbar, which opens the Geometric Tolerance dialog box, shown in Figure 14.38.

FIGURE 14.38

The Geometric Tolerance dialog box.

Use this dialog box to build the frame. The frame enables you to create two rows of two tolerances and three datum references (for up to three dimensions), as well as a projected tolerance zone value, and a symbol and datum identifier. You'll rarely, if ever, use all of the features in the frame.

Follow these steps to build the frame:

1. Click the first Sym box to open the Symbol dialog box, shown in Figure 14.39.

FIGURE 14.39

Use the Symbol dialog box to choose the symbol for the type of geometry for which you want to specify tolerance.

2. Choose the symbol for the geometric characteristic that you are tolerancing. (Table 14.1 explains these symbols.) If you don't need a symbol, click the blank box. The Symbol dialog box disappears.

3. To insert a diameter symbol before the first tolerance, click the black Dia box to the left of the text box in the Tolerance 1 section.

4. Type the tolerance value in the Value box.

5. If you want to specify a material condition, click the black MC box to the right of the text box. The Material Condition dialog box opens, as shown in Figure 14.40. Choose the symbol that you want. The dialog box disappears.

FIGURE 14.40

The Material Condition dialog box.

6. If desired, complete a second tolerance.

7. If desired, type a datum in the Datum box of the Datum 1 section, usually A.

8. If desired, add a material condition, using the same method described in Step 5.

9. If desired, type in datum references in the Datum 2 and Datum 3 sections, usually B and C with material conditions.

10. If you need to specify a projected tolerance zone for a perpendicular part, type a value in the Height box. Then click the Projected Tolerance Zone box to insert the Projected Tolerance Zone symbol.

11. Finally, if you want to specify a datum identifier, type the identifier letter in the Datum Identifier box.

12. Click OK to return to your drawing.

If you choose a material condition symbol and then change your mind, click the material condition box again and choose the blank square to delete your symbol.

TABLE 14.1

Tolerance Symbols

Symbol	Name	Symbol	Name
⊕	Position	▱	Flatness
◎	Concentricity	○	Circularity
=	Symmetry	—	Straightness
//	Parallelism	◠	Surface profile
⊥	Perpendicularity	◠	Line profile
∠	Angularity	↗	Circular runout
⌀	Cylindricity	↗↗	Total runout

Inserting the tolerance frame

After you complete the frame, you're returned to your drawing with the `Enter tolerance location:` prompt on the command line. Specify any point to insert the frame.

 You can create a matching Datum reference to place on your model by creating a tolerance frame with no symbol and only the Datum letter.

Editing a tolerance frame

To edit a geometric tolerance, double-click the tolerance frame. The Properties palette opens. To change the text click the Text Override item and then click the Ellipsis button at the right. The Geometric Tolerance dialog box opens, and you can make any changes that you need. Click OK to return to your drawing.

ON the DVD-ROM The drawing used in the following exercise on creating geometric tolerances, `ab14-g.dwg`, is in the `Drawings` folder on the DVD.

STEPS: Creating Geometric Tolerances

1. Open `ab14-g.dwg` from your DVD.
2. Save the file as `ab14-08.dwg` in your `AutoCAD Bible` folder. This drawing of a gear operator is shown in Figure 14.41. The Dim layer is current. If the Dimension toolbar is not visible, right-click any toolbar and choose Dimension. Alternatively, display the Dashboard with its Dimensions control panel. (Choose Tools ➪ Palettes ➪ Dashboard and, if necessary, right-click the Dashboard and choose Control Panels ➪ Dimensions.)

FIGURE 14.41

A mechanical drawing using geometric tolerances.

3. Choose Tolerance from the Dimension toolbar or the Dimensions control panel of the Dashboard. In the Geometric Tolerance dialog box, click the top-left box, labeled Sym.

4. The Symbol dialog box opens. Choose the top-left symbol (for position).

5. In the Tolerance 1 section of the Geometric Tolerance dialog box, click the next black box, which is the Dia box, to insert the diameter symbol. In the Value box, type **.004**. Click the next black box, which is the MC box. In the Material Condition dialog box, choose the first image tile (for Maximum material condition).

6. In the Datum 1 section, type **B** in the Datum box. Click OK.

7. At the Enter tolerance location: prompt, pick ❶ in Figure 14.41 to place the geometric tolerance.

8. Save your drawing. It should look like Figure 14.42.

FIGURE 14.42

The drawing with the added geometric tolerance frame.

Editing Dimensions

Dimensions have many properties — text size, arrowhead size, text placement, and so on. You change most of these properties by changing the dimension style — either globally changing all dimensions using that style, or overriding a dimension style setting for a particular dimension. The next chapter covers dimension styles, but here I cover several other ways to edit dimensions.

Editing associativity

By default, new drawings created in AutoCAD 2008 and AutoCAD LT 2008 are associative. However, drawings created in releases prior to 2002 are not associative.

The DIMASSOC system variable specifies whether dimensions are associative. Here are the settings:

- **0** creates exploded dimensions. Each part of the dimension is a separate object, and there is no association between the dimension and the object that it dimensions.
- **1** creates nonassociative dimensions. The dimension is all one object but is not updated if the object that it dimensions is changed.
- **2** creates associative dimensions. The dimension is all one object and is updated if the object that it dimensions is changed.

If you open old (pre-2002 release) drawings and save them as 2008 drawings, you should change the DIMASSOC system variable's value to 2.

DIMREASSOCIATE

Use the DIMREASSOCIATE command to associate dimensions with their objects. You need to use this command when you open drawings created in releases prior to 2002 in AutoCAD 2008 or AutoCAD LT 2008. You might also need to use this command when dimensions become disassociated from their objects, perhaps through some editing process, or to reassociate dimensions after you've disassociated them for some reason.

To use DIMREASSOCIATE, follow these steps:

1. Choose Dimension ⇨ Reassociate Dimensions.
2. At the `Select objects:` prompt, select the dimensions that you want to associate. Press Enter to end object selection.

   You see a prompt that varies according to the type of dimension you've selected. For example, for linear dimensions, you see the `Specify first extension line origin or [Select object] <next>:` prompt. At the same time, you see a marker in the form of an X that corresponds to the prompt, as shown in Figure 14.43. The marker indicates an *association point* (a point that connects an object and all or part of its dimension). If the X has a box around it, the dimension is already associated with the point marked by the X.

 If you use the wheel of a mouse to pan or zoom, the X disappears. Press Esc and start the command again or type 'redraw ↵.

FIGURE 14.43

When you associate a dimension with an object, an association point appears on the object.

FLAT BLANK LAYOUT

3. Use an object snap to specify the location of the X (whether the same as shown or a different location) or use the Select Object option to select an object (right-click and choose Select Object). To skip to the next prompt without associating the dimension to the marked point, press Enter.

4. Continue to respond to the prompts in turn. The command prompts you through all of the dimensions you selected.

 When specifying object snaps, be careful that you choose the point you want. For example, if you use an endpoint object snap where two lines meet, you cannot be sure of which line's endpoint you've chosen. When you move or stretch the line that you expect to be associated with the dimension, you may find that the dimension doesn't budge. That's because it's actually associated with a different line. Selecting the object itself is often a better solution, because the dimension is associated with the object.

DIMDISASSOCIATE

Occasionally, you may want to edit a dimension in such a way that you need to remove its associativity. Perhaps you need to squeeze it into a tight corner. For these times, use the DIMDISASSOCIATE command by typing it on the command line. At the prompt, select the dimensions that you want to disassociate from their objects.

NOTE You cannot disassociate dimensions that are on locked layers. Unlock the layer first and then disassociate the dimension.

DIMREGEN

The DIMREGEN command updates the locations of all associative dimensions. This command is needed only in three unusual situations:

- If you pan or zoom with a wheel mouse in a paper space layout while model space is active
- If you open a drawing containing dimensioned objects that have been edited with a previous version of AutoCAD or AutoCAD LT
- If you open a drawing containing external references that are dimensioned in the current drawing, and dimensioned objects in the external reference have been changed

Using the DIMEDIT command

The DIMEDIT command offers four ways to edit dimensions. The advantage of this command is that you can change more than one dimension at a time. Choose Dimension Edit from the Dimension toolbar. The command responds with the Enter type of dimension editing [Home/New/Rotate/Oblique] <Home>: prompt. Right-click to choose one of the options:

■ **Home:** Moves dimension text to its default position as defined by the dimension style.

■ **New:** Lets you type new text to replace the existing text. The In-Place Text Editor opens, showing zeroes to represent the dimension text. You can use this option to add a suffix, such as *TYP* (typical), to several dimensions.

■ **Rotate:** Rotates the dimension text. This works like the rotation angle for text.

■ **Oblique:** Angles the extension lines of the dimension. Use this when you have several dimensions close together that interfere with each other. Specify the final angle of the extension lines, *not* the rotation from the current angle.

The Oblique item on the Dimension menu executes the DIMEDIT command with the Oblique option.

As soon as you choose an option, DIMEDIT prompts you to select objects. You can select as many dimensions as you wish. You have the opportunity to use the DIMEDIT command in an exercise after the next section.

Using the DIMTEDIT command

The DIMTEDIT command repositions dimension text. To start the command, choose Dimension Text Edit from the Dimension toolbar. Although its name gives the impression that you can edit the text content, you can only change its position. Also, you can edit only one dimension at a time. The command responds with the Select dimension: prompt. Select a dimension.

At the Specify new location for dimension text or [Left/Right/Center/Home/Angle]: prompt, you can use the cursor to pick a text location. You can also right-click and choose one of the options:

■ **Left:** Left-justifies the text of linear, radial, or diameter dimensions.

■ **Right:** Right-justifies the text of linear, radial, or diameter dimensions.

■ **Center:** Centers the text of linear, radial, or diameter dimensions.

■ **Home:** Returns dimension text to its default position and angle.

■ **Angle:** Rotates dimension text. This option is equivalent to the Rotate option of the DIMEDIT command.

The drawing used in the following exercise on using DIMEDIT and DIMTEDIT to edit dimensions, ab14-h.dwg, is in the Drawings folder on the DVD.

STEPS: Using DIMEDIT and DIMTEDIT to Edit Dimensions

1. Open ab14-h.dwg from your DVD.

2. Save the file as ab14-09.dwg in your AutoCAD Bible folder. This is a civil engineering drawing whose dimensions need some editing (see Figure 14.44). If the Dimension toolbar isn't visible, right-click any toolbar and choose Dimension.

3. The dimension at ❶ in Figure 14.44 is not in the proper units because the text was entered explicitly as 14.41. To correct this error, choose Dimension Edit from the Dimension toolbar. At the `Enter type of dimension editing [Home/New/Rotate/Oblique] <Home>:` prompt, right-click and choose New. The In-Place Text Editor opens, showing zeroes. Because you want the original text, click OK. At the `Select objects:` prompt, pick ❶. Press Enter to end object selection. (You could correct several dimensions this way.) This action corrects the dimension, automatically creating the text in the current units.

 4. The dimension text at ❷ in Figure 14.44 is too close to the dimension line of the vertical dimension that crosses it. Choose Dimension Text Edit from the Dimension toolbar. At the `Select dimension:` prompt, pick ❷. At the `Specify new location for dimension text or [Left/Right/Center/Home/Angle]:` prompt, right-click and choose Right. This action moves the text to the right.

5. Save your drawing.

FIGURE 14.44

A dimensioned civil engineering drawing.

AUTOCAD ONLY The Express Tools command, DIMREASSOC, does the same thing that you accomplished in Step 3 of this exercise — restoring the default measurement value to modified dimension text. Choose Express ➪ Dimension ➪ Reset Dim Text Value.

Flipping dimension arrows

Sometimes you might want to place an arrow outside the extension line, but facing inward. For example, you might do this in a tight space. Figure 14.45 shows a dimension with a flipped arrow.

FIGURE 14.45

You can flip an arrow so that it displays outside the extension line pointing inward.

To flip an arrow, pick a dimension nearest the arrow that you want to flip. Then right-click and choose Flip Arrow from the shortcut menu. Repeat the process to unflip the arrow.

Editing dimension text

You can edit dimension text as you would any other multiline text object. Choose Modify ⇨ Object ⇨ Text ⇨ Edit. At the `Select an annotation object or [Undo]:` prompt, choose the dimension. The In-Place Text Editor opens. Using the In-Place Text Editor for dimension text has already been covered in this chapter under the MText option of the dimensioning commands.

Using the Properties palette to edit dimensions

You can edit dimensions by using the Properties palette just as you can edit the properties of any other object. Double-click any dimension to open the Properties palette. You see the properties of the dimensions that you can edit.

Many of these settings make more sense after you learn about dimension styles, which are covered in the next chapter. For example, the listings for Primary Units, Alternate Units, Fit, Lines & Arrows, Text, and so on duplicate the tabs on the New Dimension Style and Modify Dimension Style dialog boxes. You can change the color, layer, lineweight, and linetype. To override the automatic dimension text, enter the text in the Text Override field of the Text section of the Properties palette.

TIP You can create a background mask like the one that you can create for multiline text. (For more information, see Chapter 13.) If dimension text covers other objects, select the dimension and open the Properties palette (Ctrl+1). Choose a color from the Fill Color drop-down list in the Text section. For the background mask to work, the dimension needs to be on top of any other objects that it overlaps. To bring a dimension to the top, use the TEXTTOFRONT command.

Changing annotative scales

Dimension and multileader styles can be annotative, meaning that they can automatically change scale, based on the scale of a viewport on a layout. (I discussed viewports and layouts in Chapter 17.) I've mentioned in this chapter how to make a dimension and multileader style annotative.

You can change the annotative scales of any dimension or multileader that uses an annotative style, by using the OBJECTSCALE command. Follow these steps:

1. Select the dimension or multileader. (You can select more than one.)
2. Open the Properties palette. In the Misc section, click the Annotative Scale item to display the Ellipsis button.

3. Click the Ellipsis button to open the Annotation Object Scale dialog box.

- To add an annotation scale, click the Add button. Choose a scale from the Add Scales to Object dialog box and click OK.

- To delete an annotation scale, select it and click the Delete button.

4. Click OK.

 You can also select one or more annotative objects, right-click in the drawing area, and choose Annotative Object Scale.

Spacing dimensions equally apart

Sometimes, after you've created a number of linear or angular dimensions, you realize that they would look neater if they were equally spaced apart from each other. Rather than recreate or move them, you can use the DIMSPACE command to space existing dimensions. You can let the command decide on the spacing automatically, or you can specify a spacing.

NEW FEATURE The DIMSPACE command is new for AutoCAD and AutoCAD LT 2008.

In order for this command to work, the dimensions must meet the following conditions:

- They must be linear or angular dimensions.

- They must be a group of the same kind of dimension. For example, you might have all linear dimensions. If one is rotated, they must all be rotated; if one is aligned, they must all be aligned.

- The dimensions must be parallel (for linear) or concentric (for angular).

- The dimensions must share an extension line.

 To space dimensions, choose Dimension Space from the Dimension toolbar or Dimspace from the Dimensions control panel of the Dashboard. At the `Select base dimension:` prompt, select a dimension close to which you want to place the other dimensions. At the `Select dimensions to space:` prompt, select the rest of the dimensions that you want to space.

At the `Enter value or [Auto] <Auto>:` prompt, enter a spacing or use the Auto option to let the command figure out the spacing itself. You can use a value of 0 to align the dimensions along the same horizontal or vertical line.

Breaking dimensions

It's not good form for dimensions to cross other dimensions or objects. Many disciplines break a dimension or extension line where it crosses an object with a small space. This gives the appearance that the object is in front of the dimension. You can break dimensions or multileaders using the DIMBREAK command.

NEW FEATURE The DIMBREAK command is new for AutoCAD and AutoCAD LT 2008.

The great feature of DIMBREAK is that if you move the object to another location where it still crosses the dimension, the break moves accordingly.

 To break a dimension or multileader, choose Dimension Break on the Dimension toolbar or Dimbreak from the Dimensions control panel of the Dashboard. At the `Select a dimension or [Multiple]:` prompt, select the dimension you want to break. At the `Select object to break dimension or [Auto/Restore/Manual] <Auto>:` prompt, select the object that crosses the dimension. The `Select object to break dimension:` prompt repeats, so that you can select another object that crosses the dimension, if any. Otherwise, press Enter to end the command.

You can use the Manual option to specify two points on the dimension line or extension line. In this way, you can set the size of the break yourself. However, if you use the Manual option, the break does not update if you move the crossing object.

Use the Multiple option at the first prompt to create breaks in more than one dimension at a time. You then select the dimensions. At the `Enter an option [Break/Restore] <Break>:` prompt, choose the Break option so that you can break all of the dimensions.

If you want to remove an existing break, use the Restore option.

You can set a break size when you create a dimension or multileader style. For dimensions, use the Break Size text box on the Symbols and Arrows tab of the Modify Dimension Style dialog box. For Multileaders, use the Break Size text box on the Leader Format tab of the Modify Multileader Style dialog box.

Using Quick Dimension to edit dimensions

You can also use Quick Dimension in AutoCAD (but not AutoCAD LT) to edit dimensions, whether created with QDIM or some other dimensioning command. When you select the geometry and dimensions you want to edit, you see an X at each eligible edit point, as shown in Figure 14.46.

FIGURE 14.46

When you edit with QDIM, you see an X at eligible edit points.

Here's what you can do with QDIM:

- You can join two dimensions by removing the edit points between them.
- You can split a dimension into two dimensions by adding edit points within the existing dimension.
- You can move the dimension line.
- You can change the type of dimension.

CAUTION Editing with QDIM works best when the geometry is simple. Unless you can select only the geometry and dimensions that you want to work with, you'll end up changing dimensions that you don't want to edit.

To edit dimensions with QDIM, follow these steps:

1. Choose Quick Dimension from the Dimension toolbar or from the Dimensions control panel of the Dashboard.

2. At the Select geometry to dimension: prompt, select the geometry and the dimensions that you want to edit.

3. At the Specify dimension line position, or [Continuous/Staggered/Baseline/Ordinate/Radius/Diameter/datumPoint/Edit/seTtings] <Continuous>: prompt, right-click and choose Edit. You see a cross at each eligible edit point.

4. At the Indicate dimension point to remove, or [Add/eXit] <eXit>: prompt, you can:

   - Select the points of the dimensions you want to remove. If you see two possible edit points in line with each other that could be creating the dimension you want to remove, select both of them.
   - Right-click and choose Add. Use object snaps to add one or more points.
   - Right-click and choose Exit to continue with the command.

5. At the Specify dimension line position, or [Continuous/Staggered/Baseline/Ordinate/Radius/Diameter/datumPoint/Edit/settings] <Continuous>: prompt, right-click and choose an option if you want to change the type of dimension.

6. The prompt repeats. Pick a location for the new set of dimensions.

7. Press Enter to end the command and update the dimensions.

Using grips to edit dimensions

Grips are ideal for moving dimension lines and text. The grips at the dimension line endpoints and the text insertion point are quite useful for making adjustments in dimensions.

To move a dimension line closer or farther from the dimensioned object, pick the dimension to display the grips. Pick one of the grips at the endpoints of the dimension line to highlight it. The Specify stretch point or [Base point/Copy/ Undo/eXit]: prompt appears. Drag the dimension line to the desired location. Press Esc to remove the grips.

To move dimension text, pick the dimension to display the grips. Pick the grip on the dimension text to highlight it. Drag the dimension text to its desired location.

 TIP For best results, turn ORTHO on while trying to drag the dimension line or the dimension text. Polar tracking also works well.

You can also grip-edit multileaders in the same way. However, there are also two triangular grips that you can use to change the length of the landing line.

Editing objects and dimensions together

Dimension associativity enables you to edit objects and have the dimensions automatically adjust to the new object measurements. Stretching the object with the STRETCH command or grips is usually the best way to accomplish this. The object and the dimension adjust at the same time. Figure 14.47 shows a house plan before and after stretching to move a window 6 inches to the left. The crossing window included the entire window, and so it was simply moved. However, the crossing window crossed the walls on either side of the window and both dimensions so that they were stretched 6 inches to the left. Notice the change in the dimension text, indicating the new measurements.

FIGURE 14.47

When you stretch objects, the dimensions are automatically updated.

ON the DVD-ROM   The drawing in the following exercise on using DDEDIT, QDIM, grips, and STRETCH to edit dimensions, ab14-i.dwg, is in the Drawings folder on the DVD.

STEPS: Using DDEDIT, QDIM, Grips, and STRETCH to Edit Dimensions

1. Open ab14-i.dwg from your DVD.

2. Save the file as ab14-10.dwg in your AutoCAD Bible folder. This is a cross-section of a valve part, as shown in Figure 14.48. If the Dimension toolbar isn't visible, right-click any toolbar and choose Dimension. Alternatively, display the Dashboard with its Dimensions control panel. (Choose Tools ⇨ Palettes ⇨ Dashboard and, if necessary, right-click the Dashboard and choose Control Panels ⇨ Dimensions.)

FIGURE 14.48

A dimensioned cross-section of a valve part.

3. To replace the dimension marked Ht., choose Modify ➪ Object ➪ Text ➪ Edit. At the `Select an annotation object or [Undo]:` prompt, choose the dimension at ❶ in Figure 14.48. The In-Place Text Editor opens with the text displayed. Select the current text and type `<>`. Click OK. The command automatically creates the original measured dimension. Press Enter to end the command.

4. If you are using AutoCAD LT, skip to Step 5. Select the two dimensions marked ❷ in Figure 14.48. Also select the cyan centerline and the two green hidden lines. Choose Quick Dimension from the Dimension toolbar or from the Dimensions control panel of the Dashboard. At the first prompt, right-click and choose Edit. At the `Indicate dimension point to remove, or [Add/eXit] <eXit>:` prompt, choose the two edit points (each marked with an X) on the cyan centerline. Right-click and choose eXit. At the `Specify dimension line position, or [Continuous/Staggered/Baseline/Ordinate/Radius/Diameter/ datumPoint/Edit/seTtings] <Continuous>:` prompt, place the dimension line where it was previously. (You can use the outside arrows as a guide.)

5. Pick the dimension at ❶. Press Shift and click the grip on the text and one of the dimension's grips to activate them. Click either of the grips and drag slightly to the left to place the dimension and its text closer to the object that you are dimensioning.

6. Choose Stretch from the Modify toolbar or from the 2D Draw control panel of the Dashboard. Follow the prompts:

```
Select objects: Pick at ❸.
Specify opposite corner: Pick at ❹.
9 found
Select objects: ↵
Specify base point or [Displacement] <Displacement>: 0,-.25 ↵
Specify second point or <use first point as displacement>: ↵
```

The valve part stretches, and the dimension that measures its height changes accordingly.

7. Save your drawing. It should look like Figure 14.49.

FIGURE 14.49

The edited valve part.

Summary

The dimension features in AutoCAD and AutoCAD LT enable you to dimension almost anything. In this chapter, you read about:

- Creating linear, radial, dimension, angular, and ordinate dimensions
- Formatting and creating multileaders
- Dimensioning with the Quick Dimension feature, available in AutoCAD only
- Creating inspection dimensions
- Creating tolerances
- Editing dimensions

In the next chapter, I continue the subject of dimensions by explaining how to gain total control with dimension styles.

Chapter 15

Creating Dimension Styles

IN THIS CHAPTER

Understanding dimension styles

Defining a new dimension style

Changing dimension styles

I n Chapter 14, you drew many dimensions using the default dimension style. However, you can create your own dimension styles to control the way dimensions appear. Now that you're familiar with dimensions, you can learn how to customize them to suit your needs.

Understanding Dimension Styles

You should create your dimension styles before dimensioning. Some drawings have several dimension styles, although a drawing can look confusing if it has too many dimension styles. In general, you create a dimension style, save it in your template drawings, and (you hope) rarely have to deal with it again, except to override a setting for a unique situation.

The various disciplines each have their own standards and customs regarding dimensions. Dimension styles are flexible enough to accommodate any type of dimensioning practice.

 To create a dimension style, choose Dimension Style from the Dimension toolbar or the Dimensions control panel of the Dashboard (or choose Dimension ⇨ Dimension Style) to open the Dimension Style Manager, shown in Figure 15.1. The current dimension style is shown as Standard, which is the default dimension style.

The Dimension Style Manager is the master control room for managing dimensions. Here you create new dimension styles and modify existing ones.

The preset Standard dimension style is most appropriate for mechanical drafting. Whichever type of drafting you do, you'll probably need to make some changes to the default dimension style or create a new dimension style. A preview of the current dimension style is shown at the right side of the dialog box.

FIGURE 15.1

The Dimension Style Manager.

To create a new style, click New to open the Create New Dimension Style dialog box, shown in Figure 15.2. Type a new name in the New Style Name text box. In the Start With drop-down list, choose which existing dimension style you want to use as a basis for the new dimension style. If you have more than one to choose from, choose the style that most resembles the new style you want to create.

FIGURE 15.2

The Create New Dimension Style dialog box.

If you want dimensions that use this dimension style to be annotative, check the Annotative check box. Annotative dimensions are valuable when you will be displaying your model at more than one scale, in separate viewports.

NEW FEATURE AutoCAD 2008 and AutoCAD LT 2008 introduce *annotative* objects, which automatically scale according to the scale of a viewport on a layout. You use a layout to lay out a drawing for plotting, and viewports display various views of the drawing. Each viewport can have a different scale, and annotative objects automatically adjust in size accordingly. I discuss annotative objects more in Chapter 17.

The Use For drop-down list lets you decide whether you want to use the dimension style for all dimensions or only for a specific type of dimension; you can choose from Linear, Angular, Radius, Diameter, Ordinate, or Leaders and Tolerances. Usually, you create a dimension style for all dimension types. Later in this chapter, I explain how to create variants of dimension styles for specific types of dimensions. When you're done, click Continue.

You can also use the Dimension Style Manager to rename an existing dimension style. Click its name to select it. Click it a second time to see an edit box. Type the new name and press Enter.

Defining a New Dimension Style

Dimension styles have many components, and so the process of defining a dimension style is complex. Your task is organized for you by the tabs of the dialog box.

When you click Continue in the Create New Dimension Style dialog box, a second New Dimension Style dialog box opens, as shown in Figure 15.3.

FIGURE 15.3

The New Dimension Style dialog box with the Lines tab displayed.

The New Dimension Style dialog box has the following tabs:

- **Lines:** Sets specifications for dimension lines and extension lines.

- **Symbols and Arrows:** Sets specifications for arrowheads, center marks, the arc length symbol, the jog angle for dimensioning large radii, the linear job height factor, and the break size for breaking dimensions.

- **Text:** Determines the appearance, placement, and alignment of dimension text.

- **Fit:** Sets how text and arrows fit inside narrow dimensions, as well as where text is placed when it doesn't fit in its default position. This tab also allows you to set the scale factor for dimension features, to specify an annotative dimension style, and to specify whether to place a dimension line inside narrow dimensions.

- **Primary Units:** Determines the format and precision for the primary measuring unit for both linear and angular dimensions.

- **Alternate Units:** Determines the format and precision for secondary units, if turned on (such as metric measurements if your primary units are Imperial, or vice versa).

- **Tolerances:** Formats tolerance notation in dimensions.

Managing dimension lines

An important part of defining a dimension style is specifying how the dimension lines and extension lines look, which you do on the Lines tab of the New Dimension Style dialog box. In Chapter 14, Figure 14.1, I illustrate the parts of a dimension. Refer to that figure if you need a refresher.

Dimension lines

To set the color of the dimension line so that it differs from that of the rest of the dimension, click the Color drop-down list and choose a color. Choose Select Color to open the Select Color dialog box if you want to use a nonstandard color. Remember, a dimension is a block — that is, it is one object. The default color is ByBlock so that dimensions take on the color of the current layer or color setting. In general, you should have a separate layer for dimensions, so that the entire dimension is the color set for that layer. Use this setting only if you want the dimension lines to be a different color from your dimension layer color. The arrowheads do not have a separate color setting and always follow the dimension-line setting.

 See Chapter 11 for a discussion of how to use the Select Color dialog box. See Chapter 18 for coverage of blocks.

To specify a linetype for a dimension, choose one from the Linetype drop-down list. If the linetype that you want isn't on the list, then you need to load it. To do this, choose Other to open the Select Linetype dialog box. (For more information on loading linetypes, see Chapter 11.) The default lineweight is ByBlock, which means that it takes on the lineweight of the current layer. To set a lineweight for the dimension line, click the Lineweight drop-down list and choose a lineweight. In general, you want your objects to stand out, so dimensions should have a lineweight the same as, or narrower than, the objects that you're dimensioning.

The Extend Beyond Ticks text box determines how far the dimension lines extend past the extension lines. When you have arrowheads at the ends of the dimension lines, the Extension option is unavailable. However, if you choose Architectural Tick, Oblique, Dot Small, Integral, or None in the Arrowheads section of the dialog box, the Extend Beyond Ticks option becomes available. This type of extension is typical for architectural drafting. Figure 15.4 shows a dimension with an architectural tick and a 0.1-unit extension.

The Baseline spacing text box determines the distance between successive dimension lines when you create baseline dimensions. This specification creates evenly spaced dimension lines. (In Chapter 14, I discuss the DIMSPACE command, which lets you evenly space any linear or angular dimensions.)

FIGURE 15.4

A typical architectural dimension showing the text above one dimension line, an architectural tick, and the dimension line extending slightly beyond the extension lines.

In some dimension styles, the dimension text splits the dimension line into two parts, as shown in Figure 15.5. This creates two dimension lines. You can suppress — that is, turn off — the first or second dimension line (or both dimension lines) by checking the appropriate box (or boxes). The first line is nearest where you specified the first extension-line origin. (If you selected an object instead of specifying two extension-line origins, you may not be able to predict which dimension line is the first and which is the second. Experiment.) You would usually suppress dimension lines when they interfere with other dimensions or with objects in your drawing. (The DIMBREAK command, which I cover in Chapter 14, breaks dimensions where they cross objects. You may be able to break a dimension instead of suppressing one of the dimension lines.)

FIGURE 15.5

A typical mechanical dimension with text splitting two dimension lines.

Extension lines

As with dimension lines, you can pick a color for the extension lines that differs from that of the rest of the dimension. Click the Color drop-down list and choose a color. Choose Select Color to open the Select Color dialog box if you want a nonstandard color. The default color is ByBlock so that extensions take on the color of the current layer or color setting.

You can now choose a separate linetype for each extension line. Choose the linetype that you want from the drop-down lists. If the linetype that you want isn't listed, click Other to open the Select Linetype dialog box, where you can load the linetype that you need.

Extension lines typically extend slightly past the dimension line, as you can see in some of the figures in this chapter. Use the Extend Beyond Dim Lines text box to specify this extension distance.

Extension lines don't usually touch the object that they dimension to make it easier to distinguish the dimension from the object. Use the Offset from Origin text box to define the distance from the specified points on the object to the extension lines.

Extension lines usually vary in length throughout a drawing, depending on the shape of the objects that you're dimensioning. However, sometimes you may want the extension lines to all be the same length, even if they don't reach near their objects. This method avoids dimension lines crossing each other when you're dimensioning a complex shape.

To specify fixed-length extension lines, check the Fixed Length Extension Lines check box and specify the length in the Length text box.

You can suppress the first or second extension line (or both lines) so that either or both are not visible. To do this, check the appropriate box (or boxes). Figure 15.6 shows a dimension with the first extension line suppressed.

FIGURE 15.6

A dimension with the first extension line suppressed.

Defining symbols and arrows

The Symbols and Arrows tab organizes your settings related to arrowheads and certain dimension-related symbols, as shown in Figure 15.7. For example, you can define center marks and arc length symbols on this tab.

FIGURE 15.7

The Symbols and Arrows tab lets you define arrowheads and fine-tune dimension symbols.

Defining arrowheads

The Arrowheads section controls the arrowheads at the ends of dimension lines. You don't actually have to use arrowheads, as you saw in Figure 15.4. You can also set the first and second arrowheads individually. However, if you change the first arrowhead, the second one follows suit, assuming that you want both ends of the dimension to look the same. To specify two different arrowheads, choose an arrowhead in the first drop-down box and then in the second drop-down box.

You can create and use your own arrowhead:

1. In any drawing, create the arrowhead that you want with a unit size of 1.

2. Make a block out of it. For an arrow-shaped block, pick the point of the arrow for the insertion point and create it pointing to the right. You may have to experiment with the right insertion point. Save the block. (See Chapter 18 for instructions on creating blocks. You can't use annotative blocks as arrowheads.)

3. In the first and second drop-down lists, choose User Arrow. The Select Custom Arrow Block dialog box opens, displaying the blocks available in the drawing.

4. Choose the block that you want from the drop-down list.

5. Click OK.

Figure 15.8 shows a dimension with a user arrow.

FIGURE 15.8

A dimension with a user arrow.

> **TIP** You can set a different arrow for leaders. Choose the arrow that you want from the Leader drop-down list.

Set the size of the arrowhead in the Arrow Size text box. As explained later in this chapter in the discussion of scale, you should use the final size that you want to see when the drawing is plotted on paper.

Defining symbols

The Center Marks section of the New Dimension Style dialog box specifies how you want to mark the centers of arcs and circles when you choose Center Mark from the Dimension toolbar (the DIMCENTER command). In the Center Marks section, choose Mark to create a small cross, Line to create a cross plus four lines that cross, or None. Figure 15.9 shows a circle with centerlines and an arc with a center mark.

Specify the size of the center mark or centerline in the text box to the right of the center marks options. For center marks, the size is the distance from the intersection of the two lines to their endpoints. If you use centerlines, the size also determines the distance from the circle quadrants to the end of the centerlines.

FIGURE 15.9

A circle with a centerline and an arc with a center mark.

In the Dimension Break section, specify the break size. A dimension break is a gap in the dimension where it crosses an object. I discuss dimension breaks (the DIMBREAK command) in Chapter 14.

The Arc Length Symbol section is for specifying the location of the symbol used when you dimension arc lengths. By default, the symbol goes before the dimension value, but you can choose to put it on top or omit it completely.

The Radius Jog Dimension section lets you specify the angle used when you create a jogged dimension for circles or arcs with large radii. A jogged dimension is a small dimension that doesn't reach to the center of the circle or arc. For more information on jogged dimensions, see the section "Creating radial dimensions" in Chapter 14.

In the Linear Jog Dimension section, specify a jog height factor for linear jogs. A jog is a zigzag symbol that indicates that the object is not drawn to scale, usually due to space limitations. For more information, see the section "Creating jogged dimension lines" in Chapter 14. You specify the size in relation to the text height for the dimension. The default is 1.5 times the text height. I discuss dimension text height in the next section.

Because the Standard dimension style is closest to mechanical drafting standards, in the following exercise, you start to create an architectural dimension style using the Standard style as a base. This requires you to make a maximum number of changes, thereby letting you become as familiar as possible with the dimension style settings. Here you practice controlling dimension lines and arrows.

 The drawing used in the following exercise on controlling dimension lines and arrows, `ab15-a.dwg`, is in the `Drawings` folder on the DVD.

STEPS: Controlling Dimension Lines and Arrows

1. Open `ab15-a.dwg` from your DVD.

2. Save the file as `ab15-01.dwg` in your `AutoCAD Bible` folder. This drawing is an elevation of a garage, as shown in Figure 15.10. ORTHO and OSNAP should be on. Set running object snaps for endpoint and intersection. The Dim layer is current. If the Dimension toolbar is not visible, right-click any toolbar and choose Dimension.

3. To see what the Standard dimension style looks like, choose Linear from the Dimension toolbar. At the `Specify first extension line origin or <select object>:` prompt, pick ❶ in Figure 15.10. At the `Specify second extension line origin:` prompt, pick ❷. At the `Specify dimension line location or [Mtext/Text/Angle/Horizontal/Vertical/Rotated]:` prompt, pick a location for the dimension line below the line that you dimensioned. The arrows and text are so small that you can't even see them.

4. Use a Zoom Window to zoom in on ❶ and the left end of the dimension. Choose Zoom Previous from the Standard toolbar. Zoom in on the center of the dimension to see the text. Choose Zoom Previous again. As you can see, this dimension needs some modification.

5. Choose Dimension Style from the Dimension toolbar. The current dimension style should be Standard. Click New. In the New Style Name text box, type Arch 48 and click Continue.

6. Click the Symbols and Arrows tab if it isn't on top. In the Arrowheads section, choose Oblique from the first drop-down list. The size should be 3/16".

7. Click the Lines tab. In the Dimension Lines section, type **3/32** in the Extend Beyond Ticks text box. (Because of the units precision setting—set by choosing Format ⇨ Units—this value is rounded off to 1/8" in the display, although the value is still 3/32.) Click OK to return to the Dimension Style Manager.

FIGURE 15.10

The garage elevation.

GARAGE SOUTH ELEV 1/4" = 1'-0"

8. In the Dimension Style Manager, notice that the arrows have been changed to ticks in the preview. Click Set Current, and then click Close.

9. Select the dimension that you created in Step 3. In the Dim Style Control drop-down list on the Dimension toolbar, choose Arch 48. The dimension now has the geometry settings that you just made. To check it out, do a Zoom Window to the left end of the dimension. You can see that the oblique mark has replaced the arrow. Do a Zoom Previous.

10. Save your drawing. Keep this drawing open if you're continuing on to the next exercise.

Managing dimension text

You can format the text of the dimension for readability and to match other text in your drawing. In the New Dimension Style dialog box, the Text tab, shown in Figure 15.11, controls text appearance, placement, and alignment.

Text appearance

You have full control over dimension text appearance, as you do over any other text in your drawing. To specify a text style for your dimension text, choose a text style from the Text style drop-down list. You may want to create a special text style, such as Dim Text for dimension text, to give you the flexibility to alter dimension text without changing other text in your drawing. Create the dimension text style before creating your dimension style. If you want the dimension to be annotative, its text style should also be annotative.

CROSS-REF See the section "Understanding Text Styles" in Chapter 13 for a discussion of text styles.

FIGURE 15.11

The Text tab of the New Dimension Style dialog box.

Choose a color from the Text Color drop-down list. You can pick a color for the dimension text that differs from that of the rest of the dimension. The default color is ByBlock so that dimensions take on the color of the current layer or color setting. Use this setting only if you want the dimension text to be a different color from your dimension layer color. To choose a nonstandard color, choose Select Color from the drop-down list to open the Select Color dialog box.

You can create a block of color around the dimension text so that if other objects are behind the dimension, you can still read the dimension text clearly. To add a color, choose one from the Fill Color drop-down list.

Choose the height for your dimension text. When you set the text style height to zero, you can set the height in the New Dimension Style dialog box. Otherwise, the text style height takes over. It's much easier to make all of your dimension style adjustments in one place than to make changes in the text style as well.

If your unit type uses fractions, use the fraction height scale to set a ratio of fraction text to whole text. This option is available only if your units specify the use of fractions. You may want the fractions to be smaller than whole numbers. A scale of 0.5 makes the fractions half the size of whole numbers; the resulting overall fraction is slightly higher than the whole numbers of the dimension text.

Some dimension styles require a border around the dimension text. If you want to include a rectangular border, select the Draw Frame Around Text check box.

Text placement

The Vertical drop-down list affects how text is justified relative to the dimension line. As you make changes, be sure to look at the preview to see whether the results are what you want. You have the following options:

- **Centered:** Centers the text in the dimension line, breaking the dimension line into two. This is typical for mechanical drafting. You can see an example in Figure 15.5.

- **Above:** Places text above the dimension line. This is typical for architectural drafting. You can see an example in Figure 15.4.

- **Outside:** Places the text on the side of the dimension line that is farthest from the object that you're dimensioning.

- **JIS:** Places text in conformation to the Japanese Industrial Standards rules, which vary the placement according to the angle of the dimension line.

The Horizontal drop-down list affects the placement of dimension text between the extension lines. Here again, you have a handy visual confirmation of your choice. You have the following choices:

- **Centered:** This is the default. It centers text between the two extension lines.

- **At Ext Line 1:** Places the text next to the first extension line. The first extension line is always the first point that you specified at the `Specify first extension line origin or <select object>:` prompt. The picture and the words Horizontal Justification can be especially confusing for vertical dimensions. If you aren't consistent in how you pick your dimensions, you can get some strange results.

- **At Ext Line 2:** Places the text next to the second extension line. The comments for the previous option apply to this option as well.

- **Over Ext Line 1:** Places the text over the first extension line. The comments for the At Ext Line 1 option apply to this option as well.

- **Over Ext Line 2:** Places the text over the second extension line. The comments for the At Ext Line 1 option apply to this option as well.

Use the Offset from Dim Line text box to set the gap between the dimension text and the dimension line. This sets the DIMGAP system variable. If the dimension line is broken, the gap is the space between each side of the dimension text and the two dimension lines. If the dimension line is unbroken and the text is above the line, the gap is the space between the bottom of the text and the dimension line. The gap also controls the space between the box created for Basic tolerance dimensions and the text inside them. Basic tolerances are discussed in the "Formatting tolerances" section later in this chapter.

TIP   When trying to fit dimension text, lines, and arrows in a narrow space, AutoCAD and AutoCAD LT also use the gap (the DIMGAP value) to calculate the minimum space required on either side of the dimension text. Therefore, reducing the gap can help fit more of the dimension elements between the extension lines.

Text alignment

Different disciplines have different standards for aligning dimension text. The Text Alignment section of the Text tab affects how the text is aligned relative to the dimension line, as follows:

- **Horizontal:** Keeps text between the extension lines horizontal, regardless of the angle of the dimension line (typical of mechanical drawings).

- **Aligned with Dimension Line:** Keeps text at the same angle as the dimension line (typical of architectural drawings).

- **ISO Standard:** Uses the ISO standard, which aligns text with the dimension line when text is inside the extension lines, but aligns text horizontally when text is outside the extension lines (because of a tight fit).

ON the DVD-ROM   The drawing used in the following exercise on defining dimension text, `ab15-01.dwg`, is in the `Results` folder on the DVD.

STEPS: Defining Dimension Text

1. If ab15-01.dwg is open from the previous exercise, use it for this exercise as well. Otherwise, open ab15-01.dwg from the Results folder of the DVD. ORTHO and OSNAP should be on. Set running object snaps for endpoint and intersection. The Dim layer is current. If the Dimension toolbar is not visible, right-click any toolbar and choose Dimension.

2. Save the file as ab15-02.dwg in your AutoCAD Bible folder.

3. Choose Dimension Style from the Dimension toolbar. The Arch 48 dimension style should be current. Choose Modify to continue working on the Arch 48 dimension style. Click the Text tab.

4. In the Text Appearance section, choose ROMANS as the text style.

5. In the Text Placement section, choose Above from the Vertical drop-down list.

6. In the Text Alignment section, choose Aligned with dimension line. Although mechanical dimensions usually require horizontal text, architectural dimensions require that the text be aligned with the dimension line.

7. Click OK and then click Close to update the dimension to include the changes. The text is still too tiny to see clearly.

8. Save your drawing. Keep this drawing open if you're continuing on to the next exercise.

Fitting dimensions into tight spaces

When there is not enough room to place the arrowheads, dimension line, and text between the extension lines, some elements of the dimension need to go outside the extension lines. The Fit tab, shown in Figure 15.12, lets you specify how you want to handle this situation.

FIGURE 15.12

The Fit tab of the New Dimension Style dialog box.

Fit Options

The Fit Options section determines which elements are moved outside the extension lines — text, arrows, or both — when they can't fit inside the extension lines. These are among the hardest of the dimension styles options to understand, yet they can greatly affect how your dimensions appear.

CAUTION   The Fit options specify what goes *outside* the extension lines. For example, choose the Arrows option to place the arrows outside the extension lines if there is not enough room for them. Be careful, or you'll get a result that is the opposite of what you intended.

Here are your choices:

- **Either Text or Arrows (Best Fit):** Puts whatever fits inside the extension lines. The arrowheads might fit inside and the text might not, or the other way around. If there isn't enough room for either text or arrows, then they both go outside the extension lines. Figure 15.13 shows a dimension using this option.

FIGURE 15.13

A narrow dimension using the Either Text or Arrows (Best Fit) option.

- **Arrows:** If there is not enough room for both the text and the arrows between the extension lines, the arrows go outside and the text goes between them. Figure 15.14 shows a dimension using this option. The results of this option happen to look the same as Figure 15.13, but a different setting produced them.

FIGURE 15.14

A narrow dimension using the Arrows option.

- **Text:** If there isn't enough room for the text and the arrows between the extension lines, the text goes outside and the arrows go between them. Figure 15.15 shows a dimension using this option.

Creating Dimension Styles

A narrow dimension using the Text option.

■ **Both Text and Arrows:** Keeps the text and arrows together — between the extension lines if there is enough room, and outside the extension lines if there is not. Figure 15.16 shows a dimension using this option.

FIGURE 15.16

A narrow dimension using the Both Text and Arrows option.

■ **Always Keep Text between Ext Lines:** As it says, this option always keeps the text between the extension lines, even if they don't fit. Figure 15.17 shows a dimension using this option.

FIGURE 15.17

A narrow dimension using the Always Keep Text between Ext Lines option.

■ **Suppress Arrows If They Don't Fit Inside the Extension Lines:** Use this check box to suppress the display of arrows completely if they don't fit inside the extension lines (instead of putting them outside). This option is used together with one of the previous options. Figure 15.18 shows a dimension using this option with the Either Text or Arrows (Best Fit) option.

A narrow dimension using the Suppress Arrows If They Don't Fit Inside the Extension Lines option along with the Either Text or Arrows (Best Fit) option.

Text Placement

The Text Placement section determines where you want the dimension text when it isn't in its default position, due to a tight fit. Your options are:

■ **Beside the Dimension Line:** Places the dimension text next to the dimension line, but outside the extension lines. Figure 15.19 shows a dimension using this option, as well as the same dimension edited to move the text off the model. You can move the text anywhere to the left or the right of the dimension line, but not above or below it. Editing dimensions is covered later in this chapter.

Dimension text is placed beside the dimension line when it doesn't fit inside the extension lines. You can move the text from side to side. On the right, the text has been moved to the right slightly so that it doesn't cross the model.

■ **Over Dimension Line, with Leader:** Places the dimension text over the dimension line and between the extension lines, but above them, with a leader from the dimension line to the text. You can move the text anywhere to suit your needs and dimensioning conventions, as shown in Figure 15.20.

FIGURE 15.20

Dimension text is placed over the dimension line with a leader. On the right, the text has been moved to the right of the model.

■ **Over Dimension Line, without Leader:** Places the dimension text over the dimension line and between the extension lines, but above them, with no leader, as shown in Figure 15.21. You can move the text anywhere.

FIGURE 15.21

Dimension text is placed over the dimension line without a leader.

Scale for Dimension Features

The Scale for Dimension Features section lets you specify the scale factor. The reason you need to specify a scale factor is because you may have to scale the drawing when you plot it. The scale factor adjusts the size of dimension text (unless a nonzero text style height controls the text), arrowheads, spacing, and so on. It has no effect on the content of dimension text — that is, it does not affect actual measurements. So many size options are possible in a dimension style that you could spend all day trying to multiply each size option by the scale. Then, if you have to change the scale of the drawing, you would need to recalculate all of the size specifications. Setting the Overall Scale factor makes your life easier because AutoCAD or AutoCAD LT automatically multiplies every size specification by the scale factor.

To scale dimensions according to the scale of the layout, check the Scale Dimensions to Layout option. You would use this feature if you plan to use more than one viewport, each with a different scale factor. If not, you can choose an overall scale, which would be the scale factor that you plan to use; check the Use Overall Scale Of option and enter a scale.

The new annotative feature, which is available for text, hatches, blocks, and dimensions, replaces the previous dimension scaling. Therefore, when you check the Annotative check box, the two options become unavailable.

CROSS-REF Scale factors are discussed in detail in Chapter 5. See Chapter 17 for a discussion of scaling dimensions in a paper space layout (including the use of annotative dimensions) and placing dimensions on a layout.

In the Fine Tuning section, if you check the Place Text Manually option, the horizontal text placement settings are ignored, and the point that you pick at the `Specify dimension line location or [Mtext/Text/Angle/Horizontal/Vertical/ Rotated]:` prompt is used. Before you click, as you move the cursor along the dimension line, you can see the text following the cursor.

Check the Draw Dim Line Between Ext Lines option to force a dimension line between the extension lines, even when there isn't room for text or arrows, as shown in Figure 15.22.

FIGURE 15.22

A dimension with a forced dimension line.

ON the DVD-ROM The drawing used in the following exercise on setting dimension fit, ab15-02.dwg, is in the Results folder on the DVD.

STEPS: Setting Dimension Fit

1. If ab15-02.dwg is open from the previous exercise, use it for this exercise as well. Otherwise, open ab15-02.dwg from the Results folder of the DVD. ORTHO and OSNAP should be on. Set running object snaps for endpoint and intersection. The Dim layer is current. If the Dimension toolbar is not visible, right-click any toolbar and choose Dimension.

2. Save the file as ab15-03.dwg in your AutoCAD Bible folder.

3. Choose Dimension Style from the Dimension toolbar. Make sure that the Arch 48 dimension style is current. Choose Modify to continue working on the Arch 48 dimension style.

4. On the Fit tab, in the Text Placement section, choose Over Dimension Line, with Leader.

5. In the Fine Tuning section, check Draw Dim Line Between Ext Lines. Architectural dimensions customarily place a line between the extension lines, even if the text cannot fit.

6. Because the drawing's scale is ¼"=1', or 1:48, type **48** in the Use Overall Scale Of text box.

7. Click OK. Click Close to return to your drawing.

8. Save your drawing. You can finally see the dimension! It should look like Figure 15.23. Keep this drawing open if you're continuing on to the next exercise.

FIGURE 15.23

As a result of changing the overall scale, you can finally see the dimension.

GARAGE SOUTH ELEV 1/4" = 1'−0"

Defining primary units

The primary units define the type of units used to display the dimension in your drawing. You need to set primary units separately from the units for the drawing, which affect coordinate display but not dimensions.

Click the Primary Units tab, shown in Figure 15.24, to set the format and precision for linear and angular dimensions. You should already be familiar with setting units, which I discuss in Chapter 5. You must set your units for dimensions separately.

FIGURE 15.24

The Primary Units tab of the New Dimension Style dialog box.

Linear Dimensions

To get the look and accuracy that you want, you should specify the format and precision of your linear dimensions. The Linear Dimensions section provides settings for linear dimensions. You have the following options:

■ Choose a format from the Unit format drop-down list. You have the same choices as in the Drawing Units dialog box: Scientific, Decimal, Engineering, Architectural, and Fractional, as well as an additional option, Windows Desktop.

NOTE To see the current Windows Desktop units setting, choose Start ⇨ [Settings ⇨]Control Panel ⇨ Regional Settings (or Regional Options or Regional and Language Options, depending on your operating system). Click the Number tab. (You might have to click the Customize button on the Regional Options tab first.) The Windows Desktop setting does not give you complete control over units. However, if you need consistency with another Windows application, you might find this setting useful.

■ Choose a precision (the number of decimal points or the fraction denominator) from the Precision drop-down list.

■ Choose a fraction format from the Fraction Format drop-down list. This option is available only if the format that you chose uses fractions. Horizontal places a horizontal line between stacked numerators and denominators. Diagonal uses a diagonal slash between the stacked numerator and denominator. Not Stacked uses a diagonal line between the numerator and denominator, which are not stacked. You can see the effect of each choice in the preview box.

■ Choose a decimal separator. This option is available only if the format that you chose uses decimals. You can choose from a period, a comma, and a space.

■ Use the Round Off text box to round off linear dimension distances. For example, you can round to the nearest 0.1 unit or ½ inch.

■ Use the Prefix and Suffix boxes to add a prefix or suffix that you want to place before or after every dimension. For example, you might want to add a suffix of mm after every dimension if you're measuring in millimeters and giving the drawing to a client who usually sees dimensions in inches.

You can use the Scale Factor text box to set a scaling factor for linear dimensions, including radial and diameter dimensions, and ordinal dimensions. This factor changes the actual measurement text. For example, if you draw a line 2.5 units long and you specify a linear scale of 0.5, the object is dimensioned as 1.25 units. You could set this scale to 25.4 to use metric measurements on a drawing that you have created with U.S. measurements. This can occur if you're sending the same drawing to certain clients in the United States and other clients elsewhere in the world. You can also use this scale in conjunction with alternate units, as explained in the next section.

Check the Apply to Layout Dimension Only option to apply the linear scaling factor only to layout (paper space) dimensions.

In the Zero suppression section, choose whether you want to suppress leading and trailing zeros. If you suppress leading zeros, a number such as 0.375 appears as .375. If you suppress trailing zeros, a number such as 3.7500 appears as 3.75.

For architectural units, you can choose to suppress 0 feet and 0 inches. If you suppress 0 feet, a number such as 0'-8" becomes 8". If you suppress 0 inches, a number such as 6'-0" becomes 6'.

Angular Dimensions

To get the look and accuracy that you need for angular dimensions, you should also set their format and precision. The Angular Dimensions section of the Primary Units tab lets you format angular measurements. You have the following options:

■ Choose from Decimal Degrees, Degrees Minutes Seconds, Gradians, and Radians.

■ Choose a precision from the Precision drop-down list.

In the Zero Suppression section, choose whether you want to suppress leading and trailing zeros for angular dimensions. For example, an angle of 37.0° would appear as 37° with the trailing zero suppressed.

Defining alternate units

If you want, you can show an alternate set of units in your dimensions. The most common use of this feature is to show millimeters and inches together. Alternate units appear in square brackets. To show alternate units, click the Alternate Units tab of the New Dimension Style dialog box, as shown in Figure 15.25. Check the Display Alternate Units check box.

As you can see, this dialog box is very similar to the Primary Units tab, discussed in the previous section. Notice the default scale of 25.40 in the Multiplier for Alt Units text box. There are 25.4 millimeters to an inch. If your primary units are millimeters, you can set the linear scale to 0.03937, which is the number of inches to a millimeter. Of course, if your units are not inches but meters, miles, or something else, you need to make the appropriate calculations.

Figure 15.26 shows two dimensions with alternate units.

FIGURE 15.25

The Alternate Units tab of the New Dimension Style dialog box.

FIGURE 15.26

Dimensions showing both U.S. and metric measurements.

Thanks to Jerry Bottenfield of Clow Valve Company, Oskaloosa, Iowa, for this drawing.

In the Placement section, choose one of the options to place alternate units after or below the primary units.

ON the DVD-ROM **The drawing used in the following exercise on defining primary units,** ab15-03.dwg, **is in the** Results **folder on the DVD.**

STEPS: Defining Primary Units

1. If ab15-03.dwg is open from the previous exercise, use it for this exercise as well. Otherwise, open ab15-03.dwg from the Results folder of the DVD. ORTHO and OSNAP should be on. Set running object snaps for endpoint and intersection. The Dim layer is current. If the Dimension toolbar is not visible, right-click any toolbar and choose Dimension.

2. Save the file as ab15-04.dwg in your AutoCAD Bible folder.

3. Choose Dimension Style from the Dimension toolbar. The Arch 48 dimension style should be current. Choose Modify to continue working on this dimension style. Click the Primary Units tab.

4. In the Unit Format drop-down list, choose Architectural.

5. In the Precision drop-down list, change the precision to 0'-0 1/8".

6. In the Fraction format drop-down list, choose Diagonal.

7. In the Zero Suppression section, uncheck the 0 Inches check box because architectural dimensions sometimes show 0 inches.

8. Click the Text tab. In the Fraction Height Scale text box, type .75.

9. Click OK. In the Dimension Style Manager, click Set Current and then click Close to return to your drawing. The dimension is automatically updated and now looks appropriate for an architectural drawing.

10. To see how the stacked fractions appear, create a linear dimension from ❶ to ❷ in Figure 15.27. If necessary, zoom in to see the dimension text clearly.

FIGURE 15.27

The dimension style is now complete.

11. Return to the previous view if you zoomed in. Save your drawing. It should look like Figure 15.27.

Formatting tolerances

Tolerances are used in mechanical drafting to specify how much deviation is allowed from the exact measurement when the model is manufactured. Format the tolerance notation on the Tolerances tab of the New Dimension Style dialog box. The Tolerances tab is shown in Figure 15.28.

FIGURE 15.28

The Tolerances tab of the New Dimension Style dialog box.

CROSS-REF The Tolerances tab formats regular dimensions. You can also create special Tolerance control frames, which have the same purpose, but are separate object types. I cover them in the "Creating Geometric Tolerances" section of Chapter 14.

Use the Tolerance Format section to specify how you want the tolerances to be displayed. You can choose one of four tolerance methods from the Method drop-down list:

- **Symmetrical** tolerances have the same upper and lower amounts and are shown with a plus/minus sign, as shown in Figure 15.29. The Upper Value text box is active so that you can type in the tolerance amount.

- **Deviation** tolerances can have different upper and lower amounts and are therefore shown after separate plus and minus signs, as shown in Figure 15.30. When you choose a deviation tolerance, the Upper Value and Lower Value text boxes become active.

- **Limits** dimensions include the upper and lower tolerances in the measurement, as shown in Figure 15.31. Use the Upper Value and Lower Value text boxes to type in the upper and lower tolerance amounts.
- **Basic** dimensions place the dimension in a box, as shown in Figure 15.32.

FIGURE 15.29

Symmetrical tolerances.

FIGURE 15.30

Deviation tolerances.

FIGURE 15.31

Limits dimensions.

FIGURE 15.32

A Basic dimension.

In the Precision drop-down list, choose a precision value. Use the Upper Value text box to set the tolerance value for symmetrical tolerances. For deviation and limits tolerances, use both the Upper Value and Lower Value text boxes.

The Scaling for Height text box lets you scale the height of the tolerance relative to the dimension text height. Using smaller text for the tolerances is common. A value of 1 creates tolerance text that is equal to the dimension text height. A setting of 0.5 creates tolerance text that is half the size of regular dimension text.

Use the Vertical Position drop-down list to determine how the tolerances are aligned with the main dimension text. This setting has the greatest effect on Deviation tolerances that display two lines of text for the one dimension text line. You have the following choices:

- **Top:** Aligns the tolerance text with the top of the dimension text
- **Middle:** Aligns the tolerance text with the middle of the dimension text
- **Bottom:** Aligns the tolerance text with the bottom of the dimension text

The Vertical position setting also applies to stacked fractions, determining how the fractions are justified with the whole-number dimensions.

If you choose a Limits or Deviation tolerance, you can specify the alignment of stacked upper and lower tolerance values. You can align the values by the decimal separators (such as a decimal point) or by the operational symbols (such as the plus-minus symbol).

Use the Zero Suppression section to suppress leading or trailing zeros, or feet and inches. See the preceding explanation of the Primary Units tab for more information.

If you've turned on alternate units, you can separately set the precision and zero suppression for alternate unit tolerances in the Precision text box.

Click OK, and then click Close to return to your drawing. You're ready to start dimensioning!

Changing Dimension Styles

Just as you often need to edit objects in a drawing, you may need to edit dimension styles. Whether you want to use a different dimension style for a certain object or change the properties of a dimension style, you have the flexibility you need. You can change dimensions in the following ways:

- Choose a new dimension style
- Create a variant of a dimension style for a certain type of dimension
- Modify the characteristics of the dimension style in use
- Override the dimension style with different dimension options for one dimension that you want to be an exception

Chapter 14 covers some dimension editing techniques. This section explains how to make changes related to dimension styles.

Choosing a new current dimension style

To start using another dimension style, click the Dim Style Control drop-down list on the Styles toolbar, the Dimension toolbar, or the Dimensions control panel of the Dashboard, and choose the dimension style that you want to use.

Existing dimensions remain unchanged, but any new dimensions that you add from this point forward will use the new current dimension style.

Creating a variant of a dimension style

Create a variant of a dimension style for a specific type of dimension, such as a leader or angular dimension. You might have an architectural dimension style with ticks (rather than arrows) at the end of the dimension lines, but you might want angular dimensions to have open arrows. Here are the steps to do this:

1. Choose Dimension Style from the Dimension toolbar.
2. Click New.
3. From the Use For drop-down list, choose the type of dimension that you want to use with the new variant.
4. Click Continue.
5. Make the changes that you want, using the techniques described earlier in this chapter.

6. Click OK to return to the Dimension Style Manager. Here you see the variant listed under its base (parent) dimension style.

7. Click Close.

Dimensions of the type that you specified now take on the characteristics of the variant. For example, angular dimensions would have an open arrow.

Modifying a dimension to use a new dimension style

You can change the dimension style used by a dimension. Select the dimension and then choose a new dimension style from the Dim Style Control drop-down list on the Styles or Dimension toolbar, or in the Dimensions control panel of the Dashboard.

Another method of changing a dimension's style is to choose Properties on the Standard (or Standard Annotation) toolbar (or press Ctrl+1) and select one or more dimensions. In the Properties palette, click the Dim style item in the Misc section and choose a new dimension style from the drop-down list.

 Double-click any dimension to open the Properties palette, where you can change the properties of that dimension.

You can choose Match Properties on the Standard (or Standard Annotation) toolbar to match the properties of one dimension to those of another. Follow these steps:

1. Choose Match Properties.

2. At the `Select source object:` prompt, choose the dimension whose properties you want to copy.

3. At the `Select destination object(s) or [Settings]:` prompt, choose the dimension or dimensions to which you want to copy the properties. (Use the Settings option if you want to copy only some of the properties. Also, if the destination dimension doesn't check, use the Settings option and make sure that the Dimension check box is selected in the Special Properties section of the Property Settings dialog box.)

4. Press Enter to end the command.

Modifying dimension styles

You can easily change a dimension style. The advantage of changing a dimension style is that all dimensions using that style are automatically updated. To change a style:

1. Choose Dimension Style from the Dimension toolbar.

2. Choose the dimension style that you want to change from the list of styles.

3. Choose Modify.

4. AutoCAD opens the Modify Dimension Style dialog box, which is exactly the same as the New Dimension Style dialog box. Use the settings on all of the tabs and make the changes that you want. Click OK to close these dialog boxes and return to the Dimension Styles Manager.

5. Click Close.

All dimensions automatically change to reflect the changed dimension style.

 You can create a new dimension style from an existing dimension on the fly by using the Properties palette. Double-click a dimension to open the Properties palette. Click the arrow next to the type of change that you want to make, and make the change. After you're done, right-click in the drawing area and choose Dim Style ⇨ Save as New Style. The New Dimension Style dialog box opens so that you can give the dimension style a name. Click OK.

Overriding a dimension style

Sometimes you want to make an exception to a style for one dimension — for example, when suppressing an extension line in a tight space. It isn't often worthwhile to create a new dimension style for such a situation. To override a dimension style, simply change the properties of the dimension by using the Properties palette.

You can also create an override to the current dimension style. The override is like a subset of the dimension style. After you create the override, all new dimensions that you create using the dimension style include the override changes. To revert back to the original dimension style, you must delete the override. You also have the option to incorporate the override into the dimension style or save it as a new style.

To create a dimension style override, follow these steps:

1. Choose Dimension Style from the Dimension toolbar.
2. Choose the dimension style for which you want to create an override (if it isn't already selected).
3. In the Dimension Style Manager, click Override.
4. The Override dialog box opens, which is just like the New (or Modify) Dimension Style dialog box. Make the changes that you want using any of the tabs. Click OK.
5. In the Dimension Style Manager, you see the style override listed beneath the dimension style that you selected. Click Close.

New dimensions that you create using the dimension style that you selected now include the override properties.

To stop using the override, open the Dimension Style Manager, right-click the style override to open the shortcut menu, and do one of the following:

- Choose Delete to delete the override.
- Choose Save to Current Style to incorporate the override properties into the current dimension style.
- Choose Rename to create a new dimension style from the override. You see a selection box around the name. Type a new dimension style name and press Enter. This action removes the override and replaces it with the new dimension style.

Removing the override doesn't change dimensions that you've already created with the override.

> **TIP** To quickly override a dimension's style, select the dimension. Then right-click and choose one of four options. Dim Text Position offers four sub-options to control the position of the dimension's text. Precision lets you quickly choose from 0 to 6 decimal places. The Dim Style option creates a new style from the selected dimension. Finally, the Flip Arrow option flips the selected arrow to the outside of the extension lines.

Updating dimensions

The Dimension toolbar and the Dimensions control panel of the Dashboard include a Dimension Update button. This command updates selected dimensions so that they use the current dimension style, including any overrides that you may have just made. Use this command when you realize that you want to include some existing dimensions in the overrides that you've made.

Comparing dimension styles

You can compare a dimension style with the current dimension style. To do this, follow these steps:

1. Choose Dimension Style from the Dimension toolbar, and choose Compare. The Compare Dimension Styles dialog box opens, as shown in Figure 15.33.

2. In the Compare and With drop-down boxes, choose the two dimension styles that you want to compare. The resulting list shows the differences by system variable. For more information about system variables used in dimensions, see the sidebar, "Dimension System Variables."

FIGURE 15.33

The Compare Dimension Styles dialog box enables you to compare the properties of two dimension styles.

3. Click Close twice to return to your drawing.

TIP Click the Copy button at the right side of the Compare Dimension Styles dialog box to copy the comparison to the Clipboard. You can then paste it into another document, for example, an e-mail message to a client.

Copying dimension styles from other drawings

With proper planning, dimension styles make dimensioning much easier and produce more uniform results. Although you can save dimension styles in your templates, you may sometimes need to work with someone else's drawing or an old drawing that doesn't contain the dimension styles that you need. As explained in Chapters 11 and 13, you can use the DesignCenter to import features from other drawings. To import a dimension style, follow these steps:

1. Choose DesignCenter from the Standard or Standard Annotation toolbar (or press Ctrl+2) to open the DesignCenter.

2. In the left pane, navigate to the drawing that has the dimension style that you want.

3. Double-click the drawing icon or click its plus sign.

4. To see the list of the dimension styles, double-click the dimension style's icon in either the left or right pane.

5. Double-click the dimension style's icon to import it into your drawing.

6. If you want, click the DesignCenter's Close button to close the DesignCenter.

AUTOCAD ONLY The Express Tools offer two commands, DIMIM and DIMEX, which enable you to save (export) and retrieve (import) dimension styles. Choose Express ➪ Dimension ➪ Dimstyle Import or Dimstyle Export. For information on installing Express Tools, see Appendix A.

The drawing used in the following exercise on changing dimension styles, ab15-b.dwg, is in the Drawings folder on the DVD.

STEPS: Changing Dimension Styles

1. Open ab15-b.dwg from your DVD.

2. Save the file as ab15-05.dwg in your AutoCAD Bible folder. This is a tension arm for a commercial dryer, as shown in Figure 15.33. ORTHO and OSNAP should be on. Set running object snaps for endpoint, intersection, and center. The Dims layer is current. If the Dimension toolbar is not visible, right-click any toolbar and choose Dimension. Alternatively, you can use the Dashboard; choose Tools ➪ Palettes ➪ Dashboard. If the Dimensions control panel is not displayed, right-click the Dashboard and choose Control Panels ➪ Dimensions.

3. The current dimension style is CIR. From the Dim Style Control drop-down list, choose LIN.

4. Choose Linear from the Dimension toolbar or the Dimensions control panel of the Dashboard. At the Specify first extension line origin or <select object>: prompt, choose the endpoint at ❶ in Figure 15.34. (If necessary, press Tab until you see the endpoint tooltip.) At the Specify second extension line origin: prompt, choose the intersection at ❷. At the Specify dimension line location or [Mtext/Text/Angle/Horizontal/Vertical/ Rotated]: prompt, choose an appropriate location above the bottom-most dimension.

5. Choose Dimension Style from the Dimension toolbar or the Dimensions control panel of the Dashboard. Choose Override and click the Tolerances tab. Change the Tolerance Method to None. Click the Lines tab. In the Extension Lines section, check the Suppress: Ext Line 1 option to suppress the first extension line. Click OK. In the Dimension Style Manager, click Close.

6. Choose Linear from the Dimension toolbar or the Dimensions control panel of the Dashboard. At the Specify first extension line origin or <select object>: prompt, choose the intersection at ❷ in Figure 15.34. At the Specify second extension line origin: prompt, choose the intersection at ❸. At the Specify dimension line location or [Mtext/Text/Angle/Horizontal/Vertical/Rotated]: prompt, pick the endpoint object snap at the right side of the previous dimension's dimension line in order to align the two dimensions.

FIGURE 15.34

The tension arm needs some additional dimensions.

7. The first dimension (the one you created in Step 4) needs to be updated to remove the tolerance. Choose Dimension Update from the Dimension toolbar or the Dimensions control panel of the Dashboard. At the `Select objects:` prompt, choose the first dimension. Right-click to end object selection to update the dimension.

8. To list the overrides, choose Dimension Style. Choose Compare. In the Compare Dimension Styles dialog box, `<style overrides>` should be displayed in the Compare drop-down list, and LIN should be displayed in the With drop-down list. You see a list of the overrides, which are the only differences between the two. Click Close.

9. To remove the overrides (no tolerance and the first extension line suppressed), right-click `<style overrides>` in the Dimension Style Manager and choose Delete. You get the message, `Are you sure you want to delete "<style overrides>"?` Choose Yes. Click Close to return to the drawing.

10. Choose Linear from the Dimension toolbar or the Dimensions control panel of the Dashboard. At the `Specify first extension line origin or <select object>:` prompt, choose the intersection at ❹ in Figure 15.34. At the `Specify second extension line origin:` prompt, choose the intersection at ❺. At the `Specify dimension line location or [Mtext/Text/Angle/Horizontal/Vertical/Rotated]:` prompt, pick an appropriate location to the right of the model.

11. To compare the CIR and LIN dimension styles, choose Dimension Style. Choose Compare. LIN should appear in the Compare drop-down list. Choose CIR from the With drop-down list. The result is a list of the differences. Click Close twice to return to your drawing.

12. Save your drawing. It should look like Figure 15.35.

FIGURE 15.35

The dimensions have been added.

FLAT BLANK LAYOUT

Dimension System Variables

All of the settings that you make in the Dimension Styles dialog box are stored in a large number of system variables devoted to dimensions. (See Chapter 5 for more information about system variables.)

To read about the dimension variables, choose Help ⇨ Help and click the Contents tab. Double-click Command Reference and then double-click System Variables. Double-click D System Variables. All of the variables starting with DIM are dimension system variables.

Once upon a time, the only way to manage dimensions was by knowing all of the dimension system variables and individually setting each one. Today, the Dimension Style Manager makes it much easier to manage dimensions. However, if you want to create scripts or AutoLISP routines to manage your dimensions, you need to understand how the dimension system variables work, because scripts and AutoLISP routines cannot access dialog boxes.

You can use the DIMSTYLE command on the command line to list all of the system variable settings for a dimension style. Type **-dimstyle** at the command line. Use the STatus option to display the current style's system variable values. You can get a great education in dimension system variables by printing out and perusing this list.

The other DIMSTYLE options are:

- **ANNotative:** Saves an annotative dimension style.
- **Save:** Saves a non-annotative dimension style.
- **Restore:** Makes a dimension style current.
- **Variables:** Lists dimension variables, such as the STatus option, but lets you first choose the dimension style for which you want to list the variables.
- **Apply:** Updates dimensions to the current style, including overrides. This is equivalent to choosing Update from the Dimension toolbar.
- **?:** Lists all dimension styles in the drawing.

You can also create dimension style overrides by using the DIMOVERRIDE command (Dimension ⇨ Override). You need to know the name of the system variable and the setting code that you want. The command displays the Enter dimension variable name to override or [Clear overrides]: prompt. To create an override, type the system variable and its setting. Then select the dimensions for which you want to override dimension style settings. To clear all dimension style overrides, type **c ↵**. Then select the dimensions for which you want to remove overrides.

Summary

In this chapter, you gained a thorough understanding of how to use dimension styles to organize your dimensions. You read how to:

- Define a dimension's lines and arrows
- Define dimension text style and placement
- Create an annotative dimension style

- Fit dimensions into small spaces
- Define the primary and alternate measuring units
- Format tolerances
- Create a variant of a dimension style for specific types of dimensions
- Change dimension style used by a dimension
- Modify a dimension style and update all dimensions that use that style
- Override a dimension style for temporary changes
- Update existing dimensions
- Compare dimension styles
- Copy dimension styles from other drawings using the DesignCenter

In the next chapter, you learn how to draw complex objects.

Chapter 16

Drawing Complex Objects

utoCAD and AutoCAD LT offer a number of complex objects that can
help you create accurate, professional drawings. Polylines are single
objects that can combine line segments and arcs. Splines are mathematically controlled curves that are based on points that you specify. Regions and
boundaries create complex shapes from existing objects. Hatches create various
types of fills inside closed objects. Multilines (in AutoCAD) and dlines (in
AutoCAD LT) are sets of parallel lines. Sketching is a way to create freehand
drawings. Digitizing with a tablet is a process that is used to transfer an existing
paper drawing into your drawing. In this chapter, I introduce you to these complex objects and explain how to use them.

IN THIS CHAPTER

Creating and editing polylines

Drawing and editing splines

Creating regions and boundaries

Using hatches to fill closed areas

**Creating and editing multilines
and dlines**

Using the SKETCH command

**Digitizing drawings with the
TABLET command**

Creating and Editing Polylines

Polylines are single objects that combine line segments and arcs. In certain situations, being able to edit an entire set of lines and arcs as one object is useful.
Polylines can have a width, which can vary from the start point to the endpoint of
each segment. Polylines ensure that all of the vertices of a series of lines and arcs
actually touch. They're also useful for 3D drawing. In short, polylines are a neat,
clean way to draw. (Technically, polylines are called *lightweight polylines* to distinguish them from the type of polylines used in Release 13 of AutoCAD and earlier.)

CROSS-REF You can create 3D solids that you draw like polylines, using
the POLYSOLID command (AutoCAD only). See Chapter 24
for more information.

The RECTANG and POLYGON commands create polylines. Figure 16.1 shows a
few examples of polylines.

FIGURE 16.1

Four examples of polylines.

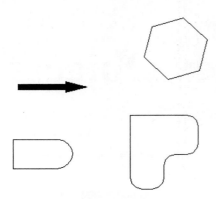

Using the PLINE command

To draw a polyline, choose Polyline from the Draw toolbar or the 2D Draw control panel of the Dashboard (or choose Draw ➪ Polyline). This starts the PLINE command. The command responds with the `Specify start point:` prompt. Specify the start point. You then see the `Specify next point or [Arc/Close/Halfwidth/Length/Undo/Width]:` prompt, which offers the following options:

- **Arc:** Draws arcs. This option opens up a set of arc suboptions, which are explained next, after this list.

- **Close:** Closes a polyline by drawing a line from the endpoint of the last line segment to the start point of the polyline. This option appears only after you've picked a second point.

- **Halfwidth:** Defines half of the width of the polyline — the distance from the center of the polyline to its edge. The option asks you for the starting halfwidth and the ending halfwidth, enabling you to create polylines that are tapered.

- **Length:** Specifies the length of the next line segment. The option draws the line segment in the same direction as the last line segment or tangent to the last arc.

- **Undo:** Undoes the last line segment.

- **Width:** Defines the width of the polyline. The option asks you for the starting width and the ending width.

- **Specify next point:** Enables you to create a line segment. This is the default option.

Like the LINE command, PLINE continues to prompt you for more points, repeating the entire prompt each time. When you're done, press Enter to end the command.

If you choose Arc, you see the `Specify endpoint of arc or [Angle/CEnter/CLose/Direction/Halfwidth/Line/Radius/Second pt/ Undo/Width]:` prompt. Although this may seem overwhelming, most of the options are similar to the ARC command options. If you need a review, see the section "Drawing Arcs" in Chapter 7. The arc options are as follows:

Generating Linetypes on Polylines

When you create a polyline with a noncontinuous linetype, you may find that the linetype doesn't appear properly along the polyline. One reason is that the segments of the polyline may be too short to fit the entire linetype definition — in this case the polyline appears continuous, even though it's defined with a dashed line or other linetype. You can choose to generate the linetype continuously along the polyline, instead of starting the linetype definition anew at each vertex. This results in a more normal-looking linetype along the polyline. To do this, you need to turn on the PLINEGEN system variable. By default, it is off (set to 0). To turn on PLINEGEN, type **plinegen** ↵ and then **1** ↵.

As explained in the section "Editing polylines with the PEDIT command" later in the chapter, you can also modify the display of linetypes for existing polylines.

- **Angle:** Specifies the included angle.
- **CEnter:** Specifies the arc's center.
- **CLose:** Closes the polyline by drawing an arc from the endpoint of the last arc to the start point of the polyline.
- **Direction:** Specifies the direction of the arc from the start point.
- **Halfwidth:** Defines half of the width of the polyline — the distance from the center of the polyline to its edge. The option asks you for the starting halfwidth and the ending halfwidth.
- **Line:** Returns you to the main polyline prompt so that you can draw line segments.
- **Radius:** Specifies the arc's radius.
- **Second pt:** Specifies the second point of the arc.
- **Undo:** Undoes the last arc.
- **Width:** Defines the width of the polyline. The option asks you for the starting width and the ending width.
- **Specify endpoint of arc:** Specifies the endpoint of the arc. This is the default. This option creates an arc tangent to the previous arc (continuing in the same direction).

PLINE continues to display the arc submenu until you use the Line suboption or end the command by pressing Enter.

 The drawing used in the following exercise on drawing polylines, ab16-a.dwg, is in the Drawings folder on the DVD.

STEPS: Drawing Polylines

1. Open ab16-a.dwg from your DVD.
2. Save the file as ab16-01.dwg in your AutoCAD Bible folder. It shows a small section of a drive block, as shown in Figure 16.2. In this exercise, you complete part of the drawing. ORTHO and OSNAP should be on. Set running object snaps to endpoint, midpoint, and intersection. Layer 3 is current. This exercise assumes that you have dynamic input (the DYN button on the status bar) on, set to the default of relative coordinates.

FIGURE 16.2

A small section of a drive block.

Thanks to Mary Redfern of the Bethlehem Corporation, Easton, Pennsylvania, for this drawing.

   3. Choose Polyline from the Draw toolbar or the 2D Draw control panel of the Dashboard. Follow the prompts:

```
Specify start point: Press Shift+right-click and choose the From
object snap.
Base point: Choose ❶ in Figure 16.2.
<Offset>: @-1/2,0 ↵
Specify next point or [Arc/ Halfwidth/Length/Undo/Width]: Move the
cursor in the 90-degree direction and type 3/32 ↵.
```

4. Type **a** ↵ to continue with an arc. At the `Specify endpoint of arc or [Angle/CEnter/ CLose/Direction/Halfwidth/Line/Radius/Second pt/Undo/Width]:` prompt, type **3/16,3/16** ↵.

5. Type **l** ↵ to continue with a linear segment. At the `Specify next point or [Arc/Close/ Halfwidth/Length/Undo/Width]:` prompt, move the cursor in the 0-degree direction and type **11/32** ↵.

6. Type **a** ↵ to continue with an arc. At the prompt, type **3/16,3/16** ↵.

7. Type **l** ↵ to continue with a linear segment. At the prompt, move the cursor in the 90-degree direction and type **6-3/32** ↵.

8. Type **a** ↵ to continue with an arc. At the prompt, type **-5/16,5/16** ↵.

9. To create the last arc, type **r** ↵. Follow the prompts:

```
Specify radius of arc: 5-5/8 ↵
Specify endpoint of arc or [Angle]: Choose the From object snap.
Base point: Choose point ❷ in Figure 16.2.
<Offset>: @0,7-1/4 ↵
```

10. Press Enter to exit the PLINE command.

11. Save your drawing. It should look like Figure 16.3.

FIGURE 16.3

The completed polyline.

ON the DVD-ROM Ar1 **creates a label of the area of an enclosed polyline. Look in** \Software\Ch16\ar1.
Note that you can also create a similar label using the area field (AutoCAD only). I cover fields
in Chapter 13.

Editing polylines with the PEDIT command

Because polylines can be quite complex, there is a special command to edit them, PEDIT. To edit a polyline,
choose Modify ➪ Object ➪ Polyline, or double-click the polyline. The command responds with the Select
polyline or [Multiple]: prompt. When you select a polyline, you see the Enter an option
[Close/Join/Width/Edit vertex/
Fit/Spline/Decurve/Ltype gen/Undo]: prompt. The options are:

- **Close:** Closes an open polyline. If necessary, it adds a segment to connect the endpoint to the
  start point. If the polyline is already closed, this prompt becomes Open. Open creates a break
  between the first and last segments of the polyline.

- **Join:** Joins touching lines, arcs, or other polylines to the polyline.

- **Width:** Enables you to specify one width for the entire polyline.

- **Edit Vertex:** Provides a set of suboptions for editing vertices. These suboptions are explained
  after this list.

- **Fit:** Turns the polyline into a curve that passes through the vertices.

- **Spline:** Creates a curve by using the vertices as control points. The curve does not usually pass
  through the vertices. This is not the mathematically exact spline that the SPLINE command produces (covered later in this chapter).

- **Decurve:** Returns a Fit or Spline curve to its original vertices.

- **Ltype gen:** Turns on continuous linetype generation for the selected polyline.

- **Undo:** Undoes the most recent edit.

TIP You can change any line or arc into a polyline. Start PEDIT and choose a line or arc. The command responds: Object selected is not a polyline. Do you want to turn it into one? <Y>. Press Enter to accept the default and turn the object into a polyline. (You can change the PEDITACCEPT system variable to 1 to suppress this prompt and automatically turn non-polyline objects that you select for the PEDIT command to polylines.) To turn a series of connected lines and arcs into a polyline, first, turn one of the objects into a polyline as I just explained. Then use the Join option and select the other objects individually or by a selection window. In order to create a polyline in this way, the individual lines and arcs must connect exactly end to end. However, if you use the Multiple option, which I explain following the current list, you can join lines that aren't exactly touching.

When you choose the Edit Vertex option, you see a new set of suboptions, with the Enter a vertex editing option [Next/Previous/Break/Insert/Move/Regen/Straighten/Tangent/ Width/eXit] <N>: prompt. You see an X at one of the vertices. This is the current vertex, which you can edit. The suboptions are as follows:

- **Next:** Moves you to the next vertex so that you can edit it.
- **Previous:** Moves you to the previous vertex.
- **Break:** Breaks the polyline. You can choose the Go suboption to break the polyline into two (although you can't see the break). You can move to another vertex using the Next or Previous suboptions and then choose Go. This option breaks the polyline between the original vertex and the vertex to which you moved. Use the eXit suboption to return to the previous prompt. (You can also use the BREAK command.)
- **Insert:** Inserts another vertex. At the prompt, specify its location.
- **Move:** Moves the vertex. At the prompt, specify its location.
- **Regen:** Regenerates the polyline.
- **Straighten:** Deletes vertices. This works like the Break option with the same Next, Previous, Go, and eXit suboptions. As soon as you move to a new vertex, the option draws a straight line between it and the original vertex. If you don't move to a new vertex, this option affects only an arc by changing it to a straight line segment.
- **Tangent:** Specifies a direction from the vertex. The command uses this information if you choose the Fit option.
- **Width:** Enables you to specify a starting and ending width of the segment, starting with the current vertex.
- **eXit:** Exits this group of suboptions.

CAUTION You can make many changes during the PEDIT session. If you return to the command line and use the U or UNDO command, the entire session is undone. If you want to undo only part of the session, use the Undo option of the PEDIT command.

You can also edit polylines with grips. A polyline has a grip at each vertex, making it easy to move vertices.

To edit multiple polylines at one time, follow these steps:

1. Start the PEDIT command.
2. Choose the Multiple option (type **m** or right-click and choose Multiple from the shortcut menu) at the first prompt.
3. At the Select objects: prompt, select the polylines.
4. You then see the Enter an option [Close/Open/Join/Width/Fit/Spline/ Decurve/Ltype gen/Undo]: prompt.

5. Choose the option that you want. For example, you can change the width of all of the selected polylines or apply the Spline option to them.

You can also join two polylines that aren't touching, if you use the Multiple option first. Select the polylines and then choose the Join option. You then need to specify two suboptions:

- **Fuzz distance:** The maximum distance that the endpoints of the polylines can be from each other. In other words, in order for the join to work, the fuzz distance must be greater than the distance of the endpoints. If you want to join the endpoints regardless, type in a very large number.

- **Jointype:** The method of joining polylines. You can use the Extend method, which extends (or trims) the segments to the nearest endpoints, or the Add method, which adds a straight segment between the two nearest endpoints. You can choose the Both suboption, which tries to extend or trim; if it can't, it adds a segment.

Editing polylines using the Properties palette

You can also edit polylines in the Properties palette. Select a polyline, and display the Properties palette.

You can choose a vertex by clicking Vertex in the Geometry section of the dialog box. An X appears on the polyline to let you know which vertex you've chosen. You can then edit the vertex's coordinates by typing them in, or by clicking the Pick a Point button that appears and then picking a point in the drawing. You can change the start and ending width and specify a global width for the entire polyline.

You can close and open a polyline in the Misc section. You can also turn on continuous linetype generation for the selected polyline by choosing Linetype generation and then choosing Enabled from the drop-down list that appears. Of course, you can also change the layer, color, linetype, lineweight, and linetype scale.

You can "paint" polyline properties from one polyline to another, using the MATCHPROP command. Select a polyline, choose Match Properties on the Standard or Standard Annotation toolbar, and then select the polyline that you want to edit. (Make sure the Polyline check box in the Property Settings dialog box is selected.)

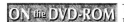 The drawing used in the following exercise on editing polylines, `ab16-b.dwg`, is in the `Drawings` folder on the DVD.

STEPS: Editing Polylines

1. Open `ab16-b.dwg` from your DVD.

2. Save the file as `ab16-02.dwg` in your `AutoCAD Bible` folder. This is a topographical drawing, as shown in Figure 16.4. The contours are polylines.

3. Choose Modify ➪ Object ➪ Polyline to start the PEDIT command. Select the polyline at ❶ in Figure 16.4.

4. At the Enter an option [Close/Join/Width/Edit vertex/Fit/Spline/Decurve/Ltype gen/Undo]: prompt, right-click and choose Width. At the Specify new width for all segments: prompt, type .5 ↵.

5. Type **e** ↵ to choose the Edit vertex option. At the `Enter a vertex editing option` `[Next/Previous/Break/Insert/Move/Regen/Straighten/Tangent/Width/eXit]` `<N>:` prompt, type **n** ↵ several times until the X mark is at ❶ in Figure 16.4. (There are many vertices, so it's not important that you find the exact one.)

The topographical drawing's contours are polylines.

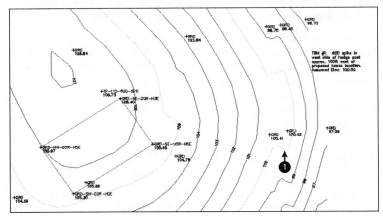

Thanks to Henry Dearborn, AIA, of Fairfield, Iowa, for this drawing.

6. Type **m** to move the vertex. At the `Specify new location for marked vertex:` prompt, pick a point slightly above the existing vertex. Then type **x** ↵ to exit the Edit vertex submenu.

7. At the main PEDIT prompt, type **s** ↵. PEDIT smoothes out the polyline.

8. Press Enter to exit the PEDIT command.

9. Save your drawing.

Drawing and Editing Splines

The SPLINE command draws a NURBS, which stands for nonuniform rational B-spline. Without becoming too technical, a *spline* is a smooth curve that is defined by a series of points. The SPLINE command provides a more precise representation of a spline than the Spline option of the PLINE command. By default, the curve passes through each point that you define. Figure 16.5 shows a beanbag chair created with two splines.

A beanbag chair created with two splines.

Creating splines

To create a spline, choose Spline from the Draw menu. The command responds with the `Specify first point or [Object]:` prompt. Use the Object option to convert a polyline that you've created with PEDIT's Spline option into a true spline. (It won't look any different, but its internal definition changes.) Otherwise, specify the first point for the spline.

If you choose a point, the command displays the `Specify next point:` prompt so that you can pick a second point. After you do so, you see the `Specify next point or [Close/Fit tolerance] <start tangent>:` prompt. Use these options as follows:

- **Close:** Closes the spline by connecting the last point with the first point in a continuous (tangent) curve. The prompt asks for a tangent direction. You can specify a direction by picking a point (watch the spline image change as you move the cursor) or pressing Enter to accept the default tangent direction.

- **Fit Tolerance:** Specifies how closely the spline comes to the points that you pick. The default, 0, creates a spline that passes through each point. If you want the curve to have a latitude of 0.5 units from the points, set the tolerance to 0.5.

- **Specify next point:** The default option is to continue entering points. Press Enter to end point selection.

- **Start tangent:** When you press Enter to complete point selection, you're prompted for start and ending tangent directions. You can press Enter at both prompts to accept the default tangents, based on the curve's current shape. You can see the effect of other tangent points by moving the cursor and watching the image change.

 The drawing used in the following exercise on drawing splines, `ab16-c.dwg`, is in the `Drawings` folder on the DVD.

STEPS: Drawing Splines

1. Open `ab16-c.dwg` from your DVD.

2. Save the file as `ab16-03.dwg` in your `AutoCAD Bible` folder. This is a topographical site map, shown in Figure 16.6. OSNAP should be on. Set a running object snap for insertion.

3. Use Zoom Window to zoom in on the area near the start of the north edge of the drive. Choose Spline from the Draw toolbar or 2D Draw control panel of the Dashboard.

4. At the `Specify first point or [Object]:` prompt, use the Insertion object snap to pick the cross at the start of the north edge of the drive, as shown in Figure 16.6. Continue to pick the crosses marked N-EDGE-DR. Choose Pan from the Standard toolbar (or choose View ⇨ Pan ⇨ Realtime) to do a real-time pan when you reach the edge of the display. Press Esc. Continue picking points until you get to the end of the north edge of the drive, as shown in Figure 16.6. Press Enter to endpoint selection.

5. At the `Specify start tangent:` and `Specify end tangent:` prompts, press Enter.

6. Start the SPLINE command again and pick points for the south edge of the drive, from the start of the south edge of the drive to the end, as shown in Figure 16.6. Pan as necessary. Again, press Enter to accept the default directions for the start and end tangents.

7. If you want, choose Zoom Previous on the Standard toolbar (or choose View ⇨ Zoom ⇨ Previous) several times until you see the original view of the drawing. Save your drawing.

 `GeomCurves.lsp` is a routine that creates various kinds of geometrical curves, such as spirals and parabolas. You can find it in the `\Software\Chapter 16\GeomCurves` folder.

FIGURE 16.6

A topographical site map. You can complete the gravel road based on surveyor's data.

Start of south edge of drive   Start of north edge of drive

End of north edge of drive

End of south edge of drive

Editing splines

Like polylines, splines have their own editing command. To understand how to edit splines, you need to understand how your drawing stores them.

When you pick points to create the spline, AutoCAD stores these points as *fit points* (or data points). If the tolerance is zero, the curve lies on these fit points. When you select a spline at the command line, grips appear at these fit points. However, when you use the SPLINEDIT command, to see the fit points as grips, you must choose the Fit Data option first. Only then can you edit the fit points.

AutoCAD and AutoCAD LT calculate *control points* based on the fit points. The spline is then calculated based on the control points, not the fit points. Most of the control points are not on the spline. When you use SPLINEDIT to edit a spline, and use the Move vertex option described later, you see the control points displayed as grips, and you can move the control points.

Figure 16.7 shows a spline created using point objects as the fit points; these are the points that were picked when creating the spline. Note that the spline passes through each fit point.

FIGURE 16.7

The point objects were used as the pick points. These are the fit points of the spline.

Figure 16.8 shows the same spline as in Figure 16.7, where it appears when selected with no command active. Notice that the grips are exactly on the fit points.

Because the spline is calculated based on the control points, the fit points are not necessary to generate the spline. In fact, if you use the Move vertex or Refine options to move or edit a control point, only the control points are needed to generate the spline, and the fit point information is discarded so that you can no longer edit it. The Fit Data option also disappears from the prompt. You can edit the fit points using grips.

FIGURE 16.8

When you select a spline with no command active, you see grips on the fit points.

To edit a spline, choose Modify ➪ Object ➪ Spline to start the SPLINEDIT command. After you select the spline, the command responds with the `Enter an option [Fit data/Close/Move vertex/Refine/ rEverse/Undo]:` prompt. Here's how to use these options:

- **Fit Data:** Fit data means the points that you've chosen, their tolerance, and the tangents. Use this option to edit fit data. This option has its own list of suboptions that are explained after this list.

- **Close/Open:** If the spline is open, this option closes it by adding a continuous (tangent) curve from the last point to the start point. If the spline is closed, this option appears as Open. If the spline was originally closed, the Open option removes the connection between the last and first points, although the spline looks the same. If the spline was originally open and you closed it, when you use the Open option, this option erases the curve that it added when you closed it.

- **Move Vertex:** This works like the Edit vertex option of PEDIT, except that this option displays the points as grips and highlights them. You can use Next and Previous suboptions, select any point to move, and pick a new location for the highlighted vertex.

- **Refine:** Enables you to refine the spline in three ways:
    - **Add control points:** This doesn't change the shape of the spline but adjusts nearby control points slightly.
    - **Elevate the order of the spline:** This adds control points throughout the spline (but once you go up, you can't go down).
    - **Change the weight of any control point:** This is like the gravity that the control point exerts on the spline. Watch the spline inch toward the control point as you increase its weight.

- **rEverse:** Reverses the direction of the spline so that the start point becomes the endpoint, and vice versa.

- **Undo:** Undoes the most recent edit operation.

When you use the SPLINEDIT command and select a spline, you see control points, not fit points. In Figure 16.9, the grips indicate the control points.

FIGURE 16.9

When you choose the SPLINEDIT command and select a spline, the grips indicate the control points, which are not generally on the spline.

Fit point

Control point

If you choose the Fit Data option, you see the `Enter a fit data option [Add/Close/Delete/ Move/Purge/Tangents/toLerance/eXit] <eXit>:` prompt. Descriptions of these options follow:

- **Add:** Adds fit data points to the curve. The prompt asks you to select a point and then automatically selects the next point as well, shown with highlighted grips. At the prompt for a new point, which must be between the two highlighted points, the spline reshapes accordingly.
- **Open/Close:** Opens or closes the spline using the fit points.
- **Delete:** Deletes a selected fit point.
- **Move:** Moves a fit point. You can use the Next or Previous suboptions or the Select Point option to select the point that you want to move. Selected points appear as highlighted grips. You get a prompt for the new fit point location. You can also use grips to edit fit points.
- **Purge:** Deletes fit point information.
- **Tangents:** Enables you to specify start and end tangents of open splines, or one tangent for closed splines. If you don't use this option, a default tangent is calculated.
- **toLerance:** Enables you to specify the tolerance, which determines how closely the spline comes to the fit points.
- **eXit:** Exits the suboption menu.

When you use SPLINEDIT and choose the Fit Data option, the grips appear on the fit points so that you can edit them, as shown in Figure 16.10.

FIGURE 16.10

When you use the Fit Data option of the SPLINEDIT command, the grips appear on the fit points.

You can edit a spline in the Properties palette. It works similarly to editing a polyline. You can choose the fit points or the control points and change them.

Creating Regions

Regions are two-dimensional surfaces. They look like closed polylines, but your drawing can calculate more information from regions than from polylines, such as the centroid, moments of inertia, and other properties relating to mass. You can also create complex shapes by combining, subtracting, and intersecting regions. The REGION command is often used as a preparation for 3D drawing.

You create a region from other objects. You can use closed polylines, closed splines, circles, ellipses, and combinations of lines, arcs, and elliptical arcs that create a closed shape. The shape cannot intersect itself like a figure 8.

Figure 16.11 shows a complex region. Although it looks like a circle with seven circles inside it, it's actually a circular surface with seven holes in it. When you select it, you can see that it's one object. The real proof is when you try to extrude it to create a 3D object out of it. You can then view it at an angle, hide background lines, and clearly see the holes, as shown in Figure 16.12.

 To create a region, choose Region from the Draw toolbar or 2D Draw control panel of the Dashboard. The prompt asks you to select objects. Select all of the objects and press Enter to end object selection. If all of the objects create a closed, nonintersecting shape, the prompt tells you:

```
1 loop extracted.
1 Region created.
```

FIGURE 16.11

A complex region.

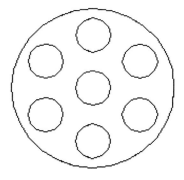

FIGURE 16.12

A region can be used to create a complex 3D object.

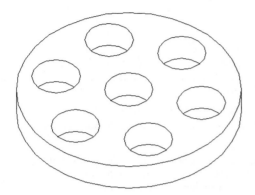

The original objects are deleted. If your objects aren't perfectly end-to-end, the prompt merely states:

```
0 loops extracted.
0 Regions created.
```

> **TIP** If you want to keep the original objects when converting closed shapes to a region, change the DELOBJ system variable to 0 (off) before you use the REGION command. The DELOBJ system variable determines whether objects that are used to create other objects are deleted.

The BOUNDARY command (see the next section) offers a way to create regions in situations where objects are not neatly drawn end to end.

If you had a hatch inside the objects, you lose hatch associativity. You can rehatch the region if you want.

> **NOTE** The XEDGES command extracts the edges of a region. For example, if you create a closed polyline of line and arc segments and make a region out of it, you can then use the XEDGES command to change the region to individual lines and arcs. (The EXPLODE command would have the same effect.) I discuss the XEDGES command more in Chapter 24, because it can also extract edges from solids.

You can combine, subtract, and intersect regions to create complex objects. The three commands to accomplish these functions are UNION, SUBTRACT, and INTERSECT. These commands are discussed in Chapter 24 because they're most often used in 3D drafting.

> **ON the DVD-ROM** The drawing used in the following exercise on creating regions, ab16-d.dwg, is in the Drawings folder on the DVD.

STEPS: Creating Regions

1. Open ab16-d.dwg from your DVD.
2. Save the file as ab16-04.dwg in your AutoCAD Bible folder.

3. Choose Region from the Draw toolbar or 2D Draw control panel of the Dashboard. At the `Select objects:` prompt, use a selection window to select the entire model, shown in Figure 16.13. Press Enter to end object selection. The prompt responds with this message:

```
7 loops extracted.
7 Regions created.
```

4. Save your drawing.

FIGURE 16.13

The outer profile and the six circles can all be turned into regions. The circles could then be subtracted from the outer profile to create a surface with six holes.

Creating Boundaries

The BOUNDARY command creates either polylines or regions from an enclosed area. This command has the capability of analyzing an area and ignoring intersecting lines that give the REGION command so much trouble. However, no spaces are allowed between objects. (Chapter 12 explains how to use the BOUNDARY command to calculate the area of a closed space.) Use the BOUNDARY command whenever you need to create a closed complex area. To create a boundary, choose Draw ➪ Boundary to open the Boundary Creation dialog box, shown in Figure 16.14.

FIGURE 16.14

The Boundary Creation dialog box.

Follow these steps:

1. If you want the command to detect internal closed areas, leave the Island Detection check box checked. Otherwise, uncheck this check box.

2. The Object Type drop-down list determines the type of object that BOUNDARY creates. Choose either Region or Polyline.

3. Choose the boundary set, which is the area to include in the analysis for the boundary. Usually, you can accept the default of Current viewport. However, if you have a very complex drawing, choose New to temporarily return to your drawing. Specify a window around the area that you want for the boundary set. The command then returns you to the dialog box.

4. To specify the enclosed area for the boundary, choose Pick Points. You return to your drawing with the `Pick internal point:` prompt.

5. Pick any point inside the closed area that you want for your boundary. The command analyzes the area that you picked.

6. You then get a prompt for another internal point. If you want to create other boundaries, continue to pick internal points. Press Enter to end point selection.

The prompt informs you of how many regions or polylines it created, and then ends the command.

When BOUNDARY creates a region or polyline, the original objects are not deleted. You end up with a region or polyline on top of your original objects.

 The drawing used in the following exercise on creating boundaries, ab16-e.dwg, is in the `Drawings` **folder on the DVD.**

STEPS: Creating Boundaries

1. Open ab16-e.dwg from your DVD.

2. Save the file as ab16-05.dwg in your AutoCAD Bible folder. This is a bushing, shown in Figure 16.15.

FIGURE 16.15

A bushing.

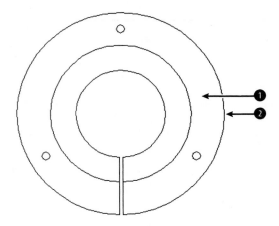

3. Choose Draw ⇨ Boundary. In the Boundary Creation dialog box, choose Region as the Object type.

4. Choose Pick Points.

5. At the `Pick internal point:` prompt, choose ❶ in Figure 16.15.

6. Press Enter to end internal point selection. The prompt responds:

   ```
   4 loops extracted.
   4 Regions created.
   BOUNDARY created 4 regions
   ```

7. To see the new region, start the MOVE command. At the `Select objects:` prompt, pick ❷. Move the region to the right; the exact distance is not important. You see both the new region and the original objects.

8. Save your drawing.

Creating Hatches

Hatches are patterns that fill in an area. Most types of drafting make use of hatching. In architectural drafting, hatched areas are used to indicate materials, such as insulation or grass. In mechanical drafting, hatching often indicates hidden areas or certain materials. AutoCAD and AutoCAD LT provide a large number of hatch patterns. Hatches are created from repeating patterns of lines. You can also create solid fills in the same way that you create hatch patterns.

CROSS-REF Chapter 31 explains how to create your own hatch patterns.

Figure 16.16 shows a drawing with a simple hatch pattern. Here the cross-section shows solid metal that is hatched to distinguish it from the holes.

FIGURE 16.16

Hatch patterns help you to distinguish different materials or textures.

Thanks to Jerry Bottenfield of Clow Valve Company, Oskaloosa, Iowa, for this drawing.

Understanding hatch patterns

Hatch patterns may seem complex, but they are easy to use, after you understand how they work. Hatch patterns have three qualities that are similar to dimensions:

- **They are blocks.** This means that all of the lines that fill in an area are one object. Blocks are covered in Chapter 18.

- **They are associative.** If you edit the object that is hatched, the hatch automatically adjusts to fit the new shape of the object.

- **They can be annotative.** If you activate the annotative property of the hatch, the hatch can automatically adjust its display scale in a viewport. (See Chapter 17 for a discussion of viewports.)

You have several ways to specify exactly which area you want to hatch. Often, the key to successful hatching lies in how you construct the area that you want to hatch. For example, you can use the BOUNDARY and REGION commands covered in previous sections of this chapter to create complex closed areas that you can hatch.

AutoCAD stores hatch pattern definitions in the `acad.pat` and `acadiso.pat` files. AutoCAD LT uses the `acadlt.pat` and `acadltiso.pat` files. If you create your own hatch patterns, you can put them in another file with the `.pat` filename extension.

> **TIP** Create a separate layer for hatch patterns. You may want to turn off or freeze your hatch layer to reduce visual clutter or assist in selecting objects. Hatches are also typically a different color than the model that you're hatching.

Defining a hatch

To hatch an area, choose Hatch from the Draw toolbar or 2D Draw control panel of the Dashboard. This starts the BHATCH command. The Hatch and Gradient dialog box opens with the Hatch tab on top, as shown in Figure 16.17. (The AutoCAD LT dialog box doesn't have a Gradient tab.)

Specifying the hatch type and pattern

Use the Hatch and Gradient dialog box to define your hatch. From the Type drop-down list, choose one of the three options:

- **Predefined:** Enables you to select any of the standard hatch patterns.
- **User-defined:** Enables you to define your own hatch pattern by specifying the angle and spacing, using the current linetype.
- **Custom:** Enables you to choose a pattern that you've created in your own `.pat` file.

Click the Pattern drop-down list to choose the hatch patterns, or click the Ellipsis button to the right to open the Hatch Pattern palette and choose from the image tiles, as shown in Figure 16.18.

FIGURE 16.17

The Hatch and Gradient dialog box with the Hatch tab on top.

FIGURE 16.18

The Hatch Pattern palette, shown with the ANSI tab on top.

In the palette, click the tabs to see the different types of hatches. Click the image tile to choose a hatch pattern and click OK. The palette is simply another method of choosing the hatch pattern — you can also choose the pattern by using the Pattern drop-down list. The swatch shows you how your chosen hatch will look.

CROSS-REF **You can drag hatches from your drawing to the Tools palette to create hatch tools that you can then drag into your drawing. See Chapter 26 for a description of the Tools palette.**

The Custom Pattern drop-down list is available only if you have chosen Custom as the pattern type. Here you choose the name of your custom hatch pattern. I explain how to create custom hatch patterns in Chapter 31.

Setting the hatch angle and scale

Use the Angle text box to rotate the angle of the hatch pattern. You can choose from the drop-down list or type an angle. Watch out here, as many of the patterns are already defined at an angle. The hatch pattern in Figure 16.19 uses a 0-degree angle because ANSI31 is defined as diagonal lines.

The Scale box determines the scale of the hatch pattern. You can choose from the drop-down list or type a scale. A scale of 1 (the default) creates the hatch as defined. A scale of 0.5 shrinks it by one-half. Figure 16.19 shows two hatch patterns using the ANSI31 pattern. The left one uses a scale of 1, and the right one uses a scale of 0.5.

FIGURE 16.19

You can scale the hatch pattern to suit your needs.

The Spacing box and the Double check box are available if you have chosen User Defined as the pattern type. A user-defined hatch uses the current linetype and creates a hatch based on the spacing and angle that you specify. Figure 16.20 shows a user-defined double hatch with an angle of 45 degrees and 0.1-unit spacing.

FIGURE 16.20

A user-defined hatch.

To define a user-defined hatch pattern:

1. Choose Hatch from the Draw toolbar or 2D Draw control panel of the Dashboard to open the Hatch and Gradient dialog box.

2. In the Type drop-down list, choose User Defined.

3. In the Angle box, type an angle or choose one from the drop-down list. When creating a user-defined hatch, you need to specify the actual angle that you want to see.

4. In the Spacing box, enter the spacing between the lines. For example, type **.5** to create a hatch pattern with lines 0.5 units apart.

5. If you want to cross-hatch so that the parallel lines are crossed by an equal number of perpendicular lines, check Double.

The ISO Pen Width box is available only for ISO predefined hatch patterns. This feature adjusts the scale of the pattern according to the pen width that you specify. When you choose a pen width from the drop-down list, the scale shown in the Scale box automatically changes to equal the pen width. Note that you still have to separately set the width of your plotter pens when you plot your drawing.

AUTOCAD ONLY The Express Tools SUPERHATCH command creates a hatch pattern from an image, block, xref, or wipeout. Choose Express ⇨ Draw ⇨ Super Hatch. For information on installing Express Tools, see Appendix A.

Setting the hatch origin

The Hatch Origin section lets you determine where the hatch pattern starts. By default, the pattern starts at the origin of the drawing, which is generally 0,0. As a result, the hatch in your object may start somewhere in the middle. This effect is very visible with certain hatch patterns, such as bricks. In Figure 16.21, you see two rectangles. The one on the left uses the default origin; the one on the right uses the lower-left corner of the rectangle as the origin.

FIGURE 16.21

You can specify where the hatch pattern starts.

To specify the hatch origin, choose the Specified Origin option. You can then click the Click to Set New Origin button to specify any point in your drawing. However, if you want the origin to be one of the corners or the center of the hatched boundary area, check the Default to Boundary Extents check box and choose one of the options from the drop-down list.

If you always want to use the same hatch origin (such as the lower-left corner of the boundary), check the Store as Default Origin check box.

Determining the hatch boundary

Hatching an entire object is the simplest way to place a hatch. However, the area that you want to hatch is often fairly complex, and the program needs to do some calculations to determine the area.

The Hatch and Gradient dialog box offers two ways to specify the hatch boundary: you can pick points inside an area and let the command try to find an enclosed boundary, or you can select objects. If you want to hatch an entire object, follow these steps:

1. Choose Add: Select Objects. You return temporarily to your drawing.
2. Select all of the objects that you want to hatch. You can use all of the standard object-selection options to select objects. Remove and Add are especially helpful.
3. Press Enter to end object selection and return to the dialog box.

If the area you want to hatch does not neatly fit into one or more objects, choose Add: Pick Points. You return to your drawing and see the following:

```
Pick internal point or [Select objects/remove Boundaries]: Selecting
everything...
Selecting everything visible...
Analyzing the selected data...
Analyzing internal islands...
Pick internal point or [Select objects/remove Boundaries]:
```

The command is determining the *boundary set,* which is simply everything visible on the screen. At the `Pick internal point or [Select objects/remove Boundaries]:` prompt, pick a point that is inside the boundary that you want to hatch. You can continue to pick internal points to hatch adjoining areas. Each boundary is helpfully highlighted. Press Enter to return to the dialog box.

 You can hatch outside the display on the screen. The hatch pattern extends to include the entire object or boundary that you specified.

Sometimes, you need more control over the boundary and also need to remove a boundary that you've selected, without starting from scratch. To remove a boundary, click the Remove Boundaries button in the dialog box. In your drawing, when you see the `Select objects or [Add boundaries]:` prompt, select the objects that you want to remove. For example, if you have an inner island that you want to hatch, then by default, the hatch excludes the island. One way to hatch the island is to remove its boundary.

If you choose the Add Boundaries option, you can either select additional objects or pick internal points. Press Enter when you're done to return to the dialog box.

While you're in your drawing, either before or after picking points or selecting objects, you can right-click to open a very useful shortcut menu. This shortcut menu enables you to manage the hatch boundary without returning to the dialog box. Choose from the following options on the shortcut menu:

- **Enter:** Returns you to the dialog box
- **Undo Last Select/Pick/Draw:** Undoes your most recent object selection, point pick, or boundary change
- **Clear All:** Undoes all of your picks/object selections
- **Pick Internal Point:** Switches to picking internal points
- **Select Objects:** Switches to selection of objects
- **Remove Boundaries:** Lets you choose boundaries to remove
- **Hatch Origin:** Lets you choose the hatch origin
- **Normal Island Detection:** Sets island detection to Normal mode
- **Outer Island Detection:** Sets island detection to Outer mode
- **Ignore Island Detection:** Sets island detection to Ignore mode
- **Preview:** Previews the hatch

Previewing the hatch before applying it is always a good idea. After previewing a hatch, right-click to accept the preview and place the hatch. Press Esc or left-click to return to the Hatch and Gradient dialog box. From the dialog box, click OK to create the hatch and return to your drawing.

> **NOTE** To display hatches, either solid fill or lines, the FILLMODE system variable must be on, which it is by default. To turn FILLMODE off, type **fillmode** ↵ and **0** ↵. You must regenerate the drawing to see the effect.

The dialog box has several other options:

- Click Preview if you want to try it before you apply it.
- Click View Selections if you want to temporarily return to your drawing and check which objects you've selected.
- Check Annotative if you want to create a hatch with the ability to automatically resize its appearance according to viewport scale.

> **NEW FEATURE** AutoCAD 2008 and AutoCAD LT 2008 introduce the new annotative property for hatches which links size to viewport scale. Annotative objects create representations at various scales that you can automatically display at those scales when you lay out your drawing for plotting.

See Chapter 5 for information on using annotative scales, and see Chapter 17 for an exercise on using annotative objects.

- Uncheck Associative if you want to create a hatch that is not associated with its object. By default, hatches are associative.
- Check Create Separate Hatches if you are selecting several separate enclosed areas and want each area to be a separate hatch object. Otherwise, you create one hatch object that hatches these separated areas.
- Choose a draw order for hatches from the Draw Order drop-down list. By default, hatches display behind their boundaries, so that when you pick a boundary, you select the boundary, not the hatch.

■ Choose Inherit Properties to use the hatch type, pattern, angle, scale, and/or spacing of an existing hatch. You return to your drawing to pick a hatch pattern. You then return to the Hatch and Gradient dialog box.

> **CAUTION** If you use the gap tolerance feature (which I cover in the "Other advanced options" section later in this chapter), subsequent hatches are set to nonassociative. If you want associative hatches for closed areas, be sure to choose Associative in the Options area of the dialog box.

Islands

Islands are enclosed areas entirely inside a hatch boundary. Islands make hatching more difficult because you may or may not want to hatch the inside of the island.

> **NOTE** Text is counted as an island, enabling you to hatch areas that contain text without hatching over the words.

Managing islands when you select objects to hatch

When you choose the hatching boundary by selecting objects, you must also select the islands. If you select the entire area by window, you automatically include the internal islands. If you need to pick individual objects, you must also pick the islands individually. If you later erase an island, you don't lose hatch associativity, and the hatch regenerates so that it covers the entire outer boundary.

The resulting hatch depends on the boundary *style*. To specify the boundary style, in the Hatch and Gradient dialog box, click the right arrow at the lower-right corner of the dialog box to display the expanded section, shown in Figure 16.22.

FIGURE 16.22

The expanded section of the Hatch and Gradient dialog box offers advanced options to refine the hatching process.

Three boundary styles affect how islands are hatched:

- **Normal:** Hatches alternating areas so that the outer area is hatched, the next inner island is not hatched, the next inner island is hatched, and so on.
- **Outer:** Hatches only the outer area and does not hatch any inner islands.
- **Ignore:** Ignores islands and hatches everything from the outside in.

Figure 16.23 shows three copies of a nut hatched in the three styles. To hatch this model, I selected the entire model, except for the spout at the bottom, with a window.

FIGURE 16.23

Hatching islands using the three boundary styles.

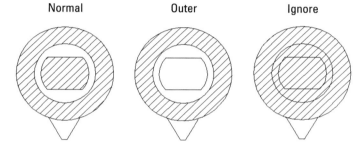

Normal   Outer   Ignore

Managing islands when you pick points to specify the hatch

When you pick points instead of selecting objects, you don't need to select the islands. Hatching detects islands by default. As soon as you pick points, the Remove Boundaries button becomes available, and you can select the islands to remove them from consideration if you want to hatch them. For example, if you remove all of the islands shown in Figure 16.23, the result is the same as using the Ignore style, where everything inside the outside boundary is hatched.

Other advanced options

When you pick points to determine the hatch boundary, the hatching process uses the same mechanism as the BOUNDARY command to temporarily create a boundary for hatching. Check Retain Boundaries in the Boundary Retention section of the expanded dialog box if you want to draw the boundary as an object, and specify whether you want it to be a region or a polyline. Otherwise, the boundary is discarded when the hatch is placed. For more information, see the discussion of the BOUNDARY command earlier in this chapter.

You can also specify a smaller boundary set than the objects that are visible on-screen. Use this when you're picking points and have such a complex drawing that the process of analyzing the visible objects takes a long time. To create a new boundary set, click the New button and specify a window in your drawing.

You can hatch areas that are not completely closed using the Gap Tolerance feature. In the Tolerance text box, enter a value greater than the size of the gap. You can use values from 0 to 5000. When you hatch an unclosed area, sometimes picking points is more successful; other times, selecting objects works best, so try both options. When you do so, the Open Boundary Warning message opens. Click Yes to hatch the open boundary. Note that the hatch is not associative, which means that if you modify your almost closed area, you need to rehatch. Using this feature sets subsequent hatches as non-associative, so be sure to recheck the Associative check box in the main part of the dialog box.

You can fine-tune how a hatch inherits properties, specifically the hatch's origin. Choose to use the current origin setting (from the left side of the dialog box) or use the setting of the source hatch.

Dragging and dropping hatch patterns

After you have spent the time creating a hatch, you may want to use that hatch in other drawings. You can open a `.pat` (hatch pattern) file from the DesignCenter, preview its hatch patterns, and drag any hatch pattern into any closed object in your current drawing. Here's how to drag a hatch pattern from the DesignCenter:

1. Click DesignCenter on the Standard (or Standard Annotation) toolbar (or press Ctrl+2) to open the DesignCenter.

2. Use the Tree view to navigate to the folder that contains your `acad.pat`, `acadlt.pat`, or other `.pat` file. If necessary, click the Desktop button and navigate from there.

 To find the location of your `.pat` files, choose Tools ➪ Options and click the File tab. Double-click the Support File Search Path option. One of the paths listed contains your hatch files.

3. Double-click the folder and select a hatch pattern (`.pat`) file. A preview of all of the hatch patterns appears in the right pane.

4. From the right pane of the DesignCenter, drag the hatch pattern that you want onto a closed object in your drawing (or an unclosed object with the gap tolerance value greater than the gap). If you need more options, right-click the pattern as you drag, then choose BHATCH from the shortcut menu to open the Hatch and Gradient dialog box, and then specify the hatch parameters in the usual way.

You can drag a hatch pattern to a tool palette to create a hatch with the properties — such as layer and angle — of the hatch in your drawing. Then you can drag that hatch tool onto any closed area in your drawing. The hatch automatically fills the area with the same properties. For more information on tool palettes, see Chapter 26.

Creating gradient fills

Gradients are fills that gradually change from dark to light or from one color to another. You can use gradients to create presentation-quality illustrations without rendering. You can also use gradients as a substitute for shading because they offer more flexible options.

AUTOCAD ONLY AutoCAD LT doesn't offer the gradient feature.

To create a gradient:

1. Choose Gradient from the Draw toolbar or 2D Draw control panel of the Dashboard to open the Hatch and Gradient dialog box with the Gradient tab on top, shown in Figure 16.24.

2. Choose One Color or Two Color.

   ■ If you choose One Color, click the ellipsis button to the right of the color swatch to open the Select Color dialog box, where you can choose the color you want. (For instructions on using this dialog box, see Chapter 11.) Then use the Shade/Tint slider to choose whether you want the gradient to range lighter or darker. You see the result in the gradient swatches below the slider.

   ■ If you choose Two Color, you see two color swatches. Click each Ellipsis button and choose a color.

FIGURE 16.24

Use the Gradient tab of the Hatch and Gradient dialog box to create gradient fills of closed objects.

3. Choose one of the nine gradient styles.

4. If you want the gradient to be symmetrical, check the Centered check box. To create a gradient that isn't symmetrical, uncheck the Centered check box. When you uncheck the Centered check box, the gradient focus moves up and to the left. (You can change this location by changing the angle, as explained in the next step.)

5. From the Angle drop-down list, choose an angle. If your gradient is centered, the gradient rotates around its center and remains symmetrical. If your gradient is not centered, the gradient rotates around the edges. Watch the gradient style tiles to see the results. You can type an angle that is not on the list.

6. Choose Add: Pick Points to pick a location inside a closed area or choose Add: Select Objects to select closed objects, as explained in the section, "Determining the hatch boundary." (The other options are the same as for hatches.) In your drawing, specify the area that you want to hatch, and then end selection to return to the dialog box.

7. To preview the gradient, click Preview. To return to the dialog box, press Esc.

8. Click OK to finalize the gradient.

You can use the Gap Tolerance feature to fill an almost-enclosed area with a gradient. For more information, see the discussion on hatches in the "Other advanced options" section earlier in this chapter.

See Figure 16.25 for an example of some gradient fills. You could turn off the boundary layer for a more realistic look.

FIGURE 16.25

The gradient on the left gives the illusion of light shining from the left. (Refer to Figure 8-26, which shows the original isometric drawing without the gradients.) On the right, you see a sophisticated use of gradients to create a presentation-quality drawing.

Thanks to James Wedding for permission to use the drawing on the right from Jones & Boyd, Inc.

Editing hatches

To edit a hatch pattern, including a solid or gradient, double-click it. The Hatch Edit dialog box opens. You can also choose Modify ➪ Object ➪ Hatch and then select a hatch object.

The Hatch Edit dialog box is exactly the same as the Hatch and Gradient dialog box, except that not all of the options are available. You can use this dialog box to change any of the hatch properties. You can change the boundary style on the expanded area of the dialog box. You can also preview the hatch. After you make your changes, click OK to return to your drawing.

Because hatches are associative (unless you explode them or choose to create them as nonassociative), when you edit their boundaries, they adjust to fit the new boundary. However, if the new boundary is no longer closed, the hatch may lose its associativity, and you see the Hatch boundary associativity removed warning message.

By default, object snaps don't work with hatch lines. This prevents you from accidentally drawing to a hatch line instead of a nearby object. If you want to snap to hatch lines, choose Tools ➪ Options, click the Drafting tab, and uncheck the Ignore Hatch Objects check box. Click OK to return to your drawing.

 You can obtain the area of a hatch in the Properties palette. Select a hatch and open the Properties palette. Look for the Area item in the Geometry section.

You can also recreate the boundary of any hatch as a polyline or region. Edit the hatch and choose Recreate Boundary in the Edit Hatch dialog box. You can use this feature to create a boundary for a hatch if you have deleted it.

You can also edit a gradient (AutoCAD only) in the Properties palette. Choose Properties on the Standard (or Standard Annotation) toolbar (or press Ctrl+1) and use the items in the Pattern section. You can change the colors, angle, type, and whether it is centered.

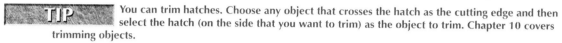

You may find it difficult to select solid fill hatches. In some locations, you can pick the solid hatch, while at other points, you get the Other corner: prompt, meaning that no object was found. If necessary, try a crossing window at the edge of the hatch. This always selects the solid hatch but also selects the boundary. Hatches have a grip at their center. If you can find the grip and include it in the window, you can easily select the solid hatch. When the hatch highlights as you hover the mouse over it, you can pick to select it.

TIP You can trim hatches. Choose any object that crosses the hatch as the cutting edge and then select the hatch (on the side that you want to trim) as the object to trim. Chapter 10 covers trimming objects.

ON the DVD-ROM The drawing used in the following exercise on creating and editing hatches, ab16-f.dwg, is in the Drawings folder on the DVD.

STEPS: Creating and Editing Hatches

1. Open ab16-f.dwg from your DVD.

2. Save the file as ab16-06.dwg in your AutoCAD Bible folder.

 3. Choose Hatch from the Draw toolbar or 2D Draw control panel of the Dashboard. On the Hatch tab of the Hatch and Gradient dialog box, choose ANSI35 from the Pattern drop-down list. From the Scale drop-down list, choose 0.5. Click Add: Select Objects.

4. You're now back in your drawing. Pick the two large circles in Figure 16.26. Right-click and choose Preview. Press Esc to return to the dialog box. Click OK to create the hatch and end the BHATCH command.

FIGURE 16.26

The result after editing the two hatches.

5. Again choose Hatch from the Draw toolbar or 2D Draw control panel of the Dashboard. From the Type drop-down list, choose User defined. Set the angle to 135 and the spacing to 0.05.

6. Choose Add: Pick Points. In your drawing, pick points ❶, ❷, ❸, and ❹ in Figure 16.26. Right-click and choose Preview. Right-click again to create the hatch and end the BHATCH command.

7. Click the circumference of the left large circle. (If necessary, zoom in to avoid selecting the hatching.) Pick the top grip to make it hot. At the Specify stretch point or [Base Point/Copy/ Undo/eXit]: prompt, type .35 ↵. Press Esc to remove the grips.

8. Double-click one of the hatches at the top of the model. Notice that this action selects all of the hatches because they were created with one command. In the Hatch Edit dialog box that opens, change the angle to 90 and the spacing to 0.04. Click OK. Your drawing should look like Figure 16.26.

9. Save your drawing.

Using the SOLID command

The SOLID command creates solidly filled 2D areas. (It is not directly related to 3D solids.) In general, BHATCH is much more flexible. Although the SOLID command is a 2D command, it's sometimes used in 3D drawing. When you create a 2D solid and give it thickness, it creates surfaces with tops and bottoms. I cover using thickness in Chapter 21.

SOLID creates straight-edged shapes. If FILLMODE is on, AutoCAD or AutoCAD LT fills in the shape with a solid fill (that's why it's called SOLID).

To draw a solid, type **solid** ↵. The command prompts you for first, second, third, and fourth points. You must specify these points in zigzag order, not around the perimeter of the shape. After the fourth point, the command continues to prompt you for third and fourth points, which you can use to create new adjacent solids. Press Enter to end the command.

Creating and Editing Multilines

Multilines are sets of parallel lines that you draw with one command. You can specify how far apart they are, and each line can have its own color and linetype. Multilines are used for drawing architectural plans where you need to draw an inner and outer wall. (I cover a 3D version, polysolids, in Chapter 24.) To draw a multiline, you first define, save, and load a multiline style. Then you can use the multiline style to draw multilines. There is a separate command for editing multilines that enables you to break multiline intersections, as you would for the doors and windows in a floor plan. Figure 16.27 shows a floor plan for an apartment drawn using multilines.

 AutoCAD LT doesn't have the Multiline feature but has a similar feature called Dlines. I cover Dlines in the section "Creating Dlines in AutoCAD LT."

FIGURE 16.27

A floor plan of an apartment that is drawn using multilines.

Thanks to Bill Wynn of New Windsor, Maryland, for this drawing.

Creating a multiline style

The first step in drawing multilines is to design the multiline style. To create a multiline style, choose Format ⇨ Multiline Style to open the Multiline Style dialog box, as shown in Figure 16.28.

The Multiline Style dialog box.

Like text styles and dimension styles, multiline styles group a set of properties under one name. The default multiline style, called Standard, defines two lines 1 unit apart. Multiline styles have two parts: element properties and multiline properties. The element properties define each individual line element. The multiline properties define properties that apply to the multiline as a whole.

Defining multiline style properties

To start defining the multiline style, click New. In the Create New Multiline Style dialog box, type a name in the New Style Name text box and click Continue. The New Multiline Style dialog box opens, as shown in Figure 16.29.

The Elements section lists the current elements of the multiline. Elements are simply the lines that make up the multiline. The offset defines the distance of the line from the start point when you start to draw. An offset of zero places the line on the start point. As you can see, the Standard multiline style has two elements, each 0.5 units from the start point. Figure 16.30 shows the Standard multiline style as it appears in relation to the start point that you pick.

 You can change the relationship of the start point and the element lines by using the Justification option when you draw the multiline, as explained later in the "Drawing multilines" section.

FIGURE 16.29

The New Multiline Style dialog box.

FIGURE 16.30

The Standard multiline style places two lines on either side of the start point.

To define the element lines of a multiline style, follow these steps:

1. In the Elements section, highlight the first element. Even if you typed a new name for the multiline style, the elements listed are the same as the current multiline style.

TIP When creating a new multiline style, first set as current the multiline style that is the most similar to the one that you want to create.

2. In the Offset box, type the offset value that you want. The offset should be zero if you want the line to appear on your pick points, a positive number (in units) if you want the line to appear above your pick points, and a negative number (in units) if you want the line to appear below your pick points. (This assumes the default of zero justification, explained later in this chapter.)

TIP When defining the multiline style elements, think of the multiline as being drawn horizontally to the right to help you visualize what *above* and *below* mean.

3. Choose Color to choose a color for the line element.

4. Choose Linetype to choose a linetype for the line element.

5. Choose Add to add a new element or Delete to delete a listed element.

6. To define the next element, select the second element in the Elements box and repeat Steps 2 through 4. Continue to define elements until you're done.

7. If you want, enter a description for the multiline style in the Description text box.

8. Click OK to return to the Multiline Style dialog box.

 A multiline style can have up to 16 elements. All 16 elements must be on the same layer, but you can vary the linetypes and colors.

Use the left side of the New Multiline Style dialog box to set the overall properties of the multiline. Caps cross the ends of multilines to close them. You can choose line or arc caps. Figure 16.31 shows the effects of all of the possible choices in this box. You can also choose a color to add a solid fill to the multiline. To display a line at the junction of each line segment, check the Display Joints check box. After you make your choices, click OK to return to the Multiline Style dialog box.

FIGURE 16.31

The results of choosing the various options in the New Multiline Style dialog box.

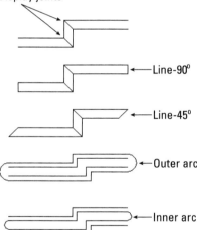

Saving a new multiline style

Before you can use the multiline style, you must save it. AutoCAD saves multiline styles in a file with the .mln filename extension. After you click Save, the Save Multiline Style dialog box opens.

In general, you can save your multiline styles in the default file, which is acad.mln. Click Save to return to the Multiline Style dialog box.

Loading a multiline style

Like linetypes, multiline styles must be loaded before you can use them. Choose Load to open the Load Multiline Styles dialog box. Choose the style that you created from the list and click OK.

You return to the Multiline Styles dialog box. You're now ready to use the multiline style. Click OK to return to your drawing.

You can also use the Multiline Style dialog box to rename multiline styles and make another multiline style current.

ON the DVD-ROM   The drawing used in the following exercise on creating a multiline style, ab16-g.dwg, is in the Drawings folder on the DVD.

STEPS: Creating a Multiline Style

1. Open ab16-g.dwg from your DVD.
2. Save the file as ab16-07.dwg in your AutoCAD Bible folder. This is a site plan, shown in Figure 16.32.

FIGURE 16.32

The parallel lines at the bottom of the site plan can be drawn by using a multiline.

3. Choose Format ⇨ Multiline Style to open the Multiline Style dialog box. Click New. In the text box, type **siteplan**. Choose Continue.
4. In the Elements section of the dialog box, the top element should be highlighted. Change the offset to 0, the color to black (it may list as white), and the linetype to DASHDOT.
5. Highlight the second element. Change the offset to –132 (11' × 12"), the color to magenta, and the linetype to continuous.
6. Click Add. Change the offset to –180 (15' × 12"), the color to red, and the linetype to center.
7. Click Add. Change the offset to –228 (19' × 12"), the color to magenta, and the linetype to continuous.
8. Click Add. Change the offset to –360 (30' × 12"), the color to black, and the linetype to dashdot.
9. Click Add. Change the offset to –480 (40' × 12"), the color to red, and the linetype to center.
10. Click OK. In the Multiline Style dialog box, click Save.

CAUTION If you are using someone else's computer, check with the owner before saving the linestyle to `acad.mln`. You can't do any damage, but the owner may not want to have your multiline style there. You can change the name in the File Name text box to something else, such as `my_mls.mln`.

11. In the Save Multiline Style dialog box, you should see `acad.mln` in the File Name text box. You can also type a new MLN filename. Choose Save.

12. With the new multiline style selected, choose Set Current, and click OK to return to your drawing.

13. Save your drawing. If you're continuing on to the next exercise, keep the drawing open.

Drawing multilines

Defining a multiline style is the hard part. As soon as the style is defined, saved, loaded, and made current, you can draw with it. You may find that you need some practice to get the hang of it because you're drawing more than one line at once. To draw a multiline, choose Draw ➪ Multiline to start the MLINE command. The command responds with the `Specify start point or [Justification/Scale/STyle]:` prompt. The prompt also displays the current justification, scale, and style. The default is to pick a point. From there you get the `Specify next point:` prompt. After the first segment, you get the `Specify next point or [Undo]:` prompt, and after the second segment, the `Specify next point or [Close/Undo]:` prompt. Here is how to use the options:

■ **Justification:** You can choose Zero, Top, or Bottom.

  ▪ Zero places the element that has a zero offset in the multiline definition at the pick point. You do not need to have a line at zero offset, as is the case with the Standard multiline style. The top example in Figure 16.33 shows the Standard multiline style with zero justification.

  ▪ Top places the line with the highest positive offset at the pick point. The middle example in Figure 16.33 shows the Standard multiline style with top justification.

  ▪ Bottom places the line with the highest negative offset at the pick point. The bottom example in Figure 16.33 shows the Standard multiline style with bottom justification.

■ **Scale:** Multiplies the offset values in the multiline definition by the scale. The Standard multiline style places two lines 1 unit apart. A scale of 6 would place them 6 units apart.

■ **Style:** Enables you to specify the current multiline style. Type ? ↵ to get a list of the available multiline styles.

FIGURE 16.33

Drawing a multiline using the Standard multiline style in zero, top, and bottom justification.

As you draw a multiline, whenever you create a corner by changing direction, the command creates a clean corner.

STEPS: Drawing Multilines

1. Continue from the previous exercise. (If you didn't do the previous exercise, you should do it to create the multiline style.) Set a running object snap for intersection. Turn on Ortho.

2. Choose Draw ➪ Multiline. The prompt displays the following message:

   `Current settings: Justification = Top, Scale = 1.00, Style = SITEPLAN`

3. At the `Specify start point or [Justification/Scale/STyle]:` prompt, press Shift + right-click and choose the From object snap. At the `Base point:` prompt, choose ❶ in Figure 16.35. (If necessary, press Tab until you get the Intersection object snap.) At the `<Offset>:` prompt, type **@0,–10'** ↵.

4. At the `Specify next point:` prompt, move the cursor to the right and type **255'** ↵. If you want, you can experiment by drawing other line segments. Press Enter to end the command. The drawing should look like Figure 16.34.

5. Save your drawing.

FIGURE 16.34

The completed multiline.

Editing multilines

No matter how many segments it contains, the entire multiline is one object. Many editing commands simply do not work with multilines. Table 16.1 shows the editing commands and whether they work with multilines.

TABLE 16.1

Using Editing Commands with Multilines

Command	Usable with Multilines	Command	Usable with Multilines
ARRAY	Yes	LENGTHEN	no
BREAK	No	MIRROR	yes
CHAMFER	No	MOVE	yes
COPY	Yes	ROTATE	yes
EXPLODE	Yes	SCALE	yes
EXTEND	Yes	STRETCH	yes
FILLET	No	TRIM	yes

You can use grips to stretch, move, copy, mirror, and rotate multilines.

To edit multilines, you use the MLEDIT command. To start MLEDIT, double-click the multiline (or choose Modify ➪ Object ➪ Multiline) to open the Multilines Edit Tools dialog box, shown in Figure 16.35.

FIGURE 16.35

The Multilines Edit Tools dialog box.

This dialog box enables you to edit multiline intersections and corners. You can also add or delete a vertex. Click one of the images, and its name appears at the bottom of the dialog box.

The first column manages crossing intersections. To edit a crossing intersection, choose one of the tiles in the first column and click OK. The command prompts you to pick a first multiline and then a second multiline. MLEDIT always cuts the first multiline that you pick. The second one may be cut if it is called for by the edit type.

 Although the command prompts you to pick two multilines, they can actually be two parts of the same multiline.

The second column manages T-shaped intersections. To edit a crossing intersection, choose one of the tiles in the second column and click OK. The command prompts you to pick a first multiline and then a second multiline. MLEDIT always cuts the first multiline that you pick. The second one may be cut if it is called for by the edit type and depending on the shape of the multiline.

The third column manages corners and vertices. The top tile creates a corner. The second tile adds a vertex, and the third deletes a vertex. Choose the edit that you want and click OK. The command prompts you to select a multiline. Be careful — you must pick the point where you want to add or delete the vertex. To see the current vertices, pick the multiline with no command active to see the grips.

The last column of the dialog box makes cuts through multilines and welds them back together again. Here's how to use these options:

- Use the top tile to make a cut through one element of a multiline.
- Use the middle tile to cut through all of the elements of a multiline.

  In both cases, you get a prompt to select a multiline and then a second point. Be careful — the point that you use to select the multiline is the first point of the cut. For a single cut, the pick point of the multiline also determines which element the command cuts.

- Use the bottom tile to remove the cuts. Removing cuts is called *welding*.

For all of these editing tools, you get prompts for further edits. Press Enter to end selection.

You can also move vertices using grips with the Stretch option.

An old command, TRACE, draws lines with width. Usually you can use polylines or multilines instead to create the same effect.

 Multiline styles are stored with the drawing, so that they can be updated and viewed, even if the multiline style file containing the multiline definition is not available.

Creating Dlines in AutoCAD LT

Dlines are the AutoCAD LT equivalent of Multilines. AutoCAD does not include dlines. Dlines (double lines) create line segments and arcs that are individual objects. The double lines and arcs have nicely finished corners and ends. You can specify the width between the lines, offset the lines from your pick points, and cap the lines with a simple square cap.

To create a dline, choose Draw ⇨ Double Line. The first prompt, `Specify start point or [Break/Caps/Dragline/Snap/Width]:`, gives you the following options:

- **Break:** Breaks the dline when it crosses other double lines, single lines, or arcs.
- **Caps:** Places a square cap at the start or end of the double line or at both the start and end. Otherwise, use the None sub-option.

- **Dragline:** Offsets the double line from your pick points. A positive value for this option offsets to the right, and a negative value offsets to the left of your pick points. By default, the double line is centered on either side of your pick points. You can also choose to use the Left or Right suboptions to align the left or right line with your pick points.

- **Snap:** Ends a double line whenever you use an object snap.

- **Width:** Specifies the distance between the double lines.

After you specify the first point, the prompt expands to give you three more options:

- **Arc:** Creates double arcs using this option. (You can't easily do this in AutoCAD!) You have suboptions that are similar to the ARC command options, including a Line option to return to drawing lines segments.

- **CLose:** Draws a double line from the last point back to the first point.

- **Undo:** Undoes the last line segment or arc.

Because dlines are individual lines and arcs, there are no special editing tools and they are easy to edit.

Using the SKETCH Command

The SKETCH command enables you to draw freehand. Freehand drawing is useful for contour lines in architectural or civil engineering drawings, for illustrative effects, and for when you're feeling artistic. Although you may get best results if you have a digitizer and a stylus pen, you can sketch with a mouse or puck as well. Figure 16.36 shows some contour lines created with SKETCH.

 AutoCAD LT does not offer the Sketch feature.

FIGURE 16.36

Contour lines drawn with SKETCH.

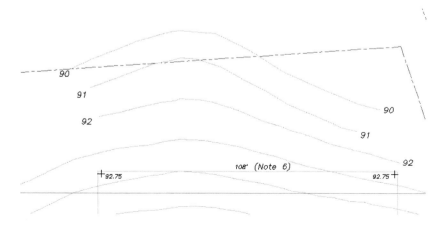

Sketch can create lines or polylines. Polylines are probably easier to work with if you need to edit the sketch later; you can use the PEDIT command. To specify whether SKETCH creates lines or polylines, set the SKPOLY system variable. A value of zero creates lines, and a value of one creates polylines.

Start the SKETCH command by typing **sketch** ↵. The command places you in a special sketch mode and displays a special menu on the command line:

```
Record increment <0.1000>: Press Enter or type a new increment.
Sketch.  Pen eXit Quit Record Erase Connect .
```

Type the record increment, which is the length of the line or polyline segment that you want to create. If the increment is too big, small movements do not create a segment at all, and the sketch line appears jagged instead of smooth. However, you need to take into account the scale of your drawing and your zoom factor. You should also turn off ORTHO and SNAP if they're on.

The pick button is equivalent to typing **p**, and toggles the pen up and down. Follow these steps to start sketching:

1. Place the cursor where you want to start drawing.
2. Press the pick button. The prompt responds with the `<Pen down>` message. You can now draw.
3. Without holding down the pick button, move the mouse or stylus to create the shape that you want. SKETCH creates a temporary green line.
4. After you finish, click the pick button again to see the `<Pen up>` message.
5. Move the mouse to the starting point of your next line or polyline. Continue in this manner until you finish sketching.
6. Type **r** to record the sketch. The prompt tells you what you created. The sketch changes to the color of the current layer and becomes permanent, as shown in this example:

   ```
   4 polylines with 238 edges recorded.
   ```
7. Type **x** to exit Sketch mode.

Here are the other options:

- **Quit:** Quits Sketch mode without saving your sketch. The temporary line disappears.
- **Erase:** Erases temporary lines.
- **Connect:** Enables you to continue drawing from the end of the last sketch. Use this when the pen is up. Type **c** and move to the endpoint of the last temporary sketch.
- **. (Period):** Enables you to draw straight line segments from the endpoint of the last sketch. While the pen is up, type a period to add a line segment from the last endpoint to your current cursor position.

 The drawing used in the following exercise on sketching, `ab16-h.dwg`, is in the `Drawings` folder on the DVD.

STEPS: Sketching

1. Open `ab16-h.dwg` from your DVD.
2. Save the file as `ab16-08.dwg` in your `AutoCAD Bible` folder. It shows the front elevation of a house. You'll add the sketched path and contours, as shown in Figure 16.37.
3. Type **skpoly** ↵. Set SKPOLY to 1 and press Enter.

4. Type **sketch** ↵. At the Record increment <0'-0">: prompt, type **1** ↵ to set the record increment to 1".

5. At the Sketch. Pen eXit Quit Record Erase Connect . prompt, move the cursor to ❶ in Figure 16.37. Click the pick button to put the pen down and draw the first line of the path. Click the pick button to put the pen up.

6. Use the same technique to draw the other lines in Figure 16.37. If you make a mistake, type **q** ↵ to quit and then start again.

7. After you're done, type **r** to record the lines.

8. Type **x** to end the SKETCH command.

9. Save your drawing.

FIGURE 16.37

A sketched path and contours.

Digitizing Drawings with the TABLET Command

In Chapter 3, I explained that you can use a digitizer to execute commands. One important use for a digitizer is to copy paper drawings into your drawing. Many companies have used this technique to copy old drawings that were drafted by hand so that they could be edited electronically. Digitizing can also be used to copy artwork and logos into a drawing.

To digitize a paper drawing, you use a special digitizing mode that turns the entire digitizer into a drawing tablet. To start the TABLET command, choose Tools ➪ Tablet and choose one of the options.

If you've been using the digitizer to execute commands, you need to reconfigure it to eliminate the command areas and enlarge the drawing area. Use the Configure option of the TABLET command and reconfigure the digitizer for 0 tablet menus. Respecify the screen pointing area so that the fixed screen pointing area covers the entire digitizing area.

Attach the paper drawing securely to the digitizer so that it won't move as you work.

To set up the digitizing mode, start the TABLET command and choose the Calibrate option. The option prompts you to pick two points on the paper drawing and specify which coordinates they represent. To do this you need to mark two points on the paper drawing; take out a ruler and measure their distance. If the drawing has a title block, two corners of the title block are distinctive points to mark and measure. If the drawing is drawn to a scale — and it probably is — the coordinates you type should be the distance in real life, not the measurement. In other words, if the two horizontal points are 1 inch apart and 1 inch represents 48 inches (a scale of 1=48), you could enter 0,0 for the first point and 48,0 for the second point. However, it is usually useful to choose points over a wider area of your drawing. You can calibrate more than two points if you want.

NOTE If your drawing is distorted or uses a perspective view that you want to straighten out, you can calibrate additional points and choose either Affine or Projective calibration to account for the distortion. Affine calibration requires at least three points and scales the X and Y axes separately. Projective calibration requires at least four points and stretches the coordinates to adjust for the perspective view. You can provide up to 31 calibration points.

After you finish specifying calibration points and coordinates, press Enter. Now your entire tablet can be used only for picking points. You can press F12 to use a menu or toolbar and press F12 again to return to picking points, or type commands on the command line.

NOTE You can turn Tablet mode on and off by starting the TABLET command and choosing the On and Off options. Tablet calibration settings are lost when you close the drawing session.

Choose the command that you need and pick points along the paper drawing. After you're done, turn off Tablet mode and do any necessary editing and cleanup.

In this exercise, you practice digitizing drawings. If you have a digitizer, you can try this exercise. Otherwise, skip it.

STEPS: Digitizing Drawings

1. Start a new drawing using `acad.dwt` or `acadlt.dwt` as your template.
2. Save the file as `ab16-09.dwg` in your `AutoCAD Bible` folder. This is a sheet metal template as shown in Figure 16.38.
3. Make a photocopy of Figure 16.38 and tape it to the active area of your digitizer.
4. Choose Tools ⇨ Tablet ⇨ Calibrate. Follow the prompts:
   ```
   Digitize point #1: Pick ❶ in Figure 16.38.
   Enter coordinates for point #1: 0,0 ↵
   Digitize point #2: Pick ❷ in Figure 16.38.
   Enter coordinates for point #2: 7,5 ↵
   Digitize point #3 (or RETURN to end): ↵
   ```
5. Type **tablet** ↵ and **on** ↵.
6. Type **line** ↵.
7. In Figure 16.38, pick ❸ with the digitizer, then ❹, and then each line endpoint in turn, counterclockwise around the figure.
8. After you reach ❺, do not digitize point ❶ again. Instead, type **c** ↵ to close the figure exactly.
9. Type **tablet** ↵. Type **off** ↵ to return the digitizer to Screen Pointing mode.
10. Save your drawing.

FIGURE 16.38

An unfolded sheet-metal template.

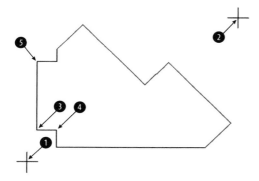

Summary

Several types of complex objects add greatly to the capabilities of AutoCAD and AutoCAD LT. In this chapter, you read about:

- Using polylines to combine lines, segments, and arcs of any width into one object
- Utilizing splines to mathematically calculate curves, fit to points that you specify
- Using regions, which are two-dimensional surfaces
- Creating regions or polylines from complex areas by using the BOUNDARY command
- Filling in an area with lines, a solid fill, or a gradient (AutoCAD only) with the hatch feature
- Drawing complex parallel lines at one time with multilines (AutoCAD only), and drawing double lines with AutoCAD LT
- Drawing freehand by using the SKETCH command, creating either lines or polylines (AutoCAD only)
- Using a digitizer in Tablet mode, when you need to copy a paper drawing into AutoCAD or AutoCAD LT

In the next chapter, I explain how to lay out and plot a drawing.

Chapter 17

Plotting and Printing Your Drawing

Most drawing jobs are not complete until you see the final result on paper. Traditionally, drawings are plotted on a plotter. However, you can also print a drawing on a regular computer printer. Many printers and plotters can handle a wide range of drawing sizes and paper types. In this chapter, I explain the process of preparing a drawing for plotting, including laying it out in paper space, more properly known as a *layout*. Finally, I cover the actual process of creating a plot.

Preparing a Drawing for Plotting or Printing

When you complete your drawing, you often have some details to finish. If you didn't start with a title block, you may need to insert one. Even if you have a title block, you may need to complete some of its annotation,such as the date that you completed the drawing. If the drawing has layers that you don't want to appear on paper, you should set their layer state to Frozen, Off, or Not Plottable.

Many architectural and mechanical drawings show several views of the model. Now is the time to check that the views are pleasingly laid out, with enough space between them for dimensions and annotation. Later in this chapter, I explain how to create viewports that lay out the drawing in various views.

Doing a draft plot

You may want to do a draft plot, either to check the drawing itself or to be sure that it will print out properly. Although you can preview the plot, sometimes the results are not what you want, and it pays to test the plot on inexpensive paper before plotting on expensive vellum. Draft plots for checking purposes can often be done on a printer. Some companies have wide-format inkjet printers that accept 17×22-inch paper and are used exclusively for check plots. Even if the final plot will be all in black, a color printer is a good choice for draft plots because you can easily check the layer scheme.

Plotting a drawing from model space

Model space refers to the mode in which you work when you draw and edit your model. Throughout this book, the discussions and exercises have assumed that you were in model space. AutoCAD and AutoCAD LT have two buttons on the status bar that let you switch between model space and a layout. When the Model button is indented, you know that you're in model space, as shown in Figure 17.1.

You can switch between two methods for displaying model and paper space (layouts). One method shows two buttons on the status bar — a model button and a button for the current layout. You can click the arrows to access a menu listing additional layouts. See Figure 17.1. This system increases the drawing area slightly.

FIGURE 17.1

You can switch between model and paper space using the buttons on the status bar.

Click to display the model and layout tabs

Additional Layouts menu

Current layout button

Model button

The other method uses tabs for model space and each of the layouts, as shown in Figure 17.2. To display the tabs instead of the buttons on the status bar, right-click either button and choose Display Layout and Model Tabs.

After you've prepared your drawing for plotting, as just discussed, you can plot your drawing. See the discussion on plotting later in this chapter.

CROSS-REF You can also plot entire sheet sets. For more information, see Chapter 26. The PUBLISH command, which I cover in Chapter 28, lets you plot multiple drawings.

Creating a Layout in Paper Space

If you're using several views of your model, you should consider creating a paper space layout. Although paper space was designed for the needs of 3D drawings, it's often used for 2D layout as well. If you want to show views of your model at different scales, paper space is indispensable. If you use a title block, paper space is a good choice, because the size of the title block needs to be appropriate for the sheet of paper on which you will plot. Paper space is a tool for laying out a drawing. It's analogous to creating a sheet of paper at the size on which you'll plot, and placing views on the paper. You place the views by means of *floating viewports.* Floating viewports on a paper space layout are windows into model space, through which you see your drawing.

A layout provides a visual environment that lets you know what your plot will look like. By creating more than one layout for a drawing, you can create more than one plot for a single drawing. For example, you can create layouts at different scales for different sheet sizes, layouts with different layer states for contractors who need to see varying aspects of a drawing, or layouts that show different sets of views of the drawing.

Entering paper space

You draw in model space, which you access by clicking the Model button on the status bar or the Model tab at the bottom of the screen. You use a paper space layout to lay out a drawing. When you're in paper space, you can view your drawing only through floating viewports.

To enter a paper space layout, simply click the layout button on the status bar. If you are using tabs, click a layout tab. By default, you see one floating viewport through which you can view your model. An example is shown in Figure 17.2. The paper space icon and the layout tab confirm that you're looking at a paper space layout.

To switch back to model space, click the Model button or tab.

FIGURE 17.2

When you display a layout, the layout is automatically created, with one floating viewport through which you can see your entire drawing.

Printable area of paper   Floating viewport

Current layout tab   Paper size of current plotter or printer

Model tab

Paper space icon

Using the Layout Wizard

The Layout Wizard guides you through the process of laying out a drawing in paper space. Although you may eventually want to lay out your drawings on your own, the Layout Wizard is one way to get started using a paper space layout.

To use the Layout Wizard, follow these steps:

1. Choose Tools ➪ Wizards ➪ Create Layout. You see the wizard screen shown in Figure 17.3, where you name the layout. This name will appear on the Additional Layouts menu on the status bar or on the layout tab at the bottom of the drawing area.

FIGURE 17.3

The first screen of the Layout Wizard.

2. Type a name for the layout and click Next.

3. The second screen asks you to choose a configured plotter. This list also includes printers. For more information on configuring a plotter or printer, see Appendix A. Click Next after you're done.

4. On the third screen, shown in Figure 17.4, specify a paper size and drawing units, and then click Next.

5. On the next screen, specify whether you want the drawing to plot in portrait or landscape orientation. The wizard rotates a letter *A* on a sheet of paper so that you can see which way your drawing will plot. Then click Next.

6. On the Title Block screen, choose a title block if you want to add one. You can add it as a block, which actually inserts the title block (see Chapter 18), or as an *external reference,* or *xref,* which references an outside drawing of a title block (see Chapter 19). Choose the option you prefer in the Type section, and click Next.

FIGURE 17.4

The Paper Size screen of the Layout Wizard.

NOTE To add your own title block, first create it as a drawing (in model space) and save it in the \Template folder, or create your own folder for your templates. (To find the location of the \Template folder, choose Tools ➪ Options and click the Files tab. Double-click Template Settings and then Drawing Template File Location. To use your own folder, change this location. The new location will become the default location for all your templates. Using your own folder reduces the chance that you'll lose your templates when you reinstall or upgrade.) If you have a template that you use for a title block, open a new drawing using that template and save it as a drawing in the \Template folder, using the same name as the template. (It now has a .dwg filename extension.) AutoCAD no longer supplies drawing files for most of the templates, and AutoCAD LT includes none, so you need to use your own.

7. On the Define Viewports screen, shown in Figure 17.5, you choose from four viewport configuration options:

   - Choose None if you want to create your own floating viewports.
   - Choose Single to create one viewport.
   - Choose Std. 3D Engineering Views to create a 2×2 array of top, front, side, and isometric views.
   - Choose Array to specify how many views you want, in rows and columns.

   You can also set the viewport scale. If you want to set the scale of each viewport individually, leave the default Scaled to Fit option for now. Then click Next.

CROSS-REF For more information on scales, see Chapter 5. Also see the discussion of viewport scales later in this chapter.

8. On the Pick Location screen, the wizard prompts you to pick two corners to define the size of the viewport configuration that you chose. If you chose more than one viewport, these two corners define the extents of all of the viewports combined, not the extents of the individual viewports. Click Next.

9. On the last screen, click Finish to close the wizard and return to your drawing.

FIGURE 17.5

The Define Viewports screen of the Layout Wizard.

Figure 17.6 shows the result of completing the wizard with a 2×1 array of viewports. Usually, you still need to pan the model and change the scale to get the view that you want in each viewport. I discuss this process later in this chapter.

FIGURE 17.6

After completing the Layout Wizard, you now see your model in the viewport(s) that you created.

Laying out a drawing in paper space on your own

The Layout Wizard is a good way to learn, but soon you'll want to create layouts on your own. The Layout Wizard only creates the floating viewports, leaving the scaling, panning, and other tasks up to you.

Managing layouts

You can have up to 256 layouts, including model space. To create a new layout, first display the tabs. (If they're not displayed, right-click the current layout button on the status bar and choose Display Layout and Model Tabs.) Right-click an existing layout tab and choose from the following options on the short-cut menu:

- **New layout:** Creates a new layout.
- **From template:** Opens the Select File dialog box in which you can choose a .dwg, .dxf, or .dwt file. Click Open. You can then choose the layout or layouts that you want from the Insert Layout(s) dialog box. When you import a template, you import everything that exists on the paper space layout, including viewports, any existing text, the title block, and so on. (You can then get rid of anything you don't want, if necessary.)

CROSS-REF If you import a layout from a drawing, any layers, linetypes, and such also come along for the ride. Use the PURGE command to get rid of anything that you don't need. See Chapter 11 for information on purging. You can also import a layout using the DesignCenter. See Chapter 26 for details.

- **Delete:** Deletes the selected layout. A warning dialog box appears. Click OK to delete the layout.
- **Rename:** Opens the Rename Layout dialog box, where you can rename the layout. Click OK.

NEW FEATURE You can also rename a layout tab by double-clicking it. Then just type the new layout name and press Enter.

- **Move or Copy:** Opens the Move or Copy dialog box. To move a layout tab, you choose the layout tab that you want the selected tab to be to the left of. You can also choose to move it to the end. Click Create a copy to copy the selected tab. (You can then rename it.) Click OK after you're done.

NEW FEATURE You can move a layout by dragging it to a new location. You see a small arrow to indicate where it will go. This method is much easier than using the Move or Copy dialog box. To copy a layout, press Ctrl and drag to a new location. The new layout takes on the same name as the original one, but with (2) added at the end of its name.

- **Select All Layouts:** Selects all layouts. You can then delete them.

TIP To select multiple layouts (but not necessarily all of them), press Ctrl and click each one that you want to select. By pressing Shift, you can select a range of layouts; click the first and then the last in the range.

- **Activate Previous Layout/Activate Model Tab:** Moves you to the last layout tab that you had displayed or to the Model tab.
- **Page Setup Manager:** Opens the Page Setup Manager, which is discussed next.
- **Plot:** Opens the Plot dialog box, which is discussed later in this chapter.
- **Publish Selected Layouts:** If two or more layouts are selected, you can use this item to start the PUBLISH command with the selected layouts in the list of sheets to publish. For more information on the PUBLISH command, see Chapter 28.
- **Hide Layout and Model Tabs:** Hides the tabs.

To move through the tabs (Model and all of the layout tabs) from left to right, press Ctrl+Page Down. To move from right to left, press Ctrl+Page Up.

Using the Page Setup Manager

When you click a new (unused) layout tab, or choose it from the layout button (or Additional Layouts menu) on the status bar, by default you see one floating viewport. However, you can create and save page setups that store many of the settings that were explained previously in the discussion of the Layout Wizard. The value in saving page setups is that the settings are attached to the layout. If you have more than one layout, each with its own page setup, then you can quickly switch the page settings as you move from layout to layout. Once you have page setups, you can manage them in the Page Setup Manager, shown in Figure 17.7.

FIGURE 17.7

The Page Setup Manager helps you to control your page setups.

 When you check the Display When Creating a New Layout check box, the Page Setup Manager automatically appears each time you display a layout for the first time. To make it display each time it does not appear, right-click the current paper space layout tab (you need a tab to do this) and choose Page Setup Manager; then check the check box. You can also specify whether you want the Page Setup Manager to appear when you click a new layout by choosing Tools ⇨ Options and clicking the Display tab. Check or uncheck the Show Page Setup Manager for New Layouts check box.

To display the Page Setup Manager, right-click the active layout tab and choose Page Setup Manager. The Page Setup Manager lists your layouts and page setups. You can create a new page setup, modify an existing setup, or set a page setup current for the active layout. Click the Import button to import a page setup from another drawing.

To create a new page setup, click New. In the New Page Setup dialog box, enter a name for the page setup. Choose an existing page setup to start from so that you don't have to change all of the settings, and click OK. The Page Setup dialog box appears, as shown in Figure 17.8.

FIGURE 17.8

The Page Setup dialog box.

Here's how to use the Page Setup dialog box:

- **Printer/Plotter:** Choose a printer or plotter from the drop-down list. For more information, see "Specifying plot settings" later in this chapter.
- **Paper size:** Choose a paper size from the drop-down list.
- **Plot area:** By default, the plot is set to the layout. However, you can choose to plot the current display, the drawing extents, a named view, or a window that you specify.
- **Plot offset:** You can move the plot from the lower-left corner. Specify the X and Y offset in inches. If you aren't plotting the layout, but rather some smaller area, check the Center the Plot check box to center the plot on the paper.
- **Plot scale:** Set the scale from the drop-down list. You can also type a scale in the text boxes. Because you scale your model in your floating viewports, you usually don't have to scale the layout as well. Therefore, you typically plot a layout in paper space at 1:1. If you're using lineweights and want to scale them, check the Scale Lineweights check box.
- **Plot style table:** Choose a plot style table if you want to use one. For more information, see the section "Working with Plot Styles" later in this chapter.
- **Shaded viewport options:** Use this feature to determine the display of the Model tab. (To set the display of a viewport on a layout, select the viewport and make the changes in the Properties palette.) With the Model tab displayed, choose one of the Shade Plot display options: As Displayed, Wireframe, Hidden, 3D Hidden, 3D Wireframe, Conceptual, Realistic, Rendered, Draft, Low, Medium, High, or Presentation. You can also choose a quality (resolution) — Draft, Preview, Normal, Presentation, Maximum, or Custom. If you choose the Custom quality, you can specify the dots per inch (dpi). (AutoCAD only.)
- **Plot options:** Clear the Plot Object Lineweights check box if you used lineweights but don't want the lineweights to be plotted. Clear the Plot with Plot Styles check box if you assigned plot styles to layers or objects but don't want to plot them. (Plot styles are discussed later in this chapter.)

Clear the Plot Paperspace Last check box in order to plot objects drawn on the paper space layout first. Check the Hide Paperspace Objects check box to hide lines of 3D objects that you created *in paper space.* (Later in this chapter, I explain how to hide lines of 3D objects that were created in model space, a more common situation.)

■ **Drawing orientation:** Choose portrait or landscape. You can also choose to plot upside-down. Use these settings to rotate a drawing when you plot it.

When you've completed your settings in the dialog box, click OK to return to the Page Setup Manager. You can see the new page setup in the list. To make the page setup active, click Set Current. Then click Close to return to your drawing.

> **NOTE** You can import settings saved in PCP or PC2 files from earlier releases of AutoCAD or AutoCAD LT. PCP and PC2 files contain plot settings that are similar to those that you set in the Page Setup dialog box. Click the layout that you want to use and choose Tools ➪ Wizards ➪ Import Plot Settings. In the Import PCP or PC2 Settings Wizard, follow the instructions to import the PCP or PC2 file.

Preparing layers

If necessary, create the layers that you need. If you want to insert a title block, create a separate layer for it. The actual viewports should also be on their own layer, because it's common to freeze that layer or set it to non-plottable, so that the borders don't show. Even if you want to plot the viewports, making them a different color from your model helps you to easily distinguish them.

Inserting a title block

Insert the title block. You can have a file that contains just the title block. You can also use a block or external reference. Putting the title block on your layout is common because it defines the edges of your paper and is not a real-life object. These qualities make it appropriate for paper space.

Creating floating viewports

Remember that you need a floating viewport to see your model on a paper space layout. The default is one floating viewport. Floating viewports have properties that are important to understand when you're creating layouts in paper space. These properties are:

■ Unlike tiled viewports (see Chapter 8), floating viewports are actual objects that you can erase, move, and stretch. They can — and should — be on separate layers, so that you can control the visibility of the viewport borders when desired. They don't need to take up the entire screen. You can change their size and location freely.

■ In paper space, the crosshairs are not limited to one floating viewport.

■ You can separately set the visibility of the UCS icon in each floating viewport.

■ You can create as many viewports as you want, but it's best to keep the drawing uncluttered.

■ After you create floating viewports, you can switch to model space and work on your models while still on the layout. To do so, double-click inside a viewport. You do this mostly to adjust the view of the model in the viewport. In model space, floating viewports are similar to tiled viewports in that only one can be active at a time.

Whatever you draw in paper space does not affect your models; it exists only in paper space and disappears when you click the Model tab or button.

Because viewports are created on the current layer, you need to make the desired layer current. Then, to create floating viewports, choose View ➪ Viewports while on a layout. Choose from the following submenu items:

- **Named Viewports:** If you've saved a tiled viewport configuration, choose this option to open the Viewports dialog box. On the Named Viewports tab, choose the configuration from the list and click OK. In other words, you can use a tiled viewport configuration for floating viewports. See Chapter 8 for a full discussion of saving viewport configurations.

- **New Viewports:** Choose this item to open the Viewports dialog box, shown in Figure 17.9. Choose one of the standard configurations, which you can see in the Preview box. Click OK to create the viewports.

TIP If you have saved named views, you can immediately display them in a viewport. Click one of the viewports in the Preview pane and choose the named view from the Change View To drop-down list. At the same time, you can specify a visual style for each viewport. (I cover visual styles in Chapter 22; visual styles are available in AutoCAD only.) You can do this for each viewport that you create.

FIGURE 17.9

Use the Viewports dialog box to choose one of the standard configurations of floating viewports.

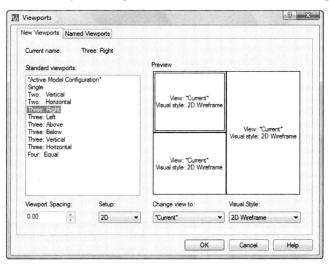

- **1 Viewport:** You see the `Specify corner of viewport or [ON/OFF/Fit/Shadeplot/ Lock/Object/Polygonal/Restore/Layer/2/3/4] <Fit>:` prompt on the command line. You can pick two diagonally opposite points or use the Fit option to create one viewport that fits the entire screen.

AUTOCAD ONLY AutoCAD LT does not include the Object or Polygonal options. You cannot create non-rectangular viewports in AutoCAD AutoCAD LT, but you can view them if you open a drawing created in AutoCAD.

- **2 Viewports:** Creates two floating viewports. You can choose a horizontal or vertical configuration. You can choose Fit to fit them to the entire screen or pick diagonal points. The diagonal points define the combined two viewports, not each viewport.

- **3 Viewports:** Creates three floating viewports. You can choose from several configurations. You can choose Fit to fit them to the entire screen or pick diagonal points. The diagonal points define the combined three viewports, not each viewport.

- **4 Viewports:** Creates four floating viewports. You can choose Fit to fit them to the entire screen or pick diagonal points. The diagonal points define the combined four viewports, not each viewport.

- **Polygonal Viewport:** Lets you create a viewport using a combination of line segments and arcs, with prompts similar to those that you see when creating a polyline (see Chapter 16 for information on creating polylines). Follow these steps to create a polygonal viewport (AutoCAD only):

  1. At the `Specify start point:` prompt, pick a point.

  2. At the `Specify next point or [Arc/Length/Undo]:` prompt, continue to specify points or right-click to choose one of the options. If you choose the Arc option, you see sub-options that are just like those you see when drawing an arc in a polyline.

  3. Press Enter to use the Close option (which appears after you've specified two or more points) to complete the viewport.

- **Object:** Select an existing closed object, such as an ellipse; the object turns into a viewport. (AutoCAD only)

You now see your drawing in the new viewport(s).

Returning to model space while on a layout

The next step is to set the view in each viewport. To do this, you need to return to model space while still on the layout, and make a viewport active. You can do this in two ways:

- If you do not have layout tabs displayed, click the Model button on the status bar. If you have layout tabs displayed, click PAPER on the status bar. (The button then says MODEL.) Then click the viewport that you want to become active.

- Double-click inside the viewport that you want to become active.

 To help you work more easily in a viewport, you can maximize the viewport temporarily without leaving the layout. Just double-click the selected viewport's border.

Another way to maximize a viewport is to right-click with the viewport border selected and choose Maximize Viewport. The viewport takes up the entire screen and you see a red border around the edge. You can draw, edit, zoom, or pan in the view as you normally would in model space; however, zooming and panning have no effect on the viewport's view or scale. When you've finished making the desired changes, right-click and choose Minimize Viewport. The commands that maximize and minimize a viewport are VPMAX and VPMIN. While you're in a layout, you can use the following buttons on the status bar:

 - Maximize Viewport: Maximizes the viewport to take up the entire screen

 - Minimize Viewport: Returns the viewport to its original size

 - Maximize Next Viewport: Switches to the next viewport, still maximized

 - Maximize Previous Viewport: Switches to the previous viewport, still maximized

You can now access your models. Working with floating viewports in model space is quite similar to working with tiled viewports. The active viewport shows a dark border.

 To cycle from viewport to viewport while in model space, press Ctrl+R. (This technique doesn't work if the viewport is maximized.)

Setting viewport scale

You'll probably want to set the zoom for each viewport to exact scale. Each viewport can have its own scale, and you can set the zoom in two ways:

- If you're still in paper space, select the viewport on its border. Choose Properties from the Standard (or Standard Annotation) toolbar (or press Ctrl+1) to open the Properties palette. Choose Standard Scale and choose one of the standard scales from the drop-down list that appears.

- From model space, choose Zoom Scale from the Zoom flyout of the Standard toolbar or choose View ⇨ Zoom ⇨ Scale. You need to use the inverse of the scale factor with the xp option of the ZOOM command. If you have an architectural drawing at a scale of 1:48, type **1/48xp ↵**. (The abbreviation *xp* stands for "times paper space.")

After you scale each viewport, you need to go back and pan until you see what you want in the viewport. If you can't get it perfectly, you can also change the size of the viewport itself.

Locking the viewport

If you remain in model space with a viewport active, and then zoom in or out, you change the displayed scale of the model. After you set the scale, you should lock it to avoid this problem. To lock a viewport, select the viewport's border (while in paper space, not model space) and display the Properties palette. Choose Display Locked and then choose Yes from the drop-down list. (You can also select the viewport, right-click, and choose Display Locked ⇨ Yes.) Now, when you zoom in and out, only paper space objects will be affected.

Setting viewport size, placement, and display

To adjust the viewports themselves, return to paper space by clicking MODEL on the status bar or by double-clicking anywhere outside a viewport (but in the drawing area). You cannot access your models anymore, but you can now move and resize the viewports if necessary. You can use grips to stretch and move them, or use the STRETCH and MOVE commands.

The VPCLIP command (available in AutoCAD only) enables you to redefine the boundary of an existing viewport. You can delete the boundary of a clipped viewport and change it to a rectangular viewport or create a polygonal boundary just as you do when creating a polygonal viewport.

To redefine the boundary of a viewport, you must be in paper space. Type **vpclip** on the command line. Select a clipped viewport boundary from paper space. At the `Select clipping object or [Polygonal/Delete] <Polygonal>:` prompt, you can select an object to use for the new boundary or press Enter to see the same prompts that you see when you create a polygonal viewport. Right-click and choose Delete to delete the boundary of a clipped viewport (one created by choosing an object or using the Polygonal option).

You can also turn viewports on and off. When a viewport is off, it doesn't display your model. Do this when the regeneration process becomes slow as a result of a large number of viewports or a complex drawing. To turn off a viewport, select it (in paper space); then right-click and choose Display Viewport Objects ⇨ No.

Controlling scale for noncontinuous linetypes

The PSLTSCALE system variable controls linetype scaling in paper space viewports. By default, it is set to 1 so that the paper space scale controls the scale of any noncontinuous linetypes. This lets you have viewports of differing scales while displaying linetypes identically. When you set PSLTSCALE to 0, linetype scales are based on the drawing units where the object was created (in either model space or paper space). Linetypes are still scaled by the LTSCALE factor. When you either change PSLTSCALE or change the zoom scale in a viewport with PSLTSCALE set to 1, you need to do a regen to update the linetype scales in each viewport.

Setting layer visibility and properties within a viewport

If you want, you can individually set layer visibility in floating viewports. For example, you might have some text or dimensions that appear in more than one floating viewport, but you may not want to show them more than once. Or perhaps you don't want a hatch to appear in one of the viewports. You must be in model space, so double-click in any viewport. To freeze a layer in an active viewport, click the Layer Control drop-down list on the Layers toolbar or the Layers control panel of the Dashboard. Find the layer that you want to freeze in that viewport and click the icon in the Freeze or Thaw in Current Viewport column. Click the top of the drop-down list to close it. That layer disappears in the active viewport.

You can also freeze/thaw layers in new viewports; these are viewports that you haven't yet created. Choose Layer Properties Manager from the Layers toolbar or the Layers control panel of the Dashboard to open the Layer Properties Manager. Click the icon for the layer that you want in the New VP Freeze column and choose OK to close the dialog box.

CROSS-REF Don't forget that layers have a plottable/not plottable state. Therefore, you can set certain layers to not plottable if you don't want them to appear on the plot. For more information, see Chapter 11.

NEW FEATURE You can now change the properties of a layer (color, linetype, lineweight, and plot style (by viewport. For example, you could make a layer that is green in model space display as blue in one of the viewports.

To set layer properties for individual viewports, follow these steps:

1. Display a layout and double-click the desired viewport to enter model space from that layout. This action makes that viewport *current;* a bold border appears around it.

2. Click Layer Properties Manager on the Layers toolbar or from the Layers control panel of the Dashboard. You now see four new columns (VP Color, VP Linetype, VP Lineweight, and VP Plot Style (as shown in Figure 17.10.

3. To override the properties of a layer for that viewport, you use the same method as for any other property. (See Chapter 11 for a full explanation of the Layer Properties Manager and layers.) For example, to override the color, click the layer's item in the VP Color column to open the Select Color dialog box, where you can choose a new color.

4. Click OK to close the Layer Properties Manager.

When you create a layer override, the Layer Properties Manager displays a cyan (turquoise) block in the columns for the layer's name, the property you overrode, and the VP column for that property, as shown in Figure 17.11. You see the same background for that layer in the Layer Control drop-down list on the Layers toolbar and in the Layers control panel of the Dashboard. The block only appears when the affected viewport is current. A new layer filter, Viewport Overrides, appears in the Layer Filter list, which displays only layers that have viewport overrides.

FIGURE 17.10

When you open the Layer Properties Manager from model space on a layout, you see columns that let you override layer properties for the current viewport.

FIGURE 17.11

A cyan block in the Layer Properties Manager denotes the override when you make the affected viewport current.

You can remove overrides in several ways, depending on whether you want to remove all of a layer's overrides and whether you want to remove overrides in all viewports (as opposed to the current one). To remove an override, open the Layer Properties Manager and do one of the following:

- To remove one property override (such as Color) for a layer, right-click the column containing the override for that layer and choose Remove Viewport Overrides For ⇨ Color ⇨ In Current Viewport Only or In All Viewports.

- To remove all property overrides for a layer (or all selected layers), right-click the layer and choose Remove Viewport Overrides For ⇨ Selected Layers ⇨ In Current Viewport Only or In All Viewports.

- To remove all property overrides, right-click any layer and choose Remove Viewport Overrides For ⇨ All Layers ⇨ In Current Viewport Only or In All Viewports.

Setting hidden and shaded views for viewports

If you have a 3D drawing, you may want to hide back lines for objects in a viewport when you plot (similar to using the HIDE command or the 3D Hidden visual style on the Model tab). This procedure lets you hide lines in one viewport but not in others. You don't see the result until you plot or display a plot preview. You can also specify shading and rendered views for each viewport, from both model space and paper space layouts, as shown in Figure 17.12.

FIGURE 17.12

In this drawing, one viewport displays a wireframe, one a hidden view, and one a rendered view.

To choose the type of shaded view, select any viewport in paper space. Right-click, and choose Shade Plot. Then choose one of the following options:

- **As Displayed:** Plots the objects as they're currently displayed.
- **Wireframe:** Plots the objects in wireframe display.
- **Hidden:** Plots the objects with back lines removed.
- **3D Hidden:** Like the Hidden option, hides the back lines. (AutoCAD only.)
- **3D Wireframe:** Plots the objects in wireframe display. (AutoCAD only.)
- **Conceptual:** Shades the model with flat colors on its faces. (AutoCAD only.)
- **Realistic:** Shades the model with a special color palette and gradients. (AutoCAD only.)
- **Rendered:** Plots objects using the default rendering settings. (See Chapter 25 for information on rendering. This option is not available in AutoCAD LT.)

AUTOCAD ONLY Express Tools include several commands for working with layouts:

- The ALIGNSPACE command (choose Express ⇨ Layout Tools ⇨ Align Space) aligns objects in different viewports.

- The VPSYNC command (choose Express ⇨ Layout Tools ⇨ Synchronize Viewports) changes the pan and zoom of a second viewport to match that of the first ("master") viewport that you select, so that the view of the objects is consistent (synchronized) from viewport to viewport.

- The VPSCALE command (choose Express ⇨ Layout Tools ⇨ List Viewport Scale) displays the scale from paper space to model space of the selected viewport.

- The LAYOUTMERGE command (choose Express ⇨ Layout Tools ⇨ Merge Layout) moves all objects on one or more layouts that you specify to a single layout.

Annotating a layout

Before plotting, you may want to add notes, dimensions, and other annotations. You also need to pay attention to the scale of certain items in your viewports to make sure that they appear properly. For example, if you have one viewport at 1:1 and another at 1:4 and you show dimensions in both viewports, the dimensions will appear at different sizes in each viewport. This makes legibility difficult. Other items that may need adjustment are text, hatches, blocks, and linetypes.

You can annotate a drawing in two different ways:

- You can use *annotative objects*, which store representations at various scales and display them according to the scale of a specific viewport. You create these objects in model space. For example, you can display objects at 1:1 in one viewport and 1:4 in another viewport, but the text will be the same size in each viewport. You can control the display of more types of objects in this way, but the process is somewhat more complex.

NEW FEATURE Annotative objects are new for AutoCAD 2008 and AutoCAD LT 2008. They automate the process of scaling certain types of objects in viewports at various scales. You can create annotation objects for text, Mtext, dimensions, tolerances, leaders, multileaders, hatches, blocks, and block attributes.

CROSS-REF I discuss how to create annotative objects in the following chapters: text and Mtext in Chapter 13; dimensions, tolerances, multileaders, and leaders in Chapters 14 and 15; hatches in Chapter 16; and blocks and attributes in Chapter 18.

- You can annotate in paper space, in which case you create the annotations at their desired plotting size, without scaling them. This method is fairly easy, but it doesn't allow control over drawing objects such as blocks, attributes, and hatches.

Before these methods were available, for each object, you needed to create a separate layer for each scale, calculate the appropriate size for each object, and freeze layers in the viewports where you didn't want certain objects to appear. For example, if you wanted one text object to appear at 1:1 in one viewport and another text object to appear at 1:4 in another viewport, you created them at the appropriate size on different layers. Then you froze one layer in one viewport and the other layer in the other viewport. As you can imagine, this was a complicated process.

Using annotation objects on a layout

The purpose of using annotation objects is to automate the process of scaling these objects when you display them at different scales in different viewports. To use this feature, each of the objects needs to be annotative; you add this property when you create the object or its style (such as a text style).

Follow these steps to create and use annotation objects:

1. For the following objects, first create an annotative style:

   - **Mtext:** Use the default Annotative text style or create an annotative text style by checking the Annotative check box in the Text Style dialog box. At the same time, you use the Paper Text Height text box to set the final height you want for your text when you plot it on paper. See Chapter 13 for details.

   - **Dimensions:** Use the default Annotative dimension style or create an annotative dimension style by checking the Annotative check box in the Create New Dimension Style dialog box or on the Fit tab of the New (or Modify) Dimension Style dialog box. See Chapter 15 for details. Note that you need an annotative text style for the text in your annotative dimensions.

   - **Multileaders:** Use the default Annotative multileader style or create an annotative multileader style by checking the Annotative check box in the Create New Multileader Style dialog box or on the Leader Structure tab of the New (or Modify) Multileader Style dialog box. See Chapter 14 for details. Note that you need an annotative text style for the text in your multileaders.

> **NOTE** You can also create annotative leaders using the QLEADER command. You don't create a special style for the leader, but you need to use an annotative text style for its text. You also need an annotative text style for block attributes (covered in Chapter 18).

2. Decide which objects you will display at which scales. If you don't know this when you draw your objects, you can add scales to them later. Remember that you might have objects that you want to appear at one scale, but not at another scale; however, you might have objects that you want to appear at more than one scale. Of course, you can change the scales of your objects later. A good way to help you figure out the scales that you need is to set up your viewports before you finish drawing, including their scales.

> **NOTE** When you turn the ANNOAUTOSCALE system variable on, it automatically adds scales to annotative objects as you add annotative scales. If you have an object that you want to have only one scale, then turn off this system variable. It's off by default. Use the icon on the right side of the status bar to the right of the Annotation Visibility button to toggle ANNOAUTOSCALE on and off. When on, there's a yellow lightning bolt; when off, the lightning bolt is gray. In general, leave ANNOAUTOSCALE off unless you want to update all of the annotative objects in your drawing to a new annotative scale.

3. You need to assign an annotation scale to all objects that you want to be annotative. You can do so as you draw, or afterwards. To set the annotation scale as you draw, click the Annotation Scale button at the right side of the status bar to display the scale list and choose the scale you want. For example, choose 1:4 if you plan to display the object in a viewport at the 1:4 scale.

> **CROSS-REF** In Chapter 5, I explain scales in general and how to edit the scale list. It's much easier to work with the scale list when it doesn't include scales that you don't use. You can also change the order of the list to place scales that you use most often at the top.

4. Create the object. The Select Annotation Scale dialog box may open, requesting that you choose an annotation scale. You can do so from the drop-down list in that dialog box. If you've already set the scale, just click OK. Remember that you can add and change annotation scales at any time.

> **NOTE** The Select Annotation Scale dialog box opens the first time in an AutoCAD or AutoCAD LT session that you create an annotation object.

5. Add other annotation scales to existing objects. You can do this in two ways:

- If ANNOAUTOSCALE is on, to add another annotation scale to existing objects, you just choose another annotation scale by clicking the Annotation Scale button on the status bar.

- If ANNOAUTOSCALE is off, you need to add annotation scales manually. Use this method if you don't want all objects to have every annotation scale that you'll be using. Select the object, right-click it, and choose Annotative Object Scale ⇨ Add/Delete Scales to open the Annotation Object Scale dialog box, shown in Figure 17.13. You can also open the dialog box by clicking the Add/Delete Scales button in the Annotation Scaling control panel of the Dashboard or by displaying the Properties palette, clicking the Annotative Scale item, and clicking the Ellipsis button that appears.

NOTE When you hover the cursor over an annotation object, you see a special annotation icon near the cursor, which lets you know that the object is annotative. If an object has two or more annotation scales, you see a double annotation icon.

FIGURE 17.13

Use the Annotation Object Scale dialog box to add or delete annotation scales for selected objects.

6. If you're manually adding an annotation scale, click the Add button. In the Add Scales to Object dialog box, choose the scale or scales that you want, and click OK twice to return to your drawing.

NOTE The ANNOALLVISIBLE system variable determines whether you see all of the scales for an object (On) or only the current scale (Off). Use the Annotation Visibility button on the status bar to the right of the Annotation Scale drop-down list. On the model tab, turn this variable on to check that objects have the multiple annotation scales that you want them to have. On a layout, you usually want to keep this variable off, because seeing multiple scales is confusing.

The SELECTIONANNODISPLAY system variable specifies whether you see alternative sizes of an annotative object when you select it. The size of the object for the current annotative scale shows whether or not the object is selected, but when you select the object, you see all sizes if this system variable is set to 1, the default. However, objects at sizes for non-current scales are dimmed.

7. Switch to a layout and create the viewports that you need at the scales that you have chosen. Pan to get the display you want. Then lock the display, as explained earlier in this chapter.

Your annotation objects now automatically scale to match the scale of their viewport. If you don't get the results you want, you can check that the viewport scale and the annotative scale match by selecting a viewport and looking on the right side of the status bar. If they don't match, change the annotative scale from the drop-down list; your objects should now scale properly.

You can change the annotative scale on the status bar.

NEW FEATURE   You can lock and unlock any selected viewport on the status bar, by using the lock icon to the left of the VP Scale drop-down list.

Adding text and dimensions in paper space

Annotation that applies to the entire drawing, such as title block text, can be, and often is, created on the paper space layout. You can change to a text layer and use the DTEXT or MTEXT command, as usual.

Sometimes you create an object in model space — perhaps some text or a logo — and want to move it to paper space, or vice versa. For example, you may want to move a text label that you inserted in model space into your title block, which you inserted in paper space. The CHSPACE command makes it easy to move objects from one space to the other, without worrying about scale differences.

To move an object in either direction, follow these steps:

1. Display a layout. You must be on a layout to use CHSPACE.
2. Switch to the space where the object that you want to move resides. For example, if you want to move text from model space to paper space, double-click inside the viewport containing the text to switch to model space.
3. Choose Modify ⇨ Change Space.
4. Select the object that you want to move.
5. Make the desired viewport active and press Enter.

The command scales objects to maintain the same visual appearance. The amount of scaling depends on the scaling of the viewport. If the viewport scale is 1:1, no scaling occurs.

In Chapters 14 and 15, I discussed dimensioning in model space, but you can dimension in paper space, as well. The Trans-Spatial Dimensioning feature automatically adjusts dimensions for the scale of the viewport. These paper space dimensions are fully associative. Dimensioning in paper space has several advantages:

- You don't have to worry about the size of the individual dimension components themselves, such as the text and the arrows. If you plot from paper space, you plot at 1:1 scale.
- If you don't need to scale other objects (such as hatches and blocks), dimensioning in paper space is probably simpler than using the annotative feature.
- You can place the dimensions outside the border of the floating viewport, which may make it easier to fit the dimensions. (On the other hand, you may find it harder to fit the dimensions if you have other viewports on the layout.)
- You can easily dimension just one view of the model.

TIP   If you create dimensions in a viewport in paper space and then zoom or pan in that viewport, the objects and the dimension get out of sync. Use the DIMREGEN command on the command line to reset the dimension to match its object.

You still need to scale the size of the dimension to your viewport scale, including the text, arrows, and so on, as follows:

1. Open the Dimension Style Manager.
2. Choose the dimension style that you want to use and click Modify.
3. On the Fit tab, choose Scale Dimensions to Layout.
4. Click OK and then click Close.

When you follow this procedure, all of the dimensions using the dimension style that you chose appear the same size on your final plot.

NOTE Drawings created in earlier releases (before AutoCAD 2002 and AutoCAD LT 2002) do not automatically have the new associative dimensions. If necessary, change the DIMASSOC system variable's value to 2. Also, you usually need to use the DIMREASSOCIATE command to associate existing dimensions to their objects. See Chapter 14 for more information on associative dimensions.

Saving a layout template

After you do all of the work to create a layout, you can save it as a template so that you can use it in other drawings. (The template includes all objects on the layout.) Here's how:

1. Type **layout** ↵ on the command line.
2. At the prompt, right-click and choose Save As.
3. At the `Enter layout to save to template <Layout2>:` prompt, press Enter to save the current layout, the name of which appears in brackets, or type the name of another layout.
4. The Create Drawing File dialog list opens, with the `Template` folder active. The Files of Type drop-down list shows AutoCAD (LT) Drawing Template File (`*.dwt`). Type a name for the drawing template and click Save.

To use the template to add a new layout in any drawing, right-click a layout tab and choose From Template, as explained earlier in this chapter.

ON the DVD-ROM The drawings used in the following exercise on laying out a drawing in paper space, ab17-a.dwg and ab-17-a-blk.dwg, are in the Drawings folder on the DVD.

STEPS: Laying Out a Drawing in Paper Space

1. Open ab17-a.dwg from your DVD.
2. Save the file as ab17-01.dwg in your AutoCAD Bible folder. This file already has a text style, dimension style, and multileader style that are annotative.
3. If you do not have tabs displayed at the bottom of the drawing area, right-click the Model button on the status bar and choose Display Layout and Model Tabs. Click the Layout1 tab. Right-click the tab and choose Page Setup Manager.
4. Click New. In the New Page Setup Name text box, type **PrinterDraft**. Click OK. The Page Setup dialog box opens.
5. In the Paper Size section, the paper size should be set to Letter (8.50 × 11 inches). (This enables you to plot to a printer if you don't have a plotter available.) In the Shaded Viewport Options section, choose Draft from the Quality drop-down list. Make sure that your printer is listed in the Name drop-down list of the Printer/Plotter section. Click OK to return to the Page Setup Manager.

6. The `PrinterDraft` page setup should be highlighted. Click Set Current. Click Close.

7. Double-click the Layout1 tab. Type **2-view** and press Enter.

8. Click the Layer Control drop-down list arrow. Choose the `TB` layer to make it current.

9. Choose Insert ⇨ Block to open the Insert dialog box. Click Browse. Choose `ab17-a-blk.dwg` from the DVD and click Open.

10. Uncheck any checked Specify On-Screen check boxes. Click OK to insert the title block, as shown in Figure 17.14.

11. Choose the `Np` layer from the Layer Control drop-down list to make it current.

12. Choose View ⇨ Viewports ⇨ 1 Viewport. At the `Specify corner of viewport or` `[ON/OFF/Fit/Shadeplot/Lock/Object/Polygonal/Restore/LAyer/2/3/4]` `<Fit>:` prompt, choose ❶ in Figure 17.14. (In AutoCAD LT, your prompt will look slightly different.) At the `Specify opposite corner:` prompt, choose ❷.

The title block inserted into paper space.

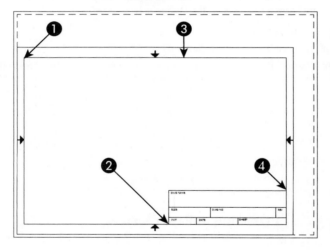

13. Right-click and choose Repeat 1 Viewport. At the prompt, choose ❸ in Figure 17.14. At the next prompt, choose ❹. You now see the drawing in the two viewports.

14. Click the border of the left viewport. Press Ctrl+1 to open the Properties palette. Choose Standard Scale from the Properties palette. Click the Standard Scale drop-down arrow and choose 1:2 from the scale list. Press Esc to deselect the top-left viewport.

15. Select the right viewport and set its standard scale to 1:1. Deselect the right viewport.

16. Double-click inside each viewport in turn to switch to model space, and pan until you see the view shown in Figure 17.15. It doesn't have to match exactly. Notice that the dimension text size is different in the two viewports.

17. Click the Model tab. Change the current layer to Hatch. Choose Hatch from the Draw toolbar or the 2D Draw control panel of the Dashboard. Leave the defaults of the ANSI31 pattern, 1.0000 Scale, and 0 Angle. In the Options section of the Hatch dialog box, check the Annotative check box. Click the Add: Pick Points button and click inside the ellipse at the lower section of the handwheel. Press Enter. Click Preview and right-click to accept the hatch.

NOTE If you pass the cursor over the hatch, you see the annotative icon. When you move the cursor over the dimensions and the multileader, you see that they are also annotative. This is because they were created using annotative styles.

18. Using the Annotation Scale list on the status bar, change the current scale to 1:2. You need to add this scale to the annotative objects. Select all of the dimensions, except the two diameter dimensions in the lower-right quadrant of the handwheel (which read Ø 1 and Ø 7/8). (Also don't include the multileader in the upper-right quadrant of the wheel that contains the text R3/8.) Right-click in the drawing area and choose Annotative Object Scale ⇨ Add Current Scale. Notice that the size of the dimensions changes.

19. Repeat Step 18 for the multileader below the handwheel. Finally, repeat Step 18 for the hatch that you just drew.

20. On the status bar, change the annotation scale back to 1:1. The dimensions, multileaders, and hatch return to their original sizes.

21. Switch to the 2-view tab. You should see that the text of the dimensions in both viewports is the same size, as is the hatch pattern. Note that the diameter dimensions in the lower-right quadrant that don't have a 2:1 annotation scale, don't appear in the left-hand viewport, which has a 2:1 annotation scale. Similarly, the multileader in the upper-right quadrant (with the text R3/8) also appears only in the right-hand 1:1 viewport because it has a 1:1 annotation scale only.

NOTE If you don't see these results, first select each viewport in turn, making sure that both the VP scale and the annotation scale are the same, and that the left viewport is set to 1:2 and the right viewport is set to 1:1. Also, return to model space, select the dimensions that appear incorrect, right-click them, and choose Annotative Object Scale ⇨ Add/Delete Scales. In the Annotation Object Scale dialog box, make sure that the scales are correct; if not, add or delete a scale as necessary.

22. Double-click the right-hand viewport to enter model space from the layout with that viewport current. You'll create a layer override for the hatch. On the Layers toolbar or the Layers control panel of the Dashboard, click the Layer Properties Manager button. In the VP Color column, click the HATCH row, which reads cyan. In the Select Color dialog box that opens, choose the Red swatch. Click OK twice to return to your drawing. The hatch now displays as red in the right viewport.

23. Double-click inside the left viewport. From the Layer Control drop-down list on the Layers toolbar or the Layers control panel of the Dashboard, click the icon in the third column (Freeze or Thaw in Current Viewport) next to the HATCH layer, to freeze that layer in the viewport.

24. From the same Layer Control drop-down list, click the name of the DIM layer to make it current. From the Dimension Style Control drop-down list in the Dimension control panel of the Dashboard or the Dimensions toolbar, choose STYLE1. This dimension style is set to be scaled to paper space.

25. Double-click outside a viewport, but in the drawing area, to enter paper space. Choose Dimension ⇨ Linear. In the left viewport, use the Quadrant object snap to create a dimension from the top quadrant to the bottom quadrant of the ellipse below the center of the handwheel.

Place the dimension to the left of the ellipse. The ellipse is correctly dimensioned at 3/4 unit, although it is zoomed in to a 2:1 scale. (It's too small, however.) Because you wouldn't dimension using annotative dimensions and also in paper space, erase the new dimension that you just created; it was just an exercise to show how dimensioning in paper space works.

26. Click the Layer Control drop-down arrow and change the current layer to TEXT. Click the Layer Control drop-down arrow again. Click the icon in the second column (Freeze or Thaw in ALL Viewports) next to the Np layer to freeze the layer containing the viewport borders. Click the top of the drop-down list to close it.

27. Choose Draw ➪ Text ➪ Single Line Text. Complete the text in the title block at the default height, as shown in Figure 17.15.

28. Save your drawing.

FIGURE 17.15

The completed drawing layout is now ready for plotting.

Working with Plot Styles

A *plot style* is an object property, like color, linetype, lineweight, or layer. Just as you can assign a color to an object and also to a layer, you can assign a plot style to an object and also to a layer. Because a plot style determines how an object is plotted, its function is to override the object's original properties. However, a plot style is more complex than a color or a linetype because it contains a set of properties, such as color-related properties, linetype, lineweight, and line styles. The use of plot styles is completely optional. Without plot styles, objects are simply plotted according to their properties.

You can use plot styles to create several types of plots for one drawing or layout. Plot styles also enable you to use some of the printer-like capabilities of plotters, such as screening and dithering.

Plot styles are stored in plot-style tables, which are files that you can create and edit. You generally follow these steps to use plot styles in your plots:

1. Create a plot-style table.
2. Attach a plot-style table to a layout.
3. Set the plot-style property for a layer or object.
4. Plot.

Setting the plot-style mode

Plot styles come in two types, color-dependent and named. Before you work with plot styles, you need to choose which type you want to use:

- **Color-dependent plot styles,** the default, are saved in color-dependent plot-style tables, which are files with a file extension of `.ctb`. You assign plotting properties based on object color. The disadvantage of color-dependent plot styles is that you can't assign different properties to two objects that have the same color.

- **Named plot styles** are saved in named plot-style tables, which are files with a file extension of `.stb`. Named plot styles let you assign plotting properties to objects regardless of their color. Therefore, two objects of the same color can be plotted differently.

 Dimensions and tables don't take full advantage of named plot styles. They support color-dependent plot styles only for their components, such as the arrows and extension lines of dimensions.

After you decide which type of plot style you want to use, you set the mode by choosing Tools ➪ Options and clicking the Plot and Publish tab. Click the Plot Style Table Settings button. In the Plot Style Tables Settings dialog box, choose either Use Color Dependent Plot Styles or Use Named Plot Styles.

In the same location, you can set the following:

- Default plot-style table (the default is `acad.stb` or `acadlt.stb` for named and `acad.ctb` or `acadlt.ctb` for color-dependent plot styles).

- Default plot style for layer 0 (the default is Normal for named plot styles and ByColor for color-dependent plot styles).

- Default plot style for objects (the default is ByLayer for named plot styles and ByColor for color-dependent plot styles).

The default plot style for objects is the current plot style for new objects, and is similar in concept to the current color, linetype, lineweight, or layer for new objects. After you're done, click OK.

It is important to understand that changing the plot style mode does not affect the current drawing. To use the new setting, you must either open a new drawing or open a drawing from a previous release that has not been saved in AutoCAD 2000/AutoCAD LT 2000 or later format. Moreover, the template that you use to open a new drawing must be set to use named plot styles. AutoCAD and AutoCAD LT come with a template called `acad -Named Plot Styles.dwt` (`acadlt -Named Plot Styles.dwt`) that you can use, or you can create your own template. Several other templates have the words "Named Plot Styles" in their title, indicating that they include the setting for named plot styles.

CAUTION   If you have color-dependent plot styles for existing pre–AutoCAD 2000/AutoCAD LT 2000 drawings (and want to keep them that way) but decide to use named plot styles for new drawings, you need to avoid opening any of the existing drawings while you're in named plot-style mode. If you do, they'll be changed to named plot-style mode. Remember that pre–Release 2000 drawings don't have any plot styles and that plot settings had to be according to color. You might consider setting the mode to color-dependent plot styles, creating a script file to open and save all of your existing drawings as AutoCAD 2007 or AutoCAD LT 2007 drawings, and only then change the mode to named plot styles. Chapter 30 explains how to create script files.

You can convert color-dependent plot style tables to named plot-style tables using the CONVERTCTB command. You can then use the CONVERTPSTYLES command to convert the drawing so that it uses named plot styles. You can also use the CONVERTPSTYLES command to convert a drawing from using named plot styles to color-dependent plot styles.

Creating a plot-style table

Each named plot-style table comes with a default plot style called Normal. By default, the plot style for each layer in a named plot style drawing is Normal. Figure 17.16 shows the Normal plot style, shown in a plot-style table with a Style1 that you can use to create a new plot style. The Normal plot style is grayed out because you cannot change it.

The Table View tab lists your plot styles side-by-side. Each plot style includes settings for the various categories that are available in a plot style.

Plot style tables are stored in the `Plot Styles` folder. The default plot-style tables are `acad.stb` or `acadlt.stb` (named plot style) and `acad.ctb` or `acadlt.ctb` (color-dependent plot style).

FIGURE 17.16

The Normal plot style is the default plot style for layers.

To find the location of the `Plot Styles` folder, choose Tools ⇨ Options and click the Files tab. Double-click Printer Support File Path and then double-click Plot Style Table Search Path.

You can use plot configuration files (PCP and PC2 files) or the Release 14 configuration file (`acadr14.cfg`) to create plot-style tables in order to import your previously created configuration information. You can also create plot-style tables from scratch.

Creating a named plot-style table

To use plot styles, you can add a plot style to an existing plot-style table or create a new plot-style table. Each plot-style table is a separate file. To create a named plot-style table, use the Add Plot Style Table Wizard. You can access this wizard in two ways:

- Choose File ⇨ Plot Style Manager to open the `\Plot Styles` folder. Then double-click the Add-A-Plot Style Table Wizard icon. From this folder you can also access existing plot-style tables for editing.
- Choose Tools ⇨ Wizards ⇨ Add Plot Style Table.

To use the wizard, follow these steps:

1. Choose Tools ⇨ Wizards ⇨ Add Plot Style Table. The wizard opens with an explanation of plot-style tables. Choose Next.

2. On the Begin screen, shown in Figure 17.17, choose the source that you want to use for the plot-style table. You can start from scratch or use an existing plot-style table. Choose Use My R14 Plotter Configuration (CFG) to use the pen assignments from the `acadr14.cfg` file. If you have a PCP (Release 12/13) or PC2 (Release 14) configuration file, you can use it to import the settings from that file into the plot-style table. Then click Next.

3. If you choose to start from scratch or to use R14 Plotter Configuration or PCP/PC2 files, choose whether you want color-dependent or named plot styles. If you chose to use an existing file as a basis for the plot-style table, choose the file. If you chose to use a CFG file, you must also specify the plotter, because the CFG file can contain information for more than one plotter. Click Next.

FIGURE 17.17

In the Begin screen of the Add Plot Style Table Wizard, choose the source that you want to use for the new plot-style table.

4. On the File Name screen, type a name for the plot-style table file. Click Next.

5. On the Finish screen, an option labeled Use this plot style table for new and pre-AutoCAD 2007 drawings may be available. If it is, then check this option to attach the plot-style table to all new drawings by default. You don't have to use the plot styles, but they will be available. Clear the option if you don't want to attach this plot-style table to new drawings by default. You can also click Plot Style Table Editor to edit plot styles immediately. You can edit plot styles at any time, as explained next. Click Finish.

Editing a plot-style table

After you create a plot-style table, you can edit it by adding, naming, and deleting its plot styles (for named plot-style tables only) and, of course, creating the settings that you want for the plot styles. To open the Plot Style Table Editor, do one of the following:

- Choose Plot Style Table Editor from the Finish screen of the Add Plot Style Table Wizard.
- Choose File ⇨ Plot Style Manager and double-click any existing CTB or STB file.
- From the Page Setup dialog box (discussed earlier in this chapter) or the Plot dialog box (discussed later in this chapter), choose the named plot-style table that you want to edit from the Plot Style Table drop-down list, and click Edit.
- From the Select Plot Style dialog box (accessed from the Layer Properties Manager after you click the Plot Style column), choose Editor.
- Choose Tools ⇨ Options and click the Plot and Publish tab. Choose Plot Style Table Settings and then choose Add or Edit Plot Style Tables.

The Plot Style Table Editor's Table View tab was shown in Figure 17.18. The Form View tab is shown in Figure 17.18. You can edit styles using either view tab. The Form View tab focuses on one style at a time and provides better visual confirmation of some of the choices. The Table View tab lets you compare your style to existing styles as you work.

A new Plot Style Table includes one default style, Normal. To add a style, click Add Style. Before you go any further, click the style name and type a more descriptive name for the style.

Creating a Color-Dependent Plot-Style Table

Prior to AutoCAD and AutoCAD LT 2000, plotting was integrally related to object color. For example, you assigned pens in a pen plotter according to color. If you want to continue to create settings based on color, you can create a color-dependent plot-style table. To do this, follow the same steps for creating a named plot-style table. On the Pick Plot Style Table screen, choose Color-Dependent Plot Style Table and click Next. The rest of the steps are the same.

The result is a CTB file with 255 styles, one for each color. You cannot add, delete, or rename these styles, but you can edit their properties. For example, you can specify that objects on color 1 should be plotted with no lineweight or a specific linetype. However, be aware that color-dependent plot styles result in slower display regeneration.

In this chapter, I focus on named plot styles. However, creating color-dependent plot styles is very similar.

FIGURE 17.18

The Form View tab of the Plot Style Table Editor.

You can't rename a plot style that is currently assigned to an object or layer, so it's best to name it when you create it. You can't change the names of styles in a color-dependent plot-style table.

Each plot style has a description area that you can use to provide a more detailed description of the plot style. For example, you could summarize a plot style as "color black & no lineweight."

Now go through each of the properties and make any changes that you want. In Table view, you need to click the property in the Plot Styles column for a drop-down list to appear. The properties are as follows:

- **Color:** You can specify a color other than the default, which is Object Color. For example, you might want to create a plot style that plots everything in black or red. For more options, choose Select Color and define a color in the Select Color dialog box. (See Chapter 11 for an explanation of how to use the Select Color dialog box.)

- **Dither:** Dithering is a method of using dot patterns to approximate a greater range of colors. Not all plotters support dithering. Dithering gives the impression of more colors but can make thin lines and dim colors look unclear.

- **Grayscale:** Converts objects to grayscale, if supported by the plotter. You could use grayscale to deemphasize certain layers or to print a draft plot on a black-and-white laser printer.

- **Pen # and Virtual Pen #:** These settings apply to pen plotters only (the Virtual Pen # setting applies to non-pen plotters that can simulate pen plotters) and specify which pen to use for the object that is assigned the plot style.

- **Screening:** Specifies the amount of ink used for a color. The range is from 0 (no ink; that is, white) to 100 (full intensity of the color). Some plotters, such as pen plotters, do not support screening. You could use a 50 percent screen to deemphasize certain layers, such as those containing proposed changes, or to save ink.

- **Linetype:** You can specify a linetype other than the default, Object Linetype, to override the object's linetype when you plot. For example, you might want to have the option to plot certain objects that are not yet approved in a dashed or dotted linetype.

- **Adaptive:** Choose On to adapt the scale of a linetype to complete the linetype pattern on the object. Choose Off if maintaining the proper linetype scale is essential.

- **Lineweight:** You can specify a lineweight other than the default, Object Lineweight. For example, if you're using heavy lineweights, you might want to specify a narrower lineweight to save ink on a draft plot.

- **Line End Style:** When you use lineweights, you need to specify how you want to end lines. You can choose from Butt, Square, Round, and Diamond. The default is Object End Style.

- **Line Join Style:** Specifies how objects with lineweights are joined. The choices are Miter, Bevel, Round, and Diamond. The default is Object Join Style.

- **Fill Style:** You can choose from Solid, Checkerboard, Crosshatch, Diamonds, Horizontal Bars, Slant Left, Slant Right, Square Dots, and Vertical Bar. The default is Object Fill Style.

To delete a style, select it and click Delete. In Table view, click a style's gray column head to select it.

After you're done, click the Save & Close button.

Attaching a plot-style table to a layout

As soon as you have your plot-style table and the plot styles that you want, you can start using the plot styles. The first step is to attach the table to a layout (including model space). Remember that you can attach different plot-style tables to different layouts (or the Model tab).

To attach a plot-style table to a layout or the Model tab, display the tabs if necessary (right-click the Model or Layout button on the status bar and choose Display Model and Layout tabs), and follow these steps:

1. Choose the Layout or Model tab.
2. Right-click the tab and choose Page Setup Manager.
3. Choose a page setup and click Modify (or click New and create a new one).
4. In the Plot Style Table section of the Page Setup dialog box, choose a plot-style table from the Plot Style Table drop-down list.
5. If you're on the Model tab, choose Yes or No to the question asking whether you want to apply the plot-style table to the Model tab only or to all layouts. If you're on a layout tab, check the Display Plot Styles check box to see the result of the plot styles in your drawing.
6. Click OK. Then click Close to return to your drawing.

To see the result, you still need to attach a plot style to a layer or object, as I explain in the next section.

Setting the plot-style property for a layer or object

To use a plot style, you need to assign it to a layer or an object. The plot style is only applied if the plot style is first defined in the plot-style table that you've assigned to a layout (or Model tab).

To set the plot style for a layer, follow these steps:

1. Make sure that the layout tab that you want to use is active.

2. Choose Layer Properties Manager from the Layers toolbar to open the Layer Properties Manager.

3. Choose the layer whose plot style you want to change, and click the Plot Style column to open the Select Plot Style dialog box.

4. Choose the plot-style table from the Active Plot Style table list at the bottom of the dialog box.

5. Choose a plot style from the Plot Styles list.

6. Click OK twice to return to your drawing.

If you checked Display Plot Styles in the Page Setup dialog box, as explained in the previous section, you should see the result of the plot style. If not, type **regenall** ⏎.

To set the plot style for an object, select the object and display the Properties palette (Ctrl+1). Choose the Plot Style item, and choose a plot style from the drop-down list. You can attach a plot style to a viewport (which is an object), but the plot style doesn't affect the objects in the viewport.

You can view the effects of plot styles in two ways:

- To display plot styles in your drawing all the time, display the layout for which you want to view the plot style. Right-click the layout's tab and choose Page Setup Manager. Then select the page setup associated with the layout and click Modify. In the Page Setup dialog box, check Display Plot Styles in the Plot Style Table section. Click OK and then click Close to return to the drawing window. (You may have to use REGENALL to see the result.)

- You can also see the effects of plot styles in a preview of your plot. Choose Plot from the Standard toolbar and click Preview.

 The drawing used in the following exercise on creating and applying a plot style, ab17-b.dwg, is in the Drawings folder on the DVD.

STEPS: Creating and Applying a Plot Style

1. With any drawing open, choose Tools ⇨ Options and click the Plot and Publish tab. Now click the Plot Style Table Settings button and take note of the current setting under Default Plot Style Behavior for New Drawings. Remember this setting so that you can set it back to its original setting at the end of the exercise.

2. Click Use Named Plot Styles (unless that is the current setting) and click OK twice.

3. Open ab17-b.dwg from your DVD.

4. Save the file as ab17-02.dwg in your AutoCAD Bible folder.

5. Choose Tools ⇨ Wizards ⇨ Add Plot Style Table. Click Next.

6. In the Begin screen, choose Start from Scratch and click Next. In the next screen, choose Named Plot Style Table (it's probably already selected) and click Next. In the File Name screen, type **ab17-02** and click Next.

7. In the Finish screen, click Finish. (Don't check Use for New and Pre-AutoCAD 2008 Drawings because this is just an exercise.)

8. Choose File ⇨ Plot Style Manager. (You could have opened the new plot-style table from the wizard, but this is how you usually do it when you haven't just finished creating a table.) Double-click ab17-02.stb.

9. In the description box of the General tab, type **AutoCAD Bible Plot Style Table.**

10. Click the Table View tab. Click the Add Style button. Click the name Style1. Type **Black color** and press Enter.

11. Click the Color row under the Black Color column, and choose Black from the drop-down list. Click Save & Close. Close the Plot Styles folder window.

12. If you don't have model and layout tabs displayed, right-click the Model or Layout button on the status bar and choose Display Layout and Model Tabs. Select Layout1, right-click it, and then choose Page Setup Manager from the shortcut menu.

13. In the Page Setup Manager, choose New. In the New Page Setup dialog box, enter **AB 2008** and click OK.

14. In the Page Setup dialog box, make sure that your printer or plotter is listed in the Printer/Plotter section. Then choose ab17-02.stb from the Plot Style Table drop-down list. Check the Display Plot Styles check box and click OK. Select AB 2008 and click Set Current. Click Close. This assigns the plot-style table to Layout1.

15. Choose Layer Properties Manager from the Layers toolbar. In the Layer Properties Manager, choose A-DETL-PATT (the layer with the magenta color). Click that layer's Plot Styles column to open the Select Plot Style dialog box. Choose Black Color and click OK. The Plot Style for the A-DETL-PATT layer now shows as Black Color. Click OK to close the Layer Properties Manager.

16. Type **regenall** ↵. The objects on A-DETL-PATT (the diagonal marks on the mirror) now show as black, and will plot as black.

17. Click PAPER on the status bar to switch to model space.

18. Select the bottom horizontal line of the sink cabinet.

19. Open the Properties palette (Ctrl+1). In the Properties palette, click Plot Style. From the drop-down list to the right, choose Black Color.

20. Press Esc so that the object is no longer highlighted. The line appears as black.

21. Choose Tools ➪ Options. On the Plot and Publish tab, click the Plot Style Table Settings button and change the Default Plot Style Behavior for New Drawings setting to what it was at the beginning of this exercise.

22. Save your drawing.

 The plot style that you created, ab17-02.stb, is in the Results folder on the DVD.

Plotting a Drawing

After you lay out your drawing, you're ready to plot it. Plotting outputs your drawing onto paper (or perhaps vellum or some other medium). Although you might go through several iterations of drawing and editing in electronic form, you eventually plot most drawings. The first step is to check the plotter or printer. It should be on, connected to your computer, and have the appropriate paper in it. Your drawing should appear on the screen.

CROSS-REF   For more information on configuring plotters, see Appendix A. For information on plotting drawing sets, see Chapter 26. I cover plotting electronically to a DWF file in Chapter 28.

To start plotting, choose Plot from the Standard toolbar to open the Plot dialog box, shown in Figure 17.19. As you can see, this dialog box is almost identical to the Page Setup dialog box.

 You can hide the right side of the Plot dialog box if you don't need the features there. Click the arrow at the lower-right corner of the dialog box.

FIGURE 17.19

The Plot dialog box.

If you set the Layout Settings in the Page Setup dialog box and set them current, those settings were saved with the tab that was current at the time. You can usually just click OK in the Plot dialog box and plot immediately. Plot settings are saved in your drawing.

Specifying plot settings

If you saved a page setup, you can choose it from the drop-down list in the Page Setup section of the dialog box. See the discussion of the Page Setup dialog box earlier in this chapter for details.

To select a plotter or printer, choose one from the drop-down list in the Printer/Plotter section of the dialog box. A plotter must be either a Windows system printer or a configured plotter. To add a system printer, choose Start ➪ Printers and Faxes (or Start ➪ Control Panel(➪ Hardware and Sound) ➪ Printers). Click or double-click Add a Printer. (The exact instructions vary with your version of Windows.) To add a configured plotter, which has a driver specifically to optimize the functioning of that plotter, use the Add Plotter Wizard. (Choose Tools ➪ Wizards ➪ Add Plotter.)

Configuring Your Plotter

Most printers and plotters have many settings that you can control from within AutoCAD or AutoCAD LT. You can also control how information about the drawing is sent to the printer or plotter. Configuring a plotter usually provides you with more options than if you choose the default Windows system printer settings. The settings that configure how your printer or plotter functions are in the Plotter Configuration Editor, as shown here.

To configure your plotter, choose File ⇨ Plotter Manager to open a window for the \Plotters folder. (To find the location of the Plotters folder, choose Tools ⇨ Options and click the Files tab. Double-click Printer Support File Path. Then double-click Printer Configuration Search Path to display the location.)

Plotter configuration settings are stored in PC3 files. Double-click the PC3 file icon for the plotter that you want to configure to open the Plotter Configuration Editor. (You can also open the Plotter Configuration Editor from the Plot dialog box by clicking Properties in the Printer/Plotter section.) Click the Device and Document Settings tab. The top section lists the possible types of settings. To open a list with a plus sign to its left, click the plus sign; sub-options appear. As you click each item on the top, the appropriate settings appear in the lower section. For example, if you want to set the color, speed, and width for each pen in a pen plotter, click physical pen characteristics. Then, in the bottom half of the Editor, you can click each pen in the carousel and change its characteristics. To specify settings for raster and vector graphics, choose Graphics; you can also merge overlapping lines. Choose Custom Paper Sizes to add custom sheet sizes; these will then appear in the Page Setup and Plot dialog boxes so that you can choose them when you plot. In each case, the Editor walks you through the choices that you need to make to configure your plotter. See Appendix A for further information.

You can filter out unused paper sizes using the Plotter Configuration Editor. However, at the end of the process, you can opt to apply the change only to the current plot. Follow these steps:

1. On the Device and Document Settings tab, choose Filter Paper Sizes.
2. In the list of paper sizes, uncheck any sizes that you don't want to display.
3. Click OK.
4. In the Changes to a Printer Configuration File dialog box, choose to apply the changes only to the current plot or to the file. When you apply the changes to the file, they are permanent until you edit the printer configuration file again.
5. Click OK.

TIP To avoid inadvertently plotting to a Windows system printer when you should be plotting to a plotter, you can hide the display of Windows system printers in the Plot and Page Setup dialog boxes. Because these printers won't appear on the list of plotters, you can't plot to them. To hide system printers, choose Tools ➪ Options and click the Plot and Publish tab. In the General Plot Options section of the dialog box, check Hide System Printers and click OK.

If you want to use a plot-style table, check that it appears in the Plot Style Table drop-down list.

To choose how many copies you want to plot, change the number in the Number of Copies text box.

Check the Plot to File check box to create a plot file rather than a paper plot. When you click OK, the Browse for Plot File dialog box opens so that you can choose a name and location. Click Save to create the plot file.

You can merge overlapping objects so that the same area is not printed more than once. To set the Merge Overlapping property:

1. Click Properties in the Printer/Plotter section of the Plot dialog box.
2. In the Plotter Configuration Editor that opens, display the Device and Document Settings tab. Click the plus sign (+) next to Graphics. If you see Merge Control in the Graphics list that opens, you can use this feature on your printer or plotter. (For more information about the Plotter Configuration Editor, see the sidebar "Configuring Your Plotter.")
3. Click Merge Control. In the Merge Control area that is displayed, choose either Lines Overwrite or Lines Merge, and click OK.
4. You then have the choice of applying the change to the current plot only or making the change permanent by editing the PC3 file that contains the parameters for your plotter or printer. Choose one of the options and click OK.

Previewing your plot

You should preview your drawing before you plot. Click the Preview button in the Plot dialog box to see exactly how your drawing will plot. You can also use the Plot Preview button on the Standard (or Standard Annotation) toolbar, which is just like the one that you use in your Windows word processor. When you choose Plot Preview, you see a preview of your plot using current plot parameters.

If you configured your plotter to merge lines, you can see the merged lines in Preview mode. For more information, see the sidebar "Configuring Your Plotter."

Right-click to open the shortcut menu that lets you plot, zoom, pan, or exit the preview.

I cover previewing a plot last because it should be the last step before you actually plot. However, it can also be the first step to help you to determine the settings that you need.

Creating a plot stamp

The PLOTSTAMP command places text in a specified corner of the plot, such as the drawing name, layout name, date and time, and so on. To create a plot stamp, enter **-plotstamp** on the command line. Use the options to specify what you want to appear, and use the On and Off options to turn the stamp on and off. You can enter **plotstamp** to set the plotstamp in a dialog box, which is easier; however, you should then look at the Plot Options section of the extended Plot dialog box to make sure that the plot stamp is on (the Plot Stamp On check box should be checked. Click the Advanced button in the Plot Stamp dialog box to specify the location, offset, and text properties of the plot stamp.

 Stmplot **stamps a drawing with its name and location, your name, the date, and the time, and starts the PLOT command. Look in** \Software\Chap17\Stmplot. **(AutoCAD only.)**

Creating the plot

To start the plotting process, simply click OK in the Plot dialog box.

You can plot *in the background,* which means that you can continue to work while your drawing is plotting. By default, background plotting is off. To turn it on, choose Tools ➪ Options and click the Plot and Publish tab. In the Background Processing Options section, check the Plotting check box. You can also separately specify background plotting for publishing, which I cover in Chapter 28. (Background plotting is on by default for publishing.)

If you're plotting in the background, you can place your cursor over the plotter icon in the status tray to view information about the status of the plot.

When the plot is finished, a notification bubble appears at the lower-right corner of your screen, as shown in Figure 17.20. As you can see, you can click the link to view the Plot and Publish Details.

FIGURE 17.20

This bubble appears when your plot is done.

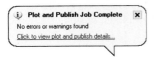

If you view the Plot and Publish Details, you see a report like the one shown in Figure 17.21. You can see details for all plots that you did in the current session of AutoCAD or AutoCAD LT.

If you need to plot large numbers of drawings or multiple layouts, use the PUBLISH command, which I cover in Chapter 28.

FIGURE 17.21

The Plot and Publish Details report tells you what happened when you plotted your drawings.

Summary

In this chapter, you learned how to lay out and plot a drawing. You discovered how to:

- Lay out a drawing in model space
- Use a paper space layout
- Create layouts, using the Layout Wizard and using the commands individually
- Use annotative objects in a viewport
- Add text and dimensions in paper space
- Use the Page Setup dialog box to specify layout settings
- Create plot-style tables and apply plot styles
- Plot a drawing

This chapter ends Part II, "Drawing in Two Dimensions." Part III, "Working with Data," explains how to integrate your drawing with data about your objects. The next chapter explains how to use blocks and attributes.

Part III

Working with Data

Part III covers the various ways that you work with data in your drawings. This part brings you to a new level of sophistication in terms of automation and interfacing with other drawings and data. Chapter 18 covers blocks and attributes, which enable you to work repetitively with objects and text. You can build intelligent, flexible blocks using the Dynamic Blocks feature. You can use attribute text to accurately place text and to create a simple database of information related to your objects. Chapter 19 explains how to refer to other drawings with external references, also called *xrefs*. Chapter 20 describes how to connect sophisticated external databases to objects in your drawings.

Chapter 18

Working with Blocks and Attributes

As you draw, you'll find that you often need to place the same group of objects several times in a drawing. An architect needs to place windows and doors many times in a plan layout of a house. An electrical engineer places electrical symbols in a drawing again and again. A mechanical model may include nuts, bolts, and surface finish symbols many times in a drawing. *Blocks* are groups of objects that you save and name so that you can insert them in your drawing whenever you need them. A block is one object, regardless of the number of individual objects that were used to create it. Because it's one object, you can easily move, copy, scale, or rotate it. However, if necessary, you can *explode* a block to obtain the original individual objects.

A great advantage of blocks is that by changing the block definition, you can update all of the instances of that block in that drawing. Another advantage of blocks is that they reduce the size of the drawing file. A drawing stores the definition of a block only once, along with a simple reference to the block each time it's inserted, instead of storing each individual object in each block in the drawing database.

As soon as you have a block in a drawing, you can work with it as with any other object. You can snap to object snaps of the individual objects within blocks, as well as trim and extend to objects within blocks, even though you can't edit the individual objects. For example, you can draw a line from the midpoint of a line in a block.

Many disciplines use *parts libraries* that may consist of thousands of items. You use the block feature to save and insert these parts. You can save many blocks in a drawing or place each in a separate file so that you can insert them in any drawing you wish.

Dynamic blocks are blocks that contain parameters for insertion and editing. You can create a dynamic block that takes the place of numerous similar regular blocks by giving it the flexibility to take on various sizes, rotations, visibility variations, and more.

You can attach *attributes* to blocks. Attributes are labels that are associated with blocks. Attributes have two main uses: to label objects and to create a simple database. If you have AutoCAD, you can use fields in your attributes to automate the generation of text. (Chapter 13 explains all about fields.)

This chapter explains how to make the most of blocks and attributes.

Combining Objects into Blocks

Any object or set of objects can be saved as a block. Creating a block is easy, but a little planning makes using it much simpler. Before you create a block, you need to understand how blocks are inserted and how you want to use the specific block that you're creating.

Understanding base points and insertion points

Figure 18.1 shows the legend for a plat drawing. Each legend symbol is a block that is then inserted in the drawing as needed. A symbol has been selected, and you can see that it has one grip at the *base point*. The base point is the point that you use to insert the block. Every block must have a base point. When you insert the block, the base point is placed at the coordinate that you specify for inserting the block — the *insertion point*. All of the objects of the block are then inserted in their proper place relative to that insertion point.

FIGURE 18.1

Each legend symbol is a block. Every block has a base point.

The base point does not have to be on the object, but it should be in a location that makes it easy to insert the block. Figure 18.2 shows a different sort of block, a title border/block. In this case, the base point is usually inserted at 0,0 of the drawing. By placing the base point at the lower-left corner of the border, you can easily place this block in any drawing. The base point is similar in concept to the justification point on text objects.

FIGURE 18.2

This title block is a block. Its base point is at the lower-left corner.

Creating a block

To create a block, first create the objects just as you want to save them. You may include other blocks as objects in your block. (A block within a block is called a *nested block*.)

After you've created the objects for your block, follow these steps:

 1. Choose Make Block from the Draw toolbar or the 2D Draw control panel of the Dashboard to start the BLOCK command and open the Block Definition dialog box, shown in Figure 18.3. The dialog box guides you through the process of defining a block.

FIGURE 18.3

The Block Definition dialog box.

2. In the Name text box, type a name for the block. The name can be up to 255 characters, and spaces are allowed.

3. Choose how you want the objects of the block to be treated:

- **Retain:** Keeps the objects that you selected as individual objects.
- **Convert to Block:** Converts the objects to a block.
- **Delete:** Deletes the objects. Use this option if you created the objects to insert them elsewhere and do not need the original objects.

4. Choose the insert units that you want to use when defining your block. (You can choose anything from microns to parsecs!) Let's say you work in kilometers and save a block with an insert unit of kilometers. When you insert a block, it will be measured in kilometers, rather than millimeters or inches. If the units aren't important to you, you can specify the units as Unitless.

5. If you want the block to be annotative, check the Annotative check box in the Behavior section of the dialog box. You can set up annotative objects to scale automatically to the scale of a viewport.

CROSS-REF   For more information on using annotative objects, see Chapter 17.

CAUTION   You cannot put annotative blocks inside other annotative blocks. Also, you shouldn't manually scale (as with the SCALE command) blocks that contain annotative objects. When you scale an annotative block, the resulting scale includes your scale as well as the current annotation scale.

6. Check the Scale Uniformly check box to force any scaling of the block to scale at equal X and Y factors. This feature prevents distortion of the block. By default, this option is not checked. However, it's not available if you choose to make the block annotative.

7. The Allow Exploding check box lets you explode the block after you insert it. This option is checked by default.

8. If you want, enter a description for the block. The description is used by the DesignCenter. You can also add a hyperlink by clicking the Hyperlink button. (See Chapter 28 for more on hyperlinks.)

9. Check the Open in Block Editor check box if you know that you want to create a dynamic block. (I explain dynamic blocks later in this chapter.) Then, when you click OK to close the dialog box, the Block Editor immediately opens.

10. If you haven't already selected objects, check the Specify On-screen checkboxes in both the Base Point and Objects sections of the dialog box. Click OK. You return to your drawing. At the `Insertion base point:` prompt: specify a base point. (If you don't check the Specify On-screen checkbox in the Base Point section, you get the default of 0,0 (or 0,0,0 for 3D drawings). Use an object snap on any of the objects in the block.

CAUTION   For precision, you should always use an object snap when defining the base point. If the base point that you need to use is not on any object, you can use the From object snap, object snap tracking, or some other means of specifying a precise coordinate.

11. At the `Select objects:` prompt, use any selection method to select the objects that you want in your block. Press Enter to end selection and complete the process. (If you select the objects before starting the command the dialog box notes how many objects are selected.) By not checking (or unchecking) the Specify On-screen check box in the Objects section, you skip this step. To filter out the selected objects, choose Quick Select, as described in Chapter 10.

12. Click OK to return to your drawing.

The definition of the block is now stored in the drawing, ready for you to insert as many times as needed. If you selected Delete, your objects disappeared. You can retrieve them by the one command with a sense of humor: OOPS. The OOPS command restores the last object or set of objects that you erased. This command works whether you used the ERASE command or created a block, and even if you used some other command in the meantime. By contrast, UNDO undoes almost all commands, but only in the order that they were executed.

 If you create a number of block definitions that you don't end up using in the drawing, use the PURGE command to delete them. This reduces the size of the drawing file.

Redefining a block

One advantage of deleting the objects is that their disappearance confirms that you selected the right objects. If you make a mistake, or if you want to change the block in some way, you can redefine it. If you just created the block, use UNDO and make any necessary changes. If you created the block earlier, follow these steps:

1. Insert the block and explode it. (Exploding is covered later in this chapter.)
2. Make the desired changes and repeat the process of defining the block, using the same name for the block.

 When you specify the name of the block, you should type it, rather than choose it from the Name drop-down list. Choosing the name from the list replaces selected objects that you wanted to be in the new version of the block with the objects from the previous block definition, and sets the insertion point to 0,0.

3. Click Yes when the message asks whether you want to redefine the block.

Redefining a block that has been inserted in your drawing updates all of the blocks in that drawing. This is a powerful technique to control your drawing. If you have repetitive symbols in your drawing, it's worthwhile to make blocks out of them just so that you can make this type of global change if necessary.

ON the DVD-ROM The drawing that you need for the following exercise on creating a block, ab18-a.dwg, is in the Drawings folder on the DVD.

STEPS: Creating a Block

1. Open ab18-a.dwg from the DVD.
2. Save the file as ab18-01.dwg in your AutoCAD Bible folder. This is a small portion of an electrical schematic drawing, as shown in Figure 18.4. OSNAP should be on. Set running object snaps for endpoint, quadrant, and intersection.

FIGURE 18.4

A portion of an electrical schematic.

3. To make a block of the 1.5-amp fuse, choose Make Block from the Draw toolbar or the 2D Draw control panel of the Dashboard.

4. In the Name text box of the Block Definition dialog box, type **1-5 amp fuse.**

5. In the dialog box's Objects section, choose Delete. The Insert Units should be Unitless. Leave the Description blank. The Open in Block Editor check box should not be checked.

6. In the Base Point and the Objects sections, check the Specify On-screen check box.

7. Click OK.

8. In the drawing, at the `Specify insertion base point:` prompt, use the Quadrant object snap to pick ❶ in Figure 18.4.

9. At the `Select objects:` prompt, select the boxed objects shown in Figure 18.4 (the two lines of text, the two circles, and the two arcs). Press Enter to end selection.

10. To check that the block has been created, choose Make Block from the Draw toolbar or the 2D Draw control panel of the Dashboard. Click the Name drop-down arrow to see your block. Click Cancel.

11. Save your drawing.

Saving blocks as files

You can use the DesignCenter to insert blocks from any drawing. Nevertheless, many users need to organize their blocks in their own files so that they can be easily stored and located. Parts and symbols libraries are made up of many individual drawing files, one for each part or symbol. These libraries are a powerful aid to drawing more efficiently.

To save a block as a file, follow these steps:

1. Type **wblock** ↵ to open the Write Block dialog box, shown in Figure 18.5, (WBLOCK stands for write block. Writing to a file is another expression for saving to a file.)

2. In the Source section, choose how you want to create the drawing file:

   ▪ **Block:** Use this option when you've already created the block and now want to save it as a drawing file. Choose the block from the drop-down list.

   ▪ **Entire drawing:** Use this option to make a copy of your drawing.

   ▪ **Objects:** Use this option to start defining the block in the same way that you define a block within a drawing. The Base Point and Objects sections become available.

3. Choose the location (drive and folder) for the file in the File Name and Path text box. If you're creating the file from objects, insert a name for the file in place of the default `New Block` at the end of the path.

4. In the Insert Units drop-down list, choose the units that you want for your block, or choose Unitless for no units.

5. After you're done, click OK to create the drawing file.

FIGURE 18.5

Use the Write Block dialog box to save a block as a separate drawing file.

When you save a drawing that you plan to insert as a block, use the BASE command to create the insertion point. By default, the base point is 0,0,0. By setting the base point to another point in the drawing, such as an object snap on one of the objects, you can more easily control how that drawing is inserted.

NEW FEATURE If you want a drawing to act like an annotative block when you insert it, set its ANNOTATIVEDWG system variable to 1.

Replacing an existing file

If you make a mistake when selecting objects to write to a file with WBLOCK, or you want to change the objects in the file, then you can replace the file. Start WBLOCK and type the name of the block file that you want to change. Be sure to choose the same file location. When you click OK, a message asks whether you want to replace the existing file. Click Yes.

ON the DVD-ROM The drawing that you need for the following exercise on saving a block to a file, ab18-b.dwg, is in the Drawings folder on the DVD.

STEPS: Saving a Block to a File

1. Open ab18-b.dwg from the DVD.

2. Save the file as ab18-02.dwg in your AutoCAD Bible folder. This is a large title block, as shown in Figure 18.6. OSNAP should be on. Set a running object snap for endpoint.

3. Type **wblock** ↵. In the Source section of the Write Block dialog box, choose Entire Drawing. Set the File Name and Path box to AutoCAD Bible\tb-f by typing the path and the filename. (Alternatively, click the ellipsis [...] button and navigate to your AutoCAD Bible folder. In the File Name text box, type **tb-f**. Click Save.) Click OK.

4. Press Enter to repeat the WBLOCK command.

5. In the Source section of the dialog box, choose Objects. In the Objects section, click Select Objects.

A title block can be saved as a file and inserted into any other drawing.

6. Use Zoom Window to zoom in on the text at the bottom-right corner of the title block. At the `Select objects:` prompt, select all of the 90°-rotated text at ❶ in Figure 18.6. Press Enter to end selection.

7. In the Base Point section, click Pick Point. Use the Endpoint object snap to pick the bottom-left corner of the box containing the text that you selected. Using this base point lets you easily place the text in the box at any time.

8. In the Objects section, choose Delete from Drawing.

9. In the File Name and Path text box, type **notes-tol** after the path, which should already be set to your `AutoCAD Bible` folder. Click OK to save the block as a file.

10. Type **oops** ↵ to bring back the text.

11. Choose Zoom Extents from the Zoom flyout of the Standard toolbar (or choose View ➪ Zoom ➪ Extents), and save your drawing.

Inserting Blocks and Files into Drawings

Blocks that are defined in a drawing are inserted in the same way as separate drawing files. After you choose the location, you can change the size and rotation of the block. This capability is ideal for parts libraries. Parts may be created at the size of 1 unit and then scaled or rotated as needed. Figure 18.7 shows a window block inserted at various scales and rotation angles. (You could also create one dynamic block with the capability of inserting it at various scales and rotation angles. I cover dynamic blocks later in this chapter.)

A block of a window inserted at various rotation angles and scales.

Using the Insert dialog box

To insert a block or file, follow these steps:

1. Choose Insert Block from the Draw toolbar or the 2D Draw control panel of the Dashboard to start the INSERT command. The Insert dialog box opens, as shown in Figure 18.8.

NOTE   If the block is annotative, you see an annotative icon next to the block's preview.

The Insert dialog box.

2. You can insert a block or a file as follows:

   ▪ To insert a block from within your drawing, click the Name drop-down list and choose one of the existing blocks.

   ▪ To insert a file, click Browse. The Select Drawing File dialog box opens. Locate the file's drive and folder, and then choose the file. A preview appears to the right. Click Open. The Insert dialog box displays the path of the file.

3. Uncheck Specify On-screen in the Insertion Point, Scale, and Rotation sections if you want to specify the insertion point, scale, and rotation angle in the dialog box. Then provide the requested information in the dialog box.

NOTE The Uniform Scale check box forces scaling to be the same for the X and Y directions. The first time in each session that you insert or create an annotative object, the Select Annotation Scale dialog box opens, where you can choose the desired annotation scale from the drop-down list.

4. Check the Explode check box if you want to insert the block as individual objects instead of as one block object. The Explode check box is disabled if you did not check the Allow Exploding check box in the Block Definition dialog box when you created the block.

5. Click OK to close the Insert dialog box.

NOTE While you're dragging the block and before you specify an insertion point, you can display the Properties palette and change general properties of the block. For example, you can choose a layer to insert the block on a layer other than the current layer.

6. If any of the Specify On-Screen check boxes were checked, the command line prompts you for the necessary information:

   ▪ At the `Specify insertion point:` prompt (which varies, depending on whether or not you checked the Explode check box in Step 4), specify the insertion point. You see the block with its base point at the cursor, and so you can judge how it looks.

TIP A Basepoint option appears with the `Specify insertion point:` prompt. When you use this option, you can move the insertion basepoint of the block to anywhere you want. Usually, you would use an object snap to specify a different point on the block.

   ▪ At the `Enter X scale factor, specify opposite corner, or [Corner/XYZ] <1>:` prompt, press Enter to accept the default scale factor of 1, or type another scale. The Specify Opposite Corner option lets you define a square box whose side defines the scale factor. A side of 1 unit results in a scale factor of 1. If you specify the X scale factor, the command line prompts you for the Y scale factor. The default is the same scale as X, but you can specify a different one. For 3D models, use the XYZ option to specify all three scale factors. (If you checked Explode, the prompt is slightly different, and you specify the scale factor for all directions at once. If the Uniform Scale check box is checked, the prompt asks you for a scale factor.)

   ▪ At the `Specify rotation angle <0>:` prompt, type in a rotation angle. You can also pick a point to use the angle from the insertion point to the point that you picked as the rotation angle. This technique is useful for aligning a block with an existing object.

After you provide all of the necessary information, the command inserts the block or file.

A negative scale factor for any of the axes creates a mirror image of the block or file. When you specify a negative X scale axis, the block is mirrored around the Y axis. When you specify a negative Y scale axis, the block is mirrored around the X axis. Figure 18.9 shows a door block inserted with positive and negative scale factors. The rotation angle of all the blocks is 0 degrees. By combining negative and positive scale factors with rotation angles, you can get any door configuration that you want. Sometimes it can be difficult to visualize the result of a negative scale combined with a rotation angle. See the sidebar, "Presetting Scale and Rotation While Inserting a Block," for a solution. Dynamic blocks also offer a way to insert blocks at various scales and rotation angles.

When you insert a drawing file, paper space objects are not included in the block definition created in your drawing. To insert paper space objects in another drawing, open the original drawing and define the objects as a block. Then use the DesignCenter to insert that block into any other drawing.

FIGURE 18.9

A door block inserted at various positive and negative scale factors, creating mirror images in different directions.

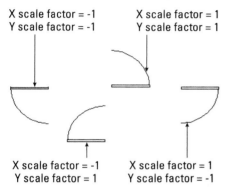

X scale factor = -1   X scale factor = 1
Y scale factor = -1   Y scale factor = 1

X scale factor = -1   X scale factor = 1
Y scale factor = 1   Y scale factor = -1

Using the DesignCenter

When you want to insert a block from within another drawing, use the DesignCenter. Any time that you need to find one block from within another drawing, you need to use the DesignCenter. For this reason, the DesignCenter is the tool to use if you have a block library containing multiple blocks within one drawing. Choose DesignCenter from the Standard or Standard Annotation toolbar (or press Ctrl+2). In the left pane, navigate to the drawing that contains the block that you want. Double-click the drawing and choose Blocks from the list that appears. In the right pane, you see a list of the blocks in that drawing. Click Preview to see a preview of each block that you select. Click Description to see a description of the block. (The description only appears if you saved one when creating the block.) There are two ways to insert the block:

- Double-click the block's icon to open the Insert dialog box so that you can specify exactly how you want to insert the block, just as I described earlier for blocks within a drawing.

- Drag the block's icon onto the drawing area to insert the block at the point where you release the mouse button, using the default scale and rotation.

You can also use the DesignCenter to insert entire drawings. In the left pane, navigate to the folder containing the drawing. The drawings are then listed in the right pane. Choose a drawing and drag it onto the drawing area. On the command line, you'll see the -INSERT command, the command-line version of INSERT. You can simply specify an insertion point, scale, and rotation, or you can use the options described in the sidebar, "Presetting Scale and Rotation While Inserting a Block."

CROSS-REF You can also insert blocks from a tool palette. You can quickly create a tool palette containing all the blocks in a folder. See Chapter 26 for details.

Presetting Scale and Rotation While Inserting a Block

When you're dragging a block on the screen to specify an insertion point, it may be helpful to see the block at the scale and rotation angle that you want. The problem is that the prompts for scale and rotation come after the prompt for the insertion point. If you use the command-line version of INSERT by typing **-insert**, you can preset the scale and rotation angle at the `Specify insertion point or [Basepoint/Scale/X/Y/Z/Rotate]:` prompt, using the options shown here. All of the prompts appear on the command line, including the prompt for the name of the block or file that you want to insert.

Option	Use
Scale	Specifies the scale factor
X	Specifies the X scale factor
Y	Specifies the Y scale factor
Z	Specifies the Z scale factor
Rotate	Specifies the rotation angle
PScale	Specifies the preliminary scale factor for the display of the block as you drag it, and prompts you again for the scale so that you can change it
PXscale	Specifies the preliminary X scale factor for the display of the block as you drag it, and prompts you again for the scale so that you can change it
PYscale	Specifies the preliminary Y scale factor for the display of the block as you drag it, and prompts you again for the scale so that you can change it
PZscale	Specifies the preliminary Z scale factor for the display of the block as you drag it, and prompts you again for the scale so that you can change it
PRotate	Specifies the preliminary rotation angle for the display of the block as you drag it, and prompts you again for the rotation angle so that you can change it

ON the DVD-ROM   The drawings that you need for the following exercise on inserting blocks, `ab14-b.dwg` and `ab18-c.dwg`, are in the `Drawings` folder on the DVD.

STEPS: Inserting Blocks

1. Open `ab18-c.dwg` from the DVD.

2. Save the file as `ab18-03.dwg` in your `AutoCAD Bible` folder. This is the floor plan of the first floor of a house, as shown in Figure 18.10. Many of the doors and a toilet need to be inserted. OSNAP should be on. Set running object snaps for endpoint and midpoint. The current layer is Door.

3. Use Zoom Window to zoom in on the left wing of the house.

FIGURE 18.10

The floor plan of the house needs some doors and a toilet.

 4. Choose Insert Block from the Draw toolbar or the 2D Draw control panel of the Dashboard. In the Name drop-down list of the Insert dialog box, choose DOOR (if it isn't already selected). Check all three Specify On-screen check boxes. Make sure that the Uniform Scale check box is not checked. Click OK to close the Insert dialog box.

> **TIP** If you make a mistake while inserting a door, press Esc if you're in the middle of the prompts. If you've completed the command, click Undo on the Standard or Standard Annotation toolbar or erase the door and start over.

5. As you move the cursor, you can see the dragged image of a door. This image shows you the block at an X and Y scale of 1, and a 0-degree rotation angle. Follow the prompts:

```
Specify insertion point or [Basepoint/Scale/X/Y/Z/Rotate]: Use the
Endpoint object snap to pick ❶ in Figure 18.10.
Enter X scale factor, specify opposite corner, or [Corner/XYZ] <1>:
-1 ↵
Enter Y scale factor <use X scale factor>: 1 ↵
Specify rotation angle <0>: 270 ↵ (You could also specify -90
degrees.)
```

6. Repeat the INSERT command. The Insert dialog box already shows the DOOR block. Click OK. Follow the prompts. You'll probably want to use Zoom Window to zoom into the area of ❷ in Figure 18.10.

```
Specify insertion point or [Basepoint/Scale/X/Y/Z/Rotate]: Pick ❷ in
Figure 18.10.
Enter X scale factor, specify opposite corner, or [Corner/XYZ] <1>:
2/3 ↵
Enter Y scale factor <use X scale factor>: ↵
Specify rotation angle <0>: 180 ↵
```

7. If you zoomed in for the previous step, return to the previous view using Zoom Previous. Zoom in to the area around ❸ in Figure 18.10. Choose Insert Block from the Draw toolbar or the 2D Draw control panel of the Dashboard. Click OK. Follow the prompts:

```
Specify insertion point or [Basepoint/Scale/X/Y/Z/Rotate]: Pick ❸ in
Figure 18.10.
Enter X scale factor or specify opposite corner, or [Corner/XYZ] <1>:
-3/4 ↵
Enter Y scale factor <use X scale factor>: 3/4 ↵
Specify rotation angle <0>: 315 ↵
```

8. Use Zoom Dynamic to zoom in to the area around ❹ and ❺ in Figure 18.10. Choose Insert Block from the Draw toolbar or the 2D Draw control panel of the Dashboard. Click OK. Follow the prompts:

```
Specify insertion point or [Basepoint/Scale/X/Y/Z/Rotate]: Pick ❹ in
Figure 18.10.
Enter X scale factor, specify opposite corner, or [Corner/XYZ] <1>: 1 ↵
Enter Y scale factor <use X scale factor>: ↵
Specify rotation angle <0>: 270 ↵
```

9. Repeat the INSERT command and click OK. Follow the prompts:

```
Specify insertion point or [Basepoint/Scale/X/Y/Z/Rotate]: Pick ❺ in
Figure 18.10.
Enter X scale factor, specify opposite corner, or [Corner/XYZ] <1>:
-1 ↵
Enter Y scale factor <use X scale factor>: 1 ↵
Specify rotation angle <0>: 90 ↵
```

10. Use Zoom Dynamic to zoom in on the area around ❻ and ❼ in Figure 18.10. Start the INSERT command and click OK. Follow the prompts:

```
Specify insertion point or [Basepoint/Scale/X/Y/Z/Rotate]: Pick ❻ in
Figure 18.10.
Enter X scale factor, specify opposite corner, or [Corner/XYZ] <1>:
-2/3 ↵
Enter Y scale factor <use X scale factor>: 2/3 ↵
Specify rotation angle: 270 ↵
```

11. Repeat the INSERT command and click OK. Follow the prompts:

```
Specify insertion point or [Basepoint/Scale/X/Y/Z/Rotate]: Pick ❼ in
Figure 18.10.
Enter X scale factor, specify opposite corner, or [Corner/XYZ] <1>:
2/3 ↵
Enter Y scale factor <use X scale factor>: ↵
Specify rotation angle: 90 ↵
```

12. Beneath the doors that you just inserted is a water closet with a toilet. Pan down to it. Erase the toilet, which is a block. Change the current layer to FIXTURE.

13. Choose DesignCenter from the Standard (or Standard Annotation) toolbar (or press Ctrl+2). (If you don't see the two panes, click Tree View Toggle on the DesignCenter toolbar.) In the left pane, navigate to your DVD drive. (You may need to use the horizontal scroll bar if the left side of the

list of drives and folders is not in view.) Double-click the DVD drive and then double-click `ab14-b.dwg`. Click Blocks from the list of named objects. On the right, you see the blocks in the drawing.

14. Double-click TOILET2. You see a preview at the bottom of the DesignCenter. (If you don't, click Preview on the DesignCenter toolbar.) The Insert dialog box opens. Because you can see the preview, you know the rotation angle is correct; you can assume that the scale is correct because toilets are generally about the same size. The Insertion Point Specify On-Screen check box should be checked. The other Specify On-Screen check boxes should be unchecked. Click OK.

15. Drag the toilet into the water closet and use a Midpoint object snap to place it at the middle of the bottom wall of the water closet. If you want, close the DesignCenter by clicking its Close button.

16. Do a Zoom Extents and save your drawing.

The MINSERT command (AutoCAD only) lets you insert blocks (but not annotative blocks) in a rectangular array. Type **minsert** ↵. MINSERT prompts you for an insertion point, scale factors, and rotation angle using the same prompts as the INSERT command, but without the dialog box. It then starts the same prompts as the Rectangular option of the ARRAY command, asking for the number of rows and columns and the distance between them. The value of MINSERT is that it reduces the size of your drawing because the array is one block object. The disadvantage is that you can't edit the individual blocks in the array or the array as a whole in any way. If you need to edit them, erase the entire array of blocks, redefine the single block, if necessary, and start over, this time using INSERT and ARRAY separately. You cannot explode a minserted block.

Managing Blocks

Several factors require care when working with blocks. Large libraries of blocks need to be well managed so that you can find the block that you need quickly. You also need to consider the issue of which layers you use when you define your blocks, so that you get the desired results when you insert them.

> **TIP** You can use the QSELECT command to select all instances of a block from a drop-down list. Choose Block Reference as the object type and Name as the property. From the Value drop-down list, choose the block that you want.

Working with layers

You may want a block to take on the current layer when inserted, or to retain its original layer. You can manage block layers along with their color and linetype properties to obtain the desired result. A block can be defined in four ways to determine which layer, color, linetype, and lineweight properties it will use when it's inserted, as shown in Table 18.1. Each method has different results when the block is inserted, although some of the differences are minor.

As you can see, careful planning of the layers that you use when creating a block is essential. As Table 18.1 makes clear, two of the methods (setting the objects to ByBlock and creating them on layer 0) create chameleon blocks that take on the properties of the current layer. Use the other two methods when you want the block to retain its properties, regardless of the current layer.

Creating blocks on layer 0 is the simplest method. If you want the blocks to have a specific color and linetype, create a layer for them and switch to that layer before inserting the blocks. You can also change the layer of a block, after it's inserted, in the same way that you change the layer of any object.

TABLE 18.1

Properties of Block Component Objects and Insertion Results

Properties of Component Objects	Insertion Results
On any layer (except layer 0), with color, lineweight, and linetype set to ByLayer	The block keeps properties of that layer. If you insert a block into another drawing without that layer, the drawing creates the layer. If you insert the block into another drawing with that layer, but the layer has a different color and linetype properties, the block takes on properties of the layer that are different from those that you created it on. If you insert the block on a different layer, the block keeps the properties of the layer on which it was created, but the Properties palette reports the block as being on the layer on which it was inserted, because it reports the layer of the insertion point, not the block objects.
On any layer (including layer 0), with color, linetype, and lineweight set explicitly	The block keeps the color, linetype, and lineweight with properties that were explicitly set. If you insert the block into another drawing, the drawing creates the layer on which original objects were made.
On any layer (except layer 0), with color, linetype, and lineweight set to ByBlock	The block takes on the color of the current color setting. (If the current color is set to ByLayer, the block will take on the current layer's color.) If you insert the block into another drawing, the drawing creates the layer on which original objects were made. *Note:* If the color, linetype, and lineweight are ByBlock when you create objects for a block, the objects are always shown with black/white color, a continuous linetype, and the default lineweight.
On layer 0 (with color, linetype, and lineweight set to ByBlock or ByLayer)	The block takes on the layer and properties of the current layer on which it's inserted. If you insert the block into another drawing, no layers are created.

ON the DVD-ROM The drawing that you need for the following exercise on working with blocks and layers, `ab18-d.dwg`, is in the `Drawings` folder on the DVD.

STEPS: Working with Blocks and Layers

1. Open `ab18-d.dwg` from the DVD.
2. Save the file as `ab18-04.dwg` in your `AutoCAD Bible` folder. This is a portion of an electrical schematic, as shown in Figure 18.11. OSNAP should be on. Set running object snaps for endpoint, midpoint, quadrant, and intersection.
3. Choose Make Block from the Draw toolbar or the 2D Draw control panel of the Dashboard. In the Name text box of the Block Definition dialog box, type **hl switch**. Make sure that the Specify On-screen check boxes in both the Base Point and Objects sections are checked. Choose Retain in the Objects section. Click OK.
4. Use the Quadrant object snap to pick the left quadrant of the left circle in the switch, at ❶ in Figure 18.11. Use a selection window to select the entire hi-limit switch box (not including the text labels). Right-click to end selection. The objects in this block were created on the Object layer, which is red with a continuous linetype. The color, linetype, and lineweight are set to ByLayer.

FIGURE 18.11

The electrical schematic has several symbols that would be useful as blocks.

5. Use a selection window to select the air damper switch. (The objects are currently on the Object layer, which is red with a continuous linetype.) Click the Color Control drop-down list from the Properties toolbar or the Object Properties control panel of the Dashboard and choose ByBlock. Do the same with the Linetype Control and the Lineweight Control drop-down lists. The switch turns black (or white if you're using a black screen). The objects are still selected.

6. Choose Make Block again from the Draw toolbar or the 2D Draw control panel of the Dashboard. In the Name text box, type **ad switch.** The dialog box says 4 objects selected. Click Pick Point. Uncheck the Specify On-screen check box in the Objects section (because the objects are already selected). Click OK. Use the Quadrant object snap to pick the left quadrant of the left circle in the switch.

7. Use a selection window to select the top conduit symbol at ❷ in Figure 18.11 (it consists of four objects). (It is currently on the Conduit layer, which is black and has a linetype of Hidden2.) Use the Color Control drop-down list to set the color to green. Use the Linetype Control drop-down list to set the linetype to Hidden2. Choose Make Block from the Draw toolbar or the 2D Draw control panel of the Dashboard. In the Name text box, type **top conduit.** The dialog box tells you that four objects are selected. The Specify On-screen check box in the Base Point section should be checked. Click OK. Use the Intersection object snap to pick ❸. The conduit appears green with the Hidden2 linetype.

8. Use a selection window to select the bottom conduit at ❹. (It is currently on the Conduit layer, which is black and has a linetype of Hidden2.) Use the Layer Control drop-down list to set the layer to 0. Choose Make Block from the Draw toolbar or the 2D Draw control panel of the Dashboard. In the block Name text box, type **bot conduit.** The dialog box tells you that four objects are selected. Click OK. Use the Intersection object snap to pick ❺. The conduit appears black with a continuous linetype.

9. Save your drawing. Choose File ➪ New. In the Select Template dialog box, click the down arrow next to the Open button. Choose one of the Open with No Template options. A new drawing opens with only one layer, layer 0. (Click the Layer Control drop-down list to check, if you want.)

10. Choose DesignCenter from the Standard (or Standard Annotation) toolbar (or press Ctrl+2). In the left pane, locate your AutoCAD Bible folder and then locate ab18-04.dwg. (You can also click the Open Drawings tab and find ab18-04.dwg there.) Double-click the drawing, and then

click Blocks. In the right pane, double-click `hl switch`. In the Insert dialog box, check Specify On-screen for Insertion Point and Scale. Click OK. Follow the prompts to insert the file anywhere in the drawing, using a scale factor of 3. The block, whose objects were created on the Object layer, retained its original color (red), linetype, and lineweight but is listed as being on layer 0. Select the block and look at the Layer Control drop-down list to verify this.

11. Check the Layer Control drop-down list. A new layer, `Object`, is the layer that the original objects were on.

12. In the right pane of the DesignCenter, double-click `top conduit`. In the Insert dialog box, click OK. Follow the prompts to insert the file anywhere in the drawing, using a scale factor of 3. Again, the object retains its explicitly set properties of green color and Hidden2 linetype but is listed as being on layer 0. Click the Layer Control drop-down list to see that the Conduit layer has been added to the drawing.

13. Click the Color Control drop-down list on the Object Properties toolbar or the Object Properties control panel of the Dashboard, and choose Cyan to make it the current color.

14. In the DesignCenter's right pane, double-click `ad switch`. In the Insert dialog box, click OK. Follow the prompts to insert the file anywhere in the drawing, using a scale factor of 3. The block (whose objects were created on the Object layer and whose properties were set to ByBlock) takes on the current color of Cyan and is listed on layer 0.

15. Choose Layer Properties Manager from the Layers toolbar or the Layers control panel of the Dashboard, and click New Layer in the Layer Properties Manager. Name the new layer **Green** and set its color to Green. Click Set Current to make it the current layer and then click OK.

16. Double-click `bot conduit`. In the Insert dialog box, click OK. Follow the prompts to insert the file anywhere in the drawing, using a scale factor of 3. The block, whose original objects were on layer 0, has the properties of layer Green and is listed on layer Green.

17. Click the DesignCenter's Close button to close the DesignCenter. Don't save this new drawing.

Exploding blocks

You can explode blocks into their original objects. You may need to do this to edit a block. If you want, you can then redefine the block, as explained earlier in this chapter. To explode a block, choose Explode from the Modify toolbar or the 2D Draw control panel of the Dashboard. (You can select objects before or after choosing the command.) You can also explode polylines, dimensions, leaders, multileaders, hatches, regions, multilines, and certain 3D objects (bodies, 3D meshes, 3D solids, various types of surfaces, poly-face meshes, and polygon meshes) into simpler types of objects. (Drawing in 3D is covered in Part IV.) Exploding a block with nested blocks explodes only the top-level block. You need to use EXPLODE again to explode the next level of blocks.

When you explode blocks that were created on layer 0 or with BYBLOCK objects, the objects return to their original status and appear black/white with a continuous linetype and default lineweight again.

If you insert a block with different X and Y scales, the command does its best to create objects based on their new shapes. For example, if you have a block that includes a circle and insert it with an X scale of 1 and a Y scale of 2, you see an ellipse. Therefore, when you explode the block, you get an ellipse from what used to be a circle.

 When you explode an annotative block, you get the components of the current scale presentation only. The components are not annotative.

Using the XPLODE command

The XPLODE command is a version of the EXPLODE command that you can use to control the final layer, color, and linetype of the objects. If you select more than one object, you can set the properties for all of the objects that you select at once (that is, *globally*) or for each object individually.

To xplode an object, type **xplode** ↵. (XPLODE is actually an AutoLISP program in AutoCAD and is also built into AutoCAD LT.) At the Select objects: prompt, select one or more blocks. If you select more than one object, XPLODE displays the XPlode Individually/<Globally>: prompt. Type **i** ↵ to get prompts for each block individually. Press Enter to accept the Globally default option. If you choose the Individually option, XPLODE highlights each block in turn so that you know which block you're working on as you respond to prompts.

At the Enter an option [All/Color/LAyer/LType/LWeight/Inherit from parent block/Explode] <Explode>: prompt, choose whether you want to specify color, layer, linetype, lineweight, or all four. If you are using AutoCAD, the Color option allows you to specify true colors using the RGB system or a color from a color book. (See Chapter 11 for more information.) The Inherit from Parent Block option works only for blocks created on layer 0 whose color and linetype were also set to ByBlock. These ByBlock objects then retain their color and linetype after you explode them.

Xplode cannot explode blocks whose X and Y scale factors have unequal absolute values. That means an X scale of 1 and a Y scale of –1 is okay, but not an X scale of 2 and a Y scale of –3.

 The drawing that you need for the following exercise on exploding and xploding blocks, ab18-e.dwg, is in the Drawings folder on the DVD.

STEPS: Exploding and Xploding Blocks

1. Open ab18-e.dwg from the DVD.
2. Save the file as ab18-05.dwg in your AutoCAD Bible folder. This is the same electrical schematic used in the previous exercise, except that the objects are now blocks that have been inserted (see Figure 18.12). OSNAP should be on. Set running object snaps for endpoint, midpoint, quadrant, and intersection. The current layer is Object.

FIGURE 18.12

The electrical schematic has several blocks that have been inserted.

3. Choose Explode from the Modify toolbar or the 2D Draw control panel of the Dashboard. At the `Select objects:` prompt, choose the air damper switch at **1** in Figure 18.12. Press Enter to end selection. The switch turns black or white (the opposite of your screen color) because it was created from objects whose color and linetype were set to ByBlock.

4. Choose Undo from the Standard (or Standard Annotation) toolbar.

5. Type **xplode** ↵. At the `Select objects:` prompt, choose the air damper switch again. Press Enter to end selection. At the `Enter an option [All/Color/LAyer/LType/LWeight/Inherit from parent block/Explode] <Explode>:` prompt, right-click and choose LAyer. At the `Enter new layer name for exploded objects <OBJECT>:` prompt, press Enter to accept the default of OBJECT, the current layer. The command line informs you that `Object exploded onto layer OBJECT`.

6. Choose the `hi-limit` switch at **2**. Choose Explode from the Modify toolbar or the 2D Draw control panel of the Dashboard. The command explodes the block onto the Object layer because these objects were created on that layer with their color and linetype set to ByLayer.

7. Type **xplode** ↵. The top conduit was created from objects set explicitly to green color and hidden2 linetype. The bottom conduit was created from objects set to layer 0. Follow the prompts:

```
Select objects: Choose the conduits at ❸ and ❹. End selection.
2 objects found.
Xplode Individually/<Globally>: ↵ to accept the default.
Enter an option [All/Color/LAyer/LType/LWeight/Inherit from parent
block/Explode] <Explode>: Right-click and choose All.
New Color [Truecolor/Colorbook] <BYLAYER>: ↵ (AutoCAD LT doesn't
include the Truecolor/COlorbook options.)
Enter new linetype name for exploded objects <BYLAYER>: ↵
Enter new lineweight < >: ↵
Enter new layer name for exploded objects <OBJECT>: conduit ↵
Objects exploded with color of BYLAYER, linetype of BYLAYER, and
layer conduit.
```

8. Save your drawing.

Editing blocks

Blocks can be complex objects. You may need to add, remove, or change a component of a block. You can also update or substitute blocks. Here are a few additional points that can help you to work with blocks.

Double-clicking to edit blocks

If you double-click a block, you open the Edit Block Definition dialog box. Choose the block from the Block to Create or Edit list and click OK to open the Block Editor. The Block Editor opens. I explain the Block Editor in detail later in this chapter in connection with dynamic blocks. However, you can use the Block Editor to edit all blocks, not just dynamic ones. Make the changes you want.

When you're done, choose Save Block Definition from the Block Editor's toolbar and click the Close Block Editor button.

Editing blocks with grips

To a certain extent, you can use grip editing with blocks. By default, when you select a block, only one grip — at the base point — is displayed. However, you can show the grips of all of the objects by choosing

Tools ⇨ Options. On the Selection tab, choose Enable Grips within Blocks and click OK. Figure 18.13 shows the results of both settings.

As a general rule, you don't want to enable grips for blocks when working with such complex blocks. However, you can turn them on to use grips to mirror, rotate, move, or scale the block if you want to use the grip of a component object as a base point for the edit.

Updating blocks

As I mentioned earlier in the chapter, when you redefine a block, all instances of that block are automatically updated. However, if you inserted a file to use as a block in a drawing and then changed that file, your current drawing has no way of knowing of the change in that drawing file. (Instead, use an external reference to solve this problem. See Chapter 19 for more on external references.)

FIGURE 18.13

By default, only one grip appears at the base point for a block. You can also choose to display the grips for all of the component objects.

Single grip at base point

Thanks to Sid Herbage of Mississauga, Ontario, for this drawing of a quadricycle engine.

To update a block that came from inserting an entire file, you can reinsert the file. Follow these steps:

1. Choose Insert Block.
2. Click Browse.
3. Choose the file that you've changed, and click Open. (You must locate the actual file rather than choose the block of the same name that already exists in the drawing.)
4. A message asks whether you want to redefine the block because that block already exists in the drawing. Choose Yes.
5. Press Esc to avoid actually inserting a new copy of the block.

The drawing updates all of the instances of the block with the new file. You can also use the DesignCenter to insert and update blocks.

NEW FEATURE You can update a block definition in your current drawing to match a block on a tool palette by right-clicking the block tool on the tool palette and clicking Redefine. All instances of the block are redefined to match the tool on the tool palette. (The block on the tool palette must be in the drawing, not an external drawing.)

Substituting blocks

You can substitute a different file as the basis for blocks in your drawing. There are three reasons for doing this:

- If you have many instances of complex blocks, you may find that regen times are slow. You can create a simple block, WBLOCK it, and substitute it for the original blocks until plotting time. This is similar to using QTEXT to replace text with rectangles (see Chapter 13).

- You can create more than one version of a drawing — for example, an office layout with various kinds of desks. You can create the drawing with one type of desk, inserting files of the desks. Substitute a file of another type of desk, and you have a new office layout design.

- Another common reason to substitute blocks is when your company switches to a different standard for a part.

To substitute blocks, follow these steps:

1. Type **-insert** ↵ on the command line.
2. Type **blockname=filename** where blockname is the name of the block and filename is the name of the file. (If the file is not in the support file search path, type the entire path.) Press Enter.

NOTE To place a folder in the support file search path, choose Tools ➪ Options and click the Files tab. Double-click Support File Search Path. Click Add, and then type the path or browse to it. After you're done, click OK to close the Options dialog box.

3. A message tells you that the block with this name already exists, and asks whether you want to redefine it. Type **y** ↵.
4. Press Esc to avoid actually inserting a new copy of the new file.

The file that you inserted replaces the current blocks.

AUTOCAD ONLY The Express Tools command BLOCKREPLACE (choose Express ➪ Blocks ➪ Replace Block with Another Block) is another way to substitute blocks. Another Express Tools command, NCOPY (choose Express ➪ Blocks ➪ Copy Nested Objects), copies objects nested inside blocks or xrefs. XLIST (choose Express ➪ Blocks ➪ List Xref/Block Properties) lists properties of nested objects within blocks. SHP2BLK (choose Express ➪ Modify ➪ Convert Shape to Block) converts a shape definition to a block. (I cover shape definitions in Chapter 32.)

Usually when you insert a file into a drawing, the block name and filename are the same. Likewise, when you WBLOCK a block, you usually name the file with the name of the block. Be aware that when you use block substitution, you have a block in your drawing that is the same as a file of a different name. For example, if you have a block in your drawing called smalldesk and substitute a file called bigdesk, you now have a block called smalldesk that is actually the same as the file bigdesk. This can become confusing, so use block substitution with care.

Creating and Using Dynamic Blocks

You probably have multiple similar blocks that you store and use on a regular basis. Moreover, you might insert these blocks at various scales and rotation angles. For example, you could have several sizes of doors that you insert at various angles, sometimes right-opening and sometimes left-opening. Dynamic blocks are blocks that contain intelligence and flexibility so that you can insert them in many variations. Potentially, you could significantly reduce the number of blocks in your block library.

Dynamic blocks let you specify the types and amounts of variations for each block. You create (author) dynamic blocks in the Block Editor. For a block to be dynamic, it must include at least one *parameter*. A parameter usually has an associated *action*.

Parameters define the special properties of the dynamic block, including locations, distances, and angles. Parameters can also constrain the values within which the parameter can function. An action specifies how a block uses its associated parameter to change in some way.

For example, you may want to move one component of a block independently of the block, such as the chair in a block containing a desk and a chair. To accomplish this, you add a point parameter that specifies a point on the chair. You then add a move action that allows you to move the chair from that point. Figure 18.14 shows a desk and a chair block that includes the following dynamic components:

- The desk has a distance parameter with a stretch action. Therefore, you can stretch the desk without affecting the chair. You would use this type of action if you have several sizes of desks that you need to include in your drawing.

- The chair contains a point parameter with a move action. As a result, you can move the chair independently of the rest of the block. If you stretch the desk, you might want to move the chair so that it remains centered in front of the desk, or you might simply want to move the chair farther away from the desk.

If you open a dynamic block in a pre-2006 release of AutoCAD or AutoCAD LT, you see the last current view of the block. You cannot use the dynamic features of the block, but you can edit it as a regular block. The block is assigned a name, such as U2.

To change the background color of the Block Editor, choose Tools ➪ Options and click the Display tab. Click the Colors button. From the Content list, choose Block Editor. Then choose Uniform Background from the Interface Element list, and choose a color from the Color drop-down list. Click Apply & Close, and then click OK.

FIGURE 18.14

This dynamic block contains components that enable you to stretch the desk's length and move the chair.

Stretch action grip   This desk is being stretched

79.1073

Polar: 11.1073 < 0°

Move action grip   The chair has been moved away from the desk

Understanding the work flow of dynamic blocks

Because defining a dynamic block takes some time — although simpler dynamic blocks are not very time-consuming to set up — the most common use for dynamic blocks is to create a block library. Normally, you define your dynamic blocks and save them for future use in your drawings. In other words, unless you need to insert a new block many times in several variations in a drawing, you won't create dynamic blocks for the current drawing on which you're working.

A block library can have two configurations:

- **One block per drawing:** You save each block in its own drawing. Use the BASE command to specify the origin of the drawing, which is usually on an object snap somewhere on the block. (I explain the BASE command in the "Saving blocks as files" section earlier in this chapter.) You use the INSERT command to insert the drawing, thereby inserting its block.

- **Many blocks per drawing:** You put a number of (usually) related blocks in a drawing. To insert the block, you use the DesignCenter to locate the drawing and find the individual block that you want. (See the section "Using the DesignCenter" earlier in the chapter for information on inserting blocks with the DesignCenter.)

The first part of the process of creating dynamic blocks is to define the block. I explain the details in the next few sections, but here I provide an overview of the workflow:

1. In your block library drawing or in a new drawing, create the block.
2. Open the Block Editor (the BEDIT command) and choose the block.
3. Add parameters and associated actions.
4. Save the block definition in the Block Editor.
5. Close the Block Editor.
6. If the drawing will contain just this block, use the BASE command to set the drawing origin where you want the insertion point to be, usually somewhere on the block.
7. Save the drawing.

You may want to follow this process for any number of blocks. When your blocks are defined, you do the following to insert your dynamic blocks.

1. In your current drawing, either use the INSERT command to insert the drawing containing the block, or use the DesignCenter to choose the block from within the drawing.

2. Select the block to see its special grips. These grips show you where you can modify the block.

3. Usually, you click and drag a grip. Some dynamic block parameters involve choosing a visibility or lookup option from a drop-down list.

Defining a dynamic block

To define a dynamic block, first create the objects that you want for the block, or display an existing block. Then choose Block Editor from the Standard (or Standard Annotation) toolbar, or choose Tools ➪ Block Editor to start the BEDIT command. In the Edit Block Definition dialog box, choose <Current Drawing> or the block's name and click OK. You can also copy and paste individual objects from the drawing into the Block Editor to create a block from those objects.

You may see a message that asks whether you want to see how dynamic blocks are created. Click Yes to open the New Features Workshop, which contains an animated tutorial on dynamic blocks. (You can access the New Features Workshop at any time from the Help menu.) Otherwise, click No. The Block Editor opens, as shown in Figure 18.15. At the same time, the Block Authoring Palettes window opens.

FIGURE 18.15

The Block Editor is a special window for authoring dynamic blocks.

Block Authoring
Palettes window

Block Editor toolbar

Before you start defining your block, you need to decide the types of variations that you want the block to have. You build flexibility into your blocks with a combination of parameters and actions. Table 18.2 lists the parameters, the actions that you can add to each parameter, and a description of the uses for those parameters and actions on the specified component of the dynamic block.

TABLE 18.2

Dynamic Block Parameters and Actions

Parameter	Available Actions	Uses
Point	Move, Stretch	Move or stretch from that point (X,Y coordinate).
Linear	Move, Scale, Stretch, Array	Move, scale, stretch, or array along the line between two points.
Polar	Move, Scale, Stretch, Polar Stretch, Array	Move, scale, stretch, stretch at an angle, or array along the line between two points and at the specified angle.
XY	Move, Scale, Stretch, Array	Move, scale, stretch, or array at the specified X and Y distance.
Rotation	Rotate	Rotate at the specified angle.
Flip	Flip	Flip along a *reflection line*. Flipping is like mirroring without retaining the original objects.
Alignment	None	Align the entire block with other objects. You can align perpendicular or tangent to other objects. No action is required.
Visibility	None	Control the visibility of components in the block. No action is required. See the section "Adding visibility parameters" later in this chapter.
Lookup	Lookup	Choose a custom property from a list or table that you define. See the section "Adding lookup parameters and actions" later in this chapter.
Base point	None	Define a base point for the dynamic block.

Adding a parameter

To create a dynamic block, you start by adding a parameter. Click the parameter that you want from the Parameters tab of the Block Authoring Palettes window. Each parameter prompts you for the information it needs. For example, the linear parameter responds with the `Specify start point or` `[Name/Label/Chain/Description/Base/Palette/Value set]:` prompt. When you specify the start point, you get a prompt for the endpoint. The flip parameter prompts you for a reflection line, which is like a mirror line.

The options for each parameter are fairly similar. Here's how to use the options:

- **Name:** You can change the name of the parameter. The name appears in the Properties palette when you select the parameter. However, you may find it confusing to change the name, because the name clearly denotes which parameter the block uses. On the other hand, if you have more than one of the same type of action, such as two stretch actions, renaming the actions to identify what they apply to can eliminate confusion. For example, you could have two Move actions, "Move table" and "Move chair."

- **Label:** The label appears in the Properties palette, but also next to the block when you have the Block Editor open. Change the label to suit your needs. For example, the linear parameter uses a label of "Distance." You might want to change that to Length, Width, or even something more specific.

- **Chain:** Sometimes, you might want one action to cause more than one change in a block. To do this, you can chain parameters. As a result, activating one parameter's actions causes the secondary parameter's action to occur. The primary parameter must have an action whose selection set includes the secondary parameter in addition to any other objects it will act on. (If the action is a stretch action, the stretch frame also needs to include the secondary parameter.) You must then set the secondary parameter's Chain property to Yes.

- **Description:** You can add a description to a parameter. This description displays in the Properties palette when you select the parameter in the Block Editor.

NEW FEATURE If you add a description, it appears as a tooltip when you select the inserted dynamic block in your drawing and hover the cursor over the parameter's grip. You could use this feature to provide brief description of the type of parameter or instructions on how to use it.

- **Base:** Creates a base point parameter, which sets a base point for the block.

- **Palette:** By default, displays parameter labels in the Properties palette when you select the block reference in a drawing. Change to No if you don't want to display the labels.

- **Value set:** You can constrain the available values for your block's size, either as increments (for example, from 3 feet to 7 feet in 6-inch increments) or by providing a list (for example, only 36", 40", and 42"). This option prompts you to choose either the increment or the list method, and then prompts you for values.

When you are finished using the options or have specified the necessary coordinates (such as a start point and endpoint for a linear parameter), the Specify label location: prompt appears. Pick a point to place the label for the parameter.

An exclamation point now appears next to the parameter. This exclamation point alerts you that you have not yet added an action to the parameter. Most parameters require an action to function properly. Figure 18.16 shows a chair with a linear parameter.

FIGURE 18.16

This chair has a linear parameter, but no action.

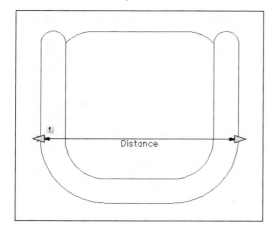

You can use the grips of the parameters as insertion points when you insert the dynamic block. During insertion, you press Ctrl to cycle among the grips if their Cycling property is set to Yes. To check, select a grip, open the Properties palette, and look for the Cycling property. You can specify the order of the cycling. Select a grip, right-click, and choose Insertion Cycling to open the Insertion Cycling Order dialog box, where you can turn cycling on or off for each grip and move the grips up and down in the order of the list.

Adding an action

When you have placed a parameter, you're ready to add an associated action. Table 18-2 lists which actions you can associate with your parameter. Click the Actions tab of the Block Authoring Palettes window, shown in Figure 18.17.

FIGURE 18.17

Use the Actions tab of the Block Authoring Palettes to associate an action with a parameter.

NOTE Sometimes the parameter and action labels become too large. When this happens, click the Update Parameter and Action Text Size button on the Block Editor's toolbar.

Sometimes, the parameter that you want to use has more grips than you need. For example, if you use a linear parameter, you end up with two grips, one at each end of the length that you define. However, you might want to stretch only in one direction; in this case, you need to have only one grip. To remove the extra grip, select the parameter, right-click, and choose Grip Display ➪ 1. The other option is to use a point parameter with a stretch action.

TIP Why would you use the linear parameter (instead of a point parameter) when you want to add a stretch action? When you stretch the inserted dynamic block, if you have Dynamic Input turned on, you see a linear tooltip that allows you to enter a total length. You can set the total length in the Properties palette, although that isn't nearly as convenient. Also, a point parameter doesn't offer the Value Set option, which lets you constrain sizes.

To add an action, choose an appropriate action for your parameter. At the Select parameter: prompt, select the parameter. Remember that you always apply an action to a parameter, rather than to an object.

However, as part of the process, you specify a selection set for the action, which means selecting the object or objects. Note that you can add more than one action to a parameter.

 Be sure to select the actual parameter, and not the object or the grip. An easy way to select the parameter is to click its label.

The next prompts depend on the action that you choose and on the parameter to which you're attaching the action. Table 18.3 explains some of the prompt options that you find for commonly used actions.

TABLE 18.3

Action Prompt Options

Action	Parameter	Option Responses
Move	Point	Select the objects.
Move	Linear, polar, or XY	Because you have more than one point, you need to specify which point you want to associate with the action. You can choose the point by moving the cursor over it; a red circle appears over the active point. You can also use the Start point/Second point options. You can press Enter to use the second point (the default), and then select the objects.
Scale	Linear, polar, or XY	You select the objects. You can also specify a dependent base (relative to the base point of the action's parameter) or an independent base point (which you specify). If you used an XY parameter, you can also specify whether the distance is the X distance, the Y distance, or the XY distance (the default).
Stretch	Point	Select the objects.
Stretch	Linear, polar, or XY	Because you have more than one point, you need to specify which point you want to associate with the action. You can choose the point by moving the cursor over it; a red circle appears over the active point. You can also use the sTart point/Second point options or press Enter to use the second point (the default), and then select the objects. Then you specify diagonal corners of a *stretch frame* that defines the area that is included in the stretch. (You can also use a Cpolygon.) Finally, you select objects. You can continue to add or remove objects, just as you do when stretching.
Polar stretch	Polar	Identical to the prompts for the Stretch parameter. In addition, you specify objects to rotate only (but not stretch).

NOTE Defining the stretch frame for a stretch action is similar to specifying a crossing selection window in the STRETCH command, except that you can create the stretch frame from left to right. For example, objects within the frame are moved, and objects that cross the frame are stretched. However, you also select objects for a stretch action. If objects are in the stretch frame but not in the selection set, they are not stretched or moved. If objects are outside the frame, but are in the selection set, they are moved. After you select objects, you can select or deselect individual objects to add them to, or subtract them from, the selection set.

The final step is to specify the location of the action's label. At this point, you can also use one of two options:

■ **Multiplier:** Multiplies the parameter value by a factor that you specify. For example, you can multiply a stretch by a factor of .5. For example, if you want to keep a circle centered inside a rectangle that you're moving or stretching, use a .5 multiplier so that the circle moves or stretches half of the distance of the rectangle, thereby remaining centered.

■ **Offset:** Changes the parameter angle by an amount that you specify. For example, you can increase an angle by 90 degrees. This allows you to move the cursor to the right (0 degrees) and stretch an object in the 90-degree direction.

CAUTION If the exclamation point doesn't disappear after you add an action, the action was not successfully added! Undo the last command (BACTIONTOOL) and try again. Usually the problem involves selecting the proper parts of the parameter and correctly selecting the applicable objects. Reducing the number of grips may also solve this problem. Select the parameter, right-click, and choose Grip Display.

Adding visibility parameters

Visibility parameters enable you to turn the visibility of a block component on and off when you insert it. You can define multiple named visibility states, thereby creating many variations of visibility or invisibility. You can use visibility parameters in two ways:

■ **Make one component visible or invisible:** You can choose to display or not display one component. For example, if you have a telephone on a desk, you can display or not display the telephone.

■ **Switch among multiple components:** You can include variations of a component, and cycle among them during insertion. For example, you can have three types of telephones (such as single-line, two-line, and multiple-line), all in the same location, with one on top of the other. When inserting the block, you can choose which telephone to display.

Visibility parameters are a very powerful way to add flexibility to a block and to reduce the number of similar blocks you store. You can add only one visibility parameter per block.

To add a visibility parameter, follow these steps:

1. Open the Block Editor in a drawing that contains the components that you need. If you want to switch among multiple components, place them on top of each other.

2. Choose Visibility Parameter from the Parameters tab of the Block Authoring Palettes, and place it near the components. Before placing the parameter, you may want to use the Label option to change the label.

3. Choose Manage Visibility States on the Block Editor toolbar (or double-click the visibility parameter) to open the Visibility States dialog box, shown in Figure 18.18.

4. Click the default visibility state (VisibilityState0) to select it. Enter a new name for your first state and press Enter. The name should relate to what the state will display. In the telephone example, you might use `telephone` or `single-line` as the state.

5. Click New to open the New Visibility State dialog box, shown in Figure 18.19.

6. Enter a new visibility state name. In the telephone example, you might use `no telephone` or `two-line`. To leave the visibility of existing objects unchanged, use the default option, Leave Visibility of Existing Objects Unchanged in New State. If you want the new state to hide all objects, choose Hide All Existing Objects in New State. To display all objects, choose Show All Existing Objects in New State. Whichever option you choose, you can change the visibility of individual objects for each state afterwards. Click OK.

FIGURE 18.18

Use the Visibility States dialog box to add and name visibility states.

FIGURE 18.19

The New Visibility State dialog box.

7. If you need more visibility states, repeat Steps 5 and 6 until you're done.

8. Click OK to close the Visibility States dialog box and return to the Block Editor.

 9. Choose the first state from the Visibility States drop-down list at the right side of the Block Editor's toolbar. For that state, select all of the objects that you want to make invisible, if any. Then click the Make Invisible button on the Block Editor's toolbar.

10. Repeat Step 9 for each state. If you chose to hide objects when you created the state, you may instead need to make certain objects visible by clicking the Make Visible button.

  If you need to select an object that's invisible, click the Visibility Mode button. The object is displayed in a light gray color so that you can see and select it.

11. Check each visibility state by choosing each state in turn from the Visibility States drop-down list and making sure that each state displays what you want it to display.

When you insert the dynamic block and select it, you see a down arrow. Click the arrow to display the list of visibility states. Choose the state that you want.

Adding lookup parameters and actions

A lookup parameter/action combination creates a table that pairs labels with values. For example, you might have a desk that comes in three sizes. You can create this desk and use the Value Set option to create a list of three sizes: 4 feet, 5 feet, and 6 feet. You can then create labels that say 4' desk, 5' desk, and 6' desk. When you insert the desk, you can choose the label that you want from a drop-down list; the desk automatically stretches to the proper size. You don't need to use the Value Set option, because you specify values in the lookup table.

Lookup tables are great when you want pre-set sizes for a block. When you insert the block, you don't even have to think about exact measurements; you just choose from a drop-down list, as shown in Figure 18.20.

FIGURE 18.20

You can specify a pre-set size by choosing from the drop-down list.

To create a lookup parameter and action, follow these steps:

1. In the Block Editor, add a parameter and action that you will use as the basis for the Lookup parameter and action. For example, add a linear parameter and a stretch action. If you add a value set (list or increment), the measurements will be available in advance when you create the lookup table.
2. From the Parameters tab of the Block Authoring Palettes, add a lookup parameter.
3. From the Actions tab, add a lookup action. At the prompt, select the lookup parameter and place the lookup action. The Property Lookup Table dialog box opens.
4. Click the Add Properties button, choose the parameter that you want to work with (for example, the linear parameter), and click OK. You return to the Property Lookup Table dialog box, as shown in Figure 18.21.
5. If you have values from a value set, you can see them by clicking the first row in the Input Properties side of the dialog box. A drop-down arrow appears. Choose the first value. If you don't have a value set, you can enter values on each row. Click the same row on the Lookup Properties side of the dialog box and enter the label that corresponds with the value. For example, in Figure 18.20, the label was Chair/Couch. Then click the next row, choose the next value, and enter the next label. Continue until you're done.
6. Click the lower-right cell in the dialog box, which says Read Only by default; it changes to read Allow Reverse Lookup. (To do this, all of the rows in the table must be unique.) You need to use this option in order to choose a value from a drop-down list of labels when you insert the block.
7. Click OK to return to the Block Editor.

FIGURE 18.21

The Property Lookup Table dialog box enables you to associate values with labels.

Now each value in the lookup table is associated with the labels that you entered. When you insert the dynamic block and select it, click the down arrow and choose from the options that drop down.

TIP To edit the lookup action, select it. In the Properties palette, click the icon next to the Lookup Table item to open the Property Lookup Table dialog box. There you can make your changes.

Using parameter sets

The Parameter Sets tab of the Block Authoring Palettes contains a number of ready-made parameter-action combinations that you can use. These sets are great for quick creation of dynamic blocks that are not complex. Hover the cursor over any parameter set to see a tooltip explaining the set's functioning.

When you place a parameter set, you see that exclamation point, because you have not yet selected the objects for the action. Double-click the action to display prompts that allow you to select objects.

TIP You can edit these parameter sets and create new ones. To create a new one, right-click the parameter set on the Parameter Sets tab and choose Copy. Then right-click the tab itself and choose Paste. To change a parameter set, right-click a parameter set and choose Properties. Then change the settings in the Tool Properties dialog box. To add an action, click the Actions item, and then click the Ellipsis button to open the Add Actions dialog box.

Saving dynamic blocks and closing the Block Editor

When you have finished creating a dynamic block, click Save Block Definition on the Block Editor toolbar. Always save the block definition before closing the Block Editor. (Click the Save Block As button to create a new dynamic block based on the existing one.) Then click the Close Block Editor button.

TIP You can use the Save Block As button to create a duplicate of any block, not just a dynamic one. You can then modify the new block to make a variation of the original block. When you close the Block Editor, you can insert that block like any other block.

If you want to put the base point for the block somewhere on the block, use the BASE command. Then save your drawing.

Inserting and modifying dynamic blocks

You insert a dynamic block in the same way that you insert a regular block: by using the Insert dialog box or the DesignCenter. For more information, see "Inserting Blocks and Files into Drawings" earlier in this chapter.

During insertion, you can press Ctrl to cycle among the grips if their Cycling property is set to Yes. Each time you press Ctrl, the cursor moves to another grip on the block. Also, before you specify the insertion point, you can open the Properties palette and specify values, such as the distance value of a length parameter.

To use the dynamic features of the block, first select the block. You see special, turquoise dynamic block grips, depending on the type of action. For example, in Figure 18.14, you see grips for stretch and move actions. You click and drag these grips in the same way that you do for regular grips; the difference is that the resulting modification is controlled by the parameters and actions that you defined. If you have created a value set, you see vertical lines at the available lengths, as shown in Figure 18.22. Lookup and visibility actions have a down arrow so that you can open a drop-down list and choose a visibility state or lookup label.

FIGURE 18.22

This block can be a chair, loveseat, or sofa. The faint vertical lines indicate the available lengths as you drag.

 ON the DVD-ROM   The drawing that you need for the following exercise on creating and inserting dynamic blocks, ab18-f.dwg, is in the Drawings folder on the DVD.

STEPS: Creating and Inserting Dynamic Blocks

1. Open ab18-f.dwg from the DVD. This is a set of office furniture, as shown in Figure 18.23.

2. Save the drawing as ab18-06.dwg in your AutoCAD Bible folder. Set an endpoint running object snap.

3. Hover the cursor over any part of the drawing. You can see that it is all one block, called DeskSet.

4. Double-click the block. In the Edit Block Definition dialog box, choose DeskSet and click OK. The Block Editor opens with the desk set (including a desk, armchair, computer, monitor, and phone) displayed. Inside the Block Editor, you work with the individual components of the DeskSet block. The Block Authoring Palettes window also opens. (You may see a window asking if you want to see how dynamic blocks are created. You can choose Yes or No.)

5. You want to be able to move the armchair separately from the rest of the block. To add a point parameter to the chair, click the Parameters tab of the Block Authoring Palettes and choose Point Parameter.

FIGURE 18.23

The office furniture is a block that can be more useful if it is dynamic.

6. Follow these prompts:

    ```
    Specify parameter location or [Name/Label/Chain/Description/Palette]:
    Right-click and choose Label.
    Enter position property label <Position>: Chair Location ⏎
    Specify parameter location or [Name/Label/Chain/Description/Palette]:
    Pick the endpoint at the middle of the front of the chair.
    Specify label location: Pick a location for the Chair Location label.
    ```

7. To add a move action to the point parameter, click the Actions tab and choose Move Action. Follow the prompts:

    ```
    Select parameter: Select the point parameter by clicking its label.
    Specify selection set for action. Select objects: Select all of the
    objects that make up the chair. (In this instance, it doesn't make
    any difference whether or not you include the actual parameter in the
    selection set.)
    Select objects: ⏎
    Specify action location or [Multiplier/Offset]: Place the action in
    the middle of the chair (or anywhere near the chair).
    ```

8. To add a linear parameter to the desk, click the Parameters tab and choose Linear Parameter. Follow the prompts:

    ```
    Specify start point or [Name/Label/Chain/Description/Base/
    Palette/Value set]: Right-click and choose Label.
    Enter distance property label <Distance>: Desk length ⏎
    Specify start point or [Name/Label/Chain/Description/Base/
    Palette/Value set]: Right-click and choose Value set.
    Enter distance value set type [None/List/Increment] <None> : Choose
    Increment from the drop-down list.
    ```

581

```
Enter distance increment: 6 ↵
Enter minimum distance: 48 ↵
Enter maximum distance: 72 ↵
Specify start point or
[Name/Label/Chain/Description/Base/Palette/Value set]: Choose the
endpoint at the upper-left corner of the desk.
Specify endpoint: Choose the endpoint at the upper-right corner of
the desk.
Specify label location: Pick a location above the desk.
```

9. We only want the right grip for the linear parameter. This makes sure that the desk can only be stretched toward the right. Select the linear parameter. Right-click and choose Grip Display ➪ 1. The left grip disappears.

10. Click the Actions tab and choose Stretch Action. Follow the prompts:

```
Select parameter: Select the linear parameter by clicking its label.
Specify parameter point to associate with action or enter [sTart
point/Second point] <Start>: Pass the cursor over the right grip and
click.
Specify first corner of stretch frame or [CPolygon]: Click at ❶ in
Figure 18.24.
Specify opposite corner: Click at ❷.
Specify objects to stretch. Select objects: Click close to but not on
top of ❷.
Specify opposite corner: Click close to but not on top of ❶. The
command line should show 52 found.
Select objects: ↵
Specify action location or [Multiplier/Offset]: Place the action
label to the right of the grip on the right side of the desk.
```

11. The block should look like Figure 18.24.

FIGURE 18.24

The DeskSet block after adding a move action to the armchair and a stretch action to the desk.

12. To allow for various size monitors, click the Parameters tab and choose Linear Parameter. Right-click and choose the Label option. Type **Monitor width** ↵.

13. At the next two prompts, pick points ❸ and ❹ in Figure 18.24. Then place the parameter label above the monitor.

14. You can also create a value set in the Properties palette. Select the `Monitor width` parameter and open the Properties palette (Ctrl+1). In the Value Set section, choose List from the `Dist Type` drop-down list. Next to the `Dist Value List` item, click the Ellipsis (. . .) button to open the Add Distance Value dialog box. The current width is already there. In the Distances to Add text box, type **18-1/2** ↵. The value changes to 1'-6 ½" and moves below to the list box. Again in the Distances to Add text box, type **20-1/2** ↵. Click OK to close the dialog box. Close or minimize the Properties palette.

15. With the linear parameter still selected, in the Properties palette, change the value of the Number of Grips item (in the Misc section) to 1.

16. Click the Actions tab on the Block Authoring Palettes and choose Stretch Action. At the `Select parameter:` prompt, select the linear parameter that you just created. At the next prompt, click the right parameter point. To specify the stretch frame, pick ❺ and then ❻ in Figure 18.24. To select objects, pick near ❻ and then near ❺. Press Enter to end selection. Specify a label location above the monitor.

17. We want to create a lookup parameter for the monitor. On the Parameters tab, choose Lookup Parameter and pick a location on the monitor. On the Actions tab, choose Lookup Action. Select the lookup parameter and select a location just below it. The Property Lookup Table dialog box opens.

18. Click Add Properties. In the Add Parameter Properties dialog box, choose the `Linear 1` parameter and click OK. Back in the Property Lookup Table dialog box, click the first row on the Input Properties side, below the Monitor width heading, and choose the first measurement from the drop-down list. In the same row on the Lookup Properties side, type **15" monitor.** (Note that monitors are measured diagonally, and so the horizontal width of a 15" monitor is not 15".) In the second row on the Input Properties side, choose the second measurement and enter **17" monitor** on the right. In the third row on the left, choose the last measurement and enter **19" monitor** on the right.

19. Click the Read Only cell; it changes to read Allow Reverse Lookup. The Property Lookup Table dialog box should look like Figure 18.25. Click OK.

20. Because some people may not have a phone, we want to create a visibility parameter and action for the phone. On the Parameters tab, choose Visibility Parameter. Follow the prompts:

```
Specify parameter location or [Name/Label/Description/Palette]:
Right-click and choose Label.
Enter visibility property label <Visibility>: Phone/No Phone ↵
Specify parameter location or [Name/Label/Description/Palette]: Pick
a location near the phone.
```

583

FIGURE 18.25

The Property Lookup Table dialog box is ready to create a lookup table for the computer monitor.

21. Choose Manage Visibility States from the Block Editor toolbar. The Visibility States dialog box opens. Click the VisibilityState0 item and type **Has phone** ↵. Click New. In the Visibility State Name text box of the New Visibility State dialog box, type **No phone** ↵. Click OK twice to return to the Block Editor.

22. From the Visibility States drop-down list, make sure that No Phone is displayed; if not, choose it. Click the Make Invisible button on the Block Editor toolbar. At the Select objects: prompt, select all of the objects of the phone and press Enter to end selection. To double-check the visibility states, choose the Has Phone state and make sure that the phone appears.

23. Your block should look like Figure 18.26. Click Save Block Definition on the Block Editor toolbar. At the message asking whether you want to update the block reference in the drawing, click Yes. Then click Close Block Editor. Save your drawing.

24. Open a new drawing based on the default template or any template that you usually use. Open the DesignCenter. In the Open Drawings pane, browse to, and double-click, ab18-06.dwg. Click Blocks. Drag the DeskSet block from the right side of the DesignCenter to your drawing.

NOTE If you create a block inside a drawing and then make it dynamic, you need to use the DesignCenter to insert it. If you try to insert the entire drawing, you see only a regular block. However, if you don't create a block in the source drawing and create the dynamic block in the Block Editor without ever creating and naming a block, you can use the INSERT command to insert the entire drawing and use the dynamic features of the block.

25. Choose Zoom ⇨ Extents. Close or minimize the DesignCenter.

26. Select the DeskSet block. It should look like Figure 18.27.

27. Click the desk's stretch grip and stretch the desk one vertical line to the left to make it 6 inches shorter. The computer moves with the desk.

28. Click the armchair's move grip and move the chair to the left so that it is still centered in front of the computer.

FIGURE 18.26

The completed dynamic block in the Block Editor.

FIGURE 18.27

When you select a dynamic block, you see grips for its dynamic features.

29. Click the monitor's lookup grip and choose 19" monitor from the drop-down list. The monitor becomes wider.

30. Click the phone's visibility grip and choose No phone from the drop-down list. The phone disappears.

31. Continue to experiment with the grips to see all of the possible variations. You do not need to save this drawing.

Using Windows Features to Copy Data

You can insert objects by copying them from other drawings and pasting them into your current drawing or using the drag-and-drop feature. You may be able to insert objects in this way without creating blocks.

Manipulating objects with the Windows Clipboard

You're probably familiar with cutting or copying data in other Windows applications and then pasting it, either within a file or from file to file. Table 18.4 compares copying, using blocks, and using the Clipboard with the CUTCLIP, COPYCLIP, and PASTECLIP commands.

TABLE 18.4

Comparison of Methods of Moving/Copying Objects

Method	Features
MOVE/COPY	Precise placement of objects; only works within a drawing.
BLOCK/WBLOCK/INSERT	Precise placement of objects; can scale and rotate; creates block definition; can insert many times, even after other commands; can insert files (other drawings) that you save permanently. With the DesignCenter or Tools palette, you can insert blocks from other drawings.
CUTCLIP/COPYCLIP/PASTECLIP	No precise placement of objects (uses bottom-left corner of extents of object(s) that you copy); creates anonymous block in file with a name like A$CE314; can scale and rotate; can both move and copy objects; can insert (paste) many times; can copy from drawing to drawing or to other Windows applications.

In general, for one-time moving or copying with a drawing, you should use the MOVE or COPY command. If you want to copy an object several times over a period of time, use a BLOCK command. Use the Clipboard when you want to insert objects into another drawing one or more times without saving the objects. Also, the Clipboard is indispensable for copying objects to other applications.

To place objects on the Clipboard, first select them. To move them, choose Cut to Clipboard on the Standard or Standard Annotation toolbar. To copy them, choose Copy. You can paste objects that you've copied to the Clipboard into the same drawing as a block using the PASTEBLOCK command; right-click and choose Paste as Block. If you want to paste the objects in another drawing, open that drawing. Choose Paste on the Standard or Standard Annotation toolbar. The command line prompts you for an insertion point.

CROSS-REF Chapter 27 covers moving and copying objects, images, and data to and from other applications.

Using drag-and-drop

The drag-and-drop feature in Windows enables you to drag another drawing file into your drawing. Your drawing then prompts you as it would if you inserted the file using the -INSERT command. You need to open either My Computer or Windows Explorer. In the following steps, I use Windows Explorer.

To insert a drawing file using drag-and-drop, follow these steps:

1. Open Windows Explorer (Choose Start ➪ All Programs ➪ Accessories ➪ Windows Explorer).
2. In the Folders window, click the folder containing the drawing file that you want to insert.
3. Locate the drawing file.
   - If the drawing window is visible, drag the drawing file into the AutoCAD or AutoCAD LT window.
   - If the drawing window is not visible, drag the drawing file onto the AutoCAD or AutoCAD LT button on the task bar, wait for your drawing to appear, and then drag the file into the drawing window.
4. Respond to the prompts of the -INSERT command on the command line.

When you drag the file into the drawing area, you see a plus sign at the cursor (or a rectangular cursor, depending on your operating system), indicating that you can drop the file.

To open a drawing file instead of inserting it, drag the file onto the application title bar at the very top of the application window, or simply double-click its icon in Windows Explorer. If you drag with the right-mouse button, when you release the mouse button in the drawing area, you have some additional options to create an external reference (Create Xref) or to create a hyperlink.

TIP If you really don't know where the file is, or you're not even sure of its name, use the Windows Find feature. Choose Start ➪ Search(➪ For Files or Folders). On the screen that appears, set the criteria for the file. For example, you could find all drawing names that start with the letter C by typing c*.dwg in the Named text box. From the resulting list, choose the drawing that you want, and drag it onto your drawing using the same steps listed previously.

Drag-and-drop is easy to use. It's a helpful tool if you aren't sure where the file that you want is located because it's easier to navigate with Windows Explorer than from the Select Drawing File dialog box.

You can also drag an object from one drawing to another. First open both drawings. It helps to be able to see them both at once. Choose Window ➪ Tile Vertically to see them side-by-side. Select the object or objects that you want to copy. Now click the object or objects again, and hold down the mouse button until the cursor displays a small rectangle. Then drag the object(s) to the other drawing.

ON the DVD-ROM The drawings that you need for the following exercise on using the Windows Clipboard and drag-and-drop, `ab18-g-1.dwg` and `ab18-g-2.dwg`, are in the `Drawings` folder on the DVD.

STEPS: Using the Windows Clipboard and Drag-and-Drop

1. Open `ab18-g-1.dwg` from the DVD. This is a set of office furniture, as shown in Figure 18.28. Before proceeding, close any other drawings that you have open.

FIGURE 18.28

A set of office furniture.

2. Pick the chair, which is a block, and choose Copy from the Standard or Standard Annotation toolbar.

3. Choose Open from the Standard or Standard Annotation toolbar. Open `ab18-g-2.dwg` from the DVD. This is the plan of an office building, as shown in Figure 18.29.

4. Save the drawing as `ab18-07.dwg` in your `AutoCAD Bible` folder.

5. Choose Paste from the Standard or Standard Annotation toolbar. At the `Specify insertion point:` prompt, pick ❶ in Figure 18.29. This action inserts the armchair in the lobby using the default scale and rotation.

6. Choose Window ➪ Tile Vertically. You can now see both drawings at once. Click in `ab18-g-1.dwg` to activate it. Select the chair. Click and hold the left-mouse button on the chair again until you see the small rectangle at the cursor. Drag the chair into `ab18-07.dwg` and place it next to the first chair.

7. Click the Close button of `ab18-g-1.dwg`. (You don't need to save any changes.) Click the Maximize button of `ab18-07.dwg`.

8. From the task bar menu, choose Start ➪ All Programs ➪ Accessories ➪ Windows Explorer. Locate `ab18-g-1.dwg` on the DVD. If necessary, resize the Exploring window so that you can see some of the drawing window.

9. Drag `ab18-g-1.dwg` from its listing in Windows Explorer onto the drawing area, and release the mouse button.

10. Use Zoom Window to zoom in to the area around ❷ in Figure 18.29. At the prompt, pick ❷.

11. Press Enter three times to accept the defaults and insert the entire drawing.

12. Choose Zoom Previous from the Standard toolbar (or choose View ➪ Zoom ➪ Previous). Save your drawing. It should look like Figure 18.30.

FIGURE 18.29

The office plan.

FIGURE 18.30

The office plan with added chairs and office furniture.

As you can see, copying to the Clipboard is ideal when you want to insert part of an existing drawing into another drawing. Drag-and-drop is also a simple way to insert one or more objects or an entire drawing.

Working with Attributes

Your drawings do not exist in a vacuum. The objects in your drawing represent real objects. These objects have characteristics that you cannot visually represent in a drawing, such as cost, manufacturer, date purchased, and so on. *Attributes* are labels that are attached to blocks. Using attributes, you can attach labels with pertinent data to blocks. You can then extract the data and import it into a database program or spreadsheet, or even redisplay the data in an AutoCAD table.

CROSS-REF You can access and link to outside databases from within AutoCAD. See Chapter 20 for more information on external databases. You can also access data from objects that are not blocks; for more information, see the section on tables in Chapter 13. Both of these features are available in AutoCAD only.

You can also use attributes to place text relative to blocks. A common example is to use attributes for completing title block information, such as the drawing name, drawing number, date, scale, revision number, drafter, and so on. In this case, your plan is not to extract the data at all; you just use the attributes to help you precisely place the text in the title block. By inserting fields into these attributes (in AutoCAD only), you can gain another benefit from attributes: automating the creation of title block text. For more information, see the discussion of fields in Chapter 13.

Attributes have several limitations. For example, they can only be attached to blocks (either regular or dynamic). However, you can create a dummy block that contains only attributes. The database features are also limited. Nevertheless, attributes are quite useful for simple database needs, as well as for placing text.

Defining an attribute creates a template into which you can place values when you insert the block. You define a tag that is equivalent to a field or category in a database. When you insert the block, you're prompted for the tag's value. For example, if your tag is COST, the value may be 865.79. This template is called an attribute definition.

Creating attribute definitions

The first procedure when working with attributes is to draw the individual objects that are to make up the block. If the block already exists, explode it, add the attributes, and then redefine the block.

The exception is when you want to create attributes without creating any other objects in the block. You might do this to extract attributes that apply to the drawing as a whole.

After you have the objects, choose Draw ➪ Block ➪ Define Attributes to start the ATTDEF command. The Attribute Definition dialog box opens, as shown in Figure 18.31.

NEW FEATURE The Dashboard has a new Block Attributes control panel, but it isn't displayed by default. To display it, right-click the Dashboard and choose Control Panels ➪ Block Attributes. You can choose Define Attributes from the Block Attributes control panel on the Dashboard to define attributes.

FIGURE 18.31

The Attribute Definition dialog box.

Mode section

The Mode section of the dialog box sets certain attribute properties, including visibility and default value. These properties are shown in Table 18.5.

TABLE 18.5

Attribute Modes

Mode	Explanation
Invisible	The attribute values that you set are not displayed in the drawing. Use this mode for attributes that you want to extract into a database but do not want to see in the drawing. Examples would be model numbers, purchase dates, cost, and so on. Of course, if you're using attributes to place text in a drawing, then you want them to be visible.
Constant	Sets a constant value for an attribute. The attribute automatically takes the attribute value that you set (in the Attribute section of the dialog box), and you do not get a prompt for a value. You might use this for the first three digits of employees' telephone numbers that have the same first three digits. You cannot edit constant attribute values.
Verify	When you insert an attribute, a prompt appears, asking you to verify the value. Use this option if you have a preset default.
Preset	Automatically inserts a default value that you specify. For example, if the most common manufacturer of a chair is American Interiors, you can specify this as a preset value. As you insert the block, this default is inserted for you, and you have to type a value only if it differs from the default. (You need to insert the attribute with the ATTDIA system variable set to 1 to get a prompt allowing you to change the value. See the explanation of ATTDIA later in this chapter.)

continued

TABLE 18.5	(continued)
Mode	**Explanation**
Lock Position	Locks the position of the attribute relative to the block. When you insert a block with attributes, locked attributes do not have their own grip and you can't move them independently from the block. Unlocked attributes have their own grip that you can use to separately move the attribute. If you want to include an attribute in the selection set of an action in a dynamic block, you must lock that attribute. You can then move them using the – ATTEDIT command on the command line.
Multiple Lines	Allows an attribute to contain multiple lines of text. An Ellipsis button appears to the right of the Default text box, which you click to open a simplified multiline text editor, as shown in Figure 18.32. The text that you enter becomes the default text, but you can change it when you insert the block. You can then specify a boundary width in the Text Settings section.

NEW FEATURE You can now create attributes that contain more than one line of text. You format them in a simplified text editor, providing more formatting options than for single-line attributes. Right-click in the text editor for additional options.

FIGURE 18.32

You can use a simplified multiline text editor to format attributes that contain multiple lines.

TIP Although by default, you see the simplified multiline text editor, you can use the full In-Place Text Editor to format multiple line attributes. Set the ATTIPE system variable to 1. However, if you need compatibility with earlier versions of AutoCAD or AutoCAD LT, you may need to return this system variable to its default value of 0. Otherwise, earlier versions may not display the attributes properly.

Attribute section

In the Attribute section of the dialog box, specify the Tag, which is the name of the attribute. You use this tag when you extract the attributes. A tag is equivalent to a field in a database. For example, if you import the data into a spreadsheet the tags would be the column heads. The tag name cannot include spaces or exclamation points (!) and is converted to uppercase letters.

The Prompt is simply a plain-English version of the tag. The prompt asks you for the value of the attribute. For example, if the tag is PUR_DATE, you could define the prompt as Date Purchased.

The Default is used for setting a default value. You can use this if the value is usually the same. To insert a field, click the Insert Field button and choose a field from the Field dialog box, as I explain in Chapter 13. When you insert the block and are prompted for a value, you can either use the field value or you can change it.

If you checked the Multiple Lines check box, the Default text box is not available; instead, click the Ellipsis button that appears and enter the default value in the simplified multiline text editor.

> **TIP** You can use the value to clarify a format that should be followed when entering information. For example, you could set the value of a date to dd/mm/yy so that users know how to format the date.

Text Settings section

Use the Text Settings section to format the text. Choose a justification and text style from the drop-down list boxes. When you set the height, be sure to take into account the scale factor if you're not using annotative attributes. You can also set a rotation angle for the text.

Check the Annotative check box to make the attribute annotative so that it will automatically scale to match the scale of the viewport. For more information on annotative objects, see Chapter 17. I discuss annotative text, which is similar, in Chapter 13.

If you checked the Multiple Lines check box, the Boundary Width text box is available so that you can specify the width of the text. However, you can also adjust the width by dragging the arrows on the ruler of the simplified multiline text editor.

Insertion Point section

In the Insertion Point section, check the Specify On-Screen check box to specify the insertion point in your drawing. Uncheck the same check box if you want to pre-specify coordinates. If you're using the attributes to place text in a schedule or title block, then the placement is obviously very important. If you're inserting invisible attributes, simply place them near the block. If you're creating more than one attribute for a block, place the attribute so that there is room for the other attributes underneath. When you've completed the dialog box, click OK. If you chose to specify the insertion point in the drawing, specify the point to insert the attribute.

> **CAUTION** If you're creating an attribute for a table or an electrical symbol, for example, you don't want the insertion point to be 0,0. Instead, you want an insertion point near the block. If you uncheck the Specify On-Screen check box and click OK to close the dialog box, the default insertion point is at 0,0. If 0,0 isn't visible on the screen, then you don't see the attribute — it seems to disappear! You can choose Undo from the Standard or Standard Annotation toolbar and create a new attribute in the right location, or move the attribute as explained in the section on editing attributes later in this chapter.

After you define one attribute, the Align Below Previous Attribute Definition check box is active. Select this option to line up succeeding attributes under the first one.

Now is the time to confirm that the attribute definitions are the way you want them. You can edit attribute definitions before they've been placed into a block in two ways:

- Choose Properties on the Standard (or Standard Annotation) toolbar (or press Ctrl+1), select one attribute definition, and edit all of its properties, such as the tag, value, prompt, and modes. You can also change properties such as the layer, text style, and so on.

- Choose Modify ➪ Object ➪ Text ➪ Edit and change the tag, the prompt, and the default (DDEDIT command).

> **TIP** If you're creating many blocks with similar attributes, you can copy just the attributes, modify them as just described, place them near other objects, and then create the blocks. This way, you don't have to define all of the attributes from scratch.

Creating the block

After you create the objects and their attribute definitions, you generally create a block. Choose Make Block from the Draw toolbar or the 2D Draw control panel of the Dashboard, and select the objects and the attributes in the block.

> **TIP** If the order of the attribute prompts is important, don't use a window to select the attributes. Select them in the order in which you want the prompts to appear. You can then use a crossing or window box to select the rest of the objects to be included in the block. The order of the attribute prompts will be important if you're taking the data for the attributes from a listing, such as a spreadsheet that you've printed out. Inserting the attribute values will be much easier if the prompts follow the order of the printed document that you're using.

Name the block and define the block's insertion point as you would normally. Generally, you want to check Delete because you don't need the block without the attribute tags in your drawing. Remember that you can make the block annotative, if you want.

Don't forget to pay attention to the layer of the attributes, just as you would the layer of the block objects. The same layer rules apply to attributes as to blocks.

> **NOTE** If you want to insert the objects and the attributes as a file instead of as a block, you don't need to create a block at all. Create a drawing that contains just the objects and its attributes. Use the BASE command to change the base point of the drawing (usually 0,0) to the desired insertion point of the block. Then save the drawing. When you insert the drawing, you are prompted for the attributes, as usual. Use this technique for blocks and attributes that you use for more than one drawing, such as a title block.

After you create the block, you cannot edit the attributes in the Properties palette. I cover other techniques for editing attributes later in this chapter.

> **ON the DVD-ROM** The drawing that you need for the following exercise on creating attributes, ab18-h.dwg, is in the Drawings folder on the DVD.

STEPS: Creating Attributes

1. Open ab18-h.dwg from the DVD. This is a plan of an office building zoomed in to one office. A file containing one set of office furniture has been inserted, as shown in Figure 18.33.

2. Save the drawing as ab18-08.dwg in your AutoCAD Bible folder.

3. Choose Explode from the Modify toolbar or the 2D Draw control panel of the Dashboard, select the furniture in the office, and press Enter. This block has nested blocks. Choose the chair and explode it again to get its component objects.

4. Choose Draw ➪ Block ➪ Define Attributes. In the Attribute Definition dialog box, check Invisible in the Mode section.

5. In the Attribute section, enter the following:

   Tag: **mfr**
   Prompt: **Manufacturer**
   Default: **American Office Furniture**

6. Leave the Text Settings as they are. Make sure that the Specify On-Screen check box is checked and click OK. Pick point ❶ in Figure 18.33.

7. Repeat the ATTDEF command. Check the Align Below Previous Attribute Definition check box. Enter the following:

Tag: **pur_date**
Prompt: **Date purchased**
Default: **3/91**

8. Click OK.

FIGURE 18.33

An office with a set of office furniture.

9. Choose Make Block from the Draw toolbar or the 2D Draw control panel of the Dashboard. In the Name text box, type **armchair.** Click Select Objects. Select the entire chair along with the two attributes. End selection. The dialog box shows that 18 objects are selected. Click Pick Point. Use the Endpoint object snap to choose ❷ as the base point. Check Delete. Click OK.

10. A message asks whether you want to redefine the block because there is already a block definition with the same name in the drawing. Choose Yes.

11. Save your drawing. If you're continuing on to the next exercise, leave the drawing open.

NOTE Redefining a block updates only block geometry, not attributes. Therefore, if you add attribute definitions to a block, only new blocks that you'll insert include the attributes. Existing blocks don't gain these new attribute definitions. To update existing blocks with their current attribute definitions, use the ATTSYNC command (AutoCAD only).

Inserting blocks with attributes

After you define a block with attributes, you insert it as you would any block. Your drawing automatically detects the existence of the attributes and prompts you for their values.

NOTE You can insert attributes either in a dialog box or on the command line. By default, you insert them on the command line. To use a dialog box, set the system variable ATTDIA to 1. You would use the command line to automate the insertion of attributes using an AutoLISP routine, menu item, or script file. When you use a dialog box, the Verify and Constant modes are not used. To skip all of the prompts and automatically use default values that you have set, set the ATTREQ system variable to 0.

ON the DVD-ROM The drawing that you need for the following exercise on inserting blocks with attributes, ab18-08.dwg, is in your AutoCAD Bible folder if you did the previous exercise. Otherwise, you can find it in the Results folder on the DVD.

STEPS: Inserting Blocks with Attributes

1. Use ab18-08.dwg if you have it open from the previous exercise. Otherwise, open it from the Results folder of the DVD.
2. Save the drawing as ab18-09.dwg in your AutoCAD Bible folder.
3. Type **attdia** ↵. If it's currently set to 0, type **1** ↵.
4. Choose Insert Block from the Draw toolbar or the 2D Draw control panel of the Dashboard. Chose ARMCHAIR from the Name drop-down list. Verify that the Specify On-screen option is checked only for Insertion Point, and click OK.
5. Pick a point in front of the desk (turn off OSNAP if necessary) to insert the armchair, and open the Enter Attributes dialog box, as shown in Figure 18.34. The values that were entered when the attributes were defined are displayed, but you can change them.

FIGURE 18.34

The Edit Attributes dialog box.

6. The default values exist because most of the furniture was purchased at one time when the office was opened. However, let's assume that this chair was purchased later. Change the purchase date to 3/05. Click OK. Because the attributes are invisible, you see only the chair, but the values do exist in the drawing database.
7. Save the drawing.

Editing attributes

You can edit the properties of the attribute tags before you create the block, by using the Properties palette or DDEDIT (choose Modify ⇨ Object ⇨ Text ⇨ Edit). If you have AutoCAD, after you create the block, use the Block Attribute Manager. The Block Attribute Manager manages all properties of block attributes in one place. Use the Block Attribute Manager and its Edit Attribute dialog box to edit any aspect of block attributes. If you have AutoCAD LT, use the Edit Attributes dialog box (ATTEDIT command).

Editing attribute properties in AutoCAD

After you insert a block and give values to its attributes, you can modify the following:

- Attribute prompt order
- Tag and prompt names
- Attribute visibility
- Text options (text style, justification, height, annotative, among others)
- Properties (layer, linetype, color, lineweight, and plot style)
- Attribute default value

After you make your changes, you can update all of the blocks in your drawing to reflect the changes.

Choose Modify ⇨ Object ⇨ Attribute ⇨ Block Attribute Manager to start the BATTMAN command and open the Block Attribute Manager, as shown in Figure 18.35.

FIGURE 18.35

The Block Attribute Manager.

From the Block drop-down list in the Block Attribute Manager, choose the block whose attribute values you want to change. You can also click Select block to select the block in your drawing. Use the Block Attribute Manager to:

- **Change the order of the attribute prompts when you insert a block with attributes.** Choose any attribute from the list in the Block Attribute Manager, and click Move Down or Move Up. Continue to use this procedure until you have the order that you want.
- **Delete an attribute.** Choose it and click Remove.

- **Change which attribute properties are listed in the Block Attribute Manager.** Click Settings. In the Block Attribute Settings dialog box, click all of the properties that you want to see listed. For example, you can include columns for layer, style (text style), and color. Click OK.

 When you add properties to the listing in the Block Attribute Manager, resize the dialog box so that you can see all of the columns.

- **Edit the attributes, including prompt, default, text display, and properties.** Click Edit to open the Edit Attribute dialog box, as shown in Figure 18.36.
- **Update all of the blocks in your drawing to reflect the changes that you've made.** Click Sync. Usually you do this after using the Edit Attribute dialog box. Because changes such as attribute order and mode affect only new insertions of the block, this update brings existing blocks into concordance with new blocks.

FIGURE 18.36

The Edit Attribute dialog box.

Use the Edit Attribute dialog box to edit all of the properties of individual attributes. This dialog box has three tabs:

- **Attribute:** Allows you to change the mode and attribute properties. For example, in the Mode section, you can change the visibility of attributes. In the Data section, you can change the tag, prompt, and default. You can right-click the Default text box and choose Insert Field to use a field. (See Chapter 13 for a discussion of fields.)
- **Text Options:** Allows you to change text style, height, justification, and so on.
- **Properties:** Allows you to change attribute layer, color, linetype, and so on.

After you finish making changes, click OK in the Edit Attribute dialog box to return to the Block Attribute Manager. Click OK to return to your drawing.

ON the DVD-ROM `Insrot` is a program that inserts a block at a specified rotation but keeps the attributes horizontal. Look in `\Software\Chapter 18\Insrot`. Attstrip removes all attributes from selected blocks. Look in `\Software\Chapter 18\attstrip`.

You may need to change the values of an attribute. Perhaps you entered the wrong purchase date or a part number has changed. Choose Modify ➪ Object ➪ Attribute ➪ Single to start the EATTEDIT command, and select the block containing the attributes that you want to change. You see the Enhanced Attribute Editor, as shown in Figure 18.37.

FIGURE 18.37

The Enhanced Attribute Editor.

As you can see, the Enhanced Attribute Editor is similar to the Edit Attribute dialog box. For example, it has the same three tabs. However, the Attribute tab enables you to change attribute values, something that you can't do in the Edit Attribute dialog box. To change an attribute's value, select it and type a new value in the Value text box. You can right-click the Value text box and choose Insert Field to use a field. (See Chapter 13 for more about fields.)

The Text Options and Properties tabs of the Enhanced Attribute Editor are the same as in the Edit Attribute dialog box.

 If you explode a block with attribute values, you lose the attribute values.

Editing attribute properties in AutoCAD and AutoCAD LT

In both AutoCAD and AutoCAD LT, you can change attribute values using the ATTEDIT command to open the Edit Attributes dialog box, as shown in Figure 18.38.

FIGURE 18.38

The Edit Attributes dialog box.

If a block has a number of attributes and you want to change them all in order, this dialog box makes it easy to go through all of the attributes quickly. Press Tab to go to the next attribute.

In AutoCAD LT, one way to change attribute properties is to explode the block and double-click the attribute. This starts the DDEDIT command and opens the Edit Attribute Definition dialog box, where you can change the tag, prompt, and default value. You can then redefine the block. This method works in AutoCAD, but is not necessary if you use the Block Attribute Manager, as explained in the previous section.

To edit attributes on the command line, type **-attedit**. At the `Edit attributes one at a time?` `[Yes/No] <Y>:` prompt, select the Yes option. This command then prompts you for changes in attribute values and properties, such as position, text style, color, and so on.

When you create invisible attributes, you can't edit them because you can't select them. The ATTDISP command controls attribute visibility globally, for all attributes in your drawing. Choose View ➪ Display ➪ Attribute Display and choose one of the following options. The currently active option is checked on the menu.

- **Normal:** Attributes that were created as visible are visible. Attributes that were created as invisible are invisible. This is the default option.
- **On:** All attributes are visible.
- **Off:** All attributes are invisible.

Changing the current option causes your drawing to regenerate.

Making global changes in attributes

In both AutoCAD and AutoCAD LT, you can also use the -ATTEDIT command on the command line to make global changes. If you answer No to the `Edit attributes one at a time? [Yes/No] <Y>:` prompt, you can make global changes to attribute values. For example, you can change all instances of A- in your part numbers to B-. You can even change invisible attribute values.

To use -ATTEDIT to make global changes, follow these steps:

1. Choose Modify ➪ Object ➪ Attribute ➪ Global.
2. At the `Edit attributes one at a time? [Yes/No] <Y>:` prompt, type **n ↵**.
3. At the `Edit only attributes visible on screen? [Yes/No] <Y>:` prompt, answer **y** or **n ↵**, as desired. If you answer **n** to edit invisible attributes, then you must know the attribute text string that you want to change because it is invisible.
4. At the `Enter block name specification <*>:` prompt, you can type a block name to limit the changes to one block, or press Enter to include any block.
5. At the `Enter attribute tag specification <*>:` prompt, you can type a tag to limit the changes to one tag type, or press Enter to include any tag.
6. At the `Enter attribute value specification <*>:` prompt, you can type a value to limit the changes to one value, or press Enter to include any value.
7. If you chose to edit only attributes that are visible on-screen, you see the `Select Attributes:` prompt. (If not, skip to Step 8.) Pick each attribute that you want to modify, or use a window. Press Enter to end selection. If you include other objects or blocks that do not fit the block name, attribute tag, or attribute value specifications that you made, then these other objects are not selected. The command line informs you of how many attributes were selected.
8. At the `Enter string to change:` prompt, type the text string (any consecutive text) that you want to change.
9. At the `Enter new string:` prompt, type the text string that will replace the old string.

If you chose to edit attributes that are not visible on the screen, the drawing regenerates, and the command line lists the changes that it made.

Redefining attributes

You can redefine a block with attributes to include different objects and attributes, using the ATTREDEF command. Redefining a block lets you add or delete attributes or redefine a block that contains attributes. Follow these steps:

AUTOCAD ONLY AutoCAD LT does not include this feature. Instead, explode the block and start from scratch. You can use the DDEDIT command to change attributes after you explode a block.

1. Explode one of the blocks with attributes. If there are nested blocks that you want to change, explode them, too.

2. If you want to add attributes, define and place them. Delete unwanted attributes. Make any other changes that you want to the objects.

3. Type **attredef** ⏎.

4. At the Enter name of block you wish to redefine: prompt, type the name of the block.

5. At the Select objects for new Block...: prompt, select the objects and the attributes that you want to include. Do not include any existing attributes that you want to delete.

6. At the Specify insertion base point of new Block: prompt, pick the base point for the block.

Here's how your drawing handles the changes:

■ If you created new attributes, the command places them for all existing blocks and gives them their default values.

■ Any attributes that you did not change retain their old values for all existing blocks.

■ Any attributes that you did not include in the new block definition are deleted from existing blocks.

ON the DVD-ROM The drawing that you need for the following exercise on editing attributes, ab18-i.dwg, is in the Drawings folder on the DVD.

STEPS: Editing Attributes

1. Open ab18-i.dwg from the DVD.

2. Save the file as ab18-10.dwg in your AutoCAD Bible folder. This is a portion of an office building plan layout, as shown in Figure 18.39.

3. Choose Modify ➪ Object ➪ Attribute ➪ Single.

   ▦ **If you have AutoCAD:** At the Select a block: prompt, pick the chair at in Figure 18.39. In the Value text box of the Enhanced Attribute Editor, change the date purchased to 4/97.

   ▦ **If you have AutoCAD LT:** At the Select block reference: prompt, pick the chair at ❶ in Figure 18.39. In the Edit Attributes dialog box, change the date purchased to 4/97.

   Notice that the manufacturer is American Office Furniture. Because these attributes are invisible, you can't see the result in the drawing. Click OK.

4. To see the attributes, choose View ➪ Display ➪ Attribute Display ➪ On. You can now see the attributes for the chair, as well as nearby attributes for the desk. To turn off the attributes, repeat the process, this time choosing the Normal option.

FIGURE 18.39

An office building plan layout.

5. Choose Modify ➪ Object ➪ Attribute ➪ Global. Follow the prompts:

```
Edit attributes one at a time? [Yes/No] <Y>: n ↵
Performing global editing of attribute values.
Edit only attributes visible on screen? [Yes/No] <Y>: n ↵
Drawing must be regenerated afterwards.
Enter block name specification <*>: armchair ↵
Enter attribute tag specification <*>: ↵
Enter attribute value specification <*>: ↵
6 attributes selected.
Enter string to change: American ↵
Enter new string: Acme ↵ (Press F2 to hide the text window if it is
open.)
```

6. Choose Explode from the Modify toolbar or the 2D Draw control panel of the Dashboard and select the chair at ❶ in Figure 18.39. Press Enter to end selection. The attributes reappear, but without their values. Choose Draw ➪ Block ➪ Define Attributes. Create an invisible attribute with a tag and prompt of Color, and a default value of Dusty Blue. Click OK and pick an insertion point underneath the other two attributes of the armchair. (You'll need to pan down a little. Exact placement is not important.)

7. To redefine the block, do one of the following:

    If you have AutoCAD: Type **attredef** ↵. Follow the prompts:

```
Enter name of Block you wish to redefine: armchair ↵
Select objects for new Block...Select objects: Use a window to select
the chair and the three attributes. Press Enter to end selection.

Specify insertion base point of new Block: Use an endpoint object
snap to pick the endpoint at ❷.
```

    If you have AutoCAD LT: Choose Make Block from the Draw toolbar. In the Name text box, enter **armchair**. Click the Pick Point button and use an endpoint object snap to pick the endpoint at ❷. Click the Select Objects button and select all of the objects that make up the chair, and then the three attributes. Press Enter to end selection. In the Objects section, choose the Delete option. Click OK. Click Yes to redefine the block.

The armchair block disappears.

8. Choose Insert Block. In the Insert dialog box, choose **armchair** from the Name drop-down list. With Specify On-screen checked only for Insertion Point, click OK. Insert the chair at ❷. In the Edit Attributes dialog box, click OK to accept the values, or press Enter to accept the values on the command line.

9. **AutoCAD only:** To verify that your drawing has redefined the block elsewhere, choose Modify ⇨ Object ⇨ Attribute ⇨ Single. Select the block at ❸. Notice that the Color tag has been added with a value of Dusty Blue. Click OK to accept the values. (In AutoCAD LT, the new attribute appears only in the block that you redefined, and new blocks that you insert.)

10. Use Zoom Window to zoom in closely to the telephone at ❹ in Figure 18.39. The telephone has a visible attribute of the phone number. The number is so small that it cannot usually be seen, and so does not interfere with the drawing.

11. To modify the properties of this attribute, do one of the following:

    If you have AutoCAD: Choose Modify ⇨ Object ⇨ Attribute ⇨ Block Attribute Manager. From the Block drop-down list, choose Phone. Click Edit. On the Attribute tab of the Edit Attribute dialog box, change the prompt to **Extension**. On the Text Options tab, choose Fit from the Justification drop-down list. On the Properties tab, choose Blue (if you're using a white background) or Cyan (if you're using a black background) from the Color drop-down list. Click OK twice to return to your drawing. The text of the phone extension is now blue and fills up the entire rectangle on the phone.

    If you have AutoCAD LT: Choose Modify ⇨ Object ⇨ Attribute ⇨ Global. Follow the prompts:

```
Edit attributes one at a time? [Yes/No] <Y>: ↵
Enter block name specification <*>: ↵
Enter attribute tag specification <*>: ↵
Enter attribute value specification <*>: ↵
Select Attributes: Select the phone number.
Select Attributes: ↵
1 attributes selected.
Enter an option [Value/Position/Height/Angle/Style/Layer/Color/Next]
<N>: c ↵
Enter new color <BYLAYER>: blue ↵ (or enter cyan if you are using a
black screen).
Enter an option [Value/Position/Height/Angle/Style/Layer/Color/Next]
<N>: ↵
```

    The phone number is now blue (or cyan).

12. Choose Zoom Previous from the Standard toolbar (or choose View ⇨ Zoom ⇨ Previous). Save the drawing.

AUTOCAD ONLY The Express Tools command BURST (choose Express ⇨ Blocks ⇨ Explode Attributes to Text) converts attributes to text. Apply the ATTOUT and ATTIN commands (choose Express ⇨ Blocks ⇨ Export Attribute Information and Express ⇨ Blocks ⇨ Import Attribute Information respectfully). Export Attribute Information and Import Attribute Information work together to enable you to edit attributes in another program. For example, ATTOUT creates a tab-delimited file that you can open in Notepad or Excel. When you use ATTIN, existing blocks are updated with the new attribute information.

Extracting a database from attributes

After you insert all of your blocks and attributes, you can extract the data using the Data Extraction Wizard, shown in Figure 18.40. To start the wizard, choose Tools ➪ Data Extraction. For information on extracting data from objects that are not blocks, see my coverage of tables in Chapter 13.

AUTOCAD ONLY The Data Extraction Wizard exists only in AutoCAD. For AutoCAD LT, you need to use the method that I explain in the sidebar, "Creating a Template File the Old-Fashioned Way."

FIGURE 18.40

The first screen of the Data Extraction Wizard.

On the Begin screen of the wizard, choose one of two options:

- **Create a new data extraction:** You can start from scratch or use a DXE or BLK file, which are templates that you create in the Data Extraction Wizard of AutoCAD 2008 or previous releases. These extraction template files save the parameters of the data extraction, so that you don't have to create them all over again.

- **Edit an existing data extraction:** Choose this option if you previously extracted data and want to modify the results.

NOTE Don't confuse the template file used for extracting attributes with the template file (with a file-name extension of .dwt) that you use as a basis for opening a drawing. Keep in mind that you can't use ASCII template files with the Data Extraction Wizard; you can only use .dxe or .blk templates.

In either case, click Next. The following instructions assume that you chose the first option.

AutoCAD saves the extraction parameters as a DXE file, and so the Save Data Extraction As dialog box opens, where you choose a location and name for the file.

 On the Define Data Source screen, choose from where you want to extract attributes. Most often, you want to select objects in the current drawing. In that case, click the Select Objects in the Current Drawing button to return to the drawing. However, you can choose other drawings (including the current drawing) or a drawing set. If you choose the current drawing and don't add any other drawings, you'll be able to extract from all objects in the drawing. On the next screen, you can individually choose which objects you want to include.

Click Settings to specify some block and block-count settings:

- **Extract Objects from Blocks:** Includes nested blocks.
- **Extract Objects from Xrefs:** Includes objects in external references (xrefs). See Chapter 19 for coverage of xrefs.
- **Include Xrefs in Block Counts:** When counting blocks, counts xrefs as blocks.

In the Extract From section, you can include all objects or only objects in model space. Then click OK.

Click Next to go to the next screen, Select Objects, as shown in Figure 18.41. Here you choose the objects with which you want to work. If you selected objects in the previous screen, you may have what you want here, but you may still find objects that you don't want to include.

NEW FEATURE You can now extract data from any object in your drawing, but attributes apply only to blocks.

If you're only interested in blocks and attributes that you've created, uncheck the Display All Object Types check box and choose the Display Blocks Only option. By checking the Display Blocks with Attributes Only check box, you can remove other blocks from your drawing. Check the Display Objects Currently In-Use Only check box to remove objects such as blocks that are defined but not inserted into the drawing, or objects from other drawings that you don't want to include. Uncheck this check box if you need to extract objects across multiple drawings and need access to certain objects not in the current drawing.

When you're done, you should see listed only the types of objects that you need. Then individually check or uncheck the objects listed. For example, you may want to extract attributes from some blocks, but not from others. Then click Next.

FIGURE 18.41

The Select Objects screen of the Data Extraction Wizard.

On the Select Properties screen, shown in Figure 18.42, you choose which properties you want to extract. If you want to extract only attributes, uncheck all the other check boxes in the Category Filter section. (I discuss the other categories more in Chapter 13.) You should be left with just the attributes that you want to extract. Click Next.

FIGURE 18.42

The Select Properties screen of the Data Extraction Wizard.

On the Refine Data screen, shown in Figure 18.43, you have three check boxes which allow you to combine (or not combine) identical rows, show (or not show) a column that counts the blocks, and show (or not show) a column that lists the name of the block. You can sort each column by clicking the column's heading. Finally, you can add a link to external data by clicking the Link External Data button. I cover this feature in Chapter 13.

You can click Full Preview to preview the resulting data. Click the window's Close button to return to the wizard. Then click Next.

FIGURE 18.43

The Refine Data screen of the Data Extraction Wizard.

On the Choose Output screen, check the output that you want to create. You can output to an AutoCAD table, an external file, or both. You can create the following types of files:

- **CSV (Comma Delimited)** (`*.csv`): Lists its attribute values with a comma between each value. Most spreadsheets and databases can import this format.
- **Tab Delimited File** (`*.txt`): This is like a CSV file, except that there is a tab between each attribute value.
- **Microsoft Excel** (`*.xls`): Creates an Excel spreadsheet.
- **Microsoft Access Database** (`*.mdb`): Creates a Microsoft Office Access database file.

If you check the Output Data to External File check box, enter the filename in the text box, or click the Ellipsis button to open the Save As dialog box, where you can browse to the desired location, name the file, and choose the file type. You choose the file type by specifying the filename extension. Click Save.

To continue, click Next.

If you chose to export to a table, on the next screen, you can choose a table title and style. If you don't have a table style (except the default, Standard), click the Table Style button to open the Table Style dialog box. Click New to create a new table style. When you have chosen a table title and style, click Next.

The Finish screen just tells you that you'll need to specify an insertion point if you chose to create a table and that your file will be saved if you chose to create an external file. Then click Finish.

If you chose to create a table, you see the table at the cursor, and the `Specify insertion point:` prompt. Specify a location to place the table. If you chose to create an external file, you see a message on the command line that looks something like the following:

```
External file "C:\AutoCAD Bible\Ch18\ab18-08.xls" was successfully
created.
```

Creating a Template File the Old-Fashioned Way

With AutoCAD's Data Extraction Wizard, you don't need to create templates "by hand." You can still create templates on your own, but you must use the ATTEXT command to extract them. If you have AutoCAD LT, you must use the following method.

Create the template file in a text editor such as Windows Notepad. The template file contains two columns. The first is the name of the attribute tag. The second is a format code that specifies whether the data is a character or number, how many spaces to allow for the data, and the decimal precision to use. The format code uses the following syntax:

TWWWPPP

where T is the data type (either N for numeral or C for character), WWW is the width, including commas and decimal points, and PPP is the precision. For integers and all character data, use 000 as the precision.

For example, you would use N006002 for costs that range up to $999.99. The N means that the data is numeric, 006 means that you will have up to six spaces, including the decimal point, and the 002 means that you have precision to two decimal places.

continued

continued

In addition to information from your attributes, you can extract certain standard fields from the drawing's database. The table that follows lists these fields and their formatting.

The block number is a number given to the blocks that you select when extracting the data. The block handle is a unique alphanumeric code given to all objects in your drawing; to see a block's handle, use the LIST command and select the block. Handles are used for referring to objects when you write AutoLISP or other programming code. The extrusion data is used for 3D drawing. See Chapter 24 for an explanation of extrusion.

Field	Format	Explanation
BL: LEVEL	NWWW000	Block nesting level
BL: NAME	CWWW000	Block name
BL: X	NWWWPPP	X coordinate of block insertion point
BL: Y	NWWWPPP	Y coordinate of block insertion point
BL: Z	NWWWPPP	Z coordinate of block insertion point
BL: NUMBER	NWWW000	Block counter
BL: HANDLE	CWWW000	Block handle
BL: LAYER	CWWW000	Block insertion layer name
BL: ORIENT	NWWWPPP	Block rotation angle
BL: XSCALE	NWWWPPP	X scale factor
BL: YSCALE	NWWWPPP	Y scale factor
BL: ZSCALE	NWWWPPP	Z scale factor
BL: XEXTRUDE	NWWWPPP	X component of Block's extrusion direction
BL: YEXTRUDE	NWWWPPP	Y component of Block's extrusion direction
BL: ZEXTRUDE	NWWWPPP	Z component of Block's extrusion direction

Template files are quite finicky. Here are the rules that you should follow:

- You must include at least one attribute tag in your template.
- Each row must be unique — don't include the same attribute more than once.
- You must use only spaces to line up the two columns — no tabs! (Lining up the two columns just makes it easier to read.)
- End each line with a return, including the last line.
- Don't put any extra spaces after any line or any extra returns after the last return that is after the last line of text.

Each row in the template file becomes a column in the resulting output file. If you choose space-delimited form for the output file, then spaces do not automatically appear between the columns; as a result, the output files are hard to read. You can place dummy rows in the template file for the purpose of creating spaces in the resulting columns. A typical dummy row looks like this:

```
DUMMY1      C002000
```

Because each row must be unique, if you need another dummy row, call it DUMMY2. This row creates a blank column of two spaces in the output file.

The figure shows a typical template file that tracks the company division, as well as the furniture's manufacturer, purchase date, cost, and color.

After you're done, save the file with a filename extension of .txt. To use the file, you must use the ATTEXT command, which opens the Attribute Extraction dialog box. In this dialog box, click Template File and choose the file that you created. Choose the file format that you want to create, and name the output file. Then click OK to extract the attributes.

 If you have AutoCAD LT, skip this exercise, and use the following exercise instead.

 The drawing that you need for the following exercise on extracting attribute data in AutoCAD, ab18-j.dwg, is in the Drawings folder on the DVD.

STEPS: Extracting Attribute Data in AutoCAD

1. Open ab18-j.dwg from the DVD. This is the same office building plan that you used earlier in this chapter, shown in Figure 18.44. Save the drawing as ab18-11.dwg in your AutoCAD Bible folder. Change the current layer to 0.

2. Choose Tools ➪ Data Extraction to open the Data Extraction Wizard.

3. The Create a New Data Extraction option should be selected on the Begin screen. Click Next.

4. The Save Data Extraction As dialog box opens. In the File Name text box, enter **ab18-11.dxe** and click Save.

5. On the Define Data Source screen, the Drawings/Sheet Set option should be selected. The Include Current Drawing check box should also be checked. Click Next.

FIGURE 18.44

The office building plan includes several blocks of armchairs with invisible attributes.

6. On the Select Objects screen, uncheck the Display All Object Types check box and check the Display Blocks Only option. Check the Display Blocks with Attributes Only check box. You should now see three objects listed, ARMCHAIR, DESK, and PHONE. Uncheck DESK and PHONE to extract the data for the armchair blocks only. Click Next.

7. On the Select Properties screen, uncheck Drawing and General in the Category Filter pane. In the Properties pane, click the Category column to sort by category. Leave only the following properties checked:

   ▪ **For the Attributes category:** COLOR, MFR, and PUR_DATE

   ▪ **For the Geometry category:** Position X and Position Y

   ▪ **For the Misc category:** Rotation

8. You can change the display name of the properties. Click in the appropriate row of the Display Name column twice to select the display name and make the following changes:

   ▪ Change COLOR to Color

   ▪ Change PUR_DATE to Purchase Date

   ▪ Change MFR to Manufacturer

   ▪ Change Position X to X Location

   ▪ Change Position Y to Y Location

9. Click Next. (If you get a message about non-uniformly scaled blocks, click OK.)

10. On the Refine Data screen, you should see the data with each attribute in its own column. You can resize the window to see all of the data. Click the Manufacturer column to sort the list by manufacturer. Note how the column names match the changes you made to the display names. Click Next.

11. In the Output Options section, check both check boxes to create both a table and an external file. Click the Ellipsis button next to the External File text box. In the Save As dialog box, navigate to your `AutoCAD Bible` folder. From the Files of Type drop-down list, choose `*.csv`. Leave the default name (`ab18-11.csv`) and click Save. (If you have Microsoft Excel or Access, you can choose the appropriate file type for one of those applications.) Click Next.

12. On the Table Style screen, type **Armchair Data** in the Enter a Title for Your Table text box. The table style should be set to Office. Click Next.

13. On the Finish screen, click Finish.

14. On the command line, you see a message that the CSV file was successfully created. You also see a `Specify insertion point:` prompt for the table. Pick a point to the right of the floor plan to insert the table.

15. To view the CSV file, open Windows Explorer and double-click `ab18-11.csv` in your `AutoCAD Bible` folder. It should open in Microsoft Excel or another application that opens CSV files on your system. The data should look like Figure 18.45.

FIGURE 18.45

The output file that results from extracting the attributes in the office building plan.

16. Save your drawing.

NOTE If you export attributes in tab-delimited (`.txt`) format, you can open the Multiline Text Editor and click Import Text to import the output file into your drawing. You can also open the output file, copy it to the Clipboard, and paste it into your drawing. The Import Text method enables you to format the text as you would any multiline text, but may take some experimenting to align the columns. You cannot format the text that you import using the Clipboard method, but it's nicely lined up in columns. Using the table option as you did in the exercise provides the best combination of formatting options.

ON the DVD-ROM The files that you need for the following exercise on extracting attribute data in AutoCAD LT, `ab18-j.dwg` and `ab18-j.txt`, are in the `Drawings` folder on the DVD.

STEPS: Extracting Attribute Data in AutoCAD LT

1. Open `ab18-j.dwg` from the DVD. This is the same office building plan that you used earlier in this chapter, shown in Figure 18.44.

2. Type **attext** ⏎ to open the Attribute Extraction dialog box.

3. Choose the Space Delimited File (SDF) option.

4. Choose Select Objects. Pick the five armchairs in the lobby and the three offices. Press Enter to end selection.

5. Choose Template File. In the Template File dialog box, navigate to and choose `ab18-j.txt` from the DVD. Click Open.

6. Choose Output File. In the Output File dialog box, choose your `AutoCAD Bible` folder and name the file `ab18-11.txt`. Click Save.

7. Click OK. The command line displays the message `8 records in extract file`.

8. To view the output file, choose Start ⏏ Run from the Windows task bar. Type **Notepad** and click Run. In Notepad, choose File ⏏ Open, and locate the `ab18-11.txt` file in your `AutoCAD Bible` folder. Click Open.

This exercise shows how to extract attributes using space-delimited format. This format is easier to import into AutoCAD by copying and pasting. However, comma-delimited format is easier to import into most spreadsheet programs.

Summary

In this chapter, I covered all of the ways that you can use blocks and attributes in your drawings. You read about:

- Combining objects into blocks in your drawings so that you can edit them as a unit
- Inserting blocks at any scale and rotation
- Saving a block as a file
- Inserting blocks with the INSERT command
- Using the DesignCenter to import blocks from other drawings
- Creating and inserting dynamic blocks
- Copying objects by using the Windows Clipboard and drag-and-drop
- Using attributes to place text and to create simple databases
- Defining attributes
- Inserting blocks with attributes and assigning values to the attributes
- Extracting attribute data in both AutoCAD and AutoCAD LT

In the next chapter, I explain how to insert references (xrefs) to other files in your drawings.

Chapter 19

Referencing Other Drawings

Sometimes you need to refer to another drawing without inserting it. You may want to use part of another drawing as an example for your current drawing, or to see how the model in your drawing fits in with models in other drawings. You may want the flexibility of seeing the other drawing sometimes, but not seeing it at other times. Using an external reference is like laying one drawing on top of another and being able to see both at the same time. You can easily load and unload the other drawing.

Understanding External References

External references, commonly called *xrefs*, enable you to view any drawing as a reference while in your current drawing. The external drawing is not part of your current drawing. The current drawing keeps track of the location and name of an external reference so that you can always reference it easily. As with blocks, you can snap to objects in the external reference, thereby using it as a reference for the drawing process. You can also change the visibility settings of the xref's layers.

Xrefs have several advantages over blocks:

- **Xrefs keep your drawing smaller than blocks.** The externally referenced drawing doesn't become part of your drawing. Your drawing maintains only a reference (name and location) to the other drawing.

- **You always have the most updated version of the xref.** Each time that you open a drawing, a current copy of the xref loads. By contrast, you would need to reinsert a file inserted as a block to see the most updated version.

- **In a team project, several people can use the same drawing as an xref, each having access to the latest changes.**

■ **Xrefs can be attached and detached easily for maximum flexibility, loaded and unloaded to display or hide them, or overlaid for temporary use.** If you're only using the xref for reference, you may detach it before plotting.

Attaching an external reference

The first step is to attach the external reference, which is just another drawing, to your current (host) drawing. When working with xrefs, you may find it useful to use the Reference toolbar. To open the Reference toolbar, right-click any toolbar and choose Reference. You can underlay DWF files, which are covered in Chapter 28, and DGN drawings. I explain underlays at the end of this chapter.

NEW FEATURE AutoCAD 2008 and AutoCAD LT 2008 can now use Version 8 DGN files, created in the Bentley Microstation(r) program, as xrefs.

To attach an xref of an AutoCAD or AutoCAD LT drawing, follow these steps:

1. Choose Attach Xref from the Reference toolbar (or choose Insert ➪ DWG Reference) to start the XATTACH command. The Select Reference File dialog box opens.

2. Choose the file you want to attach and click Open. The External Reference dialog box (shown in Figure 19.1) opens. This dialog box displays the file that you chose, along with its path (location).

FIGURE 19.1

The External Reference dialog box.

3. Choose the type of xref that you want in the Reference Type section:
   ■ **Attachment:** Use an attachment when you want to be sure that the xref will be displayed if someone else xrefs your current drawing. In other words, that person will see your current drawing, and your xref will be nested within it.
   ■ **Overlay:** Use an overlay when you're sharing drawings in a networked environment and you don't want to change your drawing by attaching an xref. If someone else attaches your drawing while you're working on it, the overlay is not displayed.

NOTE The XREFTYPE system variable determines which of these two choices, Attachment or Overlay, is automatically chosen in the Reference Type section. The default value, 0, uses the Attachment option.

4. From the Path Type drop-down list, choose the type of path that you want to use:

  - **Full path:** Specifies the full path of the xref drawing, including the drive letter (such as c:).

  - **Relative path:** Specifies only part of the xref drawing's path, assuming the current drive or folder. This option enables you to move an xref to a different drive that has the same folder structure.

  - **No path:** Uses the current folder of the host drawing. This option enables you to use an xref when you move the drawing, for example, when you send it to someone else with a different folder structure. To make sure that the drawing can find the xref, ensure that it is in the project files search path.

5. Use the bottom half of the dialog box to specify the insertion point, the X, Y, and Z scale factors, and the rotation angle, either in the dialog box or on-screen. These prompts are the same ones that you use when inserting a block or file.

NOTE A check box in the Scale section lets you specify the use of a uniform scale, so the Y and Z values are always the same as the X value. The Block Unit section displays the units set for the referenced drawing. This is the same setting you use when you create a block and allows for the automatic scaling of the drawing. You can set this value using the INSUNITS system variable or choose Format ➪ Units to set it in the Units dialog box.

6. Click OK to attach the xref.

If your current view does not show the entire xref, do a ZOOM Extents.

CROSS-REF You can also attach an xref from a tool palette. For more information on tool palettes, see Chapter 26.

After you have the xref in your drawing, you can start to work. The xref is like a block, although you cannot explode it. However, you can use object snaps on all of the objects in an xref, just as you can with blocks. This enables you to use the xref as a basis for your own drawing.

Opening an xref

Sometimes you need to open the xref to work on it directly. For example, you may see an error that you want to correct. The XOPEN command opens xrefs. (The XOPEN command is not available in AutoCAD LT.) The easiest way to use XOPEN is to click the xref to select it in your drawing, right-click, and choose Open Xref. The xref opens in its own drawing window.

Using the External References palette

To see what type of xrefs you have in your drawing, choose Tools ➪ Palettes ➪ External References. The external references are listed in the External References palette, shown in Figure 19.2. This palette shows the following types of references:

- **Drawings**
- **Images:** Any type of bitmap (raster) image that you can import. (See Chapter 27 for more information.)

- **DWF underlays:** DWF files that act like xrefs. I explain how to attach DWF underlays at the end of this chapter, and I cover creating DWF files in Chapter 28.
- **DGN underlays**: DGN files (Microstation drawings) that act like xrefs. I cover DGN files at the end of this chapter.

 The External References palette replaced the Xref Manager as of AutoCAD 2007 and AutoCAD LT 2007. You can open the earlier Xref Manager with the CLASSICXREF command.

FIGURE 19.2

The External References palette displays referenced drawings, images, DWF files, and DGN drawing files.

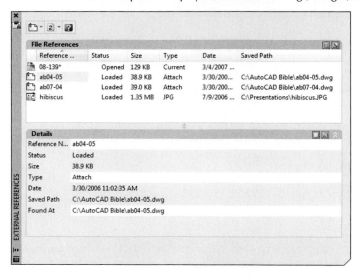

The top pane lists all the referenced drawings and files. You can choose one of two views, using the buttons at the top-right corner of the palette:

- **List view** lists all of the references along with their status, size, type, date, and time saved, as well as the saved path, if any.

- **Tree view** lists all of the references in a graphical view that shows their relationships. This view is great for understanding nested xrefs.

 You can change the width of the columns in List view by placing the cursor on a column dividing line until it changes to a two-headed arrow. Then drag in either direction.

When you click any xref, the lower panel displays one of two views, which you specify using the buttons at the right side of the panel:

- **Details** displays information about the selected reference, similar to the information you see in the top half.

- **Preview** displays a visual preview of the reference.

If you move or delete a referenced item, the External References palette notes that the file is not found. To troubleshoot, it helps to know where it searches for xrefs. The External References palette searches for references according to a specific order:

- **Path specified:** Locates the specified path xref.

- **Current folder:** Locates the current folder of the host drawing.

- **Project path:** The path for external references. To check or change the project path, choose Tools ⇨ Options and click the Files tab. Double-click Project Files Search Path. Click Add and then click Browse to navigate to a folder where you keep drawings that you may want to use as xrefs. (AutoCAD LT doesn't offer the Project Files Search Path.)

- **Support path:** The location for support files. To check or change the support path, choose Tools ⇨ Options and then click the Files tab. Double-click Support File Search Path. Click Add and then click Browse to navigate to a folder.

- **Start-in folder:** To find the start-in folder, right-click your AutoCAD 2008 or AutoCAD LT 2008 desktop shortcut and choose Properties.

 The drawings used in the following exercise on attaching xrefs, `ab19-a.dwg` and `ab19-b.dwg`, are in the `Drawings` folder on the DVD.

STEPS: Attaching Xrefs

1. Open `ab19-a.dwg` from the DVD. This is the floor plan for a house. If the Reference toolbar is not displayed, right-click any toolbar and choose Reference.

2. Open Windows Explorer (right-click Start on the task bar and choose Explore). Copy `ab19-b.dwg` from the DVD to your `AutoCAD Bible` folder.

 3. In your drawing, choose Attach Xref from the Reference toolbar. In the Select Reference File dialog box, choose `ab19-b.dwg`. Click Open.

4. In the External Reference dialog box, you see the filename displayed. Make sure that all Specify On-Screen check boxes are unchecked, and click OK. You see `ab19-b.dwg`, which is a title block, in `ab19-a.dwg`.

5. Save the drawing as `ab19-01.dwg` in your `AutoCAD Bible` folder. Click the drawing's Close box to close the drawing.

6. Start a new drawing using the `acad.dwt` or `acadlt.dwt` template. Choose Format ⇨ Units and choose Architectural. In the Units to Scale Inserted Content drop-down list, choose Inches. Click OK. Save it as `ab19-02.dwg` in your `AutoCAD Bible` folder.

7. Choose Attach Xref from the Reference toolbar. In the Select Reference File dialog box, choose `ab19-01.dwg`, which you just saved in your `AutoCAD Bible` folder. Click Open.

8. In the External Reference dialog box, you see the filename displayed. Leave the defaults and click OK. Choose View ⇨ Zoom ⇨ Extents. You see `ab19-01.dwg`, which includes both the title block and the floor plan of the house in your new drawing. The title block drawing (`ab19-b.dwg`) is a nested xref in the floor plan (`ab19-01.dwg`) xref. You see the following message (press F2 to open the Text Window so you can see the message that scrolls by):

```
Attach Xref "ab19-01": C:\AutoCAD Bible\ab19-01.dwg
"ab19-01" loaded.
Attach Xref "ab19-b": C:\AutoCAD Bible\ab19-b.dwg
"ab19-b" loaded.
```

9. To help you visualize the relationships among the three drawings, choose External References from the Reference toolbar. The External References palette lists both drawings. Click Tree View at the top-right corner of the palette. You now see the two xrefs listed in a tree structure, showing their relationship more clearly, as shown in Figure 19.3. Close or Auto-Hide the palette.

FIGURE 19.3

Tree view shows nested xrefs clearly.

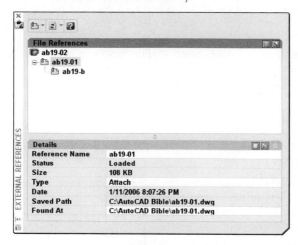

10. Save your drawing. It should look like Figure 19.4.

FIGURE 19.4

The current drawing is blank but displays an xref of a house plan that has a nested xref of a title block.

Editing an Xref within Your Drawing

While you're working in a drawing with an external reference, you may decide that the external reference needs some modification. The same may apply if you inserted a file as a block. You can make changes to the xref or block and save those changes back to the original drawing. You can even transfer objects from your drawing to the xref or block, and vice versa. This feature is called *in-place editing*.

AUTOCAD ONLY AutoCAD LT doesn't include the in-place editing feature. Instead, you need to explode the block and redefine it (for blocks) or open the original file and modify it (for xrefs). In AutoCAD, you can edit blocks using the Block Editor, which I cover in Chapter 18. When you double-click a block, the Block Editor opens.

The steps to edit an xref or block are as follows:

1. Choose the xref or block in your drawing.
2. Choose from any nested xrefs.
3. Select the objects that you want to edit to add them to the working set of objects being edited.
4. Edit the objects.
5. If desired, add or remove objects from the working set to transfer them to or from the xref or block.
6. Save the changes back to the xref or block.

Choosing the xref or block to edit

To start the process of in-place editing, double-click the xref that you want to edit. The Reference Edit dialog box opens, as shown in Figure 19.5. You can also choose Tools ➪ Xref and Block In-place Editing ➪ Edit Reference In-Place, and then select the xref that you want to edit.

FIGURE 19.5

The Reference Edit dialog box enables you to choose which reference you want to edit, including nested references.

As you click each of the available references, its preview appears at the right. If the xref has nested objects, choose one of the following options (if it does not, then ignore this section of the dialog box):

- **Automatically select all nested objects:** Includes all nested objects in the editing process.
- **Prompt to select nested objects:** Prompts you to select which nested objects you want to edit.

For more control, click the Settings tab to set the following options:

- **Create unique layer, style, and block names:** Displays layer, style, and block names with a prefix of $#$, to help distinguish them from these named items in your main drawing.
- **Display attribute definitions for editing:** Enables you to edit attribute definitions of blocks with attributes. (See Chapter 18 for details on attributes.)
- **Lock objects not in working set:** Locks objects in the host drawing so that you can't accidentally modify them.

Click OK to close the Reference Edit dialog box.

 If the reference comes from an earlier release, you see a warning that if you save your changes back to the xref, that xref will be updated to AutoCAD 2007 format (also used in AutoCAD 2008).

If you checked the Prompt to Select Nested Objects option, you see a prompt to select nested objects. Complete object selection to define the working set, that is, the objects that you can edit. Other objects are faded by 50 percent (this is the default, determined by the XFADECTL system variable).

The Refedit toolbar opens, shown in Figure 19.6, and you see the message Use REFCLOSE or the Refedit toolbar to end reference editing session on the command line. You're now ready to edit the xref or block.

FIGURE 19.6

The Refedit toolbar.

Editing the xref

There are several types of edits that you can make on the working set of objects from the xref or block:

- If you change an object's properties, such as its layer, the object will have the new object property.
- If you erase an object, the object is deleted from the xref or block.
- If you draw a new object, the object is added to the xref or block. An exception is if you create a new object by editing objects outside the working set. For example, if you break a line (not in the working set) into two lines, then nothing is added to the working set.
- You can transfer an object from the main drawing to the xref or block. Select an object and choose Add to Working Set. Remember that the working set consists of objects from the xref or block, so if you add objects to the working set, they become part of the xref or block.
- You can transfer an object from the xref or block to the main drawing. Select an object and choose Remove from Working Set. The working set consists of objects from the xref or block, so if you remove objects from the working set, they're no longer part of the xref or block; instead, they become part of your main drawing.

After you finish editing the working set, if you like what you did, choose Save Reference Edits from the Refedit toolbar. Otherwise, choose Close Reference.

When you save changes to a block, block definitions are redefined and all instances of the block are regenerated according to the new definition. If you gave an xref object properties that don't exist in the xref, such as a layer, the new property is copied to the xref so that the object can keep that property.

 The drawings used in the following exercise on editing an xref in place, ab19-a.dwg and ab19-b.dwg, are in the Drawings folder on the DVD.

STEPS: Editing an Xref in Place

1. Open ab19-a.dwg from the DVD. Save it as ab19-03.dwg in your AutoCAD Bible folder.

2. Open ab19-b.dwg from the DVD. Save it as ab19-04.dwg in your AutoCAD Bible folder. Click the Close box of ab19-04.dwg to close the drawing (but not the program), leaving ab19-03.dwg on your screen.

3. Choose Insert ⇨ DWG Reference and choose ab19-04.dwg from the AutoCAD Bible folder. Click Open. From the External Reference dialog box, uncheck all of the Specify On-Screen check boxes and click OK to insert the xref.

4. Double-click the title block. The Reference Edit dialog box opens. Choose ab19-04.dwg. It is displayed in the preview box. Click OK. The Refedit toolbar opens, and you can now edit the xref. Your screen should look like Figure 19.7.

FIGURE 19.7

The title block is an xref in the drawing of the floor plan.

5. Select the title block again and choose Explode.

6. Choose Draw ⇨ Text ⇨ Single Line Text. At the Specify start point of text or [Justify/Style]: prompt, pick ❶ in Figure 19.7. At the Specify height <0'-0 3/16">: prompt, type **10** ↵. Press Enter again for the rotation angle.

621

7. Type **Davis Floor Plan** and press Enter twice to end the command.

8. Choose the text (the name and address of the architect) at the bottom of the title block and change its color to red to make it stand out.

9. Select the letter N and arrow symbol at ❷ in Figure 19.7. To transfer these objects from the xref to the floor plan drawing, choose Remove from Working Set from the Refedit toolbar.

10. To save the changes, choose Save Reference Edits. Click OK again at the dialog box that informs you that all reference edits will be saved. You see the following information on the command line:

```
The following symbols will be permanently bound to the current
drawing:
Layers: $0$TITLEBLK
Text Styles: $0$ROMANS, $0$ROMAND
Blocks: $0$KNTITL

Enter option [Save/Discard reference changes] <Save>: _sav
Regenerating model.
11 objects added to ab19-04
1 object removed from ab19-04
1 xref instance updated
ab19-04 redefined and reloaded.
```

11. Choose External References from the Reference toolbar. In the External References palette, right-click ab19-04.dwg and choose Detach from the shortcut menu. (Detaching xrefs is covered later in this chapter.) You can now see that ab19-03.dwg includes the North symbol and letter because they were removed from the xref.

12. To see the results of the editing on the xref, open ab19-04.dwg. You can see the changes in the title block text and that the North symbol and letter are gone.

13. Close both drawings, saving changes to ab19-03.dwg.

Controlling Xref Display

You can control the display of xref layers so that you see only those layers you need. Several features let you control the process of displaying xrefs, making it easier to see only part of an xref and speeding up the display of very large xrefs.

Xrefs and dependent symbols

Dependent symbols are named items in a drawing, such as layers, text styles, dimension styles, and so on. When you attach an xref, these symbols are listed in your current drawing. For example, the Layer Control drop-down list displays the layers of the xref. Xref symbols have the format xref_name|symbol_name. This system distinguishes xref symbols from those of your current drawing and ensures that there are no duplicate symbols.

Xrefs and layers

You can turn on and off, or freeze and thaw, xref layers. You can also change an xref layer's properties in the Layer Properties Manager dialog box. By default, these changes are retained. However, you can set the VIS-RETAIN system variable to 0 to discard these changes. The next time you open the drawing or reload the xref, the original settings are restored.

Objects created on layer 0 do not take on the typical xref layer name format, but stay on layer 0. If objects in the xref are on layer 0 with the color and linetype set to ByLayer, they take on the color and linetype properties of the current layer in the current drawing. If color and linetype are set to ByBlock, then objects assume the current properties when the xref is attached. If you explicitly set color and linetype, then objects retain those settings.

The XBIND command

You can use the XBIND command to import only the symbols that you want from the external reference into the current drawing. This makes it easy to work with a consistent set of symbols in the current drawing and the xrefs. For example, you can choose to import the titleblk layer and the dec dimension style. Choose Xbind from the References toolbar or type **xbind** ↵ on the command line. The Xbind dialog box opens, listing each xref in the drawing along with its symbols in a Windows Explorer — like display, as shown in Figure 19.8.

Using the XBIND command to import symbols, such as layers, text styles, and so on.

Click the plus sign next to any symbol type to open a list of symbols. Click the one you want and choose Add to add it to the Definitions to Bind list. Click OK when you're done.

Later in this chapter, I explain how you can use the DesignCenter to move xrefs and other dependent symbols from one drawing to another.

Circular references

If drawing *a* includes drawing *b* as an xref and drawing *b* includes drawing *a* as an xref, then you have a circular reference. Circular references can exist among three or more xrefs when you have nested xrefs. The program detects circular references and loads as much as it can. If you try to load an xref in such a situation, you see the following message:

```
Warning: Circular reference from XREF to current drawing.
Circular reference(s) have been found. Continue? <N> Type y to continue
to load the xref.
Breaking circular reference from XREF to current drawing.
```

Clipping xrefs

You may want to see only part of an xref. This option is especially important when you're using very large xref drawings. The XCLIP command enables you to create a border in an xref, and hides any part of the xref outside the border.

AUTOCAD ONLY   AutoCAD LT doesn't include the xref clipping feature.

 To clip an xref, choose Modify ⇨ Clip ⇨ Xref or choose Clip Xref from the Reference toolbar. At the prompt to select objects, pick the xref you want to clip. Note that any nested xrefs are clipped with the main xref that you select.

Table 19.1 explains the options of this command.

TABLE 19.1

XCLIP Options

Option	How to Use It	
ON	Turns the clipping boundary on, displaying only the portion of the xref inside the clipping boundary. By default, the clipping boundary is on. Use this after you've turned it off to see only the clipped portion again.	
OFF	Turns the clipping boundary off, displaying the entire xref. The clipping boundary is still retained. This is somewhat like turning off a layer. You may want to see the entire xref for a while (for example, while redefining the boundary). Then you can turn the boundary back on (using the ON option) when you need only the clipped portion again.	
Clipdepth	This is used for 3D drawings only. After you set a clipping boundary, you can set front and back planes parallel to the boundary to display only the portion of the xref within that three-dimensional space. You create the front and back planes by specifying a distance from the clipping boundary. The Remove sub-option removes the clipping planes.	
Delete	Deletes the clipping boundary. The boundary is no longer retained in the drawing.	
generate Polyline	Creates a polyline from the clipping boundary, using the current layer, color, and linetype. If you want to change the clipping boundary, you can edit the polyline by using PEDIT and redefine the boundary with the new polyline.	
New boundary	This is the default option. Press Enter to see the sub-options, which follow.	
	Select polyline	Enables you to specify the clipping boundary by selecting an existing polyline. This option decurves fit-curved or arc portions of the polyline when creating the boundary.
	Polygonal	Enables you to specify a polygonal area, such as a polyline with straight edges. This option creates a rubber-band line as you pick points, keeping the polygon closed. You can use this option to create an irregularly shaped area that includes only the portion of the xref that you want to see.
	Rectangular	Enables you to pick two points on diagonally opposite corners of a rectangle, such as creating a selection window.
	Invert Clip	Enables you to hide any part of the xref inside the border. After choosing this sub-option, choose one of the previous sub-options to define the clipping boundary.

In addition to clipping xrefs, the XCLIP command can also clip blocks.

To see the clipping boundary (if you haven't used an existing polyline to define it), change the value of the XCLIPFRAME system variable to 1.

NEW FEATURE The ability to invert the xref clip (hide any part of the xref inside the border), is new for AutoCAD 2008. Select Invert Clip, and then select one of the New Boundary options.

Figure 19.9 shows an xref clipped with a polygonal boundary. Compare this to Figure 19.4, which shows the entire xref.

FIGURE 19.9

An xref clipped with a polygonal boundary.

Speeding up the display of large xrefs

In order to reduce the time needed to display large xrefs, such as those used in GIS or 3D drawings, you can use *demand loading*. This feature enables you to load only the objects necessary to display the xref in your drawing. Demand loading works together with spatial and layer indexes.

- The spatial index is created when you save a drawing. This index is used when you have enabled demand loading and attach a clipped xref that was saved with a spatial index. The index determines how much of the xref needs to be read to display it.

- The layer index is also created when you save a drawing. This index is used when you've enabled demand loading and attach an xref that was saved with a layer index and has frozen or turned off layers. The index determines how much of the xref needs to be read to display it.

To make it perfectly clear, you need all of the following in order to use demand loading:

- Demand loading must be enabled in the current drawing.
- The xref must have been saved with a spatial or layer index.
- The xref must either be clipped (for a spatial index) or have layers that are frozen or turned off (for a layer index).

CROSS-REF Demand loading is similar to partial opening and loading of drawings, explained in Chapter 8.

Demand loading

You can turn on demand loading in your current drawing. To turn on demand loading, choose Tools ➪ Options, and then click the Open and Save tab. In the Demand Load Xrefs drop-down list, choose Enabled. Others on a networked system cannot then edit the original drawing while you're referencing it. To let others edit the original drawing, choose Enabled with Copy. This option uses a copy of the referenced drawing for your xref. Click OK. You can turn on demand loading just before you attach an xref; you don't need to keep demand loading on all the time.

Spatial indexes

You save a spatial index for a drawing that you expect to use as an xref. The saving process takes a little longer, but you save time at the other end when you load a clipped xref or clip an xref for the first time. To create a spatial index in AutoCAD, choose File ➪ Save As to open the Save Drawing As dialog box. From the Tools menu at the top-right of the dialog box, choose Options to open the Saveas Options dialog box, shown in Figure 19.10 with the DWG Options tab on top.

FIGURE 19.10

The DWG Options tab of the Saveas Options dialog box enables you to save spatial and layer indexes.

From the Index type drop-down list, choose Spatial or Layer & Spatial. Click OK. Then click Save in the Save Drawing As dialog box. In AutoCAD LT, use the INDEXCTL system variable on the command line and set its value to 2 for just a spatial index, or to 3 for both spatial and layer indexes.

> **TIP** If you want to create an index for an existing drawing, click OK once to return to the Save Drawing As dialog box. Click Cancel. In other words, you don't have to actually save the drawing to set up the index, which is controlled by the INDEXCTL system variable.

After you create a spatial index, each time you save the drawing, you see the following message:

```
Updating Indexes for block *MODEL_SPACE
```

To stop saving the index each time you save in AutoCAD, choose File ➪ Save As. Choose Tools ➪ Options. In the Saveas Options dialog box, choose None from the Index Type drop-down list. Click OK and then click Cancel. In AutoCAD LT, change the value of the INDEXCTL system variable to 0.

Layer indexes

You save a layer index for a drawing that you expect to use as an xref to create an index of all of the layers in the drawing. As with a spatial index, the saving process takes a little longer, but you save time at the other end when you load an xref with frozen or turned off layers. To create a layer index in AutoCAD, choose File ➪ Save As to open the Save Drawing As dialog box. From the Tools menu at the upper-right corner of the dialog box, choose Options to open the Saveas Options dialog box, shown in Figure 19.10.

From the Index type drop-down list, choose Layer or Layer & Spatial. Click OK, and then click Cancel. In AutoCAD LT, set the INDEXCTL system variable to 1 for just a layer index, or to 3 for both layer and spatial indexes.

After you create a layer index, each time you save the drawing, you see the following message:

```
Updating Indexes for block *MODEL_SPACE
```

To stop saving the index in AutoCAD, choose File ➪ Save As. Choose Options. In the Saveas Options dialog box, choose None from the Index type drop-down list. Click OK once and then click Cancel. In AutoCAD LT, change the value of the INDEXCTL system variable to 0.

ON the DVD-ROM The drawings used in the following exercise on controlling xref display — ab19-a.dwg, ab19-b.dwg, ab19-01.dwg, and ab19-02.dwg — are in the Drawings and Results folders on the DVD.

STEPS: Controlling Xref Display

1. Open ab19-01.dwg from your AutoCAD Bible folder if you did the first exercise in this chapter.

   If you didn't do the first exercise in this chapter, use Windows Explorer to find ab19-b.dwg in the Drawings folder on the DVD and ab19-01.dwg and ab19-02.dwg in the Results folder on the DVD. Copy all three files to your AutoCAD Bible folder. In Windows Explorer, right-click each file and choose Properties. Uncheck the Read-Only option (if checked) and click OK. Then open ab19-01.dwg from your AutoCAD Bible folder. If you get a message that the drawing cannot find the xrefs, choose Tools ➪ Options and click Project Files Search Path on the Files tab. Click Add and add your AutoCAD Bible folder. You can click Browse to choose the folder from a dialog box.

2. **To create layer and spatial indexes, do one of the following:**

   ■ **If you have AutoCAD:** Choose File ➪ Save As. From the Tools menu of the dialog box, choose Options. In the Index type drop-down list of the Saveas Options dialog box, choose Layer & Spatial. Click OK. (It may already be set for these indexes.) Click Cancel.

   ■ **If you have AutoCAD LT:** On the command line, enter **indexctl** ↵. Then enter **3** ↵.

3. Choose Save from the Standard or Standard Annotation toolbar. Note the message on the command line that the indexes are being updated.

4. Close ab19-01.dwg.

5. Open ab19-02.dwg from your AutoCAD Bible folder. This drawing has an attached xref of a house plan and a nested xref of a title block, as shown in Figure 19.11.

6. Save it as `ab19-05.dwg` in your `AutoCAD Bible` folder.

7. Choose Tools ➪ Options and click the Open and Save tab. In the Demand Load Xrefs drop-down list, choose Enabled. (It may already be set to Enabled.) Click OK.

8. Click the Layer Control drop-down list. Click the On/Off icon next to the `Ab19-01|notes` layer to turn the layer back on. Click the top of the drop-down list box to close it. The notes layer displays.

FIGURE 19.11

Picking a polygonal boundary to clip an xref.

9. In AutoCAD only, choose Clip Xref from the Reference toolbar or choose Modify ➪ Clip ➪ Xref to start the XCLIP command. (If you have AutoCAD LT, skip this step.) Follow the prompts:

```
Select objects: Pick anywhere on the xref in Figure 19.11.
Select objects: ↵
Enter clipping option
[ON/OFF/Clipdepth/Delete/generate Polyline/New boundary] <New>: ↵
Specify clipping boundary:
[Select polyline/Polygonal/Rectangular/Invert clip] <Rectangular>:
Right-click and choose Polygonal.
Specify first point: Pick ❶ in Figure 19.11. (It might help to turn
off OSNAP if it is on.)
Specify next point or [Undo]: Pick ❷.
Specify next point or [Undo]: Pick ❸.
Specify next point or [Undo]: Pick ❹.
```

```
Specify next point or [Undo]: Pick ❺.
Specify next point or [Undo]: Pick ❻.
Specify next point or [Undo]: Pick ❼.
Specify next point or [Undo]: Pick ❽.
Specify next point or [Undo]: Pick ❾.
Specify next point or [Undo]: Pick ❿.
Specify next point or [Undo]: ↵
```

This action clips the xref.

10. Turn off the `Ab19-01|notes` layer again.

11. Save your drawing. It should look like Figure 19.12. (If you have AutoCAD LT, you still see the entire xref.) Keep the drawing open if you're continuing on to the next exercise.

FIGURE 19.12

The clipped xref.

Managing Xrefs

If you have many xrefs in a drawing, you need a way to keep track of them and their relationships to your drawing. You have several techniques for managing xrefs. The External References palette, DesignCenter, and the xref notification feature are all tools to help you with this task.

 Though it may be obvious, the first principle of managing xrefs is to keep them simple. Overly complex nested configurations are hard to manage, no matter what you do.

The External References palette is designed to let you manage xrefs (as well as DWF and DGN underlays, and images) from one place. The External References palette has its features explained in Table 19.2. You access these features by right-clicking a reference and choosing from the shortcut menu.

TABLE 19.2

External References Palette Features

Feature	What It Does		
Attach	Opens the External Reference dialog box so you can specify an xref to attach to your drawing, as explained earlier in this chapter.		
Detach	Detaches an xref. The xref is not displayed, and the xref definition is no longer saved in the drawing.		
Reload	Reloads the most recent version of the xref. Use this whenever the xref has changed during a session (because someone else on a networked system has edited the xref drawing) or after unloading an xref.		
Unload	Unloads the xref without detaching it. The xref is not displayed, but the xref definition is still saved in the drawing. You can then use Reload to display the xref again.		
Bind	Changes the xref to a block. Opens the Bind Xrefs dialog box, which enables you to choose to either bind or insert the xref.		
	Bind	When creating a block from the xref, this feature changes named layers, text styles, dimension styles, and so on (called *symbols*) from the format `xref_name|symbol_name` to `drawing_name$#$symbol_name`, where # is 0 if the same name does not exist in the current drawing or 1 if it already exists. In this way, no symbol names are duplicated. This method enables you to keep track of where the symbols came from.	
	Insert	When creating a block from the xref, this feature removes the `xref_name|` portion of symbol names. For example, if a layer of that name already exists in your drawing, objects on that layer take on the properties of that layer, as defined in your drawing. The same applies to text styles, dimension styles, and so on. This method removes the complexity that arises with the xref naming of these symbols.	
Open	Opens the selected xref in a new drawing window. (AutoCAD only.)		
Xref Found At	Specifies where the xref was actually found, which may be different from the saved path. You can then click Save Path to save the current path. If the location of an xref is changed and is not in the Support Files or Project Files search path, the status of the xref displays as Not Found. Use the Browse button to find and open the xref and click Save Path. Click OK to automatically reload the xref.		

NOTE   You cannot bind or detach nested xrefs without binding the parent xref.

 You can also click the Refresh button to refresh the selected reference, or use its down button to choose Reload All References.

AUTOCAD ONLY   Express Tools offer two commands that can help you work with xrefs. XLIST (choose Express ⇨ Blocks ⇨ List Xref/Block Properties) lists properties of xrefs and blocks such as object type, layer, object, and linetype. BLOCKTOXREF (choose Express ⇨ Blocks ⇨ Convert Block to Xref) replaces a block with an xref (that is, another drawing file).

Xref notification

If an xref is moved or renamed while you have it displayed in an open drawing, you need to reload it. An xref can change if someone else on your network opens and edits it while you're using it. External Reference Notification offers instant notification if an xref changes.

 When you open a drawing with an xref, the status bar displays the Manage Xrefs icon in the tray area at the right. When an xref changes, a "balloon message" or window appears to notify you, including the name of the drawing and the person who changed it, as shown in Figure 19.13. Click the link to reload the xref (or xrefs). If you want to open the External References palette, perhaps to choose which xrefs you want to reload, click the Manage Xrefs icon on the status bar.

FIGURE 19.13

If an xref changes, the balloon message appears on the status bar to notify you.

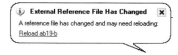

AUTOCAD ONLY In AutoCAD only, you can control and turn off notification using the XREFNOTIFY system variable.

DesignCenter

As explained in earlier chapters, you can use the DesignCenter to move named objects, including xrefs, from one drawing to another. (I cover the DesignCenter in detail in Chapter 26.) To insert an xref from another drawing, press Ctrl+2. Navigate to the drawing and double-click it to open the list of named objects. Double-click Xrefs to see a list of xrefs in the right pane, as shown in Figure 19.14.

FIGURE 19.14

You can use the DesignCenter to insert xrefs into your drawing.

Double-click the xref that you want to insert. The External Reference dialog box opens (refer to Figure 19.1) so that you can insert the xref. You can also right-click and choose Attach as Xref, or right-click and drag a drawing from the DesignCenter into your drawing.

The xref log file

If you set the XREFCTL system variable to 1 (by default, it's set to 0), a copy of all xref activity for your current drawing is saved in an ASCII text file. You can read the log to troubleshoot problems that may occur. Figure 19.15 shows part of an xref log file. The log file goes in the same folder as your drawing and uses your drawing name with the .xlg filename extension.

This file can become long. Therefore, once in a while, you should delete all or part of the file.

FIGURE 19.15

An xref log file.

CROSS-REF The Reference Manager is a stand-alone program that manages xrefs, images, fonts, and plot configurations, which are all outside files that are referenced in your drawing. See Chapter 26 for full coverage of the Reference Manager.

The drawing used in the following exercise on managing xrefs, ab19-05.dwg, is in the Results folder on the DVD.

STEPS: Managing Xrefs

1. Use ab19-05.dwg from your AutoCAD Bible folder if you did the previous exercise. Otherwise, open it from the Results folder of the DVD.

2. Save it as ab19-06.dwg in your AutoCAD Bible folder.

3. Do one of the following:

    ◾ **If you have AutoCAD:** Choose Modify ➪ Clip ➪ Xref. At the Select objects: prompt, pick the xref anywhere. Press Enter. At the Enter clipping option [ON/OFF/ Clipdepth/Delete/generate Polyline/New boundary] <New>: prompt, right-click and choose Delete to delete the clip and restore the entire view of both xrefs.

    ◾ **If you have AutoCAD LT:** If you did the previous exercise and opened ab19-05.dwg from your AutoCAD Bible folder, skip this step. If you opened ab19-05.dwg from the DVD, you have opened an AutoCAD drawing with a clipped xref. Because AutoCAD LT doesn't support clipping, you need to reattach the xref. Copy ab19-b.dwg from the \Drawings folder and ab19-01.dwg from the \Results folder (both on the DVD) to your AutoCAD Bible folder. Choose Insert ➪ External References. Choose ab19-01 and click Detach. Click Attach DWG. Select ab19-01.dwg from your AutoCAD Bible folder and click Open. In the External Reference dialog box, uncheck the Insertion Point, Scale, and Rotation Specify On-screen check boxes (if checked) and click OK to attach the xref.

4. Choose Insert ➪ External References. Click the Tree View button. Right-click ab19-b, the nested xref, and choose Unload.

5. Right-click ab19-b again. Choose Reload to reload the xref.

6. This time right-click ab19-01. Choose Bind. In the Bind Xrefs dialog box, choose Insert and click OK. This action inserts both xrefs (ab19-01 and ab19-b) as blocks. (Click the Layer Control drop-down list to see that there are no xref-type layer names.)

7. Save your drawing.

Working with DWF and DGN Underlays

You can use DWF files and DGN drawings as *underlays*, which are similar to xrefs. A DWF file is an accurate, compressed image representation of a drawing, and I explain how to create DWF files in Chapter 28. DGN files are drawings created with Bentley Microstation®, another CAD program.

Attaching a DWF underlay

Attaching a DWF file is similar to attaching an xref or inserting a block. To attach a DWF, follow these steps:

1. Choose Insert ➪ DWF Underlay (the DWFATTACH command).

2. In the Select DWF File dialog box, choose the DWF file and click Open.

3. In the Attach DWF Underlay dialog box, choose a sheet from the DWF file, if it contains more than one page.

4. From the Path Type drop-down list, choose the type of path:

   ▪ **Full path:** Specifies the full path of the xref drawing, including the drive letter (such as c:).

   ▪ **Relative path:** Specifies only part of the xref drawing's path, assuming the current drive or folder. This option enables you to move an xref to a different drive that has the same folder structure.

   ▪ **No path:** Uses the current folder of the host drawing. This option enables you to use an xref when you move the drawing, for example, when you send it to someone else with a different folder structure. To make sure that the drawing can find the xref, ensure that it is in the project files search path.

5. To specify the insertion point, scale, and rotation, uncheck the respective check boxes in the dialog box; otherwise, specify them on-screen.

6. Click OK to attach the DWF as an underlay.

If your current view does not show the entire underlay, use the ZOOM Extents command and option.

Adjusting a DWF underlay

You can change the appearance of the DWF underlay to make it more or less prominent, by using the DWFADJUST command. This command has three options:

■ **Fade:** Blends the underlay more or less with the background color. You can choose a value from 0 to 80, where 80 fades the underlay completely with the background. The default value is 25.

■ **Contrast:** Increases or decreases the contrast of the colors. The values range from 0 to 100, where 100 changes the colors to their closest primary or secondary color. The default is 75.

■ **Monochrome:** Displays the DWF as shades of gray. Choose Yes or No.

If you selected a single DWF underlay, the default values for Fade, Contrast, and Monochrome are the current property settings of the selected underlay. If you select multiple underlays, the default values for Fade, Contrast, and Monochrome remain as they were set the last time the command was used.

Clipping a DWF underlay

If the DWF underlay is large, you may not want to view all of it in your drawing. You can clip a DWF underlay in the same way that you can clip an xref or block, by using the DWFCLIP command. To access this command, select an underlay, right-click, and choose DWF Clip. The options are:

■ **ON:** Turns on an existing clipping boundary. By default, a clipping boundary is on.

■ **OFF:** Turns off an existing clipping boundary, so that you can see the entire DWF underlay.

■ **Delete:** Deletes a clipping boundary.

■ **New boundary:** Creates a new rectangular or polygonal clipping boundary.

Using a DWF underlay frame

You can frame the DWF underlay with a frame boundary or leave it without a frame. This is very similar to clipping an xref or block. If the DWF is not clipped, the frame shows the rectangular border of the entire DWF. If you clipped the DWF, the frame shows the clipping border.

To display a frame on a DWF underlay, use the DWFFRAME system variable and set its value to 1 (displays the frame and plots it) or 2 (displays the frame, but doesn't plot it). To turn off the frame, set the value to 0. Even with the frame turned off, you can select the DWF underlay.

Allow snapping to DWF object snaps

By default, you can snap to all object snaps in DWF underlays. If you need to use the object snaps of your underlay, this is the ideal setting. However, if you don't want to use them and find yourself getting "caught" on the underlay's object snaps, you can turn off this feature by setting the DWFOSNAP system variable's value to 0.

Note that even with DWFOSNAP set to 0, you can snap to the insertion point of the underlay.

NEW FEATURE AutoCAD 2008 allows you to control which layers you see for a DWF underlay. Note that this feature only works if you enable the publishing of layer information in the Publish Options dialog box when you create your DWF. See Chapter 28 for more information on DWF files.

Underlaying DGN files

To underlay a DGN file, choose Insert ➪ DGN Underlay, or choose Attach DGN from the Attach File dropdown list of the External References palette (the DGNATTACH command). The Select DGN File dialog box opens; select a DGN file and click Open. The Attach DGN Underlay dialog box opens, as shown in Figure 19.16.

FIGURE 19.16

The DGN Underlay dialog box lets you attach a Microstation drawing file as an underlay.

If the drawing has more than one model, choose the one you want to attach from the Select a Design Model from the DGN File list box. DGN files can have master units (Imperial or metric) and another set of units, called *sub units.* Choose which one you want to use. AutoCAD converts one unit (either master or sub) to one drawing unit. Click OK to attach the DGN underlay. You can allow or disallow snapping to object snaps on the underlay model. Select the object, right-click, and select or deselect the DGN Object Snap item on the shortcut menu. You can also turn this ability on or off at the command line with the DGNOSNAP command.

DGN underlays are different from xrefs in that you cannot control the display of layers, edit the file, or bind the file.

You can control visibility of the DGN by clipping it. Select the underlay, right-click, and choose DGN Clip (the DGNCLIP command). You then see prompts similar to the XCLIP command, which is discussed earlier in this chapter, but you can only create rectangular or polygonal boundaries.

When you select the DGN underlay and open the Properties palette, you can use the Underlay Adjust section to control the overall appearance of the underlay (the DGNADJUST command). You can increase or decrease the contrast and fade as well as display the underlay in monochrome.

Summary

In this chapter, I covered the techniques that you need to know to work with xrefs. You read about:

- Attaching and overlaying xrefs
- Opening an xref in its own window
- Editing xrefs and blocks from within the drawing in which they appear
- Clipping xrefs so that only the portion you need to see is displayed
- Setting spatial and layer indexes to speed up the display of large xrefs
- Deleting, unloading, and reloading xrefs
- Binding an xref to make it part of your drawing
- Working with DWF and DGN underlays

In the next chapter, I cover database connectivity, which enables you to access outside databases.

Chapter 20

Working with External Databases

The AutoCAD database connectivity feature enables you to communicate with an external database from within AutoCAD.

AUTOCAD ONLY AutoCAD LT does not include the database connectivity feature. This entire chapter applies to AutoCAD only.

Database connectivity is a powerful way to link drawing objects with data and is more flexible than using block attributes. With database connectivity, you can link data in an external database to any object in a drawing. In this chapter, I show you that database connectivity does not have to be as difficult as it often sounds.

Many AutoCAD users maintain databases separately from their drawings. You can work directly with your data by linking the rows of the database tables to objects in your drawings. The drawing objects thus become intelligent and carry these links with them in the drawing. You can also change data, such as a price or a part number, from within AutoCAD and have that change automatically applied and available in all drawing objects that are linked to that database item. Finally, you can create labels in your drawing, based on the data in the database.

CROSS-REF You can link to external Microsoft Excel spreadsheets and comma delimited (CSV) files in a table. For more information, see Chapter 13. Using that feature, you can view the external data and change it (both in the table and in Excel). Your table always displays the current data in the spreadsheet. However, the external database access feature described in this chapter offers some additional capabilities, such as linking rows of data to objects in your drawing, creating labels, and creating SQL queries.

Understanding External Database Access

Many organizations maintain extensive databases of objects that are in your AutoCAD drawings. Manufacturers maintain databases of parts, offices maintain databases of furniture, and so on. You need to keep your drawings and the databases synchronized so that the information in the databases and in the drawings is always accurate and up to date.

The linking of databases and AutoCAD drawings is referred to as *external database access*. External database access enables you to:

- Create links between AutoCAD drawing objects and the external data
- View data in external databases
- Edit data in external databases
- Display external database data in your drawing

The database connectivity feature works with the following databases:

- Microsoft Access
- dBASE
- Microsoft Excel
- Oracle
- Paradox
- Microsoft Visual FoxPro
- SQL Server

After you configure a database, as explained later in this chapter, you can access the data in the database even if you don't have the database program that created the data.

A *database* is a set of related information, usually maintained by a database management system (DBMS) — an application that manages databases. A database is stored in the form of a table that contains rows and columns. A row, also called a *record,* contains one element of data, such as the information for one desk. A column, also called a *field,* contains the attributes of the data, such as the price.

Table 20.1 shows the first three rows of the database used as an example in this chapter.

TABLE 20.1

A Simple Database Table

Part Number	Description	Dwg Size	Made/Purchased	Units
8665-023-012	Welding Wire — 0.030 StainlessB	B	P	FT
8665-023-013	Weld Rod — 0.045 Dia Stainless Steel	B	P	FT
8665-023-014	Welding — Rod 0.045 Dia S.S.	B	P	FT

A *relational database* is a type of database that contains a collection of tables. Each table represents a set of data for a defined use.

Structured Query Language (SQL — pronounced *sequel* or *S-Q-L*) was created to provide users with a database language that would be applicable across multiple platforms and database-management programs.

Some database systems use environments, catalogs, schemas, and tables to create a hierarchy of *database objects*. A database object is simply the term used to specify any of the following SQL2 objects: environment, catalog, schema, or table.

- The *environment* is the entire database system — the DBMS, the databases it can access, the users, and the programs that can access those databases.

- A *catalog* is a collection of schemas and has the same name as the folder where the database is located.

- A *schema* is a set of tables and other database components. It has the same name as the catalog subfolder where the database tables reside.

You don't need to work with these concepts if your database system does not require or specify it. AutoCAD can connect to an individual table or to a collection of tables stored in an environment, catalog, or schema.

Preparing for Database Connectivity

Database connectivity involves several components that you need to prepare in advance. When they are in place, the connection should go smoothly. In this section, I explain the necessary preparation steps.

The basic steps for starting to work with database connectivity are as follows:

1. Make sure that you have the ODBC Data Source program from Microsoft.
2. Arrange your database tables into catalogs (folders) and schemas (subfolders) appropriate for your application, if necessary.
3. Configure the appropriate database driver using Microsoft's ODBC (Open Database Connectivity) or OLE DB programs.
4. Configure your data source from within AutoCAD.
5. Start the dbCONNECT command.
6. Establish a user access name and password, if required by the database system.
7. Connect to your data source.
8. Open the Data View window containing your data table.
9. Edit the data, if desired.
10. Link database rows to objects in your drawing.
11. Create labels based on the data in your drawing, if desired.

Organizing the database structure

To connect to a database, you need to know the type of database-management system that created the database and the structure of the database itself, along with the folders that contain that structure.

In the following exercise, you create a simple structure for a Microsoft Access database table.

639

In this chapter, you cannot do the later exercises without doing the earlier ones. The later exercises depend on the setup and configuration that you create in the earlier exercises.

The file used in the following exercise on creating the structure for the database, `ab20-prt.mdb`, is in the `Drawings` folder on the DVD.

STEPS: Creating the Structure for the Database

1. Right-click Start on the task bar. Choose Explore to open Windows Explorer.

2. If your `AutoCAD Bible` folder is not displayed in the Folders window, click the plus sign (+) next to the drive containing the `AutoCAD Bible` folder.

3. Click the `AutoCAD Bible` folder and choose File ➪ New ➪ Folder from the Explorer menu. (In Windows Vista, click Organize ➪ New Folder.) A new folder appears in the right window, called `New Folder`. Type **Databases** ↵ to rename the folder.

4. If necessary, in the Folders window, click the plus sign to open the `AutoCAD Bible` folder. You should see the new `Databases` folder. (If not, press F5 to refresh the Explorer view.)

5. From the DVD, copy `ab20-prt.mdb` to the `Databases` folder that you just created. (Be sure to choose the `ab20-prt.mdb` file, not the `ab20-prt.xls` file.) The `.mdb` file is a database of parts. Figure 20.1 shows this database.

FIGURE 20.1

The Microsoft Access database.

PART_NO	DESCRIPTION	DWG_SIZE	MADE/PUR	UNITS	A
8665-023-012	WELDING WIRE	B	P	FT	
8665-023-013	WELD ROD - .04	B	P	FT	
8665-023-014	WELDING - ROD	B	P	FT	
8665-023-015	WELDING ROD	B	P	FT	
8665-023-016	WELDING ROD	B	P	FT	
8665-023-017	WELD ROD - .05	B	P	FT	
8665-073-042	NIPPLE - 1.2 X 2	C	P	EACH	
8685-079-000	TAPE	A	P	IN	
8685-092-000	TAPE - TEFLON	A	P	IN	
8685-097-002	TAPE	B	P	IN	
8685-097-003	TAPE	B	P	IN	
8685-097-004	TAPE - STRAPPI	B	P	IN	
8685-117-001	TAPE		P	IN	
8685-118-001	TAPE - DUCT	A	P	FT	
8685-119-001	TAPE - FOAM, [	B	P	IN	
8688-003-000	PIN - DOWELL	A	P	EACH	
8697-003-000	GAUGE - PRESS	A	P	EACH	
8711-001-001	TRANSFORMER	B	P	EACH	
8711-002-001	TRANSFORMER	C	P	EACH	
8711-002-002	TRANSFORMER	C	P	EACH	
8711-003-001	TRANSFORMER	C	P	EACH	
8711-003-002	TRANSFORMER	C	P	EACH	
8711-003-003	TRANSFORMER	C	P	EACH	
8711-004-001	TRANSFORMER	C	P	EACH	
8711-005-001	TRANSFORMER		P	EACH	

Record: 1 of 157   No Filter   Search

Thanks to Gary Morris of the Dexter Company, Fairfield, Iowa, for this database.

6. Because this file is coming from a DVD, you may need to change its read-only property. Still in Explorer, right-click `ab20-prt.mdb` and choose Properties from the menu. Uncheck Read-Only and click OK.

7. Click the Close button of Explorer to close it.

> **NOTE** If you have Microsoft Access 2007, you may want to open this database in Access and convert it to 2007 format. When you open the database, you'll automatically see a dialog box prompting you to convert the file.

Configuring a data source

To start working with external databases, you must tell AutoCAD how to communicate with your database, called a *data source*. AutoCAD uses ODBC and OLE DB for this communication. AutoCAD provides a sample Microsoft Access file, called `db_samples.mdb` in AutoCAD's `Sample` folder, that you can work with to get started.

First, you must install and configure the ODBC Data Source Administrator. To check if the ODBC Data Source Administrator is installed on your computer, open the Control Panel by choosing Start ⇨ Settings ⇨ Control Panel (or as required by your operating system), and look for one of the following items:

■ ODBC Data Sources (32-bit) or Data Sources (ODBC)

■ Administrative Tools ⇨ Data Sources (ODBC)

To check if you have the required drivers installed, double-click the ODBC item. In the ODBC Data Source Administrator dialog box, you'll see a list of database application drivers. Check to see that your database application is listed. A database driver contains information about how to connect to your database. In most cases, your operating system will include the ODBC Administrator. If you don't have the ODBC 32-bit Administrator, you need to install the Microsoft ODBC Driver Pack. The ODBC Driver Pack 3.0 (or later) is free from the Microsoft Web site at `msdn2.microsoft.com/en-us/data/aa937730.aspx`. The MDAC (Microsoft Data Access Components) 2.8 download should provide you with everything you need.

> **CAUTION** The 64-bit release of AutoCAD does not support these drivers for connectivity to Microsoft Access and Excel databases. The solution is to use SQL Server instead of the OLE DB driver. For more information, check AutoCAD Help in the AutoCAD 2008 Driver and Peripheral Guide ⇨ Configure External Databases. Microsoft has more information changes in its support for database access at `msdn.microsoft.com/library/default.asp?url=/library/en-us/mdacsdk/htm/mdac_deprecated_components.asp`.

The instructions to set up the database vary according to the drivers that you use. The AutoCAD online help contains help on all supported databases. Look in Help ⇨ Help and click the Contents tab. Double-click Driver and Peripheral Guide and then Configure External Databases. Click the Procedures tab and choose the link for your database.

To set up your database using ODBC, follow these steps:

1. From the Windows task bar, choose Start ⇨ Settings ⇨ Control Panel (or Start ⇨ Control Panel).

2. Double-click the Administrative Tools icon, and then double-click the Data Sources (ODBC) item. Windows opens the ODBC Data Source Administrator dialog box, shown in Figure 20.2.

3. Click the User DSN tab if it isn't already displayed. Choose Add.

4. In the Create New Data Source dialog box, choose the driver appropriate for your database and click Finish.

FIGURE 20.2

Use the ODBC Data Source Administrator dialog box, accessed from the Windows Control Panel, to choose a database driver to connect to your database.

5. In the ODBC Setup dialog box, which is now titled with the name of the driver that you chose (for example, ODBC Microsoft Access Setup), type a name for your data source in the Data Source Name text box. You can also add a description. In general, this name refers to your database program, not the individual database file.

6. Click Select and navigate to the folder containing your database. Choose the database file and click OK.

7. Click OK again in the Setup dialog box.

8. In the ODBC Data Source Administrator dialog box, your data source is listed with its appropriate driver. Click OK. Close the Administrative Tools window and the Control Panel.

You're now ready to configure your database from within AutoCAD. Follow these steps:

1. Choose Tools ➪ Palettes ➪ dbConnect to open the dbConnect Manager palette and display the dbConnect menu.

2. From the menu, choose dbConnect ➪ Data Sources ➪ Configure. (The dbConnect menu appears when you start dbConnect.) In the Configure a Data Source dialog box, type a name representing your database file. Click OK.

3. On the Provider tab of the Data Link Properties dialog box, choose Microsoft OLE DB Provider for ODBC drivers. Click Next.

4. From the Use Data Source Name drop-down list on the Connection tab, choose the name of the data source that you used in the ODBC Setup dialog box, as shown in Figure 20.3.

5. For server-based databases, enter the user name and password.

6. Click Test Connection. You should see a message saying Test Connection Succeeded. (If not, check your settings as well as the spelling and case of the name of the data source.) Click OK.

7. Click OK in the Data Link Properties dialog box.

FIGURE 20.3

Use the Data Link Properties dialog box to configure your data source within AutoCAD.

You're now ready to establish a connection between a database and an AutoCAD drawing.

ON the DVD-ROM The drawing used in the following exercise on configuring a Microsoft Access database, ab20-a.dwg, is in the Drawings folder on the DVD. This exercise requires that you have completed the steps in the previous exercises.

STEPS: Configuring a Microsoft Access Database

1. From the task bar, choose Start ➪ Settings ➪ Control Panel (or Start ➪ Control Panel). Double-click the Administrative Tools icon, and then double-click the Data Sources (ODBC) icon. (Your item may have a slightly different name.)

2. On the User DSN tab of the ODBC Data Source Administrator dialog box, choose Add.

3. In the Create New Data Source dialog box, choose Microsoft Access Driver (*.mdb), or Microsoft Access 12.0 Driver (*.mdb, *.accdb) if you have Microsoft Access 2007. Choose Finish.

4. In the Data Source Name text box of the ODBC Microsoft Access Setup dialog box, type **ab20-Access**.

5. Click Select and navigate to your AutoCAD Bible\Databases folder (which you created in the previous exercise). Choose ab20-prt.mdb and click OK.

6. Click OK twice more to exit the ODBC Data Source Administrator.

7. Close the Administrative Tools and Control Panel windows.

8. Open AutoCAD. Open ab20-a.dwg from the DVD. Save it as ab20-01.dwg in your AutoCAD Bible folder.

9. Choose Tools ⇨ Palettes ⇨ dbConnect to open the dbConnect Manager palette and display the dbConnect menu. From the menu, choose dbConnect ⇨ Data Sources ⇨ Configure. In the Configure a Data Source dialog box, type **ab20-prt**. Click OK.

10. On the Provider tab of the Data Link Properties dialog box (which opens automatically), choose Microsoft OLE DB Provider for ODBC Drivers. Click Next.

11. From the Use Data Source Name drop-down list, choose ab20-Access.

12. Click Test Connection. You see a message saying `Test Connection Succeeded`. Click OK.

13. Click OK in the Data Link Properties dialog box.

14. Keep `ab20-01.dwg` open for the next exercise.

Connecting to an Excel Spreadsheet

If you have a database in Excel and want to practice working with Excel, you can use the Excel spreadsheet database on the DVD. Remember that you can also connect to Excel data from a table, as I explain in Chapter 13. Here's how to connect to Excel data using the external database access feature:

1. Follow the steps in the exercise "Creating the Structure for the Database." In Step 5, copy the `ab20-prt.xls` file instead of the `.mdb` file. If necessary, uncheck the read-only property as described in Step 6.

2. Double-click the Administrative Tools, then Data Sources (ODBC) icons in the Control Panel to open the ODBC Data Source Administrator dialog box.

3. On the User DSN tab of the ODBC Data Source Administrator dialog box, choose Add.

4. In the Create New Data Source dialog box, choose Microsoft Excel Driver (*.xls) and choose Finish.

5. In the ODBC Microsoft Excel Setup dialog box, type **ab Excel** as the Data Source Name. (If you want, type a description.)

6. Click Select Workbook. Use the dialog box to choose the `AutoCAD Bible\databases\ ab20-prt.xls` worksheet. Click OK three times and close the Control Panel.

7. Open AutoCAD. Open `ab20-a.dwg` from the DVD. Save it as `ab20-01.dwg` in your `AutoCAD Bible` folder. Choose Tools ⇨ Palettes ⇨ dbConnect.

8. Choose dbConnect ⇨ Data Sources ⇨ Configure. In the Configure a Data Source dialog box, type **ab Excel.** Click OK.

9. On the Provider tab of the Data Link Properties dialog box, choose Microsoft OLE DB Provider for ODBC drivers. Click Next.

10. From the upper drop-down list, choose ab Excel.

11. Click Test Connection. At the `Test Connection Succeeded` message, click OK.

12. Click OK in the Data Link Properties dialog box.

You can continue the rest of the exercises, starting from "Connecting a Database to a Drawing," without change.

The equivalent of a table in Excel is a *named range.* You need to open your worksheet, select all of the data, and type a range name in the Name box at the left end of the Formula bar. To set up the database, put a field name in the first row of each column.

Connecting to Your Database

After you configure the database connectivity feature, you're ready to connect to your database. Here you actually start making connections between objects in your drawing and rows in your database.

Before connecting to your database, you should think about the relationship between the drawing and the database. For example, you should decide:

- If the data is to be in one database with many tables or in several separate databases
- Which data you want to link to which drawing objects
- If several drawing objects will be linked to one row or only one object will be linked to a row
- If you want a drawing object linked to more than one row
- Which column(s) will identify unique records

You're now ready to connect your database to your drawing.

Connecting a database to a drawing

You use the dbConnect Manager, shown in Figure 20.4, to perform all of the connectivity functions. The dbConnect Manager has its own toolbar, which becomes active when you choose a connected data source. All configured data sources are listed.

You can dock and undock the dbConnect Manager like any palette. You can also resize it by dragging its right border left or right. After you open the dbConnect Manager, you see a list of open drawings and configured data sources.

Follow these steps to connect an external database to a drawing:

1. Open the drawing that you want to connect with a database.
2. Choose Tools ➪ Palettes ➪ dbConnect (or press Ctrl+6) to open the dbConnect Manager.
3. Right-click the data source to which you want to connect. (The names listed come from the names that you entered when you configured the data source in AutoCAD.) Choose Connect.

FIGURE 20.4

The dbConnect Manager.

AutoCAD lists the database tables associated with the data source. The entire database structure is now connected, and you can view and work with the database data within AutoCAD. In order to do the following exercise, you must have completed the previous two exercises.

STEPS: Connecting a Database to a Drawing

1. You should have `ab20-01.dwg` open from the previous exercise.
2. Choose Tools ➪ Palettes ➪ dbConnect to open the dbConnect Manager.
3. Right-click `ab20-prt` and choose Connect. The dbConnect Manager lists the database table PART NO.
4. Save the drawing. Keep it open. Continue to the next exercise.

Opening a data table

After your database is connected, you choose the database table with which you want to work. If necessary, click the plus sign next to the desired database to see the actual database files that are available. The database file also displays a plus sign. If necessary, click it to display the database tables within the database file. (A database file can contain more than one table.)

You can view or edit a table in the Data View window:

- View the data when you have no need to edit it. To view your data, right-click the table that you want to view and choose View Table.
- Edit the data when you need to make changes to your database from within AutoCAD. To edit your data, right-click and choose Edit Table.

To view or edit a table, select the table. Choose View Table or Edit Table from the dbConnect Manager's toolbar. You can also right-click the table and choose View Table or Edit Table from the shortcut menu.

Figure 20.5 shows the Data View window when you choose Edit Table. (When you choose View Table, you see the same view but the data cells are gray.)

The Data View window presents your data in a grid, with each piece of data in a cell, like a spreadsheet. You can use the scroll bars to scroll through the data. To the left of the horizontal scroll bar, you can use the arrows to move from record to record. The far left and right arrows with a vertical bar move you to the first and last record, respectively.

When you open the Data View window, a new Data View item appears on the AutoCAD menu.

You can temporarily change the way the data is displayed. These changes are discarded after you close the Data View window; they don't affect the data file in your database. Here are your options:

- **Resize a column:** You may find that your data doesn't completely display in a column or that columns don't all appear in the window. Click the grid line to the right of any column header and drag it to the left or right. You can also resize the entire Data View window by dragging on its sides or bottom.
- **Move a column:** You can change the order of the columns by moving a column to another location. Click the column's header to select the column. Then click and drag the column to the location you want. A black vertical line indicates where the column will land.
- **Hide a column:** You can hide a column with which you don't need to work. This is especially helpful if you have many columns and can't fit them easily on the screen. Click the column's header to select the column. Then right-click the column header and choose Hide. To redisplay the column, right-click any column header and choose Unhide All.

■ **Sort records:** You can sort records in ascending (low to high) or descending (high to low) order. Sorting helps you to more easily find the records that you want. Right-click any column header and choose Sort to open the Sort dialog box, shown in Figure 20.6. In the Sort By drop-down list, choose the column that you want to sort by first. Then choose Ascending or Descending. This column may have duplicate records. If so, you may want to choose a secondary column for sorting in the Then By drop-down list. Choose Ascending or Descending for the secondary column. AutoCAD will then sort first by the first column and then by the secondary column. You can choose up to five columns to sort by.

■ **Freeze one or more columns:** Freezing one or more contiguous columns moves them to the left column. Select the columns by clicking their column headers. (Press Ctrl to select additional columns. You can also select one column, press Shift, and select another column to select all of the columns in-between.) Then right-click a selected column and choose Freeze. To return the column to its original location, right-click and choose Unfreeze All.

■ **Align text:** You can align text in a column or columns. By default, columns use the Standard alignment, which right-aligns numbers and left-aligns everything else. Select a column or columns by clicking the column header(s), right-click any column header, and choose Align. Then choose Standard, Left, Center, or Right.

■ **Format text:** You can format the font, font style, font size, effects (strikethrough and underline), and color of the text in the Data View window. Note that, unlike the other changes previously listed, these changes continue to affect the formatting of the Data View window the next time you open a Data View window. Choose Data View ➪ Format to open the Format dialog box. Choose the formatting that you want and then click OK.

TIP To get the Data View window out of the way, you can dock it. Right-click in the Data View window's toolbar area and choose Allow Docking. Then drag the window to the right edge of your screen (assuming your dbConnect window is on the left side of your screen).

FIGURE 20.5

The Data View window displays your data.

Grid header   Column header

Record header

FIGURE 20.6

Use the Sort dialog box to temporarily sort your data in the Data View window.

Although you can scroll through your data's records, if you have many records, this can be time-consuming. You can search for a particular record by specifying a desired value. Follow these steps:

1. Select any cell in the column that contains the record that you want to find. If you want to search the entire column, choose the first or last cell in the column.

2. Choose Data View ⇨ Find to open the Find dialog box, shown in Figure 20.7. (You can also right-click any cell in the column and choose Find.)

FIGURE 20.7

The Find dialog box.

3. In the Find what box, type a value (text, numbers, or a combination). Choose to search either Up (from the selected cell to the first record) or Down (from the selected cell to the last record). If desired, choose Match Case. Then click Find Next to find the next instance of the value. Continue to click Find Next to move to the next matching record.

> **TIP** If you want, you can copy your formatting, including sorting, to the Clipboard and paste it into your DBMS. To do this, select the records that you want to export. To export the entire database, click the grid header. Then right-click any cell and choose Copy. Open your DBMS and click Paste from the Standard toolbar.

In the following exercise, you practice using the Data View window.

STEPS: Working with the Data View Window

1. Ab20-01.dwg should still be open from the previous exercise. If there's a plus sign next to ab20-prt, click it to display the "PART NO" table. The dbConnect Manager should look similar to Figure 20.8.

Displaying a database table in the dbConnect Manager palette.

2. Right-click the table icon and choose Edit Table. The Data View window opens.
3. From the menu, choose Data View ➪ Format. (A new Data View menu item has appeared.) In the Format dialog box, choose Arial as the font and 10 as the font size. Click OK.
4. The columns are too wide and you can't see all of them. Click the grid line to the right of the PART_NO column and drag it to the left so that the width of the column just fits the width of the part numbers. Do the same with the other columns. (You can also double-click the grid line between columns to automatically resize the column to the left to the widest value.) To access the right grid line of the last column (UNITS), expand the right side of the entire window. Then resize the UNITS column and shrink the Data View window to fit. Your Data View table should look like Figure 20.9.
5. Right-click the PART_NO column's header and choose Align ➪ Right to right-align the first column.
6. To practice moving around the table, click the right-most arrow at the bottom of the Data View window (to the left of the horizontal scroll bar) to move to the last record. Use the vertical scroll bar to scroll through the database and get an idea of its contents. Click any cell. Click a row header to select an entire row. Click a column header to select an entire column.
7. To sort the records by description and help you to find all of the angles, right-click the DESCRIP-TION column header and choose Sort. In the Sort dialog box, choose DESCRIPTION from the Sort By drop-down list, and then click Ascending (if it's not already selected). Because there are a number of duplicate records in the DESCRIPTION column, choose PART_NO in the Then By drop-down list, which should also be sorted in ascending order. Click OK. AutoCAD sorts the data by description, and then by part number.
8. Say that you want to find part number 9003-242-001. Right-click the top cell in the PART_NO column. Choose Find. In the Find dialog box, type **9003-242-001** and choose Down in the Direction section. Click Find Next. AutoCAD highlights the cell containing that part number.
9. Close the Find dialog box and save your drawing. Keep it open for the next exercise.

FIGURE 20.9

The Data View table after some formatting.

Editing data in the Data View window

After you open your data in Edit mode, you can easily edit the data. You can change the value of any record. You can add or delete records to reflect new or deleted objects in your drawing. Changing a record is as simple as selecting a cell and typing a new value.

To add a new record, right-click any record (row) header and choose Add New Record. AutoCAD opens up a space for a new record at the end of the list of records. Type the data for the new record, tabbing from column to column. (You can also use the right-arrow key to move to the next column.)

To delete a record, right-click the record header of the record that you want to delete, selecting the entire record. Choose Delete Record. You need to confirm the deletion in the dialog box that pops up.

CAUTION You should not use the DBMS to edit a database separately while it is connected to AutoCAD. If you do edit the database table outside of AutoCAD during an AutoCAD connection, you may get system crashes or corrupted data. If you need to edit the database using the DBMS, make sure that you disconnect the table first in the dbConnect Manager palette.

AutoCAD doesn't save your changes until you commit them. To save your changes, right-click the *grid header* — the cell at the top-left corner of the Data View window — and choose Commit. To discard your changes, choose Restore, which restores the original values of the database when you opened the Data View window.

STEPS: Editing Data

1. With ab20-01.dwg and the Data View window still open from the previous exercise, the part number that you found in the previous exercise (9003-242-001) should still be highlighted. If not, find it following the instructions in Step 8 of the previous exercise.

2. Note that the MADE/PUR column indicates that this horizontal angle is purchased. Say that the company has decided to make this angle. Click the P in the MADE/PUR column of the 9003-242-001 record and type **M.**

3. To add a record, right-click any record (row) header and choose Add New Record. AutoCAD moves you to the end of the records with a space for a new record. Type the following, tabbing between each column:

    ```
    8665-023-018    WELDING ROD - .05 DIA S.S.    B    P    FT
    ```

4. I don't recommend saving the changes to the database because you may want to do this exercise again in the future. Right-click the grid header (in the upper-left corner of the database) and choose Restore. AutoCAD closes the Data View window.

5. Keep the drawing open for the next exercise.

Linking Data to Drawing Objects

The main purpose of using data connectivity is to link data to objects in your drawing. A row of data contains information about the real-life object that objects in your drawing represent. By connecting a row of data to an object or objects in your drawing, you can:

■   View information about the real-life object while in your drawing, such as price, source, next service date, and so on.

■   Update a drawing based on changes in the database or vice versa, to keep your drawings and your database synchronized.

■   Display a label containing data information next to a drawing object.

Creating a link template

When AutoCAD creates a link, it associates an object or objects with a row in your database. To do so, AutoCAD needs to know which field (column) to look in to identify the row. For example, let's say you want to link price information to some objects. However, several rows may contain the same price information. If you provide a field that contains no duplicate data, AutoCAD can always locate the required row. If AutoCAD finds two rows with the same data, it accesses the first row. It makes sense, therefore, to be careful to choose a column that contains no duplicate values. If your data doesn't contain such a column, most DBMSs can create an index field that ensures that each row is unique.

A *link template* identifies which fields are associated with a link between the data and a drawing object. A link template also identifies your database. After you create a link template, you can open your data directly from the template, which is listed in the dbConnect window.

If you want to associate data from more than one database table to a single object, you may need to create more than one link template for an object.

To create a link template, follow these steps:

1. Choose dbConnect ➪ Templates ➪ New Link Template.

2. If you haven't already opened a data table, AutoCAD opens the Select Data Object dialog box. Choose a table and click Continue.

3. In the New Link Template Name text box of the New Link Template dialog box, shown in Figure 20.10, type a name for the link template. AutoCAD assigns an automatic name using the name of the data source and Link1, Link2, and so on. You can use that name or type your own. If you have a previous link template that you want to use as a basis for the new template, choose it from the Start with Template drop-down list. Click Continue.

FIGURE 20.10

The New Link Template dialog box.

4. In the Link Template dialog box, check a key field. If the key field that you choose contains any duplicate rows, you should choose a second key field.

5. Click OK. AutoCAD creates the link template, which is added to the dbConnect Manager palette beneath the current drawing.

You're now ready to link data with drawing objects.

If the structure of your database changes dramatically, you may need to edit a link template. For example, a field that contained no duplicate entries might now contain some. Other changes requiring a change in the template would be a change in the name or length of a field. To edit a link template:

1. Connect to the desired database table.

2. Choose dbConnect ⇨ Templates ⇨ Edit Link Template.

3. In the Select a Database Object dialog box, choose a link template.

4. Click Continue.

5. Check one (or more) of the key fields and click OK.

You can also delete a link template by choosing dbConnect ⇨ Templates ⇨ Delete Link Template.

This exercise requires that you have completed the previous exercises in this chapter.

STEPS: Creating a Link Template

1. Continue with ab20-01.dwg from the previous exercise. In the dbConnect window, right-click "PART NO" and choose Edit Table to open the Data View window.

2. Choose dbConnect ⇨ Templates ⇨ New Link Template.

3. Select the PART_NO table and click Continue.

4. In the New Link Template dialog box, use AutoCAD's suggested name, _PART_NO_Link1. Click Continue.

5. In the Link Template dialog box, check PART_NO. This column contains no duplicate rows.

6. Click OK to return to the drawing. You see the new link template with a chain-link icon in the dbConnect Manager palette just under the name of the open drawing.

7. Save your drawing. Leave it open to continue with the next exercise.

You're now ready to link drawing objects to your database.

Creating a link

You can link a drawing object to as many records in a database as you want, and you can link one database record to several drawing objects. For example, you may want to link a record containing part-number information to the part in the drawing. However, that part may be made up of a number of objects, such as lines, arcs, and circles. You can link the record to all of those objects in your drawing that make up the part. On the other hand, if you have a database of office equipment, you may attach a row representing telephone numbers and telephones to an object in your drawing representing a phone. However, if someone has a two-line phone, you may need to attach two rows to that one telephone object in your drawing.

Here's how to create a link:

1. Open a Data View window that has a defined link template and choose a link template from the Select a Link Template drop-down list at the top of the window.
2. Select one or more records that you want to link to your drawing.
3. Choose Data View ⇨ Link and Label Settings ⇨ Create Links.
4. Choose Data View ⇨ Link! (You can also choose Link in the Data View window.)
5. AutoCAD returns you to your drawing. Select one or more objects and press Enter to end object selection.

AutoCAD provides a message on the command line, for example: 1 Record(s) linked with 1 Object(s). You now have a link between your data and your drawing.

CAUTION   If you create a link between a drawing object and a row and in a later session of AutoCAD edit that object without connecting to the database table, the link information may become corrupted.

You can delete a link by selecting a linked object and right-clicking in the drawing area. From the shortcut menu, choose Link ⇨ Delete Link.

Viewing linked objects and rows

After you create a link, you need to be able to see which rows are linked to which objects before you can make decisions regarding either the data or the drawing objects. You can view the link from either side. That is, you can select an object and see which row or rows it is linked to or you can select a row and have AutoCAD select the object or objects to which it's linked. In both cases, you need to have a Data View table displayed.

- To find out which row an object is linked to, select one or more objects. Then choose Data View ⇨ View Linked Records. AutoCAD highlights the row or rows that are linked to the selection set of objects. Later in this section, I explain how to customize the display of a row or rows.

- To find out which object a row is linked to, select one or more records. Choose Data View ⇨ View Linked Objects. AutoCAD pans, zooms (or does both so that you can see the objects in the center of the screen), and selects them. Later in this section, I explain how to customize the panning and zooming.

You'll find that the Data View window obscures your drawing. You can drag it to the bottom of your screen, resize it, or dock it.

TIP   When you use View Linked Objects, the selected objects form a selection set. You can then use the results with other commands that allow prior selection of objects. For commands that you must execute before selecting objects, type **p** ⏎ at the Select objects: prompt to use the Previous option and get the selection set.

If you want to move from object to object or row to row to view your links one after another, you should use Auto-View. The Auto-View feature automatically highlights either objects when you choose a row in the Data View window or rows when you choose objects in your drawing. However, you can work from only one side of the equation — either rows or objects — at a time. Here's how it works:

- To automatically select linked objects when you select a row, choose Data View ➪ AutoView Linked Objects (or use the AutoView Linked Objects in Drawing button in the Data View window). Then select a record (or records) by clicking the row header(s) in the Data View window. AutoCAD highlights the linked objects. You can continue to select different records to highlight their linked objects. Choose Auto-View Linked Objects (or click the button) again to turn off Auto-View.

- To automatically select linked rows when you select an object, choose Data View ➪ AutoView Linked Records (or use the AutoView Linked Records in Data View button in the Data View window). Then select an object (or objects). AutoCAD highlights the linked rows. You can continue to select different objects to highlight their linked rows. Choose Auto-View Linked Records (or click the button) again to turn off Auto-View.

When you're in Auto-View, you can't select records. If you click another record's row header to create a link, AutoCAD just tells you 0 Object(s) found matching 0 selected Record(s). Be sure to turn off Auto-View when you go on to another task.

You can customize how AutoCAD displays linked rows and how AutoCAD pans (AutoPan) and zooms (AutoZoom) to display selected objects. Choose Data View ➪ Settings. In the Record Indication Settings section of the Data View and Query Options dialog box, choose either Show Only Indicated Records or Show All Records, Select Only Indicated Records (the default). You can also choose the highlight color. To set AutoPan and AutoZoom, use the AutoPan and Zoom section of the same dialog box. Uncheck Automatically Pan Drawing and Automatically Zoom Drawing if you don't want this feature. When Automatically Zoom Drawing is checked, you can also choose a zoom percentage. You can choose from 20 to 90 percent. The default, 50 percent, means that the height (or width, if less) of the extents of the zoomed area is 50 percent of the drawing area. Click OK after you finish using the dialog box.

Editing links

After you create links in your drawing, you need to be careful how you edit your database from within AutoCAD. For example, you don't want to inadvertently delete a record that is linked to an object.

You may need to edit the key value assigned to a linked object. For example, your company may change the part-numbering scheme or you may have simply assigned the wrong part number to an object. The Link Manager enables you to edit key values for linked objects. Follow these steps:

1. Choose dbConnect ➪ Links ➪ Link Manager to open the Link Manager, shown in Figure 20.11. You can also select a linked object, right-click in the drawing area, and choose Link ➪ Link Manager.
2. At the Select an object: prompt, select an object.
3. In the Link Manager, choose the Link Template that you want to work with from the drop-down list.
4. In the Value column, type a new value, such as a new part number.
5. Click OK.

AutoCAD updates the link.

You can also click the Delete button to delete the object's link.

FIGURE 20.11

The Link Manager enables you to edit key value data for its linked object.

Exporting link information

You can export a list of links and the handle of the associated links' objects. A *handle* is a unique name that AutoCAD gives to each object in the drawing. (To view an object's handle, select it and choose Tools ⇨ Inquiry ⇨ List.) You can export the reports in the same format as your database (called the *native format*) or in space- or comma-delimited formats. You might use these reports to keep track of how many objects are linked to a row because the exported information tells you how many instances a drawing contains of a record in a database. For example, if your database lists configurations of desktop computers and you've linked each person's computer to the appropriate row in the database, the list will let you know how many people have each configuration.

Follow these steps to export links:

1. Choose dbConnect ⇨ Links ⇨ Export Links.
2. At the Select objects: prompt, choose the objects whose links you want to export. When you complete object selection, AutoCAD opens the Export Links dialog box, shown in Figure 20.12.

FIGURE 20.12

The Export Links dialog box.

3. In the Include Fields section, select the fields that you want to include.

4. In the Save In drop-down list, navigate to the folder where you want to save the file.

5. In the Save as Type drop-down list, choose one of the three options: comma-delimited format, space-delimited format, or native database format.

6. In the File Name text box, type a name for the file.

7. Click Save.

   AutoCAD creates the file.

You can use this file to create a schedule of objects with links — but it takes some work. The comma-delimited format seems to work better than the space-delimited format. You'll probably want to edit the file first to remove the object handles. You can open the Multiline In-Place Text Editor and click Import Text to import the output file into your drawing. You can also open the output file, copy it to the Clipboard, and paste it into your drawing. The Import Text method enables you to format the text as you would any multi-line text but takes some experimenting to set up in the proper columns. You can also import the file into a spreadsheet and format it before importing it into your drawing. If you used the native format, you can open it in your DBMS, format it, and import it into your drawing. (See Chapter 27 for more information on importing files.)

STEPS: Creating and Viewing Links

1. You should have `ab20-01.dwg` open from the previous exercise. The Data View window is open with the database visible. The _PART_NO_Link1 link template is current. You can see the entire drawing in Figure 20.13.

FIGURE 20.13

This drawing of a base assembly for a commercial washing machine has objects that can be linked to the database of parts.

Thanks to Robert Mack of The Dexter Company, Fairfield, Iowa, for this drawing.

2. To locate the record that you need, in the Data View window click the left-most arrow next to the horizontal scroll bar to move to the first record. Choose Data View ⇨ Find. In the Find dialog box, type **9003-242-001**. The direction should be down. Click Find Next. AutoCAD finds the record. Close the Find dialog box by clicking its Cancel button.

3. Click the row's header (the arrow to the left of the row) to select the entire row.

4. Choose Data View ⇨ Link and Label Settings ⇨ Create Links. The Create Links menu item may already be checked.

5. Choose Data View ⇨ Link!

6. AutoCAD returns you to your drawing. Use the Zoom Window to zoom into the area marked ❶ in Figure 20.13.

7. Select all of the objects that make up the angle bracket indicated by ❶ in Figure 20.13 (and which the drawing itself labels as 2), as shown in Figure 20.14. Include the two cyan hidden lines representing the hole, but not the yellow centerline. Don't select the vertical line on the right of the angle, which belongs to another part. Press Enter to end the selection. AutoCAD returns you to the Data View table and displays 1 Record(s) linked with 8 Object(s) on the command line.

8. The linked row is highlighted in yellow. Make sure that the arrow cursor in the row header points to the highlighted row. (AutoCAD moves it down one so that you can work on the next row.) To view the objects connected to the row, choose Data View ⇨ View Linked Objects. Drag the Data View window to the bottom of the screen so that you can see the drawing (or dock it). The objects that you selected in Step 7 are selected.

FIGURE 20.14

The horizontal angle.

2 1/4±1/8" TYP.

9. In the drawing, press Esc to deselect the objects and remove the grips. To check the link, click any other row in the Data View window to move the cursor. (Try to position the Data View window so that you can see both the row you were working with and the objects you linked it to at the same time.) Choose Data View ⇨ View Linked Records. At the Select objects: prompt, select one of the objects in the angle and press Enter. AutoCAD displays the correct row in the database.

10. Save your drawing and keep it open for the next exercise.

Creating Labels

A *label* is multiline text that appears in your drawing, displaying data from a row in your database. You can choose which fields from the row are displayed. There are two types of labels:

- **Attached labels** are attached to objects and are displayed with a leader pointing to the object. If you move the object, the label moves as well. Use an attached label when the row in the database applies to one or more specific objects in your drawing.

- **Freestanding labels** are independent of any object. You would use freestanding labels when your database applies to the drawing as a whole.

Creating label templates

Before creating a label, you need to create a label template. A label template specifies which fields will be included in the label as well as text formatting. Here's how to create a label template:

1. Choose dbConnect ➪ Templates ➪ New Label Template.
2. In the Select a Database Object dialog box, choose a link template to use with the label template. Click Continue.
3. In the New Label Template dialog box, shown in Figure 20.15, type a template name in the New Label Template Name text box. AutoCAD suggests a default name. If you have an existing label template that you would like to use as a basis for the new label template, choose it from the Start with Template drop-down list. Click Continue.

The New Label Template dialog box.

4. AutoCAD opens the Label Template dialog box, shown in Figure 20.16, with the Label Fields tab displayed. Use the Character and Properties tabs to format the text. (Note that this dialog box looks like the pre-2004 Multiline Text Editor.)
5. On the Label Fields tab, choose a field that you want to appear on the label from the Field drop-down list. Then click Add. Continue to add fields as desired. You can add text to this field. For example, you could type **Part No:** before the PART_NO field.

FIGURE 20.16

Use the Label Template dialog box to format and define label templates.

If you add text before or after the field, don't forget to add a space between the text and the field so that the result is Part No: 9003-242-001 rather than Part No:9003-242-001, for example.

6. Click the Label Offset tab, shown in Figure 20.17. This tab defines the placement of the label and the leader that connects the label with the object. In the Start drop-down list, choose a justification. This defines where on the object AutoCAD places the tip of the leader.

FIGURE 20.17

The Label Offset tab of the Label Template dialog box.

7. In the Leader Offset text boxes, type an X and Y offset (in units). This offset represents the X and Y distances between the point of the leader arrow and the insertion point of the text. (If this distance is too small to fit an arrow, the arrow is suppressed.)

8. In the Tip Offset text boxes, type an X and Y offset (in units). This offset represents the distance between the point of the leader arrow and the object to which it points. By default, this is set to 0,0 so that the point of the leader arrow touches its object.

9. Click OK to close the Label Template dialog box and place the label.

After you create the label template, you can create attached and freestanding labels. The settings on the Label Offset tab apply only to attached labels.

You can edit a label template to change the included fields or the formatting. To edit a label template, choose dbConnect ➪ Templates ➪ Edit Label Template. In the Select a Database Object dialog box, choose the label template that you want to edit and then click Continue. Then use the Label Template dialog box to edit the label template using the same steps that you used to create it. Click OK after you're done.

Creating attached labels

You create a link between a row and an object and an associated attached label at the same time. You need to have a table open and to have defined both a link and a label template. If you have defined more than one link or label template, choose the desired template(s) from the drop-down list at the top of the Data View window. Follow these steps:

1. Select the record that you want to link by clicking its row header in the Data View window.
2. Choose Data View ⇨ Link and Label Settings ⇨ Create Attached Labels. This puts you in Creating Attached Labels mode, which means that from now on any links that you create also create labels.
3. Choose Data View ⇨ Link!
4. At the Select objects: prompt, choose the object(s) that you want to attach to the label. End object selection.
5. AutoCAD automatically places the label based on the label template. If you selected more than one object, labels are placed on all of the objects (which can get confusing).

Of course, you can then move the labels and leaders to a more suitable location.

If you've already created a link to an object, follow the same procedure. The link is re-created along with the attached label.

Creating freestanding labels

To create a freestanding label, you need to have a table open with at least a link and a label template. If you have more than one template defined, choose the one that you want to use in the drop-down list at the top of the Data View window. Follow these steps:

1. Select the record that you want to link to the freestanding label.
2. Choose Data View ⇨ Link and Label Settings ⇨ Create Freestanding Labels.
3. Choose Data View ⇨ Link!
4. At the Specify point for label: prompt, pick a point in your drawing. AutoCAD places the freestanding label and displays this message on the command line: 1 Record(s) linked with 1 Label(s).

When you create a freestanding label, the row and the label are linked. If you select a row linked to a freestanding label and choose Data View ⇨ View Linked Objects, AutoCAD selects the label.

If the data in the database is changed from within the DBMS, the labels in your drawing may become outdated. To ensure that your labels are always accurate, you should periodically update them. To update labels, choose dbConnect ⇨ Labels ⇨ Reload Labels. In the Select a Database Object dialog box, choose the label template that you want to use and then click OK.

STEPS: Creating a Label Template and a Label

1. Continue with ab20-01.dwg from the previous exercise. The Data View window should still be open. Press Esc to make sure that no objects are still selected.
2. Choose dbConnect ⇨ Templates ⇨ New Label Template.
3. In the Select a Database Object dialog box, click Continue.

4. In the New Label Template dialog box, click Continue to use the default name.

5. In the Label Template dialog box, click the Label Fields tab. Choose PART_NO from the Field drop-down list. Click Add.

6. Choose DESCRIPTION from the Field drop-down list and then click Add.

7. Click the Label Offset tab. In the Start drop-down list, choose Top Left. Set the Leader offset X and Y values to 2.

8. Click the Character tab. Select all of the text and change the height to ⁵⁄₁₆.

9. Click OK.

10. Choose Data View ⇨ Link and Label Settings ⇨ Create Attached Labels.

11. Choose Data View ⇨ Link!

12. At the `Select objects:` prompt, choose the horizontal line marked at the top of the angle that you linked in the previous exercise. Press Enter to end object selection. AutoCAD automatically places the label.

13. The label covers existing objects. Pick the text of the label and then click its grip. Move the text to the left and pick a better location. The leader automatically changes direction and ends at the left side.

14. Save your drawing. Leave it open for the next exercise.

Querying with the Query Editor

You can use SQL (Structured Query Language) statements to gather more information about the elements in the drawing and database files. SQL is the language used by almost all database-management systems for refining the information that you get from a database.

AutoCAD uses the Query Editor to enable you to design queries. For example, you can do the following:

■ Query the contents of a database to view a specified subset of the data.

■ View a subset of records that falls into a certain range of values.

■ Access all of the tables in one data source with a series of SQL commands.

In addition, the Link Select dialog box enables you to create a selection set of objects by combining SQL queries and direct selection of objects in your drawing.

To open the Query Editor, follow these steps:

1. Choose dbConnect ⇨ Queries ⇨ New Query on a Link Template. (You can also right-click the table in the dbConnect Manager and choose New Query.)

2. In the Select a Database Object dialog box, choose the link template that you want to use and then click Continue.

3. In the New Query dialog box, shown in Figure 20.18, type a name for the new query or accept the name that AutoCAD supplies. To base a query on an existing query, choose an existing query from the drop-down list. Click Continue.

AutoCAD opens the Query Editor, shown in Figure 20.19. The Query Editor is designed to provide something for everyone — whether you're just starting out or you're an expert at SQL.

FIGURE 20.18

The New Query dialog box.

FIGURE 20.19

The Query Editor's four tabs enable you to build queries to refine how you view your database.

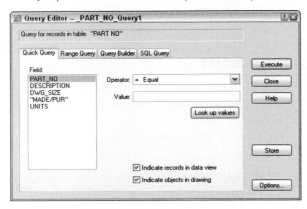

To restore the original view in the Data View window, do one of the following:

- Close the Data View window and then reopen it from the dbConnect window.
- Click the Query Builder tab and right-click any used cell. Choose Clear Grid. Click Yes at the warning message. Then click Execute.

Using the Quick Query tab

Use the Quick Query tab to create simple queries based on one field, an operator, and a single value. For example, you can create a query that finds all records from the current table where the field DWG_SIZE equals E. You can also find all records where DWG_SIZE does not equal E.

The advantage to using Quick Query over the Find dialog box, described earlier in this chapter, is that Quick Query displays all of the records matching the query and hides the rest. You don't have to click Find Next to move from record to record.

From the Field box, choose a field. In the Operator drop-down list, choose an operator, such as equal (=) or greater than (>). In the Value box, type a value for the field. If you're not sure what values are available, click Look Up Values. (This can be slow in a large database or when you're working with a database across a busy network.)

CAUTION Queries are case-sensitive. A value of "B" is not the same as "b." You need to be aware of the case used in your database. Some databases are all uppercase, making it easy to specify values. Just turn on Caps Lock and type away.

Choose Indicate Records in Data View and/or Indicate Objects in Drawing. By default, both are checked. To save the query for future use, click Store. Click Execute to see the results.

To return to the Query Editor, choose Return to Query on the Data View window toolbar.

Table 20.2 lists the available operators.

TABLE 20.2

Query Operators

Operator	Description
Equal (=)	Records that match the value exactly.
Not equal (<>)	All records except those that match the value exactly.
Greater than (>)	Records greater than the value. Includes text. For example, D is greater than B.
Less than (<)	Records less than the value.
Greater than or equal (>=)	Records that are greater than or match exactly the value.
Less than or equal (<=)	Records that are less than or match exactly the value.
Like	Records that contain the value. You must use the % wildcard (which is like the * wildcard used in Windows).
In	Records that match the values that you specify. You list the values, separated by a comma. For example, you could find records for which the field DWG_SIZE is B or D by typing **B,D** in the Value box.
Is null	Records that have no value. The Value box is unavailable. You can use this to find missing data.
Is not null	Records that have a value. You can use this to remove from view all records with missing data.

Using the Range Query tab

The Range Query tab, shown in Figure 20.20, finds records based on one field and a range of values. For example, you can find all records where the field DWG_SIZE ranges from B to D. The range can be either textual or numeric.

Use the Range Query tab to find records that match a range of values.

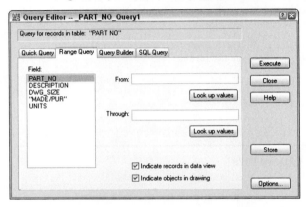

To construct a range query, choose a field from the Fields list. Then type the beginning value of the range in the From box and the ending value of the range in the Through box. In both cases, you can click Look Up Values to choose from a list of available values.

Click Store to save the query. Click Execute to execute the query.

Using the Query Builder tab

The Query Builder enables you to create multiple criteria. For example, you can create a query that finds records where the field DWG_SIZE ranges from B to D and the field PART_NO is greater than 9029-072-001. In order to build the criteria, you use Boolean operators and parenthetical grouping. This tab also enables you to specify which fields will appear in the Data View window and to sort the records. Using all of these options offers a great deal of flexibility to create a complex query without knowing SQL. Here's how it works:

- **And operator:** Displays the records that meet both the criteria before and after the And operator.
- **Or operator:** Displays records that meet either of the criteria before and after the Or operator.
- **Parenthetical grouping:** Enables you to group sets of criteria. For example, you can group two criteria that use an And operator and a second group of two criteria that use an And operator. Then you can put an Or operator between the two groups.

Figure 20.21 shows an example of a query using all three elements.

FIGURE 20.21

Use the Query Builder tab to design a query with multiple criteria.

Building a query with multiple criteria

To create a query using multiple criteria, follow these steps:

1. On the first line, choose a field from the Field column. (When you click the first cell in the Field column, a drop-down arrow appears.)

2. Choose an Operator from the Operator column.

3. Type a value in the Value cell. (An ellipsis button appears, and you can choose from all of the values in the database.)

4. Click in the Logical cell to insert the And operator. Clicking again changes the operator to Or.

5. Move to the second line and create the next row of criteria. Continue until you've specified all of the criteria that you want.

6. Add parenthetical grouping. Click to the left of the Field column of a row to insert a left parenthesis and between the Value and Logical columns to insert a right parenthesis. Continue to insert all of the parentheses that you need. You can't insert parentheses until you have enough rows defined for a parenthesis to make sense.

7. Click Store to save the query. Click Execute to execute the Query.

Specifying fields and sorting

You can also limit which fields appear in the Data View table. First define the query in the top half of the tab. The query does not need to be complex. Then select the first field from the Fields in Table list. Click Add above the Show Fields list. Continue until you have all of the fields that you want. By default, all of the fields are shown. To start from scratch, right-click in the Show fields box and choose Clear All. To remove one field, right-click it and choose Clear Field Name.

To sort the data, choose the first field that you want to sort by from the Show Fields list. (You can only sort by fields that you're showing.) Click Add above the Sort By list. By default, AutoCAD sorts by ascending order. To sort by descending order, click the Ascending/Descending button. You can click it again to change the order back to ascending. You can also repeat the process for additional fields.

Click Store to save the query. Click Execute to execute the Query.

Using the SQL Query tab

Here's where the fun is. Try creating a query in one of the first three tabs and then click the SQL Query tab. Lo and behold, there is your query in SQL language. This is a great way to learn SQL. (I'm still waiting for a macro recorder that does the same thing in VBA, such as the one contained in Microsoft Office.) Figure 20.22 shows the SQL Query tab for the same query shown in Figure 20.21.

FIGURE 20.22

The SQL Query tab enables you to create free-form SQL queries and displays queries created on the other tabs in SQL.

The SQL Query tab is the only tab you can use to create a query to search more than one database table. Choose a table in the Table section and click Add. You can build the query by specifying fields, an operator, and values. As you work, you see the results in the top box, in SQL language.

The Check button enables you to check the SQL query before executing it. Click Store to save the query. Click Execute to execute the Query.

Although complete coverage of SQL syntax is beyond the scope of this book, you may find a few rules helpful:

■ Text data must be enclosed in single quotation marks ('B').

■ Column names are not case-sensitive, but column values are.

■ There are certain SQL keywords that are used in the program. You cannot use these as table or column names. Examples include CHAR, GROUP, SQL, TABLE, USER, and CURRENT.

■ In most standard SQL syntax, you need to end each statement with a semicolon (;). However, this is not necessary in AutoCAD.

■ You cannot use AutoCAD or DOS wildcard characters, such as ? or * in column values or names.

■ To name more than one specification, separate each one by commas.

The SELECT statement is probably the most common SQL statement. The SELECT statement can retrieve a subset of the rows in one or more tables, retrieve a subset of the columns in one or more tables, or link rows in two or more tables to retrieve common data to both tables.

The following shows the syntax of the SQL SELECT statement, including modifying statements that instruct the DBMS exactly which rows to select.

```
SELECT <select list>
FROM <table name> [{,<table name>}...]
[WHERE <search condition>]
[GROUP BY <column spec>[{,<column spec>}...]
[HAVING <search condition>]
[ORDER BY <sort spec> [{,<sort spec>}...]
```

In the preceding syntax, square brackets ([]) indicate optional elements, an ellipsis (...) indicates that the statement may be repeated, and curly brackets ({}) mean that the elements are listed in sequence.

Here is the meaning of the statement functions:

- The SELECT statement specifies the columns to retrieve.
- The FROM clause specifies the tables containing the specified columns.
- The WHERE clause specifies the rows that you want to retrieve in the tables.
- The GROUP BY clause divides a table into groups. Groups are designated by a column name or by the results of computed numeric data type columns.
- The ORDER BY clause sorts results into one or more columns in either ascending (ASC) or descending (DESC) order.

STEPS: Creating a Query

1. You should still have ab20-01.dwg and the PART_NO Data View window open. Choose dbConnect ➪ Queries ➪ New Query on a Link Template.

2. In the Select a Database Object dialog box, click Continue.

3. In the New Query dialog box, click Continue to open the Query Editor.

4. Your goal is to locate the part number of a trip arm that appears in a size-B drawing that you have open because the part number has been smudged on the paper drawing. You know that arms all have a part number starting with 9001. Because you need to specify a range of part numbers, click the Range Query tab.

5. PART_NO is already selected in the Field box. In the From range, type **9001-000-000**. In the Through range, type **9001-999-999**. This will include all part numbers that start with 9001.

6. You also need to specify the drawing size. To add to the query, click the Query Builder tab. Your range query is already there. You could have built it on the Query Builder tab, but using the Range Query tab was much easier.

7. Click in the second row of the Logical column, at the end of the last existing line of the query. AutoCAD places an And operator there.

8. Click in the third row of the Field column to open the drop-down list. Choose DWG_SIZE.

9. Click in the third row of the Operator column. By default, AutoCAD places the Equal operator, which is what you want.

10. Click in the third row of the Value column. Type **B.** (Make sure that it is uppercase.)

11. Click Execute. You now have only four items in the Data View window and can easily find the trip arm's part number.

12. Save your drawing.

Creating selection sets with Link Select

Link Select enables you to create combined selection sets of objects. You can define the selection sets either by using the Query Editor or by selecting objects directly in your drawing, or you can use a combination of these two methods. You first define a selection set called A. Then you define a selection set called B. Then you combine the two selection sets using logical operators.

You need to have your links already set up so that AutoCAD knows the relationship between your records and objects in the drawing.

As you work, the status area at the bottom of the dialog box displays the results of the running Link Select operation, both in terms of the number of linked objects and the number of records that currently meet your specifications.

Table 20.3 shows how the logical operators work.

TABLE 20.3

Logical Operators for Selection Sets in Link Select

Operator	Function
Union	Combines both selection sets
Subtract A-B	Subtracts the second selection set of objects from the first
Subtract B-A	Subtracts the first selection set of objects from the second
Intersect	Selects only objects that are contained in both selection sets

The Link Select dialog box contains its own version of the Query Editor so that you can build queries without leaving the dialog box.

To use Link Select, follow these steps:

1. Choose dbConnect ⇨ Links ⇨ Link Select, to open the Link Select dialog box, shown in Figure 20.23.

2. At the top-center of the dialog box, choose either Use Query or Select in Drawing.
   - If you choose Use Query, use the Query tabs to specify a query.
   - If you choose Select in Drawing, click Select (the Execute button changes to the Select button) to return to your drawing and choose objects in the drawing at the Select objects: prompt. End object selection to return to the Link Select dialog box.

3. Click Execute to add the query or selection of objects in your drawing to the Link Select operation.

4. Create a second selection set using the same process.

5. From the Do drop-down list, choose one of the logical operators. You now have one selection set from the combined selection sets that you specified.

6. If you want, you can now create an additional selection set and use an operator to combine it with the previous selection set created in Step 5.

7. Choose Finish to complete the process.

FIGURE 20.23

Use the Link Select dialog box to create combined selection sets of objects from queries and/or direct selection in your drawing.

Working with Query Files

If you use queries a lot, you want to keep track of them. You can store, edit, rename, and delete queries. You can also import and export them for use by others. You do this by saving the information in a query file.

Storing queries

As I discussed previously, you can store a query by clicking Store on any tab. Stored queries are displayed under the drawing in the dbConnect window. To execute a stored query, choose dbConnect ➪ Queries ➪ Execute Query. Choose the query that you want to execute and click OK. It helps if the queries have names that meaningfully relate to the query.

You can also edit a query. Choose dbConnect ➪ Queries ➪ Edit Query. Choose the query and click Continue. In the Query Editor, make the desired changes and choose Store.

To rename a query, click it in the dbConnect window. Click it again to display an edit box. You can now edit the query's name. Remember that you have to name the query up front. If you're not sure what the query will consist of, use the default name, construct your query, and then rename it to something more meaningful afterward.

To delete a query, choose dbConnect ➪ Queries ➪ Delete Query. Choose the query or queries and click OK.

Importing and exporting queries

To export a query that has been saved (by clicking Store in the Query Editor), choose dbConnect ➪ Queries ➪ Export Query Set. In the Export Query Set dialog box, navigate to the desired folder and choose a name. Click Save. Queries have a .dbq filename extension.

To find the location of your queries, choose Tools ⇨ Options and click the Files tab. Double-click Data Sources Location to see the path.

To import a query that has been exported and named, choose dbConnect ⇨ Queries ⇨ Import Query Set. You need to know the name and location of the .dbq file. In the Import Query Set dialog box, locate the file and click Open. AutoCAD assigns default names to queries.

Summary

Using external databases to store data about drawing objects can reduce the size of drawings, simplify reporting, make data accessible to all users on a network, and enable you to edit a database from inside AutoCAD. In this chapter you read about:

- Configuring a data source
- Connecting a database table with your drawing
- Creating a link template
- Creating links between drawing objects and rows in the database
- Creating labels containing information from the database
- Defining SQL queries to select and sort the data that you view
- Selecting objects based on queries
- Storing and saving queries

This chapter ends Part III, "Working with Data." In Part IV, you start to draw in three dimensions. In the next chapter, I discuss how to specify 3D coordinates.

Part IV

Drawing in Three Dimensions

Part IV introduces you to three-dimensional drawing. AutoCAD creates three types of 3D objects (also called *models*): wireframes, surfaces, and solids. Wireframes, as the name implies, look like models created with wire. They don't have real surfaces or solidity. However, they're useful for creating shapes that you can turn into surfaces or solids. Surfaces, unlike wireframes, can hide objects behind them. They're especially useful for creating unusually shaped objects. Solids are defined as the entire volume of space that they enclose. You can add and subtract solids from each other, creating realistic objects.

AutoCAD LT can only create wireframes and 2D objects with thickness, which is a kind of surface. Although AutoCAD LT's 3D capabilities are quite limited, you can still create simple 3D objects. Furthermore, AutoCAD LT can open and display a drawing that contains 3D objects created in AutoCAD.

In Chapter 21, I explain the basics of 3D drawing. This includes specifying 3D coordinates, using the User Coordinate System for 3D drawing, and creating objects with elevation and thickness. Chapter 22 explains the techniques for viewing, and navigating through, 3D objects. Chapter 23 covers surface models. Chapter 24 explains how to create true solids, and covers editing in three dimensions. Chapter 25 explains how to create photorealistic views of your 3D drawings using AutoCAD's rendering feature.

Chapters 23 through 25 apply only to AutoCAD.

Chapter 21

Specifying 3D Coordinates

The topics in the previous chapters have worked with two axes, X and Y. In this chapter, I add the Z axis. When you have a drawing with 3D objects, you can view it from any angle. The view that you've been using in 2D drawings is like looking at a house from the top, which you could call a plan view or a floor plan. From this view, even a 3D drawing looks two-dimensional. But when you look at a 3D drawing from an angle, you can see that there's more to it than meets the eye. Figure 21.1 shows the plan view of an office building. Figure 21.2 shows the same drawing viewed in a perspective view from the front.

Although this drawing is quite complex, you can easily get started by working on simpler models. Three-dimensional drawing is not as difficult as it seems at first. In this chapter, I start by explaining how to work with 3D coordinates. I also cover wireframe models and 3D surfaces created with thickness and elevation. These are essentially 2D objects placed in 3D space and are therefore a good place to start when learning about drawing in 3D. Most of the features that I cover in this chapter apply to AutoCAD LT as well as AutoCAD.

FIGURE 21.1

An office building in plan view.

Thanks to Roger Cusson of Interface Architectural Software, Montreal, Quebec, for this drawing.

FIGURE 21.2

The same office building viewed from the front.

Working in a 3D Environment

AutoCAD comes with a 3D workspace and template that automatically set you up to work easily in 3D. These are not available in AutoCAD LT. To use the workspace, choose 3D Modeling from the Workspaces toolbar. (If the Workspaces toolbar is not displayed, right-click any toolbar button and choose Workspaces from the list of toolbars.)

To use the 3D template, choose File ⇨ New. In the Select Template dialog box, choose acad3D.dwt (or acadiso3D.dwt for metric drawings) and click Open. The Tool palettes and the Dashboard open as well. In Figure 21.3, you see the result, minus the Tool palettes, which I closed to display more of the drawing area.

FIGURE 21.3

The acad3D.dwt template and the 3D Modeling workspace provide a suitable environment for working in 3D.

The grid is on, by default, to give you a sense of perspective and depth. The default viewpoint helps you see your 3D objects more clearly. When you draw solids or surfaces, they display the Realistic visual style that you see in Figure 21.3. You can change every aspect of what you see, including the colors, which palettes and toolbars appear, and the viewpoint. Chapter 22 covers the ways to change the viewpoint and the visual style. Appendix A explains how to configure AutoCAD to look the way you want, including the colors of the grid and background.

Using 3D Coordinates

All of the 2D methods of specifying coordinates have their 3D counterparts. Just as you can draw a line by specifying a start point of 3,4 and an endpoint of 5,7, you can draw a 3D line by specifying a start point of 3,4,2 and an endpoint of 5,7,6. Absolute coordinates are the same in 3D — you just add a Z coordinate. In the same way, you can specify relative coordinates. In 3D drawings, you can use two new types of coordinates that are 3D counterparts of polar coordinates, *cylindrical* and *spherical*. Figure 21.4 shows the three axes X, Y, and Z. The arrows show the positive direction of the axes.

FIGURE 21.4

The three axes in a 3D drawing.

CROSS-REF Working with the User Coordinate System (UCS) is essential in 3D work. If you aren't familiar with the User Coordinate System, review the discussion in Chapter 8.

Most 2D commands accept 3D coordinates (a coordinate that includes a Z value) only on the first point. After that, you can omit the Z coordinate because the Z value will be the same as that of the first point. For example, if you draw a rectangle, you can specify its first corner as 2,3,8 but the second corner must be specified without the Z value, as in 6,7. The Z value for the opposite corner is automatically 8.

The LINE command is an exception. It is a true 3D command, so you can specify X, Y, and Z values at all points.

Absolute and relative Cartesian coordinates in 3D

You don't use absolute coordinates more in 3D than you do in 2D — in fact, you may even use them less. But understanding absolute coordinates is important to understanding the Cartesian coordinate system that defines every point in your drawing. Figure 21.5 shows a wireframe model of a square and a triangle drawn with absolute coordinates, viewed from above (plan view) and from the southeast view (above, to the right, and in front). The square is drawn in 2D — which means that the Z coordinates are all zero — to be a reference point for visualizing the 3D points of the triangle.

You can use relative coordinates in the same way by including the change in coordinates. For example, to draw the line from (3,2,1) to (6,4,3), shown in Figure 21.5, you can start with the absolute coordinate (3,2,1) and then specify 3,2,2 because that's the difference between (3,2,1) and (6,4,3).

If you are using Dynamic Input with the default settings, specifying 3,2,2 as a second point is the same as specifying @3,2,2 with Dynamic Input off. For more information on Dynamic Input, see Chapter 4.

Cylindrical and spherical coordinates

Just as polar coordinates are often more useful than Cartesian coordinates in 2D, cylindrical and spherical coordinates can be more useful in 3D. Here's how they work.

Cylindrical coordinates have the format (@)`distance<angle,distance`:

- The first distance is the number of units in the XY plane from the origin (for absolute coordinates) or your last point (for relative coordinates).
- The angle is the number of degrees from the X axis in the XY plane.
- The second distance is the number of units along the Z axis.

FIGURE 21.5

A rectangle and triangle viewed from plan view and southeast view.

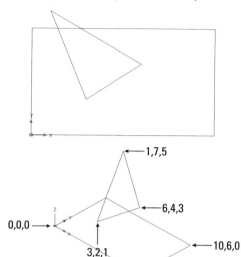

Cylindrical coordinates can be absolute or relative. Add the @ for relative coordinates. When you draw a line using cylindrical coordinates, neither distance that you specify is the length of the line. In essence, you're defining the lengths of two sides of a triangle to draw the hypotenuse. Figure 21.6 shows an example of a line drawn with cylindrical coordinates. The line was drawn from 0,0,0 to @5<30,3, which results in a line 5.8310 units long. (The @ wasn't necessary because the line was drawn from 0,0,0.)

> **NOTE** You may find that cylindrical coordinates do not work very well with dynamic input on. In that case, click the DYN button on the Status bar to turn off dynamic input.

The two sides of the triangle are 5 and 3 units long. To calculate the length of the hypotenuse, use the Pythagorean theorem, which says that $a^2 + b^2 = c^2$, where a and b are the two sides of the triangle and c is the hypotenuse. Therefore, the hypotenuse is the square root of 25 + 9 or 34, which is 5.8310. Of course, you can use the DIST or LIST command to check it out.

Spherical coordinates have the format (@)distance<angle<angle:

- The first distance is the total number of units from the origin (for absolute coordinates) or your last point (for relative coordinates).
- The first angle is the number of degrees from the X axis in the XY plane.
- The second angle is the number of degrees from the XY plane in the Z direction.

Spherical coordinates can be absolute or relative. Add the @ for relative coordinates. When you draw a line using spherical coordinates, the first distance is the actual length of the line. Figure 21.7 shows an example of a line drawn with spherical coordinates. The line was drawn from 0,0,0 to @5<15<30.

FIGURE 21.6

A line drawn using cylindrical coordinates.

FIGURE 21.7

A line drawn using spherical coordinates.

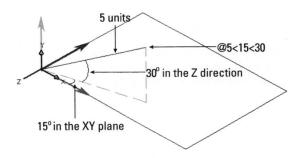

Using the Dashboard for 3D drawings

The Dashboard is a palette that contains a large number of tools and settings in one place. When you use the 3D Modeling workspace, the Dashboard contains tools especially for 3D drawings. For more information on the Dashboard, see Chapter 3.

Using editing commands with 3D wireframes

Certain 2D editing commands work well in 3D. Others have special 3D versions. Because wireframes are simply 2D objects placed in 3D space, you can generally use the familiar editing commands. For example, to move an object 3 units in the positive Z-axis direction, type **0,0,3** at the Specify base point or [Displacement] <Displacement>: prompt and press Enter twice. You can also use the 3DMOVE command, which I cover in Chapter 24.

You need to be careful when selecting objects for editing. For example, if you draw two identically sized rectangles at different Z coordinates, you see only one rectangle when you look at them from plan view. How do you know which rectangle you're selecting? By changing the angle from which you view your drawing (as I explain in the next chapter), you can see all of the parts of the drawing and can select objects easily.

CROSS-REF Multiple tiled viewports in which you view your drawing from different viewpoints can be very helpful in 3D drawing. For example, you can have a plan view in one viewport and a southeast view in another. Tiled viewports are covered in Chapter 8. You can convert solids and certain surfaces to wireframes by extracting their edges with the XEDGES command (AutoCAD only). I cover this command in Chapter 23 in the "Extracting edges from a surface or a region" section.

In the following exercise, you draw a simple wireframe piano bench and practice using 3D coordinates for both drawing and editing commands. You also view the drawing from two different angles.

ON the DVD-ROM The drawing used in the following exercise on using 3D coordinates, ab21-a.dwg, is in the Drawings folder on the DVD.

STEPS: Using 3D Coordinates

1. Open ab21-a.dwg from the DVD. This exercise assumes that you have dynamic input on, set to the default of relative coordinates. The drawing uses a 2D environment.

2. Save it as ab21-01.dwg in your AutoCAD Bible folder.

3. Choose Rectangle from the Draw toolbar. At the Specify first corner point or [Chamfer/Elevation/Fillet/Thickness/Width]: prompt, type **0,0,19** ↲. At the Specify other corner point or [Area/Dimensions/Rotation]: prompt, type **39,15** ↲. This creates a rectangle 39 units long by 15 units wide that is 19 units above the plane created by the X and Y axes. Notice that you can omit the Z coordinate for the second corner.

4. Start the COPY command. To copy the rectangle 2 units above the original rectangle, follow the prompts:

   ```
   Select objects: Pick the rectangle.
   Select objects: ↲
   Specify base point or [Displacement/mOde] <Displacement>: 0,0,2 ↲
   Specify second point or <use first point as displacement>: ↲
   ```

   You now have two rectangles, but because you're looking from the top, you see only one.

5. Choose View ➪ 3D Views ➪ SE Isometric. Now you can see the two rectangles, as shown in Figure 21.8.

6. If OSNAP is not on, click it on the status bar. Set a running object snap for endpoints.

7. Start the LINE command. Follow the prompts:

   ```
   Specify first point: Pick the endpoint at ❶ in Figure 21.8.
   Specify next point or [Undo]: #0,0,0 ↲ (The # symbol forces an
   absolute coordinate.)
   Specify next point or [Undo]: 1,0,0 ↲
   Specify next point or [Close/Undo]: 0,0,21 ↲
   Specify next point or [Close/Undo]: ↲
   ```

FIGURE 21.8

The two rectangles, shown from Southeast Isometric view.

8. Start the COPY command. At the `Select objects:` prompt, select the three lines that you just drew. End object selection. At the `Specify base point or [Displacement/mOde]` `<Displacement>:` prompt, type **38,0,0** ↵. At the `Specify second point or <use first point as displacement>:` prompt, press Enter to copy the three lines. Because the bench is 39 units long and the legs are 1 unit wide, copying the leg 38 units in the X direction places the copy in the right location.

9. Do a Zoom Extents so that you can see the entire drawing.

10. Repeat the COPY command. Use two separate crossing windows to select the first leg, then the second leg. Each window should select three objects. End object selection. At the `Specify base point or [Displacement/mOde] <Displacement>:` prompt, type **0,15,0** ↵ to copy the legs 15 units in the Y direction. Press Enter at the `Specify second point or <use first point as displacement>:` prompt to copy the legs to the back of the bench.

11. To draw an open cover for the piano bench, start the LINE command. Start it at the endpoint at ❷ in Figure 21.8. At the `Specify next point or [Undo]:` prompt, type **@15<90<45** ↵. You know the length of the line because the cover is the same as the width of the piano bench. At the `Specify next point or [Undo]:` prompt, turn on ORTHO, move the cursor parallel to the length of the bench, and type **39**. At the `Specify next point or [Close/Undo]:` prompt, use the Endpoint object snap to pick ❸. End the LINE command. Zoom out and pan so that you can see the entire bench.

12. Turn dynamic input off by clicking the DYN button on the status bar. (Dynamic input doesn't support cylindrical coordinates very well.) To draw some bracing inside the bench, start the LINE command again. At the `Specify first point:` prompt, choose the endpoint at ❹. At the `Specify next point or [Undo]:` prompt, type **@15<90,2** ↵. End the LINE command. Here, cylindrical coordinates are ideal because you don't know the length of the line but you know the change in the X and Z coordinates (the width and the height of the bench's body, respectively).

13. Save your drawing. It should look like Figure 21.9.

FIGURE 21.9

The completed wireframe piano bench.

Using point filters, object snaps, object tracking, and grips in 3D

As mentioned earlier, it's often hard to tell which point you're picking in 3D. On a flat screen, you can be sure of only two dimensions. The other dimension is, so to speak, going in or out of the screen — it could be X, Y, or Z, depending on the angle that you're using to look at the drawing. That dimension is the one that's hard to pick on the screen. You use point filters, object snaps, object tracking, and grips to be sure that you have the right point in 3D drawings.

Point filters

In Chapter 4, I discuss point filters for 2D objects. They work the same way in 3D. You usually use point filters together with object snaps. For example, for the X coordinate, you might pick the endpoint of a line. Often point filters are the only way to define a 3D point that isn't on an existing object. The point filters for 3D drawings are `.xy`, `.xz`, and `.yz`. For example, if you want to pick a point 3 units in the Z direction from the endpoint of an existing line, you can use the `.xy` point filter to choose the endpoint of the line. The prompt then asks you for the Z coordinate, which you can specify as a number or by using an object snap. You can also use point filters to specify each coordinate (X, Y, and Z) separately.

Object snaps

Object snaps are essential for 3D work. Turn on OSNAP and set running object snaps. Object snaps ensure that you're specifying the point that you want. However, don't forget that in 3D drawings, you can have two lines, one on top of the other. Use a view that enables you to see the two lines separately so that you can pick the object snap that you want. The Apparent Intersection object snap is especially useful for 3D work. You can use it to specify points that look as if they intersect from your viewpoint, even though in true 3D they would not intersect.

NOTE When you use an object snap in 3D, the Z value of the point comes from the Z value of the object. If you want to force a constant Z value, based on the current UCS or elevation, for a specific operation, temporarily change the new OSNAPZ system variable to 1. (This system variable is not available in AutoCAD LT.) I discuss UCSs in 3D and elevation later in this chapter.

TIP   You can use point objects to help you draw in 3D. Set a visible point style (Format ⇨ Point Style). Then place a point at a known coordinate. You can then use the Node object snap to access that point.

Object tracking

You can use object tracking in 3D as well. For example, if you want to draw a line starting from the middle of a box, you can acquire the midpoints of two sides and start the line there. (I cover object tracking in Chapter 4.) Object tracking in 3D improves the ease with which you can find the exact 3D point that you need.

Grips

You can use grips to edit 3D objects as well. Again, it's important to choose a view that makes the editing easy. Grip-editing wireframes is somewhat different from grip-editing solids. Chapter 24 discusses 3D editing in AutoCAD in more detail.

NOTE   Grips are shown parallel to the plane of the current User Coordinate System. When you change your viewpoint, the grips change their shape slightly to look as if they are lying on the XY plane.

ON the DVD-ROM   The drawing used in the following exercise on using point filters and object snaps with 3D wireframe objects, `ab21-b.dwg`, is in the `Drawings` folder on the DVD.

STEPS: Using Point Filters, Object Tracking, and Object Snaps with 3D Wireframe Objects

1. Open `ab21-b.dwg` from the DVD.

2. Save it as `ab21-02.dwg` in your `AutoCAD Bible` folder. OSNAP should be on. Set a running object snap for endpoint and midpoint. Make sure the OTRACK is on. This drawing uses a 3D environment, based on `acad3D.dwt`. This is the same piano bench drawn in the previous exercise, but without the cover. In this exercise, you use the bench to create a chair.

3. Choose Stretch from the Modify toolbar. Use a crossing window to select the right side of the bench. Eight objects should be selected. End object selection. At the `Specify base point or [Displacement] <Displacement>:` prompt, use the Endpoint object snap to pick ❶ in Figure 21.10. At the `Specify second point of displacement:` prompt, type **-15,0** ↵. (If you're not using Dynamic Input, type **@-15,0**.)

4. Use Pan Realtime to pan the chair to the bottom of your screen and zoom out a little to leave room for the back of the chair that you will draw next.

5. Start the LINE command. Follow the prompts:

   ```
   Specify first point: Choose ❷ in Figure 21.10.
   Specify next point or [Undo]: .xy ↵
   of Pick ❷.
   (need Z): 45 ↵
   Specify next point or [Undo]: Pass the cursor over the top endpoint
   of the line that you just drew, to acquire the point. Then pass the
   cursor over ❸ to acquire that point. Move the cursor to the approx-
   imate intersection of the two lines, until you see the Endpoint: +Z,
   Endpoint: Z tooltip, and click.
   Specify next point or [Close/Undo]: Pick ❸.
   Specify next point or [Close/Undo]: ↵
   ```

6. Repeat the LINE command. Draw a line from the midpoint of the left side of the back of the chair back to the midpoint of the right side.

FIGURE 21.10

The piano bench after being shrunk with the STRETCH command.

7. Choose Fillet from the Modify toolbar. At the Select first object or [Undo/Polyline/Radius/Trim/Multiple]: prompt, right-click and choose Radius. At the Specify fillet radius <0.5000>: prompt, type 1 ↵.

8. At the Select first object or [Undo/Polyline/Radius/Trim/Multiple]: prompt, pick ❶ in Figure 21.11. At the Select second object: prompt, pick ❷.

9. Repeat the FILLET command and pick ❷ and ❸ for the two lines.

10. Save the drawing of the chair. It should look like Figure 21.11.

FIGURE 21.11

A wireframe model of a chair.

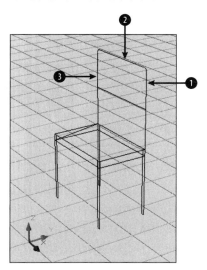

Creating 3D polylines

You've already created 3D lines by specifying 3D coordinates for the endpoints. The LINE command is a true 3D command because it accepts 3D coordinates. However, many commands cannot accept 3D coordinates. For example, you cannot place the center of a circle on one Z coordinate and the circumference on another. The whole circle must be on the same XY plane. Later in this chapter, I explain how to change the UCS to get around this restriction by changing the definition of the XY plane.

This doesn't mean that you don't use circles in 3D work. For example, you can create a circle in one XY plane and then use that circle as a base for a cylinder. The point is that the CIRCLE command itself is only a 2D command.

One command that has a 3D counterpart is PLINE. The 3D command is 3DPOLY (Draw ➪ 3D Polyline). The 3DPOLY command is like the PLINE command with a few differences:

- You cannot draw arcs.
- You cannot give the polyline a width.
- You cannot use a noncontinuous linetype.

The 3DPOLY command can accept all 3D coordinates. You can also edit it with the PEDIT command, although there are fewer options.

> **TIP**   If you want to create curved shapes in 3D space, you can create 2D polylines with a width and then add a thickness and an elevation. Elevation and thickness are both explained in the next section. Other options are available if you want to create surfaces (Chapter 23) or solids (Chapter 24).

Creating helixes

You can create a wireframe helix, or spiral, using the HELIX command. You can find this command by choosing Draw ➪ Helix or by choosing Helix on the Modeling toolbar. (It's not available in AutoCAD LT.)

When you start the command, an initial message indicates the default number of turns and the direction of the twist (clockwise or counterclockwise).

Follow the prompts:

```
Specify center point of base: Specify the center point for the base at
the bottom of the helix.
Specify base radius or [Diameter] <default>: Enter a radius (or
diameter) using the option. The default is the last radius you used.
Specify top radius or [Diameter] <default>: Enter a radius for the top
of the helix.
Specify helix height or [Axis endpoint/Turns/turn Height/tWist]
<default>: Enter a height to use the default number of turns. You can
also use the options to change the number of turns and the direction of
the twist. You can specify the height by specifying an axis endpoint
(the center of the top of the helix) or the turn height.
```

Figure 21.12 shows a helix with five turns. You can grip-edit the helix to increase its height.

FIGURE 21.12

A helix with a small base and a larger top looks like a whirlpool.

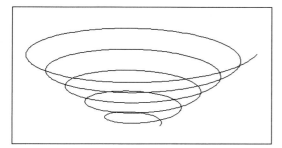

Using Elevation and Thickness

Wireframes have a number of limitations. In Figure 21.11, the chair that you drew in the previous exercise, you can see the back leg through the seat of the chair. Also, creating the detail of a real chair would be tedious if you were to use individual lines or 3D polylines. Finally, wireframes don't have any surface or solid properties. You can't display them in any realistic fashion or calculate properties, such as area, mass, and so on.

Creating surfaces with thickness

You can create simple surfaces by adding thickness to 2D objects. When you add thickness to a 2D object, the object is pushed out into the third dimension. For example, a circle becomes a cylinder and a rectangle becomes a box. Remember that you won't see the thickness if you're looking at the object from the top. Figure 21.13 shows some objects created using thickness.

FIGURE 21.13

3D surfaces created by adding thickness to 2D objects.

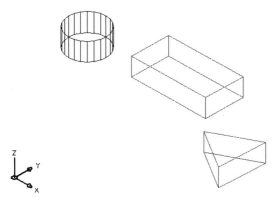

Surfaces created by adding thickness are sometimes called 2½D objects. Although they have three dimensions, the third dimension can only be a straight side perpendicular to the 2D object at the base.

The parallel lines on the cylinder are called *tessellation lines*. These lines help you to visualize curved surfaces. They aren't actually part of the cylinder; for example, you can't use object snaps on them.

To add thickness to an existing 2D object, display the Properties palette (Ctrl+1) and select the object. (You can also select the object first.) In the palette, click the Thickness property and change the number in the Thickness text box. Press Enter.

NOTE   You can use the CONVTOSURFACE command to convert open polyline figures with no width, lines, and arcs — as long as they have a thickness. You can use the CONVTOSOLID command to convert three types of closed wireframe objects with thickness to solids — polylines with a uniform width, closed polyline figures with no width, and circles. I discuss surfaces in Chapter 23 and solids in Chapter 24.

You can also change the current thickness. The current thickness affects new objects as you draw them, but not existing objects. There are two ways to change the current thickness:

- With no object selected, display the Properties palette (Ctrl+1). Click the Thickness property and type a value in the text box. Press Enter.

- Use the ELEV command (which can also change the current elevation, discussed in the next section) by typing it on the command line. The ELEV command prompts you for the current elevation and the current thickness. At the prompt for a thickness, type a number and press Enter.

In most cases, you use a positive number, which extrudes objects in the positive direction of the Z axis. However, you can use a negative number to extrude objects in the negative direction of the Z axis. As soon as you change the current thickness, all objects that you draw have that thickness.

CAUTION   Because it's easy to forget the current thickness, unless you're drawing a number of objects with the same thickness, it's usually safer to draw objects with no thickness and then change the thickness. If you do change the current thickness, don't forget to change it back to zero when you're finished creating the 3D objects.

Do Objects with Thickness Have Tops and Bottoms?

If you look carefully at Figure 21.14, you see that the cylinder has a top but the triangular prism and the box don't. AutoCAD creates top and bottom surfaces on some objects with thickness but not on others.

When you add a thickness to objects created with the SOLID command (a 2D command), circles, and wide polylines, they are surfaces with tops and bottoms.

However, if you draw a closed polyline, for example with the RECTANG or POLYGON command, and give it a thickness, there is no top or bottom surface. The same is true for a closed figure that you draw with the LINE command.

Therefore, if you want a top and bottom, use the SOLID command, draw a polyline with a width greater than zero, or draw a circle. (Hatching a closed figure with a solid fill does not have the same effect as the SOLID command.) These objects create opaque horizontal surfaces. You can see the difference when you use the HIDE command. Note that a circle doesn't display a top if you use the 3D Hidden visual style. (See Chapter 22 for more on visual styles.)

Using the HIDE command

Because objects with thickness are surfaces, not wireframes, you can use the HIDE command to hide lines that would normally be hidden from view in real life. AutoCAD and AutoCAD LT calculate which lines are behind surfaces from the current viewpoint that you're using, and hide them. Figure 21.14 shows the same objects as Figure 21.13 after using the HIDE command. You may notice that the cylinder has a top but the triangular prism and the box don't. For a further explanation, see the sidebar, "Do Objects with Thickness Have Tops and Bottoms?"

To return to the wireframe display, use the REGEN command. You use the HIDE command in AutoCAD LT or in a 2D environment in AutoCAD; in a 3D environment in AutoCAD, you use visual styles instead. I cover visual styles in Chapter 22.

FIGURE 21.14

3D surfaces after using the HIDE command.

Controlling the display of hidden lines and objects

You can control the display of polylines at the face intersections of solid and surface objects, including surfaces that you create using thickness. In a 2D environment in AutoCAD, and in AutoCAD LT, you use the HLSETTINGS command to specify settings that affect the display of hidden lines. For example, instead of hiding back lines completely, you could display them as dashed lines or in a different color. In AutoCAD, this opens the Visual Styles Manager palette; in AutoCAD LT, this opens the Hidden Line Settings dialog box.

Several system variables affect the 3D display only when you use the HIDE command or the 3D Hidden visual style. These system variables work on both solids and surfaces. Type **hlsettings** at the command prompt to open the Hidden Line Settings dialog box (AutoCAD LT) or Visual Styles Manager palette (AutoCAD), shown in Figure 21.15. Note that I cover the Visual Styles Manager for other settings in Chapter 22.

Here's how to use the Hidden Line Settings dialog box and the Visual Styles Manager palette to specify the display of hidden lines.

FIGURE 21.15

The Hidden Line Settings dialog box and the Visual Styles Manager allow you to control the display of back lines in AutoCAD LT and AutoCAD, respectively.

Use the 2D Hide - Obscured Lines section (Obscured Lines in AutoCAD LT) to choose a linetype and color for displaying hidden lines. When you choose a linetype, hidden lines are shown in the linetype that you choose. These linetypes are not affected as you zoom in or out. Choose from these linetypes:

- Off (fully hides back lines)
- Solid
- Dashed
- Dotted
- Short Dash
- Medium Dash
- Long Dash
- Double Short Dash
- Double Medium Dash
- Double Long Dash
- Medium Long Dash
- Sparse Dot

If you choose a linetype, then choose a color from the Color drop-down list. You can choose from one of the standard color index numbers (from 1 to 255). Use the 2D Hide - Intersection Edges section (Face Intersections in AutoCAD LT) to turn on the display of polylines at the intersections of 3D model faces. Then use the Color drop-down list to choose a color for the polylines.

Use the 2D Hide - Miscellaneous section (Halo Gap Percentage in AutoCAD LT) to create a gap that shortens lines at the point that they would be hidden by the HIDE command, in order to set off the lines from the unhidden portion of the model. By default, this percentage is set to 0, which creates no gap. Set the gap as a percentage of an inch. The gap doesn't change as you zoom in or out.

You can set the HIDEPRECISION system variable to 1 if you want a more exact calculation of the HIDE command results. The process takes longer but yields better results in a complex drawing with many surfaces and solids. In AutoCAD, enter **hideprecision** on the command line to set its value. The default is 0. In AutoCAD LT, you can choose the option in the Hidden Line Settings dialog box.

Use the HIDETEXT system variable to hide text behind other objects (a value of On, the default). When this system variable is set to Off, text will not hide other objects, or be hidden, unless it has a thickness. In AutoCAD LT, you can choose this option from the Hidden Line Settings dialog box.

Figure 21.16 shows a model using a halo gap value of 15; a green, dashed line to display hidden lines; and face intersections displayed in red.

FIGURE 21.16

This model uses HALOGAP, OBSCUREDLTYPE, and OBSCUREDCOLOR to display hidden lines.

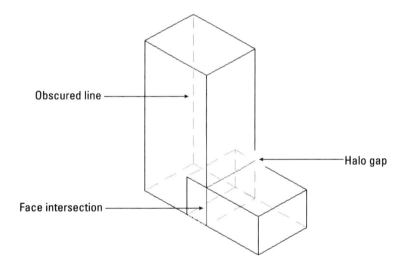

> **NOTE** The word *wireframe* is used in two ways. First, it means 3D objects that are created using only lines and 3D polylines. These objects have no surfaces or solidity. Second, it means surfaces and solids that are displayed as if they are created with lines and 3D polylines, such as the models in Figure 21.13. In this book, I usually distinguish between wireframes and wireframe display, or visual style. If the subject is surfaces and solids, the term *wireframe* generally means wireframe display.

Adding elevation to objects

Until now, I've discussed 3D objects based on 2D objects that were on the XY plane. In other words, their Z coordinate was zero. Although you generally don't want objects to float in the air, you certainly may want to place one object on top of another. To do this, you need to start the object above the XY plane (although you can also place objects below the XY plane) and give an object elevation, which is its Z coordinate.

To give elevation to an existing object, you can use several methods:

- Select the object and display the Properties palette (Ctrl+1). Click the Elevation property, type a new elevation in the text box, and press Enter.
- Move the object(s) with the MOVE command in the Z direction.
- Use the 3DMOVE command to move the object in the Z direction. I cover this command in Chapter 24, where I discuss editing in 3D.

For new objects, change the current elevation with the ELEV command as described earlier in this chapter in the discussion on thickness.

NOTE   For some objects, you can use the Properties palette (press Ctrl+1) to change the Z coordinate. This works for circles, lines, arcs, and ellipses but not for polylines. To elevate an entire line, you need to change the Z coordinate of both the start point and the endpoint.

When you change the current elevation, all objects that you create are drawn on that elevation. Remember to change the elevation back to zero when you want to draw on the XY plane again.

CAUTION   If you specify an object snap of an object on a different elevation than your current elevation (with a different Z coordinate), AutoCAD and AutoCAD LT use the elevation of the object snap, not the current elevation. However, if you specify the first point of a 2D command, such as PLINE (to create a polyline), on the current elevation, you can use object snaps at a different elevation for subsequent points. Because the entire polyline must be on the same elevation, subsequent points follow the elevation of the first point.

STEPS: Working with Elevation, Thickness, and the HIDE Command

1. Start a new drawing using the `acad.dwt` or `acadlt.dwt` template. The DUCS button on the status bar should be off (if you have AutoCAD). This template uses a 2D environment.
2. Save it as `ab21-03.dwg` in your `AutoCAD Bible` folder.
3. Start the CIRCLE command. Specify the center as 6,6 and the radius as 18.
4. Choose View ⇨ 3D Views ⇨ SE Isometric to display a 3D view.
5. Select the circle. Display the Properties palette (Ctrl+1). Click the Thickness property. In the Thickness text box, type **3** ↵.
6. Type **elev** ↵. At the `Specify new default elevation <0.0000>:` prompt, type **3** ↵. Because you just changed the existing circle's thickness to 3, you set the elevation to 3 to place an object on top of the circle. At the `Specify new default thickness <0.0000>:` prompt, type **24** ↵.
7. Start the CIRCLE command again. Specify 6,6 as the center and set the radius to 3.
8. Zoom out and pan so that you can see the entire model.
9. Type **elev** ↵. At the `Specify new default elevation <3.0000>:` prompt, type **27**. At the `Specify new default thickness <24.0000>:` prompt, type **3** ↵. This places any new object on top of the two circles that you just drew.
10. Start the CIRCLE command. Specify the center as 6,6 and the radius as 18. Because you don't specify a Z coordinate, the current elevation is used. You can verify in the Dynamic Input tooltip that the Z coordinate is 27.
11. Type **hide** ↵. You can now see the cable spool clearly.
12. Save your drawing. It should look like Figure 21.17.

FIGURE 21.17

A cable spool created by drawing 2D circles with thickness and elevation.

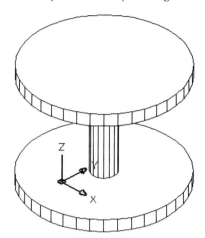

Working with the User Coordinate System

Except for certain true solids, much of 3D work starts with a 2D shape. However, the 2D drawing commands can be drawn only on, or parallel to, the XY plane. For example, the spool in Figure 21.17 consists of three circles, all parallel to the XY plane. How do you draw a circle, or any other 2D object for that matter, that is not parallel to the XY plane?

The answer is to change the User Coordinate System (UCS), thereby changing the definition of the XY plane. You can move the UCS to any location to define the XY plane in any way that you want. After you do so, you can draw a 2D object at any angle. This section offers a brief review of UCS features that are particularly useful for 3D drawing. (See Chapter 8 for complete coverage of the UCS feature.)

Using the UCS icon

Although you may have found the UCS icon an annoyance in 2D work, you should display it when working in 3D. Otherwise, it's easy to lose track of which direction is which. Remember that you can also choose the Origin option, which displays the UCS icon, if possible, at the origin. Choose View ➪ Display ➪ UCS Icon ➪ Origin.

CROSS-REF You can customize the look of the UCS icon. The 3D style is helpful when you're working in 3D. See Chapter 8 for details on customizing the UCS icon display.

UCSs and viewpoints

A plan view of the World UCS (the default) is different from the plan view of a UCS that you've created by rotating the UCS around the X axis, for example. The UCS defines the orientation and origin of the X, Y, and Z axes. On the other hand, the viewpoint shows your drawing from different angles without changing the orientation or origin of the axes. Understanding the difference between the UCS and viewpoints is important. The next chapter is all about viewpoints.

The UCS is important because it enables you to draw and edit at unusual angles. However, once you have a suitable UCS, you need to look at the drawing from the best viewpoint, one that displays the objects clearly with as little overlapping as possible.

If you want to change your UCS when you change your viewpoint, you can use the UCSORTHO system variable. When this variable is on and you switch to an orthographic viewpoint (top, bottom, left, right, front, or back), the UCS changes to match the viewpoint.

When the UCSFOLLOW system variable is on (set to 1), it switches you to plan view whenever you change the UCS. This means that whenever you change the UCS, you start by looking at your model from the top. You can then change the viewpoint to anything that you want.

NOTE   In 3D work, you usually use a 3D UCS icon display. However, if you use the 2D display, and choose a viewpoint that looks straight across the XY plane, you see a broken pencil icon, indicating that you're looking at the XY plane edge on.

AUTOCAD ONLY   Express Tools has a command, RTUCS, that enables you to rotate the UCS icon by dragging with the mouse. You can set an incremental angle for rotation and specify an active axis around which you rotate the UCS. Choose Express ⇨ Tools ⇨ Real-Time UCS.

Using UCS options to change the UCS

To change the UCS, choose one of the UCS menu items on the Tools menu. The following UCS options on the Tools ⇨ New UCS submenu are useful for 3D drawing.

Object

You can align the UCS with any existing object. Because this option orients the UCS differently for different objects, this option can sometimes be confusing. However, to modify some objects, you must be on its XY plane — a good time to use the Object option. The overall principle is that the UCS's XY plane stays parallel to the previous UCS, except for 3Dface objects. Table 21.1 explains how the Object option aligns the UCS for various kinds of objects.

TABLE 21.1

UCS Orientation with the Object Option

Object	UCS Orientation
Line	The endpoint nearest your pick point is the origin. The line lies on the X axis.
2D Polyline	The endpoint of the polyline nearest your pick point is the origin. The first segment of the polyline lies on the X axis.
Dimension	Places the origin at the midpoint of the dimension text. The X axis is parallel to the X axis that you used when you created the dimension.
Text	Places the origin at the insertion point and aligns the X axis with the rotation angle of the text. The same applies to attributes.
Block	Places the origin at the insertion point and aligns the X axis with the rotation angle of the block.
Circle	The origin is at the circle's center. The X axis is aligned with your pick point.
Arc	The origin is at the arc's center. The X axis is aligned with the endpoint closest to your pick point.

Object	UCS Orientation
Point	The origin is at the point. The X axis may be difficult to determine in advance.
Solid	Uses the first point that you specified for the origin and the first and second points to align the X axis. AutoCAD LT doesn't offer solids, but you can open AutoCAD drawings containing solids.
3Dface	Uses the first point for the origin. The X axis is aligned with the first two points. The Y axis is aligned with the first and fourth points. The new UCS may not be parallel to the prior UCS. AutoCAD LT doesn't offer 3Dfaces, but you can open AutoCAD drawings containing 3Dfaces.

Face

The Face option aligns the UCS on a face of a solid object. At the `Select face of solid object:` prompt, click within the boundary of a face or on its edge to highlight the face, and align the X axis of the UCS with the closest edge of the first face that it finds.

At the `Enter an option [Next/Xflip/Yflip] <accept>:` prompt, you can now refine the UCS. Right-click and choose Next to move the UCS to the adjacent face or the back face of the selected edge. Right-click and choose Xflip to rotate the UCS 180 degrees around the X axis. Right-click and choose Yflip to rotate the UCS 180 degrees around the Y axis. When you have the UCS that you want, press Enter to accept the current location of the UCS.

View

The View option aligns the X and Y axes with the current view. The current origin remains the same. The View option is most often used for creating text that you want to appear flat from your viewpoint of a 3D view of the drawing.

Origin

The Origin option creates a UCS parallel to the current UCS, but with a new origin that you specify. You can use the Origin option for working at a new elevation, instead of changing the current elevation.

Z Axis Vector

The Z Axis Vector option enables you to define an origin and then a point on the positive side of the Z axis. You can keep the previous origin to twist the UCS around its origin.

3Point

The first point that you specify is the origin, the second point indicates the positive direction of the X axis, and the third point indicates the positive direction of the Y axis.

X

The X option maintains the current origin and rotates the Y and Z axes around the current X axis at the rotation angle that you specify. The most common rotation is 90 degrees or a multiple of 90 degrees, but you can specify any angle.

Y

The Y option keeps the current origin and rotates the X and Z axes around the current Y axis. You specify the angle.

Z

The Z option keeps the current origin and rotates the X and Y axes around the current Z axis. You specify the angle.

The World option returns the UCS to the World Coordinate System. The Previous option switches to the previously UCS that you used.

Changing the UCS dynamically

Creating a new UCS is great if you need to work in it for a while and if you want to save it for future use. However, sometimes you just want to draw an object on a certain plane of an existing solid object. For these times, you can use the dynamic UCS feature, which creates a UCS on the fly so that you can draw on any face of an object. You can also use the dynamic UCS feature to help you specify a regular UCS.

 AutoCAD LT does not have the dynamic UCS feature.

The dynamic UCS feature works only on solids (covered in Chapter 24). You turn this feature on and off by clicking the DUCS button on the status bar (or pressing F6). You can temporarily override the DUCS feature by pressing Shift+Z.

To create a temporary UCS, follow these steps:

1. Start a command. Some commands that work with the dynamic UCS feature are:
   - Commands that draw 2D geometry, text, a table, 3D solids, or a polysolid.
   - The INSERT and XREF commands for inserting blocks or xrefs.
   - Editing commands, such as the ROTATE, MIRROR, and ALIGN commands, and grip-editing.
   - The UCS command.

2. Pass the cursor over a face of a solid. A dashed border appears on the solid's face, as shown in Figure 21.18.

3. Continue the command. For example, if you're drawing a circle, specify the center point. The UCS icon appears near the cursor in its new direction so that you can see where the XY plane is. The temporary X axis is aligned with the edge of the face and always points to the right of your screen.

NOTE   **If the grid is on, it flips to match the XY plane. This can be distracting, so you may want to turn it off.**

4. Finish the command. The UCS automatically returns to its previous setting.

FIGURE 21.18

When you pass the cursor over a face of a solid, the dashed border confirms the face, and you can temporarily draw on or edit that face.

To temporarily turn off dynamic UCS as you move your pointer over a face of a solid, press Shift+Z.

The drawing used in the following exercise on creating UCSs, ab21-c.dwg, is in the Drawings folder on the DVD.

STEPS: Creating UCSs

1. Open ab21-c.dwg from the DVD.

2. Save it as ab21-04.dwg in your AutoCAD Bible folder. This drawing contains some center-lines based on measurements of a chair. OSNAP should be on. Set running object snaps for end-point, midpoint, center, and quadrant. The UCS icon is set at the origin. This drawing starts in a 2D environment.

3. Choose Circle from the Draw toolbar. Use the From object snap to specify the center at an offset from ❶ (in Figure 21.19) of @2,0. Set the radius to 0.5.

FIGURE 21.19

These centerlines are the basis for drawing a chair.

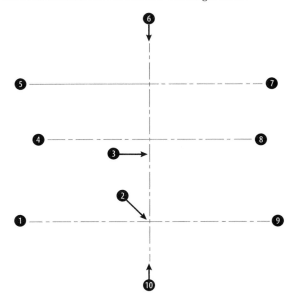

4. Display the Properties palette (Ctrl+1) and select the circle that you just drew. Change the thickness to 16. Press Enter. Close the Properties palette (or right-click its title bar and choose Auto-Hide).

5. Click ORTHO on the status bar to turn it on. Choose Mirror from the Modify toolbar. The circle should still be selected. (If it isn't, select it.) Specify the endpoint at ❷ for the first point of the mirror line. Specify any point vertical to ❷ for the second point of the mirror line. Choose not to delete the source object (the circle).

6. Repeat the MIRROR command. Select the two circles. Pick the midpoint of the line at ❸ for the first point of the mirror line. Pick any point horizontal to the first point for the second point of the mirror line. Press Enter. There are now four legs. Turn ORTHO off.

7. Type **elev** ⏎. Change the elevation to 16 and the thickness to 1.

8. Choose View ⇨ 3D Views ⇨ SE Isometric. You can now see the four chair legs.

9. Choose Polyline from the Draw toolbar. At the `Specify start point:` prompt, choose the From object snap. Use the Center object snap of the top of the circle near ❶ in Figure 21.19 for the base point and an offset of @–2,0. (You may have to press the Tab key until you get the Center object snap.) Continue to pick points ❹ through ❿. Notice that the Endpoint object snap symbol appears at the height of the first point. Then right-click and choose Close to close the polyline.

10. Choose Modify ⇨ Object ⇨ Polyline (or type **pedit** ⏎). Select the polyline. At the prompt, right-click and choose Fit to fit the polyline. Press Enter to end the command.

11. To see the result, type **hide** ⏎. Remember that the polyline has no top or bottom surface. Imagine your model as a glass-bottomed chair. It should look like Figure 21.20.

FIGURE 21.20

Part of a 3D chair.

12. Choose Tools ⇨ Inquiry ⇨ List. Select the front-left leg at ❶ in Figure 21.20. Press Enter. The center (of the circle at the bottom of the leg) is X = 3.5000; Y = –7.0000; Z = 0.0000.

13. To see the effect of a different UCS option, choose Tools ⇨ New UCS ⇨ X. To rotate the UCS around the X axis, type **90** ⏎. Again, choose Tools ⇨ Inquiry ⇨ List and select the same leg of the chair. Now the center is X = 3.5000, Y = 0.0000, Z = 7.0000. Look at the UCS icon (which is at 0,0,0) and try to visualize why the coordinates are the way they are listed.

14. Because you know the center of the circle of the front leg, you can move the UCS there. Choose Tools ⇨ New UCS ⇨ Origin. At the `Origin point <0,0,0>:` prompt, type **3.5,0,7** ⏎. This places the X axis through the center of the circle.

15. Choose Tools ➪ New UCS ➪ View. The UCS is now parallel to your current view. Choose Draw ➪ Text ➪ Single Line Text. Start the text at ❷ in Figure 21.20. Set the height to 1.0 and the rotation to 0. Type **A glass-bottomed chair**. Press Enter twice to end the command.

16. Choose Tools ➪ New UCS ➪ Object. Pick the line at ❸. Choose Tools ➪ New UCS ➪ Origin. Type **0,0,17** as the origin to place the UCS at the top of the seat.

17. Choose Tools ➪ New UCS ➪ X. Type **–10** ↵ to rotate the UCS around the X axis by –10 degrees. This enables you to create the back of the chair at a 10-degree angle. Type **plan** ↵ and press Enter again to accept the default. (This command is covered in the next chapter.) It enables you to view your drawing from plan view (in this case, relative to the current UCS).

> **TIP** Although it's not necessary for this exercise, this would be a good UCS to save (choose Tools ➪ Named UCS and rename the Unnamed current UCS to Chair Back). Now that you've gone through all of these steps, it would be a shame to have to re-create the UCS again.

18. With no objects selected, display the Properties palette (Ctrl+1). Set the thickness to 16. Close the Properties palette.

19. Start the CIRCLE command. Choose the center of the lower circle of the top-left leg (it's below the chair's seat) for the center. Accept the default radius of 0.5. Use the same technique to draw a circle at the corresponding right circle. Choose View ➪ 3D Views ➪ SE Isometric to see the results. Use the Previous option of the ZOOM command to return to your previous display.

20. Change the thickness to –5. Type **hide** ↵ so that you can see the circles that you just created more clearly.

21. Start the ARC command. The start point should be at the left quadrant of the left circle that you just drew. The second point is the intersection of the vertical centerline and the top horizontal centerline. (There is an Endpoint object snap there.) The endpoint is the right quadrant of the right circle.

22. Choose Tools ➪ New UCS ➪ World. Choose View ➪ 3D Views ➪ SE Isometric. Then type **hide** ↵ to see the final result.

23. Save your drawing. The chair should look like Figure 21.21.

FIGURE 21.21

The completed glass-bottomed chair.

A glass-bottomed chair

Summary

This chapter introduced you to 3D drawing. You read about:

- Understanding all of the types of 3D coordinates and how to use them
- Using editing commands in 3D
- Using point filters, object snaps, and grips in 3D drawings
- Utilizing elevation and thickness
- Understanding the HIDE command and the system variables that affect the hidden display
- Working with User Coordinate Systems in 3D

In the next chapter, I explain all of the ways to view 3D drawings.

Chapter 22

Viewing 3D Drawings

s soon as you start to work in three dimensions, you need to be able to see the drawing from different angles. By combining various User Coordinate Systems (UCSs) and different viewpoints, you can view and draw any object in 3D. Unless otherwise stated, the features in this chapter apply to both AutoCAD and AutoCAD LT.

Your basic point of reference is plan view in the World Coordinate System (WCS). This is the view that you use in 2D, and so it's familiar. Plan view is the view from the top. For a building, the top is obvious. However, for a bushing, which view is the top? Figure 22.1 shows a 2D drawing of a bushing. Figure 22.2 shows the 3D version. The left view of Figure 22.1 is the plan view looking down from the top. (Although your drawing calls this the plan view, engineering practice might call this the front view.)

When working in 3D, you can use many of the familiar 2D techniques for viewing your drawing:

■ Use ZOOM Previous to display the previous viewpoint.

■ Save views so that you can easily return to them.

■ Use real-time zoom and pan as well as all of the other zoom options.

■ Create tiled viewports to display more than one view at a time.

CROSS-REF You can save drawings in the 3D DWF format (in AutoCAD only) for viewing on the Web or sending to people. For more information, see Chapter 28.

IN THIS CHAPTER

Using the standard viewpoints

Using the DDVPOINT and VPOINT commands

Displaying a plan view with the PLAN command

Creating a named view with a camera

Working with visual styles

Using 3D Orbit

Walking through a model

Laying out a 3D drawing

FIGURE 22.1

The left image is the plan view, looking down from the top.

Thanks to Robert Mack, the Dexter Company, Fairfield, Iowa, for this drawing.

FIGURE 22.2

A 3D view of the bushing after using the HIDE command.

Working with the Standard Viewpoints

The View toolbar offers 10 standard viewpoints. (Right-click any toolbar and choose View to display the View toolbar.) Because these viewpoints are useful — and easy to use — they're the most commonly used viewpoints. You can do a lot of your work just using these viewpoints. The standard viewpoints show viewpoints relative only to the WCS, not the current UCS. Therefore, they're most useful when you're using the WCS.

To use a preset viewpoint, you can choose it from the View toolbar. You can also choose View ⇨ 3D Views and choose the viewpoint that you want from the submenu. Each of the preset viewpoints automatically does a Zoom Extents.

Using the VPOINT command

The VPOINT command was the original, command-line method of setting viewpoints. Now it's generally used for scripts and AutoLISP routines when you need a way to set a viewpoint from the command line. (AutoCAD LT does not support AutoLISP routines.)

The VPOINT command defines a viewpoint using X, Y, and Z vectors. The vectors for the standard viewpoints are based on a maximum of 1 unit. Imagine a model of the three axes floating out in space. You're Superman and can fly around the model from any angle. When you're over the Z axis, you can define the Z vector from 0,0,0 to your position as 1. The other vectors are 0 (zero) because you're right over them, so that 0,0,1 defines the top, or plan, view. The next section shows the vector equivalents for the standard viewpoints, to give you a feel for the vector system.

The VPOINT command also has a Rotate option that is the command-line equivalent of the DDVPOINT command's Viewpoint Presets dialog box. Using this option, you define a viewpoint by the angle from the X axis in the XY plane, and then the angle from the XY plane.

Looking at a drawing from the standard viewpoints

Showing the viewpoints is easier than describing them. In Table 22.1, I show a simple 3D house from all 10 standard viewpoints. Although the front of the house faces east, this is particular to this house. From your drawing's point of view, east is 0 degrees when looking from the top view, and 0 degrees faces to the right.

NOTE A system variable, UCSORTHO, automatically changes the UCS to match the viewpoint when you switch to one of the orthographic (top, bottom, left, right, front, and back) viewpoints. In order to distinguish between the viewpoints and UCSs, I turned UCSORTHO off for the following section.

TABLE 22.1

Standard Viewpoints

Viewpoint	Description	Example
Top (see Note at end of table)	The top view is the plan view. You're looking at the model from a bird's-eye perspective, suspended over the model. The VPOINT equivalent is 0,0,1.	
Bottom	The bottom view is the plan view for groundhogs. It's not very useful for buildings, but it may be useful for 3D mechanical drawings. The VPOINT equivalent is 0,0,–1. Notice the direction of the UCS icon. If you're using the 2D UCS icon, you'll notice that the square is missing at the axis intersection, indicating that you're viewing from the negative Z direction, or from "underneath."	

continued

TABLE 22.1 *(continued)*

Viewpoint	Description	Example
Left	The left view shows you your model from the left side, of course. In architecture it would be one of the elevation views. The VPOINT equivalent is –1,0,0. Notice that the text appears backward. This is because the text was drawn from the right view.	
Right	The right view shows you your model from the right side. Like the left view, the right view is an elevation view. The VPOINT equivalent is 1,0,0. Notice that the text now appears correctly because it was drawn from this view.	
Front	The front view, another elevation view, shows your model from the front. The VPOINT equivalent is 0,–1,0. The text, stating that the front faces the east, doesn't represent any rule in AutoCAD or AutoCAD LT. I simply use it to help you to see the differences in the sides of the house.	
Back	The back view, another elevation view, shows your model from the back. Here you see the text of the front of the house, shown backward. The VPOINT equivalent is 0,1,0.	
Southwest	The SW (southwest) isometric view shows you your model from a diagonal viewpoint in all three dimensions. Notice how one corner of the house is closest to you (the corner between the left and front views), and how you're also looking at the house from a view halfway between a side view and the top view. The isometric views are excellent for viewing all of the 3D objects in a drawing. As you can see, many more objects are visible than with the top view or any of the side views. The VPOINT equivalent is –1,–1,1.	
Southeast	The SE (southeast) isometric view also shows your model from a diagonal viewpoint in all three dimensions. Here you're looking at the house at the corner between the right and front views, as well as halfway between a side view and the top view. You see the same objects as you do in SW isometric view. However, in a drawing not as symmetrical as the house, one view may bring certain objects to the front so that you can select them. The VPOINT equivalent is 1,–1,1.	
Northeast	The NE (northeast) isometric view shows your model from the corner between the right and the back views, as well as halfway between a side view and the top view. The VPOINT equivalent is 1,1,1.	
Northwest	The NW (northwest) isometric view shows your model from the corner between the left and the back views, as well as halfway between a side view and the top view. The VPOINT equivalent is –1,1,1.	

You can also access the top view by typing **PLAN** on the command line. Note that the PLAN command does not change the UCS, even though you choose to see the plan view of a different UCS. This actually makes it very flexible because you can see what your drawing looks like from a different UCS without actually changing the UCS. The PLAN command is explained later in this chapter.

Using DDVPOINT

If the standard views aren't sufficient for your needs, DDVPOINT can give you both flexibility and precision. To use this command, choose View ➪ 3D Views ➪ Viewpoint Presets to open the Viewpoint Presets dialog box, shown in Figure 22.3. This dialog box enables you to set the view to a great degree of accuracy.

FIGURE 22.3

The Viewpoint Presets dialog box.

The left side of the dialog box determines the angle from the X axis in the XY plane. These angles work as follows:

270	Front view
0	Right view
90	Back view
180	Left view

Other angles result in viewpoints between these views. For example, an angle of 315 degrees enables you to look at your drawing from a view between front and right. If you're thinking that this is similar to the SE isometric view, you're correct.

The right side of the dialog box determines the angle from the XY plane, in the Z direction. A 0-degree angle enables you to look at your drawing from the front, back, or one side (elevation views), depending on the setting on the left part of the dialog box. Often you want to look at your drawing from above. A 90-degree angle shows you the plan view. An angle between 0 and 90 gives you a slanted view from the top, such as for one of the isometric standard views. (The isometric views set the angle from the XY plane to 35.3 degrees.)

> **TIP** There's an art to using the two dials to set the view angle that you want. If you click the inside border of either one, close to the indicator needle, you set the angle based on exactly where you clicked. This results in uneven degrees, such as 47.6. However, if you click the outside border of either image, or the numbers themselves, the angle is rounded to the value in the segment.

When you open the dialog box, the black needles indicate the angles for the current view. When you change the angles, the black (or white) needles move to the new angle, but the original needle remains to indicate the current angle. This enables you to constantly see the current angles for reference.

Beneath the dials are text boxes that reflect your choices. You can simply type the angles that you want in the text boxes.

A very handy Set to Plan View button is at the bottom of the dialog box. This enables you to quickly return to plan view when you become a little dizzy from flying around your model.

You can set the viewing angles either based on the WCS, or relative to a different UCS that you're using. It can become confusing if you have several different UCSs and start viewing them from several different viewpoints. As a result, the default is to view the drawing based on the WCS. However, sometimes you need to see your drawing relative to a UCS that you've created. To do so, click Relative to UCS.

> **TIP** Keep the number of UCSs to the minimum necessary and save them. When possible, use a new viewpoint instead of creating a new UCS. The Dynamic UCS feature (available in AutoCAD only) creates temporary UCSs; I discuss this feature in Chapter 21.

Click OK after you finish making your changes.

Creating a Named View with a Camera

A camera is a way to define and save a 3D view. When you save a named view using the VIEW command, you display the view that you want and then save it. When you use a camera, you define a location and a target to define the view. AutoCAD places a camera glyph (visual representation) in the drawing to represent the view. You can select the camera glyph and edit its properties using its grips. You can also edit the camera's properties in the Properties palette. By default, the camera glyph does not plot. Cameras are listed in the View Manager dialog box, along with other named views.

The CAMERA command is only in AutoCAD and not AutoCAD LT. When you open an AutoCAD drawing containing a camera in AutoCAD LT, the camera glyph doesn't appear.

Creating a camera

 To create a view with a camera, choose Camera from the View toolbar or the Navigate control panel of the Dashboard. At the `Specify camera location:` prompt, specify a coordinate for the camera. You can place the coordinate on the XY plane and change the height later, using the Height option. At the `Specify target location:` prompt, specify the target, which is what the camera is looking at.

The next prompt offers the following options:

- **?:** Displays the `Enter camera name(s) to list <*>:` prompt. Press Enter to list all current camera names and other named views in the drawing.
- **Name:** Lets you name the camera. If you don't use this option, the command assigns a default camera name, starting with Camera1 and so on.
- **LOcation:** Use this option to change the camera location.

- **Height:** Sets the camera height. You can use this to change the Z value of the camera after specifying its location on the XY plane.
- **Target:** Use this option to change the camera's target.
- **LEns:** Defines the field (width) of view in degrees using a camera lens length in millimeters. Table 22.2 describes the relationship between lens length and field of view.
- **Clipping:** Creates front and back clipping planes for the view.
- **View:** You can use this option to make the camera's view current. Use the Yes sub-option. This ends the command.
- **eXit:** Exits the command.

TABLE 22.2

Lens Length and Field-of-View Equivalents

Lens Length	Field of View (in degrees)
15 mm	100
20 mm	84
24 mm	74
28 mm	65
35 mm	54
50 mm	40
85 mm	24
135 mm	15
200 mm	10

You can also create a camera from the Tool palette. Display the Camera's tool palette tab. Choose one of the three cameras (Normal, Wide-angle, or Extreme Wide-angle) and drag it onto the drawing area. Release the mouse button. Then click to place the camera and click again to specify the target.

When you create the camera, you can set its view to current using the View option. After you change the view, you can get back to the view by choosing it in the View Manager and setting it to current. You can also select the camera, right-click, and choose Set Camera View.

Editing a camera

When you edit a camera, the Camera Preview window opens to show you a preview of the camera's view, as shown in Figure 22.4. You can change the visual style within the Camera Preview window, using the Visual Style drop-down list. (This doesn't change the visual style in the main drawing area.)

To edit a camera, select it and use its grips to change the camera location, target location, and lens length (field of view), as shown in Figure 22.5. Each grip has a tooltip to tell you its purpose. When you select a grip to make it hot, you can enter a new coordinate in the Dynamic Input tooltip. You can also edit the properties of a selected camera in the Properties palette.

FIGURE 22.4

The Camera Preview window shows you what the camera's view will look like.

FIGURE 22.5

Grip-editing a camera.

The drawing used in the following exercise on using standard viewpoints and DDVPOINT, `ab22-a.dwg`, is in the `Drawings` folder on the DVD.

STEPS: Using Standard Viewpoints and DDVPOINT

1. Open `ab22-a.dwg` from the DVD.

2. Save it as `ab22-01.dwg` in your `AutoCAD Bible` folder. It shows the same house used in Table 22-1, from the SE isometric view.

3. Type **ucsortho** ↵ **0** ↵ to turn off the UCSORTHO system variable. Turning off UCSORTHO prevents the UCS from changing whenever you switch to one of the six orthogonal viewpoints.

 4. Right-click any toolbar and choose View to open the View toolbar. Choose Top View from the View toolbar.

 5. Choose Bottom View from the View toolbar.

 6. Choose Front View from the View toolbar. You see the front of the house with the trees.

 7. Choose Right View from the View toolbar. You see the text "North side."

 8. Choose NW Isometric View from the View toolbar. You're looking at the back of the house.

 9. Choose SW Isometric View from the View toolbar. You're looking at the front of the house. If you want, try the rest of the standard viewpoints.

10. Choose Top from the View toolbar again.

 11. If you are using AutoCAD, choose Camera from the View toolbar. (If you are using AutoCAD LT, skip to the next step.) Follow the prompts:

```
Current camera settings: Height=40'-1 1/16" Lens Length=50.0000 mm
Specify camera location: 27',-15' ↵
Specify target location: 15',20' ↵
Enter an option
   [?/Name/LOcation/Height/Target/LEns/Clipping/View/eXit]<eXit>: n ↵
Enter name for new camera <Camera1>: thruFrontDoor ↵
Enter an option
   [?/Name/LOcation/Height/Target/LEns/Clipping/View/eXit]<eXit>: h ↵
Specify camera height <14'>: 5' ↵
Enter an option
   [?/Name/LOcation/Height/Target/LEns/Clipping/View/eXit]<eXit>: le
   ↵
Specify lens length in mm <35.0000>: 28 ↵
Enter an option
   [?/Name/LOcation/Height/Target/LEns/Clipping/View/eXit]<eXit>: v ↵
Switch to camera view? [Yes/No] <No>: y ↵
```

12. Choose View ➪ 3D Views ➪ Viewpoint Presets to open the Viewpoint Presets dialog box. Set the left dial (angle from X axis) to 315 degrees by clicking the number 315. Set the right dial (angle from XY plane) to 60 degrees by clicking the second-from-the-top segment pointed to by the number 60. Click OK. You see a view somewhat like the SE isometric view, but from much higher up.

13. Repeat the DDVPOINT command. In the X Axis text box, type **240**. In the XY Plane text box, type **5**. Click OK. You view the house from slightly off the ground, much as you might see it if you were walking up to the house.

14. If you have AutoCAD, choose View ➪ Visual Styles ➪ 3D Hidden. If you have AutoCAD LT, choose View ➪ Hide. Notice that you can see the windows on the far side through the windows on your side of the house.

15. Choose View ➪ Named Views. Click the New button. In the New View dialog box, type the name of the view, **walk up**. Click OK. Click OK again to return to your drawing. It should look like Figure 22.6.

FIGURE 22.6

The final view of the house.

16. If you're working on someone else's computer or want UCSORTHO on, type **ucsortho** ⏎ **1** ⏎ to turn it back on.

17. Save the drawing.

NOTE In AutoCAD, when you save the view, by default, you save it with the current visual style. Therefore, if you change the visual style and restore the view, the visual style changes back to the one you used when you saved the view. If you don't want to save the visual style, choose <None> from the Visual Style drop-down list in the New View dialog box.

Adding a Background to a Named View

When you save a named view using the View Manager, you can add a background. I discussed the View Manager in Chapter 8, but here I explain how to add a background. Backgrounds only apply to 3D views. They are not available in AutoCAD LT.

You can add a solid, gradient, or image background to a named view. Whenever you display that view, the background appears if the current visual style has backgrounds turned on (the VSBACKGROUNDS system variable). Backgrounds, especially image backgrounds, are usually used in the context of rendering, and I include an exercise on adding a background in Chapter 25.

To create a view with a background, choose View ➪ Named Views. In the View Manager, click the New button to define the new view. At the bottom of the New View dialog box, choose Solid, Gradient, or Image from the drop-down list.

NEW FEATURE You can specify lighting in real-world units. To turn on this feature, you set the LIGHTINGUNITS system variable to 1 or 2. By default, this feature off (set to 0). When photometry is on, you have an additional background option, Sun & Sky. If you choose this option, the Adjust Sun & Sky Background dialog box opens. The settings in this dialog box are the same for creating a sun light when photometry is on. I explain this feature, called *photometry*, in Chapter 25 where I discuss lights.

The Background dialog box opens, as shown in Figure 22.7, after you choose the Solid option and select a color.

FIGURE 22.7

The Background dialog box enables you to display a background while you work.

In the Background dialog box, you again have the opportunity to choose one of the three options. To specify the background, choose one of the following:

- **Solid background:** Choose Solid (the default) from the Type drop-down list. Click the color swatch in the Color section. In the Select Color dialog box that opens, choose a color.
- **Gradient background:** Choose Gradient from the Type drop-down list. For a two-color gradient, uncheck the Three Color check box. Click in each color swatch to open the Select Color dialog box and choose a color. To rotate the gradient, enter a rotation angle in the Rotation text box or use the arrows to change the value.

■ **Image background.** Choose Image from the Type drop-down list. Click the Browse button to choose an image file (in BMP, JPEG, TIF, PNG, TGA, GIF, or PCX format), and click Open. To adjust the position, scale, or offset of the image, click the Adjust Image button. In the Adjust Image dialog box, you can choose a position (Center, Stretch, or Tile) to specify how the image fits the viewport. You can also click the Offset or Scale option buttons and use the sliders to change the offset or scale of the image. Click OK when you're done. You can see an example of an image background in Figure 25.1.

When you specify the background, click OK to return to the View Manager and click OK again to return to your drawing.

To edit a background, choose the view from the View Manager, click the Background item in the General category, click the down arrow, drop-down list, and choose Edit. You can also choose <None> to remove the image.

Working with the Tripod and Compass

You can choose another method of defining views, using the VPOINT command. To start this command, choose View ⇨ 3D Views ⇨ Viewpoint. The tripod and compass appear, as shown in Figure 22.8.

FIGURE 22.8

The VPOINT tripod and compass define viewpoints in 3D.

If you type the VPOINT command, or press Enter to repeat the command, press Enter at the Current view direction: VIEWDIR=-1.0000,-1.0000,1.0000 Specify a view point or [Rotate] <display compass and tripod>: prompt to see the compass and tripod. (The numbers show the current viewpoint.)

Move the cursor about, and two things happen. The cursor moves within the compass, and the axes dynamically shift position.

Imagine that you take a tangerine and make a large, cross-shaped cut at the very bottom. Then you open out the bottom and remove the peel from the tangerine. Flatten the peel on the table. This is the concept of the compass, except that the outer edge is round. (The tangerine peel would have the shape of the cuts on its outer edge.) The very center of the compass — or the peel — is like the North Pole. When you're over the North Pole, you're looking straight down at your model — or the tangerine. This produces a plan view. The inner circle of the compass is where the middle of the tangerine was, at the equator. From the equator, you're looking sideways (from the front, back, or side) at your model. The outer circle of the compass represents the South Pole. From over the South Pole, you're looking at the bottom of your model — or the tangerine.

All of this is equivalent to the right image in the Viewpoint Presets dialog box that you use with the DDVPOINT command; it determines your view relative to the XY plane:

- At the center of the compass, you're right on top, looking down. This is a plan view.
- At the inner circle, you're on the side, looking at the XY plane on its edge.
- At the outer circle, you're beneath the XY plane, looking up.

The cross that goes through the compass represents the X and Y axes. If you place the cursor on the positive (right) side of the X axis, you're looking at the tangerine from its right side — this is equivalent to a right view. The position of the cursor relative to the X and Y axes is equivalent to the left image in the Viewpoint Presets dialog box that you use with the DDVPOINT command; it determines your view relative to the X axis in the XY plane. To summarize, going clockwise:

- The positive X axis gives you a right view.
- The negative Y axis is equivalent to a front view.
- The negative X axis gives you a left view.
- The positive Y axis gives you a back view.

When you have the cursor at the desired location, simply click. Your drawing displays the viewpoint that you specified.

You cannot achieve an exact viewpoint this way. However, some people find this method of defining a viewpoint more intuitive. You can also look at the tripod as the axes move about. However, be careful — sometimes it's difficult to see whether an axis is coming toward you or going away from you.

Along with the tripod and compass, you see the current UCS icon based on the current UCS to help you find your bearings. Figure 22.9 shows a cursor location that results in the viewpoint shown in Figure 22.10. This is very close to the SE isometric view.

FIGURE 22.9

This cursor location results in the viewpoint shown in Figure 22.10.

FIGURE 22.10

This viewpoint results from the cursor location on the compass shown in Figure 22.9.

Displaying a Quick Plan View

The PLAN command is a quick way to return to plan view. Type **plan** ↵. This command has three options:

- **<Current UCS>:** This is the default. You see the plan view of the current UCS.
- **UCS:** The UCS option enables you to choose a named UCS. Type **?** ↵ to see a list of the named UCSs. Otherwise, type the name of a UCS.
- **World:** This option gives you the plan view of the WCS. If your current UCS is the WCS, there is no difference between this option and the Current UCS option.

Figure 22.11 shows a sample UCS listing. The units are architectural.

Returning to Plan View When You Change the UCS

If you like plan views, you'll love UCSFOLLOW. UCSFOLLOW is a system variable that returns you to plan view whenever you change the UCS. It's for those who like to find their bearings in plan view first, before going on to change the viewpoint in another UCS.

The default value is 0 (off), which means that your drawing does not return to plan view. In other words, your display remains unchanged when you change the UCS. Type **ucsfollow** and change the value to 1 to turn UCS-FOLLOW on. From then on, your drawing automatically displays the plan view when you change the UCS.

FIGURE 22.11

A listing of saved UCSs.

```
Enter UCS name(s) to list <*>:

Current ucs name: *NO NAME*

Saved coordinate systems:

"EASTELEV"
     Origin = <0'-0",0'-0",0'-0">, X Axis = <0'-0",0'-0",0'-1">
     Y Axis = <0'-0",0'-1",0'-0">, Z Axis = <-0'-1",0'-0",0'-0">
"FRONTROOF"
     Origin = <0'-0",10'-0",0'-0">, X Axis = <0'-0",0'-0",0'-1">
     Y Axis = <0'-0 7/8",0'-0 7/16",0'-0">, Z Axis = <-0'-0 7/16",0'-0
7/8",0'-0">
"NORTHSIDE"
     Origin = <0'-0",0'-0",40'-0">, X Axis = <0'-1",0'-0",0'-0">
     Y Axis = <0'-0",0'-1",0'-0">, Z Axis = <0'-0",0'-0",0'-1">
```

AUTOCAD ONLY The Express Tools' extended PLAN command, EXPLAN, prompts you to select objects so that you can see the plan view zoomed in on those objects. Choose Express ➪ Tools ➪ Extended Plan. For information about installing Express Tools, see Appendix A.

Working with Visual Styles

Visual styles allow you to display your drawing in different ways, depending on your needs. Sometimes, you want to see the wireframes; other times, you may want a more realistic look. Visual styles are very flexible, because you can create your own styles.

NOTE Visual styles take the place of shading and the SHADEMODE command of earlier versions in AutoCAD. Visual styles are not available in AutoCAD LT. See the "Using the shading options in AutoCAD LT" section for more information about shading in AutoCAD LT.

Displaying visual styles in AutoCAD

To display a visual style in AutoCAD, choose View ➪ Visual Styles. You have the following preset options:

- **2D Wireframe:** Displays objects in the familiar wireframe display, with no shading and the 2D UCS icon. It uses the 2D model space background (black by default).

- **3D Wireframe:** Displays objects in wireframe, along with a shaded UCS icon. It uses the 3D parallel or perspective background, which by default is gray or shades of gray. (I explain these backgrounds later in this chapter.)

- **3D Hidden:** Hides the display of back edges and faces.
- **Conceptual:** Shades the objects using the *Gooch* face style, which uses a gradation of cool and warm colors. The effect is somewhat cartoon-like, but can make details of your objects easier to see.
- **Realistic:** Shades the objects. This option displays materials that you have attached to the objects if materials are turned on. (You turn materials and textures on and off in the Materials control panel of the Dashboard. I discuss materials in detail in Chapter 25.) If you are not working with materials, you'll get the clearest display with objects that are not black/white.

These visual styles are easy to access in the Visual Style control panel of the Dashboard, as shown in Figure 22.12. Any custom visual styles that you create are also available here.

FIGURE 22.12

You can switch visual styles from the Dashboard.

In a 3D environment, which uses a gray background, new objects that you draw on layer 0 (zero) are black if your 2D background is black, and white if your 2D background is white.

A number of system variables control exactly how objects are displayed. You can access these in the Visual Styles control panel of the Dashboard. For example:

- **VSINTERSECTIONEDGES:** If objects intersect, by default AutoCAD doesn't display a line between them. You can display a line by changing this system variable to 1. However, this may slow performance, due to the calculations required.

- **VSFACECOLORMODE:** This system variable modifies the face color. You can easily set this system variable in the Visual Style control panel of the Dashboard, using the Regular Face Colors flyout. The default value, 0, adds no modifying color. You can set the value to 3 to desaturate the color. This may help to make the model clearer.

- **VSOBSCUREDEDGES:** This system variable takes the place of the previous OBSCUREDCOLOR and OBSCUREDLTYPE system variables. It works with the VSOBSCUREDCOLOR and VSOBSCUREDLTYPE system variables to display back lines in a 3D Hidden visual style; for example, you can display back lines as dashed lines or in a different color from the object's main color. For more information, see Chapter 21.

- **VSFACEOPACIT** Another way to display back lines is to change the opacity of the faces. This system variable sets the opacity. The value of this system variable is a percentage of opacity. You can insert a minus sign before the value to turn off the effect. The default, -60, turns off the effect, but you can change it to 60 to quickly turn it on. You can access this system variable from the Visual Style control panel of the Dashboard, where it's called X-ray Mode. The button toggles opacity between -60 and 60.

Creating custom visual styles

The full power of visual styles is apparent when you create your own. The system variables just listed and several others combine to define a visual style. You can set these values and then save them as your own visual style.

  To create your own visual style, open the Visual Styles Manager palette, shown in Figure 22.13, from the Visual Styles control panel of the Dashboard or the Visual Styles toolbar.

FIGURE 22.13

The Visual Styles Manager enables you to create and save custom visual styles.

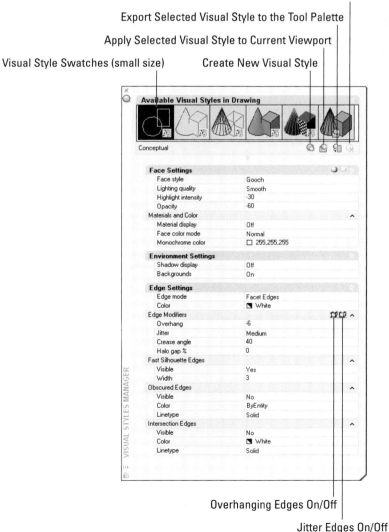

Delete Selected Visual Style

Export Selected Visual Style to the Tool Palette

Apply Selected Visual Style to Current Viewport

Visual Style Swatches (small size)   Create New Visual Style

Overhanging Edges On/Off

Jitter Edges On/Off

To create a new visual style, click the Create New Visual Style button in the Visual Styles Manager to start from default settings. To use the settings of an existing style as a basis, select the visual style that most resembles the style that you want to create, right-click it, and choose Copy. Then right-click in the Visual Styles Manager and choose Paste. Then change the settings. The settings in the Visual Styles Manager fall into three groups: Face, Environment, and Edge.

Face settings determine how the faces of 3D objects look. You can set the following options:

- **Face Style:** You can set the face style to None (like 3D Wireframe or 3D Hidden), Gooch (like Conceptual), or Real (like Realistic).
- **Lighting Quality:** By default, the lighting is smoothed over curved objects. You can turn this off for a faceted look.
- **Highlight Intensity:** Controls the size of highlights created by lighting on objects without materials. The default is -30 and the value can range from -100 to 100. Larger numbers result in larger highlights.
- **Opacity:** Sets the opacity of the faces. This is the VSFACEOPACITY system variable that I discussed in the previous section.

Environment settings affect the display of shadows and backgrounds. You can turn these on or off. You add a background using the VIEW command, as I explained earlier in this chapter.

Edge settings affect how the edges of your 3D models look. Edges are the lines or curves that border the faces. You can choose from three edge modes: Facet Edges, Isolines, or None. The 3D Wireframe visual style uses isolines to give you a better sense of curves. The 3D Hidden visual style uses facet edges to show just the edges and to provide a cleaner look. If you use isolines, you can choose the number of lines (the ISO-LINES system variable). You can also decide if the isolines are always on top, which provides edges even to shaded objects.

Two edge modifiers, jitter and overhang, help to provide a hand-drawn look. Jitter adds additional lines, as if you're sketching. Overhand extends lines past their ends, as shown in Figure 22.14.

FIGURE 22.14

You can get a hand-drawn look with the jitter and overhang features.

You can set jitter and overhang in the expanded Visual Style control panel of the Dashboard:

 To set jitter, click the Edge Jitter button to activate its control, and drag the slider in either direction.

 To set overhang, click the Edge Overhang button to activate its control, and drag the slider in either direction.

You can also set jitter and overhang in the Visual Styles Manager, when you define a visual style. Click the Overhanging Edges and Jitter Edges buttons in the Edge Modifiers section and change the values of these items.

 Fast silhouette edges are the lines or curves around the edge of a model. The 3D Hidden and Conceptual visual styles use fast silhouette edges, and you can increase their width for a bolder look. In the Dashboard, click the Silhouette Edges button and drag the slider in either direction. In the Visual Styles Manager, use the Fast Silhouette Edges section.

Intersection edges display lines where solids intersect. I explained this feature in the previous section. Figure 22.15 shows a model with a smaller box intersecting with a larger box. (They're both filleted.) The left side does not display an intersection edge between the two boxes; the right side does.

FIGURE 22.15

You can choose to display edges where solids intersect.

Intersection edge

When you're done designing your visual style, you can use the Apply Selected Visual Style to Current Viewport button to apply the visual style. The visual style also appears in the Dashboard, so you can choose it from there. You can also use the Delete the Selected Visual Style button to delete your visual styles; however, you can't delete the styles that come with AutoCAD.

Using the shading options in AutoCAD LT

The SHADEMODE command in AutoCAD LT has only two options, 2D Wireframe and Hidden. The 2D Wireframe option allows you to turn off the shading in a viewport set for one of the options only available in AutoCAD. However, AutoCAD LT has a SHADE command that provides the following options:

- **256 Color:** Displays shaded faces. Shading is flat, but curved faces give the impression of gradual shading because they're broken up into many faces, each a slightly different color.
- **256 Color Edge Highlight:** Similar to 256 Color, but highlights edges using the same color as your drawing background.
- **16 Color Hidden Line:** Looks like a hidden display. The non-hidden edges are in the object's color, and the faces are the color of the background of the drawing area.
- **16 Color Filled:** The reverse of 16 Color Hidden Line, so that the faces are in the object's color, and non-hidden edges are the background color.

You can also control the shading by using the SHADEDGE system variable.

In AutoCAD LT, you cannot edit your objects in Shaded mode, which is a better-looking version of the HIDE command. If you regenerate the drawing, the shading goes away.

Display materials, textures, and lights as you work

Materials, textures, and lights are used in rendering, which is covered in Chapter 25. You can display materials and textures that you've attached to objects, even as you work, although doing so may slow down performance. You can also display lights. To display these features, you need to use the Realistic visual style, or a visual style that uses the Real face style.

 This section applies to AutoCAD only. AutoCAD LT does not include materials, textures, or lights, which is part of the rendering capability of AutoCAD.

 To display materials and textures, click the Materials and Textures On button in the Materials control panel of the Dashboard. Figure 22.16 shows a model with the Bronze Satin material attached.

 To display lights that you have created, click the Viewport Lighting Mode button in the Lights control panel of the Dashboard so that the tooltip reads User Light/Sunlight. You can adjust the brightness and contrast of lighting in the Dashboard as well. Click the double down arrows to expand the Lights control panel, and drag the Brightness and Contrast sliders.

FIGURE 22.16

A model with the Bronze Satin material attached. (It looks better in color!)

NEW FEATURE When the photometric feature is on (the LIGHTINGUNITS system variable is set to 1 or 2), you can adjust midtones of the light, using the Drag to Change Mid Tones slider in the expanded Lights control panel of the Dashboard.

CROSS-REF If you don't see lights or materials, they may be off due to Adaptive Degradation. AutoCAD automatically turns off certain features based on the capability of your graphics card and overall computer system. For more information, see Appendix A.

ON the DVD-ROM The drawing used in the following exercise on using and creating visual styles in a drawing, `ab22-b.dwg`, is in the `Drawings` folder on the DVD.

AUTOCAD ONLY This exercise is for AutoCAD only. AutoCAD LT doesn't offer these shading options.

STEPS: Using and Creating Visual Styles

1. Open `ab22-b.dwg` from the DVD.

2. Save it as `ab22-02.dwg` in your `AutoCAD Bible` folder. This drawing should display the 3D Wireframe visual style. If the Dashboard isn't open, choose Tools ➪ Palettes ➪ Dashboard.

3. From the Visual Style control panel of the Dashboard, choose 2D Wireframe. The background color and the UCS change.

4. This time, choose 3D Hidden. Back lines disappear and the background is the same as for 3D Wireframe.

5. Choose the Conceptual visual style. The colors of the model change to blue and green.

6. Choose the Realistic visual style. This time, if your computer system can support it, you see the bronze satin material that I attached to the drawing.

7. Click Visual Styles Manager from the Visual Style control panel of the Dashboard.

8. Click the Create New Visual Style button near the top of the Visual Styles Manager palette. In the Create New Visual Style dialog box, enter **MyRealistic** in the Name text box. In the Description text box, enter **No edges;silhouette**. You want to create a visual style that doesn't show edges within the model but displays a thick silhouette around its outside. Click OK.

9. Change the following settings:
   ```
   Material display: Material and textures
   Edge Mode: None
   Fast Silhouette Edges-Visible: Yes
   Fast Silhouette Edges-Width: 9
   ```

10. Click the Apply Selected Visual Style to Current Viewport button. You see the change in the model. The internal edges disappear, but there's a thicker edge around the outside.

11. Close or hide the Visual Styles Manager. From the Dashboard, choose the Realistic visual style. Then choose the MyRealistic visual style to see the difference. Your model should look like Figure 22.17.

FIGURE 22.17

The model with the MyRealistic custom visual style.

Displaying Parallel and Perspective Projections

You may have noticed when you open AutoCAD with the default 3D environment that the grid lines look like they're receding into the distance. That's because AutoCAD is displaying a *perspective* view, which makes parallel lines converge as they get farther away. Because this is how parallel lines look in real life (try looking down a road or a railroad track into the distance), a perspective view looks more realistic than a parallel view that keeps lines parallel, regardless of their distance. However, when you zoom in, objects may appear distorted. Use a perspective view when you want to convey a realistic sense of depth. In general, perspective view is most useful in architectural settings. AutoCAD LT doesn't include perspective projections.

The PERSPECTIVE system variable controls the current view. A value of 0 (zero) turns off perspective view; 1 turns it on. You can change the view in the 3D Navigate control panel of the Dashboard:

 Click Perspective Projection to turn on a perspective view.

 Click Parallel Projection to turn on a parallel view.

Using 3D Orbit

The 3D Orbit feature is a fully interactive way to change your viewpoint in real time. Using 3D Orbit is like orbiting the earth to view any continent or ocean below. When you enter 3D Orbit mode, you cannot use other commands. In this regard, 3D Orbit is like Realtime Pan and Realtime Zoom. Similarly, you can press Esc or Enter to exit 3D Orbit mode. You access the 3D Orbit options by right-clicking in the drawing area to display the 3D Orbit shortcut menu.

AUTOCAD ONLY 3D Orbit is not available in AutoCAD LT. This entire section, including the exercise, is for AutoCAD only.

Starting 3D Orbit

To start 3D Orbit, choose View ⇨ Orbit ⇨ Constrained Orbit or choose Constrained Orbit from the Orbit flyout toolbar in the 3D Navigate control panel of the Dashboard. If another mode of 3D Orbit is active, right-click and choose Other Navigation Modes ⇨ Constrained Orbit or type **1**.

The term *constrained* means that the orbit is restricted to the XY plane or the Z direction. You enter 3D Orbit mode, and AutoCAD displays the 3D Orbit cursor, as shown in Figure 22.18.

TIP You can use 3D Orbit transparently, that is, in the middle of another command. Just press and hold Shift and your mouse's wheel (using it like a button), rotate your model as you want, and release the buttons. You then continue the command in progress. This way of using the 3DORBIT command without actually executing the command makes it very easy to navigate your model.

NEW FEATURE You can now use 3D Orbit in the Block Editor when editing 3D blocks.

Like several other modes, the 3D Orbit mode includes the ability to zoom and pan. Therefore, you can use this command for more than just orbiting.

FIGURE 22.18

3D Orbit mode allows you to change the viewpoint of your drawing in real time.

TIP For faster performance, select only the objects that you want to view with 3D Orbit before starting the command. Objects that you did not select disappear while you're in 3D Orbit mode. Of course, they reappear as soon as you leave 3D Orbit mode.

Navigating with 3D Orbit

The default 3D Orbit mode is Constrained Orbit. Drag to the left or right to rotate the model around on the XY plane, and drag up or down to rotate the model along the Z axis. You can't rotate the model upside down in Constrained Orbit mode. Drag diagonally to create isometric views.

 If you need more freedom, you can use Free Orbit mode. Choose View ⇨ Orbit ⇨ Free Orbit or choose Free Orbit from the Orbit flyout toolbar in the 3D Navigate control panel of the Dashboard. If another mode of 3D Orbit is active, right-click and choose Other Navigation Modes ⇨ Free Orbit or type **2**. In Free Orbit mode, you have less control but more options.

Free Orbit mode displays an *arcball* and has four cursors that affect how your model rotates. Each cursor is location-based. As you move your cursor to a new location, the cursor shape automatically changes, and the type of rotation changes. The arcball is shown in Figure 22.19.

FIGURE 22.19

3D Orbit's Free mode uses an arcball.

Arcball

You use the arcball in the following ways:

- **Rolling with the circular arrow cursor:** When you place your cursor outside the arcball, it takes the shape of a circular arrow. As you click and drag around the outside of the arcball, your model turns around an imaginary axis that extends from the center of the arcball outward, and perpendicular to the screen — that is, pointing at you. This type of rotation is called a *roll*.

- **Rotating freely with the sphere and lines cursor:** As soon as you move your cursor within the arcball, it takes the shape of a small sphere encircled by two lines. As you click and drag within the arcball, your model moves around the center of the arcball in the direction that you drag. Imagine that your model is encased in a transparent sphere, similar to a gerbil or hamster ball. As you drag the cursor, you're rotating the sphere around its center point. If you drag from one edge of the arcball to its opposite edge, you can release the mouse, move back to your starting point, and then click and drag again in the same direction. When you do this a few times, you rotate your model 360 degrees. You achieve the best results by dragging in a line in any direction, rather than 'round and 'round.

- **Rotating around the vertical axis with the horizontal ellipse cursor:** When you move your cursor over either the left or right quadrant circle on the arcball, it becomes a horizontal ellipse. As you click and drag from either quadrant, your model rotates around the arcball's vertical axis, which extends from the top quadrant to the bottom quadrant. Although your cursor enters the arcball, it retains its horizontal ellipse form until you release the mouse button. You can drag from one quadrant to its opposite quadrant, release the mouse button, move back to your starting point, and then click and drag again in the same direction. When you do this a few times, you rotate your model 360 degrees.

- **Rotating around the horizontal axis with the vertical ellipse cursor:** When you move your cursor over either the top or bottom quadrant circle on the arcball, it becomes a vertical ellipse. As you click and drag from either quadrant, your model rotates around the arcball's horizontal axis, which extends from the left quadrant to the right quadrant. You can drag from one quadrant to its opposite quadrant, release the mouse button, move back to your starting point, and then click and drag again in the same direction. When you do this a few times, you rotate your model 360 degrees.

Using the 3D Orbit visual aids

3D Orbit includes three visual aids that can help you find your bearings:

- **Compass:** Displays a sphere that is made up of three dashed lines labeled as the X, Y, and Z axes. The lines look like the threads of a baseball. To display the compass, right-click and choose Visual Aids ⇨ Compass from the shortcut menu.

- **Grid:** Displays a grid of lines representing the XY plane. The Z coordinate of the grid is equal to the value of the ELEVATION system variable, which is set to 0 (zero) by default. You can specify the structure of the grid with the GRIDUNIT system variable. You can set this value by choosing Tools ⇨ Drafting Settings before you use this visual aid.

- **UCS icon:** Displays a shaded, three-dimensional 3D UCS icon. The X axis is red, the Y axis is green, and the Z axis is blue.

You would rarely want to use all three visual aids. The compass and grid can both interfere with viewing your model and should be used temporarily when needed.

To display the visual aids, right-click while in 3D Orbit mode and choose Visual Aids from the shortcut menu. Then choose the aid that you want from the submenu. To turn off the visual aids, follow the same procedure — the submenu items toggle the visual aids on and off when you click them.

NOTE If you choose a visual style (other than the default 2D wireframe), the visual aids remain active after you exit 3D Orbit. You can switch to the 2D wireframe visual style, as explained earlier in this chapter, or you can re-enter 3D Orbit and turn off the visual aids.

Creating a continuous orbit

Absolutely the coolest feature of 3D Orbit — and one of the coolest features of AutoCAD as a whole — is continuous orbit. Continuous orbit enables you to choose a direction of rotation and then let go. 3D Orbit automatically continues the rotation in the same direction and continues it until you change or stop it. With continuous orbit, who needs screensavers? Here's how it works:

1. Choose View ➪ Orbit ➪ Continuous Orbit or choose Continuous Orbit from the Orbit flyout toolbar in the 3D Navigate control panel of the Dashboard. With 3D Orbit mode active, right-click and choose Other Navigation Modes ➪ Continuous Orbit or type **3**.

2. Click and drag in the direction of rotation that you want to create. The faster you drag, the faster the resulting orbit.

3. Release your mouse button. Your model continues to rotate in the same direction. All you do is watch.

Continuous orbit is an ideal way to view your model. As your model rotates, you can pick out any errors and then stop continuous orbit to fix them. You can change the direction of your continuous orbit at any time by clicking and dragging in a new direction and then releasing the mouse button. To stop continuous orbit, choose any other 3D Orbit mode or click in the drawing window.

Resetting the view

You can end up with some strange views of your model when using 3D Orbit, so AutoCAD provides a way to reset your view to the view that was current when you first started 3D Orbit. With any 3D Orbit mode active, right-click and choose Reset View from the shortcut menu.

Refining your 3D Orbit view

3D Orbit offers many options for refining your view so that you see just the view that you want. You can pan and zoom, adjust the camera distance, create parallel and perspective views, set clipping planes, or display a preset view. You can also start Walk or Fly mode, as discussed later in this chapter.

Because you cannot use other commands while in 3D Orbit mode, you must access most of these options by right-clicking in the drawing area to access the 3D Orbit shortcut menu, shown in Figure 22.20. You can also use the 3D Navigation toolbar for some of these options.

FIGURE 22.20

The 3D Orbit shortcut menu holds all the options while you are in 3D Orbit mode.

Exit		
Current Mode: Constrained Orbit		
Other Navigation Modes ▶	✓ Constrained Orbit	1
	Free Orbit	2
✓ Enable Orbit Auto Target	Continuous Orbit	3
Animation Settings ...	Adjust Distance	4
	Swivel	5
Zoom Window		
Zoom Extents	Walk	6
Zoom Previous	Fly	7
✓ Parallel	Zoom	8
Perspective	Pan	9
Reset View		
Preset Views ▶		
Named Views ▶		
Visual Styles ▶		
Visual Aids ▶		

Panning in 3D Orbit

To pan in 3D Orbit mode, right-click and choose Other Navigation Modes ⇨ Pan from the 3D Orbit short-cut menu or type **9**. You see the familiar hand cursor. Click and drag to pan, in the same way that you normally pan in real-time. To stop panning, right-click and choose another mode.

Zooming in 3D Orbit

To zoom in 3D Orbit, right-click and choose Other Navigation Modes ⇨ Zoom from the 3D Orbit shortcut menu or type **8**. You see the familiar magnifying glass cursor with a plus (+) and a minus (–) sign. Click and drag in the direction of the plus sign (toward the top of your screen) to zoom in; click and drag in the direction of the minus sign (toward the bottom of your screen) to zoom out, just as you do when you normally use zoom real-time. To stop zooming, switch to any other mode.

Using Zoom options in 3D Orbit

To zoom to a window in 3D Orbit, right-click and choose Zoom Window from the shortcut menu. Your cursor displays a small rectangle. Click and drag, and then release the mouse button to define the two corners of the window.

To zoom to drawing extents in 3D Orbit, right-click and choose Zoom Extents. To return to the previous view, right-click and choose Zoom Previous.

Adjusting the camera distance

You can adjust the distance between the viewer, called the *camera*, and the target, which by default is set to the center of the 3D view (this view may be different from the center of your model). Changing this camera distance is equivalent to zooming in and out.

To adjust the camera distance in 3D Orbit, right-click and choose Other Navigation Modes ⇨ Adjust Distance from the shortcut menu or type **4**. The cursor changes to a horizontal line with a double-headed arrow pointing up and down. Click and drag toward the top of your screen to move the camera closer to your objects — similar to zooming in. Click and drag toward the bottom of your screen to move the camera away from your objects — similar to zooming out.

Controlling view properties

When you use 3D Orbit, the Properties palette displays special properties that relate to 3D Orbit features.

- **View Height** is a way to specify the distance of the imaginary camera. In other words, you can use this property to zoom in and out on your model. A larger number makes your model look smaller because the distance (or height) of the camera from the model increases.

- **View Width** is another way to zoom in and out. Here you specify the width of the view of the imaginary camera. A larger number makes your model look smaller because the view encompasses a larger area (and your model is a smaller part of that area).

- **Lens Length** and **Field of View** define the angle of the view. I discuss these concepts in the section "Creating a Named View with a Camera" earlier in this chapter.

To change these properties, click their row in the Properties palette. Type a new value and press Enter.

Creating parallel and perspective views

To create a perspective view in 3D Orbit, right-click and choose Perspective. To return to parallel view, choose Parallel. For more information on perspective views, see the section "Displaying Parallel and Perspective Projections" earlier in this chapter.

Using a preset view

After you use 3D Orbit a few times, your model may appear askew, with no indication of how to return it to a viewpoint that you can comprehend. You can switch to any of the preset views discussed at the beginning of this chapter. From 3D Orbit, right-click and choose Preset Views from the shortcut menu. Then choose one of the standard viewpoints on the submenu list.

 The drawing used in the following exercise on working in 3D Orbit, ab22-c.dwg, is in the Drawings folder on the DVD.

STEPS: Working in 3D Orbit

1. Open ab22-c.dwg from the DVD. This is a 3D chair shown from a Northeast isometric view.
2. Choose View ⇨ Orbit ⇨ Constrained Orbit.
3. Place the mouse cursor to the right of the chair in the middle (vertically) of the screen. Drag to the left twice until the chair turns around completely and is back to approximately its original position.
4. Place the cursor below the chair and drag up until it stops. Drag down until the chair is in its original position. Place the cursor above the chair and drag down until it stops. Return the chair to its original position again.
5. Place the cursor above the chair until you are looking down at it — a Top view. The chair is still rotated. Drag from the left to the right until the chair's bottom is horizontal on the screen.
6. Right-click and choose Other Navigation Modes ⇨ Free Orbit. Place the cursor inside the arcball and drag in various directions to see that you now have more freedom to tumble the chair upside down.
7. Right-click and choose Zoom Previous to return to the Top view.
8. Type 1 to return to Constrained Orbit mode. The arcball disappears.
9. Right-click and choose Other Navigation Modes ⇨ Continuous Orbit. Click and drag with the cursor, making a small movement from right to left, and then release the mouse button. You may need to try this a couple of times to find a continuous orbit that you like. Try clicking and dragging in a different direction to change the direction of the continuous orbit, and then release the mouse button.
10. Type 1 to stop the continuous orbit.
11. Right-click and choose Reset View to re-display the chair exactly in its original view.
12. Type 9 (pan). Pan the chair to the right a little.
13. Right-click and choose Other Navigation Modes ⇨ Zoom. Zoom the chair in slightly.
14. Right-click and choose Preset Views ⇨ NW Isometric.
15. Press Esc to exit 3D Orbit mode.

Don't save your drawing.

Using Tiled Viewports

As you learned in Chapter 8, you can create multiple viewports to view your drawing at different zooms and pans. Tiled viewports are very helpful in 3D drawings as well. Although you can, and should, save UCSs and views, if you find yourself switching back and forth between two to four viewpoints, try creating two to four viewports with the different viewpoints and UCSs in them. The only disadvantage is that you have less screen real estate for each viewpoint.

Walking Through a Model

To better see what a model looks like, and to show it to clients, you can "walk" through it. This feature is most useful for architectural models, because it simulates walking through a space, such as a building. Although Walk appears as a mode on the 3D Orbit shortcut menu, it has its own unique navigational system. Walking maintains your view parallel to the XY plane, but you can use the Fly mode to move away from the XY plane.

You can record your walk-through and save it as an animation file to play back later. In addition, you can create an object that functions as a motion guide, called a motion point or path. You can then record an animation file that uses the point or path to define the walk-through.

AUTOCAD ONLY AutoCAD LT doesn't include walk- or fly-throughs, nor does it include any way to create a movie file of your drawing navigation.

Navigating in Walk mode

To enter Walk mode, choose Walk from the Walk flyout in the Navigate control panel of the Dashboard or the 3D Navigation toolbar. You can also choose View ➪ Walk and Fly ➪ Walk. This executes the 3DWALK command. From any 3D Orbit mode, right-click and choose Other Navigation Modes ➪ Walk or type **6**.

You must be in perspective view to use Walk and Fly modes. If you aren't, a message asks you whether you want to toggle to a perspective view.

The Walk and Fly Navigation Mappings window opens, as shown in Figure 22.21. Click the window's Close button to return to your drawing.

TIP Because walking through a model is sometimes a little cumbersome, depending on the capabilities of your graphics card and the complexity and size of your model, you should display your desired starting point before you enter 3DWALK. Also, switch to the visual style you want to use before entering Walk mode; you can't switch from within Walk mode.

FIGURE 22.21

The Walk and Fly Navigation Mappings window lets you know which keys to use for navigating in Walk and Fly modes.

Because you turn by dragging with the mouse, you'll probably find it easiest to use the W, A, S, and D keys with your left hand (assuming you use your right hand for your mouse). This set of keys is used for navigating in computer games and provides an easy way to move in the four directions without looking at the keys.

When you close the Walk and Fly Navigation Mappings window, the Position Locator window opens, and your cursor changes to a plus sign, as shown in Figure 22.22. The Position Locator window shows you your model from the top, so you can gauge your position.

FIGURE 22.22

The Position Locator shows you a 2D map of your model.

The best feature of the Position Locator is that you can drag the red dot that represents your position to move your current position. You can also drag the target indicator to change your view. In the General section of the Position Locator window, you can also specify the following settings:

- **Position indicator color:** You can change the color (which is red by default) to contrast better with your model.

- **Position indicator size:** You can change the indicator's size to small, medium, or large.

- **Position indicator blink:** You can make the indicator blink if you want.

- **Position Z:** Sets the Z coordinate for the current position.

- **Target indicator:** You can turn the target indicator on or off. Having it on is generally helpful because it explains what you are seeing in the main drawing area and you can drag it to change your view.

- **Target indicator color:** You can change the color (which is green by default) to contrast better with your model.

- **Target Z:** Sets the Z coordinate for the target.

- **Preview transparency:** Sets the transparency of the preview in the Position Locator window. For example, if you're in a house, as shown in Figure 22.22, you want to be able to see through the roof. You can set a number from 0 to 95. Don't include the percent (%) symbol when you enter a new number.

- **Preview visual style:** You can choose a visual style for the preview.

When you're ready to walk, press the W key or the Up arrow. You can press the key repeatedly or hold it down, but if you hold it down for a while, you'll then need to wait for the display to catch up. As you walk, you can drag to the left or right to change your viewing direction. Whenever you need to get your bearing, just look over at the Position Locator window to see where you are as well as your view's target.

NOTE The capabilities of your computer, including your graphics card, have a major effect on the performance when you walk through a model. AutoCAD needs to make many calculations each second to redisplay your screen as you change position.

Specifying Walk mode settings

 You can specify several settings that affect how Walk mode works. While in Walk mode, right-click and choose Walk and Fly Settings. At other times, choose Walk and Fly Settings from the Walk flyout in the 3D Navigate control panel of the Dashboard or choose View ⇨ Walk and Fly ⇨ Walk and Fly Settings. The Walk and Fly Settings dialog box opens, as shown in Figure 22.23.

FIGURE 22.23

The Walk and Fly Settings dialog box allows you to fine-tune the Walk mode settings.

You can choose when the instruction window displays. After a while, you know the instructions, so you probably don't want the window to display each time you enter Walk or Fly mode. You can also choose whether or not to display the Position Locator window.

To change the size of your steps and how many steps you move per section, use the settings in the Current Drawing Settings section. If you set your steps too small, walking seems too slow, but if they're too big, you don't have as much control. Click OK when you're done changing the settings.

Flying through a model

Walking through a model keeps you parallel to the XY plane. However, sometimes you may want to look at the roof of a house or go up stairs. Fly mode frees you to leave the XY plane.

 You can enter Fly mode by pressing the F key from Walk mode. From any 3D Orbit mode, right-click and choose Other Navigation Modes ➪ Fly or type 7. Otherwise, choose Fly from the Walk flyout in the 3D Navigate control panel of the Dashboard or the 3D Navigation toolbar. You can also choose View ➪ Walk and Fly ➪ Fly. This executes the 3DFLY command.

The controls are the same for Fly and Walk modes, except that when you drag the mouse forward, you go upward, away from the XY plane, and when you drag the mouse backward (toward you), you go downward. Figure 22.24 shows the process of "flying" up a flight of stairs.

FIGURE 22.24

You can use Fly mode to climb a flight of stairs.

Saving the walk as a movie file

 You can record your walk- or fly-through as you go, and save the result as a movie (video) file. Before you start, specify the movie settings by choosing Animation Settings from the expanded 3D Navigate control panel of the Dashboard. From any 3D Orbit mode, you can right-click and choose Animation Settings. The Animation Settings dialog box opens, as shown in Figure 22.25.

FIGURE 22.25

The Animation Settings dialog box specifies settings for a move that you record during Walk or Fly mode.

In the Animation Settings dialog box, you can choose a visual style or presentation level from the Visual Style drop-down list. Choose a resolution from the Resolution drop-down list. The Frame Rate (FPS) determines the number of frames per second. Finally, choose one of the four available movie formats from the Format drop-down list: AVI, MOV, MPG, or WMV (the default). Note that the first three settings greatly affect the size of the resulting movie. When you're done, click OK.

NOTE To save to the MOV format, you need to install Apple QuickTime Player. You need Microsoft® Windows Media® Player 9 or later installed to save to WMV format; if it isn't, AVI is the default format.

To start recording, click the Start Recording button in the expanded 3D Navigate control panel of the Dashboard. Then start walking or flying, following the directions in the previous sections.

When you're done, click the Save Animation button on the Dashboard. In the same locations are buttons to pause and play the recording. You can play the animation before you save it to make sure it's acceptable to you. The Animation Preview window opens and plays the animation. This playback is a preview and may not be as polished as the final version.

When you click the Save Animation button, the Save As dialog box opens, where you can save the movie. Navigate to the desired location, enter a name, and click Save. At this time, you can click the Animation Settings button and change the animation settings. The Creating Video progress meter displays to show you the progress as the movie saves. When it's done, open the movie file and watch. Bring some popcorn!

TIP If you don't like the result, choose Zoom Previous from the Standard toolbar. Your display returns to the beginning of your walk, so you can start again.

Using a motion path to save a movie file

Using Walk and Fly modes can result in some jerkiness as you make little adjustments along the way. For a smoother ride, you can draw a motion path and save a movie file that automatically runs along the path.

You need to specify both the camera and its target. They can be either a point or a path (line, arc, elliptical arc, ellipse, circle, polyline, 3D polyline, or spline), but they can't both be a point. For example:

■ If the camera is a point and the target is a circle, the resulting movie is like standing in one place and turning around.

■ If the camera is a circle and the target is a point, the result is like walking around a point (such as the center of a table) that you look at throughout.

The first step is to create one or two motion paths for the camera and/or the target. If you are using paths, a polyline is ideal if you want to add some turns, because you can only select one object.

> **TIP** You may want to create a separate layer that you can later turn off. Also, you usually want to place the height of the motion paths at eye level. You can also place the camera and target paths at different heights, or use a 3D polyline and vary the heights along the way.

Then choose View ➪ Motion Path Animations to open the Motion Path Animation dialog box, shown in Figure 22.26.

FIGURE 22.26

Specify the motion paths and movie settings before you create a motion path animation.

Follow these steps to set up the motion path animation:

1. In the Camera section, choose either Point or Path. If you choose Path, name the path or accept the default name. Then click the Select Path or Pick Point button to select an object for a motion path or to specify a point.

2. In the Target section, do the same. Remember that you can't choose a point for both the camera and the target.

3. In the Animation Settings section, set the frame rate in frames per second and the number of frames. The Duration adjusts automatically based on your choices.

4. Choose a visual style from the Visual Style drop-down list.

5. Choose a format and resolution. These settings are the same as for a walk-through animation, which I discussed in the previous section of this chapter.

6. By default, the movie slows down around corners. You can uncheck the Corner Deceleration check box if you want to. You can also check the Reverse check box to make the animation go backward.

7. Click the Preview button to preview the result. Remember that the preview may not be as good as the final movie. In my experience, the preview did not use the visual style I chose, but the final did.

8. Click OK.

9. In the Save As dialog box, navigate to the desired location. Enter a name and click Save. You can click the Animation Settings dialog box to change the settings before you save. The Creating Video progress meter shows your progress, and the Preview Animation window previews the animation.

 The drawing used in the following exercise on using Walk mode and creating animations, ab22-d.dwg, is in the Drawings folder on the DVD.

STEPS: Using Walk Mode and Creating Animations

1. Open ab22-d.dwg from the DVD.

2. Save the drawing as ab22-03.dwg in your AutoCAD Bible folder. You're inside a 3D house, looking down a hallway, in the 3D Hidden visual style, as shown in Figure 22.27. Type **ucsortho** ↵ and set its value to 0.

FIGURE 22.27

The start of a walk down a hall.

Thanks to Andrew Wilcox of Virtual Homes, Inc., Hammonds Plains, Nova Scotia, Canada, for this drawing.

 3. Display the Dashboard (Tools ➪ Palettes ➪ Dashboard). From the 3D Navigate control panel of the Dashboard, choose Walk and Fly Settings from the Walk flyout. In the Walk and Fly Settings dialog box, make sure that the Walk/fly Step Size is set to 12 drawing units and the Steps per Second is set to 2. Click OK.

 4. Choose Walk from the Walk Flyout on the Dashboard. If the message appears asking you to toggle to perspective view, click Yes. Close the Walk and Fly Navigation Mappings dialog box. The Position Locator appears, showing that you're in an open dining area, looking down a diagonal hallway. You want to go down that hallway, turn to the right, continue to the end of the hallway, and turn left into the master bedroom.

5. Press and hold the W key, or press the W key multiple times until the Position Locator indicates that you're in the narrow hallway. If necessary, let the screen redisplay the model.

6. Continue to walk to the end of the diagonal segment of hallway, as shown in the Position Locator. If necessary, drag slightly to the left or right to adjust your view. Don't mind that along the way, you may be seeing through walls.

7. Drag to the right to turn to the right, until the Position Locator shows the center target line horizontal, facing right. You should be able to see the table inside the bedroom, through a partially open door.

 8. At this point, you want to record the rest of your walk as a video file. Choose Animation Settings from the extended section of the 3D Navigate control panel of the Dashboard. Change the Visual Style to 3D Hidden and change the Frame Rate (FPS) to 15. Choose WMV or AVI as the format, depending on what you think you can play on your computer (probably either). Click OK.

9. From the Dashboard, click the Start Recording Animation button.

10. Continue to walk forward using the W key and dragging slightly to the left to keep the bed in the bedroom in the center of your view until your screen looks like Figure 22.28.

FIGURE 22.28

The master bedroom.

11. From the Dashboard, choose Play Animation to see the preview. Close the preview window.

12. From the Dashboard, choose Save Animation. In the Save As dialog box, navigate to your AutoCAD Bible folder, name the file ab22-03a.wmv (or .avi, depending on the format you chose), and click Save. The Creating Video window shows the progress.

13. In Windows Explorer, double-click the file to open it and watch the animation.

14. Now you want to create an animation from a motion path. From the Dashboard, choose Top from the Select or Manage Views in the This Drawing drop-down list. At the same time, change the visual style to 3D Wireframe. Turn the Motion Path1 and Motion Path2 layers on. You should see two motion paths in the drawing (See Figure 22.29).

You can use these two motion paths to create a video file of a walk-through.

Motion Path 1

Motion Path 2

15. Choose View ➪ Motion Path Animations. Set the Camera section to Path and click the Select Path button. Select Motion Path 1 and name it Motion Path 1. (See Figure 22.29.) Set the Target section to Path and click the Select Path button. Select Motion Path 2 and name it Motion Path 2. Set the frame rate to 15 and the number of frames to 45, which makes a 3-second movie. Set the visual style to 3D Hidden. Choose your preferred movie format and click OK. Save the movie as `ab22-03b.wmv` (or another format) in your `AutoCAD Bible` folder and click Save.

16. Double-click the movie file in Windows Explorer to view it.

17. Save your drawing.

ON the DVD-ROM You can find ab22-03a.wmv and ab22-03b.wmv in the Results folder of the DVD.

Using DVIEW to Create a Perspective View

The original command for defining views with perspective from any angle and distance was DVIEW. The newer 3D Orbit feature is easier to use than DVIEW, but you may still find DVIEW helpful for its precise ways of defining a view. DVIEW is also useful if you want to create 3D views using AutoLISP or VBA. Note that the DVIEW command has been removed from AutoCAD LT.

Like 3D Orbit, DVIEW uses the metaphor of a camera. There is a camera point (where you are standing) and a target point (what you are looking at). By defining these two points, you can create either close-up or distance views, much as you would with the zoom or panoramic lens of a camera. The DVIEW command creates both parallel and perspective views.

Using DVIEW

To create a perspective view, type **dview** ↵ on the command line. At the `Select objects or <use DVIEWBLOCK>:` prompt, select the objects that you want to include in the process of defining the perspective view.

You should select as few objects as you need to visualize the final result if you have a complex drawing. If you want to select the entire drawing, type **all** ↵ even if the current view doesn't display the entire drawing.

Press Enter if you don't want to choose any objects. The command substitutes a block called dviewblock, which is a simple house. You can use the house to set your perspective view.

TIP If you want, you can create your own block and name it dviewblock. Create it with X, Y, and Z dimensions of 1. When you press Enter at the `Select objects or <use DVIEWBLOCK>:` prompt, the command looks for dviewblock and uses it to display the results of the perspective view settings.

Understanding the DVIEW options

When you start DVIEW, you see the following prompt. You use these options to define the 3D view.

```
Enter option
[CAmera/TArget/Distance/POints/PAn/Zoom/TWist/CLip/Hide/Off/Undo]:
```

Here's how to use the DVIEW options:

- **Camera:** Specifies the angle of the camera, which represents where you're standing. You need to specify the angle from the X axis in the XY plane and the angle from the XY plane. This is very similar to the way that you specify a view using the DDVPOINT command, explained earlier in this chapter. At the `Specify camera location, or enter angle from XY plane, or [Toggle (angle in)] <35.2644>:` prompt, type in an angle from the XY plane, or move the cursor vertically to dynamically see the results. Keep in mind that moving the cursor horizontally changes the angle from the X axis in the XY plane. It can be confusing to change both angles at once, and so you can limit the effect of your cursor movement to one angle with the Toggle sub-option. At the `Specify camera location, or enter angle in XY plane from X axis, or [Toggle (angle from)] <66.12857>:` prompt, move the cursor horizontally to see your objects rotate around you at a constant altitude. Now, your cursor affects only the angle from the X axis. You can press Enter when you like what you see, or you can type in an angle.

- **Target:** Works exactly like the Camera option, except that it defines the angles for the target of your viewpoint (what you would see through the camera lens). However, the angles are relative to the camera position. If you've already set the camera angles, then the target angles default to those angles that you create by drawing a straight line from the camera angle through 0,0,0. As with the Camera option, use the Toggle sub-option to switch between the two angles that you need to specify.

- **Distance:** This option is very important because you use it to turn on Perspective mode. Before you use this option, the views that you see are parallel views. When you use the Distance option, you see a slider bar at the top of the screen. After you choose a distance, the Perspective mode icon replaces the UCS icon if your UCS display is set to 2D. At the `Specify new camera-target distance <3.0000>:` prompt, you can type a distance from the camera to the target or use the slider bar. Move the cursor to the right to zoom out. Moving the cursor to 4x is equivalent to using the ZOOM command and typing **4x** ↵. Move the cursor to the left of 1x to zoom in. The zoom factor is relative to the current display, and so 1x leaves the zoom unchanged. You can also type a distance in drawing units.

- **Points:** Define the camera and target by specifying two points. The command line displays the `Specify target point <0.3776, -0.1618, 1.0088>:` prompt. The default target point, which is different for each drawing, is the center of the current view. You see a rubber-band line from the target point, which you can use to find your bearings when choosing a new target point. You can also type a coordinate. At the `Specify camera point <-1.5628, 0.9420, 2.2787>:` prompt, pick or type a point. You can use the rubber-band line stretching from the target so that you can visualize the camera and target points. Because it's difficult to know which 3D points you're picking, you should use an object snap or XYZ point filters to pick points.

 Although it is common to choose a target point on one of the objects in your drawing, you often want the camera point to be off of the objects so that you're looking at the objects from a certain distance and angle. To pick the camera point, choose Format ⇨ Point Style (before starting DVIEW) and choose an easily visible point style. Decide which elevation you want, type elev ↵, and set a new elevation. From plan view, choose Point from the Draw toolbar and pick a point. The point is created on the current elevation. Then use the Node object snap to snap to the point when specifying the camera point in the Points option.

- **Pan:** At the `Specify displacement base point:` prompt, pick any point. At the `Specify second point:` prompt, pick the point to which you want the first point to pan. The model moves the distance and direction indicated by an imaginary line from the base point to the second point.

- **Zoom:** The Zoom option displays the same slider bar that you see with the Distance option, as I explained previously. If Perspective mode is not on, then you see the `Specify zoom scale factor <1>:` prompt, which works like the Distance option slider bar. If Perspective mode is on, then you see the `Specify lens length <50.000mm>:` prompt. A shorter lens length, such as 35mm, zooms you out, giving a wider viewing angle. A longer lens length, such as 70mm, zooms you in, giving a narrower viewing angle. Although the prompt shows a default in the form 50.000mm, you can only type in a number. Omit the mm.

- **Twist:** Turns your objects around in a circle parallel to the current view that you have defined. The default is 0 (zero) degrees, which is no twist. Assuming your current view looks at the objects right-side up, then 180 degrees turns the objects upside down, as if you had turned the camera in your hands upside down. You see a rubber-band line from the center of the view, which you can use to pick a twist point, or you can type in an angle.

- **Clip:** Enables you to create front and back planes that clip off the view. Objects in front of the front clipping plane or behind the back clipping plane are not displayed. You can use the front clipping plane to clip off a wall in front of the camera, thus letting you see through the wall to the objects beyond — a kind of CAD x-ray vision. Use the back clipping plane when you want to exclude objects in the distance from your perspective view. The clipping planes are always perpendicular to the line of sight, and so you only need to set their distance from the target point. At the `Enter clipping option [Back/Front/Off] <Off>:` prompt, specify Back or Front to set the back or front clipping planes. Specify Off to turn off all previously defined clipping planes.

NOTE **When you use the Distance option to create a perspective view, the option automatically turns on a front clipping plane at the camera point.**

  - Front sub-option: At the `Specify distance from target or [set to Eye(camera)/ON/OFF] <2.5682>:` prompt, specify Eye to set the clipping plane at the camera point. You can define the clipping plane by typing in a distance, or using the slider bar that appears at the top of your screen. As you move the cursor on the slider bar, stop to let the drawing redraw so that you can see the result.

■ Back sub-option: At the `Specify distance from target or [ON/OFF] <-5.5826>:` prompt, specify On or Off to turn the clipping plane on or off, or specify the distance as for the front clipping plane.

- **Hide:** Performs a hide, just like the HIDE command, thus letting you clearly see the results of the view that you've created.

- **Off:** Turns off Perspective mode and returns you to a parallel view. Otherwise, when you leave DVIEW after going into Perspective mode, your drawing retains the perspective view until you change the view — for example, with VPOINT.

- **Undo:** Undoes the effect of the last DVIEW option. You can undo through all of the changes that you have made in DVIEW.

Laying Out 3D Drawings

Laying out a 3D drawing on a layout tab is an important aspect of viewing a 3D drawing, because the layout determines the final output of the drawing. AutoCAD offers three commands that help you lay out your 3D drawing in paper space layouts: SOLVIEW, SOLDRAW, and SOLPROF. (Chapter 17 explains layouts.)

AUTOCAD ONLY   The three commands that I cover in this section are available only in AutoCAD.

Using SOLVIEW to lay out paper space viewports

SOLVIEW automates the process of creating floating viewports and orthogonal views (views at right angles from each other).

To start SOLVIEW, choose Draw ⇨ Modeling ⇨ Setup ⇨ View. SOLVIEW has four options:

- **UCS** enables you to choose the UCS to work from, as well as set the scale, center, and clipping corners of a floating viewport. Use this option first. After you choose a UCS, type in a scale. You can change this later if you want. SOLVIEW then prompts you for the center of the view. Pick a point and wait until the 3D model regenerates. SOLVIEW continues to prompt you for a view center, letting you pick points until you like what you see. Press Enter to continue the prompts. The clipping corners are the corners of the viewport. At the `Enter view name:` prompt, type a name. SOLVIEW creates the first viewport.

  Choose a view name that describes the view, such as Top, Side, or East Elevation. This helps you when you start creating orthogonal views.

- **Ortho** creates orthogonal views. At the `Specify side of viewport to project:` prompt, pick one of the edges of the first viewport. Again, choose a view center and clip the corners to create the viewport. Type a name for this new view.

  If you don't see the model properly when you pick the view center, continue with the prompts, picking clipping corners where you want them. (This problem can happen when you have several separate 3D objects in your drawing.) Then pick the viewport (in model space with tile off) and do a Zoom Extents. You can then pan and zoom as you want.

- **Auxiliary** creates inclined views. At the `Specify first point of inclined plane:` prompt, pick a point in one of the viewports. At the `Specify second point of inclined plane:` prompt, pick another point in the same viewport. The two points are usually at an angle to create the inclined view. At the `Specify side to view from:` prompt, pick a point. You then pick a view center and clipping corners, and then specify a view name.

■ **Section** creates cross-sections. At the `Specify first point of cutting plane:` prompt, pick a point in a viewport. At the `Specify second point of cutting plane:` prompt, pick a point on the opposite side of the model to create a cross-section. You then pick a side to view from, and enter the view scale, a view center, clipping corners, and a view name.

Figure 22.30 shows an example with a top view, an auxiliary view, and a section.

FIGURE 22.30

An example of using SOLVIEW.

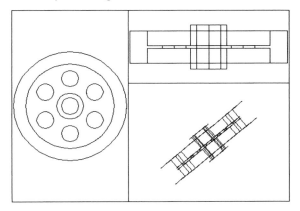

Using SOLDRAW to create hidden lines and hatching

SOLDRAW uses the views created by SOLVIEW, and creates 2D profiles that include solid and hidden lines to represent the profiles and hatching for sectional views. You must use SOLVIEW before using SOLDRAW.

To use SOLDRAW, choose Draw ➪ Modeling ➪ Setup ➪ Drawing. SOLDRAW puts you into a paper space layout and prompts you to select objects, which means floating viewports. You can select all of them if you want. SOLDRAW then proceeds to automatically create the profile views. Figure 22.31 shows an example of the hatching created for a sectional view.

FIGURE 22.31

The result of using SOLDRAW on a sectional view.

SOLDRAW uses hatch pattern defaults to define the hatch. You may have to change these settings using HATCHEDIT.

SOLVIEW creates a whole set of new layers in your drawing. SOLDRAW freezes your original layers, leaving visible only the layers that are needed to display the profile in that paper space viewport. SOLVIEW creates a special layer that you can use for dimensioning — one for each view that you create. For a view named front, the layer is named front-dim. You can use these dimensioning layers to create dimensions in paper space.

Using SOLPROF to create profiles

The SOLPROF command creates profiles like SOLDRAW, but you don't need to use SOLVIEW first. In addition, SOLPROF is more interactive than SOLDRAW. To start the command, choose Draw ⇨ Modeling ⇨ Setup ⇨ Profile. SOLPROF prompts you to select objects.

> When you start SOLPROF, you must have already created a floating viewport, and you must be in model space. Double-click any viewport to enter model space.

At the `Display hidden profile lines on separate layer? [Yes/No] <Y>:` prompt, type **Y** or **N**. By specifying Yes, you give yourself the capability of freezing or turning off the layer that contains hidden parts of the model. You can also hide other 3D objects behind the one that you're profiling.

At the `Project profile lines onto a plane? [Yes/No] <Y>:` prompt, type **Y** or **N**. If you choose Yes, SOLPROF creates 2D objects. If you choose No, SOLPROF creates 3D objects.

At the `Delete tangential edges? [Yes/No] <Y>:` prompt, type **Y** or **N**. A tangential edge is the meeting of two contiguous faces. Most drafting applications don't require you to show tangential edges.

Figure 22.32 shows the result of SOLPROF after freezing the layer that contains the original object; SOLPROF creates its own layers for the profile.

FIGURE 22.32

A profile created with SOLPROF.

Figure 22.33 shows the result of SOLPROF after also freezing the layer that SOLPROF created which contains the hidden parts of the model. In this case, the layer was named PH-159. Look for the *H,* which stands for hidden. The last part of the layer name is the handle of the object that you're profiling, and so it differs for each object.

FIGURE 22.33

A profile created with SOLPROF after freezing the layer that contains the hidden parts of the model.

You can combine viewports created with SOLPROF and viewports created with SOLVIEW and SOLDRAW. For example, you can create two orthogonal views with SOLVIEW and SOLDRAW, and then add a viewport and use SOLPROF to create another view.

 TIP As soon as you have a separate layer for the hidden portion of the model, you can modify that layer's color and/or linetype to show the hidden lines in a contrasting color or linetype.

Flattening 3D drawings

You may want to create a 2D representation of a 3D drawing. Some reasons to do this are for technical illustrations and to keep the core models of a drawing confidential. The FLATSHOT command takes all 3D objects in a drawing and makes 2D blocks from them. You can put objects that you don't want to include on off or frozen layers. This feature is available in AutoCAD only.

 Before you start, display your drawing in the desired view. If necessary, switch to parallel projection; the FLATSHOT command does not work reliably in perspective projection. Then choose Flatshot from the 3D Make control panel of the Dashboard. The Flatshot dialog box opens, as shown in Figure 22.34, where you can specify settings.

In the Destination section, you decide where the 2D objects will go. You can insert them in the current drawing as a new block, replace an existing block, or export them to a new drawing. In the Foreground Lines section, you choose the color of the lines of the objects. Foreground lines are those that would not be hidden in 3D Hidden visual style. In the Obscured Lines section, you decide how to treat lines that would be hidden in 3D Hidden visual style. You can choose not to display them, for a hidden look, or use a different color or linetype. Click OK when you're done.

If you chose to insert a new block, place the block. If you chose to export to a new file, open that file. You will probably have to Zoom to Extents to see the block. Figure 22.35 shows the results, both with and without obscured lines.

FIGURE 22.34

The Flatshot dialog box enables you to specify how the FLATSHOT command works.

FIGURE 22.35

Flatshot can create a 2D representation of 3D objects with or without hidden lines.

The FLATTEN command is an Express Tools command that also creates 2D representations of 3D objects. In addition, it reduces elevation and thickness to 0. It is available only on the command line.

Summary

In this chapter, I covered all of the ways to view your 3D drawing. You read about:

- Using the standard viewpoints on the Viewpoint flyout for a quick look.
- Utilizing the DDVPOINT command to specify exact angles.
- Creating a named 3D view with a camera.
- Adding a background to a named view.
- Using the tripod and compass for flexibility.
- Using the PLAN command to quickly return you to plan view.
- Using and creating visual styles to determine how your drawing looks. Also, using the shading options in AutoCAD LT.
- Displaying parallel and perspective projections.
- Applying 3D Orbit to view your model from any position. You can zoom and pan, create parallel and perspective views, and set clipping planes. You can also create a continuously moving orbit.
- Walking and flying through a drawing. You can navigate through a drawing and save a movie file of the result. You can also save an animation of a motion path.
- Using the DVIEW command to let you create parallel and perspective views. You set the camera and target where you can create front and back clipping planes.
- Employing the three commands — SOLVIEW, SOLDRAW, and SOLPROF — that help you lay out views of a 3D drawing for plotting.
- The FLATSHOT command, which creates 2D blocks from 3D objects.

In the next chapter, I explain how to create 3D surfaces.

Chapter 23

Creating 3D Surfaces

In this chapter, you learn to create all types of surfaces, also called *meshes*. Surfaces have a great advantage over 3D wireframe models because you can hide back surfaces and create shaded images for easier visualization of your models. Surfaces also enable you to create unusual shapes, such as for topological maps or free-form objects.

AUTOCAD ONLY This entire chapter applies to AutoCAD only. For information on surfaces that AutoCAD LT can create, see Chapter 21.

Figure 23.1 shows a lamp drawn with surfaces.

You cannot obtain information about physical properties — such as mass, center of gravity, and so on — from surfaces. Such information can be obtained only from 3D solids, which are covered in the next chapter.

AutoCAD approximates curved surfaces by creating a mesh of planes at varying angles. You see the planes because AutoCAD displays them using a web of intersecting lines. AutoCAD defines the mesh by its *vertices* — where the lines intersect. Figure 23.2 shows a mesh with its vertices.

FIGURE 23.1

A lamp drawn with surfaces.

FIGURE 23.2

A surface mesh.

Converting Objects to Surfaces

Perhaps the simplest way to create a surface is to convert an existing object to a surface. The CONVTOSUR-FACE command allows you to do just that. You can convert the following objects to surfaces:

- 2D solids created with the SOLID command
- Regions
- Zero-width polylines with thickness and that don't create a closed figure
- Lines and arcs with thickness

CAUTION By default, the original objects are deleted. You can control this using the DELOBJ system variable, which determines whether objects that are used to create other objects are deleted. To keep the original objects, change the value of DELOBJ to 0 (zero). (The default value is 1, which deletes the objects.) You can set the value to –2 to prompt you and allow you to decide if you want to delete the original objects.

To convert one of the supported objects to a surface, choose Modify ⇨ 3D Operation ⇨ Convert to Surface or enter **convtosurface** on the command line (or in the Dynamic Input tooltip). Then select the object or objects that you want to convert.

Drawing Surfaces with 3DFACE

Two-dimensional objects are often used to create three-dimensional models. In Chapter 21, I discuss how you can use 2D solids (the SOLID command), wide polylines, and circles to make horizontal surfaces when you add a thickness to them.

You can also use regions in 3D drawings. Although regions are 2D objects and cannot be given a thickness, when you use the 3D Hidden visual style, AutoCAD displays the region as a surface. When the drawing is regenerated to a wireframe display, the region is displayed as a wireframe again, losing its surface properties.

Another option is to use 3DFACE, which is a true 3D command. 3DFACE creates three- or four-sided surfaces that can be in any plane. You can place surfaces together to make a many-sided surface. While AutoCAD draws lines between these surfaces, you can make the lines invisible to create the effect of a seamless surface. You define the surface by specifying the points that create the corners of the surface. As a result, a 3D face cannot have any curves. 3DFACE only creates surfaces — you cannot give a thickness to a 3D face. However, you can create a 3D solid from a 3D face using the EXTRUDE command. 3D solids are covered in the next chapter.

Using the 3DFACE command

To create a 3D face, enter **3dface** on the command line. AutoCAD prompts you for first, second, third, and fourth points. You must specify points clockwise or counterclockwise, not in the zigzag fashion required by the SOLID command. When creating a 3D face:

- Press Enter at the `Specify fourth point or [Invisible] <create three-sided face>:` prompt to create a three-sided surface. Then press Enter again to end the command.

- To create a four-sided surface, specify a fourth point. AutoCAD repeats the `Specify third point or [Invisible] <exit>:` prompt. Press Enter to end the command.

- To create surfaces of more than four sides, continue to specify points. AutoCAD repeats the third- and fourth-point prompts until you press Enter — twice after a third point or once after a fourth point. Note that each additional set of prompts creates a separate surface object.

As you continue to add faces, the last edge created by the third and fourth points becomes the first edge of the new face so that adding a face requires only two additional points.

TIP It often helps to prepare for a complex 3D face by creating 2D objects for some or all of the faces. You can then use Endpoint object snaps to pick the points of the 3D face. Place these 2D objects on a unique layer, such as Frames or Const. You can also use point objects with a visible point style as a basis for 3D faces.

Making 3D face edges invisible

Making edges invisible makes a series of 3D faces look like one 3D face. Figure 23.3 shows three 3D faces with and without internal seams.

FIGURE 23.3

You can make internal edges of a 3D face invisible.

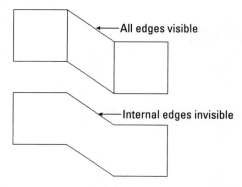

You can control the visibility of 3D face edges in several ways.

Controlling visibility during 3D face creation

While you're drawing the 3D face, you can right-click and choose Invisible before each edge. Then specify the next point. However, it's sometimes difficult to predict exactly where to indicate the invisible edge.

Using the EDGE command

After creating the entire 3D face, you can use the EDGE command. The sole purpose of the EDGE command is to make 3D face edges visible and invisible — this is probably the easiest way to control the visibility of 3D face edges.

Enter **edge** on the command line or in the Dynamic Input tooltip. Alternatively, you can choose Draw ⇨ Modeling ⇨ Meshes ⇨ Edge. At the Specify edge of 3dface to toggle visibility or [Display]: prompt, select a visible edge that you want to make invisible. AutoCAD repeats the prompt so that you can select additional edges. Press Enter to make the edges invisible. Although a visible edge might actually be two edges belonging to two adjacent 3D faces, EDGE makes them both invisible.

To make invisible edges visible, right-click and choose the Display option. AutoCAD displays all of the edges in dashed lines and shows the Enter selection method for display of hidden edges [Select/All] <All>: prompt. Press Enter to display all of the edges or use the Select option to select 3D faces (you can use windows for selection). Either way, you see the edges of the 3D face that you want to edit. AutoCAD then repeats the Specify edge of 3dface to toggle visibility or [Display]: prompt. You can now select the edge that you want to make visible. Press Enter to end the command and make the edge visible.

You may need to use the 2D Wireframe visual style to see the effect of making edges invisible. However, a plot gives the correct result.

Using the SPLFRAME system variable

Setting the SPLFRAME system variable to 1 and then regenerating the drawing makes all 3D face edges visible. (The SPLFRAME system variable also affects the display of spline-fit polylines, hence its name.) To return edges to their original setting, set SPLFRAME to 0 and do a REGEN.

 The drawing used in the following exercise on drawing 3D faces, ab23-a.dwg, is in the Drawings folder on the DVD.

STEPS: Drawing 3D Faces

1. Open ab23-a.dwg from the DVD.

2. Save it as ab23-01.dwg in your AutoCAD Bible folder. This is a blank drawing with architectural units, based on acad3D.dwt. The visual style is set to 3D Wireframe. Turn on ORTHO. OSNAP should be on. Set running object snaps for endpoints and midpoints. This exercise assumes that Dynamic Input is on and set to the default of relative coordinates.

 3. Choose Draw ⇨ Modeling ⇨ Meshes ⇨ 3D Face. Follow the prompts:

```
Specify first point or [Invisible]: 6,6 ↵
Specify second point or [Invisible]: 20,0 ↵
Specify third point or [Invisible] <exit>: 0,2' ↵
Specify fourth point or [Invisible] <create three-sided face>: -20,0 ↵
Specify third point or [Invisible] <exit>: ↵
```

4. Start the COPY command. Follow the prompts:

```
Select objects: Select the 3D face.
Select objects: ↵
Specify base point or [Displacement/mOde] <Displacement>: Pick ❶ in
    Figure 23.4.
Specify second point or <use first point as displacement>: 0,0,1.5' ↵
Specify second point or [Exit/Undo]: 0,0,3' ↵
Specify second point or [Exit/Undo]: ↵
```

If necessary, zoom and pan so that you can see all three surfaces. Your drawing should look like Figure 23.4. You now have the top, bottom, and middle shelves of the cabinet.

5. Start the 3DFACE command again. Follow the prompts:

```
Specify first point or [Invisible]: Pick the endpoint at ❶ in Figure
    23.4.
Specify second point or [Invisible]: Pick the endpoint at ❷.
Specify third point or [Invisible] <exit>: Pick the endpoint at ❸.
Specify fourth point or [Invisible] <create three-sided face>: Pick
    the endpoint at ❹.
Specify third point or [Invisible] <exit>: Pick the endpoint at ❺.
Specify fourth point or [Invisible] <create three-sided face>: Pick
    the endpoint at ❻.
Specify third point or [Invisible] <exit>: Pick the endpoint at ❼.
Specify fourth point or [Invisible] <create three-sided face>: Pick
    the endpoint at ❽.
Specify third point or [Invisible] <exit>: ↵
```

FIGURE 23.4

The three 3D faces from an isometric viewpoint.

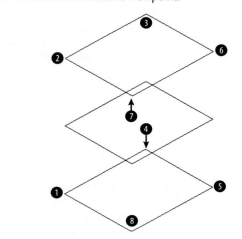

6. To draw the door of the cabinet, change the current layer to CONST. Start the LINE command and draw a line from ❷ in Figure 23.4 to 18<225. End the LINE command. Now start the COPY command and copy the line from ❷ to ❶. These two construction lines frame the door.

7. To make it easier to work on the door, choose Tools ➪ New UCS ➪ 3 Point. Follow the prompts:

```
Specify new origin point <0,0,0>: Pick the left endpoint of the
    bottom construction line.
Specify point on positive portion of X-axis <-0'-5 3/4",-0'-6
    3/4",0'-0">: Pick ❶ in Figure 23.4.
Specify point on positive-Y portion of the UCS XY plane <-0'-7
    7/16",-0'-6",0'-">: Pick the left endpoint of the top construction
    line.
```

If the grid is on, you may want to turn it off.

8. Start the LINE command again. Follow the prompts:

```
Specify first point: Choose the From object snap.
Base point: Pick the left endpoint of the top construction line.
<Offset>: @3,-3 ↵
Specify next point or [Undo]: Move the cursor to the right and type
    12 ↵.
Specify next point or [Undo]: Move the cursor down and type 30 ↵.
Specify next point or [Close/Undo]: Move the cursor to the left and
    type 12 ↵.
Specify next point or [Close/Undo]: c ↵
```

Your drawing should look like Figure 23.5.

FIGURE 23.5

The partially completed cabinet.

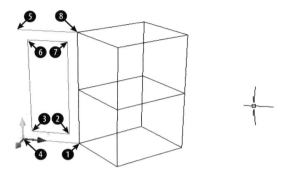

9. Change the current layer to 0. Start the 3DFACE command again. Follow the prompts:

```
Specify first point or [Invisible]: Pick the endpoint at ❶ in Figure
   23.5.
Specify second point or [Invisible]: Pick the endpoint at ❷.
Specify third point or [Invisible] <exit>: Pick the endpoint at ❸.
Specify fourth point or [Invisible] <create three-sided face>: Pick
   the endpoint at ❹. Notice the edge lines between ❶ and ❷ and
   between ❸ and ❹.
Specify third point or [Invisible] <exit>: Right-click and choose
   Invisible. Pick the endpoint at ❺.
Specify fourth point or [Invisible] <create three-sided face>: Pick
   the endpoint at ❻.
Specify third point or [Invisible] <exit>: Right-click and choose
   Invisible. Pick the endpoint at ❼.
Specify fourth point or [Invisible] <create three-sided face>: Pick
   the endpoint at ❽.
Specify third point or [Invisible] <exit>: Pick the endpoint at ❶.
Specify fourth point or [Invisible] <create three-sided face>: Pick
   the endpoint at ❷.
Specify third point or [Invisible] <exit>: ↵
```

10. Enter **edge** on the command line or in the Dynamic Input tooltip. At the Specify edge of 3dface to toggle visibility or [Display]: prompt, pick the edge between ❶ and ❷ and then the edge between ❸ and ❹. (A midpoint marker and SnapTip appear.) Press Enter. The edges disappear.

11. Choose Tools ⇨ New UCS ⇨ World.

12. Choose View ⇨ 3D Views ⇨ Viewpoint Presets to open the Viewpoint Presets dialog box. Set the From: X Axis angle to 200 degrees. Set the XY Plane angle to 35 degrees. Choose OK.

13. Choose View ⇨ Visual Styles ⇨ 3D Hidden to see the result. You can clearly see through the window of the cabinet door.

14. Save your drawing. It should look like Figure 23.6.

FIGURE 23.6

The completed kitchen cabinet, including a window in the door.

Drawing Surfaces with PFACE

PFACE draws surfaces called *polyface meshes,* which are a type of polyline. However, you cannot edit them with PEDIT. The best way to edit them is with grips. AutoCAD designed PFACE for the creation of surfaces using AutoLISP routines or other automated methods. Consequently, the input for polyface meshes is somewhat awkward. However, polyface meshes have the following advantages:

- You can draw surfaces with any number of sides, unlike 3D faces, which can have only three or four sides.
- The entire surface is one object.
- Sections that are on one plane do not show edges, so that you don't have to bother with making edges invisible.
- You can explode polyface meshes into 3D faces.
- If you create a polyface mesh on more than one plane, each plane can be on a different layer or have a different color. This can be useful for assigning materials for rendering or other complex selection processes.

On the other hand, polyface meshes are difficult to create and edit. Figure 23.7 shows two polyface meshes, one on one plane and the other on three planes.

FIGURE 23.7

You can create many-sided polyface meshes on one plane, or on several different planes. After you switch to the 3D Hidden visual style, the polyface mesh hides objects behind it.

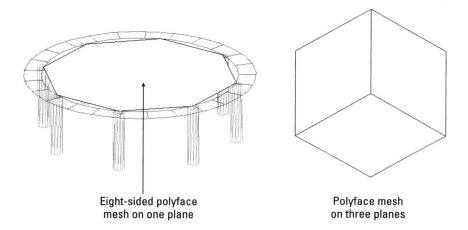

Eight-sided polyface
mesh on one plane

Polyface mesh
on three planes

The prompts for PFACE are divided into two phases. The first phase simply asks for vertices. The second phase asks you to specify which vertex makes up which face (or plane). The second phase is fairly meaningless for polyface meshes on one plane, but you have to specify the vertices anyway. Here's how to do it:

1. Type **pface** ↵.

2. At the `Specify location for vertex 1:` prompt, specify the first vertex.

3. Continue to specify vertices at the `Specify location for vertex 2 or <define faces>:` or `Specify location for vertex 3 or <define faces>:` prompts. Press Enter when you've finished.

4. At the `Face 1, vertex 1: Enter a vertex number or [Color/Layer]:` prompt, type which vertex starts the first face of the polyface mesh. It's usually vertex 1, so you type **1** ↵.

5. At the `Face 1, vertex 2: Enter a vertex number or [Color/Layer] <next face>:` prompt, type which vertex comes next on the first face. Continue to specify the vertices for the first face.

   If you're drawing a polyface mesh on one plane, continue to specify all of the vertices in order, and then press Enter twice when you're done to end the command.

   If you're drawing a polyface mesh on more than one plane, continue to specify the vertices on the first face (that is, plane) and press Enter. At the `Face 2, vertex 1: Enter a vertex number or [Color/Layer]:` prompt, type the first vertex of the second face (plane) and continue to specify vertices for the second face. Press Enter. Continue to specify vertices for all of the faces. Press Enter twice to end the command.

TIP In order to easily draw a polyface mesh with PFACE, draw 2D or point objects as a guide for picking vertices. Then you can use object snaps to pick the vertices. Also, for polyface meshes on more than one plane, draw a diagram that numbers the vertices. This helps you to specify which vertices make up which face.

During the second phase of the prompts, when PFACE asks you to define the faces, you can right-click and choose Layer or Color and specify the layer or color. Then specify the vertices that are to be on that layer or color.

In the following exercise, you draw a hexagonal night table with polyface meshes.

STEPS: Drawing Polyface Meshes

1. Open ab23-b.dwg from the DVD.

2. Save it as ab23-02.dwg in your AutoCAD Bible folder. Two hexagons have been drawn, one 24 inches above the other, on the Const layer, as shown in Figure 23.8.

FIGURE 23.8
_____

The two hexagons are the basis for a night table.

3. Type **pface** ↵. Follow the prompts. First you specify all of the vertices. Then you specify the top hexagon, then the five sides (the front is open), and finally the bottom hexagon. Unfortunately, if you make a mistake, you must start over.

```
Specify location for vertex 1: Pick ❶ in Figure 23.8.
Specify location for vertex 2 or <define faces>: Pick ❷.
Specify location for vertex 3 or <define faces>: Pick ❸.
Specify location for vertex 4 or <define faces>: Pick ❹.
Specify location for vertex 5 or <define faces>: Pick ❺.
Specify location for vertex 6 or <define faces>: Pick ❻.
Specify location for vertex 7 or <define faces>: Pick ❼.
Specify location for vertex 8 or <define faces>: Pick ❽.
Specify location for vertex 9 or <define faces>: Pick ❾.
Specify location for vertex 10 or <define faces>: Pick ❿.
```

```
Specify location for vertex 11 or <define faces>: Pick ⑪.
Specify location for vertex 12 or <define faces>: Pick ⑫.
Specify location for vertex 13 or <define faces>: ↵
Face 1, vertex 1: Enter a vertex number or [Color/Layer]: 1 ↵
Face 1, vertex 2: Enter a vertex number or [Color/Layer] <next face>:
   2 ↵
Face 1, vertex 3: Enter a vertex number or [Color/Layer] <next face>:
   3 ↵
Face 1, vertex 4: Enter a vertex number or [Color/Layer] <next face>:
   4 ↵
Face 1, vertex 5: Enter a vertex number or [Color/Layer] <next face>:
   5 ↵
Face 1, vertex 6: Enter a vertex number or [Color/Layer] <next face>:
   6 ↵
Face 1, vertex 7: Enter a vertex number or [Color/Layer] <next face>:
   ↵
Face 2, vertex 1: Enter a vertex number or [Color/Layer]: 12 ↵
Face 2, vertex 2: Enter a vertex number or [Color/Layer] <next face>:
   6 ↵
Face 2, vertex 3: Enter a vertex number or [Color/Layer] <next face>:
   5 ↵
Face 2, vertex 4: Enter a vertex number or [Color/Layer] <next face>:
   11 ↵
Face 2, vertex 5: Enter a vertex number or [Color/Layer] <next face>:
   ↵
Face 3, vertex 1: Enter a vertex number or [Color/Layer]: 5 ↵
Face 3, vertex 2: Enter a vertex number or [Color/Layer] <next face>:
   11 ↵
Face 3, vertex 3: Enter a vertex number or [Color/Layer] <next face>:
   10 ↵
Face 3, vertex 4: Enter a vertex number or [Color/Layer] <next face>:
   4 ↵
Face 3, vertex 5: Enter a vertex number or [Color/Layer] <next face>:
   ↵
Face 4, vertex 1: Enter a vertex number or [Color/Layer]: 10 ↵
Face 4, vertex 2: Enter a vertex number or [Color/Layer] <next face>:
   4 ↵
Face 4, vertex 3: Enter a vertex number or [Color/Layer] <next face>:
   3 ↵
Face 4, vertex 4: Enter a vertex number or [Color/Layer] <next face>:
   9 ↵
Face 4, vertex 5: Enter a vertex number or [Color/Layer] <next face>:
   ↵
Face 5, vertex 1: Enter a vertex number or [Color/Layer]: 3 ↵
Face 5, vertex 2: Enter a vertex number or [Color/Layer] <next face>:
   9 ↵
Face 5, vertex 3: Enter a vertex number or [Color/Layer] <next face>:
   8 ↵
Face 5, vertex 4: Enter a vertex number or [Color/Layer] <next face>:
   2 ↵
Face 5, vertex 5: Enter a vertex number or [Color/Layer] <next face>: ↵
```

```
Face 6, vertex 1: Enter a vertex number or [Color/Layer]: 8 ↵
Face 6, vertex 2: Enter a vertex number or [Color/Layer] <next face>:
   2 ↵
Face 6, vertex 3: Enter a vertex number or [Color/Layer] <next face>:
   1 ↵
Face 6, vertex 4: Enter a vertex number or [Color/Layer] <next face>:
   7 ↵
Face 6, vertex 5: Enter a vertex number or [Color/Layer] <next face>: ↵
Face 7, vertex 1: Enter a vertex number or [Color/Layer]: 7 ↵
Face 7, vertex 2: Enter a vertex number or [Color/Layer] <next face>:
   8 ↵
Face 7, vertex 3: Enter a vertex number or [Color/Layer] <next face>:
   9 ↵
Face 7, vertex 4: Enter a vertex number or [Color/Layer] <next face>:
   10 ↵
Face 7, vertex 5: Enter a vertex number or [Color/Layer] <next face>:
   11 ↵
Face 7, vertex 6: Enter a vertex number or [Color/Layer] <next face>:
   12 ↵
Face 7, vertex 7: Enter a vertex number or [Color/Layer] <next face>: ↵
Face 8, vertex 1: Enter a vertex number or [Color/Layer]: ↵
```

4. Choose View ⇨ Hide to see the final result.

5. Save your drawing. It should look like Figure 23.9.

FIGURE 23.9

The completed hexagonal night table.

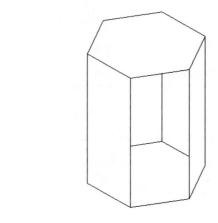

Creating Plane Surfaces

You can use the PLANESURF command to create a surface that is on the XY plane, and bounded by points that you specify. You can specify two diagonal points that define a rectangle, or select a closed object (or multiple objects that define a closed area). Figure 23.10 shows a planar surface defined by two points.

FIGURE 23.10

A planar surface between some boxes, bounded by two point objects.

The number of lines on the surface depends on the values of the SURFU and SURFV system variables. The default value for both is 6. You cannot use this command on objects created with the 3D command or on solids. Try it on closed 2D objects, including closed polylines and regions.

Creating Polygon Meshes with 3DMESH

The 3DMESH command creates polygon meshes (not to be confused with the polyface meshes created by PFACE). The 3DMESH command is used for creating irregular surfaces, vertex by vertex. The great advantage of polygon meshes is that AutoCAD considers them to be polylines, and they can therefore be edited with the PEDIT command — although in a limited manner. Figure 23.11 shows two surfaces created with 3DMESH. The surface on the right has been smoothed using PEDIT.

To use 3DMESH, enter **3dmesh** on the command line or in the Dynamic Input tooltip. You can also choose Draw ➪ Modeling ➪ Meshes ➪ 3D Mesh. AutoCAD then asks you for the Mesh M size and Mesh N size. M is the number of vertices going in the first direction. N is the number of vertices going in the other direction. Figure 23.12 shows a 3D Mesh with an M size of 5 and an N size of 3.

FIGURE 23.11

Two surfaces created with 3DMESH. The surface on the right has been smoothed using the Smooth option of PEDIT.

FIGURE 23.12

A 3D Mesh with an M size of 5 and an N size of 3, showing the vertex designations.

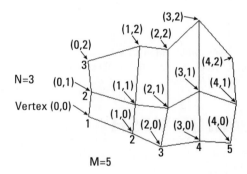

After you set the size of the 3D Mesh, you need to specify each vertex. For example, the 3D Mesh in Figure 23.12 has 15 vertices that you need to specify. AutoCAD prompts you for each vertex in order, starting with (0,0). Vertex (0,1) is the second vertex in the first column. Vertex (1,0) is the first vertex in the second column, starting from the bottom. It's a little confusing because AutoCAD starts the counting from 0 (zero), not 1. For the 3D Mesh in Figure 23.12, the last vertex is (4,2).

> **NOTE** In Figure 23.12, the 3D Mesh is five vertices wide and three vertices high as you look at it in plan view. However, you don't have to specify the vertices in the same direction. For the 3D Mesh in the figure, I started at the bottom left, continued to move up for (0,1) and (0,2), then moved to the right. However, you could start at the bottom-left and move to the right for (0,1) and (0,2), and then go back to the left either above or below (0,0) — resulting in a 3D Mesh that is three vertices wide and five vertices high as you look at it in plan view. In other words, M and N can be in any direction.

3D meshes are especially suitable for AutoLISP routines; in fact, AutoCAD supplies several. These are discussed in the next section.

To smooth a polygon mesh, start the PEDIT command and select the polygon mesh. AutoCAD responds with the Enter an option [Edit vertex/Smooth surface/Desmooth/Mclose/Nclose/Undo]: prompt. Table 23.1 explains how to use these options.

TABLE 23.1

PEDIT Options for 3D Polygon Meshes

Option	Description
Edit vertex	Displays the Current vertex (0,0). Enter an option - [Next/Previous/Left/Right/Up/Down/Move/REgen/eXit] <N>: prompt. Use the Next, Previous, Left, Right, Up, and Down sub-options to move the X marker that displays the current vertex. When you're at the vertex that you want to move, use the Move sub-option. REgen regenerates the 3D Mesh. Use eXit to return to the original prompt.
Smooth surface	Smoothes the surface according to one of three possible sets of equations — Quadratic, Cubic, or Bézier. Bézier results in the smoothest surface. Use the SURFTYPE system variable to set the type of smoothing. Set SURFTYPE to 5 to create a quadratic b-spline surface, 6 to create a cubic b-spline surface, or 7 to create a Bézier surface. Cubic (6) is the default setting. To smooth a 3D Mesh, there must be more than three vertices in both the M and N directions.
Desmooth	Removes the smoothing on the 3D Mesh surface.
Mclose	Closes the surface in the M direction by connecting the last edge to the first edge.
Nclose	Closes the surface in the N direction by connecting the last edge to the first edge.
Undo	Undoes the last option.

You can use 3DMESH to create 3D topological surfaces. You may have a surveyor's drawing that marks measurement points. Open a new drawing, using the surveyor's drawing as an xref. In plan view, create a polygon mesh. For the vertices, pick the surveyor's measurement points. (You'll need to count them first to determine a regular grid for the M and N sizes.) Then select the polygon mesh to display its grip points. Select each grip in turn, and at the prompt, type (for example) **@0,0,100.78** ↵ where the last coordinate is the measured height. When you're done, look at the surface in any nonplanar viewpoint to see the result.

Drawing Standard 3D Shapes

AutoCAD includes several AutoLISP routines that use 3D meshes to create some standard shapes. These shapes are all options of the 3D command, which you enter on the command line. You can also type **ai_** followed by the name of the shape, such as **ai_box.**

Box

Figure 23.13 shows a surface mesh box from the SE isometric viewpoint in the 3D Hidden visual style and a white background.

FIGURE 23.13

A box from an isometric viewpoint commanding the 3D Hidden visual style.

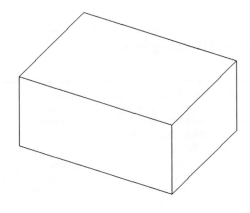

Here's how to draw a box:

1. Enter **3d** on the command line. Choose the Box option.

2. At the `Specify corner point of box:` prompt, specify the lower-left corner of the base of the box.

3. At the `Specify length of box:` prompt, specify the length of the box along the X axis. You can pick a point or enter a value.

4. At the `Specify width of box or [Cube]:` prompt, specify the width of the box along the Y axis. You can pick a point or enter a value. If you choose the Cube option, AutoCAD creates a cube with a width and height the same as the length that you just specified, and you don't see the height prompt.

5. At the `Specify height of box:` prompt, specify the height of the box along the Z axis. Pick a point or enter a value.

6. At the `Specify rotation angle of box about the Z axis or [Reference]:` prompt, specify an angle. AutoCAD rotates the box in the XY plane. Press Enter if you do not want to rotate the box. You can also use the Reference sub-option, which works like the Reference option of the ROTATE command.

As you define the box, AutoCAD draws a temporary image in yellow to show you the result of your specifications.

Wedge

Figure 23.14 shows a wedge. The prompts are the same as for the box, except that there is no Cube option. A wedge is half of a box.

FIGURE 23.14

A wedge from an isometric viewpoint in the 3D Hidden visual style.

Here's how to draw a wedge:

1. Enter **3d** on the command line. Choose the Wedge option.
2. At the `Specify corner point of wedge:` prompt, specify the lower-left corner of the base of the wedge.
3. At the `Specify length of wedge:` prompt, specify the length of the wedge along the X axis.
4. At the `Specify width of wedge:` prompt, specify the width of the wedge along the Y axis.
5. At the `Specify height of wedge:` prompt, specify the height of the wedge along the Z axis.
6. At the `Specify rotation angle of wedge about the Z axis:` prompt, specify an angle. AutoCAD rotates the wedge in the XY plane. Press Enter if you don't want to rotate the wedge.

Pyramid

You can draw pyramids with three- and four-sided bases. A pyramid with a three-sided base creates a four-sided object called a *tetrahedron*. You can top the pyramid with a point, a flat top, or, for four-sided bases, a ridge. Figure 23.15 shows the various types of pyramids that you can draw.

FIGURE 23.15

You can draw all of these pyramidal shapes.

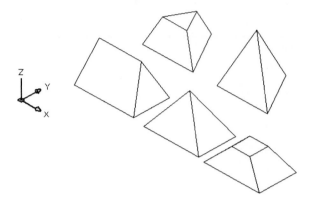

Here's how to draw the pyramids:

1. Enter **3d** on the command line. Choose the Pyramid option.

2. At the `Specify first corner point for base of pyramid:` prompt, specify the first point (any point) on the base.

3. At the `Specify second corner point for base of pyramid:` prompt, specify the second point on the base.

4. At the `Specify third corner point for base of pyramid:` prompt, specify the third point on the base.

5. At the `Specify fourth corner point for base of pyramid or [Tetrahedron]:` prompt, specify the fourth point on the base or choose the Tetrahedron option (creates a pyramid with a base of three points).

   ▪ If you chose the Tetrahedron option, at the `Specify apex point of tetrahedron or [Top]:` prompt, specify the apex (top point) or choose the Top option. AutoCAD prompts you for three top points.

   ▪ If you specified a fourth base point, at the `Specify apex point of pyramid or [Ridge/Top]:` prompt, specify the apex (top point) or choose the Ridge or Top options. If you choose the Ridge option, specify the two points for the ridge. If you choose the Top option, specify the four top points.

Specifying the apex or ridge can be tricky unless you know the absolute coordinates that you want. You can't change viewpoints during the command. However, you can easily change the points later using grips. Another trick is to start any drawing command, such as LINE, before starting the pyramid. At the `Specify first point:` prompt, pick the point that you want to use for the first base point of the pyramid. Then press Esc to cancel the command. This leaves that point as the last point specified. Now define the base of the pyramid, using the same point as the first base point. When you need to specify the apex or ridge, you can use relative coordinates from the first base point. For example, to create an apex two units directly over the first base point, specify **@0,0,2** for the apex.

When you use the Top option, AutoCAD provides a rubber-band line from each of the base corners in turn, letting you use relative coordinates from the base corners. You can also create a temporary 2D object before starting the pyramid to frame a ridge or top.

Cone

You can create full or partial cones. Figure 23.16 shows both types, as displayed in the 3D Wireframe visual style.

FIGURE 23.16

You can draw full or partial cones.

Follow these steps to create cones:

1. Enter **3d** on the command line. Choose the Cone option.

2. At the `Specify center point for base of cone:` prompt, pick the center for the circle that makes the base of the cone.

3. At the `Specify radius for base of cone or [Diameter]:` prompt, specify the radius for the circle at the base or choose the Diameter option to specify the diameter.

4. At the `Specify radius for top of cone or [Diameter] <0>:` prompt, specify the radius of the top or choose the Diameter option and specify the diameter. If you accept the default of zero, you get a complete cone. If you specify a radius or diameter, you get a truncated cone.

 You can specify the base's size to be larger than the top's size.

5. At the `Specify height of cone:` prompt, specify the height.

6. At the `Enter number of segments for surface of cone <16>:` prompt, specify the number of mesh segments. A higher number results in a smoother-looking cone.

Sphere

Drawing a sphere is quite easy. You just specify the center and radius and then the number of segments to display in each direction. Figure 23.17 shows a sphere in the 3D Wireframe visual style.

A sphere.

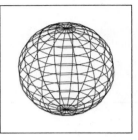

Here's how to draw a sphere:

1. Enter **3d** on the command line. Choose the Sphere option.
2. At the `Specify center point of sphere:` prompt, specify a point.
3. At the `Specify radius of sphere or [Diameter]:` prompt, specify the radius, or choose the Diameter option to specify the diameter.
4. At the `Enter number of longitudinal segments for surface of sphere <16>:` prompt, type the number of north-south lines that you want. A higher number results in a smoother-looking sphere.
5. At the `Enter number of latitudinal segments for surface of sphere <16>:` prompt, type the number of east-west lines that you want. A higher number results in a smoother-looking sphere.

The only tricky point with spheres is remembering that the center point is the center in all three dimensions. If you want to draw a ball on a table, it's easy to specify the center on the plane of the tabletop — but you end up with a ball that's half beneath the table. So plan ahead.

Dome

A dome is the top half of a sphere, as shown in Figure 23.18. The prompts are very similar to those for a sphere.

A dome.

Follow these steps to draw a dome:

1. Enter **3d** on the command line. Choose the Dome option.

2. At the `Specify center point of dome:` prompt, specify the center point of the circle that makes up the base of the dome.

3. At the `Specify radius of dome or [Diameter]:` prompt, specify the radius or use the Diameter option to specify the diameter.

4. At the `Enter number of longitudinal segments for surface of dome <16>:` prompt, type the number of north-south lines that you want. A higher number results in a smoother-looking dome.

5. At the `Enter number of latitudinal segments for surface of dome <8>:` prompt, type the number of east-west lines that you want. A higher number results in a smoother-looking dome. Notice that the default is 8 instead of 16 for the sphere because you're drawing only half of a sphere.

Dish

A *dish* is the bottom half of a sphere, as shown in Figure 23.19. Actually, a bowl would be a better name for it.

FIGURE 23.19

A dish.

Follow these steps to draw a dish:

1. Enter **3d** on the command line. Choose the Dish option.

2. At the `Specify center point of dish:` prompt, specify the center point of the circle that makes up the base of the dish.

3. At the `Specify radius of dish or [Diameter]:` prompt, specify the radius or use the Diameter option to specify the diameter.

4. At the `Enter number of longitudinal segments for surface of dish <16>:` prompt, type the number of north-south lines that you want. A higher number results in a smoother-looking dish.

5. At the `Enter number of latitudinal segments for surface of dome <8>:` prompt, type the number of east-west lines that you want. A higher number results in a smoother-looking dish. As with the dish, the default is 8 because you're drawing only half of a sphere.

As with spheres, remember that the center point is the center of the top of the dish, not its base.

Torus

A *torus* is a 3D donut, as shown in Figure 23.20.

FIGURE 23.20

A torus.

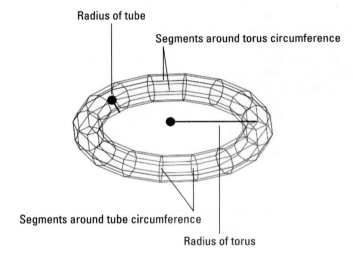

Radius of tube

Segments around torus circumference

Segments around tube circumference

Radius of torus

Follow these steps to create a torus:

1. Enter **3d** on the command line. Choose the Torus option.

2. At the `Specify center point of torus:` prompt, specify the center of the torus.

3. At the `Specify radius of torus or [Diameter]:` prompt, specify the radius of the torus, as shown in Figure 23.20, or use the Diameter option to define the diameter.

4. At the `Specify radius of tube or [Diameter]:` prompt, specify the radius of the tube or use the Diameter option to define the diameter.

5. At the `Enter number of segments around tube circumference <16>:` prompt, specify the number of segments around the tube.

6. At the `Enter number of segments around torus circumference <16>:` prompt, specify the number of segments around the torus.

As with a sphere, a torus is half above and half below the center point in the Z direction.

Mesh

The 3D command has a Mesh option that creates a 3D Mesh. All you have to do is pick the four corners and the M and N mesh sizes. This is similar to a planar surface, except that you can choose the number of mesh lines during the command.

Specify the four corner points in clockwise or counterclockwise order. Then specify the M and N mesh sizes. Figure 23.21 shows a mesh with M=8 and N=4.

FIGURE 23.21

A mesh with M=8 and N=4.

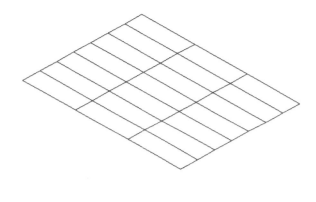

The drawing used in the following exercise on drawing 3D polygon meshes, ab23-c.dwg, is in the Drawings folder on the DVD.

STEPS: Drawing 3D Polygon Meshes

1. Open ab23-c.dwg from the DVD.

2. Save it as ab23-03.dwg in your AutoCAD Bible folder. The drawing is in architectural units. OSNAP should be on. Set running object snaps for endpoint and midpoint.

3. Enter **3d** and choose the Box option. Follow the prompts to make the tabletop:

```
Specify corner point of box: 1,1,30 ↵
Specify length of box: 4' ↵
Specify width of box or [Cube]: 3' ↵
Specify height of box: 1 ↵
Specify rotation angle of box about the Z axis or [Reference]: ↵
```

4. Do a Zoom Extents to see the entire box.

5. Start the 3D command with the Box option again. Follow the prompts to make a leg:

```
Specify corner point of box: 1,1 ↵
Specify length of box: 1 ↵
Specify width of box or [Cube]: 1 ↵
Specify height of box: 30 ↵
Specify rotation angle of box about the Z axis or [Reference]: 0 ↵
```

6. Mirror the leg, from one side of the table to the opposite side, using midpoint object snaps for the mirror line. Then mirror the two legs in the other direction, so that you have four legs. Zoom out and pan as necessary to center the table in the drawing area.

> **NOTE**   If you have trouble finding the midpoint object snaps, change the visual style to 2D Wireframe.

7. Start the 3D command with the Dish option. Follow the prompts to create a bowl on the table:

```
Specify center point of dish: 2',2',35-1/2 ↵
Specify radius of dish or [Diameter]: d ↵
Specify diameter of dish: 9 ↵
Enter number of longitudinal segments for surface of dish <16>: ↵
Enter number of latitudinal segments for surface of dish <8>: ↵
```

The dish's diameter is 9, so its height is half that, or 4½. The center of the dish is at height 35½ because the tabletop is at 31 (31 + 4½ = 35½).

8. Type **elev** ↵. Change the elevation to 31. Leave the thickness at 0 (zero).

9. Start the 3D command with the Cone option. Follow the prompts to create a salt shaker:

```
Specify center point for base of cone: 2',1'6 ↵
Specify radius for base of cone or [Diameter]: 1 ↵
Specify radius for top of cone or [Diameter] <0>: .5 ↵
Specify height of cone: 4 ↵
Enter number of segments for surface of cone <16>: 8 ↵
```

10. Start the 3D command with the Sphere option. Follow the prompts to draw an orange in the bowl:

```
Specify center point of sphere: 2',2',32-1/2 ↵
Specify radius of sphere or [Diameter]: d ↵
Specify diameter of sphere: 3 ↵
Enter number of longitudinal segments for surface of sphere <16>: 8 ↵
Enter number of latitudinal segments for surface of sphere <16>: 8 ↵
```

11. Start the 3D command with the Cone option again. Follow the prompts to make a plate.

(It may not seem logical to use a cone to make a flat plate. However, it works because you can create a truncated cone that is upside down and very shallow. It's an unusual but interesting use for the CONE command.)

```
Specify center point for base of cone: 1',1' ↵
Specify radius for base of cone or [Diameter]: 2 ↵
Specify radius for top of cone or [Diameter] <0>: 5 ↵
Specify height of cone: 1/2 ↵
Enter number of segments for surface of cone <16>: ↵
```

12. Start the 3D command with the Wedge option. Follow the prompts to make a wedge of cheese on the plate:

```
Specify corner point of wedge: 10,10 ↵
Specify length of wedge: 5 ↵
Specify width of wedge: 2 ↵
Specify height of wedge: 2 ↵
Specify rotation angle of wedge about the Z axis: 30 ↵
```

13. Start the 3D command with the Pyramid option. Follow the prompts to draw a pyramidal pepper shaker:

```
Specify first corner point for base of pyramid: 2'6,2'6 ↵
Specify second corner point for base of pyramid: 1,0 ↵
Specify third corner point for base of pyramid: 0,1 ↵
Specify fourth corner point for base of pyramid or [Tetrahedron]:
   -1,0 ↵
```

```
Specify apex point of pyramid or [Ridge/Top]: t ↵
Specify first corner point for top of pyramid: 1/4,1/4,3 ↵
Specify second corner point for top of pyramid: -1/4,1/4,3 ↵
Specify third corner point for top of pyramid: -1/4,-1/4,3 ↵
Specify fourth corner point for top of pyramid: 1/4,-1/4,3 ↵
```

14. Choose View ⇨ Visual Styles ⇨ Conceptual. Turn off the grid if it's on. You can now visualize the drawing better.

15. Save your drawing. It should look like Figure 23.22. If you look carefully, you'll see that the edge of the cheese wedge goes slightly through the plate.

FIGURE 23.22

The table with a plate, wedge of cheese, bowl, orange, and nonmatching salt and pepper shakers.

Drawing Revolved Surfaces

A common way to define a surface is to revolve an outline around an axis. You can create some very complex surfaces in this way. AutoCAD offers two ways to create surfaces from the revolution of an outline.

Understanding the REVSURF command

The REVSURF command takes an object that defines an outline or profile — AutoCAD also calls it a *path curve* — and revolves it around an axis, creating a 3D polygon mesh. Figure 23.23 shows two examples of revolved surfaces.

The path curve must be one object — a line, arc, circle, polyline, ellipse, or elliptical arc. It can be open, like the path curves shown in Figure 23.23, or closed. A closed path curve creates a model that is closed in the N direction.

> **TIP** If you have several adjoining objects that you'd like to use as one path curve, remember that you can use PEDIT to change lines and arcs to polylines and join them together. For more information, see Chapter 16. You can also use the JOIN command, which I cover in Chapter 10.

FIGURE 23.23

Two revolved surfaces.

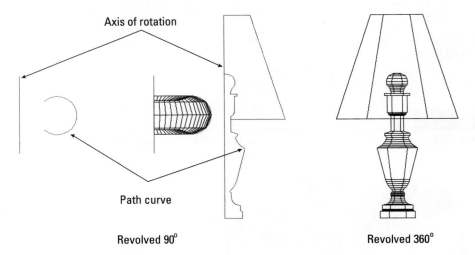

Axis of rotation

Path curve

Revolved 90°   Revolved 360°

Determining the angle of rotation

You can start the angle of rotation at any angle; it doesn't have to start on the plane of the path curve. You can rotate the path curve to any angle. Of course, rotating the path curve 360 degrees closes the model (in the M direction of the mesh).

When you rotate the path curve less than 360 degrees, you need to know which way to rotate. You can specify a positive (counterclockwise) or negative (clockwise) angle.

The point at which you pick the axis of rotation object affects the positive direction of rotation. Then you use the right-hand rule to determine which way the path curve will rotate around the axis. To do this, point your right thumb along the axis in the opposite direction from the endpoint closest to where you pick the axis. The direction in which your other fingers curl is the positive direction of rotation. Figure 23.24 shows the same model revolved in different directions. In the left model, the line of the axis was picked near the bottom endpoint. In the right model, the line of the axis was picked near the top endpoint.

Setting the number of segments

You use the SURFTAB1 and SURFTAB2 system variables to determine how AutoCAD creates the mesh. AutoCAD calls this the *wireframe density*.

- SURFTAB1 affects how the M direction — the direction of revolution — is displayed.
- SURFTAB2 affects how the N direction — the path curve — is displayed.

The higher the setting, the more lines AutoCAD uses to display the model. However, if the path curve is a polyline with straight segments, AutoCAD just displays one line at each segment vertex.

In Figure 23.24, SURFTAB1 is 6 and SURFTAB2 is 12. Figure 23.25 shows the same model with SURFTAB1 at 20 and SURFTAB2 at 5 to show the contrast between the two.

FIGURE 23.24

From the viewer's point of view, the left revolved surface was rotated back 125 degrees, and the right revolved surface was rotated forward 125 degrees.

> **NOTE** Although you count M and N mesh sizes by vertices, you specify SURFTAB1 and SURFTAB2 by the number of surface areas that you want to see.

To set these system variables, type them on the command line and specify the new value that you want.

FIGURE 23.25

The same model re-created with SURFTAB1=20 and SURFTAB2=5.

Using the REVSURF command

To create a revolved surface, follow these steps:

1. First create the path curve, which must be one object.
2. Draw the axis of revolution, usually a line.
3. Choose Draw ⇨ Modeling ⇨ Meshes ⇨ Revolved Mesh or enter **revsurf** on the command line.
4. At the `Select object to revolve:` prompt, select the path curve object.
5. At the `Select object that defines the axis of revolution:` prompt, select the axis of revolution object.

6. At the Specify start angle <0>: prompt, press Enter to accept the default of 0 (zero) or type a start angle.

7. At the Specify included angle (+=ccw, -=cw) <360>: prompt, press Enter to revolve the surface 360 degrees or type a positive or negative angle.

You may need to create the path curve and the axis in a different plane than the one you use when revolving them. You can draw the path curve and axis in one UCS and use REVSURF in another. If the object doesn't come out in the right direction, you can rotate the entire object when completed. Rotating objects in 3D is covered in the next chapter.

REVSURF retains the original path curve and axis objects. It helps to draw them in a different layer and color so that you can easily erase them afterward; otherwise, they're hard to distinguish from the revolved surface. Having the original objects on a separate layer also helps if you need to redo the revolved surface — you can more easily avoid erasing them when you erase the revolved surface.

 The drawing used in the following exercise on drawing revolved surfaces, ab23-d.dwg, is in the Drawings folder on the DVD.

STEPS: Drawing Revolved Surfaces

1. Open ab23-d.dwg from the DVD.

2. Save it as ab23-04.dwg in your AutoCAD Bible folder. The path curve and axis are already drawn. This drawing was saved using the Conceptual visual style.

3. Choose Draw ➪ Modeling ➪ Meshes ➪ Revolved Mesh.

4. At the Select object to revolve: prompt, select the polyline to the right.

5. At the Select object that defines the axis of revolution: prompt, select the line.

6. At the Specify start angle <0>: prompt, press Enter. At the Specify included angle (+=ccw, -=cw) <360>: prompt, press Enter to revolve the path curve in a full circle.

7. Save your drawing. It should look like Figure 23.26.

FIGURE 23.26

The revolved surface.

Working with the REVOLVE command

The REVOLVE command creates either a solid or a surface, depending on the source object and the axis of rotation. If the source object and the object that makes up the axis form a closed figure, REVOLVE creates a solid; otherwise, it creates a surface. When you use REVOLVE to create a surface, the prompts are similar to those of the REVSURF command. I cover the REVOLVE command more fully in the next chapter (see the "Drawing Revolved Solids" section in Chapter 24).

The REVOLVE command allows you to select more than one object to revolve, something that you can't do with the REVSURF command. The prompts of the two commands ask for the same information but in a slightly different way.

Figure 23.27 shows two examples of the REVOLVE command, one that creates a surface and the other that creates a solid. The arc is revolved around the line in each case, but when the line and the arc create a closed figure, the result is a solid.

FIGURE 23.27

When the axis does not touch the arc, the REVOLVE command creates a surface. When the axis and the arc together create a closed figure, the command creates a solid.

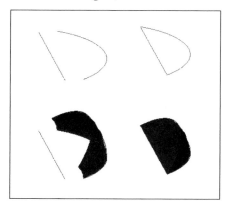

Drawing an Extruded Surface

A simple way to create a 3D object is to start with a 2D object and *extrude* it (or thrust it out). In AutoCAD, extruding refers to creating a 3D object from a 2D object. Two commands, TABSURF and EXTRUDE, allow you to extrude 2D objects to create surfaces.

Working with the TABSURF command

The TABSURF command takes an outline, or profile, which AutoCAD calls a *path curve,* and extrudes it along a vector that defines the direction and distance of the extrusion. TABSURF creates a 3D polyline mesh. The type of surface created is called a *tabulated surface.* Figure 23.28 shows two examples of extruded surfaces.

FIGURE 23.28

Two extruded surfaces created using TABSURF.

For the I-beam, you could have simply given the 2D polyline profile a thickness and achieved a similar result. However, you could not have done so with the extruded surface on the left, because the extrusion is not perpendicular to the XY plane that contains the 2D polyline profile. TABSURF can extrude a shape in any direction.

When you select the vector object, your pick point determines the direction of the extrusion. AutoCAD starts the extrusion from the end of the vector closest to the pick point.

You use the SURFTAB1 system variable to control the number of lines AutoCAD uses to display the curve. If the curve is made up of polyline segments, AutoCAD displays one line at each segment vertex.

CAUTION   Note the I-beam in Figure 23.28. If you create an object by mirroring, stretching, and so on, you'll see extra tabulation lines at the separate segments in the polyline definition. If you want a clean look, you need to draw clean. You might need to use the original shape as a guide to draw a new polyline on top of the old one, and then erase the original.

You should use a nonplanar view when using TABSURF to check that you've accurately defined the extrusion vector into the third dimension. Any of the preset isometric views will be helpful.

To draw an extruded surface, follow these steps:

1. Draw the object to extrude — a line, arc, circle, polyline, ellipse, or elliptical arc. This is the path curve.

2. Draw the vector, usually a line. If you use a 2D or 3D polyline, AutoCAD uses an imaginary line from the start point to the endpoint to determine the vector.

3. Enter **tabsurf** on the command line or in the Dynamic Input tooltip, or choose Draw ⇨ Modeling ⇨ Meshes ⇨ Tabulated Mesh.

4. At the Select object for path curve: prompt, select the path curve object.

5. At the Select object for direction vector: prompt, select the line that you're using for the vector.

ON the DVD-ROM   The drawing used in the following exercise on drawing tabulated surfaces, ab23-e.dwg, is in the Drawings folder on the DVD.

STEPS: Drawing Tabulated Surfaces

1. Open ab23-e.dwg from the DVD.

2. Save it as ab23-05.dwg in your AutoCAD Bible folder. You see a tabletop. Its bottom is at a Z height of 30. The current elevation is 30. You're looking at the table from the SE isometric view. OSNAP should be on. Set running object snaps for endpoint, midpoint, and center. The current layer is Const. The drawing is shown in Figure 23.29.

3. Start the CIRCLE command. Follow the prompts:

```
Specify center point for circle or [3P/2P/Ttr (tan tan radius)]:
    Choose the From object snap.
_from Base point: Pick the endpoint at ❶ in Figure 23.29.
<Offset>: @-1,3 ↲
Specify radius of circle or [Diameter]: .75 ↲
```

The tabletop.

4. Start the LINE command. At the Specify first point: prompt, choose the Center object snap of the circle that you just drew. At the Specify next point or [Undo]: prompt, type **3,−3,−30** ↲ to draw a line flaring out from the circle and going down to the floor. End the LINE command.

5. Enter **tabsurf** on the command line or in the Dynamic Input tooltip. At the Select object for path curve: prompt, select the circle. At the Select object for direction vector: prompt, select the line. (You can see only the top part of the line, but that's the part that you need to pick.) AutoCAD creates the tabulated surface.

6. Start the MIRROR command. Select the entire leg. Choose the midpoint of the bottom edge of both long sides of the table for the two points of the mirror line.

7. Repeat the MIRROR line and select both legs. Mirror them using the midpoints of the bottom edge of the short sides of the table for the two points of the mirror line.

8. Do a ZOOM Extents to see the entire table.

9. Save your drawing. It should look like Figure 23.30.

FIGURE 23.30

The completed table.

Working with the EXTRUDE command

The EXTRUDE command creates a surface if you start with an open 2D figure, and a solid if you start with a closed 2D figure. If you use the EXTRUDE command to create a surface, it is similar to the TABSURF command, but offers more options. I discuss the EXTRUDE command more fully in the Chapter 24, in the "Creating Extruded Solids" section.

Figure 23.31 shows an open 2D figure (an arc) and a closed figure (a line and an arc), and the results after using the EXTRUDE command.

Sweeping objects along a path

Sweeping is similar to extruding, but you have more options. Like the EXTRUDE command, the SWEEP command creates surfaces when you sweep an open profile and solids when you sweep a closed one.

Figure 23.32 shows two sweeps. On the left, an arc is swept along a helix, creating a surface. On the right, a circle is swept along the helix, creating a solid. You can scale the profile and twist it to create some very interesting models. I cover the SWEEP command fully in the next chapter, where I discuss solids. When you create a surface with this command, you create an object type called a sweptsurface.

FIGURE 23.31

On the left, the EXTRUDE command creates a surface from an arc. On the right, the command creates a solid from the closed figure of a line and an arc.

FIGURE 23.32

You can create interesting surfaces and solids using the SWEEP command.

Drawing Surfaces Between 2D Objects

If you have two existing objects, you may want to define the surface that would extend between these objects. Or, you may want to extrapolate a surface along two or more objects. You can use two commands to create these surfaces.

Creating ruled surfaces

Use the RULESURF command to create a surface that extends between two 2D objects. The objects can be lines, polylines (2D or 3D), circles, ellipses, elliptical arcs, splines, or points. The two objects must be either both open or both closed. Only one of the two can be a point.

Use the SURFTAB1 system variable to control the number of lines that AutoCAD uses to display the surface. Figure 23.33 shows some ruled surfaces.

The pick points of the two objects affect the resulting curve. If you pick them both on the same side, you get the type of curves shown in Figure 23.33. If you pick them on opposite sides, the curve intersects itself, as shown in Figure 23.34.

FIGURE 23.33

Ruled surfaces.

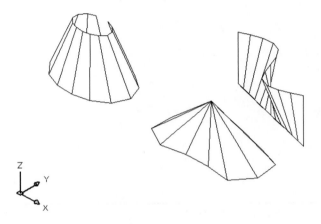

FIGURE 23.34

A self-intersecting ruled surface.

Follow these steps to draw a ruled surface:

1. Draw the two objects for the ruled surface.

2. Choose Draw ➪ Modeling ➪ Meshes ➪ Ruled Mesh, or enter **rulesurf** on the command line or in the Dynamic Input tooltip.

3. At the `Select first defining curve:` prompt, choose the first object.

4. At the `Select second defining curve:` prompt, choose the second object.

STEPS: Drawing Ruled Surfaces

1. Open `ab23-f.dwg` from the DVD.

2. Save it as `ab23-06.dwg` in your `AutoCAD Bible` folder. You see a spline, as shown in Figure 23.35. In this exercise, you use the spline to draw some drapes.

FIGURE 23.35

A spline.

3. Mirror the spline. For the mirror line, turn on ORTHO and use ❶ and ❷ as shown in Figure 23.35. Don't delete the original spline.

4. Start the COPY command and select both splines. At the `Specify base point or [Displacement/mOde] <Displacement>:` prompt, type **0,0,73** ↵ to copy the splines 73 units in the positive Z direction. Press Enter at the `Specify second point or <use first point as displacement>:` prompt.

5. Choose View ➪ 3D Views ➪ SE Isometric.

6. Enter **rulesurf** on the command line or in the Dynamic Input tooltip. At the `Select first defining curve:` prompt, choose the top-right spline near its right endpoint. At the `Select second defining curve:` prompt, choose the bottom-right spline near its right endpoint.

7. Repeat the RULESURF command. At the `Select first defining curve:` prompt, choose the top-left spline near its left endpoint. At the `Select second defining curve:` prompt, choose the bottom-left spline near its left endpoint.

8. Save your drawing. It should look like Figure 23.36.

The completed drapes.

Lofting objects

The LOFT command lets you choose two or more 2D objects and creates a new surface or solid by interpolating through them. If the 2D object is open, like an arc, the command creates surfaces; if it's closed, like a circle, the command creates solids.

Figure 23.37 shows two lofts. On the left is a surface created from four arcs. On the right is a solid created from four circles. The LOFT command has a number of parameters that you need to set. I cover this command in detail in Chapter 24. When you create a surface with this command, you create an object type called a loftedsurface.

FIGURE 23.37

You can create either a surface or a solid with the LOFT command.

Drawing Edge Surfaces

You may have several edges and want to create a surface that extends between them. You can use the EDGESURF command to create unusual surfaces bound by four touching objects. The objects can be lines, arcs, splines, or polylines (2D or 3D). EDGESURF creates a polygon mesh that approximates a Coon's surface patch mesh — a surface defined by four edges. Figure 23.38 shows an edge surface.

FIGURE 23.38

An edge surface created with the EDGESURF command.

Use the SURFTAB1 and SURFTAB2 system variables to vary the displayed lines in each direction.

Follow these steps to create an edge surface:

1. Draw the four objects to create a boundary for the surface. They must touch, so use Endpoint object snaps to create them or to move them into place.
2. Choose Draw ⇨ Modeling ⇨ Meshes ⇨ Edge Mesh, or enter **edgesurf** on the command line or in the Dynamic Input tooltip.
3. AutoCAD prompts you to select edges 1 through 4. You can select them in any order.

Creating the four edges involves moving from one UCS to another UCS because they're all in 3D. It helps to create a bounding box for your object using the BOX command. You can then use the dynamic UCS feature to temporarily change UCSs for each edge.

 The drawing used in the following exercise on drawing edge surfaces, ab23-g.dwg, is in the Drawings **folder on the DVD.**

STEPS: Drawing Edge Surfaces

1. Open ab23-g.dwg from the DVD.
2. Save it as ab23-07.dwg in your AutoCAD Bible folder. You see four curves in a bounding box, as shown in Figure 23.39. In this exercise, you use the curves to draw a dustpan.

FIGURE 23.39

The four curves are the basis for creating an edge surface.

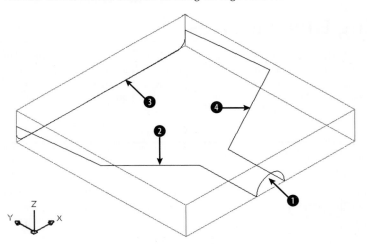

3. Freeze the Const layer.
4. Enter **edgesurf** on the command line or in the Dynamic Input interface. At the prompts, select ❶, ❷, ❸, and ❹ in Figure 23.39.
5. Choose View ⇨ Hide to see the result.
6. Save your drawing. It should look like Figure 23.40. It's either a dustpan or a starship — your choice.

FIGURE 23.40

The completed dustpan — or starship.

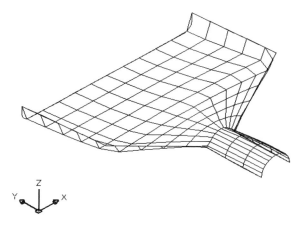

Working with Multiple Types of 3D Objects

Several commands convert one type of object to another or allow you to use multiple types of objects together. These commands mean that you don't have to choose in advance which type of object you want; if necessary, you can make changes later.

Thickening a surface into a solid

The THICKEN command allows you to add thickness to a surface and thereby turn it into a solid. You can only use it on surfaces created with the PLANESURF, EXTRUDE, SWEEP, LOFT, or REVOLVE commands. However, you can start with a region, line, or arc; for example, use CONVTOSURFACE to create a surface, and then use THICKEN to turn it into a solid.

To thicken a surface to a solid, follow these steps:

1. Choose Modify ➪ 3D Operations ➪ Thicken, or enter **thicken** on the command line (or in the Dynamic Tooltip interface).
2. Select the surface or surfaces that you want to thicken.
3. At the Specify thickness <0.0000>: prompt, enter a thickness. A positive number thickens in the positive direction of the axes; a negative number thickens in the negative direction.

Extracting edges from a surface or a region

You can turn a surface or a region into a wireframe object by extracting its edges. To extract an edge, choose Modify ➪ 3D Operations ➪ Extract Edges. The XEDGES command works only with the following surface types:

- Extrudedsurface
- Loftedsurface

- Revolvedsurface
- Planesurface

You cannot convert polygon or polyface meshes. Figure 23.40 shows edges extracted from a lofted surface.

The XEDGES command can extract edges from a surface.

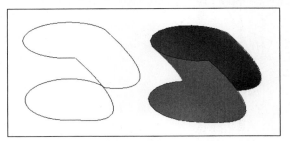

You can also select individual edges or faces to extract by pressing the Ctrl key and clicking the edges or faces that you want. Then use the XEDGES command to extract them.

Slicing solids with a surface

You can use the SLICE command to slide a solid with a surface. I cover the SLICE command in Chapter 24, in the section "Using the SLICE command."

Summary

In this chapter, you read all about 3D surfaces. You read about:

- Converting objects to surfaces
- Creating surfaces by using the 3DFACE command and controlling the visibility of the lines between the faces
- Creating polyface meshes
- Creating plane surfaces
- Drawing surfaces with 3D polygon meshes, including the basic shapes — box, wedge, pyramid, cone, sphere, dome, dish, and torus
- Making a surface by revolving a profile around an axis
- Extruding and sweeping a curve
- Creating a surface between two curves
- Making an edge surface from four curves
- Working with multiple types of 3D objects

In the next chapter, you discover how to create true solids (well, true electronic ones, at least) as well as how to edit in 3D.

Chapter 24

Creating Solids and Editing in 3D

Although you can create great-looking models with surfaces, if you want truly realistic models, you need to create solids. After all, in real life, objects have solidity. Even a thin object such as a wastepaper basket or a drape has some thickness. Solids enable you to create more realistic models than surfaces. You can also combine or subtract solids and get information about their physical properties.

AUTOCAD ONLY AutoCAD LT doesn't draw solids. For the 3D capabilities of AutoCAD LT, see Chapters 21 and 22.

Figure 24.1 shows a complex model created using solids.

As I explain in Chapter 21, when working in 3D, you should use a 3D environment. This includes the following items:

- The 3D Modeling workspace, which you choose from the Workspaces toolbar. (I explain how to customize workspaces in Appendix A.)

- The `acad3d.dwt` template (or `acadiso3d.dwt` or similar template) that turns on perspective view, the grid, and the Realistic or other 3D visual style. (I cover visual styles in Chapter 22.)

- The Dashboard palette, which combines many modeling commands and settings in one place.

To work with solids, you can display the Modeling toolbar (right-click any toolbar and choose Modeling). You can also access all of the solids commands by choosing Draw ⇨ Modeling and then choosing the specific command from the submenu that opens.

You can create complex and realistic models using solids.

Thanks to Hans-Joachim Fach, Bremen, Germany, for this drawing.

Drawing Basic Shapes

As with surfaces, AutoCAD makes it easy to create most basic geometrical shapes. These shapes are easy to draw, because you can dynamically see the result as you draw.

Drawing a box

The box is one of the most commonly used 3D objects and is often the basis for more complex models. Figure 24.2 shows a solid box shown with the 3D Hidden visual style. Visually, it looks the same as a surface box.

A solid box.

To draw a box, follow these steps:

1. Choose Box from the Modeling toolbar or the 3D Make control panel of the Dashboard.
2. At the `Specify first corner or [Center]:` prompt, specify any corner of the box, or right-click and choose Center to specify the 3D center of the box (not the center of the base).

3. If you specify the corner (the default), you then see the `Specify other corner or [Cube/Length]:` prompt.

   The default is to pick the opposite corner in the XY plane. This defines the base of the box. You can define the base just like you define any rectangle, by dragging and picking the opposite corner or by entering coordinates. At the `Specify height or [2Point]:` prompt, drag in the Z direction and pick a height or enter a height value. You can also pick two points to specify the height. This completes the box.

   If you use the Length option, AutoCAD asks you for a width and a height. If you use the Cube option, AutoCAD asks for one length and completes the box.

4. If you specify the center at the first prompt, you see the `Specify center:` prompt. Specify the center of the box. The `Specify corner or [Cube/Length]:` prompt appears.

   If you pick the corner of the box, AutoCAD then asks you for the height to complete the box.

   If you specify the length, AutoCAD then asks for a width and a height. If you use the Cube option, AutoCAD asks for a length and completes the box.

You can specify a negative length, width, or height to build the box in the negative direction. If you specify the center of the cube, don't forget that the center's Z coordinate is different from the corner's Z coordinate. AutoCAD always creates the box parallel to the XY plane.

Drawing a wedge

A wedge is a box sliced in half. The prompts are virtually the same as for the Box command. Figure 24.3 shows two wedges.

FIGURE 24.3

Two solid wedges.

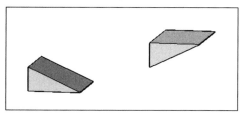

To create a wedge, follow these steps:

1. Choose Wedge from the Modeling toolbar or the 3D Make control panel of the Dashboard.
2. At the `Specify first corner or [Center]:` prompt, specify any corner of the wedge or use the Center option to specify the 3D center of the wedge.
3. If you specify the corner (the default), you then see the `Specify other corner or [Cube/Length]:` prompt.

   The default is to pick the opposite corner in the XY plane — you can also define it using coordinates. The command then asks you for the height in the Z direction. This completes the wedge.

   If you use the Length option, AutoCAD asks you for a width and a height.

If you use the Cube option, AutoCAD asks for one length and completes the wedge. For positive lengths, the wedge slopes downward in the positive X direction. (However, if you have Dynamic Input on, the slope will follow the direction of the cursor.)

4. If you specify the center, you see the `Specify center:` prompt. Specify the center point. The `Specify corner or [Cube/Length]:` prompt displays.

   If you pick the corner of the wedge, the command asks for a height.

   If you specify the length, AutoCAD then asks for a width and a height. If you use the Cube option, AutoCAD asks for a length and completes the wedge.

Drawing a cone

You can draw cones with circular or elliptical bases. By specifying a negative height, you can create an inverted cone (like an ice cream cone). By specifying the axis endpoint (the apex), you can draw cones on an angle from the XY plane. You can also specify a top radius to create a truncated cone (sometimes called a frustum cone). Figure 24.4 shows some cones.

FIGURE 24.4

Cones with varying heights and bases.

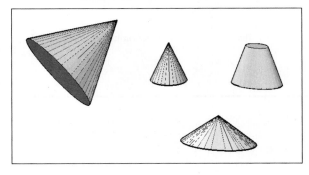

Follow these steps to draw a cone:

1. Choose Cone from the Modeling toolbar or the 3D Make control panel of the Dashboard.

2. At the `Specify center point of base or [3P/2P/Ttr/Elliptical]:` prompt, specify the center of the base if you want a circular cone. Otherwise, use the 3P, 2P, or Ttr options to define a circular base. Use the Elliptical option to define an elliptical base.

   If you specified a center point, at the `Specify base radius or [Diameter]:` prompt, specify a radius or use the Diameter option to specify the diameter.

   If you chose the Elliptical option, use the prompts to define the elliptical base. These prompts are like the prompts for the ELLIPSE command.

3. At the `Specify height or [2Point/Axis endpoint/Top radius]:` prompt, specify the height by dragging or entering a value. Use the 2Point option to specify the height by picking two points. The Axis endpoint option is another way to specify the height, and enables you to create an angled cone. (By default, the Axis endpoint is a relative coordinate, based on the center of the base.) The Top radius option creates a truncated cone.

Controlling the Display of Solids

Curved surfaces are drawn using segments. When you draw a surface sphere, AutoCAD prompts you for the number of lines to draw. The wireframe display of all of the curved solids in a drawing is controlled by the ISOLINES system variable. The default, 4, provides a bare minimum of curved lines to let you view the outlines of the curve and results in the quickest display. Increasing the ISOLINES value improves the visual result but slows down the drawing display. Generally, you can find a happy medium based on the size of your drawing, the speed of your computer, and your personal preferences. The ISOLINES variable affects only wireframe display — it has no effect when you use another visual style. Figure 24.5 shows the effect of varying the ISOLINES setting. When you change the ISOLINES value, use the REGEN command to see the result on existing objects.

The FACETRES system variable is the 3D version of VIEWRES, and it determines the display of curved surfaces and solids that are shaded or rendered. You can set FACETRES from 0.01 to 10.0. Here you see a hidden sphere at FACETRES settings of 0.05 (left) and 5.0 (right). The default is 0.5, which is generally a happy medium.

The VSEDGES system variable controls the type of edges that models display. The default value of 1 displays is 0 lines. To show more edges, you can change VSEDGES to 2, which displays facets, as you see here on the left. If you are displaying your models with some visual style (anything but wireframe or hidden), you can set VSEDGES to 0, which displays no edges. This setting provides the cleanest look, as you see on the right.

Drawing a sphere

Spheres are not used very often alone, but they can be the basis for more complex models — they certainly look pretty! Figure 24.5 shows two solid spheres. The left sphere uses the default ISOLINE value of 4. The right sphere uses an ISOLINE value of 8.

FIGURE 24.5

Two solid spheres, with ISOLINES set at 4 (left) and 8 (right).

To draw a sphere, follow these steps:

1. Choose Sphere from the Modeling toolbar or the 3D Make control panel of the Dashboard.
2. At the `Specify center point or [3P/2P/Ttr]:` prompt, specify the center of the sphere. If you want the sphere to lie on the XY plane, the Z coordinate of the center should be equal to the radius of the sphere. Use the 3P, 2P, or Ttr options to define a circle at the center of the sphere.
3. At the `Specify radius or [Diameter]:` prompt, drag and pick a point on the surface of the sphere or enter a value for the radius. You can use the Diameter option to specify the diameter instead.

Drawing a cylinder

Cylinders are very common in 3D drawing, both for building models and creating holes. Figure 24.6 shows three solid cylinders. The grid helps you to visualize the XY plane. You can draw cylinders with circular or elliptical bases. By specifying the center of the top of the cylinder separately, you can draw it at an angle.

FIGURE 24.6

Some solid cylinders.

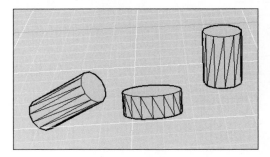

Follow these steps to draw a cylinder:

1. Choose Cylinder from the Modeling toolbar or the 3D Make control panel of the Dashboard.

2. At the `Specify center point of base or [3P/2P/Ttr/Elliptical]:` prompt, specify the center point for a circular cylinder or define the circle using the 3P, 2P, or Ttr options. You can also choose the Elliptical option to define an ellipse as a base.

   If you specified a center point, then at the `Specify base radius or [Diameter]:` prompt, specify a radius or use the Diameter option to specify the diameter.

   If you chose the Elliptical option, use the prompts to define the elliptical base.

3. At the `Specify height or [2Point/Axis endpoint]:` prompt, specify the height by dragging, entering a value, or using the 2Point option. You can create a tilted cylinder by using the Axis endpoint option to specify the center of the other end of the cylinder. (By default, the Axis endpoint is a relative coordinate, based on the center of the base.)

Drawing a torus

A *torus* is a solid 3D donut. Figure 24.7 shows some examples, and labels the parts of a torus. You can make some unusual shapes by varying the torus and tube radii. If the torus radius is negative and the tube radius is larger than the absolute value of the torus radius (for example, –2 and 3), you create a lemon (or football) shape. If the tube radius is larger than the torus radius, you create a puckered ball (or apple) shape. (You cannot get such unusual shapes using the Torus shape on the Surfaces toolbar.)

FIGURE 24.7

Varieties of the torus.

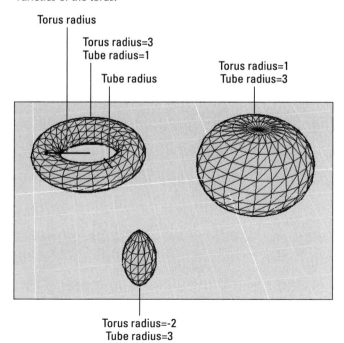

To create a torus, follow these steps:

1. Choose Torus from the Modeling toolbar or the 3D Make control panel of the Dashboard.

2. At the `Specify center point or [3P/2P/Ttr]:` prompt, specify the center of the torus (the center of the hole). You can also use the 3P, 2P, or Ttr options to define a circle as the basis for the torus.

3. At the `Specify radius or [Diameter]:` prompt, specify the radius of the entire torus or use the Diameter option to specify the diameter.

4. At the `Specify tube radius or [2Point/Diameter]:` prompt, specify the radius of just the tube or use the Diameter option to specify the tube's diameter. You can use the 2Point option to pick two points that define the tube radius.

Drawing a pyramid

You can draw pyramids with a base of 3 to 32 sides. The prompts for the base are similar to the prompts for the POLYGON command. (For more information on the POLYGON command, see the section "Drawing Polygons" in Chapter 6.) A pyramid can come to a point, or you can truncate it. You can also tilt the pyramid. Figure 24.8 shows three variations on the pyramid.

FIGURE 24.8

You can draw several types of pyramids.

Follow these steps to draw a pyramid:

1. Choose Pyramid from the Modeling toolbar or the 3D Make control panel of the Dashboard. The default number of sides is listed, as well as whether the base will be inscribed or circumscribed.

2. At the `Specify center point of base or [Edge/Sides]:` prompt, specify the center of the base. You can use the Edge option to define an edge, or the Sides option to specify the number of sides.

3. At the `Specify base radius or [Inscribed]:` prompt, drag to specify the radius or enter a value. You can use the Inscribed (or Circumscribed) option to change whether the radius is inscribed (based on the base points) or circumscribed (based on the base side midpoints).

4. At the `Specify height or [2Point/Axis endpoint/Top radius]:` prompt, drag to specify the height or enter a value. Use the 2Point option to specify the height by picking two

points. Use the Axis endpoint to specify the tip. If it isn't directly over the base's center, you tilt the pyramid. Use the Top radius to truncate the pyramid; drag or enter a value for the top's radius and then enter the height of the pyramid.

 The drawing used in the following exercise on drawing basic solids, ab24-a.dwg, **is in the** Drawings **folder on the DVD.**

STEPS: Drawing Basic 3D Solids

1. Open ab24-a.dwg from the DVD.

2. Save the file as ab24-01.dwg in your AutoCAD Bible folder. If the Modeling toolbar is not displayed, right-click any toolbar and choose Modeling. Turn on OSNAP. Set running object snaps for quadrant, and center. In this exercise, I assume that you have dynamic input on, set to the default of relative coordinates.

3. Choose Cylinder from the Modeling toolbar. Follow the prompts:

   ```
   Specify center point of base or [3P/2P/Ttr/Elliptical]: 7,6.5 ↵
   Specify base radius or [Diameter] <3.0000>: 3 ↵
   Specify height or [2Point/Axis endpoint] <1.0000>: 1 ↵
   ```

4. Repeat the CYLINDER command. Zoom closer to the top end of the lamp's arm and change the viewpoint so that you can see the end circle more clearly. Follow the prompts:

   ```
   Specify center point of base or [3P/2P/Ttr/Elliptical]: 2p ↵
   Specify first end point of diameter: Choose the bottom quadrant of
   the top end of the lamp's arm.
   Specify second end point of diameter: 3,0 ↵
   Specify height or [2Point/Axis endpoint] <17.2980>: Move the cursor
   upward and enter 2.5 ↵
   ```

5. Choose Sphere from the Modeling toolbar. Follow the prompts:

   ```
   Specify center point or [3P/2P/Ttr]: 2p ↵
   Specify first end point of diameter: Pick the left quadrant of the
   top of the cylinder that you just drew.
   Specify second end point of diameter: Pick the right quadrant of the
   top of the cylinder that you just drew.
   ```

6. Choose Cone from the Modeling toolbar. Follow the prompts:

   ```
   Specify center point of base or [3P/2P/Ttr/Elliptical]: Pick the
   center of the bottom of the cylinder.
   Specify base radius or [Diameter] <1.5000>: Pick any quadrant on the
   edge of the cylinder's bottom edge.
   Specify height or [2Point/Axis endpoint/Top radius] <4.0000>: t ↵
   Specify top radius <3.0000>: 3 ↵
   Specify height or [2Point/Axis endpoint] <4.0000>: Move the cursor
   downward and enter 4 ↵
   ```

7. Choose View ➪ Zoom ➪ Extents.

8. From the Dashboard's Visual Styles control panel, choose Conceptual from the Visual Styles drop-down list.

9. Save your drawing. It should look like Figure 24.9.

FIGURE 24.9

FIGURE 24.9

The desk lamp.

Creating Extruded Solids

The EXTRUDE command creates solids from closed 2D objects, and surfaces from unclosed 2D objects. The result is similar to adding thickness to a 2D object (discussed in Chapter 21) or using the TABSURF command (see Chapter 23). You can also extrude the face of an existing solid, as I explain later in this chapter. You can extrude lines, arcs, elliptical arcs, 2D polylines, circles, ellipses, splines, 2D solids, planar surfaces, and regions. You can use the REGION command to create one object from several objects for this purpose. You can select several objects and extrude them at one time. Figure 24.10 shows several extruded solids.

FIGURE 24.10

Some extruded solids.

Managing objects used to make other objects

When you extrude a circle to make a cylinder, for example, what should happen to the circle? Do you want to delete it because you want to turn it into a cylinder, or do you want to keep it in case your cylinder isn't just right and you need to use the circle again? The DELOBJ system variable determines whether objects used by the EXTRUDE command (as well as the REVOLVE, LOFT, SWEEP, and others) to make other objects are retained. By default, certain source objects are deleted. Therefore, when you use a 2D object to make a solid, the 2D object is deleted.

 Put source objects on a separate layer. Set DELOBJ to 0 (zero) to keep objects used to create other objects. When you're done, turn off the layer containing your source objects.

The DELOBJ system variable has the following options:

- **0:** Retains all source objects.
- **1:** Deletes profile curves. For example, if you use a circle to create a cylinder, the circle is deleted. Cross sections and guides used with the SWEEP command are also deleted. However, if you extrude along a path, the path is not deleted. This is the default option.
- **2:** Deletes all defining objects, including paths.
- **-1:** Prompts to delete profile curves. This is like 1, but you get a prompt so you can choose.
- **-2:** Prompts to delete all defining objects. This is like 2, but you get a prompt.

Using the EXTRUDE command

When you extrude an object, by default you extrude it perpendicular to the object. However, you can also taper the extrusion, as in the extruded rectangle on the right in Figure 24.10. A positive angle tapers the object inward. A negative angle tapers the object outward so it gets wider in the direction of the extrusion.

 Don't taper the object too much. If the taper angle results in the object coming to a point before its full height, AutoCAD cannot create the solid.

You can extrude the object along a path. A path can be a line, circle, arc, ellipse, elliptical arc, polyline, a spline, or even a helix. The path object must be in a different plane than the original object. Figure 24.10 shows a filleted rectangle extruded along an arc.

Not all paths are suitable for extruding objects. In the following situations, the extrusion may not work. The path should not be:

- Too close to the original object's plane
- Too complex
- Too tightly curved or bent for the size of the original object

Here are the steps for creating an extruded solid:

1. Draw the object that you want to extrude. If you want to extrude along a path, draw the path object in a different plane from the source object.

 2. Choose Extrude from the Modeling toolbar or the 3D Make control panel of the Dashboard.

3. Select the object or objects to extrude.

4. At the `Specify height of extrusion or [Direction/Path/Taper angle] <3.5226>:` prompt, specify the height of the extrusion (drag or enter a value). Use the Path option to extrude along a path object; just select the path object. The Direction option is similar to the Path option, except that you specify two points to indicate the path. Use the Taper angle option to enter a taper angle.

The drawing used in the following exercise on creating extruded solids, ab24-b.dwg, is in the Drawings folder on the DVD.

STEPS: Creating Extruded Solids

1. Open ab24-b.dwg from the DVD.

2. Save the file as ab24-02.dwg in your AutoCAD Bible folder. If the Modeling toolbar is not displayed, right-click any toolbar and choose Modeling. Make sure that OSNAP is on. Set running object snaps for endpoint and midpoint. This is a small mounting angle, shown in an edge view.

3. The angle is made up of lines and arcs. To extrude it, you need to change it into a polyline or region. To change it into a polyline, choose Modify ➪ Object ➪ Polyline. Follow the prompts:

   ```
   Select polyline or [Multiple]: Select any object on the angle.
   Object selected is not a polyline
   Do you want to turn it into one? <Y> ⏎
   Enter an option [Close/Join/Width/Edit
   vertex/Fit/Spline/Decurve/Ltype gen/Undo]: Right-click and choose
   Join.
   Select objects: Use a window to select all of the objects in the
   angle.
   Select objects: ⏎
   Enter an option [Open/Join/Width/Edit vertex/Fit/Spline/Decurve/Ltype
   gen/Undo]: Right-click and choose Enter.
   ```

4. Choose Extrude from the Modeling toolbar or the 3D Make control panel of the Dashboard. Select the mounting angle, and then right-click to end object selection. At the Specify height of extrusion or [Direction/Path/Taper angle] <-1.0800>: prompt, move the cursor up and type 3 ⏎.

5. From the Visual Styles control panel of the Dashboard, choose Conceptual from the Visual Styles drop-down list.

6. Save your drawing. It should look like Figure 24.11.

FIGURE 24.11

The completed mounting angle.

The mounting angle should have two holes in it. You would create the holes using the SUBTRACT command, which I cover later in this chapter.

Drawing Swept Solids

The SWEEP command is similar to the EXTRUDE command, but it concentrates on using paths to define the direction of the extrusion.

The SWEEP command has some great tricks up its sleeve:

1. You can draw the source object on the same plane as the path. You don't even have to place the source object on the path. The SWEEP command figures out the center of the source object. (You can use the Base point option to specify the base point for the source object.)
2. You can twist the object along the path.
3. You can scale the source object.
4. If the source object is a closed object, like a circle, you get a solid; if it's open, you get a swept surface.

The DELOBJ system variable determines what happens to the original objects; for more information, see the explanation in the previous section. Figure 24.12 shows some swept solids.

FIGURE 24.12

You can create very interesting shapes using the SWEEP command.

To create a swept solid or surface, follow these steps:

1. Draw the path that you want to sweep along.
2. In the same plane as the path, draw the object or objects that you want to sweep.
3. Choose SWEEP from the Modeling toolbar or the 3D Make control panel of the Dashboard.
4. At the `Select objects to sweep:` prompt, select the object or objects that you drew.
5. At the `Select sweep path or [Alignment/Base Point/Scale/Twist]:` prompt, select the path.
   - Use the Alignment option if you don't want to align the object perpendicular to the path. By default, the SWEEP does so; for this reason, you don't have to set up the path and the object in different planes.
   - Use the Base Point option to specify a base point on the objects to be swept, to determine the point on that object that actually lies along the path.

■ Use the Scale option to scale the object before sweeping it.

■ Use the Twist option to twist the object along the path. For example, if you specify 180°, the object twists that much from the beginning to the end of the path. This option has a sub-option, Bank, that allows you to specify if you want the object to also rotate in the 3D direction when you use a 3D sweep path (a 3D polyline, 3D spline, or helix).

 The drawing used in the following exercise on creating swept solids, ab24-c.dwg, is in the Drawings folder on the DVD.

STEPS: Creating Swept Solids

1. Open ab24-c.dwg from the DVD. This is the same drawing that was used for the exercise on drawing basic shapes; however, this time the desk lamp is missing its arm. A path is already drawn on the const layer.

2. Save the file as ab24-03.dwg in your AutoCAD Bible folder. If the Modeling toolbar is not displayed, right-click any toolbar and choose Modeling. If necessary, change the visual style to 3D Wireframe (View ➪ Visual Styles ➪ 3D Wireframe).

3. Make the const layer current. Draw a circle anywhere with a radius of 0.375 (a diameter of 0.75).

4. Switch to the object layer.

 5. Choose Sweep from the Modeling toolbar or the 3D Make control panel of the Dashboard. Follow these prompts to sweep the circle along the arm (a polyline):

```
Select objects to sweep: Select the circle.
Select objects to sweep: ↵
Select sweep path or [Alignment/Base point/Scale/Twist]: Select the
arm (the polyline).
```

6. Turn off the const layer.

7. Save your drawing. You can look back to Figure 24.9 to see what the lamp looks like.

Drawing Revolved Solids

The REVOLVE command revolves a profile around an axis. If the profile is closed, the result is a solid; if it's open, the result is a revolved surface. (When the profile is open, the result is like the REVSURF command, which I explain in Chapter 23.) You can revolve lines, arcs, elliptical arcs, 2D polylines, circles, ellipses, splines, 2D solids, planar faces, and regions.

The DELOBJ system variable affects whether the original objects are deleted. See the discussion on this system variable earlier in this chapter in the section "Managing objects used to make other objects."

Figure 24.13 shows a solid created by revolving a rectangle around a line. (You can also create this solid by drawing two circles, extruding them into cylinders, and then subtracting the smaller cylinder from the larger one — it just depends on which technique you're more comfortable with.)

FIGURE 24.13

A solid created by revolving a rectangle around a line.

Axis of revolution   Original object (rectangle)

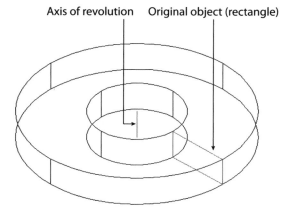

To create a revolved solid, follow these steps:

1. Choose Revolve from the Modeling toolbar or the 3D Make control panel of the Dashboard.

2. At the Select objects to revolve: prompt, select one or more objects.

3. At the Specify axis start point or define axis by [Object/X/Y/Z] <Object>: prompt, you can pick two points to create an axis of revolution. You can also select an object as an axis. Use the X, Y, or Z options to revolve the object around the respective axis.

4. At the Specify angle of revolution or [STart angle] <360>: prompt, press Enter to revolve the object 360 degrees or type an angle, either positive or negative. You can use the STart angle option to specify a start and end angle; for example, you can start at 45 degrees and end at 90 degrees.

As with the REVSURF command, you need to determine the positive direction of rotation if you're revolving less than 360 degrees. (Of course, it may be quicker to try one way and just do it the other way if it doesn't turn out right.) Here's how to figure it out:

1. First determine the positive direction of the axis. If you specify start and endpoints, the positive axis direction goes from the start point to the endpoint. If you pick an object, the positive axis direction goes from the pick point to the other endpoint. If you choose the X, Y, or Z axis, the positive direction is obvious.

2. Point your right thumb in the positive direction of the axis.

3. Look at the curl of your fingers on that hand. That's the positive direction of rotation.

Drawing Lofted Solids

The LOFT command creates a solid or surface that is interpolated from a series of profiles, or cross sections. Open profiles create a surface; closed profiles create a solid. Figure 24.14 shows some lofted solids.

Two solid and two surface lofted objects. On one of the surfaces, you can see the source cross sections (splines).

The difficult part of lofting is drawing and placing the source cross sections to get the result that you want. To create a lofted surface or solid, follow these steps:

1. Draw a series of closed (for a solid) or open (for a surface) profiles. You can start with one and then copy it to nearby locations on the path that will run centrally along the lofted object. You can then modify the copies as necessary. These cross sections become the basis for the lofted object. You need at least two cross sections.

   ▪ If you want to control the sides of the loft (generally for surfaces), draw guides on each side of your cross sections. Guides must start at the first cross section, end at the last cross section, and intersect each cross section.

   ▪ If you want to specify a path through the middle of the loft, draw a path object. The path must intersect the plane of each cross section. The resulting lofted model runs the length of the path.

2. Choose Loft from the Modeling toolbar or the 3D Make control panel on the Dashboard.

3. At the `Select cross-sections in lofting order:` prompt, choose each cross section in order, and then end selection.

4. At the `Enter an option [Guides/Path/Cross-sections only] <Cross-sections only>:` prompt, press Enter to accept the default, which uses the cross sections only to define

the loft. Use the Guides option to select guides you have drawn. Use the Path option to select a path you have drawn.

5.   If you chose the `Cross sections only` option, the Loft Settings dialog box opens. You use this dialog box to fine-tune the definition of the loft and specifically to control how the loft is curved at its cross sections.

- **Ruled:** Creates a straight (ruled) solid or surface between the cross sections and sharp edges at the cross sections.

- **Smooth Fit:** Creates a smooth solid or surface between the cross sections and sharp edges at the first and last cross section.

- **Normal to:** Defines which cross sections the solid or surface is perpendicular (normal) to — the start, end, both start and end, or all cross sections.

- **Draft Angles:** Controls the draft angle (the beginning and ending angles) at the first and last cross sections. This is similar to specifying start and end tangents on a spline. A 0° angle is the default: normal to the cross section's plane in the direction of the next cross section. A 180° angle goes outward, away from the cross section. You also define a magnitude, which is the relative distance that the solid or surface goes before bending to the next cross section. In other words, if you use a 180° angle, a large magnitude creates a large bulge.

- **Close Surface or Solid:** Closes the model.

With all these options, you may need to experiment a little. Keep the Preview Changes check box selected and watch what happens as you change the settings. After you create a loft, you can select it and make changes in the Properties palette; again, you can see the results of your changes immediately.

 The drawing used in the following exercise on creating lofted solids, `ab24-d.dwg`, is in the `Drawings` folder on the DVD.

STEPS: Creating Lofted Solids

1.   Open `ab24-d.dwg` from the DVD. This is the same drawing that was used for the exercise on drawing swept solids; again, the desk lamp's arm is missing, but it has some cross sections (on the `const` layer) that you can use to create a lofted solid. The `object` layer should be current.

2.   Save the file as `ab24-04.dwg` in your `AutoCAD Bible` folder. If the Modeling toolbar is not displayed, right-click any toolbar and choose Modeling. If necessary, change the visual style to 3D Wireframe (View ⇨ Visual Styles ⇨ 3D Wireframe).

 3.   Choose Loft from the Modeling toolbar or the 3D Make control panel of the Dashboard. Follow these prompts to loft the cross sections along the arm:

```
Select cross-sections in lofting order: Select the bottom-most cross
section (a circle).
Select cross-sections in lofting order: Continue to select all the
other cross sections, one at a time, moving upward until you select
the circle closest to the head of the lamp. Press Enter to end
selection.
Enter an option [Guides/Path/Cross-sections only] <Cross-sections
only>: c ↵
```

The Loft Settings dialog box opens. Click OK to accept all the defaults and create the lofted solid.

   4. Turn off the const layer.

   5. Change the visual style to Conceptual (View ⇨ Visual Styles ⇨ Conceptual).

   6. Save your drawing. Use the 3D Orbit override (Shift + mouse wheel) to change to a view that shows the arm more clearly. It should look like Figure 24.15.

FIGURE 24.15

The completed lamp with a lofted arm.

Drawing Polyline-Like Solids

The POLYSOLID command is helpful to architects who want to draw walls in 3D. Using POLYSOLID is like drawing a polyline with a width, or a multiline. You simply draw in plan view from point to point, but the result is a swept solid, using the width and height you specify. You can also convert existing 2D objects — lines, arcs, 2D polylines, and circles — into polysolids.

Figure 24.16 shows a simple layout, drawn using polysolids.

Follow these steps to draw a polysolid:

   1. If you want to convert a 2D object, draw the object or open a drawing containing an existing 2D object.

   2. Choose Polysolid from the Modeling toolbar or the 3D Make control panel of the Dashboard.

   3. At the Specify start point or [Object/Height/Width/Justify] <Object>: prompt, start by choosing the Height option.

   4. At the Specify height <8'-0">: prompt, enter a height.

FIGURE 24.16

You can draw walls using the POLYSOLID command.

5. The original prompt returns. Choose the Width option. At the `Specify width <0'-6">`: prompt, enter a width.

6. Again the original prompt returns.

   ■ If you want to convert an existing object, choose the Object option (you can just press Enter because it's the default option). At the `Select object:` option, select the 2D object to complete the polysolid.

   ■ If you want to draw a new polysolid, specify the start point and continue to specify segments as you would for a polyline. After you specify the first point, you can use the Arc option to create arcs. The prompts are like those for the PLINE command, but you have fewer options. The arc starts tangent to the previous segment. You can specify the direction or the second point for more control.

You can use the Close option to close the polysolid. You can also use the Justify option to determine whether the polysolid is centered around the points you specify (the default), left-justified (your points are to the left side if you're drawing upward), or right-justified.

 The drawing used in the following exercise on creating polysolids, `ab24-e.dwg`, is in the `Drawings` folder on the DVD.

STEPS: Creating Polysolids

1. Open `ab24-e.dwg` from the DVD. This drawing contains two polylines — one to turn into a polysolid and one to create a door gap.

2. Save the file as `ab24-05.dwg` in your `AutoCAD Bible` folder. If necessary, change the visual style to 3D Wireframe (View ➪ Visual Styles ➪ 3D Wireframe). The current layer should be `Walls`. If the Modeling toolbar is not visible, right-click any toolbar and choose Modeling from the list of toolbars.

3. Set the value of the DELOBJ system variable to 0 (zero) so that you don't delete the source object.

 4. Choose Polysolid from the Modeling toolbar or the 3D Make control panel of the Dashboard. Follow the prompts:

```
Specify start point or [Object/Height/Width/Justify] <Object>: h ↵
Specify height <0'-4">: 8' ↵
Specify start point or [Object/Height/Width/Justify] <Object>: w ↵
Specify width <0'-0 1/4">: 6 ↵
Specify start point or [Object/Height/Width/Justify] <Object>: ↵ to
choose the Object option.
Select object: Select the larger polyline.
```

5. Select the new polysolid and change its layer to Walls.

6. Zoom into the gap for the door. Repeat the POLYSOLID command. Follow the prompts:

```
Specify start point or [Object/Height/Width/Justify] <Object>: j ↵
Enter justification [Left/Center/Right] <Right>: r ↵
Specify start point or [Object/Height/Width/Justify] <Object>: h ↵
Specify height <8'-0">: 7' ↵
Specify start point or [Object/Height/Width/Justify] <Object>: Pick
the front endpoint on the left side of the gap.
Specify next point or [Arc/Undo]: Pick the front endpoint on the
right side of the gap.
Specify next point or [Arc/Undo]: ↵
```

7. To create a gap for a side door, you need to create a surface and slice the solid with the surface. (I discuss slicing later in this chapter.) Choose Extrude from the Modeling toolbar or the 3D Make control panel of the Dashboard. Select the smaller polyline, end selection, and drag it so that it's higher than the polysolid wall you just created. This creates an extruded surface.

8. Start the SLICE command. You can find it on the Dashboard by clicking the double down arrow in the 3D Make control panel. (I discuss this command later in this chapter.) Follow the prompts:

```
Select objects to slice: Select the first polysolid that you created.
Select objects to slice: ↵
Specify start point of slicing plane or [planar
Object/Surface/Zaxis/View/XY/YZ/ZX/3points] <3points>: s ↵
Select a surface: Select the extruded surface.
Select solid to keep or [keep Both sides] <Both>: Pick anywhere on
the main portion of the polysolid wall.
```

 NOTE If you find that this step doesn't work properly, undo it and redo the step, this time choosing the Both option. Then erase the smaller section of the polysolid in the door opening.

9. Turn off the 2D layer.

10. Save your drawing. It should look like Figure 24.17. If you want, add a polysolid over the front door and rotate the front door to open it. You should also change the DELOBJ system variable back to its original value.

FIGURE 24.17

The polysolid walls with a door and a gap.

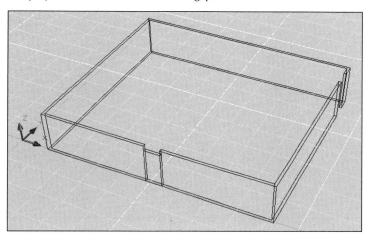

Creating Complex Solids

To create realistic objects, you usually need to edit the simple shapes that I have discussed in this chapter. You can create complex solids by adding them, subtracting them, or intersecting them. These processes are called *Boolean operations,* which in this context means using logical functions, such as addition or subtraction, on objects.

Combining solids

You use the UNION command to add two solids together, making one solid. If the solids are touching, you get a new, unified solid. If the solids are not touching, but rather completely separate, using UNION is similar to grouping, because you select them as one object.

TIP You can also use the UNION command with 2D regions, either for 2D drawings or as a basis for a 3D model.

Figure 24.18 shows the union of two solids showing in the 3D Hidden visual style.

To start the UNION command, choose Union on the Modeling toolbar or choose Modify ➪ Solid Editing ➪ Union. At the `Select objects:` prompt, select the objects that you want to unite.

CAUTION When you create complex solids, the original solids are not retained. Setting the DELOBJ system variable to 0 (zero) doesn't work because the original solids have been changed. If you want, you can copy the original objects to another location in the drawing in case you need to use them again. You can also use UNDO if the result is not what you expected.

FIGURE 24.18

The results of UNION on two solids.

Subtracting solids

You use the SUBTRACT command to subtract one solid from another. This command is most commonly used to create holes. Figure 24.19 shows the result of subtracting a small cylinder from a larger one.

FIGURE 24.19

You can create holes using the SUBTRACT command.

To subtract solids, follow these steps:

1. Choose Subtract from the Modeling toolbar or choose Modify ⇨ Solid Editing ⇨ Subtract.
2. At the following prompt, choose the solid (or region) that you want to subtract from (the one you want to keep):

   ```
   Select solids and regions to subtract from...
   Select objects:
   ```

3. At the following prompt, choose the solid (or region) that you want to subtract (the one you want to get rid of):

   ```
   Select solids and regions to subtract...
   Select objects:
   ```

Creating a solid from the intersection of two solids

You can also create a solid from the volume that two solids have in common. This volume is called their intersection. Figure 24.20 shows two solids before and after using the INTERSECT command.

FIGURE 24.20

A box and a sphere before and after using the INTERSECT command.

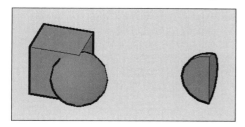

As you can see, you can create some very unusual models this way.

To use the INTERSECT command, choose Modify ➪ Solid Editing ➪ Intersect or choose Intersect from the Modeling toolbar. Just select the objects in any order. AutoCAD creates the new solid. As explained for the UNION command, the command does not save your original objects.

Creating a new solid using INTERFERE

INTERFERE is similar to INTERSECT, except that the original solids remain. AutoCAD creates a third solid from the volume that the two solids have in common. You can also use the INTERFERE command to highlight the common volume of several pairs of solids.

Figure 24.21 shows a solid that was created using INTERFERE, as well as the Interference Checking dialog box.

FIGURE 24.21

When you use INTERFERE, the original solids remain intact.

INTERFERE is useful when you have a number of interfering solids. This command enables you to divide the selection set of solids into two sets so that you can compare one against the other. For example, you can compare a box with three other solids by putting the box in one set and the other three solids in the other set.

TIP You can use INTERFERE for troubleshooting and visualizing a complex drawing. For example, you can use INTERFERE to determine which solids need to be subtracted from other solids. The new objects are created on the current layer. You can change the current layer before using INTERFERE to help you more clearly distinguish the new solid that you create.

To use INTERFERE, follow these steps:

1. Choose Modify ➪ 3D Operations ➪ Interference Checking or enter **interfere** on the command line or in the Dynamic Input tooltip.
2. At the Select first set of objects or [Nested selection/Settings]: prompt, select objects. If you want to compare only two objects, you can put them both in the first set. Otherwise, select solids for the first set and press Enter to end object selection.
3. At the Select second set of objects or [Nested selection/checK first set] <checK>: prompt, select the second set of objects and press Enter to end object selection. If you don't want a second set, press Enter to check the solids. The Interference Checking dialog box opens and the display zooms in to the model, shading the interference and showing the rest of the model in wireframe, as shown in Figure 24.21.
4. If you have more than one interference, click the Next button to display the next one. You can use the Zoom, Pan, and 3D Orbit buttons to adjust your display. Then press Esc to return to the dialog box.
5. If you want to keep the interference solid after you close the dialog box, uncheck the Delete Interference Objects Created on Close check box.
6. Click Close when you're done.

ON the DVD-ROM The drawing used in the following exercise on creating complex solids, ab24-f.dwg, is in the Drawings folder on the DVD.

STEPS: Creating Complex Solids

1. Open ab-24-f.dwg from the DVD.
2. Save the file as ab24-06.dwg in your AutoCAD Bible folder. Make sure that OSNAP is on. Set running object snaps for endpoint, midpoint, and center. This drawing is measured in millimeters. The solids have been created by drawing circles, using EXTRUDE, and moving the solids to the proper Z coordinate. The result is shown in Figure 24.22.
3. Display the Modeling toolbar by right-clicking any toolbar and choosing Modeling.
4. To create the six holes arrayed around the center plate, choose Subtract from the Modeling toolbar. Follow the prompts:

```
Select solids and regions to subtract from...
Select objects: Select the central plate at ❶ in Figure 24.22.
Select objects: Right-click.
Select solids and regions to subtract...
Select objects: Select the six circles arrayed around the plate.
Right-click to end selection.
```

FIGURE 24.22

These solids are the basis for the model.

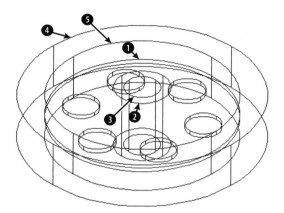

5. To create the central tube, repeat the SUBTRACT command. Follow the prompts:

   ```
   Select solids and regions to subtract from...
   Select objects: Select the outer tube at ❷.
   Select objects: Right-click.
   Select solids and regions to subtract...
   Select objects: Select the inner tube at ❸. Right-click to end
   selection.
   ```

6. To "carve out" the central disk, again repeat the SUBTRACT command. Follow the prompts:

   ```
   Select solids and regions to subtract from...
   Select objects: Select the outer circle at ❹.
   Select objects: Right-click.
   Select solids and regions to subtract...
   Select objects: Select the inner circle at ❺. Right-click to end
   selection.
   ```

7. Change the visual style to 3D Hidden (choose 3D Hidden from the Dashboard's Visual Styles control panel). This enables you to check the effects of the subtraction operations. Your drawing should look like Figure 24.23.

8. Choose Union from the Modeling toolbar. Select the three solids at ❶, ❷, and ❸ in Figure 24.23 and right-click to end selection.

9. Save your drawing.

FIGURE 24.23

The result of three subtraction operations.

3D Kitchen Plus **is a library of 3D kitchen cabinets. You can choose from several models. Look for it in** Software\Chapter 24\3D Kitchen Plus.

Pressing or pulling a region

The PRESSPULL command finds closed areas, creates a region, and then lets you extrude or "press" a hole in that region. In addition to any enclosed area that you could hatch, you can presspull segmented faces of 3D solids. For example, in Figure 24.24, you can presspull the following:

- All the enclosed objects, such as the closed spline, the circle, and the rectangles.
- The area enclosed by the overlapping rectangles.
- The triangular area on the box created by drawing a line across the top face.
- The space in the middle of the four touching boxes, which does not contain any objects.

You can use the PRESSPULL command on any face of a solid. To use the command on a 2D object, you need to move the UCS to the plane of the boundary, as if you were hatching the area.

FIGURE 24.24

You can press or pull many types of enclosed areas.

To presspull a closed area, choose Presspull from the Modeling toolbar or the 3D Make control panel of the Dashboard. At the `Click inside bounded areas to press or pull:` prompt, click inside the enclosed area. You should see the following:

```
1 loop extracted.
1 Region created.
```

You can now move the cursor up or down in either direction to press or pull the region. You can click when you like what you see, or enter a value for the height. (You can usually click and drag in one action, but sometimes AutoCAD takes some time to calculate the region; in that case, click, wait a second, and then move the cursor up or down.)

 You can press Ctrl+Alt to start the PRESSPULL command.

Using solid history

Because AutoCAD doesn't retain source objects when you use the UNION, SUBTRACT, or INTERSECT commands, it would be nice to have a way to modify the original objects separately. Solid history does just that.

 The SOLIDHIST system variable controls whether the history is maintained in the drawing. By default, this system variable is on, being set to 1.

You can also display the object's history by selecting the object and setting the Show History item in the Properties palette to Yes. For example, if you used a cylinder to make a hole in a box by using the SUBTRACT command, when you show the history, you see the original cylinder again. This display lasts even when you deselect the object, until you change the setting in the Properties palette.

More importantly, you can use solid history to edit components of a complex solid. For example, you can move or resize a hole or one part of two objects that you combined. To work with one component of a complex solid, press the Ctrl key as you pass the cursor over the object. The individual component is highlighted. Click to display grips for grip editing. I explain more about how to select individual components (*subobjects*) and grip-edit solids later in this chapter.

The new BREP command converts 3D solids into boundary representation (BREP) solids. This process deletes a solid's history and you can no longer grip-edit the solid or change its properties in the Properties palette. BREP is available on the command line only.

 The drawing used in the following exercise on using PRESSPULL and solid history, `ab24-g.dwg`, is in the `Drawings` folder on the DVD.

STEPS: Using PRESSPULL and Solid History

1. Open `ab-24-g.dwg` from the DVD.
2. Save the file as `ab24-07.dwg` in your `AutoCAD Bible` folder. This is the base of the lamp that was used for several earlier exercises in this chapter. There is a circle on the `const` layer at the top of the base. If necessary, change the visual style to 3D Wireframe (View ➪ Visual Styles ➪ 3D Wireframe).
3. Choose Presspull from the Modeling toolbar. At the `Click inside bounded areas to press or pull:` prompt, move the cursor inside the small circle until you see that it is highlighted. Click and drag downward through the thickness of the base (until you see it below the base — make it long) and then click. The cylinder jumps to the thickness of the base. You now have a hole in the base (for the arm).

4. Turn off the const layer.

5. Press the Ctrl key and pass the cursor over the center of the new hole. When you see the long cylinder that you originally pressed, click. You now see some grips.

6. Click the grip at **❶** in Figure 24.25 and drag the hole to any new location. Then click.

7. Deselect the object.

8. Save your drawing.

FIGURE 24.25

You can drag a hole to another location because composite objects retain a record of their history.

Sectioning and Slicing Solids

In many drawings, you need to show a cross section of your models. A cross section displays the inside of a 3D object. The SECTION, SECTIONPLANE, and SLICE commands create cross-section views of your 3D models.

Using the SECTION command

The SECTION command creates a 2D region from a cross-section of a 3D model along a plane that you specify. The original objects are left untouched. Figure 24.26 shows a region created using the SECTION command.

> **TIP**   The SECTION command creates the region on the current layer. Switch to a layer with a contrasting color from the object's layer so that the region is clearly visible.

To use the SECTION command, enter **section** on the command line. Select the object that you want to section. AutoCAD displays the `Specify first point on Section plane by [Object/Zaxis/View/ XY/YZ/ZX/3points] <3points>:` prompt. Use these options to define the plane of the cross section. Table 24.1 explains how to use the options.

FIGURE 24.26

The region created using SECTION is shown with a dashed line.

Region created using SECTION

TABLE 24.1

SECTION Options

Option	Description
Object	Enables you to choose a circle, ellipse, arc, spline, or 2D polyline.
Zaxis	Defines the plane by defining a Z axis. The sectioning plane is then the XY plane perpendicular to the Z axis that you defined. You define the Z axis by first specifying a point on the sectioning plane. This point is the 0,0,0 point (for purposes of this command only) where the sectioning plane and the Z axis meet. Then you pick a point on the Z axis.
View	Defines the section plane parallel to the current view at the intersection of a point that you specify.
XY	Defines the section plane parallel to the XY plane at the intersection of a point that you specify.
YZ	Defines the section plane parallel to the YZ plane at the intersection of a point that you specify.
ZX	Defines the section plane parallel to the ZX plane at the intersection of a point that you specify.
3points	This is the default. Specify three points to define the section plane. Using object snaps is a good idea.

You can move the region that you create and view it separately to spot errors in your models.

Creating an interactive section object

The SECTIONPLANE command creates a movable section object that displays the inside of a 3D model. When you turn *live sectioning* on, you can see the resulting cross section in real time as you move the section plane. You can flip the section plane to show the other half of the model. Figure 24.27 shows a section object.

You can use the SECTIONPLANE command to see various sections of a model in real time.

To create a section plane, follow these steps:

1. Choose Section Plane from the Dashboard's 3D Make control panel or choose Draw ➪ Modeling ➪ Section Plane.

2. At the `Select face or any point to locate section line or [Draw section/ Orthographic]:` prompt, do one of the following:

    ▪ Pick a face of a 3D solid. Live sectioning is turned on.

    ▪ Pick the first point of a section line. Then specify a second point at the `Specify through point:` prompt.

    ▪ Use the Draw Section option to pick several points to create a section with corners (jogs). Live sectioning is turned off.

    ▪ Use the Orthographic option to choose one of the orthographic directions. This creates a plane that applies to all 3D objects in your drawing. Live sectioning is turned on.

3. If Live sectioning is not on, you see just the section object's line. Select the line, right-click, and choose Activate Live Sectioning.

4. Use the center line end and center grips to move the section plane and adjust the sectioning of the object in real time. You can use the flip arrow to view the other side of the object. Click the drop-down arrow to display a section boundary or section volume.

You can click the live section line and right-click to access section settings. To continue working, deactivate live sectioning and deselect the section plane line, which is quite unobtrusive.

The down arrow lets you choose a section boundary or volume. The section boundary defines a plane perpendicular to the section option, underlying the visible part of the 3D model. The section volume defines a box encompassing the visible part of the model.

Using the SLICE command

The SLICE command slices a solid into two parts along a plane or surface. The original solids are modified but can be reunited with UNION. You can delete either part or keep both. Figure 24.28 shows the result of slicing a model, after one-half of the model has been deleted. This can help you to identify problems in the construction of the model. For example, this slice reveals a fault with the model — the flat disk continues through the central tube — not the desired result. However, you can also use the SLICE command to construct your models. For example, in the exercise on drawing basic solids, the lamp top was a sphere. You could slice this sphere, because the lamp should only have a top half of the sphere.

FIGURE 24.28

The result of slicing a solid and retaining one of the resulting pieces.

 To use the SLICE command, choose Slice from the expanded 3D Make control panel of the Dashboard or choose Modify ⇨ 3D Operations ⇨ Slice. Select the object that you want to slice. AutoCAD displays the `Specify start point of slicing plane or [planar Object/Surface/Zaxis/View/XY/YZ/ZX/3points] <3points>:` prompt. Use these options to define the plane of the cross section. The options are the same as for the SECTION command, except for the Surface option, and are explained in Table 24-1. (The Planar Object option is the same as the Object option in the SECTION command.)

The Surface option enables you to cut any lofted, extruded, swept, or revolved surface out of the solid. You can create some interesting shapes this way — shapes that were impossible to create in previous releases of AutoCAD.

ON the DVD-ROM The drawing used in the following exercise on slicing solids, ab24-06.dwg, is in the Results folder on the DVD.

STEPS: Slicing Solids

1. If you did the exercise on creating complex solids, open ab24-06.dwg from your AutoCAD Bible folder; otherwise, open it from the Results folder of the DVD. OSNAP should be on, with running object snaps for endpoint, midpoint, center, and quadrant. The drawing is shown in Figure 24.29.

FIGURE 24.29

The 3D model for slicing.

2. Save your drawing as ab24-08.dwg in your AutoCAD Bible folder.

3. Choose Modify ⇨ 3D Operations ⇨ Slice or choose Slice from the expanded 3D Make control panel of the Dashboard. Follow the prompts:

```
Select objects: Select the solid model.
Select objects: Right-click.
Specify start point of slicing plane or [planar
Object/Surface/Zaxis/View/XY/YZ/ZX/3points] <3points>: ↵
Specify first point on plane: Pick the quadrant at ❶ in Figure 24.29.
Specify second point on plane: Pick the quadrant at ❷.
Specify third point on plane: Pick the quadrant at ❸.
Specify a point on desired side of the plane or [keep Both sides]:
Pick the model at ❹.
```

4. As mentioned earlier, the slicing reveals an error — the disk cuts through the central tube, as shown in Figure 24.30. To fix the error, zoom in so that the model takes up the entire screen.

5. Start the CYLINDER command. Follow the prompts:

```
Specify center point of base or [3P/2P/Ttr/Elliptical]:  Pick the
midpoint at ❶ in Figure 24.30.
Specify base radius or [Diameter] <3.2605>: Pick the endpoint at ❷.
Specify height or [2Point/Axis endpoint] <9.2711>: Move the cursor
upward and enter 16 ↵
```

FIGURE 24.30

The solid after slicing and deleting one-half.

6. Choose Subtract from the Modeling toolbar. At the `Select solids and regions to sub-tract from... Select objects:` prompt, select the large solid and right-click to end object selection. At the `Select solids and regions to subtract... Select objects:` prompt, select the new cylinder that you just drew and right-click. AutoCAD subtracts the cylinder from the larger model.

7. Change the visual style to 3D Hidden (View ⇨ Visual Styles ⇨ 3D Hidden). Return to your previous view.

8. Save your drawing. If you're continuing on to the next exercise, keep the drawing open.

NOTE To correct the model, you could subtract out the circle as you just did in the exercise, mirror the entire model, and use UNION to make the two halves whole. Mirroring in 3D is covered in the next section. You could also undo the slice as soon as you saw the error and make the correction on the entire model.

Using Editing Commands in 3D

When you draw in 3D, you need to edit your models either to make corrections or as part of the construction process. A number of editing commands are exclusively for 3D or have special 3D options. In this section, you explore these special commands and options. Table 24.2 lists most of the regular editing commands and how they're used in 3D drawings.

TABLE 24.2

Editing Commands in 3D

Command	Use in 3D Drawings
ERASE	Same as for 2D.
COPY	Same as for 2D.
MIRROR	Can be used on 3D objects as long as the mirror line is in the XY plane. Otherwise, use MIRROR3D.
OFFSET	Can be used in 3D space, but only on 2D objects.
ARRAY	Can be used on 3D objects in the XY plane. Otherwise, use 3DARRAY.
MOVE	Same as for 2D; can also use the 3DMOVE command.
ROTATE	Can be used on 3D objects in the XY plane. Otherwise, use ROTATE3D, or 3DROTATE.
SCALE	Can be used on 3D objects. Scales in all three dimensions.
STRETCH	Can be used in 3D space, but only on 2D objects, wireframes, and surfaces. The results may not be what you expect because it is hard to visualize the direction of the stretch.
LENGTHEN	Can be used in 3D space, but only on 2D objects.
TRIM	Has special options for 3D, but works only on 2D objects, such as lines.
EXTEND	Has special options for 3D, but works only on 2D objects, such as lines.
BREAK	Can be used in 3D space, but only on 2D objects.
CHAMFER	Has special options for 3D.
FILLET	Has special options for 3D.
EXPLODE	Works on 3D objects — solids explode to surfaces, and surfaces explode to wireframes. Sometimes, you get regions. You can explode blocks containing 3D objects.
ALIGN	Works on 3D objects.

Grip-editing solids

You can grip-edit solids in several ways. When you select them, they show grips that allow you to stretch them in all directions. Figure 29-31 shows the grips for a solid box. The triangular grips stretch objects in the direction of the arrow. The square grips also stretch objects, usually at a corner. One grip at the center just moves the object.

Subselecting solids

You can select *subobjects* and edit them. A subobject is the face, edge, or vertex of a solid. A subcomponent of a composite solid — one that you used UNION, SUBTRACT on — is also a subobject. You can even select more than one subobject, whether on one solid or several solids.

To grip-edit a subobject, follow these steps:

1. Press Ctrl.

2. Pass the cursor over a face, edge, or vertex. Faces and edges highlight, but vertices don't.

3. Click the grip that appears.

4. Drag the grip to grip-edit the solid.

FIGURE 24.31

You can stretch a 3D solid box in many directions.

Stretch up to increase height

Move the box

Stretch down

Stretch the corner to change both the width and length

Stretch one side in the direction of the arrow

You can press Ctrl and click to select a subobject when you select objects for the MOVE, ROTATE, SCALE, or ERASE commands. You can press Ctrl and drag a selection or crossing window to select multiple subobjects.

If you want to select the back face of a solid, you can cycle through the faces by pressing and holding Ctrl and repeatedly pressing the Spacebar. Just as you can press Shift and pick to remove any object from a selection set, you can remove a subobject from a selection set by pressing and holding Ctrl and pressing Shift while you pick a subobject. Figure 24.32 shows the process of grip-stretching an edge of a box.

NEW FEATURE The LEGACYCTRLPICK system variable lets you return to the older use of Ctrl + click, which was to cycle through overlapping objects for easier selection. By default, this system variable is set to 0, which allows you to select subobjects on 3D solids. Change its value to 1 to use Ctrl + click to cycle through objects. When set to 1, you can't use Ctrl + click to select subobjects.

FIGURE 24.32

You can select subobjects and edit them separately from the solid.

Specify stretch point or   20.0248   < 109°

Using the move grip tool and the 3DMOVE command

When moving objects in 3D space, it's often hard to visualize the direction in which an object is moving as you drag it. You can use the regular MOVE command to move objects in any direction, X, Y, or Z, but entering the coordinates can be awkward. Instead, you can use the new move grip tool, with or without executing the 3DMOVE command, to interactively move objects in 3D space. Figure 24.33 shows the move grip tool.

To use the move grip tool by itself, follow these steps:

1. Select an object, with no command active. If you have a 3D visual style active (anything except 2D Wireframe), the move grip tool automatically appears.

 If you don't want the move grip tool to display automatically, set the GTAUTO system variable to 0 (zero).

2. Pass the cursor over any grip (but not an arrow); the move grip tool jumps to that grip, as shown on the left side of Figure 24.33. This temporarily places the origin of the UCS at that point.

 It is important to note the relationship between the move grip tool and the UCS icon. In any 3D visual style, the X axis of the UCS icon is red, the Y axis is green, and the Z axis is blue. The move grip tool uses the same colors to indicate the same directions.

3. You can now choose one of three setups to move the selected object:
   - **To move the selected object in any direction,** drag on the grip itself. This is no different from dragging without the move grip tool.
   - **To constrain the selected object along one axis,** pass the cursor over that axis until it turns yellow and you see a line extending to the edge of the screen on either side, as shown on the right side of Figure 24.33. Click on that axis; now you can move the object only along that axis line. Drag the object in the positive or negative direction along the line. You can use direct distance entry to move the object a specific distance, or just click where you want the grip to be.
   - **To constrain the selected object along one plane,** pass the cursor over the right-angle indicator at the intersection of any two axes (see the left side of Figure 24.33), until it turns yellow. Click on that right-angle indicator; now you can move the object only in that plane. Move the object in the desired direction. You can enter a relative coordinate or click where you want the grip to be.

FIGURE 24.33

Use the move grip tool to interactively move objects.

Right-angle indicator for the XZ plane

The 3DMOVE command also uses the move grip tool, but adds prompts similar to the MOVE command. You can find it in the 3D Make control panel of the Dashboard or the Modeling toolbar. To use the 3DMOVE command, follow these steps:

1. Start the 3DMOVE command and select objects, or select objects first and then start the command.

 If you're using the 2D Wireframe visual style, the command switches you temporarily to the 3D Wireframe visual style. When you're done, the 2D Wireframe visual style returns.

2. At the `Specify base point or [Displacement] <Displacement>:` prompt, the move grip tool appears.

   ▪ To use the **base point/second point method**, specify a base point. The move grip tool moves to the base point. You can now constrain movement to an axis or plane as described just previously in this section. Then specify a second point to move the object.

   ▪ To use the **displacement method**, enter a displacement as an X,Y or polar coordinate. At the `Specify second point or <use first point as displacement>:` prompt, press Enter to move the object and end the command. In this situation, you don't use the move grip tool because you are specifying the movement by entering coordinates.

You have a chance to use the 3DMOVE command later in this chapter in the exercise on Extending objects in 3D.

Mirroring in 3D

If the mirror line is on the XY plane, you can mirror any 3D object with the regular MIRROR command. If you want to mirror in any other plane, use MIRROR3D.

To use MIRROR3D, follow these steps:

1. Choose Modify ⇨ 3D Operations ⇨ 3D Mirror.
2. Select the object or objects that you want to mirror.
3. At the `Specify first point of mirror plane (3 points) or [Object/Last/Zaxis/ View/XY/YZ/ZX/3points] <3points>:` prompt, choose one of the options to define the mirroring plane. These are the same options described in Table 24-1 for the SECTION command. The only additional option is Last, which uses the last defined mirroring plane.
4. At the `Delete source objects? [Yes/No] <N>:` prompt, press Enter to keep the original objects, or right-click and choose Yes to delete them.

 The drawing used in the following exercise on mirroring in 3D, ab24-08.dwg, is in the Results folder on the DVD.

STEPS: Mirroring in 3D

1. If you have ab24-08.dwg open from the previous exercise, use this drawing. If you don't have it open, open it from your AutoCAD Bible folder or from the Results folder of the DVD. If necessary, change the visual style to 3D Wireframe. Make sure that OSNAP is on, and set a running object snap for endpoint. If you don't have the Modeling toolbar open, right-click any toolbar and choose Modeling from the toolbar list. The drawing is shown in Figure 24.34.

FIGURE 24.34

This 3D model was sliced and can now be mirrored.

2. Save your drawing as ab24-09.dwg in your AutoCAD Bible folder.

3. Choose Modify ⇨ 3D Operations ⇨ 3D Mirror. Follow the prompts:

   ```
   Select objects: Select the solid. Right-click to end object
   selection.
   Specify first point of mirror plane (3 points) or
   [Object/Last/Zaxis/View/XY/YZ/ZX/3points] <3points>: Pick ❶ in
   Figure 24.34.
   Specify second point on mirror plane: Pick ❷.
   Specify third point on mirror plane: Pick ❸.
   Delete source objects? [Yes/No] <N>: Right-click and choose Enter.
   ```

4. Choose Union on the Modeling toolbar. Select both solids. Right-click to end object selection. AutoCAD unites them.

5. Save your drawing.

Arraying in 3D

You can array any 3D object using the ARRAY command as long as you define the array in the current XY plane. The 3DARRAY command enables you to create a rectangular array with the normal rows and columns, but adding levels in the Z direction. For a 3D polar array, you define an axis of rotation instead of the 2D point used in the ARRAY command.

Creating 3D rectangular arrays

The rectangular array is the most common type of array. A 3D rectangular array has rows, columns, and levels. To create a 3D rectangular array, follow these steps:

1. Choose Modify ⇨ 3D Operations ⇨ 3D Array to start the 3DARRAY command.

2. Select the objects that you want to array.

3. At the `Enter the type of array [Rectangular/Polar] <R>:` prompt, right-click and choose Rectangular.

4. At the `Enter the number of rows (---) <1>:` prompt, type the total number of rows that you want. Rows are parallel to the X axis.

5. At the `Enter the number of columns (|||) <1>:` prompt, type the total number of columns that you want. Columns are parallel to the Y axis.

6. At the `Enter the number of levels (...) <1>:` prompt, type the total number of levels that you want. Levels are parallel to the Z axis.

7. At the `Specify the distance between rows (---):` prompt, type a unit distance or pick two points.

8. At the `Specify the distance between columns (|||):` prompt, type a unit distance or pick two points.

9. At the `Specify the distance between levels (...):` prompt, type a unit distance or pick two points.

 The drawing used in the following exercise on creating a rectangular array in 3D, `ab24-h.dwg`, is in the `Drawings` folder on the DVD.

STEPS: Creating a Rectangular Array in 3D

1. Open `ab24-h.dwg` from the DVD.

2. Save the file as `ab24-10.dwg` in your `AutoCAD Bible` folder. This is a drawing showing a sphere, a bead-like shape sometimes used for table legs. In this exercise, you create a 3D rectangular array to create four table legs.

3. Choose Modify ⇨ 3D Operations ⇨ 3D Array. Follow the prompts:

```
Select objects: Select the bead. Right-click to end object selection.
Enter the type of array [Rectangular/Polar] <R>: Right-click and
choose Rectangular.
Enter the number of rows (---) <1>: 2 ↵
Enter the number of columns (|||) <1>: 2 ↵
Enter the number of levels (...) <1>: 20 ↵ (The bead is 1.5 inches
high and the leg should be 30 inches high.)
Specify the distance between rows (---): 26 ↵ (This is the narrower
distance between the legs.)
Specify the distance between columns (|||): 36 ↵ (This is the wider
distance between the legs.)
Specify the distance between levels (...): 1.5 ↵ (You want the beads
to touch along the leg.)
```

4. Do a Zoom Extents to see the result. (Now you would create the tabletop.)

5. Save your drawing. It should look like Figure 24.35.

FIGURE 24.35

The four legs of a table, created by using a 3D rectangular array.

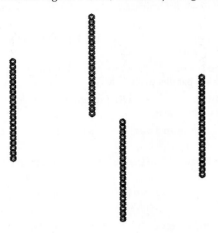

Creating 3D polar arrays

Polar arrays are not as common as rectangular arrays, either in 2D or in 3D, but in the right circumstances they can make your work a lot easier. Instead of using a center point as you do in a 2D polar array, you define a center axis. To create a 3D polar array, follow these steps:

1. Choose Modify ⇨ 3D Operations ⇨ 3D Array to start the 3DARRAY command.
2. Select the objects that you want to array.
3. At the `Enter the type of array [Rectangular/Polar] <R>:` prompt, right-click and choose Polar.
4. At the `Enter the number of items in the array:` prompt, type the total number of items that you want.
5. At the `Specify the angle to fill (+=ccw, -=cw) <360>:` prompt, press Enter to array around a full circle or type any lesser angle.
6. At the `Rotate arrayed objects? [Yes/No] <Y>:` prompt, press Enter to accept the default or type **n** ↵ if you don't want to rotate the objects as they're arrayed.
7. At the `Specify center point of array:` prompt, specify the center point of the array. This is also the first point of the axis of rotation.
8. At the `Specify second point on axis of rotation:` prompt, specify any other point on the axis of rotation.

If you rotate less than a full circle, you need to determine the positive angle of rotation. The positive direction of the axis goes from the first point that you specify (the center point) to the second point. Point your right thumb in the positive direction and follow the curl of the fingers of that hand to determine the positive angle of rotation.

ON the DVD-ROM The drawing used in the following exercise on creating 3D polar arrays, `ab24-i.dwg`, is in the `Drawings` folder on the DVD.

STEPS: Creating 3D Polar Arrays

1. Open `ab24-i.dwg` from the DVD.

2. Save the file as `ab24-11.dwg` in your `AutoCAD Bible` folder. You see part of a lamp, as shown in Figure 24.36. Make sure that OSNAP is on. Set a running object snap for endpoint.

FIGURE 24.36

A partially completed lamp.

3. To array the bracket that supports the lampshade, choose Modify ⇨ 3D Operations ⇨ 3D Array. Follow the prompts:

```
Select objects: Select the support at ❶ in Figure 24.36.
Select objects: Right-click.
Enter the type of array [Rectangular/Polar] <R>: Right-click and
choose Polar.
Enter the number of items in the array: 3 ↵
Specify the angle to fill (+=ccw, -=cw) <360>: ↵
Rotate arrayed objects? [Yes/No] <Y>: ↵
Specify center point of array: Pick the endpoint at ❷.
Specify second point on axis of rotation: Pick the endpoint at ❸.
```

4. One of the three supports cannot be seen in this view. To see all three, press Shift + mouse wheel to enter transparent 3D Orbit mode, and drag diagonally a bit until you can see all three supports.

5. Choose View ⇨ 3D Views ⇨ Top to return to plan view, and save your drawing.

Rotating in 3D

You can rotate 3D objects in the XY plane with the ROTATE command. Use ROTATE3D when you need to rotate objects in any other plane. (The 3DROTATE command, which I discuss later in this section, offers interactive rotating in 3D.) When you use the ROTATE3D command, you need to specify the axis of rotation. The ROTATE3D options are shown in Table 24.3.

TABLE 24.3

ROTATE3D Options

Option	Description
Object	Enables you to choose a line, circle, arc, or 2D polyline. If you choose a circle or arc, AutoCAD rotates around a line that starts at the object's center and extends perpendicular to the object's plane.
Last	Uses the last defined axis of rotation.
View	Defines the axis of rotation parallel to the current view at the intersection of a point that you specify.
Xaxis	The axis of rotation is parallel to the X axis and passes through a point that you specify.
Yaxis	The axis of rotation is parallel to the Y axis and passes through a point that you specify.
Zaxis	The axis of rotation is parallel to the Z axis and passes through a point that you specify.
2points	This is the default. Specify two points to define the axis. It's a good idea to use object snaps.

> **TIP** Sometimes creating an object in the XY plane and then rotating it afterward is easier. In other words, you may create an object in the wrong plane on purpose and use ROTATE3D or 3DRO-TATE later to properly place it.

To use ROTATE3D, follow these steps:

1. Enter **rotate3d** ↵ on the command line.
2. Select the object or objects that you want to rotate.
3. At the `Specify first point on axis or define axis by [Object/Last/View/Xaxis/Yaxis/Zaxis/2points]:` prompt, select one of the options explained in Table 24.3, and define the axis according to the option prompts.
4. At the `Specify rotation angle or [Reference]:` prompt, specify a positive or negative rotation angle or choose the Reference option. (The Reference option works like the Reference option for ROTATE. See Chapter 9.)

You need to determine the positive direction of rotation. Point your right thumb in the positive direction of the axis and follow the curl of your fingers. If you pick two points, the positive direction of the axis goes from the first pick point to the second pick point.

When you use the 3DROTATE command, you can rotate freely or constrain rotation around one axis. Follow these steps:

 1. Start the 3DROTATE command from the Modeling toolbar or the 3D Make control panel of the Dashboard.

> **NOTE** If you are in 2D Wireframe visual style, this command temporarily changes you to 3D Wireframe. You need to be in a non-orthogonal view to use 3DROTATE.

2. Select objects. The rotate grip tool appears, as shown in Figure 24.37.

> **NOTE** The relationship between the move grip tool and the UCS icon is significant. In any 3D visual style, the X axis of the UCS icon is red, the Y axis is green, and the Z axis is blue. The rotate grip tool uses the same colors to indicate the same directions.

3. At the `Specify base point:` prompt, specify the base point for the rotation. The rotate grip tool jumps to the base point.

4. At the `Pick a rotation axis:` prompt, hover the cursor over the ribbon that matches the axis around which you want to rotate. It turns yellow and you see an axis line, as shown in Figure 24.37. Click the yellow ribbon.

5. At the `Specify angle start point or type an angle:` prompt, you can simply enter the rotation angle that you want. For example, if you want to rotate the object 90° around an axis, enter **90** ↵. You can also enter a first point and a second point to specify the rotation angle.

FIGURE 24.37

The rotate grip tools let you constrain rotation to any axis in 3D space.

> **ON the DVD-ROM** The drawing used in the following exercise on rotating in 3D, `ab24-j.dwg`, is in the `Drawings` folder on the DVD.

STEPS: Rotating in 3D

1. Open `ab24-j.dwg` from the DVD.

2. Save the file as `ab24-12.dwg` in your `AutoCAD Bible` folder. You see the same lamp used in the previous exercise, but it has now been completed.

3. To insert the lamp in a plan view drawing of a house, you need to see it in plan view from the WCS. In other words, you should be looking down at the lamp. To do this, you need to rotate the lamp around the X axis. To visualize this, look at the UCS icon and imagine rotating the top of the lamp toward you around the horizontal (X) axis. To rotate the lamp, enter **rotate3d** ↵ on the command line. Follow the prompts:

   ```
   Select objects: Start a crossing window to select the entire lamp.
   Select objects: Right-click to end selection.
   Specify first point on axis or define axis by [Object/Last/View/
   Xaxis/Yaxis/Zaxis/2points]: Right-click and choose Xaxis.
   Specify a point on the X axis <0,0,0>: Right-click.
   Specify rotation angle or [Reference]: 90 ↵
   ```

4. Zoom to the extents of the drawing to see the entire lamp. The lamp is now rotated 90 degrees around the X axis in relation to the UCS, and you're looking at it from the top.

5. To get a better view, choose View ⇨ 3D Views ⇨ SE Isometric. Change the visual style to 3D Hidden (View ⇨ Visual Styles ⇨ 3D Hidden). The lamp should look like Figure 24.38. Remember, looking at the lamp from a different viewpoint does not change the orientation of the lamp relative to the UCS.

6. Save your drawing.

7. To try the same rotation using the 3DROTATE command, re-open `ab24-j.dwg`. You can save it again as `ab24-12.dwg`, because the result will be the same, or save it as `ab24-12-1.dwg`.

FIGURE 24.38

The lamp is now ready to place in a 3D drawing of a house.

8. Press Shift+mouse button and change the viewpoint so that you can see all three axes on the UCS icon.

 9. Choose 3D Rotate from the Modeling toolbar. At the `Select objects:` prompt, select the entire lamp and end selection.

10. At the `Specify base point:` prompt, specify the bottom corner of the lamp, using an endpoint object snap.

11. At the `Pick a rotation axis:` prompt, hover over the red (X axis) ribbon until it turns yellow, and click.

12. At the `Specify angle start point or type an angle:` prompt, enter **90** ↵.

13. Change the visual style to 3D Hidden. Save your drawing.

Aligning in 3D

I have already covered the ALIGN and the 3DALIGN commands in Chapter 10. When you work in 3D, you can use these commands to move, rotate in the XY plane, and rotate in the Z direction — all in one command. In this exercise, you use the 3DALIGN command.

> **ON the DVD-ROM** The drawing used in the following exercise on aligning in 3D, `ab24-k.dwg`, is in the `Drawings` folder on the DVD.

STEPS: Aligning in 3D

1. Open `ab24-k.dwg` from the DVD.

2. Save the file as `ab24-13.dwg` in your `AutoCAD Bible` folder. You see part of the base assembly for an industrial washer, as shown in Figure 24.39. One sidebar needs to be moved and rotated into place. Make sure that OSNAP is on; set a running object snap for endpoint.

FIGURE 24.39

Part of a base assembly for an industrial washer with a sidebar that needs to be moved and rotated into place.

Thanks to Robert Mack of the Dexter Company, Fairfield, Iowa, for this drawing.

3. Notice that it's hard to tell which way the sidebar is facing because it's displayed in wireframe. Change the visual style to 3D Hidden (View ➪ Visual Styles ➪ 3D Hidden). You can now see that **1** in Figure 24.39 is facing away from you. Switch back to the 3D Wireframe visual style.

4. Choose 3D Align from the Modeling toolbar. Follow the prompts.

```
Select objects: Select the sidebar.
Select objects: Right-click.
Specify base point or [Copy]: Pick 1 in Figure 24.39.
Specify second point or [Continue] <C>: Pick 4.
Specify third point or [Continue] <C>:  Pick 2.
Specify first destination point: Pick 3.
Specify second destination point or [eXit] <X>: Pick 5.
Specify third destination point or [eXit] <X>: Pick any point further
back than 3 on the plate.
```

The smaller bars (shown in red in the drawing) provide several endpoints that you can easily locate.

5. AutoCAD aligns the sidebar. Save your drawing. It should look like Figure 24.40.

FIGURE 24.40

The sidebar has been aligned with the rest of the model.

TIP   The trick when aligning in 3D is to properly visualize the parts. It helps to switch to 3D Hidden visual style first, as you did in the exercise. Also, take the time to find the UCS and a viewpoint that make the points that you're specifying easy to see and pick.

Trimming and extending in 3D

You can use the TRIM and EXTEND commands to trim or extend 2D objects in 3D space. AutoCAD provides the Project option for working in 3D space. The Project option has three suboptions:

- **None:** AutoCAD trims or extends only objects that actually intersect or can intersect in 3D space.
- **UCS:** This is the default. AutoCAD projects objects onto the XY plane of the current UCS. Therefore, if two lines are on different Z coordinates, you can trim and extend one of them with reference to the other, even though they do not and cannot actually meet in 3D space.
- **View:** This projects objects parallel to the current view. Objects are trimmed or extended based on the way they look on the screen. They need not (and probably won't) actually meet in 3D space.

You can also use the Extend option to trim or extend to implied intersections, as explained in Chapter 10. In the next exercise, you practice extending objects in 3D; trimming works similarly.

ON the DVD-ROM The drawing used in the following exercise on extending objects in 3D, ab24-1.dwg, is in the Drawings folder on the DVD.

STEPS: Extending Objects in 3D

1. Open ab24-1.dwg from the DVD.
2. Save the file as ab24-14.dwg in your AutoCAD Bible folder. You see a bushing, in 2D and 3D, as shown in Figure 24.41. The 3D bushing has been exploded into simple geometry — otherwise, you wouldn't be able to use it to extend the 2D lines. Display the Modeling toolbar and set a quadrant running object snap.

FIGURE 24.41

A bushing in 2D and 3D. The 3D bushing has been exploded but still looks the same. It can now be used to extend lines.

3. To turn the UCSORTHO system variable off, type **ucsortho** ↵ 0 ↵. (If its current value is 0, just press Enter at the Enter new value for UCSORTHO <0>: prompt.) You don't want the UCS to change when you change the view in Step 5.

4. Choose Extend from the Modify toolbar or choose Modify ⇨ Extend. Follow the prompts.

    ```
    Select boundary edges ...
    Select objects: Pick the 3D bushing at ❶ in Figure 24.41.
    Select objects: Right-click.
    Select object to extend or shift-select to trim or [Fence/Crossing/
    Project/Edge/Undo]: Right-click and choose Project.
    Enter a projection option [None/Ucs/View] <Ucs>: Right-click and
    choose View.
    Select object to extend or shift-select to trim or [Fence/Crossing/
    Project/Edge/Undo]: Pick the 2D bushing at ❷.
    Select object to extend or shift-select to trim or [Fence/Crossing/
    Project/Edge/Undo]: Right-click and choose Enter.
    ```

    If you have difficulty extending, change the visual style to 2D Wireframe.

5. Choose View ⇨ 3D Views ⇨ Top. You can now see that the 2D line doesn't actually meet the 3D bushing. By using the View option, you only extended the line in that view.

6. Choose Zoom Previous from the Standard toolbar.

7. Again, choose Extend from the Modify toolbar. Follow the prompts:

    ```
    Select boundary edges...Select objects: Pick the bottom edge of the
    3D bushing at ❸.
    Select objects: Right-click.
    Select object to extend or shift-select to trim or
    [Fence/Crossing/Project/Edge/Undo]: Right-click and choose Project.
    Enter a projection option [None/Ucs/View] <View>: Right-click and
    choose None.
    Select object to extend or shift-select to trim or [Fence/Crossing/
    Project/Edge/Undo]: Pick the same line that you picked in Step 4, but
    this time pick it closer to the 3D bushing, on the new length you
    created by extending it.
    Select object to extend or shift-select to trim or [Fence/Crossing/
    Project/Edge/Undo]: Right-click and choose Enter.
    ```

8. Choose View ⇨ 3D Views ⇨ Top. You can now see that the 2D line actually meets the 3D bushing.

9. Click Undo on the Standard toolbar twice to undo the viewpoint change and the extend operation.

 10. Choose 3D Move from the Modeling toolbar. Select the entire 3D bushing. At the Specify base point or [Displacement] <Displacement>: prompt, choose any quadrant at the base of the bushin At the Specify second point or <use first point as displacement>: prompt, click the blue Z axis of the move grip tool and move the cursor upward in the Z direction. Type **2** ↵. If you miss any of the objects, pick them and move them, too. This moves the entire 3D bushing 2 units in the Z direction.

11. Choose Extend from the Modify toolbar. Follow the prompts:

```
Select boundary edges...
Select objects: Pick the 3D bushing at ❸ (the bottom ring).
Select objects: Right-click.
Select object to extend or shift-select to trim or [Fence/Crossing/
Project/Edge/Undo]: Right-click and choose Project.
Enter a projection option [None/Ucs/View] <View>: Right-click and
choose Ucs.
Select object to extend or shift-select to trim or [Fence/Crossing/
Project/Edge/Undo]: Pick the same line that you extended before,
closer to its left endpoint.
Select object to extend or shift-select to trim or [Fence/Crossing/
Project/Edge/Undo]: Right-click and choose Enter.
```

12. Choose View ➪ 3D Views ➪ Top. It looks as if the 2D line now actually meets the 3D bushing.
13. Choose View ➪ 3D Views ➪ Front. (Because UCSORTHO is off, the UCS does not change.) Now you can see that the 2D line doesn't meet the 3D bushing.
14. Type **ucsortho** ↵ 1 ↵ to return UCSORTHO to its previous setting, if you changed it in Step 3.
15. Save your drawing. It should look like Figure 24.42.

FIGURE 24.42

When you use the UCS option, the lines seem to touch the boundary edge when you view the bushing from the top, but they can have different Z coordinates.

Filleting in 3D

You can fillet solids but not surfaces. If you create a 3D object from lines, you can fillet the lines. Figure 24.43 shows a 3D mechanical drawing with several filleted edges.

833

FIGURE 24.43

Filleted edges are common in 3D mechanical drawings.

Filleted edges

To use the FILLET command for solids, follow these steps:

1. Choose Fillet from the Modify toolbar or choose Modify ➪ Fillet.

2. At the `Select first object or [Undo/Polyline/Radius/Trim/Multiple]:` prompt, select the edge of the solid that you want to fillet. You cannot deselect this edge, so you must select the solid at the proper edge. Ignore the other options.

3. AutoCAD senses that you've selected a solid and responds with the `Enter fillet radius <0.5000>:` prompt. Press Enter to accept the default of 0.5 or type a new radius.

4. At the `Select an edge or [Chain/Radius]:` prompt, press Enter if you want to fillet only the one edge that you've already selected. You can also select other edges of the same solid. Press Enter to end selection of edges. AutoCAD fillets the edge or edges that you selected. You can also change the Radius setting at this prompt.

5. Use the Chain option to fillet a set of attached edges. AutoCAD responds with the `Select an edge chain or [Edge/Radius]:` prompt. Continue to pick edges that are attached to the previous edge that you picked. Press Enter to end selection of edges. AutoCAD fillets the entire chain of edges.

   You can select different radii for different edges. At the first `Enter fillet radius <0.5000>:` prompt, specify the radius for the edge you just selected. After that, use the Radius option to set the desired radius before you select the edge.

ON the DVD-ROM   The drawing used in the following exercise on filleting solids, `ab24-m.dwg`, is in the `Drawings` folder on the DVD.

STEPS: Filleting Solids

1. Open `ab24-m.dwg` from the DVD.

2. Save the file as `ab24-15.dwg` in your `AutoCAD Bible` folder. This is a solid model of a mounting angle, as shown in Figure 24.44. It needs to be filleted. Turn OSNAP off.

FIGURE 24.44

The mounting angle needs filleting.

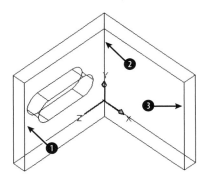

3. Choose Fillet from the Modify toolbar or choose Modify ➪ Fillet.

4. At the `Select first object or [Undo/Polyline/Radius/Trim/Multiple]:` prompt, pick the edge at **1** in Figure 24.44.

5. At the `Enter fillet radius <0.5000>:` prompt, type **.25** ↵.

6. At the `Select an edge or [Chain/Radius]:` prompt, pick **2**.

7. At the `Select an edge or [Chain/Radius]:` prompt, pick **3**. Press Enter to end the command. AutoCAD fillets all three edges.

8. Save your drawing. It should look like Figure 24.45.

FIGURE 24.45

The filleted mounting angle.

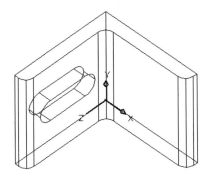

Chamfering in 3D

You can chamfer solids but not surfaces. If you create a 3D object from lines, you can chamfer the lines. Figure 24.46 shows a solid with chamfered edges. (You can see this solid as part of the wheel shown at the beginning of this chapter in Figure 24.1.)

FIGURE 24.46

A solid with chamfered edges.

To chamfer a solid, follow these steps:

1. Choose Chamfer from the Modify toolbar or choose Modify ➪ Chamfer.

2. At the `Select first line or [Undo/Polyline/Distance/Angle/Trim/mEthod/Multiple]:` prompt, select the edge that you want to chamfer. The edge is displayed as a line between two surfaces. AutoCAD highlights one of the surfaces that touch the edge you selected.

3. At the `Base surface selection...Enter surface selection option [Next/OK (current)] <OK>:` prompt, press Enter to accept the highlighted surface as the base surface. You need to define the base surface in case the two chamfering distances are not equal or if you want to chamfer a loop, which is the entire base surface. Right-click and choose Next to highlight the next surface. (Only two surfaces touch the edge that you selected.) Press Enter when the desired surface is highlighted.

4. At the `Specify base surface chamfer distance <0.5000>:` prompt, type the chamfering distance for the first surface. This is the amount that you want to cut off from that surface. (The default is the last distance you specified.)

5. At the `Specify other surface chamfer distance <0.5000>:` prompt, type the chamfering distance for the other surface. (The default is the last distance you specified.)

6. At the `Select an edge or [Loop]:` prompt, select the edge that you want to chamfer. You can also use the Loop option. AutoCAD then prompts you to select the edge loop. Select the surface, and AutoCAD chamfers all of the edges of that surface.

7. AutoCAD continues to prompt you to select edges or edge loops. Press Enter to end selection when you're finished.

ON the DVD-ROM The drawing used in the following exercise on chamfering solids, `ab24-n.dwg`, is in the `Drawings` folder on the DVD.

STEPS: Chamfering Solids

1. Open ab24-n.dwg from the DVD.

2. Save the file as ab24-16.dwg in your AutoCAD Bible folder. This is a simple box with dimensions of 233×102×12 millimeters, as shown in Figure 24.47.

You can chamfer this solid box to create a new shape.

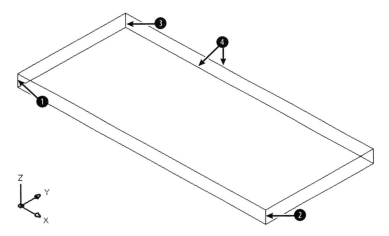

3. Choose Chamfer from the Modify toolbar or choose Modify ➪ Chamfer. Follow the prompts:

```
Select first line or [Undo/Polyline/Distance/Angle/Trim/mEthod/
Multiple]: Pick the edge at ❶ in Figure 24.47.

Base surface selection...
Enter surface selection option [Next/OK (current)] <OK>: ↵
Specify base surface chamfer distance <0.5000>: 30 ↵
Specify other surface chamfer distance <0.5000>: 30 ↵
Select an edge or [Loop]: Pick ❶.
Select an edge or [Loop]: ↵
```

You can't see the chamfer because of the viewpoint. You change the viewpoint at the end of the exercise.

4. Repeat the CHAMFER command. Do the exact same operation as in Step 3, but pick ❷.

5. Repeat the CHAMFER command. Follow the prompts:

```
Select first line or [Undo/Polyline/Distance/Angle/Trim/mEthod/
Multiple]: Pick the edge at ❸.

Base surface selection...
```

```
Enter surface selection option [Next/OK (current)] <OK>: ↵ Make sure
that the surface indicated by ❹ is highlighted. If not, type n ↵.
Then press Enter again.
Specify base surface chamfer distance <30.0000>: 233 ↵
Specify other surface chamfer distance <30.0000>: 40 ↵
Select an edge or [Loop]: Pick ❸.
Select an edge or [Loop]: ↵
```

6. Choose View3D Views ⇨ Top. This shows you the shape in profile.

7. Save your drawing. It should look like Figure 24.48.

FIGURE 24.48

The completed solid.

Exploding and converting 3D objects

The EXPLODE command has a particular effect that varies according to the type of 3D object. Table 24.4 lists the effects of exploding 3D objects.

TABLE 24.4

Using EXPLODE on 3D Objects

Object	Result
Solids	Flat surfaces become regions; curved surfaces become surfaces.
Swept, lofted, extruded, or rotated surfaces	These surfaces become 2D objects or other surfaces that you can explode again to 2D objects.
Polyface meshes	3D faces.
Polygon meshes	3D faces.
Polylines with thickness	Lines.

You can use the XEDGES command to convert solids, surfaces, and regions to 2D wireframe objects. This is another kind of exploding. To use XEDGES, choose Modify ➪ 3D Operations ➪ Extract Edges. Then select objects. You can even subselect faces and edges, as described earlier in this chapter, and use XEDGES on them.

The CONVTOSOLID command converts polylines with a uniform width, closed polylines with zero-width, and circles to solids if they have a thickness. These are all objects that look like solids anyway. Choose Modify ➪ 3D Operations ➪ Convert to Solid and select the objects. (I discuss the CONVTOSURFACE command in Chapter 23.)

The Express Tools FLATTEN command converts a 3D drawing into a 2D drawing, and changes the thickness and elevation of objects to zero. Use FLATTEN on the command line and select objects.

Using the SOLIDEDIT Command

The SOLIDEDIT command offers options to edit faces, edges, and complete solids in specific ways. This command has so many options that it might as well be several commands. Many of the options are now out of date because of the new methods of direct manipulation of solids introduced in AutoCAD 2007. On the other hand, the command still has value because it offers some options that are available nowhere else, or it makes certain edits easier.

SOLIDEDIT offers three major types of solid editing:

- **Faces:** A number of options enable you to edit the faces of solids. You can extrude, move, rotate, offset, taper, delete, copy, and color (assign a color to) faces.
- **Edges:** You can color and copy edges.
- **Bodies:** The body options apply to solids as a whole. You can imprint, separate, shell, clean, and check solids.

The easiest way to use SOLIDEDIT is to open the Solid Editing toolbar and forget the labyrinthine command line.

The next three sections explain how to edit faces, edges, and bodies.

Editing faces

A face is a surface on a solid. A face can be either flat or curved. For example, a hole in a block is a face, and many of the face-editing operations work well to modify holes. Of course, you can edit an outer face of a surface as well.

The SOLIDEDIT command supports several methods of selecting a face or faces:

- You can use the new ability to select subobjects by using the Ctrl key, as described earlier in this chapter.
- You can click within the boundary of a face. AutoCAD selects the front-most face.
- You can click on an edge to select its adjoining faces.

If you don't get the face that you want at first, at the `Select faces or [Undo/Remove]:` prompt, right-click and choose Undo to undo your last selection operation. Right-click and choose Remove to select a face to remove from the selection set. (You can also press Shift and pick a face to remove it.) The prompt then includes an Add option that you can use to start adding faces again. Then press Enter to end face selection.

You may want to perform more than one operation on a face. After you complete an operation, you can right-click to open the shortcut menu and choose another operation. To exit the command, right-click and choose Exit twice or press Enter twice.

Extruding faces

Extruding a face is like extruding a 2D object. If you're familiar with the EXTRUDE command, you'll feel comfortable extruding faces. If you just want to extrude a face more or less, without tapering it, you can grip-edit the solid, using subselection if necessary. However, this option is valuable because it enables you to easily taper the face.

To extrude a face, follow these steps:

1. Choose Extrude Faces on the Solid Editing toolbar.
2. At the `Select faces or [Undo/Remove]:` prompt, select the face or faces that you want to extrude, using the selection method(s) explained previously. After your first selection, the prompt adds the ALL option. When you're done, press Enter to end face selection.
3. At the `Specify height of extrusion or [Path]:` prompt, type a height, or right-click or choose Path to specify a path for the extrusion.
4. If you specify a height, at the `Specify angle of taper for extrusion <0>:` prompt, specify an angle. (As with the EXTRUDE command, a positive angle tapers inward.) If you choose the Path option, at the `Select extrusion path:` prompt, select an object, usually a line or arc, along which you want to extrude.
5. Press Enter twice to exit the command.

AutoCAD extrudes the face. As you exit, AutoCAD performs a validation of the solid to make sure that the solid is a valid solid if the SOLIDCHECK system variable is on. By default, SOLIDCHECK is on (set to 1) and automatically checks solids when you edit them.

Moving faces

You can move a face when a solid is complex enough to have at least two separate elements — for example, a plate with a hole in it. You can then move the hole around wherever you want. Look at the mounting angle in Figure 24.45, earlier in this chapter. You could move the hole from the left face to the right face using SOLIDEDIT. (You can also subselect the hole and move it using its grips.)

To move a face, follow these steps:

1. Choose Move Faces on the Solid Editing toolbar. AutoCAD starts the SOLIDEDIT command and automatically enters the first two prompts of the command for you.
2. Select the face or faces that you want to move, using the selection method(s) described earlier. Press Enter to end face selection.
3. At the `Specify a base point or displacement:` prompt, specify a base point if you want to pick two points, or specify a displacement, as you would with the MOVE command.

4. At the `Specify a second point of displacement:` prompt, specify a second point of displacement if you specified a base point. Otherwise, press Enter.

5. Press Enter twice to exit the command.

If you choose a face that cannot be moved, AutoCAD displays the `Modeling Operation Error: No solution for an edge` message.

Offsetting faces

You can offset a face when a solid has two separate elements, such as a wall with a window cut out of it. You can then resize the window by offsetting it. Offsetting a face increases all parts of the face equally by a distance that you specify.

Use a positive offset value to increase the volume of the solid. If your face is a solid axle in the middle of a disk, for example, and you offset the axle with a positive value, the axle gets bigger. However, if your face is a hole in the middle of a disk, a positive offset value makes the hole smaller because that makes the resulting solid bigger.

Use a negative offset value to decrease the volume of the solid. Using the same example, a negative offset value would make the axle smaller, but it would make the hole bigger.

To offset a face, follow these steps:

1. Choose Offset Faces from the Solid Editing toolbar.

2. Select the face or faces that you want to offset and press Enter to end face selection.

3. At the `Specify the offset distance:` prompt, type a positive or negative distance. You can also pick two points to specify a positive offset.

4. Press Enter twice to exit the command.

AutoCAD offsets the face. If there is no room for the offset, AutoCAD displays the message `Modeling Operation Error` on the command line.

Deleting faces

You can delete a face of a solid. This is a great way to instantly get rid of a hole, axle, or window within a solid. You can delete faces to undo the effects of both the UNION and SUBTRACT commands. You can also remove filleted and chamfered faces. AutoCAD won't delete every face; for example, you can't turn a box into a tetrahedron by deleting the box's top face. However, the capability to delete faces is a very powerful tool for editing your solids. (You can also subselect the face and press Del.)

To delete a face or faces, choose Delete Faces from the Solid Editing toolbar. Select the face or faces and press Enter. AutoCAD deletes the face or faces that you selected. If your face(s) can't be deleted, you see the message `Modeling Operation Error` on the command line.

Rotating faces

You can rotate a face when a solid is complex enough to have at least two separate elements — for example, a box with a hole in it. The prompts for rotating are very similar to those for ROTATE3D, covered earlier in this chapter. To rotate a face, follow these steps:

1. Choose Rotate Faces on the Solid Editing toolbar. AutoCAD starts the SOLIDEDIT command and automatically enters the first two prompts of the command for you.

2. Select the face or faces that you want to rotate, using the selection method(s) described earlier. Press Enter to end face selection.

3. At the `Specify an axis point or [Axis by object/View/Xaxis/Yaxis/Zaxis]` `<2points>:` prompt, specify the first point of a rotation axis or use one of the options to define an axis of rotation.

4. If you specified a first point, at the `Specify the second point on the rotation axis:` prompt, specify the second point.

5. At the `Specify a rotation angle or [Reference]:` prompt, specify a rotation angle (the right-hand rule applies in determining the direction of rotation), or use the Reference option to specify a reference (starting) angle, and then an ending angle.

6. Press Enter twice to exit the command.

AutoCAD rotates the face. If you choose a face that cannot be rotated, or if there isn't room on the solid for the rotation, AutoCAD lets you know with the message `Modeling Operation Error` on the command line. Note that you can also subselect the face and rotate it using grip-editing.

Tapering faces

You can taper an entire simple solid, such as a box, or you can taper a face that is an element within a complex solid, such as a hole or an extruded face. Tapering angles the sides of the face. To determine the direction of the taper, that is, which end gets tapered, you specify a base point and a second point. The base point side of the solid is not tapered, and AutoCAD tapers the face in the direction from the base point toward the second point. You also specify the angle of the taper. A positive taper angle tapers the face inward; a hole is tapered outward. A negative taper angle tapers the face outward; a hole is tapered inward. Figure 24.49 shows a box before and after tapering at a 15-degree angle, as well as the base point and second points that were used. All of the faces except the bottom were selected.

In general, you should use small tapering angles. If the face tapers to a point before it reaches its existing height, then AutoCAD cannot complete the taper.

To taper a face, follow these steps:

1. Choose Taper Faces on the Solid Editing toolbar. AutoCAD starts the SOLIDEDIT command and automatically enters the first two prompts of the command for you.

2. Select the face(s) that you want to taper. Press Enter to end face selection.

3. At the `Specify the base point:` prompt, pick the base point for the taper direction. Object snaps are a good idea.

4. At the `Specify another point along the axis of tapering:` prompt, specify a second point to indicate the direction of the taper. Again, use an object snap.

5. At the `Specify the taper angle:` prompt, specify an angle between –90° and +90°.

6. Press Enter twice to exit the command.

AutoCAD tapers the face. If AutoCAD can't taper the face, you see the message `Modeling Operation Error` on the command line.

FIGURE 24.49

A box before and after tapering at a 15-degree angle.

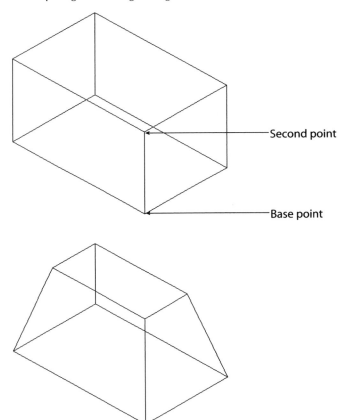

Second point

Base point

Copying faces

You can copy any face, including a hole. AutoCAD creates regions or surfaces out of the face. However, if you copy a complex face, such as a hole that may consist of several regions, you can't turn it back into a solid again.

To copy a face, follow these steps:

1. Choose Copy Faces from the Solid Editing toolbar.
2. Select the face(s) that you want to copy. Press Enter to end face selection.
3. At the `Specify a base point or displacement:` prompt, specify a base point. Object snaps are helpful.

4. At the `Specify a second point of displacement:` prompt, specify a second point to indicate the direction and distance for the copy.

5. Press Enter twice to exit the command.

AutoCAD copies the face.

Coloring faces

You can assign a color to a face of an object. You might want to color a face to make it easier to see. The color overrides the color setting for the solid's layer.

 NOTE When an object is assigned more than one material, priority goes to attachment by object, then by color, and finally by layer. If you attach a material to a solid by layer, and then attach a material to one of its faces (that you have colored) by color, both the solid and the face display their materials. For more information, see Chapter 25.

To color a face, follow these steps:

1. Choose Color Faces from the Solid Editing toolbar.
2. Select the face or faces that you want to color. Press Enter to end face selection.
3. AutoCAD opens the Select Color dialog box. Choose a color and click OK.
4. Press Enter twice to exit the command.

AutoCAD colors the face.

Attaching a material to a face

You can assign a material to a face of an object. You would do this for the purpose of displaying the object with that material in your drawing, or for rendering. For more information on materials and how to add them to your drawing, see Chapter 25.

To add a material to a face, first add the material to the drawing (as I explain in Chapter 25). Then follow these steps:

1. Start the SOLIDEDIT command. Choose the Face option, then choose the Material option.
2. Select the face or faces that you want to use. Press Enter to end face selection.
3. At the Enter new material name <ByLayer>: prompt, type the name of the material as it appears in the Materials palette.
4. Press Enter twice to exit the command.

AutoCAD adds the material to the face.

 The drawing used in the following exercise on editing solid faces, `ab24-15.dwg`, is in the `Results` folder on the DVD.

STEPS: Editing Solid Faces

1. Open `ab24-15.dwg` from the `Results` folder of the DVD. If you did the exercise on filleting solids, you can open it from your `AutoCAD Bible` folder.
2. Save the file as `ab24-17.dwg` in your `AutoCAD Bible` folder. Make sure that OSNAP is on. Set a running object snap for midpoint.

3. If the Solid Editing toolbar is not displayed, right-click any toolbar and choose Solid Editing. This is a mounting angle, shown in Figure 24.50. Note the UCS icon, which is at 0,0,0.

The mounting angle.

4. Choose Offset Faces from the Solid Editing toolbar.

5. At the Select faces or [Undo/Remove]: prompt, select the slot in the mounting angle. Selecting the slot may require a few picks to make sure that all the parts of the slot are highlighted and to remove from selection the unwanted faces of the mounting bracket that become highlighted. (*Hint:* Try picking on the cross-lines that connect the front and back of the slot. You can also press Ctrl to use the subselection feature.) To remove a face, right-click and choose Remove. Then pick on a face's edge. To add faces again, right-click and choose Add. After you're done, press Enter (or right-click and choose Enter) to end face selection.

6. At the Specify the offset distance: prompt, type **.1** ↵. AutoCAD makes the slot smaller.

7. You're still in the SOLIDEDIT command. Right-click and choose Taper. At the next prompt, select the slot and press Enter after you're done selecting.

8. At the Specify the base point: prompt, pick the midpoint at ❶.

9. At the Specify another point along the axis of tapering: prompt, pick the midpoint at ❷.

10. At the Specify the taper angle: prompt, type **10** ↵. AutoCAD tapers the slot.

11. Right-click and choose Delete. At the next prompt, select the filleted face at ❸. Right-click and choose Enter. AutoCAD removes the fillet.

12. Right-click and choose Extrude. At the next prompt, select the face at ❸ by picking inside the face. Right-click and choose Enter.

13. At the Specify height of extrusion or [Path]: prompt, type **.2** ↵.

14. At the Specify angle of taper for extrusion <0>: prompt, type **10** ↵. AutoCAD extrudes the face.

15. Press Enter twice to exit the command.

16. Save your drawing. It should look like Figure 24.51.

The edited mounting angle.

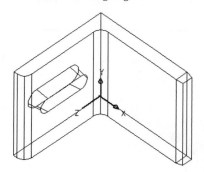

Editing edges

The two-dimensional place where two faces meet is an edge. You can perform only two editing operations on edges: you can copy them and color them.

Copying edges

When you copy an edge, you get a line, arc, circle, ellipse, or spline, depending on the shape of the solid's edge. To copy an edge, follow these steps:

1. Choose Copy Edges from the Solid Editing toolbar.
2. Select the edge or edges that you want to copy.
3. At the Specify a base point or displacement: prompt, specify a base point, preferably using an object snap or a displacement.
4. At the Specify a second point of displacement: prompt, specify a second point or press Enter if you specified a displacement in Step 2.
5. Press Enter twice to exit the command.

AutoCAD copies the edge or edges.

Coloring edges

You can color an edge to make it more visible. The color overrides the color setting for the solid's layer. To color an edge, follow these steps:

1. Choose Color Edges from the Solid Editing toolbar.
2. Select the edge or edges that you want to color. Press Enter to end edge selection.
3. AutoCAD opens the Select Color dialog box. Choose the color you want and click OK.
4. Press Enter twice to exit the command.

AutoCAD colors the edge.

Editing bodies

Several of the SOLIDEDIT options apply to solids as a whole. The operations available are imprinting, cleaning, separating, shelling, and checking. These operations are discussed in the following sections.

Imprinting solids

You can imprint an arc, circle, line, 2D polyline or 3D polyline, ellipse, spline, region, or 3D solid on a solid. The object that you're imprinting must intersect a face on the solid. The shape made by the intersection of the object is left on the solid, as if you put ink on the edges of the object and stamped it on the solid. Figure 24.52 shows an example of imprinting.

FIGURE 24.52

The ellipse was drawn on the top of the solid. After imprinting and deleting the ellipse, the shape of half of the ellipse remains on the solid.

 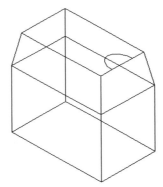

To imprint a solid, follow these steps:

1. First create one of the stampable objects previously listed so that it intersects with a solid. If you draw in top view, check in an isometric view to make sure that the intersection is where you want it.

2. Choose Imprint from the Solid Editing toolbar.

3. At the Select a 3D solid: prompt, select a solid. You can select only one.

4. At the Select an object to imprint: prompt, select the object that you want to imprint.

5. At the Delete the source object [Yes/No] <N>: prompt, type y ↵ or press Enter to indicate No.

6. AutoCAD repeats the Select an object to imprint: prompt. You can continue the command in the same way or press Enter if you're done.

7. Press Enter to exit the command.

AutoCAD imprints the solid. If you didn't delete the source object, you'll need to move it to see the result.

You can subselect an imprint and delete it or edit it in any other way. You can also use an imprint to divide a face and then use the PRESSPULL command to extrude or press that portion of the face.

Cleaning solids

After all the editing, you can end up with some pretty strange solids. Cleaning solids removes adjacent faces that share the same surface and other duplicate or unused edges, vertices, and geometry. Cleaning does not remove imprints.

 To clean a solid, choose Clean from the Solid Editing toolbar. At the `Select a 3D solid:` prompt, select a solid. AutoCAD cleans it.

Separating solids

You can separate a solid that is made up of non-touching sections. You would generally create such a solid from separate, nontouching solids, using the UNION command. The Separate option undoes the effect of the UNION command so that the solids become separate again. You can compare this operation to grouping and ungrouping objects (see Chapter 18).

 To separate a solid, choose Separate from the Solid Editing toolbar. At the `Select a 3D solid:` prompt, select the solid by picking any of its sections. AutoCAD separates the solids.

If your solid sections are even touching, you get one of the odder AutoCAD messages: `The selected solid does not have multiple lumps.`

Shelling solids

When you shell a solid, you hollow out its inside, leaving a thin wall. Think of making a drinking glass from a truncated cone (or tapered cylinder) or a room from a solid box. To shell a solid, follow these steps:

1. Choose Shell from the Solid Editing toolbar.
2. Select a solid.
3. At the `Remove faces or [Undo/Add/ALL]:` prompt, remove any face or faces that you don't want to shell. For example, if you're making a drinking glass from a truncated cone, you want to remove the larger circular face (the one you would drink out of) so that it will remain open. Otherwise, you end up with an enclosed solid that has a hollow interior. After you finish removing faces, press Enter. (The command line confirms `1 face found, 1 removed`, but there is no visual confirmation that AutoCAD has removed the correct face.)
4. At the `Enter the shell offset distance:` prompt, type the width of the wall that you want to create. A positive value creates a shell to the inside of the current solid. A negative value creates a shell to the outside of the current solid.
5. Press Enter twice to shell the solid and exit the command.

Checking solids

Checking ensures that your solid is a valid 3D solid object so that you can edit it without getting ACIS failure error messages. This might be a useful feature to put into an AutoLISP or VBA program, to make sure that it doesn't fail because of invalid solids.

 To check a solid, choose Check from the Solid Editing toolbar. At the `Select a 3D solid:` prompt, select a solid. Usually, AutoCAD replies with the message: `This object is a valid ShapeManager solid.`

 The drawing used in the following exercise on editing solid bodies, `ab24-o.dwg`, is in the `Drawings` folder on the DVD.

STEPS: Editing Solid Bodies

1. Open ab24-o.dwg from the DVD.

2. Save the file as ab24-18.dwg in your AutoCAD Bible folder. This is a simple solid box with an ellipse drawn on part of its top face.

3. Choose Imprint from the Solid Editing toolbar. Follow the prompts:

   ```
   Select a 3D solid: Select the box.
   Select an object to imprint: Select the ellipse.
   Delete the source object [Yes/No] <N>: y ↵.
   Select an object to imprint: Right-click to complete the imprint and
   end the command.
   ```

   Press Ctrl and click inside the half ellipse. Choose Presspull from the Modeling toolbar and move the cursor up. Enter .2 ↵ on the command line or Dynamic Input tooltip.

4. Choose Shell from the Solid Editing toolbar. Follow the prompts:

   ```
   Select a 3D Solid: Select the box.
   Remove faces or [Undo/Add/ALL]: Pick anywhere inside the top face.
   Remove faces or [Undo/Add/ALL]: Right-click and choose Enter.
   Enter the shell offset distance: .1 ↵
   ```

5. Press Enter twice to exit the command.

6. Choose View ➪ Visual Styles ➪ 3D Hidden. You can now see the result of the shell operation.

7. Save your drawing. It should look like Figure 24.53.

FIGURE 24.53

The shelled box.

Listing Solid Properties

The MASSPROP command provides information about regions and solids that is useful for engineering applications. The bounding box, for example, is an imaginary box that contains the solid. The calculations are based on the relationship of the solid to the UCS. If you rotate the solid or change the UCS, you get different results. For example, after running MASSPROP to find the center of gravity (centroid) and axes of your model, move the UCS to the centroid and then run MASSPROP again to identify the moments of inertia, as shown in Figure 24.54.

For 2D regions, the area moment of inertia that MASSPROP generates can be used to calculate bending and twisting stresses. You could generate a 2D region of a solid model using the SECTION command and then use the UCS command with the OBJECT option to set the UCS coplanar to the region. The MASSPROP command would then report the area moment of inertia.

AutoCAD assumes a density of 1 for all solids. You can then apply material density multipliers on the values that get reported.

FIGURE 24.54

The results of the MASSPROP command.

```
Command: massprop

Select objects: 1 found

Select objects:

---------------     SOLIDS     ---------------

Mass:              5.3869
Volume:            5.3869
Bounding box:      X: -1.5177  --  1.4823
                   Y: -1.0000  --  1.0000
                   Z: -2.3111  --  2.8889
Centroid:          X: 0.0000
                   Y: 0.0000
                   Z: 0.0000
Moments of inertia: X: 16.7389
                    Y: 19.8802
                    Z: 9.8148
Products of inertia: XY: 0.0000
                     YZ: 0.0000
                     ZX: 0.2679
Radii of gyration:  X: 1.7628
                    Y: 1.9211
                    Z: 1.3498
Principal moments and X-Y-Z directions about centroid:
Press ENTER to continue:
                    I: 16.7493 along [0.9993 0.0000 -0.0386
                    J: 19.8802 along [0.0000 1.0000 0.0000]
                    K: 9.8045 along [0.0386 0.0000 0.9993]

Write analysis to a file? [Yes/No] <N>: n
```

To list a solid's properties, choose Tools ➪ Inquiry ➪ Region/Mass Properties. Select the object that you want to list. AutoCAD opens the Text Window to display the calculations. At the Write analysis to a file? [Yes/No] <N>: prompt, press Enter to accept the No default, or right-click and choose Yes. AutoCAD prompts you for a filename and copies the data to that file.

850

Summary

In this chapter, you learned how to create and edit solids. You read about:

- Drawing basic shapes
- Creating extruded, swept, revolved, and lofted solids from 2D profiles
- Drawing polysolids
- Using UNION, SUBTRACT, and INTERSECT to create more-complex shapes
- Using the INTERFERE command to see the volume of interference between solids
- Pressing or pulling a solid
- Utilizing the SECTION, SLICE, and SECTIONPLANE commands to visualize and reshape solids
- Grip-editing and subselecting solids
- Using the move grip tool and the 3DMOVE command
- Using the special 3D editing commands MIRROR3D, 3DARRAY, ROTATE3D, and 3DROTATE
- Using the ALIGN, TRIM, EXTEND, FILLET, and CHAMFER commands for 3D editing
- Exploding into surfaces and solids into 2D objects
- Using the SOLIDEDIT command to edit faces, edges, and bodies
- Calculating a number of engineering functions on solids by using the MASSPROP command

In the next chapter, I cover rendering 3D models.

Chapter 25

Rendering in 3D

lthough 3D drawings are more realistic than those that you create in 2D, they look very artificial — they lack realistic color, shading, and lighting, for example. Rendering enables you to display a 3D drawing more realistically. Some of the more advanced features let you create shadows, make objects transparent, add backgrounds, and map 2D images onto the surface of 3D models. You can shade and render 3D surfaces and solid models. Figure 25.1 shows a whimsical rendering that uses shadows and a background.

FIGURE 25.1

This cog has been rendered with shadows and a background of clouds.

AUTOCAD ONLY AutoCAD LT does not offer any rendering features. This entire chapter applies only to AutoCAD.

Understanding Rendering

Rendering is a much more sophisticated means of visualizing a drawing than using visual styles. AutoCAD offers many settings that allow you to fine-tune the results.

Learning the steps

Rendering is a multi-step process. It generally requires a good deal of trial and error to get the exact results that you want. Here are the steps to render a drawing:

1. Start with trial rendering using the default settings. The results let you know what settings need to be changed.
2. Create lights. AutoCAD has four types of lights: default lighting, distant (including the sunlight), point, and spotlight. I explain lights in the "Creating Lights" section later in this chapter.
3. Create materials. Materials are surface characteristics and include color and/or texture, reflection (shininess), transparency, refraction, and bump maps. These characteristics are explained later in this chapter in the "Working with Materials" section.
4. Attach materials to the objects in your drawing. You can attach materials by object or layer.

CROSS-REF See the section, "Attaching a material to a face" in Chapter 24 for information on how to attach a material to the face of a solid using the SOLIDEDIT command.

5. Add a background or fog effect. I discuss these effects in the "Using backgrounds" section later in this chapter.
6. Fine-tune your rendering preferences, if desired. For example, you can render with a variety of output qualities.
7. Render the drawing.

The order of the steps is flexible. For example, you can create and attach materials before you add lights. Also, after you render, you'll probably see some room for improvement, and so you may go back and make changes.

Doing a default rendering

Doing a default rendering often helps you to decide what materials and lights you need to create for your final rendering. It also reveals any problems with the models themselves. When you render, you can open the Render toolbar, which contains most of the tools you need, or use the Dashboard, which contains more tools. Several palettes offer even more settings.

 To render a drawing using the default settings, choose Render from the Render toolbar or the Render control panel of the Dashboard. One way to get a quick rendering is to choose Render Cropped Region from the Render control panel of the Dashboard, which executes the RENDERCROP command. You define a selection window, and the command does a default rendering within that area.

TIP Choose Advanced Render Settings from the Dashboard (you need to click the double-down arrow to expand that control panel) or the Render toolbar (the RPREF command). In the Advanced Render Settings palette, use the Procedure drop-down list to choose Crop (the RENDERCROP command just mentioned) or Selection, to render just selected objects. You can also use the Destination drop-down window to choose to render in the current viewport instead of the default separate window. These settings enable you to create quick draft renderings as you test your lights and materials.

The drawing used in the following exercise on creating a default rendering, `ab25-a.dwg`, is in the `Drawings` folder on the DVD.

STEPS: Creating a Default Rendering

1. Open `ab25-a.dwg` from the DVD.
2. Save the file as `ab25-01.dwg` in your `AutoCAD Bible` folder. If the Render toolbar is not displayed, right-click any toolbar and choose Render.

3. Choose Render from the Render toolbar. Watch as the Render window opens and renders the drawing.
4. Save your drawing. It should look like Figure 25.2. As you can see, the rendering is too dark and the objects need realistic materials.

FIGURE 25.2

An initial rendering using default options and a crop window.

Thanks to Andrew Wilcox of Virtual Homes, Inc., Hammonds Plains, Nova Scotia, Canada, for this drawing.

Creating Lights

When you render using the default options, AutoCAD uses default lighting that includes two light sources that fall on the objects in the view. However, that is rarely enough, nor is it realistic. AutoCAD offers seven types of lights to give you a great deal of flexibility in creating a realistic scene. If you plan to cast shadows in your rendering, the proper placement of lights is most important.

NOTE   The default lighting uses two lights, instead of one, and must be turned off to use the lights that you create. When you create a new light, AutoCAD displays a message asking if you want to turn off the default lighting. You can also use the Default Lighting Mode button in the Lights control panel of the Dashboard to turn default lighting on and off.

 To create lights, choose one of the buttons from the Lights flyout on the Render toolbar or choose them from the Lights toolbar. You can also choose one of the individual lights in the Lights control panel of the Dashboard. If you execute the LIGHT command on the command line or in the Dynamic Input tooltip, you can choose one of the seven options to specify which type of light you want to create.

NEW FEATURE   AutoCAD 2008 offers more precise *photometry* settings for lighting, including the ability to set light intensity using real-world values, such as candela, lumen, or lux. You can also choose the type of lighting (*lamp color*), such as fluorescent, halogen, or incandescent. To use the photometry feature, you need to set the LIGHTINGUNITS system variable to 1 or 2. A value of 1 enables photometric lighting with International lighting units, and a value of 2 enables it with American lighting units. Set the value of the LIGHTINGUNITS system variable on the command line or in the Lighting section of the Units dialog box (Format ➪ Units).

Setting the default light

The default lighting consists of two lights that uniformly light up the model from all directions. You can control brightness and contrast using the sliders in the Lights control panel of the Dashboard. Remember that turning on your own lights turns off the default lighting.

NEW FEATURE   The new RENDEREXPOSURE command opens the Adjust Rendered Exposure dialog box, where you can control brightness, contrast, mid tones, exterior daylight, and processing of the background. This dialog box does a mini-rendering as you change the values, so that you can see their effect in real time.

Creating a point light

A point light is equivalent to a typical light bulb or a candle. It comes from a specific location and radiates in all directions. A point light attenuates, meaning that the intensity lessens as the distance away from the light's source increases.

 To create a new point light, choose New Point Light from the Light flyout on the Render toolbar or Create a Point Light from the expanded Lights control panel of the Dashboard. At the `Specify source location <0,0,0>:` prompt, specify the location of the light.

Use object snaps to specify the position of your lights. If there are no objects available, work out the position in advance and place an easily visible point object there; you can then snap to the point object using the Node object snap. Other options are to type the absolute coordinates or use the From object snap to specify a coordinate, based on a point on the model.

If you set the XY coordinates in plan view, be sure to set the proper Z coordinate as well. In an architectural drawing, you don't want your lights to be coming from the floor! However, in a mechanical drawing, it might be appropriate to light your model from any angle.

NOTE   If you create an opaque lampshade and place a light inside it, light will get out only through the top and bottom. If you want light to filter through the lampshade, make it partially transparent. For more information, see "Working with Materials" later in this chapter.

The next prompt depends on the value of the LIGHTINGUNITS system variable, as follows:

- If the value is 0, you see the `Enter an option to change [Name/Intensity/Status/ shadoW/Attenuation/Color/eXit] <eXit>:` prompt
- If the value is 1 or 2, you see the `Enter an option to change [Name/Intensity factor/Status/Photometry/shadoW/Attenuation/filterColor/eXit] <eXit>:` prompt

These options are discussed in the next several sections. After you create the light, you can edit these settings in the Properties palette. When you finish specifying the light's properties, press Enter to exit the command and place the point light.

Name

When you create a light, a default name is automatically created — for example, Pointlight1. Use the Name option to change the name. At the `Enter light name <Pointlight1>:` prompt, enter a name. You then return to the options prompt. Press Enter to exit the command.

If you change the name, use a name that makes it clear that the light is a point light. Keep the name short; a simple sequence of P1, P2 is often sufficient. However, you could also use P-overhd and P-door or something similar.

Intensity/Intensity factor

Use the Intensity or Intensity factor option to set the intensity, or brightness, of the light. At the `Enter intensity (0.00 – max float) <current>:` prompt, enter a number. The default is 1; higher numbers make the light brighter. Note that you can also set the brightness using the Photometry option.

Status

The Status option turns the light on and off. Choose On or Off. You can turn lights on and off to create day and night scenes or to experiment with different lighting arrangements without having to delete or move lights.

Photometry

If photometry is enabled, use this option to specify the intensity and color of the light. There are two sub-options:

- **Intensity:** You can enter an intensity in candela (abbreviated as cd) units, or you can specify flux, the perceived power of the light, or illuminance, the total flux on a surface area. You can specify illuminance in lux (abbreviated as lx) or footcandle (fc) units.
- **Color:** You can enter a color name or a Kelvin temperature value. Use the ? option and then press Enter to see a list of names, such as Fluorescent, Coolwhite, Halogen, and others. (Press F2 to open the AutoCAD Text Window, because the names scroll by too fast to see on the command line.)

Shadow

Shadows add greatly to the realism of your rendered image. They also add greatly to the rendering time. The Shadow option turns shadows on and off for that light and specifies the type of shadow. If you choose to create shadows, you can choose three types of shadows:

- **Sharp:** These are sometimes called ray-traced shadows. Use these shadows to reduce rendering time.

- **Soft Mapped:** Enter a map size from 64 to 4096. Larger map sizes are more accurate but take longer to render. At the Enter softness (1-10) <1>: prompt, enter a number from 1 to 10. The shadow softness determines the number of pixels at the edge of the shadow that are blended into the rest of the image, thus creating the soft effect.

- **Soft Sampled:** Creates a penumbra (partial shadow) effect. You can specify values for three suboptions:

  - **Shape:** Specify the shape of the shadow and its dimensions. You can choose from Linear, Disk, Rect (rectangle), Sphere, and Cylinder.

  - **sAmples:** Specify a shadow sample size. The default is 16. A larger sampling size produces a more accurate shadow.

  - **Visibility:** You can choose whether or not to make the shape you used for the shadow visible in the drawing. Choose Yes or No (the default). If you choose Yes, you see the shape around the light in the rendering.

> **TIP**
> For your practice renderings while you're creating lights and materials, turn shadows off in the Advanced Render Settings palette (RPREF command). Scroll down to the Shadows section and click the Lightbulb icon to toggle shadows on and off. Shadows significantly add to rendering time. When you're satisfied with the other settings, turn shadows on.

> **NOTE**
> The 3DCONFIG command includes a Hardware Shadows sub-option that allows you to turn shadows off. Also, the automatic adaptive degradation may affect shadows if your system is not powerful enough. For more information, see Appendix A.

Attenuation

The Attenuation option sets the *attenuation,* which is the manner in which the light loses intensity as the distance from its source increases. The Attenuation Type sub-option offers three choices:

- **None:** The light doesn't lose intensity.

- **Inverse Linear:** The light loses intensity in a linear manner, so that at 2 units from its source the light is half as intense, and at 4 units away the light is one-quarter as intense.

- **Inverse Square:** The light loses intensity at the square of the distance, so that at 2 units from its source the light is one-quarter as intense and at 4 units away the light is one-sixteenth as intense. Setting the attenuation to inverse square means that the intensity of the light drops off very quickly.

You can set a limit beyond which there is no light. The reason to do this is to improve rendering time. After a certain distance, it may make no difference if there is a little bit of light or no light, and limiting the light to that difference reduces the required calculations. Set the Use Limits sub-option to Yes if you want to use limits. Then set the Attenuation Start Limit and Attenuation End Limit values. The default start limit is 0 (zero). The end limit is a distance from the center of the light.

> **NOTE**
> The OpenGL driver (wopengl9.hdi) does not support attenuation start limits and end limits, but the Direct 3D driver (direct3d9.hdi) does support end limits. To find your driver, start the 3DCONFIG command on the command line, and click the View Tune Log button. You should find your driver under the Application Driver item.

Color/Filter Color

You can give your light any color you want. Light colors are somewhat different from pigment colors, which are more familiar. The three primary light colors are red, green, and blue (RGB). Their mixtures are different, as well; for example, red and green make yellow. White light is the sum of all colors of light together. Black is the absence of any colors of light.

Instead the RGB light color system, you can use the HLS (hue, lightness, saturation) system. Instead of mixing primary colors, you choose the color from a range of hues and then vary its lightness (brightness) and saturation (intensity).

When you use the Color option, you get the `Enter true color (R,G,B) or enter an option [Index color/Hsl/colorBook] <255,255,255>:` prompt.

- To enter RGB numbers, enter numbers from 0 to 255 for red, green, and blue. The default, 255,255,255, is white.

- To enter an ACI (AutoCAD Color Index) number, use the Index color sub-option and enter a number from 1 to 255. These are the same numbers that you find on the Index Color tab of the Select Color dialog box.

- To use the HSL system, use the Hsl option and then enter an HSL color, which is also three numbers from 0 to 255.

- To specify a color-book color, use the colorBook option.

> **TIP** An easier way to assign a light color is to place the light without changing the color, select the light, and change the color in the Properties palette. When you choose Select Color from the Color drop-down list of the Properties palette, the Select Color dialog box opens, where you can see the color swatches for each color. (See Chapter 11 for a discussion of specifying colors and using color books.)

Creating a target point light

A target point light is like a point light, but you specify a target. This helps you control the direction of the light.

> **NEW FEATURE** Target point lights are new for AutoCAD 2008. They combine features of point lights and spotlights, which I cover next.

To create a target point light, enter **targetpoint** on the command line. At the `Specify source location <0,0,0>:` enter the source of the light. At the `Specify target location <0,0,-10>:` specify the target. By default, the target is 10 units less in the Z direction than the source. The rest of the prompts are the same as for a point light.

Creating a spotlight

A spotlight differs from a point light in that it has a direction. As a result, you not only specify its location but also its target — two coordinates instead of one. In addition, a spotlight has a brighter center called the *hotspot*. Outside the center is a ring of lesser brightness called the *falloff*. Figure 25.3 shows the same scene used previously in this chapter, but with one overhead spotlight.

FIGURE 25.3

A rendering with one spotlight overhead. Here the hotspot angle is 45° and the falloff angle is 70°.

 To create a new spotlight, choose New Spotlight from the Light flyout on the Render toolbar or Create a Spotlight from the Lights control panel of the Dashboard. At the `Specify source location <0,0,0>:` prompt, enter the spotlight's location. In most cases, you don't want the Z value to be 0 (zero). At the `Specify target location <0,0,-10>:` prompt, specify the light's target.

The prompt that you now see depends on the value of the LIGHTINGUNITS system variable (discussed earlier in this chapter), which turns the photometry feature on and off:

- If the value is 0, you see the `Enter an option to change [Name/Intensity/Status/ Hotspot/Falloff/shadoW/Attenuation/Color/eXit] <eXit>:` prompt.

- If the value is 1 or 2, you see the `Enter an option to change [Name/Intensity factor/Status/Photometry/Hotspot/Falloff/shadoW/Attenuation/ filterColor/eXit]`

  `<eXit>:` prompt.

All of these options are the same as for a point light, except the Hotspot and Falloff options. (See the previous section, "Creating a point light," for details.)

Hotspot and falloff

Set the hotspot and falloff angles for the spotlight. These angles emanate from the spotlight in the direction of the light's target. The maximum angle for both is 160 degrees. If the hotspot and falloff angles are the same, there is no falloff — the entire spotlight is bright. The defaults are 44 degrees for the hotspot and 50 degrees for the falloff. This does not leave very much falloff area. You may need to experiment to get the desired result. When you're done creating the spotlight, press Enter to exit the command.

Creating a Free spotlight

A free spotlight is like a spotlight, but it has no target. From this perspective, it's like a point light, bit you can specify a hotspot and falloff, like you can with a spotlight.

Using Web Lights

Photometric web lights are a new concept in AutoCAD 2008. They provide a representation of the way a light's intensity varies in 3D space. You would use a web light when you have data about the way a real light's intensity is distributed. The result is a very precise rendering of the effect of the light. However, this result is only approximate in the viewport.

In order to use web lights, you need to turn on the photometry feature by setting the value of the LIGHTING-UNITS system variable to 1 or 2.

You can insert web lights into your drawing by using the following commands:

- **Weblight:** Use the WEBLIGHT command on the command line. A web light is similar to a spotlight, because it has a target. The options are the same as for spotlights, except for an added Web option.

- **Freeweb:** Use the FREEWEB command on the command line. A freeweb light is similar to a point light, because it has only a source location. The options are the same as for point lights, except for an added Web option.

The Web option lets you specify a file that contains light distribution information at various directions from the light in the IES (Illuminating Engineering Society) LM-63-1991 format. IES is a text-file format for describing this type of information. Light manufacturers provide these IES files (sometimes called photometric data) for their lights. You can also specify individual X, Y, and Z data for the light.

After you place a web light, you can select it and use the Web File item in the Properties palette to load an IES file. By default, these web files are in the WebFiles folder. To find the exact location, choose Tools ⇨ Options and click the Files tab. Double-click the Web File Search Path item. You can change that location or add additional locations.

NEW FEATURE   The free spotlight is a new light type for AutoCAD 2008.

To create a free spotlight, enter **freespot** on the command line. At the `Specify source location <0,0,0>:` enter the location for the light. The rest of the prompts are the same as for a spotlight.

Creating a distant light

A distant light is similar to the sun. Its rays come from so far away that, for all practical purposes, they're parallel. A distant light does not attenuate (unless you're drawing a model on Pluto). Before inserting a distant light, it is recommended that you set the LIGHTINGUNITS system variable to 0 to turn off the photometric units, or lower the distant light's intensity.

 To create a new distant light, choose New Distant Light from the Light flyout on the Render toolbar or Create a Distant Light from the Lights control panel of the Dashboard. At the `Specify light direction FROM <0,0,0>` or `[Vector]:` prompt, specify the source of the light. At the `Specify light direction TO <1,1,1>:` prompt, specify the light direction. You can specify a point or use the vector system that I discuss in the "Using the VPOINT command" section of Chapter 22. If you use the Vector option, you only set the direction of the light. AutoCAD places the light outside the model, and there is no light glyph. The rest of the options are the same as for creating a point light, which I discuss earlier in this chapter. When you are finished specifying the light, press Enter to exit the command.

Simulating the sun

You can simulate the sun by specifying a geographic location for your model and setting specific properties for the sun. In this way, you can get very realistic lighting. When you use the sun tools, you are creating a special type of distant light.

Set the geographic location

To set the geographic location, choose Geographic Location from the extended Lights control panel of the Dashboard (click the double down arrow to extend that control panel). You can also find this command (the GEOGRAPHICLOCATION command) on the Lights toolbar. The Geographic Location dialog box opens, as shown in Figure 25.4.

FIGURE 25.4

Use the Geographic Location dialog box to specify the latitude and longitude for a specific location.

To specify the location, follow these steps in the Geographic Location dialog box:

1. If you know the latitude and longitude, enter them in the Latitude and Longitude sections, and skip to Step 3; otherwise, choose the continent from the Region drop-down list. (India and Canada are also separately listed among the continents.) You see the map for the region you chose.

2. If your model is in a large city, select the Nearest Big City check box. The marker will then jump to the city nearest to the point you click. You can also choose a city from the Nearest City drop-down list. If you're not in a city, just click on the map.

 The time zone automatically adjusts to the location you chose. However, you can separately set the time zone using the TIMEZONE system variable.

3. In the North Direction section, specify the angle that represents north in your drawing. Setting the north location is important to get accurate sun results. By default, north is the positive Y direction in the World Coordinate System (WCS). To change the default, type a new angle in the Angle box, or click the compass face to specify the new angle. The positive Y axis is at 0 degrees, the positive X axis is at 90 degrees, and so on clockwise.

4. Click OK. You may see a notice about the time zone, which is automatically calculated. Check the time zone and click OK to close the notice.

Set sun properties

To set properties for the sun, such as the date and time, choose Edit the Sun from the expanded Lights control panel of the Dashboard (the SUNPROPERTIES command) to open the Sun Properties palette, as shown in Figure 25.5.

FIGURE 25.5

The Sun Properties palette keeps all of the settings for the sun in one place.

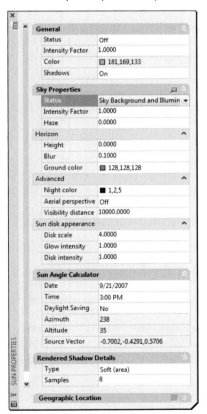

The first set of properties is the same as the options for the POINTLIGHT command. See the section "Creating a point light" earlier in this chapter for more details.

The next four sections only appear if you are using photometric lighting (which means that the LIGHTIN-UNITS system variable is 1 or 2).

NEW FEATURE   The Sky Properties, Horizon, Advanced, and Sun Disk Appearance sections for the Sun Properties palette are new for AutoCAD 2008.

The Sky Properties section allows you to add a background and illumination effect for the sky when you render the drawing. You don't see any effect in the regular viewport. You can turn the sky off, choose just a sky background effect, or choose both the sky background and the illumination effect. You can add an intensity factor for the sky. The default value is 1. Changing it to 2 will significantly brighten your sky!

CROSS-REF   To specify these sky properties for a background, turn on photometric lighting and create a new named view. At the bottom of the New Named View dialog box, choose the Sun & Sky option. See Chapter 22 for more details on creating a new view with a background.

The Haze setting creates a scattering effect. The default is 0.0 and the maximum is 15.0. A setting of 15.0 will create an effect of looking through haze.

The Horizon section controls the horizon, which is where the ground meets the sky. In order to see the horizon, you need a viewpoint that shows the horizon. If your viewport is too close to plan view, you won't see the horizon, because you'll be looking down instead of outward. You can set the following properties:

- **Height:** Sets the position of the ground plane relative to the zero value of the Z axis. Set this in real-world units. For example, 24 would be 2 feet high.
- **Blur:** Creates a blur at the junction between the ground and the sky. You can see this effect in your drawing (not only when you render), especially if the ground color contrasts with the sky color.
- **Ground Color:** Choose a color for the ground.

The Advanced section includes three "artistic" effects. First, you can choose a night color. You can also turn aerial perspective on. (It's off by default.) Aerial perspective is a bluing and slight blurring effect that creates the impression of distance. Finally, you can set the visibility distance, which is the distance at which 10% haze kicks in, reducing clarity. This setting also gives an impression of distance.

The Sun Disk Appearance section affects only the appearance of the sun, not the overall light. You can see the results of the changes you make here more clearly in the New View dialog box, which I explain in Chapter 22. The Disk Scale item specifies a scale for the sun disk itself; a value of 1 is normal size. The Glow Intensity item changes the glow around the disk; 1 is the default value. The Disk Intensity value changes the intensity of the sun disk itself; again 1 is the default value.

The Sun Angle Calculator section allows you to enter a date and time and to specify whether or not you're using Daylight Savings Time. To change the date, click the Date item, and then click the Ellipsis button. A little calendar opens. Navigate to the desired date and double-click it. The calendar closes. Choose a time from the drop-down list. Choose Yes or No from the Daylight Saving drop-down list.

NOTE   You can also set the date and time in the Lights control panel of the Dashboard, using the sliders or text boxes.

The next three settings are not changeable; they're based on the location you specified in the Geographic Location dialog box:

- The *azimuth* is the angle in the XY plane — North is located at 0 degrees. Use a positive angle to move clockwise from North, and a negative angle to move counterclockwise from North. Values can range from −180 to 180. (Both −180 and 180 would represent South.)

- The *altitude* is the angle from the XY plane. You can type in angles from −90 to 90. (An altitude of −90 would mean that the light was coming from beneath the model.)

- The *source vector* is the coordinates that represent the sun's direction. For more information on the vector system, see "Using the VPOINT command" in Chapter 22.

The Rendered Shadow Details section offers the same settings I discussed earlier in the "Creating a point light" section. However, when photometric lighting is on, the only shadow choice is Soft (Area), which creates sampled shadows. Shadows need to be on in the General section for these settings to be available.

Managing lights

 To keep track of and manage your lights, you use the Lights in Model palette. Choose Light List (the LIGHTLIST command) from the Lights control panel of the Dashboard or from the Lights toolbar. The Lights in Model palette is shown in Figure 25.6.

FIGURE 25.6

The Lights in Model palette lists all of your lights.

Lights can be difficult to select; they may be inside a lamp or high up, out of your current display. Distant lights don't have a glyph that you can click on to select them. The List in Model palette helps you select, modify, and delete lights. To select a light, choose it in the palette.

You can now edit the light either with grips or in the Properties palette. Figure 25.7 shows a selected spotlight. You can easily change the spotlight's location, target, hotspot, and falloff using grips. To change its status (on or off), color, and other properties, use the Properties palette.

To delete a light, choose it in the Lights in Model palette and press Del. You don't delete the sun, you just turn it off. (Good night!)

FIGURE 25.7

You can grip-edit a light using the grips on the light glyph.

 NOTE You may have lights that you created in AutoCAD versions prior to 2007 that you want to use in 2008 drawings. Use the CONVERTOLDLIGHTS command to convert your lights. You may have to adjust their intensity. To do so, select them and change the intensity in the Properties palette. In addition, the 3DCONVERSIONMODE system variable converts material and light definitions to the latest release. This system variable allows you to keep your definitions up to date with each new release.

ON the DVD-ROM The drawing used in the following exercise on creating lights and shadows, ab25-a.dwg, is in the Drawings folder on the DVD.

STEPS: Creating Lights and Shadows

1. Open ab25-a.dwg from the DVD. OSNAP should be on. Set running object snaps for endpoint and center. This exercise does not use the photometric feature; make sure that the value of the LIGHTINGUNITS system variable is set to 0.

2. Save the file as ab25-02.dwg in your AutoCAD Bible folder. If the Lights toolbar is not open, right-click any toolbar and choose Lights.

3. Choose New Point Light from the Lights toolbar. At the Viewport Lighting Mode message, click Yes to turn off default lighting.

4. Pan to the right until you see the floor lamp, as shown in Figure 25.8.

   ```
   Follow the prompts: Specify source location <0,0,0>: Pick the
   endpoint shown in Figure 25.8.
   Enter an option to change
   [Name/Intensity/Status/shadoW/Attenuation/Color/eXit]
   <eXit>: n ↵
   Enter light name <Pointlight1>: p1 ↵
   Enter an option to change
   [Name/Intensity/Status/shadoW/Attenuation/Color/eXit]
   <eXit>: i ↵
   Enter intensity (0.00 - max float) <1.0000>: 3 ↵
   Enter an option to change
   [Name/Intensity/Status/shadoW/Attenuation/Color/eXit]
   <eXit>: x ↵
   ```

5. Choose Light List from the Lights toolbar. In the Lights in Model palette, click the new p1 light listed there to select the light.

6. Open the Properties palette. Click the Filter Color item and choose Yellow from the drop-down list. Click the Shadows item and choose On from the drop-down list (if it's not already on).

FIGURE 25.8

Picking the point light location.

7. Choose Zoom Previous from the Zoom flyout of the Standard toolbar to return to your previous view.

8. Choose New Spotlight from the Lights toolbar. Follow the prompts:

```
Specify source location <0,0,0>: _Shift+right-click and choose From
from the OSNAP list.
from Base point: Use the Center object snap of the top edge of the
round table.
<Offset>: @0,0,5' ↵ (This places the light 5 feet directly over the
table, like a light hanging from the ceiling.)
Specify target location <0,0,-10>: Use the Center object snap of the
top of the table.
of Point to the edge of the round table.
Enter an option to change
[Name/Intensity/Status/Hotspot/Falloff/shadoW/Attenuation/Color/eXit]
<eXit>: n ↵
Enter light name <Spotlight1>: s1 ↵
Enter an option to change
[Name/Intensity/Status/Hotspot/Falloff/shadoW/Attenuation/Color/eXit]
<eXit>: f ↵
Enter falloff angle (0.00-160.00) <50>: 70 ↵
Enter an option to change
[Name/Intensity/Status/Hotspot/Falloff/shadoW/Attenuation/Color/eXit]
<eXit>: h ↵
```

```
Enter hotspot angle (0.00-160.00) <3'-9">: 40 ↵
Enter an option to change
[Name/Intensity/Status/Hotspot/Falloff/shadoW/Attenuation/Color/eXit]
<eXit>: w ↵
Enter shadow settings [Off/Sharp/soFtmapped/softsAmpled] <Sharp>: f ↵
Enter map size [64/128/256/512/1024/2048/4096] <256>: ↵
Enter softness (1-10) <1>: 5 ↵
Enter an option to change
[Name/Intensity/Status/Hotspot/Falloff/shadoW/Attenuation/Color/eXit]
<eXit>: x ↵
```

9. Choose Geographic Location from the Lights toolbar. Set the latitude to 41.00 and the longitude to 91.57. The two drop-down list boxes below should read North and West. (The cross should indicate southeast Iowa.) In the North Direction section, type **90** in the text box. Click OK. Click OK at the Time Zone Updated message. (The time zone should be Central.)

10. Click Sun Properties on the Lights toolbar. In the Sun Properties palette, set the date to 9/1. Set the time to 8:00 in the morning. (You're having breakfast.) Set the Daylight Savings item to Yes.

11. Close the Sun Properties and Lights in Model palettes (or auto-hide them).

12. Choose Advanced Render Settings from the Render toolbar. In the Shadows section of the Advanced Render Settings palette, click the Specifies If Shadows Are Computed Lightbulb icon, making sure that it is deselected.

13. Click Render on the Render toolbar or in the Advanced Render Settings palette. The rendering should take less than a minute, and it should look like Figure 25.9. There is more than enough light this time — but remember, you wouldn't normally eat breakfast with all of the lights on. Notice the effect of the yellow point light; it makes the blue floor and walls look green.

FIGURE 25.9

A rendering with lights but no shadows.

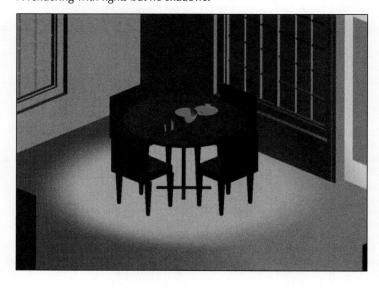

14. Choose Advanced Render Settings from the Render toolbar again. Click the Specifies If Shadows Are Computed lightbulb icon in the Shadows section. Click Render. Notice that the rendering takes much longer. Lots of shadows this time! This rendering also makes it clear that no light is coming through the windows. (See the "Working with Materials" section to learn how to make materials transparent.) The rendering should look like Figure 25.10.

15. Save your drawing. If you're continuing on to the next exercise, keep this drawing open.

FIGURE 25.10

The same rendering with shadows.

Working with Materials

Materials in AutoCAD are representations of actual materials on objects, such as glass, metal, fabric, wood, and others. Using materials is an important part of the rendering process and greatly affects the results. Materials interact with lights. For example, shiny materials reflect light differently than dull materials because shiny materials create highlights.

 You can display materials as you work. Although this requires more resources from your computer, you can see some results immediately, without rendering. Rendering always produces a more accurate result. To display materials, click the Materials and Textures button in the Materials control panel of the Dashboard, and choose Materials and Textures On from the button's drop-down toolbar. You need to be in the Realistic visual style to see the result.

> **NOTE** The Adaptive Degradation process may turn off materials automatically if your graphics card is not certified. You can turn the display of materials on manually using the 3DCONFIG command. For more information, see Appendix A.

Attaching a material from the Tool Palettes window

The easiest way to attach a material to an object is to use the collection of materials on the Tool Palettes window. To get an idea of the available materials, open the Tool Palettes window (Ctrl+3) and click the overlapping tabs at the bottom of the window, to display the full list of tabs, as shown in Figure 25.11. Notice that there are tabs that contain material samples and others that contain a materials library.

 You can click the main icon of the Materials control panel in the Dashboard to open the Tool Palettes window with the Materials group current.

To add a material to an object, choose a palette (tab) and click a material swatch on the tool palette. At the `Select objects:` prompt, select the objects for the material. You should see the change immediately if you have materials and textures set to display.

 The drawing used in the following exercise on attaching materials from the Tool Palettes window, ab25-02.dwg, is in the `Results` folder on the DVD.

FIGURE 25.11

The Tool Palettes window contains a large collection of materials.

```
Modeling
Annotation
Architectural
Mechanical
Electrical
Civil
Structural
Hatches and Fills
Tables
Command Tool Samples
Leaders
Draw
Modify

Concrete - Materials Sample
Doors and Windows - Materials Sample
Fabric - Materials Sample
Finishes - Materials Sample
Flooring - Materials Sample
Masonry - Materials Sample

Metals - Materials Sample
Woods and Plastics - Materials Sample
Generic Lights
Fluorescent
High Intensity Discharge
Incandescent
Low Pressure Sodium
Cameras
Visual Styles
```

STEPS: Attaching Materials from the Tool Palettes Window

1. If you have ab25-02.dwg open, use this file. Otherwise, open it from your AutoCAD Bible folder or the Results folder on the DVD.

2. Save the file as ab25-03.dwg in your AutoCAD Bible folder.

3. If the Dashboard isn't displayed, enter **dashboard** ↵ on the command line or in the Dynamic Input tooltip. In the Materials control panel of the Dashboard, click the Materials and Textures button in the Materials control panel of the Dashboard, and choose Materials and Textures On from the button's drop-down toolbar.

4. From the Dashboard's Visual Styles control panel, choose Realistic from the Visual Styles drop-down list.

5. Display the Tool Palettes window (Ctrl+3). Click the overlapping tabs at the bottom and choose Woods and Plastics - Materials Sample.

6. Click the Woods - Plastics.Finish Carpentry.Wood.Maple tool. At the Select objects: prompt, select the table top. The table top changes color, but still doesn't look very much like wood. In the next exercise, you'll fix that. Press Enter to end object selection.

Using the Materials palette

To manage and modify materials, choose Materials from the Render toolbar or the Materials control panel of the Dashboard to open the Materials palette, shown in Figure 25.12.

NEW FEATURE You can also access the properties of a material by right-clicking the material in the Tool Palettes window and choosing Properties to open a dialog box for that material.

The top section of the Materials palette displays all of the materials currently in the drawing. You can use the Toggle Display Mode to switch between showing one material and rows of materials. You can select any material to see and change its properties.

You can right-click any material in the preview area and do the following from the shortcut menu:

- Create a new material.
- Apply the material to selected objects.
- Select objects that use the material.
- Edit the material's name and description.
- Purge the material if it's not in use.
- Export the material to the active tool palette so that you can attach the material from there.
- Copy the material (so that you can create a new material based on the old one).
- Change the size of the material swatches. If you have a lot of materials, use the small size.

To edit an existing material, select the material and adjust its properties. I explain the properties in the next section. When you have the materials you need, you attach them to objects. See the section "Attaching materials" for details.

FIGURE 25.12

The Materials palette lets you manage materials. Note that the properties available vary with the material's template.

Checkered Underlay On/Off — Toggle Display Mode

Swatch Geometry — Preview Swatch Lighting — Preview area

Create New Material
Purge from Drawing
Indicate Materials in Use
Remove Materials from Selected Objects
Apply Materials to Objects

Material Type
Template
Color

Material Properties

Creating your own materials

 To create your own material, click the Create New Material button in the Materials palette. In the Create New Material dialog box, enter a name and description for the material and click OK. A new swatch appears in the Materials palette. You can now specify the properties for that material.

Note that you can also modify an existing material or copy an existing material and modify that copy. In fact, to get the results that you want, you often need to modify an existing material in some way. To copy a material, select it, right-click, and choose Copy. Then right-click and choose Paste.

Choose a material template

The first step is to choose a material type. A material type provides you with the basic properties that are common to that class of materials. Choose the type you want from the Type drop-down list. AutoCAD has the following basic material types:

- **Realistic:** The main template for most materials. It has moderate shininess, and zero refraction, translucency, and self-illumination. I explain these terms in the next section.
- **Realistic Metal:** The main template for metals. It has moderate shininess and no self-illumination. Translucency and refraction are not available.
- **Advanced:** Like realistic, but offers the ability to separately specify ambient, diffuse, and specular colors. I explain these terms in the next section.
- **Advanced Metal:** Like Realistic Metal, but offers the ability to separately specify ambient and diffuse colors.

In addition, there are over 15 templates that are more specific (wood, water, and so on) and assist you in creating your own materials by providing many settings for you. Choose these from the Template drop-down list, or choose User-Defined to specify properties from scratch.

NEW FEATURE You can force materials to be two-sided. This option is available in the Advanced Render Settings palette, which I cover later in this chapter. By default, this setting is on. If you turn it off, when you create a material, you can check or uncheck the Two Sided Material check box in the Materials palette. One-sided materials take less time to render.

Choose a material color

The next step is to specify the properties for your new material. The section of the Materials palette just below the Template drop-down list varies, depending on the template you chose. Figure 25.13 shows this section for the Advanced template. This section offers one, two, or three kinds of colors that you can apply to the material.

Use this section of the Materials palette to specify colors for your material.

The first set of properties includes basic colors that apply to the material. These colors are:

- **Ambient:** This is the color that appears on objects lighted by ambient light alone. Ambient light is turned off when you turn on lights that you add to the drawing; when you turn off all lights (or if you don't add any), the ambient light applies. This setting is available for the Advanced and Advanced Metal templates.

- **Diffuse:** This is the main color of the object. All templates allow you to set the diffuse color. Note that colored lights have a significant effect on the apparent color of a material.

- **Specular:** This is the color of a highlight on a shiny material. For example, a shiny metal may have a white highlight. The higher the shininess of the material, the bigger the highlight gets. Only the Advanced template has the specular setting.

For all three settings, click the gray box next to that setting to open the Select Color dialog box where you can choose a color. When you use either the Advanced or Advanced Metal template, you can lock the Ambient color to the Diffuse color by clicking the lock between the two. You can also specify that the color be the same as the object color by clicking the By Object check box. The object color is usually the color of the layer where the object resides. The Advanced template also lets you lock the Specular color to the Diffuse color.

Choosing other material properties

The next set of properties includes the overall properties that affect how the material looks and reflects light. These properties vary according to the material type, and so you may not see some of these options. They are the following:

- **Shininess:** This affects the highlight on an object. Higher shininess creates a brighter, but smaller highlight. Lower shininess creates a larger, softer highlight.

- **Opacity:** Sets the opacity (or transparency) of the object. Zero opacity creates a transparent material.

- **Reflection:** Specifies the reflectivity of the material. A material with a reflection of 100 is like a mirror.

- **Refraction Index:** Refraction specifies how light bends when it passes through a translucent material, creating a distorted effect. Glass refracts very little, but a crystal ball refracts quite a bit. If you don't want any refraction, use a 1.0 setting, the refraction of air.

- **Translucency:** This is the amount that light passes through an object. The value is a percentage. A value of 0.0 means that the object is opaque. A value of 100.0 means that the object is as transparent as possible.

- **Self-illumination:** This makes the object appear to have its own light, regardless of the lights that you add. You could represent a glowing log in a fireplace in this way.

When you create materials, try varying these settings until you get the results you want.

Adding textures, opacity, and bump maps

The bottom section of the Materials palette allows you to add three types of 2D image files that map an image onto a 3D model, to add interest to your materials. You choose these from the drop-down lists:

- **Diffuse map:** There are eight kinds of diffuse maps. Texture maps allow you to add any type of pattern to a plain color. For example, you can add a bitmap image of a plaid to a fabric material. The other seven types of maps are *procedural maps,* which allow you to specify a variety of settings to define the map. You can choose from Checker, Marble, Noise, Speckle, Tiles, Waves, and Wood.

NEW FEATURE Most of these maps are new for AutoCAD 2008. They're called *procedural maps,* and they use mathematical algorithms rather than bitmaps to define a material, thus giving you many more options.

- **Reflection map:** This is available if you choose the Advanced or Advanced Metal material type. You have the same options as for diffuse maps. Reflection maps simulate outside objects reflected on the surface of a shiny object, such as a room seen on a shiny, brass doorknob.

- **Opacity map:** Mimics areas of opacity and transparency when a material needs to vary in opacity. Anywhere that the opacity map is applied is transparent, while other areas are opaque. You can choose from the same types listed for diffuse maps.

- **Bump map:** Creates the effect of varying heights, that is, bumps. An image used for a bump map is usually black and white, and meshes with a texture map to simulate changes in height. You have the same types as for diffuse maps.

For each type, choose the Click for [map type] Settings button (where map type is the option you chose from the drop-down list) to display the controls for the settings. Then choose the same button, which is now labeled Up One Level to Parent Map, to return to the main section of the Materials palette. There, you can use the slider to specify the percent of the map that shows. If you drag the slider to the left, you see no effect; drag the slider to the right for the full effect. Click the Select button to choose the image that you want to map onto the material.

Click the Delete Map Information from Material button to delete the image and return to the underlying definition of the material.

You can use JPEG, BMP, TIF, GIF, PNG, TGA, or PCX image files for textures maps. AutoCAD comes with a large selection of map files. To find them, choose Tools ➪ Options and click the Files tab in the Options dialog box. Expand the Texture Maps Search Path item to find the location.

TIP You can use your own photographs for texture maps. For example, you could take a photo of some wood, stone, or pebbles and use it to create a material.

You can adjust these effects in the Material Scaling & Tiling and the Material Offset & Preview sections of the Materials palette, shown in Figure 25.14.

If you choose a texture map, the Material Scaling & Tiling section appears, where you can scale and tile the image. You can choose a unit from the Scale Units drop-down list to scale in real units or leave it unitless. If you choose a unit, you can set the width and height to Tile, Mirror, or None (no tiling or mirroring). Then enter a value in the Width and Height text boxes. Click the lock to make sure the scaling is the same in both directions. Select Fit to Gizmo from the Scale Units drop-down list to avoid scaling the pattern and instead fit it to the object. (Fitting to an object is always unitless.)

NOTE U and V are directions, like X and Y, but they follow the image. For example, if you rotate the object that contains the material, the U and V directions follow along; they are not tied to the User Coordinate System.

In the Material Offset & Preview section, you can change the offset of the pattern (move it) by dragging the preview directly or using the U Offset and V Offset text boxes or arrows. Finally, you can rotate the pattern using the Rotation text box or arrows. You can also right-click in the preview area and drag to rotate the pattern.

FIGURE 25.14

You can adjust the scale, tiling, offset, and rotation of any map that you use for a material.

Adjusting the mapping

The way in which a material, especially one with a texture, maps onto an object may not be suitable for that object's shape. For example, mapping a floral pattern onto a flat surface is different from mapping it onto the wall of a cylindrical shape. If the pattern has a direction, you may want to rotate it.

Use the MATERIALMAP command to fine-tune the mapping of a material. You can easily access the options on the Mapping toolbar or use the Mapping flyout of the Render toolbar. Choose one of the options (Box, Planar, Cylindrical, or Spherical) to specify which type of geometry you want to use. You can then move or rotate the texture, using the Move Grip or Rotate Grip tool.

NOTE You may have materials that you created in previous releases that you would like to use. The new materials use a different system, and so you have to convert them. Use the CONVERT-OLDMATERIALS command for this purpose. You may need to adjust the mapping, using the Adjust Bitmap dialog box, as described in the previous section. In addition, the 3DCONVERSIONMODE system variable converts material and light definitions to the latest release. This system variable allows you to keep your definitions up to date with each new release.

Adjusting lighting effects

The Advanced Lighting Override section of the Materials palette lets you change properties of a material for Realistic and Realistic Metal material types. (For other types, this section doesn't display.) These properties specify the effects of reflected and indirect light. You can set the following properties:

■ **Color Bleed Scale:** Color bleeding is the effect of light on nearby surfaces. For example, a blue carpet may make the white wall appear blue. Drag the slider to increase or decrease color bleeding.

■ **Indirect Bump Scale:** If you added a bump map, you can use this slider to adjust the effect in areas lit by indirect light.

■ **Reflectance Scale:** Reflectance is the amount of diffuse light that a material reflects. Use the slider to adjust the value.

■ **Transmittance Scale:** Transmittance is the amount of light transmitted through a material and is related to transparency. An opaque material has 0% transmittance. Use the slider to adjust this value.

 The drawing used in the following exercise on modifying and creating materials, ab25-03.dwg, is in the Results folder on the DVD.

STEPS: Modifying and Creating Materials

1. If you have ab25-03.dwg open from the previous exercise, use this file. Otherwise, open it from your AutoCAD Bible folder (if you did the exercise) or the Results folder of the DVD.

2. Save the file as ab25-04.dwg in your AutoCAD Bible folder.

3. If the Dashboard isn't displayed, enter **dashboard** ↵ on the command line or in the Dynamic Input tooltip. If you can't see the beige color on the table top, in the Materials control panel of the Dashboard, click the Materials and Textures button in the Materials control panel of the Dashboard, and choose Materials and Textures On from the button's drop-down toolbar. From the Dashboard's Visual Styles control panel, choose Realistic from the Visual Styles drop-down list.

4. Choose Tools ➪ Palettes ➪ Materials to open the Materials palette. Click the maple wood swatch.

 5. In the Maps section of the Materials palette, click the Click for Texture Map Settings button. Click the double-down arrow of the Scaling & Tiling section, and select the Fit to Gizmo option. You can now see the wood grain on the table. From the U Tile and V Tile drop-down lists, choose None. To make the grain smaller, change the values in the U Tile and V Tile text boxes to 0.5. Click the Up One Level to Parent Map button.

 6. We want to create a material for the wedge of cheese on the plate. In the Materials palette, click Create New Material. In the Create New Material dialog box, name the material **Yellow Cheese**. For the description, enter **yellow plastic plus bumps**. Click OK. A new preview swatch appears for Yellow Cheese. From the Swatch Geometry drop-down list, choose the cube.

7. Use the following settings for Yellow Cheese:

   ▪ **Type:** Realistic.

   ▪ **Template:** User-Defined.

   ▪ **Diffuse:** If the By Object check box is checked, uncheck it. Click the color swatch. From the Index Color tab of the Select Color dialog box, choose Index Color 51, a light yellow. Click OK.

   ▪ **Shininess:** Drag the Shininess slider down to about 20. Cheese isn't very shiny.

   ▪ **Bump Map:** In the Maps section, click the Select Image button below the Bump Map check box. From the Textures\Bump folder, choose Finishes.Painting.Paint.bump.jpg. Click Open. Then drag the bump map slider all the way to the right.

> **NOTE**   If the Select Image File dialog box doesn't open to the right folder, you may need to navigate to it. To check the folder, close the dialog box and choose Tools ⇨ Options. On the Files tab, expand the Texture Maps Search Path item to find the location of textures and bump maps.

8. Click the double-down arrow of the Material Scaling & Tiling section. Set the Scale Units to Inches, and the height and width to 0.5. The Width and Height drop-down boxes should be set to Tile.

9. Right-click the Yellow Cheese material swatch and choose Apply Material. At the `Select objects:` prompt, select the wedge on the plate to attach the Yellow Cheese material. Press Enter to end object selection.

> **NOTE**   You may not be able to see the bump map in your drawing. To see it, choose Render from theRender control panel of the Dashboard. By default, the rendering appears in a separate application window.

10. Save your drawing.

Attaching materials

After you import, create, and modify the materials that you need, you can attach them to objects. AutoCAD lets you attach materials by object or layer. In fact, these two options allow you to attach a material to the following:

- An entire object by selecting the object
- Any objects on a specified layer, including layers of objects within a block
- A face on an object (by subselecting the face)

I've already discussed how to attach materials from the Tool Palettes window in the "Attaching a material from the Tool Palettes window" section earlier in this chapter. To attach any material to an object from the Materials palette, follow these steps:

1. Choose Materials from the Render toolbar or the Materials control panel of the Dashboard to open the Materials palette.

2. Choose the material from the swatches.

 3. Click the Apply Material to Objects button.

4. At the `Select objects:` prompt, select the objects. You can use subselection (press Ctrl) to select a face of a solid.

> **TIP**   An easy way to attach a material is to select an object and choose the material you want from the Material property in the Properties palette. You can also select an object and apply a material in the Properties palette.

 To attach a material to all objects on a layer, you use the MATERIALATTACH command, which you can find in the Materials control panel of the Dashboard. The Material Attachment Options dialog box opens, as shown in Figure 25.15.

Drag any material on the left to a layer on the right to attach the material. To detach a material from a layer, click the Detach button (the X).

> **TIP**   Attaching materials by layer can be a very efficient method, but it requires some planning in advance. For example, if you have a block that is a chair, you can create it so that the legs are on one layer and the seat and back are on a different layer; then you can easily attach a wood-like material to the legs and a decorative pattern to the seat and back.

FIGURE 25.15

Use the Material Attachment Options dialog box to attach a material to all objects on a layer.

Using backgrounds

You can add a background to a rendering by saving a view that includes a background. In Chapter 22, I explain how to add a background using the VIEW command. For example, you can place a picture of the sky in the background (see Figure 25.1 in this chapter).

NOTE Versions of AutoCAD prior to 2007 included a scenes feature that allowed you to save views and light settings. Scenes are gone since AutoCAD 2007. Also, landscape objects, which included trees and other objects, are no longer available.

ON the DVD-ROM The files used in the following exercise on attaching materials and adding a background, ab25-b.dwg and bluesky.jpg, are in the Drawings folder on the DVD.

STEPS: Attaching Materials and Adding a Background

1. Open ab25-b.dwg from the DVD. Use Windows Explorer to copy bluesky.jpg from the Drawings folder of the DVD to your AutoCAD Bible folder.

2. Save the file as ab25-05.dwg in your AutoCAD Bible folder. If the Render toolbar is not open, right-click any toolbar and choose Render. This is the same drawing used earlier in the chapter, but all of the materials have been imported and modified, and some materials have been attached to objects. Also, the table and chairs have been separated into appropriate layers.

3. If you're not in the Realistic visual style, display the Dashboard (type **dashboard** ↵) and choose Realistic from the Visual Styles control panel of the Dashboard.

4. Choose Attach By Layer from the Materials control panel of the Dashboard. In the Material Attachment Options dialog box, drag the light wood material from the Material Name list onto the LEGS layer. (To more easily find the layer, click the Layer heading in the right pane to alphabetize the layers.) Then drag the striped fabric material onto the CUSHIONS layer. Click OK.

Foggy Landscapes

Fog is used to give a sense of distance by making objects in the distance less clear than those close up. To add a fog effect, choose Render Environment from the Render toolbar to open the Render Environment dialog box. Choose On from the Enable Fog drop-down list. You set the color (a gray color by default), near and far distances (where the fog starts and ends), and near and far percentages of fog (how much fog there should be at the near and far distances). You can also apply the fog to the background (the Fog Background setting), which turns the entire background the color of the fog. To use fog, you need to set front and back clipping on, using the 3DCLIP command. Move the front clipping plane in front of the nearest object and the back clipping plane behind the farthest object. You then need to render to see the results; you can't see them in the drawing viewport.

5. In the Materials palette, choose GREEN GLASS and click the Apply Material to Objects button. At the Select objects: prompt, select the plate on the table and press Enter to end selection.

6. Choose View ⇨ Named Views. In the View Manager, click New. In the New View dialog box's View Name text box, enter **render with background**. In the Background section, select Image from the drop-down list. The Background dialog box opens.

7. Click the Browse button. In the Select Image File dialog box, you may need to change the Files of Type drop-down list to All Image Files. Select bluesky.jpg and click Open.

8. In the Background dialog box, click Adjust Image. From the Image Position drop-down list, choose Stretch. You can see how the image improves. Click OK three times to return to the View Manager. Click Set Current and click OK to return to your drawing. You should see the image appear through the windows. (If not, you may need to render the drawing.)

9. Save your drawing. Keep it open if you're continuing to the next exercise.

Doing the Final Render

You're finally ready for your final rendering. Preparing to render can be a long process. At this time, you may want to look at some of the more specialized settings for rendering in the Advanced Render Settings palette, shown in Figure 25.16.

To open the Advanced Render Settings palette (the RPREF command), choose Advance Render Settings from the Render toolbar or the expanded Render control panel of the Dashboard. Here I highlight some of the more common settings.

At the top of the Advanced Render Settings palette is the drop-down list of the render presets. Render presets are groups of settings that you can use when you don't want to customize the settings. You can choose from Draft, Low, Medium (the default), High, and Presentation. (You can customize the presets themselves, using the RENDERPRESETS command.) The choice you make depends on your situation — how much you need to see, whether you're doing a draft or final rendering, and the capabilities of your computer system, especially its graphics card and memory.

FIGURE 25.16

FIGURE 25.16

The Advanced Render Settings palette lets you set many rendering options. This figure shows about half of the available settings.

The **Render Context** section contains settings that relate to the rendering as a whole. This section allows you to choose how your model gets rendered. Here are your options:

■ **Save File:** Click the Determines If File Is Written button if you want to save the resulting rendering to a file. Click the same button to cancel saving to a file.

■ **Procedure:** You can render the current view, crop to a window, or render selected objects.

■ **Destination:** You can render to the current viewport or to a separate window.

■ **Output File Name:** If you chose to save a file, click this item, then click the Ellipsis button to navigate to a location, and enter a filename. You can save renderings as BMP, TIF, JPEG, PNG, TGA, or PCX files.

■ **Output Size:** Choose an output size (in pixels) from the drop-down list or choose Specify Output Size to customize your size settings.

■ **Exposure Type:** Choose Automatic or Logarithmic. Automatic exposure is the normal output of previous releases. The Logarithmic setting is useful when you want more control over exposure, but are not using photometric lighting.

- **Physical Scale:** This setting helps to reduce artifacts (imperfections) caused by changes in exposure. The default value is 1500. If you see artifacts, you need to experiment to find a value that works for you; the best value will be different in a drawing with a sun from a drawing with just point lights.

The Materials section has settings relating to materials. You can specify the following:

- **Apply Materials:** Turns materials on and off.
- **Texture Filtering:** Samples textures by area to avoid aliasing, which results in artifacts, such as a jagged or moiré effect.
- **Force 2-Sided:** Renders both sides of faces, even those facing away from the view. You can turn this off to speed up rendering.

The Sampling section offers settings to control sampling, which is the precision with which the rendering deals with each pixel. A lower minimum sampling rate is quicker but less accurate. A 1/4 sampling rate (the default) makes one calculation for every four pixels. The maximum sampling rate applies when the neighboring pixels are different enough (have enough contrast) to require more precise sampling. The default is 1, which is one calculation per pixel. The contrast colors control the contrast values used to determine how much sampling to do, based on the minimum and maximum rates.

The Shadows section has a Lightbulb button that turns shadows on and off. You can turn shadows off to speed up rendering. The Mode determines the order in which shadows are computed — Simple (randomly), Sort (from an object to the light), and Segments (along the light ray). The Sampling Multiplier limits sampling for shadows throughout the drawing. Use this feature to create draft renders. Lower values mean less sampling; higher values produce more accurate results. Values range from 0 to 2.

Shadow Map turns on shadow mapping. When this is off, shadows are ray-traced, which results in sharper and more accurate outlines. Shadow maps allow for soft shadows.

The Ray Tracing section affects how the renderer calculates ray-traced shadows. The Lightbulb button turns ray tracing on and off. The Max Depth setting controls how many reflections and refractions can be calculated. You can also individually set the maximum reflections and refractions that are calculated.

The Indirect Illumination section has three subsections — all relate to subtle light effects in addition to direct lights that you create. These settings control *radiosity,* the simulation of multiple reflections of light as they interact with each other, to create more natural lighting. For example, Global Illumination creates color bleeding, which occurs when the color of one surface affects the color of a nearby surface. Final Gather adds an additional calculation to eliminate dark corners and other artifacts, but adds greatly to rendering time. The Light Properties section has controls that affect lights that you create when you use indirect illumination. You can increase the accuracy and brightness of lights with these settings, but doing so increases rendering time.

The Diagnostic section helps troubleshoot the rendering results. You can turn on the display of a grid to help understand how the renderer is placing an object. You may have noticed that when you render, the rendering appears tile by tile. You can change the size of this tile, the order of the tiling, and the maximum memory used during the rendering process.

To render, choose Render from the Render toolbar or the Render control panel of the Dashboard. The model is rendered according to the settings in the Advanced Render Settings palette.

NEW FEATURE You can now use the RENDER command on the command line by typing -render ↵. You can choose a render quality and output location.

ON the DVD-ROM The drawing used in the following exercise on creating a final rendering, ab25-05.dwg, is in the Results folder on the DVD.

STEPS: Creating a Final Rendering

1. If you have ab25-05.dwg open, use this file. Otherwise, open it from your AutoCAD Bible folder if you did the previous exercise, or from the Results folder of the DVD.

2. Save the file as ab25-06.dwg in your AutoCAD Bible folder.

3. Choose Light List from the Render toolbar or the Lights control panel of the Dashboard. In the Lights in Model palette, choose P1. Display the Properties palette (Ctrl+1), change the intensity to 2, and press Enter. This is the type of adjustment you often make when doing the final rendering.

4. Choose Advanced Render Settings from the Render toolbar or the Render control panel of the Dashboard. In the Advanced Render Settings palette, change the Shadow Map setting to On. This results in softer shadows. (You can try it both ways to see the difference.)

5. Choose Render from the Render toolbar or the Render control panel of the Dashboard.

6. The Rendering window should open. Wait until AutoCAD finishes the rendering. Look at those shadows! Can you see the orange in the transparent green bowl? Note the sky image outside the window.

7. The rendering should look like Figure 25.17, only a lot better because you see it in color on your screen. Save your drawing.

FIGURE 25.17

The final rendering with shadows, transparent objects, and a background.

Remember that rendering is a trial-and-error process. Don't expect to get it right the first time. You can probably see several areas that require improvement. At this point, you would go back and tweak the lights, materials, and so on until you were satisfied.

ON the DVD-ROM **AccuRender is a rendering program that offers additional rendering capabilities. Look for it in** Software\Chapter 25\AccuRender.

Statistics

When you render to the render window, the right pane lists a number of statistics relating to your rendering. You can use these statistics to troubleshoot or compare results among renderings. The bottom pane shows your rendering history.

Saving rendered images

You can save your rendered images and redisplay them at another time. You can also use saved rendered images in other applications and print them from those applications. Here are the steps to saving a rendering to an image file:

1. Render the image.
   - After rendering to a viewport, choose Tools ➪ Display Image ➪ Save.
   - After rendering to a render window, choose File ➪ Save from that window's menu.
2. In the Render Output File dialog box, choose a file type, enter a file name, and click Save. In the Render Output File dialog box, choose a file type from the File of Type drop-down list. Choose a location and enter a name for the file.
3. Depending on the image type that you choose, you'll see a dialog box offering options such as the number of colors and the quality. Choose the options you want and click OK to save the image.

You can import these saved rendered images back into your drawing. Figure 25.18 shows three floating viewports. One of the views shows the rendered image.

CROSS-REF See Chapter 27 for detailed instructions on importing images. You can plot rendered viewports, as I explain in Chapter 17.

FIGURE 25.18

You can include your rendered images in your drawings.

Summary

In this chapter, I covered the process of rendering. You read about the following:

- Creating lights
- Importing and creating materials
- Attaching materials
- Using backgrounds
- Rendering a drawing

This chapter ends Part IV, "Drawing in Three Dimensions." Part V, "Organizing and Managing Drawings," explains how to manage drawings, work with other applications and file types, and use AutoCAD on the Internet.

Part V

Organizing and Managing Drawings

Part V is all about how to manage drawings. In Chapter 26, I discuss ways to keep control of your drawings, including features such as the DesignCenter, tool palettes, and the Communication Center. I also explain how to set and maintain standards, keep track of your drawings, handle errors and crashes, and work with prior AutoCAD releases. Finally, I thoroughly cover how to organize your drawings into sheet sets.

Chapter 27 explains how to interface with other applications and file formats, including raster (bitmap) images. Finally, Chapter 28 covers placing your drawings on the Internet, using hyperlinks, and the DWF file format.

Chapter 26

Keeping Control of Your Drawings

When you create a drawing, you not only create objects, but you also create a complex structure to support those objects. You create named blocks, layers, layouts, text styles, dimension styles, and linetypes to help define those objects. And you spend a lot of time creating them! All of these named drawing components can be reused and organized for greater efficiency, using the DesignCenter.

Tool palettes are a multifaceted solution that enables you to execute commands, as well as to insert hatches and blocks. You can also insert tables, xrefs, images, gradients, and more.

Having standards for named drawing components, such as layers and text styles, is important for consistency and readability. AutoCAD offers a comprehensive system for maintaining CAD standards. Security is also important, and AutoCAD offers excellent features to help you with this. AutoCAD LT does not contain all of these features.

Sheet sets enable you to manage sets of drawings. You can automate the placement of viewports, as well as view and call out labels. You can plot or publish sheet sets as one group. AutoCAD LT does not offer the sheet-set feature.

You also need to keep track of your drawings and make sure that they're accessible. Archiving and repair procedures are important in any CAD environment. This chapter covers all of these topics to help you keep control of your drawings and their content.

Accessing Drawing Components with the DesignCenter

I mention the DesignCenter many times in this book — for example, in Chapter 11 on layers and Chapter 18 on blocks. In this chapter I cover the DesignCenter in detail. You can use the DesignCenter to easily drag named drawing components from one drawing to another. You can even drag raster images directly into your drawing. You can access this *drawing content* from drawings on your hard drive, on a network drive, or over the Internet. You never need to re-create them again.

You can do the following with the DesignCenter:

- Browse and insert named drawing components, including blocks (and dynamic blocks), xrefs, layers, text styles, table styles, dimension styles, linetypes, and layouts. You can also access custom objects that are created by third-party applications.
- Create shortcuts to drawings and locations that you use most often.
- Search for drawings and named drawing components.
- Open drawings by dragging them into the drawing area.
- Create tools for your tool palettes.
- View and insert raster image files by dragging them into the drawing area.

Navigating with the DesignCenter

 To open the DesignCenter, choose DesignCenter from the Standard (or Standard Annotation) toolbar, or choose Tools ⇨ Palettes ⇨ DesignCenter. As a shortcut, press Ctrl+2. The DesignCenter appears as shown in Figure 26.1. Four tabs provide access to folders, open drawings, history, and DC Online, where you can find content provided by Autodesk, manufacturers, and other users.

FIGURE 26.1

The DesignCenter with the Folders tab displayed.

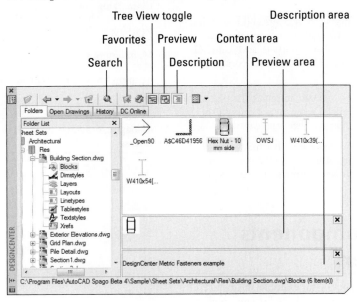

The Folders tab displays a tree view of any location—your hard drive, network, or the Internet—that you can access. This tree view is very similar to that of Windows Explorer. Click the plus sign next to a drive or folder to display its contents. Use the vertical scroll bar to display any location.

A selected drawing displays its named components in the content area on the right side of the palette. (Use the Views drop-down list to choose the type of display that you want.) You can also click the plus sign next to a drawing to display these components in the tree view. Then click a component type, such as blocks, to see a list of the blocks in the drawing, as shown in Figure 26.1. Click Preview on the DesignCenter toolbar to see a preview in the preview pane of blocks, drawings, and raster images. Click Description to display a description, if one is saved.

 After you narrow your search, you may want to click Tree View Toggle to toggle off the tree view, thus hiding the navigation pane. By default, the navigation pane displays your desktop, including the files and folders on your hard drive and network. To narrow your search, you can click two other tabs from the DesignCenter:

■ The Open Drawings tab displays currently open drawings.

■ The History tab displays the most recently opened drawings.

Finding named components and drawings

What do you do if you don't know the location of the drawing that you want? Suppose you know the name of the layer but not the name of the drawing that contains that layer. The DesignCenter includes a Search feature to help you.

 Choose Search from the DesignCenter toolbar to open the Search window, shown in Figure 26.2. (You can also right-click in the Content area and choose Search.)

FIGURE 26.2

Use the Search window to locate drawings and drawing components.

Here's how to use the Search window:

- Click the Look For drop-down list to choose what you're looking for. You can look for blocks, dimension styles, drawings, drawings and blocks, hatch pattern files, hatch patterns, layers, layouts, linetypes, table styles, text styles, and xrefs.

- Click the In drop-down list to specify the drive that you want to search. By default, the Search subfolders check box is checked so that the search looks in all folders and subfolders within the drive.

- Use the tabbed area to specify the name of the components that you want. The tab's name and content change, depending on what you chose in the Look For drop-down list. For example, if you chose Layers, the tab is called Layers and asks you for the name of the layer. If you're looking for drawings, you have three tabs to work with:

  - The **Drawings** tab enables you to look for a drawing by filename (the default), title, subject, author, or keywords. Choose one of these options in the In the Field(s) drop-down list. Then type the text that you want to look for in the Search for the Word(s) text box. You can use the wildcards * (to substitute for any number of characters), and ? (to substitute for any one character). Specifying a drawing's title, subject, and keywords is discussed later in this chapter.

  - The **Date Modified** tab enables you to search by the last date that the file was saved or modified. You can specify a range of dates, or look in the last x days or months.

  - The **Advanced** tab enables you to search for text in drawing descriptions, block names, attribute tags, and attribute values. You can also search here by drawing size.

- When you've created your specifications, click Search Now.

CROSS-REF See Chapter 18 for information on creating block descriptions when you create a block. The main reason for creating a block description is to display it in the DesignCenter and use it in a search on the Advanced tab, as just described.

For more information on searching for drawings, see the section "Finding drawings" later in this chapter.

Using the Favorites folder

The Favorites folder is a Windows convention that helps you to find files that you use often. This folder contains shortcuts to actual files. The files remain in their original locations. You'll find an Autodesk subfolder within the Favorites folder, where you can store shortcuts to drawings and other files that you use often. You can then easily open the Favorites folder and find these files. Favorites is one possible place to keep drawings that contain block libraries.

To add a shortcut to Favorites, right-click the drawing (or other file) in the DesignCenter and choose Add to Favorites.

CAUTION If you right-click in the Content pane and choose Add to Favorites, the DesignCenter adds a shortcut to the entire content of the folder. This is great for adding all of the items in a folder at once, but if you do it inadvertently, you could end up with more files than you want in Favorites. To add one item, remember to select it first.

 To access the drawings in Favorites, click Favorites on the DesignCenter toolbar. You can also right-click the content pane and choose Favorites. The Favorites folder appears in the content pane.

To move, copy, or delete shortcuts from Favorites, right-click the content pane and choose Organize Favorites.

Accessing named drawing components

As soon as you have the item that you need in the Content area, you need to insert it into your drawing. If you used the Search window to locate a file, then you can also insert directly from the results that you find. You can either drag the item onto the drawing area or right-click it and choose an option. Sometimes these two methods provide slightly different results. In this section, I explain how to insert drawing components into your drawing.

Inserting drawings

You can insert an entire drawing into your drawing. Choose the drawing's folder in the navigation pane so that the drawing appears in the content area. Drag the drawing's icon onto the drawing area. The command line prompts you for an insertion point, scale, and rotation angle, using the -INSERT command (the command-line version of the INSERT command).

If you right-click the drawing, you can choose to insert the drawing as a block, or attach it as an xref.

Opening drawings

You can open a drawing using the DesignCenter. Display the drawing in the content pane, right-click it, and choose Open in Application Window. The drawing opens, keeping your current drawing open as well.

Inserting blocks

In Chapter 5, I explain that you can use the Units dialog box (choose Format ➪ Units) to set a unit, such as inches, for automatically scaling drawings when they're inserted from the DesignCenter.

You can insert blocks in two ways:

- If you drag the block's icon onto the drawing area, the drawing uses *Autoscaling,* which compares the current drawing's units with those of the block, and scales the block appropriately, using the value set in the Units dialog box. The block takes on default scale and rotation.

- If you double-click the block's icon or right-click it and choose Insert as Block, the Insert dialog box opens, where you can specify the insertion point, scale, and rotation.

Inserting raster images

A raster image is a bitmap graphic file. You can insert raster images directly into your drawing (in AutoCAD only).

CROSS-REF See Chapter 27 for more information on raster images, including determining which type of files you can import, attaching images, clipping images, and controlling how they're displayed.

To attach a raster image, drag its icon onto the drawing area. The command line prompts you for an insertion point, scale, and rotation angle.

TIP Knowing the appropriate scale of an image before inserting it is often difficult. When you move the cursor at the Specify scale factor or [Unit] <1>: prompt, you can see a bounding box that will help you visualize the resulting size of the image.

Attaching an xref

To attach or overlay an xref, right-click its icon and choose Attach as Xref to open the External Reference dialog box. Choose either Attachment or Overlay in the Reference Type section. Specify an insertion point, scale, and rotation (or choose to specify them on-screen), and click OK.

If you drag the xref onto the drawing area, you see prompts on the command line that are similar to those of the INSERT command.

Inserting layers and styles

To insert a layer, layout, linetype, text style, table style, or dimension style into a drawing, drag its icon onto the drawing area. Of course, these items don't appear in your drawing area, but they're added to the drawing's database.

You can drag multiple items at one time. To select a contiguous group, click the first item, press and hold Shift, and click the last item. To select individual multiple items, click the first item, press and hold Ctrl, and click any other item that you want to insert. You can also double-click an item to insert it.

CAUTION The insertion process does not check for duplicate layer names. If you try to insert a layer with the same name as a layer in your current drawing, you see a message: Layer(s) added. Duplicate definitions will be ignored. You should check for duplicate layer names before trying to insert layers from the DesignCenter.

Inserting content from DC Online

The DC Online tab provides access to online resources, including standard parts and manufacturers' information. Figure 26.3 shows some of the DC Online content. To insert any content, select it and drag it into your drawing. Follow the prompts for insertion point, scale, and rotation.

FIGURE 26.3

The DC Online tab of the DesignCenter offers a large selection of content that you can drag into your drawing.

Controlling the DesignCenter display

The DesignCenter provides several controls that help you manage its display.

 A great feature of the DesignCenter is the preview pane. Click Preview and select the item in the content pane. You may or may not see a preview of a block. (A preview icon is created automatically when you use the Block Definition dialog box to create a block.) Usually, you'll see a preview of drawings and raster images. No previews exist for layers, linetypes, text styles, and so on.

 If you have old blocks that don't have preview icons, use the BLOCKICON command and press Enter at the first prompt to automatically create preview icons of all the blocks in a drawing.

 If you saved a description with a block, select the block in the content pane and click Description on the DesignCenter toolbar to see the description.

 To set the view, choose Views from the DesignCenter toolbar. The drop-down arrow lets you choose from four types of displays: large icons, small icons, list, and details.

If you make changes in the structure of a folder while the DesignCenter is open — for example, by deleting a drawing using Windows Explorer — right-click the navigation or content pane and choose Refresh. The DesignCenter re-reads the data and refreshes the list.

 To dock the DesignCenter, right-click the title bar and choose Allow Docking. Then choose Anchor Left or Anchor Right to dock it to the left or right of your drawing window. To collapse the DesignCenter down to its title bar when you're not using it, right-click the title bar and choose Auto-Hide; whenever you move the mouse cursor off the DesignCenter, it collapses. Just move the cursor back onto the title bar to expand it again. You can anchor the DesignCenter at the same side as other palettes; its title bar becomes shorter to fit. When you expand it, it rolls down to its full length. To avoid unwanted docking, either uncheck Allow Docking on its title bar or press Ctrl as you drag. These instructions apply to all palettes in AutoCAD and AutoCAD LT.

ON the DVD-ROM The drawings used in the following exercise on using the DesignCenter, `ab26-a.dwg` and `ab26-b.dwg`, are in the `Drawings` folder on the DVD.

STEPS: Using the DesignCenter

1. Open `ab26-a.dwg` from the DVD.

2. Save the file as `ab26-01.dwg` in your `AutoCAD Bible` folder. This drawing needs an updated set of layers and a title block. It is shown in Figure 26.4.

3. Choose Tools ➪ Palettes ➪ DesignCenter. If the navigation pane is not displayed, click the Folders tab and then click Tree View Toggle on the DesignCenter toolbar.

4. In the navigation pane, locate `ab26-b.dwg` on the DVD. Click its plus sign.

5. Choose Blocks. The `ansi_d` block appears in the content pane. Double-click `ansi_d`. Uncheck all Specify Onscreen check boxes and click OK.

6. Do a Zoom Extents.

7. In the navigation pane, click Layers for `ab26-b.dwg`.

8. In the content pane, click the first layer, press and hold Shift, and click the last layer to select all of the layers. Drag them onto the drawing area to import the layers.

9. Save your drawing.

FIGURE 26.4

This drawing needs updated layers and a title block.

Thanks to Vladimir Sevastyanov of Ukraine for this drawing of a gyrating swivel that feeds oil to an uncoiling machine used in the cold rolling of metal.

Accessing Drawing Content with Tool Palettes

The Tool Palettes window is a tabbed palette that can contain drawings, blocks, hatches, images, gradients (AutoCAD only), drawing objects, xrefs, tables, and commands. By default, the Tool Palettes window contains over three dozen tabs in AutoCAD and ten tabs in AutoCAD LT with sample content and commands. Each tab is considered a separate tool palette within the main Tool Palettes window. Figure 26.5 shows the default Tool Palettes window with the Draw tab on top. To open the Tool Palettes window, choose Tool Palettes Window on the Standard (or Standard Annotation) toolbar, choose Tools ➪ Palettes ➪ Tool Palettes, or press Ctrl+3.

The tool palettes are meant to be customized with your own content. You can easily create new tabs with your own blocks and other types of content, objects, or commands. After you create the tab, you can drag the items into your drawing. A *tool* is any item on a tool palette, and is represented by an icon.

NOTE Because there are so many tabs, several of the tabs overlap together at the bottom so that you can't see their titles. When you click these tabs, a menu pops up, listing the names of all of the tabs. Click the tab you want from the menu to display that tab. Materials used for rendering are on several palettes; other palettes contain visual style, light, and camera tools.

Creating a new tool palette

When you create a new tool palette, you add a tab to the Tool Palettes window. To create an empty tool palette, right-click in the Tool Palettes window and choose New Palette. A label appears so that you can name the tool palette. Type the name and press Enter. When you have a new tool palette, you're ready to add tools to the palette, as I explain in the following sections.

FIGURE 26.5

The standard Tool Palettes window has many tabs, each with a different category of commands or insertable content.

CROSS-REF You can also create a new, empty tool palette by using the Customize dialog box. See the "Customizing Tool Palettes" section in Chapter 29 for details.

You can add descriptive text and separator bars to any tool palette. For example, you can include instructions that explain a tool and organize commands into groups using separator bars. To add text or separators, right-click any tool palette and choose Add Text or Add Separator from the shortcut menu.

Adding content tools

The easiest way to create a new tool palette is from the DesignCenter, discussed in the previous section of this chapter. When you use this method, you simultaneously create not only the tool palette but also its contents. To create a new tool palette, follow these steps:

1. Open the DesignCenter.
2. In the tree view or content area, navigate to a folder, drawing file, block icon, graphic image file, or hatch icon.
3. Right-click the item and choose Create Tool Palette.
   - If you select a folder or drawing, choose Create Tool Palette of Blocks.
   - If you select a hatch file (*.pat), choose Create Tool Palette of Hatch Patterns.

After a few seconds, the new tool palette tab displays, showing each drawing, block, or hatch on the tab:

- If you chose a folder, the tab includes all drawing files in the folder.
- If you chose a drawing file, the tab includes all blocks in the drawing.
- If you chose a block icon, the tab includes the block.
- If you chose a hatch pattern file, the tab includes all hatch patterns in the `.pat` file. (See Chapter 31 for more information about creating hatch patterns in `.pat` files.)
- If you chose a hatch icon, the tab includes the hatch pattern.

Another way to add content tools is to drag content directly from an open drawing. This method is the only way to add gradients to a tool palette, but it works with any other type of content as well. Just select the object, then click and drag it onto the tool palette. The tool palette assigns a name, but you can change it to anything you want. Right-click the tool and choose Rename. Type the new name and press Enter.

NEW FEATURE   You can drag content over a tab that is not on top; that tab then becomes active so that you can add the content to it.

When you drag content from your drawing, you're creating a tool *by example*. The properties of the tool match those of the object in your drawing. For example, if you drag a hatch on layer `object` onto a tool and then use that tool to hatch a closed object in your drawing, you create a hatch on layer `object`.

Adding command tools

You can add commands to tool palettes. You choose your method depending on the amount of customization that you want and how you want to organize your commands. You can add commands by dragging objects from a drawing, buttons from a toolbar, or commands from the Commands List pane in the Customize User Interface editor.

Dragging objects from your drawing

You can drag drawing objects, such as circles, text, and so on onto a tool palette. AutoCAD creates a command tool that draws an object with the same properties as the original object. For example, if you regularly need to enter text on the Annotation layer using the Annotation text style, select some existing text with those properties, and drag it onto a tool palette. The tool is now called simply MText. Right-click, choose Rename, and enter Annotation or another meaningful name. This command tool contains the properties of the object that you used.

NOTE   When you click the selected object to start dragging it, don't click it on the grip handles. When you click, after a moment you'll see the drag-and-drop arrow cursor, and then you can drag the object to the tool palette. To drag a table, you must drag-and-drop with the *right* mouse button; otherwise, you simply select one of the table cells.

When you create certain types of command tools, the tool palette recognizes the command as one of a group of commands, and creates an entire group, or *flyout*, of command tools that all use the same properties as the original. This technique works with dimensions and common drawing geometry objects, such as lines and circles. Figure 26.6 shows an example of such a flyout on a custom tool palette. Note, however, that the tool palettes include these flyouts by default.

FIGURE 26.6

Creating one dimension tool automatically creates a flyout of all of the dimension tools.

Dragging buttons from a toolbar

You can drag buttons from a toolbar onto a tool palette. These can be the standard toolbar buttons or custom buttons that you've created. To transfer toolbar buttons to a tool palette, follow these steps:

1. Display the toolbar that you want to use.

2. Choose Tools ➪ Customize ➪ Tool Palettes or right-click in the Tool Palettes window and choose Customize Palettes. The Customize dialog box opens.

3. One by one, drag the buttons that you want onto the tool palette. (The Customize dialog box doesn't seem to have any function here, but you can't drag buttons off of a toolbar without it.)

> **TIP** You can add commands from the Command List pane of the Customize User Interface dialog box. Right-click the Tool Palettes window and choose Customize Commands. Then drag any command from the dialog box to any Tool Palette tab.

Copying a tool

You can copy an existing tool to create a new tool, whether a content tool or a command tool. You can then change the tool properties. You can use this technique to create related, but slightly different, tools. For example, you could include a hatch on two different layers. You could also include variations of a dynamic block.

To copy a tool, right-click the tool and choose Copy from the shortcut menu. Then right-click again and choose Paste. The next section explains how to change tool properties.

Setting tool properties

Each tool on a tool palette has properties that you can set. The available properties vary slightly, depending on the type of tool. The properties specify how that tool is inserted into a drawing. Tools inherit their properties from the object that you dragged onto the tool palette. However, you can change the properties. To set the properties of a tool, right-click it and choose Properties to open the Tool Properties dialog box. Figure 26.7 shows the Tool Properties dialog box for a hatch tool.

FIGURE 26.7

The Tool Properties dialog box for a hatch pattern.

The middle section of the dialog box contains Insert, Attach, or Pattern properties (depending on the type of content), and the bottom of the dialog box displays General properties.

To specify any property, click the right column for that property. Either type a new value or choose from the drop-down list. After you're done, click OK to close the Tool Properties dialog box.

 You can select multiple tools and change their common properties at one time. To select multiple tools, press Ctrl and click the tools that you want to change.

Adjusting the scale of inserted content

The tools that you create by dragging content from a drawing take their properties from that object, and so they may contain an inherent scale. For example, your hatches, blocks, and xrefs have a certain size. If you need to adjust a scale, you can do so, based on one of the following:

- **Your overall dimension scale:** You set the dimension scale on the Fit tab of the Modify Dimension Style dialog box. The value is stored in the DIMSCALE system variable.
- **Your plot scale:** You set the plot scale in the Plot dialog box.

To set the scale of a hatch, block, or xref tool, right-click the tool and choose Properties. Click the Auxiliary Scale item. Then click the down arrow that appears at the right, and choose either Dimscale or Plot Scale. Click OK. From now on, the block or xref comes into your drawing at the scale that you've set in your drawing.

Moving, deleting, and renaming tools and tool palettes

You can change the order of both tool palettes (tabs) in the Tool Palettes window and of tools on a palette.

- To move a tool on a palette, drag the tool. A horizontal cursor appears to show you where the tool will go.
- To move a palette, right-click the tab itself and choose Move Up or Move Down.

You can also move or copy a tool (drawing, block, or hatch) from one tool palette to another. Follow these steps:

1. Display the tool palette (tab) that contains the item that you want to move.
2. Right-click the item and choose Cut (to move it) or Copy (to copy it).
3. Display the tool palette (tab) where you want to place the item.
4. Right-click any blank area on the tab and choose Paste.

You can use this method to consolidate tabs or reorganize the tools on a tab.

To delete a tool palette, right-click the palette and choose Delete Palette. A warning message is displayed, explaining that you cannot recover the deleted tool palette unless you export it to a file. To delete a tool on a tool palette, right-click the tool and choose Delete. Here, too, you need to confirm the deletion when a warning message appears.

To export a tool palette, you save it to a file. You can then share tool palettes with others. You import and export tool palettes on the Tool Palettes tab in the Customize dialog box. See "Customizing Tool Palettes" in Chapter 29 for details.

To rename a tool palette, right-click the palette and choose Rename Palette. To rename a tool, right-click the tool and choose Rename. In both situations, type a new name and press Enter.

Updating tools

If the source of a tool changes, its icon does not automatically change to match. In this situation, the icon will not accurately represent its tool. To update an icon, use one of the following methods:

- Right-click the tool and choose Properties. Click the Source File (or Pattern Name) item, then use the Ellipsis button to choose any other file, block, or hatch pattern, and then immediately choose the correct item again. This technique updates the icon for the tool.
- Delete the tool and reinsert it.

If you change a block or dynamic block, you can update its image. Right-click the image and choose Update Tool Image from the shortcut menu.

NEW FEATURE You can specify any image for a tool. Perhaps you want to create your own image. Most images are 32 pixels x 32 pixels. To specify an image, right-click the tool and choose Specify Image. Choose the image you want, and click Open. By default, tool palette images are stored in the `ToolPalette\Palette\Images` folder. To find the location of the `ToolPalette` folder, use the OPTIONS command to open the Options dialog box. On the Files tab, expand the Tool Palettes File Locations item.

If you move the source file for a tool, you need to update the tool with the new location:

1. Right-click the tool and choose Properties.
2. In the Tool Properties dialog box, use the Ellipsis button to choose the file again.
3. Click OK.

Setting tool palette options

To work most comfortably with the Tool Palettes window, you can adjust its display options. Right-click any empty area on the tool palette (except the tab itself) and choose from the following options:

- **Allow Docking:** Enables you to dock the tool palette on the left or right side of the drawing area.
- **Anchor Left** or **Anchor Right:** Docks the tool palette on the left or right.
- **Auto-Hide:** Collapses the tool palette to just its title bar when the mouse cursor is off the Tool Palettes window. Pass the mouse cursor back over the title bar to expand the tool palette again. You can store the collapsed tool palette outside the application window (if it isn't fully maximized).
- **Transparency:** Opens the Transparency dialog box. When the tool palette is transparent, you can see the drawing through it. You can specify the amount of transparency or turn it off. Then click OK.

NOTE Transparency is available only when hardware acceleration is off (which it is by default). Hardware acceleration is governed by your computer's video card and helps to speed up the display. If you want to use the transparency feature, you can use software acceleration instead (and see if it affects your display speed). Choose Tools ⇨ Options and click the System tab. In the 3D Performance section, click Performance Settings. In the Hardware and Performance Tuning section, click Manual Tune. In the Hardware Settings section, uncheck the Enable Hardware Acceleration check box. Click OK three times to close all of the dialog boxes. Transparency is available only when the palette is not docked. This feature is not available for AutoCAD LT.

- **View Options:** Opens the View Options dialog box. You can change the size and layout of the tool icons on a tool palette. Use the slider to change the size of the icons. Choose from the following display styles:
  - **Icon only:** You see the icon displaying the drawing, block, or hatch, but no text.
  - **Icon with text:** Text is displayed beneath each icon, and the icons are arranged in columns. This option displays much more on a tab than the list view.
  - **List view:** You see one column of icons, with the text to the right of each icon.
- You can choose to apply the changes to the current tool palette or to all tool palettes.

Click OK when you're done.

Organizing tool palettes

You may have one set of tool palettes for architectural work and another for mechanical work. For whatever reason, you may want to display one set of tool palettes at one time and another set at another time. For this purpose, you organize tool palettes into groups. I explain how to create these groups in Chapter 29.

To display the various groups, right-click the title bar of the tool palette and choose the group that you want. Using groups helps to avoid clicking through too many tool palettes. After all, the point is instant access. However, you can always display all of the palettes by right-clicking and choosing All Palettes.

Using a tool palette

Inserting a tool from a tool palette is as simple as dragging the tool onto the drawing area. The tool is inserted using the properties specified in the Tool Properties dialog box (discussed previously in this section).

Tools know how to behave. Drag a gradient or hatch into an enclosed area and it automatically fills the area. Drag an xref onto a drawing and you get a prompt, at the command line, for the insertion point. Tools automatically use their properties so that you get a circle on its proper layer or a hatch with the proper scale.

If you want the flexibility to insert a block or hatch with more than one setting, you can insert another copy of the item onto a tool palette. For example, you can place two copies of a hatch pattern on a tool palette and set their properties to different spacing. You would then rename the tools to make the differences clear (for example, lightning1 and lightning 2). You can also copy a tool and then modify it, as I explain in the section "Copying a tool" earlier in this chapter.

NEW FEATURE You can use the new TPNAVIGATE command on the command line to display a tool palette or group, if you know its name. This command is probably designed for programming purposes.

ON the DVD-ROM The drawings used in the following exercise on creating and using a tool palette, ab26-c.dwg and ab26-d.dwg, are in the Drawings folder on the DVD.

STEPS: Creating and Using a Tool Palette

1. Open ab26-c.dwg from the DVD.
2. Save the file as ab26-02.dwg in your AutoCAD Bible folder. This drawing, shown in Figure 26.8, needs some blocks and a hatch pattern inserted. You'll also add a dimension.

FIGURE 26.8

This back porch needs some columns (which are blocks), some hatching, and a dimension.

3. Choose Tools ⇨ Palettes ⇨ Tool Palettes.
4. Choose Tools ⇨ Palettes ⇨ DesignCenter. In the DesignCenter's Folder List, navigate to the Drawings folder of your DVD and click the plus sign to the left of ab26-d.dwg. Click the Blocks item to display the two blocks (post and post-structural) in the content area on the right side of the DesignCenter.
5. Right-click any empty area of the tool palette, and choose New Palette. A label appears. Type **2d arch** and press Enter. You now have a new tool palette named 2d arch.

903

6. From the content area of the DesignCenter, drag each of the blocks to the new tool palette. An icon appears on the tool palette for each block.

7. In the Folder List of the DesignCenter, navigate to `acad.pat` or `acadlt.pat`, which contains hatch patterns. Click `acad.pat` or `acadlt.pat` to display the hatch patterns in the content area.

8. Drag User Defined, one of the hatch patterns, to the tool palette. (This hatch pattern is equivalent to choosing User Defined as the Hatch Type in the Hatch and Gradient dialog box. See the section "Creating Hatches" in Chapter 16 for details.) The tool palette now has three items on it. Close or Auto-Hide the DesignCenter.

9. Right-click the User-defined hatch icon and choose Properties to open the Tool Properties dialog box. You want to specify settings so that this hatch pattern will look like scored concrete for the porch floor.

10. In the Tool Properties dialog box, make the following changes and then click OK:
    - For the Angle, type **45**.
    - For the Spacing, type **2'** (or **24**).
    - Click the Double item at the bottom of the Pattern section and then click the arrow at the right side of the row. Choose Yes from the drop-down list.
    - Click the Layer item in the General section and choose FLOOR from the drop-down list. (You may have to drag the bottom edge of the dialog box down to see the layer item.)

11. Right-click the hatch tool and choose Rename. Type **porch tile** and press Enter.

12. Drag the User Defined hatch icon to ❶ in Figure 26.8. Then do the same for ❷ and ❸. These areas are hatched, as shown in Figure 26.9.

13. Choose the Command Tool Samples tab and click the small arrow to the right on the Linear Dimension tool to see the flyout. (If you don't see the Command Tool Samples tab, click the overlapping tabs at the bottom of the palette window and choose Command Tool Samples from the list of tabs.) To place a linear dimension, click the main linear dimension icon. Follow the prompts:

```
Specify first extension line origin or <select object>: Pick the
    upper-left corner of the porch.
Specify second extension line origin: Pick the upper-right corner of
    the porch.
Specify dimension line location or
    [Mtext/Text/Angle/Horizontal/Vertical/Rotated]: Pick any location
    for the dimension line above the steps.
```

14. Choose Zoom Window from the Zoom flyout on the Standard toolbar (or choose View ⇨ Zoom ⇨ Window), and zoom into the central area of the drawing so that you can still see the double doors at the bottom and the steps at the top.

15. Switch back to the `2d arch` tab and click the Post icon. At the `Specify insertion point:` prompt, pick the intersection at ❹ in Figure 26.8. Click the Post-Structural icon. At the prompt, pick the upper-right corner of the post block, as shown in Figure 26.9.

16. Click the Post icon. At the prompt, pick **5** in Figure 26.8. Use the same technique to place the Post-Structural icon at the upper-right corner of the post block. (The posts would then need to be spaced and mirrored to the other side of the porch, but these tasks are not necessary for this exercise.)

17. Right-click the tool palette's title bar. If Allow Docking is checked, click Allow Docking to uncheck this item. If Auto-Hide is not checked, click Auto-Hide to enable this feature. Move the mouse off the tool palette. It collapses to its title bar. Move the tool palette to the right side of your screen.

18. If you're working on someone else's computer, you should delete the tool palette. Move the cursor over the palette to display it. Right-click any blank area and choose Delete Palette. Click OK to confirm the deletion.

19. Save your drawing. It should look like Figure 26.9.

FIGURE 26.9

The drawing now has hatches and blocks inserted from the tool palette. It also has a new dimension.

Setting Standards for Drawings

One person rarely has complete control over a drawing. You may xref in other drawings, or others may xref in your drawings. Several people may work on one drawing. You may send a drawing to a client who may work on it as well. More and more, working on a drawing is becoming a collaborative effort — and it can get out of control.

One way to maintain control is to set standards for drawings, and to issue those standards so that everyone involved has access to them. If you don't have agreed-upon standards, you not only waste time changing layers, text styles, and so on, but your drawings become very complicated. You should set standards for the following:

- Drawing names and property summaries
- Blocks, including names, layers, and insertion points
- Layers, including uses, names, colors, linetypes, and lineweights
- Text styles, including uses, names, and properties
- Table styles

- Dimension styles and tolerances, if any
- Multileader styles
- Multiline styles
- Units settings
- Plot styles
- Layouts

In some cases, your standards are set by outside conventions. For example, the American Institute of Architects (AIA) and the Construction Standards Institute (CSI) publish layering standards for members.

Using the CAD Standards tools

The CAD Standards tools facilitate the process of checking drawings against standards. You can check the following in a drawing:

- Layers
- Text styles
- Linetypes
- Dimension styles

AUTOCAD ONLY   The CAD Standards feature is not available in AutoCAD LT.

AutoCAD checks for both names, such as layer names, and properties, such as layer color and linetype.

Here's the general procedure for setting and maintaining standards with the CAD manager's tools:

1. Create a standards file (*.dws).
2. Associate the standards file with a drawing or template.
3. Test the drawing against its standards file.

You can test drawings against a standards file one by one (interactively) or as a group (batch auditing).

Creating a standards file

You use a standards file to set standards for drawings. A standards file has a file name extension of .dws. Unlike many of the support files used in AutoCAD, a standards file is not a text file; rather, it is similar to a drawing file. You create a standards file by creating a drawing that contains the standards — layers, linetypes, text styles, and dimension styles — that you want.

To create a standards file from scratch, follow these steps:

1. Choose File ➪ New.
2. Choose a template, or click the Open button's down arrow and choose one of the Open with No Template options.
3. Create the layers, linetypes, dimension styles, and text styles that you want to place in the standards file.
4. Choose File ➪ Save As. In the File Name text box, type a name for the standards file.
5. In the Files of Type list, select AutoCAD Drawing Standards (*.dws).

6. In the Save In drop-down list, choose a location for the file.

7. Click Save.

AutoCAD saves the drawing standards file.

You can use an existing drawing for your standards file (in fact, this method is probably easier). However, be careful to purge all layers, linetypes, dimension styles, and text styles that you don't want.

Associating a standards file with a drawing

As soon as you have your standards file, you associate it with a drawing or template that you want to check, using the STANDARDS command.

 TIP If you use a template to start new drawings, open the template and associate the standards file with your template. Then, every drawing that you start based on the template is associated with the standards file.

To associate a standards file with the current drawing, follow these steps:

1. On the CAD Standards toolbar, click Configure Standards. (You can also choose Tools ⇨ CAD Standards ⇨ Configure or type **standards** ↵.)

2. On the Standards tab of the Configure Standards dialog box, shown in Figure 26.10, click the + button.

FIGURE 26.10

Use the Configure Standards dialog box to associate a standards file with a drawing.

3. In the Select Standards File dialog box, choose the standards file that you want to use and click Open. You can associate more than one standards file with the drawing; continue to click the + button and choose more standards files.

4. Click the Plug-ins tab and click any standards that you don't want to check. All four standards types — Dimension Styles, Layers, Linetypes, and Text Styles — are initially checked. (The choices that you make persist for future standards checks until you change them.)

5. Click OK to close the Configure Standards dialog box and return to your drawing.

Checking a drawing against standards

 To check a drawing against its associated standards file, choose Check Standards from the CAD Standards toolbar to start the CHECKSTANDARDS command (or choose Tools ➪ CAD Standards ➪ Check) and open the Check Standards dialog box, shown in Figure 26.11.

 If you just finished associating a standards file with a drawing, you can click Check Standards in the Configure Standards dialog box.

FIGURE 26.11

The Check Standards dialog box guides you through the process of checking a drawing against a standards file.

The Check Standards dialog box lists all of the problems — items in the drawing that don't match the standards file — that it finds, one by one. Here's the procedure for using this dialog box:

1. You see the first problem in the Problem section of the dialog box.

2. Use the Replace With section to choose a replacement for the nonstandard item. This section contains all eligible replacements according to the standards file.

3. Look at the Preview of Changes section to see how the replacement will affect your drawing.

4. To make the replacement and standardize your drawing, click the Fix button.

To ignore the problem and go on to the next one, click the Next button.

AutoCAD continues to display problems that you can fix or ignore. After you're done, you see the Checking is complete message, along with a short report explaining how all of the problems were handled, as shown in Figure 26.12. You can click the Next button again to recheck the drawing.

5. Click Close to return to your drawing.

908

FIGURE 26.12

The completed standards check report.

For information on *batch checking* (checking standards for many drawings at once), see the "Checking Standards for Multiple Drawings" sidebar in this chapter.

When you fix nonstandard objects — for example, layers or linetypes with nonstandard names — AutoCAD purges these objects from the drawing. For example, after you change the layer Layer1 to the layer Notes, objects on Layer1 are changed to the layer Notes, and Layer1 is purged.

Specifying CAD standards settings

You can specify how the CAD standards feature functions to provide real-time notification and automatic repair. To specify CAD standards settings, choose Tools ⇨ CAD Standards ⇨ Configure and click the Settings button to open the CAD Standards Settings dialog box, as shown in Figure 26.13. (You can also click Settings from the Check Standards dialog box.)

FIGURE 26.13

Use the CAD Standards Settings dialog box to specify how you want CAD standards checking to work.

In the top section, Notification Settings, choose one of the following:

- **Disable standards notifications:** No real-time notification of standards violations. You can still check standards using the Check Standards dialog box at any time.
- **Display alert upon standards violation:** Displays a message if your drawing is associated with a standards file and you make a change that puts the drawing in noncompliance with the standards file, as shown in Figure 26.14.
- **Display standards status bar icon:** Displays an icon on the AutoCAD status bar. The icon has an exclamation point if there is a nonstandard object in the drawing. A balloon appears to notify you that a standards violation has occurred. Click the Run Check Standards text or the icon to open the Check Standards dialog box so that you can fix the problems.

FIGURE 26.14

The alert message notifies you of a standards violation.

In the bottom section, Check Standards Settings, check Automatically Fix Non-standard Properties to fix non-compliant drawings automatically. Automatic fixing applies only to a situation where a drawing object has a name that matches a standard but has different properties. For example, if a standards file contains a layer named OBJ that has a blue color and the current drawing has an object on the OBJ layer that is red, the object will be changed to blue, to match the color of the OBJ layer in the standards file.

Check Show Ignored Problems to display any problems that were not fixed in the standards check report.

From the Preferred Standards File to Use for Replacements drop-down list, choose a standards file to use by default in the Replace With section of the Check Standards dialog box. This standards file is used only if you choose to automatically fix nonstandard properties and the associated standards file for the drawing does not provide a suitable replacement.

Using layer notification

Layers are an important part of maintaining drawings standards. Many people have strict rules about which layers are allowed in a drawing. Xrefs can be especially troublesome in this regard, because layers from the external drawings are added to your drawing. AutoCAD can notify you when new layers are added to a drawing. This notification is based on the layers existing when you open the drawing, not on a standards file.

NEW FEATURE The layer notification feature is new for AutoCAD 2008 and AutoCAD LT 2008. This feature lets you specify when you're notified and under which circumstances. You can then decide to keep or change the layers.

Checking Standards for Multiple Drawings

What do you do if you want to check standards for hundreds of drawings at once? For this scenario, AutoCAD has created Batch Standards Checking, shown here. Here's how to use the Batch Standards Checker:

1. From the Windows taskbar, choose Start ➪ All Programs ➪ Autodesk ➪ AutoCAD 2008 ➪ Batch Standards Checker. The Batch Standards Checker, shown in the following figure, appears.

2. On the Drawings tab, click the + button and select the drawings that you want to include. Click Open. After you click Open, you can click the + button again and add drawings from a different folder. Use the Remove Drawing (Delete) button to delete drawings and the Move Up and Move Down buttons to change the order of the drawings. If you also want to check external references, check the Check External References of Listed Drawings check box. Note that you can't check password-protected drawings.

3. On the Standards tab, choose to check each drawing against its associated standards file if you have associated standards files for all of your drawings. Otherwise, choose to check the drawings against the standards file(s) that you select. To select a standards file, click the + button, choose a standards file (.dws), and click Open.

4. On the Plug-ins tab, choose the standards that you want to check. This tab is the same as the Plug-ins tab of the Configure Standards dialog box, discussed earlier in this section.

continued

continued

5. Click Save on the Batch Standards Checker toolbar. In the Batch Standards Checker — File Save dialog box, save the standards check file. A standards check file (.chx) contains information about which drawings and standards files you're using for the batch standards check. AutoCAD gives the file a default name, but you can change the name if you want.

6. To start checking the drawings, click Start Check on the Batch Standards Checker toolbar. (You can click Stop Check to stop the check at any time during its progress.) The Batch Standards Checker starts checking your drawings. You can click the Progress tab to see what is happening. When the checking is done, your Standards Audit Report is displayed. An example is shown here. Standards Audit Reports appear in your Internet browser.

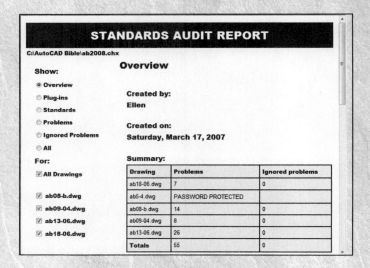

Here are some other features of the Batch Standards Checker:

- To open an existing standards check file, click Open on the Batch Standards Checker toolbar. Choose the check file and click Open.

- To view an existing batch audit report, open an existing standards check file and click the View Report button on the toolbar.

- Use the Notes tab of the Batch Standards Checker to add notes that will appear on the batch audit report.

- You can export the Standards Audit Report to HTML format. Click Export Report on the Batch Standards Checker toolbar. You can then easily e-mail the report to others. You can also copy and paste the table portion of the report into a spreadsheet program.

To set up layer notification, open the Layer Properties Manager and click the Settings button to open the Layer Settings dialog box, as shown in Figure 26.15.

FIGURE 26.15

Use the Layer Settings dialog box to specify when and how you receive notification about new layers in your drawing.

By default, layer notification only applies when xrefs add new layers to a drawing, because xrefs are the most common means of adding layers without your knowledge. However, you can choose the Evaluate All New Layers option, especially if you use templates that already contain all the desired layers.

The Notify When New Layers Are Present check box and the other check boxes below it determine if and when you see a notification window. For example, if you choose to evaluate all new layers and specify notification when you save, when you add a layer and save the drawing, you see the notification balloon shown in Figure 26.16. Click the link in the bubble to open the Layer Properties Manager.

FIGURE 26.16

This bubble tells you that new layers have been added to the drawing.

 You can uncheck the Notify When New Layers Are Present check box and still check for new layers by right-clicking the Unreconciled New Layers alert icon on the right side of the status bar and choosing View Unreconciled New Layers. The Layer Properties Manager opens.

When you open the Layer Properties Manager in this way, you see only *unreconciled* layers. (AutoCAD activates the Unreconciled New Layers filter for your layers.) These are layers that have been added to the drawing (either consciously or via xrefs) but that you haven't yet reviewed. You can perform one of three actions:

- **Leave the layer unreconciled.**
- **Reconcile the layer.** Right-click the layer in the Layer Properties Manager and choose Reconcile Layer.
- **Delete the layer.**

 The layer notification settings are saved with the drawing, and so each drawing can have its own settings.

When you create a template (as I explain in Chapter 2), after saving, the Template Options dialog box opens. Here you can decide if you want drawings created from that template to use reconciled or unreconciled layers. If you choose the default option, Save All Layers As Unreconciled, you can add layers without notification until you save the drawing. Saving the drawing creates a baseline, after which the notification starts. If you save layers as reconciled, then any new layers are considered unreconciled and you'll be notified about them according to your settings in the Layer Settings dialog box.

Translating layers

If you receive drawings from clients or colleagues, you might find that their layer system doesn't suit yours. Manually translating one set of layers to another to fit your layer standards could be a tedious job. The LAYTRANS command changes the layers of objects by specifying sets of "from" and "to" layers. For example, you can change all objects on `layer1` to the layer `objects`. Use this feature to maintain layer standards.

AUTOCAD ONLY The Layer Translation feature is not available in AutoCAD LT.

Setting up the layer mapping

 To translate one layer to another, choose Layer Translate from the CAD Standards toolbar (or choose Tools ⇨ CAD Standards ⇨ Layer Translator). The Layer Translator, shown in Figure 26.17, opens.

On the Translate From side of the dialog box, you see the layers in the drawing. (Layers with a white icon to their left are not being used. You can right-click them and choose Purge Layers to purge them from the drawing.) Select layers by clicking them. You can also select multiple layers. You can type a selection filter in the Selection Filter text box to select certain layers.

CROSS-REF See the section "Filtering the layer list" in Chapter 11 for more information about filtering layer lists.

To load existing layers, click Load. In the Select Drawing File dialog box, you can choose a drawing, a drawing template, or a drawing standards file. Click Open. The layers from that file now appear in the Translate To list. Select the layer to which you want to translate.

To define a new layer, click New. In the New Layer dialog box, type a name for the new layer and specify its color, linetype, lineweight, and plot style. Click OK.

FIGURE 26.17

The Layer Translator.

To specify how layers are translated, *map* layers in the current drawing (listed in the Translate From list) to the layers to which you want to convert (listed in the Translate To list). Select a layer in the Translate From list, then select a layer in the Translate To list, and then click Map. The mapping appears below in the Layer Translation Mappings list. Finally, you're ready to translate your layers. Click Translate, and AutoCAD takes care of the rest. All objects on the Translate From layers are now on the Translate To layers. The translation process also purges unused layers from the drawing.

> **TIP** You can select more than one layer from the Translate From list by pressing Ctrl for each additional layer. You can select a contiguous group of layers by clicking the first layer in the group, holding Shift, and selecting the last layer in the group. Then, from the Translate To list, select the layer that you want to map that group of layers to, and click Map. You can also quickly map all layers with the same name by choosing Map Same.

Managing layer translations

After you create your mappings, you can edit, remove, or save them:

- To edit a mapping, select it and click Edit. In the Edit Layer dialog box, you can choose a new layer, color, linetype, lineweight, or plot style.
- To remove a mapping, select it and click Remove.
- To save a mapping, click Save. You can choose to save a mapping as a drawing standards file (.dws) or as an actual drawing file (.dwg). Type a filename, choose a location, and click Save. (If you don't save your layer mapping, AutoCAD prompts you to do so.)
- Click Settings to customize the translation process. Here are your options:
    - The first two options in the Settings dialog box force objects to take on their layer's assigned color and linetype. Check these two settings to enforce consistency in your layer properties.
    - The Translate Objects in Blocks item determines whether layer mappings are applied to objects within blocks. See Chapter 18 for more about blocks.

- Check Write Transaction Log to create a `.log` file in the same folder as the drawing that you're translating (the current drawing). The log file lists the details of the translation and can help you troubleshoot problems later.

- Check Show Layer Contents When Selected to help you figure out which objects are on which layers. If you check this item and then select a layer translation in the Translate From or Layer Translation Mappings list, only objects on that layer are shown.

After you finish specifying the translation settings, click OK to close the Settings dialog box.

 The drawings used in the following exercise on managing CAD standards, `ab26-e.dwg` **and** `ab26-e.dws`, **are in the** `Drawings` **folder on the DVD.**

STEPS: Managing CAD Standards

1. Open `ab26-e.dwg` from the DVD.

2. Save the file as `ab26-03.dwg` in your `AutoCAD Bible` folder.

3. Open the Layer Properties Manager by clicking the Layers button on the Layers toolbar or the Layers control panel of the Dashboard. Click the Settings button.

4. To try out the layer notification feature, click the Evaluate All New Layers option and check the Save check box. Click OK.

5. In the Layer Properties Manager dialog box, click the New Layer button. Leave the default properties unchanged and click OK.

6. Save the drawing. The Unreconciled New Layers bubble appears. Click the link in the bubble to open the Layer Properties Manager dialog box, showing the new layer. Click the Delete Layer button and click OK to close the dialog box.

7. Click the Linetype Control drop-down list on the Properties toolbar. (If this toolbar is not displayed, right-click any toolbar and choose Properties from the list of toolbars.) Notice the Borderx2, Centerx2, Hiddenx2, and Phantom2 linetypes.

 8. Right-click any toolbar and choose CAD Standards to open the CAD Standards toolbar. Choose Configure from the toolbar.

9. In the Configure Standards dialog box, click the + button. Find and choose `ab26-e.dws`, a drawing standards file, on the DVD. Click Open to associate `ab26-e.dws` with `ab26-03.dwg`.

10. In the same dialog box, click Check Standards to open the Check Standards dialog box.

11. The first standards problem, `Layer 'AME_FRZ' Name is non-standard`, is listed in the Problem box. Click the Next button to ignore this problem.

12. The next problem is `Layer 'CEN' Properties are non-standard`. Choose CEN from the Replace With list and click the Fix button.

13. Continue to make the following changes, clicking the Fix button after each one:

LINETYPE	BORDERX2	BORDER
LINETYPE	CENTERX2	CENTER
LINETYPE	HIDDENX2	HIDDEN
LINETYPE	PHANTOM2	PHANTOM
TEXTSTYLE	ZONE	ROMAND
TEXTSTYLE	TECHNIBOLD	ROMANS

14. The Checking Complete dialog box appears with a summary of the standards check. Click OK.

15. Click Close.

16. Open the Linetype Control drop-down list again. The "x2" linetypes have been purged.

 17. Click Layer Translator on the CAD Standards toolbar.

18. On the right side of the Layer Translator dialog box, click Load. From the Files of Type drop-down list, choose Standards (*.dws). Choose ab26-e.dws, the same standards file that you used previously in this exercise, and click Open.

19. In the Translate From box, click CEN. Hold down the Ctrl key and click HAT.

20. In the Translate To box, click HID.

21. Click Map. This will map the layers CEN and HAT to the HID layer.

22. Click Translate to translate the mappings.

23. At the message asking whether you want to save mapping information, click No. All objects on the CEN and HAT layers are now on the HID layer.

24. Save your drawing.

The Communication Center

The Communication Center feature notifies you about updates, product support, tips, articles, and so on. An icon to the right of the InfoCenter and the Search text box connects you to the Communication Center.

To access the information for the first time, click the icon and click InfoCenter icon and then the Settings button to open the InfoCenter Settings dialog box. You can set the following:

- **General:** Your country and how often you want the Communication Center to check for new content.

- **Search Results:** Specify which locations you want to include in the results when you enter a question in the search box. I discuss using the search box in Chapter 3.

NOTE In order to configure the Communication Center, you need to install Autodesk CAD Manager Tools. For more information, see Appendix A. You then need to choose Start ➪ Autodesk ➪ CAD Manager Tools ➪ CAD Manager Control Utility to configure the Communication Center panel. In the CAD Manager Control Utility dialog box use the Info Center tab to enable the sections of the Communication Center.

- **Communication Center:** This item displays a CAD Manager Channel, a URL of an RSS news feed that a CAD Manager can use to make content available to AutoCAD users. You need to enable the CAD Manager Channel and enter the feed URL in the CAD Manager Control Utility.

- **Autodesk Channels:** If you have enabled information channels in the CAD Manager Control Utility, you can choose which Autodesk channels you want to see here. Available channels include Live Update maintenance patches, subscription announcements (for those users on AutoCAD's subscription program), articles and tips, featured technologies and content, and product support information.

- **Balloon Notification:** Choose if you want to see a balloon pop up to notify you of new content, and for which type of type of content.

- **RSS Feeds:** Use the New and Remove buttons to add or remove RSS feeds. RSS feeds are files that contain notification of new content, such as for blogs. You need to know the full URL of the RSS feed's file. (The URL of my AutoCAD Tips Newsletter RSS feed is http://www.ellenfinkelstein.com/autocad_tips_newsletter.xml.)

Click OK when you're done. After you specify the settings, click the Communication Center icon to open the Communication Center window, shown in Figure 26.18. From this window, you can click any link to access its source on the Internet.

Renaming named objects

Drawings contain many named objects, such as layers, text styles, dimension styles, and so on. Sometimes you need to rename these objects in order to maintain CAD standards and consistency. To rename objects, type **rename** on the command line and press Enter. The Rename dialog box opens, as shown in Figure 26.19.

FIGURE 26.18

Click any item to access it.

FIGURE 26.19

The Rename dialog box.

To rename objects, follow these steps:

1. Choose the type of object that you want to rename from the Named Objects list.

2. Choose the item that you want to rename from the Items list. This item appears in the Old Name text box.

3. In the Rename To text box, type the new name for the item.

   ▪ If you want to change only one item, click OK to close the dialog box.

   ▪ If you want to change more than one item, click Rename To. The dialog box remains open so that you can make other changes. Click OK after you're finished.

Working with Sheet Sets

Many AutoCAD users create sets of drawings that need to be delivered to a client. In an architectural setting, a set of drawings includes a cover page, floor plans, elevations, and sections, and may include additional sheets of sections, notes, and so on. In an engineering setting, a set of drawings may include a top view, a side view, and a section, in addition to schedules and other data. Organizing and managing all of these drawings can be a huge task. Because the sheets are numbered and reference each other, one change can involve renumbering and re-referencing the entire set of drawings.

AUTOCAD ONLY   The sheet set feature is available in AutoCAD only.

The sheet set feature offers a major rethinking of how you work with drawings. You still create your drawings in much the same way, but then you define *sheets* — paper space layouts — into sheet sets. You can do the following with sheet sets:

- **Number them.** Each sheet can have a number so that you can easily reorder them. Using fields, you can automate the process of placing the sheet number on each sheet. Changes in the sheet-set order automatically change the number on the sheets (after reloading or regenerating the drawing).

- **Plot and publish them.** You can plot or publish the entire sheet set or any selection set of sheets, all at once.

- **Associate them with a template.** You can ensure that every sheet uses the same template, or organize them so that certain sheets use certain templates. By associating a standards file with the template, you can also ensure standards compliance.

- **Manage, open, and find them.** From the Sheet Set Manager, you can easily open or find any of the drawings in the set. You can also delete any sheet.

- **Transmit and archive them.** You can eTransmit the entire sheet set, along with any dependent files. You can also create an archive package for backup purposes.

- **Facilitate multiple-user access.** Although only one drawing can be open at a time, multiple people can have access to the sheet-set information.

- **Create an index sheet.** You can create a table for an index sheet that lists all of the sheets in the sheet set.

- **Automate the creation of viewports.** You can use named views in model space to create views in viewports on a paper space layout, and specify the scale as you place the viewport.

- **Automate the completion of text in a title block.** You can use fields to automatically place text in each title block of the sheet set.

- **Automate labeling and referencing.** Using fields, you can automate the process of creating sheet labels and callouts. Labels and callouts contain numbers that are updated when sheets are reordered. Callouts are hyperlinks so that you can immediately go to the view that the callout references.

As you can see, sheet sets are a tool for managing and automating many of the organizational tasks that you need to do every day if you work with groups of drawings.

Understanding sheet sets

The drawings that you need to deliver may have one drawing with three layouts, another with one layout, and a third with four layouts. You need to deliver sheets, which are layouts, but they can be hard to manage when some layouts are in one drawing, some in another, and so on.

When you work with sheet sets, you can pull content from resource drawings that have many layouts or a few, but you create new sheets, and each sheet is a drawing. For this reason, the sheet-set structure creates new drawings, each with one layout.

You manage sheet sets and their individual sheets in the Sheet Set Manager, shown in Figure 26.20. The Sheet Set Manager is a palette like the Properties palette. For example, you can auto-hide it in the same way. To open the Sheet Set Manager, choose Tools ⇨ Palettes ⇨ Sheet Set Manager, click the Sheet Set Manager button on the Standard (or Standard Annotation) toolbar, or press Ctrl+4.

FIGURE 26.20

The Sheet Set Manager is the home base for your sheet sets.

The Sheet Set Manager has three tabs:

- **Sheet List** contains the sheets that you create for the sheet set. You use this tab to manage and organize the sheet set. You can set properties for the sheet set, for subsets (categories), and for individual sheets. You can use this tab to add and remove sheets, and to import a layout from another drawing as a sheet. You can also use it to plot, publish, eTransmit, or archive an entire sheet set or a selection of sheets, to rename and renumber sheets, and to close the sheet set. You can also open any sheet, which is the same as opening the drawing. Figure 26.20 shows the Sheet List tab.

- **Sheet Views** contains a list of paper space views, which are viewports on a layout. A layout can have more than one viewport. You can create view categories, such as elevation and floor plan. You can display the view from this tab. You also use this tab to rename and renumber your views within a layout, as well as to place label blocks that label a view and callout blocks that reference other views. See Figure 26.21 on the left.

- **Model Views** lists the drawings that are the source of your sheets, as well as their model space views, as shown in Figure 26.21 on the right.

FIGURE 26.21

On the left, you see the Sheet Views tab, which displays the views on your sheets. On the right, you see the Model Views tab, which contains the source drawings for your sheet set.

Creating a sheet set

Many AutoCAD users who work with multiple drawings create a folder structure to help organize the drawings. Sheet sets work the same way. You should start by creating a folder for your sheet set. If you want, you can create folders for categories. In the architectural example shown in Figures 26.20 and 26.21, the categories are Floor Plans, Elevations, and Sections. These become *subsets* in your sheet set. Finally, you should create a subfolder for your model space drawings, which are the drawings that you'll use to create the sheet set.

If you plan to use existing layouts as sheets, they should ideally have only one layout, especially if more than one person sometimes accesses drawings. Only one sheet in a drawing can be open at a time. Also, before you import existing layouts or create new sheets, you should first prepare your template — as I explain in the "Setting up sheet-set references" section — especially if you plan to use the automatic numbering and referencing features of sheet sets.

To create a sheet set, open the Sheet Set Manager and choose New Sheet Set from the drop-down list at the top of the palette. The Create Sheet Set Wizard opens with the Begin pane displayed, as shown in Figure 26.22.

You can choose to use an example sheet set that you've already created or that comes with AutoCAD, in order to use its structure. If you want to work with existing drawings, choose the Existing Drawings option. Then click Next. If you chose to use an example, the next screen allows you to choose the sheet set. Choose one and click Next.

FIGURE 26.22

The Create Sheet Set Wizard helps you to create sheet sets.

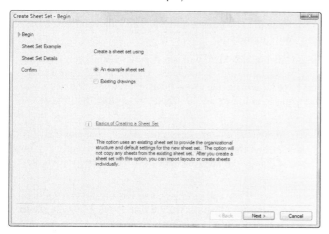

On the Sheet Set Details pane, shown in Figure 26.23, you name the sheet set, add an optional description, and specify the location of the file that contains the data for the sheet set; the default location is automatically entered for you but you can change it. Sheet-set files have a `.dst` filename extension, and you can store them in the same folder as the sheets. Click the Ellipsis button to open the Browse for Sheet Set Folder dialog box. There you can navigate to a folder or create a new folder by clicking the Create New Folder button. Then click Open to return to the wizard.

You can click the Sheet Set Properties button at this point to specify various settings, but you have access to these properties from the Sheet Set Manager, and so you can skip the properties at this stage. Then click Next.

FIGURE 26.23

You need to name the new sheet set and specify the location of its DST file.

If you chose the Existing Drawings option on the first pane, you now see the Choose Layouts pane of the wizard. Click Browse to add existing drawings that have layouts that you want to include in the sheet set. If you've created only model space drawings and want to create new sheets rather than including layouts from these drawings, you can skip this pane and click Next. However, if you have layouts that you've already set up, browse to a folder and click OK. You can continue to click Browse and add more folders if you want. You can then uncheck any folders that you don't want to include.

Click Import Options to open the Import Options dialog box. Here you can decide whether you want the sheet name to include the drawing name before the layout name. You can also choose to use your folder structure to create subsets. For example, if you have folders named Floor Plans, Elevations, and Sections, you could automatically create the subsets that you see in Figure 26.20. Click OK to close the Import Options dialog box and return to the wizard.

Click Next to display the Confirm pane of the wizard. This pane summarizes the choices that you made in the wizard. If you want to change something, click Back. Otherwise, click Finish. You can change everything later except for the sheet-set filename and location. Clicking Finish creates the DST file in the location that you chose.

The Sheet Set Manager now displays your new sheet set. If you didn't import any layouts, all you see is the Sheet List tab with the name of the sheet set. If you did import layouts, they're listed. You're now ready to set the properties of your sheet set.

Setting properties

Before you go any further, you need to set the properties of your sheet set. These properties ensure that every aspect of the sheet set works the way that you want it to. You can separately set properties for the sheet set as a whole, for subsets, and for individual sheets. To set sheet-set properties, right-click the name of the sheet set at the top of the Sheet List tab of the Sheet Set Manager, and choose Properties to open the Sheet Set Properties dialog box, shown in Figure 26.24.

FIGURE 26.24

The Sheet Set Properties dialog box.

The Sheet Set Properties dialog box always contains the sheet-set name and DST file location. Complete the rest of the properties as follows:

- **Description:** Click this item and type a new description, or edit an existing description.

- **Model view:** Click this item to display the Ellipsis button. Click the button and then click Add to browse to a folder containing drawings that you want to use for your sheets. Click Open and then click OK to return to the Sheet Properties dialog box. You can add more than one location. These drawings contain model space content that you want to place on layouts for your sheets. For easy organization, create a Model views folder inside the sheet-set folder, and place your drawings there. The folders that you enter here appear on the Model Views tab of the Sheet Set Manager.

- **Label block for views:** A label block labels a view and usually includes the view name, view number, and scale. To choose a label block, click this item and click the Ellipsis button. In the Select Block dialog box, click the Ellipsis button to choose a drawing that contains the block that you want. (If your block is in your template, choose AutoCAD Drawing Template [*.dwt] from the Files of Type drop-down list.) Click Open. If the drawing contains only that block (in other words, if the drawing is the block that you want to use), choose the Select the Drawing File as a Block option. If the drawing contains several blocks, use the Choose Blocks in the Drawing File option. You then see a list of the blocks in the drawing. Choose the block that you want (you can choose only one label block) and click OK. If you want to use the automatic numbering and referencing feature of sheet sets, you need to set up this block, as I explain later in this chapter, in the "Setting up sheet-set references" section. If you want different blocks for different subsets, or if you don't use a label block, leave this item blank.

- **Callout blocks:** Callout blocks point to other drawings. For example, on a floor plan, a callout block marks the location of a section view that is on another sheet. To choose a callout block, click this item and click the Ellipsis button. In the List of Blocks dialog box, click the Add button. Then, in the Select Block dialog box, click the Ellipsis button to choose a drawing from the Select Drawing dialog box that contains the blocks that you want. (For a template, choose AutoCAD Drawing Template [*.dwt] from the Files of Type drop-down list.) Click Open. If the drawing contains only that block (in other words, if the drawing is the block that you want to use), choose the Select the Drawing File as a Block option. If the drawing contains several blocks, use the Choose Blocks in the Drawing File option. You then see a list of the blocks in the drawing. You can choose multiple callout blocks, because many drawings contain variations of this type of block. Click OK twice to return to the Sheet Set Properties dialog box. If you want to use the automatic numbering and referencing feature of sheet sets, you need to set up this block, as I explain later in this chapter, in the "Setting up sheet-set references" section. If you want different blocks for different subsets, or if you don't use callout blocks, leave this item blank.

- **Page setup overrides file:** You may want to override page setups (which I explain in Chapter 17) if you imported layouts with varying setups. You may want to plot the entire sheet set with one page setup, rather than use page setups that came with individual layouts. You save these page setups in a template. Click this item, click the Ellipsis button that appears, choose a template, and click Open. You can create this template later and then go back and specify it.

- **Project control:** This feature provides a location to enter project information, including a project number, name, phase, and milestone. This information then appears in the Details section of the Sheet List tab of the Sheet Set Manager.

- **Sheet storage location:** This folder defines where sheets are stored. If you didn't specify this location when you created the sheet set, click this item, click the Ellipsis button, choose a folder, and click Open. Note that if the sheet set already contains sheets, changing this location doesn't move existing sheets; it only affects the location of new sheets that you create.

■ **Sheet creation template:** Click this item and then the Ellipsis button. Then click the Ellipsis button in the Select Layout as Sheet Template dialog box. Choose a template (or a drawing or standards file) and click Open. You can then click a layout in the template. Click OK.

> **CAUTION**   If you want to use the automatic numbering and referencing features of sheet sets, don't create any sheets before you've set up this template.

■ **Prompt for template:** If you want your sheets to automatically use the template, this item should be set to No. If you sometimes vary your templates, set this item to Yes so that you can choose a different template when you want.

You can create custom properties. You create custom properties to automatically insert text in your title block, using AutoCAD's field feature. After you create these properties, they become fields that you can insert. (See "Inserting Fields" in Chapter 13 for a discussion of fields.) A custom property can apply to a sheet set or an individual sheet. Common sheet-set custom properties are client name, project name, or project address. A typical sheet custom property would be the drawer's or proofer's initials, if more than one person works on the sheets in the sheet set.

To add custom properties, click the Edit Custom Properties button. In the Custom Properties dialog box, click Add. Then enter a name and a default value, and choose whether the property is for a sheet or a sheet set. (Adding a default value helps you test the fields when you set up your title block.) Click OK. Continue to click Add and define custom properties. When you're done, click OK to return to the Sheet Set Properties dialog box.

> **CAUTION**   Once you create custom properties, you can't change their name. To do so, you would need to delete and recreate the properties.

When you finish setting your sheet-set properties, click OK to return to the Sheet Set Manager and your drawing.

Creating subsets

Subsets are categories that you can use to help you organize your sheets. They may or may not have corresponding folders where you keep sheets. To create a subset, right-click the sheet-set name and choose New Subset. In the Subset Properties dialog box, name the subset and specify the location of the sheet drawings files for that subset as well as the template. The default location for both is the same as for the entire sheet set.

After you've created subsets, you can change their properties by right-clicking any subset and choosing Properties from the shortcut menu.

When you create your sheets, you can set sheet properties in the same way, by right-clicking and choosing Properties.

Setting up sheet-set references

One of the more exciting features of sheet sets is the ability to automate the completion of text in the title block, as well as the numbering of sheets, title blocks, and callout blocks. However, this feature is also fairly complex. You can omit this feature and still get significant benefits from sheet sets, such as the ability to plot the entire sheet set all at once and automate the creation of viewports. In this section, I explain how to configure the label and callout blocks so that the automation features work properly. If you don't want to use these features, you can skip this section.

The secret of this feature is the use of fields, which I cover in Chapter 13 (in the "Inserting Fields" section). You can use the fields in two ways:

- Place the fields in Mtext, which you insert in your title block, label block, and callout blocks.
- Place the fields using attributes that you associate with these blocks. I cover attributes and blocks in Chapter 18.

The advantage of using attributes is that text cannot easily be changed. If you're a CAD Manager and want to reduce errors, you might choose to use attributes. Of course, if you already use attributes, you might find it simpler to continue to use them.

On the other hand, you might want the increased flexibility and simplicity of Mtext, especially if you don't currently use attributes. One of the reasons for using attributes is to place text; using Mtext with fields works just as well to specify text placement.

Configuring title-block text

There are many ways of creating a title block. In this section, I assume that you have a template that contains a title block that you've inserted on a layout. Of course, this template also contains your text styles, table styles, dimension styles, layers, and so on.

TIP To configure your template, don't open it directly. Instead, create a new sheet in your sheet set. This sheet will automatically be based on the template that you specified in the Sheet Set Properties dialog box. When you finish configuring this sheet, you will save it as a template. To create the sheet, right-click the sheet-set name and choose New Sheet. Give the sheet a name that indicates that it will become a template, such as `WillBeTemplate`. This technique allows you to test your fields as you work, because the sheet is part of the sheet set (unlike a template that you open directly). Thanks to Heidi Hewett of Autodesk for this tip.

At this point, you should look at your title block and determine any custom properties that you need, as I explained in the previous section. You should set up these properties before you go on.

Create a new sheet on the Sheet List tab of the Sheet Set Manager. Double-click the sheet to open it. You should now see your template with its title block. If the title-block text is part of a block, whether Mtext or attributes, explode the title block.

TIP Don't try to edit attributes or blocks using the Block Attribute Manager (BATTMAN command) or the REFEDIT command, because the existing block's text will not be updated with the new field values. Instead, explode the block, change the text to fields, and redefine the block. Thanks to Heidi Hewett of Autodesk for this tip.

Double-click the Mtext or attribute text to open the In-Place Text Editor or the Edit Attribute Definition dialog box. To replace the text with a field, follow these steps:

1. Select the text.
2. Right-click and choose Insert Field to open the Field dialog box.
3. Choose one of the following fields:
   - **CurrentSheetCategory:** The view category for the current sheet.
   - **CurrentSheetCustom:** Custom properties that apply to individual sheets.
   - **CurrentSheetDescription:** The description that you entered for a sheet.
   - **CurrentSheetIssuePurpose:** The purpose property for a sheet.
   - **CurrentSheetNumber:** The sheet number.
   - **CurrentSheetNumberandTitle:** The sheet number and name.
   - **CurrentSheetRevisionDate:** The revision date for the current sheet.

- **CurrentSheetRevisionNumber:** The revision number for the current sheet.
- **CurrentSheetSet:** The name of the sheet set.
- **CurrentSheetSetCustom:** Custom properties that apply to the sheet set.
- **CurrentSheetSetDescription:** The sheet-set description that you specified.
- **CurrentSheetSetProjectMilestone:** The milestone value from the Project Control section of the Sheet Set Properties dialog box.
- **CurrentSheetSetProjectName:** The project name from the Project Control section of the Sheet Set Properties dialog box.
- **CurrentSheetSetProjectNumber:** The project number from the Project Control section of the Sheet Set Properties dialog box.
- **CurrentSheetSetProjectPhase:** The project phase value from the Project Control section of the Sheet Set Properties dialog box.
- **CurrentSheetSetSubSet:** The name of the subset that the current sheet is in.
- **CurrentSheetTitle:** The name of the sheet.
- **Sheet Set:** The name of the sheet set.
- **CreateDate:** Places the current date. (Unlike the Date field, this field doesn't update each time you open or regenerate the drawing.)

You may find other fields that are useful for your title block.

4. Choose a format from the Format list.
5. If you chose one of the custom fields, choose the specific field from the Custom Property Name drop-down list.

> **NOTE** You should immediately see the value of your field, either in your drawing or in the Edit Attribute Definition dialog box.

6. Click OK. Repeat Steps 1 through 5 to continue to add fields for the entire title block in this way.
7. Choose File ➪ Save As. From the Files of Type drop-down list, choose AutoCAD Drawing Template (`*.dwt`). Specify the location that you want for your sheet-set template. (The `Template` folder has a `SheetSets` subfolder that you can use.) Click Save. Usually, you're overwriting an existing template, so confirm the overwrite. Enter a description in the Template Description dialog box and click OK.
8. You can now delete the sheet from the sheet set. Deleting a sheet doesn't delete the drawing. Right-click the sheet and choose Remove Sheet. Click OK to confirm. The drawing is still open.
9. The template is now open on your screen. If you exploded the title block, you need to redefine the block. If you're using attributes for your text, you need to include the text as attribute definitions.
10. Select all of the objects in your title block. Choose Make Block from the Draw toolbar. In the Block Definition dialog box, enter the name of your title-block block in the Name text box. Click OK.

You can now immediately define label and callout blocks directly in the template. If you don't need these blocks, skip the next section and close the template.

Configuring label and callout blocks

Label blocks can automatically display the sheet number, sheet name, and scale. Callout blocks can automatically display the view number (often called the detail number), as well as the sheet number. In addition, callout blocks can contain a hyperlink to the view that they reference so that users can immediately display that view. You can see an example of label and callout blocks in Figure 26.26.

To set up your label and callout blocks, the simplest solution is probably to work directly in the template. When you're done, you'll delete the inserted blocks to keep only their definitions. If you want to store these blocks in a separate drawing, open the drawing. Follow these steps:

1. Choose Insert ➪ Block and choose your label block. Click OK and specify any insertion point.

2. Explode the block.

3. Double-click the text that contains the view number. (This is often called the detail number and will number a floating viewport containing one view of the drawing.) The In-Place Text Editor opens (the Edit Attribute Definition dialog box opens if the text is an attribute).

4. Select the text. (In the Edit Attribute Definition dialog box, select the text in the Default text box.) Right-click and choose Insert ➪ Field. The Field dialog box opens.

5. From the Field Names list, choose SheetSetPlaceholder. From the Placeholder Type list, choose View Number.

6. Repeat Steps 3 through 5 for the view name and the view scale, using the ViewTitle and the ViewportScale types of the SheetSetPlaceholder field, respectively.

7. To redefine the block, select all of the objects, choose Make Block from the Draw toolbar, and type the title-block name in the Name text box. When the label block is automatically inserted into the drawing, its insertion point will be at the lower-left corner of the view, and so you need to define the base point of the block slightly above the block's left edge. Click OK and then click Yes to confirm the redefinition of the block.

 You can use the Block Editor to edit the block. Then you don't have to explode or redefine the block.

NOTE If your text is composed of attributes, choose Modify ➪ Object ➪ Attributes ➪ Block Attribute Manager to open the Block Attribute Manager. Choose each field, click Edit, check the Preset check box, and click OK twice to return to your drawing. You want attributes that are fields to be preset because you'll define their value using the Sheet Set Manager; you don't want the Edit Attributes dialog box to pop up to ask for a value whenever you insert a title block. You can also select the attribute, open the Properties palette, and change the Preset item's value to Yes.

8. If you didn't choose the Delete option in the Block Definition dialog box, delete the block. The block definition stays in the template's database and will be available to any drawing that you base on that template.

9. Repeat Steps 1 through 8 for your callout blocks. For these blocks, you use the SheetSetPlaceholder field with the ViewNumber and SheetNumber field types. However, for callout blocks, be sure to check the Associate Hyperlink check box in the Field dialog box, so that the callout bubble will link to the view (detail) that it references.

10. Save the template and close it.

You're now ready to use your sheet set.

Adding and managing sheets

After you've configured your sheet-set properties, you're ready to use your sheet set. The first step is to specify the value of any custom properties that you have defined so that they'll appear in your title-block text property. On the Sheet List tab, right-click the sheet-set name and choose Properties. Click Edit Custom Properties and set the values that you want.

You can now add sheets. Each sheet will be a separate drawing with one layout tab. To add a sheet, follow these steps:

1. Display the Sheet List tab of the Sheet Set Manager.
2. Right-click the sheet-set name and choose New Sheet.
3. In the New Sheet dialog box, give the sheet a number and a name.
4. The name of the drawing is automatically completed, using both the number and the name of the sheet.

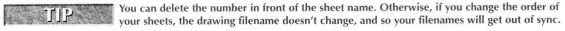 You can delete the number in front of the sheet name. Otherwise, if you change the order of your sheets, the drawing filename doesn't change, and so your filenames will get out of sync.

5. Click OK. The new sheet appears on the Sheet List tab.
6. If you created sheet properties, right-click the sheet name and choose Properties. Change the values of any custom properties that are specific for that sheet.

NEW FEATURE You can import a layout as a sheet by displaying the layout and dragging from the layout tab to the Sheet List tab of the Sheet Set Manager.

To organize your sheets, you can create subsets. A subset is just an organizational tool, although you can create a folder structure that matches your subsets. You can also assign different templates to sheets in different subsets. To add a subset, right-click the sheet-set name and choose New Subset. You can also right-click an existing subset and choose New Subset to create a nested subset. In the Subset Properties dialog box, name the subset. You can also assign a template and folder location. Click OK.

On the Sheet List tab, you can also do the following with sheets:

- **Move sheets:** You can place sheets in a different order by dragging them. You can drag multiple sheets to a new location or subset.
- **Remove sheets:** Right-click any sheet and choose Remove Sheet. You can also select multiple sheets to remove all of the selected sheets. Click OK to confirm.
- **Change a sheet's name and number:** Right-click a sheet and choose Rename & Renumber. Type a new number, a new name, or both, and click OK. Note that renumbering a sheet doesn't change its order on the Sheet List. Two sheets can have the same number. You can use any numbering system that you want.

NOTE When changing a sheet's name, you have an option to also change the name of the associated drawing file to match the new sheet name.

- **Change sheet properties:** Right-click a sheet and choose Properties. Make any changes that you want in the Sheet Properties dialog box and click OK.
- **Import a sheet:** You can create a sheet by importing a layout tab of an existing drawing. On the Sheet List tab, right-click the sheet-set name and choose Import Layout as Sheet. In the Import Layouts as Sheets dialog box, click the Browse for Drawings button. Navigate to a drawing and click Open. Then choose the layouts in that drawing that you want to import. Click the Import Checked button.

NOTE To import a layout as a sheet, you must have displayed a layout tab in that drawing; otherwise you get a message that the drawing does not contain any initialized layouts. To remedy the situation, open the drawing, click the layout tab, and save the drawing. Then close the drawing. You can now import the layout into your sheet set.

The drawings and files used in the following exercise on creating and configuring a sheet set, `ab26-f-1.dwg`, `ab26-f-2.dwg`, `ab26-f-3.dwg`, and `ab26-f.dwt`, are in the `Drawings` folder on the DVD.

STEPS: Creating and Configuring a Sheet Set

Note: This is a long exercise. You should leave yourself 45 to 60 minutes to complete it.

1. Open Windows Explorer. (Right-click the Windows Start button and choose Explore.) In the folder pane, locate and click the `AutoCAD Bible` folder that you created for the exercises in this book. From the menu, choose File ➪ New ➪ Folder and name the new folder `AB 2008 Sheet Set`.

2. Click the new `AB 2008 Sheet Set` folder and again choose File ➪ New ➪ Folder. Name the new folder `Model View Drawings`.

3. Copy `ab26-f-1.dwg`, `ab26-f-2.dwg`, `ab26-f-3.dwg`, and `ab26-f.dwt` (a template file) from the DVD of this book to the `Model View Drawings` folder.

4. Open a new drawing, based on any template. (You need a drawing open to create a new sheet set, although not to open an existing one.)

5. Choose Tools ➪ Palettes ➪ Sheet Set Manager. From the drop-down list at the top, choose New Sheet Set to open the Create Sheet Set Wizard.

6. On the Begin pane, choose Existing Drawings and click Next.

7. In the Name of New Sheet Set text box, type **ab26-f**. In the Description text box, type **AB Residence, size A**. (You wouldn't normally use size A sheets for architectural drawings, but using this size enables you to print the sheets on your printer if you don't have a plotter available.) In the Store Sheet Set Data File (`.dst`) Here box, click the Ellipsis button and navigate to the `AutoCAD Bible\AB 2008 Sheet Set` folder that you created in Step 1. Click Open and then click Next.

8. On the Choose Layouts pane, click Next. You're going to create the sheets from scratch rather than import them. (You will use the existing drawings for the model view, but you won't use them as the sheets themselves.)

9. On the Confirm pane, read the information. If it's correct, click Finish. (Otherwise, click Back and make any corrections that you want.)

10. Click the Sheet List tab of the Sheet Set Manager if it isn't already on top. You should see your sheet set listed. Right-click the sheet-set name and choose Properties from the shortcut menu.

11. In the Sheet Set Properties dialog box, set the following items:

    - **Model view:** Click the Ellipsis button. Click Add. Navigate to the `AutoCAD Bible\AB 2008 Sheet Set\Model View Drawings` folder that you created in Step 2. Click Open. Click OK to return to the Sheet Set Properties dialog box.

    - **Label block for views:** Click the Ellipsis button. In the Select Block dialog box, click the Ellipsis button again. If necessary, choose AutoCAD Drawing Template (`*.dwt`) from the Files of Type drop-down list. Navigate to the `AutoCAD Bible\AB 2008 Sheet Set\Model View Drawings` folder and choose `ab26-f.dwt`. Click Open. Choose the Choose Blocks in the Drawing File option. Choose the `view label` block. Click OK.

    - **Callout blocks:** Click the Ellipsis button. In the List of Blocks dialog box, click Add. In the Select Block dialog box, click the Ellipsis button. If necessary, choose AutoCAD Drawing Template (`*.dwt`) from the Files of Type drop-down list. Navigate to the `AutoCAD Bible\AB 2008 Sheet Set\Model View Drawings` folder and choose `ab26-f.dwt`. Click Open. Choose the Choose Blocks in the Drawing File option. Choose the `Callout button-left arrow` block. Click OK twice.

▪ **Sheet creation template:** Click the Ellipsis button. In the Select Layout as Sheet Template dialog box, click the Ellipsis button. If necessary, choose AutoCAD Drawing Template (`*.dwt`) from the Files of Type drop-down list. Navigate to the `AutoCAD Bible\AB 2008 Sheet Set\Model View Drawings` folder and choose `ab26-f.dwt`. Click Open. (If the template contained more than one layout, you would choose the layout of the template that you want to use.) Click OK.

▪ **Prompt for template:** Choose No from the drop-down list if this value is set to Yes.

12. Click Edit Custom Properties. Click Add. In the Add Custom Property dialog box, add the following custom properties:

   ▪ Customer Name, with a value of CustomerName, sheet set
   ▪ Customer Address 1, with a value of CustomerAddress1, sheet set
   ▪ Customer Address 2, with a value of CustomerAddress2, sheet set
   ▪ Drawn By, with a value of DB, sheet
   ▪ Checked By, with a value of CB, sheet

   Click OK to close the Custom Properties dialog box. Click OK again to close the Sheet Set Properties dialog box and return to your drawing.

13. Right-click the sheet-set name and choose New Subset. Type **Floor Plans** and click OK. Repeat this process to add subsets for Elevations and Sections.

14. To configure the title-block text, right-click the sheet-set name and choose New Sheet. Because you'll later save this sheet as a template and then delete it, number it XX and name it WILL BE TEMPLATE. (This technique helps you to confirm your fields.) Delete the XX from the front of the filename and click OK.

15. Double-click the new sheet to open it. You should see the template's title block.

16. Double-click the text `CustomerName` to open the In-Place Text Editor. Select the text, right-click, and choose Insert Field. Choose SheetSet from the Field Category drop-down list to filter the fields that you see on the Field Names list. Choose CurrentSheetSetCustom (check the field name carefully, because there are many similar fields), set the format to Title case, and choose Customer Name from the Custom Property Name drop-down list. Click OK. You now see the text surrounded by the gray field box. Click OK to close the In-Place Text Editor. In the same way, set the following other fields:

   ▪ **CustomerAddress1:** CurrentSheetSetCustom, Title case, Customer Address 1
   ▪ **CustomerAddress2:** CurrentSheetSetCustom, Title case, Customer Address 2
   ▪ **DB:** (Drawn By) CurrentSheetCustom, Uppercase, Drawn By
   ▪ **CB:** (Checked By) CurrentSheetCustom, Uppercase, Checked By
   ▪ **P-01:** CurrentSheetNumber, Uppercase

   You can now see the values of all the fields in the title block.

17. The Layout tab takes on the name of the sheet, which is WILL BE TEMPLATE. If your drawing window displays the Layout tab, double-click the Layout tab to rename it. If your drawing window doesn't display the Layout tab (the default), first right-click the layout's button on the status bar and click Display Layout and Model Tabs. Name the Layout tab **Titleblock.**

18. Choose File ⇨ Save As. From the Files of Type drop-down list, choose AutoCAD Drawing Template (*.dwt). Navigate to your AutoCAD Bible\AB 2008 Sheet Set\Model View Drawings folder. Name the template ab26-f.dwt and click Save. Click Yes to replace the existing template. Click OK to accept the description. (Because you have now changed the template, if you want to do the exercise again, you must recopy the template from the DVD.)

19. You no longer need the WILL BE TEMPLATE sheet. Right-click the sheet and choose Remove Sheet. Click OK to confirm. (Removing the sheet does not remove the drawing or templates.)

20. The template is still open. Make sure that the current layer is 0.

21. To configure the label and callout blocks, choose Insert Block from the Draw toolbar and choose the view label block from the Name drop-down list. Make sure that only the Insertion Point Specify On-Screen check box is checked, and click OK. Pick any insertion point. If the Edit Attributes dialog box opens, click OK. If the attribute prompts appear on the command line (and in the Dynamic Input tooltip), press Enter until the command is completed.

22. In the same way, insert the callout bubble-left arrow block.

23. Select the view label block and click Block Editor on the Standard (or Standard Annotation) toolbar. In the Edit Block Definition dialog box, with the view label block highlighted, click OK.

24. Double-click the V# text inside the circle. The Edit Attribute Definition dialog box opens. Select the text in the Default text box. Right-click in the Default text box and choose Insert Field. In the Field dialog box, choose SheetSetPlaceholder as the Field Name and View Number as the Placeholder Type. (If you use view numbers that include letters, choose Uppercase as the Format.) Click OK twice to return to the Block Editor.

 You don't see the gray field box yet, because you haven't yet inserted the attribute as part of a block.

25. Use the same procedure to add SheetSetPlaceholder fields for VIEWNAME (use the ViewTitle type and Title case format) and SCALE (use the ViewportScale type and choose the format that you want). Press Enter to end the DDEDIT command.

26. Select the attributes. Display the Properties palette and change the Preset item's value to Yes.

27. Click Save Block Definition and click Close Block Editor to return to your drawing.

28. Repeat Steps 23 through 27 for the callout bubble-left arrow block. For the top text, use the ViewNumber placeholder type. For the bottom text, use the SheetNumber placeholder type. This time, be sure to check the Associate Hyperlink check box in the Field dialog box.

29. Delete both blocks. Then save and close the template.

30. Before you create new sheets, specify the values of the sheet-set level custom properties. Right-click the sheet-set name on the Sheet List tab of the Sheet Set Manager and choose Properties. The Sheet Set Custom Properties section lists the sheet-set properties that you created earlier. (You might have to scroll down in the Sheet Set Properties dialog box to see them.) For Customer Name, type **AB Residence**. For Customer Address 1, enter any address. For Customer Address 2, enter any city, state, and ZIP or postal code. Click OK to return to your drawing.

31. On the Sheet List tab of the Sheet Set Manager, right-click the Floor Plans subset and choose New Sheet. Number the new sheet 1 and name it Basement Floor Plan. Delete the number 1 from the filename and click OK. In the same way, create a sheet 2 named 1st Floor Plan, and a sheet 3 named 2nd Floor Plan.

32. In the same way, add four new sheets to the Elevations subset:

- 4: East Elevation
- 5: North Elevation
- 6: West Elevation
- 7: South Elevation

33. In the same way, add two new sheets to a new Sections subset: a sheet 8 called Internal Sections and a sheet 9 called External Sections.

34. Right-click each sheet that you've created and choose Properties. Change the values for the DB and CB sheet properties to any initials.

35. Leave AutoCAD and the Sheet Set Manager open for the next exercise.

Using a sheet set

When your sheet set is configured and you've created your sheets, you're ready to use your sheet set. You can create viewports on your sheets, insert callout blocks, plot or publish sheets, archive and eTransmit sheets, and create a table that lists all of the sheets.

Creating viewports from named views

A major feature of a sheet set is the ability to create viewports on your sheets. You do this by creating named views in model space in your resource drawings. Then you place the view onto a layout to create a viewport. (For information on named views, see the section "Creating Named Views" in Chapter 8. For coverage of viewports, see the section "Creating a Layout in Paper Space" in Chapter 17.) When you place the view, you can specify the scale that you need.

If you don't already have the named view that you need, click the Model Views tab and double-click the drawing containing the content that you need. This opens the drawing. (If necessary, click the plus sign next to the resource location to display the available drawings.) Click the Model button on the status bar (or the Model tab if it's displayed), define the named view, and then save and close the drawing.

The Model Views tab now lists the named view under the drawing. (Again, you may have to click the plus sign next to the drawing to display the view.)

To create a viewport based on a named view, follow these steps:

1. Click the Sheet List tab. Double-click the sheet on which you want to place a viewport, to open the drawing with the layout displayed.

2. Click the Model Views tab.

3. Right-click the named view that you want to use, and choose Place on Sheet.

4. Move the cursor onto the drawing area. The command line displays the `Specify insertion point:` prompt, and you can see the view on the layout. AutoCAD calculates a standard scale, based on the size of the layout and the size of the view.

5. To change the scale, right-click in the drawing area. A list of scales appears. Choose the scale that you want.

6. Click to specify the insertion point that you want, and place the viewport. If you've specified a label block, the block automatically appears with its insertion point at the lower-left corner of the view.

Use this procedure to place viewports on all of your sheets. Your views now appear on the Sheet Views tab. If you want to place callout or label blocks that use the ViewNumber field, you need to number these views. Right-click a view on the Sheet Views tab and choose Rename & Renumber. Enter a number and a name and click OK. To see the result in an existing field, regenerate the drawing to update the fields.

Inserting callout blocks

If you've set up callout blocks, as I describe in the "Configuring label and callout blocks" section earlier in this chapter, now is the time to place them. A callout block references another sheet that contains a detail or a different view. Follow these steps:

1. On the Sheet List tab of the Sheet Set Manager, double-click the sheet on which you want to place the callout block, to open the layout.

2. Click the Sheet Views tab, which contains all of the model views that you have on your layouts, and right-click the view that you want to reference. Choose Place Callout Block and choose the block. (If you see a Select Blocks submenu item, choose it, choose the block that you want, and click OK to select the block that you want to use. This makes the block available on the menu. Then right-click the view again, choose Place Callout Block, and choose the block.)

3. At the prompt, pick an insertion point to place the block. The block should display the correct view (detail) and sheet number.

Plotting and publishing

Automation of plotting and publishing is one of the advantages of sheet sets. You can plot or publish an entire sheet set or just part of it, directly from the Sheet Set Manager.

 To plot the entire sheet set, click the sheet-set name and choose Publish ⇨ Publish to Plotter. Your sheet set plots according to the settings in the template. To apply page-setup overrides, choose Publish Using Page Setup Override.

 To publish the sheet set, click the sheet-set name and choose Publish to DWF. If you plan to publish to DWF format, choose Sheet Set Publish Options from the Publish drop-down list. The Sheet Set Publish Options dialog box opens, where you can specify options for publishing to DWF. For example, you can decide whether you want to publish to single-sheet or multi-sheet DWF format. You can also specify a password and decide how much data you want to make available. For more information about the PUBLISH command and the DWF format, see Chapter 28.

NEW FEATURE The PUBLISHCOLLATE system variable determines whether a sheet set is published as a single plotting job or as separate jobs for each sheet. The default value, 1, publishes the sheets as a single job. However, to publish sheets as a single job, all sheets must be the same size, and you need to choose the Publish Using Page Setup Override option from the Publish drop-down list on the Sheet List tab of the Sheet Set Manager. Change the value to 0 if you might need to have other plotting jobs interrupt the sheet set. You can also publish the sheet set in reverse order; choose Publish in Reverse Order from the Publish drop-down list. On the same menu, you have options to add a plot stamp, manage plot setups, and open the PUBLISH dialog box.

To plot or publish a subset or sheet, right-click the subset or sheet and use the options on the shortcut menu.

 You can create selection sets of sheets and save them. Then you can plot or publish the selection set of sheets. To create a selection set of sheets, select the sheets that you want to include and click Sheet Selections ⇨ Create. Name the selection set and click OK. After that, you can choose the selection set from the Sheet Selections drop-down list to select the sheets that you need. Then you can choose to plot or publish them.

Archiving and eTransmitting sheet sets

Archive your sheets sets to save them in ZIP format (by default). You can use the ZIP file for transmittal or backup purposes. (For more information about the archiving process, see the discussion on eTransmitting drawings in Chapter 28.) To archive a sheet set, follow these steps:

1. Right-click the sheet-set name and choose Archive.
2. In the Archive a Sheet Set dialog box, you can add notes that will go in the archive report, use the tabs to review the files that will be included, view the archive report, and modify current archive settings. Then click OK.
3. Choose a location for the archive file and click Save.

You create a transmittal when you want to e-mail your sheet set along with all necessary dependent drawings and files. I cover eTransmitting drawings in Chapter 28. To eTransmit a sheet set, follow these steps:

1. Right-click the sheet-set name and choose eTransmit.
2. In the Create Transmittal dialog box, you can add notes, use the tabs to review the files that will be included, view the transmittal report, and choose a transmittal setup that you've saved. Click OK.
3. Choose a location for the file and click Save.

Creating a list of sheets

A sheet set often has an index sheet that contains a table of contents. Using AutoCAD's table feature, you can automatically generate a table that lists all of the sheets in the sheet set. To create a table listing the sheets, follow these steps:

1. Create a new sheet. You can number it sheet 1 or sheet 0.
2. Double-click the sheet to open its drawing.
3. Right-click the sheet-set name and choose Insert Sheet Set Table to open the Insert Sheet List Table dialog box, shown in Figure 26.25.

FIGURE 26.25

Use the Insert Sheet List Table dialog box to create a table that lists all of the sheets in your sheet set.

4. From the Table Style Name drop-down list, choose any table style that you've saved in your template. You can click the Ellipsis button to open the Table Style dialog box and define a table style.

5. Check the Show Subheader check box if you want to show your sheets divided by subsets.

6. In the Title Text text box, enter a name to appear as the title of the table. You may want to use the name of the sheet set here, instead of the default text.

7. In the Column Settings section, you specify what data you want to show and how you want to title each column. On the left, you can choose the data from the drop-down lists. On the right, you can change the text. For example, for the Sheet Title item, you may want the title to appear as "Sheet Name." Click Add to add a new column, or click Remove to remove a column. You can also change the order of the columns.

8. Click OK.

9. A message appears, explaining what happens if you manually make changes in the table — the changes are lost when you update the table. Click OK.

10. If Ortho is on, turn it off. At the `Specify insertion point:` prompt, pick a location for the table on your index sheet.

If you make any changes in your sheet set, such as adding or renumbering sheets, you should update the table. Select the table by clicking on any outside border, right-click, and choose Update Sheet List Table.

ON the DVD-ROM The drawings and files used in the following exercise on using a sheet set, `ab26-f-1.dwg`, `ab26-f-2.dwg`, and `ab26-f-3.dwg`, are in the `Drawings` folder on the DVD. The `ab26-f.dwt` file is in the `Results` folder. (It's called `ab26-f.dwt after exercise.dwt` because it contains the results of the previous exercise. Ideally, you should do the previous exercise and use the template that you saved in that exercise.)

STEPS: Using a Sheet Set

1. You should do the previous exercise before doing this exercise to set up and configure your sheet set and the blocks. If the Sheet Set Manager is not open, choose Tools ➪ Palettes ➪ Sheet Set Manager, click Open, and open the `ab26-f` sheet set from the `AutoCAD Bible\AB 2008 Sheet Set` folder.

2. Click the Model Views tab of the Sheet Set Manager. Click the plus sign next to the folder name at the top to display the list of the three drawings in the `Model View Drawings` folder. Click the plus sign next to each drawing to display their model space named views.

3. Click the Sheet List tab. Double-click `1 - Basement Floor Plan`. You see the title block displayed with all of the title-block fields completed.

4. Change the current layer to `viewport`.

5. Click the Model Views tab again. (You may want to auto-hide the Sheet Set Manager at this point.) Right-click `Floor - Basement` and choose Place on Sheet. Move the cursor onto the drawing area. Right-click and choose 1/16"=1'. Place the viewport all the way to the left of the layout. (The view doesn't fit perfectly, but that's okay for this exercise.) The result should look like Figure 26.26, except without the callout block. (If you want, continue to place the floor-plan views on the floor-plan sheets, matching the 1st- and 2nd-floor views to the 1st- and 2nd-floor sheets. You can also do the same for the four elevation views.)

6. On the Sheet List tab, double-click the External Sections sheet to open it. Make `viewport` the current layer. Click the Model Views tab. Right-click the `Section 2` view and choose Place on Sheet. In the drawing area, right-click and choose 1/16"=1' and pick a point for the view.

FIGURE 26.26

The basement floor plan.

7. Click the Sheet Views tab to see the views that you've placed. To number these views, right-click each view and choose Rename & Renumber. Because you're placing only one view on a sheet, number each view 1 and click OK.

8. To place a callout bubble on the basement floor plan that references the Exterior Section sheet, choose that drawing from the Window menu. Click the Sheet Views tab. This tab now lists the views that you just placed. Right-click the `Section 2` view (the one that you're pointing to) and choose Place Callout Blocks ➪ `callout bubble-left arrow`. At the prompt, pick **1** in Figure 26.26. The fields in the callout block show the correct view and sheet numbers.

9. If you have a printer or plotter available, click the Sheet List tab. Select the Basement Floor Plan and Exterior Sections sheets. Click the Sheet Selections button and choose Create. Name the selection **basement-exterior sections** and click OK.

10. Choose Publish ➪ Publish to Plotter. The two sheets are plotted.

NOTE   If you have any difficulty plotting/printing, you may need to change the page setup to point to your plotter or printer.

11. To create a table that lists all of the sheets, first create a new sheet. On the Sheet List tab, right-click the sheet-set name and choose New Sheet. Number it 0 and name it Index Sheet. Delete the 0 from the filename and click OK.

12. Double-click the new sheet's name to open it.

13. Right-click the sheet-set name and choose Insert Sheet List Table. From the Table Style Name drop-down list, choose Sheet Set List. (This table style was saved with the template.) The Show Subheader check box should be checked. In the Title Text box, type **AB26-f Sheets**. For the column settings, set up the following columns. If necessary, click Add to add a column.

Sheet Number	Sheet No.
Sheet Title	Sheet Name
Drawing Author	By

14. Click OK to return to your drawing. Pick an insertion point for the table.

15. Save and close any open drawings.

Organizing Your Drawings

Some offices keep track of thousands of drawings. You must not only track your drawings' names and other properties, but also make sure that you don't lose them! Archiving and finding drawings are important procedures in any CAD environment.

Archiving drawings

You should use the Autosave feature to regularly save a backup of the drawing to the hard drive. The default time is set to 10 minutes, but automatic backups can still be useful. Choose Tools ➪ Options, click the Open and Save tab, and change the Automatic Save setting. Click OK. Of course, you shouldn't rely on Autosave; instead, save your drawing frequently by clicking the Save button.

The Autosave time counts from the most recent time you saved your drawing. Therefore, if you manually save more often than every 10 minutes, the feature doesn't create an Autosave file.

Backing up to the hard drive doesn't provide sufficient security. Hard drives can fail. Every time you exit AutoCAD or AutoCAD LT, you should back up every drawing that you worked on to some type of external storage medium. Backing up drawings for storage is called *archiving*.

ON the DVD-ROM On the DVD, I include an AutoLISP program, `savea.lsp`, which backs up to the `a:` drive without leaving your drawing. (You can change it to back up to any drive.) This enables you to back up while working on a drawing. See the `Software\Chapter 01\Savea` folder of the DVD. This program works with AutoCAD only.

You'll probably want to invest in one of the many types of removable backup systems. These come in six main types:

- **Tape drives** (internal or external) are cheap and good for entire hard-drive backups.
- **Disk cartridge drives** offer the convenience of a floppy disk but with more capacity.
- **Read/write DVD-ROM or DVD drives** enable you to write to a DVD or DVD.
- **Flash drives** are easy to use, and you can take them home with you because they're so small.
- **External hard drives** can back up your entire hard drive, and you can take them with you if you travel or to take them off-site.
- **Optical drives** have the longest life (at least 30 years) and resist accidental erasure.

If your drawings are *really* important to you, back them up twice and store one backup set off-site. This way, if your office burns down, you haven't lost everything. Remote backup services provide this type of archiving for you, and you can access your files through the Internet.

The secret to backing up is to create a schedule and then stick to it. For example, you may do a complete hard-drive backup once a week, and do drawing backups at the end of each day. Many software backup programs exist that let you choose what you want to back up and reduce the process to the click of a button. Each situation is different, but take the time to think about your needs, create a system, and let everybody know about it. Then do it.

Finding drawings

Let's say your client calls and says, "I want to see the apartment building on Fourth Street that you did three years ago." How do you find the drawing? One low-tech way is to keep a book of 8¹/₂×11 plots. Using the PUBLISH command (which I explain in Chapter 28), you can plot out a week's drawings overnight and put them in a book. Amazingly, it doesn't take that long to leaf through even a few hundred pages. (You usually have *some* idea of when you did the drawing.)

> **TIP**   Use the PLOTSTAMP command to label each drawing. Or place the drawing name and date written in large text on a separate layer in the drawing. Set the Plot property of the layer to Not Plottable while you work and for regular plotting. Set it to Plottable for your batch plots. Then, even when it is reduced, you'll know the drawing name when you look at the drawing in the book.

A number of third-party drawing management programs are available. Some of these enable you to view and manage drawings created in other CAD programs as well. Some also manage workflow by letting you route drawings to team members.

Here's a short selection of the many drawing management programs that are available:

- **AutoEDMS:** www.acssoftware.com
- **Synergis-Adept:** www.synergis-adept.com
- **Cyco AutoManager Workflow EDM:** www.cyco.com
- **Columbus:** www.oasys-software.com

You can store and manage drawings online. Web-based services, such as Autodesk Buzzsaw (www.buzzsaw.com), let you store drawings online, view them, mark them up, organize and track them, and access them.

Before backing up drawings, purge any unused layers, blocks, text styles, and so on to reduce file size.

If you know that a drawing is on the hard drive, then you can use the Find function from within AutoCAD or AutoCAD LT. Click Open on the Standard (or Standard Annotation) toolbar. In the Select File dialog box, choose Tools ➪ Find to open the Find dialog box, as shown in Figure 26.27. Use the Name & Location tab to set criteria according to the filename, file type, and location. Use the Date Modified tab to set criteria by the date that the file was saved.

FIGURE 26.27

You can use the Find dialog box to set criteria for finding drawings.

You can use Windows' Search feature to search for text inside drawings.

To search for drawings using Windows' Search feature, choose Start ➪ Search. In the Search window, enter the word or phrase that you want to look for in the Containing Text text box, and click Search Now. Using this technique, you can find not only MText and other text objects but names of layers and other named objects that match your search word or phrase.

Specifying drawing properties

You can specify drawing properties, similar to the way you can in Microsoft Office. You can use these properties not only in the DesignCenter but also in Windows Explorer. These properties are therefore available to people who can access your drawings but who don't have AutoCAD or AutoCAD LT.

You can specify a title, subject, author, and keywords. You can also write comments. At the bottom of the dialog box, you can specify a base for relative hyperlinks in the drawing. For example, you could use `www.companyname.com` as the base. AutoCAD or AutoCAD LT would then attach this base to the beginning of links in the drawing.

To specify drawing properties, choose File ➪ Drawing Properties to open the Properties dialog box.

In general, you'll find the Summary tab very useful. However, you can also use the Custom tab to create custom properties and give them values. This lets you create a simple database of your drawings that you can search using the DesignCenter's Find dialog box. When you're done, click OK.

To access a drawing's properties in Windows Explorer, navigate to the drawing and right-click it. Choose Properties from the shortcut menu.

AUTOCAD ONLY The Express Tools contain a command, PROPULATE (choose Express ➪ File Tools ➪ Update Drawing Property Data), which automatically creates or updates Property data for one or more drawings.

Maintaining Security

In these days of collaboration and interconnectivity, maintaining security is an important issue. Two features help you to keep your designs secure: password protection and digital signatures.

Password protection

Password protection ensures that unauthorized people don't open your drawings. You create a password when you save a drawing.

AUTOCAD ONLY AutoCAD LT does not offer password protection.

To create a password for a drawing, type **securityoptions** ↵ on the command line. If you're saving a drawing for the first time, you can also click the Tools drop-down list and choose Security Options. The Security Options dialog box opens.

CAUTION Before adding a password, save the drawing under another name or in a different location so that you have a copy. If you lose or forget the password, you won't be able to open the drawing. You can turn password protection off for network installations of AutoCAD.

To password-protect a drawing:

1. Type a password in the text box.
2. If you also want to encrypt drawing properties that identify the drawing, such as the title, author, subject, and keywords, check the Encrypt Drawing Properties check box.
3. Click OK.
4. The Confirm Password dialog box appears. Retype the password.
5. Click OK.

You can also change or remove a password:

1. Open the Security Options dialog box.
2. Type a new password or delete the current password. Click OK.
3. If you type a new password, reconfirm the password and click OK.

The dialog box displays the current encryption type. To specify a different encryption, click Advanced Options. Choose a new encryption type from the list and a key length, and then click OK.

When a password-protected drawing is opened, the Password dialog box appears. To open the drawing, type the password and click OK.

Digital signatures

A digital signature uses software that confirms who signed the drawing and that it has not been changed, as well as non-repudiation (so that signers cannot claim that they never signed the drawing). To use a digital signature, you need to purchase a digital ID. You can use digital IDs in both AutoCAD and AutoCAD LT.

Generally, you would use a digital signature when you send a drawing to someone else. That person can then verify that the drawing is from you and has not been changed. If the person sends the drawing back to you, you can verify that the person has not changed the drawing, because changing the drawing invalidates the digital signature.

To attach a digital signature to a drawing, follow these steps:

1. Choose Tools ➪ Options and click the Open and Save tab. Click Security Options and then the Digital Signature tab.
2. Check the Attach Digital Signature after Saving Drawing check box and choose a digital signature.
3. To place a time stamp on the drawing, choose one of the options from the Get Time Stamp From drop-down list.
4. To add a comment (that appears when the drawing is opened), type the text in the Comment text box.
5. Click OK.

When a digitally signed drawing is opened, the Digital Signature Contents dialog box appears, verifying the digital signature and the fact that the drawing has not been changed since it was signed. Click Close to close the dialog box.

Note that making any changes to the drawing invalidates the digital ID. If you make changes or try to save a drawing with an attached digital signature, a message appears asking you whether you want to continue. When you re-open the drawing, the Digital Signature Contents dialog box appears, displaying the fact that the digital signature is invalid.

Get a Trial Digital Signature from VeriSign

The Digital Signatures tab of the Security Options dialog box contains a link to VeriSign, a company that sells digital certificates. You can obtain a 60-day free trial or purchase a digital ID at one of several levels of security. If you don't have a digital signature and want to get the trial from VeriSign, follow these steps:

1. Choose Tools ➪ Options and click the Open and Save tab.
2. Click Security Options and then the Digital Signature tab. A message displays, explaining that you don't have a digital ID.
3. Click Get a Digital ID to go to VeriSign's Web site.
4. On the VeriSign Web site, click the Managed PKI Services link, then click the PKI Applications link.
5. Click the Digital IDs for Secure Email link.
6. Click the Buy Now button twice.
7. Choose your browser, and complete a short form. Then choose the I'd Like to Test Drive a 60-Day Trial Digital Id for Free option. You can then omit the credit card information and accept the license agreement.
8. Follow the instructions to install the digital signature.

The final instructions assume that you want to use the digital ID for e-mail; you can ignore those instructions.

A drawing with a valid digital signature has a checkmark attached to its icon in Windows Explorer. The drawing itself also sports an icon in the status bar.

NOTE Users who don't have the Digital Signature feature can download the Digital Signature Verifier, a free application to verify digital signatures on signed drawings. The Digital Signature Verifier is available from the Autodesk Web site at http://usa.autodesk.com/adsk/item/0,,877495-123112-587113,00.html. (You can also go to www.autodesk.com and do a search on Digital Signature Verifier.)

Keeping Track of Referenced Files

A drawing references several types of outside files, and you often need to keep track of these files, especially when you send a drawing to someone else or move it to another computer. Also, the referenced files may be moved, even if the drawing stays in the same place. Without these outside files, the drawing is not complete.

AUTOCAD ONLY AutoCAD LT does not include the Reference Manager.

Outside files include:

- Other drawings (xrefs, and DWF and DGN underlays)
- Text fonts
- Shape files
- Images
- Plot configurations

The Reference Manager not only lists referenced files, but also enables you to change saved reference paths so that the drawing can find the needed files. You don't even need to open the AutoCAD drawing, because the Reference Manager is a stand-alone application.

CROSS-REF   The new External References palette helps you manage xrefs. For more information, see Chapter 19.

To open the Reference Manager, choose Start ⇨ [All] Programs ⇨ Autodesk ⇨ AutoCAD 2008 ⇨ Reference Manager. The Reference Manager is shown in Figure 26.28.

FIGURE 26.28

The Reference Manager.

To add drawings to the Reference Manager, click Add Drawings and select the drawings. If a drawing has xrefs, you see a message asking whether you want to add the xrefs. To add them, click Yes.

The left pane of the Reference Manager contains a tree view of the drawings that you've added and external references, if any. The right pane is a Reference list and displays the specific external files associated with the added files. You can choose View ⇨ Options in the Reference Manager to customize how the Reference Manager displays files.

NOTE   Reference Manager does not find text fonts that are not used in a text style, TrueType fonts that are not saved in the Windows `Fonts` folder, OLE links, hyperlinks, database file links, PMP files, and external references to URLs on the Web.

To modify the path of an external reference so that a drawing can find it, follow these steps:

1. Close any drawings or files that you might need to access.
2. Choose a drawing in the left pane.
3. Right-click the external reference in the Reference list that you want to change, and choose Edit Selected Paths. (You can also choose Edit Selected Paths from the Reference Manager's toolbar.)

TIP   You can also choose Find and Replace to change all references that use a certain saved path, and replace them with a new path. Use this feature when you have a large number of drawings that need paths to changed referenced files.

4. Type in a new path, or use the Ellipsis button to browse to the location. Click OK.
5. From the Reference Manager's toolbar, choose Apply Changes. A summary message appears to confirm that the drawing has been updated.

To create a list of references, choose Export Report. In the Export Report dialog box, choose the file type that you want to create from the Files of Type drop-down list. You can create the following file types:

- Comma-separated values report file (*.csv)
- Extensible Markup Language report file (*.xml)
- Microsoft Excel Workbook (*.xls)

Choose a name and a location for the file and then click Save.

 The Express Tools contain a command, REDIR (choose Express ➪ File Tools ➪ Redefine Path), that redefines paths for xrefs, images, shapes, and fonts.

Handling Errors and Crashes

Although AutoCAD 2008 and AutoCAD LT 2008 are stable, nothing can eliminate the occasional crash. Knowing how to reopen a drawing after a crash can save hours of work.

Taking care of temporary files

When AutoCAD or AutoCAD LT is loaded, it opens one or more temporary files as part of its normal functioning. Note the following two points regarding these files:

- You need to leave room on your hard drive for these files — 50MB is a good starting point.
- Never erase current temporary files if you're on a network, because someone else might be using them.

CAUTION Never erase temporary files (they have an extension of .ac$) while AutoCAD or AutoCAD LT is open. Normally, they're erased when you close a drawing. Others are erased when you close the program.

However, if the program or your entire computer crashes, you may be left with one or more .ac$ files. A good guideline for erasing .ac$ files is to only erase those from yesterday or earlier. Leave today's alone.

TIP If you don't see the date and time of the files in Windows Explorer, choose View ➪ Details.

You can also specify where you want these temporary files. You might want to place them on a hard drive with more room. If you're on a network, you might want to place them on your local drive so that there is less traffic back and forth on the network. To find or change the current location, follow these steps:

1. Choose Tools ➪ Options. Click the Files tab.
2. Click the plus sign next to Temporary Drawing File Location to display the current location.
3. If you want to change the location, click Browse.
4. In the Browse for Folder list, find and choose the desired folder and click OK.
5. Click OK to close the Options dialog box.

Repairing corrupted drawing files

The most common cause for a corrupted drawing file is a program crash, but power surges and system crashes can also be causes. If AutoCAD or AutoCAD LT detects an error in a file during loading, it attempts to fix the problem automatically. In many cases, it is successful.

When it isn't, you can try the AUDIT or RECOVER commands. These commands search the database for errors and try to fix them. If they cannot fix an error, they simply move on, letting you recover at least part of the file.

If you have a drawing open and see an error message that AutoCAD or AutoCAD LT can't read the file or part of it, follow these steps:

1. Choose File ➪ Drawing Utilities ➪ Audit.
2. At the `Fix any errors detected? [Yes/No] <N>:` prompt, type **y** ↵ to fix any errors.
3. Watch the screen as it displays messages for errors.

Use RECOVER when you can't even load the drawing. Follow these steps:

1. Open a new drawing.
2. Choose File ➪ Recover.
3. In the Select File dialog box, choose the corrupted drawing file and click Open. The recovery process starts and displays the results in the Text Window.

NEW FEATURE The RECOVERALL command lets you select a drawing and run recover on that drawing as well as all associated xref files. (See Chapter 19 for more on xrefs.)

The DWGCHECK system variable controls how your drawings open when they have errors. Look up this system variable in Help to find a setting that gives you the information and control that you need. Here are some other tips for opening a recalcitrant drawing:

- Open a new drawing and choose Insert ➪ Block. Click Browse and insert the problem drawing as a block. (See Chapter 18 for more information on blocks.) Then use the AUDIT command.
- Open a new drawing and choose Insert ➪ DWG Reference. Locate and attach the problem drawing as an external reference. (See Chapter 19 for more information on external references.) Then use the AUDIT command.
- If the drawing crashes just when it looks like it has almost loaded, try again; however, this time, press Esc repeatedly until the loading is complete. This procedure aborts the regeneration of the drawing, which may be causing the crash due to corrupt objects. Then use the AUDIT command.
- If you can open the drawing but objects are not displayed, try the following:
  - Choose File ➪ Save As and save it as a new drawing.
  - Use the WBLOCK command to save the drawing as a new file.
  - Save the drawing as a DXF file. (See Chapter 27 for more on the DXF file format.)
  - Use File ➪ Save As or save as a DXF format, but to an earlier version of AutoCAD or AutoCAD LT.

Thanks to Darren Young of Minnesota CADWorks, Inc. (www.mcwi.com) for these suggestions.

Using backup drawings

If you can't repair a drawing, perhaps you have an archived copy that you can use. If not, AutoCAD and AutoCAD LT automatically create backup drawings that have the same name as your drawings, but with a .bak filename extension. You can change the extension to .dwg and open it. You may also find one of the .ac$ drawings. You can also try changing the extension of this file to .dwg.

TIP If your computer doesn't show filename extensions for BAK and AC$ drawings, open Windows Explorer and choose Tools ⇨ Folder Options. Click the File Types tab. Choose BAK from the list of extensions. Then click the Advanced button and check the Always Show Extension check box. Click OK. Do the same for the AC$ extension. Click OK (or Close).

If you want to troubleshoot a persistent crash, try turning on the log file. Choose Tools ⇨ Options and choose the Open and Save tab. Check Maintain a Log File. This log file lists all of your activity and can be used to try to determine what actions caused a crash. You can also customize the log file's location using the Files tab of the Options dialog box. In the same location, you can turn on or off the saving of backups.

AUTOCAD ONLY The Express Tools contain a command, MOVEBAK (choose Express ⇨ File Tools ⇨ Move Backup Files), that moves backup files (*.bak) to a folder that you specify, and there-after saves the backup files in that folder every time you save your drawing.

Recovering from a crash

Yes, AutoCAD does occasionally crash. The Drawing Recovery Manager tries to makes recovering from a crash easy by displaying available backup drawings for you. If you crash, you first see the message shown in Figure 26.29.

FIGURE 26.29

When you crash, you see a Drawing Recovery message explaining that you can recover your drawing.

The Drawing Recovery Manager palette then opens, where you see a list of drawings. You can select one to see it in the drawing area. In Figure 26.30, you can see that there are three versions of the drawing named ab21-04.dwg.: the recovered version, the Autosave version, and the original drawing. You can easily and quickly choose any one of these and open them to see which one you want to continue working with. AutoCAD automatically deletes old drawing recovery files.

After a crash, the AutoCAD Error Report window opens so that you can send information to Autodesk about the crash. This information helps Autodesk design AutoCAD to be more stable.

FIGURE 26.30

The Drawing Recovery Manager displays backup drawings in one place so that you can open them after a crash.

Managing Drawings from Prior Releases

When you upgrade to a new release, you need to understand how to work with drawings from earlier releases. Also, you may need to send drawings to clients or colleagues who have an earlier release. AutoCAD 2008 uses the same format as 2007 (which introduced a new file format), and the same goes for AutoCAD LT. Therefore, AutoCAD 2008 and AutoCAD LT 2008 save in the 2007 format. You can open a 2008 drawing in 2007, but not in earlier releases. You can save your AutoCAD 2008 drawings in the following earlier drawing formats:

- AutoCAD 2004/AutoCAD LT 2004 Drawing (*.dwg). This format includes AutoCAD and AutoCAD LT 2005 and 2006.
- AutoCAD 2000/LT 2000 Drawing (*.dwg). This format includes 2000, 2000i, and 2002.
- AutoCAD R14/LT98/LT97. This is the earliest version you can save to in DWG format.
- AutoCAD R12/LT 2 DXF (*.dxf). To go back earlier than AutoCAD R14/AutoCAD LT 97, you need to save to DXF format. See the "Exporting to DXF format" section in the next chapter for more about the DXF format.

Choose File ⇨ Save As and choose the file type in the Save As Type drop-down list. Then click Save.

Summary

In this chapter, I covered various methods for managing drawings. You read about the following:

- Using the DesignCenter to access drawing components
- Using the new tool palettes to access drawings, blocks, and hatches
- Maintaining CAD standards, including checking a drawing against a standards drawing and translating layers
- Understanding the new Communication Center
- Renaming named objects
- Working with sheet sets
- Organizing your drawings, including archiving drawings, finding them, and setting properties for them
- Maintaining security of your drawings with a password and digital signatures
- Using the Reference Manager to keep track of external files referenced in a drawing
- Handling errors and crashes
- Managing drawings from prior releases

In the next chapter I cover how to use AutoCAD or AutoCAD LT with other applications.

Chapter 27

Working with Other Applications

IN THIS CHAPTER

Coordinating AutoCAD and AutoCAD LT with other data

Importing from, and exporting to, other file formats, including DGN, DXF, and PDF

Working with raster images

Pasting, linking, and embedding objects

Your drawing is not a world unto itself. Many times, you need to work with files or data from other applications. Here are some possibilities:

- Working for a client who uses another CAD program
- Placing a logo into your title block
- Inserting a drawing into a report
- Inserting a spreadsheet into your drawing
- Using a satellite photo as a basis to create a map

You have several ways of working with other applications:

- You can import another file format so that the entire file is brought into your drawing.
- You can export to another file format so that the entire drawing can be imported into another application.
- You can export to an image format that others can view.
- You can import a *raster* image (bitmap) without changing any file format. A raster image is made up of dots, called *pixels*, as opposed to vectors. AutoCAD and AutoCAD LT are vector programs.
- You can import, or export to, a DXF file, which is a way of interchanging drawings between AutoCAD or AutoCAD LT and other CAD programs.

As you can imagine, the possibilities are endless. This chapter explains how to work with other applications.

Importing and Exporting Other File Formats

You can export to several other file formats, thereby enabling you to save the file in another format. You can also import several formats. This section explains how to do both.

Exporting drawings

You usually export objects to an image format and then use that format in another application. You may also export a drawing to import it into another CAD program. The method you use depends on the type of format that you want. Table 27.1 shows the file formats that AutoCAD and AutoCAD LT can create. Except as noted, you are prompted to select objects to export.

TABLE 27.1

Export File Formats

Format	Description
WMF	Windows Metafile Format — a Windows vector format.
ACIS	A solid modeling file format stored as .sat files, in text (ASCII) form. (AutoCAD only.)
STL	Exports a single solid in a format usable with stereolithography. (AutoCAD only.)
BMP	Windows bitmap — a raster format.
EPS	Encapsulated PostScript — a format used by certain printers to create high-quality text and images. Exports all objects. (AutoCAD only.)
DXF	Drawing Interchange Format is a text format for CAD drawings that most CAD programs accept. You can choose from Releases 2007, 2004, 2000, and 12 DXF file formats. Exports the entire drawing.
DXB	Another format for transferring CAD drawings, but in binary format (not text). Used less often than the DXF format.
DWF	Design Web Format — a format for placing a drawing on a Web site.
DGN	Format of Bentley Microstation drawings. You can export the entire drawing as a Version 8 DGN file.
JPG	Joint Photographic Expert Group — a raster (bitmap) format commonly used on the Web. It can be compressed, but will lose some detail. Often used for photographs because it supports many colors.
TIF	Tagged Image File Format — a raster (bitmap) format often used for scanned images. Provides good quality.
PNG	Portable Network Graphics — a raster (bitmap) format that supports many colors and also compresses well without losing detail. It also supports transparency.
PDF	Adobe Acrobat Portable Document Format.

 CROSS-REF For more information on the DWF file format, see the next chapter. The DWF format is a way to share your drawings with others either directly or on the Internet.

Exporting to DXF format

The DXF (drawing interchange file) format is a text file that contains all of the information in a 2D drawing. Because most CAD programs accept this format, you can export to DXF and send the file to someone else who can then import it into another CAD program. Figure 27.1 shows the part of a DXF file that defines a line. Not only are objects defined, but all layers, linetypes, and other settings are defined, as well. The file lists codes that specify a certain type of data (for example, the X coordinate of a line's endpoint), followed by the values for the codes (for example, 7.55).

FIGURE 27.1

Most CAD programs accept the DXF file format.

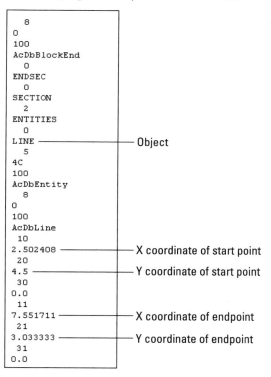

```
    8
    0
  100
AcDbBlockEnd
    0
ENDSEC
    0
SECTION
    2
ENTITIES
    0
LINE ——————————— Object
    5
   4C
  100
AcDbEntity
    8
    0
  100
AcDbLine
   10
2.502408 ————————— X coordinate of start point
   20
4.5 ————————————— Y coordinate of start point
   30
0.0
   11
7.551711 ————————— X coordinate of endpoint
   21
3.033333 ————————— Y coordinate of endpoint
   31
0.0
```

To create a DXF file, choose File ⇨ Save As. Choose one of the DXF formats in the Files of type drop-down list. You can save in DXF formats for Releases 12, 2000 (which includes Releases 2000i and 2002), 2004 (which includes Releases 2005 and 2006), and 2007 (which includes Release 2008). Click Save.

Exporting to DGN format

Many users work with companies that use other CAD products, such as Bentley Microstation. The DGN-EXPORT command allows you to translate your drawing file (and any xrefs) according to your preferences. (I cover xrefs in Chapter 19.) To export a drawing to DGN format, choose File ⇨ Export to open the Export Data dialog box, shown in Figure 27.2.

NEW FEATURE Exporting to DGN format is new for AutoCAD 2008 and AutoCAD LT 2008.

The Export Data dialog box.

Choose a location and filename, and click Save. The Export DGN Settings dialog box opens, as shown in Figure 27.3.

The Export DGN Settings dialog box lets you fine-tune your DGN export.

In the Export DGN Settings dialog box, you can specify the following settings:

- **External DWG References:** You specify whether you want to translate external references in AutoCAD DWG format into DGN references. You can keep them as external references, combine them into one drawing, or ignore them.

- **External DGN References:** You may have DGN drawings in your AutoCAD drawing as underlays. You can choose whether or not to include DGN underlays.

- **Seed File:** You can choose a seed file from available samples in the Template folder or from another location.

- **Master Units or Sub Units:** A DGN file can have two sets of measurement units (master and sub. Choose which units you want to use.

 A *seed file* for a DGN file is similar to a drawing template file. It contains settings such as the measurement units (Imperial or Metric), the Origin, and whether the file is 2D or 3D.

Keep in mind that some objects and properties are not translated properly. Examples are:

- 3D solids and surfaces

- Annotative properties

- Layer property overrides by viewport

- Custom AutoCAD objects (such as those created by related Autodesk products or third-party applications)

- Objects with Z values other than 0, when you use a 2D seed file

Exporting to PDF format

Many AutoCAD and AutoCAD LT users like to use the DWF format to share drawings when they don't want to send the drawing itself — whether for security reasons or because a colleague doesn't have the program. DWF files display the drawing in a free viewer or on the Web, and support zooming, panning, layers, named views, and so on. I cover the DWF format in Chapter 28.

However, non-CAD users, such as clients, may not want to install software to view DWF files, or they may simply feel more comfortable with an Adobe Acrobat PDF (Portable Document Format) file. The Adobe Acrobat Reader, which is the viewer for PDF files, is widely available and free.

NEW FEATURE The new DWFx format, version 7, will create files whose 2D data will conform to Microsoft's XPS format. This format is an image format similar to PDF. Windows Vista comes with an XPS reader, and so people with Windows Vista will be able to view the new DWF files without a separate reader. People with Windows XP and Microsoft .NET Framework 3.0 will also be able to view DWFx files.

To export to the PDF format, you use the PLOT command and plot to a file using a plotter configuration (PC3) file. (See the sidebar "Configuring Your Plotter" in Chapter 17 and the section "Configuring a Plotter" in Appendix A for more information.) Follow these steps:

1. Display the drawing that you want to export.
2. Start the PLOT command.
3. In the Printer/Plotter section of the Plot dialog box, click the Name drop-down list and choose DWG To PDF.pc3.

4. Make any other adjustments that you want to make in the Plot dialog box and click OK.

5. In the Browse for Plot File dialog box, name the PDF file (or accept the default) and choose a location.

6. Click OK.

You can now view your drawing in the Adobe Acrobat Reader.

CROSS-REF The PUBLISH command, covered in Chapter 28, also can create PDF files. Finally, you can publish from a sheet set, as I explain in Chapter 26, and create a multi-page PDF file of the sheets.

Exporting to other file formats

To export to JPG, PNG, or TIF formats, use the JPGOUT, PNGOUT, or TIFOUT command on the command line. Then, choose a folder, click Save, and select objects at the prompt.

When you want to export a drawing to another file format, whether to create an image file or import that file into another application, you export the drawing. WMF, which is a vector image file, is probably the most commonly used format. In AutoCAD, you can also export to a BMP file. (AutoCAD LT users need to use the BMPOUT command to export to a BMP file.) To export a drawing to another format (except for JPG, PNG, and TIF), follow these steps:

1. Choose File ⇨ Export to open the Export Data dialog box.

2. Choose the file format that you want in the Files of Type drop-down list.

3. Find the desired folder using the Save In drop-down list and the Folder box.

4. Click Save.

NOTE You can also export to 3D DWF format. See Chapter 28 for more information on DWF files.

Controlling the display of exported WMF files

The WMFBKGND system variable controls the background of WMF files that you export, whether using the Export Data dialog box, copying and pasting, or dragging and dropping. When the value of this system variable is Off (the default), the background color of the file is transparent, so that it doesn't interfere with the background on which it is pasted. You can set it to On so that the background is the same as that of the drawing background.

The WMFFOREGND system variable works in tandem with the WMFBKGND system variable. It controls the foreground (line) color of objects when you export WMF files. WMFFOREGND takes effect only when you set WMFBKGND to 0, which makes the background color transparent. A value of 0, the default, swaps foreground and background colors, if necessary, to make the foreground color (the objects) darker than the background color. A value of 1 does the opposite — the foreground color is lighter than the background color.

 The drawing used in the following exercise on exporting a WMF file, ab27-a.dwg, is in the Drawings folder on the DVD.

STEPS: Exporting a WMF File

1. Open ab27-a.dwg from the DVD.

2. Save the file as ab27-01.dwg in your AutoCAD Bible folder. You can see it in Figure 27.4.

FIGURE 27.4

The Easy Cotton Mills logo.

3. Choose File ⇨ Export. The Files of Type drop-down list should say Metafile (*.wmf). The file name automatically reads ab27-01.wmf.

4. If necessary, locate your AutoCAD Bible folder. Click Save.

5. At the Select objects: prompt, make a window around the red rectangle to include all three objects. End object selection to end the command.

You've created a WMF file.

Importing files

For most file formats, choose Insert from the menu and then choose Raster Image Reference or the file type that you want to import. Find the file in the dialog box and click Open. Generally, the command line then prompts you for an insertion point, X and Y scale factors, and a rotation angle, just as for block insertion. You can also find some of these file types by choosing File ⇨ Import.

In the following exercise, you practice importing a WMF file.

The file used in the following exercise on importing a WMF file, ab27-01.wmf, **is in the** Results **folder on the DVD. If you did the previous exercise, you can also find the file in your** AutoCAD Bible **folder.**

STEPS: Importing a WMF File

1. Open a new drawing using the acad.dwt or acadlt.dwt template.

2. Save the file as ab27-02.dwg in your AutoCAD Bible folder.

3. Choose Insert ⇨ Windows Metafile.

4. If you did the previous exercise, locate your AutoCAD Bible folder in the Import WMF dialog box. Choose ab27-01.wmf. If you didn't do the previous exercise, find ab27-01.wmf in the Results folder of the DVD. In the Import WMF dialog box, choose Tools ⇨ Options. Check Wire Frame (No Fills), uncheck Wide Lines if necessary, and click OK. Click Open.

5. At the `Specify insertion point or [Basepoint/Scale/X/Y/Z /Protate]:` prompt, pick any point near the top of your screen. Notice that the insertion point is at the top-left corner of the image.

6. Press Enter to accept the defaults for X and Y scales and rotation angle. Notice that you've lost the solid fill in the logo. The red rectangle came in fine. Also, you may see an added rectangle around the extents of the image where the extents of the screen were when the WMF file was created.

7. Pick the image. Notice that everything is selected with one grip at the insertion point. Choose Explode from the Modify toolbar.

8. Choose Tools ⇨ Inquiry ⇨ List, and pick any part of the logo. Press Enter. Notice from the listing that the logo is now made up of polylines. Repeat the LIST command with the text. It has been converted to a TEXT object. (If the text was based on a SHX font, it would be converted to polylines.) Because WMF files convert to drawing objects, you can edit them, but they may require a good deal of cleanup to attain a pleasing result.

9. Choose Insert ⇨ Windows Metafile. Choose `ab27-01.wmf`. Click Options to open the Import Options (WMF In) dialog box. This time, check Wide Lines, uncheck Wire Frame (No Fills), and click OK. In the Import WMF dialog box, click Open to import the file. Pick in a different location in your drawing, and accept the defaults.

10. Explode the inserted image. (You may have to pick it at its edge.) Erase the rectangle and the line at the right that remains. Now you have an image that is very close to the original. The text comes in with the Bookman Old Style font (or the font that you used — the same font as the original), although the spacing is not exact. Also, the logo now has its solid fill. It should look like Figure 27.5.

11. Save your drawing.

FIGURE 27.5

An imported WMF file.

Importing a DGN file

If someone sends you a file in DGN (Bentley Microstation) format, you can now import this file by choosing File ⇨ Import (the DGNIMPORT command). In the Import File dialog box, choose V8 DGN (*.dgn) from the Files of Type drop-down list and select the file.

NEW FEATURE Importing DGN files is new for AutoCAD 2008 and AutoCAD LT 2008.

The Import DGN Settings dialog box opens, where you can specify the following settings:

- **Select a design model from the DGN file:** A design model is like AutoCAD's model space. A DGN drawing may have multiple model spaces. You can only import one at a time; if you need more than one, you need to import them separately.

- **External DGN References:** You can choose to ignore any xrefs, translate all xrefs into individual files, or keep the references as DGNs and use them as underlays. (See Chapter 19 for more information about DGN underlays.)

- **Explode text nodes to text elements:** Text nodes are multiple lines of text in one object, such as AutoCAD's Mtext. Text elements would be single lines of text, such as Dtext. If you want to keep the file looking the same as the original, especially around curves and arcs, then you should check this option.

- **Conversion units:** The DGN has a master unit and a sub-unit (such as feet and inches or meters and millimeters). The dialog box displays the units, and you choose which one to import as one unit. For example, if you choose to import the file using master units of feet, it will appear 1/12 the size of the same drawing using sub-units (inches). Be sure to measure and make sure that you chose the right units.

Click OK when you're done to import the drawing.

CROSS-REF You can attach DWF files and DGN files (Microstation drawings) to your drawing. When you attach a file, you are not importing it; rather, you are just displaying it along with your drawing. These files are similar to xrefs, and so I discuss them in Chapter 19, where I cover xrefs.

Inserting a DXF file

If someone sends you a file in DXF format, it probably contains a drawing that was created in another CAD program. You can open that drawing in AutoCAD or AutoCAD LT. You can import a DXF file in two ways:

- To import a DXF file into a new drawing, use the OPEN command to open a new drawing, choose DXF in the Files of Type drop-down list, choose the DXF file, and click Open.

- To insert a DXF file into an existing drawing, choose Insert ➪ Block. In the Insert dialog box, click Browse. Then choose DXF in the Files of Type drop-down list, choose the DXF file, and click Open.

Working with Raster Images

You can easily import scanned images, digital photographs, and other image files into your drawings. You can use these images to insert a logo, show a photo or artist's rendering of your model, and for many other uses. Although raster (bitmap) images are generally much larger files than vector drawings, you can easily zoom and pan throughout your drawing. You can usually plot these raster images, as well. Table 27.2 shows the raster formats that AutoCAD 2008 supports.

AUTOCAD ONLY You cannot insert raster images into AutoCAD LT. However, you can open an AutoCAD drawing that contains images and view the image. You can also use the EXTERNALREFERENCES command to obtain information about the image. You can copy, move, and resize the image.

TABLE 27.2

Raster Formats Supported by AutoCAD 2008

File Type	File Extension	Comments
BMP	.bmp, .dib, .rle	Windows and OS/2 bitmap
CALS1	.gp4, .mil, .rst, .cg4, .cal, .cals	Mil-R-Raster 1
GIF	.gif	CompuServe Graphics Exchange Format
GeoSPOT	.bil	GeoSPOT (used in GIS applications); HDR and PAL files with correlation data must be in the same folder
JFIF or JPEG	.jpg	Joint Photographic Expert Group
FLIC	.flc, .fli	Autodesk Animator FLIC
IG4	.ig4	Image Systems Group 4
PCX	.pcx	Paintbrush
PICT	.pct, .pict	Macintosh picture
PNG	.png	Portable Network Graphic
RLC	.rlc	Run-Length Compressed
TARGA	.tga	True Vision Raster-Based Data Format
TIF	.tif, .tiff	Tagged Image File Format

Inserting images

It's easy to insert an image into your AutoCAD drawing. After you insert the image, you can manipulate it in a number of ways. To insert an image, choose Insert ➪ Raster Image Reference to open the Select Image File dialog box.

Locate the image that you want to insert and click Open. The Image dialog box opens, as shown in Figure 27.6; this dialog box lets you specify how to insert the image. You can specify the insertion point, scale, and rotation in the dialog box or on-screen. This dialog box is very similar to the Insert dialog box that you use when inserting drawings and blocks.

TIP You can specify a relative path (instead of the full path) for an image. A relative path stores only the relationship between the drawing and the image. If you put the image in the same folder as the drawing, only the drawing name is stored. Using a relative path and placing the image in the same folder as the drawing is ideal when you need to share drawings with people who don't have the same folder structure as you.

FIGURE 27.6

The Image dialog box.

Click Details to open the bottom of the dialog box. Here the dialog box lists the resolution (number of pixels) per drawing unit and the size in pixels, as well as the size in drawing units. The Current AutoCAD Unit is based on the specification in the Units dialog box. (See Chapter 5 for more information.) This information is helpful in deciding how to scale an image. Click OK to insert the image.

NOTE   Raster images usually don't scale up very well. If you enlarge them too much, the dots get too far apart, and the image looks grainy. However, the higher the resolution, the better the image will look when enlarged.

You can also use the DesignCenter to insert raster images, as described in Chapter 26.

AUTOCAD ONLY   The Express Tools contain a command, IMAGEEDIT (choose Express ⇨ File Tools ⇨ Edit Image), that opens a selected image in a specified image-editing application.

Managing images

As with xrefs, you may need a way to keep track of your images, especially if you insert many of them. Choose Insert ⇨ External References to open the External References palette, as shown in Figure 27.7. The External References palette enables you to manage the images (as well as external drawing references, and both DWF and DGN underlays) in your drawing. You can insert images from this palette, as well.

FIGURE 27.7

The External References palette.

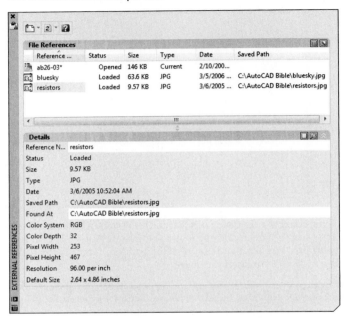

You can use the List view and Tree view buttons at the top-right corner of the File References pane to view your images as a *flat* list or a hierarchical (tree) format. Use the Details and Preview buttons at the top-right corner of the bottom pane to view either file details or a preview. Here are the other options:

- Choose **Attach Image** from the drop-down list at the top of the palette (or right-click any item) to insert an image, opening the Image dialog box (refer to Figure 27.6).

- Right-click any item and choose **Detach** to delete the image from your drawing and all references to it in the drawing database.

- Right-click any item and choose **Unload** to remove the display of the image but retain the reference to it. Later, you can reload the image to redisplay it.

- Right-click any item and choose **Reload** to redisplay an image after you've unloaded it or made changes to it.

TIP You can attach rendered images that you've saved as PCX, JPG, JPEG, PNG, TIF, TGA, or BMP files. A great way to do this is to create a floating viewport in paper space for the rendered image, letting your clients see not only the regular drawing, but also the rendered result on one sheet of paper. (Figure 25.18 in Chapter 25 was created this way.) Remember that you can plot shaded and rendered images. See Chapter 17 for details.

Clipping images

A powerful feature of AutoCAD lets you clip images just as you clip external references. Large images can slow down your drawing display. You may also simply find it distracting to see parts of an image that you don't need for your work. For example, if you attach an aerial photograph of a city block but want only one house, being able to clip around the house and not display the rest of the image is a great advantage.

To clip an image, follow these steps:

1.   Insert an image.
2.   Choose Modify ➪ Clip ➪ Image (the IMAGECLIP command).
3.   At the `Select image to clip:` prompt, select the image. Pick the image at its border.
4.   At the prompt, press Enter to accept the default of creating a new clipping boundary.
5.   At the `Enter clipping type [Polygonal/Rectangular] <Rectangular>:` prompt, press Enter to create a rectangular clip, or right-click and choose Polygonal to create a multisided boundary.

   - For a rectangular boundary, pick a first point and the opposite corner to create the boundary.
   - For a polygonal boundary, specify the first point and then use the `Specify next point or [Undo]:` prompt to pick points until you've completed the boundary. You can use the Undo option to undo the last pick, or the Close option (which appears after you pick three points) to close the final boundary. AutoCAD creates a rubber-band boundary as you pick points so that you can see the result. Press Enter when you're done.

At the `Enter image clipping option [ON/OFF/Delete/New boundary] <New>:` prompt, you can also use the following options:

■   Choose ON to turn on a boundary that you previously turned off.
■   Choose OFF to turn off a boundary and redisplay the entire image.
■   Choose Delete to delete the clipping boundary.

 Images are 2D objects. The clipping boundary must be parallel to the plane of the image.

Controlling image display

You can control several aspects of image display using the commands detailed in this section. Control the image display to adjust the properties that control how the image looks.

Image display

The IMAGEADJUST command lets you change the brightness, contrast, and fade of an image. Choose Modify ➪ Object ➪ Image ➪ Adjust to start the IMAGEADJUST command and open the Image Adjust dialog box, as shown in Figure 27.8.

This dialog box enables you to dynamically change the brightness, contrast, and fade of the image, using the slider bars or text boxes. You immediately see the results in the preview box. Choose Reset to return the image to its original status.

FIGURE 27.8

The Image Adjust dialog box.

Image quality

Choose Modify ➪ Object ➪ Image ➪ Quality to start the IMAGEQUALITY command. AutoCAD displays the `Enter image quality setting [High/Draft] <High>:` prompt. Choose either High or Draft. This command affects the display of all of the images in a drawing. Use it when a high-quality image slows down performance. A regen is not necessary after you change this setting. Plotting is always done at high quality.

Image transparency

If the image format that you're using supports transparent pixels, you can use the TRANSPARENCY command to create a transparent background for your image. This works for bi-tonal or grayscale images. (*Bi-tonal* images have only a foreground and a background color.) By default, transparency is off.

To turn transparency on, choose Modify ➪ Object ➪ Image ➪ Transparency and select the image(s) that you want to change. At the `Enter transparency mode [ON/OFF] <OFF>:` prompt, type **on** ↵ and do a regen. Other objects in your drawing will now be visible through the background of your image.

Image frame

The IMAGEFRAME command controls the frame that surrounds all images in a drawing. Choose Modify ➪ Object ➪ Image ➪ Frame. Choose one of three settings:

- **0:** Turns off the frame, both in the drawing display and when plotting.
- **1:** Turns on the frame, both in the drawing display and when plotting.
- **2:** Displays the frame in the drawing, but doesn't plot it.

Turning off the frame often improves the way the image looks. However, you select an image by clicking its frame. Therefore, an Off setting means that you cannot select the image, except when using commands specific to images, such as TRANSPARENCY, IMAGEADJUST, and IMAGECLIP.

When an image has a border, the border displays the properties of the layer that was current when the image was inserted.

Draw order

The DRAWORDER command (Tools ➪ Draw Order) changes the display order of objects, including raster and OLE objects. (OLE is discussed later in this chapter.) This command is very helpful when working with raster and OLE objects, where you may or may not want to hide the other objects in your drawing. You can move an object to the top or bottom or change its order in relation to another object — above or below it. To change an object's display order, choose Tools ⇨ Draw Order and choose one of the submenu options. At the prompt, select the objects you want. Draw order settings are saved with the drawing.

TIP The TEXTTOFRONT command controls the order of both text and dimensions. Use this command to ensure that text is always on top and never obscured by other objects. In Chapter 13, I explain how to use a background mask to make text more legible.

ON the DVD-ROM The drawing used in the following exercise on working with raster images, ab27-b.dwg, and the images ab27-b.tif and ab27-b1.bmp, are in the Drawings folder on the DVD. This exercise works with AutoCAD only.

STEPS: Working with Raster Images

1. Open ab27-b.dwg from the DVD.
2. Save the file as ab27-03.dwg in your AutoCAD Bible folder.
3. Choose View ⇨ 3D Views ⇨ Top.
4. Choose Insert ⇨ Raster Image Reference.
5. In the Select Image File dialog box, choose ab27-b.tif from the DVD. Click Open. Click Details. Notice that the image is 1 × 0.61 units. Compared to the house, it is tiny.
6. In the Image dialog box, uncheck Specify on-screen for the Scale factor (if it's checked), and change the scale factor to 5. Click OK.
7. At the Specify insertion point <0,0>: prompt, pick any point on the left side of the screen. The image is still tiny, but that's okay. Choose Zoom Window from the Zoom flyout of the Standard toolbar (or choose View ⇨ Zoom ⇨ Window) to zoom closely into the image.
8. Choose Modify ⇨ Object ⇨ Image ⇨ Adjust. At the Select image(s): prompt, select the image by picking its frame. Press Enter. In the Image Adjust dialog box, change the Contrast to 60 and the Brightness to 40. Choose OK.
9. Choose Modify ⇨ Clip ⇨ Image. At the Select image to clip: prompt, select the image again, which is shown in Figure 27.9. Follow the prompts:

```
Enter image clipping option [ON/OFF/Delete/New boundary] <New>: ↵
Enter clipping type [Polygonal/Rectangular] <Rectangular>: ↵
Specify first corner point: If OSNAP is on, turn it off. Pick ❶ in
   Figure 27.9.
Specify opposite corner point: Pick ❷.
```

FIGURE 27.9

Clipping the raster image.

10. If necessary, use Zoom Realtime to zoom out so that you have room to insert another image. Choose Insert ➪ Raster Image Reference and attach ab27-b1.bmp (located on the DVD) with a scale factor of 5. Insert it below the first image.

11. Click the Layout1 tab (or the Layout1 button on the Status bar) to enter paper space, which has three floating viewports. Double-click the bottom-left viewport. Choose View ➪ 3D Views ➪ Top. You should now see the images as a small dot to the left of the house. Use Zoom Window to zoom into the rendered table. Your drawing should now look like Figure 27.10.

FIGURE 27.10

The drawing with a rendered view in one viewport.

12. Click the right viewport. If necessary, pan the house to the right until you can see the two images that you attached. Move the Cottonmill Houses image to ❶ in Figure 27.10. Use the SCALE command to scale it, using a base point at its lower-left corner and a scale factor of 25. Move it until it fits nicely in the upper-right corner of the floor plan. Pan again to center the house in the viewport. (If it disappears, do a Zoom Extents.)

13. Choose Modify ➪ Object ➪ Image ➪ Frame. Enter 0 ↵. AutoCAD removes the frames from the two images.

14. Save your drawing.

Pasting, Linking, and Embedding Objects

To maximize the data that you have in your drawing and other documents, you can insert objects from other applications into your drawing. For example, you may have a description of your drawing in a word-processing application or a table in a spreadsheet. You can use the Windows Clipboard to share data between applications.

CROSS-REF In Chapter 18, I explain how to use the Windows Clipboard to copy and move material from one drawing to another. Chapter 13 includes a discussion of several techniques for importing text into your drawing.

You can insert data (text or images) that was created with other applications into a drawing in three ways:

- **Embed** the object if you want to be able to return to the source application to edit the object. When you double-click the object, the source application opens so that you can edit the object.

- **Paste** the object when you don't need any connection with the source application.

- **Link** the object when you want to retain a permanent link to the source file so that when the source file is changed, the change is updated in your drawing.

You can use the Clipboard to move material from one application to another and take advantage of the special options for pasting, linking, and embedding data. Linking and embedding are often referred to as Object Linking and Embedding, or OLE. You can also use drag-and-drop between applications.

The instructions that follow assume that the *source application* (the application that contains the data that you want to insert) is also a Windows application.

Embedding objects into a drawing

You have three ways to embed data from other applications. Each method has its advantages and disadvantages.

Here's the first way:

1. From your drawing, choose Insert ⇨ OLE Object to open the Insert Object dialog box, as shown in Figure 27.11. This starts the INSERTOBJ command. (The entries listed in this dialog box depend on the applications that you have installed on your computer.)

2. If you want to create a new file in the other application, choose Create New. Choose the application that you want to use from the Object Type list, and click OK. The other application opens, so that you can create the new data. When you're done, choose File ⇨ Update from the other application's menu. (This menu item can vary, depending on the application.) Click the Close button at the top-right corner of the application to close it and return to your drawing. If the OLE Properties dialog box appears, specify how you want the object to appear, and click OK. The new file is inserted.

FIGURE 27.11

The Insert Object dialog box.

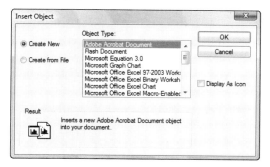

3. If you want to choose an existing file, choose Create from File. Click Browse to find the file. Click Open. You return to the Insert Object dialog box, where you can choose Link to link the data (described in the next section of this chapter). Choose OK. The file appears at the top-left corner of your screen with handles that you can use to move and/or resize the object.

Here's the second way:

1. Open the source application, select the data, and copy it to the Clipboard. (Click Copy on the Standard toolbar or choose Edit ➪ Copy.) Leave the source application open.

2. If your drawing is open, switch to it by choosing its button on the task bar. Otherwise, open it.

3. In your drawing, choose Edit ➪ Paste Special.

4. In the Paste Special dialog box, choose the first option, which lets you embed the object as an object of the source application. Click OK.

5. You can now close the other application.

The third way to insert data is to use drag-and-drop:

1. If your drawing is not open, open it. Open the drawing where you want to embed the data.

2. Open the source application and select the data.

3. Press Ctrl and click the selected data again, holding down the mouse button.

4. Drag the data to the AutoCAD or AutoCAD LT button on the Windows task bar and continue to hold down the mouse button until your drawing displays.

5. Drag the data to the desired location in your drawing.

Using INSERTOBJ gives you the option of creating a new file on the spot in the other application. You don't have to keep the other application open when you return to your drawing. Note that you cannot create a link if you're creating a new file.

Using the Clipboard enables you to insert part of a file — for example, part of a spreadsheet — which can be a great advantage. You need to keep the other application open until you paste the object into your drawing.

You can control the size of text and the plot quality of OLE objects. Choose Tools ➪ Options and click the Plot and Publish tab, where you can set the default OLE plot quality. To change the plot quality, select the OLE object and change the quality in the Plot Quality item of the Properties palette. Text is automatically scaled to approximate the size in the original application. To change the text size, select the OLE object and right-click. Choose OLE ➪ Text Size. In the OLE Text Size dialog box, you can change the text size by entering a new number in the Text Height text box. Click OK.

OLE objects have a few limitations:

- If they're contained in a block or an external reference, they may not be displayed or plotted.
- In certain cases, OLE objects can be printed out only on Windows system printers. You can usually configure your plotter to be the system printer.
- OLE objects don't rotate with your drawing when you use a PLOT rotation. To work around this, you can use the system printer's Landscape setting.

TIP If you don't mind a few steps, you can sometimes get good results importing large Excel spreadsheets by way of Microsoft Word, as follows: In Excel, use Save As to save the spreadsheet in Text (Tab delimited) format. Insert the file into Word (choose Text Files from the Open dialog box's Files of Type drop-down list). Select the entire file and choose Table ➪ Convert ➪ Text to Table. Change the Page Setup to accommodate the large size of the table, using a custom paper size. Format the table if you want. Copy it to the Clipboard. In your drawing, choose Paste on the Standard toolbar.

> **TIP** If you try to use HIDE on a 3D model that contains OLE objects, the OLE objects disappear! The solution is to insert them in paper space. You can then hide the 3D model in one floating viewport and display the OLE object in another.

Using Paste Special

When you copy data to the Clipboard, it's stored in several formats, depending on the type of data. You can then choose which format you want to use when you paste it into your drawing, using the PASTESPEC command. Choosing the right format can make a big difference, by enabling you to edit the data in your drawing as you wish.

Pasting data into your drawing

To paste data using PASTESPEC, open the source application, select the data, and copy it to the Clipboard. (Click Copy on the Standard toolbar or choose Edit ➪ Copy.) Leave the source application open.

If your drawing is open, choose its button on the task bar. If not, open it. In your drawing, choose Edit ➪ Paste Special. This opens the Paste Special dialog box, shown in Figure 27.12. In this figure, you see the options that are available when you paste in a range of cells from a spreadsheet.

FIGURE 27.12

The Paste Special dialog box after copying spreadsheet data to the Clipboard.

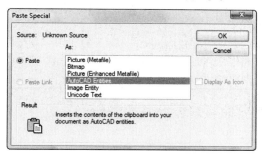

The choices that you see in the As box of the Paste Special dialog box depend on the type of data that you copied. In most cases, you can paste as an object of the source application, as a picture (metafile), as a bitmap, and as text. Table 27.3 describes the characteristics of the choices that are available in the example in Figure 27.12.

Paste Special Data Types

Data Type	Characteristics
Object of source application	The object is inserted at the top-left corner of your drawing. You cannot explode the object, but you can select it and then resize it or move it using its handles. This is an embedded object — if you double-click it, the source application opens, letting you edit the object using the source application's tools.
Picture (Metafile or Enhanced Metafile)	The object is inserted at the top-left corner of your drawing. You cannot explode the object, but you can select it and then resize it or move it using its handles. You cannot edit the object. It maintains good quality when scaled up.
Bitmap	The object is inserted at the top-left corner of your drawing. You cannot explode the object, but you can select it and then resize it or move it using its handles. You cannot edit the object.
AutoCAD Entities	You see prompts for an insertion point, scale factor, and rotation angle. You can explode the object into drawing objects. (Objects were once called *entities* in AutoCAD and AutoCAD LT.) Text objects maintain their original font and formatting.
Image Entity	You see prompts for an insertion point, scale factor, and rotation angle. The object is inserted as approximately a 1×1 unit square. It is a kind of bitmap. You can explode it, but then you lose the image!
(Unicode) Text	The object is inserted at the top-left corner of your drawing. You can explode it, but the text then loses the original formatting and font.

The best choice depends on the type of data that you're pasting. For a spreadsheet, the Picture, Bitmap, and Image Entity choices aren't useful, but they would be quite appropriate if you were pasting in an image.

 XL2CAD 1.0 **helps you to insert Microsoft Excel spreadsheets into your AutoCAD LT drawing.** XL2CAD 2.0 **does the same for AutoCAD. See** \Software\Chapter 27\Xl2CAD1 **and** \Software\Chapter 27\Xl2CAD2.

Pasting drawing objects into another application

You can also copy drawing objects to the Clipboard and paste them into another application, such as a word-processing document, a spreadsheet, or a presentation program. Figure 27.13 shows a PowerPoint slide that includes a model from an AutoCAD drawing. To paste drawing objects into another application, select the objects that you want to copy. Click Copy on the Standard toolbar. Load the other application (in this case PowerPoint), create a document or file (in this case a slide), and click Paste from the application's Standard toolbar.

FIGURE 27.13

Placing part of a drawing on a PowerPoint slide.

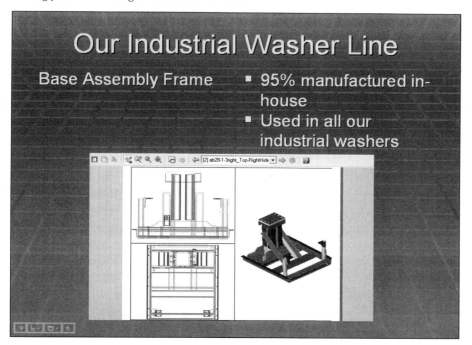

TIP You can hide a 3D view and copy and paste the view into another application. However, you cannot copy and paste a rendered view. To bring a rendered view into another application, save it as an image and import it. Chapter 25 covers saving rendered images. You can freeze any layers that you don't want to include, such as dimension and text layers.

Inserting AutoCAD as an ActiveX Component into PowerPoint

When you insert or paste AutoCAD objects into another document, such as a Word document or PowerPoint presentation, the objects are static images. What if you could display your AutoCAD drawing dynamically, with zooming and panning? You could then show your intended audience all of the detail you want.

continued

continued

It turns out that you can. You can use the DWF format (covered in more detail in Chapter 28) and insert it into any version of Word, Excel, or PowerPoint that supports ActiveX components. Viewers need the free Autodesk Design Review, which they can download at `www.autodesk.com/designreview`. Here are instructions for PowerPoint:

1. Create the DWF file. (See Chapter 28 for instructions.)

2. In PowerPoint, choose a slide layout that gives you room for the DWF file.

3. Choose Insert ⇨ Object. (In PowerPoint 2007, choose Object on the Insert tab.)

4. Click Create New and then choose Autodesk DWF Viewer Control. Click OK. You see a box with handles on your slide.

5. If you want, resize or move the box. (If you deselect the box, it may disappear. Click inside the box to select it again.)

6. Right-click the box and choose Autodesk DWF Viewer Control Object ⇨ Properties.

7. In the Autodesk DWF Viewer Control Properties dialog box, on the SourcePath tab, type the path to the DWF file or click browse to browse to the file. Click OK.

8. In your PowerPoint presentation, choose View ⇨ Slide Show to enter Slide Show view. (In PowerPoint 2007, choose Slide Show on the View tab.) You can now pan, zoom, turn layers on and off, print, and so on from within your presentation.

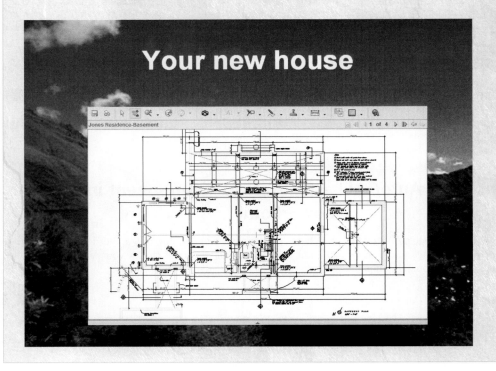

Linking data

You can insert data from a spreadsheet or text document and maintain a link to the original file, so that if the original file changes, the inserted data is updated as well, very similar to xrefs. For example, you could use this feature to place a schedule of doors and windows in an architectural drawing or a bill of materials in a mechanical drawing. You have two ways to link data.

CROSS-REF You can also create a link to an Excel spreadsheet. You can even change the Excel spreadsheet from within AutoCAD. In other words, you have a link in both directions. For more information, see Chapter 13.

First, you can link data using INSERTOBJ, as described earlier in this chapter. Second, you can use the Clipboard, by following these steps:

1. Open the source application, select the data, and copy it to the Clipboard. (Click Copy on the Standard [or Standard Annotation] toolbar or choose Edit ⇨ Copy.)
2. If your drawing is open, choose its button on the task bar. If not, open it.
3. In your drawing, choose Edit ⇨ Paste Special.
4. In the Paste Special dialog box, choose Paste Link. Click OK.

When you create a link, you don't have all of the format options that you do when you simply paste. You can create a link in the source application's format only.

When you open a drawing containing a link, a message appears, asking whether you want to update the links. In this way, you can update the links whenever you open the drawing. You can manage links by choosing Edit ⇨ OLE Links, to open the Links dialog box, as shown in Figure 27.14.

FIGURE 27.14

Use the Links dialog box to manage your links.

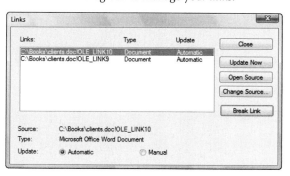

The Links dialog box enables you to manually update the links at any time by choosing Update Now. You may want to do this if you know that someone has changed the source of the link during your drawing session. You can also break the link, open the source, or change the source in this dialog box.

Remember that if you give a drawing to someone else, you also need to include any attached images or embedded objects. If the person does not have the source application for an embedded object, you can paste it in as an image.

The drawing, ab27-c.dwg, and the file, ab27-c.xls, used in the following exercise on pasting, linking, and embedding objects are in the Drawings folder on the DVD.

To do the following exercise, you need a spreadsheet application. I use Microsoft Excel in this exercise, but you can use another spreadsheet if you prefer.

STEPS: Pasting, Linking, and Embedding Objects

1. Open ab27-c.dwg from the DVD.
2. Save the file as ab27-04.dwg in your AutoCAD Bible folder.
3. Choose Insert ➪ OLE Object. Choose Create New and choose your worksheet application from the list. Click OK. Your worksheet program opens.
4. Create the worksheet shown in Figure 27.15. Adjust the width of the columns to fit the data.
5. In the spreadsheet application, choose File ➪ Update and then choose File ➪ Exit. The worksheet appears in the drawing, as shown in Figure 27.16.

FIGURE 27.15

Create this worksheet to insert into your AutoCAD drawing.

	A	B	C	D
1	Tag	Part No.	Description	
2	11	9075-052-002	Collar-Shaft	
3	17	9029-072-001	Bracket-Tube Assembly	
4	19	9081-114-001	Channel Motor Mtg. Rod	
5				

FIGURE 27.16

The spreadsheet inserted into the drawing.

Tag	Part No.	Description
11	9076-052-002	Collar-Shaft
17	9029-072-001	Bracket-Tube Assembly
19	9081-114-001	Channel Motor Mtg. Rod

6. Open your spreadsheet application and open ab27-c.xls from the DVD. Select the data in the last three columns, as shown in Figure 27.17. Click Copy on the spreadsheet's Standard toolbar.

FIGURE 27.17

Selecting part of a file to insert into your drawing.

	A	B	C	D	E	F	G
1	Qty.	Tag	Part No.	Description	Dwg. Size	Pur/Made	Units
2	2	19	9081-114-001	CHANNEL-MOTOR MTG ROD	B	P	EACH
3	2	17	9029-072-001	BRACKET-TUBE ASSY	D	M	EACH
4	2	11	9076-052-002	COLLAR-SHAFT	B	M	EACH

7. Leave your spreadsheet open and click the AutoCAD or AutoCAD LT button on the Windows task bar. Choose Edit ➪ Paste Special. Although you could insert this as an Excel Worksheet (or object from your spreadsheet application), to try another method, choose AutoCAD (LT) Entities and click OK. Pick an insertion point near the right of the existing OLE object.

8. The spreadsheet is inserted as a table object, but is very small. Click outside the table to close the In-Place Text Editor. Zoom in on the table. Click the lower-right corner of the table and drag its handle down and to the right until the table is the same height as the spreadsheet to its left.

9. Click inside the upper-left cell, press Shift, and click inside the lower-right cell. Display the Properties palette (Ctrl+1) and change the Text Height to .6800. Change the Text Style to WMF-Arial0. (This text style was created when you imported the spreadsheet, to match the original text in the spreadsheet.) Change the Alignment to Middle Center.

10. Choose Edit ➪ Paste Special again. Choose Paste Link. Now you can paste in your spreadsheet's format or as AutoCAD (LT) Entities (which creates a linked table). Click OK. Pick an insertion point. Pick the lower-right corner of the spreadsheet and drag its handle down and to the right to enlarge the table.

11. Note that the first row of data has a "P" in the Pur/Made column. Return to your spreadsheet and change cell F2 (which now says P) to M, and press Enter. Go back to your drawing and note that the P has changed to an M. Because the data are linked, any changes made to the spreadsheet are updated in your drawing.

12. Save your drawing. Close your spreadsheet program without saving the change that you made.

Summary

In this chapter, you read about the following:

- Importing and exporting other file formats, including both vector and bitmap (raster) formats
- Attaching DGN files
- Working with DXF files
- Managing images and controlling their display
- Pasting, linking, and embedding objects into your drawing

The next chapter discusses how to integrate AutoCAD and AutoCAD LT with the Internet.

Getting on the Internet

utoCAD and AutoCAD LT offer many ways to integrate your drawings with the Internet. You can open drawings from a Web site, hyperlink objects to anywhere on the Web, and publish drawings in DWF format on a Web site. When you access a Web site (perhaps your company's intranet), you can find blocks or other data, and drag them into your drawing. This chapter covers all of the ways to connect your drawings with the Internet.

You can share your 3D drawings in the 3D DWF format. The DWF format is not only for use on the Internet; your colleagues can also view your DWF files using the Autodesk Design Review.

Sending Drawings

You can instantly send your drawings to others on your team or to your clients, by either faxing or e-mailing them, just as you fax and e-mail other documents. You can fax a drawing if the recipient doesn't have AutoCAD or AutoCAD LT and wants to quickly see the drawing on paper. (Later in this chapter, I explain how someone can use Autodesk Design Review to view AutoCAD or AutoCAD LT drawings.)

Use e-mail if the recipient has AutoCAD or AutoCAD LT and may need to edit the drawing. You can also send a drawing to an FTP site. Another option is to create a PDF file from the drawing and e-mail the PDF file. I explain how to create a PDF file from a drawing in Chapter 27.

Using eTransmit

The eTransmit feature packs together all associated files with your drawing so that you can e-mail it to colleagues, clients, customers, and so on. To start a transmission, choose File ➪ eTransmit. The Create Transmittal dialog box opens, as shown in Figure 28.1, with the Files Tree tab on top and all the file items expanded.

FIGURE 28.1

The Create Transmittal dialog box enables you to create a transmittal file that you can attach to an e-mail message. The transmittal file contains a drawing, along with its associated files.

You can write a note to the recipient in the Notes section. The content of the Notes section becomes part of the transmittal report, a separate file that is included in the EXE or ZIP file. If you send an e-mail message, the note becomes the body of the message.

Specifying transmittal settings

If you have a saved transmittal setting, choose it from the Select a Transmittal Setup box and click OK. Otherwise, click Transmittal Setups to open the Transmittal Setups dialog box. To create a new setup, click New, name the setup, and click Continue. To modify an existing setup, select the setup and click Modify. In both cases, you end up in the Modify Transmittal Setup dialog box, as shown in Figure 28.2.

From the Transmittal Package Type drop-down list, choose one of the following types of transmittals:

- **Folder (set of files):** Creates a folder that includes all of the files in the transmittal. The files are not compressed.
- **Self-extracting executable (*.exe):** Creates a compressed EXE file. Recipients can double-click the file to decompress and extract the files.

WARNING   Some people won't open EXE files for fear of computer viruses, so you might need to notify your recipient in advance that you're sending the EXE file. Also, some e-mail programs block EXE attachments.

- **Zip (*.zip):** Creates a compressed ZIP file. Recipients need WinZip, or a similar decompression application.

FIGURE 28.2

Use the Modify Transmittal Setup dialog box to specify how to structure your transmittal.

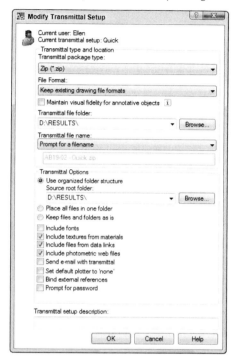

From the File Format drop-down list, you can choose to save files in earlier release formats if you want. From the Transmittal File Folder drop-down list, choose a location to save the transmittal files, or click Browse to specify another location. You can leave this item blank to save the files in the same folder as the first drawing on the list in the Create Transmittal dialog box. If you're transmitting a sheet set (AutoCAD only), the transmittal file goes in the same file as the drawing set data (DST) file.

For drawings with annotative objects, you can check or uncheck the Maintain Visual Fidelity for Annotative Objects check box. This sets the SAVEFIDELITY system variable which determines what happens when someone views the drawing in earlier releases. By default, this system variable is on (the check box is checked), which saves each scale representation as a separate block on a separate layer. This allows users in previous versions to choose which version they want by turning off layers or deleting blocks. If you work in model space and don't need layouts to look the same as in 2008, you should uncheck this check box to avoid creating all the additional layers and blocks.

If you create an EXE or ZIP file, you can use the Transmittal File Name drop-down list to choose how you want to name the file. You can choose to be prompted for a filename, have eTransmit assign a name and overwrite any existing file with that name, or have eTransmit assign a name and increment the filename (add a number) to avoid overwriting an existing file.

TIP Because you often don't need the transmittal file after you've sent it (you already have all of the files), you can put it in the `Windows\Temp` file or another location where you place files that you'll delete.

At the bottom of the dialog box are several Transmittal Options:

- Choose one of the following folder structure options:
    - The Use Organized Folder Structure option creates a hierarchical folder structure based on the structure of the files in the transmittal package. You can specify the root folder for this structure. When the recipient opens the transmittal package, all of these folders are created.
    - The Place All Files in One Folder option puts all of the files in one folder that the recipient specifies.
    - The Keep Files and Folders As Is option retains the exact paths of the existing files and folders.
- The Include Fonts check box includes the AutoCAD fonts in the transmittal. If your drawing only uses fonts included in a normal installation of AutoCAD or AutoCAD LT, you can probably assume that your recipients have them. TrueType fonts aren't included because they're proprietary.
- The Include Textures from Materials check box includes texture files that you have used as the basis for materials. Materials are used in rendering. (See Chapter 25 for more information on rendering.)
- The Include Files from Data Links check box includes Excel or CSV files that you have linked to in the drawing. (See Chapter 13 for a discussion of data links.)
- The Include Photometric Web Files check box includes web files that contain photometric data. (See Chapter 25 for more information.)
- The Send E-mail with Transmittal check box opens your e-mail program and creates a new message with the files as attachments, and the notes as the body of the message. Using this feature makes sending your drawings very easy.
- The Set Default Plotter to 'None' check box removes the plotter information from the drawings, because it's probably not useful to your recipient.
- The Bind External References check box binds xrefs to their host drawings.
- The Prompt for Password check box opens a dialog box (after you save the transmittal file) where you can specify a password. Be sure to tell your recipient the password.

At the bottom of the dialog box, you can add a description for the transmittal. Then click OK. The Transmittal Setups dialog box reappears, where you can choose the transmittal setup that you want. Then click Close.

You're now back in the Create Transmittal dialog box. Click the Files Table tab to see the files that will be included in your transmittal. The normal files are `acad.fmp` or `acadlt.fmp` (the font map that specifies font substitutions), SHX files (usually compiled fonts), and any xrefs, raster images, or standards files that are attached to the drawing.

CAUTION The eTransmit feature does *not* include files referred to by hyperlinks. Therefore, if you want hyperlinks to work, you need to add the referenced files.

To add files, click Add File, navigate to the desired file, select it, and click Open. To see the Transmittal Report, click the View Report button. The report includes your Notes and instructions to the recipient for using the associated files. For example, there are instructions for where to place SHX files and xrefs. Choose Save As to create an additional copy of the report for your own records.

When you're done, click OK. If you checked Send E-mail, your e-mail program opens, and you can send an e-mail message and the files. Either way, eTransmit creates the type of transmittal files that you requested.

Opening Drawings from the Web

You can access drawings, blocks, and so on from the Internet in the same way that you currently access them on your hard drive or network. Sharing drawings around the world can be as easy as opening a drawing on your hard drive. You have two methods for bringing objects from the Internet into your drawings.

Using the Browse the Web – Open dialog box

You can directly open a drawing from the Web within the Select File dialog box (choose File ➪ Open) by using the Search the Web button. As long as you have an active connection to the Internet, the Browse the Web – Open dialog box opens and functions as a browser. In this way, you can access drawings and other files over the Internet.

Using i-drop to drag objects into a drawing

An i-drop-enabled Web site displays the i-drop cursor when you pass the cursor over an image, as shown in Figure 28.3. This cursor indicates that you can drag the object represented by the image into your drawing. For more information on creating i-drop-enabled Web sites, go to http://idrop.autodesk.com. The Publish to Web feature, covered later in this chapter, also contains i-drop capability.

FIGURE 28.3

Dragging an object from an i-drop-enabled Web site.

Thanks to Eric Stover of Autodesk for permission to display this i-drop example from the Autodesk i-drop Web site.

If you drag with the right mouse button, a prompt asks you whether you want to save associated blocks or data when you drag with the right mouse button. Also, inserted blocks automatically include a hyperlink to the source of the content.

Creating Object Hyperlinks

You can hyperlink objects in your drawing to files or Web sites that may be located anywhere on the Internet, a network, or your own hard drive. A hyperlink creates a permanent connection between your drawing and other files that may provide supporting documentation or additional information.

When you follow a hyperlink, the appropriate application is opened with the specified file. For example, a Web site is opened in your Web browser, or a word-processing document is opened in your word-processing application.

Creating a hyperlink

Before you create your hyperlink, consider the environment in which it will be used. The file or Web page that you're linking to must be available for the hyperlink to work. For example, if you send a drawing with hyperlinks to a colleague, be sure to include the files to which the hyperlinks refer. If you're posting the drawing on a Web site as a DWF file, you need to upload the files that the hyperlinks refer to, along with the DWF file.

Here's how you create a hyperlink:

1. Select one or more objects in your drawing. The hyperlink will be attached to these objects.

2. Choose Insert ➪ Hyperlink (or Ctrl+K) to open the Insert Hyperlink dialog box, shown in Figure 28.4. (If you start the command first, select objects at the prompt.)

The Insert Hyperlink dialog box attaches hyperlinks to objects in your drawing.

3. Use the Link To list to choose the type of hyperlink that you want to create. The central portion of the dialog box changes, depending on which of these options you choose: a Web page, named view, or e-mail address.

   ▪ **Existing File or Web Page:** Creates a hyperlink to another file (on your own computer, network, intranet, or the Internet) or a Web page. You can choose from Recent Files, Browsed Pages, or Inserted Links.

   ▪ **View of This Drawing:** Creates a hyperlink to a named view, camera, or layout in the open drawing. (I explain cameras in Chapter 22. A camera is a type of 3D named view.) You can use this option to help viewers navigate to detail views or schedules (tables of data) in the drawing.

   ▪ **E-mail Address:** Opens the viewer's e-mail program and starts a new message to the specified address.

4. To help you specify the file or Web page, click either the File button or the Web Page button at the right side of the dialog box. To specify a named view in a drawing, click the Target button. In the Select Place in Document dialog box, click the plus sign next to the layout and select a view. Click OK.

5. In the Text to Display text box, type a short description of the hyperlink. The description is displayed as the tooltip. If you don't create a description, when you pass the cursor over the hyperlink, the tooltip lists the URL or file name. If the URL or filename is confusing, use a description instead.

6. Uncheck the Use Relative Path for Hyperlink check box if you want to use the entire path that you placed in the Type the File or Web Page Name text box. A relative path uses a base as a given, and requires you to specify only the part of the path after the base. Use relative paths when the hyperlinked file is in the same folder as the drawing.

NOTE You can set the base path using the HYPERLINKBASE system variable. By default, the base is the folder of the current drawing.

7. Uncheck the Convert DWG Hyperlinks to DWF check box if you don't want to convert drawing hyperlinks to DWF hyperlinks. For example, if this box is checked, a hyperlink to mydrawing.dwg becomes a hyperlink to mydrawing.dwf. If you plan to create a DWF file from the drawing that you're hyperlinking to, leave this check box checked.

8. Click OK to create the hyperlink.

Check the hyperlink by passing the cursor over the object to which you attached the hyperlink. You see the Web cursor, as shown in Figure 28.5.

FIGURE 28.5

The Web cursor appears when you pass the cursor over a hyperlinked object.

Using a hyperlink

After you create a hyperlink, you can use it at any time to open the associated file or to move to the associated location within the drawing. If you use a dial-up connection to the Internet and open a drawing with hyperlinks to the Internet while not connected, you're prompted to connect.

To open a file associated with a hyperlink, Ctrl+click any hyperlinked object. Remember that you can't just click a hyperlink as you do on a Web site, because that just selects the object in your drawing. Make sure that the hyperlink icon appears before you click, because pressing Ctrl and clicking is also a way to select edges and faces of 3D solids.

Editing a hyperlink

To edit any feature of a hyperlink, select the hyperlinked object and choose Insert ➪ Hyperlink. You can also right-click and choose Hyperlink ➪ Edit Hyperlink. The Edit Hyperlink dialog box opens. This dialog box is the same as the Insert Hyperlink dialog box and lets you edit the hyperlink. Click OK when you're done.

ON the DVD-ROM The files used in the following exercise on creating hyperlinks, ab28-a.dwg, ab28-a1.dwg, and ab28-a2.dwg, are in the Drawings folder on the DVD.

STEPS: Creating Hyperlinks

1. Open ab28-a.dwg from the DVD.

2. Save the file as ab28-01.dwg in your AutoCAD Bible folder. This is a 3D drawing of a base assembly frame for an industrial washer, shown in Figure 28.6.

FIGURE 28.6

The base assembly frame.

Thanks to Robert Mack of the Dexter Company, Fairfield, Iowa, for this drawing.

3. Copy ab28-a1.dwg, and ab28-a2.dwg from the DVD to your AutoCAD Bible folder. (You can use Windows Explorer to drag the files.)

4. Choose Insert ⇨ Hyperlink. At the Select objects: prompt, pick ❶ and ❷ in Figure 28.6. The Insert Hyperlink dialog box opens.

5. Click File. Choose ab28-a1.dwg in your AutoCAD Bible folder. Click Open. Click OK in the Insert Hyperlink dialog box.

6. Repeat the HYPERLINK command. This time, attach ❸ and ❹ in Figure 28.6 to ab28-a2.dwg in your AutoCAD Bible folder. Click OK to close the dialog box.

7. Ctrl-click the hyperlink at ❶. The ab28-a1.dwg file should open. Close it. In the same way, test the hyperlink at ❷. Do the same with the hyperlinks at ❸ and ❹.

8. Save your drawing. Keep it open if you're going on to the next exercise.

AUTOCAD ONLY The Express Tools contain three commands to help you find and change URLs that you create with hyperlinks. SHOWURLS (choose Express ⇨ Web Tools ⇨ Show URLs) lists all of the hyperlinks in your drawing, can show you the objects to which they are linked, and enables you to edit them. CHURLS (choose Express ⇨ Web Tools ⇨ Change URLs) prompts you to select a hyperlinked object so that you can change the hyperlink. REPURLS (choose Express ⇨ Web Tools ⇨ Find and Replace URLs) replaces the existing hyperlink URL of a selected hyperlinked object.

Publishing Drawings

You can save drawings as DWF (Design Web Format) files. You can use DWF files as a way to deliver files to clients and colleagues. If you place a DWF drawing on a Web site, others can view the drawing in their browser. They can also zoom, pan, and print the drawing. You can place hyperlinks in your drawing so that viewers can jump to supporting data, to other DWF drawings, or to other Web sites. Using the Autodesk Design Review, others can view DWF files on their computer; as a result, the DWF format is not limited to use on a Web site.

You can publish both 2D and 3D DWF files in AutoCAD. (AutoCAD LT does not create 3D DWF files.) DWF files are similar to 2D DWFs, but they have some limitations. The Autodesk Design Review can display 3D DWFs and includes a 3D Orbit viewing option. I explain 3D DWF files later in this chapter.

Understanding DWF files

DWF files are an image format for drawings. The DWF format allows for multiple pages. You can include as many drawings as you want, including the layouts you've created for each drawing.

The DWF format has several advantages:

- **It is a vector format.** Viewers can zoom in closely and see the details clearly.
- **2D DWF files are 2D representations, similar to a plot.** The actual objects are not available to the viewer. They cannot edit the drawing and you can restrict access to object information such as layers, object coordinates, and so on. This feature maintains security for the creator of the drawing.
- **3D DWF files do not expose the actual objects.** Viewers can view the model from any angle but cannot access object information.
- **DWF files are compressed while being transmitted.** Their small size reduces the time it takes to download and view them.
- **The Autodesk Design Review enables people without AutoCAD or AutoCAD LT to view your drawings.** You can also post DWF drawings on a Web site.
- **Viewers of 2D DWFs can zoom to named views.** Some drawing information is available. For both 2D and 3D DWF files, you can choose to allow viewers to turn layers on and off, see block properties and attributes, and display sheet set information. You have full control over whether you want to enable this information.
- **2D DWF files support hyperlinks to other drawings, data, or files.** You can provide the viewer with supporting schedules, and so on. (3D DWFs don't support hyperlinks.)

Creating 2D DWF files

To create a DWF file for a set of drawings, you use the PUBLISH command to do the following:

- Create the drawing set; that is, the list of drawings and layouts to include in the DWF file
- Specify a Page Setup for each drawing
- Save the list of drawings or load an existing list

The PUBLISH command creates the multipage DWF format. The PUBLISHTOWEB command, which creates DWF files (but can also create JPEG or PNG files), is different — it uses a wizard and a template to format a Web page containing images of your drawings. The PUBLISHTOWEB command is covered later in this chapter. Before using the PUBLISH command, save your drawing.

Starting the PUBLISH command

Start the PUBLISH command by choosing Publish on the Standard toolbar. The Publish dialog box opens, as shown in Figure 28.7, after clicking the Show Details button. You see the model and layout tabs of the current drawing displayed.

FIGURE 28.7

The PUBLISH command opens the Publish Drawing Sheets dialog box, listing the model and layout tabs of the current drawing.

Adding drawings to the drawing list

The next step is to add any other drawings and layouts that you want to include in the drawing list. The PUBLISH command streamlines the process of defining scale and plot area for each drawing by using the page-setup information defined with the layouts. Because layouts include this information, you can quickly create drawing sets for many drawings without individually deciding how to plot each drawing. You can specify a saved page setup for individual drawings for more control. (For more information on page setups and layouts, see Chapter 18.)

NOTE By default, the Publish dialog box initially lists all sheets, model, and layout, for all open drawings. To list only the sheets of the current drawing, change the value of the PUBLISHALLSHEETS system variable to 0.

You can add new drawings and layouts to the drawing list using any of the following methods:

- Drag drawings directly from Windows Explorer. You can add large numbers of drawings this way — in any folder, click the first drawing, press Shift, and click the last drawing.

- Click Add Sheets and choose drawings from the Select Drawings dialog box.

- Click Load Sheet List and choose a saved drawing list.

To save a drawing list, click Save Sheet List. The Save List As dialog box opens. Change the name if you want, choose a location, and click Save. Drawing lists have a .dsd extension. (DSD stands for Drawing Set Description.)

You can use the +PUBLISH command, a variant of the PUBLISH command that lets you start with a saved DSD file instead of with the current, or all open, drawings. The Select List of Sheets dialog box opens. Choose a DSD file and click Select. You can use the –PUBLISH command with a saved DSD file to publish DWF files from a script file. In the script file, set the FILEDIA system variable to 0 to suppress the display of the Select List of Sheets dialog box. You're then prompted for the DSD file. The process automatically generates a log file (with the name of the drawing list and an extension of .csv) that you can look at in case there are errors.

Removing model space or layout tabs from the drawing list

By default, the model tab and layouts tabs for each drawing are all included in the drawing list. If you don't want to see the model tab for drawings, uncheck the Model Tab check box in the Publish dialog box. Likewise, you can uncheck the Layout Tabs check box. After you change this setting, new drawings that you add to the drawing set will not include the tab that you unchecked.

Editing the drawing list

After you have the drawings and layouts that you want, you can modify the list in several ways:

- **Change the sheet name:** The sheet names are generated automatically from the drawing and layout names, but you might want to use a different name. Click the drawing's row and then click the sheet name one time. Enter a new name.

If you aren't in the habit of renaming your layout tabs, you might find that your sheet names are rather unhelpful. Handwheel-Layout1 doesn't explain very much. To rename a layout tab, right-click it and choose Rename. In the Rename Layout dialog box, enter a new name and click OK. (You need to display layout tabs to rename a layout. If you don't see tabs, right-click the Layout button on the status bar and choose Display Layout and Model Tabs.)

- **Page setup:** If you've specified a page setup, you can assign it to any drawing. (You can apply model page setups to model listings and layout page setups to layout listings.) Click the drawing's page setup and then click the down arrow that appears. From the drop-down list, you can choose a page setup from the drawing or import a page setup.

- **Change drawing order:** The drawing order defines how the drawings in the DWF file will be listed in the viewer. Choose a drawing and use the Move Sheet Up and Move Sheet Down buttons.

 - **Remove drawings:** To remove one or more items from the list, select them and click Remove Sheets.

Defining the output

When your list is complete, you decide on the output. From the Publish To section of the Publish dialog box, you can choose two types of output:

- **DWF File:** When you want to create a DWF file for viewing, choose this option. By default, the name of the file is the same as the name of the drawing (and in the same location), but with a .dwf extension. To password-protect the DWF file, enter a password. Don't forget this password!

- **Plotters Named in Page Setup:** Choose this option to plot all of the layouts in the list. This is essentially a batch plot. Each item in the drawing set is plotted to the plotter named in its page setup, including the default page setup. The folder setting is used if you've saved a plotter configuration file that plots drawings to a file.

The AutoCAD LT Publish dialog box does not contain the option to publish to a plotter. You can only create DWF files with the PUBLISH command in AutoCAD LT.

Note that plotting, or your last setting, is the default option. Be careful, or you may end up plotting when you want to publish.

Setting publish options

Click the Publish Options button to open the Publish Options dialog box, where you can specify how the DWF file will be published. You can do the following:

- Specify the location of the DWF file.
- Choose the type of DWF file — single-sheet or multi-sheet. You would use a single-sheet format for people using an older viewer that doesn't support the multi-sheet format.
- Specify the DWF filename now, or ask to be prompted when you click the Publish button.
- Create a password.
- Include layer information. If you include layer information, the viewer can turn layers on or off.
- Include block information, including a template file for extracting attributes. (See Chapter 18 for more about block template files.)
- Include sheet set and sheet information if you are publishing a sheet set.
- For 3D DWF files, list files by their xref hierarchy and include materials.

Publishing

When you've created your drawing list and defined your output, you're ready to publish. Click the Publish button. You may see a message asking whether you want to save the list of sheets. Choose Yes or No. When the publishing process is completed, you see the Plot and Publish Complete notification bubble at the lower-right corner of your screen. (I explain this bubble in Chapter 17.)

You can customize several settings for DWF files, such as the resolution and background color (for example, black or white). You can also create your own ePlot plotter configuration file. For more information, see the "Customizing DWF Settings" sidebar.

Creating DWF files from other applications

You can create a DWF file from a Microsoft Word document, an Excel spreadsheet, or any other Windows application using the DWF Writer. You can download the DWF Writer for free from www.autodesk.com/ dwfwriter. The DWF Writer works as a printer driver. For example, in Microsoft Word, choose File ⇨ Print and choose Autodesk DWF Writer from the Printer Name drop-down list. Then click OK to create a DWF file from your current document. You can view this document in the DWF Viewer, as I explain in the section "Viewing DWF drawings" later in this chapter.

Auto-publishing

The AUTOPUBLISH command is a way to quickly publish to a DWF file. To specify the settings that this command uses, choose Tools ⇨ Options and click the Plot and Publish tab. In the Auto Publish section, click the Automatic DWF Publish Settings button. There you can specify settings similar to those you set by clicking the Publish Options button in the Publish dialog box, as previously described.

The AUTODWFPUBLISH system variable turns the AutoPublish feature on and off. When you turn this system variable on (set its value to 1), AutoCAD executes the AUTOPUBLISH command every time you save or close the drawing. You can also turn this system variable on in the Auto Publish section of the Plot and Publish tab of the Options dialog box by checking the Automatic DWF Publish check box. Turn on AUTODWFPUBLISH if you need to keep DWF files always synchronized with your drawings.

ON the DVD-ROM The drawing used in the following exercise on creating a 2D DWF File, ab28-01.dwg, is in the Results folder on the DVD. If you did the previous exercise, you also have this file in your AutoCAD Bible folder.

STEPS: Creating a 2D DWF File

1. If you did the previous exercise, use ab28-01.dwg. If not, open it from the Results folder on the DVD and save it to your AutoCAD Bible folder. Although this drawing is a 3D drawing, you can make a 2D DWF file from it, especially if you want to preserve the hyperlinks.

2. Close any other drawings that you may have open. Choose Publish from the Standard (or Standard Annotation) toolbar.

3. Choose ab28-01-Model and click Remove Sheets.

4. In the Publish To section, make sure the DWF File option is selected. Click Publish to create the DWF file.

5. In the Select DWF File dialog box, enter ab28-02.dwf and AutoCAD Bible for the file location. Click Select.

6. A Save Sheet List dialog box opens and asks whether you want to save the current list of sheets. Click No. If you see the Processing Background Job message telling you that your job is processing in the background, click OK.

Creating 3D DWF files

You use the PUBLISH command to create 3D DWF files in the same way that you create 2D DWF files, as explained previously in this chapter. (AutoCAD LT doesn't contain this feature.) You don't need to specify that the file is a 3D drawing. You can also use the 3DDWF command to create a 3D DWF file and immediately open it in the Autodesk Design Review. This method has fewer options but is quicker. You can also choose File ➪ Export and choose 3D DWF (*.dwf) from the Files of Type drop-down list.

Either way, a dialog box opens where you can specify the name and location of the file. To set a few options, choose Tools ➪ Options. The 3D DWF Publish dialog box opens, as shown in Figure 28.8.

FIGURE 28.8

The 3D DWF Publish dialog box sets options for 3D DWF files.

Customizing DWF Settings

You can modify the PC3 file that defines the DWF file to specify certain settings that you might want, including compression, resolution, and whether to include layer information. The DWF file format follows the specification of the DWF6 ePlot.pc3 file. For safety, it's good to make a backup of the PC3 file before modifying it. To find the PC3 file, choose File ⇨ Plotter Manager. Double-click DWF6 ePlot.pc3. Right-click the file and choose Copy. Right-click in the file listing and choose Paste. Rename the copy (perhaps DWF6 ePlot-original.pc3). If you don't like the results of your editing, delete the DWF6 ePlot.pc3 file and remove -original from the name of the copy.

To modify the PC3 file, follow these steps:

1. Choose File ⇨ Plotter Manager.
2. Double-click DWF6 ePlot.pc3.
3. Click the Device and Document Settings tab and choose Custom Properties. In the middle of the dialog box, click the Custom Properties button to open the DWF6 ePlot Properties dialog box.

You can specify the following settings:

- **Resolution (dpi):** Defines the resolution for vector, gradient, and raster (bitmap) graphics. Of course, a higher resolution results in a larger file size. You can choose from the drop-down lists or choose Custom and enter a custom resolution. For plotting, you can use a resolution that matches the output of your plotter or printer. Use high resolutions for viewing highly detailed drawings.

- **Font Handling:** Specifies how many fonts can be included in the file. Use this setting to reduce file size by limiting the number of possible fonts.

  - Use the Capture None setting if you're sure that the viewer's computer has all of the fonts that the DWF file needs to display.

  - Use the Capture Some setting to specify which fonts the DWF file includes. Then click Edit Font List and deselect all of the fonts that you don't need. The fonts that are still selected will display properly, even if they aren't on the viewer's computer.

  - Use the Capture All setting if you want to include all fonts from the drawing in the DWF file. When you choose this option, the As Geometry option becomes available. This includes fonts as geometry (objects) in your drawing and requires plotting the drawing at 1:1 or better to achieve good-quality output.

- **DWF Format:** Specifies the compression format. Compressed binary is the recommended format and the default. The Zipped ASCII Encoded 2D Stream (advanced) option is an ASCII (text) format that can be uncompressed using WinZip or a similar program.

- **Background Color Shown in Viewer:** Specifies the background color shown in the viewer. Click the Color drop-down list. If you change the background from black to white, make sure that the objects are still easily visible. (Yellow doesn't show up very well on white.) If viewers will be plotting from Autodesk Design Review, change the background color to white, or their plots will print out with a black background! If the background color is set to black, color 7 objects are plotted in white. For all other background colors, color 7 objects are plotted in black.

- Edit **Virtual Pens:** If, and only if, in the Plotter Configuration File dialog box, for Vector Graphics, you chose 255 Virtual Pens in the Color Depth drop-down list, you'll see an option to edit virtual pen-set patterns. You can set the color, width, and other properties of virtual pens.

- **Include Layer Information:** Includes layer information so that viewers can turn layers on and off. This option is off by default. You can set this option in the Publish Options dialog box, as explained earlier in this section.

- **Show Paper Boundaries:** This displays a paper boundary such as the one you see on a layout tab. It's on by default and not editable.

- **Save Preview in DWF:** This option is only for viewing the DWF on Buzzsaw.com; a small preview is always saved with the DWF file.

When you finish specifying the DWF format, click OK. You then see a message asking whether you want to apply the changes for the current plot only (which creates an override of the configuration file but doesn't change it), or to save the changes to the file (which changes the configuration file, although you can always change it back).

Choose whether you want to publish all objects or just selected objects, and how you want to organize xrefs in the drawing—along with other objects or by their xref hierarchy. You can also choose to publish materials that you've attached to objects or layers. Then click OK to create the DWF file. A message appears asking whether you want to view the file. Click Yes to open the Autodesk Design Review.

The 3D DWF files (for AutoCAD only) are similar to 2D DWF files, but the following items are not displayed:

- Images and other inserted (OLE) objects
- Hyperlinks
- Bold and italic fonts
- Gradients
- Certain rendering features, such as lights, shadows, and certain types of materials
- Rays and xlines
- Named views and cameras
- Hidden edges

Using the Publish to Web Wizard

The Publish to Web feature creates HTML pages that display your drawings in DWF, JPEG, or PNG format. Through the use of templates, you can upload drawings without getting involved in Web-design issues.

To publish drawings to the Web, first prepare your drawings and decide how many you want to publish. Then follow these steps:

1. Choose File ➪ Publish to Web to open the Begin page of the Publish to Web Wizard.

2. Choose to create a new Web page or edit an existing one. Then click Next.

3. On the Create Web Page screen, shown in Figure 28.9, type a filename for the Web page. (This action creates a folder with this name and places all of the files for the Web page in the folder.) Then click the ellipsis button (...) to navigate to where you want to create this file. If you already store Web page files on your system, you can use the same location. Finally, add a description that will appear on the Web page. Click Next.

4. On the Select Image Type screen, choose the type of image that you want to create, whether DWF, JPEG, or PNG. As you choose each type from the drop-down list, a description appears on the screen. For JPEG and PNG, also click the image size that will appear on the Web page. Click Next.

5. On the Select Template screen, choose a template that structures your Web page, and click Next. You have four choices:

   - **Array of Thumbnails:** Creates a set of thumbnail images. Clicking any image displays a larger image.

   - **Array plus Summary:** Creates a set of thumbnail images. Adds information from the Summary tab of the Drawing Properties dialog box, displayed when the mouse cursor is over a thumbnail. (Choose File ➪ Drawing Properties to create summary information.)

   - **List of Drawings:** Creates a list of drawings and a frame displaying a drawing image. Users select a drawing from the list to update the image in the frame.

   - **List plus Summary:** Creates a list of drawings, an image frame, and summary information from the Summary tab of the Drawing Properties dialog box, displayed when the mouse cursor is over a thumbnail. (Choose File ➪ Drawing Properties to create summary information.)

FIGURE 28.9

On the Create Web Page screen, specify where you want to create your Web page on your own computer system, and create a description of the page.

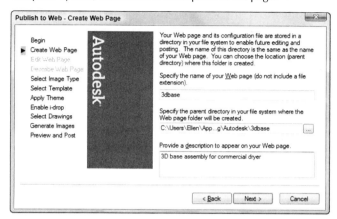

6. On the Apply Theme screen, choose one of the preset themes that control colors and fonts on your Web page. You see an example in the preview pane. Click Next.

7. On the Enable i-drop screen, choose whether you want to create an i-drop Web page so that users can drag actual drawings from the Web page into a drawing. Click Next.

8. On the Select Drawings screen, shown in Figure 28.10, choose the drawings that you want to publish. If the drawing is open, you can select it from the Drawing drop-down list. Select each drawing, choose a layout (or model) from the Layout drop-down list, type a label, and type a description to appear on the Web page. Then click Add. (If the drawing is not open, click the ellipsis button, navigate to the drawing, and click Open. Enter a label and description and then click Add.) Click Next.

9. On the Generate Images screen, choose to regenerate either all images or only those that have changes. (There is no difference if you're creating a new Web page.) Click Next and wait for the plotting process to complete.

10. On the Preview and Post screen, click Preview to preview what the Web page will look like. Your Web browser opens and displays a fully functional Web page, including links, if any. Figure 28.11 shows an example.

11. Click Post to post your new Web page. The Posting Web dialog box opens, which is like the Save As dialog box. In the Save In drop-down list, choose the desired location. To use FTP to post directly to a server, choose FTP locations or choose FTP from the Places list. (If you're saving to an intranet, you'll choose a location designated by your network administrator.) Double-click the FTP location and wait until you see the folder structure of your Web site. If you want, double-click one of the folders to save there. (The Publish to Web process creates a number of files. You probably don't want them all in the root of your Web site.) Click Save. You should see a File Upload dialog box showing the progress of the file transfer. If everything goes well, you'll see a success message that posting has been successfully completed.

NOTE   Remember to also upload any files that you have hyperlinked to in your drawing.

12. If you want, click Send Email to notify people of the URL to the new Web page.

13. To find your new page, look for a file named `acwebpublish.htm`.

FIGURE 28.10

On the Select Drawings screen, add each drawing that you want to include on the Web page, and specify a layout, label, and description for each.

FIGURE 28.11

A preview of some drawings using the Array of Thumbnails template and DWF files. You can click on any thumbnail to see the full-size DWF file. Note the i-drop icons.

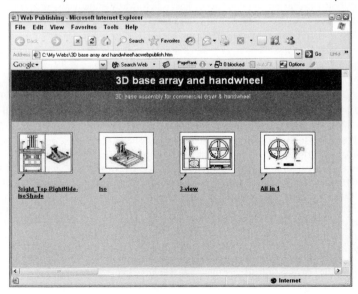

You can always upload the files by yourself, using your own FTP program or whatever other means you usually use to post to the Web site.

Posting DWF files directly

You don't need to use the Publish to Web Wizard to place DWF files on a Web site. You can upload 2D and 3D DWF files directly, and give people the URL or place a link to them on another page. You can also create JPG or PNG images on your own, as I explained in Chapter 27, and use them to display an image of the DWF.

Editing Web pages

You can edit your Web page — for example, you can delete existing drawings and add new ones. Start the Publish to Web command and choose Edit Existing Web Page on the first screen. Click Next and choose the Web page that you want to edit by choosing a PTW (Publish to Web) file. Click Next again. From this point on, you can change any existing information.

On the Select Drawings screen, click Update to update a drawing that has changed since the last time that you created the Web page. Click Remove to remove a drawing. To add a new drawing, follow the same procedures described in the previous section.

To change the order of the drawings, select a drawing from the list and click Move Up or Move Down until you have the results that you want. Continue through the wizard and re-post your drawings.

Viewing DWF drawings

The final step is to view the drawings. If you use the Publish to Web Wizard to create JPEG or PNG drawings, you simply view them like any other image. However, DWF drawings, whether viewed locally on a computer or from a Web site, can be panned and zoomed and offer other viewing options as well. To view a DWF drawing, you need Autodesk Design Review. Autodesk Design Review is free and is automatically installed when you install AutoCAD or AutoCAD LT. It is also available as a free download from the Autodesk Web site at www.autodesk.com/designreview. Autodesk Design Review replaces Autodesk DWF Viewer, which was used with earlier versions of DWF files.

NEW FEATURE Windows Vista contains an image viewer called XPS Viewer. XPS is an image type similar to Adobe's PDF. Autodesk is planning to make the 2D DWF format compliant with XPS, so that users with Windows Vista will not need any special viewer to view 2D DWF files.

Autodesk Design Review can function in two ways:

- **As a stand-alone reader,** it opens like any other program. (You can generally find it by choosing Start ⇨ [All] Programs ⇨ Autodesk ⇨ Autodesk Design Review.) Choose File ⇨ Open to open a DWF file. You can also double-click the DWF file in Windows Explorer. Use the reader in this way to view DWF files without using AutoCAD or AutoCAD LT.

- **As an ActiveX component,** Autodesk Design Review functions within Microsoft Internet Explorer. Use the reader within Internet Explorer when you've posted DWF files on a Web site. When you enter the URL in the browser, the DWF file appears. (The ActiveX doesn't work in the Firefox Web browser. Instead, the browser offers to download the file or open it, using your local DWF Viewer software.)

If you send DWF files to clients or colleagues, you can send them the Install file for Autodesk Design Review as well.

If you've given a DWF file a password, a dialog box opens, requesting the password before the DWF file is displayed.

Using view options

To view any sheet in the DWF file, choose it from the list at the left, or use the Next and Previous buttons on the viewer's toolbar. Choose the Views item to display any named views that were saved with the drawing. You can use saved views to help a customer focus on certain details and provide information about the views that you saved.

By default, layer information is not included in the DWF format. As explained earlier in this chapter, you can include layer information if you want. If the DWF file includes layer information, viewers can choose the Layers item, where they can choose to click the On or Off toggle next to a layer.

Viewers have complete freedom to pan and zoom however they want. Note that if you're sending a DWF file to a client who doesn't use AutoCAD or AutoCAD LT, the controls may not be obvious, so you may need to provide an explanation. The controls are as follows:

- Fit to Window is equivalent to a Zoom Extents. The button looks like the Zoom Extents button.
- Zoom Rectangle does a Zoom Window.
- For 3D DWFs only, the Orbit option functions somewhat like the 3D Orbit feature. (See Chapter 22 for an explanation of 3D Orbit.) Drag to tumble the model in any direction, as shown in Figure 28.12. Press Ctrl as you drag to constrain the tumbling to the vertical direction. Press Shift as you drag to tumble only horizontally. Press Ctrl and Shift together as you drag to constrain the view to rolling.

 The Orbit option works better if you first use the Zoom Rectangle option. Otherwise, the model tends to disappear from view as you drag.

FIGURE 28.12

You can use the Orbit option to tumble a 3D DWF in any direction.

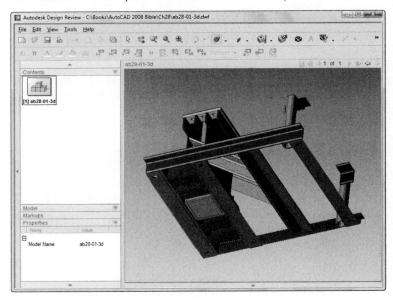

- Zoom enables you to zoom. Drag up to zoom in, and drag down to zoom out.
- Pan enables you to pan. Drag in any direction to pan in that direction.

A mouse with an IntelliMouse wheel works just as it would in AutoCAD or AutoCAD LT. Zoom in by scrolling forward, and zoom out by scrolling backward. Press the wheel and drag to pan.

If the DWF file has hyperlinks, when your cursor passes over a URL area, you can click to follow the link, as shown in Figure 28.13.

FIGURE 28.13

Passing over a URL in a DWF file.

Printing and plotting

You can print/plot drawings from Autodesk Design Review. The print options are somewhat like those in Microsoft Word because they take into account the fact that the DWF file can have many pages. Click the Print button to open the Print dialog box, as shown in Figure 28.14.

The Print dialog box offers the following features:

- **Printer:** In the Printer section, choose the printer or plotter that you want to use. Click Properties to specify how the printer/plotter functions. The features depend on the device that you choose. You can also select the Print to File check box to print to a file.
- **Paper Size:** Choose the page size from the drop-down list. The available paper sizes vary, depending on your printer or plotter.
- **Print Range:** You can choose to print all pages, or you can specify the pages. You can also choose Full Page or Current View from the View drop-down list. (Remember that 3D DWF files can only have one page.)

- **Page Handling:** Choose the number of copies you want to print and whether you want to collate them.
- **Scaling and Alignment:** You can fit to the page or specify a scale. If you scale, you can tile or clip the pages. If you clip them, you can align to one corner of the paper or center the drawing.
- **Orientation:** Choose Portrait or Landscape.
- **Color Setting:** You can print in color, black and white, or grayscale.

 On the toolbar's drop-down list of sheets in the drawing set, each layout is numbered. You can use these numbers to specify which pages you want to print.

The Preview pane lets you visualize what the output will look like. If you choose All or multiple pages in the Print Range section, you can use the arrows to scroll through each page in a multi-page DWF file.

Click OK to print. If you choose a size that doesn't fit on one sheet of paper, you see a message saying that the drawing may print across several pages.

FIGURE 28.14

The Print dialog box helps you to print or plot drawings from Autodesk Design Review.

STEPS: Viewing a DWF Drawing

1. If you didn't do the exercise on creating a 2D DWF file, copy ab28-02.dwf from the DVD to your AutoCAD Bible folder. Open Windows Explorer and navigate to ab28-02.dwf. Double-click the file to open it in Autodesk Design Review.

 If the DWF file were on a Web site, you would view it by typing the URL in your browser.

2. Autodesk Design Review opens automatically and displays the DWF file that was created in the previous exercise. From the Contents item on the left pane of the Autodesk Design Review, choose the second sheet, labeled [2]ab28-01-Iso (11.0 x 8.5 in), as shown in Figure 28.15.

FIGURE 28.15

The DWF file as seen in Autodesk Design Review.

3. Right-click in the drawing to open the shortcut menu. Choose Zoom Rectangle. Drag a window to zoom in. Choose Pan from the menu, and pan to the left. Choose Fit in Window to return to the previous view.

4. To print the drawing to the system printer, click Print on the toolbar. In the Print dialog box, click the All option in the Print Range section. Click OK.

5. Close Autodesk Design Review.

Summary

In this chapter, you discovered how to integrate your drawings with the Internet. You read about the following:

- Faxing, e-mailing, and eTransmitting drawings
- Opening drawings from anywhere on the Internet
- Creating hyperlinks in your drawings
- Using the PUBLISH command to create DWF files
- Creating 3D DWF files
- Using the Publish to Web Wizard to create Web pages with DWF, JPEG, or PNG images
- Utilizing Autodesk Design Review to view DWF files

This chapter ends Part V, "Organizing and Managing Drawings." Part VI, "Customizing AutoCAD," shows you the inner workings of AutoCAD and AutoCAD LT so that you can work in the way that best suits your needs. Chapter 29 explains how to create customized command shortcuts and toolbars.

Part VI

Customizing AutoCAD and AutoCAD LT

In Part VI, you discover how to make AutoCAD work the way you want. Customizing AutoCAD can speed up your work, make it easier, create standards for all drawings where you work, and automate often-used or repetitive tasks. You can customize the process of issuing commands as well as customize toolbars and tool palettes (Chapter 29), create macros and slide shows with script files (Chapter 30), create your own linetypes and hatch patterns (Chapter 31), create your own fonts and other shapes (Chapter 32), and customize AutoCAD's menus (Chapter 33).

Chapter 29

Customizing Commands, Toolbars, Tool Palettes, and the Dashboard

Customizing AutoCAD and AutoCAD LT can increase your efficiency and productivity. The time spent in preparation will be paid back many times. Before you start customizing, you need to know some basics that apply to almost all customization. After you understand these basics, the process becomes much easier.

Overall, AutoCAD LT offers less customizability than AutoCAD; however, most of the features in this chapter apply to both AutoCAD and AutoCAD LT.

Working with Customizable Files

The capability to customize AutoCAD and AutoCAD LT is based on the fact that most of the support files are text files that you can edit yourself. The menu and tool palettes are in XML files that you customize using the Customize User Interface dialog box and the Customize dialog box. Table 29.1 lists the most important files and their functions.

Figure 29.1 shows a portion of one of these files, `acad.pgp`, which lists command shortcuts, or aliases. The equivalent file for AutoCAD LT is `acadlt.pgp`.

FIGURE 29.1

You can edit the acad.pgp file to create keyboard shortcuts for AutoCAD commands.

TABLE 29.1

Customizable Files

AutoCAD File Name	AutoCAD LT Filename	Function
sample.cus	sample.cus	Custom dictionary file. You can add words to the custom dictionary for use with the SPELL command.
acad.pgp	acadlt.pgp	Program parameters file. This file is generally used to create keyboard shortcuts (called aliases) for commands.
acad.cui	acadlt.cui	Customization file. You modify this file using the Customize User Interface dialog box.
acad.mnl	N/A	AutoLISP routines used by AutoCAD's main menu. If you create your own menus, you can have an MNL file with the same name as your menu for AutoLISP routines. AutoCAD only.
acad2008.cfg	acadlt2008.cfg	Configuration file for storing digitizer and other settings. Usually, you should use the Options dialog box to make these selections, instead of manually editing this file. See Appendix A for more information about this file.

AutoCAD File Name	AutoCAD LT Filename	Function
acad.dcl	acadlt.dcl	Dialog Control Language (DCL) file. This file describes dialog boxes. You usually don't edit this file, but you can write your own DCL files to create dialog boxes.
acad.lin and acadiso.lin	acadlt.lin and acadltiso.lin	Linetype definition file. You can also create your own linetype definition (LIN) files or add your own definitions to acad.lin.
acad.lsp and acaddoc.lsp	N/A	AutoCAD's AutoLISP files. You create these files from scratch. You can edit or add to these files to automatically load AutoLISP routines. Other customizable LSP files are discussed in Chapter 35. AutoCAD only.
acad.mln	N/A	AutoCAD's multiline library file. AutoCAD only.
acad.pat and acadiso.pat	acadlt.pat and acadltiso.pat	AutoCAD's hatch pattern file. You can also create your own.
*.pc3	*.pc3	Plot configuration files. You can also create your own. A PC3 file contains all configuration settings for a plotter. This is not a text file; you customize it using a dialog box. For more information, see Chapter 17 and Appendix A.
acad.fmp	acadlt.fmp	Font mapping file. Use this file to specify substitute fonts, whether or not the original fonts are available on your system.
acad.psf	acadlt.psf	PostScript support file. It is used for the PSOUT and PSFILL commands.
acad.slb	acadlt.slb	Slide library file, used for hatch pattern examples in menus. You can use this file or create your own slide libraries. This is not a text file; see Chapter 30 for an explanation of how to create a slide library.
*.scr	*.scr	A script file that you create and name. Script files are macros of commands and options that run automatically.
*.shp	*.shp	A shape file that you create and name. Shape files usually hold fonts, but can hold other shapes as well. A shape file is then compiled into a file with an SHX extension for more efficient use.
acad.rx	N/A	A list of ARX (an interface for programming AutoCAD) applications that load automatically. AutoCAD only.
mtextmap.ini	mtextmap.ini	Font mapping for the appearance of text in the MTEXT editor.
acad.unt	acadlt.unt	A file that defines every conceivable type of unit.

Editing customizable files

To customize AutoCAD or AutoCAD LT, you edit a text file, use the Customize User Interface dialog box, or use the Customize dialog box. To edit files in text-only (ASCII) format, you need a text editor, which is like a word processor but does not place any codes in the file. For most of the ASCII files, you can use Notepad, which comes with Windows. All major word processors let you save documents as text documents — just remember not to click that Save button until you've specified the right file format. Files that are not in ASCII format generally have an interface, such as a dialog box, in the program for editing them.

Backing up customizable files

Before editing any preexisting files, back them up. The system of editing menus and toolbars in a dialog box helps to protect your system from errors that you might make when customizing, but if you want to undo all of your changes, you need a backup. You should back up in three stages:

- Back up the original file as it came out of the box. Keep a disk with all of the customizable files that you might ever edit in their original form.

- After you edit the file, back it up before each editing session. This way you always have your most recent version of the file. If you make a mistake, it's easy to copy that file on top of the one with the mistake and put everything back to normal.

- After you edit a file, back it up again so that you have it in case your hard drive crashes, or you need to reinstall AutoCAD or AutoCAD LT.

NOTE   To find `acad.cui` or `acadlt.cui`, choose Tools ➪ Options and click the Files tab. Open the Customization Files item, and then open the Main Customization File item. The location of this file is listed there.

This means that you should have two disks, one with the original customizable files and one with your most recent versions of them. At the very least, these disks should contain the following files:

- `acad.lin` and `acadiso.lin`/`acadlt.lin` and `acadltiso.lin`
- `acad.lsp` and `acaddoc.lsp` (AutoCAD only)
- `acad.mln` (AutoCAD only)
- `acad.mnl` (AutoCAD only)
- `acad.cui`/`acadlt.cui`
- `acad.pat` and `acadiso.pat`/`acadlt.pat` and `acadltiso.pat`
- `acad.pgp`/`acadlt.pgp`

You may also want to back up templates that you've created.

TIP   If you get into trouble, you can find an original copy of many of the customizable files at `C:\Program Files\AutoCAD 2008\UserDataCache\Support` for AutoCAD and `C:\Program Files\AutoCAD LT 2008\UserDataCache\Support` for AutoCAD LT (if you used the default installation location).

You'll use these disks not only when you make a mistake, but also whenever you need to reinstall AutoCAD or AutoCAD LT, whether due to hard-disk failure, a virus on your system, the replacement of your old computer with a new one, or some other reason. Also, when you upgrade AutoCAD or AutoCAD LT to the next release, you can usually continue to work with your familiar, customized files.

CROSS-REF   In Appendix A, I discuss the Migrate Custom Settings dialog box that appears when you install or upgrade AutoCAD or AutoCAD LT. This dialog box helps you to bring existing customizable files into your new installation of AutoCAD or AutoCAD LT.

Using the command line form of commands

For many customization tasks, you need to work with commands. When you create a *script file,* which is a series of commands, or when you edit the menu file, you need to type out the commands that you want to execute. In these cases, the customizable files can only contain the command line form of the commands.

As a result, you need to learn a whole new way of working — the old-fashioned way, by typing commands on the command line.

TIP If you're not sure of the command name but you know the menu or toolbar item, execute the command on the menu or toolbar and then press Esc. You see the command name on the command line.

A number of commands have a non-dialog-box version. Many commands can also be executed in their command line version by placing a hyphen (-) before the command name. For some commands that have no command line equivalent, you can use system variables to create the same effect. Table 29.2 lists command line versions of commands that you can use for customization.

TABLE 29.2

Command Line Forms of Commands

Command	Command Line Form
3DCONFIG	-3DCONFIG
ARCHIVE	-ARCHIVE (AutoCAD only)
ARRAY	-ARRAY
ATTDEF	-ATTDEF
ATTEDIT	-ATTEDIT
ATTEXT	-ATTEXT
BEDIT	-BEDIT
BHATCH	-BHATCH
BLOCK	-BLOCK
BOUNDARY	-BOUNDARY
COLOR	-COLOR
COPYTOLAYER	-COPYTOLAYER
DATAEXTRACTION	-DATAEXTRACTION
DDPTYPE	PDMODE, PDSIZE
DDVPOINT	VPOINT
DGNADJUST	-DGNADJUST
DGNATTACH	-DGNATTACH
DIMINSPECT	-DIMINSPECT
DIMSTYLE	-DIMSTYLE
DSETTINGS	ORTHO, SNAP, GRID, ISOPLANE, AUTOSNAP, SNAPTYPE, DYNMODE, DYNPROMPT
DWFADJUST	-DWFADJUST
DWFATTACH	-DWFATTACH
EATTEXT	-EATTEXT (AutoCAD only)
ETRANSMIT	-ETRANSMIT

continued

TABLE 29.2

Command	Command Line Form
EXPORT	DXFOUT, STLOUT (AutoCAD only), BMPOUT, PSOUT, ACISOUT (AutoCAD only), 3DSOUT (AutoCAD only), WMFOUT
FIELD	-FIELD
GROUP	-GROUP
HATCHEDIT	-HATCHEDIT
HYPERLINK	-HYPERLINK
IMAGE	-IMAGE
IMAGEADJUST	-IMAGEADJUST
INSERT	-INSERT
INTERFERE	-INTERFERE
LAYDEL	-LAYDEL
LAYER	-LAYER
LAYMCH	-LAYMCH
LAYMRG	-LAYMRG
LAYOUT	-LAYOUT
LINETYPE	-LINETYPE
LWEIGHT	-LWEIGHT
MLEDIT	-MLEDIT (AutoCAD Only)
MTEXT	-MTEXT
OPENSHEETSET	-OPENSHEETSET
OSNAP	-OSNAP
PAN	-PAN
PARTIALOAD	-PARTIALOAD (AutoCAD only)
PARTIALOPEN	-PARTIALOPEN (AutoCAD only)
PLOT	-PLOT
PLOTSTAMP	-PLOTSTAMP
PLOTSTYLE	-PLOTSTYLE
PROPERTIES	CHANGE, CHPROP, -COLOR, -LAYER, -LINETYPE, -LTSCALE, CELTYPE, CELTSCALE, ELEV, THICKNESS
PUBLISH	-PUBLISH, +PUBLISH
PURGE	-PURGE
REFEDIT	-REFEDIT (AutoCAD only)
RENAME	-RENAME
RENDER	-RENDER (AutoCAD only)
SCALELISTEDIT	-SCALELISTEDIT

Command	Command Line Form
STYLE	-STYLE
TABLE	-TABLE
TEXT	-TEXT
TOOLBAR	-TOOLBAR
UNITS	-UNITS
VBALOAD	-VBALOAD (AutoCAD only)
VBARUN	-VBARUN (AutoCAD only)
VIEW	-VIEW
VISUALSTYLES	-VISULSTYLES (AutoCAD only)
VPORTS	-VPORTS
WBLOCK	-WBLOCK
XBIND	-XBIND
XREF	-XREF

In addition, you can use the dimension variables to format dimensions in place of using the DIMSTYLE command, which opens the Dimension Style Manager dialog box. See the discussion of the -DIMSTYLE command in Chapter 15.

The FILEDIA system variable determines whether a dialog box opens for commands, such as SAVEAS and OPEN, that request filenames. When FILEDIA is set to 1, the default dialog boxes open.

NOTE Even if FILEDIA is set to 1, if a script or AutoLISP/ObjectARX program is active, the command prompt is used instead of a dialog box. You can still set the FILEDIA system variable to 0, but be sure to change it back again at the end of your script or program. (Scripts are available in AutoCAD LT, but not AutoLISP or ObjectARX programs.)

Documenting your files

Placing comments in customized files to explain how you customized them is standard practice. Although your customizations may seem obvious at the time, if you go back to a file later, you may not understand what you were trying to accomplish. Also, other people may need some explanation.

You can place comments in many of the customizable files by placing a semicolon (;) before any line of text.

Now that you know the basics of customizing files, you can move on to creating keyboard shortcuts and customizing toolbars.

Creating Shortcuts for Commands

You can create keyboard shortcuts for commands, thereby enabling you to enter commands on the command line without remembering and typing the full command name. Shortcuts are stored in the acad.pgp file for AutoCAD and the acadlt.pgp file for AutoCAD LT. You can use this file for three purposes:

- To create shortcuts to Windows programs (AutoCAD only)
- To create shortcuts to DOS commands (AutoCAD only)
- To create keyboard shortcuts for AutoCAD and AutoCAD LT commands

The auto-complete feature completes commands that you start to type in the dynamic input tooltip or on the command line. Type as many letters as you know, and then press Tab to cycle through all of the commands that start with those letters.

CROSS-REF   You can also create keyboard shortcuts, such as Ctrl+G or F11, for commands. See Chapter 33 for more information. The shortcuts in `acad.pgp` and `acadlt.pgp` use only letters and numbers.

Creating shortcuts to Windows programs

In AutoCAD, you can use the `acad.pgp` file to create shortcuts to Windows programs. For example, you may often open Notepad while customizing files. The `acad.pgp` file includes the following three shortcuts to Windows programs:

```
EXPLORER, START EXPLORER, 1,,
NOTEPAD,  START NOTEPAD, 1,*File to edit: ,
PBRUSH,   START PBRUSH,  1,,
```

AUTOCAD ONLY   The AutoCAD LT `acadlt.pgp` file does not support shortcuts to Windows programs.

The first column is the command name that you type at the command line. The second column is the command that you want Windows to execute. The number 1 specifies to start the application but not to wait until you've finished using it. This lets you return to your drawing at any time. After the 1, you can finish with two commas. However, notice that the Notepad entry has `*File to edit:` before the last comma. This is a prompt that you see on the command line. Type the name of the file to edit, and Windows opens it in Notepad. (You need to type in the complete path of the file.) To open Notepad without a file, press Enter at the `*File to edit:` prompt.

Creating keyboard shortcuts to commands

Most of the `acad.pgp` or `acadlt.pgp` files contain aliases, or keyboard shortcuts, for common commands. You can change these or add your own. After you become used to them, it's often faster to type shortcuts at the command line than to click the toolbar button or menu item, especially if your hands are already on the keyboard. You cannot include a command option in the `acad.pgp` file. To do that, you need to create a menu item, toolbar button, or AutoLISP routine.

AUTOCAD ONLY   The Express Tools contain an Alias Editor that enables you to edit the `acad.pgp` file through a dialog box interface. Choose Express ⇨ Tools ⇨ Command Alias Editor.

ON the DVD-ROM   `Quickkey` is an expanded replacement for `acad.pgp` that supports commands with their options, such as ZOOM Previous. Look in `\Software\Chapter 29\Quickkey`.

The format for creating an alias is as follows:

```
Shortcut,*Full command name
```

Refer back to Figure 29.1 for some examples of shortcuts. Note that the space between the columns is not necessary — it simply improves readability.

> **NOTE** The `acad.pgp` and `acadlt.pgp` files contain a special User Defined Command Aliases section at the end for creating your own aliases. Aliases in this section override aliases in the main section.

You can use aliases transparently if the command itself can be used transparently. Aliases cannot be used in script files or menus. Note that you cannot use control or function keys in command aliases in the PGP file.

> **CAUTION** If you're working on someone else's computer, don't do the following exercise without that person's permission. It isn't good computer etiquette to modify other people's files without asking first.

STEPS: Customizing the acad.pgp File

1. Start AutoCAD or AutoCAD LT.

2. Place a blank CD in your CD drive (or use another backup medium). Do one of the following:

   - If you have AutoCAD, type **explorer** ↵. After opening a preliminary window, the acad.pgp shortcut opens Windows Explorer.

   - If you have AutoCAD LT, open Windows Explorer by right-clicking the Windows Start button and choosing Explore.

> **NOTE** To find the location of `acad.pgp` or `acadlt.pgp`, choose Tools ➪ Options and click the Files tab. Double-click Support File Search Path to display the location of the support files.

3. Find `acad.pgp` or `acadlt.pgp`, click it, and drag it to the drive (in the Folders window) that contains your CD or another backup medium. Windows copies `acad.pgp` or `acadlt.pgp` to the disk. If you haven't already backed up your other customizable files, copy `acad.lin`, `acad.lsp`, `acad.mln`, `acad.mnl`, `acad.cui`, and `acad.pat` to the disk as well, if you're using AutoCAD. If you're using AutoCAD LT, back up the `acadlt.lin`, `acadlt.cui`, and `acadlt.pat` files. (If they don't fit, you may need to use two disks or a DVD.) Remove the disk and label it "AutoCAD *or* AutoCAD LT customizable files — original form."

4. In AutoCAD or AutoCAD LT, choose Tools ➪ Customize ➪ Edit Program Parameters to open `acad.pgp` or `acadlt.pgp`.

5. In AutoCAD only, scroll down roughly two screens until you see the three Windows commands, as shown in Figure 29.2. Place the cursor at the end of the PBRUSH line and press Enter.

FIGURE 29.2

The Windows commands in the `acad.pgp` file.

```
; Examples of external commands for Windows
; See also the (STARTAPP) AutoLISP function for
an alternative method.

EXPLORER,   START EXPLORER, 1,,
NOTEPAD,    START NOTEPAD,  1,*File to edit: ,
PBRUSH,     START PBRUSH,   1,,
```

6. In AutoCAD only, type the following and press Enter (the uppercase format and spaces are used to match the format of the rest of the file):

```
WORDPAD,   START WORDPAD, 1,,
```

7. Look at the next section of `acad.pgp` or `acadlt.pgp`. Read the guidelines for creating new aliases.

8. Scroll down until you see the following two lines:

```
CH,     *PROPERTIES
-CH,    *CHANGE
```

The alias for the CHANGE command follows the guideline of using a hyphen to distinguish command line versions of commands. Suppose you have trouble finding that hyphen quickly (you end up typing =ch instead). You want to change the alias to cg (with no hyphen).

9. Scroll down to the end of the file until you see the User Defined Command Aliases section. Place the cursor at the very end of the file and press Enter. Type the following and press Enter (don't worry about the spaces; I've matched the spacing of the `acad.pgp` or `acadlt.pgp` file):

```
CG,     *CHANGE
```

10. Choose File ⇨ Save.

11. Close Notepad. Generally, `acad.pgp` or `acadlt.pgp` is accessed only when you load a new or existing drawing. However, you can use the REINIT command to reload the file at any time. Type **reinit** ↵. The Re-initialization dialog box opens, as shown in Figure 29.3.

FIGURE 29.3

The Re-initialization dialog box.

---

12. Check the PGP File check box and click OK. In your drawing, draw any line.

13. Type **cg** ↵. The CHANGE command starts. Select the line, right-click to end selection, and pick a new endpoint location. The endpoint of the line changes accordingly.

14. Do not save your drawing.

ON the DVD-ROM The edited `acad.pgp` file is on the DVD in the `Results` folder. Although you made only two changes, if you want, you can copy the `acad.pgp` file from the DVD over your original `acad.pgp` file. Of course, you can make additional changes to suit your needs.

Customizing Toolbars

In the Windows environment, you frequently find yourself using toolbar buttons for many of your tasks. Nevertheless, how many times have you found yourself typing a command because you couldn't quickly find an equivalent button on a toolbar, or because it was on a flyout that was too annoying to deal with? In addition, think of how often you start a command with a toolbar button, only to return to the keyboard to type in a simple option.

You can customize the toolbars to make your work easier and faster. You can create new toolbars from scratch, or edit existing ones. You can even create your own toolbar buttons. When you create a toolbar button, you can attach any sequence of commands to it, such as a complex macro or even an AutoLISP expression (for AutoCAD only).

Using the Customize User Interface dialog box

The Customize User Interface dialog box (choose Tools ➪ Customize ➪ Interface, or type **cui** ↵), shown in Figure 29.4, combines all of the tools that you need to manage toolbars. You can create new toolbars, delete toolbars, and customize existing toolbars.

CROSS-REF The Customize User Interface dialog box controls customization of many aspects of the user interface. When you make a change and click Apply or OK, all aspects of the interface are updated, including the Workspaces feature, which provides a way to create and save multiple interface displays. Therefore, you may find various toolbars, palettes, and Dashboard control panels suddenly open when you return to your drawing. To learn how to control workspaces, see Appendix A.

NEW FEATURE Typing QUICKCUI opens a simplified view of the Customize User Interface dialog box. You can also access this simplified view by right-clicking toolbars, tool palettes, or Dashboard panels and choosing Customize (or Customize Commands). Click the right arrow at the bottom of the dialog box to expand it to its full size.

FIGURE 29.4

The Customize User Interface dialog box with the Toolbars item selected.

Removing buttons from an existing toolbar

You can customize any existing toolbar by removing buttons that you rarely use. To remove buttons from a toolbar, follow these steps:

1. Choose Tools ➪ Customize ➪ Interface to display the Customize User Interface dialog box.
2. In the Customizations In All CUI Files pane, with All Customization Files selected in the drop-down list, double-click the Toolbars item to expand the list of all of the toolbars.
3. Double-click the toolbar that you want to work with to expand its list of buttons.
4. Right-click the button that you want to delete, and choose Delete from the shortcut menu.

Creating a new toolbar

You may want to create your own toolbar from scratch that contains buttons for commands that you use often. To avoid changing the main menu, you should use the `custom.cui` file. This file is a separate *partial customization file*. Using a partial customization file helps you to keep your customization files separate from the standard menu file (`acad.cui` or `acadlt.cui`). For more information on partial customization files, see Chapter 33.

To create a new toolbar, first choose `custom.cui` from the drop-down list at the top of the Customizations in All CUI Files pane of the Customize User Interface dialog box. Then right-click the Toolbars item and choose New Toolbar.

> **TIP**   You can also create a new partial customization file. On the Transfer tab of the Customize User Interface dialog box, choose New from the Customizations In drop-down list. From the drop-down list, choose Save As. In the Save As dialog box, name the new file. Make sure that you use a name that is different from all other CUI files. To use the file, go to the Customize tab and choose Main CUI File from the drop-down list in the Customizations in All CUI Files pane. Then click the Load Partial Customization File button to the right of the drop-down list. In the Open dialog box, locate the partial CUI file and click Open. Again choose Main CUI File from the drop-down list. You should now see the new file listed under the expanded Partial CUI Files item.

A new toolbar appears under the Toolbars item, called Toolbar1. You can immediately rename this toolbar or right-click it and choose Rename. If you click Apply, a small, new toolbar appears on the screen, as shown in Figure 29.5.

The new toolbar is just a baby, but as you add buttons to it, it grows automatically.

Adding buttons

Once you've created a new toolbar, you need to add buttons to it. One method is to add a command from the Command List pane of the Customize User Interface dialog box. Follow these steps:

1. In the Customizations in All CUI Files pane, choose All Customization Files from the drop-down list.
2. If you are working in a partial customization file, double-click the Partial CUI Files item to expand it.

3. Expand the Toolbars item to display the list of toolbars.

4. Select the toolbar that you want to add buttons to.

5. From the Categories drop-down list of the Command List pane, choose All Commands or a category that displays the command that you want to add.

6. Drag the command from the list to the toolbar item in the Customizations in All CUI Files pane until you see an arrow pointing to the toolbar, as shown in Figure 29.6.

NEW FEATURE When you create a new toolbar, it appears in the Toolbar Preview pane. You can drag commands from the Command List to the preview of the toolbar. (However, for the first button, you need to use the method just previously described.) Also, to quickly add a new button to an existing toolbar, you can right-click the toolbar and choose Customize from the bottom of the list of toolbars. The simplified view of the Customize User Interface dialog box opens, listing all of the commands. You can then drag the command you want to the desired location on the toolbar.

FIGURE 29.5

The new toolbar shown in the Toolbar list and on the screen (on the left).

FIGURE 29.6

To add a button to a toolbar, you can drag a command from the Command List to a toolbar in the Customize User Interface dialog box.

You can also move a button from one toolbar to another. In the Customize User Interface dialog box, expand the toolbar that contains the button that you want to move. Then drag the button to your new toolbar or to any other toolbar. This moves the button, deleting it from the original toolbar.

To copy a button from another toolbar, use the same technique as for moving a button, but hold down the Ctrl key as you drag a button from one toolbar to another toolbar. This procedure leaves the first toolbar intact. You can also copy a button by right-clicking over the button, choosing Copy, and then pasting it into the desired location.

TIP   To help organize your toolbars, you can add separator spaces. With the toolbar expanded, right-click the button above where you want to add the space and choose Add Separator. You can also drag buttons to change their order, either in the Customizations in All CUI Files pane or in the Toolbar Preview pane.

Creating your own button definition

You can also create your own button definition from scratch. Follow these steps:

1. In the Customizations in All CUI Files pane, double-click the Toolbars item and choose the toolbar that you want to work with.

2. In the Command List pane, click the Create a New Command button. The Properties pane shows the properties of the new toolbar button, as shown in Figure 29.7.

FIGURE 29.7

You define a toolbar button in the Properties pane of the Customize User Interface dialog box.

3. In the Name text box, replace the default name (Command1) with your own name for the button. This name appears as a tooltip, so don't make it too long.

4. Type a helpful description in the Description text box. This text appears on the status line to further explain the function of the button.

5. Write the macro in the Macro text box. The ^C^C cancels any other command that may be active when you use the button. After that, place any valid menu command string as it would be typed on the command line, or even an AutoLISP expression (for AutoCAD only).

CROSS-REF You need to use menu syntax for the macro. I explain the details of creating command strings in Chapter 33, where I cover customizing menus.

6. From the Categories drop-down list, choose Custom Commands. Drag the new command onto a toolbar.

7. Select the button in the Customizations in All CUI Files pane. In the Button Image pane, choose a button icon from the list of button icons, or click Edit to create your own button, as explained in the next section.

8. Click Apply and click the OK button of the Customize User Interface dialog box to close it.

TIP To check the results of your customization before closing the Customize User Interface dialog box, click Apply and then move the dialog box so that it doesn't cover the new toolbar. If you are satisfied, click OK to close the dialog box.

Using the Button Editor

The Button Editor, shown in Figure 29.8, enables you to make your own button icons. In the Customizations in All CUI Files pane of the Customize User Interface dialog box, select the toolbar command that you want to work with. Open the Button Editor by clicking Edit in the Button Image pane of the Customize User Interface dialog box. You can choose one of the provided buttons and edit it — which I recommend — or start from scratch if you have artistic tendencies.

NEW FEATURE To help you find the right button to edit, each button in the Button Image pane shows a tooltip with the name of its icon file. When you click an image, the larger preview also displays the name of the icon file.

FIGURE 29.8

The Button Editor lets you design your own toolbar buttons.

The center of the editing area shows an enlarged view of the button. You see the button's actual size at the top-left corner of the dialog box. Check the Grid check box to show a grid of pixels — this is just a drawing aid. Choose a color from the color palette and then choose one of the four tools at the top of the dialog box:

- The Pencil tool draws any shape. To draw, click anywhere to draw pixel by pixel, or drag across the editing area.
- Click and drag the Line tool to draw a straight line.
- The Circle tool draws circles and ellipses. You click the center and drag out to the circumference to indicate the radius.
- The Erase tool erases. You can click to erase pixel by pixel, or drag to erase a series of pixels.

Here are the other features of the Button Editor:

- Click Clear to clear the editing area and start from scratch.
- Click Open to open an existing button for editing. Button icons are stored as BMP files.
- Click Undo to undo your most recent action.

- Click Save As to save an existing BMP file under a new name. If you create a new (or edited) button, use the Save As button and remember where you saved the BMP file. The default location is the Icons folder, which you can find by expanding Customization Files and then Custom Icon Location on the Files tab of the Options dialog box (Tools ➪ Options).

- Click Save to save the button icon as a BMP file.

- Click Close to close the Button Editor.

- Click More to select a standard index color or true color. (True colors are available in AutoCAD only.)

If you edited an existing button and saved the changes, then you're done. However, if you saved your button image under another file name (using the Save As button), you need to associate the new filename with the toolbar button. In the Properties pane, click the Small Image text box, and then click the Ellipsis (. . .) button. Browse to the BMP file and choose it. Click Open. The file location appears in the Small Image text box. You can now click Apply, or if you want to return to your drawing, click OK.

> **TIP** You can import icon images into the palette of images in the Button Image pane. Right-click the image palette and choose Import Image. After browsing to the image and importing it, you can assign it to any toolbar button.

If you think you might ever want to display large toolbar buttons, do the same for the Large Image text box. By default, when you create a button image, the Both option button is selected in the Button Image section, and so you create both a small and a large image. To display large toolbar buttons, choose Tools ➪ Options and click the Display tab. In the Window Elements section, check the Use Large Buttons for Toolbars check box.

Creating flyouts

You can use the Customize User Interface dialog box to create your own flyouts, or you can use one of the existing flyouts. To use an existing flyout, you just drag one toolbar onto another one. Expand the Toolbars item in the Customizations in All CUI Files pane. Then expand the toolbar that you want to work with. In the same pane, locate the toolbar that you want to turn into a flyout, and drag it to any location on the expanded toolbar.

To create your own flyout from scratch, follow these steps:

1. Expand the Toolbars item in the Customizations in All CUI Files pane.

2. Right-click any toolbar and choose New Flyout.

3. Right-click the new flyout (named Toolbar1 by default) and choose Rename. Type a name for the flyout.

4. From the Command List pane, drag commands to the flyout, using the same technique as described in the "Adding buttons" section earlier in this chapter.

The following exercise loads a partial customization file on top of the main customization file. After the exercise, I explain how to undo the changes if you want. If you're working on someone else's computer, don't do this exercise without that person's permission. I explain more about main and partial customization files in Chapter 33.

STEPS: Customizing Toolbars

1. Open Windows Explorer. Copy acad.cui (for AutoCAD) or acadlt.cui (for AutoCAD LT) to a floppy disk, a CD-ROM, or your AutoCAD Bible folder as a backup. If you use a folder on your hard drive, be sure to press the Ctrl key as you drag the file so that you copy it instead of moving it. If you don't do this step, you won't have a way to undo the changes that you make to the menu file.

NOTE To find the location of these files, choose Tools ⇨ Options and click the Files tab. Double-click the Customization Files item, and then double-click the Main Customization File item to display the location of the menu file.

2. Start a new drawing using any template. Save the file as ab29-01.dwg in your AutoCAD Bible folder.

3. Choose Tools ⇨ Customize ⇨ Interface to open the Customize User Interface dialog box. You should see All Customization Files in the drop-down list. Double-click the Toolbars item to expand it. Scroll down, and double-click the Zoom toolbar to expand it.

4. To delete a button from the Zoom toolbar, right-click the Zoom Center button (or the button that you use least) and choose Remove. Note that you can preview the results in the Toolbar Preview pan. Double-click the Toolbars item again to collapse it. Click the Save All Current Customization Files button to the right of the drop-down list.

5. To create a new toolbar, start by creating a new partial customization file. Click the Transfer tab of the Customize User Interface dialog box.

6. From the drop-down list in the Customizations in Main CUI (left) pane, choose New. From the drop-down list, choose Save As. In the Save As dialog box, type **ab29-01** in the File Name text box and click Save. (This should save the file in the Support folder, which is the default location for CUI files; if not, navigate to that folder.)

7. To load the new partial customization file, ab29-01.cui, click the Customize tab. Make sure that All Customization Files shows in the Customizations in All CUI Files pane drop-down list. If it doesn't, choose it. To the right of the drop-down list, click the Load Partial Customization File button. In the Open dialog box, choose ab29-01.cui and click Open. You see the filename in the drop-down list.

NOTE You may see a warning that workspace information in partial CUI files is ignored. This file doesn't have any workspace information in it, so click OK. I discuss workspaces in Appendix A.

8. To check that the new partial CUI file is loaded along with the main CUI file, choose Main CUI File from the drop-down list. Double-click the Partial CUI files item. You should see ab29-01 on the list.

9. In the Customizations in All CUI Files pane, choose All Customization Files from the drop-down list. Double-click the Partial CUI Files item and then double-click the AB29-01 item. Right-click the Toolbars item and choose New Toolbar. Type **Special** and press Enter. (If the toolbar name is not selected and editable, right-click the new toolbar and choose Rename. Then enter the new name.)

10. From the Command list drop-down list, choose All Commands. Find the Donut item and drag it to the new Special toolbar. You should see a left-pointing arrow when you have dragged the command onto the toolbar.

11. From the Categories drop-down list in the Command List pane, choose the Modify category and find Polyline Edit. (This is the PEDIT command.) Drag it to your new toolbar.

> **TIP** To find a command in the long list, click any command and type the first letter of the command you want. The list jumps to the first command with that letter. You can then scroll down and quickly find the command you want.

12. With All Commands displayed in the Categories List, drag the HIDE command (for AutoCAD LT) or Visual Styles Hidden (for AutoCAD) to the toolbar.

13. To create a custom command, click the Create a New Command button to the right of the All Commands drop-down list. You see the new command listed as Command1 in the Properties pane.

14. Complete the Properties pane as shown in Figure 29.9. Type the macro as follows after the ^C^C (which is already there), being careful to also include the spaces:

    ```
    pedit \w .1 ;
    ```

15. Select the Special toolbar item. From the Categories drop-down list, choose Custom Commands. Drag the `pline_tenth` command to the Special toolbar.

16. With the `pline_tenth` button selected, in the Button Image pane, click the PEDIT icon. (It looks similar to the icon in Figure 29.10; its tooltip is RCDATA_16_PEDIT.) Then choose Edit to open the Button Editor.

FIGURE 29.9

The completed Properties pane for the custom command.

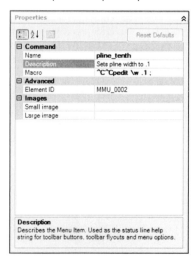

17. You want to change the button so that it looks as if a zero-width polyline is being changed to a wider polyline, because that's what the macro does. Click the red color. Choose the Pencil tool (by default, it is already chosen). Click the Grid check box to help you work. Click (or drag) the point of the Pencil tool in each box, using Figure 29.10 as a guide. (Figure 29.10 shows the button in black and white.) When you're done, click Save As.

> **TIP** If you make a mistake, it's easy to correct it. If you place a red pixel over an existing black pixel, choose black and redraw the black pixel. If you place a red pixel in a wrong spot, choose the Erase tool and click the pixel.

18. In the Create File dialog box, type **pline_tenth** in the File Name text box and click Save. (Note that the file is saved in the Support\Icons folder by default.) Click Close.

FIGURE 29.10

You can create a new button in the Button Editor.

---

19. To assign the icon to the button, in the Properties pane, click the Small Image item, and then scroll down to the bottom of the button image palette and choose the icon where it appears as the last button. (Another method is to click the Ellipsis button to the right of the Small Image item. In the Support\Icons folder where you saved the icon file, choose pline_tenth.bmp and click Open.)

20. Click Apply. If necessary, move the dialog box so that you can see the new toolbar. If it seems okay, click OK to close the Customize User Interface dialog box. (If not, continue to make changes in the dialog box.) The toolbar should look like Figure 29.11.

 NOTE   If you don't see the toolbar when you close the Customize User Interface dialog box, right-click in any empty toolbar area (off all toolbars) and choose AB29-01 ⇨ Special to display the toolbar.

FIGURE 29.11

The custom toolbar contains four buttons.

---

21. Choose Polyline from the Draw toolbar and draw any series of polyline segments. Choose the Pline_tenth button from the new toolbar. At the Select polyline or [Multiple]: prompt, pick the polyline. Its width changes to 0.1. (If it doesn't work, return to the Customize User Interface dialog box and check the macro.)

22. Save your drawing.

Undoing Toolbar Changes

To undo the changes that you made, you need to take two steps. To unload the partial customization file, right-click it in the Customizations in All CUI Files pane and choose Unload CUI File. This file is separate from the main customization file, and so it doesn't affect the main customization file directly.

To undo the changes that you made to the main customization file (`acad.cui` or `acadlt.cui`), copy the original file over the new one. To find the location of this file, choose Tools ➪ Options and click the Files tab. Double-click the Customization Files item, and then double-click the Main Customization File item.

Close AutoCAD. In Windows Explorer, locate the backup copy that you made in Step 1 of the previous exercise. Expand the location of the current main customization file. Press Ctrl and drag the backup file to the current file of the same name.

When you open AutoCAD again, it will load the backup copy of the main customization file.

Here's how the `pedit` macro that you used in the previous exercise works:

```
pedit \w .1 ;
```

1. `Pedit` issues the PEDIT command. The space after `pedit` is equivalent to pressing Enter after you've typed the command on the command line. The PEDIT command then displays the `Select polyline or [Multiple]:` prompt.

2. The backslash (`\`) is a special character that pauses the macro for your input. When you select the polyline, the macro continues, displaying the `Enter an option [Close/Join/Width/Edit vertex/Fit/Spline/Decurve/Ltype gen/Undo]:` prompt.

3. The `w` then specifies the Width option. The space following it is like pressing Enter. The PEDIT command then displays the `Specify new width for all segments:` prompt.

4. The macro then specifies 0.1. The space after it is like pressing Enter again. The PEDIT command then issues the `Enter an option [Close/Join/Width/Edit vertex/Fit/Spline/Decurve/Ltype gen/Undo]:` prompt.

5. The macro then uses a semicolon, which is used to specify pressing Enter at the end of a menu macro. This ends the command.

Customizing Tool Palettes

Tool palettes give you quick access to blocks, hatches, and commands. I cover tool palettes in Chapter 26. You can perform some customization directly on the tool palettes themselves. Here I explain the procedure for customizing the tool palettes using the Customize dialog box.

To customize tool palettes, choose Tools ➪ Customize ➪ Tool Palettes to display the Customize dialog box, shown in Figure 29.12. The current tool palettes are listed. Remember that each tab on the Tool Palette window is considered a separate tool palette.

FIGURE 29.12

The Tool Palettes tab of the Customize dialog box.

Use the Customize dialog box to customize tool palettes as follows:

- **Change the order of the tool palette tabs:** Select one of the tabs in the Tool Palettes list and drag it up or down. You can also move the tabs directly on the Tool Palette by right-clicking the tab name and choosing Move Up or Move Down.

- **Create a new tool palette:** Right-click and choose New Palette. Enter a name and press Enter. To create a new tool palette on the palette itself, right-click anywhere on the palette and choose New Palette.

- **Rename a tool palette:** Click the palette's name to select it, and then click it again so that you see a border around the name. Enter a new name and press Enter. To rename a tool palette on the palette itself, right-click on the tab's name and choose Rename Palette.

- **Delete a tool palette:** Select the tool palette, right-click and choose Delete. In the Confirm Palette Deletion dialog box, which warns you that deletion is permanent unless you first export the tool palette, click OK to delete the tool palette. You can also right-click any tool palette and choose Delete Palette.

- **Import a tool palette or group:** Right-click a palette or group and choose Import. In the Import Palette dialog box, locate the XTP file and click Open.

- **Export a tool palette group:** Right-click a palette or group and choose Export. In the Export Palette dialog box, choose the location for the file. You can change the name if you want. The tool palette is saved as an XTP file. Click Save.

- **Organize tool palettes into groups:** In the Palette Groups area, right-click and choose New Group. Enter a name for the group and press Enter. From the Palettes list on the left side of the dialog box, drag one or more tool palettes under the group name on the right, as you see in Figure 29.12.

Note that the tool palettes come with a large number of materials, as well as some visual styles, lights, and cameras. (AutoCAD only).

Customizing the Dashboard

The Dashboard gives you quick access to commonly used tools and controls. Related items are grouped together in control panels. I talk about using the Dashboard in Chapter 3.

NEW FEATURE You can now customize the Dashboard, adding control panels (called panels in the Customize User Interface dialog box), adding commands (tools) to the panels, and rearranging them to suit your needs. Note that the Dashboard was introduced in AutoCAD 2007, but is completely new for AutoCAD LT.

You can quickly control the visibility of the available control panels by right-clicking the Dashboard, choosing Control Panels, and checking or unchecking one of the items. AutoCAD comes with preconfigured panels, but you can add your own, or modify existing ones, in the Customize User Interface dialog box.

Create a new control panel

To create a new control panel, open the Customize User Interface dialog box (the CUI command), right-click the Dashboard Panels item in a full or partial CUI file, and choose New Panel. Enter a new name for the control panel. Add commands to the control panel by dragging them from the Command List pane onto Row 1 in the Customizations in All CUI Files pane.

TIP When a Dashboard panel is selected in the Customizations in All CUI Files pane, you see the Panel Preview pane. You can also drag commands directly onto the preview.

Within the Customizations in All CUI Files pane, you can also drag a toolbar onto your panel.

Most Dashboard control panels have more than one row. To add a new row, right-click the panel's name and choose New Row. As you may have noticed, some control panels have a double-down arrow that you can click to expand the panel. Expanding the panel displays additional tools. To add rows in this secondary section, click the panel's plus sign to expand the panel. You see a star and the words <PANEL SEPARATOR>. Any tools below the separator will appear in the expanded section of the control panel. Click the separator and choose New Row; the row appears below the separator. You can then add tools to that row.

Just as each Dashboard control panel has an icon, your custom control panel needs an icon. You can most easily create this icon using the Button Editor, covered earlier in this chapter. Save the new image. In the Button Image pane, select the new image (now at the bottom of the palette of icons) to the Panel Preview pane.

TIP To match the color of the other Dashboard control panel icons, click More under the color palette colors in the Button Editor. Then choose color 153, a gray-blue tint.

Modify a control panel

When you've added tools to your panel, you can rearrange them in the Panel Preview pane by dragging them around. You can also drag rows up and down in the Customizations in All CUI Files pane. To remove a button, drag it off the panel in the Panel Preview pane, or right-click any tool in the Customizations in All CUI Files pane and choose Remove. You can modify any existing control panel in the same way.

Figure 29.13 shows a custom Dashboard control panel that contains tools for working with blocks, both in the Panel Preview pane in the Customize User Interface dialog box and in the Dashboard itself.

FIGURE 29.13

A custom Dashboard control panel containing tools related to blocks.

Summary

In this chapter, I covered the basics of customizing AutoCAD and AutoCAD LT. You started to customize by:

- Creating command shortcuts (aliases) in the `acad.pgp` or `acadlt.pgp` file
- Creating your own toolbars that can contain any command sequence that you need
- Customizing tool palettes, including importing, exporting, and creating groups
- Customizing the Dashboard, including creating and modifying control panels

In the next chapter, you read about how to create macros with script files.

Chapter 30

Creating Macros and Slide Shows with Script Files

IN THIS CHAPTER

Automating commands with script files

Creating slide shows

Creating slide libraries for menu customization

Script files are like macros that you create in your word processor or spreadsheet. They automatically execute a series of commands. You can use script files to automate plotting, set up a drawing, clean up a drawing, create a slide show, or do any repetitive task. By running a script file on a number of drawings, you can complete a time-consuming task in a fraction of the time.

If you need to put together just a few commands that you might use another time for other drawings, you may want to consider creating a menu item or toolbar button instead. Chapter 29 explains how to customize toolbars, and Chapter 33 explains how to customize menus.

Creating Macros with Script Files

A script file contains a list of commands and options. To create a script file, you need to think out the commands that you want to execute, as well as their options and prompts. Then you create the text for the script file. Script files have the following characteristics:

- They must use the .scr filename extension.
- They are text-only (ASCII) files.
- They must use command-line syntax only (which can include AutoLISP expressions).

Creating the script file

You can create the script file using a text editor, such as Notepad. For early practice with script files, type each command on its own line. A blank space is equivalent to pressing Enter. End each line by pressing Enter (also called Return), without extra blank spaces. If you need two returns, one after another, at the end of a line, use a blank line for the second return. Every space is meaningful; getting those spaces and blank lines right is probably the hardest part of creating a script file. One technique is to start your script files in a word-processing program that can display nonprinting characters (blank spaces and returns). You can either save the script file in text format or copy it into Notepad. Some tips to help you create successful script files with the least aggravation are as follows:

- Before creating the script file, go through the steps once using only the command line. Turn off the Dynamic Input feature for this purpose, because it doesn't always include all of the command-line content. (Click the DYN button on the status bar.)

- If the script includes commands that open a dialog box that asks for files, set the system variable FILEDIA to zero (off) before experimenting with the commands that you'll use in the script file. This setting lets you practice the keystrokes without opening dialog boxes. You can also practice using the version of the command with the hyphen in front of it (such as -layer); however, in most cases, you don't need the hyphen in the actual script file.

> **NOTE** Script files automatically run as if FILEDIA were off, even if it's set to 1 (on). The FILEDIA system variable determines whether dialog boxes appear for commands that let you open or select files.

- For commands that require inputting text such as layer names or filenames, enclose the names in quotation marks. Then, for the next use of Enter, press Enter and go to the next line in the script instead of using a space. Otherwise, AutoCAD may misinterpret a space as a space in the layer name or filename, rather than an Enter.

- Place comments in your script file to explain what you're doing. A comment is any line that starts with a semicolon.

- Keep Notepad open as you work. When you've completed a set of keystrokes that you want, open the AutoCAD Text Window (press F2), select the command string that you want, right-click, choose Copy, switch back to Notepad, and paste. Then cut out all of the prompts, leaving only the keyboard entry. You'll probably have to readjust the spaces between the words.

- You can press End to check for blank spaces at the end of a line. Pressing Ctrl+End moves the cursor to the end of the document; this is useful for checking for extra spaces and lines at the end of a script.

Remember, you can open Notepad from within AutoCAD by typing **Notepad** at the command line. At the File to edit: prompt, press Enter to open a new file. (In AutoCAD LT, you need to start Notepad from Windows.)

Another option is to write down what you type at the command line. As you write, use an underscore to represent each space. It's very hard to remember that you left three spaces between two words unless you see three underscores. Of course, when you create the script file, you must use spaces, not underscores.

As soon as you complete the script file, save it with any name that is meaningful to you, plus an extension of .scr.

Here's an example of a script file that draws a series of circles:

```
circle 2,2 1.5
circle 6,2 1.5
circle 10,2 1.5
circle 14,2 1.5
```

This script file starts the CIRCLE command, specifies a center point, and specifies a radius, four times. The results are shown in Figure 30.1.

Running a script file created this drawing.

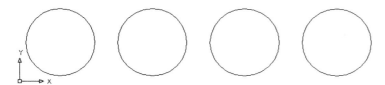

Running a script file

You can run a script file from within a drawing. Use this technique when you want the script to apply only to that drawing. However, you can also start a script within a drawing, then close the drawing and continue on to open and run the same script in other drawings.

You can also run a script file when loading AutoCAD or AutoCAD LT. You would do this when you want the script file to apply to more than one drawing. For example, you could use script files in the following situations:

- You want to use a script file to set up every drawing that you open. Although the script file applies to only one drawing at a time, you use it on a different drawing each time.

- You want to use a script file to clean up a list of drawings in one batch, such as thawing all layers on all of the drawings in a folder.

Running a script file from within a drawing

If you want the script to apply only to the current drawing, then start the script from within your drawing. To run a script from within a drawing, follow these steps:

1. Choose Tools ➪ Run Script. This opens the Select Script File dialog box.
2. Choose the script file that you want.
3. Click Open. AutoCAD or AutoCAD LT runs the script file.

Running a script when loading AutoCAD or AutoCAD LT

To run a script when loading AutoCAD or AutoCAD LT, change the target expression that Windows uses to open AutoCAD or AutoCAD LT. The easiest way to do this is to use the shortcut to AutoCAD or AutoCAD LT on your desktop and modify the target there. Right-click the AutoCAD or AutoCAD LT shortcut and choose Properties. Click the Shortcut tab, shown in Figure 30.2.

The Target text box displays the command expression that Windows uses to open AutoCAD or AutoCAD LT. Don't make any change to the current expression — just add to it. If you're using AutoCAD LT, substitute `acadlt.exe` for `acad.exe` and your AutoCAD LT program location in the following examples. The format for starting a script file is:

```
drive:\path\acad.exe drive:\path\drawingname.dwg /b script_file
```

FIGURE 30.2

The Shortcut tab of the AutoCAD 2008 Properties dialog box.

For example, if your current target reads C:\Program Files\AutoCAD 2008\acad.exe and you want to open a drawing named ba-349.dwg in c:\drawings and run a script file named pre-plot.scr, your target should read:

```
"C:\Program Files\AutoCAD 2008\acad.exe" c:\drawings\ba-349.dwg
    /b pre-plot
```

You don't need to add the .scr extension after the script filename. Long file and folder names that contain spaces must be enclosed in quotation marks, both in the target and in the actual script file. You need to include the full path of the drawing. If the script file is not in the support file search path, include the entire path. For example:

```
"C:\Program Files\AutoCAD 2008\acad.exe" "c:\aec\drc\Dobbs Ferry
    Apts.dwg" /b c:\aec\drc\cleanup
```

If you want to start a new drawing, you might want to specify a template. In the preceding format, replace the drawing filename with:

```
/t template_name
```

CROSS-REF   In Appendix A, I explain more about changing the target expression to open AutoCAD or AutoCAD LT the way you want.

When you've finished typing your additions in the Target text box, click OK. Now, when you start AutoCAD or AutoCAD LT, the drawing or template opens, and the script starts.

From within a script file, you can open (and close) other drawings. In this way, you can run a script file on as many drawings as you want. Figure 30.3 shows a script file, `multi-cleanup.scr`, that you could use when loading AutoCAD or AutoCAD LT. The target is set to `Apt 1A.dwg`.

FIGURE 30.3

A script file that cleans up three drawings.

```
chprop all  c bylayer

-layer f no-plot

qsave
close
open "f:\aec\Apt 1B"
chprop all  c bylayer

-layer f no-plot

qsave
close
open "f:\aec\Apt 1C"
chprop all  c bylayer

-layer f no-plot
qsave
```

NOTE Use the CLOSE command to close each drawing after your script file has finished working on it. If you don't, you may end up with 100 drawings open at once, and probably a major computer crash as well!

Here's how `multi-cleanup.scr` works:

1. The CHPROP command selects all objects and sets their color to BYLAYER.
2. The LAYER command freezes the layer named `no-plot`.
3. The script file saves the drawing.
4. The script file closes the drawing and opens the next drawing.
5. This process is repeated until the last drawing is edited and saved. The last drawing is left open.

TIP It's helpful to leave the last drawing open so that when you return to see the results, you can see that the last drawing has been properly edited. You then feel pretty sure that all of the previous drawings were similarly edited.

Notice the quotation marks around the filenames in the script file. These are necessary because the drawing filenames include spaces.

In the following exercise, you practice creating and using a script file similar to the multi-cleanup script file used in the previous example, but for only one drawing.

ON the DVD-ROM The drawing used in the following exercise on creating and using a script file, `ab30-a.dwg`, is in the `Drawings` folder on the DVD.

STEPS: Creating and Using a Script File

1. Open ab30-a.dwg from the DVD.

2. Save the file as ab30-01.dwg in your AutoCAD Bible folder.

3. In Windows, choose Start ➪ Run. (In Windows Vista, type **notepad** in the Start Search box.) Type **notepad** and click OK.

4. Type the following, replacing the underscores with spaces. Note that there should be two spaces between all and c. Press Enter after the qsave line.

   ```
   chprop_all__c_bylayer

   -layer_f_no-plot

   qsave
   ```

5. Save the file as cleanup.scr in your AutoCAD Bible folder. Close Notepad. The script file changes the color property of all objects to ByLayer and freezes the no-plot layer. Notice that the drawing has some text that has been set to a blue color (maybe to make it more readable). The title block is on the no-plot layer.

6. Choose Tools ➪ Run Script.

7. In the Select Script File dialog box, find cleanup.scr in your AutoCAD Bible folder and click Open. The script runs, changing the text's color to ByLayer (green) and freezing the no-plot layer. It also saves the drawing.

   If the script file doesn't work, press F2 to open the Text Window and see where the file got hung up. This will help you see where to correct the script file. Reopen it and make the correction. Save the file, close it, and try again.

8. Save your drawing.

Taking Script Files to the Max

What if you want to execute that multi-cleanup script file on 200 drawings? Typing in all of those filenames would take so long that you would wonder if you were saving any time.

However, you *can* save time. First, you need to find a text editor or word processor that can create vertical blocks of text. This means that you can select columns of text rather than lines of text. You can do this in Microsoft Word by holding down Alt and dragging down the text. (Use a fixed-width font, such as Courier New, to make selecting columns of text easier.) Then, you need to format the script file so that the entire set of commands is in one row, as in the figure shown here. In Microsoft Word, you can use Page Setup to set the paper to landscape and make it as wide as you need so that the text doesn't wrap. (Of course, you type the script once, and then copy the line and paste it as many times as you need.) You do this so that all of the filenames will be in one column. Here you see the path but no filename at the end of each line. The filename will be inserted before the quotation mark at the end of each line.

```
chprop all  c bylayer  -layer f no-plot  qsave close open "f:\aec\ "
chprop all  c bylayer  -layer f no-plot  qsave close open "f:\aec\ "
chprop all  c bylayer  -layer f no-plot  qsave
```

Now, open a DOS window. (From the Windows taskbar, choose Start ⇨ (All) Programs ⇨ Accessories ⇨ Command Prompt.) Use the DOS cd command to navigate to the folder where all of your drawings are located. (They should all be in one folder.) Type **dir *.dwg /b >dwglst.txt** and press Enter. This creates a listing of all of the files in that folder and places it in a text file named dwglst.txt. The /b parameter creates a file that contains only the names of the drawings.

Open the file in a text editor or word processor that can create vertical blocks. Create a vertical block over the drawing names and copy it to the Clipboard.

Open the script file in the same text editor or word processor, place the cursor at the top-left corner of the vertical block, and paste. You should get all of the drawing names inserted in the right place, as shown here with two drawings. If you're in a word processor, don't forget to save the file as a Text Only document.

```
chprop all  c bylayer  -layer f no-plot  qsave close open "f:\aec\ Apt 1B"
chprop all  c bylayer  -layer f no-plot  qsave close open "f:\aec\ Apt 1C"
chprop all  c bylayer  -layer f no-plot  qsave
```

Used in this way, the script files feature can be an extremely powerful tool for editing large numbers of drawings in one batch.

Creating Slide Shows

You can create an image from the display on your screen and save it as a slide. You can use several of these images to create a slide show. You can then use script files to direct the timing and order of the slide show. You first save a view of a drawing as a slide, create a slide library from the slides, and then show the slides one after another automatically.

 You can save any drawing as an image file and import it into a presentation program. You can add text and special effects to create a professional slide show. For more information, see Chapter 27.

Creating slides

Creating a slide is like capturing a screen shot of your drawing. AutoCAD or AutoCAD LT makes a simplified vector file from the current viewport in model space, or from all viewports in paper space layouts. You can create a slide of a *wireframe* or hidden display. However, you cannot make a slide of a shaded or rendered display.

To create a slide, follow these steps:

1. Display the view of the drawing that you want to save as a slide.
2. Type **mslide** ⏎.
3. In the Create Slide File dialog box, choose a location and name for the slide. Its file extension will automatically be .sld.
4. Choose Save.

Viewing slides

After you have created your slides, you will want to look at them! To view a slide, follow these steps:

1. Type **vslide** ↵.
2. In the Select Slide File dialog box, choose the slide that you want to view.
3. Choose Open to display the slide.

Do a Redraw to return to your drawing. You cannot draw in or edit a slide.

 The drawing used in the following exercise on creating and viewing slides, ab30-b.dwg, is in the Drawings folder on the DVD.

STEPS: Creating and Viewing Slides

1. Open ab30-b.dwg from the DVD.
2. Save the file as ab30-02.dwg in your AutoCAD Bible folder.
3. Type **hide** ↵ to hide the drawing.
4. Type **mslide** ↵. In the Create Slide File dialog box, click the Save In drop-down menu and select your AutoCAD Bible folder, if it isn't already selected. In the File Name text box, change the name from its default of ab30-02.sld to ab30-02a.sld. Click Save.
5. Choose View ➪ 3D Views ➪ Viewpoint Presets. Change the value in the From XY Plane text box to 60, and then click OK. (In AutoCAD LT, use the HIDE command to restore the hidden view.)
6. Issue the MSLIDE command again. This time, save the slide as ab30-02b.sld.
7. Choose View ➪ 3D Views ➪ Viewpoint Presets again. Change the value in the From XY Plane text box to 90 and click OK. (In AutoCAD LT, use the HIDE command to restore the hidden view.)
8. Issue the MSLIDE command again and save the slide as ab30-02c.sld.
9. Click Zoom Previous on the Standard or Standard Annotation toolbar (or choose View ➪ Zoom ➪ Previous) until you see the message No previous view saved.
10. Type **vslide** ↵. In the Select Slide File dialog box, choose the first slide, ab30-02a.sld. Click Open. AutoCAD displays the slide.
11. Repeat the VSLIDE command and display ab30-2b.sld. Do the same with ab30-02c.sld.
12. Enter **redraw** ↵ on the command line.
13. Save your drawing.

Using scripts to create slide shows

You can create a script file that displays slides one after another, resulting in a slide show. You can use two special script file commands for this purpose:

- DELAY *nnnn* pauses the script for the number of milliseconds that you specify. For example, DELAY 3000 pauses the script for 3 seconds.
- RSCRIPT repeats the script from the beginning. Use this command to create a continuously running script. To stop the script (whether repeating or not), press Esc or backspace, or drop down any menu.
- RESUME restarts a script file after you've stopped it.

The VSLIDE command, which displays a slide, can also be used to preload the next slide into memory. You use this command to preload a slide while viewers are looking at the previous slide. This reduces the waiting time between slides. To use this feature, put an asterisk (*) before the filename in the VSLIDE command. The next VSLIDE command detects that a slide has been preloaded and displays it without asking for the slide name. Here's how it works:

```
1 vslide ab30-02a
2 vslide *ab30-02b
3 delay 3000
4 vslide
5 vslide *ab30-02c
6 delay 3000
7 vslide
8 rscript
```

This script file does the following:

Line 1 displays ab30-02a.sld.

Line 2 preloads ab30-02b.sld.

Line 3 waits 3 seconds, displaying ab30-02a.sld.

Line 4 displays ab30-02b.sld.

Line 5 preloads ab30-02c.sld.

Line 6 waits 3 seconds, displaying ab30-02b.sld.

Line 7 displays ab30-02c.sld.

Line 8 repeats the script from the beginning.

 The Dynamic Input feature sometimes interferes with a slide show. If so, turn off Dynamic Input (click the DYN button on the status bar) before running the slide show.

STEPS: Creating a Slide Show

1. Open Notepad and type the following script:

```
vslide ab30-02a
vslide *ab30-02b
delay 3000
vslide
vslide *ab30-02c
delay 3000
vslide
delay 3000
rscript
```

2. Remember to press Enter at the end of the last line. Save the file as ab30-02.scr in your AutoCAD Bible folder. Close Notepad.

3. To ensure that AutoCAD can find the slide files, place your AutoCAD Bible folder in the support file search path. To do this, choose Tools ➪ Options and click the Files tab. Click Support File Search Path and then click Add. Click Browse and find your AutoCAD Bible folder. Click OK twice.

4. In any drawing, choose Tools ➪ Run Script. Locate ab30-02.scr in your AutoCAD Bible folder and click Open. The slide show runs. Notice that the last slide still takes a while to display.

5. Let the slide show run through twice. The last slide displays a little more quickly the second time. Press Esc to stop the slide show.

6. Don't save your drawing.

> **TIP** When running a slide show, you might want to maximize the screen area by reducing menu and command-line space. You can use the CLEANSCREEN command (press Ctrl+0) to toggle the toolbars and palette windows on and off. You can also hide (and redisplay) the command-line window by pressing Ctrl+9.

Creating Slide Libraries

You can organize your slides into slide libraries. Slide libraries have a .slb file extension. One reason for creating slide libraries is to create image tiles when you're customizing your menu. If you're using AutoCAD, then you can see an example of an image tile menu by entering the following AutoLISP code at the command line:

(menucmd "I=ACAD.image_3dobjects")↵

```
(menucmd "I=ACAD.*")   ↵
```

These image tiles are created with slides organized into libraries.

To view slides in a library, use the following format:

```
library(slidename)
```

For example, you can place the three slides that you used in the preceding exercise in a slide library called 3dmodel.slb. You can then use the following command in the script file to preload the second slide (the second line of the script file):

```
vslide *3dmodel(ab30-02b)
```

To create a slide library, you need to use the DOS prompt. You use the SLIDELIB utility, which you can find in your AutoCAD 2008 or AutoCAD LT 2008 folder.

To get to the DOS prompt, choose Start ➪ (All) Programs ➪ Accessories ➪ Command Prompt.

Follow these steps to create a slide library:

1. Create a text file (you can use Notepad) that contains the names of the slide files. Include the paths of the slide files if they're not in the support file search path. Place each slide filename on a new line. Save the file as ab30sld.lst.

> **TIP** SLIDELIB can read a listing that was created using DOS's dir command with the /b parameter, which creates a simple listing of just the filenames. Therefore, you can place all of the slide files in a folder and redirect the dir listing to a file. For example, you can create a list named ab30sld.lst by typing the following at the DOS prompt:

```
dir *.sld /b >ab30sld.lst
```

This creates the list in the same folder as the slide files.

2. Assuming that you're still in the same folder where you created the slide file list and you want to create a library called `ab30sld.slb` in the same folder, type the following at the DOS prompt (substituting the actual path to your AutoCAD or AutoCAD LT program):

```
"c:\Program Files\ AutoCAD 2008\slidelib" ab30sld < ab30sld.lst
```

 SLIDELIB cannot accept filenames with spaces, but it can handle long filenames, provided that you use a character, such as an underscore, where you might normally have a blank space.

Summary

This chapter explained how to create script files to automate repetitive commands. You read about the following:

- Creating script files that contain commands, options, and values in command-line format
- Running script files from within a drawing or when loading AutoCAD or AutoCAD LT
- Creating slides from the display in your viewport and creating a script file that displays several slides, one after another, thus resulting in a slide show
- Organizing your slides into slide libraries

In the next chapter, you read about how to create your own linetypes and hatch patterns.

Chapter 31

Creating Your Own Linetypes and Hatch Patterns

AutoCAD and AutoCAD LT come with a large number of linetypes and hatch patterns. However, when these do not serve your particular needs, you can create your own linetypes and hatch patterns. You can then use them in your drawings in the same way that you use the linetypes and hatch patterns that come with the software.

Linetypes are useful whenever you don't want a continuous linetype. They apply not only to lines, but also to polylines, arcs, ellipses, wire-frames, and solids — in fact, to most objects. You use hatch patterns to fill in closed (or almost closed) areas. Hatch patterns often represent textures or materials.

> **IN THIS CHAPTER**
>
> **Creating linetypes**
>
> **Creating hatch patterns**

Creating Linetypes

There are two types of linetypes: simple and complex. Simple linetypes consist of only dashes and dots. Complex linetypes usually have dashes and/or dots, but also contain text and/or shapes.

The default linetype file is `acad.lin` for AutoCAD and `acadlt.lin` for AutoCAD LT. You can add your own linetype definitions to this file or create your own linetype files. Linetype files are text files and must have a `.lin` file extension. Of course, be sure to make a backup copy of `acad.lin` or `acadlt.lin` before you edit it. You commonly use Notepad to edit a linetype file.

Creating simple linetypes

In the syntax for creating simple linetypes, each linetype is defined using two lines of text. The first line contains the linetype name and an optional description, formatted as follows:

```
*linetype name[, description]
```

Here are some points to remember:

- Always start the definition with an asterisk.
- The description is limited to 47 characters.
- If you include a description, precede it with a comma.

The second line of the linetype syntax is its definition. With simple linetypes, you're limited to dashes, dots, and spaces, which are measured in units and specified as follows:

- A dash is indicated by a positive number.
- A dot is indicated by a 0.
- A space is indicated by a negative number.
- Each item is separated by a comma, there are no spaces, and the maximum line length is 80 characters.
- Each line must start with the letter A.

The following definition creates a line with two dashes of 0.25 units, followed by two dots, all separated by spaces of 0.1 units.

```
*seeingdouble, Future hedge line
A,.25,-.1,.25,-.1,0,-.1,0,-.1
```

The result is shown in Figure 31.1.

FIGURE 31.1

The `seeingdouble` linetype.

If you feel quite confident, you can even create linetypes on the fly, using the command-line form of the LINETYPE command. Type **-linetype** ↵ and use the Create option. Follow the prompts and type the linetype definition on the command line. If you make a mistake, you must open the linetype file in a text editor to make your corrections.

TIP   If your linetype definition will include both dashes and dots, you'll get the best results when you start the linetype definition with a dash. Starting the definition with a dash is a matter of aesthetics, perhaps, but such a line connects better to other lines.

STEPS: Creating a Simple Linetype

1. Create a drawing using the `acad.dwt` or `acadlt.dwt` template.
2. Save your drawing as `ab31-01.dwg` in your `AutoCAD Bible` folder.
3. In Windows, choose Start ⇨ Run. Type **notepad** and click OK to open Notepad.
4. Type the following:

   ```
   *3dotsandadash, temporary fencing
   A,.5,-.25,0,-.1,0,-.1,0,-.25
   ```

5. Press Enter after the last line. Save the file as `ab31-01.lin` in your `AutoCAD Bible` folder and close Notepad.

6. In your drawing, choose Layer Properties Manager on the Layers toolbar (or choose Format ➪ Layer), and then click the New Layer icon. Name the new layer `tfence`. Set its color to red.

7. Click Continuous in the Linetype column to open the Select Linetype dialog box. Click Load.

8. In the Load or Reload Linetypes dialog box, click File. In the Select Linetype File dialog box, find `ab31-01.lin` in your `AutoCAD Bible` folder, choose it, and click Open.

9. Back in the Load or Reload Linetypes dialog box, choose `3dotsandadash` and click OK.

10. Again, in the Select Linetype dialog box, choose `3dotsandadash` and then click OK. The layer `tfence` now shows the correct linetype. Click Set Current and then click OK.

11. Start the LINE command and turn on ORTHO. Draw any line to see the linetype. Save your drawing. The linetype should look like Figure 31.2.

FIGURE 31.2

The `3dotsandadash` linetype.

Creating complex linetypes

A complex linetype includes either shapes or text in the linetype definition. Complex linetype definitions are similar to those for simple linetypes, except that they add a definition for a shape or text. Figure 31.3 shows an example of each type.

FIGURE 31.3

Complex linetypes include shapes or text.

Shapes are covered in the next chapter. At this point, you only need to know that shapes are contained in files with the file extension `.shx`.

The first line of the linetype definition is the same as for simple linetypes. The second line of the definition can contain all of the same features as those for a simple linetype. However, you add the special shape or text definition in square brackets:

- **Syntax for shapes:** `[shapename,shxfilename,details]`
- **Syntax for text:** `["text string",textstyle,details]`

`details` refers to an optional series of rotation, scale, and offset specifications that you can add to the definition. Table 31.1 describes these specifications.

The following complex linetype definition uses a shape and has no details:

```
*TEMPFENCE, FENCE SHAPE AND DASH
A,.5,-.25,[FENCE,"C:\AUTOCAD BIBLE\FENCE.SHX"],-.5
```

The specification for the shape is simply part of the rest of the definition that includes a dash and spaces before and after the shape. The shape is enclosed in both commas and square brackets. The first part of the shape definition is the name of the shape (which is defined in the shape's definition file), and the second part is the name of the shape file. In this case, the shape file is not in the support file search path, so the entire path needs to be specified. Don't forget to use quotation marks around the shape filename if the folder name or filename contains embedded spaces.

> **TIP**   Note that the space after the shape (created with the –.5 code) is larger than the space before it (created with the –.25 code). You need to allow for the space that the shape takes up. This is largely a matter of trial and error, but if you know the shape definition well, you can make a good estimate. If you need to go back and change the linetype definition, don't forget to reload the linetype (using the Load option).

The following complex linetype definition uses text and has no details:

```
*TFENCE, DASH & TEXT
A,.5,-.25,["TEMP FENCE",FENCE],-1.5
```

Again, the specification for the text is placed within a linetype definition that includes a dash and spaces. The first part of the text definition is the text string, which is always in quotation marks. The second part of the definition is the text style. As with the previous linetype definition containing a shape, the space after the text is larger than the space before in order to leave enough room for the text.

You must define the text style in the drawing before you load the linetype.

Table 31.1 lists the details that you can add to both the shape and text parts of complex linetype definitions.

TABLE 31.1

Optional Details for Shapes and Text in Complex Linetype Definitions

Detail	Syntax	Description
Relative rotation	R=##	Rotates the shape or text relative to the angle of the line that you draw. This number is in degrees unless you put a g (for grads) or r (for radians) after it.
Absolute rotation	A=##	Rotates the shape or text based on the World Coordinate System, regardless of the angle of the line. Because the default is a relative rotation of 0, you can use absolute rotation to keep the text facing upright, regardless of the direction of the line. This number is in degrees unless you put a g (for grads) or r (for radians) after it.*
Scale	S=##	Scales the text or shape. This scale is multiplied by any scale that is contained in a shape definition or height in a text style. If you use a text style with a height of 0, this scale number defines the text's height.

Detail	Syntax	Description
X offset	X=##	A positive number moves the shape or text toward the endpoint of the line. A negative number moves the shape or text toward the start point of the line. You can use an X offset to place a shape or text along a continuous linetype. You can also use an X offset to adjust the spacing of a shape or text between dashes, instead of changing the spaces before or after the dashes.
Y offset	Y=##	Moves the shape or text perpendicular to the direction of the line. A positive number moves the shape or text up if the line is drawn from left to right. Use a Y offset to center text and shapes along a linetype.

* Although using an absolute rotation of 0 might sound like a good idea for complex linetypes with text, if you use the linetype at varying angles or on curves, you may find that the text shifts to an undesirable location due to the text's justification point.

Here is a definition that includes a shape with a scale and a Y offset:

```
*TEMPFENCE, FENCE SHAPE AND DASH
A,.5,-.25,[FENCE,"C:\AUTOCAD BIBLE\FENCE.SHX",S=.025,Y=-.07],-.5
```

This shape definition scales the shape to 0.025 of its original size. This results in the linetype shown in Figure 31.4. Of course, in order to scale the shape, you need to know its original size. You can use the SHAPE command to insert a shape and get an idea of what it looks like. In this case, the shape's original definition is much too large for a linetype and needs to be scaled down.

FIGURE 31.4

The TEMPFENCE linetype.

The shape definition also moves the shape in the minus Y direction by 0.07 units. This centers the shape nicely within the linetype.

CAUTION When you create drawings using shapes or custom fonts, as in the case of complex linetypes, you need to include the shape files or font files when you distribute the drawings to others.

By including more involved shapes in a complex linetype and not much else, you can create a linetype that is mostly a series of shapes displayed one after the other. You can create some interesting effects in this way.

You can find several complex linetypes at the end of the acad.lin or aclt.lin linetype definition file. Look at their definitions and try them out to get ideas for your own complex linetypes. The Express Tools installation (in AutoCAD only) has a command, MKLTYPE (choose Express ➪ Tools ➪ Make Linetype) that automatically creates linetypes, even complex ones.

NOTE To find the location of acad.lin or acadlt.lin, choose Tools ➪ Options and click the Files tab. Double-click the first item, Support File Search Path, to display the location of the support files.

ON the DVD-ROM The drawing used in the following exercise on creating a complex linetype, ab31-a.dwg, is in the Drawings folder on the DVD.

STEPS: Creating a Complex Linetype

1. Open ab31-a.dwg from the DVD.

2. Save the file as ab31-02.dwg in your AutoCAD Bible folder. This drawing is a simple plan for a trailer park.

3. Choose Format ➪ Text Style. Click New and type **TVCABLE** for the Style Name. Click OK. In the Font Name drop-down list, choose Arial. Click Apply and then click Close.

4. In Windows, choose Start ➪ Run. Type **notepad** and click OK. Notepad opens. Type the following:

```
*TV, Buried television cable
A,.5,-.5,["TV",TVCABLE,S=.3,X=-.1,Y=-.15],-.75 ↵
```

5. Choose File ➪ Save and save it in your AutoCAD Bible folder as ab31-02.lin.

6. Choose Layer Properties Manager from the Layers toolbar. Choose Buried_cable and click its Continuous linetype in the Linetype column. In the Select Linetype dialog box, choose Load. Click File. Find ab31-02.lin in your AutoCAD Bible folder, choose it, and click Open.

7. In the Load or Reload Linetypes dialog box, choose TV and click OK. Do the same in the Select Linetypes dialog box. Click Set Current. Click OK.

8. Click Linetype Control from the Properties toolbar and choose Other. In the Linetype Manager, click Show Details to display the Details section. Change the Global Scale Factor to 192. Click OK.

9. Draw some lines or polylines. Zoom in to see the linetype more clearly. Figure 31.5 shows the resulting linetype.

10. Save your drawing.

FIGURE 31.5

The TV linetype.

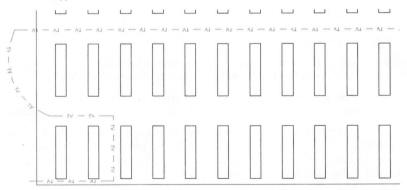

Creating Hatch Patterns

Hatch patterns are sets of line patterns that are used to fill an enclosed area. Although the part of the hatch pattern definition that defines each line is similar to a linetype definition, you also need to specify the angle and spacing of the lines. You cannot include text or shapes in hatch patterns.

Hatch patterns are stored in files with a file extension of .pat. The acad.pat or aclt.pat file includes a large number of hatch patterns. You can add to or edit this file, or create your own .pat file. As always, don't forget to make a copy of acad.pat or aclt.pat before you edit it. When creating your own .pat file, remember the following:

- If you aren't adding patterns to acad.pat or aclt.pat, you can put only one hatch pattern in a custom .pat file. The filename and pattern name must be the same.
- You can insert comments in your .pat file after a semicolon.
- You must press Enter after the end of the last line of the hatch definition.

 To find the location of acad.pat **or** acadlt.pat, **choose Tools ⊏ Options and click the Files tab. Double-click the Support File Search Path item, to display the location of the support files.**

The syntax for hatch patterns is as follows:

```
*pattern-name[, description]
angle, x-origin,y-origin, delta-x,delta-y [, dash1, dash2, ...]
```

Here are some general points for hatch-pattern definitions:

- The pattern name cannot have spaces.
- The description is optional.
- Add the dash specifications only for noncontinuous lines.
- You can have more than one definition line (the second line in the syntax I just showed), creating sets of hatch definitions that combine to create the hatch pattern.
- Each definition line can be no more than 80 characters.
- You can include a maximum of six dash specifications (which include spaces and dots).
- You can add spaces in the definition lines for readability.

Table 31.2 describes the features of a hatch-pattern definition.

TABLE 31.2

Hatch-Pattern Definitions

Specification	Explanation
Angle	Defines the angle of the lines in the hatch pattern. If you also specify an angle in the Boundary Hatch dialog box (when you are placing the hatch), the two angles are added. For example, if a hatch pattern defines lines at 105 degrees and you specify a hatch angle of 30 degrees, you end up with lines running at 135 degrees.
X-origin	Specifies the X coordinate of the base point of the hatch pattern. Your hatch probably won't go through 0,0; however, this point lines up sets of lines in hatch patterns, as well as aligning hatch patterns in different areas. Because all hatch patterns are calculated from the base point, they're always aligned, no matter where they actually appear in the drawing.
Y-origin	Specifies the Y coordinate of the base point of the hatch pattern.

continued

TABLE 31.2	(continued)
Specification	**Explanation**
Delta-x	Specifies the offset of successive lines. This applies only to dashed lines and is measured along the direction of the lines. Specifying a delta-x staggers each successive line by the amount that you specify so that the dashes don't line up.
Delta-y	Specifies the distance between lines, measured perpendicular to the direction of the lines. This applies to both continuous and dashed lines.
Dash	Defines a noncontinuous line using the same system as linetype definitions: positive for a dash, negative for a space, and 0 for a dot.

The hatch pattern shown in Figure 31.6 is the simplest form of hatch pattern.

FIGURE 31.6

The ftrailer hatch pattern with continuous lines.

Although you could specify this simple hatch pattern in the Hatch and Gradient dialog box (the Hatch dialog box if you are using AutoCAD LT), by specifying a user-defined hatch with an angle and spacing, the example that follows shows the syntax clearly. The lines are at an angle of 105 degrees; the hatch pattern starts at 0,0; and the spacing between the lines is 0.5 units. The lines are continuous.

```
*ftrailer, proposed future trailers
105, 0,0, 0,0.5
```

By adding one level of complexity, you can make the lines in the hatch pattern noncontinuous, as follows:

```
*ftrailer, proposed future trailers
105, 0,0, 0,0.5, .5,-.25,0,-.1,0,-.25
```

Note that this definition uses the maximum of six dash specifications (the dash, space, dot, space, dot, and space).

A close-up of this hatch pattern is shown in Figure 31.7.

FIGURE 31.7

The ftrailer hatch pattern with a dash and two dots.

If you add a delta-x of 0.25, the lines in the pattern are staggered by 0.25 units, along the direction of the lines, as shown in this code and in Figure 31.8:

```
*ftrailer, proposed future trailers
105, 0,0, 0.25,0.5, .5,-.25,0,-.1,0,-.25
```

You might wonder why the pattern staggers downward after adding a positive delta-x. The answer is that the direction of the lines (in this case, 105 degrees) becomes the X axis for this calculation. Figure 31.9 shows a zoomed-in display of the hatch pattern around 0,0, which is the base point. The hatch pattern is being generated up and to the left. The first line starts at 0,0, and the second line starts to the left by 0.5 units (the delta-y) and up by 0.25 units (the delta-x), as shown by the dimensions.

FIGURE 31.8

The ftrailer hatch pattern with an added delta-x.

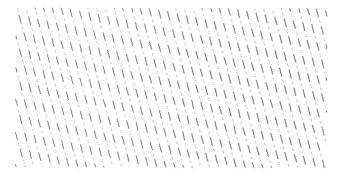

FIGURE 31.9

Calculating how the delta-x and delta-y affect a hatch pattern.

Finally, you can add additional definition lines. One of the definition lines should start at 0,0, but the others may start anywhere. Here is the definition for the pattern in Figure 31.10. It actually creates the shape of the trailers. Although you see the rectangular shape, the hatch pattern is created from four separate lines, two at 0 degrees and two at 90 degrees. Note that the two 0-degree lines are the same, except that they start at different base points. The same is true for the two 90-degree lines.

```
*trail, whole trailers-proposed
0, 0,0, 0,2, .5,-1
90, 0,0, 0,1.5, .5,-.25,0,-.25,.5,-.5
90, .5,0, 0,1.5, .5,-.25,0,-.25,.5,-.5
0, 0,1.5, 0,2, .5,-1
```

FIGURE 31.10

The trail hatch pattern looks like trailers.

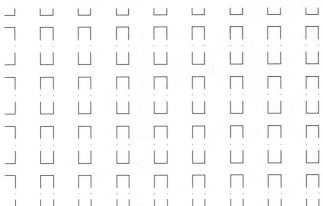

STEPS: Creating and Using a Hatch Pattern

1. Create a drawing using any template.

2. Save the file as ab31-03.dwg in your AutoCAD Bible folder.

3. In Windows, choose Start ⇨ Run. Type **notepad** and click OK. Notepad opens. (In Windows Vista, choose Start and type **notepad** in the Start Search text box and press Enter.)

4. Type the following:

```
*lightning, interwoven lightning
90, 0,0, 0,.5, .5,-.25
0, -.25,.5, 0,.75, .25,-.25
90, -.25,.5, 0,.5, .5,-.25
```

5. Press Enter after the last line. Save the file as lightning.pat in your AutoCAD Bible folder. Close Notepad.

6. If you haven't already done so, you need to add your AutoCAD Bible folder to the support file search path. Choose Tools ⇨ Options and click the Files tab. Click the plus sign to the left of Support File Search Path. Choose Add. Choose Browse. Find your AutoCAD Bible folder and click OK. Click OK again to close the Options dialog box.

7. Choose Rectangle from the Draw toolbar. At the first prompt, type **0,0** ↵. At the Specify other corner point or [Area/Dimensions/Rotation]: prompt, type **10,6** ↵.

8. Choose Hatch from the Draw toolbar. In the Type drop-down menu, choose Custom.

9. Click the ellipsis to the right of the Custom Pattern text box. Choose the lightning.pat file that you just created. Click OK.

10. Choose Add: Select Objects and pick the rectangle in your drawing. Press Enter. Click OK. The rectangle fills with the lightning hatch, as shown in Figure 31.11.

FIGURE 31.11

The lightning hatch pattern.

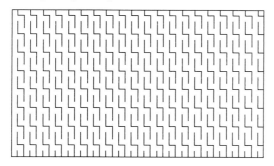

11. Save your drawing.

Check out the acad.pat or acadlt.pat file for some ideas on how to create your own hatch-pattern definitions.

Summary

In this chapter, you discovered how to create your own linetypes and hatch patterns. You read about the following:

- Creating simple linetypes that contain only dashes, dots, and spaces
- Making complex linetypes that include shapes and text
- Constructing your own hatch patterns that are made up of sets of lines

In the next chapter, you read about how to create shapes and fonts.

Chapter 32

Creating Shapes and Fonts

S hapes are text files that define a shape, or figure, that you can insert into your drawing. Shapes are similar to blocks in that you create, store, and insert them. They are different from blocks in the following ways:

- Shapes are much harder to create.
- Shapes are compiled into a format that conserves storage space, memory, and regeneration time.
- You can use shapes to create fonts, and you can insert them into linetypes.
- Like fonts, shape files are support files. If you distribute a drawing, then be sure to include any font or shape files that the drawing uses.

You can use shapes for simple outlines that you need to quickly insert many times. Some examples are shapes that are inserted into complex linetypes and font characters.

AUTOCAD ONLY AutoCAD LT doesn't offer the Shape feature. This entire chapter applies to AutoCAD only.

Creating Shapes

Shape files are used for both shapes and fonts. You create them with a text editor and save them with the `.shp` file extension. You then use the COMPILE command (on the command line), which opens the Select Shape or Font File dialog box, shown in Figure 32.1.

Choose the `.shp` file and click Open. AutoCAD automatically compiles the file into a new file with the same name but with the `.shx` file extension. It then displays a message on the command line that the compilation has succeeded.

The Select Shape or Font File dialog box.

Using shape files

After you have a compiled a shape file, you must load it with the LOAD command before you can place it in a drawing. The Select Shape File dialog box opens. Choose the `.shx` file and click Open. Font files don't have to be loaded because they're automatically referenced by text styles that use the font files.

To insert a shape, use the SHAPE command prompts as follows:

> `Enter shape name or [?]:` Type the name of the shape, or type ? ↵ to get a list of loaded shapes.
>
> `Specify insertion point:` Pick a point on the screen. AutoCAD drags the shape as you move the cursor.
>
> `Specify height <1.0000>:` This functions like a scale factor. For example, type **.5** ↵ to insert the shape at one-half its original size.
>
> `Specify rotation angle <0>:` Type a rotation angle.

Creating shape files

Shape files and font files are essentially the same. In this section, I explain how to create shapes. At the end of the chapter, I explain the few distinctions necessary to create a font file.

As with most customizable files, you use a text editor to create shape files. You can add comments by preceding them with a semicolon. A shape definition has the following syntax:

```
*shapenumber,#ofspecs,SHAPENAME
spec1,spec2,...,0
```

The definition must start with an asterisk. Each line cannot contain more than 128 characters. Table 32.1 explains the parts of this shape definition.

TABLE 32.1

The Parts of a Shape Definition

Item	Explanation
shapenumber	You can use any number from 1 to 255. Each shape in a file must have a unique number.
#ofspecs	This is the number of specifications in the second line of the definition, including the mandatory 0 at the end.
SHAPENAME	You must use uppercase for the shape name. This is the name you use with the SHAPE command.
spec1...	This is a code that defines the actual shape. Each specification code defines a part of the shape, such as a line segment or an arc. Together, all of the specifications draw the shape.
0	The definition must end with a 0.

Using length and direction codes

You can use two sets of codes to define a shape. The first set, the length and direction codes, only allows you to draw straight line segments. You use this system to create specifications in the three-character hexadecimal format.

- The first character is 0, which tells AutoCAD that the next two characters are hexadecimal values.
- The second character is a length in units. The maximum is 15 units. The number values can range from 0 to 9. For values from 10 to 15, use A to F. Keep in mind that the length is measured along the nearest X or Y distance. Therefore, diagonal lengths are not true lengths.
- The third character is a direction code. Figure 32.2 shows how this code works. Use the code that represents the desired direction of the line from the start point.

FIGURE 32.2

The direction codes.

Here is the code for the shape shown in Figure 32.3:

```
*2,4,PENNANT
044,02F,029,0
```

FIGURE 32.3

The PENNANT shape.

Here's how this shape works:

- 2 is the shape's unique number.
- 4 is the number of bytes (specifications) on the second line of the definition.
- PENNANT is the shape's name.
- 044 draws the pole, a line that is 4 units in the vertical direction.
- 02F draws the top line of the pennant, a line that is approximately 2 units in the F direction. (See the following note.)
- 029 draws the bottom line of the pennant, a line that is approximately 2 units in the 9 direction. (See the following note.)

 Although the length of the two diagonal lines was specified as 2, they're actually about 2.22 units long because the line endpoints snapped to the nearest imaginary grid point.

Using supplemental shape codes

The length and direction codes have a number of limitations:

- You can draw in only 16 directions.
- The maximum length of a line is 15 units.
- You can draw only straight line segments.
- The shape has to be continuous; you cannot lift the "pen" up and start in a new place.

The second set of codes, called the supplemental shape codes, brings additional flexibility (and complexity) to your shapes. Table 32.2 lists these codes, which can be in either hexadecimal or decimal format.

TABLE 32.2

Supplemental Shape Codes

Hexadecimal Code	Decimal Code	Explanation
000	0	Specifies the end of the shape definition.
001	1	Starts draw mode (puts the "pen" down).
002	2	Ends draw mode (lifts the "pen" up) so that you can move to a new location.
003	3	Divides the vector lengths by the specification that follows, as in 3,5 to divide the lengths by 5. This scales down the shape. You should reverse this at the end of the shape by using the 4 code.
004	4	Multiplies the vector lengths by the specification that follows, as in 4,2 to multiply the lengths by 2. This scales up the shape. You should reverse this at the end of the shape by using the 3 code.
005	5	Saves the current position so that you can return to it later in the shape definition. You must use (restore) every position that you save (with a maximum of four).
006	6	Restores the last saved position.
007	7	Draws another shape that is defined within the shape file whose number follows. For example, use 7,230 to draw shape 230. When the other shape is complete, AutoCAD returns to the current shape definition.
008	8	Draws a line specified by X and Y displacements that follow the code. For example, 8,(8,–12) draws a line whose endpoint is 8 units to the right and 12 units down from the current coordinate. You can add parentheses to your shape codes for readability.
009	9	Draws multiple X,Y displacements. You end this code with a displacement of 0,0. For example, 9,(8,–12),(1,0),(0,12),(–8,0),(0,0) draws four X,Y displacements. You can add parentheses to your shape codes for readability.
00A	10	Draws an octant arc specified by its radius (ranging from 1 to 255), and a second code in the syntax (–)0SC. In the second code, the minus sign is optional, and indicates a clockwise arc, the 0 is mandatory, the S specifies the starting octant, and the C specifies the number of octants that the arc covers. An octant is an eighth of a circle. Figure 32.4 shows the octant codes that you must use for the starting octant. For example, 10,(2,014) indicates an arc with a radius of 2 that is drawn counterclockwise from octant 1 and covers 4 octants (ending at octant 5). This is a semicircle.

continued

TABLE 32.2	(continued)	
Hexadecimal Code	**Decimal Code**	**Explanation**
00B	11	Draws a fractional arc that is not limited by octants specified by the five following codes in the syntax:

start_offset,end_offset,high_radius,radius,(-)0SC.

The start offset specifies how far past an octant the arc begins and is calculated as follows: (starting degrees – degrees of the last octant passed) * 256/45.

The end offset specifies how far past an octant the arc ends and is calculated as follows: (ending degrees – degrees of the last octant passed) * 256/45.

For both the start and the end of the arc, the last octant passed is specified in degrees, not the numbers in Figure 32.4, and is always a multiple of 45.

The high radius is 0 unless the radius is more than 255. If your radius is larger, the high radius is the maximum number of 256 multiples in the value of the radius (for example, 2 if your radius is 600). The difference (the radius minus 256 times the high radius value, or 88 if your radius is 600) is placed in the radius specification.

The radius is just the radius of the arc.

The (-)0SC part of the code is the same as for code 10 (00A), except that S is the octant that the arc starts in and C is the number of octants that the arc covers.

00C	12	Draws an arc using a system of X,Y displacement and bulge using the syntax X-displacement, Y-displacement, and bulge. These three codes can range from –127 to +127. The X and Y displacements just specify the endpoint of the arc. The bulge equals ((2 * H/D) * 127) where D is the *chord length* (the distance from the start point to the endpoint) and H is the height measured from the midpoint of the chord to the circumference of the arc. The bulge should be negative if the arc is drawn clockwise.
00D	13	Draws multiple arcs using the X,Y displacement and bulge system. End the arcs with (0,0). You can use 0 for a bulge to place a line segment in the midst of several arcs.
00E	14	This code is used only for text fonts that can be used in the vertical orientation (where each letter is drawn under the previous letter). When the vertical orientation is chosen, the specifications after this code are used. Use this code to move the starting and ending point of letters to a point appropriate for vertical orientation (that is, on top of and below the letter). See the "Creating Fonts" section later in this chapter for more information.

FIGURE 32.4

The codes for octant arcs.

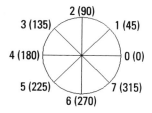

The most common use for shapes is to create fonts. Here are a few examples:

```
*3,22,ALEF
010,07E,010,2,8,(-6,5),1,8,(-2,-4),01C,2,8,(5,2),1,8,(2,4),014,0
```

This is a squared-off alef, the first letter of the Hebrew alphabet, as shown in Figure 32.5. Displaying non-Roman fonts is a common use for shapes.

FIGURE 32.5

A squared-off alef.

Planning in advance is almost essential. A common technique is to draw the shape in a drawing on a grid set to 1-unit spacing. You can use only integers in your shape codes, so you must often scale the shape up so that the smallest line segment is 1 unit.

Here's how the code for the alef works:

- The shape starts at the top left. The code 010 is a hexadecimal length and direction code that specifies a line with a length of 1 unit and a direction of 0 degrees.

- The second code, 07E, is also a hexadecimal length and direction code. It specifies a line with a length of 7 units in the E direction (315 degrees). Although the line is not actually 7 units long, its X (and in this case Y) distance is 7.

- The third code, 010, is the same as the first code and ends the first set of line segments.
- The fourth code, 2, lifts up the pen so that you can move to the start of the next line.
- The fifth code, 8, indicates that the following two codes will be an X,Y displacement.
- The sixth and seventh codes (-6,5) are placed in parentheses for readability. They move the pen (while it is up) -6 units in the X direction and +5 units in the Y direction from the end of the last line to the start of the next line. (Count the grid dots to find it.)
- The eighth code, 1, puts the pen down so that you can draw.
- The ninth code, 8, is the same as the fifth code.
- The tenth and eleventh codes (-2,-4) draw the first segment of the second line so that the end-point is -2 units in the X direction and -4 units in the Y direction from the start point.
- The twelfth code, 01C, is a hexadecimal code and finishes the second line with a 1-unit line segment in the C direction (270 degrees).
- The thirteenth code, 2, lifts up the pen again.
- The fourteenth code, 8, is the same as the fifth code.
- The fifteenth and sixteenth codes (5,2) move the pen (which is up) +5 units in the X direction and +2 units in the Y direction.
- The seventeenth code, 1, puts the pen down again.
- The eighteenth code, 8, is the same as the fifth code.
- The nineteenth and twentieth codes (2,4) draw a line whose endpoint is 2 units in the X direction and 4 units in the Y direction from its start point.
- The twenty-first code, 014, is a hexadecimal length and vector code that draws a 1-unit line in the 4 (90-degree) direction.
- The twenty-second code, 0, ends the shape definition.

Here's another example, a script alef, which is shown in Figure 32.6:

```
*4,10,S-ALEF
06C,2,8,(6,5),1,10,(3,016),0
```

FIGURE 32.6

A script alef.

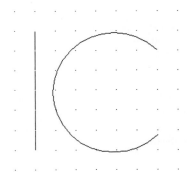

Here's the explanation of the code for the script alef:

- The first code, 06C, creates the line on the left, starting at the top and making it 6 units long.
- The second code, 2, lifts up the pen.
- The third code, 8, specifies an X,Y displacement, with the pen up.
- The fourth and fifth codes (6,5) move the pen 6 units to the right and 5 units up, to the start of the arc.
- The sixth code, 10, introduces an octant arc.
- The seventh and eighth codes (3,016) specify an arc with a radius of 3 units that starts at octant 1 and covers 6 octants (to octant 7). (See Figure 32.4 to review the octant codes.)
- The last code, 0, ends the definition.

 The Express Tools contain a command, MKSHAPE (choose Express ➪ Tools ➪ Make Shape), which makes shapes for you. You simply draw the objects, and use the command to name the shape. You can then immediately use the SHAPE command to insert the shape.

ON the DVD-ROM The drawing used in the following exercise on creating a shape, ab32-a.dwg, is in the Drawings folder on the DVD.

STEPS: Creating a Shape

1. Open ab32-a.dwg from the DVD.
2. Save the file as ab32-01.dwg in your AutoCAD Bible folder. This drawing shows an upper-case P, with dashed lines to indicate space before and after the letter, as shown in Figure 32.7. This is the type of drawing that you might use as a basis for creating a shape definition.

FIGURE 32.7

An uppercase P.

3. Type **notepad** ↵ on the command line and press Enter at the `File to edit:` prompt to open a new file.

4. Type the following in Notepad:

```
*80,15,UCP
2,030,1,0E4,020,12,(0,-8,-127),028,2,8,(9,-6),0
```

5. Press Enter at the end of the last line. Choose File ➪ Save in Notepad and save the file in your `AutoCAD Bible` folder as `ab32-01.shp`. Close Notepad.

6. In AutoCAD, type **compile** ↵. Double-click `ab32-01.shp`. AutoCAD compiles the `.shp` file. AutoCAD confirms on the command line that the compilation succeeded. (Press F2 to open the Text Window if necessary.)

7. Type **load** ↵ and choose `ab32-01.shx`. Click Open. Type **shape** ↵. To insert the shape, follow the prompts:

```
Enter shape name or [?]: ucp ↵
Specify insertion point: Pick any point.
Specify height <1.0000>: ↵
Specify rotation angle <0>: ↵
```

8. Save your drawing. It should look like Figure 32.8.

FIGURE 32.8

The picture and shape of the letter P.

Editing shape files

You don't often get a shape right the first time, and you don't see the result until after you've compiled, loaded, and inserted the shape. Editing shape files involves the following steps:

1. Erase all copies of the shape.

2. Purge the `.shx` file by using the PURGE command and choosing Shapes in the dialog box. (You may sometimes need to purge more than once.) This step removes the existing shape definition from the drawing. If you forget this step, when you try to insert the corrected shape, AutoCAD uses the old definition!

3. Edit the `.shp` file. Don't forget to change the `#ofspecs` value in the first line if necessary. Save the file.

4. Recompile the `.shp` file.

5. Reload the `.shx` file.

6. Reinsert the shape using the SHAPE command.

Creating Fonts

AutoCAD's support for TrueType fonts makes so many fonts available that the need to create your own is certainly less than with earlier versions. However, you might want to add special symbols to some existing fonts, especially if you often use these symbols within text.

Font files use the same codes to define the characters as shape files. They have the following unique characteristics:

- The `shapenumber` part of the definition must correspond to the ASCII code value for the character you're defining. To find these codes, look at the sample fonts in the Help file (choose Help ⇨ Help ⇨ Contents ⇨ Customization Guide ⇨ Shapes and Shape Fonts ⇨ Create Shape Definition Files ⇨ Sample Files). Fonts generally use either hexadecimal or decimal format.

- The `shapename` part of the definition is lowercase and is usually used to label the character. For example, it uses `ucp` for uppercase *p* and `lcr` for lowercase *r*. The sample files mentioned in the previous item use these codes.

- The file must include a special shape number 0 that defines the entire font, using the following syntax:

  ```
  *0,4,font-name
  above,below,modes,0
  ```

  The `above` value specifies how far above the baseline that uppercase letters extend. The `below` value specifies how far below the baseline that lowercase letters, such as *p* or *q*, extend. Together, these two values define the size of the characters. AutoCAD uses these values to scale letters when you define a text height for the font. Modes should be 0 for a horizontal font and 2 for a font that supports both horizontal and vertical orientations. For example, a header for a font named `arch` with capital letters 21 units high and lowercase letters that extend 7 units below the line could be:

  ```
  *0,4,arch
  21,7,0,0
  ```

- You must define the line feed (LF), which drops down one line without drawing so that lines of text can be placed beneath each other. The line feed is ASCII code 10.

- You need to create a start point and endpoint with the pen up to create spacing between letters. See the previous exercise for an example.

As with all shapes, you probably want to use AutoCAD to draw all of the characters on a grid with a spacing of 1. Decide on the height of the letters and be consistent.

Big Fonts and Unicode Fonts

The Japanese and Chinese written languages use fonts with thousands of characters, because each character represents a word. AutoCAD uses big fonts to support these languages. It is beyond the scope of this book to go into detail about how to create these fonts, but a short explanation is useful. Big font files use special codes to allow for the larger number of shapes. Big fonts allow up to 65,535 shape numbers.

Unicode fonts support the ISO10646 standard, which uses 16-bit encoding to support many languages in one font file. If you open one of the .shp files, you'll see characters for all of the letters that may have accents in French, Spanish, and so on. All of the fonts in AutoCAD are now compliant with this standard.

The advantage of Unicode fonts is that characters that you type appear the same in all systems and countries. This is important if you exchange drawings with clients or colleagues in other countries. Unicode fonts use a special header that includes two extra codes.

Unicode special characters can be inserted by typing \u+ and the hexadecimal Unicode value in the font file. (For this reason, Unicode font files use hexadecimal shape numbers.) For example, the hexadecimal code for the plus/minus sign is 00B1. If you type \u+00b1 and press Enter (using DTEXT in this example), you get the plus/minus sign. (It works with multiline text, too.)

If you don't need the additional capabilities of big fonts or Unicode fonts, you can create fonts without them.

Summary

In this chapter, you read about how to create shapes. You discovered how to:

- Use shape files when you need to insert a shape many times, while using as little storage space as possible
- Create fonts using shape files with a few special codes that define both the font as a whole and each character

In the next chapter, I explain how to customize menus.

Chapter 33

Customizing Menus

You probably use the AutoCAD and AutoCAD LT menus all the time. (If you don't, you can skip this chapter.) Although the menus are designed to be useful for most people, the whole point of customization is that everyone has different needs. You can probably draw easier and faster by customizing the menus to suit your own individual requirements. Not only can you add commands to a menu, but you can also add menu items consisting of a series of commands that run just like a macro. If you're using AutoCAD, you can even add AutoLISP routines to your menus. You can edit the default menu or create your own menu. You may want to create specialized menus that are used only for one drawing — for example, a menu to help clients view a drawing. Menu customization includes the drop-down menu, mouse or puck buttons, toolbars and the Dashboard (both covered in Chapter 29), shortcut menus, image-tile menus, keyboard shortcuts, temporary override keys, and the double-click function. The only limits are your imagination and the time that you can devote to customization.

Working with the Customization File

The AutoCAD or AutoCAD LT menu is contained in a file that you don't edit directly; instead, you use the Customize User Interface, or CUI, dialog box to modify the menu.

> **NOTE** In AutoCAD 2008 and AutoCAD LT 2008, the entire menu file is in XML format. This change occurred in AutoCAD 2006 and AutoCAD LT 2006. If you're upgrading from an earlier release, you'll see that in place of the MNU, MNS, and MNC files is one file in XML format, `acad.cui` or `acadlt.cui`. Instead of editing the file directly, you use a dialog box.

Understanding the menu file

The main menu file is `acad.cui` in AutoCAD, and `acadlt.cui` in AutoCAD LT. You can either customize this file, or load another CUI file. I discuss using this file to customize toolbars and the Dashboard in Chapter 29. In this chapter, I cover customization of the menu, including the drop-down menu, shortcut (right-click) menus, mouse buttons, keyboard shortcuts (including temporary override keys), tablet menus, image-tile menus, and double-click behavior.

CAUTION Don't even think about customizing the menu until you've backed up at least `acad.cui` or `acadlt.cui`. It is possible to corrupt the menu file.

TIP If you get into a problem with your menu, then you can restore your most recently saved menu by right-clicking the menu's name at the top of the Customizations In pane and choosing Restore ACAD.CUI (or ACADLT.CUI). You can also go back to the original menu that came with AutoCAD by right-clicking the menu name and choosing Reset ACAD.CUI. Another way to find the original menu is to look in `C:\Program Files\AutoCAD 2008\UserDataCache\Support` (if you used the default installation location).

In addition to the main menu file, AutoCAD and AutoCAD LT use these other files:

- `custom.cui`: This file is specifically meant to be used for customization. It is a *partial* customization file, which means that you use it to add on to the main customization file. For example, you can add a toolbar and a menu that you use with the regular menu.
- `acad.mnr` or `acadlt.mnr`: This file contains bitmap images used by the menu, such as toolbar icons and icons on menus.
- `acad.mnl`: This file contains AutoLISP routines used by the menu. If you create a new menu file that contains AutoLISP routines, then AutoCAD creates this file automatically. (AutoCAD only.)

You can create your own full or partial menu files using any name that you want. You'll have the best results if you place all of your menu files in the same folder as the main customization file.

NOTE To find the location of `acad.cui` or `acadlt.cui`, choose Tools ▷ Options and then click the Files tab. Expand the Customization Files item, and then expand the Main Customization File item. Browse to that location in Windows Explorer.

Loading and unloading customization files

There are two types of customization files: partial and main (full). A partial customization file usually has only one or two drop-down menus (or toolbars). You can then load this partial menu along with your regular menu. If your menu customization consists of simply adding a few menu items, then you may want to create a partial customization file and add it to your current menu.

On the other hand, you may also want to have complete alternate menus, in which case you can customize the main menu. Perhaps two different people work on one computer and have different menu needs. For example, you may find it useful to have one menu for architectural drawings, another for mechanical drawings, and a third for electrical schematics. Of course, you can customize your one main menu to better suit your needs.

Loading and unloading a main customization file

Using your own customization file is a good way to keep the original file safe, in case you want to go back to it. Generally, you start by making a copy of the default main customization file, `acad.cui` or `acadlt.cui`.

You can copy the main customization file (or any file, for that matter) in Windows Explorer. Right-click the file and choose Copy. Then right-click in any blank space in the Explorer window and choose Paste. The new file appears at the bottom of the list of files. Click the file to select it, and then click it again to change its name. Enter the new name, and then press Enter.

You can use only one main customization file at a time. If you want to work with your own customization file, you first need to unload the current customization file. Use the CUILOAD command on the command line both to unload and load a customization file. The Load/Unload Customizations dialog box opens, as shown in Figure 33.1. Choose the main customization file that you want to unload, and click Unload. (There is also a CUIUNLOAD command; it opens the same dialog box as the CUILOAD command.)

FIGURE 33.1

The Load/Unload Customizations dialog box.

To load a new main customization file, follow these steps:

1. In the Load/Unload Customizations dialog box, choose the current main customization file and click Unload.

2. Click the Browse button.

3. Navigate to and select the new main customization file. Click Open.

4. In the Load/Unload Customizations dialog box, click Load.

5. Click Close to close the dialog box.

TIP You can also use the MENU command to load a new main customization file; this method does not require you to unload the main customization file.

6. Choose Tools ➪ Customize ➪ Interface (or type **cui** on the command line or in the dynamic input tooltip).

7. In the Customizations In pane, the top drop-down list should show All Customization Files or Main CUI File. The top item in the pane lists the current main customization file. It may still show the customization file that you unloaded; in that case, right-click it and choose Rename. Enter the name of the customization file that you loaded, and press Enter to match the customization group name to the filename.

When you start AutoCAD or AutoCAD LT, the last customization file that you used, the name of which is stored in the Windows registry, is loaded. If you want to use a new menu while in AutoCAD or AutoCAD LT, unload the current customization file and load the new one.

Loading and unloading partial customization files

You can use the Custom partial customization file that comes with AutoCAD (or AutoCAD LT), or create your own partial customization files. To create a new partial customization file, follow these steps:

1. On the Transfer tab of the Customize User Interface dialog box, click the Create a New Customization File button to the right of the Customizations In drop-down list.

2. From the drop-down list, choose Save As. Enter a name for the new file in the Save As dialog box. Make sure that you use a name that is different from all other CUI files.

3. To use the file, go to the Customize tab and choose Main CUI File from the drop-down list in the Customizations In pane. Then click the Load Partial Customization File button to the right of the drop-down list. In the Open dialog box, locate the partial CUI file and click Open.

4. Choose Main CUI File again from the drop-down list. You should now see the new file listed under the expanded Partial CUI Files item.

You can load more than one partial customization file along with the main customization file. For example, you might have one partial customization file for 2D work and another for 3D work; sometimes, you might want both of them.

You can load and unload partial customization files in two ways:

- Use the CUILOAD command as explained in the previous section.

- Use the CUI command to open the Customize User Interface dialog box. To load a file, click the Load Partial Customization File button in the Customizations In pane. Select the file and click Open. In the Customize User Interface dialog box, click Apply.

After you have loaded a partial customization file, check to make sure that it has been loaded. In the Customize User Interface dialog box, choose Main CUI File from the top drop-down list. Expand the Partial CUI Files item in the Customizations in Main CUI pane, and make sure that your partial CUI file is listed.

To unload a partial customization file, use one of these methods:

- Use the CUIUNLOAD command. Follow the instructions for unloading a main CUI file described in the previous section.

- In the Customize User Interface dialog box, right-click the file and choose Unload CUI File.

Transferring customization between files

You can also move customization items between customization files, using the Transfer tab of the Customize User Interface dialog box. You can transfer items from a loaded file to any menu file. You can also transfer items between partial customization files or between a main customization file and a partial one.

When you display the Transfer tab, the current customization file is listed in the left pane. To open another file, click the Open Customization File button in the right pane, choose the file that you want to use, and click Open.

In each pane, expand the element that you want to transfer. For example, if you want to transfer menus, expand the menu item on each side. You then see the actual menus in each file that is listed. To transfer an item, drag it from one pane to the other. Make sure that you are dragging to the same type of item, that is, menu to menu or toolbar to toolbar.

When you're done, click OK to close the Customize User Interface dialog box.

Working with Menu Files from Previous Releases

How do you bring your extensively customized menus from prior releases (2005 and earlier) into the new menu system for 2008? It's easy, because AutoCAD and AutoCAD LT take care of this for you.

To convert your MNU or MNS files to CUI files, open the Customize User Interface dialog box and click the Transfer tab. From the Customizations in New CUI File drop-down list, choose Open. Select the menu file and click Open. You now see the file, with the same name as before, but with a .cui filename extension. You still need to load the file, as explained earlier in this chapter.

You might want to continue to work with your MNU and MNS files if you are in an office that uses more than one version of AutoCAD, and everyone needs to share the same file. In that case, use the MENU command to open the Select Customization File dialog box. Choose Legacy Menu Template (*.mnu) or Legacy Menu File (*.mns) from the Files of Type drop-down list. AutoCAD creates a CUI file from your MNU or MNS file. In AutoCAD LT, use the CUILOAD command again. Select the menu and click Unload. Then browse to the legacy menu you want to use and click Load. Then click Close.

Customizing a Menu

When you first start customizing a customization file, the process may seem overwhelming. However, even small changes can be very useful. Start simple and take it from there.

Menu files include the following types of customizable content:

- Toolbars let you choose commands from buttons. I discuss customizing toolbars in Chapter 29.
- Dashboard control panels also let you choose commands from buttons, as well as specify settings using special controls. Dashboard customization is covered in Chapter 29.
- Menus are the drop-down menus at the top of your screen.
- Keyboard shortcuts come in two varieties. Regular keyboard shortcuts, such as Ctrl+C for the COPYCLIP command, execute commands.
- Temporary override keys (which I explain how to use in Chapter 4) are another kind of keyboard shortcut, but they temporarily override settings, such as OSNAP and ORTHO.
- Shortcut menus appear when you click the right mouse button. (See Chapter 3 and "The User Preferences tab" section in Appendix A for more information on right-clicking.)
- Double-click actions control what happens when you double-click an object.
- Button menus control the buttons on your mouse.
- Tablet menus control the menu that can be overlaid on a digitizing tablet.
- Tablet buttons control the multiple buttons on a puck that you use with a digitizing tablet.
- The screen menu is AutoCAD's original menu that used to appear at the right side of your screen. (This section does not exist in AutoCAD LT.) By default, it is not displayed, but it still exists in the menu file. In AutoCAD, you can display it by choosing Tools ➪ Options, clicking the Display tab, and checking the Display Screen Menu check box.
- Image-tile menus create dialog boxes with images.

Looking at a drop-down menu

The best way to start customizing a menu is to look at a drop-down menu and its corresponding representation in the Customize User Interface dialog box. Each type of menu content has its own unique features, but certain features apply to most, if not all, menu types.

Figure 33.2 shows the AutoCAD Format drop-down menu. (AutoCAD LT's Format menu is slightly different.)

FIGURE 33.2

The AutoCAD Format drop-down menu.

Figure 33.3 shows the same menu as displayed in the Customize User Interface dialog box. Compare this list to the menu shown in Figure 33.2.

In Figure 33.3, the Layer item is selected, and the right side of the Customize User Interface dialog box shows the information relating to that item. Note that menu items have seven elements:

- **Name:** The name is what you actually see on the menu. The ellipsis (. . .) after a menu item provides a visual cue on the menu that these items open dialog boxes. The ampersand (&) places an underscore under the following letter. You can then type the letter to execute the menu item (instead of clicking the menu item with your mouse). The mouse buttons, tablet buttons, tablet menus, shortcut menus, and double-click actions do not display the name, but the name is required. (This was called a label in older releases.)

- **Command Name:** This is the name of the command. Usually, it's the same as the display name.

- **Description:** For drop-down menus, shortcut menus, and toolbars, the description appears on the status bar when you hover the cursor over the menu item or button. The other menu elements don't use the description, although some of them let you enter one.

- **Macro:** The macro is the command that the item executes. In the next section, I explain how to write menu macros. This can be a simple command, any group of commands, or an AutoLISP expression if you're using AutoCAD. The following conventions are recommended:

  - Add an apostrophe (') before commands that can be used transparently. (Otherwise, the commands won't work transparently when chosen from the menu.)

All other commands start with ^C^C, which is equivalent to pressing Esc twice. This cancels any other command that may be active. One Esc is generally enough, but occasionally two are necessary. (In rare situations, more might be needed.)

The underscore is used before each command. This allows translation of the command into other languages. Your menus would automatically be translated into the equivalent French command in France!

■ **Key(s):** Shortcut keys and temporary override keys have a Key item, which specifies which key combination you use to execute the macro.

■ **Element ID:** This is a unique identifier that the program assigns automatically. In previous releases, it was used to link drop-down menu items and toolbar buttons to their status-bar help, and to link a keyboard shortcut to a menu item. You can still use this identifier for programming purposes. You cannot change the ID of an existing command, but you should add one for new commands that you create.

■ **Images:** Toolbar buttons and some menu items have images. Most people use only the small image, but you can specify large images on the Display tab of the Options dialog box (Tools ➪ Options). You can choose an image from the Button Image pane, or create your own image using the Button Editor. I cover the Button Editor in Chapter 29.

Drop-down and shortcut menus (the entire menu, not their items) also have aliases that you use when referring to the menu. You can add an alias by clicking the Ellipsis button to the right of the alias item.

FIGURE 33.3

The Format menu in the Customize User Interface dialog box.

In Windows 2000 and XP, by default, the underscores appear only if you access the menu using the keyboard. To access a menu, press Alt and the underscores appear. Then type the underscored letter to open the menu. To choose a menu item, type its underscored letter. To disable this behavior and display the underscores all of the time, choose Start ⇨ Control Panel and choose Display. If you have Windows XP, choose the Appearance tab and click the Effects button. Then uncheck the Hide Underlined Letters for Keyboard Navigation Until I Press the Alt Key check box. If you have Windows 2000, choose the Effects tab. Then uncheck the Hide Keyboard Navigation Indicators Until I Use the Alt Key check box. In Windows Vista, choose Appearance and Personalization from the Control Panel Home display. In the Ease of Access Center category, click Underline Keyboard Shortcuts and Access Keys. Check the Underline Keyboard Shortcuts and Access Keys check box. Click Save.

Writing menu macros

The menu macro is the heart of the menu. To enter a macro, click the text box to the right of the Macro item and start typing. If your macro is long, click the Ellipsis button at the right of the text box to open the Long String Editor dialog box. You need to know a number of special characters and conventions in order to write menu macros. Table 33.1 lists some of the most common ones.

TABLE 33.1

Special Characters for Menu Macros

Character	Description
;	Equivalent to pressing Enter. The end of a line in a menu macro is also equivalent to pressing Enter. Use the semicolon when you need two returns at the end of a line, or when you want to indicate pressing Enter. Some commands, such as DTEXT/TEXT, also require a return to complete. You can also use ^M.
Space	Similar to pressing Enter, except when entering text (to create a text object) that contains spaces (such as between words). Use between the command and its options. Note that you can even use a space on the command line for most commands.
\	Pauses for user input, such as picking a point or typing a value.
+	Used at the end of a line to continue the macro on the next line.
*	Placed at the beginning of a macro (before the ^C^C), this character repeats the macro until you end it by pressing Esc or choosing another menu item. For example, the POINT command works this way.
^P	Turns on and off (toggles) the display of the menu macro, including menu prompts, on the command line.

Because the backslash pauses for user input, you cannot use it to specify a path, as in C:\Program Files\AutoCAD 2008\Support. Use the regular slash (/) instead.

Here is one macro from the Draw drop-down menu — Arc: Start, Center, Angle — that uses the backslash and the space:

```
^C^C_arc \_c \_a
```

Here's how this command works:

^C^C	Cancels any previous command.
_arc	Starts the ARC command (enables translation to another language version of AutoCAD or AutoCAD LT).
Space	Equivalent to pressing the spacebar, which is the same as pressing Enter after typing **arc** on the command line. The command line displays the Specify start point of arc or [Center]: prompt.
\	The backslash pauses the macro to let you specify a start point.
_c	Chooses the Center option, and enables translation to another language.
Space	Equivalent to pressing the spacebar, which is the same as pressing Enter after typing c on the command line (for the Center option). The command line displays the Specify center point of arc: prompt.
\	The backslash pauses the macro to let you specify a center point.
_a	Chooses the Angle option. Because this is at the end of the command, you don't need to specify a pause. The user specifies an angle and presses Enter, thus ending the command and drawing the arc.

The backslash allows for only one input, except when used with the SELECT command. Therefore, you can use the SELECT command in menu macros to collect a selection set, and then use another command with the Previous option to act on the entire selection set. For example:

```
^C^Cselect \move previous ;.1,0 ;
```

This macro cancels any existing command, starts the SELECT command, and lets you select as many objects as you want. You end object selection by pressing Enter. Then the macro automatically moves those objects to the right by 0.1 units. Using the All selection option is another way to select more than one object in a menu macro.

Here are a few more examples of macros from earlier chapters.

- You could place this macro on a drop-down menu to make a selected polyline 0.1 units wide:
  ```
  ^C^Cpedit \w .1 ;
  ```
- You would use the following macro to automatically draw four circles with the specified centers and radius.
  ```
  ^C^Ccircle 2,2 1.5 circle 6,2 1.5 circle 10,2 1.5 circle 14,2 1.5
  ```
- You could use this macro to clean up a drawing. It uses CHPROP to select all of the objects in a drawing, and the Color option to change their color to ByLayer. Then it uses the LAYER command to freeze the layer named no-plot and saves the drawing.
  ```
  ^C^Cchprop all  c bylayer  -layer f no-plot  qsave
  ```

Swapping menus

Sometimes you want a menu item to display another menu item. This is called *menu swapping*. Here is an example of swapping in the Mouse Buttons ➪ Shift+Click ➪ Button 2: Snap Menu item:

```
$P0=SNAP $p0=*
```

This menu introduces some new special characters that are used in the menus. Because you cannot customize the pick button (which is button 1), the first button listed is the second button. In this case, pressing Shift and the second button (the right button on a two-button mouse) opens the Object Snap menu (as you probably already know).

The Object Snap menu is in the Object Snap Cursor menu, which is a shortcut menu. For the sake of compatibility with previous menus, this menu has an alias of POP0. This menu item switches you to the Object Snap shortcut menu and displays that menu.

The special syntax is as follows:

```
$section=menugroup.menuname $section=menugroup.*
```

If the menu group is the same as that of the menu where you're placing the macro, you can leave it out. The menu group name is the same as the customization group name, which is usually the name of the file — for example, ACAD for acad.cui. The menu name is either the menu's label or an alias. The different sections or menu types have their own special abbreviations for menu swapping, as shown in Table 33.2.

TABLE 33.2

Menu-Section Abbreviations for Menu Referencing

Abbreviation	Menu Section
A1–A4	The AUX menus 1 through 4
B1–B4	The BUTTONS menus 1 through 4
P0–P16	The drop-down menus
I	The IMAGE menu
T1–T4	The TABLET menus 1 through 4

> **TIP** You could use this technique for a custom menu that swaps to an image menu that inserts commonly used blocks. However, the tool palettes, which I cover in Chapter 26, are an easier way to accomplish a similar result.

Customizing mouse buttons and tablet buttons

Although the Customizations In pane lists sections for both mouse buttons and tablet (puck) buttons, these sections are identical. You can add as many menu items as your input device has buttons. To add a button, right-click a mouse button section, such as Click or Shift+click, and choose New Button.

To add a command to a button, drag the command from the Command List pane to the mouse button in the Customizations In pane.

> **NOTE** You can customize the Mouse Buttons and Tablet Buttons sections for full menus only, not for partial menus.

Here is the default Mouse Buttons Click section:

- **Button 2: Grips Menu:** To see the macro for this item, select it and look in the Macro text box. The second button usually functions as a return (the semicolon at the end of the macro represents the return). The first part of the macro includes an expression in a programming language called

DIESEL (which is beyond the scope of this book). However, its purpose is to display the Grips shortcut menu. The Grips shortcut menu only appears if you have a hot grip in your drawing.

- **Button 3: Snap Menu:** The third button, if you have one, displays the Object Snap menu. You can change this to whatever you want.
- **Button 4: Cancel:** ^C^C, is equivalent to pressing Esc twice.
- **Button 5: Toggle Snap:** The macro, ^B, is equivalent to pressing Ctrl+B, which turns Snap on and off.
- **Button 6: Toggle Ortho:** ^O, is equivalent to pressing Ctrl+L, which turns Ortho on and off. (Once upon a time, before Windows, Ctrl+O toggled Ortho on and off.)
- **Button 7: Toggle Grid:** ^G, is equivalent to pressing Ctrl+G, which turns the grid on and off.
- **Button 8: Toggle Coords:** Toggles the coordinate display mode.
- **Button 9: Toggle Isoplane:** ^E, is equivalent to pressing Ctrl+E, which switches to the next isometric plane.
- **Button 10: Toggle Tablet:** ^T, is equivalent to pressing Ctrl+T, which turns the tablet on and off.

If you have a number of buttons on your pointing device, you can leave these macros as they are or change them to suit your needs.

TIP You can pan and zoom with the IntelliMouse. The MBUTTONPAN system variable controls the third button or wheel on your pointing device. By default, it's set to 1, which supports panning and zooming. Set it to 0 to support the definition in the customization file.

The following exercise shows you how you can customize even a two-button device. Because you may be working on someone else's computer, the exercise undoes the customization at the end.

STEPS: Customizing the Buttons Menu

1. Back up your menu files. (By default, these are `acad.cui` for AutoCAD and `acadlt.cui` for AutoCAD LT.)

CAUTION Don't continue this exercise until you've completed Step 1. If you're working on someone else's computer, ask permission before doing this exercise.

2. To make a duplicate of `acad.cui` or `acadlt.cui`, right-click the file in Windows Explorer and choose Copy from the shortcut menu. Right-click again and choose Paste. Windows places a copy of the file in the same folder.

NOTE To find the location of your menu files, choose Tools ⬦ Options and click the Files tab. Double-click Customization Files ⬦ Main Customization File to display the location of the menu files.

3. Click the copied menu file and rename it `ab1.cui` (that's the number 1, not the letter *L*). Press Enter.
4. Open a drawing using any template. On the command line or in the dynamic input tooltip, type **cuiload** ↵. In the Load/Unload Customizations dialog box, choose ACAD (or ACADLT) and click Unload. Most of your menus and all of your toolbars disappear!
5. Click Browse. In the Select Customization File dialog box, choose `ab1.cui` and click Open. Back in the Load/Unload Customizations dialog box, click Load. All of your menus and toolbars reappear. Click Close to return to your drawing.

6. On the command line or in the dynamic input tooltip, type cui ↵. In the Customizations In pane of the Customize User Interface dialog box, right-click ACAD (or ACADLT) and choose Rename. Type **ab1** ↵ to change the customization name to match the filename.

7. If you use a system mouse, double-click the Mouse Buttons item, and then double-click the Ctrl+Click item. If you use a digitizing tablet or other non-system input device, double-click Legacy, double-click Tablet Buttons, and then double-click the Ctrl+Click item. Click the Button 2 item (the right mouse button on a two-button mouse).

8. In the Command List pane, click the Create a New Command button. In the Name text box of the Properties pane, enter **Toggle Snap Mode** ↵. This lets you turn Snap on and off using Ctrl plus the right button on your pointing device. Change the current macro to **^B**. In the Element ID text box, type **MMU_0010** ↵ to ensure that the new command has a unique ID.

NOTE If your menu doesn't list a button for Ctrl+Click, then right-click this item and choose New Button.

9. Find the new Toggle Snap Mode command in the Command List pane's list of commands and drag it to the Button 2 item. You should see a small left-facing arrow pointing directly to the Button 2 item.

10. Double-click Ctrl+Shift+Click in the Customizations In pane and click the Button 2 item. Again click the Create a New Command button in the Command List pane. In the Name text box of the Properties pane, type **Toggle Ortho Mode** ↵. This lets you turn Ortho on and off using Ctrl+Shift+right-click. (Notice that the Element ID is now MMU_0011.) In the Macro text box, type **^O** ↵.

11. Find the new Toggle Ortho Mode command in the Command List pane's list of commands and drag it to the Ctrl+Shift+Click Button 2 item. You should see a small left-facing arrow pointing directly to the Button 2 item.

12. Click OK to return to your drawing.

13. Press and hold Ctrl and click the right button. The SNAP button on the status bar turns on (looks pushed in). Move your cursor around to verify that Snap is on. (If the cursor doesn't snap to points, then PolarSnap is on. Right-click SNAP on the status bar and choose Grid Snap On.)

14. Hold Ctrl+Shift and click the right button. Orthomode turns on if it's currently off or turns off if it's currently on.

15. Hold Ctrl+Shift and click the right button again to toggle Orthomode again.

16. To return to your original menu, enter **cuiload** ↵ on the command line or in the dynamic input tooltip to open the Load/Unload Customizations dialog box. Choose AB1 and click Unload. Click Browse, choose acad.cui (or acadlt.cui), and click Open. Click Load, and then click Close.

17. Again, try using Ctrl plus the right button and Ctrl+Shift+right-click. The button no longer works as before. Instead, both key combinations open the OSNAP shortcut menu.

Don't save your drawing.

Customizing drop-down menus

The Menus section controls the drop-down (or pull-down) menus, which are the menus along the top of your screen. You can customize existing menus or add your own menu to the main customization file. You can also create a partial customization file with one or more menus. Figure 33.4 shows the Edit menu in AutoCAD.

FIGURE 33.4

The Edit menu.

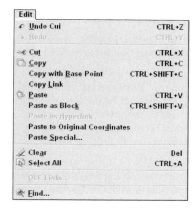

Figure 33.5 shows the Edit menu in the Customize User Interface dialog box. Compare it to Figure 33.4. Look for the separator lines and underscored letters.

FIGURE 33.5

The Edit menu in the Customize User Interface dialog box.

Here are the basic procedures for creating drop-down menus:

- To add a menu, right-click the Menus item in the Customizations In pane and choose New Menu. The menu appears at the bottom of the list of menus. You can immediately edit the default name. Press Enter.

The name of a menu appears as the menu title. Keep these fairly short to keep the menu titles from running into each other. Don't place spaces in menu title names — it becomes hard to distinguish where one menu ends and the next one starts.

- To add a command (an item) to a menu, drag the command from the Command List pane to the menu's name. If you already have items on the menu, you can drag above or below an existing item. You can also duplicate an existing command on a menu: right-click the item in the Customizations In pane and choose Duplicate. To make sure that all commands are available, choose All Customization Files or Main CUI File from the Customizations In drop-down list, and choose All Commands from the Categories drop-down list.

To quickly locate a command in the Command List, click any command and type the first letter of the command. You automatically jump to commands starting with that letter. You can then scroll down to find the command that you need, which is nearby.

To find any command that you're looking for, use the new Find Command or Text button at the top of the Command List pane. The Find and Replace dialog box opens. Enter some text and click Find Next. Commands also now show a tooltip of their macro in the Command List pane. There's also a new Search Command List text box at the bottom of the Command List pane. You can type in text to display only matching commands in the list.

- To add a separator line below any item, right-click that item and choose Insert Separator from the shortcut menu. You also see a separator line [--] in several places in Figures 33.4 and 33.5. The separator helps to organize a menu into logical sections.
- To delete an item, right-click the item and choose Remove. Choose Yes in the confirmation message box.

Creating sub-menus

Sub-menus help you to organize your menu so that related commands stay together. Figure 33.6 shows the Draw menu, which has a number of sub-menus.

To add a sub-menu, right-click any menu item and choose New Sub-menu. Name the sub-menu the same way that would you name a regular menu. You also add commands to a sub-menu in the same way that you add commands to a menu.

Creating custom commands

You can create a custom command and place it on an existing menu or a new menu that you create, in either a main or a partial customization file. To create a custom command on a menu, do the following:

1. Choose the menu in the Customizations In pane.
2. Click the Create a New Command button in the Command List pane.
3. In the Properties pane, shown in Figure 33.7, complete the following:
   - In the Name text box, replace the default name (Command1) with your own name for the command.
   - Type a help description in the Description text box. This text appears on the status bar to further explain the function of the command when you hover the mouse cursor over the menu item.

FIGURE 33.6

The AutoCAD Draw menu with the Modeling and Meshes sub-menus displayed.

FIGURE 33.7

Specify the properties of a new command in the Properties pane.

     ▨   Write the macro in the Macro text box, using the macro syntax described in this chapter.

NEW FEATURE   **You can duplicate existing commands and then edit the macro of the duplicate. To duplicate a command, right-click it in the Command List pane and choose Duplicate. Click the duplicate command and edit its macro in the Macro text box of the Properties pane.**

     ▨   New commands need an Element ID, but you can accept the default one that AutoCAD or AutoCAD LT provides. You can change the ID if you want to. You could use the ID for programming purposes.

   4.   From the Categories drop-down list, choose Custom Commands so that you can find the command more easily. Drag the new command onto the menu.

   5.   If you want, you can associate an image with the command, although this is more commonly done for toolbar buttons. The image will appear to the left of the command name on the menu. I explain how to use the Button Image pane and the Button Editor in Chapter 29.

   6.   Click OK.

STEPS: Creating a Drop-Down Partial Menu

   1.   If you haven't already done so, back up the menu files. (These are the `acad.cui`, `acad.mnr`, and `acad.mnl`, or `acadlt.cui` and `acadlt.mnr` files.)

CAUTION   **Don't continue with this exercise until you've completed Step 1. If you're working on someone else's computer, ask permission before doing this exercise. To find the location of your menu files, choose Tools ➪ Options and click the Files tab. Double-click Customization Files ➪ Main Customization File.**

   2.   Open a drawing using any template. Type **cui** ↵ on the command line or in the dynamic input tooltip.

   3.   To create a new partial customization file, click the Transfer tab of the Customize User Interface dialog box, and click the Create a New Customization File button in either pane.

   4.   From the drop-down list next to the Create a New Customization File you clicked, choose Save As. In the Save As dialog box, enter **ab2** in the File Name text box. Click Save.

   5.   Click the Customize tab. The drop-down list in the Customizations In pane should show All Customization Files. Then click the Load Partial Customization File button to the right of the drop-down list. In the Open dialog box, locate the `ab2.cui` file and click Open. (If you see a Warning about Workspaces message, click OK.)

   6.   Choose All Customization Files from the drop-down list. Expand the Partial CUI Files item; you now see AB2 listed. Double-click the AB2 item to expand it.

   7.   Right-click the AB2 item and choose New Menu. Enter **AB2** ↵ to rename the menu.

   8.   To create a sub-menu, right-click the new AB2 menu and choose New Sub-menu. Enter **&Special Edits** ↵ to rename the sub-menu. (The ampersand allows you to open the menu by pressing Alt+S.)

   9.   To create the first custom menu item, click the Create a New Command button in the Command List pane. In the Properties pane, enter the following:

```
Name: Move .1 right
Description: Moves objects .1 unit to the right
Macro (after ^C^C): _select;\_move;_previous;;.1,0;;
Element ID: AB_002a
```

In the Command List pane, choose the Move .1 right command, which is now highlighted, and drag it to the Special Edits sub-menu. As you do this, you should see a small, left-pointing arrow. When you release the mouse button, the command should appear just below the sub-menu.

10. To allow keyboard access, click the Name property for the Move .1 right command in the Properties pane and type **&** in front of the name.

11. To create another custom command, again click Create a New Command in the Command List pane. In the Properties pane, enter the following:

    Name: **Pedit .1**
    Description: **Sets polyline width to .1**
    Macro (after ^C^C): **_pedit;\w;.1;;**
    Element ID: AB_002b

    Drag the new command below the previous custom command.

12. To allow keyboard access, click the Name property for the Pedit .1 command in the Properties pane and type **&** in front of the name.

13. To add a separator line, right-click the AB2 menu (under the Menus item) and choose Insert Separator.

14. To add an existing command to the main part of the menu (not the sub-menu), choose Customize . . . from the Command List pane. Drag it up under the separator. (If it pops above the sub-menu, drag it down.)

15. To add one more custom command, click Create a New Command. In the Properties pane, enter the following:

    Name: **Cleanup**
    Description: **Cleans up drawing before plotting**
    Macro (after ^C^C): *Click this item and then click the Ellipsis button at the end of the Macro text box. Enter the macro shown in Figure 33.8. Then click OK.*
    Element ID: AB_002c

    Drag this new command to the bottom of your new menu.

16. To allow keyboard access, click the Name property for the Cleanup command in the Properties pane and type **&** in front of the name.

FIGURE 33.8

The custom Cleanup command's macro in the Long String Editor.

17. Click the Save All Current Customization Files button in the Customizations In pane. Your pane should look like Figure 33.9.

FIGURE 33.9

The new partial menu in the Customizations In pane of the Customize User Interface dialog box.

18. Click Apply and then click OK to close the Customize User Interface dialog box.

 If the AB2 menu doesn't appear, type cuiload ↲. Unload and then reload AB2.

19. Open ab33-a.dwg from the DVD. Save it as ab33-01.dwg in your AutoCAD Bible folder.
20. Look at the menu. It should look like Figure 33.10. Notice the sub-menu and the separator line. (If you don't see it, you may need to re-display your current workspace, which you can do from the Workspaces toolbar.)

FIGURE 33.10

The AB2 menu, including the sub-menu.

21. To try out the menu, choose AB2 ➪ Special Edits ➪ Move .1 Right. At the Select objects: prompt, pick the vertical red line and right-click to end object selection. The menu macro moves the line 0.1 units to the right.
22. Choose AB2 ➪ Special Edits ➪ Pedit .1. At the Select polyline or [Multiple]: prompt, choose the green polyline. The polyline becomes 0.1-unit wide.
23. Choose AB2 ➪ Cleanup. The color of all of the objects changes to ByLayer, and the no-plot layer disappears.
24. Enter **cuiload** ↲ and unload AB2. Close the Load/Unload Customizations dialog box.
25. Save your drawing.

 If some of the items don't work properly, edit the macros and try again.

Customizing shortcut menus

The shortcut menus appear at the cursor. In addition to the Object Snap menu, which appears when you press Shift and the right mouse button, and the Grips menu, which appears when there is a hot grip and you right-click, there are several other shortcut menus.

You access a shortcut menu by using the buttons on your mouse or puck. Therefore, the shortcut menus are accessed from the Buttons menu by swapping, as described earlier in this chapter.

You can customize shortcut menus that are specific to a command or to a selected object. For example, if you right-click when a polyline is selected, the shortcut menu includes a Polyline Edit item. However, if you right-click when a spline is selected, the shortcut menu includes a Spline Edit item instead. Because the appropriate shortcut menu appears depending on the context, that is, the object that is selected, shortcut menus are *context-sensitive*. For this reason, they are sometimes called context menus. You can create your own context menus.

To create a shortcut menu, you specify the following:

- **Name:** Although no name appears at the top of a shortcut menu (unlike a drop-down menu), a name is required.

- **Description:** The description is optional. The description would only appear if you turned the shortcut menu into a sub-menu, which you can do by dragging a shortcut menu in the Customize User Interface dialog box to a menu.

- **Aliases:** Aliases are used to reference the shortcut menu from elsewhere in the menu. Aliases are assigned automatically, but you need to add an alias in a special format if you create your own shortcut menu. To specify the alias, click in the Alias text box, and then click the Ellipsis button to open the Aliases dialog box. Click at the end of the current line and press Enter to start a new line. Enter the new alias in the format appropriate for that type of shortcut menu, and then click OK to close the dialog box. See the next two sections for a description of these formats.

- **Element_ID:** An ID is required, but is assigned automatically. Change this if you want to refer to the shortcut menu in program code that you write.

> **TIP** Although the examples shown here use both the initial underline to allow for translation and the ampersand to allow for keyboard entry, you don't need to use these if you don't want to. When was the last time that you used the keyboard to choose a menu item on a shortcut menu?

You can create two kinds of context-sensitive menus: object menus and command menus. The context-sensitive menus work only for full menus.

> **NOTE** If you've turned on time-sensitive right-clicking, remember to hold down the right mouse button long enough to open the shortcut menu. See Chapter 3 for details.

Object menus

The Edit mode shortcut menu appears when you right-click in the drawing area while one or more objects are selected but no command is active, as shown in Figure 33.11. Note that this menu includes the most common editing commands.

FIGURE 33.11

The Edit mode shortcut menu.

You can create *object menus* that are specific to a type of object. You might want to add certain commands that you use often with that type of object. The commands that you add to an object menu are appended to the Edit mode shortcut menu so that the result is a menu that contains the Edit mode shortcut menu, plus any additional commands that you've added for that type of object.

To create an object menu, you must assign the menu an alias of either OBJECT_objectname (used when one object of a type is selected) or OBJECTS_objectname (used when more than one object of a type is selected). The object name is the DXF name of the object, with the following five exceptions:

■ BLOCKREF for a block insertion with no attributes

■ ATTBLOCKREF for a block insertion with attributes

■ DYNBLOCKREF for a dynamic block insertion with no attributes

■ ATTDYNBLOCKREF for a dynamic block insertion with attributes

■ XREF for an xref

 To find out the object name of an object in AutoCAD, type the following on the command line:

```
(cdr (assoc 0 (entget (car (entsel))))) ↵
```

That's five closing parentheses at the end. AutoCAD then prompts you to select an object. As soon as you do, you see the object's name on the command line. See Chapters 34 and 35, which cover AutoLISP and Visual LISP, for an explanation of the parts of this AutoLISP expression. AutoLISP is not available for AutoCAD LT. In AutoCAD LT, you can create a drawing with only the one object whose name you want to know, and save it as a DXF file. Scroll down to the ENTITIES section in the DXF file to find the object's name. See Chapter 27 for more information about DXF files.

For example, to create an object menu that appears when one or more circles are selected, create an object shortcut menu with an alias of OBJECTS_CIRCLE. Open the Customize User Interface dialog box and look at the shortcut menus in `acad.cui` or `acadlt.cui` for examples to help you create your own menus. Figure 33.12 shows the Hatch Object shortcut menu in the Customize User Interface dialog box with the one added command selected.

FIGURE 33.12

The Hatch Object shortcut menu adds one command, HATCHEDIT, that appears when you right-click with a hatch selected.

Figure 33.13 shows how this shortcut menu appears when you select a hatch object. As you can see, the menu adds one item, which executes the HATCHEDIT command. (If the hatch is annotative, there's an additional Annotative Object Scale item.)

FIGURE 33.13

The Hatch Object shortcut menu is like the Edit mode shortcut menu but adds a Hatch Edit item that executes the HATCHEDIT command.

Command menus

The Command mode shortcut menu appears when you right-click in the drawing area while a command is active. You can create command menus that are specific to a command. The contents of the menu are appended to the Command mode shortcut menu; the result is a menu that contains the Command mode shortcut menu, plus any additional commands that you've added for that command. The default main customization file doesn't include any specific command menus. To create a command menu, you must assign the menu an alias COMMAND_commandname, where commandname is any valid command, including any custom or third-party command. After you name the menu, you can add commands to it that you would like to have available in the middle of the command just by right-clicking. Here are a couple of possibilities:

- For the LINE command, you might want to add the PLINE command to the shortcut menu, so that you can change your mind mid-command and create a polyline instead of a line. Of course, you can execute the PLINE command with one pick from the Draw toolbar, but the shortcut menu is closer.

- For the ROTATE command, you might want to add the ALIGN command (available in AutoCAD only), in case you realize that you need to align an object instead of just rotating it. You can see this customized shortcut menu in Figure 33.14.

A custom command menu that appears when you right-click during the ROTATE command; the ALIGN command is at the bottom.

STEPS: Creating an Object Shortcut Menu

1. If you did the exercise on Customizing the Buttons Menu, open Windows Explorer and find `ab1.cui`. Right-click it and choose Copy. Right-click again and choose Paste. Rename the copy `ab3.cui`. If you have AutoCAD, also find `ab1.mnl` and rename it `ab3.mnl`. If you didn't do that exercise, back up `acad.cui` or `acadlt.cui`. Then use the method just described to make a copy of `acad.cui` or `acadlt.cui`, and name it `ab3.cui`.

 To find the location of your menu files, choose Tools ⇨ Options and click the Files tab. Double-click Customization Files ⇨ Main Customization File.

 Don't continue with this exercise without first completing Step 1. If you're working on someone else's computer, ask permission before doing this exercise.

2. Open a drawing using any template. Type **cuiload** on the command line or in the dynamic input tooltip to open the Load/Unload Customizations dialog box. Choose ACAD and click Unload. Click Browse, browse to `ab3.cui`, and click Open. Click Load. When the file has finished loading, click Close to return to your drawing.

3. Type **cui** to open the Customize User Interface dialog box. The main customization file is listed as AB1 if you copied `ab1.cui`, or ACAD (ACADLT) if you copied `acad.cui (acadlt.cui)`. Right-click the customization file and choose Rename. Rename it **AB3**.

4. Right-click Shortcut Menus and choose New Shortcut Menu. The new menu appears, ready to be named. Type **Table Object Menu** ↵.

5. In the Description text box of the Properties panel, type **Context menu for Table object**.

6. Click the Aliases text box and then click the Ellipsis button on the right. In the Aliases dialog box, click at the end of the current alias, and press Enter to start a new line. Type **OBJECT_ACAD_ TABLE**. Click OK. Your Customize User Interface dialog box should look like Figure 33.15.

FIGURE 33.15

The Table Object Menu, a shortcut menu, has two aliases and one command.

7. From the Command list, find the EXPLODE command and drag it to your new shortcut menu.

8. Click OK to close the Customize User Interface dialog box.

9. Choose Table from the Draw toolbar and click OK in the Table dialog box to create the default table. Pick an insertion point to place the table and click outside the Multiline Text Editor. Click the edge of the table to select it so that you can see that the table is one object. Deselect the table.

10. Select the table. Right-click and choose Explode from the shortcut menu. Click anywhere on the table to see that the table is now just a collection of lines.

> **NOTE**   If you have difficulty displaying the shortcut menu and you have Time-Sensitive Right-clicking turned on, you may have better results by turning it off. Choose Tools ➪ Options, click the User Preferences tab, and click the Right-Click Customization button.

11. To return to your original menu, type **cuiload**. Unload ab3, browse to `acad.cui` or `acadlt.cui`, and click Open. Click Load, and then click Close to return to your drawing.

12. Draw a new table, select it, and right-click. You no longer have the Explode option. Press Esc. Do not save your drawing.

Customizing image-tile menus

Image-tile menus are menus that contain slides. The image tile displays the contents of the slides. The main use of image-tile menus is to insert blocks. You could use tool palettes in the same way, and tool palettes are easier to create. I cover slides in Chapter 30 and tool palettes in Chapter 26. AutoCAD LT doesn't

Creating Toggles on Drop-Down Menus

By examining `acad.cui` or `acadlt.cui`, you can accomplish some interesting things with your menus, even if you don't understand the code. You may have noticed that when the UCS icon is displayed, the View ⇨ Display ⇨ UCS Icon ⇨ On menu item shows a checkmark. If you choose this item again, not only does the UCS icon disappear, but the checkmark does, too. This is called a *toggle* and is created using the DIESEL programming language, a language that enables you to customize the command line and that works only with text strings. However, you can use it for your own menus, even if you don't know any DIESEL, simply by examining the code and making a few educated guesses. Here is the code:

```
$M=$(if,$(and,$(getvar,ucsicon),1),^C^C_ucsicon _off,
^C^C_ucsicon _on)
```

First, you see the UCSICON system variable mentioned in the expression `(getvar,ucsicon)`. Then you see the two commands at the end that issue the UCSICON system variable and turn it off and on.

Perhaps you could use a similar example in your own menu. For example, when customizing AutoCAD, you often have to turn the FILEDIA system variable on and off. Perhaps you always forget whether it's FILEDIA or DIAFILE and then have to look it up, and so you'd like to put it on your menu. First, create a custom command. For the label, you need to add some code like the following:

```
$(if,$(getvar,filedia),!.)FileDia
```

You can replace `filedia` with any system variable. The exclamation point (!) followed by a period marks the menu item with a checkmark. The text at the end is what displays on the menu.

For the command, you would use code similar to the following:

```
$M=$(if,$(and,$(getvar,filedia),1),^C^C_filedia 0,^C^C_filedia 1)
```

To use a different system variable, substitute it in the three places where `filedia` appears. If your system variable's values are off and on, you need to use those instead of 0 and 1.

All you've done is substitute FILEDIA for UCSICON in two places and the new commands at the end (you use 0 and 1 for FILEDIA instead of `off` and on). You've also created the special label.

include any image-tile menus, but you can create them. Image-tile menus are not easy to create, and you can probably use a tool palette instead. They're an old menu technology. Before you create your own image-tile menus, you need to create the slides. In order that they fit into the image tiles properly, you should create a floating viewport that is 3 units wide by 2 units high (or any multiple thereof, to maintain the proportion), center the drawing so that it takes up most of the viewport, and create the slide. Then create the slide library, as explained in Chapter 30.

To create a new image-tile menu, follow these steps:

1. Open the Customize User Interface dialog box.
2. Double-click the Legacy item in any menu to expand it.
3. Right-click the Image Tile Menus item and choose New Image Tile Menu.
4. Name the image-tile menu. The name will appear at the top of the dialog box.
5. Add a description if you want.

6. Add an alias. You will need to use this alias in the menu macro that displays the image-tile dialog box.

7. Either drag an existing command to the new image-tile menu, or create a custom command and drag that to the menu. (I explain how to create custom commands in the "Creating custom commands" section earlier in this chapter.)

8. In the Slide Library text box, enter the slide library name. The slide library is the name of the SLB file that contains the slides.

9. In the Slide Label text box, enter the label that you want to appear in the image-tile dialog box, which should also be the name of the slide (SLD) file.

As explained in the earlier section on menu swapping, you display an image-tile menu from another menu. For example, to display the 3D Objects menu (which is no longer available on the menu), AutoCAD used the following code:

```
$I=ACAD.image_3dobjects $I=ACAD.*
```

This would swap to the 3D Objects image-tile menu and display it. Remember that the customization name (ACAD in the previous example) is not necessary, if both the menu that you're referring to and the menu that you're placing the item on are the same. You can create a partial menu that displays an image-tile menu. Therefore, you need to add a menu item somewhere that displays your image-tile menu. For example, if your image-tile menu's alias is MyBlocks, you could use the following macro:

```
$I=MyBlocks $I=*
```

When you're done, click OK to close the Customize User Interface dialog box. Choose the new menu item that references the image-tile menu, and the image-tile dialog box appears. AutoCAD or AutoCAD LT automatically creates the dialog box. If it has more than 20 items, AutoCAD or AutoCAD LT creates Previous and Next boxes as well. To use one of the images, choose it either from the listing or from the image tiles and click OK.

Figure 33.16 shows an image-tile menu that inserts the symbols shown.

FIGURE 33.16

An Image Tile dialog box created from an image-tile menu.

Customizing tablet menus

Tablet menus are straightforward. Figure 33.17 shows the default tablet arrangement. You can print out this tablet drawing, AutoCAD 2008\Sample\Tablet.dwg or AutoCAD LT 2008\Sample\ Tablet Overlay.dwg, and compare it to the Tablet Menus item in the Legacy section. The entire first section, Tablet Menu 1, is left blank for you to configure. Although this menu section lists 25 rows and 25 columns, to match Tablet.dwg, use 9 rows and 25 columns. If you configure this menu area (using the TABLET command) to contain 9 rows and 25 columns, you can place your own macro in each of these boxes.

CROSS-REF For information on digitizing drawings and calibrating a tablet, including an exercise, see Chapter 16.

The syntax of the Tablet menu is very simple; you just need a name and the menu macro itself, although you can add a description.

NOTE If you customize the Tablet menu, don't forget to also open Tablet.dwg (for AutoCAD) or Tablet Overlay.dwg (for AutoCAD LT). Make the corresponding changes, and print it out to overlay on your digitizer so that the drawing that you place on your tablet reflects the menu properly.

FIGURE 33.17

The standard digitizer Tablet menu and its four parts.

Tablet 1   Tablet 3

Tablet 2   Tablet 4

Working with the Screen menu

I don't spend much time on the Screen menu here because it's no longer used very much and will probably disappear in the not-too-distant future. If you're interested in customizing it, click the Screen Menu item in the Legacy section and click the Learn More about Screen Menus link. AutoCAD LT doesn't contain a Screen menu.

Creating keyboard shortcuts

The Keyboard Shortcuts section has two subsections. Shortcut keys are a way to speed up your work. You can add keyboard shortcuts for commands that you use often. Temporary override keys are keyboard combinations that temporarily affect commonly used drafting settings, such as object snap and ORTHO. Note that keyboard shortcuts are different from aliases, which I explain in Chapter 29.

> **TIP**   To print a list of shortcut keys or temporary overrides, click either section and click the Print button in the Shortcuts pane. You can also copy the list to the clipboard by clicking the Copy to Clipboard button. You can then paste the list into another document.

Working with shortcut keys

You can create a keyboard shortcut for any command. Before adding a keyboard shortcut for a command, check to see that one doesn't already exist. In the Customize User Interface dialog box, expand the Keyboard Shortcuts item, and then the Shortcut Keys section to see the current list. To create a new keyboard shortcut, follow these steps:

1. Open the Customize User Interface dialog box.
2. Expand the Keyboard Shortcuts item, and then the Shortcut Keys section.
3. From the Command List, drag a command to anywhere in the Shortcut Keys section. The location doesn't matter.
4. In the Properties pane, click the Key(s) text box, and then click the Ellipsis button to the right to open the Shortcut Keys dialog box, as shown in Figure 33.18.

FIGURE 33.18

You assign shortcut keys to commands in the Shortcut Keys dialog box.

5. Click in the Press New Shortcut Key text box and press the keyboard combination that you want to use on your keyboard. Table 33.3 lists the keys that you can use to create shortcuts. When you include a *modifier,* such as Ctrl or Ctrl+Alt, with another key, you need to hold down the modifier or modifiers as you press the key. If the keyboard combination is already assigned to another command, then you see that command below the text box. If you want, you can choose another combination, or keep the one that you chose, thus overriding the original shortcut.

6. Click OK to close the dialog box.

7. Click OK to close the Customize User Interface dialog box. Try out your new keyboard shortcut!

 You should not reassign the commonly used Windows shortcuts, such as Ctrl+C (to copy data to the Clipboard), Ctrl+V (to paste data from the Clipboard), and so on.

TABLE 33.3

Allowable Modifier and Key Combinations for Keyboard Shortcuts

Modifier	Key
Ctrl	Any letter, number, or function key
Ctrl+Alt	Any letter, number, or function key
Shift	Any letter, number, or function key
Shift+Alt	Any letter, number, or function key
Ctrl+Shift	Any letter, number, or function key
Ctrl+Shift+Alt	Any letter, number, or function key

To remove a keyboard shortcut, right-click the shortcut in the Shortcut Keys section of the Customize User Interface dialog box and choose Delete. Confirm the deletion.

Working with temporary override keys

Temporary override keys are keyboard combinations that toggle drafting settings, such as OSNAP settings. AutoCAD and AutoCAD LT define most of these for you, which is helpful, because the required macros are complex. Most of them also have keyboard combinations, but several don't, and you can easily add them. I explain how to use the existing temporary override keys in Chapter 4.

To see the current temporary override keys, open the Customize User Interface dialog box. In the Customizations In pane, double-click the Keyboard Shortcuts item, and then the Temporary Override Keys item. Click any individual temporary override to see its properties in the Properties pane. Keyboard combinations can include function keys, or the Shift key with any letter, number, or function key. Some of the temporary overrides have two or three keyboard combinations, one for the left hand, one for the right hand, and perhaps a function key.

To create a new temporary override key, follow these steps:

1. In the Customize User Interface dialog box, expand the Keyboard Shortcut item in the Customizations In pane.

2. Right-click the Temporary Override Keys item and choose New Temporary Override. Enter a new name for the temporary override. This name doesn't have to be unique. In fact, if you want a temporary override to have two keyboard combinations, you need to create two temporary overrides with the same name and macro.

3. In the Properties pane, enter a description, if you want one. Enter a macro in the Macro 1 (Key Down) text box. You can also enter a second macro in the Macro 2 (Key Up) box, which is executed when the keyboard combination is released. Most temporary overrides don't have a macro here; in this case, releasing the keys restores the settings prior to using the temporary override.

> **TIP**   To make a copy of an existing temporary override (in order to add a second key combination), copy the existing macro and paste it into the Macro 1 (Key Down) text box of your new temporary override.

4. Click the Key(s) text box and then click the Ellipsis button. In the Shortcut Keys dialog box, click in the Press New Shortcut Key text box and press the keyboard combination that you want to use on your keyboard. The message below the text box indicates whether the keyboard combination is assigned. To accept the keyboard combination, click OK.

> **NOTE**   Make sure that Caps Lock is off; otherwise, you won't be able to add a Shift to your temporary override.

You can now use your temporary override.

> **ON the DVD-ROM**   The file used in the following exercise on creating keyboard shortcuts, ab3.cui, is in the Results folder on the DVD.

STEPS: Creating Keyboard Shortcuts

1. Back up your menu files, if you have not already done so. (By default, these are acad.cui for AutoCAD and acadlt.cui for AutoCAD LT.)

> **CAUTION**   Don't continue this exercise until you've completed Step 1. If you're working on someone else's computer, ask permission before doing this exercise.

2. To do this exercise, copy ab3.cui and rename it as ab4.cui. If you didn't do the exercise "Creating an Object Shortcut Menu," first copy ab3.cui from the Results folder of the DVD to the default location for customization files. Right-click ab3.cui in Windows Explorer, and choose Copy from the shortcut menu. Right-click again and choose Paste. Rename the new file ab4.cui.

> **NOTE**   To find the location of your customization files, choose Tools ➪ Options and click the Files tab. Double-click Customization Files and Main Customization File to display the location of the menu files.

3. Create a drawing using acad.dwt or acadlt.dwt.

4. On the command line or in the dynamic input tooltip, type **cuiload** ↵. In the Load/Unload Customizations dialog box, choose ACAD (or the currently loaded main customization file) and click Unload. Most of your menus and all of your toolbars disappear.

5. Click Browse. In the Select Customization File dialog box, choose ab4.cui and click Open. Back in the Load/Unload Customizations dialog box, click Load. All of your menus and toolbars reappear. Click Close to return to your drawing.

6. On the command line or in the dynamic input tooltip, type **cui** ↵. In the Customizations In pane of the Customize User Interface dialog box, right-click ACAD (or the previously loaded main customization file) and choose Rename. Type **ab4** ↵ to change the customization name to match the filename.

7. In the Customizations In pane, double-click Keyboard Shortcuts and then Shortcut Keys to expand those items.

8. From the Command List, drag the Deselect All command to any location on the Shortcut Keys list.

> **CAUTION**   In the next few steps, you assign Ctrl+Shift+D, Ctrl+Shift+F12, and Shift+1 to commands. If these shortcuts are assigned on your system, try various combinations until you find an unassigned shortcut.

9. In the Properties pane, click the Key(s) text box, and then click the Ellipsis button. In the Shortcut Keys dialog box, click the Press New Shortcut Key text box. On your keyboard, press Ctrl+Shift+D. Click OK. (This command is equivalent to pressing the Esc key when grips are active.)

10. In the Command List, choose the Pedit .1 command. (This custom command was created in the exercise on Customizing the Buttons Menu.) Drag it anywhere in the Shortcut Keys list.

11. In the Properties pane, click the Key(s) text box, and then click the Ellipsis button. In the Shortcut Keys dialog box, click the Press New Shortcut Key text box. On your keyboard, press Ctrl+Shift+F12 (the function key). Click OK.

12. Double-click the Temporary Override Keys item in the Customizations In pane to expand it. Scroll down and choose Object Snap Override: Intersection, which doesn't have a default temporary override key. In the Properties pane, click the Key(s) text box, and then click the Ellipsis button. In the Shortcut Keys dialog box, click the Press New Shortcut Key text box. On your keyboard, press Shift+1. Click OK.

13. Click OK to save the changes to the customization file and return to your drawing.

14. Draw a polyline that contains segments that intersect each other. Turn off OSNAP, if it is on. To test the intersection object snap shortcut key, start the LINE command and pick any point off the polyline for the first point. At the `Specify next point or [Undo]:` prompt, press and hold Shift+1. Pass the cursor over the intersection of the polyline segment. When you see the Intersection marker (an X) and tooltip, click and end the LINE command.

15. The Pedit .1 custom command issues the PEDIT command, waits for you to select a polyline, and then sets its width to .1. To test the keyboard shortcut, press Ctrl+Shift+F12. The PEDIT command starts. Select the polyline. Its width changes to .1.

16. Select the polyline. To test the Deselect All command, press Ctrl+Shift+D. The polyline is deselected.

17. Type **cuiload**. In the Load/Unload Customizations dialog box, choose AB4 and click Unload. Click Browse, choose `acad.cui` or `acadlt.cui`, and click Open. Click Load and then click Close to return to your drawing.

18. Draw another intersecting polyline. Press Ctrl+Shift+F12. Nothing happens. Select the polyline and press Ctrl+Shift+D; it stays selected. Try to draw a line to the intersection, using Shift+1. It doesn't work.

Don't save your drawing.

Customizing the double-click behavior

When you double-click an object, you usually see either the Properties palette or a specific dialog box that helps you edit that object. In the "Double-Clicking to Edit Objects" section in Chapter 10, I explain this process. You can now customize what happens when you double-click an object.

To see the current double-click settings, open the Customize User Interface dialog box and expand (or, appropriately, double-click) the Double Click Actions item. You see a list of objects. Expand any object and select the item beneath it. In the Properties pane, you see the current action, usually a command, in the Macro field.

For example, if you choose the Hatch object, the item beneath is labeled Hatch Edit, and you can see that it executes the HATCHEDIT command, which opens the Hatch Edit dialog box.

To change the double-click behavior for an object, follow these steps:

1. Start the CUI command to open the Customize User Interface dialog box.
2. Expand the Double Click Actions item and expand an object type.
3. Select the item beneath the object.
4. In the Properties pane, change the current macro field and press Enter. You can also drag a command from the Command List.

NOTE You can disable all double-click action for editing by unchecking the Double Click Editing check box on the User Preferences tab of the Options dialog box (Tools ⇨ Options). This controls the DBLCLKEDIT system variable.

Summary

In this chapter, you read about how to customize the menu to suit your situation and speed up your everyday work. Specifically, you learned the following:

- How to load and unload main and partial customization files
- How to write menu macros
- How to customize mouse and tablet buttons
- All about customizing drop-down menus
- How to create custom commands
- How to create custom shortcut menus
- How to create image-tile menus
- About customizing the tablet menu
- How to create keyboard shortcuts, including shortcut keys and temporary override keys
- How to customize what happens when you double-click an object

This chapter ends Part VI, "Customizing AutoCAD and AutoCAD LT." Part VII challenges you to go further in your customization of AutoCAD by starting to program with AutoLISP and Visual Basic for Applications.

Part VII

Programming AutoCAD

Part VII invites you to go the distance and start programming AutoCAD with AutoLISP, Visual LISP, and Visual Basic for Applications (VBA). AutoLISP is a powerful programming language that lets you quickly create your own commands and routines that are tailored to your needs. Visual LISP adds an easy-to-use interface to AutoLISP programming.

VBA is a programming language that is supported by many Windows applications. You can create programs and dialog boxes for AutoCAD with VBA. Using ActiveX, you can write programs that integrate AutoCAD with other applications.

Unfortunately, AutoCAD LT doesn't support either AutoLISP or VBA. Therefore, this entire part applies only to AutoCAD.

Due to space constraints, Chapter 37 was moved to the DVD. Look for it there in the Chapter 37 folder.

Chapter 34

Understanding AutoLISP and Visual LISP Basics

utoLISP is a programming language supported by AutoCAD that can greatly enhance your productivity by automating often-used or repetitive tasks. AutoLISP provides a glimpse into the inner workings of AutoCAD and can serve as an excellent stepping-stone to learning more advanced automation methods, such as ObjectARX and VBA. An AutoLISP routine gives you complete control over its interaction with the user and what it does after it's loaded.

You can type AutoLISP expressions on the command line in response to prompts, or you can save your code to a file that you can load and use when needed. AutoLISP offers wide and varied possibilities for shortcuts. Best of all, you can customize AutoLISP to any level of complexity.

AutoLISP intimidates many AutoCAD users, but this fear is unwarranted. The many benefits of AutoLISP well justify the initial time that you invest to learn this rich and full-featured programming language.

You can also find a tremendous number of AutoLISP routines on the Internet. Many CAD Web sites offer huge libraries of AutoLISP routines as free downloads. (For more details, see Appendix B.) Every office with more than a trivial number of AutoCAD workstations has probably created at least one AutoLISP routine to expedite some common task.

Many of the commands that you already use in AutoCAD are AutoLISP routines, including 3DARRAY, MVSETUP, AI_BOX, and others. You can often find examples of how to handle complex problems by reviewing these applications.

LISP stands for *List Processing* (not Lists in Silly Parentheses, as some say!), and as you'll see in the next chapter, the understanding of lists is crucial to using AutoLISP.

Most AutoLISP routines define a command name, which you then type at the command line in AutoCAD to run the routine. Some routines include a dialog box to help you choose options and specifications.

IN THIS CHAPTER

Understanding AutoLISP programming and the Visual LISP environment

Working with the Visual LISP interface

Getting help in Visual LISP

Creating your own AutoLISP expressions

Using AutoLISP on the command line

Introducing Visual LISP

Visual LISP (VLISP) is an integrated development environment (IDE) that provides an easy-to-use interface to help you create code, debug errors, and test programs. You can write AutoLISP code in Notepad or any text editor, but the Visual LISP interface offers many advantages.

Some useful Visual LISP features include the following:

- Syntax checker, color coding, and highlighting to help correct syntax errors
- File compilation for security and faster execution
- Debugger, with support for stepping through source code to find errors
- Helpful Inspect and Watch windows for querying a value or examining a variable during execution
- Context-sensitive help
- Management of multiple file applications from a project window
- Console history, which makes it possible to recall previously entered information

Opening Visual LISP

To start Visual LISP, you can either type **Vlide** ↵ at the AutoCAD command prompt, or choose Tools ➪ AutoLISP ➪ Visual LISP Editor. At any time, you can switch to Visual LISP using either of these methods. Figure 34.1 shows the Visual LISP screen with an AutoLISP file open.

AutoLISP and Visual LISP are discussed throughout this chapter, as well as Chapters 35 and 36. Although this book does not provide complete coverage of either AutoLISP or Visual LISP, many of the major features are explained within these three chapters.

Opening and loading an AutoLISP file with Visual LISP

As soon as you're in the Visual LISP environment, you can create a new AutoLISP file or open an existing file.

To edit or view a file in the Visual LISP text editor, follow these steps:

1. Choose File ➪ Open File from the Visual LISP menu.
2. In the Open File to Edit/View dialog box, locate and choose the file that you want to open.
3. Click Open. Visual LISP opens the file in its own window, as shown in Figure 34.1.

When you open a file, the title bar of its window displays a blank paper icon to show that the file has not been changed. If you make any changes to the file, Visual LISP adds a pencil to the image to show that you've edited the file.

You can open as many files as you want.

FIGURE 34.1

An AutoLISP file open in its own window in the Visual LISP window.

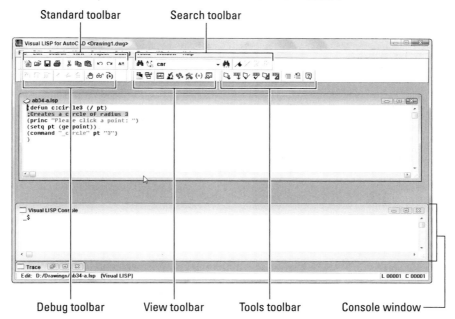

Standard toolbar   Search toolbar

Debug toolbar   View toolbar   Tools toolbar   Console window

Loading an AutoLISP file

To use the AutoLISP program in AutoCAD, you must load it. You can load it from within Visual LISP or from within AutoCAD.

 If you have a file open in Visual LISP, choose Tools ➪ Load Text in Editor or choose Load Active Edit Window from the Tools toolbar.

If you're in AutoCAD, you can load AutoLISP files into AutoCAD in two ways. One method is on the command line. To load `circle3.lsp` from the command line, type (**load "circle3"**) ↵. The parentheses are required, as they indicate that you're entering an AutoLISP expression. AutoLISP requires the quotation marks because you're specifying a filename. AutoCAD responds with `C:CIRCLE3` because `circle3` is the name of the command that `circle3.lsp` creates.

When you enter the command to load `circle3.lsp`, AutoCAD searches all of the support paths for a file called `circle3.lsp`. At installation time, AutoCAD automatically configures the support file search path to include the path of `AutoCAD 2008\Support`. For a full list of folders in the support file search path, choose Tools ➪ Options and click the Files tab. Double-click the Support File Search Path item.

NOTE AutoLISP files have the extension of `.lsp`. However, for security and speed, you can compile AutoLISP routines as `.fas` or `.vlx` project application files. AutoCAD loads `.vlx` first, then `.fas`, and `.lsp` files last. For example, if you have both a `redline.vlx` file and a `redline.lsp` file, AutoCAD loads the `redline.vlx` file. If, however, the `.lsp` file is newer than the `.fas` file, AutoCAD will load the `.lsp` file. If an AutoLISP routine is associated with a menu, it has a `.mnl` extension. For more information, see Chapter 33.

If your file is not in a folder in AutoCAD's support file search path, then you must specify the full path name. To specify the full path to the routine type, you would enter:

```
(load "c:/Program Files/AutoCAD 2008/Support/circle3") ↵
```

or

```
(load "c:\\Program Files\\AutoCAD 2008\\Support\\circle3") ↵
```

The backslash (\) has special meaning in AutoLISP, so you need to use two of them or a regular slash (/) when specifying a path. (The backslash character tells AutoLISP to interpret the following character as a special control code. For example, to use a double quote in an AutoLISP expression, precede it with a back-slash.)

You can also load AutoLISP routines with the APPLOAD command by choosing Tools ➪ Load Application or by typing **appload** ↵ at the command line. AutoCAD opens the Load/Unload Applications dialog box. By choosing AutoLISP Files (*.lsp) from the Files of Type drop-down list, you can limit the list to only LSP files, as shown in Figure 34.2.

FIGURE 34.2

The Load/Unload Applications dialog box.

If you check Add to History, AutoCAD lists previously loaded applications in the dialog box — just click the History list tab. Locate and choose the file you want to load, and click Load.

> **TIP**   If you want to use the routine regularly, you can add it to the Startup Suite to load the routine whenever you start AutoCAD. Find the file in the Load/Unload Applications dialog box and drag it to the Startup Suite area of the dialog box.

Using an AutoLISP routine in AutoCAD

After you load an AutoLISP routine, you can use it. How you use the routine depends on the routine. If the program creates a function, then you can type the function's name on the command line like any other AutoCAD command. Most routines contain prompts to guide you in their use.

 The AutoLISP file used in the following exercise on loading and using an AutoLISP routine, `circle3.lsp`, is in the `Drawings` folder on the DVD.

STEPS: Loading and Using an AutoLISP Routine

1. Use Windows Explorer to copy `circle3.lsp` from the DVD to your `AutoCAD 2008\Support\` folder, or to a folder that you added to the support file search path.
2. Create a new drawing using any template.
3. Choose Tools ➪ AutoLISP ➪ Visual LISP Editor. The Visual LISP IDE opens.
4. If any AutoLISP files are displayed in the main area, click their Close boxes.
5. Choose Open on the Standard Visual LISP toolbar. In the Open File to Edit/View dialog box, navigate to the folder where you saved `circle3.lsp` and double-click it. It appears in the Visual LISP window.

6. Choose Load Active Edit Window from the Visual LISP Tools toolbar. The Visual LISP Console window confirms that `circle3.lsp` has been loaded.

7. Choose Activate AutoCAD from the Visual LISP View toolbar. Visual LISP returns you to AutoCAD.
8. Now that `circle3` has been loaded, at the command prompt, type **circle3** ↵.
9. At the `Please click a point:` prompt, pick any point on-screen. You see a 3-unit radius circle with its center at the point that you picked, as shown in Figure 34.3.

FIGURE 34.3

The circle was drawn using the `circle3` AutoLISP routine.

10. Save your drawing in your `AutoCAD Bible` folder as `ab34-01.dwg`.

Looking at an AutoLISP routine

To examine the contents of the `circle3.lsp` file, open it in the Visual LISP editor. Figure 34.4 shows the `circle3` routine. At this point, ignore the color formatting, which is discussed later in this chapter.

The circle3 AutoLISP routine.

```
circle3.lsp
(defun c:circle3 (/ pt) ;Creates a circle of radius 3
  (prompt "\nPlease click a point: ")
  (setq pt (getpoint))
  (command "_circle" pt "3")
)
```

This figure illustrates several general characteristics of AutoLISP routines:

- As in many programming languages, indentation is used in AutoLISP to make it easier to read the code. It has no effect on the operation of the routine.

- The returns at the end of each line also make it easier to read and understand the code. All five lines could be placed on a single line, and the program would work exactly the same way.

- All AutoLISP statements are placed in parentheses. Therefore, whenever you open a parenthesis, you must close it. Every AutoLISP routine must have the same number of left and right parentheses. The physical location of a right parenthesis is not relevant; it can be placed on a new line or positioned several spaces away from the left parenthesis. In both cases, the pair is interpreted the same way.

- You interpret AutoLISP from the innermost parenthetical elements first. For example, on line 3 of the code shown in Figure 34.4, (getpoint) is done first, and then the result is used for the (setq pt (getpoint)) expression. This is analogous to mathematics, as in the expression (3 + (5 × 4)), where 5 × 4 is computed first, and the result is added to 3.

- At the end of the first line is a comment, ;Creates a circle of radius 3. The program ignores any text preceded by a semicolon. Use this technique to place explanations in your routines to help you and others understand what the routine is doing.

The following explains the routine in Figure 34.4 line by line:

- Line 1 begins with an open parenthesis that is balanced with the one on line 5. This pair of parentheses delineates the body of the function. The line begins with defun, which stands for *define function,* and the function is called c:circle3. When you prefix the function with c:, you can use it in AutoCAD by just entering **circle3** at the command line like any other AutoCAD command. (The c: stands for command and has no relation to your hard drive, which is also usually called c:.) You could use just circle3, but you would have to type **(circle3)** at the command line to use the routine. The last item on Line 1 is (/ pt). The pt after the slash means that pt is a *local variable.* A variable stores a value for later use in the routine. A local variable is used only in its own routine and is not retained for use in other routines. If you replaced (/ pt) with simply ( ), the pt variable would be available to other AutoLISP routines as well.

- Line 2 is the simplest line in this routine. It simply prints the statement Please click a point: at the command line. Anything in the quotes after prompt will be printed on the AutoCAD command line. The statement is used as a prompt to tell the user to pick a point. Putting \n before the prompt puts it on a new line and is for readability purposes.

- Line 3 is typical of AutoLISP routines that contain nested parentheses. Remember to read from the innermost parenthetical element outward. Thus, reading from the innermost parenthetical element, you have first (getpoint). This means to simply get a point. Any of the AutoCAD input methods work, such as clicking the screen, typing coordinates for a point, or using object snaps. Reading outward you have `(setq pt (getpoint))`. The statement `setq` means that the variable `pt` is set to whatever comes back from `getpoint`. Therefore, if you enter the coordinates 2,2 by typing them or selecting them on the screen, the variable `pt` equals 2,2.

■ Line 4 reads `(command "_circle" pt "3")`. The command function in AutoLISP is one of the easier functions to understand. It simply executes whatever AutoCAD command is specified in the quotes that follow, using all subsequent arguments. When the CIRCLE command is invoked in AutoCAD, it asks for the center point first and then the radius. Line 4 starts the CIRCLE command, uses for the center point whatever is assigned to the variable `pt`, and sets the radius to 3 units.

NOTE An underscore precedes the CIRCLE command so that it can be translated into other language versions of AutoCAD.

Using the Visual LISP interface

The Visual LISP window contains a number of tools that make your programming life simpler. These tools represent the difference from the old way of writing AutoLISP code, which involved creating text files in a text editor. The visual way involves working with tools that help you format and complete your code. Some of the more useful tools include:

 ■ **Format Edit Window:** Choose Format Edit Window on the Tools toolbar (or choose Tools ➪ Format Code in Editor) to indent code (and comments) so that it's more readable. Indenting code helps you to understand the levels of nested parentheses more clearly. Of course, you can indent your code manually, but automatic indenting is a boon to all AutoLISP programmers.

 ■ **Format Selection:** Select the code that you want to format. Then choose Format Selection on the Tools toolbar (or choose Tools ➪ Format Code in Selection) to indent only the selected code.

 ■ **Check Edit Window:** Choose Check Edit Window from the Tools toolbar (or choose Tools ➪ Check Text in Editor) to perform a preliminary evaluation prior to loading the file. This evaluation checks the code for unbalanced parentheses, invalid function definition formatting (an attempt to redefine a built-in or protected function), and many other common errors. Visual LISP opens the Build Output window to show you the results.

 ■ **Check Selection:** Select the code that you want to check. Choose Check Selection from the Tools toolbar (or choose Tools ➪ Check Selection) to perform a preliminary evaluation on selected code. Visual LISP opens the Build Output window to show you the results.

■ **Parentheses Matching:** The most common error for an AutoLISP programmer is incorrect parentheses matching. Visual LISP enables you to jump between matching parentheses and to quickly check your current nesting level as you develop your application. While you can use the menu items (choose Edit ➪ Parentheses Matching ➪ Match Forward and Match Backward), you'll find that the keyboard shortcuts distract you less from the code that you're viewing. To find a matching right parenthesis, press Ctrl+]. To find a left matching parenthesis, press Ctrl+[.

TIP You can highlight all of the code between matching parentheses. To highlight from left to right, place the cursor in front of a left parenthesis and press Ctrl+Shift+] or simply double-click. To highlight from right to left (backwards), place the cursor after a right parenthesis and press Ctrl+Shift+[or double-click.

 ■ **Load Selection:** You've already seen how to load the code in the active window. You can also load selected code. Select the code that you want to load and choose Load Selection from the Tools toolbar or choose Tools ➪ Load Selection.

■ **Comment Block:** In Figure 34.4, you see an example of a comment. Visual LISP supports several comment styles, which Chapter 35 covers. Visual LISP simplifies the addition of a three-semicolon comment. To place a three-semicolon comment, highlight the text that you want to change into a comment and click Comment Block on the Tools toolbar. See Chapter 35 for more information on creating comments.

 ■ **Uncomment Block:** To remove a three-semicolon comment, click Uncomment Block on the Tools toolbar.

Another feature of Visual LISP is the Console window. The Console window usually resides at the bottom of the Visual LISP window. The Console window is similar to the AutoCAD command line. Just as you can enter AutoLISP expressions on the AutoCAD command line, as explained later in this chapter, you can also enter AutoLISP expressions in the Console window and see the results. Each line uses a _$ prompt.

A nice feature of the Console window is that Visual LISP remembers everything that you enter. You can retrieve it by pressing Tab for a forward history or Shift+Tab for a backward history.

Closing a file and Visual LISP

To close a file within Visual LISP, click its Close button. (You can also press Ctrl+F4.) To exit Visual LISP, click its Close button or press Alt+F4. As with AutoCAD, Visual LISP warns you about saving your changes.

 The file used in the following exercise on using the Visual LISP interface, ab34-a.lsp, is in the Drawings folder on the DVD.

STEPS: Using the Visual LISP Interface

1. From AutoCAD, choose Tools ➪ AutoLISP ➪ Visual LISP Editor to open Visual LISP.

2. Choose Open File on the Visual LISP Standard toolbar, and open ab34-a.lsp from the DVD. Save the file as ab34-01.lsp in your AutoCAD Bible folder.

3. Choose Format Edit Window on the Tools toolbar. AutoCAD automatically formats the code.

4. Select the line of the code that reads:
   ```
   (command "_circle" pt "3")
   ```

 5. Choose Comment Block. AutoCAD places three semicolons before the text and shades it. Choose Uncomment Block. AutoCAD returns the code to its previous state.

 6. Choose Check Edit Window on the toolbar. AutoCAD opens the Build Output window and issues the Check done message.

 7. Click anywhere in the edit window to activate it. Choose Load Active Edit Window on the toolbar. AutoCAD loads the routine.

8. In the Visual LISP Console window, type **(c:circle3)** and press Enter. Visual LISP returns you to AutoCAD and starts the program. Pick a point. When you're done, you're automatically returned to the Visual LISP window.

9. Click the text editor window and choose Save File. Click the Close button at the top-right corner of the text editor window to close the routine.

10. Click the Close button at the top-right corner of your screen to close Visual LISP.

Getting Help in Visual LISP

Visual LISP offers two ways for you to get help while writing AutoLISP code: context-sensitive help on any term that you select, and the overall Help system.

 To get help on any AutoLISP function in your code, select the function (either in the edit window or in the Console window) and choose Help on the Visual LISP Tools toolbar. Figure 34.5 shows the screen that appears when you select setq and choose Help.

FIGURE 34.5

When you select any AutoLISP function in your code and choose Help, Visual LISP opens the help page for that function.

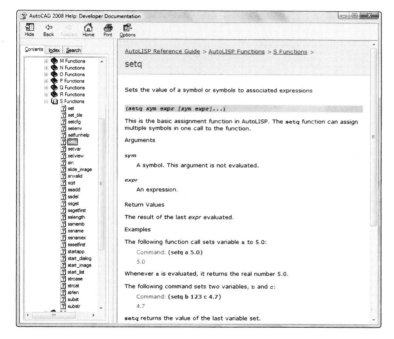

To open the entire Visual LISP and ActiveX Help system, choose Help ⇨ Visual LISP Help Topics on the Visual LISP menu or Press F1. Visual LISP displays the screen shown in Figure 34.6.

All of these help features can be a bit overwhelming, but for AutoLISP and Visual LISP you basically have three choices:

- **AutoLISP Reference:** This guide is equivalent to the Command Reference in AutoCAD's Help system. Here you'll find an alphabetical list of all AutoLISP functions.

- **AutoLISP Developer's Guide:** This guide is equivalent to the AutoCAD User's Guide. It contains all of the basic topics that you need to know to program in Visual LISP.

- **AutoLISP Tutorial:** This is a tutorial that creates a garden path.

FIGURE 34.6

The main help page of Visual LISP's Help system.

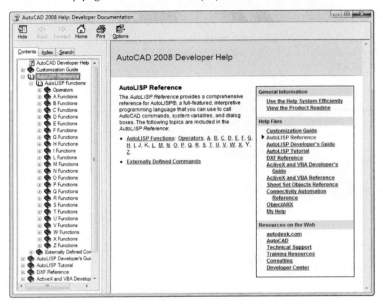

Working with AutoLISP Expressions

As with any programming language, AutoLISP has its own functions and syntax. This section explains how to start writing AutoLISP code. One big advantage to AutoLISP is that you can test your code immediately, unlike the case with languages that you need to compile first. For compiled languages, such as ObjectARX, every time a code change is made, the code must be recompiled and re-linked before you can see the changes in AutoCAD.

Understanding AutoLISP syntax

In AutoLISP's syntax, an operator always comes first, followed by a number of operands. An operator can be thought of as a function that does something, and the operands are the elements on which the function operates. Place a space between each component of the statement.

Another way to describe the syntax of AutoLISP is that, within each set of parentheses, the first item is a function, and what follows are parameters or arguments to that function.

Working with numbers and text

Table 34.1 lists the basic arithmetic functions. You can use these functions on anything that has a value. For example, if you create a variable with a value of 2, you can use that variable with the arithmetic functions.

TABLE 34.1

Basic Arithmetic Functions

Function	Description
+	Addition
–	Subtraction
*	Multiplication
/	Division
Sqrt	Square root

Table 34.1 lists only a few fundamental arithmetic operators (or functions). You can find more operators in the AutoLISP Function Synopsis under the Appendixes topic of the AutoLISP Developer's Guide, under Basic Functions ⇨ Arithmetic Functions.

Some fundamental arithmetic operations can provide a feel for the fundamentals. If you type (+ 2 3) ↵ on the AutoCAD command line (being careful to put a blank space after the + and the 2), AutoLISP responds with 5. This syntax of having the operator (the plus sign) come before the operands (2 and 3) is different from that of many languages but is important to understand in AutoLISP.

To nest expressions, simply add another set of parentheses to enclose the nested expression. For example, when you enter (* 5 (+ 2 3)), AutoCAD responds with 25. The nested expression is evaluated from the innermost parenthesis pair out; first 2 and 3 are added, and then that sum is multiplied by 5.

Working with floating-point numbers (numbers with decimal points) is as easy as working with integers. If you type (/ 7.3 5.84) ↵, then AutoLISP responds with 1.25.

 If you're using a number less than 1, you must include the leading 0, as in (+ 2.5 0.5).

Working with text is as easy as working with numbers. In AutoLISP, a *string* is simply a series of text characters. Table 34.2 lists some common string functions.

TABLE 34.2

Basic String Functions

Function	Description
STRCAT	Concatenates (attaches) strings to one another.
SUBSTR	Returns (provides you with) a substring (a portion) of a string. The first argument is the string, the second is an integer that specifies the position of the first character that you want, and the third (optional) is the number of characters that you want.
STRLEN	Calculates string length; returns the number of characters, including spaces in the string.

Here are two examples:

```
(strcat "Today is " "a good day" ".")
"Today is a good day."
(substr "Today is a good day." 12 4)
"good"
```

STRCAT stands for *string concatenate* and appends one string with another. Any number of strings can come after the STRCAT function. (There are three strings enclosed in quotes in the above STRCAT example.)

SUBSTR stands for *substring*, and in the above example, it returns the four characters starting at position 12.

 The first character of the string for SUBSTR is number 1. However, other functions that process elements of a list (such as NTH) count the first element as 0.

Table 34.3 offers you a few more functions that work with numbers and strings.

TABLE 34.3

AutoLISP Functions for Numbers and Strings

Function	Description
ABS	Returns the absolute value of the argument. (ABS -76) returns 76.
ASCII	Returns the ASCII code of a character. (ASCII "B") returns 66.
CHR	Returns the text string for an ASCII code. (CHR 66) returns "B". (Stands for character.)
ATOI	Converts a string to an integer. (ATOI "2.7") returns 2. (Stands for ASCII to integer.)
ATOF	Converts a string to a real number. (ATOF "7.6") returns 7.6. (Stands for ASCII to float, as in floating point — that is, a real number.)
ITOA	Converts an integer to a text string. (ITOA 76) returns "76". (Stands for integer to ASCII.)
RTOS	Converts a real number to a text string, enclosed in quotes. You can add a mode (1=scientific, 2=decimal, 3=engineering, 4=architectural, 5=fractional) and a precision. Otherwise, RTOS uses the current settings. (RTOS 87.3 2 2) returns "87.30". (RTOS stands for real to string.)
=	Equal to. Returns T for true if all arguments are numerically equal. (= 3 3.0) returns T. If the arguments are not equal, it returns nil.
/=	Not equal to. Returns T if all arguments are not numerically equal. (/= 5 6) returns T. If they are equal, it returns nil.
<	Less than. Returns T if each argument is numerically less than the next argument. Otherwise returns nil.
>	Greater than. Returns T if each argument is numerically greater than the next argument. Otherwise returns nil.
>=	Greater than or equal to. Returns T if each argument is numerically greater than or equal to the next argument. Otherwise returns nil.
<=	Less than or equal to. Returns T if each argument is numerically less than or equal to the next argument. Otherwise returns nil.

Using AutoLISP on the Command Line

You can use AutoLISP on the fly in AutoCAD because it is *interpreted*. By typing an expression on the command line, you get the result immediately. An interpreted language is one in which a single source statement is translated to machine language and executed, and then each subsequent source statement is operated on in the same way. This enables interactive entry of AutoLISP code into AutoCAD.

The output of an AutoLISP expression can be used in response to AutoCAD prompts as well. For example, you can type **(+ 1 7)** at the Diameter/<Radius>: prompt of the CIRCLE command for a circle with a radius of 8 units. This capability to place AutoLISP expressions into AutoCAD commands is a very powerful tool.

If you leave out a closing parenthesis, AutoCAD returns (_> when you press Enter. This tells you that one open parenthesis has not been closed. If two open parentheses remain to be closed, AutoCAD responds with ((_>. Just type the correct number of closing parentheses at the command line and press Enter. AutoCAD accepts the expression.

STEPS: Working with Numbers and Text on the Command Line

1. Open a new drawing using any template.
2. Type **circle** ↵. Follow the prompts:

   ```
   Specify center point for circle or [3P/2P/Ttr (tan tan radius)]: Pick
       any point.
   Specify radius of circle or [Diameter]: (- 5 3) ↵
   ```

   AutoCAD draws a circle with a radius of 2.
3. Type **(strcat "This is an example of " "regular text.")** ↵. Don't forget the space between *of* and the quotation mark. When the two phrases are put together, this creates the space between *of* and *regular*. AutoCAD returns "This is an example of regular text."
4. Press the up-arrow key. AutoCAD repeats the last line. Press the left-arrow key to move to the right of the last *r* in *regular*, and press Backspace to delete the word *regular*. Type **italic** ↵. AutoCAD returns the new string concatenation.
5. Save the drawing in your AutoCAD Bible folder as ab34-02.dwg.

NOTE When you create AutoLISP expressions on the command line or in the Console window, they aren't saved with the drawing. They have the same status as any input that you type at the command line.

Creating AutoLISP Files

If you want to use your AutoLISP expressions more than a couple of times, you should save them in a file. Create the routine in Visual LISP and choose Save File.

TIP A common practice is to consolidate all AutoLISP routines in one folder to make it easier to store and find them. To do this, you can create a folder called LISP in any drive or folder where you keep files that you create, and then choose Tools ⇨ Options. On the Files tab, expand the Support File Search Path and click Add. Add the path by typing it directly in the edit box or by clicking Browse and navigating to it.

Because AutoCAD can open multiple drawings, you need to organize your AutoLISP routines based on whether you want them to apply to all drawings or just the first drawing that you open.

AutoCAD offers two LSP files that you can use for your AutoLISP routines:

■ `acad.lsp`: Use this file for routines that customize the initialization of AutoCAD. `acad.lsp` is not automatically loaded for every consecutive drawing. For example, if you want to load a special menu for only a specific drawing, you could put the routine in `acad.lsp`. (You can choose to load `acad.lsp` with every drawing. Choose Tools ➪ Options and click on the System tab. In the General Options section, check the Load `acad.lsp` with Every Drawing check box.)

■ `acaddoc.lsp`: Use this file for routines that customize the initialization of individual drawings. This file is loaded every time a drawing is opened. If you have a menu that contains AutoLISP macros that include variables that you want to be available for all of your drawings, put the AutoLISP routines used by the menu in `acaddoc.lsp`.

Each drawing contains its own AutoLISP environment. AutoLISP files that you load in one drawing, along with their variables, won't be accessible to another drawing. To share functions, use `(vl-load-all "filename")` instead of `(load "filename")`, where `filename` is the name of the AutoLISP file. This enables you to "populate" every current drawing, as well as any new drawing that you may create. The VL-LOAD-ALL function is equivalent to placing an AutoLISP routine in `acaddoc.lsp`.

 To create a new Visual LISP file, open the Visual LISP Editor (choose Tools ➪ AutoLISP ➪ Visual LISP Editor) and choose New File on the Standard toolbar. Visual LISP opens an untitled document, as shown in Figure 34.7. You can now start typing code in the new document. When you start typing, you immediately notice that your code looks different than it would if you had typed it in a text editor — it's in color! Visual LISP can distinguish certain features in your code, and colors it accordingly. Table 34.4 lists the colors and their meanings.

FIGURE 34.7

A new AutoLISP document in the Visual LISP editor.

TABLE 34.4

Visual LISP Editor Coloring System

Color	AutoLISP Syntax Element
Blue	Built-in functions and protected symbols
Magenta	Text strings
Green	Integers
Teal	Real numbers
Purple on gray background	Comments
Red	Parentheses
Black	Unrecognized items, such as variables that you've created

If you want, you can customize these colors. From the Visual LISP menu, choose Tools ⇨ Window Attributes ⇨ Configure Current. In the Window Attributes dialog box, choose an element from the drop-down box and pick a color from the color swatches. You can also change the left margin and the tab width in this dialog box.

STEPS: Creating a New Visual LISP File

1. Start a new drawing using any template. You shouldn't have any other drawings open.
2. Choose Tools ⇨ AutoLISP ⇨ Visual LISP Editor.
3. Choose New File from the Visual LISP Standard toolbar.
4. Type the following:

```
draws a horizontal line 3 units long
(defun c:line3 (/ pt)
(prompt "\nPlease pick a point: ")
(setq pt (getpoint))
(command "_line" pt "@3,0" "")
)
```

5. Select the first line of text and choose Comment Block from the Tools toolbar.
6. Choose Format Edit Window from the Tools toolbar to format the code.
7. Choose Check Edit Window and look at the result in the Build Output window.
8. Click the Visual LISP Editor to activate it again.
9. Choose Load Active Edit Window to load the routine.
10. Choose Activate AutoCAD from the View toolbar.
11. On the command line or at the dynamic input tooltip, type **line3** ↵.
12. At the Please pick a point: prompt, use any method to specify a point. AutoCAD draws a horizontal line 3 units long.
13. Use the Windows task bar to return to the Visual LISP window.
14. Click the Visual LISP Editor to activate it. Choose Save File on the Visual LISP Standard toolbar. Save the routine as ab34-02.lsp in your AutoCAD Bible folder.
15. Close the Visual LISP window by clicking its Close button. Do not save your drawing.

Summary

This chapter covers the fundamentals of AutoLISP programming and the Visual LISP environment. You read about:

- How to open the Visual LISP interface and load and use AutoLISP files
- How to use AutoLISP on the command line
- What AutoLISP routines look like
- How to get help in Visual LISP
- The basic structure of AutoLISP syntax, as well as how to work with numbers and text

In the next chapter, you examine how to create variables, work with AutoCAD commands and system variables, modify AutoCAD objects (or entities, as they're often still called in AutoLISP), and work with the fundamental units of AutoLISP, known as lists.

Chapter 35

Exploring AutoLISP Further

AutoLISP offers many features that enable you to create sophisticated programs. These include variables, functions, and conditional structures. You can use these features to easily work with drawing coordinates. You can retrieve information about drawing objects and then modify them. As a result, getting input from the user makes your programs more interactive.

AUTOCAD ONLY AutoCAD LT does not support AutoLISP. This entire chapter is for AutoCAD only.

Creating Variables

You can't do anything very useful in programming without using variables. A *variable* is a symbolic name that a program operates on. An important part of the usefulness of variables is that you can assign values to them. You use the SETQ function to name and assign a value to a variable.

The following example sets the value of 3 to a variable named radius.

```
(setq radius 3)
3
```

You can try this example out in Visual LISP in the Console window. If you want to use this variable on the AutoCAD command line, precede it with an exclamation point (!). For example:

```
Command: !radius
3
```

The exclamation point before a variable evaluates the value that is stored in the variable and returns it to the command line. When you use a variable in the Console window that you've already set, you don't need the exclamation point. The Console treats everything that you type there as an AutoLISP expression.

IN THIS CHAPTER

Creating variables and functions

Working with AutoCAD commands and system variables

Working with lists

Setting conditions and creating loops

Managing drawing objects

Getting input from the user

Assigning strings to a variable is as easy as assigning numerals to a variable:

```
(setq name "Robin")
"Robin"
```

You can also nest AutoLISP expressions by placing one expression inside the other.

```
(setq radius (+ 2 1))
3
```

As explained in the previous chapter, AutoLISP evaluates LISP expressions from the innermost set of parentheses outward. In the above example, AutoLISP evaluates (+ 2 1) first and then assigns the result to the variable radius.

STEPS: Using AutoLISP Variables from within AutoCAD

1. Open a drawing using the acad.dwt template.
2. Type **(setq radius (+ 2 1))** ↵. AutoLISP returns 3.
3. Start the CIRCLE command. Specify any center point. At the Specify radius of circle or [Diameter]: prompt, type **!radius** ↵. AutoCAD draws a circle with a radius of 3 units.
4. Type **(setq color "green")** ↵. AutoLISP returns "green".
5. Type **-color** ↵. At the Enter default object color [Truecolor/Colorbook] <BYLAYER>: prompt, type **!color** ↵.
6. Draw a circle. The circle is green because the current color is now green.
7. Save your drawing in your AutoCAD Bible folder as ab35-01.dwg.

Working with AutoCAD Commands

Accessing AutoCAD commands from within AutoLISP is a powerful way to automate commonly used functions. By combining access to commands from AutoLISP with variables as described in the previous section, you gain a great deal of flexibility.

Accessing AutoCAD commands

In the previous chapter, when you looked at an AutoLISP routine (see Figure 34-4), you saw an example of the COMMAND function. You use the COMMAND function in AutoLISP to execute AutoCAD commands. This function treats all subsequent operands as if they were typed at the command line interactively. When programming COMMAND functions in AutoLISP, exactly duplicate what you would do at the command line. For example, to draw a line, you follow the steps shown in the following table. The second column shows how you would perform the same action in an AutoLISP routine.

Enter **line** at the command line	"line" (or "_line")
Specify the start point for the line	Use a variable, actual coordinates, or pause for user input.
Specify the endpoint	Use a variable, actual coordinates, or pause for user input.
Press Enter to end the LINE command	Use an empty set of two quotation marks to represent pressing Enter either within a command or to end a command.

For example, if you're using the variables startpt and endpt for the start point and endpoint of a line, here's how you would access the LINE command in an AutoLISP expression:

```
(command "_line" startpt endpt "")
```

Creating functions

Functions always begin with the operator DEFUN. You can define three principal types of functions:

- The type that you have been using thus far precedes the command name defined by DEFUN with c:, which is interpreted by AutoCAD as a command and enables you to use the function by name at the AutoCAD command line. The function becomes usable like any other AutoCAD command.

- You can also create a function definition without preceding the name with c:. This type is most valuable when it's called by other AutoLISP operations. If you need to execute it at the command line, you must enclose the function name in parentheses. Similarly, you can execute functions prefixed with a c: as an AutoLISP expression by enclosing the functions in parentheses, as in (c:circle3).

- The third type is S::STARTUP. By defining a function (usually in acaddoc.lsp, which is loaded into every drawing) with the name S::STARTUP, every AutoLISP function in the routine will automatically execute after the drawing has fully initialized. The reason for the S::STARTUP function is to ensure that AutoLISP routines that use the COMMAND function run only after AutoCAD fully initializes the components that can execute commands.

When you create an S::STARTUP function, you need to decide where to put it. Chapter 34 briefly explained the difference between acad.lsp and acaddoc.lsp. The need for two files arose because AutoCAD includes MDI, which enables you to open more than one drawing at a time. For more information, see the "Automatically Loading LSP Files" sidebar. S::STARTUP is a great tool for enhancing productivity. In this way, you can automate whatever general setup operations you normally do at the beginning of a drawing session, or for every drawing that you open.

Here's an AutoLISP routine that uses both the DEFUN and COMMAND functions:

```
(defun c:redline (/ startpt endpt)
  (terpri)
  (setq startpt (getpoint "Select the redline start point:"))
  (terpri)
  (setq endpt (getpoint startpt "Select the redline end point:"))
  (command "_line" startpt endpt "")
  (command "_chprop" "_last" "" "_color" "red" "")
)
```

Here's an explanation of this routine:

- The first line of this routine defines a function called redline. Because redline is preceded by c:, you can type **redline** at the command line when using it within AutoCAD. As you may remember from the discussion of the circle3 routine, the expression (/ startpt endpt) means that redline has two local variables that are available only to this routine. These variables are used in the next two lines.

- The new instruction, terpri, on the second and fourth lines, tells AutoCAD to print a blank line at the command line. You can use this instruction to improve readability of the prompts. Otherwise, two or more prompts run together on one line.

- Reading the third line from the innermost parenthesis pair outward, AutoCAD obtains the red line's start point from the user with the prompt Select the redline start point: and sets the variable startpt equal to that start point's value. Similarly, the fifth line obtains the red line's endpoint and sets the variable endpt to that value. By first getting the start point, you see a rubber-band effect between the start and endpoints that you specify.

Automatically Loading LSP Files

AutoCAD automatically loads four AutoLISP files. Two files, acad2008.lsp and acad2008doc.lsp, are specific to AutoCAD 2008. Autodesk recommends that you reserve these files for AutoCAD use. The acad2008.lsp file is loaded only once per AutoCAD session when you first load AutoCAD, while the acad2008doc.lsp file is loaded in the initial session and then each time a drawing is opened.

The other two automatically loaded AutoLISP files are reserved for you, the user. These files are acad.lsp, which is loaded once per AutoCAD session, and acaddoc.lsp, which is loaded every time a drawing is opened. What this means to you is that you can place different initialization routines in each file—one for AutoCAD initialization (acad.lsp), and the other for the initial drawing as well as future drawings. You can place an S::STARTUP function in both acad.lsp and acaddoc.lsp. However, be aware that placing different S::STARTUP functions in both files effectively disables the S::STARTUP function defined in acad.lsp.

You must create both acad.lsp and acaddoc.lsp. However, after you create any AutoLISP routine and save it under either name, you can add additional routines to the same file. AutoCAD automatically loads these files, as long as they exist.

The load order of these initialization files is:

1. acad2008.lsp: Loaded by AutoCAD 2008
2. acad.lsp: User-defined initialization file loaded once, upon loading AutoCAD 2008
3. acad2008doc.lsp: Document-level initialization file loaded by AutoCAD 2008
4. acaddoc.lsp: User-defined document-level initialization file

- Line 6 uses the AutoLISP COMMAND function. It issues the LINE command, specifies the start point and endpoint, and uses a set of empty quotation marks to replicate pressing Enter to end the LINE command.

- Line 7 uses the same syntax for the CHPROP command. It does the following: issues the CHPROP command; selects the line that you just used by using the Last Selection option; ends object selection by using the empty set of quotation marks; specifies the Color option; and sets the color to red. Another empty set of quotation marks ends the command.

- Line 8 ends the redline routine with a closing parenthesis.

To use this routine, you would follow these steps:

1. Open Visual LISP and start a new file.
2. Type the routine.
3. Save the routine as redline.lsp and place it in AutoCAD's Support folder or any other folder that you may have created for AutoLISP routines, and added to AutoCAD's support file search path.
4. Load the routine.
5. Switch to AutoCAD.
6. At the command prompt, type **redline** ↵.
7. In response to the prompts for the start point and endpoint of the redline, choose any two points on-screen. AutoCAD draws a red line between the two selected points.

ON the DVD-ROM The file `redline.lsp` is in the `Results` folder on the DVD. Feel free to copy it to your system and play around with it. For example, using your knowledge of the `circle3` routine discussed in Chapter 34, you could create a red circle.

Here is another example of an AutoLISP routine that creates an s::STARTUP function. It uses several of the features that I've been discussing in this chapter.

```
(defun s::startup ()
  (setq old_osmode (getvar "osmode"))
  (setvar "osmode" 0)
  (command "_rectang" "_width" "0.1" "0,0" "10,10")
  (command "_text" "8,1" "0.2" "0" "name")
  (command "_text" "8,0.7" "0.2" "0" "date")
  (command "_text" "8,0.4" "0.2" "0" "revision")
  (command "_zoom" "_extents")
  (setvar "osmode" old_osmode)
)
```

This routine creates a simple title block and border each time you open a new drawing, as shown in Figure 35.1. It turns object snaps off (the OSMODE system variable) so that all the text doesn't snap to the same location. But first it saves the current OSMODE value. At the end, the routine returns OSMODE to its original setting.

FIGURE 35.1

The result of the s::STARTUP routine.

In order to use this routine — or one of your own — you can add it to the end of `acaddoc.lsp`. AutoCAD 2008 does not come with this file, and so the first time that you want to use it, you must create it.

CAUTION Before using the s::STARTUP function, be sure that an s::STARTUP function does not already exist in the file. Other applications that you may have purchased or downloaded may include an s::STARTUP file. Adding a second s::STARTUP could possibly interfere with the operation of these other applications. In Notepad, choose Edit ➪ Find and type s::startup in the Find What text box. Click Find Next. If an s::STARTUP routine already exists, then add the body of your s::STARTUP function (minus the first line, which already exists) to the end of the existing s::STARTUP routine and save the file.

Creating functions with arguments

You can create functions that accept arguments, sometimes called parameters. An *argument* is a value that must be supplied with the function. The function then uses the value of that argument in its operation.

Earlier in this chapter, I explained that local variables are placed in parentheses after a slash. Arguments go in the same set of parentheses, but before the slash. If there are no local variables, you don't need the slash. Here is an example of a function with one argument:

```
(defun chg2red (selected_object)
...
)
```

To actually use this routine in AutoCAD or within another AutoLISP routine, use the format (chg2red selected_object). The argument is sent to the chg2red routine by adding the argument after the function name, all enclosed in parentheses.

Whenever you use the chg2red function within a routine, you must follow it by its argument. You can obtain the argument by using a variable whose value you've set in the routine, by obtaining a value through user input, or by typing in a specific value when you use the function.

The following exercise uses a function that is called from within the routine.

ON the DVD-ROM The file used in the following exercise on using AutoLISP functions and commands, ab35-a.lsp, is in the Drawings folder on the DVD. If you haven't already done so, place the DVD in your DVD drive.

STEPS: Using AutoLISP Functions and Commands

1. Start a new drawing using any template.
2. Use Windows Explorer to copy ab35-a.lsp from the DVD to AutoCAD's Support folder, or any folder that you've created for AutoLISP routines and added to AutoCAD's support file search path. This file is shown in Figure 35.2.

FIGURE 35.2

An AutoLISP routine to change an object's color to red.

```
(defun chg2red (selected_object)
       (command "_chprop" selected_object "" "_color" "red" "")
)
(defun c:chgcolor (/ selected)
       (terpri)
       (setq selected (entsel "Select an object to change to red:"))
       (chg2red selected)
)
```

3. Choose Tools ⇨ AutoLISP ⇨ Visual LISP Editor. In Visual LISP, open ab35-a.lsp. The routine appears in the Edit window.
4. Choose Load Active Edit Window.
5. Choose Activate AutoCAD.
6. Draw any object.
7. At the command line, type **chgcolor** ⏎.
8. At the Select an object to change to red: prompt, select the object that you drew in Step 6. Watch its color change to red.

Don't save the routine or your drawing.

Here's how the routine works:

■ This routine defines a function, chg2red, which is not preceded by c:. It has one argument, selected_object.

■ What AutoLISP actually ran when you typed **chgcolor** in Step 7 is the function c:chgcolor on the fourth line of the routine. In the last AutoLISP statement in that function — (chg2red selected) — the variable selected is derived from the previous step as a result of the operation entsel (entity select).

■ The variable selected is the argument passed to the function chg2red. The function chg2red now knows what object to operate on.

■ The function chg2red then uses the CHPROP command to change the object's color to red.

> **NOTE** To actually call this function at the command line, you would need to type (chg2red arg) where arg is an argument (in this case, it must be an entity name). Entity names are discussed later in this chapter.

Working with system variables

AutoCAD has a wide variety of system variables to control the drawing environment. Thankfully, the creators of AutoLISP enabled the AutoLISP programmer to automate setting and retrieving AutoCAD system variables.

Don't confuse the terms *variable* and *system variable*. A variable is a value that is stored for use in a routine. A system variable is an AutoCAD setting that changes how AutoCAD works.

To set or retrieve AutoCAD system variables, you use two operators, SETVAR and GETVAR, which can be used on AutoCAD system variables. (You can use SETVAR only on system variables that are not read-only.) Here's how they work:

■ SETVAR stands for *set variable*. You use SETVAR to change a system variable. Place the system variable in quotes, followed by the new value, as in (setvar "cmdecho" 0).

■ GETVAR stands for *get variable*. It enables you to obtain the value of any system variable. As soon as you have the value, you can set it to a variable. This is often done so that you can return a system variable to its previous value if you've changed it during a routine. Place the system variable in quotes after using GETVAR, as in (getvar "cmdecho").

Although you can use SETVAR and GETVAR on many system variables, here are two system variables that are often changed in an AutoLISP routine:

■ In all of the AutoLISP routines created thus far, AutoCAD's command responses could be seen scrolling off the command-line window. The CMDECHO system variable determines whether you see prompts and input during the functioning of AutoLISP's COMMAND function. By default, echoing is on (set to 1). If you set it to 0, you do not see prompts and input, and the functioning of the AutoLISP routine looks cleaner and runs slightly faster.

■ The FILEDIA system variable turns on and off the display of dialog boxes that enable you to choose files. Turning off this system variable enables you to work with files on the command line in AutoLISP routines.

> **ON the DVD-ROM** The file used in the following exercise on using AutoLISP to work with system variables, ab35-a.lsp, is in the Drawings folder on the DVD.

STEPS: Using AutoLISP to Work with System Variables

1. If you did the previous exercise and copied ab35-a.lsp to AutoCAD's Support folder (or another folder that you created for AutoLISP routines, and added to AutoCAD's support file search path), open it from that folder. If you did not do the previous exercise, copy ab35-a.lsp from the DVD to AutoCAD's Support folder, or another folder in AutoCAD's support file search path.

2. Start a new drawing using the acad.dwt template. Choose Tools ⇨ AutoLISP ⇨ Visual LISP Editor to open Visual LISP. Click Open and open ab35-a.lsp. Edit it to read as follows:

```
(defun chg2red (selected_object)
  (command "_chprop" selected_object "" "_color" "red" "")
)
(defun c:chgcolor (/ selected old_cmdecho)
  (setq old_cmdecho (getvar "cmdecho"))
  (setvar "cmdecho" 0)
  (terpri)
  (setq selected (entsel "Select an object to change to red:"))
  (chg2red selected)
  (setvar "cmdecho" old_cmdecho)
)
```

3. Save the file as ab35-01.lsp in the same location.

4. Choose Load Active Edit Window to load the routine.

5. Draw any object.

6. At the command line, type **chgcolor** ↵.

7. At the Select an object to change to red: prompt, select the object that you drew in Step 5. You no longer see the prompts scrolling by. The object that you select turns red, and AutoCAD immediately displays the command prompt.

Don't save your drawing.

Here's how this routine works. This discussion assumes that you have already read the discussion of the previous routine, which was very similar.

- First, you added a new variable, old_cmdecho, to the chgcolor function.

- In the following line, you set this variable to the current value of the CMDECHO system variable. You obtained this current value using GETVAR.

- You then used SETVAR to set the AutoCAD system variable CMDECHO to 0.

- You may need to see the commands echoed for debugging purposes, and so it would prove best to return CMDECHO to the value that it was set to before running the routine. Therefore, in the last line, you use SETVAR again to reset CMDECHO to the variable old_cmdecho, which stored the original value of CMDECHO.

As a result of these changes, the chgcolor program always sets the CMDECHO system variable back to the value it had before being run.

Working with Lists

Lists are the primary structures that you work with while programming in AutoLISP. As you work in this chapter, you'll begin to understand the use of lists to modify objects (also called *entities*) in the AutoCAD database, and in a variety of other contexts with AutoLISP. AutoCAD represents all object data in a list that contains many smaller lists, but the lists are simple to use and manipulate.

Using lists for coordinates

A list is always enclosed in parentheses with spaces between the elements of the list. One common use for lists is for coordinates, as shown in the following example:

    (1.0 3.5 2.0)

This list represents the X,Y,Z coordinates 1.0,3.5,2.0. You often need to extract one or more of the elements in a list. Table 35.1 shows the common list-extraction functions using the example list (1.0 3.5 2.0).

TABLE 35.1

Basic List-Extraction Functions

Function	Pronunciation	Example Output	Description
CAR	Car	1.0	Returns the first element in a list
CDR	Could-er	(3.5 2.0)	Removes the first element from a list
CADR	cad-er	3.5	Returns the second element in a list
CADDR	ca-did-der	2.0	Returns the third element in a list

For more flexibility, you can use the NTH function. Use the NTH function to access any element in a list by passing two arguments that specify the number of the element (items are numbered starting from 0) and the list that you want.

The name of the list is usually a variable set with SETQ:

    (setq corner (list 1.0 3.5 2.0))

In this example, (nth 0 corner) returns 1.0 because 1.0 is the first item in the list corner.

The LIST function creates a list. If all of the items in a list are constant values (not variables), you can use the QUOTE function to create a list. You can use a single quote (the same as an apostrophe on the keyboard) as a shortcut for the QUOTE function. The following two functions are equivalent:

    (setq corner (list 1.0 3.5 2.0))
    (setq corner '(1.0 3.5 2.0))

Many more AutoLISP list-extraction functions are detailed in the AutoLISP Function Synopsis Appendix of the Visual LISP Developer's Guide. Look under Basic Functions, then List Manipulation Functions. However, you can go a long way by remembering the functions listed here.

Creating dotted pairs

A *dotted pair* is a special type of list that contains only two elements. Some AutoLISP functions do not accept dotted pairs as an argument, but they're used to represent AutoCAD database objects. To construct a dotted pair, use the CONS function:

```
(cons 2.1 4.5)
```

This example returns (2.1 . 4.5). This list type is known as a dotted pair because it contains exactly two elements, and the elements are separated by a period or dot.

STEPS: Working with AutoLISP Lists

1. Start a new drawing using the acad.dwt template.
2. Choose Tools ⇨ AutoLISP ⇨ Visual LISP Editor to open Visual LISP.
3. In the Visual LISP Console window, type **(setq endpt '(3.5 2.0 1.4))** ↵. AutoLISP returns (3.5 2.0 1.4).
4. Continue in the Visual LISP Console. Type **(car endpt)** ↵. AutoLISP returns 3.5.
5. Type **(cadr endpt)** ↵. AutoLISP returns 2.0.
6. Type **(cdr endpt)** ↵. AutoLISP returns (2.0 1.4).
7. Type **(nth 1 endpt)** ↵. AutoLISP returns 2.0.

Don't save your drawing.

Setting Conditions

Often, you want to execute a procedure based on a certain condition. One way of doing this is with the IF statement, which does one thing if a statement is true and another thing if it's false. In other words, the operation is conditioned on the truth of a certain statement.

Looping is an important part of programming. Frequently, you want to execute a procedure over and over until the routine has finished operating on all of the target objects or items. Looping sets up the condition that determines when the operation starts, the number of objects upon which the routine operates, and when the operation ends.

Conditional structures

Conditional structures enable program flow to be determined, based on the outcome of a given decision. These decisions result in the return of either T, meaning true, or nil, meaning false. To try out the following statements, type them in the Visual LISP Console window. For instance, for the statement

```
(< 3 5)
T
```

AutoLISP returns T for true, having determined that 3 is less than 5. For the statement

```
(> 3 5)
nil
```

AutoLISP returns `nil` for false, having determined that 3 is not greater than 5. For the statement

```
(= 3 5)
nil
```

AutoLISP returns `nil`. Here, we've determined that 3 is not equal to 5. Because these statements return either `T` or `nil`, you can use the IF statement. The general syntax of the IF statement is (`if conditional-test if-true if-false`).

For example, you may want to find circles whose radius is less than 0.25. In this case, you could use the following IF statement. In this example, `radius` is a variable that has been previously set.

```
(if (< radius 0.25)
  (princ  "\nThe radius is less than .25")
  (princ  "\nThe radius is not less than .25")
)
```

The conditional test is (`< radius 0.25`). The if-true statement is (`princ "\nThe radius is less than .25"`). The if-false statement is (`princ "\nThe radius is not less than .25"`). This IF statement is equivalent to saying, "If the radius is less than .25, print 'The radius is less than .25' but if not, print 'The radius is not less than .25.'"

You can leave out the if-false statement. In this case, AutoLISP executes the if-true statement if the conditional statement is true and does nothing if it's false, and continues on to the rest of the program. In the following exercise, you see both types of IF statements, one nested inside the other.

STEPS: Using the IF Statement

1. Start a new drawing in AutoCAD using the `acad.dwt` template.
2. Open Visual LISP, start a new file, and type the following:

```
(defun c:compare2three (/ entered_num)
  (setq entered_num (getint "\nEnter an integer: "))
  (if (< entered_num 3)
    (princ "\nThe entered number is less than 3.")
    (if (= entered_num 3)
      (princ "\nThe entered number is equal to 3.")
      (princ "\nThe entered number is greater than 3.")
      )
    )
  (princ)
  )
```

The GETINT function gets an integer from the user and is covered later in this chapter. The PRINC function prints a text string on the command line. The \n before the `Enter an integer:` prompt starts a new line; it's similar to using (`terpri`). Using (`princ`) at the end of a routine is also covered later in this chapter.

3. Choose Check Edit Window. If you see any error message in the Build Output window, check your typing, make any necessary corrections, and try again.
4. Save the file as `ab35-02.lsp` in a folder that is in the support file search path, or in `AutoCAD 2008\Support`.

5. Choose Load Active Edit Window and then choose Activate AutoCAD.

6. To try out the IF statement, type **compare2three** ↵. At the Enter an integer: prompt, type 5 ↵. AutoCAD displays: The entered number is greater than 3.

7. Repeat the COMPARE2THREE command. At the Enter an integer: prompt, type **3** ↵. AutoCAD displays: The entered number is equal to 3.

8. Repeat the COMPARE2THREE command. At the Enter an integer: prompt, type **2** ↵. AutoCAD displays: The entered number is less than 3.

Don't save your drawing.

Loop structures

Looping provides the capability to execute a step or a number of steps a given number of times, based on an evaluation that you make in your application. One way to do this is with the WHILE function.

The format of the WHILE function is:

```
(while conditional-test-if-true
        then-perform- following-code-until-condition-is-false)
```

One method that can be useful with a WHILE conditional-test-if-true is to include a *counter* for the WHILE expression. A counter counts how many times an operation is executed. You can then end the operation when the counter reaches a certain number. To create a counter, set a variable (perhaps named "counter") to the number at which you want to start. Then write the code for one pass through the operation. Then set the counter to the next higher number using an expression, such as the following:

```
(setq counter (+ 1 counter))
```

The routine then loops back over the operation until the counter reaches the value that you set.

Here's a simple example:

```
(defun c:process (/ counter)
  (setq counter 1)
  (while (< counter 6)
    (princ "\nProcessing number ")
    (princ counter)
    (terpri)
    (setq counter (+ 1 counter))
  )
)
```

In this example, the process function starts by setting the variable counter to 1. Then you start the WHILE statement and specify that the counter must be less than 6. Within the WHILE statement, you print the text string "Processing number" and then the value of the counter variable. You use (terpri) so that each text string starts on a new line. Then you set the counter to the next higher number. Each time through the WHILE loop, the value of the counter is incremented by 1. Without the increment statement, line 3 would always evaluate to true, and the WHILE loop would never exit because the counter would always be 1.

If you accidentally program an infinite loop like this, you can stop the execution of your AutoLISP routine by pressing Esc, pressing Ctrl+Break, or choosing Debug ⇨ Abort Evaluation from the Visual LISP menu.

In the preceding example, the WHILE loop continues as long as the counter is less than 6. When the counter reaches 6, the routine stops. The WHILE statement returns the last value of the routine, and so AutoCAD prints 6 on the last line. Figure 35.3 shows the result.

1124

FIGURE 35.3

The result of the process function.

```
Command: process
Processing number 1
Processing number 2
Processing number 3
Processing number 4
Processing number 5
6
```

When using WHILE, you may want to combine several operations under the condition. The IF function normally evaluates one then expression if the test expression is true. Suppose you want an IF expression that processes various tasks if the test condition is true. An IF expression, as previously mentioned, processes a "do-if-true" and "do-if-false." Therefore, to process more than one "do-if-true" expression, you need to separate the "do-if-true" processes from the "do-if-false" processes. To accomplish this, use PROGN (short for *program nest*) to include (or nest) all items that you want executed when the test is true. In general, PROGN evaluates all of the statements within its parentheses and returns the last evaluation as if it were one statement, as the following example demonstrates.

In the following example, you see the same IF statements used in an earlier example. However, after the second IF statement, you want your routine to print two lines if the entered number equals 3. You can do this by enclosing the two lines of code (plus a terpri) within a PROGN statement:

```
(defun c:compare2three (/ entered_num)
  (setq entered_num (getint "\nEnter an integer: "))
  (if (< entered_num 3)
    (princ "\nThe entered number is less than 3.")
    (if (= entered_num 3)
      (progn
        (princ "\nThe entered number is equal to 3.")
        (terpri)
        (princ "\nThis is the one we are looking for.")
      )
      (princ "\nThe entered number is greater than 3.")
    )
  )
  (princ)
)
```

ON the DVD-ROM The file used in the following exercise on using WHILE, IF, PROGN, and a counter, ab35-b.lsp, is in the Drawings folder on the DVD.

STEPS: Using WHILE, IF, PROGN, and a Counter

1. Start a new drawing in AutoCAD with any template.
2. Open Visual LISP.
3. Click Open File on the Visual LISP Standard toolbar, and open ab35-b.lsp from the DVD.
4. Save the file as ab35-03.lsp in AutoCAD 2008\Support or any folder in the support file search path. Figure 35.4 shows this routine.

FIGURE 35.4

The PRINT0TO10 routine.

```
(defun c:print0to10 (/ counter halfway)
  (setq counter 0                          ; initial value of counter
        halfway 5                          ; initial value of halfway
        )
  (terpri)
  (while (< counter 11)                    ; as long as counter is less than 11
    (if (= counter halfway)
        (progn                             ; process this if the variable halfway is 5
               (princ "Hey The halfway mark is: ")
               (princ halfway)
               (terpri)
        )
        (progn                             ; otherwise just show the present counter value
               (princ "The Counter value is: ")
               (princ counter)
               (terpri)
        )
    )
    (setq counter (+ counter 1))           ; Increment the value of counter
  )
)
```

5. Load ab35-03.lsp. Return to AutoCAD.

6. Type **print0to10** ↵. Press F2 to open the AutoCAD Text Window and see the result, shown in Figure 35.5.

FIGURE 35.5

The result of the PRINT0TO10 function.

```
Command: print0to10

The Counter value is: 0
The Counter value is: 1
The Counter value is: 2
The Counter value is: 3
The Counter value is: 4
Hey The halfway mark is: 5
The Counter value is: 6
The Counter value is: 7
The Counter value is: 8
The Counter value is: 9
The Counter value is: 10
11
```

Don't save your drawing.

Managing Drawing Objects

The real power of AutoLISP is in manipulating drawing objects. This section reveals how many of the AutoLISP routines perform their magic. You can find information about an object and then use that information to change the object. You can also create selection sets of objects.

Getting information about an object

Every object in the AutoCAD database has an entity name. This name enables you to reference that object anywhere in your AutoLISP application. To see an example of an entity name, type the following after starting a new drawing:

```
(command "_line" "3,3" "5,5" "")
(entlast)
```

AutoLISP responds with an Entity name such as <Entity name: 2ed0520>.

The numbers will probably differ on your system, but using the information returned from ENTLAST enables you to programmatically get or set a variety of options on any given database object by referencing its entity name.

The ENTGET (entity get) function is the key to making modifications to the drawing database. The ENTGET function takes an entity name as its one and only argument. After drawing the line in the preceding steps, type the following:

```
(setq myline (entget (entlast)))
```

AutoLISP responds with:

```
((-1 . <Entity name: 15ac558>) (0 . "LINE") (330 . <Entity name:
15ac4f8>)(5 . "2B") (100 . "AcDbEntity") (67 . 0)
(410 . "Model") (8 . "0")(100 . "AcDbLine") (10 3.0 3.0 0.0) (11 5.0
5.0 0.0) (210 0.0 0.0 1.0))
```

This is a representation of how the line is stored in the AutoCAD drawing database. AutoLISP returned one large list that contains 12 smaller lists. Each of the smaller lists is referred to as a group indexed by the first element. The entity name is in group –1. Each of the initial numbers in the small lists represents a different quality of the line. These numbers are called *object group codes*. The object group codes used most often are listed in Table 35.2.

TABLE 35.2

Commonly Used AutoCAD Object Group Codes

Group Code	Description
–1	Entity name
0	Entity type
1	Text value
8	Layer
10	Start point (or center)
11	Endpoint (or alignment point)
38	Elevation
39	Thickness
40	Radius (or height of text)
62	Color
67	Paper space flag

As you can see from the 10, 11, and 40 codes, the meaning of the group codes can change, depending on the type of object that it's used for.

You can also use Visual LISP to examine an AutoCAD object. Begin by choosing View ➪ Browse Drawing Database ➪ Browse Selection. At this point, Visual LISP will display a pickbox in your drawing so that you can select an object.

After you end object selection, you're returned to Visual LISP, where you see the Inspect dialog box. Select the name of the entity and right-click while the cursor is over the selected text. Choose Inspect to see information about the object. Figure 35.6 shows information about an arc.

FIGURE 35.6

Getting information about a drawing object from Visual LISP.

Not all of these group codes are present in the line that you drew. For instance, group 62 (color) is absent in the list returned by AutoLISP. Every time you draw a line, you don't explicitly set its color. As a result, it defaults to the current color. In the same way, AutoLISP doesn't explicitly set every attribute of every group. In this case, the color is ByLayer and the current layer is 0. AutoLISP returned (8 . "0") in the preceding list to signify that the line is on layer 0.

There are many other group codes than the ones listed in Table 35-2, and they can be found in the Visual LISP Help system. From Visual LISP, choose Help ➪ Visual LISP Help Topics. From the Contents tab, double-click DXF Reference. (Because the group codes are also used for DXF files, they're found in the DXF Reference.) Double-click ENTITIES Section. You can then either choose Common Group Codes for Entities or choose the specific entity that you want to look up. In many cases, one group code can have different meanings, depending on the entity in which it appears. For example, in the list representing the line that you drew, group 10 is represented by (10 3.0 3.0 0.0), which means that the start point of the line is at X = 3.0, Y = 3.0, Z = 0.0. If group 0 were a circle instead, the coordinates of group 10 would specify the center point of the circle.

To manipulate a given attribute of an object, two important functions are ASSOC and SUBST:

- ASSOC returns a list that finds the entry associated with an item in a list. It takes two arguments: the item in the list and the list itself. For example, if you specify the group code (such as 10) as the first argument, it returns the code's value (which would be the start point of a line).Or, if a list named myobject contains three groups, as in ((0 . "group 0") (1 1.0 2.0) (3 4.2 1.5 6.75)), then (assoc 1 myobject) would return (1 1.0 2.0).

- SUBST substitutes a value for every occurrence in a list. The SUBST function takes three arguments. To make the substitution, the first argument specifies what to substitute with, the second argument specifies what to substitute for, and the third argument specifies on what list to perform this operation.

To manipulate the start point of your line, first get the start point:

```
(setq startpt (assoc 10 myline))
```

AutoLISP responds:

```
(10 3.0 3.0 0.0)
```

To modify the start point of your line, use:

```
(setq new_startpt '(10 6.5 1.0 0.0))
(setq myline (subst new_startpt startpt myline))
```

AutoLISP responds:

```
((-1 . <Entity name: 15ac558>) (0 . "LINE") (330 . <Entity name:
15ac4f8>)(5 . "2B") (100 . "AcDbEntity") (67 . 0)
(410 . "Model") (8 . "0")(100 . "AcDbLine") (10 6.5 1.0 0.0) (11 5.0
5.0 0.0) (210 0.0 0.0 1.0))
```

In this case, the new_startpt is substituted for the existing startpt in the object myline. No changes to the line are yet apparent. To commit the change, you need the ENTMOD function.

Modifying objects

The key to modifying objects is the ENTMOD (entity modify) function. The list returned by AutoLISP can be modified and then passed to ENTMOD as an argument to update the AutoCAD database. Continuing with the previous example, if you enter:

```
(entmod myline)
```

AutoLISP responds:

```
((-1 . <Entity name: 15ac558>) (0 . "LINE") (330 . <Entity name:
15ac4f8>) (5 ."2B") (100 . "AcDbEntity") (67 . 0)
(410 . "Model") (8 . "0") (100."AcDbLine") (10 6.5 1.0 0.0)
(11 5.0 5.0 0.0) (210 0.0 0.0 1.0))
```

The AutoCAD database is changed as well, and the start point of your line is now at X = 6.5, Y = 1.0, Z = 0.0.

Creating selection sets

A selection set is created with the SSGET (selection set get) function. This prompts the user with the familiar Select objects: prompt. Table 35.3 shows commonly used selection-set functions.

TABLE 35.3

Common AutoCAD Selection-Set Functions

Function	Description
SSGET	Obtains a selection set from the user.
SSLENGTH	Returns the number of objects in a selection set. It takes one argument, which is the selection set.
SSNAME	Returns the entity name of a given object in a selection set. It takes two arguments: the selection set and the number of the object in the selection set. The first item number is 0, the second is 1, and so on.

You can use a maximum of 256 selection sets at any given time. To release a selection set back to AutoLISP so that it can be used again, set the selection set to nil, as in (setq ss nil).

For example, you can enter the following in a new drawing:

```
(command "_circle" "3,3" "2")
nil
(command "_circle" "4,4" "3")
nil
(command "_line" "7,2" "6,6" "3,4" "5,5" "")
nil
(setq mysset (ssget))
Select objects: all ↵
5 found
Select objects: ↵
<Selection set 1>
```

Now mysset is set to the selection set specified by all, which includes the three line segments and the two circles. To see what you have in your selection set, type the following, either on the command line or in the Visual LISP Console:

(sslength mysset)
5

You now know that you have five objects in your selection set. The first object is number 0, and the fifth object is number 4. To see what the first object is, enter the following:

(ssname mysset 0)
<Entity name: 3fe0550>

To get the database data on the object, enter:

(entget (ssname mysset 0))

Visual LISP responds:

```
((-1 . <Entity name: 1601580>) (0 . "LINE") (330 . <Entity name:
16014f8>)(5 . "30") (100 . "AcDbEntity") (67 . 0) (410 . "Model") (8 .
"0")(100 . "AcDbLine") (10 3.0 4.0 0.0) (11 5.0 5.0 0.0) (210 0.0 0.0
1.0))
```

By stepping through each of the entity names returned by SSNAME from 0 to 4, you can manipulate each of the objects in the selection set.

STEPS: Creating Selection Sets

1. Start a new drawing using the acad.dwt template, and type the following in a new file in the Visual LISP edit window. Save it as ab35-04.lsp in your AutoCAD 2008Support folder or any folder in the support file search path.

```
(defun c:listsset (/ mysset counter)
 (setq mysset (ssget))
 (setq counter 0)
 (while (< counter (sslength mysset))
   (terpri)
```

```
      (princ (cdr (assoc 0 (entget (ssname mysset counter)))))))
      (setq counter (+ counter 1))
  )
  (princ)
)
```

2. Load ab35-04.lsp.

3. Activate AutoCAD and draw any number of objects on-screen — at least two different types of objects.

4. Type **listsset** ↵. AutoCAD prompts you to select objects (because of the SSGET function).

5. Select all of the objects in your drawing. The routine prints the type of each object that you selected. (Press F2 to open the AutoCAD Text Window to see the entire results.) Figure 35.7 shows the results. Of course, your results will be different because you probably drew different types of objects.

FIGURE 35.7

One possible result of the LISTSSET routine.

```
Command: listsset

Select objects: all
5 found

Select objects:

LWPOLYLINE
CIRCLE
TEXT
LINE
LINE
```

Here's a breakdown of the routine in Step 1:

- **Line 1** creates a function and declares two variables, mysset and counter.
- **Line 2** sets the mysset variable equal to the selection set that the user provides using SSGET.
- **Line 3** sets the counter variable to 0, because selection sets work on a zero-based index (the first item is 0).
- **Line 4** starts a WHILE loop. Working from the innermost set of parentheses, you first obtain the number of objects in the mysset selection set, using SSLENGTH. Then you specify that the WHILE loop will continue as long as the counter is less than the number of objects in the mysset selection set. In other words, when the routine has cycled through all of the objects in the selection set, it stops.
- **Line 5** uses TERPRI to start a new line before printing out the list of objects.
- **Line 6** prints the list. Working from the innermost set of parentheses, the routine first obtains the name of the object in the mysset selection set whose number is equal to the variable counter. The routine then gets that object using ENTGET. The routine then gets the name of that object using ASSOC with the 0 group code. The result is a dotted-pair list whose second item is the name of the object. The CDR function eliminates the first item in the dotted-pair list, leaving just the name of the object, which is what you want. The routine then prints the result.

- **Line 7** sets the counter up one to repeat the WHILE loop for the next object.
- **Line 8** closes the WHILE loop.
- **Line 9** exits the routine quietly. (I discuss exiting quietly later in the chapter.)
- **Line 10** closes the entire function.

Getting Input from the User

The course of your AutoLISP routines may often depend on user input. To satisfy this need, AutoCAD has a family of functions prefaced with the word GET. You have seen GETVAR for obtaining system variable information. Table 35.4 shows some other useful GET functions.

TABLE 35.4

Basic User-Input Functions

Function	Description
GETDIST	Returns the distance between two points
GETINT	Returns an integer
GETREAL	Returns a real number (which can be a non-integer, negative, and so on)
GETSTRING	Returns a text string

Within the COMMAND function, you can use the PAUSE function to pause the operation of the routine and enable user input, such as picking a point or typing a value. For example, the expression (command "circle" pause "3") pauses to let the user specify a center point and then creates a circle with a radius of 3.

Notice the function ENTSEL in the next exercise. This is a type of shorthand for SSGET. Use it when you want to limit the user to selecting a single object. ENTSEL returns an entity name and the coordinates of your pick point in a dotted-pair list. Therefore, you can use CAR before ENTSEL to get the entity name for ENTGET.

There is also a new argument for getstring, T. If you use this argument and it isn't nil, users can place spaces in the input. Using this argument enables users to type a text value that includes more than one word. Without the T, AutoLISP would interpret a space as equivalent to pressing Enter.

STEPS: Getting User Input

1. Start a new drawing using the acad.dwt template.
2. Start Visual LISP, open a new file, and enter the following routine. Save it as ab35-05.lsp in AutoCAD 2008\Support or a folder that you've added to the support file search path.

```
(defun c:chgmytext (/ src_object new_ht new_str)
(setq src_object (entget (car (entsel))))
(setq new_ht (getreal "\nWhat is the new height? "))
(setq new_str (getstring T "\nWhat is the new text value? "))
(setq src_object
(subst  (cons 40 new_ht)  (assoc 40 src_object ) src_object)
)
```

```
(setq src_object
(subst  (cons 1 new_str)  (assoc 1 src_object) src_object)
)
(entmod src_object)
(princ)
)
```

3. Choose Format Edit Window from the Tools toolbar.

4. Load `ab35-05.lsp`.

5. Create some text using either the DTEXT or the TEXT command and run `chgmytext` on it. AutoCAD changes the text object's height and content to the values that you input in response to the prompts.

Don't save your drawing.

Here's a breakdown of the routine in Step 2:

- **Line 1** defines the function and declares the three variables.
- **Line 2** uses ENTSEL to let the user select one object. As explained earlier, CAR enables you to get just the entity name. ENTGET gets this entity name so that you can modify it. Finally, this line sets the resulting entity name equal to the variable `src_object`.
- **Line 3** prompts the user for a new height for the text and sets the entered number equal to the `new_ht` variable.
- **Line 4** prompts the user for a new text value (a new string) and sets the entered text value equal to the `new_str` variable.
- **Line 5** starts the process of substituting the new values for the old values. Here the routine starts to set the new value for `src_object`.
- **Line 6** uses SUBST to substitute the new text height for the old text height for the object `src_object`. (Group code 40 represents text height.)
- **Line 7** closes the SETQ function.
- **Line 8** is the same as line 5. You'll be repeating the process of lines 5 through 7 for the new text (string) value.
- **Line 9** uses SUBST to substitute the new text value for the old text value. (Group code 1 represents the text value.)
- **Line 10** closes the SETQ function.
- **Line 11** uses ENTMOD on `src_object` to make the change in the drawing database.
- **Line 12** exits quietly.
- **Line 13** closes the entire function.

Putting on the Finishing Touches

You have a number of finishing touches that you should add to a routine before you can call it complete. All AutoLISP expressions return a value, and the last expression returns its value on the command line. You've noticed the PRINC function at the end of several routines. PRINC returns a blank line and, therefore, ensures that no extraneous evaluation return values are echoed on the command line. Using the PRINC function in this way is called *exiting cleanly* or *exiting quietly*.

Using AutoLISP to Match Properties

This routine modifies the layer of objects to match the layer of one other object. This powerful routine was a mainstay of many AutoCAD users before the MATCHPROP command was introduced in AutoCAD R14. The general method used here for matching layers can be used to change any properties that you want on any AutoCAD object.

```
;;;Matches the layer of one selected source object in any number of
destination objects.
(defun c:matchlayer (/ src_object mysset counter cur_ent ent_layer)
  (prompt "\n*** Select Source object to match ***")   ; prompt the user
  (if (setq src_object (car (entsel)))       ; select the object
    (progn
      (setq src_layer (assoc 8 (entget src_object)))  ; get the object's
layer
      ;; prompt the user
      (prompt "\n*** Select Destination objects to match layer ***")
      ;; collect some objects using ssget
(if (setq mysset (ssget))       ; verify the user selected something
    (progn     ; if the user selected some items do the following
      (setq counter 0)
      (while (< counter (sslength mysset))

        (setq cur_ent (entget (ssname mysset counter)))
        (setq ent_layer (assoc 8 cur_ent))
        (entmod (subst src_layer ent_layer cur_ent))
        (setq counter (+ counter 1))
        )
      )
    (prompt "\nYou did not select any items")  ; prompt the user
    )        ;_end of if verification
    )        ;_end of progn for the selection of object to match
    ;; prompt the user they did not select a source object
    (prompt "\nSorry you did not select an Object")
    )        ;_end of if
  (princ)
  )          ;_end of function c:matchlayer
```

This routine uses the PROMPT function to prompt you to select the source and destination objects; the PROMPT function is similar to the PRINC function but creates a nicer prompt in the dynamic input tooltip. Then the routine gets the name of the selected object with (car (entsel)). It determines the object's layer by using ENTGET on the object name and using ASSOC with the 8 group code. It then gets a selection set of the Destination objects. It creates a loop that cycles through these objects, gets their layers (the ent_layer variable), and uses ENTMOD and SUBST to change the object's current layer to the source object's layer.

Each selection of objects (the source object and the destination objects) is enclosed in an IF function whose if-false statement prints an error message telling users that they did not select an object (or objects).

Most of the AutoLISP applications covered thus far do not include much in the way of error handling. A new function called EQUAL is used on line 4 of the final routine in the next exercise. EQUAL is different than = in that EQUAL returns true only if two expressions are equal (each of the two objects tested for equality are evaluated before checking whether they're equal). A simple rule of thumb is to use EQUAL for list comparisons and = for numeric comparisons.

In the routine in the next exercise, if you select an object that is not a text object, the program jumps to line 18 and prints the error message You must select a text object.

A similar type of error handling is to enclose the selection of objects in an IF function. The IF function's test condition has to exist in order for the IF function to work. Therefore, if your user doesn't select an object, the test evaluates as false. You can place an error message as the if-false part of the IF function to catch this type of error.

This type of error handling is crucial to making your AutoLISP programs look finished and function properly.

Another way to finish off your routine is to add comments. Start with a comment at the beginning that states the purpose and function of the routine. This helps others understand what the routine does and can help you as well when you look at the routine again a few months later! Comments are prefaced with a semicolon.

Continue to make comments throughout your code. A lack of comments can make even the most useful code useless. Most professional programmers fully comment and document a function's purpose and behavior by placing comments within the code.

Visual LISP supports several commenting styles. When you click Format Edit Window on the Tools toolbar, Visual LISP uses these styles to automatically format your code. Here's how they work:

- **;;; Triple semicolon:** When you type a comment with three semicolons, Visual LISP places the comment at the left margin. You can use a triple semicolon comment at the beginning of your routine to describe its overall purpose and what it does.

- **;; Double semicolon:** Visual LISP indents a comment with two semicolons at the current nesting level, flush with the next level of parentheses. You can use this type of comment to explain the next line or lines of code.

- **; Single semicolon:** By default, Visual LISP indents a comment with one semicolon by 40 spaces. Choose Tools ➪ Environment Options ➪ Visual LISP Format Options to open the Format Options dialog box, shown in Figure 35.8, and change this value if you want. You can use this type of comment for running comments at the right side of your code. Because they're indented, they stand out from the body of your code.

- **;| |; Inline comment:** Place an inline comment within any line of code so that it has code both before and after it. An inline comment is formatted as follows: ;|This is a comment|;. You use the pipe symbol (usually over the backslash) along with the semicolon. You can use an inline comment to explain a small section of code within a line, or to span comments over several lines without adding a semicolon before each line.

- **;_ End-of-line comment:** Place an end-of-line comment at the end of any line of code. An end-of-line comment is formatted as follows: ;_ This is an end-of-line comment. You use the underscore symbol along with the semicolon. You can use an end-of-line comment to explain which function is matched to which closing parenthesis. This is especially useful for conditional functions where one closing parenthesis can be several lines from the opening parenthesis.

FIGURE 35.8

Use the Format Options dialog box to format margins and indentation in the Visual LISP editor.

See the "Using AutoLISP to Match Properties" sidebar for several examples of comment styles.

STEPS: Putting on the Finishing Touches

1. Load the application that was completed in the previous exercise. If you didn't do the previous exercise, enter the text of the chgmytext routine from that exercise in Visual LISP's edit window, and save it as ab35-05.lsp in AutoCAD 2008\Support or a folder that you've added to the support file search path. Then load it with any drawing that you open in AutoCAD.

2. Now run chgmytext and choose an object that is not a text object (such as a circle) in response to the Select object: prompt. Answer the prompts for new height and new text values.

   If the selected object is a circle, you see its radius change to match the value that you specified to be the new text height. This is definitely not what you intended when writing this program.

3. Modify the program so that it reads as follows, and save it as ab35-06.lsp:

```
;;;modifies text height and content (value)
(defun c:chgmytext (/ src_object new_ht new_str)
    (terpri)
    (setq src_object (entget (car (entsel))))
    (if (equal (assoc 0 src_object) '(0 . "TEXT"))
        (progn
            (prompt "\nWhat is the new height for the text? ")
            (setq new_ht (getreal))
            (prompt "\nWhat is the new text value? ")
            (setq new_str (getstring))
            (setq src_object
            (subst (cons 40 new_ht) (assoc 40 src_object)
src_object)
            )
```

```
                    (setq src_object
                          (subst (cons 1 new_str) (assoc 1
    src_object)src_object)
                    )
                    (entmod src_object)
              )
              (princ"\n You must select a text object.")
        )
      (princ)
)
```

4. Load `ab35-06.lsp`. Start `chgmytext` and try out the routine again with a circle or other non-text object.

Don't save your drawing.

Summary

In this chapter, you learned:

- How to create variables
- How to create AutoLISP functions
- How to work with AutoCAD commands and system variables
- About extending AutoLISP's power by using lists and looping
- How to modify and get information about drawing objects
- How to create selection sets
- About obtaining user input
- Tools for finishing off your AutoLISP routines by adding some error handling, making sure the routine exits quietly, and adding helpful comments about the routine's function

In the next chapter, you read about some of the more advanced features of Visual LISP.

Chapter 36

Exploring Advanced AutoLISP Topics

T his chapter builds on the previous two chapters and introduces you to a
few advanced AutoLISP topics, including local and global variables,
ActiveX, and debugging.

AUTOCAD ONLY AutoCAD LT does not support AutoLISP, and so this entire
chapter is for AutoCAD only.

Understanding Local and Global Variables

In this section, you read how local and global variables are accessed within a
function, as well as some common syntax. You also discover what can happen
when global variables are not properly documented.

Chapter 35 explained that a *variable* is a symbolic name that can be operated on
in a given program. An important part of using variables is being able to assign
values to them. There are two types of variables, global and local.

A *global* variable is exposed, or available, to all AutoLISP functions that you've
loaded into your drawing. A global variable retains its value after the program
that defined it is finished. You use a global variable when you want its value to be
available across an entire project, as opposed to just one function within a project. This allows you to retain a fixed value that might be used and assigned by
different functions, or for debugging. Any variable that you don't specifically
define as a local variable is a global variable.

A *local* variable is temporarily assigned a value during a function's execution.
After the function completes executing, the local variable value is discarded.
AutoLISP can now use the memory that was taken up by that local variable. You
use a local variable when you want to be sure that you don't have variable values
floating around and interfering with other functions. Local variables are also

IN THIS CHAPTER

**Understanding local and global
variables**

**Working with Visual LISP
ActiveX functions**

Debugging code

Using the Error Trace window

Using the Watch window

easier to debug because they affect only the code within their function. In general, most of your variables should be local. You create a local variable and declare it in the DEFUN statement after the slash and a space, as in this example:

```
(defun list-objects ( / counter sset)...
```

> **CAUTION**   Global variables can be tricky. For example, they can easily cause bugs. This is because their values persist and can be hard to debug because the values are hard to find. A common syntax for global variables is to prefix and suffix the variable with an asterisk, as in *aGlobal*. In this way, you can easily identify global variables in your code. Keep your use of global variables to a minimum, and carefully document those that you do use. Failure to follow these simple rules could result in undesirable and difficult-to-trace bugs.

STEPS: Using Local and Global Variables

1. Start a new drawing using the acad.dwt template. You should not have any other drawing open.

2. Open the Visual LISP Editor.

3. In the Console window, type the following line and then press Ctrl+Enter. You use Ctrl+Enter in the Console window to enter in code of more than one line. This line declares one local variable:

   (defun local-variable (/ var1)

4. Type the second line of code in the Console window as follows:

   (setq var1 "I'm local")) ↵

   This sets the local variable to the string that you typed. The Console returns the name of the function:

   LOCAL-VARIABLE

5. Before you test this function, you can check out the current value of the local variable, var1. Type **var1** ↵ in the Visual LISP Console. The Console returns:

   nil

   As you can see, the value is nil.

6. Test the local-variable function to check the value that it sets to the var1 variable. In the Console, type **(local-variable)** ↵. The Console returns:

   "I'm local"

   You now know that the local-variable function definitely assigns the value of "I'm local" to the variable var1.

7. To create a global variable, type **(setq var1 "I'm global")** ↵ in the Console. The Console returns:

   "I'm global"

   You know that the value of var1 is now "I'm global".

8. Test the local variable again by typing **(local-variable)** in the Console. The Console returns "I'm local" because it executes the local-variable function.

9. Test the variable var1 to see what its value is now. In the Console, type **var1** ↵. The Console returns "I'm global". The local variable was not retained when the function used the variable because the variable was local to the function. However, the global variable's value persisted.

Working with Visual LISP ActiveX Functions

ActiveX is an interface that exposes objects to the user, a programmer, or an application. AutoLISP supports ActiveX, giving you more information and flexibility in working with your drawings. You can also use ActiveX to work with objects in other Windows applications that support ActiveX. ActiveX is a *programming interface* that is used within a programming language that supports it. For example, you can also use ActiveX with Visual Basic for Applications (see the next chapter) and C++.

 In ActiveX, objects are structured in a hierarchy. You need to understand this structure before working extensively with ActiveX. Chapter 37 covers this hierarchical structure in more detail.

ActiveX enables you to get information about objects (called *get functions*) and modify them (called *put functions*). The next section first reviews how you create these two functions in AutoLISP.

Reviewing AutoLISP retrieval and modification

In this section, you look at developing a small routine, written in AutoLISP, that mimics ActiveX properties and methods. This will help you to compare how AutoLISP works compared to ActiveX.

To understand Visual LISP's ActiveX features, you need to know how AutoCAD exposes an object's properties in AutoLISP. The following examples work with a line that is 10 units long, and created using the following AutoLISP function:

```
;;; This function creates a line using the AutoLISP
;;; command function and returns nil.
(defun make-aLine ()
  (command "_line" "5,5" "15,5" "")
)
```

 The uppercase letter (in the function name) is used for readability, but you can type all lowercase letters if that's easier for you.

After loading it, you can use this function (that is, draw the line) by typing the following in the Visual LISP Console:

(make-aLine)

As explained in Chapter 35, to retrieve the last object that was created (the line), you use ENTLAST, as shown in the following code fragment. The next expression assigns the value of the last created entity, as an entity name, to the variable LineEntity. To try this out, type the following code in the Console:

(setq LineEntity (entlast))

Visual LISP responds with the entity name. As soon as you receive the entity name, you can use ENTGET to retrieve the object property list of the line entity name. The following code fragment places the property list value in the variable LinePropertyList. If you type the following in the Console and press Enter, Visual LISP responds with the property list:

(setq LinePropertyList (entget LineEntity))

Here is an example of a property list, which is formatted for readability:

```
((-1 . <Entity name: 1456d60>)
 (0 . "LINE")
```

```
(330 . <Entity name: 1456cf8>)
(5 . "2C")
(100 . "AcDbEntity")
(67 . 0)
(410 . "Model")
(8 . "0")
(100 . "AcDbLine")
(10 5.0 5.0 0.0)
(11 15.0 5.0 0.0)
(210 0.0 0.0 1.0))
```

As you can see, ENTGET returns an entity's properties as a collection of lists, all of which have a distinctive number at their first position. Some of these group codes (also commonly known as DXF fields, because you can also find them in DXF files) were listed in Table 35-2 in Chapter 35. For this exercise, you just need to remember that the 10 group code is associated with the start point of a line.

Having the entity list and knowing which values to retrieve, you can use the AutoLISP function ASSOC, which returns an associated item from a property list.

To retrieve the start point of the line, you would use the following code, which you can type in the Console:

```
(setq StartofLineList (assoc 10 LinePropertyList))
```

The Console returns the list that is associated with the 10 group code, including the group code and the coordinates:

```
(10 5.0 5.0 0.0)
```

Because the only value that you require is the start point of the line object, use the function CDR to remove the first element of the list, as shown in the following code.

```
(setq StartofLine (cdr (assoc 10 LinePropertyList)))
```

This code returns only the start point coordinate:

```
(5.0 5.0 0.0)
```

This review of how to retrieve a value from an AutoCAD object shows that retrieving information from an associated list is relatively straightforward. But how about retrieving more than one property at a time? As you can see from the preceding example, you'd have to repeat the same body of code many times over to retrieve any information. Knowing this, you could write a simple *interface function*, putting together all of the steps that I have just explained, to retrieve any group code — not just the 10 group code — from an object.

> **NOTE** An interface function is a function that hides a complex behavior from the user. The user needs to provide only basic information, but the function uses the information in several steps to obtain the desired result.

An example of an interface function is shown in the following lines:

```
;;; returns any group code value if it is present in the entity
;;; the required parameters are an entity name and a group code.
(defun Get-A-Group-Code (EntityName GroupCode)
 (cdr (assoc GroupCode (entget EntityName)))
 )
```

After you create this function and load it, you can test it out in the Console as follows, using the LineEntity variable that was previously defined:

```
(Get-A-Group-Code LineEntity 10) ↵
(5.0 5.0 0.0)
```

As you can see, the function returns only the value of the 10 group code.

You can refine this small interface by defining a separate 10 group code function, such as the following. The only required parameter is an entity name. The group code is included in the call to Get-A-Group-Code. You could do the same for an 11 group code, if you want.

```
(defun Get-Group-10-Code (anEntityName)
 (Get-A-Group-Code anEntityName 10)
 )
```

After loading, test the function, as follows:

```
(Get-Group-10-Code LineEntity) ↵
```

Visual LISP returns the start point of the line:

```
(5.0 5.0 0.0)
```

These examples summarize how you would create a simple function to get the start point of a line using AutoLISP. What if you need to change an object's property? You can do this by using the functions CONS, SUBST, and ENTMOD, which Chapter 35 covers.

CONS constructs a list. Use it when you want to create new values for a group code within an entity list, as in the following example, which you can type in the Console window:

(setq NewStartPoint (cons 10 '(0 0 0))) ↵

Visual LISP returns the following:

```
(10 0 0 0)
```

Using the variables NewStartPoint and LinePropertyList, you can now substitute the newly created group 10 code. You do this using the SUBST function. The following code substitutes the new group 10 code that is represented by the variable NewStartPoint for the 10 association in LinePropertyList in the list called LinePropertyList.

```
(Setq LinePropertyList
       (subst NewStartPoint (assoc 10 LinePropertyList)
   LinePropertyList)
   )
```

To test this out, type the preceding code in the Console window. To see the new start point, you need to scroll all the way to the right. The list (nicely formatted here) now has a new group 10 value (the start point), shown on the third-to-last line that follows:

```
((-1 . <Entity name: 1456d60>)
 (0 . "LINE")
 (330 . <Entity name: 1456cf8>)
 (5 . "2C")
 (100 . "AcDbEntity")
```

```
(67 . 0)
(410 . "Model")
(8 . "0")
(100 . "AcDbLine")
(10 0 0 0)
(11 15.0 5.0 0.0)
(210 0.0 0.0 1.0))
```

To reflect the modification of this line in AutoCAD, you can now use the function ENTMOD, by typing it in the Console, as follows. This code actually changes the start point of the line. (You can return to AutoCAD to check it out.)

```
(entmod LinePropertyList) ↵
```

As you can see from this example, getting object properties and modifying them can be a tedious and time-consuming process. Here is an example of an interface function that modifies any group code that is contained in any object.

```
(defun put-group-code-value (Entityname Groupcode Value /
  PropertyList)
(setq PropertyList (entget EntityName))
(setq PropertyList
    (subst
    (cons GroupCode Value)
    (assoc GroupCode PropertyList)
    PropertyList
    )
)
(entmod PropertyList)
)
```

This function combines all of the preceding steps into one function. Here's how it works:

- **Line 1** defines the function with three arguments: the entity name, a group code, and a new value for the group code. It also declares a local variable, PropertyList, which is the property list of the object.
- **Line 2** sets the property list equal to the ENTGET of the entity name.
- **Line 3** starts the process of setting the same property list to the new value.
- **Lines 4 through 7** execute the substitution. They substitute the new group, created by (cons GroupCode Value), for the current group value, created with the ASSOC function, in the property list named PropertyList.
- **Line 8** closes the SUBST function.
- **Line 9** closes the second SETQ function.
- **Line 10** modifies the drawing database using ENTMOD.
- **Line 11** closes the DEFUN function.

Using the preceding function, you now have a much simpler interface for modifying any group code. Next, you use the function Put-Group-Code-Value to modify the 10 group code of the line object.

After entering and loading the preceding function, you can test the function by typing the following in the Console:

```
(Put-Group-Code-Value LineEntity 10 '(5 5 0))
```

This function changes the start point of the line to 5,5,0.

Using the same logic to write the GET functions, you can now define a separate 10 group code modifier function. You can do the same for any group code.

```
(defun Put-Group-10-Code (EntityName Value)
  (Put-Group-Code-Value EntityName 10 Value)
)
```

After entering and loading this function, type the following in the Console to change the start point of the line to 15,–5,0.

```
(Put-Group-10-Code LineEntity '( 15 -5 0 ))
```

Activate AutoCAD to check that the line has been changed.

Using ActiveX with Visual LISP

ActiveX enables you to retrieve and modify objects similar to the method used in the previous section of this chapter, but it requires some preparation. The following section explains how you can use ActiveX functions to create, retrieve, and modify an object.

Retrieving and modifying object information with ActiveX

Visual LISP enables you to retrieve and modify any AutoCAD object using AutoCAD's ActiveX interface. That is to say, AutoCAD exposes all of its objects to ActiveX-enabled applications. This includes Visual LISP as ActiveX objects, all of which expose their properties, including PUT (modify) and GET (retrieve) functions.

Using Visual LISP to communicate with AutoCAD is very straightforward. You must first load all of the ActiveX functions using the VL-LOAD-COM function within Visual LISP. You need to load the VL-LOAD-COM function only once each time that you open AutoCAD, because VL-LOAD-COM loads the ActiveX functions for the entire drawing session. (However, using VL-LOAD-COM more than once doesn't cause any harm.) To load VL-LOAD-COM, enter it in the Visual LISP console window:

```
(vl-load-com)
```

After the ActiveX interface is loaded, you can interrogate the line that you created previously, but first you need to convert the entity name into a vla-object. A vla-object is no different from an entity name, except that the ActiveX object exposes certain properties that its AutoLISP counterpart does not. To convert the entity name into a vla-object, you use the function VLAX-ENAME->VLA-OBJECT, as shown here:

```
(setq vla-line (vlax-ename->vla-object (entlast)))
```

Visual LISP returns the following (your object name will be different):

```
#<VLA-OBJECT IAcadLine 03612b14>
```

As you can see by the return value of vlax-ename->vla-object, the value of the variable vla-line contains a vla-object. At this point, you can visually inspect the variable by selecting it and choosing View ➪ Inspect. Although you see the line's property in a dialog box, you can also "dump" its property and values to the Console by using the VLAX-DUMP-OBJECT Visual LISP function as follows:

```
(vlax-dump-object vla-line)
```

1145

This causes Visual LISP to display the following:

```
;  IAcadLine: AutoCAD Line Interface
;  Property values:
;    Angle (RO) = 1.5708
;    Application (RO) = #<VLA-OBJECT IAcadApplication 00af9594>
;    Delta (RO) = (0.0 10.0 0.0)
;    Document (RO) = #<VLA-OBJECT IAcadDocument 038be900>
;    EndPoint = (15.0 5.0 0.0)
;    Handle (RO) = "89"
;    HasExtensionDictionary (RO) = 0
;    Hyperlinks (RO) = #<VLA-OBJECT IAcadHyperlinks 01011d44>
;    Layer = "0"
;    Length (RO) = 10.0
;    Linetype = "ByLayer"
;    LinetypeScale = 1.0
;    Lineweight = -1
;    Normal = (0.0 0.0 1.0)
;    ObjectID (RO) = 2130009736
;    ObjectName (RO) = "AcDbLine"
;    OwnerID (RO) = 2130009336
;    PlotStyleName = "ByLayer"
;    StartPoint = (15.0 -5.0 0.0)
;    Thickness = 0.0
;    TrueColor = #<VLA-OBJECT IAcadAcCmColor 01015170>
;    Visible = -1
T
```

You'll probably have to resize the window to see all of these properties. Notice the similarities between the named properties shown here, such as EndPoint and StartPoint, and the line's group codes that you retrieve using AutoLISP. As you can see, one of the advantages of using an ActiveX-enabled object is that ActiveX exposes more information to the programmer than standard AutoLISP. One of the benefits of using ActiveX is its interface. Previously, you queried and modified a line object's start point and endpoint by using the 10 and 11 group codes. Using ActiveX to query the start point and endpoint is very straightforward. However, ActiveX returns these points in a data type called a *variant* that you need to convert to the familiar coordinate format.

To get the start point of an object, you use the VLA-GET-STARTPOINT function. In the current example, the line has been set to vla-line, and so you would type the following expression:

(setq Starting (vla-get-startpoint vla-line)) ↵

Visual LISP responds as follows:

```
#<variant 8197 ...>
```

To convert the start point from the variant data type to a usable coordinate format, you would type the following line:

(safearray-value (vlax-variant-value Starting))

Visual LISP responds with a coordinate:

```
(15.0 -5.0 0.0)
```

To modify the StartPoint property of a line to (0,0,0), you would use the following expression:

```
(vla-put-startpoint vla-line (vlax-3d-point '(0 0 0)))
```

You can return to AutoCAD to check out the line. To verify the new StartPoint, you can also use the VLA-GET-STARTPOINT function:

```
(safearray-value (vlax-variant-value (vla-get-StartPoint vla-line)))
```

Visual LISP returns the start point of the line:

```
(0.0 0.0 0.0)
```

As you can see, this is very similar to the small routine that was developed in AutoLISP earlier in this chapter.

STEPS: Retrieving and Modifying Objects with ActiveX

1. To start a new drawing session, open AutoCAD. If AutoCAD is already open, close and re-open it.
2. Start a new drawing using the `acad.dwt` template.
3. Draw any line. Neither the start point nor the endpoint should be 0,0,0.
4. Choose Tools ⇨ AutoLISP ⇨ Visual LISP Editor.
5. In the Console window, type (**vl-load-com**) ↵ to load the ActiveX functions.
6. To convert the entity name into a vla-object, type (**setq vla-line (vlax-ename->vla-object (entlast)**)) ↵.
7. To view the line's properties, type (**vlax-dump-object vla-line**) ↵.
8. To get the start point of the line, type (**setq Starting (vla-get-startpoint vla-line**)) ↵.
9. To convert the start point from the variant data type to coordinate format, type (**safearray-value (vlax-variant-value Starting**)) ↵.
10. To change the line's start point to 0,0,0, type (**vla-put-startpoint vla-line (vlax-3d-point '(0 0 0)**)) ↵.
11. Choose Activate AutoCAD on the Visual LISP View toolbar to check out the line. Its start point is now 0,0,0.

Creating objects with ActiveX

This section looks at functions that create objects. When you work with ActiveX, you need to retrieve objects in their hierarchical order. This hierarchy concept is discussed in more detail in the next chapter. For this chapter, you need to know that before you can retrieve an object, you need to retrieve the following:

- **Acad-object:** Represents the AutoCAD application.
- **ActiveDocument:** Represents your drawing.
- **ModelSpace/PaperSpace:** Represents the type of space that you want to use within the AutoCAD application.

In AutoLISP, you first retrieve the space (model or paper), then your drawing, and finally the AutoCAD application. Here you take the simple line command used earlier in this chapter and convert it using ActiveX:

```
;;; This function creates a line using Visual LISP
;;; ActiveX and returns the line object as a vla-object.
```

```
(defun ax-make-aLine ()
  (vla-AddLine
    (vla-get-ModelSpace                 ; retrieve the model
                                        ; space object
      (vla-get-ActiveDocument           ; get the current
                                        ; active document
        (vlax-get-acad-object)          ; get the acad object
      )
    )
    (vlax-3d-point '(5 5 0))            ; starting point
    (vlax-3d-point '(15 5 0))          ; ending point
  )
)
```

You can type this code in the Visual LISP Editor and load it. To try it out, type the following in the Console:

(ax-make-aLine)

Visual LISP responds with the following:

```
#<VLA-OBJECT IAcadLine 03614934>
```

This might seem a little cumbersome — as if it might be a lot of work to create a line — but it's actually quite flexible.

To locate other ActiveX functions that create objects, you need to look in the AutoCAD ActiveX and VBA Reference. In Visual LISP, choose Help, Visual LISP Help Topics. From the Contents tab, double-click ActiveX and VBA Reference, and then Methods. You immediately see an alphabetical list with the A's displayed. Here are all of the VBA methods that add drawing objects. To create a Visual LISP function, add VLA-before the method. For example, to add a circle, you would use VLA-AddCircle.

 You immediately know whether the function is correct, because it turns from black to blue as you enter it.

Debugging Code

Because few people can write perfect code on their first try, there's always a need to *debug* code. Debugging is simply the process of trying to locate and correct mistakes. This section looks at some simple examples, using some of the debugging tools that Visual LISP has to offer.

In the first example, you define a function that is guaranteed to fail. You can type this code in the Visual LISP editor and load it:

```
;;; The function below will produce an error
;;; because strcat concatenates strings.
(defun Error-Prone-Code ()
  (strcat "This is will never print the number: " 1)
)
```

Before you continue, you need to choose Debug ⇨ Break on Error. When you select this menu option, Visual LISP enables you to jump to the error in your source code automatically.

Using the function `Error-Prone-Code` produces an error because `strcat` concatenates strings, as the following demonstrates. You can type this at the console:

> **(Error-Prone-Code)** ⏎

Visual LISP responds with the following:

> ; error: bad argument type: stringp 1

 After you receive the error, choose Last Break on the Debug toolbar. Visual LISP places you in the line of the code where the error occurred.

How can you find the source of the problem in a routine? To answer this question, you often need to perform some detective work. Visual LISP provides a wealth of debugging tools, which you can leverage when you encounter an unplanned "enhancement" or bug.

STEPS: Finding the Last Break

1. Start a drawing in AutoCAD using the `acad.dwt` template.
2. Start Visual LISP and start a new file.
3. In the Visual LISP Editor, type the following:

```
;;; The function add-3-numbers will not produce
;;; an error if all of its arguments are numbers.
(defun add-3-numbers (num1 num2 num3)
   (+ num1 num2 num3)
)
```

4. Choose Load Active Edit Window on the Tools toolbar.
5. In the Console window, type the following:

```
(add-3-numbers 1 2 3) ⏎
```

Visual LISP returns 6.

6. However, if you substitute a string for one of its arguments, an error occurs. Type the following in the Console window:

```
(add-3-numbers 1 "a" 3)⏎
```

Visual LISP returns the following:

```
error: bad argument type: numberp: "a"
```

7. Choose Debug ➪ Break on Error. Look again to confirm that Break on Error is checked.
8. Choose Last Break on the Debug toolbar. Visual LISP places you in the function `add-3-numbers`, with `(+ num1 num2 num3)` as the cause of the error.

To continue after turning on Break on Error, click Reset on the Debug toolbar.

Using the Error Trace window

Any time an error occurs, you can use the last break along with the Visual LISP Error Trace window. To display the Error Trace window, choose View ➪ Error Trace to see an error list, as shown in Figure 36.1.

FIGURE 36.1

To help you debug your code, the Error Trace window displays every function call before the error, as well as where the error occurred.

```
Error trace                                    ⊠
<1> :ERROR-BREAK
[2] (+ 1 "a" 3)
[3] (ADD-3-NUMBERS 1 "a" 3)
[4] (#<USUBR @02c6f9b0 -top->)
<5> :USER-INPUT (add-3-numbers 1 "a" 3
<6> :CALLBACK-ENTRY
[7] (C:VLIDE)
<8> :CALLBACK-ENTRY
<9> :ARQ-SUBR-CALLBACK
```

The item numbered <5> in Figure 36.1 is what you entered in the Console. The item labeled [2] (+ 1 "a" 3) is where the error occurred, while <1> :ERROR-BREAK signaled the function's termination because of the error.

Visual LISP enables you to find the source *position* (the line of code that produced the error) and the *call source point* (the position in your code where the function was called) for the error. To find them, right-click the third item in the Error Trace window. From the shortcut menu, you can choose either Source Position or Call Source Point. Jumping to the position in your code where the function was called is extremely handy when debugging a large application.

Working with break points

Sometimes when you choose Last Break to highlight an error, you find that a great deal of code is highlighted, which is not very helpful for finding the error. This is where break points come in handy. *Break points* are locations in your code, specified by you, that signal Visual LISP to stop and wait until you're ready to continue processing the code. Visual LISP executes your code and stops at each break point to wait for your instructions. Break points enable you to break down your code into smaller pieces and watch what's going on piece-by-piece so that you can more easily find the error.

To place a break point, position your cursor to the left of an opening parenthesis or to the right of a closing parenthesis, and press F9. Visual LISP places a temporary red mark in your code.

After creating your break points, you need to reload your code to tell Visual LISP about your break points. Then try to execute the function again. Notice that the Debug toolbar buttons become available. Visual LISP executes your code up to the first break point.

You can now use the Debug toolbar to help find your error. The first three buttons offer three different ways to move through your code:

 ■ **Step Into:** Use this button to "step in" one expression from the innermost nested expression (from opening to closing parentheses) to the outermost, one at a time.

 ■ **Step Over:** Use this button to ignore the nested expressions; that is, step over the highlighted expression.

 ■ **Step Out:** Use this button to move to the end of the function. You can ignore the entire function that is being debugged.

To remove break points, choose View ➪ Breakpoints Window. The Breakpoints dialog box opens, as shown in Figure 36.2.

FIGURE 36.2

Use the Breakpoints dialog box to remove, show, or disable break points.

In the Breakpoints dialog box, you can do the following:

- Delete all break points by clicking Delete all.
- Delete individual break points by choosing a break point and clicking Delete.
- Jump to a break point by choosing a break point and clicking Show. Visual LISP places a blinking cursor at the break point.
- Edit a break point by choosing a break point and clicking Edit. Visual LISP then lets you disable, delete, or show the break point.

ON the DVD-ROM The file used in the following exercise on working with break points, `ab36-a.lsp`, is in the `Drawings` folder on the DVD.

STEPS: Working with Break Points

1. Open AutoCAD and start a drawing using any template.
2. Start the Visual LISP Editor. Open `ab36-a.lsp` from the DVD. Choose File ➪ Save As and save it as `ab36-01.lsp` in the `AutoCAD 2008\Support` folder or in another folder that you've added to the support file search path.
3. Choose Load Active Edit Window from the Tools toolbar.
4. Read through the code. This routine creates a vertical list of numbers. The new FOREACH function steps through each item in a list. The comments explain why it contains a bug.
5. If you didn't do the previous exercise, choose Debug ➪ Break on Error. (Don't do anything if the Break on Error item is already checked.)
6. Type the following in the Console window:

```
(list-beautify-with-bug '(1 2 3 4 5 )) ⏎
```

The Console returns the following:

```
(1
; error: bad argument type: FILE 1
```

7. Choose Last Break on the Debug toolbar to jump to the error in the source code.

8. To place a break point in the code, place the cursor after `(princ (chr 40))`. Press F9. Visual LISP marks the break with a red box.

9. Place another break point after `(princ (car aList))`. Finally, place a third break point after the closing parenthesis on the line that follows `(princ item 1)`. Your code should look like Figure 36.3.

Your code should look like this after you place three break points.

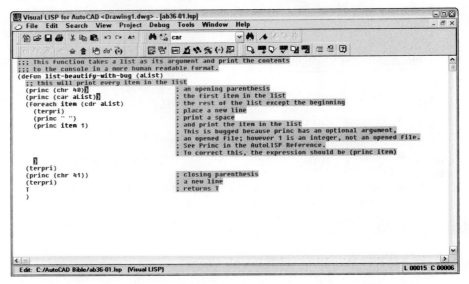

10. After the code produces an error, you need to reset. Click Reset on the Debug toolbar.

11. Click the Visual LISP Editor window and reload the function into Visual LISP. (Choose Load Active Edit Window on the Tools toolbar.)

12. Type the same expression that produced the error in the Console:

`(list-beautify-with-bug '(1 2 3 4 5 ))` ↵

 13. Visual LISP highlights the expression `(princ (chr 40))`. Choose Step Into on the Debug toolbar. Visual LISP highlights `(princ (car aList))`.

14. Choose Step Into. Now only `(car aList)` is highlighted.

15. Choose Step Into until you reach the error, `(princ item 1)`.

16. Edit `(princ item 1)` so that it reads `(princ item)`.

17. Click Reset again.

18. Choose Debug ➪ Clear All Breakpoints. Click Yes to confirm.

19. Activate the Editor window and reload the function.

20. In the Console, type (**list-beautify-with-bug** '(1 2 3 4 5)) ↵.

21. Activate the Editor window and save the file.

 If you have difficulty in fixing this bug, you can find the "repaired" version in the `Results` folder on the DVD, with the filename `list-beautify-without-bug.lsp`.

Using the Watch window

The Watch window enables you to examine expressions and variable values as they're being evaluated. To watch a variable, select it in the code and choose Debug ➪ Add Watch, or press Ctrl+W. Visual LISP opens the Watch window listing the expression or variable and displaying its value after an equal sign. If you select an expression or nothing is selected and you press Ctrl+W, the Add Watch dialog box opens. If it is not already displayed, enter the expression that you want to watch and click OK. For example, if you add a watch for (`princ (chr 40)`), the Watch window displays (`PRINC (CHR 40)`) = "(" because (`princ (chr 40)`) is another way of telling AutoLISP to print a left parenthesis. After the Watch window is open, you can add expressions or variables by selecting them and choosing Add Watch on the Watch window toolbar.

If you have a routine with arguments, you can execute the function with various arguments and see the results on your watched expressions and variables in the Watch window.

Furthermore, you can add any expression to the Watch window and alter the contents of any variable while debugging a function.

 The file used in the following exercise on using the Watch window, `ab36-01.lsp`, is in the `Results` folder on the DVD.

STEPS: Using the Watch Window

1. Open AutoCAD and start a drawing using the `acad.dwt` template.

2. Start the Visual LISP Editor. Open `ab36-01.lsp` from the `Results` folder of the DVD. If you did the previous exercise, you can open it from your `AutoCAD Bible` folder.

3. Select the expression (`princ (chr 40)`). Choose Debug ➪ Add Watch. Click OK in the Add Watch dialog box. Visual LISP opens the Watch window and displays the expression, as well as its value.

 4. To add a variable to the Watch window, select `item` to the right of the FOREACH function and choose Add Watch in the Watch window. The Watch window should look like Figure 36.4.

FIGURE 36.4

The Watch window shows an expression and a variable, and displays their values.

5. Add a break point after (princ item) by placing the cursor there and pressing F9.

6. Choose Load Active Edit Window from the Tools toolbar.

7. To examine the Watch window display as the function list-beautify-with-bug is evaluated, type the following in the Visual LISP Console:

   (list-beautify-with-bug '(1 2 3 4 5)) ↵

8. The (princ item) expression should be highlighted. Choose Step Into on the Debug toolbar. The item variable in the Watch window should now display its current value. Continue to click Step Into, watching the value of item increase in the Watch window each time you step through the cycle.

9. In the Visual LISP console, type **aList** ↵ after the last prompt. This is a variable argument that is used in the function list-beautify-with-bug. The Console returns:

   (1 2 3 4 5)

   As you can see, you can interrogate any variable while debugging the function.

10. To add a new expression to the Watch window, select the variable aList and press Ctrl+W.

11. To change the value of aList, return to the Console window and type the following:

    (setq aList (list 6 7 8 9 10)) ↵

    The Console responds as follows:

    (6 7 8 9 10)

    Notice the change in the Watch window.

12. To remove the break point, choose View ➪ Breakpoints Window to open the Breakpoints dialog box. Click Delete All to delete the break point. Visual LISP automatically closes the dialog box.

13. Click Reset on the Debug toolbar.

14. Close the Watch window and the Visual LISP IDE without saving the file.

As you can see, Visual LISP is not just an editor; it's a full-featured, integrated development environment for AutoLISP.

Summary

In this chapter, you examined some of the advanced features of AutoLISP and Visual LISP. You read about:

- Global and local variables
- Some of the features of ActiveX
- How to use some of Visual LISP's debugging features, including the Error Trace window, break points, and the Watch window

On the DVD, you read about the basics of Visual Basic for Applications, another programming language that you can use with AutoCAD. See Chapter 37 on the DVD.

Part VIII

Appendixes

The three appendixes in Part VIII provide important additional information. Although these appendixes are especially useful when you first start to use AutoCAD 2008 or AutoCAD LT 2008, they offer a great deal of information for ongoing use as well.

Appendix A runs you through the process of installing and configuring AutoCAD and AutoCAD LT to suit your personal needs. Many new features appear in the Options dialog box that I cover here. I also explain the important Workspaces feature.

Appendix B lists numerous additional resources, where you can find information on AutoCAD and AutoCAD LT, including discussion groups, Web sites, and blogs.

Appendix C explains what is on the DVD and how to use the files there.

Appendix A

Installing and Configuring AutoCAD and AutoCAD LT

Installing AutoCAD and AutoCAD LT, once something to avoid as long as possible, is now a breeze. For all practical purposes, all that you need to do is to put the CD-ROM or DVD into your CD-ROM or DVD drive and follow the instructions. Nevertheless, I provide some helpful tips and comments in this appendix. As with all software that comes with an installation program, you should close all other applications before starting, including antivirus software.

In this appendix, I also cover many ways to configure AutoCAD and AutoCAD LT so that these programs function best for your circumstances.

Installing AutoCAD and AutoCAD LT

The installation process involves some preparation, the actual installation, and finally authorization.

Preparing to install

Before you install, make sure that your system meets the minimum, and preferably the recommended, requirements:

- **Operating system:** Windows 2000 SP4; Windows XP (Home, Professional, or Tablet PC) with Service Pack 2; Windows Vista (Home Basic, Enterprise, Business, Home Premium, or Ultimate).

NEW FEATURE AutoCAD 2008 also offers a 64-bit version that is available for Windows XP Professional x64 Edition and for Windows Vista.

- **Processor speed:** III, IV or better, 800 MHz minimum, but I would recommend 2.0 GHz as a minimum. For 3D work, 3.0 GHz or greater is recommended.
- **RAM (memory):** 512MB, but I would recommend 1GB, with 2GB for 3D work; however, 512MB is acceptable for most AutoCAD LT work.

IN THIS APPENDIX

Installing AutoCAD and AutoCAD LT

Configuring workspaces

Creating multiple and customized configurations

Configuring AutoCAD and AutoCAD LT with the Options dialog box

Configuring a plotter

- **Video:** 1024×768 VGA or higher with true color. For 3D work in AutoCAD, you should have at least 128MB of RAM on a Direct3D or Open-GL capable, workstation-class graphics card. Autodesk certifies specific graphics cards for use with AutoCAD's 3D features. To see which cards are certified, use the 3DCONFIG command. In the Adaptive Degradation and Performance Tuning dialog box, click the Check for Update button to go to a Web page on Autodesk's Web site that lists graphics cards and their test results.

NEW FEATURE   Using the 3DCONFIG command, you can now specify either Direct3D or OpenGL hardware acceleration. Windows Vista does not support OpenGL.

NOTE   If your graphics card is not certified, your computer won't explode, but it could crash when using some effects, display artifacts (extra visual effects), or fail to display some features, such as materials and lights.

- **Hard disk:** 750MB free for installation (750MB for 64-bit version); for permanent storage, 750MB for 2D features, 2GB for 3D features, and 550MB for AutoCAD LT
- **Pointing device:** Mouse, trackball, digitizer puck, or other device
- **CD-ROM/DVD drive:** Any speed (for installation only)
- **Browser:** Internet Explorer 6.0 SP1 minimum; in most cases, you can use other browsers as well
- **Optional equipment:** A printer or plotter; a digitizing tablet; a network interface card if you're using the network version of AutoCAD, or Internet-enabled features of AutoCAD

In order to install AutoCAD or AutoCAD LT, you may need administrator permission to write to the folder where you're installing AutoCAD, the system registry, and the Windows System folder.

NOTE   AutoCAD 2008 and AutoCAD LT 2008 can coexist with earlier versions of both programs. When you install, the Migrate Custom Settings feature detects if you have an earlier version on your computer and guides you through the process of migrating custom features. Nevertheless, if you have customized files that you want to keep, it's always good to back them up before installation. To read the ReadMe file before starting to install, use Windows Explorer to open readme.chm from the Docs folder of the AutoCAD 2008 DVD or the AutoCAD LT 2008 CD-ROM. You can also read the ReadMe file during and at the end of installation.

Starting installation

You're now ready to install AutoCAD 2008 or AutoCAD LT 2008. Here are the steps:

1. Place the DVD or CD-ROM in your DVD/CD-ROM drive and close the drive door. In most cases, the setup procedure starts automatically. If it does not, choose Start ➪ Run. In the text box, type **d:\setup ↵** where **d** is your DVD/CD-ROM drive.

2. When the Welcome screen appears, click the type of installation that you want:
   - **Install Products:** One seat (location) standard installation.
   - **Create Deployments:** Set configurations to distribute to client workstations.
   - **Install Tools and Utilities:** Administrative, reporting, and network licensing tools (AutoCAD only). The CAD Manager Tools are also here (and included in AutoCAD LT as well). See the section later in this chapter on the tools and utilities.

3. The Install screen provides links to all of the installation tasks and information that you need, as shown in Figure A.1. In these steps, I clicked Install Products (for a stand-alone installation). You can click the View the Readme button at this point to read that file.

NOTE Some plotter manufacturers, such as Hewlett-Packard, offer a special driver that optimizes the plotter for use with AutoCAD. Check the manufacturer's Web site for the latest driver.

FIGURE A.1

The initial screen of the Installation Wizard.

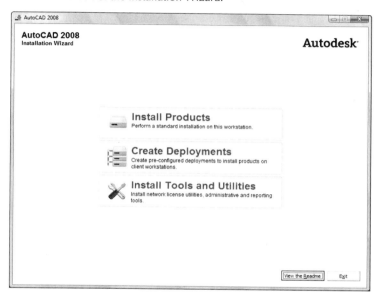

4. The Welcome screen advises you to close applications. Antivirus software can especially be a problem; you should disable it during installation. Click Next.

5. On the next screen, you select the products you want to install. The choices are AutoCAD 2008 or AutoCAD LT 2008 and DWF Viewer. Click Next.

6. Read the software license agreement. Click the Print button if you want to print the agreement. Click "I accept," and then click Next.

7. On the Personalize the Products screen, enter your name and organization. In AutoCAD only, this information is permanent and you can't change it without uninstalling AutoCAD. In AutoCAD LT, you can change this information on the System tab of the Options dialog box (OPTIONS command). Click Next.

8. On the Review-Configure-Install screen you review the installation settings. To use these default values, click Install and wait while the software installs. To change them, click the Configure button. If you chose to configure, note the information pane on the left. You can click these items to get information about your choices before you make them.

9. If you choose to configure, on the Specify User Preferences screen, choose the default text editor. Click Notepad or the Ellipsis button to choose another application. Also choose if you want a desktop shortcut. Click Next. On the next pane, you select the License Type: stand-alone or network license. Click Next. On the last configuration pane, you select the installation type: You can choose typical or custom. You can also choose whether or not to install the Express Tools (highly

recommended) and the material library (used for 3D rendering). If you choose a custom installation, you can choose which of the following items you want by checking or unchecking their check box. Then click Next.

- **CAD Standards:** For more information, see Chapter 26. (AutoCAD only.)
- **Database:** External database connectivity. For more information, see Chapter 20. (AutoCAD only.)
- **Dictionaries:** For more information, see Chapter 13.
- **Drawing encryption:** Password protection. For more information, see Chapter 26. (AutoCAD only.)
- **Express Tools:** Supplemental commands. (AutoCAD only.)
- **Fonts:** For more information, see Chapter 13.
- **Autodesk Impression Toolbar:** Allows you to export a view to Autodesk Impression, another Autodesk product that creates a hand-drawn look.
- **Material Library:** You use materials for rendering. (AutoCAD only.) This item is not checked by default.
- **New Features Workshop:** For more information, see Chapter 1.
- **Portable License Utility:** Tools to transfer a stand-alone license among computers.
- **Migrate Custom Settings**: A utility to help you to keep your custom settings when you upgrade.
- **Reference Manager:** Manages external files connected to a drawing. For more information, see Chapter 27. (AutoCAD only.)
- **Samples:** Sample drawings that you can use for your reference.
- **Tutorials:** Mostly programming tutorials. (AutoCAD only.)
- **VBA:** Support. Microsoft Visual Basic for Application support files. (AutoCAD only.)

You can go back later and add items if you decide that you need an item that you didn't initially install. When you're done, click Configuration Complete. You return to the Review-Configure-Install pane. Click Install. This takes a few minutes. You can take a break or watch the status bar that appears during the process.

10. You're now done, and you have an opportunity to read the README file — always a good idea — by checking the appropriate check box. Click Finish. The README file opens if you have asked for it. (If you want to read it later, in AutoCAD or AutoCAD LT choose Help ⇨ Help and click the Contents tab. Then choose User's Guide ⇨ Get Information ⇨ Find the Information You Need ⇨ View the Product Readme.)

 You may see a dialog box asking you to restart your computer. Because you shouldn't have any other applications open, you can do so immediately.

Don't forget to re-enable your antivirus software.

You're done! You can now choose Start ⇨ (All) Programs ⇨ Autodesk ⇨ AutoCAD 2008 or AutoCAD LT 2008 to see the sub-menu. The sub-menu includes some or all of the following items:

- **Attach Digital Signatures:** A security feature for attaching a digital signature to a drawing (see Chapter 26).
- **AutoCAD 2008 or AutoCAD LT 2008:** Starts AutoCAD or AutoCAD LT.
- **Batch Standards Checker:** Checks CAD standards for a group of drawings (see Chapter 26). (AutoCAD only.)

- **Portable License Utility:** Helps you move a license from one computer to another.
- **Reference Manager:** Manages and reports on xrefs, images, and other files associated with a drawing (see Chapter 26). (AutoCAD only.)
- **Migrate Custom Settings:** Contains the Migrate From a Previous Release item that launches the Migrate Custom Settings dialog box to help you to keep your custom settings as you upgrade. This stand-alone application usually runs automatically when you install the software. From the sub-menu, you can also select items that allows you to import and export custom settings between different computers running the same release.

NEW FEATURE The Import and Export Custom Settings tools are new. You can export setting and files for use on another computer. You can then import those settings to the destination computer.

Installing network licenses and CAD Manager tools

If you have multiple licenses, you may want to use the network license utilities. Network licenses allow you to more flexibly manager multiple seats of AutoCAD. At the first screen of the Installation Wizard, choose Install Tools and Utilities. Here you can install the Network License Manager and Network License Activation Utility. There's also a reporting utility, SAMreport-Lite, for tracking network license usage.

The Autodesk CAD Manager Tools 4.0 feature allows CAD Managers to control certain general features of AutoCAD and AutoCAD LT, including which content is available in the Communication Center. This feature is therefore essential for stand-alone installations as well.

Check the items that you want to install and click Next. Then follow the instructions, which vary according to your choices. For information about networking licensing, click the Documentation link on the installation screen and open the Network Licensing Guide. There are also guides for stand-alone installations.

Changing an installation

After you install AutoCAD or AutoCAD LT, you can add features by using the following procedure:

1. Choose Start ➪ Settings ➪ Control Panel (or Start ➪ Control Panel) and double-click Add/Remove Programs, Add or Remove Programs, or Uninstall a Program (depending on your version of Windows). (If you're not using the Classic view, you need to choose a category first, such as Programs.)
2. In the dialog box, choose AutoCAD 2008 or AutoCAD LT 2008 and then click Change, Change/Remove, or Uninstall/Change (depending on your version of Windows).
3. The software Setup Initialization feature starts. Click Add or Remove Features.
4. In the dialog box, check a feature, or uncheck an existing feature. Click Next.
5. Click Next again. The software is updated.
6. Click Finish.

You may be prompted to restart your computer.

Authorizing AutoCAD and AutoCAD LT

As with earlier versions, for security purposes, Autodesk requires that you activate AutoCAD and AutoCAD LT. (Certain customers, such as subscription customers, are exempt from the activation process.) When you first open AutoCAD or AutoCAD LT, the Product Activation dialog box opens. First, enter your serial number or Group ID. You receive this number with your product or subscription.

Then choose to activate the software or run it without activating it, while you're waiting for an activation code. To activate and register, leave the Activate the Product option checked and click Next. Then choose Get an Activation Code or Enter an Activation Code. Click Next and follow the instructions for your choice.

You can use the product for 30 days while waiting for the activation code. When you get it, choose the Enter an Activation Code option and either paste it from the Clipboard or type it in.

AutoCAD or AutoCAD LT is now ready to use. By default, your system is configured to use the current system pointing device and the current system printing device. You can further configure AutoCAD by choosing Tools ⇨ Options and using the Options dialog box. This dialog box is covered in detail later in this appendix.

NOTE If you installed the Express Tools, then the Express Tools menu and toolbars are automatically installed. Express Tools includes three toolbars. To display these toolbars, right-click in any toolbar area that doesn't contain a toolbar, such as the area to the right of the Standard Annotation toolbar. Choose Express and then choose a toolbar from the sub-menu. This applies to AutoCAD only.

If your Express Tools don't appear, you may need to activate them. Enter expresstools ⏎ on the command line. If the Express menu doesn't appear, enter expressmenu ⏎.

When you first open AutoCAD or AutoCAD LT, if you have an earlier version of AutoCAD or AutoCAD LT on your system, the Migrate Custom Settings dialog box opens. This gives you a chance to keep many of your custom settings. Choose the options that you want to keep.

Also when you start AutoCAD or AutoCAD LT for the first time, the New Features Workshop opens. You can choose to view it right away, later (meaning that it opens each time you start the program), or not at all. You can always access it by choosing Help ⇨ New Features Workshop. The tutorials review the basics of new features, as shown in Figure A.2.

FIGURE A.2

The New Features Workshop contains explanations, tutorials, and videos to help you learn about new capabilities.

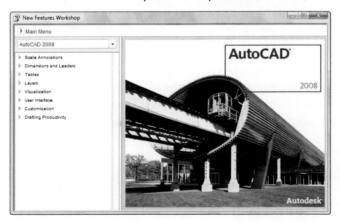

Configuring and Using Workspaces

A *workspace* is a configuration of toolbars, menus, and dockable windows (palettes, including the Dashboard, and the command line window). You can create workspaces so that you can quickly switch from one configuration to another. For example, when you are drawing in 3D, you might want the Modeling toolbar and the Dashboard displayed. On the other hand, when you are creating, organizing, and saving blocks, you might want the DesignCenter and Tool Palettes window displayed.

AutoCAD comes with three default workspaces: AutoCAD Classic, 2D Drafting & Annotation, and 3D Modeling. AutoCAD LT comes with two workspaces, 2D Drafting & Annotation and AutoCAD LT Classic. In many cases, you will want to change these workspaces to suit your drawing needs.

Creating and modifying a workspace

The easiest way to create a workspace is to display toolbars, menus, and palettes the way you want them, and then choose Save Current As from the drop-down list of the Workspaces toolbar, shown in Figure A.3. In the Save Workspace dialog box, name the workspace and then click Save. You can use this same method to modify an existing workspace. Make the changes and choose the current workspace in the Name drop-down list of the Save Workspace dialog box. Click Save, and then Click Yes when asked whether you want to replace the workspace.

FIGURE A.3

The Workspaces toolbar makes changing and saving workspaces easy.

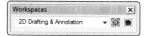

If you want to make sure that you don't forget anything, you can use the Customize User Interface dialog box. This method lets you pick and choose from the complete list of menus, toolbars, and dockable windows. Follow these steps:

1. Type **cui** ↵ to open the Customize User Interface dialog box.
2. In the Customizations In All CUI Files pane, double-click the Workspaces item to expand it.
3. To create a new workspace, right-click the Workspaces item and choose New Workspace. Then choose the new workspace to specify its settings. To edit an existing workspace, choose that workspace. The Workspace Contents pane appears to the right.
4. In the Workspace Contents pane, click the Customize Workspace button. All the menus and toolbars in the Customizations In pane now have check boxes next to them.
5. To add (display) or remove (hide) toolbars, menus, and dashboard panels, expand those items. Check or clear checkboxes to specify which toolbars, menus, and dashboard panels you want to display or hide for that workspace. Don't forget to expand the Partial CUI Files item so that you can specify the toolbars, menus, and dashboard panels for those files as well. As you add or remove items, they appear or disappear from the list in the Workspace Contents pane.

6. To specify the details of how each item should appear, click the item to show its properties in the Properties pane, where you can edit such properties as the location of a toolbar, its orientation (floating or docked), and its X and Y position. You can't edit menu properties.

7. To specify dockable window settings, which don't appear in the Customizations In All CUI Files pane, double-click the Palettes item in the Workspace Contents pane. Choose any window to edit its properties in the Properties pane.

8. To save your changes, click the Customize Workspace button at the top of the Workspace Contents pane.

9. Click OK to close the Customize User Interface dialog box.

Switching between workspaces

To switch between workspaces, choose Tools ➪ Workspaces and choose from the list of saved workspaces, or choose a workspace from the Workspaces toolbar.

If you make changes to the interface display, such as displaying a toolbar, this change does not automatically become part of the workspace. However, AutoCAD remembers that last state of the interface, and if you close and re-open AutoCAD, that toolbar is displayed.

You can specify that you want to save changes that you make to the interface display to the workspace. Choose Tools ➪ Workspaces ➪ Workspace Settings to open the Workspace Settings dialog box. Choose the Automatically Save Workspace Changes option and click OK. If you want to choose which changes are saved, keep the default Do Not Save Changes to Workspace option, and manually modify the current workspace, replacing the current one, as explained in the previous section. You can also use the Workspace Settings dialog box to organize the list of workspaces, by changing their order in the list and adding separators to group certain workspaces together.

Use the My Workspace drop-down list in the dialog box to assign a workspace to the My Workspace button on the Workspaces toolbar. This button makes it easy to return to the workspace of your choice at any time, without using the drop-down list.

You can control AutoCAD's settings (but not AutoCAD LT's) with profiles, which are different from workspaces. I discuss profiles later in this appendix.

Configuring AutoCAD and AutoCAD LT

AutoCAD and AutoCAD LT have many options and settings that you can modify to suit your particular needs. Because you usually configure the software once when you first install, and only go back to these settings occasionally, it is easy to forget them. Knowing the available options is worthwhile; sometimes these options can make your life so much easier.

Customizing the status bar

You can customize what appears in the status bar of the application window. For example, if you never use lineweights, you can remove the LWT button on the status bar.

To customize the status bar, click the down arrow at the right end of the status bar to display the status bar menu. Click any item to hide the item if it's checked or to display the item if it isn't checked. For each additional item, you need to click the down arrow again to re-open the menu.

Configuring options

You configure the application using the Options dialog box. Choose Apply to configure a setting and keep the dialog box open. Choose OK to configure a setting and close the dialog box.

NOTE   In the Options dialog box, items that are saved with the drawing display the blue and yellow drawing icon next to them. These settings change when you open other drawings that have different settings. Other settings are saved in the Windows Registry and do not change from drawing to drawing.

Take the time to browse through all of the tabs in the Options dialog box so that you know what is available. You change many of these settings only rarely after the initial run-through. Choose Tools ➪ Options to open the Options dialog box.

TIP   A quick way to access the Options dialog box is to right-click in the drawing or command line areas with no objects selected, and choose Options.

The Files tab

The Files tab lets you configure search paths, as well as specify file names and locations. You'll probably most often use the Support File Search Path, which contains a listing of the folders that AutoCAD uses to search for menus, fonts, linetypes, and hatch patterns. Rather than add your customized menus, hatches, and so on to an existing support folder, you can create a folder especially for these files and add the folder to the Support File Search Path.

The default location for support files is the first listing under the Support File Search Path item. This location may vary, depending on your operating system. However, you can also use `Program Files\ AutoCAD 2008\Support` or `Program Files\AutoCAD LT 2008\Support`, which is listed as one of the support locations.

As you click an item in the main listing of the dialog box, you see an explanation at the bottom. To edit the item, double-click the item or click the plus sign to the left of the item. You can then click a sub-item and remove it, or click Add to add a sub-item. Click Browse to find a folder or file rather than type it. Some other commonly used settings on the File tab are:

- **Project Files Search Path:** The search path for xrefs. (AutoCAD only.)
- **Automatic Save File Location:** Where the software automatically saves files if you don't.
- **Template Settings:** Default locations for various templates. You can set the default template for the QNEW command here. When you do so, clicking the QNew button on the Standard toolbar automatically opens a new drawing with this template.

The Display tab

The Display tab, shown in Figure A.4, contains settings related to the display that you see on your screen.

The Windows Elements section determines whether you see scroll bars, the screen menu, large toolbar buttons, and tooltips. (The screen menu is not available in AutoCAD LT.) You can also set the colors and fonts for the various screen elements. For example, by clicking Colors, you can change the background color of the Model or Layout tabs.

NOTE   AutoCAD 2008 contains special background settings for 3D environments, with separate settings for parallel and perspective projections.

FIGURE A.4

The Display tab of the Options dialog box.

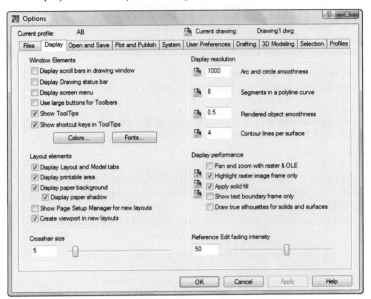

The Layout Elements section creates display settings for paper space layouts. Most are checked by default. You can set the following items:

- The Display Layout and Model Tabs option determines if you see the tabs at the bottom of the drawing area. By default, this check box is checked in AutoCAD 2008. If you uncheck this box, you see the Model and Layout buttons on the status bar. You can switch between these settings without using the Options dialog box, by right-clicking the tabs or the buttons.

- Uncheck the Display Printable Area option to hide the dashed line that you usually see around a layout. The dashed line represents the margin of the paper and, therefore, shows you the printable area.

- Uncheck the Display Paper Background option to avoid seeing the edge of the paper and the gray background. This setting makes a layout tab look very much like the model tab. If this item is checked, you can uncheck the Display Paper Shadow item to get rid of the shadow effect that makes the paper look like it's slightly above the surface of the gray background.

- Check the Show Page Setup Manager for New Layouts option to display the Page Setup Manager when you click a new layout tab. (See Chapter 17 for information on the Page Setup Manager.) This item is unchecked by default.

- Uncheck the Create Viewport in New Layouts option to display layouts with no viewport. This setting is useful if you always want to set up your own viewport configurations.

The Crosshair Size section sets the size of the crosshairs as a percentage of the entire screen. The default is 5. You can type a new number in the text box or drag the slider bar. To create crosshairs that cover the entire screen, use a setting of 100.

The Display Resolution section sets arc and circle smoothness (also accessible using the VIEWRES command), the number of segments in a polyline curve (the SPLINESEGS system variable), rendered object smoothness (the FACETRES system variable), and contour lines per surface (the ISOLINES system variable). The last two items are not available in AutoCAD LT, because they apply to 3D objects.

The Display Performance section offers settings that you can use to increase display speed. For example, several settings affect the way AutoCAD displays raster images. You can turn off FILLMODE, which applies solid fill in wide polylines, donuts, and hatched objects. AutoCAD LT has only the text boundary and solid fill items.

The Reference Edit fading intensity setting applies to objects during in-place reference editing. This setting affects how much objects that you are *not* editing are faded, compared to objects that you *are* editing. The default is 50 percent. For more information, see Chapter 19. This setting applies to AutoCAD only.

The Open and Save tab

The Open and Save tab, shown in Figure A.5, contains settings related to opening the program and files, as well as saving drawings.

FIGURE A.5

The Open and Save tab.

The File Save section specifies the default drawing type and whether or not a thumbnail preview image is saved. You can see this preview when you want to open a new drawing and set the view to Preview. You can separately specify thumbnails for sheet sets.

Annotative scaling is a new feature in AutoCAD 2008 and AutoCAD LT 2008 that is not supported in older releases. As a result, an option has been added to specially preserve those scales when opening the file in older versions of AutoCAD and AutoCAD LT. When you check Maintain Visual Fidelity for Annotative Objects, each scale representation of your annotative objects is saved as a separate block on a separate layer. These layers are automatically frozen according to which annotation scale is current (visible). If you don't use this option, the older drawing will only have objects from the annotative scale on the Model tab. More objects could appear in model space (depending on the ANNOALLVISIBLE system variable) and paper space viewports in varying sizes. This option is checked by default to facilitate using annotative objects in earlier releases.

Setting the Incremental Save percentage enables you to control when AutoCAD or AutoCAD LT saves the entire drawing, as opposed to just your changes — an incremental save. The default is 50 percent, which avoids too many long, full saves.

In the File Safety Precautions section, set the default time between automatic saves. The other settings in this section are:

- **Create Backup Copy with Each Save:** By default, AutoCAD and AutoCAD LT create backup drawings whenever you save a drawing. Backup drawings have the same name as your drawing, but with an extension of .bak. Although you probably spend some time erasing these drawings, they can be very useful if a drawing becomes corrupted. You can change their extension to .dwg and open them as drawing files. However, you can also turn off this feature. Unfortunately, you can't control where the backup files are stored.

- **Full-Time CRC Validation:** Check this item if data that you import is becoming corrupted and you suspect a hardware problem. A cyclic redundancy check performs a validation during the importing process and can help you troubleshoot this problem. (AutoCAD Only.)

- **Maintain a Log File:** Keeps a log file that records the contents of the text window. Each time you work in AutoCAD, the new material is added to the end of the existing log file, and so you should periodically edit or delete material from the log file. Use the Files tab to control the log file location.

- **File Extension for Temporary Files:** Sets the filename extension for temporary files that are created while you're working. By default, the extension for these files is .ac$. Use the Files tab to control the temporary file location.

Use the Security Options button to set options for passwords and digital signatures. See Chapter 26 for more details. AutoCAD LT doesn't include the password feature.

In the File Open section, you can set how many of the most recently used drawings you want to see at the bottom of the File menu. The default is nine, which is also the maximum setting. You can also choose whether or not you want to see the full path on the File menu listing and on the application window title bar.

In the External References (Xrefs) section, you can turn on and off demand loading of external references. When the Retain Changes to Xref Layers setting is checked (which it is by default), any changes that you made to xref layer properties and states (such as freezing a layer) are saved. When you reopen the drawing containing the xref, these changes are retained. Finally, in AutoCAD only, you can set whether the current drawing can be edited in-place when someone else is referencing it. For more information, see Chapter 19.

In the ObjectARX Applications section (AutoCAD only), you have settings related to ObjectARX applications and proxy graphics created by ObjectARX applications. ObjectARX is a programming interface for creating applications that work with AutoCAD. By default, the application is loaded when you either use one of the application's commands, or open a drawing containing a custom object created by the application.

You can further restrict when the application is loaded to reduce demands on memory. In the Proxy Images for Custom Objects drop-down list, you can control how custom objects created by an ObjectARX application are displayed.

The Plot and Publish tab

The Plot and Publish tab, shown in Figure A.6, contains settings related to plotting and publishing, including plot style table settings. Later in this appendix, I explain how to configure a plotter.

FIGURE A.6

The Plot and Publish tab.

In the Default Plot Settings for New Drawings section, you set the default plotter/printer for new drawings and whether or not to use the same settings that you used the last time you plotted. As soon as you create plot settings for a drawing, those settings are saved with the drawing. Click Add or Configure Plotters for access to the Add-a-Plotter Wizard and existing plot configuration files. If you use a template, the plot settings in the template take precedence over the settings here.

The Plot to File section sets the default location for the file when you plot to a file. The Background Processing Options section determines whether plotting and publishing occur in the background (so that you can continue to work) or in the foreground. By default, background plotting is off for plotting and on for publishing (using the PUBLISH command). The Plot and Publish Log File section specifies whether to create a log file specifically for plotting and publishing operations.

In the Auto Publish section, you can set options for automatically creating DWF files every time you save or close a drawing. You do this to make sure that your DWF files are always up to date with your drawings. Click the Automatic DWF Publish Settings button to open the Auto Publish Options dialog box. I describe these settings in Chapter 28. Then check the Automatic DWF Publish check box.

In the General Plot Options section, you can choose whether to keep the paper size specified on the layout tab or use the plotter's default paper size when you change plotters. You can also decide whether AutoCAD alerts you and creates an error log when the drawing is spooled through a system printer because of a port conflict.

In the same section, you can set a value for the quality of plotted OLE objects. You can choose from Monochrome, Low Graphics, High Graphics and Automatically Select. The default is Automatically Select. Check the Use OLE Application When Plotting OLE Objects check box for the best quality when plotting OLE objects. Check the Hide System Printers check box to repress the display of Windows system printers on the list of printers in the Plot and Page Setup dialog boxes, so you that can't inadvertently print to your printer instead of to your plotter.

The Specify Plot Offset Relative To section determines how plot offsets (which you set in the Plot or Page Setup dialog boxes) work. Click the Plot Stamp Settings button to specify what you want to include if you add a plot stamp when plotting.

Click the Plot Style Table Settings button to decide whether to use color-dependent or named plot styles for new drawings, and choose a default plot style table. You can also set default plot styles for layer 0 and objects. Click the Add or Edit Plot Style Tables button to go to the Plot Styles folder where the plot style tables are stored. You can then double-click the Add-A-Plot Style Table Wizard to create a new table or open an existing table for editing. For more information on plotting and plot style tables, see Chapter 17.

The System tab

The System tab contains a number of settings that affect how your computer works with AutoCAD or AutoCAD LT, as well as some general settings. Figure A.7 shows the System tab.

FIGURE A.7

The System tab.

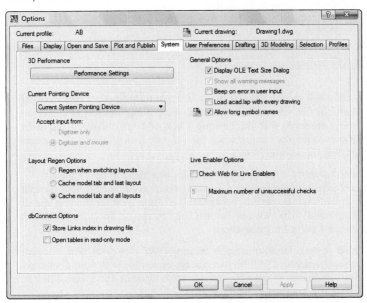

In the 3D Performance Settings section (AutoCAD only), click the Performance Settings button to open the Adaptive Degradation and Performance Tuning dialog box, shown in Figure A.8.

NOTE   AutoCAD 2008 analyzes your computer system and degrades the display, based on the settings in this dialog box. For example, if your graphics card is not certified, materials and textures do not display by default. (You can easily turn them on. See the "Display materials, textures, and lights as you work" section in Chapter 22 for more information.)

FIGURE A.8

The Adaptive Degradation and Performance Tuning dialog box allows you to specify how AutoCAD displays 3D features in relation to your computer system's capabilities.

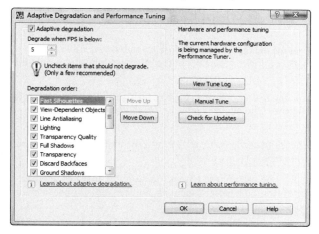

On the left side of the dialog box, you can turn Adaptive Degradation off by unchecking the check box at the top. Then you can set the level at which degradation starts to function. By default, this is five frames per second, which refers to the speed at which your monitor refreshes the display. In the Degradation Order box, you can do two things:

- **Uncheck items that you don't want to degrade.** For example, you may always want to see materials and textures.

- **Change the order of degradation.** Items at the top degrade first. Select an item and click the Move Up or Move Down button to change the order.

You may need to see the results you get before making these decisions.

The right side of the dialog box contains information about performance tuning. Click View Tune Log to see the Performance Tuner Log window. Here you can see if your graphics card is certified, which just means that Autodesk has tested it and recommends it. The bottom of the window shows the effects on specific features, such as geometry acceleration, smooth line display, the Gooch shader, and full-shadow display.

Click the Manual Tune button to change the settings. For example, you can choose to enable *hardware acceleration,* even if your graphics card is not certified. Hardware acceleration means that your graphics card's capabilities are used. (When hardware acceleration is turned off, AutoCAD uses *software acceleration* to try to display the screen properly.) Autodesk says that you do this at your own risk, but you may find that this works for you. For example, you may have an excellent graphics card, but Autodesk may not have tested and certified it yet. You can also turn off specific features, such as full shadows, which involve intensive computer capabilities.

In the lower section of the dialog box, you can adjust features that don't require hardware acceleration, such as the display of backward-facing faces of solids, transparency, and tessellation lines (the apparent smoothness of curved objects created by using many short lines or triangles). The Tessellation cache is useful if you are displaying 3D objects in more than one viewport. You can also reset the setting to their recommended values. Click OK when you're done.

So, how do you know which graphics cards are certified? Click the Check for Updates button in the Adaptive Degradation and Performance Tuning dialog box to go to Autodesk's Web site and see a list of recommended cards. When you're done with the Adaptive Degradation and Performance Tuning dialog box, click OK to return to the Options dialog box.

In the Current Pointing Device section of the Options dialog box, you choose Wintab Compatible Digitizer ADI 4.2 if you have a digitizer. If you have a digitizing device, you can choose to accept input from only the digitizer, or both the digitizer and the mouse.

 If you're installing a digitizer, follow the instructions provided by the digitizer manufacturer to configure Windows for the Wintab driver. The digitizer must be configured to work with Windows.

In the Layout Regen Options section, you can choose to cache (save in memory) the model and layout tabs to avoid regenerations when you switch among the tabs. (AutoCAD only.)

In the dbConnect Options section (AutoCAD only), you can choose whether to store the index of database links in the drawing file to enhance performance during Link Select functions. You can also choose to open database tables in read-only mode; however, you won't be able to edit them.

AutoCAD LT has a User Name section that contains your name and organization. This is derived from the information that you provided at installation. You can change this name. The REVDATE command, which is available only in AutoCAD LT, uses this name to place a time stamp on your drawing.

In the General Options section, you can do the following:

- Turn off the display of the OLE Properties dialog box when inserting OLE objects into AutoCAD drawings.
- Bring back dialog boxes that have a Don't Display This Warning Again check box (that you checked).
- Tell AutoCAD to beep (or to remain silent) when it detects an invalid entry.
- Determine whether AutoLISP loads `acad.lsp` into every drawing that you open. By default, this box is not checked, meaning that only `acaddoc.lsp` is loaded into every drawing. (AutoCAD only.)
- Disable long names for layers, dimension styles, blocks, linetypes, text styles, layouts, UCS names, views, and viewport configurations, for compatibility with prior releases and customization.

In the Live Enabler Options section, you can decide when you want to check for object enablers. Object enablers let the user display and use custom objects in drawings, even when the application that created them is unavailable. For example, if you send a customer who is using Release 2000 a drawing with associative dimensions, that customer can use an object enabler to view those dimensions.

The User Preferences tab

The User Preferences tab, shown in Figure A.9, offers a variety of preference settings.

In the Windows Standard Behavior section, you can turn double-click editing on or off. Double-click editing determines what happens when you double-click an object. (You can customize this process in the Customize User Interface dialog box, as I explain in Chapter 33.) You can also disable the shortcut menus that appear when you right-click in the drawing or command areas. A right-click is then equivalent to pressing Enter.

FIGURE A.9

The User Preferences tab.

You can customize what happens when you right-click. Click Right-Click Customization to open the dialog box shown in Figure A.10.

At the top of the Right-Click Customization dialog box, you can turn on the time-sensitive right-click feature.

With time-sensitive right-clicking, a quick right-click is equivalent to pressing Enter. For example, it repeats the last command, or ends the LINE command (and other commands that require Enter to end). A longer right-click (hold your finger on the mouse slightly longer) opens the shortcut menu. You can specify the length of time required for the longer right-click, which is 250 milliseconds by default.

FIGURE A.10

The Right-Click Customization dialog box.

In the Default Mode section, if you haven't turned on time-sensitive right-clicking, then you can choose the Repeat Last Command option if you don't want to use shortcut menus. In the Edit Mode section, you can choose the Repeat Last Command option to disable the shortcut menus only when one or more objects are selected, but no command is in progress. When you do this, right-clicking automatically repeats the most recent command. In the Command Mode section, you have three choices if you haven't turned on time-sensitive right-clicking:

- Choose the ENTER option to disable the shortcut menus whenever a command is in progress. You then have to use the keyboard to choose command options.

- Choose the Shortcut Menu: Always Enabled option to always have the shortcut menu available.

- Choose the Shortcut Menu: Enabled When Command Options Are Present option as an in-between option. The shortcut menu is now available when the command has options, but when the command has no options, right-clicking is like pressing Enter.

Click Apply & Close to close the Right-Click Customization dialog box and return to the User Preferences tab of the Options dialog box.

In the Insertion Scale section of the User Preferences tab, you can specify default units for inserted objects (*source contents units*) and drawings (*target drawing units*) when dragging objects into a drawing from the DesignCenter or i-drop, or using commands like INSERT or XATTACH. When you don't use the INSUNITS system variable (saved in your drawing), this setting determines the units to apply. You can choose anything from inches to parsecs!

In the Fields section, you can turn on and off the gray border around fields. (The border doesn't plot; it just indicates to you that the text is a field.) Click the Field Update Settings button to specify when fields are automatically updated. By default, they update when you open, save, plot, eTransmit, or regenerate a drawing. AutoCAD LT, which doesn't have the field feature, only includes the ability to turn the background on and off. (AutoCAD LT can read fields created in AutoCAD drawings.)

Click the Lineweight Settings button to open the Lineweight Settings dialog box shown in Figure A.11. For more information on lineweights, see Chapter 11.

FIGURE A.11

The Lineweight Settings dialog box.

In the Lineweights list you can set the current lineweight. There are three standard lineweight styles: `ByLayer`, `ByBlock`, and `Default`. The `Default` value is 0.01 inches or 0.25 mm. All new layers have a default setting of `Default`. You can also set any specific width that you want. In the Units for Listing section, choose Millimeters or Inches. The default is Millimeters, probably because pen widths for pen plotters are traditionally defined in millimeters. Checking the Display Lineweight check box is equivalent to clicking the LWT button on the status bar. In the Default drop-down list, you can change the default lineweight that new layers automatically use.

With the Adjust Display Scale slider, you can control how lineweights are displayed on the Model tab. (Lineweights on a paper space layout are displayed in real-world units.) On the Model tab, lineweights are displayed in pixels using a proportion of pixel width to real-world unit value. Depending on the resolution of your monitor, you may want to adjust the display scale to better see different lineweights.

 You can see the results of any display scale change immediately in the Lineweights list on the left of the dialog box. Scroll down to the bottom to see the difference for wider lineweights.

Click Apply & Close to return to the User Preferences tab of the Options dialog box.

Click the Edit Scale List button to open the Edit Scale list dialog box. Here you can customize the list of scales so that you always have the scales that you need (and don't have the scales that you never use). I discuss the scale list in Chapter 5.

In the Priority for Coordinate Data Entry section, you specify which has priority: running object snaps or keyboard entry. By default, keyboard entry has priority except in scripts, and so you can use running object snaps when picking points on the screen, but override them when you want to type in coordinates.

In the Associative Dimensioning section, choose whether you want new dimensions to be *associative* and thus automatically adjusting as their associated objects change size.

In the Hyperlink section, you can disable the hyperlink cursor (which appears when you pass the cursor over a hyperlink) and the hyperlink shortcut menu, as well as the hyperlink tooltip that appears when you pass the cursor over a hyperlink.

The Undo/Redo section has only one setting: you can choose to combine consecutive zooms and pans into one command when you use the U or UNDO command. You may do several zooms and pans together, but you probably don't want to step backward through each one individually. This feature is on by default.

The Drafting tab

The Drafting tab, shown in Figure A.12, includes AutoSnap and AutoTrack settings. In the AutoSnap Settings section, you can disable the marker (that visually indicates each object snap), the magnet (that draws the cursor to the object snap), and the tooltip (that says which object snap you've found). By default, the aperture is not displayed with AutoSnap markers because the combination can be confusing. You can also choose a color for the AutoSnap marker. Click the Colors button to change the color of the AutoSnap marker item. You can also change the marker size by dragging the control bar.

FIGURE A.12

The Drafting tab.

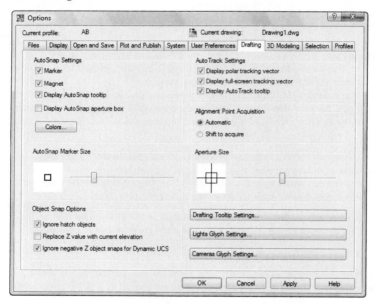

In the Object Snap Options section, you can turn off the option to ignore hatch objects. By default, you cannot snap to hatch objects. If you want to snap to hatch objects, uncheck the check box. You can also choose the Replace Z Value with Current Elevation option (AutoCAD only) to specify that object snaps use the current elevation for the Z value instead of the Z value of the object snap's point on the object.

You can also specify how the Dynamic UCS feature works with object snaps (in AutoCAD only). By default, when you're in a Dynamic UCS, you don't snap to object snaps with negative Z values, so that you can easily draw on the temporary XY plane. Uncheck the Ignore Negative Z Object Snaps for Dynamic UCS to enable snapping to all object snaps.

In the AutoTrack Settings section, you control the visual elements for AutoTracking:

- Uncheck the **Display Polar Tracking Vector** check box to disable the vector that appears when you move the cursor along a polar angle. You still see the tooltip.

- Uncheck the **Display Full-Screen Tracking Vector** check box to see only a localized vector when using object snap tracking — the vector appears between the acquired points, instead of crossing the entire screen.

- Uncheck the **Display AutoTrack Tooltip** check box to disable the tooltip that tells you which object snaps you've tracked.

In the Alignment Point Acquisition section, you can require pressing the Shift key to acquire points. You might do this if you find yourself acquiring points by accident, which can result in annoying tracking vectors.

You can set the aperture size for picking an object snap. However, the aperture box is off by default. (You can turn it on in the AutoSnap Settings section, as previously described.)

Click the Drafting Tooltip Settings button to open the Tooltip Appearance dialog box. Here you can set the color, size, and transparency for tooltips. You can also choose to apply these settings to all tooltips or only to the Dynamic Input tooltip.

Click the Light Glyph Settings button (AutoCAD only) to open the Light Glyph Appearance dialog box, where you can determine how light glyphs look. You can change their color and size.

Click the Camera Glyph Settings button (AutoCAD only) to open the Camera Glyph Appearance dialog box. Here, too, you can change the size and color of the glyphs.

The 3D Modeling tab

This tab, available in AutoCAD only, contains settings specific to 3D modeling. The 3D Modeling tab is shown in Figure A.13.

In the 3D Crosshairs section, you can specify the look of the 3D crosshairs. You can choose to show the Z axis (on by default) and to label the axes. If you show labels, you can customize them. You can also show labels for a Dynamic UCS.

In the Display UCS Icon section, you can decide when you want to see the icon. Some people don't want it in 2D model space, for example, but want it on for 3D work.

In the Dynamic Input section, you can display a Z field for pointer input. If you leave this item unchecked (the default), you can always display it simply by entering a comma and a third (Z) coordinate value.

In the 3D Objects section, you can set a separate visual style while you are creating 3D solids and extruded solids and surfaces. By default, the current visual style (ByViewport) is used, but you may want a special one for the creation process.

The Deletion Control While Creating 3D Objects drop-down list sets the DELOBJ system variable, which I discuss in the "Managing objects used to make other objects" section of Chapter 24.

The two isoline drop-down lists control the SURFU and SURFV system variables, which I cover in the "Creating Plane Surfaces" section of Chapter 23. These set the default number of isolines on surfaces and meshes.

The 3D Modeling tab.

The 3D Navigation section contains settings related to 3D Navigation. You can reverse the direction that you scroll the mouse wheel to zoom in and out to match other software that may be the opposite of AutoCAD. You can set walk and fly settings as well as animation settings here. I cover these settings in Chapter 22.

The Selection tab

The Selection tab contains settings that control how you select objects. This tab is shown in Figure A.14.

The options in the Selection Modes and Pickbox Size sections, which customize object selection, are discussed in detail in Chapter 9. The options in the Grips and Grip Size sections are covered in Chapter 10.

The Selection Preview section lets you specify what happens when you pass the cursor over an object to see what object you would select if you clicked your mouse. By default, objects are highlighted and you can customize the look of this highlighting. I cover this section in Chapter 9.

The Profiles tab

The Profiles tab, shown in Figure A.15, enables you to create user profiles. AutoCAD LT does not offer this feature (or the tab). A profile is a group of settings, most of which you set in the Options dialog box. It can include all settings that are saved in the Windows Registry. Settings that are saved in the current drawing (indicated in the Options dialog box by the blue drawing marker) are not included in a profile. If you share your system with someone else and you each want to store different settings, or if you want different settings for different projects, you can create a profile and make it current when you open AutoCAD.

FIGURE A.14

The Selection tab.

FIGURE A.15

The Profiles tab with the default and one custom profile.

Whatever settings you create with the Options dialog box are automatically part of the default profile, which starts out with the unexciting name of Unnamed Profile. Here's how you create a new profile:

1. Click Add to List to open the Add Profile dialog box. Type in a profile name and description and click Apply & Close. This adds a new profile that is a duplicate of the current profile.
2. On the Profiles tab, click the new profile and choose Set Current.
3. Go through the other tabs and make the changes that you want. Be sure to click Apply on each tab.
4. Click OK to close the Options dialog box.

Whenever you make changes in AutoCAD settings that affect the Windows Registry, those changes become part of the current profile.

To use the profile or another profile, choose Tools ➪ Options and click the Profiles tab. Choose the profile and click Set Current, or double-click the profile. Click OK to return to your drawing. You see the results immediately. Of course, some settings are not visible but make themselves evident in other ways, such as right-click functioning and the creation of a log file.

> **TIP** To start AutoCAD with a specific profile, you can specify a profile using a command line switch, as explained in the next section. You can also export a profile (click the Export button) to share it with colleagues or use it on another computer. To use an exported profile, click the Import button on the Profiles tab of the Options dialog box.

Starting AutoCAD Your Way

When you choose the AutoCAD icon to open AutoCAD, Windows notwithstanding, you execute a statement similar to the one that old-timers once typed at the DOS prompt. This is called a *command line statement.* By default, it looks something like c:\Program Files\AutoCAD 2008\acad.exe or c:\Program Files\AutoCAD LT 2008\acadlt.exe. Your exact command line statement depends on where you installed AutoCAD or AutoCAD LT.

Using command line switches

You can add parameters, called *switches,* to the end of this command line that control what happens when you start the program. Always add a space between the acad.exe or aclt.exe command and a switch. Before any switch, you can add the name of a drawing to open that drawing. You need quotation marks around any path or drawing name that contains spaces. Table A.1 lists the available command line switches and their functions.

You can combine switches. For example, the following command line statement opens the drawing "Union Hill Apts" in the front view and runs the setup script.

```
C:\Program Files\AutoCAD 2008\acad.exe "c:\drawings\Union Hill
Apts.dwg" /v front /b setup
```

To change the command line switch, follow these steps:

1. Right-click the shortcut to AutoCAD or AutoCAD LT on your desktop.
2. Choose Properties.
3. Click the Shortcut tab.
4. In the Target text box, add your switches to the end of the current command line statement.
5. Click OK.

TABLE A.1		

Command Line Switches

Switch	Example	Function
/c	/c c:\steve\steve.cfg	Specifies the location and, optionally, the filename of the hardware configuration file that you want to use. Configuration files are discussed in the next section.
/s	/s c:\steve	Specifies support folders for fonts, menus, AutoLISP files, linetypes, and hatch patterns. Use this when you want to use support files that are not in AutoCAD's support file search path. You can specify up to 15 folders, separated by semicolons without spaces. (AutoCAD only.)
/b	"c:\drawings\ Union Hill Apts.dwg" /b setup	Opens a drawing (here named "Union Hill Apts") and runs a script (here named "setup"). The full drawing path is required. Omit the drawing to run the script with a new drawing.
/t	/t a-tb	Opens a new drawing based on a template file (here named "a-tb").
/nologo		Starts AutoCAD or AutoCAD LT without displaying the splash screen at startup.
/v	"c:\drawings\Union Apts" / v front	Opens a drawing and immediately displays the specified view (here named "front"). The full drawing path is required.
/r	/r	Resets AutoCAD to the default configuration (acad2008.cfg) for the default system pointing device. (AutoCAD only.)
/p	/p steve	Specifies an existing profile to use when starting AutoCAD. This profile is used only for the current session. You can also change profiles using the Profile tab of the Options dialog box. Use quotation marks around the name if it contains spaces. (AutoCAD only.)
/nossm	/nossm	Opens AutoCAD without the Sheet Set Manager. (AutoCAD only.)
/set	/set ab26-f	Opens AutoCAD and the named sheet set (here called "ab26-f"). (AutoCAD only.)
/w	/w ab_3d	Opens AutoCAD with the specified workspace.
/ld	/ld balloon.dbx	Loads an ARX or DBX file. (AutoCAD only.)
/nohardware	/nohardware	Disables hardware acceleration. (AutoCAD only.)
/pl	/pl garage.dsd	Publishes a drawing set description (DSD) file. (AutoCAD only.)

Understanding configuration files

Every time you open AutoCAD, a configuration file is created. By default, this file (acad2008.cfg for AutoCAD or acadlt2008.cfg for AutoCAD LT) is an ASCII file containing mostly hardware-configuration information for your mouse and digitizer. Figure A.16 shows the beginning of the default file.

If you use multiple pointing devices — for example, a large and a small digitizer — you may want to create more than one configuration file to make it easy to switch from one configuration to another.

You should not edit the configuration file; instead, let AutoCAD create it for you. The problem is that AutoCAD assumes one configuration file and overwrites the previous one whenever you make changes that affect the file — such as adding a pointing device.

FIGURE A.16

The acad2008.cfg file.

Remember that you can use the /c command line switch to specify a configuration file. To create a new file, follow these steps:

1. Use Windows Explorer to back up your current configuration file under a new name, such as acad2008-orig.cfg.

 To find the location of acad2008.cfg, choose Tools ⇨ Options and click the Files tab. Double-click Help and Miscellaneous Files, and then double-click Configuration File. (AutoCAD only.)

2. Open AutoCAD and make the pointer change that you want on the System tab of the Options dialog box. (If you're installing a new digitizer, follow the manufacturer's instructions to install the digitizer.) Click OK.

3. Close AutoCAD.

4. In Explorer, find the new acad2008.cfg file that AutoCAD created. Change its name, using something meaningful, such as LargeDigitizer.cfg.

5. If you want to keep the original acad2008.cfg file, change its name back to acad2008.cfg.

You now have two configuration files. (You can create more if you want.) To use them, you can change the command line switch as needed, but there's an easier way, as explained in the next section.

Creating multiple configurations

This appendix has discussed three different ways to create session configurations:

- Profiles
- Configuration files
- Command line switches

You can use command line switches to specify a profile and a configuration file, as well as to configure AutoCAD in other ways, such as opening a drawing with a certain template or running a script file when you open a drawing.

If you regularly use these features, you should create multiple configurations to make it easy to open AutoCAD the way that you want by doing the following:

- Create the profiles and configuration files that you need.
- Make as many shortcuts as you need.

NOTE To create a new shortcut, use Explorer to find acad.exe (usually in AutoCAD 2008) or acadlt.exe (usually in AutoCAD LT 2008). Right-click it and choose Create Shortcut from the menu. Drag this to your desktop and rename it.

- Change the command line switches to specify the profiles and configuration files that you want, and add any other command line switches that you need.

For example, here are command lines for two separate AutoCAD desktop shortcuts. You could make similar command lines for AutoCAD LT.

```
C:\Program Files\AutoCAD 2008\acad.exe /t acad /nologo
C:\Program Files\AutoCAD 2008\acad.exe /p steve /c steve.cfg /t arch
```

The first command line statement opens drawings using the acad.dwt template and doesn't display the logo. It also uses the default profile and configuration file.

The second command line statement opens drawings using the arch.dwt template and displays the logo. It also uses the steve profile and the steve configuration file.

You could also have each configuration run different script files. This technique takes some time to set up, but after it's done, it saves you time and reduces errors each time you open AutoCAD or AutoCAD LT.

Configuring a Plotter

Windows supports many printers. To add a printer supported by Windows, choose Start ➪ Settings ➪ Printers (and Faxes) (or Start ➪ Printers and Faxes) and double-click Add Printer. A printer added in this way is called a *Windows system printer.*

The Windows system printer drivers are great for small desktop printers because that's their intended use, but they aren't optimized for pen plotters or large-format plotters. For this purpose, AutoCAD and AutoCAD LT come with *nonsystem drivers.* These drivers are specially designed for CAD. You cannot use them with other Windows applications.

Using the Plotter Manager

To configure a non-system plotter, use the Plotter Manager. (You can also use the Plotter Manager to create custom settings for a system printer.) You have several ways to open the Plotter Manager:

- From Windows, choose Start ➪ Settings ➪ Control Panel (or Start ➪ Control Panel) and double-click Autodesk Plotter Manager. (If you're not using the Classic view, click Printer, or Printers and Other Hardware, to see the shortcut for the Autodesk Plotter Manager.)
- From within AutoCAD or AutoCAD LT, choose File ➪ Plotter Manager.
- From within AutoCAD or AutoCAD LT, choose Tools ➪ Options. On the Plot and Publish tab, click Add or Configure Plotters.

The Plotter Manager has a wizard (double-click Add-A-Plotter Wizard) that guides you through the process of configuring a printer. Follow the instructions on each page, which vary based on your previous choices.

For more information, see the "Use Plotters and Printers" section in the Help system. Choose Help ➪ Help and then choose Driver and Peripheral Guide from the Contents tab.

During the process of configuring a plotter, you can import a PCP or PC2 configuration file that was created with an earlier release.

The result of configuring a plotter is a plotter configuration file that has a file name extension of `.pc3`. These PC3 files are saved in the `Plotters` folder. (To find the PC3 files, choose Tools ➪ Options and click the Files tab. Double-click Printer Support File Path and then double-click Printer Configuration Search Path.) You can share configured plot files with colleagues or copy them to another computer, such as a notebook computer. You can configure more than one plotter. You can also create more than one configuration for a single plotter. To use a PC3 file, choose it from the Name drop-down list under the Printer/Plotter section of the Plot dialog box.

At the end of the Plotter Manager Wizard, you can click Edit Plotter Configuration to change the default settings for your plotter. You can also click Calibrate Plotter to test that the plotter plots accurately.

Editing a plotter configuration

You can edit a plotter configuration and change its original settings. You can access the file in several ways:

- As just mentioned, click Edit Plotter Configuration at the end of the Plotter Manager Wizard.
- From within AutoCAD or AutoCAD LT, choose File ➪ Page Setup Manager. Click Modify. In the Page Setup dialog box, choose the plotter that you want and click Properties.
- From within AutoCAD or AutoCAD LT, click Plot on the Standard (or Standard Annotation) toolbar. Choose the plotter that you want and click Properties.
- From Windows Explorer, double-click a PC3 file. The location of the PC3 files is listed on the Files tab of the Options dialog box, under Printer Support File Path ➪ Printer Configuration Search Path.

A PC3 file is not an ASCII file. When you open a PC3 file, you see the Plotter Configuration Editor dialog box, as shown in Figure A.17.

The General tab lists basic information about the plotter. This tab does not contain any options that you can configure, although you can add a description of the plotter and its settings.

The Ports tab enables you to choose to plot through a port (the usual situation), plot to a file, or use AutoSpool to plot to a printer spooler. If more than one port is available, then you can choose and configure the port.

FIGURE A.17

The Plotter Configuration Editor is the place to change settings related to your printer or plotter.

The Device and Document Settings tab contains plotting options, depending on your plotter.

As you select an item from the top part of the Plotter Configuration Editor, the appropriate options become available on the bottom of the dialog box. You can configure the following (your plotter will probably show different options):

- **Media:** The source and size of the paper.

- **Physical Pen Configuration:** Correction for filled areas (for extra accuracy), pen optimization for faster plotting, pen color, pen speed, and pen width.

- **Graphics:** Color depth (the number of colors), monochrome, resolution, and dithering.

- **Custom properties:** Vary by plotter. For Windows system printers, you might find settings such as draft printing and grayscale (for color printers).

- **Initialization Strings:** Rarely used nowadays. If you're plotting to an unsupported plotter, you may be able to prepare the plotter for printing, set options, and restore the plotter to its original state using ASCII text initialization strings.

- **User-Defined Paper Sizes and Calibration:** Calibrate a plotter, create custom paper sizes, and change the plottable area of standard paper sizes.

When you finish making changes, click OK to save the changes to the PC3 files. You can also click Save As to create a new PC3 file. Click Default to return all settings to their defaults.

Appendix B

AutoCAD and AutoCAD LT Resources

A side from this book, you have many other resources for learning about AutoCAD. These resources range from AutoCAD's New Features Workshop to Web sites and include everything else in between.

This book's DVD contains a document containing clickable links for the Internet resources in this appendix. Look in the Links folder.

IN THIS APPENDIX

Learning AutoCAD or AutoCAD LT

Accessing technical support

Joining Autodesk user groups

Finding Internet resources

Discovering AutoCAD and AutoCAD LT

AutoCAD and AutoCAD LT are not programs that you can easily pick up as you work with them. You'll need some formal education, whether by using this book, taking a course, or a combination of methods.

Using AutoCAD and AutoCAD LT Help resources

AutoCAD's own Help resources are a good place to start when you have a question. In Chapter 3, I explain how to use Help. You can also try the New Features Workshop, which includes explanations and demonstrations that are related to the new 2008 features. Choose Help ➪ New Features Workshop.

Learning from your dealer

You're supposed to learn AutoCAD from your dealer. Most dealers include some training when you purchase AutoCAD. However, the amount of training and follow-up support varies greatly, and so does the price. If you have more than one AutoCAD dealer nearby, check not only the cost of AutoCAD but also the cost of training.

Unlike AutoCAD, AutoCAD LT is often sold online without any training. Keep in mind that AutoCAD LT is not a simple program either, and some training will definitely help you get more out of the program.

Dealers usually offer upgrade seminars and courses when you upgrade. If you're already using AutoCAD or AutoCAD LT, you may be able to take a course that focuses on the new features.

If you're going to use third-party applications that work with AutoCAD or other Autodesk products, check how much experience the dealer has with these products and what kind of support the dealer offers.

Autodesk has an Autodesk Training Center program that certifies trainers. Your dealer may or may not be an Autodesk Training Center; remember to ask. Premier Training Centers offer additional training in certain disciplines, thus offering solutions that are more specialized to their customers.

Taking a course

You may be able to take a course in AutoCAD at a local college or Autodesk Training Center. Many universities and community colleges offer courses in AutoCAD. Such courses may fit your schedule because they're often offered in the evening, over a period of several weeks. Of course, that may not work if you need to get up and running very quickly. AutoCAD LT courses are less common, but you can check out your local colleges. However, a course on AutoCAD would certainly help you to learn AutoCAD LT.

Autodesk holds a once-a-year conference, called Autodesk University, which offers classes that are taught by top AutoCAD experts. For more information, go to www.autodesk.com/au. AUGI (www.augi.com) offers one-day seminars around the United States.

Autodesk sells short, self-paced courses on both AutoCAD and AutoCAD LT. From the Autodesk home page (www.autodesk.com), click Store, and then choose your location. Click the link for the division of interest to you under Learning and Training to find more information.

If you are a Subscription member, you have access to special courses. For more information about the Subscription program, go to www.autodesk.com and click the Subscription link.

Learning from other users

If you work in an office with several AutoCAD or AutoCAD LT users, you'll find that they're usually happy to share information and tips with you. This won't generally get you started from scratch, but it's great for rounding out your knowledge.

Reading magazines and newsletters

Cadalyst (phone: 888-527-7008) covers AutoCAD as well as other CAD programs. It is published in both print and Web versions and includes many helpful articles (as well as advertisements, of course). In addition, *Cadalyst* has an extensive Web site (www.cadalyst.com), but I discuss that later.

Autodesk User Group International (AUGI) has a couple of great publications, including AUGIWorld magazine. You can find out more at www.augi.com. A free registration is required. Then click the Publications link.

If you're interested in the CAD industry in general, try Ralph Grabowski's weekly *upFront.eZine*, which you can subscribe to by sending the e-mail message "subscribe upfront" to ralphg@xyzpress.com.

I offer a monthly e-mail newsletter, *AutoCAD Tips Newsletter*. You can sign up at www.ellen finkelstein.com.

Accessing Technical Support

Autodesk has always referred customers to their dealer for technical support. As with training, you should check out the provisions of the technical support. Some dealers charge for each phone call, while others provide free support to all customers for as long as Autodesk supports the product.

However, Autodesk offers its own support. For an overview of support options, click Support from the Autodesk home page (www.autodesk.com), select AutoCAD or AutoCAD LT in the Select a Product drop-down list, and then choose one of the Support options. The Autodesk Web site offers a large number of technical documents that answer many common questions. From Autodesk's home page, choose Support, select AutoCAD from the Technical Support drop-down list, and then choose Knowledge Base.

The Autodesk Web site offers discussion groups. From Autodesk's home page, choose Support, choose Discussion Groups, and then choose AutoCAD or AutoCAD LT under Product Discussions. You can ask questions and receive answers from other users as well as from Autodesk employees.

Autodesk User Groups

Autodesk User Groups (AUGs) meet regularly, offer courses and seminars, bring in speakers, and generally offer the types of resources that all AutoCAD users need.

The AUGI (Autodesk User Group International) Web site is at www.augi.com. AUGI is also now offering its own technical support and training (AUGI forums). You can find a lot of information and educational resources there, as well as AutoCAD and AutoCAD LT forums, which have their own easy entrance via the AutoCAD Community at www.augi.com/autocad/.

A number of the local user groups have their own Web sites. For example, the Vancouver AutoCAD Users Society (VAUS) was the first AUG. Its Web site is www.vaus.org.

Internet Resources

The Internet is a rich source of knowledge regarding AutoCAD. Autodesk administers its own discussion groups accessible from a news reader at news://discussion.autodesk.com or from a web browser at http://discussion.autodesk.com/. There are discussion groups on several versions of AutoCAD and AutoCAD LT.

The Internet sports hundreds of CAD-related Web sites. Here are some of the most prominent:

- The Autodesk Web site, at www.autodesk.com, contains a lot of product and support resources on AutoCAD and other Autodesk products. At www.autodesk.com/autocad, AutoCAD's home page, you can find a great deal of information about AutoCAD, including training and upgrade information. For information on AutoCAD LT, go to www.autodesk.com.

- The *Cadalyst* Web site, at www.cadalyst.com, shown in Figure B.1, is another important resource. Here you can find news, events, links, products, downloads, and so on. The *Cadalyst* files offer all of the AutoLISP code that the magazine has published since 1993.

FIGURE B.1

The Cadalyst Web site.

- The CAD Depot, at `www.caddepot.com`, has a great collection of freeware and shareware, articles, news, and links. To find downloads applicable to AutoCAD LT, you can perform a search on AutoCAD LT.

- TenLinks.com, at `www.tenlinks.com`, is a wide-ranging directory and news source, with a daily e-mail newsletter.

- CADwire.net, at `www.cadwire.net`, offers news, articles, and directories.

- CADInfo.net, at `www.cadinfo.net`, has software libraries, links, and articles on various CAD-related topics.

The Web has many, many more AutoCAD sites, but most of them are more specialized. Table B.1 lists some useful sites. If you don't have this list when you access the Internet, just type **AutoCAD** into any major search engine. One Web site will lead to another until you find what you need. Enjoy!

TABLE B.1

Useful AutoCAD Web Sites

Name	URL	Description
AUGI	`www.augi.com`	AutoCAD User Group International. This site includes a lot of information on AutoCAD, connections to local groups, and a newsletter.
Better Than Nothing AutoLISP	`http://home.pacifier.com/~nemi`	Leonid Nemirovsky's AutoLISP routines are useful and are free to download. I put several of them on the CD-ROM of this book. Leonid wrote two (`It.lsp` and `Idt.lsp`) at my request, for which I'm grateful.

Name	URL	Description
CAD Forum	www.cadforum.cz/cadforum_en/	This site offers loads of tips on both AutoCAD and AutoCAD LT.
Dotsoft	www.dotsoft.com	Terry Dotson's site offers AutoCAD-related software for sale, along with a lot of freebies and tips.
EllenFinkelstein.com	www.ellenfinkelstein.com/autoCAD.html	My site contains information about the latest AutoCAD features, tips, tutorials, and links to buy my books. You can sign up for the monthly AutoCAD Tips Newsletter or read my AutoCAD Tips Blog.
HyperPics	www.hyperpics.com	Lee Ambrosius's site offers AutoCAD and AutoCAD LT tips and tricks, with a lot of information on customization.
ManuSoft	www.manusoft.com	This site offers a good collection of software for AutoCAD — some for free, others to buy.
University of New South Wales	www.fbe.unsw.edu.au/Learning/AutoCAD/	UNSW has placed some of its AutoCAD courses on its Web site, and they are available for Release 2000; even better, they are free.
upfront.eZine	www.upfrontezine.com/	Besides the current issue of Ralph Grabowski's ezine, you can purchase his eBooks.
CADTutor	www.cadtutor.com	Free tutorials and articles on AutoCAD.

A number of AutoCAD blogs have sprung up — and more keep coming. If you want the latest news, tips, and information every day, try one of these:

- **Between the Lines** by Autodesk employee Shaan Hurley at autodesk.blogs.com/between_the_lines.
- **RobiNZ CAD Blog** by Robin Capper at rcd.typepad.com/rcd.
- **Beyond the UI** by Lee Ambrosius (the technical editor of this book) at hyperpics.blogs.com/beyond_the_ui.
- **Lynn Allen Blogs** by Autodesk employee Lynn Allen at lynn.blogs.com/lynn_allens_blog.
- **In the Dynamic Interface** by Mark Douglas at mdouglas.blogs.com/in_the_dynamic_interface.
- **AutoCAD Insider** by Autodesk employee Heidi Hewitt at heidihewett.blogs.com/my_weblog.
- **Beth's CAD Blog** by Beth Powell at bethscadblog.blogspot.com.
- **CAD Panacea** by R. K. McSwain at rkmcswain.blogspot.com.
- **JTB World Blog** by Jimmy Bergmark at jtbworld.blogspot.com.
- **Mistress of the Dorkness** by Melanie (Stone) Perry (who helped me update some of the chapters of this book) at mistressofthedorkness.blogspot.com.
- **The Mad Cadder** by Michael Rotolo at themadcadder.blogs.com/my_weblog.
- **CAD-e-Corner** by Ward Romberger at cadecorner.blogspot.com.
- **AutoCAD Tips Blog** (my own) at www.ellenfinkelstein.com/autocad_tips_blog.html.

Appendix C

What's on the DVD

The *AutoCAD 2008 and AutoCAD LT 2008 Bible* DVD contains all of the drawings and files that you need to do the exercises in the book, as well as the results of those exercises. In addition, I've tried out many useful shareware programs and AutoLISP routines to see whether they work with AutoCAD 2008 and AutoCAD LT and then selected those that I felt would be most useful. Although AutoCAD LT doesn't support AutoLISP routines, a couple of the programs work with AutoCAD LT as well. You can also find the entire book in non-printable PDF format and a document of links to Internet resources. I hope that you find this DVD a valuable addition to your AutoCAD arsenal.

CROSS-REF The drawings on the DVD are also available on the publisher's Web site at www.wiley.com/go/autocad2008bible. Click the Downloads link.

This appendix provides you with information on the contents of the DVD that accompanies this book. For the latest and greatest information, please refer to the README file located at the root of the DVD. Here is what you'll find:

- System requirements for the DVD
- Using the DVD with Windows
- What's on the DVD
- Troubleshooting

System Requirements

Make sure that your computer meets the minimum system requirements listed in this section. If your computer doesn't match up to most of these requirements, you may have a problem using the contents of the DVD:

- Windows 2000, Windows XP, or Windows Vista
- PC with a Pentium processor running at 200 MHz or faster

IN THIS APPENDIX

Using the DVD

Accessing the software

Using the e-book version

Troubleshooting tips

- At least 64MB of total RAM installed on your computer; for best performance, I recommend at least 128MB

- Ethernet network interface card (NIC) or modem with a speed of at least 28,800 bps

- A DVD drive

For system requirements for AutoCAD 2008 and AutoCAD LT 2008, see Appendix A.

Using the DVD with Microsoft Windows

You can copy certain items from the DVD to your hard drive. Follow these steps:

1. Insert the DVD into your computer's DVD drive.
2. The DVD interface will appear. The interface provides a simple point-and-click way to explore the contents of the DVD. Click one of the buttons to continue.

If the DVD interface does not appear, follow these steps to access the DVD:

1. Click the Start button on the left end of the taskbar.
2. Choose Run from the menu that pops up. (In Windows Vista, skip this step.)
3. In the dialog box that appears, type **d:\setup.exe**. (If your DVD drive is not drive d, fill in the appropriate letter in place of d.) This brings up the DVD interface described in the preceding set of steps. (In Windows Vista, type d:\setup.exe in the Start Search text box.)

What's on the DVD

The following sections provide a summary of the software and other materials that you'll find on the DVD.

Using the Drawings folder

I've placed all of the files that you need for the exercises in the Drawings folder of the DVD. Almost all of these files are named as in the following examples: ab15-a.dwg, ab15-b.dwg, ab15-c.dwg, and so on. In these examples, the number 15 corresponds to the chapter number, and the letters correspond to the first, second, and third drawings that you need to open.

A few files have other names, such as bluesky.jpg and others. In each case, I provide you with the name of the file to open. You can easily find these files with Windows Explorer, because Explorer automatically alphabetizes the files. (If they aren't alphabetized, click the Name column of the right-hand window. If Explorer alphabetizes them in reverse order, click Name one more time.)

Using the Results folder

The Results folder offers you the results of all of the exercises. You may want to check your work in the exercise against these results. You may also sometimes use the result of one exercise as the basis for a second exercise (although I try not to require this very often). In this situation, if you haven't done the previous exercise, you can access the resulting file from the Results folder and use it for the next exercise. If you have any difficulty opening a drawing from the Results folder, copy it to your hard drive and remove its read-only attribute, as described in the "Changing the Windows Read-Only Attribute" sidebar.

Changing the Windows Read-Only Attribute

You can use the exercise drawings directly from the DVD, but you might get better results by copying them to your hard drive. In most cases, the exercises instruct you to do this.

To use the software from the DVD, copy the files to a folder in AutoCAD's support-file search path.

Initially, you might run into the problem of not being able to access files on the DVD after you copy the files to your computer. After you copy or move a file from the DVD to your hard disk or another storage medium (such as a Zip drive), you may see the following error message when you attempt to open or save a file with its associated application:

```
[Application] is unable to open the [file].
Please make sure the drive and file are writable.
```

Windows recognizes all files on a DVD drive as read-only. Normally, this makes sense, because a DVD is a read-only medium — that is, you can't write data back to the disc. However, when you copy a file from a DVD to your hard disk or to a Zip drive, Windows may not automatically change the file attribute from read-only to writable. Installation software normally takes care of this chore for you, but when the files are to be manually copied to your disk, you may have to change the file attribute yourself. Luckily, this is easy:

1. Choose Start ➪ (All) Programs ➪ Accessories ➪ Windows Explorer.
2. Highlight the filename(s).
3. Right-click the highlighted filename(s) to display a shortcut menu.
4. Choose Properties to display the Properties dialog box.
5. Click the Read-Only check box so that it's no longer checked.
6. Click OK.

You should now be able to use the file(s) with the specific application without seeing the annoying error message.

Using the Chapter 37 folder

Due to space constraints (due to this book getting longer and longer), Chapter 37, "Programming with Visual Basic for Applications," was moved to the DVD. It is in PDF format. You can print it out (unlike the rest of the book that is in PDF format on this DVD).

Using the Links folder

Appendix B contains numerous links to AutoCAD resources. The Links folder contains these resources as live links to make it easy for you to navigate to them with a single click.

Using the Software folder

I have assembled what I think is an excellent collection of software that works with AutoCAD 2008, and a couple of applications that work with AutoCAD LT 2008. The Software folder is divided into subfolders by chapter. Not all chapters have software, and so subfolders appear only for the chapters that have software. This makes it easy for you to find software by function. For example, you can find software for text objects by looking in the Chapter 13 subfolder because Chapter 13 covers text. Table C.1 at the end of this appendix lists the software alphabetically so that you can review it at a glance. Within each chapter's subfolder, you'll find subfolders for each program or AutoLISP routine.

I'm very pleased to include 30-day trial versions of AutoCAD 2008 and AutoCAD LT 2008 with this book. These trial versions are in the `Software` folder. You cannot install them directly from the DVD-ROM. Double-click the EXE file. In the WinZip Self-Extractor dialog box that opens, click the Unzip button to decompress the file onto your own hard drive. When this process is completed, the installation process should automatically start; if not, double-click `setup.exe` in the folder you unzipped to.

 Trial versions are also available from Autodesk's Web site. For AutoCAD, go to www.autodesk. com/autocad-trial. For AutoCAD LT, go to www.autodesk.com/autocadlt-trial.

To find out in detail what each software program or AutoLISP routine does, read the text (TXT) file if there is one. It provides details about what the software does and how to install it. Sometimes details are at the beginning of the LSP file. You can open and read it.

Most of the software on the DVD is *freeware* — you can use it at no cost. Most of the software consists of AutoLISP routines. However, some of it is *shareware*. Here's the scoop on shareware: You try it out and if you like it, you buy it. It works on the honor system, so please be honorable and pay for the shareware that you use. All shareware comes with a text file that explains how much to pay for it, what you get when you register, and where to send your payment. Often, you can access additional features when you register.

The DVD also has one or two demo programs. Demos are not fully functional — usually they either shut down after a short time, or they don't work to their fullest extent. Demos are not shareware — they demonstrate regular software programs that you must buy.

Using Adobe Reader

Adobe Reader is included on the DVD to enable you to read this book in its electronic form. You can find it in the `\Software\Adobe Reader` folder. Follow these steps to install the software:

1. Start Windows Explorer and open the `Software\Adobe Reader` folder on the DVD.
2. In the `Software\Adobe Reader` folder, locate the EXE file and double-click it.
3. Follow the instructions on-screen to install the software.
4. To view this book in its electronic form, start Windows Explorer and open the `eBook` folder from the DVD.
5. Double-click the book's PDF file in the `eBook` folder.

Using AutoLISP routines

AutoLISP routines are easy to install. (AutoCAD LT does not support AutoLISP.) Follow these steps:

1. Copy the LSP file to AutoCAD's `Support` folder or to a folder that you've placed in AutoCAD's support file search path.

NOTE To add a folder to AutoCAD's support file search path, choose Tools ⇨ Options and click the plus sign (+) next to Support File Search Path on the Files tab. Choose Add. Type in a folder path or choose Browse to locate one.

2. In AutoCAD, type **(load "file name")** where **file name** is the name of the LSP file. You don't need the `.lsp`, but don't forget the parentheses or the quotation marks. Alternatively, choose Tools ⇨ Load Application to use a dialog box. AutoCAD responds with the name of the last function that was defined in the routine.
3. Type the name of the function to use the AutoLISP routine.

If no text file explains how to use the program, brief instructions may be displayed on the command line. If not, type the name of the file, such as **atc**, and press Enter.

Using VBA programs

To load a VBA program, copy it to a folder in AutoCAD's support file search path. (AutoCAD LT does not support VBA.) Choose Tools ➪ Macro ➪ Load Project. Locate the VBA program (a DVB file), select it, and click Open. AutoCAD displays a message telling you that the VBA program contains macros and allowing you to disable them. Of course, the VBA program doesn't work if you disable the macros. If you want, you can check the file with a virus-checker first. To enable the macros, choose Enable Macros. AutoCAD loads the VBA program.

To use a VBA program, choose Tools ➪ Macro ➪ Macros. Select the VBA program and click Run. For more information on VBA programs, see Chapter 37.

Using a setup or install file

If you see a setup or install file (such as setup.exe), use it to install the software. You might need to remove the read-only attribute first, as explained in the "Changing the Windows Read-Only Attribute" sidebar earlier in this appendix. Copy all of the files to a folder in the support file search path. In Windows Explorer, double-click the setup or install file, and the process should start automatically. The user can also install everything from within the DVD interface.

Applications

The following applications in Table C.1 are in the \Software folder on the *AutoCAD 2008 and AutoCAD LT 2008 Bible* DVD. The Subfolder column lets you know which subfolder to look in. These subfolders correspond to the chapters of the book. Where possible, I also give you a Web site where you can find more information.

TABLE C.1

The DVD Software

Name	Type	Chapter	Description
3D Kitchen Plus, from Doug Morris	Demo	24	A library of 3D kitchen cabinets.
3dspiral, from Autodesk, Inc.	Open Source	21	Constructs 2D and 3D spirals.
AccuRender, from Robert McNeel & Associates	Evaluation	25	Advanced rendering program. For more information, go to www.mcneel.com.
Adobe Reader, from Adobe Systems, Inc.	Freeware		View electronic content in PDF format. For more information, go to www.adobe.com.
Ar1, from Leonid Nemirovsky	Freeware	16	Creates a label of the area of an enclosed polyline. For more information, go to http://home.pacifier.com/~nemi/.
Arcsum, from Dotsoft	Freeware	12	Lists the total length of a selection set of arcs. For more information, see www.dotsoft.com.

continued

TABLE C.1 *(continued)*

Name	Type	Chapter	Description
Attstrip, from Dotsoft	Freeware	18	Removes all attributes from selected blocks. For more information, see www.dotsoft.com.
AutoCAD 2008, from Autodesk, Inc.	30-day trial		Design, visualize, and document your ideas clearly and efficiently with AutoCAD® 2008 software. It enables you to create, edit, and develop design alternatives using realistic solids and surfaces in an updated design environment. Communicate your ideas with powerful sketch, shadow, and rendering tools, including intuitive walk-through animations.
AutoCAD LT 2008, from Autodesk, Inc.	30-day trial		AutoCAD LT® software, the world's number one–selling 2D drafting and detailing product, includes dynamic blocks, Express Tools for better layer management, and other drafting enhancements to boost productivity. Full DWG file format compatibility, DGN support, and access to attached drawings add to design process efficiency.
Br, from Leonid Nemirovsky	Freeware	10	Draws a break symbol. For more information, go to http://home.pacifier.com/~nemi/.
GeomCurves, from Eugeny Kalney	Freeware	16	Creates a variety of mathematically defined curves.
Idt, from Leonid Nemirovsky	Freeware	13	Lets you specify spacing between lines of dtext. For more information, go to http://home.pacifier.com/~nemi/.
Insrot, from DotSoft	Freeware	18	Inserts rotated blocks while maintaining attributes horizontal. For more information, see www.dotsoft.com.
It, from Leonid Nemirovsky	Freeware	13	Lets you specify spacing between lines of text. For more information, go to http://home.pacifier.com/~nemi/.
Keypad, from ManuSoft	Freeware	33	Creates a keypad toolbar. For more information, see www.manusoft.com.
Layerhtm, from DotSoft	Freeware	11	Displays a copy of the Layer Properties Manager dialog box in your browser so that you can print it.
Linesum, from DotSoft	Freeware	12	Provides the total length of selected lines. For more information, see www.dotsoft.com.

Name	Type	Chapter	Description
Mhatch, from DotSoft	Freeware	16	Creates solid fills for a selection of closed objects. For more information, see `www.dotsoft.com`.
Mmt, from Leonid Nemirovsky	Freeware	13	Merges two Mtext objects. For more information, go to `http://home.pacifier.com/~nemi/`.
Mpe-arch, from Henry Dearborn	Freeware	18	Mechanical and electrical components for architectural drawings.
North, from DotSoft	Freeware	18	A collection of North symbols for architectural drawings. For more information, see `www.dotsoft.com`.
Paper Space Manager Utilities, from Leonid Nemirovsky	Freeware	17	Automates the setting of scales for paper space, creating viewports, and switching between viewports and corresponding views in model space. For more information, go to `http://home.pacifier.com/~nemi/`.
Pend, from Leonid Nemirovsky	Freeware	10	Creates a pipe break symbol in a line. For more information, go to `http://home.pacifier.com/~nemi/`.
Polydis, from DotSoft	Freeware	12	Reports the length of a selected polyline. For more information, see `www.dotsoft.com`.
Quickkey, from DotSoft	Freeware	29	"Super-Alias" replacement for `acad.pgp` that supports command options like ZOOM Previous. For more information, see `www.dotsoft.com`.
Recent, from DotSoft	Freeware	2	Adds a Recent pull-down menu that displays the last 26 drawings that were opened. For more information, see `www.dotsoft.com`.
Rtltscal, from Dotsoft	Freeware	11	Provides real-time linetype scale control. For more information, see `www.dotsoft.com`.
Savea, from the author	Freeware	1	Saves a drawing to the `a:` drive.
Sfld, from Leonid Nemirovsky	Freeware	13	Creates custom fields. For more information, go to `http://home.pacifier.com/~nemi/`.
Stmplot, from Leonid Nemirovsky	Freeware	17	Adds drawing information to plots. For more information, go to `http://home.pacifier.com/~nemi/`.
Txt2mtxt, from DotSoft	Freeware	13	Converts single-line text to Mtext. For more information, see `www.dotsoft.com`.
Txtexprt, from DotSoft	Freeware	13	Exports Text objects to a text file. For more information, see `www.dotsoft.com`.

continued

TABLE C.1	*(continued)*		
Name	**Type**	**Chapter**	**Description**
Txtstack, from DotSoft	Freeware	13	Adjusts spacing between lines of single-line text. For more information, see `www.dotsoft.com`.
Wb, from Leonid Nemirovsky	Freeware	13	Creates a list of blocks in a folder, and wblocks the blocks to that folder. For more information, go to `http://home.pacifier.com/~nemi/`.
Wblockm, from DotSoft	Freeware	18	Creates individual drawings (write blocks) of all of the blocks in a drawing, in a folder that you specify. For more information, see `www.dotsoft.com`.
WinRAR, from Softronic Oy (Rarsoft)	Trial Version		A compression and decompression program. For more information, go to `www.rarlab.com`.

Shareware programs are fully functional, trial versions of copyrighted programs. If you like particular programs, register with their authors for a nominal fee and receive licenses, enhanced versions, and technical support. *Freeware programs* are copyrighted games, applications, and utilities that are free for personal use. Unlike shareware, these programs do not require a fee or provide technical support. *GNU software* is governed by its own license, which is included inside the folder of the GNU product. See the GNU license for more details.

Trial, demo, or evaluation versions are usually limited either by time or functionality (such as being unable to save projects). Some trial versions are very sensitive to system date changes. If you alter your computer's date, the programs will "time out" and will no longer be functional.

Using the e-Book version of *AutoCAD 2008 and AutoCAD LT 2008 Bible*

You can now have access to *AutoCAD 2008 and AutoCAD LT 2008 Bible* without lugging around a heavy book. The complete text of this book is on the DVD in the `\eBook` folder in Adobe's Portable Document Format (PDF). The PDF format displays a picture of the pages of the book. To read and search the book in this format, you need the Adobe Reader for Windows, which is on the DVD in the `\Software\Adobe Reader` folder.

You can put Adobe Reader on your laptop and read while you travel. You can refer to the book when you're in the field or on-site. You cannot print the ebook.

Troubleshooting

If you have difficulty installing or using any of the materials on the companion DVD, try the following solutions:

- **Turn off any antivirus software that you may have running.** Installers sometimes mimic virus activity and can make your computer incorrectly believe that a virus is infecting it. (Be sure to turn the antivirus software back on later.)

- **Close all running programs.** The more programs that you're running, the less memory is available to other programs. Installers also typically update files and programs; if you keep other programs running, installation may not work properly.

- **Reference the README:** Please refer to the README file located at the root of the DVD for the latest product information at the time of publication.

- **If you are trying to use an AutoCAD drawing, copy it to your local hard drive and remove its Read-Only attribute, as described in the sidebar, "Changing the Windows Read-Only Attribute."**

There is no way to install the DVD as a whole; you can only install individual software applications on the DVD or copy drawing files. For AutoLISP and VBA software, see information in the "Using the Software folder" section of this appendix.

Customer Care

If you have trouble with the DVD, please call the Wiley Product Technical Support phone number at (800) 762-2974. Outside the United States, call 1(317) 572-3994. You can also contact Wiley Product Technical Support at http://support.wiley.com. John Wiley & Sons will provide technical support only for installation and other general quality control items. For technical support on the applications themselves, consult the program's vendor or author.

To place additional orders or to request information about other Wiley products, please call (877) 762-2974.

Index

Symbols and Numerics

A

D

W

Wiley Publishing, Inc.
End-User License Agreement

READ THIS. You should carefully read these terms and conditions before opening the software packet(s) included with this book *"AutoCAD 2008 and AutoCAD LT 2008 Bible"*. This is a license agreement "Agreement" between you and Wiley Publishing, Inc. "WPI". By opening the accompanying software packet(s), you acknowledge that you have read and accept the following terms and conditions. If you do not agree and do not want to be bound by such terms and conditions, promptly return the Book and the unopened software packet(s) to the place you obtained them for a full refund.

1. **License Grant.** WPI grants to you (either an individual or entity) a nonexclusive license to use one copy of the enclosed software program(s) (collectively, the "Software") solely for your own personal or business purposes on a single computer (whether a standard computer or a work-station component of a multi-user network). The Software is in use on a computer when it is loaded into temporary memory (RAM) or installed into permanent memory (hard disk, CD-ROM, or other storage device). WPI reserves all rights not expressly granted herein.

2. **Ownership.** WPI is the owner of all right, title, and interest, including copyright, in and to the compilation of the Software recorded on the disk(s) or CD-ROM "Software Media". Copyright to the individual programs recorded on the Software Media is owned by the author or other authorized copyright owner of each program. Ownership of the Software and all proprietary rights relating thereto remain with WPI and its licensers.

3. **Restrictions on Use and Transfer.**
   (a) You may only (i) make one copy of the Software for backup or archival purposes, or (ii) transfer the Software to a single hard disk, provided that you keep the original for backup or archival purposes. You may not (i) rent or lease the Software, (ii) copy or reproduce the Software through a LAN or other network system or through any computer subscriber system or bulletin-board system, or (iii) modify, adapt, or create derivative works based on the Software.

   (b) You may not reverse engineer, decompile, or disassemble the Software. You may transfer the Software and user documentation on a permanent basis, provided that the transferee agrees to accept the terms and conditions of this Agreement and you retain no copies. If the Software is an update or has been updated, any transfer must include the most recent update and all prior versions.

4. **Restrictions on Use of Individual Programs.** You must follow the individual requirements and restrictions detailed for each individual program in the "What's on the CD-ROM" appendix of this Book. These limitations are also contained in the individual license agreements recorded on the Software Media. These limitations may include a requirement that after using the program for a specified period of time, the user must pay a registration fee or discontinue use. By opening the Software packet(s), you will be agreeing to abide by the licenses and restrictions for these individual programs that are detailed in the "What's on the CD-ROM" appendix and on the Software Media. None of the material on this Software Media or listed in this Book may ever be redistributed, in original or modified form, for commercial purposes.

5. **Limited Warranty.**
   (a) WPI warrants that the Software and Software Media are free from defects in materials and workmanship under normal use for a period of sixty (60) days from the date of purchase of this Book. If WPI receives notification within the warranty period of defects in materials or workmanship, WPI will replace the defective Software Media.

(b) WPI AND THE AUTHOR(S) OF THE BOOK DISCLAIM ALL OTHER WARRANTIES, EXPRESS OR IMPLIED, INCLUDING WITHOUT LIMITATION IMPLIED WARRANTIES OF MERCHANTABILITY AND FITNESS FOR A PARTICULAR PURPOSE, WITH RESPECT TO THE SOFTWARE, THE PROGRAMS, THE SOURCE CODE CONTAINED THEREIN, AND/OR THE TECHNIQUES DESCRIBED IN THIS BOOK. WPI DOES NOT WARRANT THAT THE FUNCTIONS CONTAINED IN THE SOFTWARE WILL MEET YOUR REQUIRE-MENTS OR THAT THE OPERATION OF THE SOFTWARE WILL BE ERROR FREE.

(c) This limited warranty gives you specific legal rights, and you may have other rights that vary from jurisdiction to jurisdiction.

6. **Remedies.**

(a) WPI's entire liability and your exclusive remedy for defects in materials and workmanship shall be limited to replacement of the Software Media, which may be returned to WPI with a copy of your receipt at the following address: Software Media Fulfillment Department, Attn.: *AutoCAD 2008 and AutoCAD LT 2008 Bible*, Wiley Publishing, Inc., 10475 Crosspoint Blvd., Indianapolis, IN 46256, or call 1-800-762-2974. Please allow four to six weeks for delivery. This Limited Warranty is void if failure of the Software Media has resulted from accident, abuse, or misapplication. Any replacement Software Media will be warranted for the remainder of the original warranty period or thirty (30) days, whichever is longer.

(b) In no event shall WPI or the author be liable for any damages whatsoever (including without limitation damages for loss of business profits, business interruption, loss of business information, or any other pecuniary loss) arising from the use of or inability to use the Book or the Software, even if WPI has been advised of the possibility of such damages.

(c) Because some jurisdictions do not allow the exclusion or limitation of liability for consequential or incidental damages, the above limitation or exclusion may not apply to you.

7. **U.S. Government Restricted Rights.** Use, duplication, or disclosure of the Software for or on behalf of the United States of America, its agencies and/or instrumentalities "U.S. Government" is subject to restrictions as stated in paragraph (c)(1)(ii) of the Rights in Technical Data and Computer Software clause of DFARS 252.227-7013, or subparagraphs (c) (1) and (2) of the Commercial Computer Software - Restricted Rights clause at FAR 52.227-19, and in similar clauses in the NASA FAR supplement, as applicable.

8. **General.** This Agreement constitutes the entire understanding of the parties and revokes and supersedes all prior agreements, oral or written, between them and may not be modified or amended except in a writing signed by both parties hereto that specifically refers to this Agreement. This Agreement shall take precedence over any other documents that may be in conflict herewith. If any one or more provisions contained in this Agreement are held by any court or tribunal to be invalid, illegal, or otherwise unenforceable, each and every other provision shall remain in full force and effect.